FOURTH EDITION

Cognitive Neuroscience

The Biology of the Mind

MICHAEL S. GAZZANIGA

University of California, Santa Barbara

RICHARD B. IVRY

University of California, Berkeley

GEORGE R. MANGUN

University of California, Davis

With special appreciation for the Fourth Edition to Rebecca A. Gazzaniga, M.D.

W·W·NORTON

NEW YORK · LONDON

W. W. Norton & Company has been independent since its founding in 1923, when William Warder Norton and Mary D. Herter Norton first published lectures delivered at the People's Institute, the adult education division of New York City's Cooper Union. The firm soon expanded its program beyond the Institute, publishing books by celebrated academics from America and abroad. By midcentury, the two major pillars of Norton's publishing program—trade books and college texts—were firmly established. In the 1950s, the Norton family transferred control of the company to its employees, and today—with a staff of four hundred and a comparable number of trade, college, and professional titles published each year—W. W. Norton & Company stands as the largest and oldest publishing house owned wholly by its employees.

Editors: Aaron Javsicas and Sheri Snavely

Development Editor: Michael Zierler

Project Editor: Diane Cipollone

Electronic Media Editor: Callinda Taylor

Editorial Assistant: Shira Averbuch

Marketing Manager, Psychology: Lauren Winkler

Production Manager: Eric Pier-Hocking

Photo Editor: Stephanie Romeo

Photo Researcher: Elyse Rieder

Permissions Manager: Megan Jackson

Permissions Clearing: Bethany Salminen

Art Director: Rubina Yeh

Designer: Lisa Buckley

Composition: TSI Graphics

Manufacturing: Quad Graphics

The text of this book is composed in Epic with the display set in Mr Eaves San, Mr Eaves XL San, Franklin Gothic Std.

Library of Congress Cataloging-in-Publication Data.
Gazzaniga, Michael S.
   Cognitive neuroscience : the biology of the mind / Michael S. Gazzaniga, University of California, Santa Barbara; Richard B. Ivry, University of California, Berkeley; George R. Mangun, University of California, Davis. – Fourth edition.
        pages cm
   Includes bibliographical references and index.
   ISBN 978-0-393-91348-4 (hardcover)
   1. Cognitive neuroscience. I. Ivry, Richard B. II. Mangun, G. R. (George Ronald), 1956- III. Title.
   QP360.5.G39 2013
   612.8'233–dc23

                          2013027471

W. W. Norton & Company, Inc., 500 Fifth Avenue, New York, NY 10110-0017
wwnorton.com

W. W. Norton & Company Ltd., Castle House, 75/76 Wells Street, London W1T 3QT
1 2 3 4 5 6 7 8 9 0

For Lilly, Emmy, Garth, Dante, and Rebecca
M.S.G.

For Henry and Sam
R.B.I.

For Nicholas and Alexander
G.R.M.

Brief Overview

Contents

PART I   Background and Methods

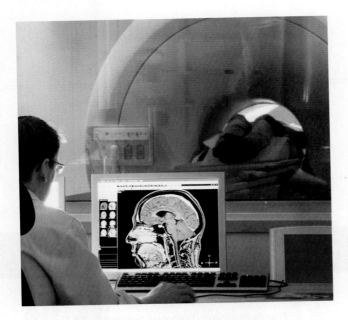

PART II   Core Processes

PART III Control Processes

14 Consciousness, Free Will, and the Law   604

Boxes

Preface

Welcome to the fourth edition! When cognitive neuroscience emerged in the late 1970's, it remained to be seen if this new field would have "legs." Today, the answer is clear: the field has blossomed in spectacular fashion. Cognitive neuroscience is well represented at all research universities, providing researchers and graduate students with the tools and opportunities to develop the interdisciplinary research programs that are the mainstay of the field. Multiple journals, some designed to cover the entire field, and others specialized for particular methodologies or research themes, have been launched to provide venues to report the latest findings. The number of papers rises at an exponential rate. The annual meeting of the Cognitive Neuroscience Society has also flourished. While 400 pilgrims attended the first meeting in 1993, the 20th anniversary meeting in 2013 was attended by almost 2000 people.

The fundamental challenge we faced in laying the groundwork for our early editions was to determine the basic principles that make cognitive neuroscience distinct from physiological psychology, neuroscience, cognitive psychology, or neuropsychology. It is now obvious that cognitive neuroscience overlaps with, and synthesizes, these disciplinary approaches as researchers aim to understand the neural bases of cognition. In addition, however, cognitive neuroscience is increasingly informing and informed by disciplines outside the mind-brain sciences, as exemplified by our new Chapter 14: "Consciousness, Free Will, and the Law"

As in previous editions, we continue to seek a balance between psychological theory, with its focus on the mind, and the neuropsychological and neuroscientific evidence about the brain that informs this theory. We make liberal use of patient case studies to illustrate essential points and observations that provide keys to understanding the architecture of cognition, rather than providing an exhaustive description of brain disorders. In every section, we strive to include the most current information and theoretical views, supported by evidence from the cutting-edge technology that is such an important part of cognitive neuroscience. In contrast to purely cognitive or neuropsychological approaches, this text emphasizes the convergence of evidence that is a crucial aspect of any science, particularly studies of higher mental function. We also provide examples of research using computational techniques to complete the story.

Teaching students to think and ask questions like cognitive neuroscientists is a major goal of our text. As cognitive neuroscientists, we examine mind–brain relationships with a wide range of techniques, such as functional and structural brain imaging, neurophysiological recording in animals, human EEG and MEG recording, brain stimulation methods, and analysis of syndromes resulting from brain damage. We highlight the strengths and weaknesses of these methods to demonstrate how these techniques must be used in a complementary manner. We want our readers to learn what questions to ask, how to choose the tools and design experiments to answer these questions, and how to evaluate and interpret the results of those experiments. Despite the amazing progress of the neurosciences, the brain remains a great mystery, with each insight inspiring new questions. For this reason, we have not used a declarative style of writing throughout the book. Instead, we tend to present results that can be interpreted in more than one way, helping the reader to recognize that there are possible alternative interpretations.

Since the first edition, there have been many major developments, both methodological and theoretical. There has been an explosion of brain imaging studies—almost 1,500 a year for the last decade. New technologies, such as transcranial magnetic stimulation, diffusion tensor imaging and optogenetics have been added to the arsenal of the cognitive neuroscientist. New links to genetics, comparative anatomy, computation and robotics have emerged. Parsing all of these studies and deciding which ones should be included has been a major challenge for us. We firmly believe that technology is a cornerstone of scientific advancement. As such, we have felt it essential to capture the cutting-edge trends in the field, while keeping in mind that this is an undergraduate survey text that needs to be completed in a quarter or semester.

The first three editions have provided compelling evidence that our efforts have led to a highly useful text for undergraduates taking their first course in cognitive neuroscience, as well as a concise reference volume for graduate students and researchers. Over 400 colleges and universities worldwide have adopted the text. Moreover, instructors tell us that in addition to our interdisciplinary approach, they like that our book has a strong narrative voice and offers a manageable number of chapters to teach in a one-semester survey course.

Still, we have had to do some pruning for the 4th edition in order to present both the foundations of cognitive neuroscience and the latest the field has to offer; in general, we have opted to take a leaner approach than in previous editions, providing the necessary updates on new developments while streamlining the descriptions of experimental results. Inspired by feedback from our adopters, we have also made some changes to make the text even more user friendly. Highlights of the fourth edition include the following:

- All the chapters have been rewritten. In order to add new findings but maintain a reasonable sized text, we had to trim out some of the older material and streamline our presentations. Careful attention has been paid to the chapter's heading and subheading structure to provide a roadmap to the essential themes of the chapters.
- The illustrations have been redrawn. The stunning new art program is designed to facilitate student understanding, and now includes a "hand-pointer" feature that draws students' attention to the most important figure elements.
- We have added an "anatomical orientation" figure at the beginning of each chapter to orient students to the brain regions that will be major players throughout the chapter.
- Key points to remember have been interspersed after major sections throughout the text instead of being stacked at the end of the chapter.
- The chapters on cellular mechanisms and neuroanatomy have been combined, providing a concise presentation of the basic concepts that are most essential for cognitive neuroscience. The focus of the field is more at the systems level of analysis, and this has led us to leave the more detailed study of cellular and molecular topics to texts dedicated to these levels of analysis.
- We have eliminated the chapter on the evolutionary perspective and instead have sprinkled discussions of this topic throughout the text.
- An extensive section on decision-making has been added to the cognitive control chapter.
- The chapter on emotion has been expanded and includes extensive discussion of the fine interplay between affective and cognitive neurosciences.
- We have added a new chapter that tackles the important, yet elusive problem of consciousness, taking on issues such as free will and how cognitive neuroscience can have practical applications for informing public policy and the law.

The new edition also offers an even more generous suite of instructor ancillaries:

- Lecture PowerPoints, new to this edition, feature text and images as well as instructor-only lecture notes and suggestions.
- Art PowerPoints and JPEGs provide all the art and tables from the book in easily adaptable formats.
- The Test Bank for *Cognitive Neuroscience*, Fourth Edition, has been developed using the Norton Assessment Guidelines. Each chapter of the Test Bank includes five question types classified according to the first five levels of Bloom's taxonomy of knowledge types.
- The Studying the Mind DVD includes exclusive Norton interviews with leading cognitive neuroscience researchers on key aspects of how we study the human mind.
- The Cognitive Neuroscience Patient Interviews DVD presents original footage of interviews with patients suffering from a variety of cognitive and neurological disorders, and bring to life the cognitive models, concepts, and research methodologies discussed in the text. Several new videos have been added for the fourth edition.

As with each edition, this book has required a laborious interactive effort among the three of us, along with extensive discussions with our colleagues, our students, and our reviewers. The product has benefited immeasurably from these interactions. Of course we are ready to modify and improve any and all of our work. In our earlier editions, we asked readers to contact us with suggestions and questions, and we do so again. We live in an age where interaction is swift and easy. We are to be found as follows: gazzaniga@psych.ucsb.edu; mangun@ucdavis.edu; ivry@socrates.berkeley.edu.

Good reading and learning!

Acknowledgments

Once again, we are indebted to a number of people. First and foremost we would like to thank Rebecca A. Gazzaniga, M.D. for her extensive and savvy editing of the Fourth Edition. She mastered every chapter, with an eye to make sure the story was clear and engaging. We could not have completed this edition without her.

We are also especially grateful to Tamara Y. Swaab, Ph.D. (University of California, Davis), for the language chapter in this and prior editions, Michael B. Miller, Ph.D. (University of California, Santa Barbara), for contributions to the chapter on hemispheric lateralization, Stephanie Cacioppo, Ph.D. (University of Chicago), for contributions to the chapter on emotion, and Jason Mitchell, Ph.D. (Harvard University), for contributions to the social cognition chapter. For answering miscellaneous questions that cropped up in the methods chapter we would like to tip our hats to Scott Grafton (University of California, Santa Barbara) and Danielle Bassett.

For work on the previous editions that continues to play an active part in this new edition we thank again Megan Steven (Dartmouth College) for her writing skills, Jeff Hutsler (University of Nevada, Reno) and Leah Krubitzer (University of California, Davis) for evolutionary perspectives, Jennifer Beer (University of Texas, Austin) for insights on social cognition, and Liz Phelps for her work on emotion. Tim Justus (Pitzer College), Chadd Funk, Adam Riggal, Karl Doron, Kristin McAdams, and Todd Heatherton (Dartmouth College) who are all to be thanked for sharing their advice and wisdom and for helping along the way. We thank Frank Forney for his art in the previous editions, and Echo Medical Media for the new art in this edition. We also thank our many colleagues who provided original artwork or scientific figures. We would also like to thank our readers Annik Carson and Mette Clausen-Bruun who took the time to point out typos in our previous edition, to anatomist Carlos Avendaño, who alerted us to some anatomical errors, and to Sophie van Roijen, who suggested the very good idea of adding an index of abbreviations.

Several instructors took time from their busy schedules to review our previous edition and make suggestions for this edition. We thank Joy Geng, University of California, Davis; Brian Gonsalves, University of Illinois; Roger Knowles, Drew University; Sam McClure, Stanford University; John McDonald, Simon Fraser University; Kathleen Taylor, Columbia University; and Katherine Turner, San Diego State University.

In addition, we are indebted to many scientists and personal friends. Writing a textbook is a major commitment of time, intellect, and affect! Those who helped significantly are noted below. Some reviewed our words and critiqued our thoughts. Others allowed us to interview them. To all we owe our deep gratitude and thanks.

Eyal Aharoni, Rand University; David G. Amaral, University of California, Davis; Franklin R. Amthor, University of Alabama, Birmingham; Michael Anderson, St. Andrews University; Adam Aron, University of California, San Diego; Ignacio Badiola, Florida International University; David Badre, Brown University; Juliana Baldo, VA Medical Center, Martinez, California; Gary Banker, Oregon Health Sciences University; Horace Barlow, Cambridge University; Kathleen Baynes, University of California, Davis; N. P. Bechtereva, Russian Academy of Science; Mark Beeman, Northwestern University; Marlene Behrmann, Carnegie Mellon University; Robert S. Blumenfeld, University of California, Davis; Elizabeth Brannon, Duke University; Rainer Breitling, San Diego State University; Silvia Bunge, University of California, Berkeley; Valerie Clark, University of California, Davis; Clay Clayworth, VA Medical Center, Martinez, California; Asher Cohen, Hebrew University; Jonathan Cohen, Princeton University; Roshan Cools, Radboud University; J. M. Coquery, Université des Sciences et Technologies de Lille; Michael Corballis, University Auckland; Paul Corballis, Georgia Tech University; Clayton Curtis, New York University; Anders Dale, Massachusetts General Hospital; Antonio Damasio, University of Southern California; Hanna Damasio, University of Southern California; Lila Davachi, New York University; Daniel C. Dennett, Tufts University; Michel Desmurget, Centre de Neuroscience Cognitive; Mark D'Esposito, University of California, Berkeley; Joern Diedrichsen, University College London; Nina Dronkers, University of California, Davis; Paul Eling, Radboud University Nijmegen; Russell Epstein, University of Pennsylvania; Martha Farah, University of Pennsylvania; Harlen Fichtenholtz, Duke University; Peter T. Fox, University of Texas; Karl Friston, Institute of Neurology, London; Rusty Gage, Salk Institute; Jack Gallant, University of California, Berkeley; Vittorio Gallese, University of Parma, Italy; Isabel

Gauthier, Vanderbilt University; Priyanka Ghosh; Christian Gerlach, University of Southern Denmark; Robbin Gibb, University of Lethbridge; Mitchell Glickstein, University College London and Dartmouth College; Gail Goodman, University of California, Davis; Elizabeth Gould, Princeton University; Jay E. Gould, University of West Florida; Scott Grafton, University of California, Santa Barbara; Charlie Gross, Princeton University; Nouchine Hadjikhani, Massachusetts General Hospital; Peter Hagoort, Max Planck Institute for Psycholinguistics; Todd Handy, University of British Columbia; Eliot Hazeltine, University of Iowa; Hans-Jochen Heinze, University of Madgeberg; Arturo Hernandez, University of Houston; Laura Hieber, University of California, Berkeley; Steven A. Hillyard, University of California, San Diego; Hermann Hinrichs, University of Madgeberg; Jens-Max Hopf, University of Magdeburg; Joseph Hopfinger, University of California, Davis; Richard Howard, National University of Singapore; Drew Hudson, University of California, Berkeley; Akira Ishiguchi, Ochanomizu University; Lucy Jacobs, University of California, Berkeley; Amishi Jha, University of California, Davis; Cindy Jordan, Michigan State University; Tim Justus, VA Medical Center, Martinez, California; Nancy Kanwisher, Massachusetts Institute of Technology; Larry Katz, Duke University; Steven Keele, University of Oregon; Leon Kenemans, University of Utrecht; Steve Kennerley, University of California, Berkeley; Alan Kingstone, University of British Columbia; Robert T. Knight, University of California, Berkeley; Talia Konkle, Harvard University; Stephen M. Kosslyn, Harvard University; Neal Kroll, University of California, Davis; Leah Krubitzer, University of California, Davis; Marta Kutas, University of California, San Diego; Ayelet Landau, University of California, Berkeley; Joseph E. Le Doux, New York University; Matt Lieberman, University of California, Los Angeles; Steven J. Luck, University of California, Davis; Jennifer Mangels, Graduate Center at the City University of New York; Chad Marsolek, University of Minnesota; Nancy Martin, University of California, Davis; James L. McClelland, Stanford University; George A. Miller, Princeton University; Teresa Mitchell, Duke University; Ryan Morehead, University of California, Berkeley; Amy Needham, Duke University; Kevin Ochsner, Columbia University; Ken A. Paller, Northwestern University; Jasmeet K. Pannu, University of Arizona; Galina V. Paramei, Liverpool Hope University; Steven E. Petersen, Washington University School of Medicine; Steven Pinker, Harvard University; Lara Polse, University of California, San Diego; Michael I. Posner, University of Oregon; David Presti, University of California, Berkeley; Robert Rafal, University of Bangor; Marcus Raichle, Washington University School of Medicine; Charan Ranganath, University of California, Davis; Patricia Reuter-Lorenz, University of Michigan; Jesse Rissman, University of California, Los Angeles; Matthew Rushworth, University of Oxford; Alexander Sack, Maastricht University; Mikko E. Sams, University of Tampere; Donatella Scabini, University of California, Berkeley; Daniel Schacter, Harvard University; Ariel Schoenfeld, University of Magdeburg; Michael Scholz, University of Magdeberg; Art Shimamura, University of California, Berkeley; Michael Silver, University of California, Berkeley; Michael Silverman, Oregon Health Sciences University; Noam Sobel, Weizmann Institute of Science; Allen W. Song, Duke University; Larry Squire, University of California, San Diego; Alit Stark-Inbar, University of California, Berkeley; Michael Starks, 3DTV Corporation; Thomas M. Talavage, Massachusetts General Hospital; Keiji Tanaka, Riken Institute; Michael Tarr, Brown University; Ed Taylor; Jordan Taylor, Princeton University; Sharon L. Thompson-Schill, University of Pennsylvania; Roger Tootell, Massachusetts General Hospital; Anne M. Treisman, Princeton University; Carrie Trutt, Duke University; Endel Tulving, Rotman Research Institute, Baycrest Center; John Vollrath; John Wallis; C. Mark Wessinger, University of Nevada, Reno; Susanne Wiking, University of Tromsø; Kevin Wilson, Gettysburg College; Ginger Withers, Oregon Health Sciences University; Marty G. Woldorff, Duke University; Andrew Yonelinas, University of California, Davis.

Often we forget to thank the many people, some of whom have generously given hundreds of hours of their time, for being participants in the research work that we discuss; without their contributions, cognitive neuroscience would not be where it is today.

Finally, we would like to thank the outstanding editorial and production team at W. W. Norton, Michael Zierler, Diane Cipollone, Aaron Javsicas, Sheri Snavely, Callinda Taylor, Shira Averbuch, and Eric Pier-Hocking, whose sharp eyes and wise counsel have helped us produce this exciting new edition of our textbook.

FOURTH EDITION

Cognitive Neuroscience

The Biology of the Mind

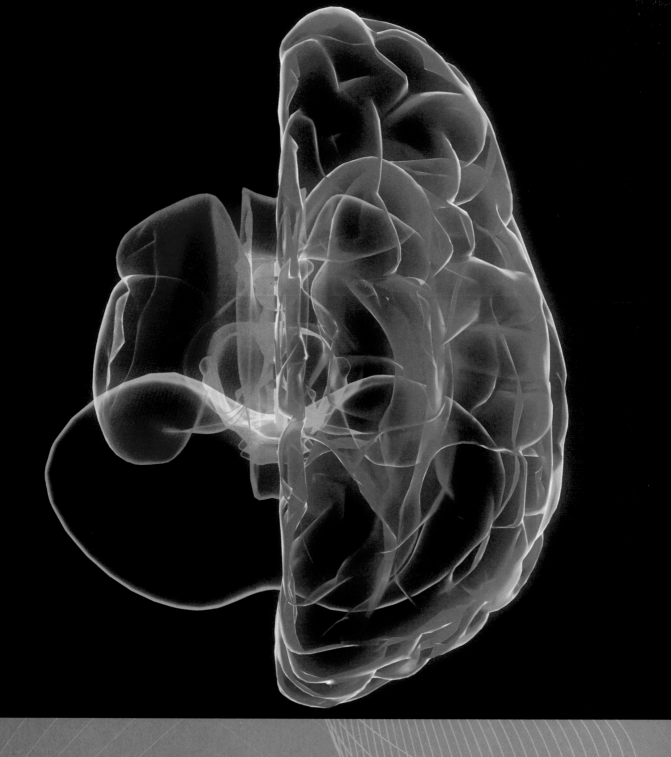

In science it often happens that scientists say, "You know that's a really good argument; my position is mistaken," and then they actually change their minds and you never hear that old view from them again. They really do it. It doesn't happen as often as it should, because scientists are human and change is sometimes painful. But it happens every day. I cannot recall the last time something like that happened in politics or religion.

~Carl Sagan, 1987

A Brief History of Cognitive Neuroscience

AS ANNE GREEN WALKED to the gallows in the castle yard of Oxford, England, in 1650, she must have been feeling scared, angry, and frustrated. She was about to be executed for a crime she had not committed: murdering her stillborn child. Many thoughts raced through her head, but "I am about to play a role in the founding of clinical neurology and neuroanatomy" although accurate, certainly was not one of them. She proclaimed her innocence to the crowd, a psalm was read, and she was hanged. She hung there for a full half hour before she was taken down, pronounced dead, and placed in a coffin provided by Drs. Thomas Willis and William Petty. This was when Anne Green's luck began to improve. Willis and Petty were physicians and had permission from King Charles I to dissect, for medical research, the bodies of any criminals killed within 21 miles of Oxford. So, instead of being buried, Anne's body was carried to their office.

An autopsy, however, was not what took place. As if in a scene from Edgar Allan Poe, the coffin began to emit a grumbling sound. Anne was alive! The doctors poured spirits in her mouth and rubbed a feather on her neck to make her cough. They rubbed her hands and feet for several minutes, bled five ounces of her blood, swabbed her neck wounds with turpentine, and cared for her through the night. The next morning, able to drink fluids and feeling more chipper, Anne asked for a beer. Five days later, she was out of bed and eating normally (Molnar, 2004; Zimmer, 2004).

After her ordeal, the authorities wanted to hang Anne again. But Willis and Petty fought in her defense, arguing that her baby had been stillborn and its death was not her fault. They declared that divine providence had stepped in and provided her miraculous escape from death, thus proving her innocence. Their arguments prevailed. Anne was set free and went on to marry and have three more children.

This miraculous experience was well publicized in England (Figure 1.1). Thomas Willis (Figure 1.2) owed much to Anne Green and the fame brought to him by the events of her resurrection. With it came money he desperately needed and the prestige to publish his work and disseminate his ideas, and he had some good ones. An inquisitive neurologist, he actually coined the term *neurology* and became one of the best-known doctors of his time. He was the first anatomist to link abnormal human behaviors to changes in brain structure. He drew these conclusions after treating patients throughout their

FIGURE 1.1 An artistic rendition of the miraculous resurrection of Anne Green in 1650.

arises from awareness, perception, and reasoning), and *neuroscience* (the study of how the nervous system is organized and functions). This seemed the perfect term to describe the question of understanding how the functions of the physical brain can yield the thoughts and ideas of an intangible mind. And so the term took hold in the scientific community.

FIGURE 1.2 Thomas Willis (1621–1675), a founder of clinical neuroscience.

When considering the miraculous properties of brain function, bear in mind that Mother Nature built our brains through the process of evolution; they were not designed by a team of rational engineers. While life first appeared on our 4.5-billion-year-old Earth approximately 3.8 billion years ago, human brains, in their present form, have been around for only about 100,000 years, a mere drop in the bucket. The primate brain appeared between 34 million and 23 million years ago, during the Oligocene epoch. It evolved into the progressively larger brains of the great apes in the Miocene epoch between roughly 23 million and 7 million years ago. The human

lives and autopsying them after their deaths. Willis was among the first to link specific brain damage to specific behavioral deficits, and to theorize how the brain transfers information in what would later be called *neuronal conduction*.

With his colleague and friend Christopher Wren (the architect who designed St. Paul's Cathedral in London), Willis created drawings of the human brain that remained the most accurate representations for 200 years (Figure 1.3). He also coined names for a myriad of brain regions (Table 1.1; Molnar, 2004; Zimmer, 2004). In short, Willis set in motion the ideas and knowledge base that took hundreds of years to develop into what we know today as the field of *cognitive neuroscience*.

In this chapter, we discuss some of the scientists and physicians who have made important contributions to this field. You will discover the origins of cognitive neuroscience and how it has developed into what it is today: a discipline geared toward understanding how the brain works, how brain structure and function affect behavior, and ultimately how the brain enables the mind.

A Historical Perspective

The scientific field of **cognitive neuroscience** received its name in the late 1970s in the back seat of a New York City taxi. One of us (M.S.G.) was riding with the great cognitive psychologist George A. Miller on the way to a dinner meeting at the Algonquin Hotel. The dinner was being held for scientists from Rockefeller and Cornell universities, who were joining forces to study how the brain enables the mind—a subject in need of a name. Out of that taxi ride came the term *cognitive neuroscience*—from *cognition*, or the process of knowing (i.e., what

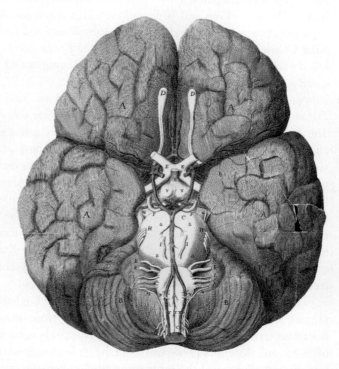

FIGURE 1.3 The human brain (ventral view) drawn by Christopher Wren for Thomas Willis, published in Willis's *The Anatomy of the Brain and Nerves*.

TABLE 1.1 A Selection of Terms Coined by Thomas Willis

Term	Definition
Anterior commissure	Axonal fibers connecting the middle and inferior temporal gyri of the left and right hemispheres.
Cerebellar peduncles	Axonal fibers connecting the cerebellum and brainstem.
Claustrum	A thin sheath of gray matter located between two brain areas: the external capsule and the putamen.
Corpus striatum	A part of the basal ganglia consisting of the caudate nucleus and the lenticular nucleus.
Inferior olives	The part of the brainstem that modulates cerebellar processing.
Internal capsule	White matter pathways conveying information from the thalamus to the cortex.
Medullary pyramids	A part of the medulla that consists of corticospinal fibers.
Neurology	The study of the nervous system and its disorders.
Optic thalamus	The portion of the thalamus relating to visual processing.
Spinal accessory nerve	The 11th cranial nerve, which innervates the head and shoulders.
Stria terminalis	The white matter pathway that sends information from the amygdala to the basal forebrain.
Striatum	Gray matter structure of the basal ganglia.
Vagus nerve	The 10th cranial nerve, which, among other functions, has visceral motor control of the heart.

lineage diverged from the last common ancestor that we shared with the chimpanzee somewhere in the range of 5–7 million years ago. Since that divergence, our brains have evolved into the present human brain, capable of all sorts of wondrous feats. Throughout this book, we will be reminding you to take the evolutionary perspective: Why might this behavior have evolved? How could it promote survival and reproduction? WWHGD? (What would a hunter-gather do?) The evolutionary perspective often helps us to ask more informed questions and provides insight into how and why the brain functions as it does.

During most of our history, humans were too busy to think about thought. Although there can be little doubt that the brains of our long-ago ancestors could engage in such activities, life was given over to more practical matters, such as surviving in tough environments, developing ways

to live better by inventing agriculture or domesticating animals, and so forth. Nonetheless, the brain mechanisms that enable us to generate theories about the characteristics of human nature thrived inside the heads of ancient humans. As civilization developed to the point where day-to-day survival did not occupy every hour of every day, our ancestors began to spend time looking for causation and constructing complex theories about the motives of fellow humans. Examples of attempts to understand the world and our place in it include *Oedipus Rex* (the ancient Greek play that deals with the nature of the child–parent conflict) and Mesopotamian and Egyptian theories on the nature of religion and the universe. Although the pre-Socratic Greek philosopher, Thales, rejected supernatural explanations of phenomena and proclaimed that every event had a natural cause (presaging modern cognitive neuroscience), the early Greeks had one big limitation: They did not have the methodology to explore the mind systematically through experimentation.

It wasn't until the 19th century that the modern tradition of observing, manipulating, and measuring became the norm, and scientists started to determine how the brain gets its jobs done. To understand how biological systems work, a laboratory is needed and experiments have to be performed to answer the questions under study and to support or refute the hypotheses and conclusions that have been made. This approach is known as the scientific method, and it is the only way that a topic can move along on sure footing. And in the case of cognitive neuroscience, there is no end to the rich phenomena to study.

The Brain Story

Imagine that you are given a problem to solve. A hunk of biological tissue is known to think, remember, attend, solve problems, tell jokes, want sex, join clubs, write novels, exhibit bias, feel guilty, and do a zillion other things. You are supposed to figure out how it works. You might start by looking at the big picture and asking yourself a couple of questions. "Hmmm, does the blob work as a unit with each part contributing to a whole? Or, is the blob full of individual processing parts, each carrying out specific functions, so the result is something that looks like it is acting as a whole unit?" From a distance the city of New York (another type of blob) appears as an integrated whole, but it is actually composed of millions of individual processors—that is, people. Perhaps people, in turn, are made of smaller, more specialized units.

This central issue—whether the mind is enabled by the whole brain working in concert or by specialized parts of the brain working at least partly independently—is what fuels much of modern research in cognitive neuroscience.

FIGURE 1.4 Franz Joseph Gall (1758–1828), one of the founders of phrenology.

As we will see, the dominant view has changed back and forth over the years, and it continues to change today.

Thomas Willis foreshadowed cognitive neuroscience with the notion that isolated brain damage (biology) could affect behavior (psychology), but his insights slipped from view. It took another century for Willis's ideas to resurface. They were expanded upon by a young Austrian physician and neuroanatomist, Franz Joseph Gall (Figure 1.4). After studying numerous patients, Gall became convinced that the brain was the organ of the mind and that innate faculties were localized in specific regions of the cerebral cortex. He thought that the brain was organized around some 35 or more specific functions, ranging from cognitive basics such as language and color perception to more ephemeral capacities such as affection and a moral sense, and each was supported by specific brain regions. These ideas were well received, and Gall took his theory on the road, lecturing throughout Europe.

Building on his theories, Gall and his disciple Johann Spurzheim hypothesized that if a person used one of the faculties with greater frequency than the others, the part of the brain representing that function would grow (Gall & Spurzheim, 1810–1819). This increase in local brain size would cause a bump in the overlying skull. Logically, then, Gall and his colleagues believed that a careful analysis of the skull could go a long way in describing the personality of the person inside the skull. Gall called this technique *anatomical personology* (Figure 1.5). The idea that character could be divined through palpating the skull was dubbed **phrenology** by Spurzheim and, as you may well imagine, soon fell into the hands of charlatans. Some employers even required job applicants to have their skulls "read" before they were hired.

Gall, apparently, was not politically astute. When asked to read the skull of Napoleon Bonaparte, Gall did not ascribe to his skull the noble characteristics that the future emperor was quite sure he possessed. When Gall later applied to the Academy of Science of Paris, Napoleon decided that phrenology needed closer scrutiny and ordered the Academy to obtain some scientific evidence of its validity. Although Gall was a physician and neuroanatomist, he was not a scientist. He observed correlations and sought only to confirm, not disprove, them. The Academy asked physiologist Marie-Jean-Pierre Flourens (Figure 1.6) to see if he could come up with any concrete findings that could back up this theory.

Flourens set to work. He destroyed parts of the brains of pigeons and rabbits and observed what happened. He was the first to show that indeed certain parts of the brain were responsible for certain functions. For instance, when he removed the cerebral hemispheres, the animal no longer had perception, motor ability, and judgment.

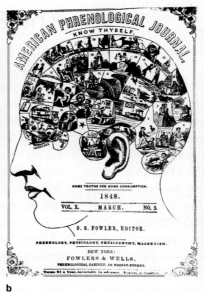

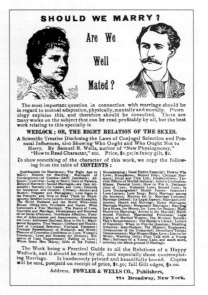

a   b   c

FIGURE 1.5 **(a)** An analysis of Presidents Washington, Jackson, Taylor, and McKinley by Jessie A. Fowler, from the *Phrenological Journal*, June 1898. **(b)** The phrenological map of personal characteristics on the skull, from the *American Phrenological Journal*, March 1848. **(c)** Fowler & Wells Co. publication on marriage compatibility in connection with phrenology, 1888.

a   b

FIGURE 1.6 **(a)** Marie-Jean-Pierre Flourens (1794–1867), who supported the idea later termed the *aggregate field theory*. **(b)** The posture of a pigeon deprived of its cerebral hemispheres, as described by Flourens.

Without the cerebellum, the animals became uncoordinated and lost their equilibrium. He could not, however, find any areas for advanced abilities such as memory or cognition and concluded that these were more diffusely scattered throughout the brain. Flourens developed the notion that the whole brain participated in behavior, a view later known as the **aggregate field theory**. In 1824, Flourens wrote, "All sensations, all perceptions, and all volitions occupy the same seat in these (cerebral) organs. The faculty of sensation, percept and volition is then essentially one faculty." The theory of localized brain functions, known as localizationism, fell out of favor.

That state of affairs didn't last for too long, however. New evidence obtained through clinical observations and autopsies started trickling in from across Europe, and it helped to swing the pendulum slowly back to the localizationist view. In 1836 a neurologist from Montpellier, Marc Dax, provided one of the first bits of evidence. He sent a report to the Academy of Sciences about three patients, noting that each had speech disturbances and similar left-hemisphere lesions found at autopsy. At the time, a report from the provinces got short shrift in Paris, and it would be another 30 years before anyone took much notice of this observation that speech could be disrupted by a lesion to one hemisphere only.

Meanwhile, in England, the neurologist John Hughlings Jackson (Figure 1.7)

FIGURE 1.7 John Hughlings Jackson (1835–1911), an English neurologist who was one of the first to recognize the localizationist view.

began to publish his observations on the behavior of persons with brain damage. A key feature of Jackson's writings was the incorporation of suggestions for experiments to test his observations. He noticed, for example, that during the start of their seizures, some epileptic patients moved in such characteristic ways that the seizure appeared to be stimulating a set map of the body in the brain; that is, the clonic and tonic jerks in muscles, produced by the abnormal epileptic firings of neurons in the brain, progressed in the same orderly pattern from one body part to another. This phenomenon led Jackson to propose a *topographic* organization in the cerebral cortex—that is, a map of the body was represented across a particular cortical area, where one part would represent the foot, another the lower leg, and so on. As we will see, this proposal was verified over a half century later by Wilfred Penfield. Jackson was one of the first to realize this essential feature of brain organization.

Although Jackson was also the first to observe that lesions on the right side of the brain affect visuospatial processes more than do lesions on the left side, he did not maintain that specific parts of the right side of the brain were solely committed to this important human cognitive function. Being an observant clinical neurologist, Jackson noticed that it was rare for a patient to lose a function completely. For example, most people who lost their capacity to speak following a cerebral stroke could still say some words. Patients unable to direct their hands voluntarily to specific places on their bodies could still easily scratch those places if they itched. When Jackson made these observations, he concluded that many regions of the brain contributed to a given behavior.

Meanwhile, the well-known and respected Parisian physician Paul Broca (Figure 1.8a) published, in 1861, the results of his autopsy on a patient who had been nicknamed Tan—perhaps the most famous neurological case in history. Tan had developed aphasia: He could understand language, but "tan" was the only word he could utter. Broca found that Tan (his real name was Leborgne) had a syphilitic lesion in his left hemisphere in the inferior frontal lobe. This region of the brain has come to be called *Broca's area*. The impact of this finding was huge. Here was a specific aspect of language that was impaired by a specific lesion. Soon Broca had a series of such patients. This theme was picked up by the German neurologist Carl Wernicke. In 1876, Wernicke reported on a stroke victim who (unlike Broca's patient) could talk quite freely but made little sense when he spoke. Wernicke's patient also could not understand spoken or written language. He had a lesion in a more posterior region of the left hemisphere, an area in and around where the temporal and parietal lobes meet, which is now referred to as *Wernicke's area* (Figure 1.8b).

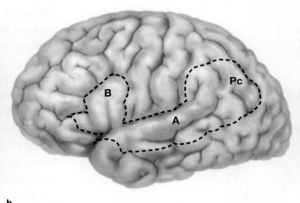

a

b

FIGURE 1.8 (a) Paul Broca (1824–1880). **(b)** The connections between the speech centers, from Wernicke's 1876 article on aphasia. A = Wernicke's sensory speech center; B = Broca's area for speech; Pc = Wernicke's area concerned with language comprehension and meaning.

Today, differences in how the brain responds to focal disease are well known (H. Damasio et al., 2004; R. J. Wise, 2003), but a little over 100 years ago Broca's and Wernicke's discoveries were earth-shattering. (Note that people had largely forgotten Willis's observations that isolated brain damage could affect behavior. Throughout the history of brain science, an unfortunate and oft repeated trend is that we fail to consider crucial observations made by our predecessors.) With the discoveries of Broca and Wernicke, attention was again paid to this startling point: Focal brain damage causes specific behavioral deficits.

As is so often the case, the study of humans leads to questions for those who work on animal models. Shortly after Broca's discovery, the German physiologists Gustav Fritsch and Eduard Hitzig electrically stimulated discrete parts of a dog brain and observed that this stimulation produced characteristic movements in the dog. This discovery led neuroanatomists to more closely analyze the cerebral cortex and its cellular organization; they wanted support for their ideas about the importance of local regions. Because these regions performed different functions, it followed that they ought to look different at the cellular level.

Following this logic, German neuroanatomists began to analyze the brain by using microscopic methods to view the cell types in different brain regions. Perhaps the most famous of the group was Korbinian Brodmann, who analyzed the cellular organization of the cortex and characterized 52 distinct regions (Figure 1.9). He published his cortical maps in 1909. Brodmann used tissue stains, such as the one developed by Franz Nissl, that permitted him to visualize the different cell types in different brain regions. How cells differ between brain regions is called **cytoarchitectonics**, or *cellular architecture*.

Soon many now-famous anatomists, including Oskar Vogt, Vladimir Betz, Theodor Meynert, Constantin von

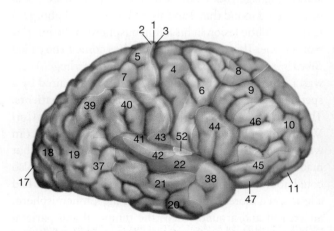

FIGURE 1.9 Sampling of the 52 distinct areas described by Brodmann on the basis of cell structure and arrangement.

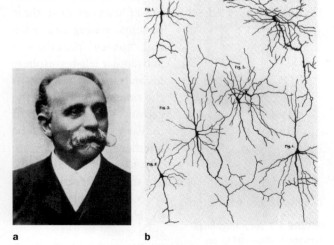

a

b

FIGURE 1.10 (a) Camillo Golgi (1843–1926), cowinner of the Nobel Prize in 1906. **(b)** Golgi's drawings of different types of ganglion cells in dog and cat.

Economo, Gerhardt von Bonin, and Percival Bailey, contributed to this work, and several subdivided the cortex even further than Brodmann had. To a large extent, these investigators discovered that various cytoarchitectonically described brain areas do indeed represent functionally distinct brain regions. For example, Brodmann first distinguished area 17 from area 18—a distinction that has proved correct in subsequent functional studies. The characterization of the primary visual area of the cortex, area 17, as distinct from surrounding area 18, remarkably demonstrates the power of the cytoarchitectonic approach, as we will consider more fully in Chapter 2.

Despite all of this groundbreaking work in cytoarchitectonics, the truly huge revolution in our understanding of the nervous system was taking place elsewhere, in Italy and Spain. There, an intense struggle was going on between two brilliant neuroanatomists. Oddly, it was the work of one that led to the insights of the other. Camillo Golgi (Figure 1.10), an Italian physician, developed one of the most famous cell stains in the history of the world: the silver method for staining neurons—*la reazione nera*, "the black reaction," that impregnated individual neurons with silver chromate. This stain permits visualization of individual neurons in their entirety. Using Golgi's method, Santiago Ramón y Cajal (Figure 1.11) went on to find that, contrary to the view of Golgi and others, neurons were discrete entities. Golgi had believed that the whole brain was a **syncytium**, a continuous mass of tissue that shares a common cytoplasm. Ramón y Cajal, who some call the father of modern neuroscience, was the first to identify the unitary nature of neurons and to articulate what came to be known as the **neuron doctrine**, the concept that the nervous system is made up of individual cells. He also recognized that the transmission of electrical information

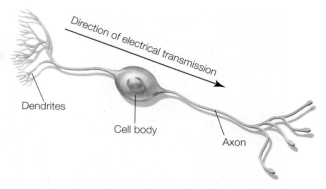

FIGURE 1.12 A bipolar retinal cell, illustrating the dendrites and axon of the neuron.

went in only one direction, from the dendrites down to the axonal tip (Figure 1.12).

Many gifted scientists were involved in the early history of the neuron doctrine (Shepherd, 1991). For example, Jan Evangelista Purkinje (Figure 1.13), a Czech, not only described the first nerve cell in the nervous system in 1837 but also invented the stroboscope, described common visual phenomena, and made

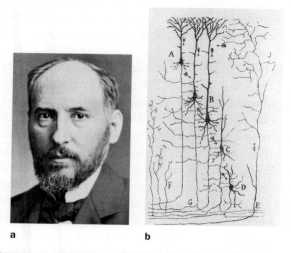

FIGURE 1.11 (a) Santiago Ramón y Cajal (1852–1934), cowinner of the Nobel Prize in 1906. (b) Ramón y Cajal's drawing of the afferent inflow to the mammalian cortex.

FIGURE 1.13 (a) Jan Evangelista Purkinje (1787–1869), who described the first nerve cell in the nervous system. (b) A Purkinje cell of the cerebellum.

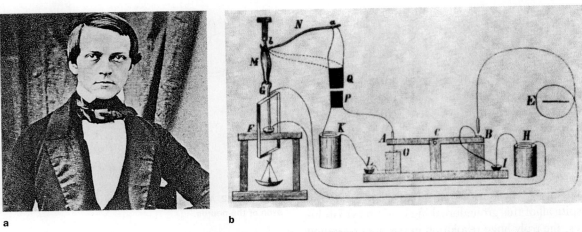

FIGURE 1.14 (a) Hermann Ludwig von Helmholtz (1821–1894). **(b)** Helmholtz's apparatus for measuring the velocity of nerve conduction.

a host of other major discoveries. Hermann von Helmholtz (Figure 1.14) figured out that electrical current in the cell was not a by-product of cellular activity, but the medium that was actually carrying information along the axon of a nerve cell. He was also the first to suggest that invertebrates would be good models for studying vertebrate brain mechanisms. British physiologist Sir Charles Sherrington vigorously pursued the neuron's behavior as a unit and, indeed, coined the term *synapse* to describe the junction between two neurons.

With Golgi, Ramón y Cajal, and these other bright minds, the neuron doctrine was born—a discovery whose importance was highlighted by the 1906 Nobel Prize in Physiology or Medicine shared by Golgi and Ramón y Cajal, and later by the 1932 Nobel Prize awarded to Sherrington.

As the 20th century progressed, the localizationist views were mediated by those who saw that, even though particular neuronal locations might serve independent functions, the network of these locations and the interaction between them are what yield the integrated, holistic behavior that humans exhibit. Once again this neglected idea had previously been discussed nearly a century earlier by the French biologist Claude Bernard, who wrote in 1865:

> If it is possible to dissect all the parts of the body, to isolate them in order to study them in their structure, form and connections it is not the same in life, where all parts cooperate at the same time in a common aim. An organ does not live on its own, one could often say it did not exist anatomically, as the boundary established is sometimes purely arbitrary. What lives, what exists, is the whole, and if one studies all the parts of any mechanisms separately, one does not know the way they work.

Thus, scientists have come to believe that the knowledge of the parts (the neurons and brain structures) must be understood in conjunction with the whole (i.e., what the parts make when they come together: the mind). Next we explore the history of research on the mind.

The Psychological Story

Physicians were the early pioneers studying how the brain worked. In 1869 a Dutch ophthalmologist, Franciscus Donders, was the first to propose the now-common method of using differences in reaction times to infer differences in cognitive processing. He suggested that the difference in the amount of time it took to react to a light and the amount of time needed to react to a particular color of light was the amount of time required for the process of identifying a color. Psychologists began to use this approach, claiming that they could study the mind by measuring behavior, and experimental psychology was born.

Before the start of experimental psychological science the mind had been the province of philosophers, who wondered about the nature of knowledge and how we come to know things. The philosophers had two main positions: **rationalism** and **empiricism**. Rationalism grew out of the Enlightenment period and held that all knowledge could be gained through the use of reason alone: Truth was intellectual, not sensory. Through thinking, then, rationalists would determine true beliefs and would reject beliefs that, although perhaps comforting, were unsupportable and even superstitious. Among intellectuals and scientists, rationalism replaced religion and became the only way to think about the world. In particular, this view, in one form or another,

MILESTONES IN COGNITIVE NEUROSCIENCE
Interlude

In textbook writing, authors use broad strokes to communicate milestones that have become important to people's thinking over a long period of time. It would be folly, however, not to alert the reader that these scientific advances took place in a complex and intriguing cultural, intellectual, and personal setting. The social problems that besieged the world's first scientists remain today, in full glory: Issues of authorship, ego, funding, and credit are all integral to the fabric of intellectual life. Much as teenagers never imagine that their parents once had the same interests, problems, and desires as they do, novitiates in science believe they are tackling new issues for the first time in human history. Gordon Shepherd (1991), in his riveting account *Foundations of the Neuron Doctrine*, detailed the variety of forces at work on the figures we now feature in our brief history.

Shepherd noted how the explosion of research on the nervous system started in the 18th century as part of the intense activity swirling around the birth of modern science. As examples, Robert Fulton invented the steam engine in 1807, and Hans Christian Ørsted discovered electromagnetism. Of more interest to our concerns, Leopoldo Nobili, an Italian physicist, invented a precursor to the galvanometer—a device that laid the foundation for studying electrical currents in living tissue. Many years before, in 1674, Anton van Leeuwenhoek in Holland had used a primitive microscope to view animal tissue (Figure 1). One of his first observations was of a cross section of a cow's nerve in which he noted "very minute vessels." This observation was consistent with René Descartes's idea that nerves contained fluid or "spirits," and these spirits were responsible for the flow of sensory and motor information in the body (Figure 2). To go further, however, this revolutionary work would have to overcome the technical problems with early microscopes, not the least of which was the quality of glass used in the lens. Chromatic aberrations made them useless at higher magnification. It was not until lens makers solved this problem that microscopic anatomy again took center stage in the history of biology.

FIGURE 1 (a) Anton van Leeuwenhoek (1632–1723). (b) One of the original microscopes used by Leeuwenhoek, composed of two brass plates holding the lens.

FIGURE 2 René Descartes (1596–1650). Portrait by Frans Hals.

was supported by René Descartes, Baruch Spinoza, and Gottfried Leibniz.

Although rationalism is frequently equated with logical thinking, the two are not identical. Rationalism considers such issues as the meaning of life, whereas logic does not. Logic simply relies on inductive reasoning, statistics, probabilities, and the like. It does not concern itself with personal mental states like happiness, self-interest, and public good. Each person weighs these issues differently, and as a consequence, a rational decision is more problematic than a simple logical decision.

Empiricism, on the other hand, is the idea that all knowledge comes from sensory experience, that the brain began life as a blank slate. Direct sensory experience produces simple ideas and concepts. When simple ideas interact and become *associated* with one another, complex ideas and concepts are created in an individual's knowledge system. The British philosophers—from

FIGURE 1.15 Edward L. Thorndike (1874–1949).

Thomas Hobbes in the 17th century, through John Locke and David Hume, to John Stuart Mill in the 19th century—all emphasized the role of experience. It is no surprise, then, that a major school of experimental psychology arose from this associationist view. Psychological associationists believed that the aggregate of a person's experience determined the course of mental development.

One of the first scientists to study **associationism** was Hermann Ebbinghaus, who, in the late 1800s, decided that complex processes like memory could be measured and analyzed. He took his lead from the great psychophysicists Gustav Fechner and Ernst Heinrich Weber, who were hard at work relating the physical properties of things such as light and sound to the psychological experiences that they produce in the observer. These measurements were rigorous and reproducible. Ebbinghaus was one of the first to understand that mental processes that are more internal, such as memory, also could be measured (see Chapter 9).

Even more influential to the shaping of the associationist view was the classic 1911 monograph *Animal Intelligence: An Experimental Study of the Associative Processes in Animals*, by Edward Thorndike (Figure 1.15). In this volume, Thorndike articulated his law of effect, which was the first general statement about the nature of associations. Thorndike simply observed that a response that was followed by a reward would be stamped into the organism as a habitual response. If no reward followed a response, the response would disappear. Thus, rewards provided a mechanism for establishing a more adaptive response.

Associationism came to be dominated by American behavioral psychologist John B. Watson (Figure 1.16), who proposed that psychology could be objective only if it were based on observable behavior. He rejected Ebbinghaus's methods and declared that all talk of mental processes, which cannot be publicly observed, should be avoided. Associationism became committed to an idea widely popularized by Watson that he could turn any baby into anything. Learning was the key, he proclaimed, and everybody had the same neural equipment on which learning could build. Appealing to the American sense of equality, American psychology was giddy with this idea of the brain as a *blank slate* upon which to build through learning and experience, and every prominent psychology department in the country was run by people who held this view.

Behaviorist–associationist psychology went on despite the already well-established position—first articulated by Descartes, Leibniz, Kant, and others—that complexity is built into the human organism. Sensory information is merely data on which preexisting mental structures act. This idea, which dominates psychology today, was blithely asserted in that golden age, and later forgotten or ignored.

Although American psychologists were focused on behaviorism, the psychologists in Britain and Canada were not. Montreal became a hot spot for new ideas on how biology shapes cognition and behavior. In 1928, Wilder Penfield (Figure 1.17), an American who had studied neuropathology with Sir Charles Sherrington at Oxford,

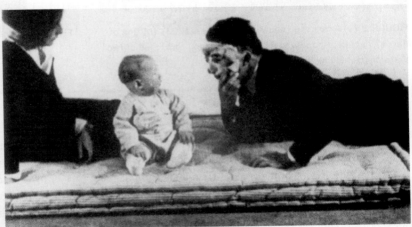

a   b

FIGURE 1.16 (a) John B. Watson (1878–1958). **(b)** Watson and "Little Albert" during one of Watson's fear-conditioning experiments.

FIGURE 1.17 Wilder Penfield
(1891–1976).

FIGURE 1.18 Donald O. Hebb
(1904–1985).

FIGURE 1.19 Brenda Milner
(1918–).

FIGURE 1.20 George A. Miller
(1920–2012).

became that city's first neurosurgeon. In collaboration with Herbert Jasper, he invented the **Montreal procedure** for treating epilepsy, in which he surgically destroyed the neurons in the brain that produced the seizures. To determine which cells to destroy, Penfield stimulated various parts of the brain with electrical probes and observed the results on the patients—who were awake, lying on the operating table under local anesthesia only. From these observations, he was able to create maps of the sensory and motor cortices in the brain (Penfield & Jasper, 1954) that Hughlings Jackson had predicted over half a century earlier.

Soon he was joined by a Nova Scotian psychologist, Donald Hebb (Figure 1.18), who spent time working with Penfield studying the effects of brain surgery and injury on the functioning of the brain. Hebb became convinced that the workings of the brain explained behavior and that the psychology and biology of an organism could not be separated. Although this idea—which kept popping up only to be swept under the carpet again and again over the past few hundred years—is well accepted now, Hebb was a maverick at the time. In 1949 he published a book, *The Organization of Behavior: A Neuropsychological Theory* (Hebb, 1949), that rocked the psychological world. In it he postulated that learning had a biological basis. The well-known neuroscience mantra "cells that fire together, wire together" is a distillation of his proposal that neurons can combine together into a single processing unit and the connection patterns of these units make up the ever-changing algorithms determining the brain's response to a stimulus. He pointed out that the brain is active all the time, not just when stimulated by an impulse, and that inputs from the outside can only modify the ongoing activity. Hebb's theory was subsequently used in the design of artificial neural networks.

Hebb's British graduate student, Brenda Milner (Figure 1.19), continued the behavioral studies on Penfield's patients, both before and after their surgery.

When patients began to complain about mild memory loss after surgery, she became interested in memory and was the first to provide anatomical and physiological proof that there are multiple memory systems. Brenda Milner, 60 years later, is still associated with the Montreal Neurological Institute and has seen a world of change sweep across the study of brain, mind, and behavior. She was in the vanguard of cognitive neuroscience as well as one of the first in a long line of influential women in the field.

The true end of the dominance of **behaviorism** and stimulus–response psychology in America did not come until the late 1950s. Psychologists began to think in terms of cognition, not just behavior. George Miller (Figure 1.20), who had been a confirmed behaviorist, had a change of heart in the 1950s. In 1951, Miller wrote an influential book entitled *Language and Communication* and noted in the preface, "The bias is behavioristic." Eleven years later he wrote another book, called *Psychology, the Science of Mental Life*—a title that signals a complete rejection of the idea that psychology should study only behavior.

Upon reflection, Miller determined that the exact date of his rejection of behaviorism and his cognitive awakening was September 11, 1956, during the second Symposium on Information Theory, held at the Massachusetts Institute of Technology (MIT). That year had been a rich one for several disciplines. In computer science, Allen Newell and Herbert Simon successfully introduced Information Processing Language I, a powerful program that simulated the proof of logic theorems. The computer guru John von Neumann wrote the Silliman lectures on neural organization, in which he considered the possibility that the brain's computational activities were similar to a massively parallel computer. A famous meeting on artificial intelligence was held at Dartmouth College, where Marvin Minsky, Claude Shannon (known as the father of information theory), and many others were in attendance.

FIGURE 1.21 Noam Chomsky (1928–).

FIGURE 1.22 Patricia Goldman-Rakic (1937–2003).

Big things were also happening in psychology. Signal detection and computer techniques, developed in World War II to help the U.S. Department of Defense detect submarines, were now being applied by psychologists James Tanner and John Swets to study perception. In 1956, Miller wrote his classic and entertaining paper, "The Magical Number Seven, Plus-or-Minus Two," in which he showed that there is a limit to the amount of information that can be apprehended in a brief period of time. Attempting to reckon this amount of information led Miller to Noam Chomsky's work (Figure 1.21; for a review see Chomsky, 2006), where he came across, perhaps, the most important development to the field. Chomsky showed him how the sequential predictability of speech follows from adherence to grammatical, not probabilistic, rules. A preliminary version of Chomsky's ideas on syntactic theories, published in September 1956 in an article titled, "Three Models for the Description of Language," transformed the study of language virtually overnight. The deep message that Miller gleaned was that learning theory—that is, associationism, then heavily championed by B. F. Skinner—could in no way explain how language was learned. The complexity of language was built into the brain, and it ran on rules and principles that transcended all people and all languages. It was innate and it was universal. Thus, on September 11, 1956, after a year of great development and theory shifting, Miller realized that, although behaviorism had important theories to offer, it could not explain all learning. He then set out to understand the psychological implications of Chomsky's theories by using psychological testing methods. His ultimate goal was to understand how the brain works as an integrated whole—to understand the workings of the brain *and* the mind. Many followed his new mission, and a few years later a new field was born: cognitive neuroscience.

What has come to be a hallmark of cognitive neuroscience is that it is made up of an *insalata mista* ("mixed salad") of different disciplines. Miller had stuck his nose into the worlds of linguistics and computer science and come out with revelations for psychology and neuroscience. In the same vein, in the 1970s Patricia Goldman-Rakic (Figure 1.22) put together a multidisciplinary team of people working in biochemistry, anatomy, electrophysiology, pharmacology, and behavior. She was curious about one of Milner's memory systems, working memory, and chose to ignore the behaviorists' claim that the prefrontal cortex's higher cognitive function could not be studied. As a result, she produced the first description of the circuitry of the prefrontal cortex and how it relates to working memory (Goldman-Rakic, 1987). Later she discovered that individual cells in the prefrontal cortex are dedicated to specific memory tasks, such as remembering a face or a voice. She also performed the first studies on the influence of dopamine on the prefrontal cortex. Her findings caused a phase shift in the understanding of many mental illnesses—including schizophrenia, which previously had been thought to be the result of bad parenting.

The Instruments of Neuroscience

Changes in electrical impulses, fluctuations in blood flow, and shifts in utilization of oxygen and glucose are the driving forces of the brain's business. They are also the parameters that are measured and analyzed in the various methods used to study how mental activities are supported by brain functions. The advances in technology and the invention of these methods have provided cognitive neuroscientists the tools to study how the brain enables the mind. Without these instruments, the discoveries made in the past 40 years would not have been possible. In this section, we provide a brief history of the people, ideas, and inventions behind some of the noninvasive techniques used in cognitive neuroscience. Many of these methods and their current applications are discussed in greater detail in Chapter 3.

The Electroencephalograph

In 1875, shortly after Hermann von Helmholtz figured out that it was actually an electrical impulse wave that carried messages along the axon of a nerve, British scientist Richard Canton used a galvanometer to measure continuous spontaneous electrical activity from the cerebral cortex and skull surface of live dogs and apes. A fancier version, the "string galvanometer," designed by a Dutch physician, Willem Einthoven, was able to make photographic recordings of the electrical activity. Using this apparatus, the German psychiatrist Hans Berger published a paper describing recordings of a human brain's electrical currents in 1929. He named the recording an electroencephalogram. Electroencephalography remained the sole technique for noninvasive brain study for a number of years.

Measuring Blood Flow in the Brain

Angelo Mosso, a 19th-century Italian physiologist, was interested in blood flow in the brain and studied patients who had skull defects as the result of neurosurgery. During these studies, he recorded pulsations as blood flowed around and through their cortex (Figure 1.23) and noticed that the pulsations of the brain increased locally during mental activities such as mathematical calculations. He inferred that blood flow followed function. These observations, however, slipped from view and were not pursued until a few decades later when in 1928 John Fulton presented the case of patient Walter K., who was evaluated for a vascular malformation that resided above his visual cortex (Figure 1.24). The patient men-

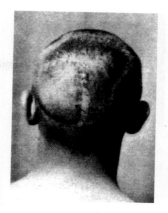

FIGURE 1.24 Walter K.'s head with a view of the skull defect over the occipital cortex.

FIGURE 1.25 Seymour S. Kety (1915–2000).

tioned that at the back of his head he heard a noise that increased when he used his eyes, but not his other senses. This noise was a bruit, the sound that blood makes when it rushes through a narrowing of its channel. Fulton concluded that blood flow to the visual cortex varied with the attention paid to surrounding objects.

Another 20 years slipped by, and Seymour Kety (Figure 1.25), a young physician at the University of Pennsylvania, realized that if you could perfuse arterial blood with an inert gas, such as nitrous oxide, then the gas would circulate through the brain and be absorbed independently of the brain's metabolic activity. Its accumulation would be dependent only on physical parameters that could be measured, such as diffusion, solubility, and perfusion. With this idea in mind, he developed a method to measure the blood flow and metabolism of the human brain as a whole. Using more drastic methods in animals (they were decapitated; their brains were then removed and analyzed), Kety was able to measure the blood flow to specific regions of the brain (Landau et al., 1955). His animal studies provided evidence that blood flow was related directly to brain function. Kety's method and results were used in developing positron emission tomography (described later in this section), which uses radiotracers rather than an inert gas.

Computerized Axial Tomography

Although blood flow was of interest to those studying brain function, having good anatomical images in order to locate tumors was motivating other developments in instrumentation. Investigators needed to be able to obtain three-dimensional views of the inside of the human body. In the 1930s, Alessandro Vallebona developed tomographic radiography, a technique in which a series of transverse sections are taken. Improving upon these

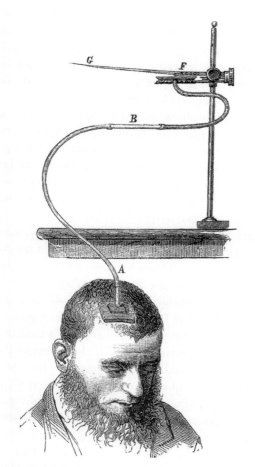

FIGURE 1.23 Angelo Mosso's experimental setup was used to measure the pulsations of the brain at the site of a skull defect.

FIGURE 1.26 Irene Joliot-Curie (1897–1956).

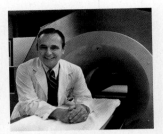

FIGURE 1.27 Michel M. Ter-Pogossian (1925–1996).

FIGURE 1.28 Michael E. Phelps (1939–).

initial attempts, UCLA neurologist William Oldendorf (1961) wrote an article outlining the first description of the basic concept later used in computerized tomography (CT), in which a series of transverse X-rays could be reconstructed into a three-dimensional picture. His concept was revolutionary, but he could not find any manufacturers willing to capitalize on his idea. It took insight and cash, which was provided by four lads from Liverpool, the company EMI, and Godfrey Newbold Hounsfield, a computer engineer who worked at the Central Research Laboratories of EMI, Ltd. EMI was an electronics firm that also owned Capitol Records and the Beatles' recording contract. Hounsfield, using mathematical techniques and multiple two-dimensional X-rays to reconstruct a three-dimensional image, developed his first scanner, and as the story goes, EMI, flush with cash from the Beatles' success, footed the bill. Hounsfield performed the first computerized axial tomography (CAT) scan in 1972.

Positron Emission Tomography and Radioactive Tracers

While CAT was great for revealing anatomical detail, it revealed little about function. Researchers at Washington University, however, used CAT as the basis for developing positron emission tomography (PET), a noninvasive sectioning technique that could provide information about function. Observations and research by a huge number of people over many years have been incorporated into what ultimately is today's PET. Its development is interwoven with that of the radioactive isotopes, aka "tracers," that it employs. We previously noted the work of Seymour Kety done in the 1940s and 1950s. A few years earlier, in 1934, Irene Joliot-Curie (Figure 1.26) and Frederic Joliot-Curie discovered that some originally nonradioactive nuclides emitted penetrating radiation after being irradiated. This observation led Ernest O. Lawrence (the inventor of the

cyclotron) and his colleagues at the University of California, Berkeley to realize that the cyclotron could be used to produce radioactive substances. If radioactive forms of oxygen, nitrogen, or carbon could be produced, then they could be injected into the blood circulation and would become incorporated into biologically active molecules. These molecules would concentrate in an organ, where the radioactivity would begin to decay. The concentration of the tracers could then be measured over time, allowing inferences about metabolism to be made.

In 1950, Gordon Brownell at Harvard University realized that positron decay (of a radioactive tracer) was associated with two gamma particles being emitted at 180 degrees. Using this handy discovery, a simple positron scanner with a pair of sodium iodide detectors was designed and built, and it was scanning patients for brain tumors in a matter of months (Sweet & Brownell, 1953). In 1959, David E. Kuhl, a radiology resident at the University of Pennsylvania, who had been dabbling with radiation since high school (did his parents know?), and Roy Edwards, an engineer, combined tomography with gamma-emitting radioisotopes and obtained the first emission tomographic image.

The problem with most radioactive isotopes of nitrogen, oxygen, carbon, and fluorine is that their half-lives are measured in minutes. Anyone who was going to use them had to have their own cyclotron and be ready to roll as the isotopes were created. It happened that Washington University had both a cyclotron that produced radioactive oxygen-15 (^{15}O) and two researchers, Michel Ter-Pogossian and William Powers, who were interested in using it. They found that when injected into the bloodstream, ^{15}O-labeled water could be used to measure blood flow in the brain (Ter-Pogossian & Powers, 1958). Ter-Pogossian (Figure 1.27) was joined in the 1970s by Michael Phelps (Figure 1.28), a graduate student who had started out his career as a Golden Gloves boxer. Excited about X-ray CT, they thought that they could adapt the technique to reconstruct the distribution within an organ of a short-lived "physiological" radionuclide from its emissions. They designed and constructed the first positron emission tomograph, dubbed PETT (positron emission transaxial tomography; Ter-Pogossian et al., 1975), which later was shortened to PET.

Another metabolically important molecule in the brain is glucose. Under the direction of Joanna Fowler and Al

Wolf, using Brookhaven National Laboratory's powerful cyclotron, ^{18}F-labeled 2-fluorodeoxy-D-glucose (2FDG) was created (Ido et al., 1978). [18]F has a half-life that is amenable for PET imaging and can give precise values of energy metabolism in the brain. The first work using PET to look for neural correlates of human behavior began when Phelps joined Kuhl at the University of Pennsylvania and together, using 2FDG, they established a method for imaging the tissue consumption of glucose. Phelps, in a leap of insight, invented the block detector, a device that eventually increased spatial resolution of PET from 3 centimeters to 3 millimeters.

Magnetic Resonance Imaging

Magnetic resonance imaging (MRI) is based on the principle of nuclear magnetic resonance, which was first described and measured by Isidor Rabi in 1938. Discoveries made independently in 1946 by Felix Bloch at Harvard University and Edward Purcell at Stanford University expanded the understanding of nuclear magnetic resonance to liquids and solids. For example, the protons in a water molecule line up like little bar magnets when placed in a magnetic field. If the equilibrium of these protons is disturbed by zapping them with radio frequency pulses, then a measurable voltage is induced in a receiver coil. The voltage changes over time as a function of the proton's environment. By analyzing the voltages, information about the examined tissue can be deduced.

In 1971, while Paul Lauterbur (Figure 1.29) was on sabbatical, he was thinking grand thoughts as he ate a fast-food hamburger. He scribbled his ideas on a nearby napkin, and from these humble beginnings he developed the theoretical model that led to the invention of the first magnetic resonance imaging scanner, located at The State University of New York at Stony Brook (Lauterbur, 1973). (Lauterbur won the 2003 Nobel Prize in Physiology or Medicine, but his first attempt at publishing his findings was rejected by the journal *Nature*. He later quipped, "You could write the entire history of science in the last 50 years in terms of papers rejected by *Science* or *Nature*" [Wade, 2003]). It was another 20 years, however, before MRI was used to investigate brain function. This happened when researchers at Massachusetts General Hospital demonstrated that following the injection of contrast material into the bloodstream, changes in the blood volume of a human brain, produced by physiological manipulation of blood flow, could be measured using MRI (Belliveau et al., 1990). Not only were excellent anatomical images produced, but they could be combined with physiology germane to brain function.

FIGURE 1.29 Paul Lauterbur (1929–2007).

Functional Magnetic Resonance Imaging

When PET was introduced, the conventional wisdom was that increased blood flow to differentially active parts of the brain was driven by the brain's need for more oxygen. An increase in oxygen delivery permitted more glucose to be metabolized, and thus more energy would be available for performing the task. Although this idea sounded reasonable, little data were available to back it up. In fact, if this proposal were true, then increases in blood flow induced by functional demands should be equivalent to the increase in oxygen consumption. This would mean that the ratio of oxygenated to deoxygenated hemoglobin should stay constant. PET data, however, did not back this up (Raichle, 2008). Instead, Peter Fox and Marc Raichle, at Washington University, found that although functional activity induced increases in blood flow, there was no corresponding increase in oxygen consumption (Fox & Raichle, 1986). In addition, more glucose was being used than would be predicted from the amount of oxygen consumed (Fox et al., 1988). What was up with that? Raichle (2008) relates that oddly enough, a random scribble written in the margin of Michael Faraday's lab notes in 1845 (Faraday, 1933) provided the hint that led to the solution of this puzzle. It was Linus Pauling and Charles Coryell who somehow happened upon this clue.

Faraday had noted that dried blood was not magnetic and in the margin of his notes had written that he must try fluid blood. He was puzzled because hemoglobin contains iron. Ninety years later, Pauling and Coryell (1936), after reading Faraday's notes, became curious too. They found that indeed oxygenated and deoxygenated hemoglobin behaved very differently in a magnetic field. Deoxygenated hemoglobin is weakly magnetic due to the exposed iron in the hemoglobin molecule. Years later, Kerith Thulborn (1982) remembered and capitalized on this property described by Pauling and Coryell, realizing that it was feasible to measure the state of oxygenation in vivo. Seiji Ogawa (1990) and his colleagues at AT&T Bell Laboratories tried manipulating oxygen levels by administering 100 % oxygen alternated with room air (21 % oxygen) to human subjects who were undergoing MRI. They discovered that on room air, the structure of the

Air   **O₂**

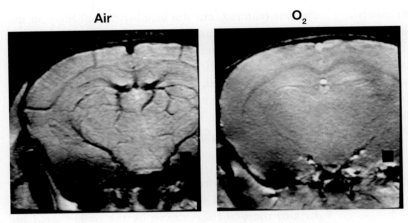

FIGURE 1.30 Images of a mouse brain under varying oxygen conditions.

venous system was visible due to the contrast provided by the deoxygenated hemoglobin that was present. On 100% O_2, however, the venous system completely disappeared (Figure 1.30). Thus contrast depended on the blood oxygen level. BOLD (blood oxygen level–dependent) contrast was born. This technique led to the development of functional magnetic resonance imaging (fMRI). MRI does not use ionizing radiation, it combines beautifully detailed images of the body with physiology related to brain function, and it is sensitive (Figure 1.31). With all of these advantages, it did not take long for MRI and fMRI to be adopted by the research community, resulting in explosive growth of functional brain imaging.

Machines are useful, however, only if you know what to do with them and what their limitations are.

Raichle understood the potential of these new scanning methods, but he also realized that some basic problems had to be solved. If generalized information about brain function and anatomy were to be obtained, then the scans from different individuals performing the same tasks under the same circumstances had to be comparable. This was proving difficult, however, since no two brains are precisely the same size and shape. Furthermore, early data was yielding a mishmash of results that varied in anatomical location from person to person. Eric Reiman, a psychiatrist working with Raichle, suggested that averaging blood flow across subjects might solve this problem. The results of this approach were clear and unambiguous (Fox, 1988). This landmark paper presented the first integrated approach for the design, execution, and interpretation of functional brain images.

But what can be learned about the brain and the behavior of a human when a person is lying prone in a scanner? Cognitive psychologists Michael Posner, Steve Petersen, and Gordon Shulman, at Washington University, developed innovative experimental paradigms, including the cognitive subtraction method (first proposed by Donders), for use while PET scanning. The methodology was soon applied to fMRI. This joining together of cognitive psychology's experimental methods with brain imaging was the beginning of human functional brain mapping. Throughout this book, we will

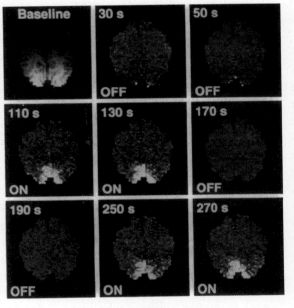

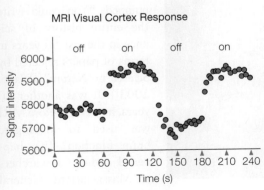

MRI Visual Cortex Response

a   b

FIGURE 1.31 An early set of fMRI images showing activation of the human visual cortex.

draw from the wealth of brain imaging data that has been amassed in the last 30 years in our quest to learn about how the brain enables the mind.

The Book in Your Hands

Our goals in this book are to introduce you to the big questions and discussions in cognitive neuroscience and to teach you how to think, ask questions, and approach those questions like a cognitive neuroscientist. In the next chapter, we introduce the biological foundations of the brain by presenting an overview of its cellular mechanisms and neuroanatomy. In Chapter 3 we discuss the methods that are available to us for observing mind–brain relationships, and we introduce how scientists go about interpreting and questioning those observations. Building on this foundation, we launch into the core processes of cognition: hemispheric specialization, sensation and perception, object recognition, attention, the control of action, learning and memory, emotion, and language, devoting a chapter to each. These are followed by chapters on cognition control, social cognition, and a new chapter for this edition on consciousness, free will, and the law.

Each chapter begins with a story that illustrates and introduces the chapter's main topic. Beginning with Chapter 4, the story is followed by an anatomical orientation highlighting the portions of the brain that we know are involved in these processes, and a description of what a deficit of that process would result in. Next, the heart of the chapter focuses on a discussion of the cognitive process and what is known about how it functions, followed by a summary and suggestions for further reading for those whose curiosity has been aroused.

Summary

Thomas Willis first introduced us, in the mid 1600s, to the idea that damage to the brain could influence behavior and that the cerebral cortex might indeed be the seat of what makes us human. Phrenologists expanded on this idea and developed a localizationist view of the brain. Patients like those of Broca and Wernicke later supported the importance of specific brain locations on human behavior (like language). Ramón y Cajal, Sherrington, and Brodmann, among others, provided evidence that although the microarchitecture of distinct brain regions could support a localizationist view of the brain, these areas are interconnected. Soon scientists began to realize that the integration of the brain's neural networks might be what enables the mind.

At the same time that neuroscientists were researching the brain, psychologists were studying the mind. Out of the philosophical theory of empiricism came the idea of associationism, that any response followed by a reward would be maintained and that these associations were the basis of how the mind learned. Associationism was the prevailing theory for many years, until Hebb emphasized the biological basis of learning, and Chomsky and Miller realized that associationism couldn't explain all learning or all actions of the mind.

Neuroscientists and psychologists both reached the conclusion that there is more to the brain than just the sum of its parts, that the brain must enable the mind—but how? The term *cognitive neuroscience* was coined in the late 1970s because fields of neuroscience and psychology were once again coming together. Neuroscience was in need of the theories of the psychology of the mind, and psychology was ready for a greater understanding of the working of the brain. The resulting marriage is cognitive neuroscience.

The last half of the 20th century saw a blossoming of interdisciplinary research that produced both new approaches and new technologies resulting in noninvasive methods of imaging brain structure, metabolism, and function.

So welcome to cognitive neuroscience. It doesn't matter what your background is, you're welcome here.

Key Terms

aggregate field theory (p. 7)
associationism (p. 12)
behaviorism (p. 13)
cognitive neuroscience (p. 4)

cytoarchitectonics (p. 8)
empiricism (p. 10)
Montreal procedure (p. 13)
neuron doctrine (p. 9)

phrenology (p. 6)
rationalism (p. 10)
syncytium (p. 9)

Thought Questions

1. Can we study how the mind works without studying the brain?

2. Will modern brain-imaging experiments become the new phrenology?

3. How do you think the brain might be studied in the future?

4. Why do good ideas and theories occasionally get lost over the passage of time? How do they often get rediscovered?

Suggested Reading

Kass-Simon, G., & Farnes, P. (1990). *Women of science: Righting the record.* Bloomington: Indiana University Press.

Lindzey, G. (Ed.). (1936). *History of psychology in autobiography* (Vol. 3). Worcester, MA: Clark University Press.

Miller, G. (2003). The cognitive revolution: A historical perspective. *Trends in Cognitive Sciences, 7,* 141–144.

Raichle, M. E. (1998). Behind the scenes of functional brain imaging: A historical and physiological perspective. *Proceedings of the National Academy of Sciences, USA, 95,* 765–772.

Shepherd, G. M. (1991). *Foundations of the neuron doctrine.* New York: Oxford University Press.

Zimmer, C. (2004). *Soul made flesh: The discovery of the brain—and how it changed the world.* New York: Free Press.

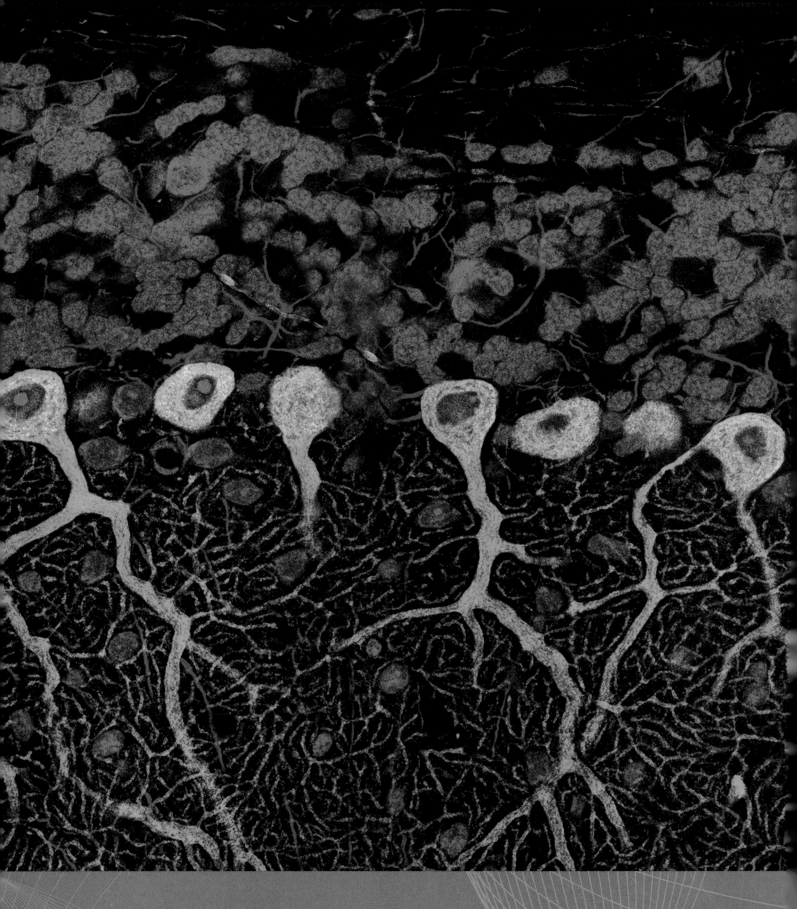

You shake my nerves and you rattle my brain.

Jerry Lee Lewis

Structure and Function of the Nervous System

ONE DAY IN 1963, neuroscientist Jose Delgado coolly stood in a bullring in Cordoba, Spain, facing a charging bull. He did not sport the Spanish matador's typical gear of toreador pants, jacket, and sword, however. No theoretical scientist he, Delgado stepped into the ring in slacks and a pullover sweater while holding a small device in his hand (and a cape, for good effect). He was about to see if it worked. As the bull came charging toward him, Delgado stood his ground, trigger finger itchy on the device's button. And then he calmly pushed it. The bull slammed on the brakes and skidded to a stop, standing a few feet before the scientist (Figure 2.1). The bull placidly looked at the smiling Delgado. Seemingly, this was no ordinary bull; but yet it was. One odd thing about this bull, however, gave Delgado his confidence: An electric stimulator had been surgically implanted in its caudate nucleus. The device in Delgado's hand was a transmitter he had built to activate the stimulator. By stimulating the bull's caudate nucleus, Delgado had turned off its aggression.

Years before, Delgado had been horrified by the increasingly popular frontal lobotomy surgical procedure that destroyed brain tissue and function. He was interested in finding a more conservative approach to treating mental disorders through electrical stimulation. Using his knowledge of the electrical nature of neurons, neuroanatomy, and brain function, he designed his devices, the first neural implants ever to be used. Exceedingly controversial at the time, his devices were the forerunners of the now common intracranial devices used for stimulating the brain to treat disorders like Parkinson's disease, chronic pain, and other maladies.

Delgado understood that our nervous system uses electrochemical energy for communication and that nerves can be thought of as glorified electrical cables running to and from our brains. He also understood that inside our brains, neurons form an intricate wiring pattern: An electrical signal initiated at one location could travel to another location to trigger a muscle to contract or initiate a behavior, such as aggression, to arise or cease. Delgado was banking on the hope that he had figured out the correct circuit involved in aggressive behavior. Delgado's device was built with the knowledge that neurons use electrochemical signals to communicate. This knowledge is the foundation on which all theories of neuronal signaling are built. Thus, for us, it is important to understand the basic physiology of neurons and the anatomy of the nervous system, which is what this chapter discusses. In many of the following chapters, we will look at what

FIGURE 2.1 Jose Delgado halting a charging bull by remote control.

results from the activity within and among specific circuits (i.e., perception, cognition, emotion, action).

Since all theories of how the brain enables the mind must ultimately mesh with the actual nuts and bolts of the nervous system, we need to understand the basics of its organizational structure, function, and modes of communication. In this chapter, we begin with the anatomy of the neuron and an overview of how information is transferred both within a neuron, and from one neuron to the next. Then, we turn to the bigger picture. Our neurons are strung together into circuits that form the brain and extend out to form the entire nervous system. We survey the anatomy and functions of the brain and the nervous system. Finally, we look at the development of the nervous system—prenatally, in the years following birth, and in adults.

The Structure of Neurons

The nervous system is composed of two main classes of cells: neurons and glial cells. **Neurons** are the basic signaling units that transmit information throughout the nervous system. As Ramón y Cajal and others of his time deduced, neurons take in information, make a "decision" about it following some relatively simple rules, and then, by changes in their activity levels, pass it along to other neurons. Neurons vary in their form, location, and interconnectivity within the nervous system (Figure 2.2), and these variations are closely related to their functions.

Glial cells are nonneural cells that serve various functions in the nervous system, some of which are only now being elucidated. These include providing structural support and electrical insulation to neurons, and modulating neuronal activity. We begin with a look at neuronal structure and function, and then we return to glial cells.

The standard cellular components found in almost all eukaryotic cells are found in neurons as well. A cell membrane encases the cell body (in neurons, it is sometimes called the

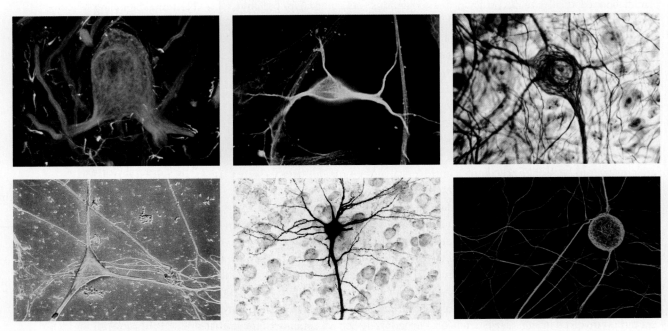

FIGURE 2.2 Mammalian neurons show enormous anatomical variety.
(Clockwise from upper left) Neuron from the vestibular area of the brain—glial cells are the thin white structures (confocal light micrograph); Hippocampal neuron (fluorescent micrograph); Mouse neuron and spinal cord ganglia (transmission electron micrograph); Multipolar neuron cell body from human cerebral cortex (scanning electron micrograph); Neuron from the brain; Nerve culture from dorsal root ganglia of an embryonic rat (fluorescent micrograph).

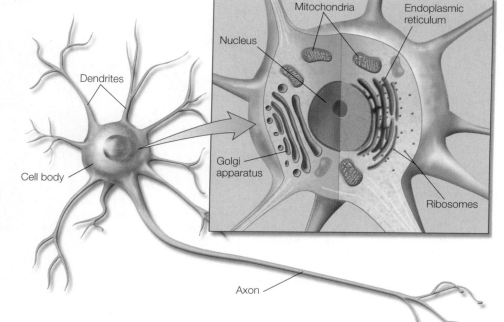

FIGURE 2.3 Idealized mammalian neuron.
A neuron is composed of three main parts: a cell body, dendrites, and an axon. The cell body contains the cellular machinery for the production of proteins and other cellular macromolecules. Like other cells, the neuron contains a nucleus, endoplasmic reticulum, ribosomes, mitochondria, Golgi apparatus, and other intracellular organelles (inset). The dendrites and axon are extensions of the cell membrane and contain cytoplasm continuous with that in the cell body.

soma; Greek for "body"), which contains the metabolic machinery that maintains the neuron: a nucleus, endoplasmic reticulum, a cytoskeleton, mitochondria, Golgi apparatus, and other common intracellular organelles (Figure 2.3). These structures are suspended in cytoplasm, the salty intracellular fluid that is made up of a combination of ions, predominantly ions of potassium, sodium, chloride, and calcium, as well as molecules such as proteins. The neuron, like any other cell, sits in a bath of salty extracellular fluid, which is also made up of a mixture of the same types of ions.

Neurons, unlike other cells, possess unique cytological features and physiological properties that enable them to transmit and process information rapidly. The two predominant cellular components unique to neurons are the dendrites and axon. **Dendrites** are branching extensions of the neuron that receive inputs from other neurons. They take many varied and complex forms, depending on the type and location of the neuron. The arborizations may look like the branches and twigs of an old oak tree, as seen in the complex dendritic structures of the cerebellar Purkinje cells (Figure 2.4),

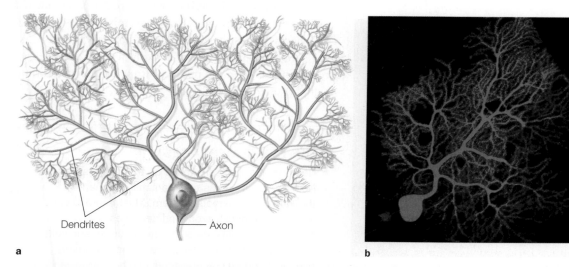

a

b

FIGURE 2.4 Soma and dendritic tree of a Purkinje cell from the cerebellum.
The Purkinje cells are arrayed in rows in the cerebellum. Each one has a large dendritic tree that is wider in one direction than the other. **(a)** Sagittal section through a cerebellar cortex showing a Purkinje cell. **(b)** Confocal micrograph of a Purkinje cell from mouse cerebellum. The cell is visualized using flourescence methods.

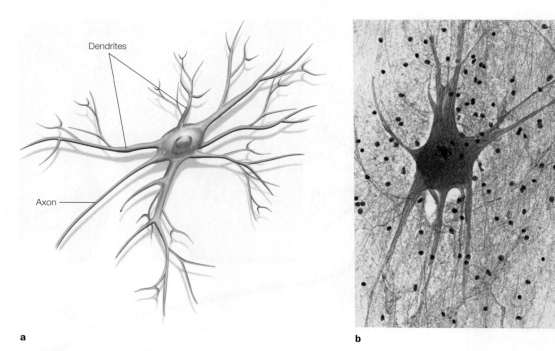

Dendrites

Axon

a

b

FIGURE 2.5 Spinal motor neuron.
(a) Neurons located in the ventral horn of the spinal cord send their axons out the ventral root to make synapses on muscle fibers. **(b)** A spinal cord motor neuron stained with cresyl echt violet stain.

or they may be much simpler, such as the dendrites in spinal motor neurons (Figure 2.5). Many dendrites also have specialized processes called **spines**, little knobs attached by small necks to the surface of the dendrites, where the dendrites receive inputs from other neurons (Figure 2.6).

The **axon** is a single process that extends from the cell body. This structure represents the output side of the neuron. Electrical signals travel along the length of the axon to its end, the axon terminals, where the neuron transmits the signal to other neurons or other cell types. Transmission occurs at the **synapse**, a specialized structure where two neurons come into close contact so that chemical or electrical signals can be passed from one cell to the next. Some axons branch to form **axon collaterals** that can transmit signals to more than one cell (Figure 2.7). Many axons are wrapped in layers of a fatty substance called **myelin**. Along the length of the axons, there are evenly spaced gaps in the myelin. These gaps are commonly referred to as the **nodes of Ranvier** (see Figure 2.11), named after the French histologist and anatomist Louis-Antoine Ranvier, who first described them. Later, when we look at how signals move down an axon, we will explore the role of myelin and the nodes of Ranvier in accelerating signal transmission.

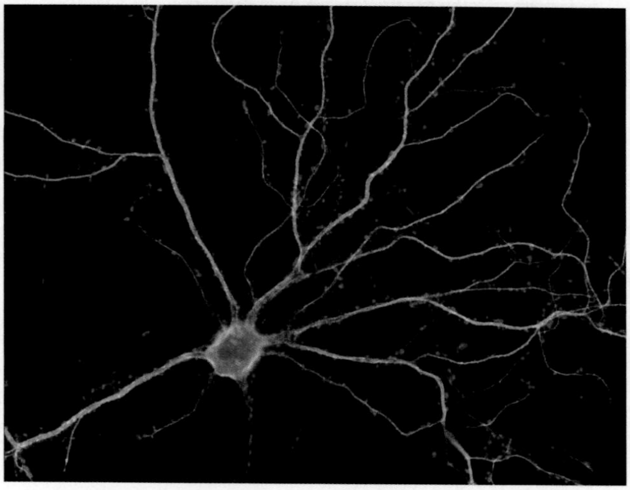

FIGURE 2.6 Dendritic spines on cultured rat hippocampal neurons.
Neuron has been triple stained to reveal the cell body (blue), dendrites (green), and the spines (red).

TAKE-HOME MESSAGES

- Neurons and glial cells make up the nervous system.
- Neurons are the cells that transmit information throughout the nervous system. Most neurons consist of a cell soma (body), axon, and dendrites.
- Neurons communicate with other neurons and cells at specialized structures called synapses, where chemical and electrical signals can be conveyed between neurons.

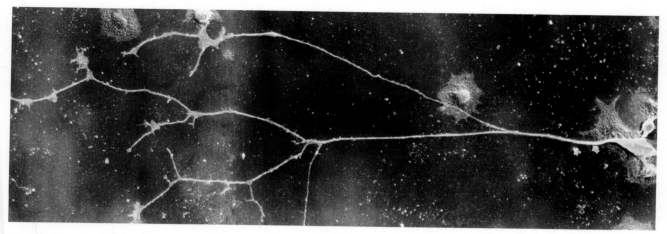

FIGURE 2.7 Axons can take different forms.
A neuron and its axon collaterals are shown stained in yellow. The cell body **(far right)** gives rise to an axon, which branches forming axon collaterals that can make contact with many different neurons.

Neuronal Signaling

Neurons receive, evaluate, and transmit information. This process is referred to as *neuronal signaling*. Information is transferred across synapses from one neuron to the next, or from a neuron to a non-neuronal cell such as those in muscles or glands. It is also conveyed within a neuron, being received at synapses on dendrites, conducted within the neuron, transmitted down the axon, and passed along at synapses on the axon terminals. These two types of transport, within and between neurons, are typically handled in different ways. Within a neuron, transferring information involves changes in the electrical state of the neuron as electrical currents flow through the volume of the neuron. Between neurons, information transfer occurs at synapses, typically mediated by chemical signaling molecules (neurotransmitters) but, in some cases, also by electrical signals. Regarding information flow, neurons are referred to as either presynaptic or postsynaptic in relation to any particular synapse. *Most neurons are both presynaptic and postsynaptic*: They are **presynaptic** when their axon makes a connection onto other neurons, and **postsynaptic** when other neurons make a connection onto their dendrites.

The Membrane Potential

The process of signaling has several stages. Let's return to Delgado's bull, because his neurons process information in the same way ours do. The bull may have been snorting about in the dirt, his head down, when suddenly a sound wave—produced by Delgado entering the ring—courses down his auditory canal and hits his tympanic membrane (eardrum). The resultant stimulation of the auditory receptor cells (auditory hair cells) generates neural signals that are transmitted via the auditory pathways to the brain. At each stage of this ascending auditory pathway, neurons receive inputs on their dendrites that typically cause them to generate signals that are transmitted to the next neuron in the pathway.

How does the neuron generate these signals, and what are these signals? To answer these questions, we have to understand several things about neurons. First, energy is needed to generate the signals; second, this energy is in the form of an electrical potential across the neuronal membrane. This electrical potential is defined as the difference in the voltage across the neuronal membrane, or put simply, the voltage inside the neuron versus outside the neuron. Third, these two voltages depend on the concentrations of potassium, sodium, and chloride ions as well as on charged protein molecules both inside and outside of the cell. Fourth, when a neuron is not actively signaling—what we call its resting state—the inside of a neuron is more negatively charged than the outside. The voltage difference across the neuronal membrane in the resting state is typically –70 millivolts (mV) inside, which is known as the *resting potential* or **resting membrane potential**. This electrical potential difference means that the neuron has at its disposal a kind of battery; and like a battery, the stored energy can be used to do work— signaling work (Figure 2.8).

How does the neuron generate and maintain this resting potential, and how does it use it for signaling? To answer these questions about function, we first need to examine the structures in the neuron that are involved in signaling. The bulk of the *neuronal membrane* is a bilayer of fatty lipid molecules that separates the cytoplasm from the extracellular milieu. Because the membrane is composed of lipids, it does not dissolve in the

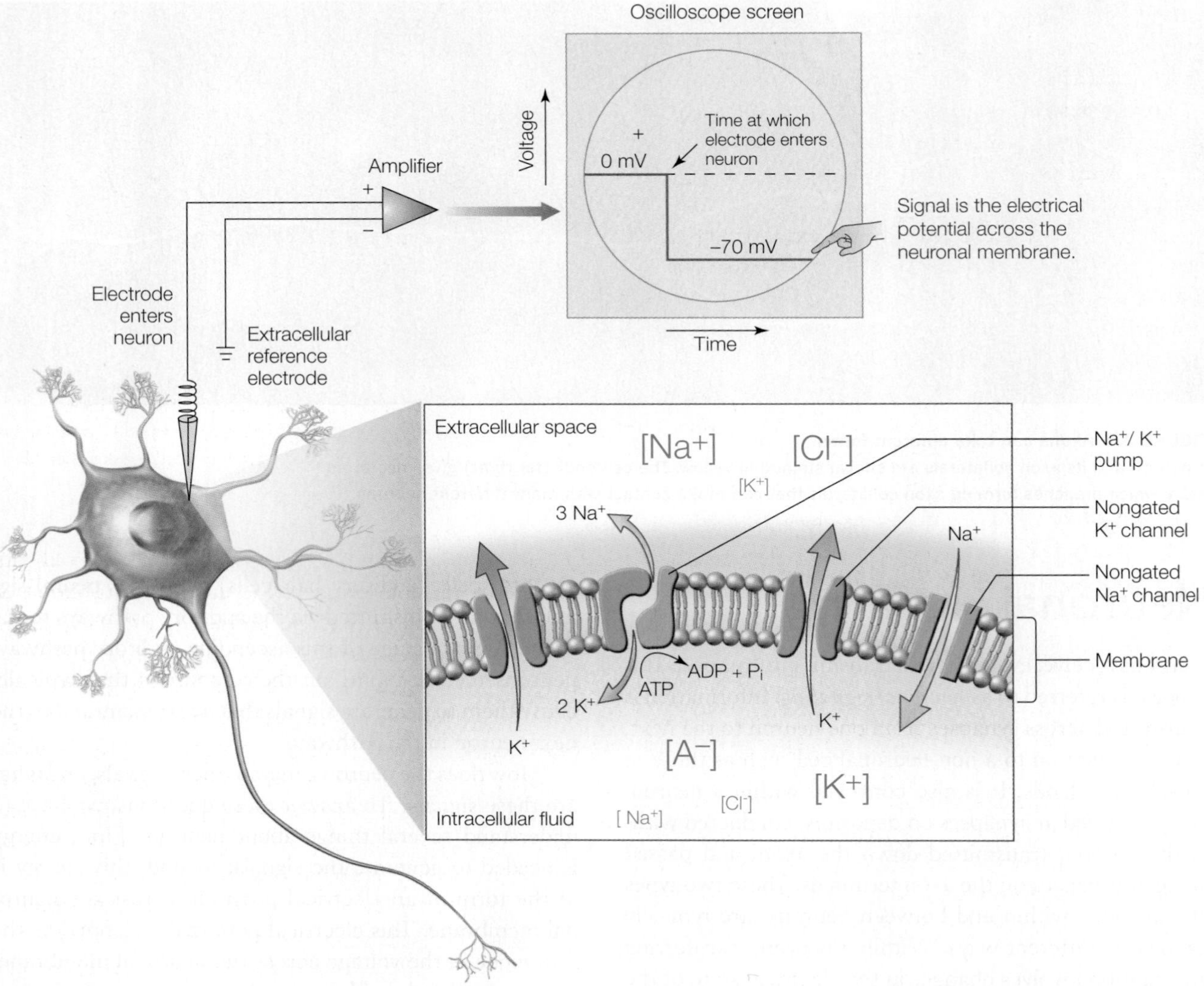

FIGURE 2.8 Ion channels in a segment of neuronal membrane and measuring resting membrane potential.

Idealized neuron **(left)** shown with intracellular recording electrode penetrating the neuron. The electrode measures the difference between the voltage inside versus outside the neuron and this difference is amplified and displayed on an oscilloscope screen **(top)**. The oscilloscope screen shows voltage over time, and shows that prior to the electrode entering the neuron, voltage between the electrode and the extracellular reference electrode is zero, but when the electrode is pushed into the neuron, the difference becomes −70 mV, which is the resting membrane potential. The resting membrane potential arises from the asymmetric distribution of ions of sodium (Na^+), potassium (K^+), and chloride (Cl^-), as well as of charged protein molecules (A^-), across the neuron's cell membrane **(inset)**.

watery environments found inside and outside of the neuron. The lipid membrane blocks the flow of water-soluble substances between the inside and the outside of the neuron. It also prevents ions (molecules or atoms that have either a positive or negative electrical charge), proteins, and other water-soluble molecules from moving across it. To understand neuronal signaling, we must focus on ions. This point is important: The lipid membrane maintains the separation of intracellular and extracellular ions and electrical charge that ultimately permits neuronal communication.

The neuronal membrane, though, is not merely a lipid bilayer. The membrane is peppered with transmembrane proteins that serve as conduits for ions to move across the neuronal membrane (Figure 2.8, inset). There are two main types of these proteins: ion channels and ion pumps. **Ion channels**, as we shall see, are proteins with a pore through their centers, and they allow certain ions to flow down their concentration gradients. **Ion pumps** use energy to actively transport ions across the membrane against their concentration gradients, that is, from regions of low concentration to regions of higher concentration.

Ion Channels The transmembrane passageways created by ion channels are formed from the three-dimensional structure of these proteins. These hydrophilic channels selectively permit one type of ion to pass through the membrane. The ion channels of concern to us—the ones found in neurons—are selective for either sodium, potassium, calcium, or chloride ions (Na^+, K^+, Ca^{2+}, and Cl^-, respectively; Figure 2.8, inset). The extent to which a particular ion can cross the membrane through a given ion channel is referred to as its **permeability**. This characteristic of ion channels gives the neuronal membrane the attribute of *selective permeability*. (Selective permeability is actually a property of all cells in the body; as part of cellular homeostasis, it enables cells to maintain internal chemical stability.) The neuronal membrane is more permeable to K^+ than to Na^+ (or other) ions, a property that contributes to the resting membrane potential, as we shall learn shortly. The membrane permeability to K^+ is larger because there are many more K^+-selective channels than any other type of ion channel.

Unlike most cells in the body, neurons are excitable, meaning that they can change the permeability of their membranes. This is brought about by ion channels that are capable of changing their permeability for a particular ion. Such proteins are called *gated ion channels*. They open or close based on changes in nearby transmembrane voltage, or as a response to chemical or physical stimuli. In contrast, ion channels that are unregulated, and hence always allow the associated ion to pass through, are known as *nongated ion channels*.

Ion Pumps Under normal conditions, there are concentration gradients of different ions across the neuronal membrane. Specifically, Na^+ and Cl^- concentrations are greater outside of the cell, and K^+ concentrations are greater inside the cell. Given that the neuronal membrane contains ion channels that permit the different ions inside and outside of the cell to flow across the neuronal membrane, how does the neuron maintain different concentrations of ions inside compared with outside of the cell? Put another way, why don't K^+ ions flow out of the neuron—down their concentration gradient—until the K^+ ion concentrations inside and outside the cell are equal? We can ask the same questions for all other ions. To combat this drive toward equilibrium, neurons use *active transport* proteins, known as *ion pumps*. In particular, neurons use a Na^+/K^+ pump that pumps Na^+ ions out of the cell and K^+ ions into the cell. Because this process is transporting ions up their concentration gradients, the mechanism requires energy. Each pump is an enzyme that hydrolyzes adenosine triphosphate (ATP). For each molecule of ATP that is hydrolyzed, the resulting energy is used to move three Na^+ ions out of the cell and two K^+ ions into the cell

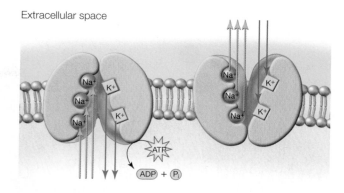

Extracellular space

Intracellular fluid

FIGURE 2.9 Ion channels pump ions across the membrane. The Na^+–K^+ pump preserves the cell's resting potential by maintaining a larger concentration of K^+ inside the cell and Na^+ outside the cell. The pump uses ATP as energy.

(Figures 2.8, inset and 2.9). The concentration gradients create forces—the forces of the unequal distribution of ions. The force of the Na^+ concentration gradient wants to push Na^+ from an area of high concentration to one of low concentration (from outside to inside), while the K^+ concentration gradient acts to push K^+ from an area of high concentration to an area of low concentration (from inside to outside)—the very thing the pump is working against. Since there are both positively and negatively charged ions inside and outside the cell, why is there a difference in voltage inside versus outside the neuron?

The inside and outside voltages are different because the membrane is more permeable to K^+ than to Na^+. The force of the K^+ concentration gradient pushes some K^+ out of the cell, leaving the inside of the neuron slightly more negative than the outside. This creates another force, an **electrical gradient**, because each K^+ ion carries one unit of positive charge out of the neuron as it moves across the membrane. These two gradients (electrical and ionic concentration) are in opposition to one another with respect to K^+ (Figure 2.10). As negative charge builds up along the inside of the membrane (and an equivalent positive charge forms along the extracellular side), the positively charged K^+ ions outside of the cell are drawn electrically back into the neuron through the same ion channels that are allowing K^+ ions to leave the cell by diffusion. Eventually, the force of the concentration gradient pushing K^+ out through the K^+ channels is equal to the force of the electrical gradient driving K^+ in. When that happens, the opposing forces are said to reach *electrochemical equilibrium*. The difference in charge thus produced across the membrane is the resting membrane potential, that –70 mV difference. The value for the resting membrane potential of any cell can be calculated by using knowledge from electrochemistry, provided that the concentrations of the ions inside and outside the neuron are known.

Extracellular space

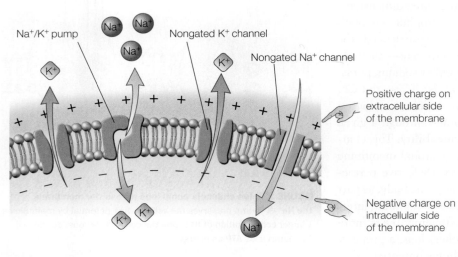

Intracellular fluid

FIGURE 2.10 Selective permeability of the membrane.
The membrane's selective permeability to some ions, and the concentration gradients formed by active pumping, lead to a difference in electrical potential across the membrane; this is the *resting membrane potential.* The membrane potential, represented here by the positive charges outside the neuron along the membrane and the negative charges inside along the membrane, is the basis for the transmembrane voltage difference shown in Figure 2.8. Because the concentration gradient for K⁺ forces K⁺ out of the cell, a net negative charge develops inside the neuron.

The Action Potential

We now understand the basis of the energy source that neurons can use for signaling. Next we want to learn how this energy can be used to transmit information within a neuron, from its dendrites that receive inputs from other neurons, to its axon terminals where it makes synapses on the next neurons in the chain. The process begins when *excitatory postsynaptic potentials* (EPSPs) at synapses on the neuron's dendrites cause ionic currents to flow in the volume of the cell body. If these currents are strong enough to reach the axon terminals, then the processes of neuronal signaling could be completed. Unfortunately, in the vast majority of cases, this distance is too great for the EPSP to have any effect. Why is this the case?

The small electrical current produced by the EPSP is passively conducted through the cytoplasm of the dendrite, cell body, and axon. Passive current conduction is called **electrotonic conduction** or *decremental conduction.* Decremental, because it diminishes with distance from its origin—the synapse, in this case. The maximum distance a passive current will flow is only about 1 millimeter. In most cases, a millimeter is too short to be effective for conducting electrical signals, but in a structure like the retina, a millimeter is enough to permit neuron-to-neuron communication. Most of the time, however, the reduction in signal intensity makes it unlikely that a single EPSP will be enough to trigger the firing of its own cell, much less

transmit the signal to another cell (your toes would be in trouble, for example, because they are 1 meter from the spinal cord and close to 2 meters from the brain). How does the neuron solve this problem of decremental conduction and the need to conduct over long distances?

Neurons evolved a clever mechanism to regenerate and pass along the signal initiated in the synapse. It works something like 19th-century firefighters in a bucket brigade, who handed buckets of water from one person to the next along a distance from the source of water to where it was needed at the fire. This regenerative process is an active membrane mechanism known as the **action potential**. An action potential is a rapid depolarization and repolarization of a small region of the membrane caused by the opening and closing of ion channels.

An action potential is an entirely different animal from the EPSP. Unlike a postsynaptic potential, it doesn't decrement after only 1 millimeter. Action potentials can travel for meters with no loss in signal strength, because they continuously regenerate the signal. This is one reason there can be giraffes and blue whales. It is, however, metabolically expensive, and it contributes to the inordinate amount of the body's energy used by the brain.

The action potential is able to regenerate itself due to the presence of **voltage-gated ion channels** located in the neuronal membrane (Figure 2.11a, inset). These are found at the **spike-triggering zone** in the **axon hillock** and along the axon. In myelinated axons, these voltage-gated ion channels are confined to the axon hillock and the nodes of Ranvier (Figure 2.11a). As its name denotes, the spike-triggering zone initiates the action potential. (The term *spike* is shorthand for an action potential, because when viewed as a recording displayed on an oscilloscope screen, the action potential looks like a little spike in the recorded signal.) How does the spike-triggering zone initiate an action potential?

The passive electrical currents that are generated following EPSPs on multiple distant dendrites sum together at the axon hillock. This current flows across the neuronal membrane in the spike-triggering zone, depolarizing the membrane. If the depolarization is strong enough, meaning the membrane moves from its resting potential of about –70 mV to a less negative value of approximately

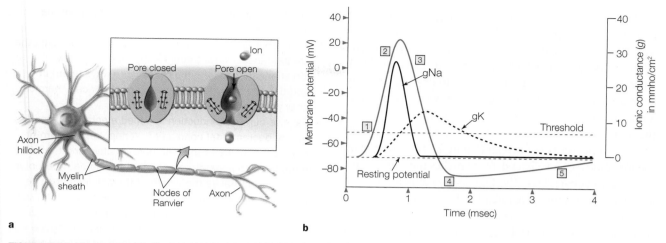

FIGURE 2.11 The neuronal action potential, voltage-gated ion channels, and changes in channel conductance.

(a) An idealized neuron with myelinated axon and axon terminals. Voltage-gated ion channels located in the spike-triggering zone at the axon hillock, and along the extent to the axon, open and close rapidly, changing their conductance to specific ions (e.g., Na⁺), alerting the membrane potential and resulting in the action potential **(inset)**. **(b)** Relative time course of changes in membrane voltage during an action potential, and the underlying causative changes in membrane conductance to Na⁺ (gNa) and K⁺ (gK). The initial depolarizing phase of the action potential (red line) is mediated by increased Na⁺ conductance (black line), and the later repolarizing, descending phase of the action potential is mediated by an increase in K⁺ conductance (dashed line) that occurs when the K⁺ channels open. The Na⁺ channels have closed during the last part of the action potential, when repolarization by the K⁺ current is taking place. The action potential undershoots the resting membrane potential at the point where the membrane becomes more negative than the resting membrane potential.

−55 mV, an action potential is triggered. We refer to this **depolarized** membrane potential value as the **threshold** for initiating an action potential. Figure 2.11b illustrates an idealized action potential. The numbered boxes in the figure correspond to the numbered events in the next paragraph. Each event alters a small region of the membrane's permeability for Na⁺ and K⁺ due to the opening and closing of voltage-gated ion channels.

When the threshold (Figure 2.11 b, label 1) is reached, voltage-gated Na⁺ channels open and Na⁺ flows rapidly into the neuron. This influx of positive ions further depolarizes the neuron, opening additional voltage-gated Na⁺ channels; thus, the neuron becomes more depolarized (2), continuing the cycle by causing even more Na⁺ channels to open. This process is called the Hodgkin–Huxley cycle. This rapid, self-reinforcing cycle, lasting only about 1 millisecond, generates the large depolarization that is the first portion of the action potential. Next, the voltage-gated K⁺ channels open, allowing K⁺ to flow out of the neuron down its concentration gradient. This outward flow of positive ions begins to shift the membrane potential back toward its resting potential (3). The opening of the K⁺ channels outlasts the closing of the Na⁺ channels, causing a second repolarizing phase of the action potential; and this drives the membrane potential toward the equilibrium potential of K⁺, which is even more negative

than the resting potential. The **equilibrium potential** is the particular voltage at which there is no net flux of ions. As a result, (4) the membrane is temporarily hyperpolarized, meaning that the membrane potential is even farther from the threshold required for triggering an action potential (e.g., around −80 mV). Hyperpolarization causes the K⁺ channels to close, resulting in (5) the membrane potential gradually returning to its resting state. During this transient **hyperpolarization** state, the voltage-gated Na⁺ channels are unable to open, and another action potential cannot be generated. This is known as the *absolute refractory period*. It is followed by the *relative refractory period*, during which the neuron can generate action potentials, but only with larger-than-normal depolarizing currents. The **refractory period** lasts only a couple of milliseconds and has two consequences. One is that the neuron's speed for generating action potentials is limited to about 200 action potentials per second. The other is that the passive current that flows from the action potential cannot reopen the ion-gated channels that generated it. The passive current, however, does flow down the axon with enough strength to depolarize the membrane a bit farther on, opening voltage-gated channels in this next portion of the membrane. The result is that the action potential is propagated down the axon in one direction only—from the axon hillock toward the axon terminal.

So that is the story of the self-regenerating action potential as it propagates itself down an axon (sometimes traveling several meters). But traveling far is not the end of the story. Action potentials must also travel quickly if a person wants to run, or a bull wants to charge, or a very large animal (think blue whale) simply wants to react in a reasonable amount of time. Accelerated transmission of the action potential is accomplished in myelinated axons. The thick lipid sheath of myelin (Figure 2.11a) surrounding the membrane of myelinated axons makes the axon super-resistant to voltage loss. The high electrical resistance allows passive currents generated by the action potential to be shunted farther down the axon. The result is that action potentials do not have to be generated as often, and they can be spread out along the axon at wider intervals. Indeed, action potentials in myelinated axons need occur only at the nodes of Ranvier, where myelination is interrupted. This creates the appearance that the action potential is jumping down the axon at great speed, from one node of Ranvier to the next. We call this **saltatory conduction**. (Saltatory conduction is derived from the Latin word *saltare*, to jump or leap.) The importance of myelin for efficient neuronal conduction is notable when it is lost, which is what happens when a person is afflicted with multiple sclerosis (MS).

There is one interesting tidbit left concerning action potentials. Action potentials are always the same amplitude; therefore, they are said to be *all or none* phenomena. Since one action potential is the same amplitude as any other, the strength of the action potential does not communicate anything about the strength of the stimulus. The intensity of a stimulus (e.g., a sensory signal) is communicated by the *rate of firing* of the action potentials: More intense stimuli elicit higher action potential firing rates.

So, we see how the neuron has solved the problem of long-distance communication as well as communication speed. When the action potential reaches the axon terminal, the signal is now strong enough to cause depolarization of the presynaptic membrane and to trigger neurotransmitter release. The signal is ready to be transferred to the next neuron across the **synaptic cleft**, the gap between neurons at the synapse.

TAKE-HOME MESSAGES

- The presynaptic cell is located before the synapse with respect to information flow; the postsynaptic cell is located after the synapse with respect to information flow. Nearly all neurons are both pre- and postsynaptic, since they both receive and transmit information.
- The resting membrane potential is the difference in the voltage across the neuronal membrane during rest (i.e., not during any phase of the action potential).
- The electrical gradient results from the asymmetrical distribution of ions across the membrane. The electrical difference across the membrane is the basis of the resting potential.
- Ion channels are formed by transmembrane proteins that create passageways through which ions can flow.
- Ion channels can be either passive (always open) or gated (open only in the presence of electrical, chemical, or physical stimuli).
- Passive current conduction is called electrotonic conduction or decremental conduction. A depolarizing current makes the inside of the cell more positive and therefore more likely to generate an action potential; a hyperpolarizing current makes the inside of the cell less positive and therefore less likely to generate an action potential.
- Action potentials are an all-or-none phenomena: The amplitude of the action potential does not depend on the size of the triggering depolarization, as long as that depolarization reaches threshold for initiating the action potential.
- Voltage-gated channels are of prime importance in generating an action potential because they open and close according to the membrane potential.
- Myelin allows for the rapid transmission of action potentials down an axon.
- Nodes of Ranvier are the spaces between sheaths of myelin where voltage-gated Na^+ and K^+ channels are located and action potentials occur.

Synaptic Transmission

A neuron communicates with other neurons, muscles, or glands at a synapse, and the transfer of a signal from the axon terminal to the next cell is called *synaptic transmission*. There are two major kinds of synapses—chemical and electrical—each using very different mechanisms for synaptic transmission.

Chemical Transmission

Most neurons send a signal to the cell across the synapse by releasing neurotransmitters into the synaptic cleft. The general mechanism is as follows. The arrival of the action potential at the axon terminal leads to the depolarization of the terminal membrane, causing voltage-gated Ca^{2+} channels to open. The opening of these channels triggers small **vesicles** containing neurotransmitter to fuse with the membrane at the synapse and release the transmitter into the synaptic cleft. The transmitter diffuses across the cleft and, on reaching the postsynaptic membrane, binds with specific receptors embedded in the postsynaptic membrane (Figure 2.12). Neurotransmitter binding induces a change in the receptor, which opens specific ion channels and results in an influx of ions leading to either depolarization (excitation) or hyperpolarization (inhibition) of the postsynaptic cell (Figure 2.13). Hyperpolarization of the postsynaptic neuron produces an inhibitory postsynaptic potential (IPSP).

Neurotransmitters

The process just described brings us to a hot topic of the popular press: **neurotransmitters**. While you may have heard of a few of them, more than 100 neurotransmitters have been identified. What makes a molecule a neurotransmitter?

- It is synthesized by and localized within the presynaptic neuron, and stored in the presynaptic terminal before release.
- It is released by the presynaptic neuron when action potentials depolarize the terminal (mediated primarily by Ca²⁺).
- The postsynaptic neuron contains receptors specific for the neurotransmitter.
- When artificially applied to a postsynaptic cell, the neurotransmitter elicits the same response that stimulating the presynaptic neuron would.

Biochemical Classification of Neurotransmitters Some neurotransmitters are amino acids: aspartate, gamma-aminobutyric acid (GABA), glutamate, and glycine. Another category of neurotransmitters, called *biogenic amines*, includes dopamine, norepinephrine, and epinephrine (these three are known as the *catecholamines*), serotonin (5-hydroxytryptamine), and histamine. Acetylcholine (ACh) is a well-studied neurotransmitter that is in its own biochemical class. Another large group of neurotransmitters consists of slightly larger molecules, the *neuropeptides* (made up of strings of amino acids). More than 100 neuropeptides are active in the mammalian brain, and they are divided into five groups:

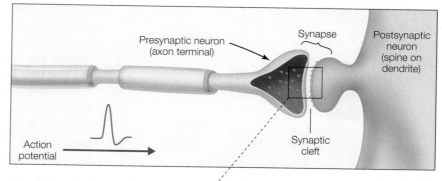

Action potential

① Action potential depolarizes the terminal membrane, which causes Ca²⁺ to flow into the cell

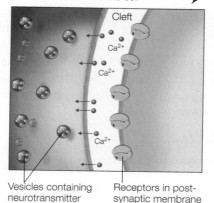

Cleft

Vesicles containing neurotransmitter

Receptors in post-synaptic membrane

② Ca²⁺ causes vesicles to bind with cell membrane

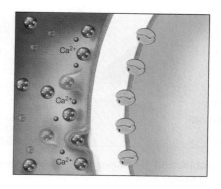

③ Release of neurotransmitter by exocytosis into the synaptic cleft

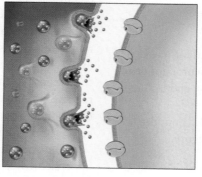

④ Transmitter binds with receptor

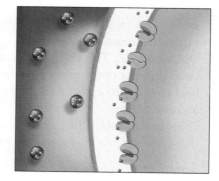

FIGURE 2.12 Neurotransmitter release at the synapse, into synaptic cleft. The synapse consists of various specializations where the presynaptic and postsynaptic membranes are in close apposition. When the action potential invades the axon terminals, it causes voltage-gated Ca²⁺ channels to open (1), which triggers vesicles to bind to the presynaptic membrane (2). Neurotransmitter is released into the synaptic cleft by exocytosis and diffuses across the cleft (3). Binding of the neurotransmitter to receptor molecules in the postsynaptic membrane completes the process of transmission (4).

1. *Tachykinins* (brain-gut peptides). This group includes substance P, which affects vasoconstriction and is a spinal neurotransmitter involved in pain.
2. *Neurohypophyseal hormones.* Oxytocin and vasopressin are in this group. The former is involved in mammary functions and has been tagged the "love hormone" for its role in pair bonding and maternal behaviors; the latter is an antidiuretic hormone.
3. *Hypothalamic releasing hormones.* This group includes corticotropin-releasing hormone, involved

Before transmitter release

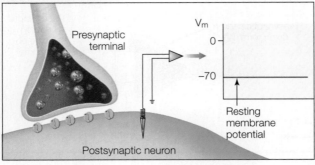

After transmitter release

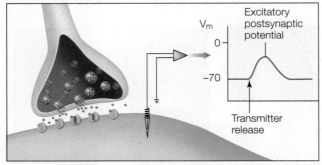

FIGURE 2.13 Neurotransmitter leading to postsynaptic potential. The binding of neurotransmitter to the postsynaptic membrane receptors changes the membrane potential (V_m). These postsynaptic potentials can be either excitatory (depolarizing the membrane), as shown here, or inhibitory (hyperpolarizing the membrane).

in the stress response, and somatostatin, an inhibitor of growth hormone.

4. *Opioid peptides.* This group is so named for its similarity to opiate drugs, permitting the neuropeptide to bind to opiate receptors. It includes the endorphins and enkephalins.

5. *Other neuropeptides.* This group includes peptides that do not fit neatly into another category.

Some neurons produce only one type of neurotransmitter, but others produce multiple kinds of neurotransmitters. In the latter case, the neurotransmitters may be released together or separately, depending on the conditions of stimulation. For example, the rate of stimulation by the action potential can induce the release of a specific neurotransmitter.

Functional Classification of Neurotransmitters

As mentioned earlier, the effect of a neurotransmitter on the postsynaptic neuron is determined by the postsynaptic receptor rather than by the transmitter itself. That is, the same neurotransmitter released from the same presynaptic neuron onto two different postsynaptic cells might cause one to increase firing and the other to decrease firing, depending on the receptors that the

transmitter binds to. The effects of a neurotransmitter also depend on the connections of the neurons that use the transmitter. Nevertheless, neurotransmitters can be classified not only biochemically but also by the *typical effect* that they induce in the postsynaptic neuron.

Neurotransmitters that usually have an excitatory effect include ACh, the catecholamines, glutamate, histamine, serotonin, and some of the neuropeptides. Usually inhibitory neurotransmitters include GABA, glycine, and some of the peptides. Some neurotransmitters act directly to excite or inhibit a postsynaptic neuron, but other neurotransmitters act only in concert with other factors. These are sometimes referred to as *conditional neurotransmitters*; that is, their action is conditioned on the presence of another transmitter in the synaptic cleft or activity in the neuronal circuit. These types of mechanisms permit the nervous system to achieve complex modulations of information processing by modulating neurotransmission.

Inactivation of Neurotransmitters after Release

Following the release of neurotransmitter into the synaptic cleft and its binding with the postsynaptic membrane receptors, the remaining transmitter must be removed to prevent further excitatory or inhibitory signal transduction. This removal can be accomplished (a) by active reuptake of the substance back into the presynaptic terminal, (b) by enzymatic breakdown of the transmitter in the synaptic cleft, or (c) merely by diffusion of the neurotransmitter away from the region of the synapse or site of action (e.g., in the case of hormones that act on target cells distant from the synaptic terminals).

Neurotransmitters that are removed from the synaptic cleft by reuptake mechanisms include the biogenic amines (dopamine, norepinephrine, epinephrine, histamine, and serotonin). The reuptake mechanism is mediated by active transporters, which are transmembrane proteins that pump the neurotransmitter back across the presynaptic membrane.

An example of a neurotransmitter that is eliminated from the synaptic cleft by enzymatic action is ACh. The enzyme acetylcholinesterase (AChE), which is located in the synaptic cleft, breaks down ACh after it has acted on the postsynaptic membrane. In fact, special AChE stains (chemicals that bind to AChE) can be used to label AChE on muscle cells, thus revealing where motor neurons innervate the muscle.

To monitor the level of neurotransmitter in the synaptic cleft, presynaptic neurons have autoreceptors. These autoreceptors are located on the presynaptic terminal and bind with the released neurotransmitter, allowing the presynaptic neuron to regulate the synthesis and release of the transmitter.

Electrical Transmission

Some neurons communicate via electrical synapses. These synapses are very different from chemical synapses—in electrical synapses, no synaptic cleft separates the neurons. Instead, the neuronal membranes are touching at specializations called *gap junctions*, and the cytoplasms of the two neurons are essentially continuous. These gap junction channels create pores connecting the cytoplasms of the two neurons (Figure 2.14). As a result, the two neurons are *isopotential* (i.e., have the same electrical potential), meaning that electrical changes in one are reflected instantaneously in the other. Following the principles of electrotonic conduction, however, the passive currents that flow between the neurons when one of them is depolarized (or hyperpolarized) decrease and are therefore smaller in the postsynaptic neuron than in the presynaptic neuron. Under most circumstances, the communication is bidirectional; however, so-called rectifying synapses limit current flow in one direction, as is typical in chemical synapses.

Electrical synapses are useful when information must be conducted rapidly, such as in the escape reflex of some invertebrates. Groups of neurons with these synapses can activate muscles quickly to get the animal out of harm's way. For example, the well-known tail flip reflex of crayfishes involves powerful rectifying electrical synapses. Electrical synapses are also useful when groups of neurons should operate synchronously, as with some hypothalamic neurosecretory neurons. Electrical

synapses also have some limitations: They are much less plastic than chemical synapses, and they cannot amplify a signal (whereas an action potential that triggers a chemical synapse could cause a large release of neurotransmitter, thus amplifying the signal).

TAKE-HOME MESSAGES

- Synapses are the locations where one neuron can transfer information to another neuron or specialized non-neuronal cell. They are found on dendrites and at axon terminals but can also be found on the neuronal cell body.
- Chemical transmission results in the release of neurotransmitters from the presynaptic neuron and the binding of those neurotransmitters on the postsynaptic neuron, which in turn causes excitatory or inhibitory postsynaptic potentials (EPSPs or IPSPs), depending on the properties of the postsynaptic receptor.
- Classes of neurotransmitters include amino acids, biogenic amines, and neuropeptides.
- Neurotransmitters must be removed from the receptor after binding. This removal can be accomplished by (a) active reuptake back into the presynaptic terminal, (b) enzymatic breakdown of the transmitter in the synaptic cleft, or (c) diffusion of the neurotransmitter away from the region of the synapse.
- Electrical synapses are different than chemical synapses as they operate by passing current directly from one neuron (presynaptic) to another neuron (postsynaptic) via specialized channels in gap junctions that connect the cytoplasm of one cell directly to the other.

The Role of Glial Cells

The other type of cell in the nervous system is the **glial cell** (also called *neuroglial cell*). There are roughly as many glial cells in the brain as there are neurons. Located throughout the nervous system, they may account for more than half of the brain's volume. The term *neuroglia* means, literally, "nerve glue," because anatomists in the 19th century believed that the main role of neuroglial cells in the nervous system was structural support. While glial cells do provide structural support, they also carry out other roles in the nervous system, such as helping to form the blood–brain barrier and aiding in the speed of information transfer. More recently, glial cells have revealed a bit of a surprise: They appear to have a previously unrecognized role in modulating neural activity.

The central nervous system has three main types of glial cells: astrocytes, microglial cells, and oligodendrocytes (Figure 2.15). *Astrocytes* are large glial cells with round

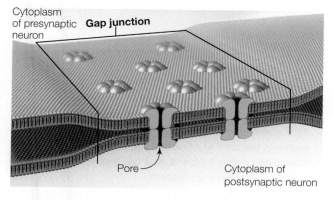

FIGURE 2.14 Electrical synapse between two neurons. Electrical synapses are formed by gap junctions, places where multiple transmembrane proteins in the pre- and postsynaptic neurons connect to create pathways that connect the cytoplasms of the two neurons.

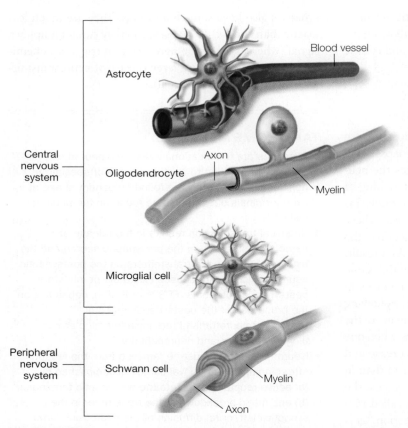

FIGURE 2.15 Various types of glial cells in the mammalian central and peripheral nervous systems.
An astrocyte is shown with end feet attached to a blood vessel. Oligodendrocytes and Schwann cells produce myelin around the axons of neurons—oligodendrocytes in the central nervous system, and Schwann cells in the peripheral nervous system. A microglial cell is also shown.

or radially symmetrical forms; they surround neurons and are in close contact with the brain's vasculature. An astrocyte makes contact with blood vessels at specializations called *end feet*, which permit the astrocyte to transport ions across the vascular wall. The astrocytes create a barrier, called the **blood–brain barrier** (**BBB**), between the tissues of the central nervous system and the blood. The BBB restricts the diffusion of microscopic objects (such as most bacteria) and large hydrophilic molecules in the blood from entering the neural tissue, but it allows the diffusion of small hydrophobic molecules such as oxygen, carbon dioxide, and hormones. For example, many drugs and certain neuroactive agents, such as dopamine and norepinephrine, when placed in the blood, cannot cross the BBB. Thus, it plays a vital role in protecting the central nervous system from blood-borne agents such as chemical compounds, as well as pathogens that might unduly affect neuronal activity.

Astrocytes are recognized for their supporting roles, so to speak, but recent evidence suggests that they have an active role in brain function. *In vitro* studies indicate that they respond to and release neurotransmitters and other neuroactive substances that affect neuronal activity and modulate synaptic strength. More recently, *in vivo* studies found that when astrocyte activity is blocked, neural activity increases. This finding supports the notion that neural activity is moderated by astrocyte activity (Schummers et al., 2008). It is hypothesized that astrocytes either directly or indirectly regulate the reuptake of neurotransmitters.

Microglial cells, which are small and irregularly shaped (Figure 2.15), come into play when tissue is damaged. They are phagocytes, literally devouring and removing damaged cells. Unlike many cells in the central nervous system, microglial cells can proliferate even in adults (as do other glial cells).

Glial cells are also the myelin formers in the nervous system. In the central nervous system, *oligodendrocytes* form myelin; in the peripheral nervous system, *Schwann cells* carry out this task (Figure 2.15). Both glial cell types create myelin by wrapping their cell membranes around the axon in a concentric manner during development and maturation. The cytoplasm in that portion of the glial cell is squeezed out, leaving primarily the lipid bilayer of the glial cell sheathing the membrane. Myelin is a good electrical insulator because the layers of cell membrane are composed of lipid bilayers, which are themselves poor electrical conductors.

TAKE-HOME MESSAGES

- An astrocyte is a type of glial cell that helps form the blood–brain barrier.
- Astrocytes have an active role in modulating neural activity.
- Glial cells aid in the speed of information transfer by forming myelin around the axons of the neurons.
- An oligodendrocyte is a type of glial cell that forms myelin in the central nervous system.
- A Schwann cell is a type of glial cell that forms myelin in the peripheral nervous system.
- As part of the immune response of the nervous system, microglial cells are phagocytic cells that engulf damaged cells.

The Bigger Picture

Until now, we have been talking about only one or two neurons at a time. This approach is useful in understanding how neurons transmit information, but it fails to illuminate how the nervous system and the brain function. Neurons rarely work in isolation. Neural communication depends on patterns of connectivity in the nervous system, the neural "highways" that allow information to get from one place to another. Identifying these patterns of connectivity in the nervous system in order to map out the neural highways is tricky because most neurons are not wired together in simple, serial circuits. Instead, neurons are extensively connected in both serial and parallel circuits. A single cortical neuron is likely to be innervated by (i.e., receive inputs from) a large numbers of neurons: A typical cortical neuron has between 1,000 and 5,000 synapses, while a Purkinje neuron may have up to 200,000 synapses. The axons from these input neurons can originate in widely distributed regions. Thus, there is tremendous *convergence* in the nervous system. There is also *divergence*, in which a single neuron can project to multiple target neurons in different regions. Although most axons are short projections from neighboring cortical cells, some are quite long, originating in distant cortical regions. These may reach their target only after descending below the cortical sheath into the white matter, traveling through long fiber tracts, and then entering another region of cortex, subcortical nucleus, or spinal layer to synapse on another neuron. Thanks to this extensive interconnectivity, each neuron is only a few synapses away from any other given neuron, and each neuron makes a small contribution to overall function. Connections between two cortical regions are referred to as *corticocortical connections*, following the convention that the first part of the term identifies the source and the second part identifies the target. Inputs that originate in subcortical structures such as the thalamus would be referred to as *thalamocortical connections*; the reverse are *corticothalamic*, or more generally, *corticofugal projections* (projections extending from more central structures, like cortex, outward toward the periphery).

Groups of interconnected neurons that process specific kinds of information are referred to as **neural circuits**. Neural circuits have many different forms and purposes. Some are involved in reflexes, such as the "knee-jerk reflex"—a tap by your doctor on your patellar tendon at the knee sends a sensory signal to the spinal cord which stimulates motor neurons to fire action potentials leading to muscle contraction and the brief knee jerk. This is an example of a monosynaptic reflex arc, stimulation of which is used by all physicians to test the integrity of

different parts of the nervous system. Other neural circuits throughout the nervous system perform other functions.

In general though, neural circuits share some basic features. They take in information (afferent inputs), they evaluate the input either at a synapse or within one or a group of neurons (local circuit neurons), and they convey the results to other neurons, muscles, or glands (efferent outputs).

One characteristic of some neural circuits is that they show plasticity. The patterns of activation within a neural circuit can change. This is what happens with learning and during development.

Neural circuits, in turn, can be combined to form **neural systems**. For example, the visual system is composed of many different neural circuits organized in both hierarchical and parallel processing streams to enable vision, and to provide outputs to cognitive and motor systems. Neural circuits involved in the visual system include such things as the retinogeniculostriate circuit that brings information from the eye to the visual cortex. Later in the book we will refer to *visual areas*, such as visual area V1, which is the striate (primary) visual cortex. Areas are intermediate between neural circuits and systems. That is, the visual system comprises neurons, neural circuits, and visual areas.

But before we can talk about neural circuits, systems, areas, or anything else about the brain for that matter, we need to get some neuroanatomy under our belts. Understanding anatomy is important for understanding function. So, next we present a tour of neuroanatomy, including a bit of function to put the brain anatomy into the context of cognitive neuroscience. For a brief discussion of celebral vasculature, see the box "How the Brain Works: Blood Supply and the Brain."

Early in each of Chapters 4 through 14, there is a box called Anatomical Orientation, containing one or a few illustrations of the brain. This box highlights the anatomy that is relevant to the cognitive functions discussed in that chapter. The anatomy presented here and in the coming chapters will help you see how the structures of the brain are related to the functions of the mind.

Overview of Nervous System Structure

The nervous system is composed of the **central nervous system** (**CNS**), consisting of the brain and spinal cord, and the **peripheral nervous system** (**PNS**), consisting of the nerves (bundles of axons and glia) and ganglia (clumps

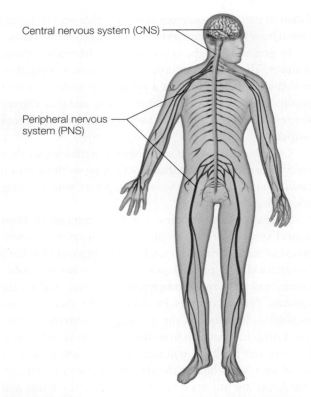

Central nervous system (CNS)

Peripheral nervous
system (PNS)

FIGURE 2.16 The peripheral and central nervous systems of the human body.
The nervous system is generally divided into two main parts. The central nervous system includes the brain and spinal cord. The peripheral nervous system, comprising the sensory and motor nerves and associated nerve cell ganglia (groups of neuronal cell bodies), is located outside the central nervous system.

of nerve cell bodies) outside of the CNS (Figure 2.16). The CNS can be thought of as the command-and-control center of the nervous system. The PNS represents a courier network that delivers sensory information to the CNS and carries the motor commands from the CNS to the muscles. These activities are accomplished through two systems, the *somatic motor system* that controls the voluntary muscles of the body and the *autonomic motor system* that controls visceral functions. Before we concentrate on the CNS, a word about the autonomic nervous system.

The Autonomic Nervous System

The **autonomic nervous system** (also called the autonomic, or visceral, motor system) is involved in controlling the involuntary action of smooth muscles, the heart, and various glands. It has two subdivisions: the *sympathetic* and *parasympathetic* branches (Figure 2.17). The sympathetic system uses the neurotransmitter norepinephrine, and the parasympathetic system uses acetylcholine as its transmitter. The two systems frequently

operate antagonistically. For example, activation of the sympathetic system increases heart rate, diverts blood from the digestive tract to the somatic musculature, and prepares the body for action (fight or flight) by stimulating the adrenal glands to release adrenaline. In contrast, activation of the parasympathetic system slows heart rate, stimulates digestion, and in general helps the body with functions germane to maintaining the body.

In the autonomic system, a great deal of specialization takes place that is beyond the scope of this chapter. Still, understanding that the autonomic system is involved in a variety of reflex and involuntary behaviors, mostly below the level of consciousness, is useful for interpreting information presented later in the book. In Chapter 10, on emotion, we will discuss arousal of the autonomic nervous system and how changes in a number of psychophysiological measures tap into emotion-related changes in the autonomic nervous system. For example, changes in skin conductance are related to sweat gland activity, and sweat glands are under the control of the autonomic nervous system.

In the rest of this chapter, we focus on the CNS in order to lay the groundwork for the studies of cognition that compose the rest of the book. But to talk about brain anatomy, we need some standard terminology that places parts of the brain in proper three-dimensional space. For that, please take a look at the box "Navigating the Brain."

The Central Nervous System

The CNS is made up of the delicate brain and spinal cord, each encased in its protective, bony shell and suspended in a sea of cerebrospinal fluid (CSF). Both the brain and the spinal cord are covered with three protective membranes—the meninges. The outer membrane is the thick **dura mater**; the middle is the *arachnoid mater*; and the inner and most delicate is the *pia mater*, which firmly adheres to the surface of the brain. The CSF occupies the subarachnoid space between the arachnoid membrane and the pia mater, as well as the brain ventricles, cisterns and sulci, and the central canal of the spinal cord (see "How the Brain Works: The Chambers of the Mind").

In the CNS, neurons are bunched together in various ways (Figure 2.18). Two of the most common organizational clusters are in a **nucleus** or in a **layer**. A nucleus is a relatively compact arrangement of nerve cell bodies and their connections, ranging from hundreds to millions of neurons, with functionally similar inputs and outputs. They are located throughout both the brain and the spinal cord. The outer layer of the brain, the **cerebral cortex**, on the other hand, has billions of neurons. They are arranged in layers of thin sheets, folded across the surfaces of the cerebral hemispheres like a

Parasympathetic branch

Sympathetic branch

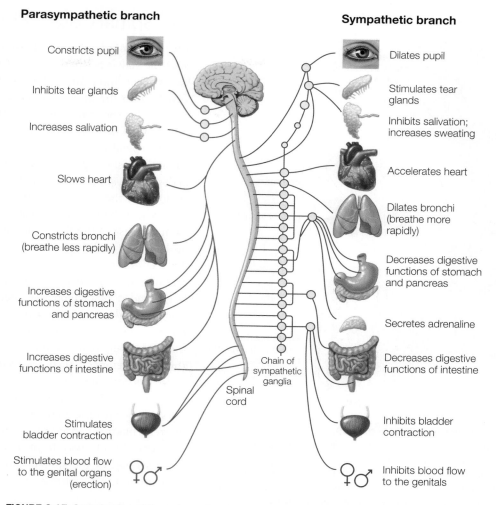

Constricts pupil

Inhibits tear glands

Increases salivation

Slows heart

Constricts bronchi
(breathe less rapidly)

Increases digestive
functions of stomach
and pancreas

Increases digestive
functions of intestine

Stimulates
bladder contraction

Stimulates blood flow
to the genital organs
(erection)

Dilates pupil

Stimulates tear
glands

Inhibits salivation;
increases sweating

Accelerates heart

Dilates bronchi
(breathe more
rapidly)

Decreases digestive
functions of stomach
and pancreas

Secretes adrenaline

Decreases digestive
functions of intestine

Inhibits bladder
contraction

Inhibits blood flow
to the genitals

Chain of
sympathetic
ganglia

Spinal
cord

FIGURE 2.17 Organization of the autonomic nervous system, showing sympathetic and parasympathetic branches.
Please see the text for details.

handkerchief. When we look at a slice of the brain, we see the cortex as a thin grayish layer overlaying the whitish interior. The **gray matter** is composed of neuronal cell bodies, and the **white matter** consists of axons and glial cells. Much like nerves in the PNS, these axons are grouped together in **tracts** that run in *association tracts* from one region to another within a hemisphere, or may cross into the other hemisphere in tracts called **commissures**. The largest of all the fiber tracts is the main commissure crossing between the hemispheres, the **corpus callosum**. Finally, there are *projection tracts* that run from the cerebral cortex to the deeper subcortical structures and the spinal cord.

TAKE-HOME MESSAGES

- The central nervous system consists of the brain and spinal cord. The peripheral nervous system consists of all nerves and neurons outside of the central nervous system.

- The autonomic nervous system is involved in controlling the action of smooth muscles, the heart, and various glands. It includes the sympathetic and parasympathetic systems.
- The sympathetic system uses the neurotransmitter norepinephrine. This system increases heart rate, diverts blood from the digestive tract to the somatic musculature, and prepares the body for fight-or-flight responses by stimulating the adrenal glands.
- The parasympathetic system uses acetylcholine as a neurotransmitter. It is responsible for decreasing heart rate and stimulating digestion.
- Groups of neurons are called ganglia.
- The cerebral cortex is a continuous sheet of layered neurons in each hemisphere.
- The axons of cortical neurons and subcortical ganglia travel together in white matter tracts that interconnect neurons in different parts of the brain and spinal cord.
- The corpus callosum is the main fiber tract that connects the two hemispheres of the brain.

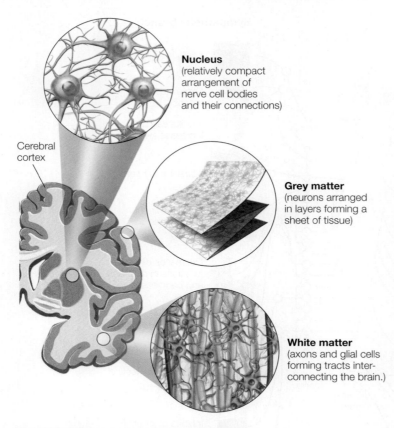

Nucleus
(relatively compact arrangement of nerve cell bodies and their connections)

Cerebral cortex

Grey matter
(neurons arranged in layers forming a sheet of tissue)

White matter
(axons and glial cells forming tracts interconnecting the brain.)

FIGURE 2.18 Organization of neurons in the CNS.
In the CNS, neurons can be organized in clumps called nuclei (top—not to be confused with the nucleus inside each neuron), which are most commonly found in subcortical and spinal structures, or sheets called layers (middle), which are most commonly found in the cortex. The cell bodies of glial cells are located in the white matter (e.g., oligodendrocytes), and in the cortex.

A Guided Tour of the Brain

When we see a brain, the cerebral cortex, the outer layer, is most prominent. But for the brain, the cerebral cortex is the frosting on the cake—it's the last thing to develop from an evolutionary, as well as an embryological, point of view. Deep within, at the base of the brain, are structures that are found in most vertebrates and have evolved for hundreds of millions of years. These parts of the brain control our most basic survival functions, such as breathing, heart rate, and temperature. In contrast, the prefrontal cortex, which is found only in mammals, is evolutionarily the youngest part of our brain. Damage to the prefrontal cortex may not be immediately fatal, but it will likely affect such things as our ability to make decisions as well as other behaviors that we consider to be most advanced in humans. We begin our tour of the CNS with a brief look at the spinal cord.

The Spinal Cord

The spinal cord takes in sensory information from the body's peripheral sensory receptors, relays it to the brain, and conducts the final motor signals from the brain to muscles. In addition, each level of the spinal cord has reflex pathways, such as the knee-jerk reflex mentioned earlier.

The spinal cord runs from the brainstem at about the first spinal vertebrae to its termination in the *cauda equina* (meaning "horse's tail"). It is enclosed in the bony *vertebral column*—a stack of separate bones, the *vertebrae*, that extend from the base of the skull to the fused vertebrae at the *coccyx* (tailbone). The vertebral column is divided into sections: cervical, thoracic, lumbar, sacral, and coccygeal. The spinal cord is similarly divided (excluding the coccygeal region, since we no longer have tails) into 31 segments. Each segment has a right and a left *spinal nerve* that enters and exits from the vertebral column through openings called *foramen*. Each spinal nerve has both sensory and motor axons: one afferent neuron carries sensory input through the dorsal root into the spinal cord, and the other efferent neuron carries motor output through the ventral root away from it. In looking at a cross section of the spinal cord (Figure 2.19), we can see the peripheral region is made up of

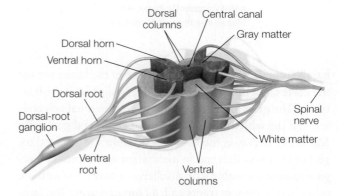

Dorsal columns

Central canal

Gray matter

Dorsal horn

Ventral horn

Dorsal root

Dorsal-root ganglion

Ventral root

Ventral columns

Spinal nerve

White matter

FIGURE 2.19 Gross anatomy of the spinal cord.
This cross-sectional and three-dimensional representation of the spinal cord shows the central butterfly-shaped gray matter, which contains neuronal cell bodies, and the surrounding white matter axon tracts, which convey information down the spinal cord from the brain to the peripheral neurons and up the spinal cord from peripheral receptors to the brain. The dorsal and ventral nerve roots are shown exiting and entering the cord; they fuse to form peripheral nerves. The cell bodies of peripheral sensory inputs reside in the dorsal-root ganglion and project their axons into the central nervous system via the dorsal root. The ventral horn of the spinal cord houses motor neurons that project their axons out the ventral roots to innervate peripheral muscles.

For anatomists, the head is merely an appendage to the body, so the terms that are used to describe the orientation of the head and its brain are in relation to the body. Confusion arises due to differences in how the head and body are arranged in animals that walk on four legs versus humans, who are upright. Let's first picture the body of the cutest kind of dog, an Australian shepherd, looking off to the left of the page (Figure 1, top). The front end is the *rostral* end, meaning "nose." The opposite end is the *caudal* end, the "tail." Along his back is the *dorsal* surface, just like the dorsal fin is on the back of a shark. The bottom surface along the dog's belly is the *ventral* surface. We can refer to the dog's nervous system by using the same coordinates (Figure 1, bottom). The part of the brain toward the front is the rostral end (toward the frontal lobes); the posterior end is the caudal end (toward the occipital lobe). Along the top of his head is the *dorsal* surface, and the bottom surface of the brain is the *ventral* surface.

We humans are atypical animals because we stand upright and, therefore, tilt our heads forward in order to be parallel with the ground. Thus, the dorsal surface of the body and brain are now at right angles to each other (Figure 2). Luckily, we have a cerebral cortex that can understand this. In humans, we also use the terms *superior* and *inferior* to refer to the top and bottom of the brain, respectively.

Similarly, along with the terms *rostral*, which still means "toward the frontal pole," and *caudal*, which still means "toward the occipital pole," *anterior* and *posterior* are also used to refer to the front and back of the brain, respectively.

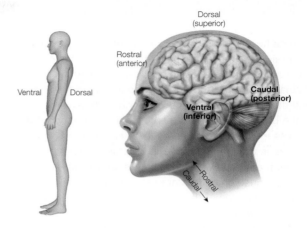

FIGURE 2 Navigating the human brain.

When we consider the spinal cord, the coordinate systems align with the body axis. Thus, in the spinal cord, *rostral* means "toward the brain," just as it does in the dog.

Throughout this book, pictures of brain slices usually will be in one of three planes (Figure 3). If we slice it from nose to tail, that is a *sagittal* section. When that slice is directly through the middle, it is a *midsagittal* or *medial* section. If it is off to the side, it is a *lateral* section. If sliced from top to bottom, separating the front of the brain from the back, we have made a *coronal* section. If we slice in a plane that separates dorsal from ventral, that is known as either an *axial*, *transverse*, or *horizontal* section.

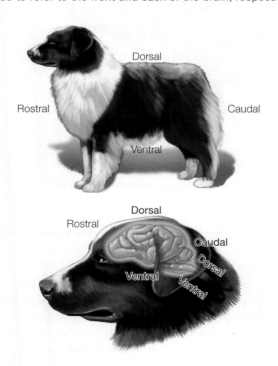

FIGURE 1 A dog brain in relation to the body.

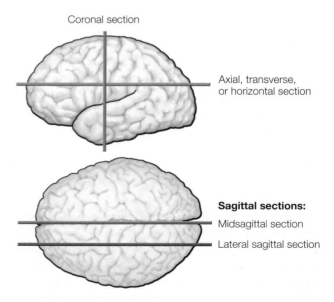

FIGURE 3 Three orthogonal planes through the brain.

HOW THE BRAIN WORKS
The Chambers of the Mind

Scientists have understood for many decades that neurons in the brain are functional units, and that how they are interconnected yields specific circuits for the support of particular behaviors. Centuries ago, early anatomists, believing that the head contained the seat of behavior, examined the brain to see where the conscious self (soul, if you wish) was located. They found a likely candidate: Some chambers in the brain seemed to be empty (except for some fluid) and thus were possible containers for higher functions. These chambers are called *ventricles* (Figure 1). What is the function of these chambers within the brain?

The brain weighs a considerable amount but has little or no structural support; there is no skeletal system for the brain. To overcome this potential difficulty, the brain is immersed in a fluid called *cerebrospinal fluid* (CSF). This fluid allows the brain to float to help offset the pressure that would be present if the brain were merely sitting on the base of the skull. CSF also reduces shock to the brain and spinal cord during rapid accelerations

or decelerations, such as when we fall or are struck on the head.

The ventricles inside the brain are continuous with the CSF surrounding the brain. The largest of these chambers are the lateral ventricles, which are connected to the third ventricle in the brain's midline. The cerebral aqueduct joins the third to the fourth ventricle in the brainstem below the cerebellum. The CSF is produced in the lateral ventricles and in the third ventricle by the choroid plexus, an outpouching of blood vessels from the ventricular wall. Hence, CSF is similar to blood, being formed from an ultrafiltrate of blood plasma; essentially, CSF is a clear fluid containing proteins, glucose, and ions, especially potassium, sodium, and chloride. It slowly circulates from the lateral and third ventricles through the cerebral aqueduct to the fourth ventricle and on to the subarachnoid space surrounding the brain, to be reabsorbed by the arachnoid villi in the sagittal sinus (the large venous system located between the two hemispheres on the dorsal surface; not shown).

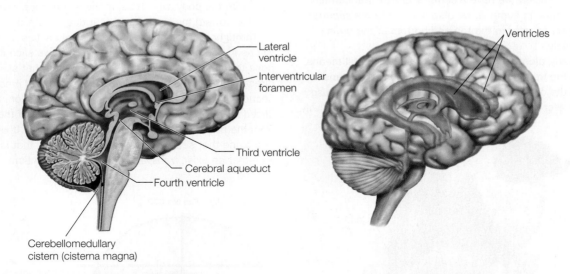

Lateral ventricle
Interventricular foramen
Third ventricle
Cerebral aqueduct
Fourth ventricle
Cerebellomedullary cistern (cisterna magna)
Ventricles

FIGURE 1 Ventricles of the human brain.
(left) Midsagital section showing the medial surface of the left hemisphere. **(right)** Transparent brain showing the ventricular system in 3D view.

white matter tracts. The more centrally located gray matter, consisting of neuronal bodies, resembles a butterfly with two separate sections or horns: the *dorsal horn* and *ventral horn*. The ventral horn contains the large motor neurons that project to muscles. The dorsal horn contains sensory neurons and interneurons. The interneurons

project to motor neurons on the same (*ipsilateral*) and opposite (*contralateral*) sides of the spinal cord to aid in the coordination of limb movements. The gray matter surrounds the *central canal*, which is an anatomical extension of the ventricles in the brain and contains cerebrospinal fluid.

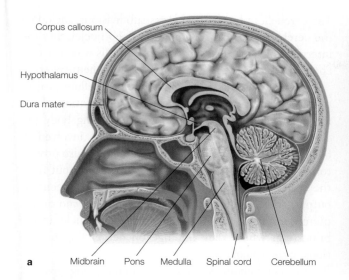
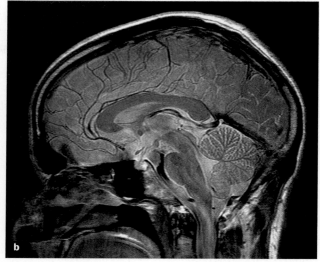

FIGURE 2.20 Gross anatomy of a brain showing brain stem.
(a) Midsagittal section through the head, showing the brainstem, cerebellum, and spinal cord. (b) High-resolution structural MRI obtained with a 4-tesla scanner, showing the same plane of section as in (a).

The Brainstem: Medulla, Pons, Cerebellum, and Midbrain

We usually think of the **brainstem** as having three main parts: the medulla (myelencephalon), the pons and cerebellum (metencephalon), and the midbrain (mesencephalon). These three sections form the central nervous system between the spinal cord and the diencephalon. Though the brainstem is rather small compared to the vast bulk of the forebrain (Figures 2.20 and 2.21), it plays a starring role in the brain. It contains groups of motor and sensory nuclei, nuclei of widespread modulatory neurotransmitter systems, and white matter tracts of ascending sensory information and descending motor signals.

Damage to the brainstem is life threatening, largely because brainstem nuclei control respiration and global states of consciousness such as sleep and wakefulness. The medulla, pons, and cerebellum make up the hindbrain, which we look at next.

Medulla The brainstem's most caudal portion is the **medulla**, which is continuous with the spinal cord (Figure 2.21). The medulla is essential for life. It houses the cell bodies of many of the 12 cranial nerves, providing sensory and motor innervations to the face, neck, abdomen, and throat (including taste) as well as the motor nuclei that innervate the heart. The medulla controls vital functions such as respiration, heart rate, and arousal. All of the ascending somatosensory information entering from the spinal cord passes through the medulla via two bilateral nuclear groups, the *gracile* and *cuneate nuclei*. These projection systems continue through the brainstem

to synapse in the thalamus en route to the somatosensory cortex. Another interesting feature of the medulla is that the corticospinal motor axons, tightly packed in a pyramid-shaped bundle (called the *pyramidal tract*), cross here to form the *pyramidal decussation*. Thus, the motor neurons originating in the right hemisphere cross to control muscles on the left side of the body, and vice versa. Functionally, the medulla is a relay station for sensory and motor information between the body and brain; it is the crossroads for most of the body's motor fibers;

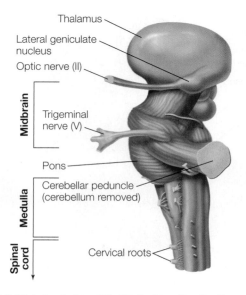

FIGURE 2.21 Lateral view of the brainstem showing the thalamus, pons, medulla, midbrain, and spinal cord.
Anterior in the brain is at the top, and the spinal cord is toward the bottom in this left lateral view. The cerebellum is removed in this drawing.

it controls several autonomic functions, including the essential reflexes that determine respiration, heart rate, blood pressure, and digestive and vomiting responses.

Pons The **pons**, Latin for "bridge," is so named because it is the main connection between the brain and the cerebellum. Sitting anterior to the medulla, the pons is made up of a vast system of fiber tracts interspersed with nuclei (Figure 2.21). Many of the cranial nerves synapse in the pons; these include the sensory and motor nuclei from the face and mouth and the visuomotor nuclei controlling some of the extraocular muscles. Thus, the pons is important for some eye movements as well as those of the face and mouth. In addition, some auditory information is channeled through another pontine structure, the superior olive. This level of the brainstem contains a large portion of the reticular formation that modulates arousal. Interestingly, the pons is also responsible for generating rapid eye movement (REM) sleep.

Cerebellum The **cerebellum** (literally, "small cerebrum" or "little brain"), which clings to the brainstem at the level of the pons, is home to most of the brain's neurons (see Figures 2.20 and 2.22). Visually, the surface of the cerebellum appears to be covered with thinly spaced, parallel grooves; but in reality, it is a continuous layer of tightly folded neural tissue (like an accordion). It forms the roof of the fourth ventricle and sits on the cerebellar *peduncles* (meaning "feet"), which are massive input and output fiber tracts of the cerebellum (see Figure 2.21).

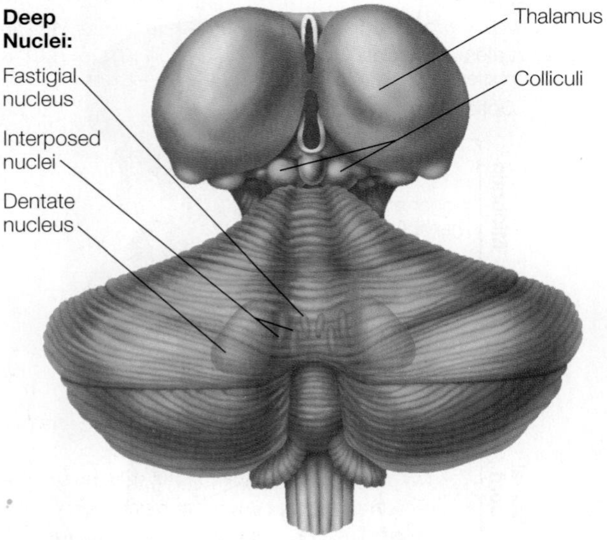

Deep Nuclei:
Fastigial nucleus
Interposed nuclei
Dentate nucleus
Thalamus
Colliculi

FIGURE 2.22 Gross anatomy of the cerebellum.
Anterior in the brain is at the top, and the spinal cord is toward the bottom (not shown). This dorsal view of the cerebellum shows the underlying deep nuclei in a see-through projection.

The cerebellum has several gross subdivisions, including the cerebellar cortex, four pairs of deep nuclei, and the internal white matter (Figure 2.22). In this way, the cerebellum resembles the forebrain's cerebral hemispheres.

Most of the fibers arriving at the cerebellum project to the cerebellar cortex, conveying information about motor outputs and sensory inputs describing body position. Inputs from vestibular projections involved in balance, as well as auditory and visual inputs, also project to the cerebellum from the brainstem. The output from the cerebellum originates in the deep nuclei. Ascending outputs travel to the thalamus and then to the motor and premotor cortex. Other outputs project to nuclei of the brainstem, where they impinge on descending projections to the spinal cord.

The cerebellum is critical for maintaining posture, walking, and performing coordinated movements. It does not directly control movements; instead, it integrates information about the body, such as its size and speed, with motor commands. Then, it modifies motor outflow to effect smooth, coordinated movements. It is because of the cerebellum that Yo-Yo Ma can play the cello and the Harlem Globetrotters can dunk a ball with such panache. If your cerebellum is damaged, your movements will be uncoordinated and halting, and you may not be able to maintain balance. In Chapter 8, we look more closely at the cerebellum's role in motor control. In the 1990s, it was discovered that the cerebellum is involved with more than motor functions. It has been implicated in aspects of cognitive processing including language, attention, learning, and mental imagery.

Midbrain The mesencephalon, or **midbrain**, lies superior to the pons and can be seen only in a medial view. It surrounds the cerebral aqueduct, which connects the third and fourth ventricles. Its dorsal portion consists of the *tectum* (meaning "roof"), and its ventral portion is the *tegmentum* ("covering"). Large fiber tracts course through the ventral regions from the forebrain to the spinal cord, cerebellum, and other parts of the brainstem. The midbrain also contains some of the cranial nerve ganglia and two other important structures: the superior and inferior colliculi (Figure 2.23). The *superior colliculus* plays a role in perceiving objects in the periphery and orienting our gaze directly toward them, bringing them into sharper view. The *inferior colliculus* is used for locating and orienting toward auditory stimuli. Another structure, the *red nucleus*, is involved in certain aspects of motor coordination. It helps a baby crawl or coordinates the swing of your arms as you walk. Much of the midbrain is occupied by the mesencephalic reticular formation, a rostral continuation of the pontine and medullary reticular formation.

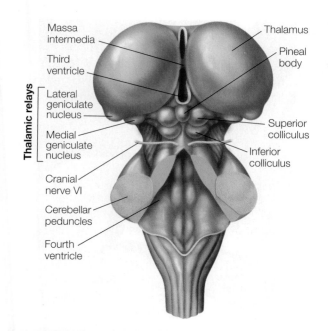

FIGURE 2.23 Anatomy of the midbrain.
The dorsal surface of the brainstem is shown with the cerebral cortex and cerebellum removed.

TAKE-HOME MESSAGES

- The spinal cord conducts the final motor signals to the muscles, and it relays sensory information from the body's peripheral receptors to the brain.
- The brainstem's neurons carry out many sensory and motor processes, including visuomotor, auditory, and vestibular functions as well as sensation and motor control of the face, mouth, throat, respiratory system, and heart.
- The brainstem houses fibers that pass from the cortex to the spinal cord and cerebellum, and sensory fibers that run from spinal levels to the thalamus and then to the cortex.

- Many neurochemical systems have nuclei in the brainstem that project widely to the cerebral cortex, limbic system, thalamus, and hypothalamus.
- The cerebellum integrates information about the body and motor commands and modifies motor outflow to effect smooth, coordinated movements.

The Diencephalon: Thalamus and Hypothalamus

After leaving the brainstem, we arrive at the diencephalon, which is made up of the **thalamus** and **hypothalamus**. These subcortical structures are composed of groups of nuclei with interconnections to widespread brain areas.

Thalamus Almost smack dab in the center of the brain and perched on top of the brainstem (at the rostral end; see Figure 2.21), the thalamus is the larger of the diencephalon structures. The thalamus is divided into two parts—one in the right hemisphere and one in the left—that straddle the third ventricle. In most people, the two parts are connected by a bridge of gray matter called the *massa intermedia* (see Figure 2.23). Above the thalamus are the fornix and corpus callosum; beside it is the *internal capsule*, containing ascending and descending axons running between the cerebral cortex and the medulla and spinal cord.

The thalamus has been referred to as the "gateway to the cortex" because, except for some olfactory inputs, all of the sensory modalities make synaptic relays in the thalamus before continuing to the primary cortical sensory receiving areas (Figure 2.24). The thalamus is involved in relaying primary sensory information. It also receives inputs from the basal ganglia, cerebellum, neocortex, and medial temporal lobe and sends projections back to these structures to create circuits involved in many different functions. It also relays

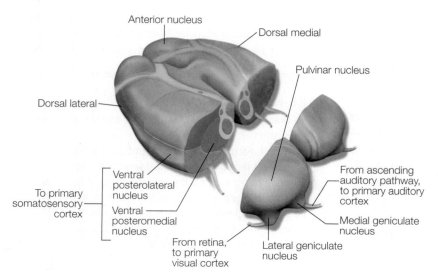

FIGURE 2.24 The thalamus, showing inputs and outputs and major subdivisions.
The various subdivisions of the thalamus serve different sensory systems and participate in various cortical–subcortical circuits. The posterior portion of the thalamus (**lower right**) is cut away in cross section and separated from the rest of the thalamus to reveal the internal organization of the thalamic nuclei (**upper left**).

most of the motor information that is on its way to the spinal cord. Thus, the thalamus, a veritable Grand Central Station of the brain, is considered a relay center where neurons from one part of the brain synapse on neurons that travel to another region. In the thalamus, information can be reorganized and shuttled, like in a train station switching yard, according to the connection patterns formed by the neurons.

The thalamus is divided into several nuclei that act as specific relays for incoming sensory information (Figure 2.24). The *lateral geniculate nucleus* receives information from the ganglion cells of the retina and sends axons to the primary visual cortex. Similarly, the *medial geniculate nucleus* receives information from the inner ear, via other brainstem nuclei in the ascending auditory pathway, and sends axons to the primary auditory cortex. Somatosensory information projects via the *ventral posterior (medial and lateral) nuclei of the thalamus* to the primary somatosensory cortex. Sensory relay nuclei of the thalamus not only project axons to the cortex but also receive heavy descending projections back from the same cortical area that they contact. Located at the posterior pole of the thalamus is the *pulvinar nucleus*, which is involved in attention and in integrative functions involving multiple cortical areas.

Hypothalamus The main link between the nervous system and the endocrine system is the hypothalamus, which is the main site for hormone production and control. Easily located, it lies on the floor of the third ventricle (see Figure 2.20a). The two bumps seen on the ventral surface of the brain, the *mammillary bodies*, belong to the small collection of nuclei and fiber tracks contained in the hypothalamus (Figure 2.25). It receives inputs from the limbic system structures and other brain areas. One of its jobs is to control circadian rhythms (light–dark cycles) with inputs from the mesencephalic reticular formation, amygdala, and the retina. Extending from the hypothalamus are major projections to the prefrontal cortex, amygdala, spinal cord, and pituitary gland. The pituitary gland is attached to the base of the hypothalamus.

The hypothalamus controls the functions necessary for maintaining the normal state of the body (homeostasis). It sends out signals that drive behavior to alleviate such feelings as thirst, hunger, and fatigue, and it controls body temperature and circadian cycles. You would not want to be in the broiling hot desert without your hypothalamus. It accomplishes much of this work through the endocrine system and via control of the **pituitary gland**.

The hypothalamus produces hormones, as well as factors that regulate hormone production in other parts of the brain. For example, hypothalamic neurons send axonal projections to the *median eminence*, an area bordering the pituitary gland. There it releases peptides (releasing factors) into the circulatory system of the

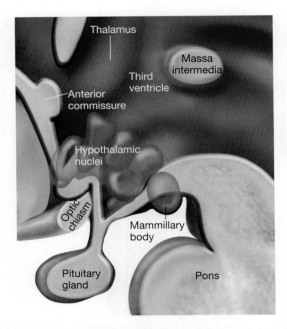

FIGURE 2.25 Midsagittal view of the hypothalamus. Various nuclear groups are shown diagrammatically. The hypothalamus is the floor of the third ventricle, and, as the name suggests, it sits below the thalamus. Anterior is to the left in this drawing.

anterior pituitary gland. These in turn trigger (or inhibit) the release of a variety of hormones from the anterior pituitary into the bloodstream, such as growth hormone, thyroid-stimulating hormone, adrenocorticotropic hormone, and the gonadotropic hormones.

Hypothalamic neurons in the anteromedial region, including the *supraoptic nucleus* and *paraventricular nuclei*, send axonal projections into the posterior pituitary gland. There they stimulate the gland to release the hormones vasopressin and oxytocin into the blood to regulate water retention in the kidneys, milk production, and uterine contractility, among other functions. Circulating peptide hormones in the bloodstream can also act on distant sites and influence a wide range of behaviors, from the fight-or-flight response to maternal bonding. The hypothalamus can itself be stimulated by hormones circulating in the blood that were produced in other regions of the body.

TAKE-HOME MESSAGES

- The thalamus is the relay station for almost all sensory information.
- The hypothalamus is important for the autonomic nervous system and endocrine system. It controls functions necessary for the maintenance of homeostasis. It is also involved in control of the pituitary gland.
- The pituitary gland releases hormones into the bloodstream where they can circulate to influence other tissues and organs (e.g., gonads).

The Telencephalon: Limbic System, Basal Ganglia, and Cerebral Cortex

Toward the front of and evolutionarily newer than the diencephalon, the telencephalon develops into the cerebrum, which includes the cerebral cortex, the limbic system, and the basal ganglia. Compared to the diencephalon, the anatomy (and functions) of the forebrain above the thalamus are less straightforward. Instead of a rather linear stacking of structures, it forms a clump of structures found deep within the cerebral hemispheres nestled over and around the diencephalon. In the 17th century, Thomas Willis observed that the brainstem appeared to sport a cortical border encircling it and named it the *cerebri limbus* (in Latin, *limbus* means "border"). For better or for worse, in a move that began to tie the area with specific functioning, Paul Broca in 1878 renamed it the *grand lobe limbique* and suggested that it was a primary player in olfaction.

Limbic System The "classical" limbic lobe (Figure 2.26) is made up of the *cingulate gyrus* (a band of cerebral cortex that extends above the corpus callosum in the anterior–posterior direction and spans both the frontal and parietal lobes), the hypothalamus, anterior thalamic nuclei, and the **hippocampus**, an area located on the

ventromedial aspect of the temporal lobe. In the 1930s James Papez (pronounced "payps") first suggested the idea that these structures were organized into a system for emotional behavior, which led to the use of the term *Papez circuit*. It was named the **limbic system** by Paul MacLean in 1952 when he suggested the addition of more brain areas, such as the amygdala and prefrontal cortex. Note that the limbic system is neither anatomically nor functionally organized to the degree that other systems are in the brain. In fact, some researchers feel that the limbic system is sufficiently nebulous that the concept should be discarded or reevaluated. The classical limbic system, as noted earlier, has been extended to include the **amygdala**, a group of neurons anterior to the hippocampus, along with the orbitofrontal cortex and parts of the basal ganglia (see Figure 2.26). Sometimes the medial dorsal nucleus of the thalamus is also included. The organization and role of the limbic system are described in more detail in Chapter 10.

Basal Ganglia The **basal ganglia** are a collection of nuclei bilaterally located deep in the brain beneath the anterior portion of the lateral ventricles, near the thalamus (Figure 2.27). These subcortical nuclei, the *caudate nucleus, putamen, globus pallidus, subthalmic nucleus,* and *substantia nigra,* are extensively interconnected. The caudate nucleus together with the putamen is

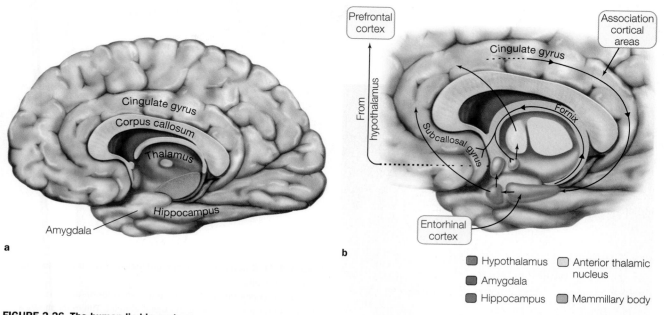

FIGURE 2.26 The human limbic system.
(a) Anatomy of the limbic system. **(b)** Major connections of the limbic system, shown diagrammatically in a medial view of the right hemisphere. The figure zooms in on the region in purple in (a). The basal ganglia are not represented in this figure, nor is the medial dorsal nucleus of the thalamus. More detail is shown here than needs to be committed to memory, but this figure provides a reference that will come in handy in later chapters.

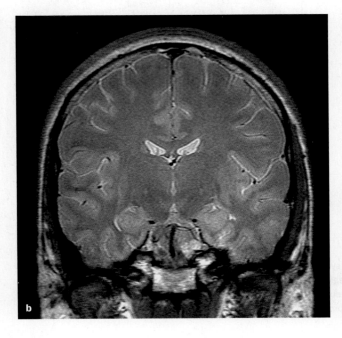

Level of anterior commissure

Longitudinal fissure
Corpus callosum
Lateral ventricles

Caudate nucleus ⎫
Putamen   ⎬ Neostriatum   Basal ganglia
Globus pallidus

Anterior commissure

Basal ganglia

Corpus callosum
Caudate nucleus

Thalamus
Putamen
Globus pallidus
Subthalamic nucleus
Substantia nigra
Amygdala

Mammillary bodies

a   Level of mammillary bodies

b

FIGURE 2.27 Coronal and transparent views of the brain showing the basal ganglia.
(a) Cross sections through the brain at two anterior–posterior levels (as indicated), showing the basal ganglia. The inset shows a transparent brain with the basal ganglia in 3D in blue. (b) Corresponding high-resolution, structural MRI (4-tesla scanner) taken at approximately the same level as the more posterior drawing in (a). This image also shows the brainstem as well as the skull and scalp, which are not shown in (a).

known as the *striatum*. The basal ganglia receive inputs from sensory and motor areas, and the striatum receives extensive feedback projections from the thalamus. A comprehensive understanding of how these deep brain nuclei function remains elusive. They are involved in a variety of crucial brain functions including action selection, action gating, motor preparation, timing, fatigue, and task switching (Cameron et al., 2009). Notably, the basal ganglia have many dopamine receptors. The dopamine signal appears to represent the *error* between predicted future reward and actual reward (Shultz et al., 1997), and plays a crucial role in motivation and learning. The basal ganglia may also play a big role in reward-based learning and goal-oriented behavior. One summary of basal ganglia function proposes that it combines an organism's sensory and motor context with reward information and passes this integrated information to the motor and prefrontal cortex for a decision (Chakravarthy et al., 2009).

TAKE-HOME MESSAGES

- The limbic system includes subcortical and cortical structures that are interconnected and play a role in emotion.
- The basal ganglia are involved in a variety of crucial brain functions, including action selection, action gating, reward-based learning, motor preparation, timing, task switching, and more.

The Cerebral Cortex

The crowning glory of the cerebrum is its outermost tissue, the cerebral cortex. It is made up of large sheets of (mostly) layered neurons, draped and folded over the two symmetrical hemispheres like frosting on a cake. It sits over the top of the core structures that we have been discussing, including parts of the limbic system and basal ganglia, and surrounds the structures of the diencephalon. The term *cortex* means "bark," as in tree bark, and in higher mammals and humans it contains many infoldings, or convolutions (Figure 2.28). The infoldings of the cortical sheet are called **sulci** (the crevices) and **gyri** (the crowns of the folded tissue that one observes when viewing the surface).

The folds of the human cortex serve several functions. First, they enable more cortical surface to be packed into the skull. If the human cortex were smoothed out to resemble that of the rat, for example, humans would need to have very large heads. The total surface area of the human cerebral cortex is about 2,200 to 2,400 cm², but because of extensive folding, about two thirds of this area is confined within the depths of the sulci. Second, having a highly folded cortex brings neurons into closer three-dimensional relationships to one another, reducing axonal distance and hence neuronal conduction time between different areas. This savings occurs because the axons that make long-distance corticocortical connections run under the cortex through the white matter and do not follow the foldings of the cortical surface in their paths to

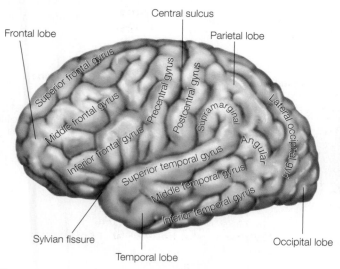

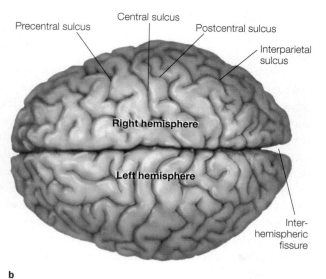

a

b

FIGURE 2.28 The human cerebral cortex.
Lateral view of the left hemisphere (**a**) and dorsal view of the brain (**b**) in humans. The major features of the cortex include the four cortical lobes and various key gyri. Gyri are separated by sulci and result from the folding of the cerebral cortex that occurs during development of the nervous system, to achieve economies of size and functionality.

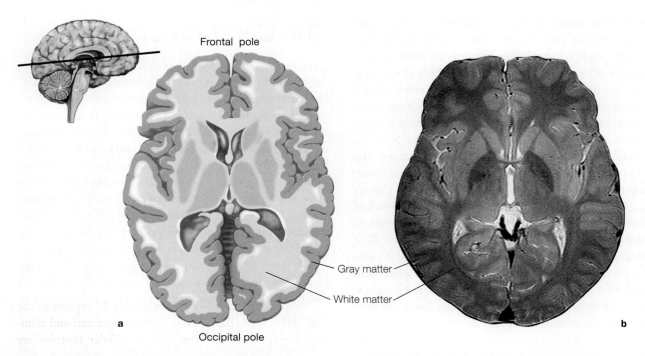

FIGURE 2.29 Cerebral cortex and white matter tracts.
(a) Horizontal section through the cerebral hemispheres at the level indicated at upper left. White matter is composed of myelinated axons, and gray matter is composed primarily of neurons. This diagram shows that the gray matter on the surface of the cerebral hemispheres forms a continuous sheet that is heavily folded. (b) High-resolution structural MRI in a similar plane of section in a living human. This T2 image was obtained on a 4-tesla scanner (a high-magnetic-field scanner). Note that on T2 images, the white matter appears darker than the gray matter, but this is due to the imaging technique, not the actual appearance.

distant cortical areas. Third, by folding, the cortex brings some nearby regions closer together; for example, the opposing layers of cortex in each gyrus are in closer linear proximity than they would be if the gyri were flattened.

The cortex ranges from 1.5 to 4.5 mm in thickness, but in most regions it is approximately 3 mm thick. The cortex contains the cell bodies of neurons, their dendrites, and some of their axons. In addition, the cortex includes axons and axon terminals of neurons projecting to the cortex from other brain regions, such as the subcortical thalamus. The cortex also contains blood vessels. Because the cerebral cortex has such a high density of cell bodies, it appears grayish in relation to underlying regions that are composed primarily of the axons that connect the neurons of the cerebral cortex to other locations in the brain. These appear slightly paler or even white (Figure 2.29) because of their lipid sheaths (myelin). As described earlier, for this reason anatomists used the terms *gray matter* and *white matter* when referring to areas of cell bodies and axon tracts, respectively.

Dividing the Cortex Anatomically

The cerebral hemispheres have four main divisions, or lobes, that are best seen in a lateral view: the **frontal, parietal, temporal,** and **occipital lobes** (Figure 2.30).

These names are derived from names given to the overlying skull bones; for example, the temporal lobe lies underneath the temporal bone. The skull bones themselves are named for their locations. The temporal bone lies under the temple, where the passage of time can be

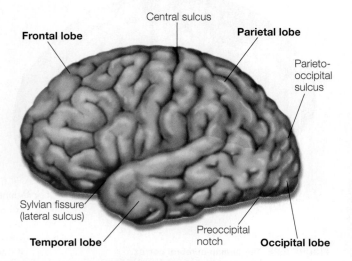

FIGURE 2.30 The four lobes of the cerebral cortex.
This is a lateral view of the left hemisphere showing the four major lobes of the brain, and some of the major landmarks that separate them.

observed first in the graying of hair. The word temporal derives from Latin "tempora," meaning "time."

The lobes can usually be distinguished from one another by prominent anatomical landmarks such as pronounced sulci. The **central sulcus** divides the frontal lobe from the parietal lobe, and the **Sylvian (lateral) fissure** separates the temporal lobe from the frontal and parietal lobes. The occipital lobe is demarcated from the parietal and temporal lobes by the *parieto-occipital sulcus* on the brain's dorsal surface and the *preoccipital notch* located on the ventrolateral surface. The left and right cerebral hemispheres are separated by the *interhemispheric fissure* (also called the *longitudinal fissure*; see Figure 2.28b) that runs from the rostral to the caudal end of the forebrain.

Hidden from the lateral surface view are other parts of the cerebrum, not all of which are conveniently contained in the four lobes. For instance, the **insula** is located between the temporal and frontal lobe, and is, as its name implies, an island of folded cortex hidden deep in the lateral sulcus. The insula, which is surprisingly large, is divided into the larger anterior insula and smaller posterior insula.

Connections between the cerebral hemispheres are via axons from cortical neurons that travel through the corpus callosum, which, as previously mentioned, represents the largest white matter commissure in the nervous system. As we will discuss in Chapter 4, the corpus callosum carries out valuable integrative functions for the two hemispheres.

Dividing the Cortex Cytoarchitectonically

The cerebral cortex can be more finely divided, both anatomically and functionally. We will take a look at both.

Cytoarchitectonics uses the microanatomy of cells and their organization to subdivide the cortex (*cyto*– means "cell" and *architectonics* means "architecture"). Using histological analysis, tissue regions are defined in which the cellular architecture looks similar, and therefore might indicate areas of homogeneous function. This work began in earnest with Korbinian Brodmann at the beginning of the 20th century.

Brodmann identified approximately 52 regions of the cerebral cortex. These areas were categorized and numbered according to differences in cellular morphology and organization (Figure 2.31). Other anatomists further subdivided the cortex into almost 200 cytoarchitectonically defined areas. A combination of cytoarchitectonic and functional descriptions of the cortex is probably the most effective way of dividing the cerebral cortex into

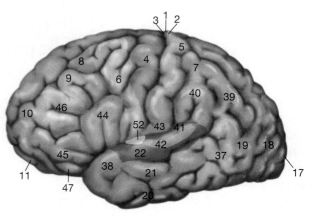

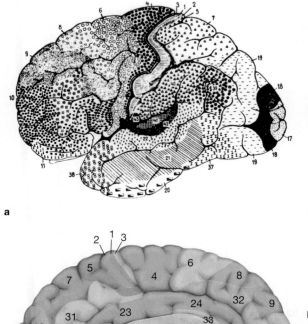

FIGURE 2.31 Cytoarchitectonic subdivisions of the human cerebral cortex.
(a) Brodmann's original cytoarchitectonic map from his work around the start of the 20th century. Different regions of cortex have been demarcated by histological examination of the cellular microanatomy. Brodmann divided the cortex into about 52 areas. (b) Lateral view of the right hemisphere showing Brodmann's areas color coded. Over the years, the map has been modified, and the standard version no longer includes some areas. (c) Medial view of the left hemisphere showing Brodmann's areas. Most of Brodmann's areas are symmetrical in the two hemispheres.

meaningful units. In the sections that follow, we use Brodmann's numbering system and anatomical names to describe the cerebral cortex.

The Brodmann system often seems unsystematic. Indeed, the numbering has more to do with the order in which Brodmann sampled a region than with any meaningful relation between areas. Nonetheless, in some regions the numbering system roughly corresponds with the relations between areas that carry out similar functions, such as vision—e.g., Brodmann areas 17, 18, and 19. Unfortunately, the nomenclature of the cortex (and indeed the nervous system) is not fully standardized. Hence, a region might be referred to by its Brodmann name, a cytoarchitectonic name, a gross anatomical name, or a functional name. For example, let's consider the first area in the cortex to receive visual inputs from the thalamus—the primary sensory cortex for vision. The Brodmann name is area 17 (or Brodmann area 17; i.e., BA17), another cytoarchitectonic name is *striate cortex* (owing to the highly visible stripe of myelin in cross sections of this cortex, known

as the *Stria of Gennari*), the gross anatomical name is *calcarine cortex* (the cortex surrounding the calcarine fissure in humans), and the functional name is *primary visual cortex*, which has been labeled area V1 (for "visual area 1") based on studies of the visual systems of monkeys. We chose primary visual cortex as an example here, because all these different terms refer to the same cortical area. Unfortunately, for much of the cortex, this is not the case; that is, different nomenclatures often do not refer to precisely the same area with a one-to-one mapping. For example, BA18 of the visual system is not fully synonymous with V2 (for "visual area 2").

Using different anatomical criteria, it is also possible to subdivide the cerebral cortex according to the general patterns of layering (Figure 2.32a, b). Ninety percent of cortex is composed of **neocortex:** *cortex that contains six cortical layers or that passed through a developmental stage involving six cortical layers.* Neocortex includes areas like primary sensory and motor cortex and association cortex (areas not obviously primary sensory or motor).

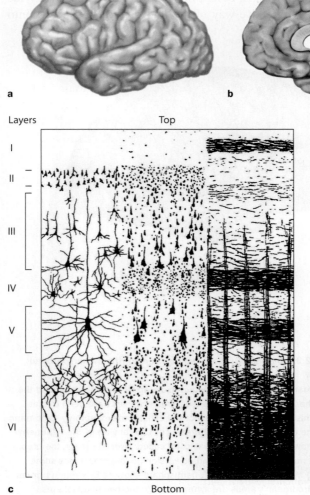

a
b

Layers   Top

I

II

III

IV

V

VI

c   Bottom

FIGURE 2.32 Cerebral cortex, color-coded to show the regional differences in cortical layering that specify different types of cortex.
(a) The lateral surface of the left hemisphere. (b) The medial surface of the right hemisphere. Neocortex is shown in red, mesocortex in blue, and allocortex in green. (c) Idealized cross section of neocortex showing a variety of cell types and the patterns of three different types of staining techniques. On the left, the Golgi preparation is apparent: Only a few neurons are stained, but each is completely visualized. In the middle, we see primarily cell bodies from the Nissl stain. On the right, we see the fiber tracks in a Weigert stain, which selectively stains myelin.

Mesocortex is a term for the so-called paralimbic region, which includes the cingulate gyrus, parahippocampal gyrus, insular cortex, and orbitofrontal cortex. Mesocortex is interposed between neocortex and allocortex and usually has six layers. *Allocortex* typically has only one to four layers of neurons and includes the hippocampal complex (sometimes referred to as *archicortex*) and primary olfactory cortex (sometimes referred to as *paleocortex*).

In neocortex the cortical layers numbered 1–6 (or for the more classically minded users, I–VI) are sheets of neurons neatly stacked on top of each other. The neurons of each layer are typically similar within a layer, but different between layers. For instance, neocortical layer 4 is packed with stellate neurons, and layer 5 is predominantly pyramidal neurons (Figure 2.32c). The deeper layers, 5 and 6, mature earlier during gestation and project primarily to targets outside the cortex. Layer 4 is typically the input layer, receiving information from the thalamus as well as information from other, more distant cortical areas. Layer 5, on the other hand, is typically considered an output layer that sends information from the cortex back to the thalamus, facilitating feedback. The superficial layers mature last and primarily project to targets within the cortex. It has been suggested that the superficial layers and the connections they form within the cortex participate in the higher cognitive functions.

The neurons in any one sheet, while interwoven with the other neurons in the same layer, are also lined up with the neurons in the sheets above and below it, forming columns of neurons running perpendicular to the sheets. These columns are known as *minicolumns* or *microcolumns*. These columns are not just an anatomical nicety. The neurons within a column synapse with those from the layers above and below them, forming an elemental circuit, and appear to function as a unit. Neuronal columns are the fundamental processing unit within the cerebral cortex, and bundles of microcolumns assembled together, dubbed *cortical columns*, create functional units in the cortex.

Functional Divisions of the Cortex

The lobes of the cerebral cortex have a variety of functional roles in neural processing. Sometimes we get lucky, and the gross anatomical subdivisions of the cerebral cortex can be related fairly to specific functions, such as in the precentral gyrus where the primary motor cortex resides. More typically, however, cognitive brain systems are often composed of networks whose component parts are located in different lobes of the cortex. In addition, most functions in the brain—whether sensory, motor, or cognitive—rely on both cortical and subcortical components. Thus, it can be daunting to reveal relationships between cognitive functions and locations within the brain where they occur. The detailed functional anatomy of the brain will be revealed to you in the next twelve chapters. The rest of this section, however, provides a beginner's guide to the functional anatomy of the cortex.

Motor Areas of the Frontal Lobe Among many other functions, the frontal lobe plays a major role in the planning and execution of movements. It has two main subdivisions: the prefrontal cortex and the motor cortex (Figure 2.33a). The motor cortex sits in front

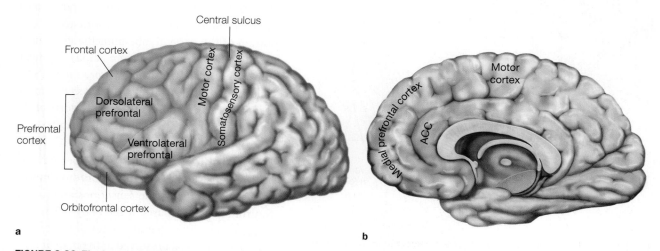

FIGURE 2.33 The human frontal cortex.
(a) Divisions of the frontal cortex. The frontal lobe contains both motor and higher order association areas. For example, the prefrontal cortex is involved in executive functions, memory, decision making, and other processes. (b) Midsagital section of the brain showing the medial prefrontal regions, which include the anterior cingulate cortex (ACC). Also visible is the supplementary motor area.

of the central sulcus, beginning in the depths of the sulcus and extending anteriorly. The primary motor cortex (M1) corresponds to BA4. It includes the anterior bank of the central sulcus and much of the precentral gyrus (the prefix *pre-* in neuroanatomy means "in front of"). Anterior to this area are two more main motor areas of cortex (within BA6; see Figure 2.31 for BA locations): the premotor cortex on the lateral surface of the hemisphere, and the supplementary motor cortex that lies dorsal to the premotor area and extends around to the hemisphere's medial surface. These motor cortical areas contain motor neurons whose axons extend to the spinal cord and brainstem and synapse on motor neurons in the spinal cord. The output layer of primary motor cortex contains some of the most amazing neurons in the nervous system: the large pyramidal neurons known as *Betz's cells*, named after Vladimir Aleksandrovich Betz, the Russian anatomist who described them in the 19th century. Betz's cells are the largest neurons in the cerebral cortex. They reach 60 to 80 microns in diameter at the cell body, and some of them send axons several feet long down the spinal cord.

Prefrontal Cortex The more anterior regions of the frontal lobe, the **prefrontal cortex**, take part in the more complex aspects of planning, organizing, and executing behavior—tasks that require the integration of information over time. Because of its facility with these tasks, the frontal lobe is often said to be the center of executive function. People with frontal lobe lesions often have difficulty reaching a goal. They may know the steps that are necessary to attain it, but they just can't figure out how to put them together. Another problem associated with frontal lobe lesions is a lack of motivation to initiate action, to modulate it, or to stop it once it is happening. The main regions of the prefrontal cortex are the *dorsolateral prefrontal cortex*, the *ventrolateral prefrontal cortex*, the *orbitofrontal cortex* (Figure 2.33a), and the *medial prefrontal regions*, including the *anterior cingulate cortex* (Figure 2.33b).

Somatosensory Areas of the Parietal Lobe The parietal lobe receives sensory information from the outside world, sensory information from within the body, and information from memory, and integrates it. Parietal lobe lesions result in all sorts of odd deficits relating to sensation and spatial location: People think that parts of their body are not their own or parts of space don't exist for them, or they may recognize objects only from certain viewpoints, or they can't locate objects in space at all. Stimulating certain regions of the parietal lobe causes people to have "out of body" experiences (Blanke et al., 2002).

Sensory information about touch, pain, temperature sense, and limb proprioception (limb position) is received via receptor cells on the skin and converted to neuronal impulses that are conducted to the spinal cord and then to the somatosensory relays of the thalamus (Figure 2.34). From the thalamus, inputs travel to the *primary somatosensory cortex* (or S1), a portion of the parietal lobe immediately caudal to the central sulcus (see Figure 2.33a). The next stop is the *secondary somatosensory cortex* (S2), which is located ventrally to S1; S2 receives most of its input from S1. Together, these cortical regions are known as the *somatosensory cortex*.

Topographical Mapping The specific cortical regions of the somatosensory and motor cortices that process the sensations and motor control of specific parts of the body have been mapped out. The spatial relationships of the body are fairly well preserved in the map of neural representations draped across these cortices, by using a principle known as **topography** (see "How the Brain Works: Cortical Topography").

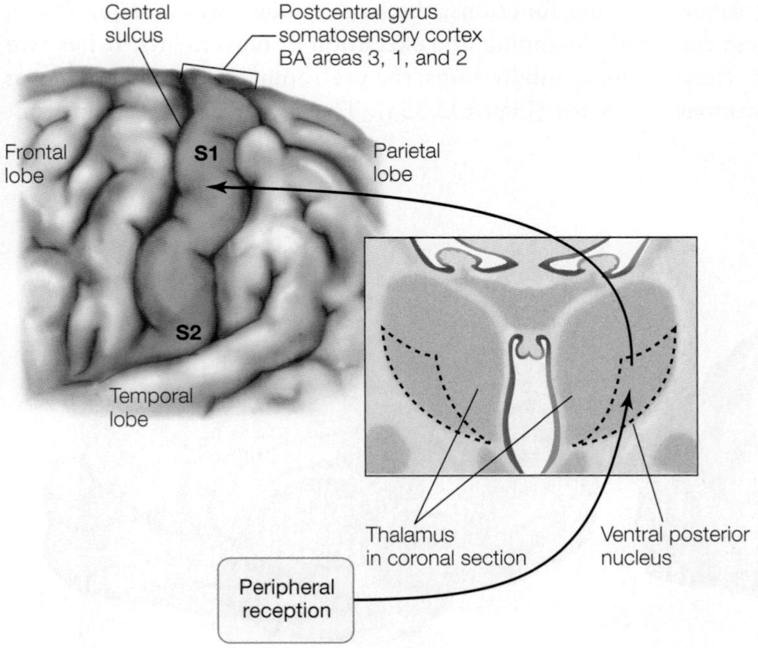

FIGURE 2.34 The somatosensory cortex, which is located in the postcentral gyrus.
Inputs from peripheral receptors project via the thalamus (shown in cross section) to the primary somatosensory cortex (S1). Secondary somatosensory cortex (S2) is also shown.

HOW THE BRAIN WORKS
Cortical Topography

Early insights into human cortical organization were made possible by studies that involved direct stimulation of the cortex of humans undergoing brain surgery while they were awake. Because there are no pain receptors in the central nervous system, patients experience no discomfort from stimulation. Thus, stimulation can be applied even when they are awake and fully conscious, enabling researchers to gather the patient's subjective experiences—a relative impossibility in animal studies. Wilder Penfield and Herbert Jasper (1954) at the Montreal Neurological Institute carried out such pioneering work in the 1940s. Taking advantage of the fact that the cortex is exposed during surgery, these surgeons removed damaged brain tissue and during the same procedure, systematically explored the effects of small levels of electrical current applied to the cortical surface.

In their studies, Penfield and his associates found a topographic correspondence between cortical regions and body surface with respect to somatosensory and motor processes. This correspondence is represented in Figure 1 by overlaying drawings of body parts on drawings of coronal sections of the motor and somatosensory cortex. These coronal sections are from the regions indicat ed by the color codes in the lateral view of the whole brain at the top of the figure (only one hemisphere is shown here). The resulting map of the body surface on the cortex is some-

times called a *homunculus*, because it is an organized representation of the body across a given cortical area. Note that there is an indirect relation between the actual size of body parts and the cortical representation of the body's parts. For example, areas within the motor homunculus that activate muscles in the fingers, mouth, and tongue are much larger than would be expected if the representation were proportional. The large drawings of the fingers and mouth indicate that large areas of cortex are involved in the fine coordination required when we manipulate objects or speak.

Is the representation of the homunculus in the figure correct? Recent evidence from brain-imaging studies using functional magnetic resonance imaging (fMRI; described in Chapter 3) suggests that it may not be. Ravi Menon and his colleagues (Servos et al., 1999) in Canada stimulated the foreheads and chins of healthy volunteers while their brains were being scanned. In contrast to the results of the electrical-stimulation studies, the researchers found that stimulating the forehead produced activity in a region that was below (inferior to) the region for activity related to chin stimulation—the reverse of the drawing in the figure based on the work of Penfield and his colleagues. If the latter pattern from neuroimaging turns out to be accurate, it will constitute a dramatic example of scientific revisionism.

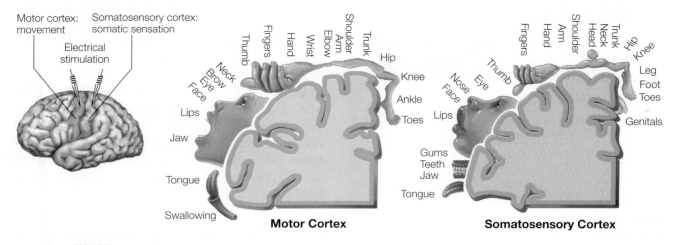

FIGURE 1

Topographic correspondence between cortical regions and body surface with respect to somatosensory and motor processes.

For example, within the somatosensory cortex, neurons that respond to touch of the index finger are adjacent to those that respond to touch of the middle finger, which are also next to neurons that respond to touch of the ring finger. Similarly, the hand area as a whole is adjacent to the lower arm area, which is near the upper arm, and so forth. This mapping of specific parts of the body to areas of the cortex is known as **somatotopy**, resulting in somatotopic maps in the cortical areas. It is interesting to ask why such maps exist, since there is no inherent necessity for the organization. Yet topographic maps are a common feature of the nervous system (see Chapter 5), perhaps reflecting the fact that neighboring body parts are frequently co-recruited, as when we're gripping a ball or stroking a favorite pet.

Visual Processing Areas in the Occipital Lobe

The business of the occipital lobes is vision. The primary visual cortex is where the cerebral cortex begins to process visual information. As mentioned earlier, this area is also known as *striate cortex*, V1 for visual area 1, or BA17. It receives visual information relayed from the lateral geniculate nucleus of the thalamus (Figure 2.35). In humans, the primary visual cortex is on the medial surface of the cerebral hemispheres, extending only slightly onto the posterior hemispheric pole. Thus, most of the primary visual cortex is effectively hidden from view, between the two hemispheres. The cortex in this area has six layers and begins the cortical coding of visual features like luminance, spatial frequency, orientation, and motion—features that we will take up in detail in Chapters 5 and 6.

Visual information from the outside world is processed by multiple layers of cells in the retina and transmitted via the optic nerve to the lateral geniculate nucleus of the thalamus, and from there to V1—a pathway often referred to as the *retinogeniculostriate*, or primary visual pathway. The retina also sends projections to other subcortical brain regions by way of secondary projection systems. The superior colliculus of the midbrain is the main target of the secondary pathway and participates in visuomotor functions such as eye movements. In Chapter 7, we will review the role of the cortical and subcortical projection pathways in visual attention.

Surrounding the striate cortex is a large visual cortical region called the *extrastriate* ("outside the striate") visual cortex (sometimes referred to as the *prestriate* cortex in monkeys, to signify that it is anatomically anterior to the striate cortex). The extrastriate cortex includes BA18 and BA19 and other areas.

Auditory Processing Areas in the Temporal Lobe

The auditory cortex lies in the superior part of the temporal lobe in a region known as *Heschl's gyrus* within the Sylvian fissure (Figure 2.36) and roughly corresponds with Brodmann areas 41 and 42. The auditory cortex has a tonotopic organization, meaning that the physical layout of the neurons is based on the frequency of sound. Neurons in the auditory cortex that respond best to low frequency are at one end of the cortex, and those that respond to high frequencies are at the other. The projection from the cochlea (the auditory sensory organ in the inner ear) proceeds through the subcortical relays to the medial geniculate of the thalamus and then to Heschl's gyri, the primary auditory cortex (A1) in the supratemporal cortex. Surrounding and posterior to A1 is A2, the auditory association area. BA22, which surrounds the auditory cortex, aids in the perception of auditory inputs; when this area is stimulated, sensations of sound are produced in humans.

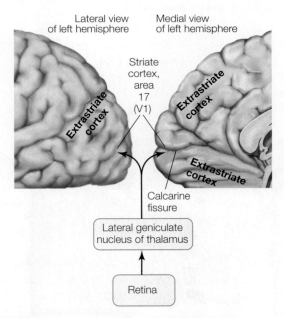

FIGURE 2.35 The visual cortex, which is located in the occipital lobe.
Brodmann area 17, also called the *primary visual cortex*, visual area 1 (V1), and striate cortex, is located at the occipital pole and extends onto the medial surface of the hemisphere, where it is largely buried within the calcarine fissure.

Association Cortex The portion of the neocortex that is neither sensory nor motor cortex has traditionally been termed the **association cortex**. These regions, which surround the identified sensory or motor cortical

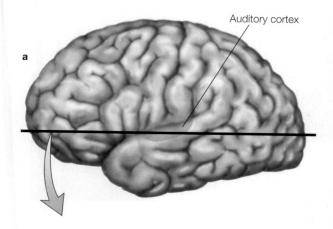

Auditory cortex

a

b

FIGURE 2.36 The human auditory cortex.
(a) Primary auditory cortex, which is located in the superior temporal lobe. The primary auditory cortex and surrounding association auditory areas contain representations of auditory stimuli and show a tonotopic organization. (b) This MRI shows areas of the superior temporal region in horizontal section that have been stimulated by tones of different frequencies (shown in red vs. blue) and show increased blood flow as a result of neuronal activity.

regions, contain cells that may be activated by more than one sensory modality. Association cortex receives and integrates inputs from many cortical areas; for example, inputs of the various qualities of a particular stimulus (e.g., pitch, loudness, timbre of a voice) are integrated with other sensory inputs, memory, attention, emotion, and so forth to produce our experience of the world. They are also the areas responsible for all of our high-end human abilities, such as language, abstract thinking, designing such things as a Maserati, and most important, vacation planning.

Each sense has a sensory association area. For example, though the primary visual cortex is necessary for normal vision, neither it nor the extrastriate cortex is the sole locus of visual perception. Regions of visual association cortex in the parietal and temporal lobes

process information from the primary visual cortex about color, simple boundaries, and contours to enable people to recognize these features as a face, or a petunia, or that Maserati. Moreover, visual association cortex can be activated during mental imagery when we call up a visual memory even in the absence of visual stimulation. Or, in the case of the auditory system, the auditory association area is necessary to recognize sounds. If that area is damaged, a person can still hear sound but is unable to tell a dog's bark from a piano concerto. As another example, the association areas of the parietal–temporal–occipital junction of the left hemisphere have a prominent role in language processing, whereas this region in the right hemisphere is implicated in attentional orienting (see Chapter 7). Thus, higher mental processes are the domain of the association cortical areas, in interaction with sensory and motor areas of cortex (Figure 2.37; "How the Brain Works: Billions and Billions").

This wraps up our whirlwind tour of the brain, but leaves us with the question of how this complicated structure—the brain—is formed in the first place. We conclude this chapter with a brief look at brain development.

TAKE-HOME MESSAGES

- Gyri are the protruding areas seen on the surface of the cortex; sulci, or fissures, are the enfolded regions of cortex.
- Brodmann divided the brain into distinct regions based on the underlying cytoarchitectonics.
- The lobes of the brain include the frontal, parietal, temporal, and occipital lobes.
- The frontal lobe is for planning, cognitive control, and execution of movements. The parietal lobe receives sensory input about touch, pain, temperature, and limb position, and it is involved in coding space and coordinating actions.
- The temporal lobe contains auditory, visual, and multimodal processing areas. The occipital lobe processes visual information. The limbic lobe (not really a lobe) is involved in emotional processing, learning, and memory.
- Topography is the principle that the anatomical organization of the body is reflected in the cortical representation of the body, both in the sensory cortex and motor cortex.
- Association cortices are those regions of cortex outside the sensory specific and motor cortical regions. Association cortex receives and integrates input from multiple sensory modalities.

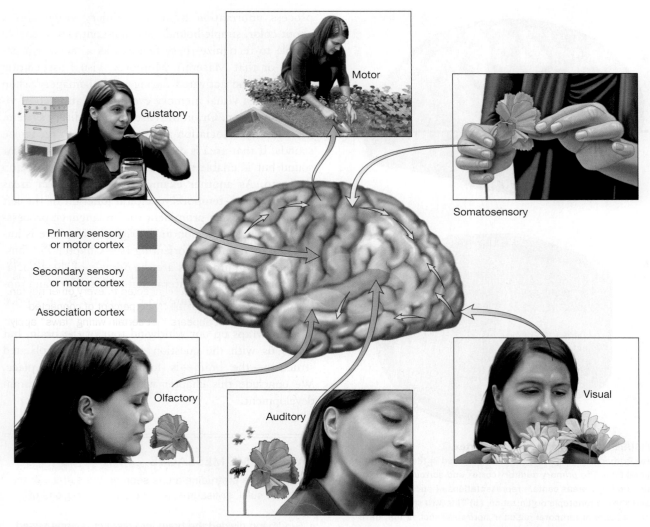

FIGURE 2.37 Primary sensory and motor cortex and surrounding association cortex.
The blue regions show the primary cortical receiving areas of the ascending sensory pathways and the
primary output region to the spinal cord. The secondary sensory and motor areas are colored pink. The
remainder is considered association cortex.

HOW THE BRAIN WORKS
Billions and Billions: Brain Size, Complexity, and Human Cognition

In 2009, the big brain theory, the idea that humans were more intelligent and could credit all their high end abilities to the fact that they have a proportionately larger brain for their body than the other great apes, hit a wall. Although it had some major chinks in its armor already, for instance, the fact that Neanderthals had bigger brains than humans without possessing our scope of abilities, and that after split brain surgery the isolated left brain (with half the acreage) is just as intelligent as a whole brain, it still garnered quite a few fans. But then Suzana Herculano-Houzel (2009) and her coworkers stepped in using a new technique to more accurately count neuron numbers and found that the

human brain is a proportionately scaled-up primate brain, no bigger than what you would expect for an ape of our size. It turns out that the human brain has on average 86 billion neurons, with 69 billion of them located in the cerebellum. The entire cortex, the area that we think is responsible for human thought and culture, has only 17 billion (19% of all the neutrons in the brain and similar to the percent found in other mammals), leaving only one billion for the entire rest of the brain. Not only that, but the visual and other sensory areas and the motor cortex have way more neurons than the frontal lobes (including the prefrontal cortex—that part of the human brain that is involved with all the high end abilities such as memory and planning, cognitive flexibility, abstract thinking, initiating appropriate behavior and inhibiting inappropriate behavior, learning rules, and picking out relevant information perceived through the senses). So what accounts for increased abilities?

Interestingly, the volume of the human cerebral cortex is 2.75 times larger than in chimpanzees, but has only 1.25 times more neurons (Shariff, 1953). One thing that neuro-anatomists have discovered is that the dendritic tips of the front lobe neurons are more arborized: They are chock full of branches with the resulting possibility of increased neuronal connections. This suggests that it may be the connectivity patterns of the neurons themselves that is different.

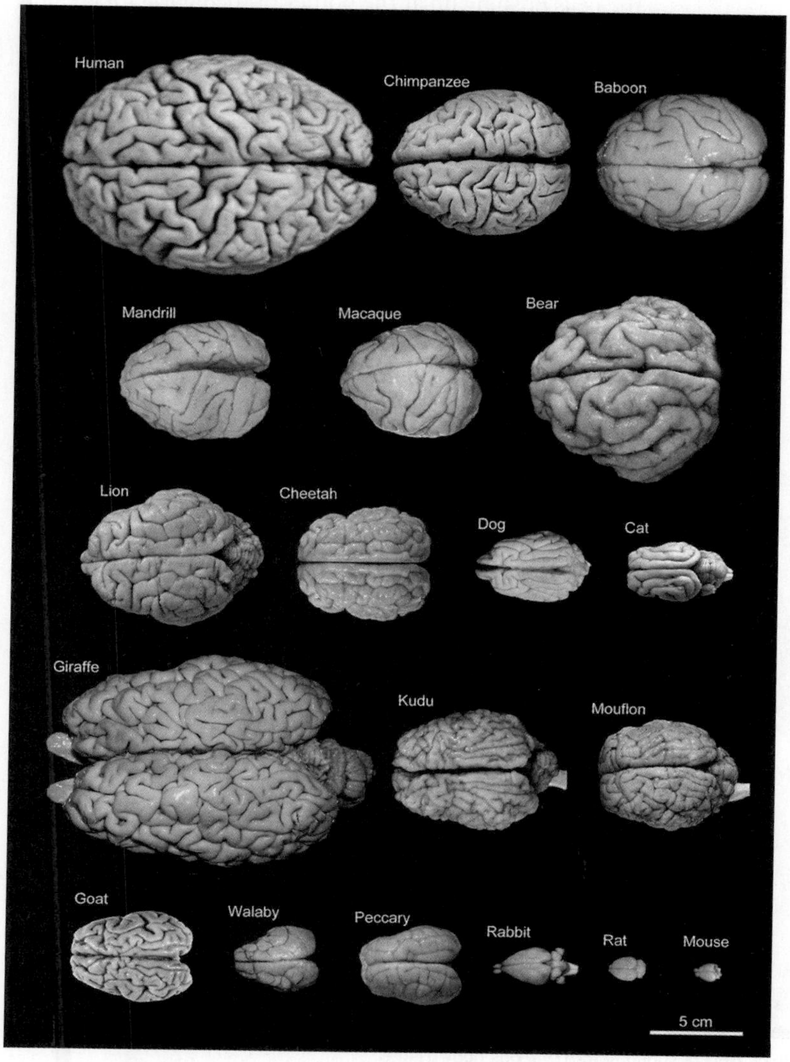

FIGURE 1 Variability of brain size and external topography.

Generally in the brain, the larger an area is, the better connected it is with more neurons, and more neurons connected to each other, but there is a limit. If our brains were fully connected, each neuron connected to every other one, our brains would have to be 20 kilometers in diameter (Clark & Sokoloff, 1999) and would require so much energy that all our time (and then some) would be spent eating. Big heads, indeed! With such distances for axons to travel across the brain, the processing speed would be slowed down, no doubt creating an uncoordinated body and rather dull witted person. So, as the primate brain evolved and the number of neurons increased, not every neuron connected to every other neuron. This resulted in an actual fall in the percent of connectedness. It appears that certain wiring "laws" apply to the evolutionary development of the large human brain (Striedter, 2005).

- *Decreased long distance brain connectivity with increasing size.* The number of neurons that an average neuron connects to actually does not change with increasing brain size. By maintaining absolute connectivity, not proportional connectivity, large brains became less interconnected. No need to worry about this, because evolution came up with two clever solutions.
- *Minimizing connection lengths.* Short connections keep processing localized, with the result that less space is needed fro the shorter axons, less energy is required, and signaling is faster over shorter distances. This organization set the stages for local networks to divide up and specialize, forming multiple clusters of processing modules.
- *Not all connections are minimized, but some very long connections between distant sites are retained.* Primate brains in general, and human brains in particular, have developed what is known as "small-world architecture," which is common to many complex systems, including human social relations. This type of organizational structure combines many short fast local connections with a few long distance ones to communicate the results of the local processing. It also has the advantage that a smaller number of steps connect any two processing units. This design allows both a high degree of local efficiency and at the same time, quick communication to the global network.

Development of the Nervous System

Thus far, we have been discussing the neuroanatomy of the developed adult brain. In humans and many other species, the fetal brain is well developed and shows cortical layers, neuronal connectivity, and myelination; in short, it is already extremely complex, although by no means completely developed. To find out how this complex brain develops prenatally and to uncover the rules governing development, let's examine the development of the nervous system and give special attention to the neocortex.

Overview of Gross Development

From a single fertilized egg, an organism made up of billions of cells with specialized functions will arise. This complexity clearly peaks in the nervous system. Fertilization is followed by a series of events leading to the formation of a multicellular blastula, which has already begun to specialize. The blastula contains three main cell lines, which after a few days form three layers: the ectoderm (outer layer) that will form the nervous system and the outer skin, lens of the eye, inner ear, and hair; the mesoderm (middle layer) that forms the skeletal system and voluntary muscle; and the endoderm (inner layer) that will form the gut and digestive organs. The early processes that go into forming the nervous system are called neurulation (Figure 2.38). During this stage, the ectodermal cells on the dorsal surface form the neural plate.

As the nervous system continues to develop, the cells at the lateral borders of the neural plate push upward. (Imagine joining the long sides of a rectangular piece of dough to form a tube.) This movement causes the more central cells of the neural plate to invaginate, or dip inward, to form the *neural groove*. As the groove deepens, the cells pushing up at the border of the neural fold region eventually meet and fuse, forming the *neural tube* that runs anteriorly and posteriorly along the embryo. The adjacent nonneural ectoderm then reunites to seal the neural tube within an ectodermal covering that surrounds the embryo.

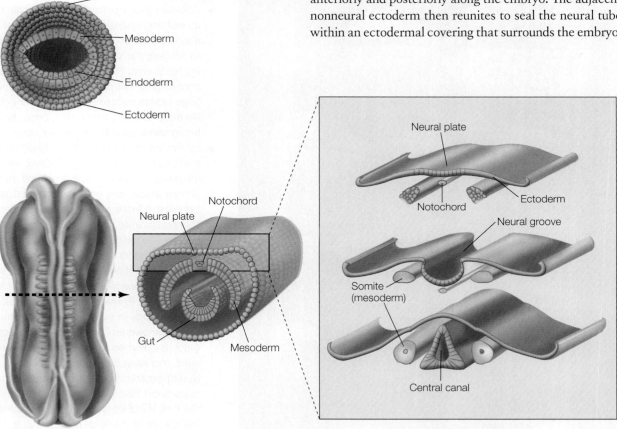

FIGURE 2.38 Development of the vertebrate nervous system.
Cross sections through the blastula and embryo at various developmental stages during the first 21 days of life. Early in embryogenesis, the multicellular blastula (**top**) contains cells destined to form various body tissues. Migration and specialization of different cell lines leads to formation of the primitive nervous system around the neural groove and neural tube on the dorsal surface of the embryo. The brain is located at the anterior end of the embryo and is not shown in these more posterior sections, which are taken at the level of the spinal cord.

Blood Supply and the Brain

Approximately 20% of the blood flowing from the heart is pumped to the brain. A constant flow of blood is necessary, because the brain has no way of storing glucose or extracting energy without oxygen. When the flow of oxygenated blood to the brain is disrupted for only a few minutes, unconsciousness and death can result. Two sets of arteries bring blood to the brain: the vertebral arteries, which supply blood to the caudal portion of the brain, and the internal carotid arteries, which supply blood to wider brain regions (Figure 1). Although the major arteries sometimes join together and then separate again, little mixing of blood occurs between the rostral and caudal arterial supplies or between the right and left sides of the rostral portion of the brain. As a safety measure, in the event of a blockage or ischemic attack, blood should be rerouted to reduce the probability of loss of blood supply; but in practice, this rerouting of the blood supply is relatively poor.

Blood flow in the brain is tightly coupled with metabolic demand of the local neurons. Hence, increases in neuronal activity lead to a coupled increase in regional cerebral blood flow. Increased blood flow is not primarily for increasing the delivery of oxygen and glucose to the active tissue, but rather to hasten removal of the resultant metabolic by-products of the increased neuronal activity. The precise mechanisms for altering blood flow, however, remain hotly debated. These local changes in blood flow permit regional cerebral blood flow to be used as a measure of local changes in neuronal activity, and serve as the basis for some types of functional neuroimaging. Particular examples are positron emission tomography, using techniques such as the ^{15}O-water method, and functional magnetic resonance imaging, which is sensitive to changes in the concentration of oxygenated versus deoxygenated blood in the region of active tissue.

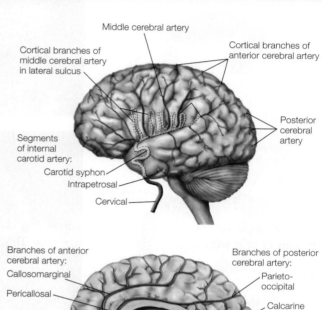

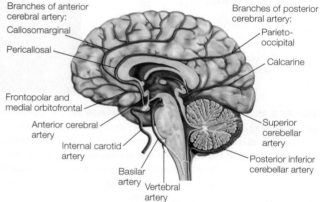

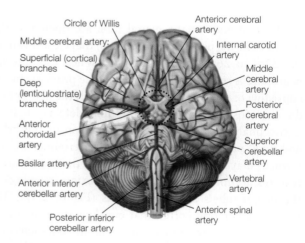

FIGURE 1 Blood supply and the brain.

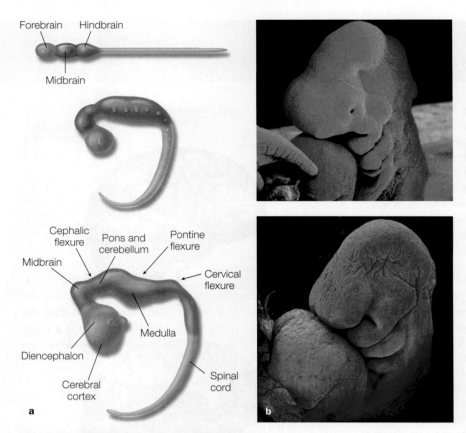

FIGURE 2.39 Early stages of embryonic development in mammals.
(a) Developing embryo. The embryo goes through a series of folds, or flexures, during development. These alterations in the gross structure of the nervous system give rise to the compact organization of the adult brain and brainstem in which the cerebral cortex overlays the diencephalon and midbrain within the human skull. **(b)** There is significant similarity between the gross features of the developing fetuses of mammals, as shown by this comparison of a human fetus (**top**) and pig fetus (**bottom**).

after birth (but see the section called "Birth of New Neurons Throughout Life," later in this chapter). Although axonal myelination continues for some period postnatally (e.g., until adulthood in the human frontal lobe), the newborn has a well-developed cortex that includes the cortical layers and areas characterized in adults. For instance, BA17 (the primary visual cortex) can be distinguished from the motor cortex by cytoarchitectonic analysis of its neuronal makeup.

Neural Proliferation and Migration of Cortical Cells The neurons that form the brain arise from a layer of precursor cells in *proliferative zones* located adjacent to the ventricles of the developing brain. The cortical neurons arise from the *subventricular zone*, and those that form other parts of the brain arise from precursor cells in the *ventricular zone*. For this discussion, refer to Figure 2.40, which shows a cross section through the cortex and the precursor cell layers at various times during gestation. We will now concentrate on the cells that form the cortex. The *precursor cells* are undifferentiated cells from which all cortical cells, including neuronal subtypes and glial cells, arise through cell division and differentiation. For the first five to six weeks of gestation, the cells in the subventricular zone divide in a symmetrical fashion. The result is exponential growth in the number of precursor cells.

At the end of six weeks, when there is a stockpile of precursor cells, asymmetrical division begins. After every cell division, one of the two cells formed becomes a migratory cell destined to be part of another layer; the other cell remains in the subventricular zone, where it continues to divide asymmetrically. Later in gestation, the proportion of migratory cells increases until a laminar (i.e., layered) cortex made up of the migratory cells is formed. This cortex has a foundational epithelial layer that becomes the cell lining of the ventricles and is known as the *ependymal cell layer*.

The migratory cells travel outward from the subventricular zone by moving along peculiar cells known as radial glial cells, which stretch from the subventricular zone to the surface of the developing cortex. The work

At both ends of the neural tube are openings (the anterior and the posterior neuropores) that close on about the 23rd to 26th day of gestation. When the anterior neuropore is sealed, this cavity forms the primitive brain, consisting of three spaces, or ventricles. If the neuropores do not close correctly, neural tube defects such as anencephaly (absence of a major portion of the brain and skull) or spina bifida (some of the vertebrae are not formed) may result. From this stage on, the brain's gross features are formed by growth and flexion (bending) of the neural tube's anterior portions (Figure 2.39). The result is a cerebral cortex that envelops the subcortical and brainstem structures. The final three-dimensional relations of the brain's structures are the product of continued cortical enlargement and folding. The posterior portion of the neural tube differentiates into a series of repeated segments that form the spinal cord.

In primates, almost all neurons are generated prenatally during the middle third of gestation. The entire adult pattern of gross and cellular neural anatomical features is present at birth, and there is little generation of neurons

of radial glial cells does not end with development. These cells are transformed into astrocytes in the adult brain, helping to form part of the blood–brain barrier.

As the first migrating neurons approach the surface of the developing cortex—a point known as the *cortical plate*—they stop short of the surface. Neurons that migrate later pass beyond the termination point of the initial neurons and end up in more superficial positions—positions nearer the outer cortical surface. Thus, it is said that the cortex is built from the inside out, because the first neurons to migrate lie in the deepest cortical layers, whereas the last to migrate move farthest out toward the cortical surface.

Neuronal Determination and Differentiation The cortex is made up of many different types of neurons organized in a laminar fashion. Layer IV, for example, contains large pyramidal cells, layer III is populated primarily by stellate cells, and so on. You may be wondering how that population of virtually identical precursor cells gives rise to the variety of neurons and glial cells in the adult cortex. What determines the type of neuron that a migrating cell is fated to become? The answer lies in the timing of neurogenesis. Experimental manipulation of developing cells has shown that the differentiated cell type is not hardwired into the code of each developing neuron. Neurons that are experimentally prevented from migrating, by exposing them to high-energy X-rays, eventually form cell types and patterns of connectivity that would be expected from neurons that were created at the same gestational stage. Even though the thwarted neurons might remain in the ventricular zone, they display interconnections with other neurons that would be normal had they migrated to the cortical layers normally.

The timeline of cortical neurogenesis differs across cortical cytoarchitectonic areas, but the inside-out pattern is the same for all cortical areas. Because the timeline of cortical neurogenesis determines the ultimate pattern of cortical lamination, anything that affects the genesis of cortical neurons will lead to an ill-constructed cortex. A good example of how neuronal migration can be disrupted in humans is *fetal alcohol syndrome*. In cases of chronic maternal alcohol abuse, neuronal migration is severely disrupted and results in a disordered cortex, leading to a plethora of cognitive, emotional, and physical disabilities.

The Radial Unit Hypothesis We now have a picture of how cortical neurons are born and how they migrate radially from the ventricular zone toward the surface of the developing cortex. The neurons migrate along the radial glial cells that form a pathway for them. Because the radial glial highway is organized in a straight line from the ventricular zone to the cortical surface, there is a topographic relation between the precursor and proliferating neurons in the ventricular area and the cortical neurons that they yield in the adult. Hence, cells born next to each other in the ventricular zone end up near each other (in the plane perpendicular to the surface of cortex) in the cortex. In addition, cells derived from precursor cells distant from one another will ultimately be distant in the cortex.

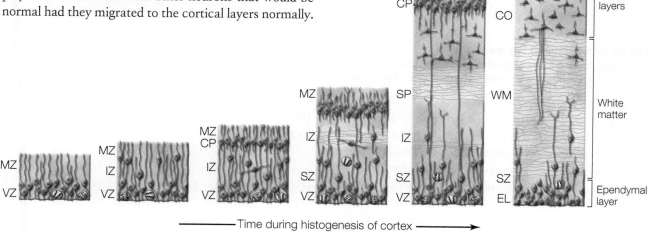

FIGURE 2.40 Histogenesis of the cerebral cortex.
Cross-sectional views of developing cerebral cortex at early **(left)** and late **(right)** times during histogenesis. The mammalian cortex develops from the inside out as cells in the ventricular zone (VZ) divide, and some of the cells migrate to the appropriate layer in the cortex. Radial glial cells form a superhighway along which the migrating cells travel en route to the cortex. CO = cortex; CP = cortical plate; EL = ependymal layer; IZ = intermediate zone; ML = molecular layer; MZ = marginal zone; SP = subplate; SZ = subventricular zone; WM = white matter.

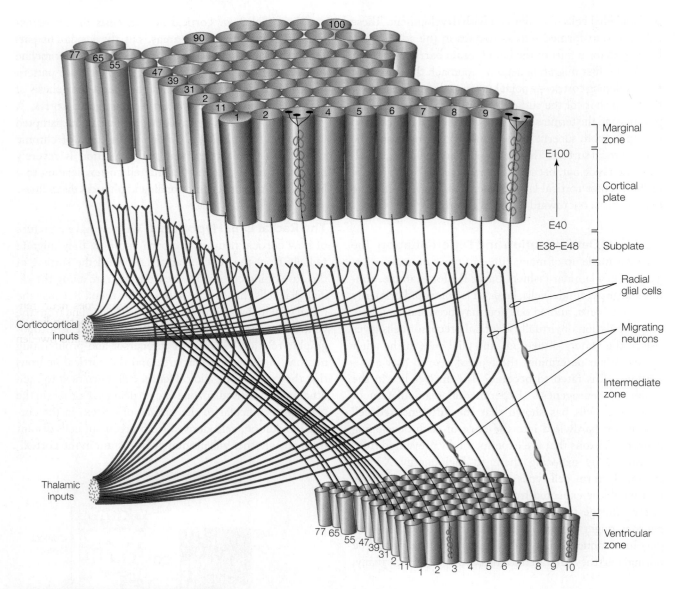

FIGURE 2.41 Radial unit hypothesis.
Radial glial cells in the ventricular zone project their processes in an orderly map through the various cortical
layers, thus maintaining the organizational structure specified in the ventricular layer. (E = Embryonic day.)

According to this concept, termed the *radial unit hypothesis* by neuroscientist Pasko Rakic (1995) of Yale University, the columnar organization in the adult cortex is derived during development from cells that divide in the ventricular region (Figure 2.41). The cortical column is thus a principal unit of organization that has functional consequences and a developmental history. The radial unit hypothesis also provides a method for the evolutionary expansion of cortical size: Each unit is not enlarged; instead, the number of units increases. The radial unit and the cortical columns that arise from these groupings have functional and anatomical consequences in the adult. For example, the intracortical interconnectivity of local neurons appears to be well suited to the sizes of cortical columns, which vary in adults from about 100 μm to 1 μm on a side, depending on the species and cortical area.

Birth of New Neurons Throughout Life

One principle about the human brain that, until recently, dominated in the neuroscience community, is the idea that the adult brain produces no new neurons (Figure 2.42). This view has been held despite a variety of claims of neurogenesis in the brain in histological studies dating as far back as the time of Ramón y Cajal. Recent studies using an array of modern neuroanatomical techniques have challenged this belief.

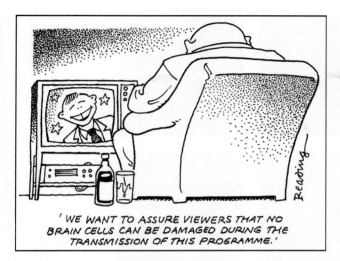

FIGURE 2.42 This cartoon exposes the commonly held belief that once we lose neurons, they can never be replaced.
© Bryan Reading/www.cartoonstock.com.

Neurogenesis in adult mammals has now been well established in two brain regions: the hippocampus and the olfactory bulb. Neurogenesis in the hippocampus is particularly noteworthy because it plays a key role in learning and memory (see Chapter 9). In rodents, studies have shown that stem cells in a region of the hippocampus known as the *dentate gyrus* produce new neurons in the adult, and these can migrate into regions of the hippocampus where similar neurons are already functioning. It is important to know that these new neurons can form dendrites and send out

axons along pathways expected of neurons in this region of the hippocampus, and they can also show signs of normal synaptic activity. These findings are particularly interesting because the number of new neurons correlates positively with learning or enriched experience (more social contact or challenges in the physical environment) and negatively with stress (e.g., living in an overcrowded environment). Moreover, the number of newborn neurons is related to hippocampal-dependent memory (Shors, 2004).

Other investigators have found that these new neurons become integrated into functional networks of neurons and participate in behavioral and cognitive functions in the same way that those generated during development do (Ramirez-Amaya et al., 2006). Future work will be required to establish whether adult neurogenesis occurs more broadly in the mammalian brain or is restricted to the olfactory bulb and hippocampus.

What about the adult *human* brain? Does neurogenesis also occur in mature humans? In a fascinating line of research, a team of scientists from California and Sweden (Eriksson et al., 1998) explored this question in a group of terminally ill cancer patients. As part of a diagnostic procedure related to their treatment, the patients were given BrdU, a synthetic form of thymidine used as a label to identify neurogenesis. The purpose was to assess the extent to which the tumors in the cancer patients were proliferating; tumor cells that were dividing would also take up BrdU, and this label could be used to quantify the progress of the disease.

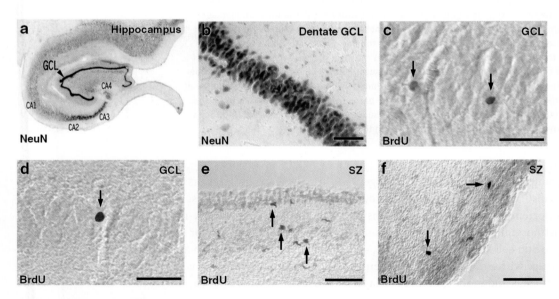

FIGURE 2.43 Newly born neurons in adult human.
(a) The hippocampus of the adult human brain, stained for a neuronal marker (NeuN). (b) The dentate gyrus granule cell layer (GCL) in a NeuN-stained section. (c) Bromodeoxyuridine (BrdU)-labeled nuclei (arrows) in the granule cell layer of the dentate gyrus. (d) BrdU-labeled cells (arrow) in the granule cell layer of the dentate gyrus. (e) BrdU-stained cells (arrows) adjacent to the ependymal lining in the subventricular zone (SZ) of the human caudate nucleus. These neurons have elongated nuclei resembling the migrating cells that typically are found in the rat subventricular zone. (f) BrdU-stained cells (arrows) with round to elongated nuclei in the subventricular zone of the human caudate nucleus. The horizontal black bars are scale bars representing 50 μm.

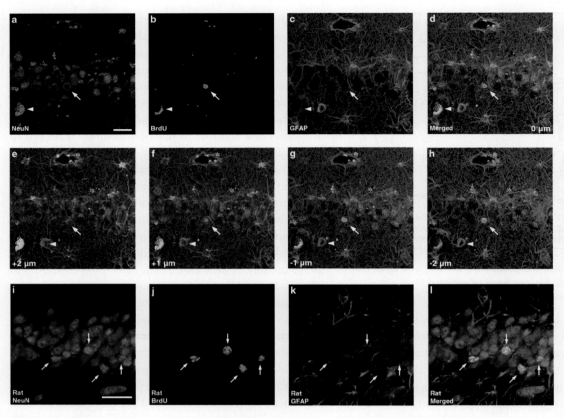

FIGURE 2.44 The birth of new neurons in the dentate gyrus of the adult human (a–h) compared to those in the adult rat (i–l).
New neurons show simultaneous labeling for different stains. **(a)** A neuron is labeled for NeuN, a neuronal marker. **(b)** The same cell is labeled with BrdU, indicating that it is newly born (full arrow). (Note that the lone arrowheads in (a) through (d) are pointing to neurons that are fluorescing red or green, owing to nonspecific staining; i.e., these are not newly born neurons). **(c)** This same cell is not stained by glial fibrillary acidic protein (GFAP), indicating that it is not an astrocyte. **(d)** The three stained sections are merged. The image shows that a BrdU-labeled cell could specifically coexpress NeuN without expressing GFAP. Confocal microscopy permits examination of the coexpression of NeuN and BrdU in the neuron by focusing the image above **(e, f)** and below **(g, h)** the level of the section shown in panel (d). Note that red blood cells and endothelial cells, present in several small blood vessels, show nonspecific staining, as indicated by the asterisks in (e) through (h). Panels **(i)** through **(l)** show the similarity of the BrdU-labeled neurons in rat dentate gyrus. Note: The scale bar in (a) is 25 μm, and the scale is the same for panels (a) through (h). The scale bar in panel (i) is also 25 μm and is the scale for (i) through (l), but the magnification for (i) through (l) is higher than for (a) through (h).

Neurons undergoing mitotic division during neurogenesis in these patients also took up the BrdU, which could be observed in postmortem histological examinations of their brains. The postmortem tissue was immunostained to identify neuron-specific cell surface markers. The scientists found cells labeled with BrdU in the subventricular zone of the caudate nucleus and in the granular cell layer of the dentate gyrus of the hippocampus (Figure 2.43). By staining the tissue to identify neuronal markers, the researchers showed that the BrdU-labeled cells were neurons (Figure 2.44). These findings demonstrate that new neurons are produced in the adult human brain, and that our brains renew themselves throughout life to an extent not previously thought possible.

These exciting results hold great promise for the future of neuroscience. Research is under way to investigate the functionality of new neurons in the adult brain and to determine whether or not such neuronal growth can be facilitated in order to ameliorate brain damage or the effects of diseases such as Alzheimer's.

The Baby Brain: Ready to Rock 'n' Roll?

A host of behavioral changes takes place during the first months and years of life. What accompanying neurobiological changes enable these developments? Even if we assume that neuronal proliferation continues, we know that at birth the human brain has a fairly full complement of neurons, and these are organized to form a human nervous system that is normal, even if not complete in all details. What details are incomplete, and what is known about the time course of the maturation of the brain?

Although the brain nearly quadruples in size from birth to adulthood, it is not because of an increase in neuron number. A substantial amount of that growth comes from **synaptogenesis** (the formation of synapses) and the growth of dendritic trees. Synapses in the brain begin to form long before birth—prior to week 27 in humans (counting from conception)—but they do not reach peak density until after birth, during the first 15 months of life. Synaptogenesis is more pronounced early in the deeper cortical layers and occurs later in more superficial layers, following the pattern of neurogenesis described earlier. At roughly the same time that synaptogenesis is occurring, neurons of the brain are increasing the size of their dendritic arborizations, extending their axons, and undergoing myelination. Synaptogenesis is followed by **synapse elimination** (sometimes called *pruning*), which continues for more than a decade. Synapse elimination is a means by which the nervous system fine-tunes neural connectivity, presumably eliminating the interconnections between neurons that are redundant, unused, or do not remain functional. An example comes from primary visual cortex (BA17): Initially, there is overlap between the projections of the two eyes onto neurons in BA17. After synapse elimination, the cortical inputs from the two eyes within BA17 are nearly completely segregated. The axon terminals relaying information from each eye form a series of equally spaced patches (called *ocular dominance columns*), and each patch receives inputs from predominantly one eye.

One of the central hypotheses about the process of human synaptogenesis and synapse elimination is that the time course of these events differs in different cortical regions. The data suggest that in humans, synaptogenesis and synapse elimination peak earlier in sensory (and motor) cortex than in association cortex. By contrast, in the brain development of other primates, synaptogenesis and pruning appear to occur at the same rates across different cortical regions. Differences in methodology, however, must be resolved before these interspecies variations will be wholly accepted. Nonetheless, compelling evidence suggests that different regions of the human brain reach maturity at different times.

The increase in brain volume that occurs postnatally is also a result of both myelination and the proliferation of glial cells. White matter volume increases linearly with age across cortical regions (Giedd et al., 1999). In contrast, gray matter volume increases nonlinearly, showing a preadolescent increase followed by a postadolescent decrease. In addition, the time course of gray matter increase and decrease are not the same across different cortical regions. In general, these data support the idea that postnatal developmental changes in the human cerebral cortex may not occur with the same time course across all cortical regions (see also Shaw et al., 2006).

TAKE-HOME MESSAGES

- The nervous system develops from the ectoderm, which forms a neural plate. The neural plate becomes the neural groove and eventually the neural tube.
- Neuronal proliferation is the process of cell division in the developing embryo and fetus. It is responsible for populating the nervous system with neurons.
- Neurons and glial cells are formed from precursor cells. After mitosis, these cells migrate along the radial glial cells to the developing cortex.
- The type of cell that is made (e.g., a stellate or pyramidal cell) appears to be based on when the cell is born (genesis) rather than when it begins to migrate.
- The radial unit hypothesis states that the columnar organization in the adult cortex is derived during development from cells that divide in the ventricular region.
- A belief strongly held by most neuroscientists was that the adult brain produces no new neurons. We now know that this is not the case; new neurons form throughout life in certain brain regions.
- Synaptogenesis is the birth of new synapses; neurogenesis is the birth of new neurons.

Summary

In terms of evolution, the oldest parts of the brain, which make up the brain stem structures, control our most basic survival functions, such as breathing, heart rate, and temperature. The more rostral structures evolved more recently and mediate more complex behaviors. The most rostral and youngest structure is the prefrontal cortex and is found only in mammals.

In the brain and the rest of the nervous system, nerve cells (neurons) provide the mechanism for information processing. Neurons can receive and process sensory inputs, plan and organize motor acts, and enable human thought. At rest, the neuronal membrane has properties that allow some materials (primarily ions) dissolved in intracellular and extracellular fluids to pass through more easily than others. In addition, active transport processes pump ions across the membrane to separate different species of ions, thereby setting the stage for differences in electrical potential inside and outside the neuron. These electrical differences are a form of energy that can be used to generate electrical currents that, via action potentials, can travel great distances down axons away from the neuron's cell body. When the action potential reaches an axon terminal, it prompts the release of chemicals at a specialized region, the synapse, where the neuron contacts another neuron, muscle, or gland.

These chemicals (neurotransmitters) diffuse across the synaptic cleft between the neurons and contact receptor molecules in the next (postsynaptic) neuron. This chemical transmission of signal leads to the generation of currents in the postsynaptic neuron and the continuation of the signal through the system of neurons that make up a neuronal circuit. Ion channels are the specialized mediators of neuronal membrane potential. They are large transmembrane proteins that create pores through the membrane. Transmembrane proteins also form receptors on postsynaptic neurons. These are the receptors that bind with neurotransmitters, leading to changes in the membrane potential. Neurotransmitters come in a large variety of forms. Small-molecule transmitters include amino acids, biogenic amines, and substances like ACh; large-molecule transmitters are the neuropeptides.

Neuronal circuits are organized to form highly specific interconnections between groups of neurons in subdivisions of the central nervous system. The functions might be localized within discrete regions that contain a few or many subdivisions, identifiable either anatomically or functionally, but usually by a combination of both approaches. Brain areas are also interconnected to form higher level circuits or systems that are involved in complex behaviors such as motor control, visual perception, or cognitive processes such as memory, language, and attention. Neurodevelopment begins at an early stage in fetal growth and continues through birth and adolescence. New research also suggests that new neurons and new synapses form throughout life, allowing, at least in part, for cortical plasticity.

Key Terms

action potential (p. 30)
amygdala (p. 47)
association cortex (p. 56)
autonomic nervous system (p. 38)
axon (p. 26)
axon collateral (p. 26)
axon hillock (p. 30)
basal ganglia (p. 47)
blood–brain barrier (BBB) (p. 36)
brainstem (p. 43)
central nervous system (CNS) (p. 37)
central sulcus (p. 51)
cerebellum (p. 44)
cerebral cortex (p. 38)
commissure (p. 39)
corpus callosum (p. 39)
cytoarchitectonics (p. 51)
dendrite (p. 25)
depolarize (p. 31)

dura mater (p. 38)
electrical gradient (p. 29)
electrotonic conduction (p. 30)
equilibrium potential (p. 31)
frontal lobe (p. 50)
glial cell (p. 35)
gray matter (p. 39)
gyrus (p. 49)
hippocampus (p. 47)
hyperpolarization (p. 31)
hypothalamus (p. 45)
insula (p. 51)
ion channel (p. 28)
ion pump (p. 28)
layer (p. 38)
limbic system (p. 47)
medulla (p. 43)
midbrain (p. 44)
myelin (p. 26)

neocortex (p. 52)
neural circuit (p. 37)
neural system (p. 37)
neuron (p. 24)
neurotransmitter (p. 33)
node of Ranvier (p. 26)
nucleus (p. 38)
occipital lobe (p. 50)
parietal lobe (p. 50)
peripheral nervous system (PNS)
    (p. 37)
permeability (p. 29)
pituitary gland (p. 46)
pons (p. 44)
postsynaptic (p. 27)
prefrontal cortex (p. 54)
presynaptic (p. 27)
refractory period (p. 31)
resting membrane potential (p. 27)

Thought Questions

1. If action potentials are all or none, how does the nervous system code differences in sensory stimulus amplitudes?

2. What property (or properties) of ion channels makes them selective to only one ion, such as K^+, and not another, such as Na^+? Is it the size of the channel, other factors, or a combination?

3. Given that synaptic currents produce electrotonic potentials that are decremental, how do inputs located distantly on a neuron's dendrites have any influence on the firing of the cell?

4. What would be the consequence for the activity of a postsynaptic neuron if reuptake or degradation systems for neurotransmitters were damaged?

5. What are glial cells and what are their functions?

6. What region of the cerebral cortex has increased in size the most across species during evolution? What function does this brain region carry out in humans that is absent or reduced in animals?

7. Why are almost all sensory inputs routed through the thalamus on the way to cortex? Wouldn't it be faster and therefore more efficient to project these inputs directly from sensory receptors to the primary sensory cortex?

8. What brain areas have been associated with the creation of new neurons and what functions are they thought to perform?

Suggested Reading

Aimone, J. B., Deng, W., & Gage, F. H. (2010). Adult neurogenesis: Integrating theories and separating functions. *Trends in Cognitive Sciences, 14*(7), 325–337. Epub 2010 May 12.

Bullock, T. H., Bennett, M. V., Johnston, D., Josephson, R., Marder, E., & Fields, R. D. (2005). The neuron doctrine, redux. *Science 310,* 791. doi:10.1126/science .1114394

Haeusser, M. (2000). The Hodgkin–Huxley theory of the action potential. *Nature Reviews Neuroscience, 3,* 1165.

Mesulam, M.-M. (2000). Behavioral neuroanatomy: Large-scale networks, association cortex, frontal syndromes, the limbic system, and hemispheric specialization. In Shaw, P., Greenstein, D., Lerch, J., Clasen, L., Lenroot, R., Gogtay, N., et al. (2006). Intellectual ability and cortical development in children and adolescents. *Nature, 440,* 676–679.

Shepherd, G. M. (1988). *Neurobiology* (2nd ed.). New York: Oxford University Press.

Shors, T. J. (2004). Memory traces of trace memories: Neurogenesis, synaptogenesis and awareness. *Trends in Neurosciences, 27,* 250–256.

Streidter, G. (2005). *Principles of brain evolution,* pps. 217–53. Sunderland, MA: Sinawer.

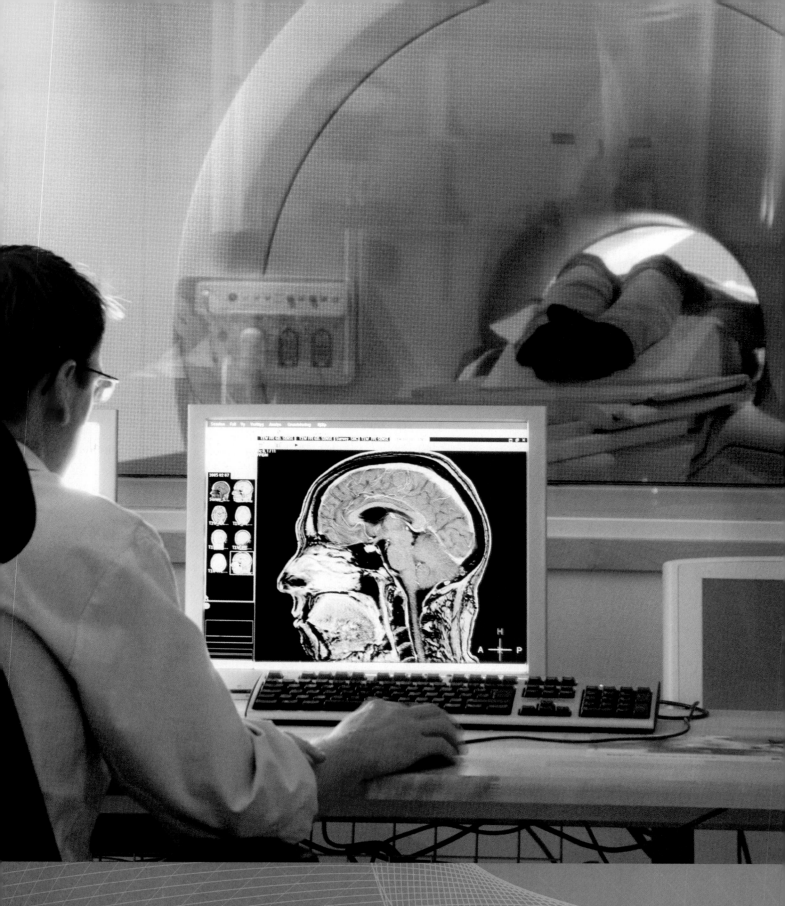

Though this be madness, yet there is method in't.

William Shakespeare

Methods of Cognitive Neuroscience

IN THE YEAR 2010, *Halobacterium halobium* and *Chlamydomonas reinhardtii* made it to prime time as integral parts of the journal *Nature*'s "Method of the Year." These microscopic creatures were hailed for their potential to treat a wide range of neurological and psychiatric conditions: anxiety disorder, depression, and Parkinson's disease, just to name a few. Not bad for a bacterium that hangs out in warm brackish waters and an alga more commonly known as pond scum.

Such grand ambitions for these humble creatures likely never occurred to Dieter Oesterhelt and Walther Stoeckenius (1971), biochemists who wanted to understand why the salt-loving *Halobacterium*, when removed from its salty environment, would break up into fragments, and why one of these fragments took on an unusual purple hue. Their investigations revealed that the purple color was due to the interaction of retinal (a form of vitamin A) and a protein produced by a set of "opsin genes." Thus they dubbed this new compound bacteriorhodopsin. The particular combination surprised them. Previously, the only other place where the combined form of retinal and an opsin protein had been observed was in the mammalian eye, where it serves as the chemical basis for vision. In *Halobacterium*, bacteriorhodopsin functions as an ion pump, converting light energy into metabolic energy as it transfers ions across the cell membrane. Other members of this protein family were identified over the next 25 years, including channelrhodopsin from the green algae *C. reinhardtii* (Nagel et al., 2002). The light-sensitive properties of microbial rhodopsins turned out to provide just the mechanism that neuroscientists had been dreaming of.

In 1979, Francis Crick, a codiscoverer of the structure of DNA, made a wish list for neuroscientists. What neuroscientists really need, he suggested, was a way to selectively switch on and off neurons, and to do so with great temporal precision. Assuming this manipulation did not harm the cell, a technique like this would enable researchers to directly probe how neurons functionally relate to each other in order to control behavior. Twenty years later, Crick (1999) proposed that light might somehow serve as the switch, because it could be precisely delivered in timed pulses. Unknown to him, and the neuroscience community in general, the key to developing this switch was moldering away in the back editions of plant biology journals, in the papers inspired by Oesterhelt and Stoeckenius's work on the microbial rhodopsins.

A few years later, Gero Miesenböck provided the first demonstration of how photoreceptor proteins could control neuroactivity. The key challenge was getting the proteins into the cell. Miesenböck accomplished this feat by inserting genes that, when expressed, made targeted cells light responsive (Zemmelman et al., 2002). Expose the cell to light, and the neuron would fire. With this methodological breakthrough, **optogenetics** was born (Figure 3.1).

Miesenböck's initial compound proved to have limited usefulness, however. But just a few years later, two graduate students at Stanford, Karl Deisseroth and Ed Boyden, became interested in the opsins as possible neuronal switches (Boyden, 2011). They focused on channelrhodopsin-2 (ChR-2), since a single gene encodes this opsin, making it easier to use molecular biology tools. Using Miesenböck's technique, a method that has come to be called viral transduction, they spliced the gene for ChR-2 into a neutral virus and then added this virus to a culture of live nerve cells growing in a petri dish. The virus acted like a ferry, carrying the gene into the cell. Once the ChR-2 gene was inside the neurons and the protein had been expressed, Deisseroth and Boyden performed the critical test: They projected a light beam onto the cells. Immediately, the targeted cells began to respond. By pulsing the light, the researchers were able to do exactly what Crick had proposed: precisely control the neuronal activity. Each pulse of light stimulated the production of an action potential; and when the pulse was discontinued, the neuron shut down.

Emboldened by this early success, Deisseroth and Boyden set out to see if the process could be repeated in live animals, starting with a mouse model. Transduction methods were widely used in molecular biology, but it was important to verify that ChR-2 would be expressed in targeted tissue and that the introduction of this rhodopsin would not damage the cells. Another challenge these scientists faced was the need to devise a method of delivering light pulses to the transduced cells. For their

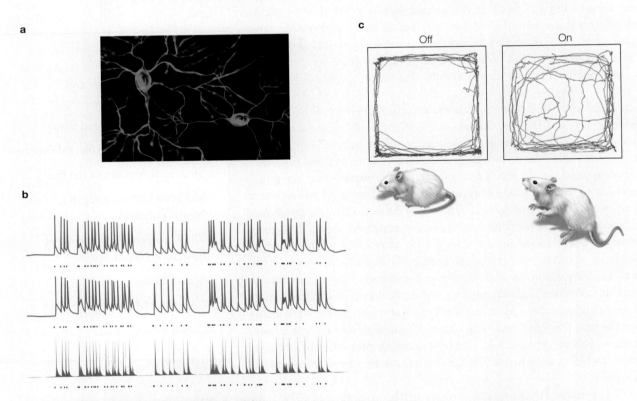

FIGURE 3.1 Optogenetic control of neural activity.
(a) Hippocampal neuron that has been genetically modified to express Channelrhododopsin-2, a protein which forms light-gated ion channels. **(b)** Activity in three neurons when exposed to a blue light. The small grey dashes below each neuron indicate when the light was turned on (same stimulus for all three neurons). The firing pattern of the cells is tightly coupled to the light, indicating the experimenter can control, to a large extent, the activity of the cells. **(c)** Behavioral changes resulting from optogenetic stimulation of cells in a subregion of the amygdala. When placed in an open, rectangular arena, mice generally stay close to the walls. With amygdala activation, the mice become less fearful, venturing out into the open part of the arena.

THE SCIENTIFIC METHOD

The overarching method that neuroscientists use, of course, is the scientific method. This process begins with an observation of a phenomenon. Such an observation can come from various types of populations: animal or human, normally functioning or abnormally functioning. The scientist devises a hypothesis to explain an observation and makes predictions drawn from the hypothesis. The next step is designing experiments to test the hypothesis and its predictions.

Such experiments employ the various methods that we discuss in this chapter. Experiments cannot prove that a hypothesis is true. Rather, they can provide support for a hypothesis. Even more important, experiments can be used to disprove a hypothesis, providing evidence that a prevailing idea must be modified. By documenting this process and having it repeated again and again, the scientific method allows our understanding of the world to progress.

initial in vivo study, they implanted a tiny optical fiber in the part of the brain containing motor neurons that control the mouse's whiskers. When a blue light was pulsed, the whiskers moved (Aravanis et al., 2007). Archimedes, as well as Frances Crick, would have shouted, "Eureka!"

Optogenetic techniques are becoming increasingly versatile (for a video on optogenetics, see http://spie.org/x48167.xml?ArticleID=x48167). Many new opsins have been discovered, including ones that respond to different colors of visible light. Others respond to infrared light. Infrared light is advantageous because it penetrates tissue, and thus, it may eliminate the need for implanting optical fibers to deliver the light pulse to the target tissue. Optogenetic methods have been used to turn on and off cells in many parts of the brain, providing experimenters with new tools to manipulate behavior. A demonstration of the clinical potential of this method comes from a recent study in which optogenetic methods were able to reduce anxiety in mice (Tye et al., 2011). After creating light-sensitive neurons in their amygdala (see Chapter 10), a flash of light was sufficient to motivate the mice to move away from the wall of their home cage and boldly step out into the center. Interestingly, this effect worked only if the light was targeted at a specific subregion of the amygdala. If the entire structure was exposed to the light, the mice remained anxious and refused to explore their cages.

Theoretical breakthroughs in all scientific domains can be linked to the advent of new methods and the development of novel instrumentation. Cognitive neuroscience is no exception. It is a field that emerged in part because of the invention of new methods, some of which use advanced tools unavailable to scientists of previous generations (see Chapter 1; Sejnowski & Churchland, 1989). In this chapter, we discuss how these methods work, what information can be derived from them, and their limitations. Many of these methods are shared with other players in the neurosciences, from neurologists

and neurosurgeons to physiologists and philosophers. Cognitive neuroscience endeavors to take advantage of the insights that each approach has to offer and combine them. By addressing a question from different perspectives and with a variety of techniques, the conclusions arrived at can be made with more confidence.

We begin the chapter with cognitive psychology and the behavioral methods it uses to gain insight into how the brain represents and manipulates information. We then turn to how these methods have been used to characterize the behavioral changes that accompany neurological insult or disorder, the subfield traditionally known as neuropsychology. While neuropsychological studies of human patients are dependent on the vagaries of nature, the basic logic of the approach is now pursued with methods in which neural function is deliberately perturbed. We review a range of methods used to perturb neural function. Following this, we turn to more observational methods, first reviewing ways in which cognitive neuroscientists measure neurophysiological signals in either human or animal models, and second, by examining methods in which neural structure and function are inferred through measurements of metabolic and hemodynamic processes. When studying an organ with 11 billion basic elements and gazillions of connections between these elements, we need tools that can be used to organize the data and yield simplified models to evaluate hypotheses. We provide a brief overview of computer modeling and how it has been used by cognitive neuroscientists, and we review a powerful analytical and modeling tool—brain graph theory, which transforms neuroimaging data into models that elucidate the network properties of the human brain. The interdisciplinary nature of cognitive neuroscience has depended on the clever ways in which scientists have integrated paradigms across all of these fields and methodologies. The chapter concludes with examples of this integration. *Andiamo!*

Cognitive Psychology and Behavioral Methods

Cognitive neuroscience has been informed by the principles of **cognitive psychology**, the study of mental activity as an information-processing problem. Cognitive psychologists are interested in describing human performance, the observable behavior of humans (and other animals). They also seek to identify the internal processing—the acquisition, storage, and use of information—that underlies this performance. A basic assumption of cognitive psychology is that we do not directly perceive and act in the world. Rather, our perceptions, thoughts, and actions depend on internal transformations or computations. Information is obtained by sense organs, but our ability to comprehend that information, to recognize it as something that we have experienced before and to choose an appropriate response, depend on a complex interplay of processes. Cognitive psychologists design experiments to test hypotheses about mental operations by adjusting what goes into the brain and then seeing what comes out. Put more simply, information is input into the brain, something secret happens to it, and out comes behavior. Cognitive psychologists are detectives trying to figure out what those secrets are.

For example, input this text into your brain and let's see what comes out:

> ocacdrngi ot a sehrerearc ta maccbriegd ineyurvtis, ti edost'n rttaem ni awth rreod eht tlteser ni a rwdo rea, eht ylon pirmtoatn gihtn si atth het rifts nda satl ttelre eb tat het ghitr clepa. eht srte anc eb a otlta sesm dan ouy anc itlls arde ti owtuthi moprbel. ihst si cebusea eth nuamh nidm sedo otn arde yrvee telrte yb stifle, tub eth rdow sa a lohew.

Not much, eh? Now take another shot at it:

> Aoccdrnig to a rseheearcr at Cmabrigde Uinervtisy, it deosn't mttaer in waht oredr the ltteers in a wrod are, the olny iprmoatnt tihng is taht the frist and lsat ltteer be at the rghit pclae. The rset can be a total mses and you can sitll raed it wouthit porbelm. Tihs is bcuseae the huamn mnid deos not raed ervey lteter by istlef, but the wrod as a wlohe.

Oddly enough, the second version makes sense. It is surprisingly easy to read the second passage, even though only a few words are correctly spelled. As long as the first and last letters of each word are in the correct position, we can accurately infer the correct spelling, especially when the surrounding context helps generate expectations for each word. Simple demonstrations like this one help us discern the content of mental representations,

and thus, help us gain insight into how information is manipulated by the mind.

Cognitive neuroscience is distinctive in the study of the brain and behavior, because it combines paradigms developed in cognitive psychology with methods employed to study brain structure and function. Next, we introduce some of those paradigms.

Ferreting Out Mental Representations and Transformations

Two key concepts underlie the cognitive approach:

1. Information processing depends on internal representations.
2. These mental representations undergo transformations.

Mental Representations We usually take for granted the idea that information processing depends on internal representations. Consider the concept "ball." Are you thinking of an image, a word description, or a mathematical formula? Each instance is an alternative form of representing the "circular" or "spherical" concept and depends on our visual system, our auditory system, our ability to comprehend the spatial arrangement of a curved drawing, our ability to comprehend language, or our ability to comprehend geometric and algebraic relations. The context would help dictate which representational format would be most useful. For example, if we wanted to show that the ball rolls down a hill, a pictorial representation is likely to be much more useful than an algebraic formula—unless you are doing your physics final, where you would likely be better off with the formula.

A letter-matching task, first introduced by Michael Posner (1986) at the University of Oregon, provides a powerful demonstration that even with simple stimuli, the mind derives multiple representations (Figure 3.2). Two letters are presented simultaneously in each trial. The participant's task is to evaluate whether they are both vowels, both consonants, or one vowel and one consonant. The participant presses one button if the letters are from the same category, and the other button if they are from different categories.

One version of this experiment includes five conditions. In the physical-identity condition, the two letters are exactly the same. In the phonetic-identity condition, the two letters have the same identity, but one letter is a capital and the other is lowercase. There are two types of same-category conditions, conditions in which the two letters are different members of the same category. In one, both letters are vowels; in the other, both letters are consonants.

Experiments like the one represented in Figure 3.2 involve manipulating one variable and observing its effect on another variable. The variable that is manipulated is called the independent variable. It is what *you* (the researcher) have changed. In this example, the relationship of the two letters is the independent variable, defining the conditions of the experiment (e.g., Identical, Same letter,

Both vowels, etc.). The dependent variable is the event being studied. In this example, it is the response time of the participant. When graphing the results of an experiment, the independent variable is displayed on the horizontal axis (Figure 3.2b) and the dependent variable is displayed on the vertical axis. Experiments can involve more than one independent and dependent variable.

Finally, in the different-category condition, the two letters are from different categories and can be either of the same type size or of different sizes. Note that the first four conditions—physical identity, phonetic identity, and the two same-category conditions—require the "same" response: On all three types of trials, the correct response is that the two letters are from the same category. Nonetheless, as Figure 3.2b shows, response latencies differ significantly. Participants respond fastest to the physical-identity condition, next fastest to the phonetic-identity condition, and slowest to the same-category condition, especially when the two letters are both consonants.

The results of Posner's experiment suggest that we derive multiple representations of stimuli. One representation is based on the physical aspects of the stimulus. In this experiment, it is a visually derived representation of the shape presented on the screen. A second representation corresponds to the letter's identity. This representation reflects the fact that many stimuli can correspond to the same letter. For example, we can recognize that *A*, *a*, and *a* all represent the same letter. A third level of abstraction represents the category to which a letter belongs. At this level, the letters *A* and *E* activate our internal representation of the category "vowel." Posner maintains

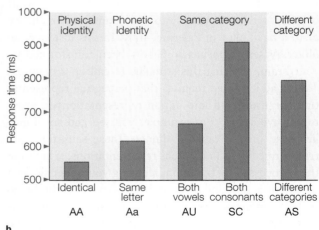

FIGURE 3.2 Letter-matching task.
(a) Participants press one of two buttons to indicate if the letters are the same or different. The definition of "same" and "different" is manipulated across different blocks of the experiment. **(b)** The relationship between the two letters is plotted on the x-axis. This relationship is the independent variable, the variable that the experimenter is manipulating. Reaction time is plotted on the y-axis. It is the dependent variable, the variable that the experimenter is measuring.

that different response latencies reflect the degrees of processing required to perform the letter-matching task. By this logic, we infer that physical representations are activated first, phonetic representations next, and category representations last.

As you may have experienced personally, experiments like these elicit as many questions as answers. Why do participants take longer to judge that two letters are consonants than they do to judge that two letters are vowels? Would the same advantage for identical stimuli exist if the letters were spoken? What about if one letter were visual and the other were auditory? Cognitive psychologists address questions like these and then devise methods for inferring the mind's machinery from observable behaviors.

In the letter-matching task, the primary dependent variable was reaction (or response) time, the speed with which participants make their judgments. Reaction time experiments use the chronometric methodology. *Chronometric* comes from the Greek words *chronos* ("time") and *metron* ("measure"). The chronometric study of the mind is essential for cognitive psychologists because mental events occur rapidly and efficiently. If we consider only whether a person is correct or incorrect on a task, we miss subtle differences in performance. Measuring reaction time permits a finer analysis of the brain's internal processes.

Internal Transformations The second critical notion of cognitive psychology is that our mental representations undergo transformations. For instance, the transformation of mental representations is obvious when we consider how sensory signals are connected with stored information in memory. For example, a whiff of garlic may transport you to your grandmother's house or to a back alley in Palermo, Italy. In this instance, an olfactory sensation has somehow been transformed by your brain, allowing this stimulus to call up a memory. Taking action often requires that perceptual representations be translated into action representations in order to achieve a goal. For example, you see and smell garlic bread on the table at dinner. These sensations are transformed into perceptual representations, which are then processed by the brain, allowing you to decide on a course of action and to carry it out—pick up the bread and place it in your mouth. Take note, though, that information processing is not simply a sequential process from sensation to perception to memory to action. Memory may alter how we perceive something. When you see a dog, do you reach out to pet it, perceiving it as cute, or do you draw back in fear, perceiving it as dangerous, having been bitten when you were a child? The manner in which

information is processed is also subject to attentional constraints. Did you register that last sentence, or did all the talk about garlic cause your attention to wander as you made plans for dinner? Cognitive psychology is all about how we manipulate representations.

Characterizing Transformational Operations Suppose you arrive at the grocery store and discover that you forgot to bring your shopping list. You know for sure that you need coffee and milk, the main reason you came; but what else? As you cruise the aisles, scanning the shelves, you hope something will prompt your memory. Is the peanut butter gone? How many eggs are left?

This memory retrieval task draws on a number of cognitive capabilities. As we have just learned, the fundamental goal of cognitive psychology is to identify the different mental operations or transformations that are required to perform tasks such as this.

Saul Sternberg (1975) introduced an experimental task that bears some similarity to the problem faced by an absentminded shopper. In Sternberg's task, however, the job is not recalling items stored in memory, but rather comparing sensory information with representations that are active in memory. In each trial, the participant is first presented with a set of letters to memorize (Figure 3.3a). The memory set could consist of one, two, or four letters. Then a single letter is presented, and the participant must decide if this letter was part of the memorized set. The participant presses one button to indicate that the target was part of the memory set ("yes" response) and a second button to indicate that the target was not part of the set ("no" response). Once again, the primary dependent variable is reaction time.

Sternberg postulated that, to respond on this task, the participant must engage in four primary mental operations:

1. *Encode.* The participant must identify the visible target.
2. *Compare.* The participant must compare the mental representation of the target with the representations of the items in memory.
3. *Decide.* The participant must decide whether the target matches one of the memorized items.
4. *Respond.* The participant must respond appropriately for the decision made in step 3.

By postulating a set of mental operations, we can devise experiments to explore how these putative mental operations are carried out.

A basic question for Sternberg was how to characterize the efficiency of recognition memory. Assuming that all items in the memory set are actively represented, the recognition process might work in one of two ways:

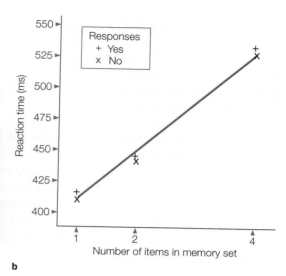

a

b

FIGURE 3.3 Memory comparison task.
(a) The participant is presented with a set of one, two, or four letters and asked to memorize them. After a delay, a single probe letter appears, and the participant indicates whether that letter was a member of the memory set. **(b)** Reaction time increases with set size, indicating that the target letter must be compared with the memory set sequentially rather than in parallel.

A highly efficient system might simultaneously compare a representation of the target with all of the items in the memory set. On the other hand, the recognition process might be able to handle only a limited amount of information at any point in time. For example, it might require that each item in memory be compared successively to a mental representation of the target.

Sternberg realized that the reaction time data could distinguish between these two alternatives. If the comparison process can be simultaneous for all items—what is called a *parallel* process—then reaction time should be independent of the number of items in the memory set. But if the comparison process operates in a sequential, or *serial*, manner, then reaction time should slow down as the memory set becomes larger, because more time is required to compare an item with a large memory list than with a small memory list. Sternberg's results convincingly supported the serial hypothesis. In fact, reaction time increased in a constant, or linear, manner with set size, and the functions for the "yes" and "no" trials were essentially identical (Figure 3.3b).

Although memory comparison appears to involve a serial process, much of the activity in our mind operates in parallel. A classic demonstration of parallel processing is the word superiority effect (Reicher, 1969). In this experiment, a stimulus is shown briefly and participants are asked which of two target letters (e.g., *A* or *E*) was presented. The stimuli can be composed of words, nonsense letter strings, or letter strings in which every letter is an *X*

except for the target letter (Figure 3.4). Brief presentation times are used so that errors will be observed, because the critical question centers on whether context affects performance. The *word superiority effect* (see Figure 3.4 caption) refers to the fact that participants are most accurate in identifying the target letter when the stimuli are words. As we saw earlier, this finding suggests that we do not need to identify all the letters of a word before we recognize the word. Rather, when we are reading a list of words, representations corresponding to the individual letters and to the entire word are activated in parallel for each item. Performance is facilitated because both representations can provide information as to whether the target letter is present.

Does the stimulus contain an A or an E?		
Condition	**Stimulus**	**Accuracy**
Word	RACK	90%
Nonsense string	KARC	80%
Xs	XAXX	80%

FIGURE 3.4 Word superiority effect.
Participants are more accurate in identifying the target vowel when it is embedded in a word. This result suggests that letter and word levels of representation are activated in parallel.

Constraints on Information Processing

In the memory search experiment, participants are not able to compare the target item to all items in the memory set simultaneously. That is, their processing ability is constrained. Whenever a constraint is identified, an important question to ask is whether the constraint is specific to the system that you are investigating (in this case, memory) or if it is a more general processing constraint. Obviously, people can do only a certain amount of internal processing at any one time, but we also experience task-specific constraints. Processing constraints are defined only by the particular set of mental operations associated with a particular task. For example, although the comparison (item 2 in Sternberg's list) of a probe item to the memory set might require a serial operation, the task of encoding (item 1 in Sternberg's list) might occur in parallel, so it would not matter whether the probe was presented by itself or among a noisy array of competing stimuli.

Exploring the limitations in task performance is a central concern for cognitive psychologists. Consider a simple color-naming task—devised in the early 1930s by J. R. Stroop, an aspiring doctoral student (1935; for a review, see MacLeod, 1991)—that has become one of the most widely employed tasks in all of cognitive psychology. We will refer to this task many times in this book. The Stroop task involves presenting the participant with a list of words and then asking her to name the color of each word as fast as possible. As Figure 3.5 illustrates, this task is much easier when the words match the ink colors.

The Stroop effect powerfully demonstrates the multiplicity of mental representations. The stimuli in this task appear to activate at least two separable representations. One representation corresponds to the color of each stimulus; it is what allows the participant to perform the task. The second representation corresponds to the color concept associated with each word. Participants are slower to name the colors when the ink color and words are mismatched, thus indicating that the second representation is activated, even though it is irrelevant to the task. Indeed, the activation of a representation based on the word rather than the color of the word appears to be automatic.

The Stroop effect persists even after thousands of trials of practice, because skilled readers have years of practice in analyzing letter strings for their symbolic meaning. On the other hand, the interference from the words is markedly reduced if the response requires a key press rather than a vocal response. Thus, the word-based representations are closely linked to the vocal response system and have little effect when the responses are produced manually.

Color matches word	Color without word	Color doesn't match word
RED	XXXXX	GREEN
GREEN	XXXXX	BLUE
RED	XXXXX	RED
BLUE	XXXXX	BLUE
BLUE	XXXXX	GREEN
GREEN	XXXXX	RED
BLUE	XXXXX	GREEN
RED	XXXXX	BLUE

FIGURE 3.5 Stroop task.
Time yourself as you work through each column, naming the color of the ink of each stimulus as fast as possible. Assuming that you do not squint to blur the words, it should be easy to read the first and second columns but quite difficult to read the third.

TAKE-HOME MESSAGES

- Cognitive psychology focuses on understanding how objects or ideas are represented in the brain and how these representations are manipulated.
- Fundamental goals of cognitive psychology include identifying the mental operations that are required to perform cognitive tasks and exploring the limitations in task performance.

Studying the Damaged Brain

An integral part of cognitive neuroscience research methodology is choosing the population to be studied. Study populations fall into four broad groups: animals and humans that are neurologically intact, and animals and humans in which the neurological system is abnormal, either as a result of an illness or a disorder, or as a result of experimental manipulation. The population a researcher picks to study depends, at least in part, on the questions being asked. We begin this section with a discussion of the major natural causes of brain dysfunction. Then we consider the different study populations, their limitations, and the methods used with each group.

Causes of Neurological Dysfunction

Nature has sought to ensure that the brain remains healthy. Structurally, the skull provides a thick, protective encasement, engendering such comments as "hardheaded" and "thick as a brick." The distribution of arteries is extensive, ensuring an adequate blood supply. Even so, the brain is subject to many disorders, and their rapid treatment is frequently essential to reduce the possibility of chronic, debilitating problems or death. We discuss some of the more common types of disorders.

Vascular Disorders   As with all other tissue, neurons need a steady supply of oxygen and glucose. These substances are essential for the cells to produce energy, fire action potentials, and make transmitters for neural communication. The brain, however, is a hog. It uses 20% of all the oxygen we breathe, an extraordinary amount considering that it accounts for only 2% of the total body mass. What's more, a continuous supply of oxygen is essential: A loss of oxygen for as little as 10 minutes can result in neural death. **Angiography** is a clinical imaging method used to evaluate the circulatory system in the brain and diagnose disruptions in circulation. As Figure 3.6 shows, this method helps us visualize the distribution of blood by highlighting major arteries and veins. A dye is injected into the vertebral or carotid artery and then an X-ray study is conducted.

Cerebral vascular accidents, or strokes, occur when blood flow to the brain is suddenly disrupted. The most frequent cause of stroke is occlusion of the normal passage of blood by a foreign substance. Over years, atherosclerosis, the buildup of fatty tissue, occurs in the arteries. This tissue can break free, becoming an embolus that is carried off in the bloodstream. An embolus that enters the cranium may easily pass through the large carotid or vertebral arteries. As the arteries and capillaries reach the end of their distribution, however, their size decreases. Eventually, the embolus becomes stuck, or infarcted, blocking the flow of blood and depriving all downstream tissue of oxygen and glucose. Within a short time, this tissue will become dysfunctional. If the blood flow is not rapidly restored, the cells will die (Figure 3.7a).

The onset of stroke can be quite varied, depending on the afflicted area. Sometimes the person may lose consciousness and die within minutes. In such cases the infarct is usually in the vicinity of the brainstem. When the infarct is cortical, the presenting symptoms may be striking, such as sudden loss of speech and comprehension. In other cases, the onset may be rather subtle. The person may report a mild headache or feel clumsy in using one of his or her hands. The vascular system is fairly consistent between individuals; thus, stroke of a particular artery typically leads to destruction of tissue in a consistent anatomical location. For example, occlusion of the posterior cerebral artery invariably leads to deficits in visual perception.

There are many other types of cerebral vascular disorders. Ischemia can be caused by partial occlusion of an artery or a capillary due to an embolus, or it can arise from a sudden drop in blood pressure that prevents blood from reaching the brain. A sudden rise in blood pressure can lead to cerebral hemorrhage (Figure 3.7b), or bleeding over a wide area of the brain due to the breakage of blood vessels. Spasms in the vessels can result in irregular blood flow and have been associated with migraine headaches.

Other disorders are due to problems in arterial structures. Cerebral arteriosclerosis is a chronic condition in which cerebral blood vessels become narrow because of thickening and hardening of the arteries. The result can be persistent ischemia. More acute situations can arise if a person has an aneurysm, a weak spot or distention in a blood vessel. An aneurysm may suddenly expand or even burst, causing a rapid disruption of the blood circulation.

Tumors   **Brain lesions** also can result from tumors. A *tumor*, or *neoplasm*, is a mass of tissue that grows abnormally and has no physiological function. Brain tumors are relatively common; most originate in glial cells and other supporting white matter tissues. Tumors also can develop from gray matter or neurons, but these are much less common, particularly in adults. Tumors are classified as benign when they do not recur after removal and tend to remain in the area of their germination (although they can become quite large). Malignant, or cancerous, tumors are likely

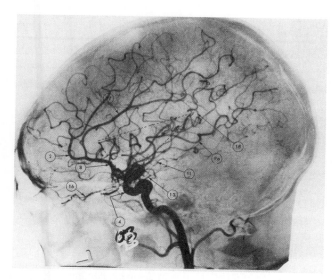

FIGURE 3.6 The brain's blood supply.
The angiogram provides an image of the arteries in the brain.

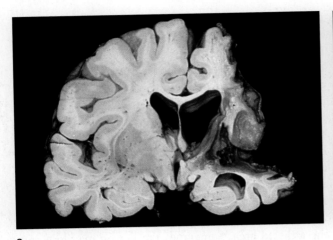
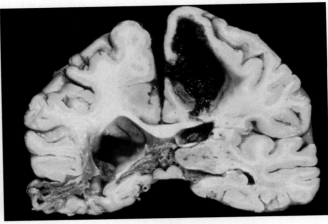

a   b

FIGURE 3.7 Vascular disorders of the brain.
(a) Strokes occur when blood flow to the brain is disrupted. This brain is from a person who had an occlusion of the middle cerebral artery. The person survived the stroke. After death, a postmortem analysis shows that almost all of the tissue supplied by this artery had died and been absorbed. **(b)** Coronal
section of a brain from a person who died following a cerebral hemorrhage. The hemorrhage destroyed
the dorsomedial region of the left hemisphere. The effects of a cerebrovascular accident 2 years before
death can be seen in the temporal region of the right hemisphere.

to recur after removal and are often distributed over several different areas. With brain tumors, the first concern
is not usually whether the tumor is benign or malignant,
but rather its location and prognosis. Concern is greatest
when the tumor threatens critical neural structures. Neurons can be destroyed by an infiltrating tumor or become
dysfunctional as a result of displacement by the tumor.

Degenerative And Infectious Disorders Many neurological disorders result from progressive disease. Table 3.1
lists some of the more prominent degenerative and infectious disorders. In later chapters, we will review some of

these disorders in detail, exploring the cognitive problems
associated with them and how these problems relate to underlying neuropathologies. Here, we focus on the etiology
and clinical diagnosis of **degenerative disorders**.

Degenerative disorders have been associated with
both genetic aberrations and environmental agents. A
prime example of a degenerative disorder that is genetic
in origin is Huntington's disease. The genetic link in
degenerative disorders such as Parkinson's disease and
Alzheimer's disease is weaker. Environmental factors are
suspected to be important, perhaps in combination with
genetic predispositions.

TABLE 3.1 Prominent Degenerative and Infectious Disorders of the Central Nervous System

Disorder	Type	Most Common Pathology
Alzheimer's disease	Degenerative	Tangles and plaques in limbic and temporoparietal cortex
Parkinson's disease	Degenerative	Loss of dopaminergic neurons
Huntington's disease	Degenerative	Atrophy of interneurons in caudate and putamen nuclei of basal ganglia
Pick's disease	Degenerative	Frontotemporal atrophy
Progressive supranuclear palsy (PSP)	Degenerative	Atrophy of brainstem, including colliculus
Multiple sclerosis	Possibly infectious	Demyelination, especially of fibers near ventricles
AIDS dementia	Viral infection	Diffuse white matter lesions
Herpes simplex	Viral infection	Destruction of neurons in temporal and limbic regions
Korsakoff's syndrome	Nutritional deficiency	Destruction of neurons in diencephalon and temporal lobes

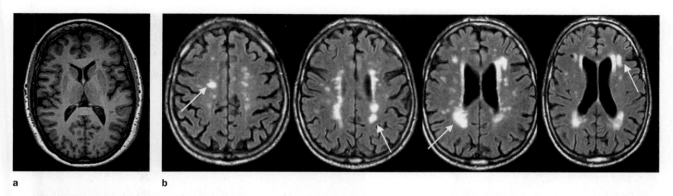

a   b

FIGURE 3.8 Degenerative disorders of the brain.
(a) Normal brain of a 60-year-old male. **(b)** Axial slices at four sections of the brain in a 79-year-old
male with Alzheimer's disease. Arrows show growth of white matter lesions.

Although neurologists were able to develop a taxonomy of degenerative disorders before the development of neuroimaging methods, diagnosis today is usually confirmed by MRI scans. The primary pathology resulting from Huntington's disease or Parkinson's disease is observed in the basal ganglia, a subcortical structure that figures prominently in the motor pathways (see Chapter 8). In contrast, Alzheimer's disease is associated with marked atrophy of the cerebral cortex (Figure 3.8).

Progressive neurological disorders can also be caused by viruses. The human immunodeficiency virus (HIV) that causes dementia related to acquired immunodeficiency syndrome (AIDS) has a tendency to lodge in subcortical regions of the brain, producing diffuse lesions of the white matter by destroying axonal fibers. The herpes simplex virus, on the other hand, destroys neurons in cortical and limbic structures if it migrates to the brain. Viral infection is also suspected in multiple sclerosis, although evidence for such a link is indirect, coming from epidemiological studies. For example, the incidence of multiple sclerosis is highest in temperate climates, and some isolated tropical islands had not experienced multiple sclerosis until the population came in contact with Western visitors.

Traumatic Brain Injury More than any disease, such as stroke or tumor, most patients arrive on a neurology ward because of a traumatic event such as a car accident, a gunshot wound, or an ill-advised dive into a shallow swimming hole. **Traumatic brain injury (TBI)** can result from either a closed or an open head injury. In closed head injuries, the skull remains intact, but mechanical forces generated by a blow to the head damage the brain. Common causes of closed head injuries are car accidents and falls, although researchers are now recognizing that closed head TBI can be prevalent in people who have been near a bomb blast or participate in contact sports. The damage may be at the site of the blow, for example,

just below the forehead—damage referred to as a coup. Reactive forces may also bounce the brain against the skull on the opposite side of the head, resulting in a countercoup. Certain regions are especially sensitive to the effects of coups and countercoups. The inside surface of the skull is markedly jagged above the eye sockets; and, as Figure 3.9 shows, this rough surface can produce extensive tearing of brain tissue in the orbitofrontal region.

An imaging method, diffusion tensor imaging (discussed later in the chapter), can be used to identify anatomical damage that can result from TBI. For example, using this method, researchers have shown that professional boxers have sustained damage in white matter tracts, even if they never had a major traumatic event (Chappell et al., 2006, Figure 3.10). Similarly, evidence is mounting that the repeated concussions suffered by football and soccer players may cause changes in neural connectivity that produce chronic cognitive problems (Shi et al., 2009).

Open head injuries happen when an object like a bullet or shrapnel penetrates the skull. With these injuries, the penetrating object may directly damage brain tissue, and the impact of the object can also create reactive forces producing coup and countercoup.

Additional damage can follow a traumatic event as a result of vascular problems and increased risk of infection. Trauma can disrupt blood flow by severing vessels, or it can change intracranial pressure as a result of bleeding. People who have experienced a TBI are also at increased risk for seizure, further complicating their recovery.

Epilepsy Epilepsy is a condition characterized by excessive and abnormally patterned activity in the brain. The cardinal symptom is a seizure, a transient loss of consciousness. The extent of other disturbances varies. Some epileptics shake violently and lose their balance. For others, seizures may be perceptible only to the most attentive friends and family. Seizures are confirmed by electroencephalography

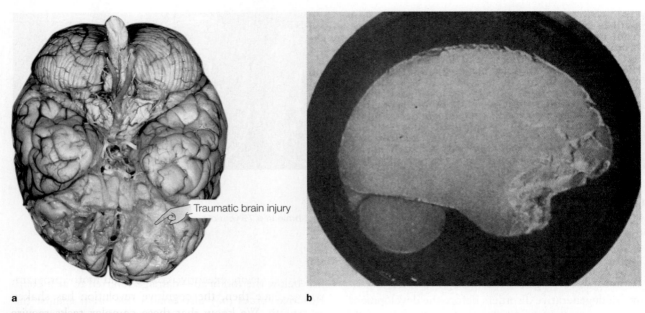

a   b

FIGURE 3.9 Traumatic brain injury.
Trauma can cause extensive destruction of neural tissue. Damage can arise from the collision of the brain
with the solid internal surface of the skull, especially along the jagged surface over the orbital region.
In addition, accelerative forces created by the impact can cause extensive shearing of dendritic arbors.
(a) In this brain of a 54-year-old man who had sustained a severe head injury 24 years before death,
tissue damage is evident in the orbitofrontal regions and was associated with intellectual deterioration
subsequent to the injury. **(b)** The susceptibility of the orbitofrontal region to trauma was made clear by A.
Holbourn of Oxford, who in 1943 filled a skull with gelatin and then violently rotated the skull. Although
most of the brain retains its smooth appearance, the orbitofrontal region has been chewed up.

(EEG). During the seizure, the EEG profile is marked by
large-amplitude oscillations (Figure 3.11).

The frequency of seizures is highly variable. The most
severely affected patients have hundreds of seizures each

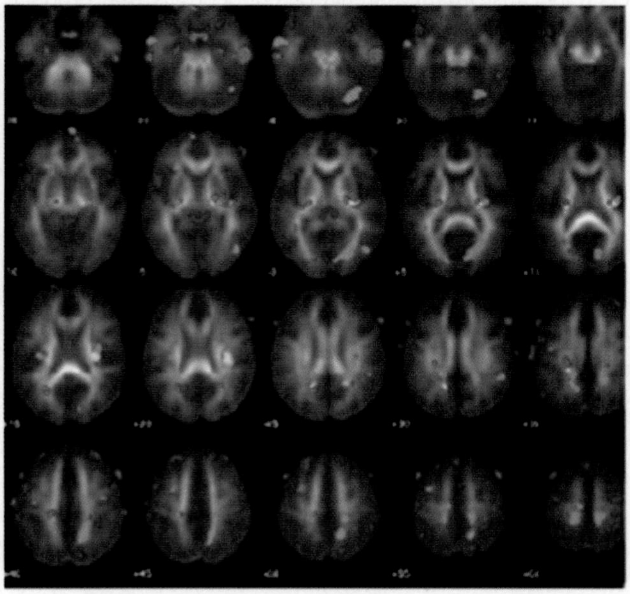

day, and each seizure can disrupt function for a few minutes.
Other epileptics suffer only an occasional seizure, but it may
incapacitate the person for a couple of hours. Simply having
a seizure, however, does not mean a person has epilepsy.
Although 0.5% of the general population has epilepsy, it
is estimated that 5% of people will have a seizure at some
point during life, usually triggered by an acute event such as
trauma, exposure to toxic chemicals, or high fever.

TAKE-HOME MESSAGES

■ Brain lesions, either naturally occurring (in humans) or
experimentally derived (in animals), allow experimenters
to test hypotheses concerning the functional role of the
damaged brain region.

■ Cerebral vascular accidents, or strokes, occur when blood
flow to the brain is suddenly disrupted. Angiography is
used to evaluate the circulatory system in the brain.

■ Tumors can cause neurological symptoms either by damaging neural tissue or by producing abnormal pressure
on spared cortex and cutting off its blood supply.

■ Degenerative disorders include Huntington's disease,
Parkinson's disease, Alzheimer's disease, and AIDS-
related dementia.

■ Neurological trauma can result in damage at the site of
the blow (coup) or at the site opposite the blow because

FIGURE 3.10 Sports-related TBI.
Colored regions show white matter tracts that are abnormal in the
brains of professional boxers.

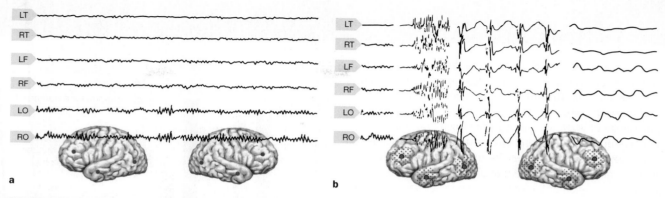

FIGURE 3.11 Electrical activity in a normal and epileptic brain.
Electroencephalographic recordings from six electrodes, positioned over the temporal (T), frontal (F), and occipital (O) cortex on both the left (L) and the right (R) sides. **(a)** Activity during normal cerebral activity. **(b)** Activity during a grand mal seizure.

of reactive forces (countercoup). Certain brain regions such as the orbitofrontal cortex are especially prone to damage from trauma.

- Epilepsy is characterized by excessive and abnormally patterned activity in the brain.

Studying Brain–Behavior Relationships Following Neural Disruption

The logic of using participants with brain lesions is straightforward. If a neural structure contributes to a task, then a structure that is dysfunctional through either surgical intervention or natural causes should impair performance of that task. Lesion studies have provided key insights into the relationship between brain and behavior. Fundamental concepts, such as the left hemisphere's dominant role in language or the dependence of visual functions on posterior cortical regions, were developed by observing the effects of brain injury. This area of research was referred to as behavioral neurology, the province of physicians who chose to specialize in the study of diseases and disorders that affect the structure and function of the nervous system.

Studies of human participants with neurological dysfunction have historically been hampered by limited information on the extent and location of the lesion. Two developments in the past half-century, however, have led to significant advances in the study of neurological patients. First, with neuroimaging methods such as computed tomography and magnetic resonance imaging, we can precisely localize brain injury in vivo. Second, the paradigms of cognitive psychology have provided the tools for making more sophisticated analyses of the behavioral deficits observed following brain injury. Early work focused on localizing complex tasks such as

language, vision, executive control, and motor programming. Since then, the cognitive revolution has shaken things up. We know that these complex tasks require integrated processing of component operations that involve many different regions of the brain. By testing patients with brain injuries, researchers have been able to link these operations to specific brain structures, as well as make inferences about the component operations that underlie normal cognitive performance.

The lesion method has a long tradition in research involving laboratory animals, in large part because the experimenter can control the location and extent of the lesion. Over the years, surgical and chemical lesioning techniques have been refined, allowing for ever greater precision. Most notable are neurochemical lesions. For instance, systemic injection of 1-methyl-4-phenyl-1,2,3,6-tetrahydropyridine (MPTP) destroys dopaminergic cells in the substantia nigra, producing an animal version of Parkinson's disease (see Chapter 8). Other chemicals have reversible effects, allowing researchers to produce a transient disruption in nerve conductivity. As long as the drug is active, the exposed neurons do not function. When the drug wears off, function gradually returns. The appeal of this method is that each animal can serve as its own control. Performance can be compared during the "lesion" and "nonlesion" periods. We will discuss this work further when we address pharmacological methods.

There are some limitations in using animals as models for human brain function. Although humans and many animals have some similar brain structures and functions, there are notable differences. Because homologous structures do not always have homologous functions, broad generalizations and conclusions are suspect. As neuroanatomist Todd Preuss (2001) put it:

The discovery of cortical diversity could not be more inconvenient. For neuroscientists, the fact of diversity means that broad generalization about cortical

Consider a study designed to explore the relationship of two aspects of memory: when we learned something and how familiar it is. The study might be designed around the following questions: Is familiarity dependent on our knowledge of when we learned something? Do these two aspects of memory depend on the same brain structures? The working hypothesis could be that these two aspects of memory are separable, and that each is associated with a particular region of the brain. A researcher designs two memory tests: one to look at memory of when information was acquired—"Do you remember when you learned that the World Trade Center Towers had been attacked?" and the second to look at familiarity—"What events occurred and in what order?"

Assuming that the study participants were selectively impaired on only one of the two memory tests, our researcher would have observed a **single dissociation** (Figure 1a). In a single dissociation study, when two groups are each tested on two tasks, a between-group difference is apparent in only one task. Two groups are necessary so that the participants' performance can be compared with that of a control group. Two tasks are necessary to examine whether a deficit is specific to a particular task or reflects a more general impairment. Many conclusions in neuropsychology are based on single dissociations. For example, compared to control participants, patients with hippocampal lesions cannot develop long-term memories even though their short-term memory is intact. In a separate example, patients with Broca's aphasia have intact comprehension but struggle to speak fluently.

Single dissociations have unavoidable problems. In particular, although the two tasks are assumed to be equally sensitive to differences between the control and experimental groups, often this is not the case. One task may be more sensitive than the other because of differences in task difficulty or sensitivity problems in how the measurements are obtained. For example, a task that measures familiarity might require a greater degree of concentration than the one that measures when a memory was learned. If the experimental group has a brain injury, it may have produced a generalized problem in concentration and the patient may have difficulty with the more demanding task. The problem, however, would not be due to a specific memory problem.

A **double dissociation** identifies whether two cognitive functions are independent of each other, something that a single association cannot do. In a double dissociation, group 1 is impaired on task X (but not task Y) and group 2 is impaired on task Y (but not task X;

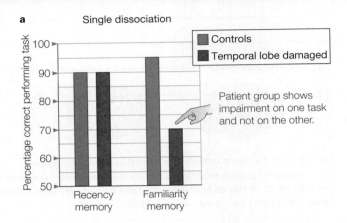

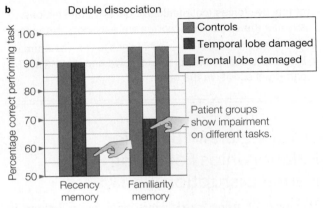

FIGURE 1 Single and double dissociations.
(a) In the single dissociation, the patient group shows impairment on one task and not on the other. (b) In the double dissociation, one patient group shows impairment on one task, and a second patient group shows impairment on the other task. Double dissociations provide much stronger evidence for a selective impairment.

Figure 1b). Either the performances of the two groups are compared to each other, or more commonly, the patient groups are compared with a control group that shows no impairment in either task. With a double dissociation, it is no longer reasonable to argue that a difference in performance results merely from the unequal sensitivity of the two tasks. In our memory example, the claim that one group has a selective problem with familiarity would be greatly strengthened if it were shown that a second group of patients showed selective impairment on the temporal-order task. Double dissociations offer the strongest neuropsychological evidence that a patient or patient group has a selective deficit in a certain cognitive operation.

organization based on studies of a few "model" species, such as rats and rhesus macaques, are built on weak foundations.

In both human and animal studies, the lesion approach itself has limitations. For naturally occurring lesions associated with strokes or tumors, there is considerable variability among patients. Moreover, researchers cannot be confident that the effect of a lesion eliminates the contribution of only a single structure. The function of neural regions that are connected to the lesioned area might also be altered, either because they are deprived of their normal neural input or because their axons fail to make normal synaptic connections. The lesion might also cause the individual to develop a compensatory strategy to minimize the consequences of the lesion. For example, when monkeys are deprived of sensory feedback to one arm, they stop using the limb. However, if the sensory feedback to the other arm is eliminated later, the animals begin to use both limbs (Taub & Berman, 1968). The monkeys prefer to use a limb that has normal sensation, but the second surgery shows that they could indeed use the compromised limb.

The Lesion Approach in Humans Two methodological approaches are available when choosing a study population of participants with brain dysfunction. Researchers can either pick a population with similar anatomical lesions or assemble a population with a similar behavioral deficit. The choice will depend, among other things, on the question being asked. In the box "The Cognitive Neuroscientist's Toolkit: Study Design," we consider two possible experimental outcomes that might be obtained in neuropsychological studies, the single and double dissociation. Either outcome can be useful for developing functional models that inform our understanding of cognition and brain function. We also consider in that box the advantages and disadvantages of conducting such studies on an individual basis or by using groups of patients with similar lesions.

Lesion studies rest on the assumption that brain injury is eliminative—that brain injury disturbs or eliminates the processing ability of the affected structure. Consider this example. Suppose that damage to brain region A results in impaired performance on task X. One conclusion is that region A contributes to the processing required for task X. For example, if task X is reading, we might conclude that region A is critical for reading. But from cognitive psychology, we know that a complex task like reading has many component operations: fonts must be perceived, letters and letter strings must activate representations of their corresponding meanings, and syntactic operations must link individual words into

a coherent stream. By merely testing reading ability, we will not know which component operation or operations are impaired when there are lesions to region A. What the cognitive neuropsychologist wants to do is design tasks that will be able to test specific hypotheses about brain-function relationships. If a reading problem stems from a general perceptual problem, then comparable deficits should be seen on a range of tests of visual perception. If the problem reflects the loss of semantic knowledge, then the deficit should be limited to tasks that require some form of object identification or recognition.

Associating neural structures with specific processing operations calls for appropriate control conditions. The most basic control is to compare the performance of a patient or group of patients with that of healthy participants. Poorer performance by the patients might be taken as evidence that the affected brain regions are involved in the task. Thus, if a group of patients with lesions in the frontal cortex showed impairment on our reading task, we might suppose that this region of the brain was critical for reading. Keep in mind, however, that brain injury can produce widespread changes in cognitive abilities. Besides having trouble reading, the frontal lobe patient might also demonstrate impairment on other tasks, such as problem solving, memory, or motor planning. Thus the challenge for the cognitive neuroscientist is to determine whether the observed behavioral problem results from damage to a particular mental operation or is secondary to a more general disturbance. For example, many patients are depressed after a neurological disturbance such as a stroke, and depression is known to affect performance on a wide range of tasks.

Functional Neurosurgery: Intervention to Alter or Restore Brain Function

Surgical interventions for treating neurological disorders provide a unique opportunity to investigate the link between brain and behavior. The best example comes from research involving patients who have undergone surgical treatment for the control of intractable epilepsy. The extent of tissue removal is always well documented, enabling researchers to investigate correlations between lesion site and cognitive deficits. But caution must be exercised in attributing cognitive deficits to surgically induced lesions. Because the seizures have spread beyond the epileptogenic tissue, other structurally intact tissue may be dysfunctional owing to the chronic effects of epilepsy. One method used with epilepsy patients compares their performance before and after surgery. The researcher can differentiate changes associated with the surgery from those associated with the epilepsy. An especially fruitful paradigm for cognitive neuroscience has involved the study of patients who have had the fibers of the corpus callosum severed. In these patients, the two hemispheres have been disconnected—a procedure referred to as a *callosotomy* operation or, more informally, the *split-brain* procedure. The relatively few patients who have had this procedure have been studied extensively, providing many insights into the roles of the two hemispheres on a wide range of cognitive tasks. These studies are discussed more extensively in Chapter 4.

In the preceding examples, neurosurgery was eliminative in nature, but it has also been used as an attempt to restore normal function. Examples are found in current treatments for Parkinson's disease, a movement disorder resulting from basal ganglia dysfunction. Although the standard treatment is medication, the efficacy of the drugs can change over time and even produce debilitating side effects. Some patients who develop severe side effects are now treated surgically. One widely used technique is **deep-brain stimulation** (**DBS**), in which electrodes are implanted in the basal ganglia. These devices produce continuous electrical signals that stimulate neural activity. Dramatic and sustained improvements are observed in many patients (Hamani et al., 2006; Krack et al., 1998), although why the procedure works is not well understood. There are side effects, in part because more than one type of neuron is stimulated. Optogenetics methods promise to provide an alternative method in which clinicians can control neural activity. While there are currently no human applications, this method has been used to explore treatments of Parkinson's symptoms in a mouse model of the disease. Early work here suggests that the most effective treatments may not result from the stimulation of specific cells, but rather the way in which stimulation changes the interactions between different types of cells (Kravitz et al., 2010). This finding underscores that many diseases of the nervous system are not usually related to problems with neurons per se, but rather with how the flow of information is altered by the disease process.

TAKE-HOME MESSAGES

- Research involving patients with neurological disorders is used to examine structure–function relationships. Single and double dissociations can provide evidence that damage to a particular brain region may result in a selective deficit of a certain cognitive operation.

- Surgical procedures have been used to treat neurological disorders such as epilepsy or Parkinson's disease. Studies conducted in patients before and after surgery have provided unique opportunities to study brain-behavior relationships.

Methods to Perturb Neural Function

As mentioned earlier, patient research rests on the assumption that brain injury is an eliminative process. The lesion is believed to disrupt certain mental operations while having little or no impact on others. The brain is massively interconnected, however, so just as with lesion studies in animals, structural damage in one area might have widespread functional (i.e., behavioral) consequences; or, through disruption of neural connections, the functional impact might be associated with a region of the brain that was not itself directly damaged. There is also increasing evidence that the brain is a plastic device: Neural function is constantly being reshaped by our experiences, and such reorganization can be quite remarkable following neurological damage. Consequently, it is not always easy to analyze the function of a missing part by looking at the operation of the remaining system. You don't have to be an auto mechanic to understand that cutting the spark plug wires or cutting the gas line will cause an automobile to stop running, but this does not mean that spark plug wires and the gas line do the same thing; rather, removing either one of these parts has similar functional consequences.

Many insights can be gleaned from careful observations of people with neurological disorders, but as we will see throughout this book, such methods are, in essence, correlational. Concerns like these point to the need for methods that involve the study of the normal brain.

The neurologically intact participant, both human and nonhuman, is used, as we have already noted, as a control when studying participants with brain injuries. Neurologically intact participants are also used to study intact function (discussed later in this chapter) and to investigate the effects of transient perturbations to the normal brain, which we discuss next.

One age-old method of perturbing function in both humans and animals is one you may have tried yourself: the use of drugs, whether it be coffee, chocolate, beer, or something stronger. Newer methods include transcranial magnetic stimulation and transcranial direct current stimulation. Genetic methods, used in animal models, provide windows into the molecular mechanisms that underpin brain function. Genomic analysis can also help identify the genetic abnormalities that contribute to certain diseases, such as Huntington's. And of course, optogenetics, which opened this chapter, has enormous potential for understanding brain structure–function connections as well as managing or curing some devastating diseases.

We turn now to the methods used to perturb function, both at the neurologic and genetic levels, in normal participants.

Pharmacology

The release of neurotransmitters at neuronal synapses and the resultant responses are critical for information transfer from one neuron to the next. Though protected by the blood–brain barrier (BBB), the brain is not a locked compartment. Many different drugs, known as psychoactive drugs (e.g., caffeine, alcohol, and cocaine as well as the pharmaceutical drugs used to treat depression and anxiety), can disturb these interactions, resulting in changes in cognitive function. **Pharmacological studies** may involve the administration of agonist drugs, those that have a similar structure to a neurotransmitter and mimic its action, or antagonist drugs, those that bind to receptors and block or dampen neurotransmission.

For the researcher studying the impacts of pharmaceuticals on human populations, there are "native" groups to study, given the prevalence of drug use in our culture. For example, in Chapter 12 we examine studies of cognitive impairments associated with chronic cocaine abuse.

Besides being used in studies of chronic drug users, neurologically intact populations are used for studies in which researchers administer a drug in a controlled environment and monitor its effects on cognitive function. For instance, the neurotransmitter dopamine is known to be a key ingredient in reward-seeking behavior. One study looked at the effect of dopamine on decision making when a potential monetary reward or loss was involved. One group of participants received the dopamine receptor antagonist haloperidol; another received the receptor agonist L-DOPA, the metabolic precursor of dopamine (though dopamine itself is unable to cross the BBB, L-DOPA can and is then converted to dopamine). Each group performed a computerized learning task, in which they were presented with a choice of two symbols on each trial. They had to choose between the symbols with the goal of maximizing payoffs (Figure 3.12; Pessiglione et al., 2006). Each symbol was associated with a certain unknown probability of gain or no gain, loss or no loss, or no gain or loss. For instance, a squiggle stood an 80% chance of winning a pound and a 20% chance of winning nothing, but a figure eight stood an 80% of losing a pound and a 20% chance of no loss, and a circular arrow resulted in no win or loss. On gain trials, the L-DOPA-treated group won more money than the haloperidol-treated group, whereas on loss trials, the groups did not differ. These results are consistent with the hypothesis that dopamine has a selective effect on reward-driven learning.

A major drawback of drug studies in which the drug is injected into the bloodstream is the lack of specificity. The entire body and brain are awash in the drug, so it is unknown how much drug actually makes it to the site of

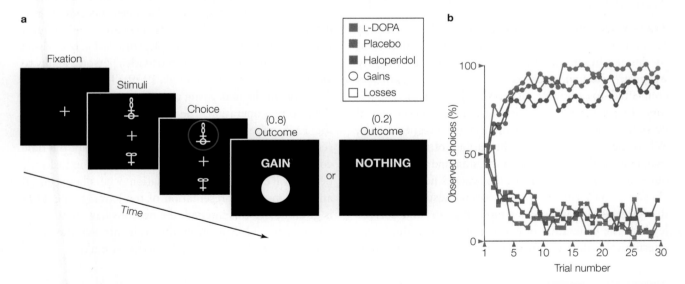

FIGURE 3.12 Pharmacological manipulation of reward-based learning.
(a) Participants chose the upper or lower of two abstract visual stimuli and observed the outcome. The selected stimulus, circled in red, is associated with an 80% chance of winning $1 and a 20% chance of winning nothing. The probabilities are different for other stimuli. **(b)** Learning functions showing probability of selecting stimuli associated with gains (circles) or avoid stimuli associated with losses (squares) as a function of the number of times each stimulus was presented. Participants given L-DOPA (green), a dopamine agonist, were faster in learning to choose stimuli associated with gains, compared to participants given a placebo (gray). Participants given haloperidol (red), a dopamine antagonist, were slower in leaning to choose the gain stimuli. The drugs did not affect how quickly participants learned to avoid the stimuli associated with a cost.

interest in the brain. In addition, the potential impact of the drug on other sites in the body and the dilution effect confound data analysis. In some animal studies, direct injection of a study drug to specific brain regions helps obviate this problem. For example, Judith Schweimer (2006) examined the brain mechanisms involved in deciding how much effort an individual should expend to gain a reward. Do you stay on the couch and watch a favorite TV show, or get dressed up to go out to a party and perhaps make a new friend? Earlier work showed that rats depleted of dopamine are unwilling to make effortful responses that are highly rewarding (Schweimer et al., 2005) and that the anterior cingulate cortex (ACC), a part of the prefrontal cortex, is important for evaluating the cost versus benefit of performing an action (Rushworth et al., 2004). Knowing that there are two types of dopamine receptors in the ACC, called D1 and D2, Schweimer wondered which was involved. In one group of rats, she injected a drug into the ACC that blocked the D1 receptor; in another, she injected a D2 antagonist. The group that had their D1 receptors blocked turned out to act like couch potatoes, but the rats with blocked D2 receptors were willing to make the effort to pursue the high reward. This dissociation indicates that dopamine input to the D1 receptors within the ACC is critical for effort-based decision making.

Transcranial Magnetic Stimulation

Transcranial magnetic stimulation (**TMS**) offers a method to noninvasively produce focal stimulation of the human brain. The TMS device consists of a tightly wrapped wire coil, encased in an insulated sheath and connected to a source of powerful electrical capacitors. Triggering the capacitors sends a large electrical current through the coil, generating a magnetic field. When the coil is placed on the surface of the skull, the magnetic field passes through the skin and scalp and induces a physiological current that causes neurons to fire (Figure 3.13a). The exact mechanism causing the neural discharge is not well understood. Perhaps the current leads to the generation of action potentials in the soma; alternatively, the current may directly stimulate axons.

The area of neural activation will depend on the shape and positioning of the coil. With currently available coils, the area of primary activation can be constrained to about 1.0 to 1.5 cm^3, although there are also downstream effects (see Figure 3.13b).

When the TMS coil is placed over the hand area of the motor cortex, stimulation will activate the muscles of the wrist and fingers. The sensation can be rather bizarre. The hand visibly twitches, yet the participant is aware that the movement is completely involuntary! Like many research tools, TMS was originally developed for clinical purposes. Direct stimulation of the motor cortex provides a relatively simple way to assess the integrity of motor pathways because muscle activity in the periphery can be detected about 20 milliseconds (ms) after stimulation.

TMS has also become a valuable research tool in cognitive neuroscience because of its ability to induce "virtual lesions" (Pascual-Leone et al., 1999). By stimulating the brain, the experimenter is disrupting normal activity in a selected region of the cortex. Similar to the logic in lesion studies, the behavioral consequences of the stimulation are used to shed light on the normal function of the disrupted tissue. This method is appealing because the technique, when properly conducted, is safe and noninvasive, producing only a relatively brief alteration in neural activity. Thus, performance can be compared between stimulated and nonstimulated conditions in the same individual. This, of course, is not possible with brain-injured patients.

The virtual-lesion approach has been successfully employed even when the person is unaware of any effects from the stimulation. For example, stimulation over visual cortex (Figure 3.14) can interfere with a person's ability to identify a letter (Corthout et al., 1999). The synchronized discharge of the underlying visual neurons interferes with their normal operation. The timing between the onset of the TMS pulse and the onset of the stimulus (e.g., presentation of a letter) can be manipulated to plot the time course of processing. In the letter identification task, the person will err only if the stimulation occurs between 70 and 130 ms after presentation of the letter. If the TMS is given before this interval, the neurons have time to recover; if the TMS is given after this interval, the visual neurons have already responded to the stimulus.

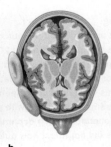

a　　　　　　　　　　**b**

FIGURE 3.13 Transcranial magnetic stimulation.
(a) The TMS coil is held by the experimenter against the participant's head. Both the coil and the participant have affixed to them a tracking device to monitor the head and coil position in real time. **(b)** The TMS pulse directly alters neural activity in a spherical area of approximately 1 cm^3.

become hyperpolarized and are less likely to fire. tDCS will alter neural activity over a much larger area than is directly affected by a TMS pulse.

tDCS has been shown to produce changes in behavioral performance. The effects can sometimes be observed within a single experimental session. Anodal tDCS generally leads to improvements in performance, perhaps because the neurons are put into a more excitable state. Cathodal stimulation may hinder performance, akin to TMS, although the effects of cathodal stimulation are generally less consistent. tDCS has also been shown to produce beneficial effects for patients with various neurological conditions such as stroke or chronic pain. The effects tend to be short-lived, lasting for just a half hour beyond the stimulation phase. If repeatedly applied, however, the duration of the benefit can be prolonged from minutes to weeks (Boggio et al., 2007).

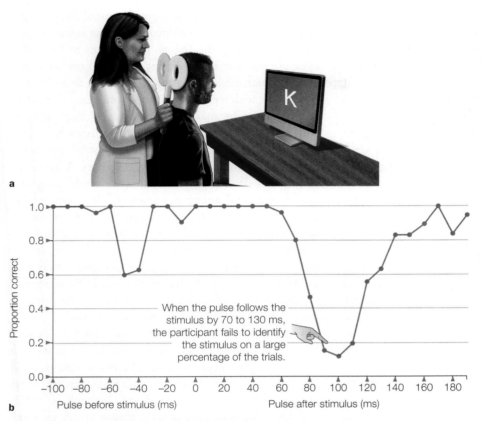

FIGURE 3.14 Transcranial magnetic stimulation over the occipital lobe.
(a) The center of the coil is positioned over the occipital lobe to disrupt visual processing. The participant attempts to name letters that are briefly presented on the screen. A TMS pulse is applied on some trials, either just before or just after the letter. **(b)** The independent variable is the time between the TMS pulse and letter presentation. Visual perception is markedly disrupted when the pulse occurs 80–120 ms after the letter due to disruption of neural activity in the visual cortex. There is also a drop in performance if the pulse comes before the letter. This is likely an artifact due to the participant blinking in response to the sound of the TMS pulse.

Transcranial Direct Current Stimulation

Transcranial direct current stimulation (tDCS) is a brain stimulation procedure that has been around in some form for the last two thousand years. The early Greeks and Romans used electric torpedo fish, which can deliver from 8 to 220 volts of DC electricity, to stun and numb patients in an attempt to alleviate pain, such as during childbirth and migraine headache episodes. Today's electrical stimulation uses a much smaller current (1–2 mV) that feels like a tingling or itchy feeling when it is turned on or off. tDCS sends a current between two small electrodes—an anode and a cathode—placed on the scalp. Physiological studies show that neurons under the anode become depolarized. That is, they are put into an elevated state of excitability, making them more likely to initiate an action potential when a stimulus or movement occurs (see Chapter 2). Neurons under the cathode

TMS and tDCS give cognitive neuroscientists safe methods for transiently disrupting the activity of the human brain. An appealing feature of these methods is that researchers can design experiments to test specific functional hypotheses. Unlike neuropsychological studies in which comparisons are usually between a patient group and matched controls, participants in TMS and tDCS studies can serve as their own controls, since the effects of these stimulation procedures are transient.

Genetic Manipulations

The start of the 21st century witnessed the climax of one of the great scientific challenges: the mapping of the human genome. Scientists now possess a complete record of the genetic sequence on our chromosomes. We have only begun to understand how these genes code for all aspects of human structure and function. In essence, we now have a map containing the secrets to many treasures: What causes people to grow old? Why are some people more susceptible to certain cancers than other people?

What dictates whether embryonic tissue will become a skin cell or a brain cell? Deciphering this map is an imposing task that will take years of intensive study.

Genetic disorders are manifest in all aspects of life, including brain function. As noted earlier, diseases such as Huntington's disease are clearly heritable. By analyzing individuals' genetic codes, scientists can now predict whether the children of individuals carrying the HD gene will develop this debilitating disorder. Moreover, by identifying the genetic locus of this disorder, scientists hope to devise techniques to alter the aberrant genes, either by modifying them or by figuring out a way to prevent them from being expressed.

In a similar way, scientists have sought to understand other aspects of normal and abnormal brain function through the study of genetics. Behavioral geneticists have long known that many aspects of cognitive function are heritable. For example, controlling mating patterns on the basis of spatial-learning performance allows the development of "maze-bright" and "maze-dull" strains of rats. Rats that quickly learn to navigate mazes are likely to have offspring with similar abilities, even if the offspring are raised by rats that are slow to navigate the same mazes. Such correlations are also observed across a range of human behaviors, including spatial reasoning, reading speed, and even preferences in watching television (Plomin et al., 1990). This finding should not be taken to mean that our intelligence or behavior is genetically determined. Maze-bright rats perform quite poorly if raised in an impoverished environment. The truth surely reflects complex interactions between the environment and genetics (see "The Cognitive Neuroscientist's Toolkit: Correlation and Causation").

To understand the genetic component of this equation, neuroscientists are now working with many animal models, seeking to identify the genetic mechanisms of both brain structure and function. Dramatic advances have been made in studies with model organisms like the fruit fly and mouse, two species with reproductive propensities that allow many generations to be spawned in a relatively short time. As with humans, the genomes for these species have been sequenced, which has provided researchers the opportunity to explore the functional role of many genes. A key methodology is to develop genetically altered animals, using what are referred to as **knockout procedures.** The term *knockout* comes from the fact that specific genes have been manipulated so that they are no longer present or expressed. Scientists can then study the knockout strains to explore the consequences of these changes. For example, *weaver* mice are a knockout strain in which Purkinje cells, the prominent cell type in the cerebellum, fail to develop. As the name implies, these mice exhibit coordination problems.

At an even more focal level, knockout procedures have been used to create strains that lack a single type of postsynaptic receptor in specific brain regions, while leaving intact other types of receptors. Susumu Tonegawa at the Massachusetts Institute of Technology (MIT) and his colleagues developed a mouse strain in which N-methyl-D-aspartate (NMDA) receptors were absent in cells within a subregion of the hippocampus (Wilson & Tonegawa, 1997; also see Chapter 9). Mice lacking these receptors exhibited poor learning on a variety of memory tasks, providing a novel approach for linking memory with its molecular substrate (Figure 3.15). In a sense, this approach constitutes a lesion method, but at a microscopic level.

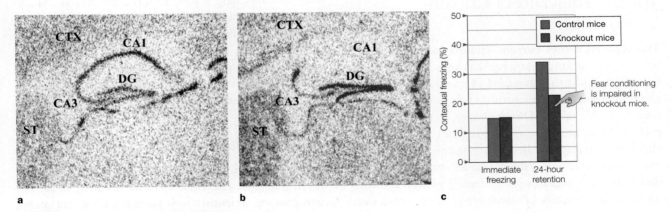

a　　　　　　　　**b**　　　　　　　　**c**

FIGURE 3.15 Fear conditioning in knockout mice.
Brain slices through the hippocampus, showing the absence of a particular receptor in genetically altered mice (CTX = cortex; DG = dentate gyrus; ST = striatum). **(a)** Cells containing the gene associated with the receptor are stained in black. **(b)** These cells are absent in the CA1 region of the slice from the knockout mouse. **(c)** Fear conditioning is impaired in knockout mice. After receiving a shock, the mice freeze. When normal mice are placed in the same context 24 hours later, they show strong learning by the large increase in the percentage of freezing responses. This increase is reduced in the knockout mice.

Neurogenetic research is not limited to identifying the role of each gene individually. Complex brain function and behavior arise from interactions between many genes and the environment. As our genetic tools become more sophisticated, scientists will be better positioned to detect the polygenetic influences on brain function and behavior.

TAKE-HOME MESSAGES

- Brain function can be perturbed by drugs, magnetic or electrical stimulation, and through genetic manipulations.

- A major drawback of drug studies, in which the drug is injected into the bloodstream, is the lack of specificity.

- Transcranial magnetic stimulation (TMS) uses magnetic pulses to transiently alter local brain physiology.

- Gene knockout technology allows scientists to explore the consequences of the lack of expression of a specific gene in order to determine its role in behavior.

Structural Analysis of the Brain

We now turn to the methods used to analyze brain structure. Structural methods take advantage of the differences in physical properties that different tissues possess. For instance, when you look at an X-ray, the first thing you notice is that bones appear starkly white and the surrounding structures vary in intensity from black to white. The density of biological material varies, and the absorption of X-ray radiation is correlated with tissue density. In this section, we introduce computed tomography (CT), magnetic resonance imaging (MRI), and diffusion tensor imaging (DTI).

Computed Tomography

Computed tomography (**CT** or **CAT** scanning), introduced commercially in 1983, has been an extremely important medical tool for structural imaging of neurological damage in patients. While conventional X-rays compress three-dimensional objects into two dimensions, CT scanning allows for the reconstruction of three-dimensional space from compressed two-dimensional images. Figure 3.16a depicts the method, showing how X-ray beams are passed through the head and a two-dimensional (2-D) image is generated by sophisticated computer software. The sides of the CT scanner rotate, X-ray beams are sequentially projected, and 2-D images are collected over a 180° arc. Finally, a computer constructs a three-dimensional X-ray image from the series of 2-D images.

Figure 3.16b shows a CT scan of a healthy individual. Most of the cortex and white matter appear as homogeneous gray areas. The typical spatial resolution for CT scanners is approximately 0.5 to 1.0 cm in all directions. Each point on the image reflects an average density of that point and the surrounding 1.0 mm of tissue. Thus, it is not possible to discriminate two objects that are closer than approximately 5 mm. Because the cortex is only 4 mm thick, it is very difficult

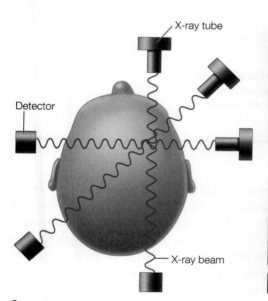
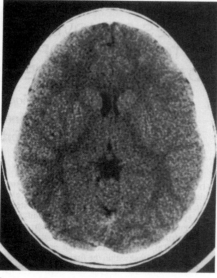

a   **b**

FIGURE 3.16 Computed tomography provides an important tool for imaging neurological pathology. As with standard clinical X-rays, the absorption of X-ray radiation in a CT scan is correlated with tissue density. High-density material, such as bone, absorbs a lot of radiation and appears white. Low-density material, such as air or cerebrospinal fluid, absorbs little radiation. The absorption capacity of neural tissue lies between these extremes. **(a)** The CT process is based on the same principles as X-rays. An X-ray is projected through the head, and the recorded image provides a measurement of the density of the intervening tissue. By projecting the X-ray from multiple angles combined with the use of computer algorithms, a three-dimensional image based on tissue density is obtained. **(b)** In this transverse CT image, the dark regions along the midline are the ventricles, the reservoirs of cerebrospinal fluid.

The issue of causation is important to consider in any discussion of scientific observation. Consider a study that examined the relationship between drinking habits and personal income (Peters & Stringham, 2006). Self-reported drinkers earned about 10% more than self-reported abstainers. Those who drank in bars earned an additional 7%. The research team offered the counterintuitive conclusion that the increase in alcohol consumption played a causative role in the higher income levels, at least in men. In their view, social drinking increases social networking, and this networking has the benefit of increasing income. Although this causal chain is

reasonable, there are certainly alternative ways to account for the relationship between drinking and income. For example, individuals who make a lot of money can afford to go to bars at night and spend their income on drinks. In elementary statistics courses, we learn to be wary about inferring causation from correlation, but the temptation can be strong.

The tendency to infer causation from correlation can be especially great when we're comparing the contribution of nature and nurture to brain and behavior. A good example comes from work examining the relationship of chronic stress and the hippocampus, a part of the brain

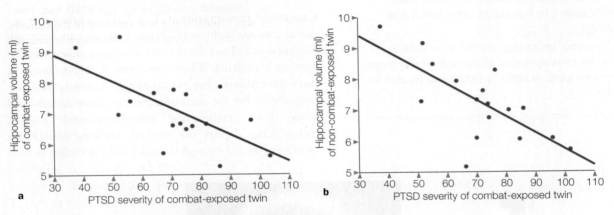

Figure 1 Exploring the relationship between PTSD and hippocampal size.
Scatter plots illustrate the relationship of symptom severity in combat veterans with PTSD to **(a)** their own hippocampal volumes and **(b)** the hippocampal volumes of their identical twin brothers who were not exposed to combat. Symptom severity represents the total score received on the Clinician-Administered PTSD Scale (CAPS).

to see the boundary between white and gray matter on a CT scan. The white and gray matter are also of very similar density, further limiting the ability of this technique to distinguish them. Larger structures, however, can be identified easily. The surrounding skull appears white due to the high density of bone. The ventricles are black owing to the low density of cerebrospinal fluid.

Magnetic Resonance Imaging

Although CT machines are still widely used, many hospitals now also own a **magnetic resonance imaging** (**MRI**) scanner, which can produce high-resolution images of soft tissue. MRI exploits the magnetic properties of atoms that make up organic tissue. One such atom that is pervasive in the brain, and indeed in all organic tissue, is hydrogen.

The proton in a hydrogen atom is in constant motion, spinning about its principal axis. This motion creates a tiny magnetic field. In their normal state, the orientation of a population of protons in tissue is randomly distributed, unaffected by the weak magnetic field created by Earth's gravity (Figure 3.17). The MRI scanner creates a powerful magnetic field, measured in tesla units. Whereas gravitational forces on the Earth create a magnetic field of about 0.001 tesla, the typical MRI scanner produces a magnetic field from 0.5 to 1.5 teslas. When a person is placed within the magnetic field of the MRI machine, a significant proportion of their protons become oriented in the direction parallel to the strong magnetic force of the MRI machine. Radio waves are then passed through the magnetized regions, and as the protons absorb the energy in these waves, their orientation is perturbed in a

that is critical for learning and memory. From animal studies, we know that exposure to prolonged stress, and the resulting increase in glucocorticoid steroids, can cause atrophy in the hippocampus (Sapolsky et al., 1990). With the advent of neuroimaging, we have also learned that people with chronic posttraumatic stress disorder (PTSD) have smaller hippocampi then individuals who do not suffer from PTSD (Bremner et al., 1997; M. B. Stein et al., 1997). Can we therefore conclude that the stress that we know is associated with PTSD results, over time, in a reduction in the hippocampal volume of people with PTSD? This certainly seems a reasonable way to deduce a causal chain of events between these observations.

It is also important, however, to consider alternative explanations. For instance, the causal story may run in the opposite direction: Individuals with smaller hippocampi, perhaps due to genetic variation, may be more vulnerable to the effects of stress, and thus be at higher risk for developing PTSD. What study design could distinguish between two hypotheses—one that emphasizes environmental factors (e.g., PTSD, via chronic stress, causes reduction in size of the hippocampus) and one that emphasizes genetic factors (e.g., individuals with small hippocampi are at risk for developing PTSD)?

A favorite approach of behavioral geneticists in exploring questions like these is to study identical twins. Mark Gilbertson and his colleagues (2002) at the New Hampshire Veterans Administration Medical Center studied a cohort of 40 pairs of identical twins. Within each twin pair, one member had experienced severe trauma during a tour of duty in Vietnam. The other member of the pair had not seen active duty. In this way, each high-stress participant had a very well-matched control, at least in terms of genetics: an identical twin brother.

Although all of the active-duty participants had experienced severe trauma during their time in Vietnam (one of the inclusion criteria for the study), not all of these individuals had developed PTSD. Thus, the experimenters could look at various factors associated with the onset of PTSD in a group of individuals with similar environmental experiences. Consistent with previous studies, anatomical MRIs showed that people with PTSD had smaller hippocampi than unrelated individuals without PTSD had. The same was also found for the twin brothers of the individuals with PTSD; that is, these individuals also had smaller hippocampi, even though they did not have PTSD and did not report having experienced unusual trauma in their lifetime. Moreover, the severity of the PTSD was negatively correlated with the size of the hippocampus in both the patient with PTSD (Figure 1a) and the matched twin control (Figure 1b). Thus, the researchers concluded that small hippocampal size was a risk factor for developing PTSD and that PTSD alone did not cause the decreased hippocampal size.

This study serves as an example of the need for caution: Experimenters must be careful when making causal inferences based on correlational data. This study also provides an excellent example of how scientists are studying interactions between genes and the environment in influencing behavior and brain structure.

---

predictable direction. When the radio waves are turned off, the absorbed energy is dissipated and the protons rebound toward the orientation of the magnetic field. This synchronized rebound produces energy signals that are picked up by detectors surrounding the head of the participant. By systematically measuring the signals throughout the three-dimensional volume of the head, an MRI system can then construct an image based on the distribution of the protons and other magnetic agents in the tissue. The hydrogen proton distribution is determined largely by the distribution of water throughout the brain, enabling MRI to distinguish clearly the brain's gray matter, white matter, ventricles, and fiber tracts.

As Figure 3.17b shows, MRI scans provide a much clearer image of the brain than is possible with CT scans. This improvement occurs because the density of protons is much greater in gray matter compared to white matter. With MRI, it is easy to see the individual sulci and gyri of the cerebral cortex. A sagittal section at the midline reveals the impressive size of the corpus callosum. The MRI scans can resolve structures that are much smaller than 1 mm, allowing elegant views of small, subcortical structures such as the mammillary bodies or superior colliculus.

Diffusion Tensor Imaging

A variant of traditional MRI scanners is now used to study the anatomical structure of the axon tracts that form the brain's white matter; that is, it can offer information about anatomical connectivity between regions. This method, called **diffusion tensor imaging (DTI)**, is performed with an MRI scanner that measures the density

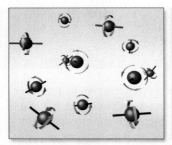

In normal state, the orientation of spinning protons is randomly distributed.

Exposure to the magnetic field of the MRI scanner aligns the orientation of the protons.

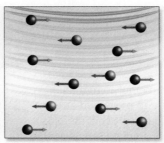

When a radio frequency pulse is applied, the axes of the protons are shifted in a predictable manner and put the protons in an elevated energy state.

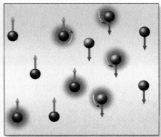

When the pulse is turned off, the protons release their energy as they spin back to the orientation of the magnetic field.

a

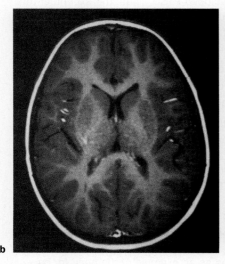
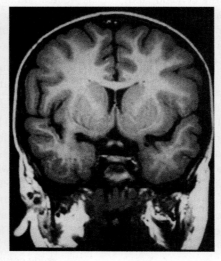
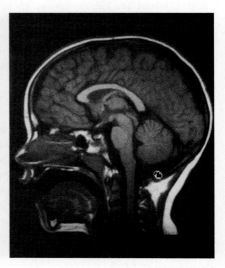

b

FIGURE 3.17 MRI.
Magnetic resonance imaging exploits the fact that many organic elements, such as hydrogen, are magnetic. **(a)** In their normal state, the orientation of these hydrogen atom nuclei (i.e., protons) is random. When an external magnetic field is applied, the protons align their axis of spin in the direction of the magnetic field. A pulse of radio waves (RF) alters the spin of the protons as they absorb some of the RF energy. When the RF pulse is turned off, the protons emit their own RF energy, which is detected by the MRI machine. The density of hydrogen atoms is different in white and gray matter, making it easy to visualize these regions. **(b)** Transverse, coronal, and sagittal images. Comparing the transverse slice in this figure with the CT image in Figure 3.16 reveals the finer resolution offered by MRI. Both images are from about the same level of the brain.

and the motion of the water contained in the axons. DTI uses the known diffusion characteristics of water to determine the boundaries that restrict water movement throughout the brain (Behrens et al., 2003). Free diffusion of water is *isotropic*; that is, it occurs equally in all directions. Diffusion of water in the brain, however, is *anisotropic*, or restricted, so it does not diffuse equally in all directions. The reason for this anisotropy is that the axon membranes restrict the diffusion of water; the probability of water moving in the direction of the axon is thus greater than the probability of water moving perpendicular to the axon (Le Bihan, 2003). Within the brain, this anisotropy is greatest in axons because myelin creates a nearly pure lipid boundary, which limits the flow of water

much more than gray matter or cerebrospinal fluid does. In this way, the orientation of axon bundles within the white matter can be imaged (DaSilva et al., 2003).

MRI principles can be combined with what is known about the diffusion of water to determine the diffusion anisotropy within the MRI scan. By introducing two large pulses to the magnetic field, MRI signals can be made sensitive to the diffusion of water (Le Bihan, 2003). The first pulse determines the initial position of the protons carried by water. The second pulse, introduced after a short delay, detects how far the protons have moved in space in the specific direction being measured. Since the flow of water is constrained by the axons, the resulting image reveals the major white matter tracts (Figure 3.18).

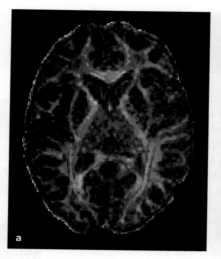 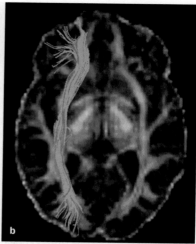

FIGURE 3.18 Diffusion tensor imaging.
(a) This axial slice of a human brain reveals the directionality and connectivity of the white matter. The colors correspond to the principal directions of the white matter tracts in each region. **(b)** DTI data can be analyzed to trace white matter connections in the brain. The tracts shown here form the inferior fronto-oc-cipital fasciculus, which, as the name suggests, connects the visual cortex to the frontal lobe.

TAKE-HOME MESSAGES

- Computed tomography (CT or CAT) uses X-rays to image the 3-D structure of the brain.
- Magnetic resonance imaging (MRI) exploits the magnetic properties of the organic tissue of the brain to image its structure. The spatial resolution of MRI is superior to CT.
- Diffusion tensor imaging (DTI), performed with magnetic resonance scanners, is used to measure white matter pathways in the brain and thus can offer information about anatomical connectivity between regions.

Methods for the Study of Neural Function

The development of electrodes and recording systems that can measure the electrical activity within a single neuron or from a small group of neurons was a turning point for neurophysiology and related fields. We open this section with a brief discussion of the single-cell recording method and provide some examples of how it is used to understand cognitive functions. We then turn to the blossoming number of methods used to study brain function during cognitive processing. In this section, we introduce some of the technologies that allow researchers to directly observe the electrical activity of the healthy brain in vivo. After that, we turn to methods that measure physiological changes resulting from neural activity and, in particular, changes in blood flow and oxygen utilization that arise when neural activity increases.

Single-Cell Recording in Animals

The most important technological advance in **neurophysiology**—perhaps in all of neuroscience—was the development of methods to record the activity of single neurons in laboratory animals. With these methods, the understanding of neural activity advanced by a quantum leap. No longer did the neuroscientist have to be content with describing nervous system action in terms of functional regions. **Single-cell recording** enabled researchers to describe the response characteristics of individual elements.

In single-cell recording, a thin electrode is inserted into an animal's brain. When the electrode is in the vicinity of a neuronal membrane, changes in electrical activity can be measured (see Chapter 2). Although the surest way to guarantee that the electrode records the activity of a single cell is to record intracellularly, this technique is difficult, and penetrating the membrane frequently damages the cell. Thus single-cell recording is typically done extracellularly, with the electrode situated on the outside of the neuron. There is no guarantee, however, that the changes in electrical potential at the electrode tip reflect the activity of a single neuron. More likely, the tip will record the activity of a small set of neurons. Computer algorithms are subsequently used to differentiate this pooled activity into the contributions from individual neurons.

The neurophysiologist is interested in what causes change in the synaptic activity of a neuron. She seeks to determine the response characteristics of individual neurons by correlating their activity with a given stimulus pattern or behavior. The primary goal of single-cell recording experiments is to determine what experimental manipulations produce a consistent change in the response rate of an isolated cell. For instance, does the cell increase its firing rate when the animal moves its arm? If so, is this change specific to movements in a particular direction? Does the firing rate for that movement depend on the outcome of the action (e.g., a food morsel to be reached or an itch to be scratched)? Equally interesting, what makes the cell decrease its response rate? These measurements of

The data from single-cell recording studies is commonly graphed as a raster plot, which shows action potentials as a function of time (Figure 1). The graph includes data from before the start of the trial, providing a picture of the baseline firing rate of the neuron. The graph then shows changes in firing rate as the stimulus is presented and the animal responds. Each line of a raster plot represents a single trial, and the action potentials are marked as ticks in the column. To give a sense of the average response of the neuron over the course of a trial, the data are summed and presented as a bar graph known as a peristimulus histogram. A histogram allows scientists to visualize the rate and timing of neuronal spike discharges in relation to an external stimulus or event.

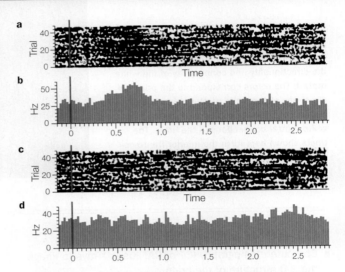

FIGURE 1 Graphing the data from single-cell recording experiments. Raster plots show the timing of action potentials. It can be called a spike raster, raster plot, or raster graph. Here is a raster plot of a face selective cell during forty different trials presenting either a threatening face (a) or a non face stimulus (c). Stimulus onset is marked by the vertical red line. The trials are plotted on the y-axis and time is plotted on the x-axis. Each dot in the raster plot marks the time of occurrence of a single AP spike. (b) and (d) are histograms.

changes are made against a backdrop of activity, given that neurons are constantly firing even in the absence of stimulation or movement. This baseline activity varies widely from one brain area to another. For example, some cells within the basal ganglia have spontaneous firing rates of over 100 spikes per second, whereas cells in another basal ganglia region have a baseline rate of only 1 spike per second. Further confounding the analysis of the experimental measurements, these spontaneous firing levels fluctuate.

Single-cell recording has been used in almost all regions of the brain across a wide range of nonhuman species. For sensory neurons, the experimenter might manipulate the input by changing the type of stimulus presented to the animal. For motor neurons, output recordings can be made as the animal performs a task or moves about. Some significant advances in neurophysiology have come about recently as researchers probe higher brain centers to examine changes in cellular activity related to goals, emotions, and rewards.

In a typical experiment, recordings are obtained from a series of cells in a targeted area of interest. Thus a functional map can describe similarities and differences between neurons in a specified cortical region. One area

where the single-cell method has been used extensively is the study of the visual system of primates. In a typical experiment, the researcher targets the electrode to a cortical area that contains cells thought to respond to visual stimulation. Once a cell has been identified, the researcher tries to characterize its response properties.

A single cell is not responsive to all visual stimuli. A number of stimulus parameters might correlate with the variation in the cell's firing rate; examples include the shape of the stimulus, its color, and whether it is moving (see Chapter 5). An important factor is the location of the stimulus. As Figure 3.19 shows, all visually sensitive cells respond to stimuli in only a limited region of space. This region of space is referred to as that cell's **receptive field**. For example, some neurons respond when the stimulus is located in the lower left portion of the visible field. For other neurons, the stimulus may have to be in the upper right (Figure 3.19b).

Neighboring cells have at least partially overlapping receptive fields. As a region of visually responsive cells is traversed, there is an orderly relation between the receptive-field properties of these cells and the external

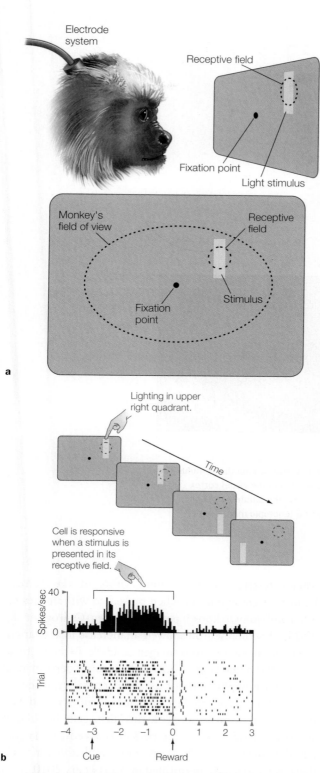

FIGURE 3.19 Electrophysiological methods are used to identify the response characteristics of cells in the visual cortex.
(a) While the activity of a single cell is monitored, the monkey is required to maintain fixation, and stimuli are presented at various positions in its field of view. (b) The vertical lines to the right of each stimulus correspond to individual action potentials. The cell fires vigorously when the stimulus is presented in the upper right quadrant, thus defining the upper right as the receptive field for this cell.

world. External space is represented in a continuous manner across the cortical surface: Neighboring cells have receptive fields of neighboring regions of external space. As such, cells form a topographic representation, an orderly mapping between an external dimension such as spatial location and the neural representation of that dimension. In vision, topographic representations are referred to as **retinotopic**. Cell activity within a retinotopic map correlates with the location of the stimulus (Figure 3.20a,b).

There are other types of topographic maps. In Chapter 2, we reviewed the motor and somatosensory maps along the central sulcus that provide topographic representations of the body surface. In a similar sense, auditory areas in the subcortex and cortex contain tonotopic maps, in which the physical dimension reflected in neural organization is the sound frequency of a stimulus. With a tonotopic map, some cells are maximally activated by a 1000-Hz tone and others by a 4000-Hz tone (Figure 3.20c). In addition, neighboring cells tend to be tuned to similar frequencies. Thus, sound frequencies are reflected in cells that are activated upon the presentation of a sound. Tonotopic maps are sometimes referred to as *cochleotopic* because the cochlea, the sensory apparatus in the ear, contains hair cells tuned to distinct regions of the auditory spectrum.

When the single-cell method was first introduced, neuroscientists had high hopes that the mysteries of brain function would finally be solved. All they needed was a catalog of contributions by different cells. Yet it soon became clear that, with neurons, the aggregate behavior of cells might be more than just the sum of its parts. The function of an area might be better understood by identifying the correlations in the firing patterns of groups of neurons rather than identifying the response properties of each individual neuron. This idea has inspired single-cell physiologists to develop new techniques that allow recordings to be made in many neurons simultaneously—what is called **multiunit recording**.

Bruce McNaughton and colleagues at the University of Arizona studied how the rat hippocampus represents spatial information by simultaneously recording from 150 cells (Wilson & McNaughton, 1994). By looking at the pattern of activity over the group of neurons, the researchers were able to show how the rat coded spatial and episodic information differently. Today, it is common to record from over 400 cells simultaneously (Lebedev & Nicolelis, 2006). As we will see in Chapter 8, multiunit recordings from motor areas of the brain are now being used to allow animals to control artificial limbs just by thinking about movement. This dramatic medical advance may change the way rehabilitation programs are designed for paraplegics. For example, multiunit recordings can be obtained while people think about actions they would like

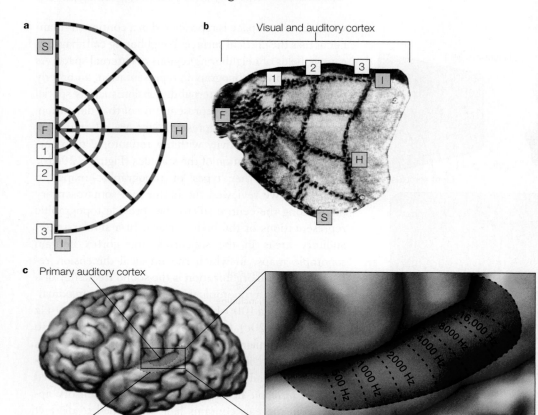

FIGURE 3.20 Topographic maps of the visual and auditory cortex.
In the visual cortex, the receptive fields of the cells define a retinotopic map. While viewing the stimulus
(a), a monkey was injected with a radioactive agent. **(b)** Metabolically active cells in the visual cortex
absorb the agent, revealing how the topography of the retina is preserved across the striate cortex.
(c) In the auditory cortex, the frequency-tuning properties of the cells define a tonotopic map. Topographic maps are also seen in the somatosensory and motor cortex.

to perform, and this information can be analyzed by computers to control robotic or artificial limbs.

Single-Cell Recordings in Humans

Single-cell recordings from human brains are rare. When
surgical procedures are required to treat cases of epilepsy
or to remove a tumor, however, intracranial electrodes may
be inserted as part of the procedure to localize the abnormality in preparation of the surgical resection. In epilepsy,
the electrodes are commonly placed in the medial temporal lobe (MTL), where the focus of generalized seizures is
most frequent. Many patients with implanted electrodes
have given generously of their time for research purposes,
engaging in experimental tasks so that researchers can
obtain neurophysiological recordings in humans.

Itzhak Fried and his colleagues have found that MTL
neurons in humans can respond selectively to specific
familiar images. For instance, in one patient a single
neuron in the left posterior hippocampus was activated

when presented with different views of the actress
Jennifer Aniston but not when presented with images of
other well-known known people or places (Quiroga et al.,
2005). Another neuron showed an increase in activation
when the person viewed images of Halle Berry or read
her printed name (Figure 3.21). This neuron corresponds
to what we might think of as a conceptual representation, one that is not tied to a particular sensory modality
(e.g., vision). Consistent with this idea, cells like these
are also activated when the person is asked to imagine
Jennifer Aniston or Halle Berry, or to think about movies
these actresses have performed in (Cerf et al., 2010).

Electroencephalography

Although the electrical potential produced by a single
neuron is minute, when populations of neurons are
active together, they produce electrical potentials large
enough to be measured by non-invasive electrodes
that have been placed on the scalp, a method known

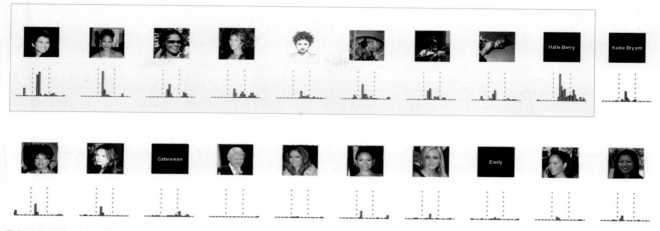

FIGURE 3.21 The Halle Berry neuron?
Recordings were made from a single neuron in the hippocampus of a patient with epilepsy. The cell activity to each picture is shown in the histograms, with the dotted lines indicating the window within which the stimulus was presented. This cell showed prominent activity to Halle Berry stimuli, including photos of her, photos of her as Catwoman, and even her name.

as **electroencephalography (EEG)**. These surface electrodes, usually 20 to 256 of them embedded in an elastic cap, are much bigger than those used for single-cell recordings (Figure 3.22). The electrical potential can be recorded at the scalp because the tissues of the brain, skull, and scalp passively conduct the electrical currents produced by synaptic activity. The fluctuating voltage at each electrode is compared to the voltage at a reference electrode, which is usually located on the mastoid bone at the base of the skull. The recording from each electrode reflects the electrical activity of the underlying brain region. The record of the signals is referred to as an *electroencephalogram.*

EEG yields a continuous recording of overall brain activity. Because we have come to understand that predictable EEG signatures are associated with different behavioral states, it has proved to have many important clinical applications (Figure 3.23). In deep sleep, for example, the EEG is characterized by slow, high-amplitude

oscillations, presumably resulting from rhythmic changes in the activity states of large groups of neurons. In other phases of sleep and in various wakeful states, the pattern changes, but always in a predictable manner. Because normal EEG patterns are well established and consistent among individuals, EEG recordings can be used

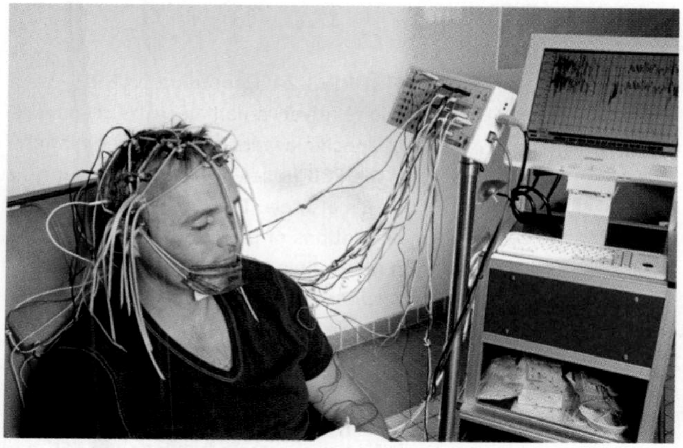

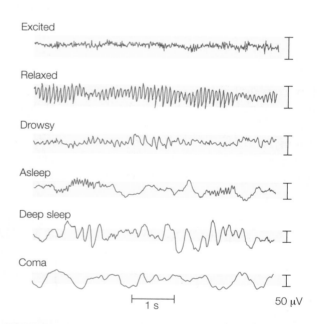

Excited

Relaxed

Drowsy

Asleep

Deep sleep

Coma

1 s   50 μV

FIGURE 3.23 EEG profiles obtained during various states of consciousness.
Recorded from the scalp, the electrical potential exhibits a waveform with time on the x-axis and voltage on the y-axis. Over time, the waveform oscillates between a positive and negative voltage. Very slow oscillations dominate in deep sleep, or what is called the delta wave. When awake, the oscillations occur much faster when the person is relaxed (alpha) or reflect a combination of many components when the person is excited.

FIGURE 3.22 Person wired up for an EEG study.

THE COGNITIVE NEUROSCIENTIST'S TOOLKIT
ERP Recordings

ERP graphs show the average of EEG waves time-locked to specific events such as the onset of a stimulus or response. Time is plotted on the x-axis and voltage on the y-axis. The ERP is composed of a series of waves with either positive or negative polarities (see Figure 3.24 for an example). The components of the waveform are named according to its polarity, N for negative and P for positive, and the time the wave appeared after stimulus onset. Thus, a wave tagged N100 is a negative wave that appeared 100 milliseconds after a stimulus. Unfortunately, there are some idiosyncrasies in the literature (see Figure 3.25). Some components are labeled to reflect their order of appearance. Thus, N1 can refer to the first negative peak. Care must also be used when looking at the wave polarity, because some researchers plot negative in the upward direction and others in the downward direction.

Some components of the ERP have been associated with psychological processes:

- After a stimulus, the earliest components are connected with sensory processing and occur within

the first 100 ms. This trait has made them an important tool for clinicians evaluating sensory systems.

- Waves that occur 100 ms after the stimulus presentation are no longer solely derived from sensory processing, but are modulated by attention. The N100 and P100 waves are associated with selective attention.
- The N200 wave is known as the mismatch negativity component. It is found when a stimulus is physically deviant from the preceding stimuli, such as when a G tone is heard after a series of C tones.
- The P300 wave is seen when an attended stimulus is presented, especially if the stimulus is relatively rare.
- The N400 component is observed when a stimulus is unexpected. It differs from the N200 in that the surprise event here might be a violation of semantics (e.g., "The cow jumped over the banana"), rather than a physical change.

---

to detect abnormalities in brain function. For example, EEG provides valuable information in the assessment and treatment of epilepsy (see Figure 3.10b).

Event-Related Potential

EEG reveals little about cognitive processes, because the recording tends to reflect the brain's global electrical activity. Another approach used by many cognitive neuroscientists focuses on how brain activity is modulated in response to a particular task. The method requires extracting an evoked response from the global EEG signal.

The logic of this approach is as follows: EEG traces recorded from a series of trials are averaged together by aligning them relative to an external event, such as the onset of a stimulus or response. This alignment eliminates variations in the brain's electrical activity that are unrelated to the events of interest. The evoked response, or **event-related potential** (**ERP**), is a tiny signal embedded in the ongoing EEG that was triggered by the stimulus. By averaging the traces, investigators can extract this signal, which reflects neural activity that is specifically related to the sensory, motor, or cognitive event that evoked it—hence the name *event-related potential* (Figure 3.24).

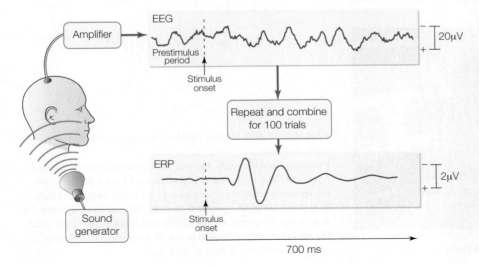

FIGURE 3.24 Recording an ERP.
The relatively small electrical responses to specific events can be observed only if the EEG traces are averaged over a series of trials. The large background oscillations of the EEG trace make it impossible to detect the evoked response to the sensory stimulus from a single trial. Averaging across tens or hundreds of trials, however, removes the background EEG, leaving the event-related potential (ERP). Note the difference in scale between the EEG and ERP waveforms.

ERPs provide an important tool for clinicians. For example, the visual evoked potential can be useful in diagnosing multiple sclerosis, a disorder that leads to demyelination. When demyelination occurs in the optic nerve, the electrical signal does not travel as quickly, and the early peaks of the visual evoked response are delayed in their time of appearance. Similarly, in the auditory system, tumors that compromise hearing by compressing or damaging auditory processing areas can be localized by the use of auditory evoked potentials (AEPs) because characteristic wave peaks and troughs in the AEP are known to arise from neuronal activity in specific anatomic areas of the ascending auditory system. The earliest of these AEP waves indicates activity in the auditory nerve, occurring within just a few milliseconds of the sound. Within the first 20 to 30 ms after the sound, a series of AEP waves indicates, in sequence, neural firing in the brainstem, then midbrain, then thalamus, and finally the cortex (Figure 3.25).

Note that these localization claims are based on indirect methods, because the electrical recordings are actually made on the surface of the scalp. For early components related to the transmission of signals along the sensory pathways, the neural generators are inferred from the findings of other studies that use direct recording techniques as well as considerations of the time required for neural signals to travel. This approach is not possible when researchers look at evoked responses generated by cortical structures. The auditory cortex relays its message to many cortical areas, which all contribute to the measured evoked response, making it much harder to localize these components.

ERPs are thus better suited to addressing questions about the time course of cognition rather than to localizing the brain structures that produce the electrical events. For example, as we will see in Chapter 7, evoked responses can tell us when attention affects how a stimulus is processed. ERPs also provide physiological indices of when a person decides to respond or when an error is detected.

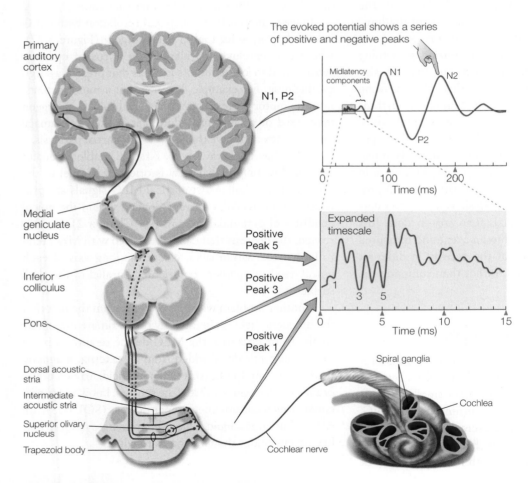

FIGURE 3.25 Measuring auditory evoked potentials.
The evoked potential shows a series of positive (P) and negative (N) peaks at predictable points in time.
In this auditory evoked potential, the early peaks are invariant and have been linked to neural activity
in specific brain structures. Later peaks are task dependent, and localization of their source has been a
subject of much investigation and debate.

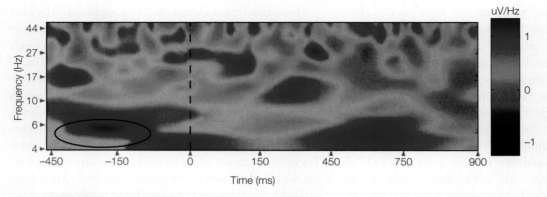

FIGURE 3.26 Time-frequency analysis plot.
Stimulus is presented at time 0. The color represents "power," or the activity (as indicated at the bar on the right, where blue is the lowest activity and red is the highest) of a particular frequency at various times both before and after the stimulus is presented. Alpha rhythm (8–12 Hz; circled lower left) is strong prior to the onset of a stimulus. Following the stimulus, there is a shift in the EEG waveform with increasing power at lower frequencies, as well as higher frequencies (not shown).

Lately, researchers also have been interested in the event-related oscillatory activity in the EEG signal. The waves of the EEG signal represent a number of rhythms, reflecting the synchronized and oscillatory activity of groups of neurons. Presumably, recognizing something requires not only that individual neurons fire but also that they fire in a coherent manner. This coherent firing is what produces the rhythms of the brain. The rhythms are defined by the frequency of the oscillations; thus, alpha refers to frequencies around 10 Hz, or 10 times per second (Figure 3.26). **Time-frequency analysis** refers to the fact that the amplitude (i.e., power) of a wave in different frequency regions varies over the course of processing. Thus time-frequency analysis is a way to characterize two-dimensional signals that vary in time. Just as with ERP, activity is linked to an event and measured over time; but the strength of the activity in different EEG frequencies is measured, rather than summing the signal of all of the activity.

Magnetoencephalography

A technique related to the ERP method is **magnetoencephalography**, or **MEG**. The electrical current associated with synaptic activity produces small magnetic fields that are perpendicular to the current. As with EEG, MEG traces can be recorded and averaged over a series of trials to obtain event-related fields (ERFs). MEG provides the same temporal resolution as with ERPs, but it can be used more reliably to localize the source of the signal. Unlike electrical signals, magnetic fields are not distorted as they pass through the brain, skull, and scalp. Modeling techniques, similar to those used in EEG, are necessary to localize the source of the electrical activity. With MEG data, however, the solutions are more accurate.

Indeed, the reliability of spatial resolution with MEG has made it a useful tool in neurosurgery (Figure 3.27), where it is employed to identify the focus of epileptic seizures and to locate tumors in areas that present a surgical dilemma. For example, learning that a tumor extends into the motor cortex of the precentral sulcus, a surgeon may avoid or delay a procedure if it is likely to damage motor cortex and leave the person with partial paralysis.

MEG has two drawbacks. First, it is able to detect current flow only if that flow is oriented parallel to the surface of the skull. Most cortical MEG signals are produced by intracellular current flowing within the apical dendrites of pyramidal neurons (see Chapter 2). For this reason, the neurons that can be recorded with MEG tend to be located within sulci, where the long axis of each apical dendrite tends to be oriented parallel to the skull surface.

Another problem with MEG stems from the fact that the magnetic fields generated by the brain are extremely weak. To be effective, the MEG device requires a room that is magnetically shielded from all external magnetic fields, including the Earth's magnetic field. To detect the brain's weak magnetic fields, the sensors, known as superconducting quantum interference devices (SQUIDS), are encased in large, liquid-helium-containing cylinders that keep them colder than 4 degrees Kelvin.

Electrocortogram

An **electrocortogram (ECoG)** is similar to an EEG, except that the electrodes are placed directly on the

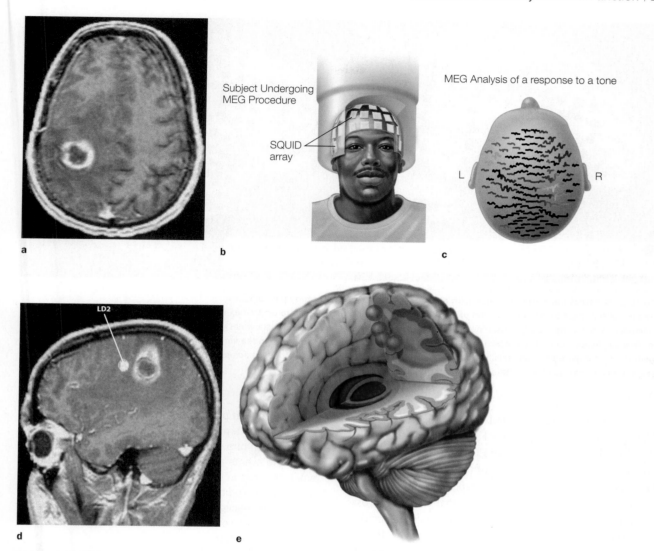

FIGURE 3.27 Magnetoencephalography as a noninvasive presurgical mapping procedure.
(a) This MRI shows a large tumor in the vicinity of the central sulcus. **(b)** Device used to record MEG showing location of the SQUIDS. **(c)** These event-related fields (ERFs) were produced following repeated tactile stimulation of the index finger. Each trace shows the magnetic signal recorded from an array of detectors placed over the scalp. **(d)** Inverse modeling showed that the dipole (indicated by LD2) producing the surface recordings in part (a) was anterior to the lesion. **(e)** This three-dimensional reconstruction shows stimulation of the fingers and toes on the left side of the body in red and the tumor outlined in green.

surface of the brain, either outside the dura or beneath it. Thus, ECoG is appropriate only for people who are undergoing neurosurgical treatment. The ECoG recordings provide useful clinical information, allowing the surgical team to monitor brain activity to identify the location and frequency of abnormal brain activity. Since the implants are left in place for a week, there is time to conduct experiments in which the person performs some sort of cognitive task. ECoG electrodes measure electrical signals before they pass through the scalp and skull. Thus, there is far less signal distortion compared

with EEG. This much cleaner signal results in excellent spatial and temporal resolution. The electrodes can also be used to stimulate the brain and to map and localize cortical and subcortical neurologic functions, such as motor or language function. Combining seizure data with the knowledge of what structures will be affected by surgery permits a risk–benefit profile of the surgery to be established.

ECoG is able to detect high-frequency brain activity, information that is attenuated or distorted in scalp EEG recordings. The experimental question in ECoG studies,

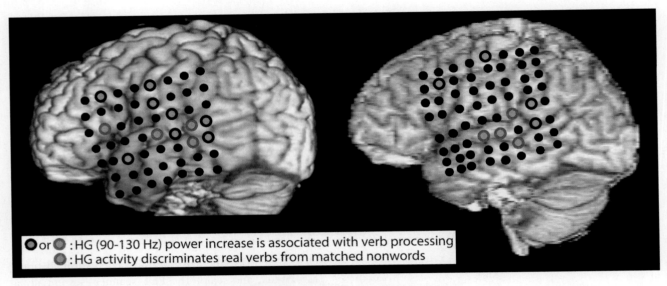

: HG (90-130 Hz) power increase is associated with verb processing
: HG activity discriminates real verbs from matched nonwords

FIGURE 3.28 Structural MRI renderings with electrode locations for four study participants.
Structural MRI images to indicate position of electrode grid on four patients. Electrodes that exhibited an increase in high frequency (gamma) power following the presentation of verbs are shown in green. Red circles indicate electrodes in which the increase in gamma was also observed when the verb condition was compared to acoustically matched nonwords. Verb processing is distributed across cortical areas in the superior temporal cortex and frontal lobe.

however, is frequently dictated by the location of the ECoG grid. For example, Robert Knight and his colleagues (2007) studied patients who had ECoG grids that spanned temporal and frontal regions of the left hemisphere. They monitored the electrical response when people processed words. By examining the signal changes across several frequency bands, the researchers could depict the successive recruitment of different neural regions (Figure 3.28). Shortly (100 ms) after the stimulus was presented, the signal for very high-frequency components of the ECoG signal (high gamma range) increased over temporal cortex. Later on, the activity change was observed over frontal cortex. By comparing trials in which the stimuli were words and trials in which the stimuli were nonsense sounds, the researchers could determine the time course and neural regions involved in distinguishing speech from nonspeech.

TAKE-HOME MESSAGES

- Single-cell recording allows neurophysiologists to record from individual neurons in the animal brain in order to understand how increases and decreases in the activity of neurons correlate with stimulation of one of the senses or behavior.
- With multiunit recording, the activity of hundreds of cells can be recorded at the same time.
- Electroencephalography (EEG) measures the electrical activity of the brain. The EEG signal includes endogenous changes in electrical activity as well as changes triggered by specific events (e.g., stimuli or movements).

- An event-related potential (ERP) is a change in electrical activity that is time-locked to specific events, such as the presentation of a stimulus or the onset of a response. When the events are repeated many times, the relatively small changes in neural activity triggered by these events can be observed by averaging of the EEG signals. In this manner, the background fluctuations in the EEG signal are removed, revealing the event-related signal with great temporal resolution.
- Electrocortogram (ECoG) is similar to an EEG, except that the electrodes are placed directly on the surface of the brain.
- Magnetoencephalography (MEG) measures the magnetic signals generated by the brain. The electrical activity of neurons also produces small magnetic fields, which can be measured by sensitive magnetic detectors placed along the scalp. MEG can be used in an event-related manner similar to ERPs, with similar temporal resolution. The spatial resolution can be superior because magnetic signals are minimally distorted by organic tissue such as the brain or skull.

The Marriage of Function and Structure: Neuroimaging

The most exciting advances for cognitive neuroscience have been provided by imaging techniques that allow researchers to continuously measure physiological changes in the human brain that vary as a function of a person's perceptions, thoughts, feelings, and actions (Raichle, 1994). The most prominent of these neuroimaging methods are **positron emission tomography**, commonly referred to as **PET**, and **functional magnetic resonance imaging**, or **fMRI**. These methods detect changes in metabolism or blood flow in the brain while the participant is engaged in cognitive tasks. They enable researchers to identify brain regions that are activated during these tasks and to test hypotheses about functional anatomy.

Unlike EEG and MEG, PET and fMRI do not directly measure neural events. Rather, they measure metabolic changes correlated with neural activity. Like all cells of the human body, neurons require oxygen and glucose to generate the energy to sustain their cellular integrity and perform their specialized functions. As with all other parts of the body, oxygen and glucose are distributed to the brain by the circulatory system. The brain is a metabolically demanding organ. The central nervous system uses approximately 20 % of all the oxygen that we breathe. Yet the amount of blood supplied to the brain varies only a little between times when the brain is most active and when it is quiescent. (Perhaps this is so because what we regard as active and inactive in relation to behavior does not correlate with active and quiescent in the context of neural activity.) Thus, the brain must regulate how much or how fast blood flows to different regions depending on need. When a brain area is active, more oxygen and glucose are provided by increasing the blood flow to that active region, at the expense of other parts of the brain.

Positron Emission Tomography

PET activation studies measure local variations in cerebral blood flow that are correlated with mental activity (Figure 3.29). A radioactive substance is introduced into the bloodstream. The radiation emitted from this "tracer" is monitored by the PET instrument. Specifically, the radioactive isotopes within the injected substance rapidly decay by emitting a positron from their atomic nuclei. When a positron collides with an electron, two photons, or gamma rays, are created. The two photons move in opposite directions at the speed of light, passing unimpeded through brain tissue, skull, and scalp. The PET scanner—essentially a gamma ray detector—determines where the collision took place. Because these tracers are in the blood, a reconstructed image shows the distribution of blood flow: Where there is more blood flow, there will be more radiation.

The most common isotope used in cognitive studies is ^{15}O, an unstable form of oxygen with a half-life of 123 seconds. This isotope, in the form of water ($H_2^{15}O$), is injected into the bloodstream while a person is engaged in a cognitive task. Although all areas of the body will use some of the radioactive oxygen, the fundamental

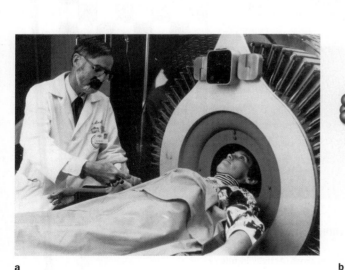

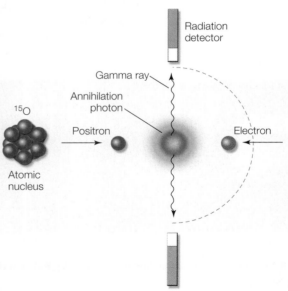

a

b

FIGURE 3.29 Positron emission tomography.
(a) PET scanning allows metabolic activity to be measured in the human brain. **(b)** In the most common form of PET, water labeled with radioactive oxygen, ^{15}O, is injected into the participant. As positrons break off from this unstable isotope, they collide with electrons. A by-product of this collision is the generation of two gamma rays, or photons, that move in opposite directions. The PET scanner measures these photons and calculates their source. Regions of the brain that are most active will increase their demand for oxygen, hence active regions will have a stronger PET signal.

assumption of PET is that there will be increased blood flow to the brain regions that have heightened neural activity. Thus PET activation studies measure relative activity, not absolute metabolic activity. In a typical PET experiment, the injection of tracer is administered at least twice: during a control condition and during one or more experimental conditions. The results are usually reported as a change in **regional cerebral blood flow** (**rCBF**) between the control and experimental conditions.

PET scanners are capable of resolving metabolic activity to regions, or **voxels**, of approximately 5 to 10 mm³. Although this volume includes thousands of neurons, it is sufficient to identify cortical and subcortical areas of enhanced activity. It can even show functional variation within a given cortical area, as the images in Figure 3.30 demonstrate.

PiB: A Recent Addition to the PET Tracer Family

Recognizing that PET scanners can measure any radioactive agent, researchers have sought to develop specialized molecules that might serve as biomarkers of particular neurological disorders and pathologies.

One important result has been the synthesis of PiB, or Pittsburgh Compound B, a radioactive agent developed by Chester Mathis and William Klunk at the University of Pittsburgh when they were looking for new ways to diagnosis and monitor Alzheimer's disease. Historically, Alzheimer's has been a clinical diagnosis (and frequently misdiagnosed), because a definitive diagnosis required sectioning brain tissue postmortem to identify the characteristic beta-amyloid plaques and neurofibrillary tangles. A leading hypothesis for the cause of Alzheimer's disease is that the production of amyloid, a ubiquitous protein in tissue, goes awry and leads to the characteristic plaques. Beta-amyloid plaques in particular appear to be a hallmark of Alzheimer's disease. Mathis and Klunk set out to find a radioactive compound that would specifically label beta-amyloid. After testing hundreds of compounds, they identified **PiB**, a protein-specific, carbon[11]-labeled dye that could be used as a PET tracer (Klunk et al., 2004). PiB binds to beta-amyloid (Figure 3.31), providing physicians with an in vivo assay of the presence of this biomarker. PET scans can now be used to measure beta-amyloid plaques, thus adding a new tool for

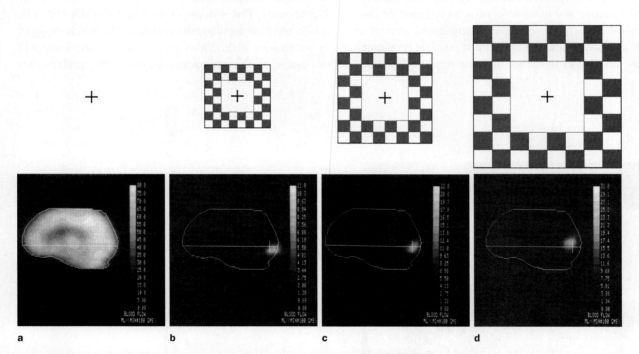

a b c d

FIGURE 3.30 Measurements of cerebral blood flow using PET to identify brain areas involved in visual perception.
(a) Baseline condition: Blood flow when the participant fixated on a central cross. Activity in this baseline condition was subtracted from that in the other conditions in which the participant views a checkerboard surrounding the fixation cross to help participants from moving their eyes. The stimulus is presented at varying positions, ranging from near the center of vision to the periphery **(b–d)**. A retinotopic map can be identified in which central vision is represented more inferiorly than peripheral vision. Areas that were more active when the participant was viewing the checkerboard stimulus will have higher counts, reflecting increased blood flow. This subtractive procedure ignores variations in absolute blood flow between the brain's areas. The difference image identifies areas that show changes in metabolic activity as a function of the experimental manipulation.

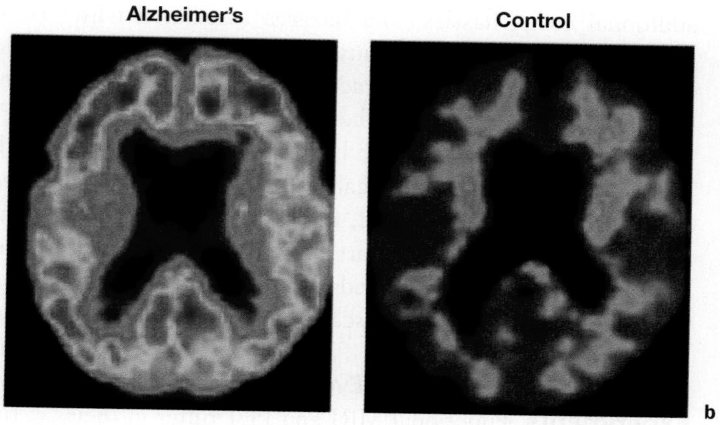

Alzheimer's   Control

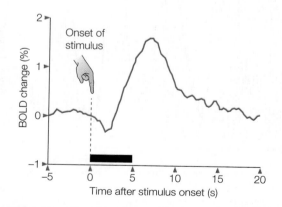

FIGURE 3.31 Using PiB to look for signs of Alzheimer's disease.

PiB is a PET dye that binds to beta-amyloid. The dye was injected into a man with moderate symptoms of Alzheimer's disease **(a)** and into a cognitively-normal woman **(b)** of similar age. **(a)** The patient with Alzheimer's disease shows significant binding of PiB in the frontal, posterior cingulate, parietal, and temporal cortices, as evidenced by the red, orange, and yellow. **(b)** The control participant shows no uptake of PiB in her brain.

diagnosing Alzheimer's. What's more, it can be used to screen people showing very early stages of cognitive impairment, or even people who are asymptomatic, to predict the likelihood of developing Alzheimer's. Being able to diagnose the disease definitively is a boon to patient treatment—because of the previously substantial risk of misdiagnosis—and to research, as scientists develop new experimental drugs designed either to disrupt the pathological development of plaques or to treat the symptoms of Alzheimer's.

Functional Magnetic Resonance Imaging

As with PET, functional magnetic resonance imaging (fMRI) exploits the fact that local blood flow increases in active parts of the brain. The procedure is essentially identical to the one used in traditional MRI. Radio waves cause the protons in hydrogen atoms to oscillate, and a detector measures local energy fields that are emitted as the protons return to the orientation of the magnetic field created by the MRI machine. With fMRI, however, imaging is focused on the magnetic properties of the deoxygenated form of hemoglobin, deoxyhemoglobin. Deoxygenated hemoglobin is paramagnetic (i.e., weakly magnetic in the presence of a magnetic field), whereas oxygenated hemoglobin is not. The fMRI detectors measure the ratio of oxygenated to deoxygenated hemoglobin; this value is referred to as the **blood oxygen level–dependent**, or **BOLD**, effect.

Intuitively, it might be expected that the proportion of deoxygenated hemoglobin will be greater in the area surrounding active brain tissue, given the intensive metabolic costs associated with neural function. fMRI results, however, are generally reported as an *increase* in the ratio of oxygenated to deoxygenated hemoglobin. This change occurs because, as a region of the brain becomes active, the amount of blood being directed to

that area increases. The neural tissue is unable to absorb all of the excess oxygen. Functional MRI studies measure the time course of this process. Although neural events occur on a timescale measured in milliseconds, changes in blood flow are modulated much more slowly. In Figure 3.32, note that following the presentation of a stimulus (in this case, a visual stimulus), an increase in the BOLD response is observed after a few seconds, peaking 6 to 10 seconds later. Thus, fMRI can be used to obtain an indirect measure of neuronal activity by measuring changes in blood flow.

Functional MRI has led to revolutionary changes in cognitive neuroscience. Just over 20 years from when the first neuroimaging study appeared in the early 1990s, fMRI papers now fill the pages of neuroscience journals. Functional MRI offers several advantages over PET. MRI scanners are much less expensive and easier to maintain; fMRI uses no radioactive tracers, so it does not incur the

FIGURE 3.32 Functional MRI signal observed from visual cortex in the cat with a 4.7-tesla scanner.

The black bar indicates the duration of a visual stimulus. Initially there is a dip in the blood oxygen level–dependent (BOLD) signal, reflecting the depletion of oxygen from the activated cells. Over time, the BOLD signal increases, reflecting the increased hemodynamic response to the activated area. Scanners of this strength are now being used with human participants.

additional costs, hassles, and hazards associated with handling these materials. Because fMRI does not require the injection of radioactive tracers, the same individual can be tested repeatedly, either in a single session or over multiple sessions. Thus, it becomes possible to perform a complete statistical analysis on the data from a single participant. In addition, the spatial resolution of fMRI is superior to PET, in part because high-resolution anatomical images are obtained (using traditional MRI) while the participant is in the scanner.

Block Design Versus Event-Related Design Experiments Functional MRI and PET differ in their temporal resolution, which has ramifications for study designs. PET imaging requires sufficient time to detect enough radiation to create images of adequate quality. The participant must be engaged continually in a single given experimental task for at least 40 s, and metabolic activity is averaged over this interval. Because of this time requirement, block design experiments must be used with PET. In a **block design experiment**, the recorded neural activity is integrated over a "block" of time during which the participant either is presented a stimulus or performs a task. The recorded activity pattern is then compared to other blocks that have been recorded while doing the same task or stimulus, a different task or stimulus, or nothing at all. Because of the extended time requirement, the specificity of correlating activation patterns with a specific cognitive process suffers.

Functional MRI studies frequently use either a block design, in which neuronal activation is compared between experimental and control scanning phases (Figure 3.33), or an **event-related design**. Similar to what we saw before in ERP studies, the term *event-related* refers to the fact that, across experimental trials, the BOLD response will be linked to specific events such as the presentation of a stimulus or the onset of a movement. Although metabolic changes to any single event are likely to be hard to detect among background fluctuations in the brain's hemodynamic response, a clear signal can be obtained by averaging over repetitions of these events. Event-related fMRI improves the experimental design because experimental and control trials can be presented randomly. Researchers using this approach can be more confident that the participants are in a similar attentional state during both types of trials, which increases the likelihood that the observed differences reflect the hypothesized processing demands rather than more generic factors, such as a change in overall arousal. Although a block design experiment is better able to detect small effects, researchers can use a greater range of experimental setups with event-related design; indeed, some questions can be studied only by using event-related fMRI (Figure 3.34).

A powerful feature of event-related fMRI is that the experimenter can choose to combine the data in many different ways after scanning is completed. For example, consider memory failure. Most of us have

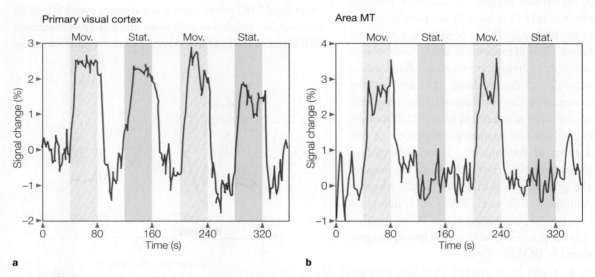

a   b

FIGURE 3.33 Functional MRI measures time-dependent fluctuations in oxygenation with good spatial resolution.
The participant in this experiment viewed a field of randomly positioned white dots on a black background. The dots would either remain stationary or move along the radial axis. The 40-s intervals of stimulation (shaded background) alternated with 40-s intervals during which the screen was blank (white background). **(a)** Measurements from primary visual cortex (V1) showed consistent increases during the stimulation intervals compared to the blank intervals. **(b)** In area MT, a visual region associated with motion perception (see Chapter 5), the increase was observed only when the dots were moving.

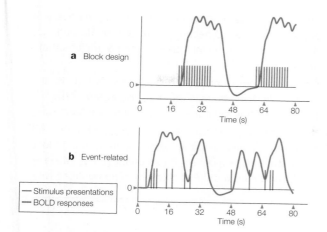

a Block design

Time (s)

b Event-related

— Stimulus presentations
— BOLD responses

Time (s)

FIGURE 3.34 Block design versus event-related design.

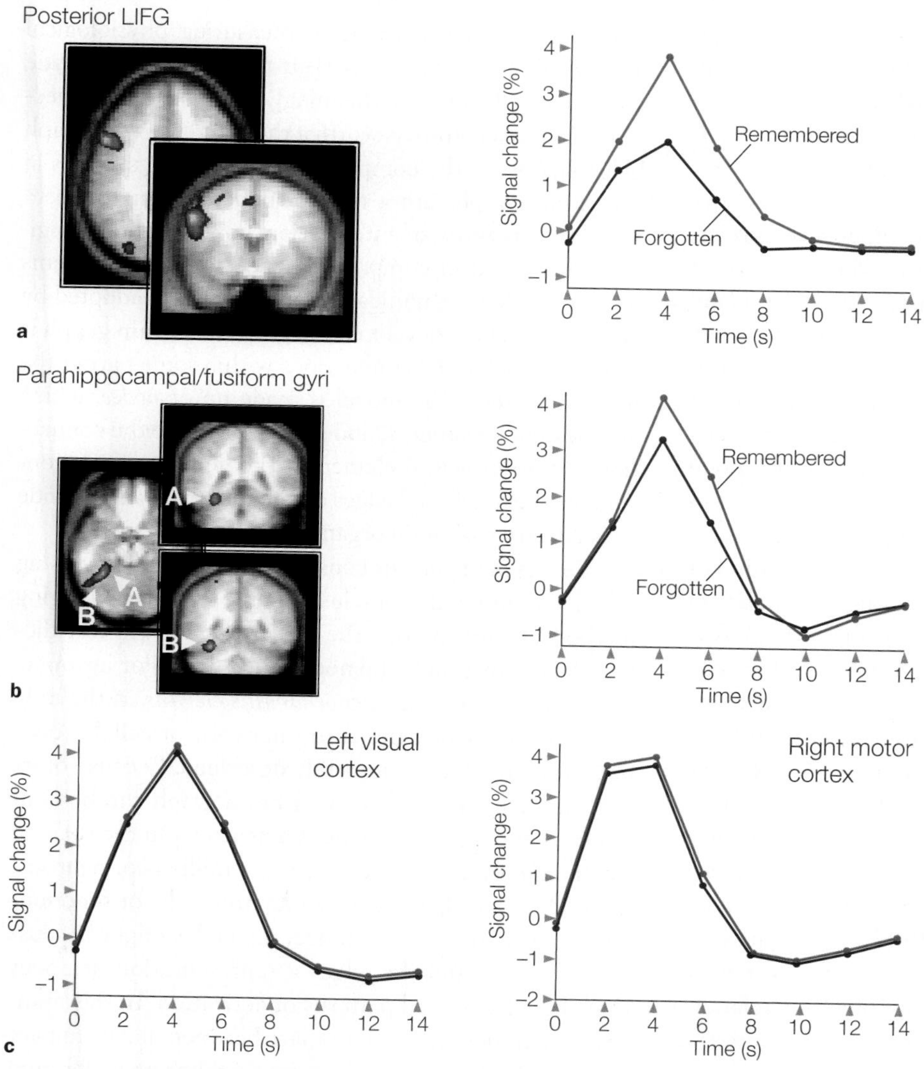

experienced the frustration of being introduced to someone at a party and then being unable to remember the person's name just 2 minutes later. Is this because we failed to listen carefully during the original introduction, so the information never really entered memory? Or did the information enter our memory stores but, after 2 minutes of distraction, we were unable to access the information? The former would constitute a problem with memory encoding; the latter would reflect a problem with memory retrieval. Distinguishing between these two possibilities has been difficult, as evidenced by the thousands of articles on this topic that have appeared in cognitive psychology journals over the past 100 years.

Anthony Wagner and his colleagues at Harvard University used event-related fMRI to take a fresh look at the question of memory encoding versus retrieval (Wagner et al., 1998). They obtained fMRI scans while participants were studying a list of words, where one word appeared every 2 seconds. About 20 minutes after completing the scanning session, the participants were given a recognition memory test. On average, the participants correctly recognized 88% of the words studied during the scanning session. The researchers then separated the trials on the basis of whether a word had been remembered or forgotten. If the memory failure was due to retrieval difficulties, no differences should be detected in the fMRI response to these two trials, since the scans were obtained only while the participants were reading the words. If the memory failure was due to poor encoding, however, the researchers would expect to see a different fMRI pattern following presentation of the words that were later remembered compared to those that were forgotten. The results clearly favored the encoding-failure hypothesis (Figure 3.35). The BOLD signal recorded from two areas, the prefrontal cortex and

Posterior LIFG

a

Parahippocampal/fusiform gyri

b

Left visual cortex

Right motor cortex

c

FIGURE 3.35 Event-related fMRI study showing memory failure as a problem of encoding.
Both the left inferior frontal gyrus (LIFG) **(a)** and the parahippocampal region **(b)** in the left hemisphere exhibit greater activity during encoding for words that are subsequently remembered compared to those that are forgotten. (A = parahippocampal region; B = fusiform gyrus.) **(c)** Activity over the left visual cortex and right motor cortex is identical following words that subsequently are either remembered or forgotten. These results demonstrate that the memory effect is specific to the frontal and hippocampal regions.

the hippocampus, was stronger following the presentation of words that were later remembered. (As we'll see in Chapter 9, these two areas of the brain play a critical role in memory formation.) The block design method could not be used in a study like this, because the signal is averaged over all of the events within each scanning phase.

Limitations of PET and fMRI

It is important to understand the limitations of imaging techniques such as PET and fMRI. First, PET and fMRI have poor temporal resolution compared with single-cell recordings or ERPs. PET is constrained by the decay rate of the radioactive agent (on the order of minutes), and fMRI is dependent on the hemodynamic changes (on the order of seconds) that underlie the BOLD response. A complete picture of the physiology and anatomy of cognition usually requires integrating results obtained in ERP studies with those obtained in fMRI studies.

A second difficulty arises when interpreting the data from a PET or fMRI study. The data sets from an imaging study are massive, and often the comparison of experimental and control conditions produces many differences. This should be no surprise, given what we know about the distributed nature of brain function. For example, asking someone to generate a verb associated with a noun (experimental task) likely requires many more cognitive operations than just saying the noun (control task). As such, it is difficult to make inferences about each area's functional contribution from neuroimaging data. Correlation does not imply causation. For example, an area may be activated during a task but not play a critical role in performance of the task. The BOLD signal is primarily driven by neuronal input rather than output (Logothetis et al., 2001); as such, an area showing increased activation may be downstream from brain areas that provide the critical computations. Rather than focus on local changes in activity, the data from an fMRI study can be used to ask whether the activation changes in one brain area are correlated with activation changes in another brain area—that is, to look at what is called *functional connectivity* (Sun et al., 2004). In this manner, fMRI data can be used to describe networks associated with particular cognitive operations and the relationships among nodes within those networks. This process is discussed next.

TAKE-HOME MESSAGES

- Positron emission tomography (PET) measures metabolic activity in the brain by monitoring the distribution of a radioactive tracer. The PET scanner measures the photons that are produced during decay of the tracer. A popular tracer is ^{15}O because it decays rapidly and the distribution of oxygen increases to neural regions that are active.

- Pittsburgh Compound B (PiB) is a tracer that binds to beta-amyloid and is used as an in vivo assay of the presence of this biomarker for Alzheimer's disease.

- Functional magnetic resonance imaging (fMRI) uses MRI to measure changes in the oxygen content of the blood (hemodynamic response). These changes are assumed to be correlated with local changes in neuronal activity.

Brain Graphs

Whether counting neurons or measuring physiological and metabolic activity, it is clear that the brain is made up of networks of overwhelmingly complicated connections. Just as a picture is worth a thousand words, a graph helps illuminate the complex communication systems in the brain. Graphs are a tool for understanding connections and patterns of information flow. Methods originally developed in computer science to study problems like air traffic communication are now being adopted by neuroscientists to develop brain graphs. A **brain graph** is a visual model of the connections within some part of the nervous system. The model is made up of *nodes*, which are the neural elements, and *edges*, which are the connections between neural elements. The geometric relationships of the nodes and edges define the graph and provide a visualization of brain organization.

Neuroscientists can construct brain graphs by using the data obtained from just about any neuroimaging method (Figure 3.36). The selected data set will dictate what constitutes the nodes and edges. For instance, the nematode worm, *Caenorhabditis elegans*, is the only organism for which the entire network of cellular connections have been completely described. Because of its very limited nervous system, a brain graph can be constructed in which each node is a neuron. On the scale of the human brain, however, with its millions of neurons, the nodes and edges represent anatomically or functionally defined units. For instance, the nodes might be clusters of voxels and the edges a representation of nodes that show correlated patterns of activation. In this manner, researchers can differentiate between nodes that act as hubs, sharing links with many neighboring nodes, and nodes that act as connectors, providing links to more distant clusters. Beyond simply showing the edges, a brain graph can also depict the relative strength, or weighting, of the edges.

Brain graphs are a valuable way to compare results from experiments using different methods (Bullmore &

Bassett, 2011). For instance, graphs based on anatomical measures such as diffusion tensor imaging (DTI) can be compared with graphs based on functional measures such as fMRI. Brain graphs also provide ways to visualize the organizational properties of neural networks. For instance, three studies employing vastly different data sets to produce graphical models have reported similar associations between general intelligence and topological measures of brain network efficiency (van den Heuvel et al., 2009; Bassett et al., 2009; Li et al. 2009).

Brain graphs promise to provide a new perspective on neurological and psychiatric disorders. The neurological problems observed in patients with traumatic brain injury (TBI) likely reflect problems in connectivity, rather than restricted damage to specific brain regions. Even when the pathology is relatively restricted, as in stroke, the network properties of the brain are likely disrupted (Catani & ffytche, 2005).

Brain graphs can be used to reveal these changes, providing a bird's-eye view of the damaged landscape.

TAKE-HOME MESSAGE

- A brain graph is a visual model of brain organization, and can be defined either with structural or functional data. Because it can be constructed from data obtained through different types of neuroimaging methods, a brain graph is a valuable way to compare results from experiments using different methods.

Computer Modeling

Creating computer models to simulate postulated brain processes is a research method that complements the other methods discussed in this chapter. A **simulation** is an imitation, a reproduction of behavior in an alternative medium. The simulated cognitive processes are commonly referred to as *artificial intelligence*—artificial in the sense that they are artifacts, human creations—and intelligent in that the computers perform complex functions. The simulations are designed to mimic behavior and the cognitive processes supporting that behavior. The computer is given input and then must perform internal operations to create a behavior. By observing the behavior, the researcher can assess how well it matches behavior produced by a real mind. Of course, to get the computer to succeed, the modeler must specify how information is represented and transformed within the program. To do this, he or she must generate concrete hypotheses regarding the "mental" operations needed for the machine. As such, computer simulations provide a useful tool for testing theories of cognition. The success and failure of various models yields valuable insight into the strengths and weaknesses of a theory.

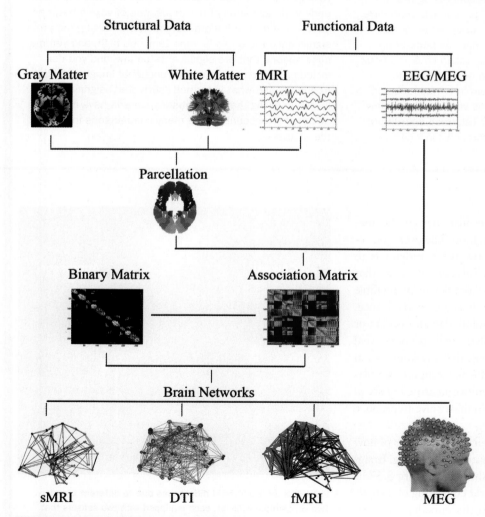

FIGURE 3.36 Constructing a human brain network.
A brain network can be constructed with either structural or functional imaging data. The data imaging methods such as anatomical MRI or fMRI can be divided into regions of interest. This step would already be performed by the sensors in EEG and MEG studies. Links between the regions of interest can then be calculated, using measures like DTI strength or functional connectivity. From these data, brain networks can be constructed.

THE COGNITIVE NEUROSCIENTIST'S TOOLKIT
Analyzing Brain Scans

In general, brains all have the same components; but just like fingerprints, no two brains are exactly the same. Brains vary in overall size, in the size and location of gyri, in the size of individual regions, in shape, and in connectivity. As a result, each brain has a unique configuration, and each person solves problems in different ways. This variation presents a problem when trying to compare the structures and functions of one brain with another.

One solution is to use mathematical methods to align individual brain images into a common space, building on the assumption that points deep in the cerebral hemispheres have a predictable relationship to the horizontal planes running through the anterior and posterior commissures, two large white matter tracts connecting the two cerebral hemispheres. In 1988, Jean Talairach and Pierre Tournoux published a standardized, three-dimensional, proportional grid system to identify and measure brain components despite their variability (Talairach & Tournoux, 1988). Using the postmortem brain of a 60-year-old French woman, they divided the brain into thousands of small, volume-based units, known as voxels (think of tiny cubes). Each voxel was given a 3-D **Talairach coordinate** in relation to the anterior commissure, on the x (left or right), y (anterior or posterior), and z (superior or inferior) axes. By using these standard anatomical landmarks, researchers can take individual brain images obtained from MRI and PET scans, and morph them onto standard Talairach space as a way to combine information across individuals.

There are limitations to this method, however. To fit brains to the standardized atlas, the images must be warped to fit the standard template. The process also requires **smoothing**, a method that is somewhat equivalent to blurring the image. Smoothing helps compensate for the imperfect alignment, but it can also give a misleading picture of the extent of activation changes among the voxels. The next step in data analysis is a statistical comparison of activation of the thousands of voxels between baseline and experimental conditions. Choosing the proper significance threshold is important. Too high, and you may miss regions that are significant; too low, and you risk including random activations. Functional imaging studies frequently use what is termed "corrected" significance levels, implying that the statistical criteria have been adjusted to account for the many comparisons involved in the analysis.

Computer models are useful because they can be analyzed in detail. In creating a simulation, however, the researcher must specify explicitly how the computer is to represent and process information. This does not mean that a computer's operation is always completely predictable and that the outcome of a simulation is known in advance. Computer simulations can incorporate random events or be on such a large scale that analytic tools do not reveal the solution. The internal operations, the way information is computed, however, must be known. Computer simulations are especially helpful to cognitive neuroscientists in recognizing problems that the brain must solve to produce coherent behavior.

Braitenberg (1984) provided elegant examples of how modeling brings insight to information processing. Imagine observing the two creatures shown in Figure 3.37 as they move about a minimalist world consisting of a single heat source, such as a sun. From the outside, the creatures look identical: They both have two sensors and four wheels. Despite this similarity, their behavior is distinct: One creature moves away from the sun, and the other homes in on it. Why the difference? As outsiders with no access to the internal operations of these creatures, we

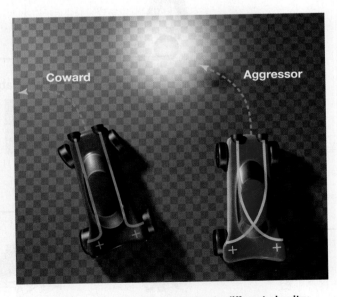

FIGURE 3.37 Behavioral differences due to different circuitry. Two very simple vehicles, each equipped with two sensors that excite motors on the rear wheels. The wheel linked to the sensor closest to the sun will turn faster than the other wheel, thus causing the vehicle to turn. Simply changing the wiring scheme from uncrossed to crossed radically alters the behavior of the vehicles. The "coward" will always avoid the source, whereas the "aggressor" will relentlessly pursue it.

might conjecture that they have had different experiences and so the same input activates different representations. Perhaps one was burned at an early age and fears the sun, and maybe the other likes the warmth.

As their internal wiring reveals, however, the behavioral differences depend on how the creatures are wired. The uncrossed connections make the creature on the left turn away from the sun; the crossed connections force the creature on the right to orient toward it. Thus, the two creatures' behavioral differences arise from a slight variation in how sensory information is mapped onto motor processes.

These creatures are exceedingly simple—and inflexible in their actions. At best, they offer only the crudest model of how an invertebrate might move in response to a phototropic sensor. The point of Braitenberg's example is not to model a behavior; rather, it represents how a single computational change—from crossed to uncrossed wiring—can yield a major behavioral change. When interpreting such a behavioral difference, we might postulate extensive internal operations and representations. When we look inside Braitenberg's models, however, we see that there is no difference in how the two models process information, but only a difference in their patterns of connectivity (see the preceding section, on Brain Graphs).

Representations in Computer Models

Computer models differ widely in their representations. Symbolic models include, as we might expect, units that represent symbolic entities. A model for object recognition might have units that represent visual features like corners or volumetric shapes. An alternative architecture that figures prominently in cognitive neuroscience is the **neural network**. In neural networks, processing is distributed over units whose inputs and outputs represent specific features. For example, they may indicate whether a stimulus contains a visual feature, such as a vertical or a horizontal line.

Models can be powerful tools for solving complex problems. Simulations cover the gamut of cognitive processes, including perception, memory, language, and motor control. One of the most appealing aspects of neural networks is that the architecture resembles the nervous system, at least superficially. In these models, processing is distributed across many units, similar to the way that neural structures depend on the activity of many neurons. The contribution of any unit may be small in relation to the system's total output, but complex behaviors can be generated by the aggregate action of all the units. In addition, the computations in these models are simulated to occur in parallel. The activation levels of the units in the network can be updated in a relatively continuous and simultaneous manner.

Computational models can vary widely in the level of explanation they seek to provide. Some models simulate behavior at the systems level, seeking to show how cognitive operations such as motion perception or skilled movements can be generated from a network of interconnected processing units. In other cases, the simulations operate at a cellular or even molecular level. For example, neural network models have been used to investigate how variation in transmitter uptake is a function of dendrite geometry (Volfovsky et al., 1999). The amount of detail that must be incorporated into the model is dictated largely by the type of question being investigated. Many problems are difficult to evaluate without simulations, either experimentally because the available experimental methods are insufficient, or mathematically because the solutions become too complicated given the many interactions of the processing elements.

An appealing aspect of neural network models, especially for people interested in cognitive neuroscience, is that "lesion" techniques demonstrate how a model's performance changes when its parts are altered. Unlike strictly serial computer models that collapse if a circuit is broken, neural network models degrade gracefully: The model may continue to perform appropriately after some units are removed, because each unit plays only a small part in the processing. Artificial lesioning is thus a fascinating way to test a model's validity. Initially, a model is constructed to see if it adequately simulates normal behavior. Then "lesions" can be included to see if the breakdown in the model's performance resembles the behavioral deficits observed in neurological patients.

Models Lead to Testable Predictions

The contribution of computer modeling usually goes beyond assessing whether a model succeeds in mimicking a cognitive process. Models can generate novel predictions that can be tested with real brains. An example of the predictive power of computer modeling comes from the work of Szabolcs Kali of the Hungarian Academy of Sciences and Peter Dayan at the University College London (Kali & Dayan, 2004). Their computer models were designed to ask questions about how people store and retrieve information in memory about specific events—what is called *episodic memory* (see Chapter 9). Observations from the neurosciences suggest that the *formation* of episodic memories depends critically on the hippocampus and adjacent areas of the medial temporal lobe, whereas the *storage* of such memories involves the neocortex. Kali and Dayan used a computer model to explore a specific question: How is access to stored memories maintained in a system where the neocortical connections are ever changing (see the discussion on cortical plasticity in Chapter 2)? Does the maintenance of memories over time require the reactivation of hippocampal–neocortical connections, or can neocortical representations remain stable despite fluctuations and modifications over time?

The model architecture was based on anatomical facts regarding patterns of connectivity between the hippocampus and neocortex (Figure 3.38). The model was then trained on a set of patterns that represented distinct episodic memories. For example, one pattern of activation might correspond to the first time you visited the Pacific Ocean; another pattern, to the lecture in which you first learned about the Stroop effect. Once the model had mastered the memory set by showing that it could correctly recall a full episode when given only partial information, Kali and Dayan tested it on a consolidation task. Could old memories remain after the hippocampus was disconnected from the cortex if cortical units continued to follow their initial learning rules? In essence, this was a test of whether lesions to the hippocampus would disrupt long-term episodic memory. The results indicated that episodic memory became quite impaired when the hippocampus and cortex were disconnected. Thus the model predicts that hippocampal *reactivation* is necessary for maintaining even well-consolidated episodic memories. In the model, this maintenance process requires a mechanism that keeps hippocampal and neocortical representations in register with one another, even as the neocortex undergoes subtle changes associated with daily learning.

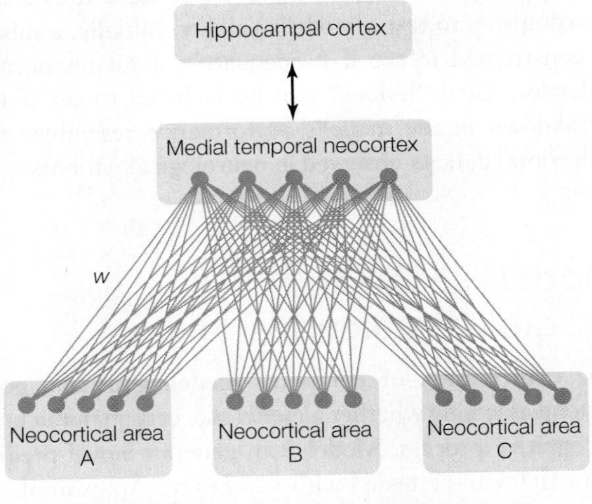

This modeling project was initiated because research on people with lesions of the hippocampus had failed to provide a clear answer about the role of this structure in memory consolidation. The model, based on known principles of neuroanatomy and neurophysiology, could be used to test specific hypotheses concerning one type of memory, episodic memory, and to direct future research. Of course, the goal here is not to make a model that has perfect memory consolidation. Rather, it is to ask how human memory works.

The contribution of computer simulations continues to grow in the cognitive neurosciences. The trend in the field is for modeling work to be more constrained by neuroscience. Researchers will replace generic processing units with elements that embody the biophysics of the brain. In a reciprocal manner, computer simulations provide a useful way to develop theory, which may then aid researchers in designing experiments and interpreting results.

FIGURE 3.38 Computational model of episodic memory. "Neurons" (●) in neocortical areas A, B, and C are connected in a bidirectional manner to "neurons" in the medial temporal neocortex, which is itself connected bidirectionally to the hippocampus. Areas A, B, and C represent highly processed inputs (e.g., inputs from visual, auditory, or tactile domains). As the model learns, it extracts categories, trends, and correlations from the statistics of the inputs (or patterns of activations) and converts these to weights (*w*) that correspond to the strengths of the connections. Before learning, the weights might be equal or set to random values. With learning, the weights become adjusted to reflect correlations between the processing units.

TAKE-HOME MESSAGE
- Computer models are used to simulate neural networks in order to ask questions about cognitive processes and generate predictions that can be tested in future research.

Converging Methods

As we've seen throughout these early chapters, cognitive neuroscience is an interdisciplinary field that draws on ideas and methodologies from cognitive psychology, neurology, the neurosciences, and computer science. Optogenetics is a prime example of how the paradigms and methods from different disciplines have coalesced into a startling new methodology for cognitive neuroscientists and, perhaps soon, for clinicians. The great strength of cognitive neuroscience lies in how diverse methodologies are integrated.

Many examples of convergent methods will be evident as you make your way through this book. For example, the interpretation of results from neuroimaging studies is frequently guided by other methodologies. Single-cell recording studies of primates can be used to identify regions of interest in an fMRI study of humans. Imaging studies can be used to isolate a component operation that might be linked to a particular brain region based on the performance of patients with injuries to that area.

In turn, imaging studies can be used to generate hypotheses that are tested with alternative methodologies. A striking example of this method comes from work asking how people identify objects through touch. An fMRI study on this problem revealed an unexpected result: tactile object recognition led to pronounced activation of the visual cortex, even though the participants' eyes were shut during the entire experiment (Deibert et al., 1999; Figure 3.39a). One possible reason for visual cortex activation is that the participants identified the objects through touch and then generated visual images of them. Alternatively, the participants might have constructed visual images during tactile exploration and then used the images to identify the objects.

A follow-up study with transcranial magnetic stimulation (TMS) was used to pit these hypotheses against one another (Zangaladze et al., 1999). TMS stimulation over the visual cortex impaired tactile object recognition. The disruption was observed only when the TMS pulses were delivered 180 ms after the hand touched the object; no effects were seen with earlier or later stimulation (Figure 3.39b). The results indicate that the visual

representations generated during tactile exploration were essential for inferring object shape from touch. These studies demonstrate how the combination of fMRI and TMS allows investigators to test causal accounts of neural function as well as make inferences about the time course of processing. Obtaining converging evidence from various methodologies enables neuroscientists to make the strongest conclusions possible.

One of the most promising methodological developments in cognitive neuroscience is the combined use of imaging, behavioral, and genetic methods. This approach is widely employed in studies of psychiatric conditions known to have a genetic basis. Daniel Weinberger and his colleagues at the National Institutes of Health have proposed that the efficacy of antipsychotic medications in treating schizophrenia varies as a function of how a particular gene is expressed, or what is called a *polymorphism* (Bertolino et al., 2004; Weickert et al., 2004). In particular, when given an antipsychotic drug, schizophrenics, who have one variant of a gene linked to the release of dopamine in prefrontal cortex, show improved performance on tasks requiring working memory and correlated changes in prefrontal activity. In contrast, schizophrenics with a different variant of the gene did not respond to the drugs.

The logic underlying these clinical studies can also be applied to ask how genetic differences within the normal population relate to individual variations in brain

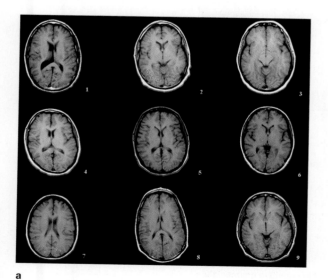

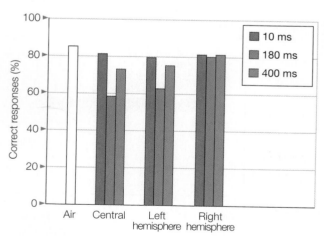

a

b

FIGURE 3.39 Combined use of fMRI and TMS to demonstrate the role of the visual cortex in tactile perception.

(a) Functional MRI showing areas of activation in nine people during tactile exploration with the eyes closed. All of the participants show some activation in striate and extrastriate cortex. (b) Accuracy in judging orientation of tactile stimulus that is vibrated against the right index finger. Performance is disrupted when the pulse is applied 180 ms after stimulus onset, but only when the coil is positioned over the left occipital lobe or at a midline point, between the left and right sides of the occipital lobe.

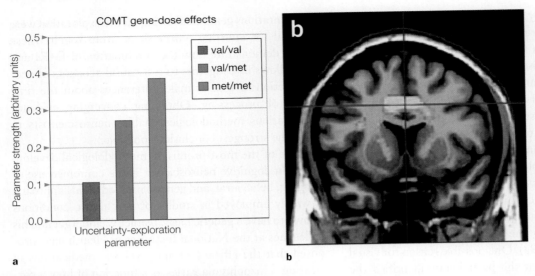

a

b

FIGURE 3.40 Genetic effects on decision making.
(a) Participants were divided into three groups based on a genetic analysis of the COMT gene. They performed a decision-making task and a model was used to estimate how likely they were to explore new, but uncertain choices. Those with the met/met allele were more likely to explore compared to those with the val/val allele. **(b)** Allele differences in the DRD4 gene influenced the level of conflict-related activity in the anterior cingulate cortex (region highlighted in yellow-orange).

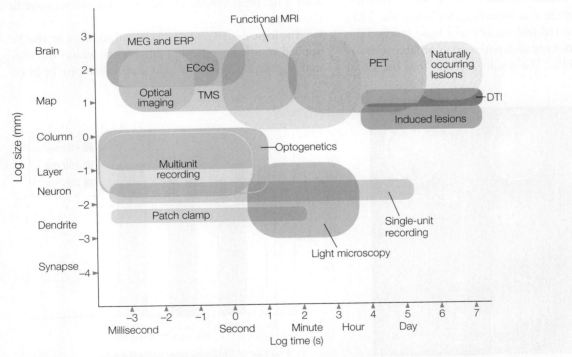

FIGURE 3.41 Spatial and temporal resolution of the prominent methods used in cognitive neuroscience.
Temporal sensitivity, plotted on the *x*-axis, refers to the timescale over which a particular measurement is obtained. It can range from the millisecond activity of single cells to the behavioral changes observed over years in patients who have had strokes. Spatial sensitivity, plotted on the *y*-axis, refers to the localization capability of the methods. For example, real-time changes in the membrane potential of isolated dendritic regions can be detected with the patch clamp method, providing excellent temporal and spatial resolution. In contrast, naturally occurring lesions damage large regions of the cortex and are detectable with MRI.

function and behavior. A common polymorphism in the human brain is related to the gene that codes for monoamine oxidase A (MAOA). Using a large sample of healthy individuals, Weinberger's group found that the low-expression variant was associated with increased tendency toward violent behavior as well as hyperactivation of the amygdala when the participants viewed emotionally arousing stimuli (Meyer-Lindenberg et al., 2006). Similarly, variation in dopamine-related genes (COMT and DRD4) have been related to differences in risk taking and conflict resolution: Does an individual stick out her neck to explore? How well can an individual make a decision when faced with multiple choices? Phenotypic differences correlate with the degree of activation in the anterior cingulate, a region associated with the conflict that arises when having to make such choices (Figure 3.40; for a review, see Frank & Fosella, 2011).

TAKE-HOME MESSAGE

- Powerful insights into the structural and functional underpinnings of cognitive behavior can be gained from experiments that combine methods such as genetic, behavioral, and neuroimaging techniques.

Summary

Two goals have guided our overview of cognitive neuroscience methods presented in this chapter. The first was to provide a sense of how various methodologies have come together to form the interdisciplinary field of cognitive neuroscience (Figure 3.41). Practitioners of the neurosciences, cognitive psychology, and neurology differ in the tools they use—and also, often, in the questions they seek to answer. The neurologist may request a CT scan of an aging boxer to determine if the patient's confusional state is reflected in atrophy of the frontal lobes. The neuroscientist may want a blood sample from the patient to search for metabolic markers indicating a reduction in a transmitter system. The cognitive psychologist may design a reaction time experiment to test whether a component of a decision-making model is selectively impaired. Cognitive neuroscience endeavors to answer all of these questions by taking advantage of the insights that each approach has to offer and using them together.

The second goal of this chapter was to introduce methods that we will encounter in subsequent chapters. These chapters focus on content domains such as perception, language, and memory, and on how these tools are being applied to understand the brain and behavior. Each chapter draws on research that uses the diverse methods of cognitive neuroscience. The convergence of results obtained by using different methodologies frequently offers the most complete theories. A single method often cannot bring about a complete understanding of the complex processes of cognition.

We have reviewed many methods, but the review is incomplete. Other methods include patch clamp techniques to isolate restricted regions on the neuron, enabling studies of the membrane changes that underlie the flow of neurotransmitters, and laser surgery can be used to restrict lesions to just a few neurons in simple organisms, providing a means to study specific neural interactions. New methodologies for investigating the relation of the brain and behavior spring to life each year. Neuroscientists are continually refining techniques for measuring and manipulating neural processes at a finer and finer level. Genetic techniques such as knockout procedures have exploded in the past decade, promising to reveal the mechanisms involved in many normal and pathological brain functions. Optogenetics, which uses light to control the activity of neurons and hence to control neural activity and even behavior, has given researchers a new level of control to probe the nervous system.

Technological change is also a driving force in our understanding of the human mind. Our current imaging tools are constantly being refined. Each year, more sensitive equipment is developed to measure the electrophysiological signals of the brain or the metabolic correlates of neural activity, and the mathematical tools for analyzing these data are constantly becoming more sophisticated. In addition, entire new classes of imaging techniques are beginning to gain prominence.

We began this chapter by pointing out that paradigmatic changes in science are often fueled by technological developments. In a symbiotic way, the maturation of a scientific field such as cognitive neuroscience provides a tremendous impetus for the development of new methods. Obtaining answers to the questions neuroscientists ask is often constrained by the tools available, but such questions promote the development of new research tools. It would be naïve to imagine that current methodologies will become the status quo for the field. We can anticipate the development of new technologies, making this an exciting time to study the brain and behavior.

Key Terms

angiography (p. 79)

block design experiment (p. 108)

blood oxygen level–dependent (BOLD) (p. 107)

brain graph (p. 110)

brain lesion (p. 79)

cerebral vascular accident (79)

cognitive psychology (p. 74)

computed tomography (CT, CAT) (p. 91)

deep-brain stimulation (DBS) (p. 86)

degenerative disorder (p. 80)

diffusion tensor imaging (DTI) (p. 93)

double dissociation (p. 84)

electrocortogram (ECoG) (p. 102)

electroencephalography (EEG) (p. 99)

event-related design (p. 108)

event-related potential (ERP) (p. 100)

functional magnetic resonance imaging (fMRI) (p. 105)

knockout procedure (p. 90)

magnetic resonance imaging (MRI) (p. 92)

magnetoencephalography (MEG) (p. 102)

multiunit recording (p. 97)

neural network (p. 113)

neurophysiology (p. 95)

optogenetics (p. 72)

pharmacological studies (p. 87)

PiB (p. 106)

positron emission tomography (PET) (p. 105)

receptive field (p. 96)

regional cerebral blood flow (rCBF) (p. 106)

retinotopic (p. 97)

simulation (p. 111)

FIGURE 4.2 The block design test.
The pattern in red on the right is the shape that the patient is trying to create with the blocks given to him. **(a)** With his right hand (left hemisphere), he is unable to duplicate the pattern. **(b)** With his left hand (right hemisphere), he is able to perform the task correctly.

After the first testing session revealed this separation so clearly, investigators arranged to film W.J. carrying out tasks. The scientists knew a young fashion photographer, Baron Wolman, who dabbled in filmmaking (and would later help found *Rolling Stone* magazine); he was invited to come to a session during which the whole test was carried out again. Wolman could not believe his eyes. During filming, W.J.'s right hand attempted to arrange the blocks, and his left hand kept trying to intervene. Mind Right saw

the problem, knew the solution, and tried to help out just like a good friend. W.J. had to sit on his left hand so that the inadequate but dominant right hand could at least try.

For the film's final scene, they decided to see what would happen if both hands were allowed to arrange the blocks. Here they witnessed the beginning of the idea that Mind Left can have its view of the world with its own desires and aspirations, and Mind Right can have another view. As soon as Mind Right, working through the left hand, began to arrange the blocks correctly, Mind Left would undo the good work. The hands were in competition! The specializations of each hemisphere were different, and growing out of that difference were the behaviors of each half of the brain. These results raised all sorts of questions. Are there two selves? If not, why not? If so, which one is in charge? Do the two sides of the brain routinely compete? Which half decides what gets done and when? Are consciousness and our sense of self located in one half of the brain? And why do split-brain patients generally feel unified and no different even though their two hemispheres do not communicate? Such questions gave birth to the field of human **split-brain research**.

The popular press picked up these findings, and the concept that the "right brain" and "left brain" think differently about the world made its way into the mainstream. This led to the boiled-down notion that the left hemisphere is analytical and logical while the right hemisphere is creative, musical, and intuitive. Many general interest books have been written based on this naïve view: that artists, musicians, and poets mostly use their right hemisphere while lawyers, mathematicians, and engineers mostly use their left hemisphere (Figure 4.3).

FIGURE 4.3 Books perpetuating the common idea that the left brain is analytic and the right brain is creative.

ANATOMICAL ORIENTATION

The hemispheres of the brain

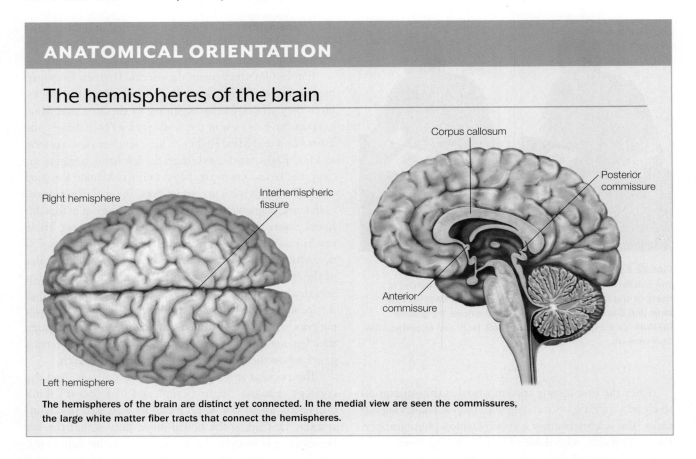

The hemispheres of the brain are distinct yet connected. In the medial view are seen the commissures, the large white matter fiber tracts that connect the hemispheres.

In reality, the science has shown this to be a gross exaggeration of the findings on hemispheric specialization. It turns out that most cognitive processes are redundant and that each hemisphere is capable of carrying out those processes. As we learn in this chapter, however, the hemispheres have some fundamental differences that can help us understand the organization of the cerebral cortex, the evolutionary development and purpose of certain specializations, and the nature of the mind.

You should keep in mind, however, that despite all we have learned about hemispheric differences and specializations, the fundamental mystery, first discovered in the surgeries of the 1940s, remains today. That is, patients who undergo split-brain surgery report no change in their mental status, even though their "speaking" left hemisphere has been irretrievably isolated from their right hemisphere and all of the special properties that it may include. These two separate but coexisting brains do not result in split personalities, nor do they fight over control of the body. In short, the individual with the split brain does not feel conflicted. At the end of this chapter, we examine why this is the case and revisit what clues it may offer about our general conscious experience (also see Chapter 14, where these ideas are discussed in more detail).

We will find that research on laterality has provided extensive insights into the organization of the human brain, and that the simplistic left-brain/right-brain claims distort the complex mosaic of mental processes that contribute to cognition. Split-brain studies profoundly demonstrate that the two hemispheres do not represent information in an identical manner. Complementary studies on patients with focal brain lesions underscore the crucial role played by lateralized processes in cognition. This research and recent computational investigations of lateralization and specialization have advanced the field far beyond the popular interpretations of left-brain/right-brain processes. They provide the scientific basis for future explorations of many fascinating issues concerning cerebral lateralization and specialization.

In this chapter, we examine the differences between the right and left cerebral hemispheres using data from studies of split-brain patients as well as those with unilateral brain lesions. We also examine the evolutionary reasons for lateralization of functions, and as noted, the chapter ends with some musing about what split-brain research has to say about the conscious experience. We begin, however, at the beginning: the anatomy and physiology of the two halves and their interconnections.

Anatomy of the Hemispheres

Anatomical Correlates of Hemispheric Specialization

For centuries, the effects of unilateral brain damage have revealed major functional differences between the two hemispheres. Most dramatic has been the effect of left-hemisphere damage on language functions. In the late 1950s, the dominant role of the left hemisphere in language was confirmed by employing the **Wada test**, pioneered by Juhn A. Wada and Theodore Rasmussen. This test is often used before elective surgery for the treatment of disorders such as epilepsy to determine in which hemisphere the speech center is located. A patient is given an injection of **amobarbital** into the carotid artery, producing a rapid and brief anesthesia of the ipsilateral hemisphere (i.e., the hemisphere on the same side as the injection; Figure 4.4). Then the patient is engaged in a series of tests related to language and memory. The Wada test has consistently revealed a strong bias for language lateralization to the left hemisphere, because when the injection is to the left side, the patient's ability to speak or comprehend speech is disrupted for several minutes. Functional neuroimaging techniques, such as positron emission tomography (PET) and functional magnetic resonance imaging (fMRI), have further confirmed that language processing is preferentially biased to the left hemisphere (Binder & Price, 2001). Regions of the right hemisphere, however, are also engaged, especially for language tasks that require higher-level comprehension (Bookheimer, 2002). Since functional lateralization of language processes clearly exists, can we identify anatomical correlates that account for these lateralized functions?

Macroscopic Anatomical Asymmetries The major lobes (occipital, parietal, temporal, and frontal; see Figure 2.00) appear, at least superficially, to be symmetrical, and each half of the cerebral cortex of the human brain is approximately the same size and surface area. The two hemispheres are offset, however. The right protrudes in front, and the left protrudes in back. The right is chubbier (actually has more volume) in the frontal region, and the left is larger posteriorly in the occipital region, frequently nudging the right hemisphere off center and bending the longitudinal fissure between the two hemispheres to the right (Figure 4.5).

Anatomists of the nineteenth century observed that the **Sylvian fissure** (also called the *lateral fissure*)—the large sulcus that defines the superior border of the temporal lobe—has a more prominent upward curl in the right hemisphere than it does in the left hemisphere, where it is relatively flat. This difference in the shape of the Sylvian fissure between the two cerebral hemispheres is directly related to subsequent reports of size differences in adjacent cortical regions buried within the fissure. At Harvard

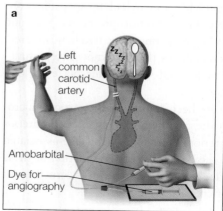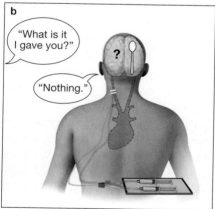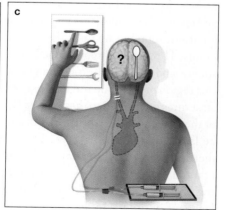

FIGURE 4.4 Methods used in amobarbital (Amytal) testing.
(a) Subsequent to angiography, amobarbital is administered to the left hemisphere, anesthetizing the language and speech systems. A spoon is placed in the left hand, and the right hemisphere takes note. **(b)** When the left hemisphere regains consciousness, the subject is asked what was placed in his left hand, and he responds, "Nothing." **(c)** Showing the patient a board with a variety of objects pinned to it reveals that the patient can easily point to the appropriate object, because the right hemisphere directs the left hand during the match-to-sample task.

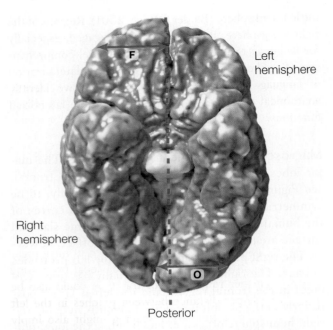

FIGURE 4.5 Anatomical asymmetries between the two cerebral hemispheres.
View looking at the inferior surface of the brain; note that the left hemisphere appears on the right side of the image. In this computer-generated reconstruction, the anatomical asymmetries have been exaggerated.

Medical School in the 1960s, Norman Geschwind examined brains obtained postmortem from 100 people known to be right-handed (Geschwind & Levitsky, 1968). After slicing through the lateral fissure, Geschwind measured the temporal lobe's surface area and discovered that the **planum temporale**, the cortical area at the center of Wernicke's area (involved with the understanding of written and spoken language), was larger in the left hemisphere—a pattern found in 65% of the brains. Of the remaining brains, 11% had a larger surface area in the right hemisphere and 24% had no asymmetry. The asymmetry in this region of the temporal lobe may extend to subcortical structures connected to these areas. For example, portions of the thalamus (the lateral posterior nucleus) also tend to be larger on the left. Because these temporal lobe asymmetries seem to be a characteristic of the normally lateralized brain, other investigators have explored whether the asymmetry is absent in individuals with developmental language disorders. Interestingly, MRI studies reveal that the area of the planum temporale is approximately symmetrical in children with dyslexia—a clue that their language difficulties may stem from the lack of a specialized left hemisphere. Interestingly, an MRI study on adults with dyslexia found that the typical medial temporal lobe asymmetries were reversed in dyslexic adults (Casanova et al., 2005).

The asymmetry of the planum temporale is one of the few examples in which an anatomical index is correlated with a well-defined **functional asymmetry**. The complex functions of language comprehension presumably require more cortical surface. Some questions remain, however, concerning both the validity and the explanatory power of this asymmetry. First, although the left-hemisphere planum temporale is larger in 65% of right-handers, functional measures indicate that 96% of right-handers show left-hemisphere language dominance. Second, there is a suggestion that the apparent asymmetries in the planum temporale result from the techniques and criteria used to identify this region. When three-dimensional imaging techniques—techniques that take into account asymmetries in curvature patterns of the lateral fissures—are applied, hemispheric asymmetries become negligible. Whether or not this view is correct, the anatomical basis for left-hemisphere dominance in language may not be fully reflected in gross morphology. We also need to examine the neural circuits within these cortical locations.

Microscopic Anatomical Asymmetries By studying the cellular basis of hemispheric specialization, we seek to understand whether differences in neural circuits between the hemispheres might underlie functional asymmetries in tasks such as language. Perhaps specific organizational characteristics of local neuronal networks—such as the number of synaptic connections—may be responsible for the unique functions of different cortical areas. In addition, regions of the brain with greater volume may contain more minicolumns and their connections (Casanova & Tillquist, 2008; see Chapter 2, p. 53). A promising approach has been to look for specializations in cortical circuitry within **homotopic areas** (meaning areas in corresponding locations in the two hemispheres) of the cerebral hemispheres that are known to be functionally asymmetrical—and what better place to look than in the language area?

Differences have been found in the cortical microcircuitry between the two hemispheres in both anterior (Broca's) and posterior (Wernicke's) language-associated cortex. We leave the discussion of the function of these areas to Chapter 11; here, we are merely concerned about their structural differences.

As we learned in Chapter 2 (p. 38), the cortex is a layered sheet of tightly spaced columns of cells, each comprising a circuit of neurons that is repeated over and over across the cortical surface. From studies of visual cortex, we know that cells in an individual column act together to encode relatively small features of the visual world. Individual columns connect with adjacent and distant columns to form ensembles of neurons that can encode more complex features.

In language-associated regions, several types of micro-level asymmetries between the hemispheres have been identified. Some of these asymmetries occur at the level of the individual neurons that make up a single cortical column. For instance, the left hemisphere has greater high-order dendritic branching than that of their homologs in the right hemisphere, which have more low-order dendritic branching (Scheibel et al., 1985). Other asymmetries are found in the relationships between adjacent neuronal columns: Within Wernicke's area in the left hemisphere, for example, columns are spaced farther from each other, possibly to accommodate additional connectional fibers between the columns. Asymmetries also are found in larger ensembles of more distant cortical columns (Hutsler & Galuske, 2003). Individual cells within a column of the left primary auditory cortex have a tangential dendritic spread that accommodates the greater distance between cell columns, but secondary auditory areas that show the same increase in distance between the columns do not have longer dendrites in the left hemisphere. The cells in these columns contact fewer adjacent cell columns than do those in the right hemisphere.

Additional structural differences have been documented in both anterior and posterior language cortex. These asymmetries include cell size differences between the hemispheres, such as those shown in Figure 4.6, and may suggest a greater long-range connectivity in the language-associated regions of the left hemisphere. Asymmetries in connectivity between the two hemispheres have been demonstrated directly by tracing the neuronal connections within posterior language-associated regions using dyes that diffuse through postmortem tissue. Such dyes show a patchy pattern of connectivity within these regions of each hemisphere; but within the left hemisphere, these patches are spaced farther apart than those in the right hemisphere (Galuske et al., 2000).

What is the functional significance of these various asymmetries within cortical circuitry, and how might these changes specifically alter information processing in the language-dominant hemisphere? Most interpretations of these findings have focused on the relationship between adjacent neurons and adjacent columns, highlighting the fact that differences in both columnar spacing and dendritic tree size would cause cells in the left hemisphere to connect to fewer neurons. This structural specialization might underlie more elaborate and less redundant patterns of connectivity, which in turn might give rise to better separation between local processing streams. Further refinement of this type could also be driving the larger distance between patches in the left hemisphere, since this larger spacing might also imply more refined connections.

A thorough understanding of the anatomy and physiology of language-associated cortices could shed considerable light on the cortical mechanisms that facilitate linguistic analysis and production, which we will discuss in Chapter 11. Because cortical areas have a basic underlying organization, documenting cortical locations involved in certain functions should distinguish, in terms of form and variety, between the neural structures common to all regions and the structures critical for a region to carry out particular cognitive functions. These questions hold importance not only for the greater understanding of species-specific adaptations such as language, but also for understanding how evolution may build functional specialization into the framework

Right hemisphere

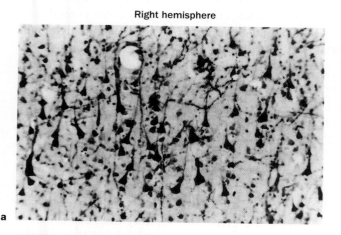

Left hemisphere

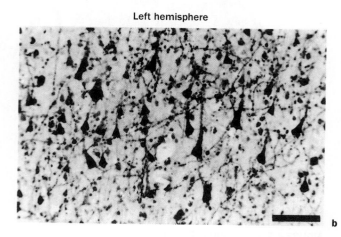

a

b

FIGURE 4.6 Layer III pyrimidal cell asymmetry.
Visual examination reveals a subtle difference in the sizes of the largest subgroups of layer III pyramidal cells (stained here with acetylthiocholinesterase): in the left hemisphere they are larger (b) compared to the right (a).

of cortical organization. There are also implications for developmental problems such as dyslexia and autism. For instance, minicolumns in autism are reduced in size and increased in numbers. If changes in these parameters occur early during development, then they would provide for basic alterations in corticocortical connections and information processing (Casanova et al., 2002; 2006).

The Anatomy of Communication

The corpus callosum. The left and right cerebral hemispheres are connected by the largest white matter structure in the brain, the **corpus callosum**. It is made up of approximately 250 million axonal fibers that cross from one side of the brain to the other, facilitating interhemispheric communication. It is located beneath the cortex and runs along the longitudinal fissure. The corpus callosum is divided on a macroscopic level into the anterior portion, called the *genu*, the middle portion, known as the *body*, and the posterior portion, called the **splenium** (Figure 4.7). The neuronal fiber sizes vary across the corpus callosum: Smaller fibers (~0.4 μm) are located anteriorly, fitfully grading to larger fibers (5 μm) located more posteriorly (Aboitiz et al., 1992). The prefrontal and temporoparietal visual areas are connected by the small-diameter, slow-conducting fibers, and the large fibers connect sensorimotor cortices in each hemisphere (Lamantia & Rakic, 1990). As with many parts of the brain, the fiber tracts in the corpus callosum maintain a topographical organization (Zarei et al., 2006).

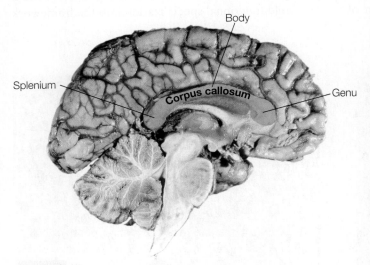

FIGURE 4.7 The corpus callosum.
A sagittal view of the left hemisphere of a postmortem brain. The corpus callosum is the dense fiber tract located below the folds of the cortex. The anterior portion is the genu, the middle portion is the body, and the posterior portion is the splenium.

By using the MRI technique known as diffusion tensor imaging (DTI; see Chapter 3), researchers have traced the white fiber tracks from one hemisphere across the corpus callosum to the other hemisphere. The results indicate that the corpus callosum can be partitioned into vertical segments carrying homotopic and heterotopic connections between specific regions of each hemispheric cortex (Hofer & Frahm, 2006). Heterotopic fibers connect different areas between the hemispheres. Figure 4.8 shows a segmentation of the corpus callosum containing fibers projecting into the prefrontal, premotor, primary motor, primary sensory, parietal, temporal, and occipital areas. As can be clearly seen in the figure, almost all of the visual information processed in the occipital, parietal, and temporal cortices is transferred to the opposite hemisphere via the posterior third of the corpus callosum, whereas premotor and supplementary motor information is transferred across a large section of the middle third of the corpus callosum.

Many of the callosal projections link homotopic areas (Figure 4.9). For example, regions in the left prefrontal cortex project to homotopic regions in the right prefrontal cortex. Although this pattern holds for most areas of the association cortex, it is not always seen in primary cortex. Callosal projections connecting the two halves of the primary visual cortex link only those areas that represent the most eccentric regions of space; and in both the primary motor and the somatosensory cortices, homotopic callosal projections are sparse (Innocenti et al., 1995). Callosal fibers also connect **heterotopic areas** (regions with different locations in the two hemispheres). These projections generally mirror the ones found within a hemisphere. For instance, a prefrontal area sending projections to premotor areas in the same hemisphere is also likely to send projections to the analogous premotor area in the contralateral hemisphere. Yet, heterotopic projections are usually less extensive than are projections within the same hemisphere.

The commissures. A much smaller band of fibers connecting the two hemispheres is the **anterior commissure**. It is about one tenth the size of the corpus callosum, is found inferior to the anterior portion of the corpus callosum, and primarily connects certain regions of the temporal lobes, including the two amygdalae (Figure 4.10). It also contains decussating fibers from the olfactory tract and is part of the neospinothalamic tract for pain. Even smaller is the **posterior commissure**, which also carries some interhemispheric fibers. It is above the cerebral aqueduct at the junction of the third ventricle

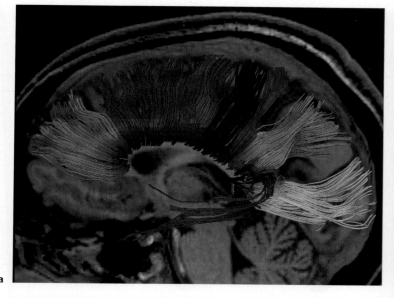

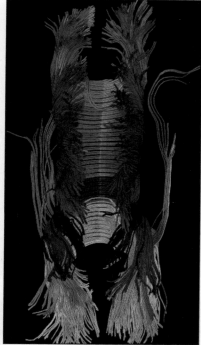

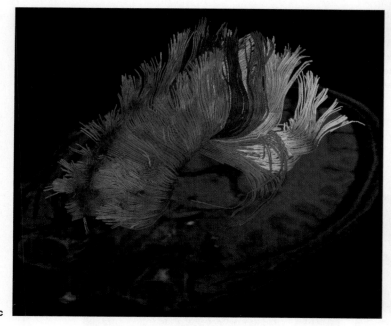

FIGURE 4.8 3-D reconstruction of transcallosal fiber tracts placed on anatomical reference images.
(a) Sagittal view: callosal fiber bundles projecting into the prefrontal lobe (coded in green), premotor and supplementary motor areas (light blue), primary motor cortex (dark blue), primary somatosensory cortex (red), parietal lobe (orange), occipital lobe (yellow), and temporal lobe (violet). **(b)** Top view. **(c)** Oblique view.

(Figure 4.10). It contains fibers that contribute to the papillary light reflex.

Function of the Corpus Callosum

The corpus callosum is the primary communication highway between the two cerebral hemispheres. Researchers, of course, are interested in exactly what is being communicated and how. Several functional roles have been proposed for callosal connections. For instance, some researchers point out that in the visual association cortex, receptive fields can span both visual fields. Communication across the callosum enables information from both visual fields to contribute to the activity of these cells.

Indeed, the callosal connections could play a role in synchronizing oscillatory activity in cortical neurons as an object passes through these receptive fields (Figure 4.11). In this view, callosal connections facilitate processing by pooling diverse inputs. Other researchers view callosal function as predominantly inhibitory (See the box "How the Brain Works: Interhemispheric Communication"). If the callosal fibers are inhibitory, they would provide a means for each hemisphere to compete for control of current processing. For example, multiple movements might be activated, all geared to a common goal; later processing would select one of these candidate movements (see Chapter 8). Inhibitory connections across the corpus callosum might be one contributor to this selection process.

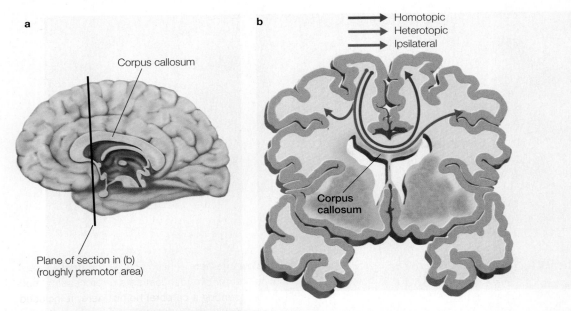

FIGURE 4.9 Tracing connections between and within the cerebral cortices.
(a) Midsagittal view of the right cerebral hemisphere, with the corpus callosum labeled. **(b)** The caudal surface of a coronal section of brain roughly through the premotor cortical area. Homotopic callosal fibers (blue) connect corresponding sections of the two hemispheres via the corpus callosum; heterotopic connections (green) link different areas of the two hemispheres of the brain. In primates, both types of contralateral connections (blue and green), as well as ispilateral connections (red), start and finish at the same layer of neocortex.

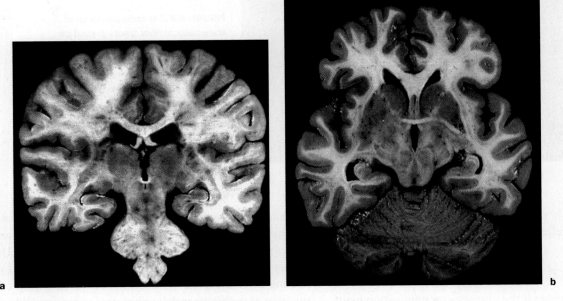

FIGURE 4.10 Coronal sections at **(a)** the level of the posterior commissure and **(b)** the anterior commissure.

HOW THE BRAIN WORKS
Interhemispheric Communication: Cooperation or Competition?

Theories of callosal function generally have focused on the idea that this massive bundle of axonal fibers provides the primary pathway for interhemispheric transfer. For example, in Chapter 6 we will discuss Warrington's model of object recognition. In her view, the right hemisphere performs a specialized operation essential for perceptual categorization. This operation is followed by a left-hemisphere operation for semantic categorization. Interhemispheric communication is essential in this model for shuttling the information through these two processing stages.

On the other hand, interhemispheric communication need not be a cooperative process. Connections across the corpus callosum may underlie a competition between the hemispheres. Indeed, the primary mode of callosal communication may be inhibitory rather than excitatory. By this view, we need not assume that interhemispheric communication is designed to share information processing within the two hemispheres to facilitate concurrent, and roughly identical, activity in homologous regions. Similar to the way in which split-brain behavior is assumed to reflect the independent operation of the two hemispheres, behavior produced by intact brains may also reflect the (fluctuating) dominance of one or the other hemisphere.

One challenge for a cooperative system is that there must be a means to ensure that the two hemispheres are operating on roughly the same information. Such coordination might be difficult, given that both the perceptual input and the focus of our attention are constantly changing. Although computers can perform their operations at lightning speed, neural activity is a relatively slow process. The processing delays inherent in transcallosal communication may limit the extent to which the two hemispheres can cooperate.

A number of factors limit the rate of neural activity. First, to generate an action potential, activity within the receiving dendritic branches must integrate tiny inputs across both space and time in order to reach threshold. Second, the rate at which individual neurons can fire is limited, owing to intrinsic differences in membrane properties, tonic sources of excitation and inhibition, and refractory periods between spike-generating events. Third, and most important, neural signals need to be propagated along axons. These conduction times can be quite substantial, especially for the relatively long fibers of the corpus callosum.

James Ringo and his colleagues (1994) at the University of Rochester provided an interesting analysis of this problem. They began by calculating estimates of transcallosal conduction delays. Two essential numbers were needed: the distance to be traveled, and the speed at which the signal would be transmitted. If the distances were direct, the average distance of the callosal fibers would be short. Most axons follow a circuitous route, however. Taking this point into consideration, a value of 175 mm was used as representative of the average length of a callosal fiber in humans. The speed at which myelinated neural impulses travel is a function of the diameter of the fibers. Using the limited data available from humans, in combination with more thorough measures in the monkey, the average conduction speed was estimated to be about 6.5 m/s. Thus to travel a distance of 175 mm would take almost 30 ms. Single-cell studies in primates have confirmed that interhemispheric processing entails relatively substantial delays.

Ringo used a neural network to demonstrate the consequences of slow interhemispheric conduction times. The network consisted of two identical sets of processing modules, each representing a cerebral hemisphere. It included both intrahemispheric and interhemispheric connections; the latter were much sparser to reflect the known anatomy of the human brain. This network was trained to perform a pattern recognition task. After it had learned to classify all of the patterns correctly, the interhemispheric connections were disconnected. Thus, performance could now be assessed when each hemisphere had to operate in isolation.

The critical comparison was between networks in which the interhemispheric conduction times during learning had been either slow or fast. The results showed that, for the network trained with fast interhemispheric connections, the disconnection procedure led to a substantial deterioration in performance. Thus, object recognition was dependent on cooperative processing for the network with fast interhemispheric connections. In contrast, for the network trained with slow interhemispheric connections, performance was minimally affected by the disconnection procedure. For this network, recognition was essentially dependent only on intrahemispheric processing. These results led Ringo to conclude that a system with slow interhemispheric conduction delays—for example, the human brain—ends up with each hemisphere operating in a relatively independent manner.

Interestingly, these delays could be reduced if the callosal fibers were larger because the larger size would increase conduction speed. Larger fibers, however, would require a corresponding increase in brain volume. For example, reducing the conduction delay by a factor of two would lead to a 50% increase in brain volume. Such an increase would have severe consequences for metabolic demands as well as for childbirth. The brain appears to have evolved such that each hemisphere can have rapid access to information from either side of space, but with limited capability for tasks that would require extensive communication back and forth across the corpus callosum. The delays associated with transcallosal communication not only might limit the degree of cooperation between two hemispheres but also might have provided an impetus for the development of hemispheric specialization. Independent processing systems would be more likely to evolve non-identical computational capabilities.

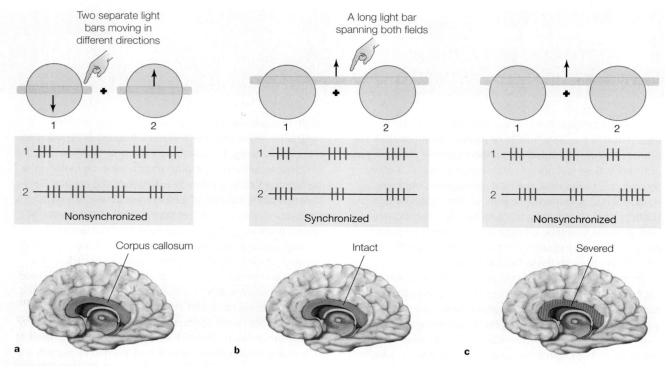

FIGURE 4.11 Synchrony in cortical neurons.
(a) When receptive fields (1 and 2) on either side of fixation are stimulated by two separate light bars moving in different directions (as indicated by the arrows), the firing rates of the two cells are not correlated. **(b)** In animals with an intact corpus callosum, cells with spatially separate receptive fields fire synchronously when they are stimulated by a common object, such as a long light bar spanning both fields. **(c)** In animals whose corpus callosum has been severed, synchrony is rarely observed.

Callosal connections in the adult, however, are a scaled-down version of what is found in immature individuals. In developing animals, callosal projections are diffuse and more evenly distributed across the cortical surface. Cats and monkeys lose approximately 70% of their callosal axons during development; some of these transient projections are between portions of the primary sensory cortex that, in adults, are not connected by the callosum. Yet this loss of axons does not produce cell death in each cortical hemisphere. This is because a single cell body can send out more than one axon terminal: one to cortical areas on the same side of the brain, and one to the other side of the brain. Thus, loss of a callosal axon may well leave its cell body—with its secondary collateral connection to the ipsilateral hemisphere—alive and well, just like pruning a bifurcating peach tree branch leaves the branch thriving. The refinement of connections is a hallmark of callosal development, just as such refinement characterizes intrahemispheric development (see Chapter 2).

In general terms, hemispheric specialization must have been influenced and constrained by callosal evolution. The appearance of new cortical areas might be expected to require more connections across the callosum (i.e., expansion). In contrast, lateralization might have been facilitated by a lack of callosal connections. The resultant isolation would promote divergence among the functional capabilities of homotopic regions, resulting in **cerebral specializations**.

As with the cerebral hemispheres, researchers have investigated functional correlates of anatomical differences in the corpus callosum. Usually, investigators measure gross aspects like the cross-sectional area or shape of the callosum. Variations in these measures are linked to gender, handedness, mental retardation, autism, and schizophrenia. Interpretation of these data, however, is complicated by methodological disagreements and contradictory results. The underlying logic of measuring the corpus callosum's cross-sectional area relies on the relation of area to structural organization. Callosal size could be related to the number and diameter of axons, the proportion of myelinated axons, the thickness of myelin sheaths, and measures of nonneural structures such as the size of blood vessels or the volume of extracellular space with resultant functional differences. Among large samples of callosal measurements from age-matched control subjects, sex-based differences are seen in the shape of the midsagittal sections of the callosum but not in its size. More recently, studies looking at the parasagittal size and asymmetry of the corpus callosum have found an increased rightward callosal asymmetry in males compared to females (Lunder et al., 2006). That is, a larger chunk of the callosum bulges off to the right side in males. It may be that what side of the hemispheric fence the major part of the callosum sits on is the important factor. Thus, this sexually dimorphic organization of the corpus callosum (more on the right than the left in males) may involve not just the corpus callosum, but asymmetric hemispheric development also, reflected in the distribution of parasagittal callosal fibers (Chura et al., 2009). This structure could in turn account for the observed patterns of accelerated language development in females, who have more acreage in the left hemisphere, and the enhanced performance in males during visuospatial tasks and increased rate of left-handedness in males thanks to their rightward bulge. Tantalizing research by Linda Chura and her colleagues found that with increasing levels of fetal testosterone, there was a significantly increasing rightward asymmetry (e.g., right > left) of a posterior subsection of the callosum, called the isthmus, that projects mainly to parietal and superior temporal areas.

TAKE-HOME MESSAGES

- The Wada test is used to identify which hemisphere is responsible for language before brain surgery is performed.
- The two halves of the cerebral cortex are connected primarily by the corpus callosum, which is the largest fiber system in the brain. In humans, this bundle of white matter includes more than 250 million axons.
- Two smaller bands of fibers, the anterior and posterior commissures, also connect the two hemispheres.
- The corpus callosum has both homotopic and heterotopic connections. Homotopic fibers connect the corresponding regions of each hemisphere (e.g., V1 on the right to V1 on the left), whereas heterotopic fibers connect different areas (e.g., V1 on the right to V2 on the left).
- Differences in neural connectivity and organization may underlie many of the gross asymmetries between the hemispheres.
- Ninety-six percent of humans, regardless of which hand is dominant, have a left-hemisphere specialization for language.
- The planum temporale encompasses Wernicke's area and is involved in language. The asymmetry of the planum temporale is one of the few examples in which an anatomical index is correlated with a well-defined functional asymmetry.
- Differences have been found in the specifics of cortical microcircuitry between the two hemispheres in both anterior (Broca's) and posterior (Wernicke's) language-associated cortex.

Splitting the Brain: Cortical Disconnection

Because the corpus callosum is the primary means of communication between the two cerebral hemispheres, we learn a great deal when we sever the callosal fibers. This approach was successfully used in the pioneering animal studies of Ronald Myers and Roger Sperry at the California Institute of Technology. They developed a series of animal experiments to assess whether the corpus callosum is crucial for unified cortical function. First, they trained cats to choose a "plus" stimulus versus a "circle" stimulus randomly alternated between two doors. When a cat chose correctly, it was rewarded with food. Myers and Sperry made the startling discovery that when the corpus callosum and anterior commissure were sectioned, such visual discriminations learned by one hemisphere did not transfer to the other hemisphere. Further studies done on monkeys and chimpanzees showed that visual and tactile information lateralized to one hemisphere did not transfer to the opposite hemisphere, thus corroborating the results from cats.

This important research laid the groundwork for comparable human studies initiated by Sperry and one of the authors (MSG; Sperry et al., 1969). Unlike lesion studies, the split-brain operation does not destroy any cortical tissue; instead, it eliminates the connections between the two hemispheres. With split-brain patients, functional inferences are not based on how behavior changes after a cortical area is eliminated. Rather, it becomes possible to see how each hemisphere operates in relative isolation.

The Surgery

Corpus callosotomy, or split-brain surgery, is used to treat intractable epilepsy when other forms of treatment, such as medication, have failed. This procedure was first performed in 1940 by a Rochester, New York, surgeon, William Van Wagenen. One of Van Wagenen's patients, who had a history of severe epileptic seizures, improved after developing a tumor in his corpus callosum (Van Wagenen & Herren, 1940). Epileptic seizures are the result of abnormal electrical discharges that zip across the brain. The improvement in his patient's condition gave Van Wagenen the idea that if he were to sever the patient's corpus callosum, perhaps the electrical impulses causing seizures would be unable to spread from one hemisphere to the other: The epileptogenic activity would be held in check, and a generalized seizure would be prevented. The idea was radical, particularly when so little was really understood about brain function. The surgery itself was also painstaking, especially without today's microsurgical techniques, because only a thin wall of cells separates the ventricles from the corpus callosum. With the limited treatment options available at the time, however, Van Wagenen had desperate patients; and to twist a phrase, they called for desperate measures. One great fear loomed: What would be the side effect—a split personality with two minds fighting for control over one body? To everyone's relief, the surgery was a great success. Remarkably, the patients appeared and felt completely normal. The seizures typically subsided immediately, even in patients who, before the operation, experienced up to 15 seizures per day. Eighty percent of the patients enjoyed a 60% to 70% decrease in seizure activity, and some were free of seizures altogether (Akelaitis, 1941). Everyone was happy, yet puzzled. Twenty of the surgeries were performed without any discernible psychological side effects: no changes to the psyche, personality, intellect, sensory processing, or motor coordination. Akelaitis concluded:

> The observations that some of these patients were able to perform highly complex synchronous bilateral activities as piano-playing, typewriting by means of the touch system and dancing postoperatively suggests strongly that commissural pathways other than the corpus callosum are being utilized. (Akelaitis, 1943, p. 259)

Methodological Considerations in Studying Split-Brain Patients

A number of methodological issues arise in evaluations of the performance of split-brain patients. First, bear in mind that these patients were not neurologically normal before the operation; they were all chronic epileptics, whose many seizures may have caused neurologic damage. Therefore, it is reasonable to ask whether they provide an appropriate barometer of normal hemispheric function after the operation. There is no easy answer to this question. Several patients do display abnormal performance on neuropsychological assessments, and they may even be mentally retarded. In some patients, however, the cognitive impairments are negligible; these are the patients studied in closest detail.

Second, it is important to consider whether the **transcortical** connections were completely sectioned, or whether some fibers remained intact. In the original California operations, reviewing surgical notes was the only way to determine the completeness of the surgical sections. In recent years though, MRIs, such as in Figure 4.12, diffusion tensor imaging, and electrical brain-mapping techniques have provided a more accurate representation of the extent of surgical sections. Accurate documentation of a callosal section is crucial for learning about the organization of the cerebral commissure.

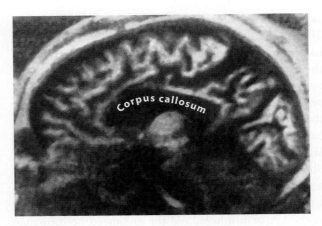

FIGURE 4.12 This MRI shows a sagittal view of a brain in which the corpus callosum has been entirely sectioned.

The main methods of testing the perceptual and cognitive functions of each hemisphere have changed little over the past 30 years. Researchers use primarily visual stimulation, not only because of the preeminent status of this modality for humans but also because the visual system is more strictly lateralized (see Figure 4.1) than are other sensory modalities, such as the auditory and olfactory systems.

The visual stimulus is restricted to a single hemisphere by quickly flashing the stimulus in one visual field or the other (Figure 4.13). Before stimulation, the patient is required to fixate on a point in space. The brevity of

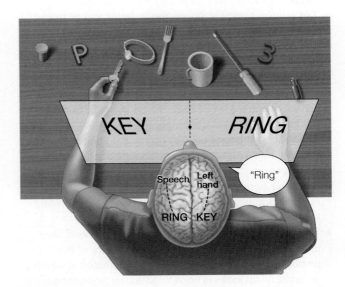

FIGURE 4.13 Restricting visual stimuli to one hemisphere. The split-brain patient reports through the speaking hemisphere only the items flashed to the right half of the screen and denies seeing left-field stimuli or recognizing objects presented to the left hand. Nevertheless, the left hand correctly retrieves objects presented in the left visual field, about which the patient verbally denies knowing anything.

stimulation is necessary to prevent eye movements, which would redirect the information into the unwanted hemisphere. Eye movements take roughly 200 ms, so if the stimulus is presented for a briefer period of time, the experimenter can be confident that the stimulus was lateralized. More recent image stabilization tools—tools that move in correspondence with the subject's eye movements—allow a more prolonged, naturalistic form of stimulation. This technological development has opened the way for new discoveries in the neurological and psychological aspects of hemisphere disconnection.

Functional Consequences of the Split-Brain Procedure

The results of testing done on the patient W.J. were contrary to the earlier reports on the effects of the split-brain procedure as reported by A. J. Akelaitis (1941), who had found no significant neurological and psychological effects after the callosum was sectioned. Careful testing with W.J. and other California patients, however, revealed behavioral changes similar to those seen in split-brain primates (see below). Visual information presented to one half of the brain was not available to the other half. The same principle applied to touch. Patients were able to name and describe objects placed in the right hand but not objects presented in the left hand. Sensory information restricted to one hemisphere was also not available to accurately guide movements with the ipsilateral hand. For example, when a picture of a hand portraying the "OK" sign was presented to the left hemisphere, the patient was able to make the gesture with the right hand, which is controlled from the left half of the brain. The patient was unable to make the same gesture with the left hand, however, which is controlled from the disconnected right hemisphere.

From a cognitive point of view, these initial studies confirmed long-standing neurological knowledge about the nature of the two cerebral hemispheres, which had been obtained earlier from patients with unilateral hemispheric lesions: The left hemisphere is dominant for language, speech, and major problem solving. Its verbal IQ and problem-solving capacity (including mathematical tasks, geometric problems, and hypothesis formation) remain intact after callosotomy (Gazzaniga, 1985). Isolating half the brain, cutting its acreage by 50%, causes no major changes in cognitive function—nor do the patients notice any change in their abilities. The right hemisphere is impoverished in its ability to perform cognitive tasks, but it appears specialized for visuospatial tasks such as drawing cubes and other three-dimensional patterns. The split-brain patients cannot name or describe visual and tactile stimuli presented to the right hemisphere, because the sensory information is disconnected from the dominant left (speech) hemisphere. This does not mean that *knowledge* about the stimuli is absent in the right hemisphere, however. Nonverbal response techniques are required to demonstrate the competence of the right hemisphere. For example, the left hand can be used to point to named objects or to demonstrate the function of depicted objects presented in the left visual field.

Split-Brain Evidence for Callosal Function Specificity We have seen that when the corpus callosum is fully sectioned, little or no perceptual or cognitive interaction occurs between the hemispheres. Surgical cases in which callosal section is limited or part of the callosum is inadvertently spared have enabled investigators to examine specific functions of the callosum by region. For example, when the splenium, the posterior area of the callosum that interconnects the occipital lobe, is spared, visual information is transferred normally between the two cerebral hemispheres (Figure 4.14). In these instances, pattern, color, and linguistic information presented anywhere in either visual field can be matched with information presented to the other half of the brain. The patients, however, show no evidence of interhemispheric transfer of tactile information from touched objects. Tactile information turns out to be transferred by fibers in a region just anterior to the splenium, still located in the posterior half of the callosum.

Surgeons sometimes perform the split-brain procedure in stages, restricting the initial operation to the front (anterior) or back (posterior) half of the callosum. The remaining fibers are sectioned in a second operation

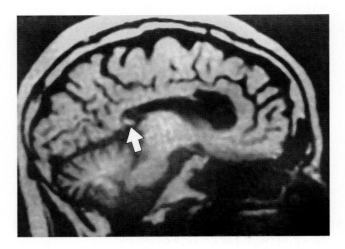

FIGURE 4.14 An incomplete corpus callostomy.
MRI scan showing that the splenium (*arrow*) was spared in the split-brain procedure performed on this patient. As a result, visual information can still be transferred between the cerebral hemispheres.

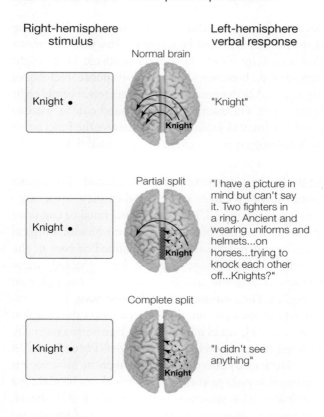

Right-hemisphere stimulus — Left-hemisphere verbal response

Normal brain

Knight •   "Knight"

Partial split

Knight •   "I have a picture in mind but can't say it. Two fighters in a ring. Ancient and wearing uniforms and helmets...on horses...trying to knock each other off...Knights?"

Complete split

Knight •   "I didn't see anything"

FIGURE 4.15 Schematic representation of split-brain patient J.W.'s naming ability for objects in the left visual field at each operative stage.

only if the seizures continue to persist. This two-stage procedure offers a unique glimpse into what the anterior and posterior callosal regions transfer between the cerebral hemispheres. When the posterior half of the callosum is sectioned, transfer of visual, tactile, and auditory sensory information is severely disrupted, but the remaining intact anterior region of the callosum is still able to transfer higher order information. For example, one patient (J.W.) was able to name stimuli presented in the left visual field following a resection limited to the posterior callosal region. Close examination revealed that the left hemisphere was receiving higher order cues about the stimulus without having access to the sensory information about the stimulus itself (Figure 4.15). In short, the anterior part of the callosum transfers semantic information about the stimulus but not the stimulus itself. After the anterior callosal region was sectioned in this patient, this capacity was lost.

TAKE-HOME MESSAGES

- In some of the original animal studies on callosotomies, Myers and Sperry demonstrated that visual discrimination learned by one hemisphere did not transfer to the other hemisphere when the hemispheres were disconnected.

- The splenium is the most posterior portion of the corpus callosum. When the posterior half of the callosum is sectioned in humans, transfer of visual, tactile, and auditory sensory information is severely disrupted. The anterior part of the callosum is involved in the higher order transfer of semantic information.

Hemispheric Specialization

Evidence from Split-Brain Patients

As we saw in Chapter 1, the history of cerebral specialization—the notion that different regions of the brain have specific functions—began with Franz Joseph Gall in the early 1800s. Although it fell repeatedly in and out of fashion, this idea could not be discounted, because so many clinical findings, especially in patients who had suffered strokes, provided unassailable evidence that it was so. Over the last 50 years, studies done with split-brain patients have demonstrated that some of the brain's processing is lateralized. In this section, we review some of these findings. The most prominent lateralized function in the human brain is the left hemisphere's capacity for language and speech, which we examine first. We also look at the lateralization of visuospatial processing, attention and perception, information processing, and how we interpret the world around us.

Language and Speech When we are trying to understand the neural bases of language, it is useful to distinguish between grammatical and lexical functions. The grammar–lexicon distinction is different from the more traditional syntax–semantics distinction commonly invoked to improve understanding of the differential effects of brain lesions on language processes (see Chapter 11). *Grammar* is the rule-based system that humans have for ordering words to facilitate communication. For example, in English, the typical order of a sentence is subject (noun)—action (verb)—object (noun). The *lexicon* is the mind's dictionary, where words are associated with specific meanings. A "dog" is, well, associated with a dog; but so is a *chien* and a *cane*, depending on the language that you speak.

The grammar–lexicon distinction takes into account factors such as memory, because, with memory, word strings as idioms can be learned by rote. For example, "How are you?" or "Comment allez-vous?" is most likely a single lexical entry. Although the lexicon cannot possibly encompass the infinite number of unique phrases and sentences that humans can generate—such as the one you are now reading—memory does play a role in many short phrases. When uttered, such word strings do not reflect an underlying interaction of syntax and semantic systems; they are, instead, essentially an entry from the lexicon. This is more apparent when you are learning a new language. You often learn stock phrases that you speak as a unit, rather than struggle with the grammar. With this in mind, it might be predicted that some brain areas ought to be wholly responsible for grammar, whereas the lexicon's location ought to be more elusive, since it reflects learned information and thus is part of the brain's general memory and knowledge systems. The grammar system, then, ought to be discrete and hence localizable, and the lexicon should be distributed and hence more difficult to damage completely.

Language and speech are rarely present in both hemispheres; they are either in one or the other. While it is true that the separated left hemisphere normally comprehends all aspects of language, the linguistic capabilities of the right hemisphere do exist, although they are uncommon. Indeed, out of dozens of split-brain patients who have been carefully examined, only six showed clear evidence of residual linguistic functions in the right hemisphere. And even in these patients, the extent of right-hemisphere language functions is severely limited and restricted to the lexical aspects of comprehension.

Interestingly, the left and right lexicons of these special patients can be nearly equal in their capacity, but they are organized quite differently. For example, both hemispheres show a phenomenon called the *word superiority effect* (see Chapter 5). Normal English readers are better able to identify letters (e.g., *L*) in the context of real English words (e.g., *belt*) than when the same letters appear in pseudowords (e.g., *kelt*) or nonsense letter strings (e.g., *ktle*). Because pseudowords and nonwords do not have lexical entries, letters occurring in such strings do not receive the additional processing benefit bestowed on words. Thus, the word superiority effect emerges.

While the patients with right-hemisphere language exhibit a visual lexicon, it may be that each hemisphere accesses this lexicon in a different way. To test this possibility, investigators used a letter-priming task. Participants were asked to indicate whether a briefly flashed uppercase letter was an *H* or a *T*. On each trial, the uppercase letter was preceded by a lowercase letter that was either an *h* or a *t*. Normally, participants are significantly faster, or primed, when an uppercase *H* is preceded by a lowercase *h* than when it is preceded by a lowercase *t*.

The difference between response latency on compatible (*h–H*) versus incompatible (*t–H*) trials is taken to be a measure of letter priming. J.W., a split-brain participant, performed a lateralized version of this task

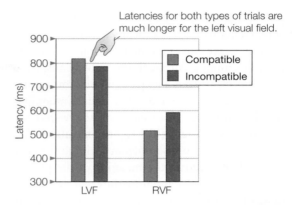

FIGURE 4.16 Letter priming as a function of visual field in split-brain patients.
The graph shows the response latencies for compatible and incompatible pairs of letters in the left and right visual fields (LVF and RVF, respectively). The latencies for both types of trials are much longer for the left visual field (right hemisphere).

in which the prime was displayed for 100 ms to either the right or the left visual field, and 400 ms later the target letter appeared in either the right or the left visual field. The results, shown in Figure 4.16, provide no evidence of letter priming for left visual field (LVF) trials but clear evidence of priming for trials of the right visual field (RVF). Thus, the lack of a priming phenomenon in the disconnected right hemisphere suggests a deficit in letter recognition, prohibiting access to parallel processing mechanisms. J.W. exhibited a variety of other deficiencies in right-hemisphere function as well. For example, he was unable to judge whether one word was superordinate to another (e.g., *furniture* and *chair*), or whether two words were antonyms (e.g., *love* and *hate*).

In sum, there appear to be two lexicons, one in each hemisphere. The right hemisphere's lexicon seems organized differently from the left hemisphere's lexicon, and these lexicons are accessed in different ways. These observations are consistent with the view that lexicons reflect learning processes and, as such, are more widely distributed in the cerebral cortex. A long-held belief has been that in the general population, the lexicon appears to be in the left hemisphere. Recent evidence from functional-imaging studies, however, suggests a broader role for the right hemisphere in language processing, although the precise nature of that role remains to be defined. Some theorists have suggested that the language ability of the left hemisphere gives it a superior ability to perform higher cognitive functions like making inferences and solving mathematics problems. Split-brain patients who have an extensive right-brain lexicon, however, do not show any attendant increase in their right brain's ability to perform these tasks (Gazzaniga & Smylie, 1984).

In contrast, generative syntax is present in only one hemisphere. Generative syntax means that by following rules of grammar, we can combine words in an unlimited number of meanings. Although the right hemisphere of some patients clearly has a lexicon, it performs erratically on other aspects of language, such as understanding verbs, pluralizations, the possessive, or active–passive differences. In these patients, the right hemisphere also fails to use word order to disambiguate stimuli for correct meaning. For instance, the meaning of the phrase "The dog chases the cat" cannot be differentiated from the meaning of "The cat chases the dog." Yet these right hemispheres can indicate when a sentence ends with a semantically odd word. "The dog chases cat the" would be flagged as wrong. What's more, right hemispheres with language capacities can make grammar judgments. For some peculiar reason, although they cannot use syntax to disambiguate stimuli, they can judge that one set of utterances is grammatical while another set is not. This startling finding suggests that patterns of speech are learned by rote. Yet recognizing the pattern of acceptable utterances does not mean that a neural system can use this information to understand word strings (Figure 4.17).

A hallmark of most split-brain patients is that their speech is produced in the left hemisphere and not the right. This observation, along with amobarbital studies (see Wada and Rasmussen, 1960) and functional imaging studies, confirms that the left hemisphere is the dominant hemisphere for speech production in most (96%) of us. Nonetheless, there are now a handful of documented cases of split-brain patients who can produce speech from both the left and the right hemispheres. Although speech is restricted to the left hemisphere following callosal bisection, in these rare patients the capacity to make one-word utterances from the disconnected right hemisphere has emerged over time. This intriguing development raises the question of whether information is somehow transferring to the dominant hemisphere for speech output or whether the right hemisphere itself is capable of developing speech production. After extensive testing, it became apparent that the latter hypothesis was correct.

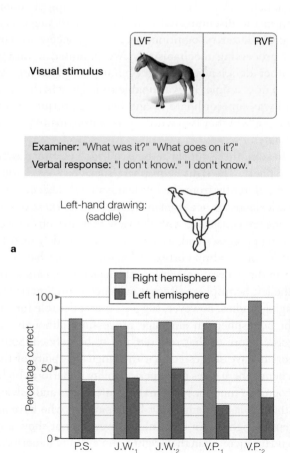

a

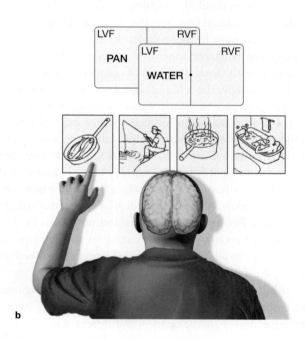

b

FIGURE 4.17 Cognitive abilities of the right hemisphere.
(a) The right hemisphere is capable of understanding language but not syntax. When presented with a horse stimulus in the left visual field (right hemisphere), the subject maintains through the left hemisphere that he saw nothing. When asked to draw what goes on the object, the left hand (right hemisphere) is able to draw a saddle. **(b)** The capacity of the right hemisphere to make inferences is extremely limited. Two words are presented in serial order, and the right hemisphere (left hand) is simply required to point to a picture that best depicts what happens when the words are causally related. The left hemisphere finds these tasks trivial, but the right cannot perform the task. **(c)** Data from three patients show that the right hemisphere is more accurate than the left in recognizing unfamiliar faces.

c

For example, the patients were able to name an object presented in the left field, say a spoon, and in the right field, a cow, but were not able to judge whether the two objects were the same. Or, when words like *father* were presented such that the fixation point fell between the *t* and the *h*, the patients said either "fat" or "her," depending on which hemisphere controlled speech production. These findings illustrate that an extraordinary plasticity lasts sometimes as long as 10 years after callosal surgery. In one patient, in fact, the right hemisphere had no speech production capability for approximately 13 years before it "spoke."

Finally, note that although most language capabilities are left lateralized, the processing of the emotional content of language appears to be right lateralized. It is well known that patients with damage to certain regions of the left hemisphere have language comprehension difficulties. Speech, however, can communicate emotion information beyond the meanings and structures of the words. A statement, such as "John, come here," can be interpreted in different ways if it is said in an angry tone, a fearful tone, a seductive tone, or a surprised tone. This nonlinguistic, emotional component of speech is called *emotional prosody*. One patient with left-hemisphere damage reportedly has difficulty comprehending words but shows little deficit in interpreting the meaning of emotional prosody (Barrett et al., 1999). At the same time, several patients with damage to the temporoparietal lobe in the right hemisphere have been shown to comprehend the meaning of language perfectly but have difficulty interpreting phrases when emotional prosody plays a role (Heilman et al., 1975). This double dissociation between language and emotional prosody in the comprehension of meaning suggests that the right hemisphere is specialized for comprehending emotional expressions of speech.

Visuospatial Processing Early testing of W.J. made it clear that the two hemispheres have different visuospatial capabilities. As Figure 4.2 shows, the isolated right hemisphere is frequently superior on neuropsychological tests such as the block design task, a subtest of the Wechsler Adult Intelligence Scale. In this simple task of arranging red and white blocks to match a given pattern, the left hemisphere of a split-brain patient performs poorly while the right hemisphere easily completes the task. Functional asymmetries like these, however, have proven to be inconsistent. In some patients, performance is impaired with either hand; in others, the left hemisphere is quite adept at this task. Perhaps a component of this task, rather than the whole task, is lateralized. Additional testing has shown that patients who demonstrate a right-hemisphere superiority for the block design task exhibit no asymmetry on the perceptual aspects of the task (contrary to what you may have predicted). If a picture of the block design pattern is lateralized, either hemisphere can easily find the match from a series of pictures. Since each hand is sufficiently dexterous, the crucial link must be in the mapping of the sensory message onto the capable motor system.

The right hemisphere is also specialized for efficiently detecting upright faces and discriminating among similar faces (Gazzaniga & Smylie, 1983). The left hemisphere is not good at distinguishing among similar faces, but it is able to distinguish among dissimilar ones when it can tag the feature differences with words (blond versus brunette, big nose versus button nose). As for the recognition of familiar faces in general, the right hemisphere outperforms the left hemisphere in this task (Turk, 2002).

What about that most familiar of faces, one's own? In one study, software was used to morph the face of one split brain patient J.W. in 10% increments, into that of a familiar other, Mike (Figure 4.18). The faces were

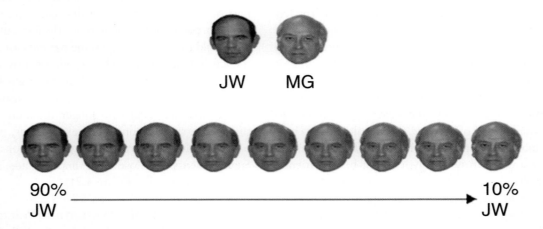

FIGURE 4.18 Morphed images of J.W. and M.G.
The image on the far left contains 10% M.G. and 90% J.W. and changes in 10% increments from left to right, to 90% M.G. and 10% J.W. on the far right. The two original photographs of M.G. and J.W. pictured above and these nine morphed images were presented to each hemisphere randomly.

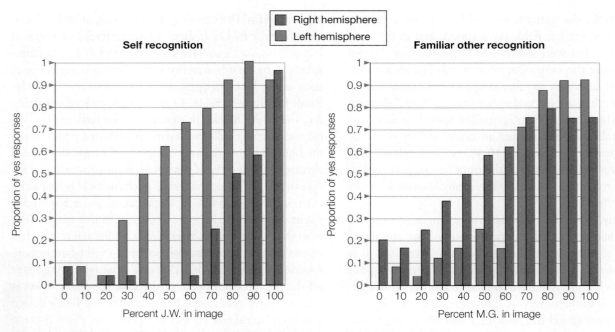

FIGURE 4.19 Left hemisphere is better at recognizing self, and right hemisphere is superior to recognizing familiar other.
The proportion of "yes" responses to recognition judgments are plotted on the y-axis as a function of the percentage of the individual contained in the image and the cerebral hemisphere to which the image was presented.

flashed randomly to J.W.'s separated hemispheres. Then that hemisphere was asked, in the first condition, "Is that you?" and, in another condition, "Is that Mike?" A double dissociation was found (Figure 4.19). The left hemisphere was biased towards recognizing one's own face, while the right hemisphere had a recognition bias for familiar others (Turk et al., 2002).

Both hemispheres can generate spontaneous facial expressions, but you need your left hemisphere to produce voluntary facial expressions. Indeed, people appear to have two neural systems for controlling facial expressions (Figure 4.20; Gazzaniga & Smylie, 1990). The left hemisphere sends its messages directly to the contralateral facial nucleus via cranial nerve VII, which in turn innervates the right facial muscles. At the same time, it also sends a command over the corpus callosum to the right half of the brain. The right hemisphere sends the message down to the left facial nucleus, which in turn innervates the left half of the face. The result is that a person can make a symmetrical voluntary facial response, such as a smile or frown. When a split-brain patient's left hemisphere is given the command to smile, however, the lower right side of the face responds first while the left side responds about 180 msec later. Why does the left side respond at all? Most likely the signal is rerouted through secondary ipsilateral pathways that connect to both facial nuclei, which then eventually send the signal over to the left-side facial muscles.

Unlike voluntary expressions, which only the left hemisphere can trigger, spontaneous expressions can be managed by either half of the brain. When either half triggers a spontaneous response, the pathways that activate the brainstem nuclei are signaled through another pathway—one that does not course through the cortex. Each hemisphere sends signals straight down through the midbrain and out to the brainstem nuclei, which then signal the facial muscles. Clinical neurologists know of the distinction between these two ways of controlling facial muscles. For example, a patient with a lesion in the part of the right hemisphere that participates in voluntary expressions is unable to move the left half of the face when told to smile. But the same patient can easily move the left half of the face when spontaneously smiling, because those pathways are unaffected by right-hemisphere damage. In contrast, patients with Parkinson's disease, whose midbrain nuclei no longer function, are unable to produce spontaneous facial expressions, whereas the pathways that support voluntary expressions work fine. Such patients can lose their masked-face appearance when asked to smile (Figure 4.21).

The Interactions of Attention and Perception The attentional and perceptual abilities of split-brain patients have been extensively explored. After cortical disconnection, perceptual information is not shared between the two cerebral hemispheres. Sometimes the supporting

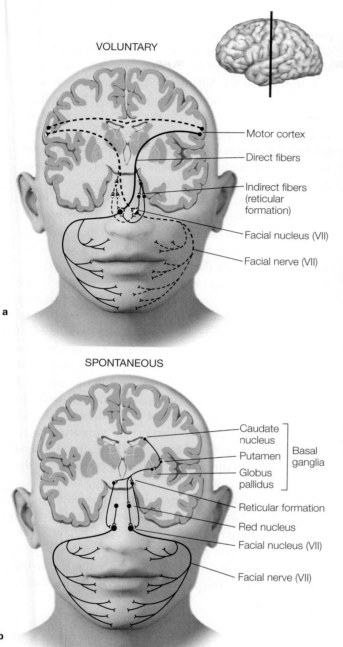

FIGURE 4.20 **The neural pathways that control voluntary and spontaneous facial expression are different.**
(a) Voluntary expressions that can signal intention have their own cortical networks in humans. (b) The neural networks for spontaneous expressions involve older brain circuits and appear to be the same as those in chimpanzees. (inset) The location of the section that has been overlaid onto each face.

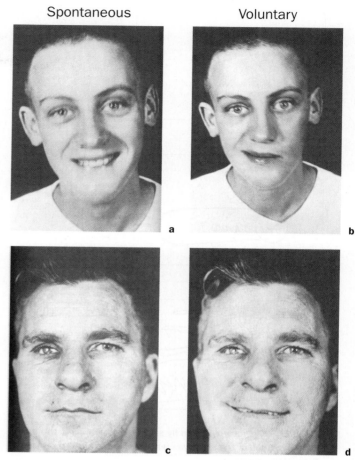

FIGURE 4.21 **Facial expressions of two kinds of patients.**
The patient in the upper row suffered brain damage to the right hemisphere. (a) The lesion did not interfere in spontaneous expression but (b) it did interfere with voluntary expression. (c) This Parkinson's disease patient has a typical masked face. Because Parkinson's disease involves the part of the brain that controls spontaneous facial expression, the faces of these patients, when they are told to smile (d), light up because the other pathway is still intact.

cognitive processes of attentional mechanisms, however, do interact. Some forms of attention are integrated at the subcortical level, and other forms act independently in the separated hemispheres.

We noted earlier that split-brain patients cannot integrate visual information between the two visual fields. When visual information is lateralized to either the left or the right disconnected hemisphere, the unstimulated hemisphere cannot use the information for perceptual analysis. This is also true for certain types of somatosensory information presented to each hand. Although touching any part of the body is noted by either hemisphere, patterned somatosensory information is lateralized. Thus, when holding an object in the left hand, a split-brain patient is unable to find an identical object with the right hand. Some investigators argue that higher order perceptual information is integrated by way of subcortical structures, but others have not replicated these results.

For example, split-brain patients sometimes drew pictures that combined word information presented to the two hemispheres. When "ten" was flashed to one

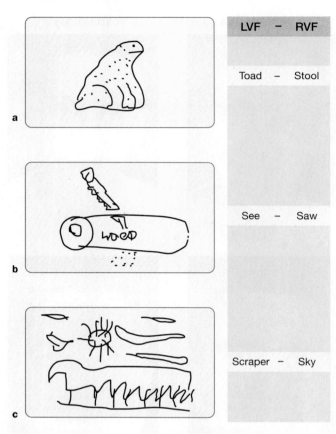

LVF	–	RVF
Toad	–	Stool
See	–	Saw
Scraper	–	Sky

FIGURE 4.22 Pictures drawn by split-brain participant J.W.'s left hand in response to stimuli presented to the left and right visual fields (LVF and RVF).
(a) Drawing of the LVF word *Toad* (ipsilateral to the drawing hand).
(b) Drawing of the RVF *Saw* (contralateral to the drawing hand).
(c) Drawing combining both words: *Scraper* and *Sky* (ipsilateral + contralateral).

hemisphere and "clock" was flashed to the other, the patient drew a clock set at 10. This outcome initially seemed to imply that subcortical transfer of higher order information was taking place between the hemispheres. Subsequent observations (Figure 4.22; Kingstone & Gazzaniga, 1995), however, suggested that it actually reflects dual hemispheric control of the drawing hand (with control biased to the left hemisphere). When conceptually ambiguous word pairs, such as *hot dog*, were presented, they were always depicted literally (e.g., a dog panting in the heat) and never as emergent objects (e.g., a frankfurter). This suggests that no transfer of higher order information occurred. Moreover, right- and left-hand drawings often depicted only the words presented to the left hemisphere. *The subcortical transfer of information is more apparent than real.*

We have seen that *object identification* seems to occur in isolation in each hemisphere of split-brain patients. In other studies, evidence suggested that crude information concerning *spatial locations* can be integrated

between the hemispheres. In one set of experiments, the patient fixated on a central point located between two 4-point grids, one in each visual field (Holtzman, 1984). In a given trial, one of the positions on one of the grids was highlighted for 500 msec. Thus information went in to either the left hemisphere or the right hemisphere, depending on which grid was illuminated. For example, in Figure 4.23a, the upper-left point of the grid in the left visual field was highlighted. This information would be registered in the right hemisphere of the subject. After 1 sec, a tone sounded and the subject was asked to move her eyes to the highlighted point *within* the visual field with the highlighted stimulus. The results were as expected. Information from the left visual field that went to the right hemisphere guided eye movement back to the same location where the light flashed. In the second condition, the subject was required to move her eyes to the relative point in the visual field opposite to the one with the highlighted stimulus (Figure 4.23b). If she could do this, it would mean that information about the location of light stimulus was coming in to the left hemisphere from the right visual field and was guiding her eye movement to the analogous location in the right-brain-controlled left visual field. Split-brain subjects did this task easily. So some type of spatial information is transferred and integrated between the two half brains, enabling attention to be transferred to either visual field. The ability remained intact even when the grid was randomly positioned in the test field.

These results raised a question: Are the attentional processes associated with spatial information affected by cortical disconnection? As we will see in Chapter 7, surprisingly, split-brain patients can use either hemisphere to direct attention to positions in either the left or the right visual field. This conclusion was based on studies

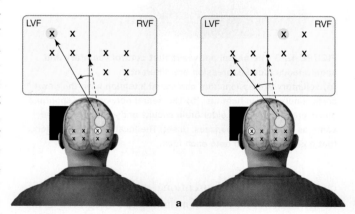

FIGURE 4.23 Cross-integration of spatial information.
(a) On within-field trials, the eye moved to the stimulus that was surrounded by the probe. **(b)** On between-field trials, the eye moved to the corresponding stimulus in the other hemifield.

using a modified version of the spatial cuing task (see Figure 7.8 on page 279). In this task, participants respond as quickly as possible upon detecting a target that appears at one of several possible locations. The target is preceded by a cue, either at the target location (a valid cue) or at another location (an invalid cue). Responses are faster on valid trials, indicating spatial orienting to the cued location. In split-brain patients, as with normal participants, a cue to direct attention to a particular point in the visual field was honored no matter which half of the brain was presented with the critical stimulus (Holtzman et al., 1981). These results suggest that the two hemispheres rely on a common orienting system to maintain a single focus of attention.

The discovery that spatial attention can be directed with ease to either visual field raised the question of whether each separate cognitive system in the split-brain patient, if instructed to do so, could independently and simultaneously direct attention to a part of its own visual field. Can the right hemisphere direct attention to a point in the left visual field while the left hemisphere attends to a point in the right visual field? Normal subjects cannot divide their attention that way, but perhaps the split-brain operation frees the two hemispheres from this constraint. As it turns out, the answer is no. The integrated spatial attention system remains intact following cortical disconnection (Reuter-Lorenz & Fendrich, 1990). *Thus, as in neurologically intact observers, the attentional system of split-brain patients is unifocal.* They, like us, are unable to prepare simultaneously for events taking place in two spatially disparate locations.

The dramatic effects on perception and cognition of disconnecting the cerebral hemispheres initially suggested that each hemisphere has its own attentional resources (Kinsbourne, 1982). If that model were true, then the cognitive operations of one hemisphere, no matter what the difficulty, would have little influence on the cognitive activities of the other. The left brain could be solving a differential equation while the right brain was planning for next weekend. The alternative view is that the brain has limited resources to manage such processes: If most of our resources are being applied to solving our math problems, then fewer resources are available for planning the weekend's activities. This phenomenon has been studied extensively, and all of the results have confirmed that the latter model is correct: Our central resources are limited.

Attentional resources are shared. The concept that attentional resources are limited should be distinguished from limitations in processing that are a result of other properties of the sensory systems. Even though the overall resources that a brain commits to a task appear constant,

the method of deploying them can vary depending on the task. For example, the time needed to detect a complex object increases as more items are added to the display. Normal control subjects require an additional 70 ms to detect the target when two extra items are added to the display, and another 70 ms for each additional pair of items. In split-brain patients, when the items are distributed across the midline of the visual field (so that objects are in both visual fields—that is, a bilateral array), as opposed to all being in one visual field, the increase in reaction time to added stimuli is cut almost in half (Figure 4.24) (Luck et al., 1989). Two half brains working separately can do the job in half the time that one whole brain can. Division of cognitive resources improved performance. Separation of the hemispheres seems to have turned a unified perceptual system into two simpler perceptual systems that, because they are unable to communicate, don't "interfere" with each other. The large perceptual problem, which the normal brain faces, is broken down into smaller problems that a half brain

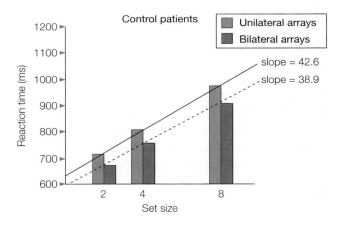

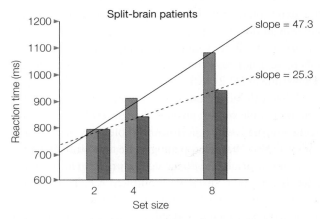

FIGURE 4.24 Division of cognitive resources in split brain patients improved visual search performance.
As more items are added to a set, for split brain patients the increase in reaction time for bilateral arrays is only half as fast as when all objects are confined to one side.

can solve when each hemisphere perceives only half the problem. It appears as if the patient's total information processing capacity has increased so that it is superior to that of normal participants. How can this be, if resources remain constant? This conundrum forces us to consider where resources are applied in a perceptual–motor task.

It appears that each hemisphere employs a different strategy to examine the contents of its visual field. The left hemisphere adopts a helpful cognitive strategy in solving the problem, whereas the right hemisphere does not possess those extra cognitive skills. This phenomenon was shown in a different experiment. Here, the task was to find a black circle in a field of equally numbered black squares and gray circles. Randomly interspersed through the trials were "guided" trials, where the search for the black circle had a guide—that is, a clue: There were fewer black squares in a ratio of about 2:5. A cognitive or "smart" approach would be to use the clue: concentrating on the black colored figures should enable a subject to complete the task faster than concentrating on the circular shaped figures. In two out of three split-brain patients, the left, dominant hemisphere used the clue, which decreased its reaction time in the guided trials, but the right hemisphere did not (Kingstone et al., 1995). In control groups, 70% of people have a faster reaction time to guided trials and use the "smart" strategy. This result indicates that not all people use guided search; but when they do, their left hemisphere is using it. This apparent discrepancy supports other evidence that multiple mechanisms of attention operate at different stages of visual search processing from early to late, some of which might be shared across the disconnected hemispheres and others of which might be independent. *Thus, each hemisphere uses the available resources but at different stages of processing.*

What's more, using a "smart strategy" does not mean the left hemisphere is always better at orienting attention. It depends on the job. For instance, the right hemisphere, superior in processing upright faces, automatically shifts attention to where a face is looking; but the left hemisphere does not have the same response to gaze direction (Kingstone et al., 2000).

When thinking about neural resources and their limitations, people often consider the mechanisms that are being engaged while performing voluntary processing. For example, what is happening as we try to rub our stomach, pat our head, and do a calculus problem at the same time? Searching a visual scene, however, calls upon processes that may well be automatic, built-in properties of the visual system itself. Indeed, the hemispheres interact quite differently in how they control reflex and voluntary attention processes. It appears that reflexive automatic attention orienting is independent in the two hemispheres, as the right hemisphere's automatic shifting of

FIGURE 4.25 Global and local representations.
We represent information at multiple scales. At its most global scale, this drawing is of a house. We can also recognize and focus on the component parts of the house.

attention to gaze direction indicates. Voluntary attention orienting, however, is a horse of a different color. Here, it appears, the hemispheres are competing, and the left has more say (Kingstone et al., 1995). That these systems are distinct is reflected in the discovery that splitting brains has a different effect on the processes.

Global and local processing. What is the picture in Figure 4.25? A house, right? Now describe it more fully. You might note its architectural style, and you might point out the detailing on the front door, the double hung windows running across the front façade, and the shingled roof. In recounting the picture, you would have provided a hierarchical description. The house can be described on multiple levels: Its shape and attributes indicate it is a house. But it is also a specific house, with a specific configuration of doors, windows, and materials. This description is hierarchical in that the finer levels of description are embedded in the higher levels. The shape of the house evolves from the configuration of its component parts—an idea that will be developed in Chapter 6.

David Navon (1977) of the University of Haifa introduced a model task for studying **hierarchical structure**. He created stimuli that could be identified on two different levels (e.g., Figure 4.26). At each level, the stimulus contains an identifiable letter. The critical feature is that the letter defined by the global shape is composed of smaller letters (the local shape). In Figure 4.26a, for example, the global *H* is composed of local *F*s.

Navon was interested in how we perceive hierarchical stimuli. He initially found that the perceptual system first extracted the global shape. The time required to

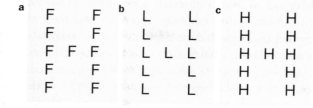

FIGURE 4.26 Local and global stimuli used to investigate hierarchical representation.
Each stimulus is composed of a series of identical letters whose global arrangement forms a larger letter. The participants' task is to indicate whether the stimulus contained an *H* or an *L*. When the stimulus set included competing targets at both levels **(b)**, the participants were instructed to respond either to local targets only or to global targets only. Neither target is present in **(e)**.

identify the global letter was independent of the identity of the constituent elements, but when it came to identifying the small letters, reaction time was slowed if the global shape was incongruent with the local shapes. Subsequent research qualified these conclusions. Global precedence does depend on object size and the number of local elements. Perhaps different processing systems are used for representing local and global information. Lynn Robertson and her colleagues (1988) found evidence that supports this hypothesis. Patients who have a lesion in either the left or right hemisphere were presented with local and global stimuli in the center of view (the critical laterality factor was whether the lesion was in the left or right hemisphere). Patients with left-side lesions were slow to identify *local* targets, and patients with right-side lesions were slow with *global* targets, demonstrating that the left hemisphere is more adept at representing local information and the right hemisphere is better with global information.

Keep in mind that both hemispheres can abstract either level of representation, but they differ in how *efficiently* local and global information are represented. The right is better at the big picture, and the left is more detail oriented. Thus, patients with left-hemisphere lesions are able to analyze the local structure of a hierarchical stimulus, but they must rely on an intact right hemisphere, which is less efficient at abstracting local information. Further support for this idea comes from studies of local and global stimuli with split-brain patients

(Robertson et al., 1993). Here, too, patients generally identify targets at either level, regardless of the side of presentation. As with normal participants and patients with unilateral lesions, however, split-brain patients are faster at identifying local targets presented to the right visual field (i.e., the left hemisphere) and global targets presented to the left visual field (i.e., the right hemisphere).

Theory of Mind

Theory of mind refers to our ability to understand that other individuals have thoughts, beliefs, and desires. In terms of laterality, theory of mind is an interesting case. You might expect theory of mind to be another hemispheric specialization, lateralized to the left hemisphere like language is, given its dependency on reasoning. Much of the prevailing research on theory of mind, however, suggests that if it is lateralized at all, it is lateralized to the right hemisphere. Many neuroimaging studies show a network of regions in both hemispheres engaged in theory of mind tasks, including the medial prefrontal cortex (PFC), posterior superior temporal sulcus (STS), precuneus, and the amygdala–temporopolar cortex (Figure 4.27). Rebecca Saxe and her colleagues (2009), however, have demonstrated in several fMRI studies, using a version of the false belief task (see Chapter 13), that the critical component of theory of mind, the attribution of beliefs to another person, is localized to the temporal parietal junction in

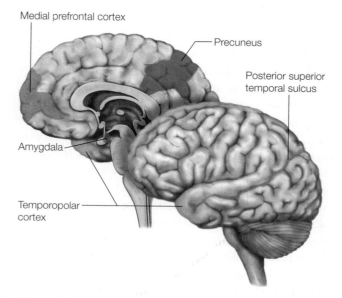

FIGURE 4.27 Theory of mind tasks activate a network of regions bilaterally.
These include the medial prefrontal cortex, posterior superior temporal sulcus, precuneus (hidden in the medial longitudinal fissure in the parietal lobe), and the amygdala-temporopolar cortex. The attribution of beliefs is located in the right hemisphere's temporal parietal junction.

the right hemisphere. This finding may sound merely interesting to you, but to split-brain researchers it was shocking. Think about it for a second. If this information about the beliefs of others is housed in the right hemisphere, and if, in split-brain patients, it isn't transferred to the speaking, left hemisphere, wouldn't you expect that these patients would suffer a disruption in social and moral reasoning? Yet they don't. Split-brain patients act like everyone else. Do these findings also suggest that the recursive nature of thinking about the beliefs of another person is lateralized to the right hemisphere?

A split-brain study by Michael Miller and colleagues at UCSB may provide some insight into these questions (M. Miller et al., 2010). They tested three full-callosotomy patients and three partial-callosotomy patients on a moral reasoning task that depended on the ability to attribute beliefs to another person (the same task, used above by Saxe and colleagues, that produced activations in the right hemisphere). The task involved hearing a scenario in which the actions of an agent conflicted with the beliefs of the agent. For example: Grace works in a chemical plant, and she is fixing coffee for her friend. She adds a white powder to her friend's coffee, believing that the white powder is sugar. The white powder was mislabeled, however, and was actually quite toxic. Her friend drinks the coffee and dies. After hearing the scenario, the subject is asked this question: Was it morally acceptable for Grace to give the coffee to her friend? Participants with an intact corpus callosum would typically say that it was morally acceptable to give her friend the coffee, because they think Grace believed that the white powder was sugar and intended no harm. That is, they realize that Grace had a false belief.

If the special mechanisms that attribute belief are lateralized to the right hemisphere, then the speaking left hemisphere of the split-brain patients should be cut off from those mechanisms. Split-brain patients would thus respond in a way that relies on the outcome of the actions (i.e., her friend died) and is not based on the beliefs of the actors. Children younger than age 4 typically respond in this way (because they do not yet have a fully developed theory of mind). Indeed, Miller and colleagues found that all of the split-brain patients responded that Grace's action was morally unacceptable.

This intriguing result leaves open a question: If split-brain patients are cut off from this important theory-of-mind mechanism, then why don't they act like severely autistic patients, who are unable to comprehend the thinking and beliefs of other people? Some scientists have suggested that the specialized mechanism observed in the right hemisphere may be used for the fast, automatic processing of belief attributions, and that slower, more deliberate reasoning mechanisms of the left hemisphere could perform the same function given time for deliberation. In fact,

Miller and colleagues observed that patients in the moral reasoning study were often uncomfortable with their initial judgments. They would offer spontaneous rationalizations for responding in a particular way. For example, in another scenario, a waitress *knowingly* served sesame seeds to somebody who she believed was highly allergic to them. The outcome, however, was harmless, because the person was not allergic. The patient judged the waitress's action to be morally acceptable. Some moments later, however, he appeared to rationalize his response by saying, "Sesame seeds are tiny little things. They don't hurt nobody." This patient had to square his automatic response, which did not benefit from information about the belief state of the waitress, with what he rationally and consciously knew is permissible in the world. This brings us to a discussion of the left brain interpreter mechanism.

The Interpreter

A hallmark of human intelligence is our ability to make causal interpretations about the world around us, to formulate hypotheses and predictions about the events and actions in our lives, and to create a continuous sensible narrative about our place in the world. This ability allows us to adapt to a constantly changing world and easily solve problems that may arise. We make the causal interpretations almost on a moment-to-moment basis without realizing it. Imagine going to a movie on a sunny afternoon. Before entering the theater, you notice that the street and parking lot are dry, and only a few clouds are in the sky. Once the movie is over, however, and you walk back outside, the sky is gray and the ground is very wet. What do you instantly assume? You would probably assume that it rained while you were watching the movie. Even though you did not witness the rain and nobody told you that it had rained, you make that interpretation based on the evidence of the wet ground and gray skies. This ability to make interpretations is a critical component of our intellect.

After a callosotomy surgery, the verbal intelligence and problem-solving skills of a split-brain patient remain relatively intact. There may be minor deficits, including free recall ability, but for the most part intelligence remains unchanged. An intact intelligence, however, is true only for the speaking left hemisphere, not for the right hemisphere. The intellectual abilities and problem-solving skills of the right hemisphere are seriously impoverished. A large part of the right hemisphere's impoverishment can be attributed to the finding that causal inferences and interpretations appear to be a specialized ability of the left hemisphere. One of the authors (MSG) has referred to this unique specialization as the **interpreter**.

The interpreter has revealed itself in many classic experiments over the years. A typical observation is when the speaking left hemisphere offers up some kind of rationalization to explain the actions that were initiated by the right hemisphere, but whose motivation for the actions are unknown to the left hemisphere. For example, when the split-brain patient P.S. was given the command to stand up in a way that only the right hemisphere could view, P.S. stood up. When the experimenter asked him why he was standing, P.S.'s speaking left hemisphere immediately came up with a plausible explanation: "Oh, I felt like getting a Coke." If his corpus callosum were intact, then P.S. would have responded that he stood up because that was the instruction he had received.

The effects of the interpreter manifest itself in a number of ways. Sometimes it interprets the actions initiated by the right hemisphere, as in the example just described, but sometimes it interprets the moods caused by the experiences of the right hemisphere. Emotional states appear to transfer between the hemispheres subcortically, so severing the corpus callosum does not prevent the emotional state of the right hemisphere from being transferred to the left hemisphere, even though all of the perceptions and experiences leading up to that emotional state are still isolated. One of the authors (MSG) reported on a case in which he showed some negatively arousing stimuli to the right hemisphere alone. The patient denied seeing anything; but at the same time, she was visibly upset. Her left hemisphere felt the autonomic response to the emotional stimulus, but had no idea what had caused it. When asked what was upsetting, her left brain responded that the experimenter was upsetting her. In this case, the left hemisphere felt the valence of the emotion but was unable to explain the actual cause of it, so the interpreter constructed a theory from the available information.

Probably the most notable example of the interpreter at work is an experiment done by Gazzaniga and Joseph LeDoux (1978) using a simultaneous concept task. A split-brain patient was shown two pictures, one exclusively to the left hemisphere and one exclusively to the right. Then he was asked to choose, from an array of pictures placed in full view in front of him, those that were associated with the pictures lateralized to the left and right sides of the brain (Figure 4.28). In one example of this kind of test, a picture of a chicken claw was flashed to the left hemisphere and a picture of a snow scene to the right hemisphere. Of the array of pictures placed in front of the subject, the obviously correct association is a chicken for the chicken claw and a shovel for the snow scene. Patient P.S. responded by choosing the shovel with the left hand and the chicken with the right. When asked why he chose these items, he (his left hemisphere) replied, "Oh, that's simple. The chicken claw goes with the chicken, and you need a shovel to clean out the chicken shed." Remember that the left brain has

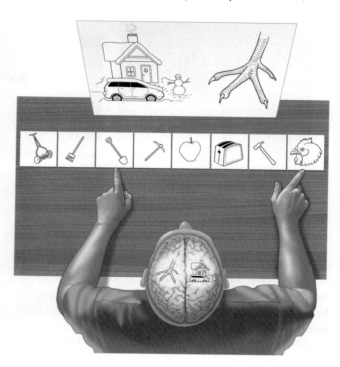

FIGURE 4.28 The Interpreter at work.
Split brain patient P.S. His left hemisphere had seen a chicken claw and his right hemisphere had seen a snow scene. When asked to point to a picture associated with the image he had just seen, his right hand (guided by his left hemisphere) pointed to the chicken (to go with the claw), and his left hand pointed to the shovel ("to clean out the chicken shed").

no knowledge about the snow scene or why he picked the shovel. The left brain, having seen the left hand's response, has to interpret that response in a context consistent with what it knows. What it knows is that there is a chicken, and his left hand is pointing to a shovel. It does not have a clue about a snow scene. What is the first sensible explanation it can come up with? Ahh—the chicken shed is full of chicken manure that must be cleaned out.

The interpreter can affect a variety of cognitive processes. For example, it may be a major contributor to the distortion of memories. In a study by Elizabeth Phelps and one of the authors (MSG), split-brain patients were asked to examine a series of pictures that depicted an everyday storyline, such as a man getting out of bed and getting ready for work (Phelps & Gazzaniga, 1992). During a recognition test, the patients were shown an intermingled series of photos that included the previously studied pictures, new pictures unrelated to the storyline, and new pictures that were closely related to the storyline (Figure 4.29). The left hemisphere falsely recognized the new pictures related to the story, while the right hemisphere rarely made that mistake. Both hemispheres were equally good at recognizing the previously studied pictures and rejecting new unrelated pictures. The right

Distractor picture (not related to story)   Distractor picture (related to story)

FIGURE 4.29 Split-brain patients first examined a series of pictures that told the story of a man getting up in the morning and getting ready to go to work. A recognition test was done a while later testing each hemisphere separately. In this test the patients were shown a stack of pictures that included the original pictures and other pictures, some that had no relation to the story and others that could have been part of the story but weren't.

hemisphere, however, was more accurate at weeding out the new related pictures. Because of the left hemisphere's tendency to make an inference that something must have occurred since it fit with its general schema of the event, it falsely recognized new related photos.

George Wolford and colleagues at Dartmouth College also demonstrated this phenomenon using a probability-guessing paradigm (Wolford et al., 2000). Participants were presented with a simple task of trying to guess which of two events would happen next. Each event had a different probability of occurrence (e.g., a red stimulus might appear 75% of the time and a green one 25% of the time), but the order of occurrence of the events was entirely random. There are two possible strategies for responding in this task: *matching* and *maximizing*. In the red–green example, frequency matching would involve guessing red 75 % of the time and guessing green 25% of the time. Because the order of occurrence was random, this strategy potentially would result in a great number of errors. The second strategy, maximizing, involves simply guessing red every time. That approach ensures an accuracy rate of 75% because red appeared 75 % of the time. Animals such as rats and goldfish maximize. Humans match. The result is that nonhuman animals perform better than humans in this task. The humans' use of this suboptimal strategy has been attributed to a propensity to try to find patterns in sequences of events, even when we are told that the sequences are random. In Las Vegas casinos, the house maximizes; you don't. We all know how that ends up.

Wolford and colleagues tested each hemisphere of split-brain patients using the probability-guessing paradigm.

They found that the left hemisphere used the frequency-matching strategy, whereas the right hemisphere maximized. When patients with unilateral damage to the left or right hemisphere were tested on the probability-guessing paradigm, the findings indicated that damage to the left hemisphere resulted in use of the maximizing strategy, whereas damage to the right hemisphere resulted in use of the suboptimal frequency-matching strategy.

Together, these findings suggest that the right hemisphere outperforms the left hemisphere because the right hemisphere approaches the task in the simplest possible manner, with no attempt to form complicated hypotheses about the task. The left hemisphere, on the other hand, engages in the human tendency to find order in chaos. The left hemisphere persists in forming hypotheses about the sequence of events, even in the face of evidence that no pattern exists. Although this tendency to search for causal relationships has many potential benefits, it can lead to suboptimal behavior when there is no simple causal relationship. Some common errors in decision making are consistent with the notion that we are prone to search for and posit causal relationships, even when the evidence is insufficient or random. This search for causal explanations appears to be a left-hemisphere activity and is the hallmark of the interpreter.

Note, however, that the right hemisphere is not devoid of causal reasoning. Matt Roser and colleagues (2005) discovered that while judgments of *causal inference* are best when the information is presented in the right visual field to the left hemisphere, judgments of *causal perception* are better when the information is presented in the left visual field. In one experiment, Roser had both control and split-brain participants watch a scenario in which two switches are pressed, either alone or together. When switch A is pressed, a light goes on; when B is pressed, it does not go on; when both are pressed, it does come on. When asked what caused the light to come on, only the left brain could make the *inference* that it was switch A. In a separate test, Roser had the same participants look at films of two balls interacting. Either one ball hits the second and it moves; one hits the second and there is a time gap before it moves; or one comes close, but there is a space gap, and the second one moves. The subject is asked if one ball caused the other to move. In this case, the right brain could determine the causal nature of the collision. These results suggest that the right hemisphere is more adept at detecting that one object is influencing another object in both time and space—computations essential for causal perception.

To perceive objects in the environment as unified, the visual system must often extrapolate from incomplete information about contours and boundaries. Paul Corballis and colleagues (1999) used stimuli containing illusory contours to reveal that the right hemisphere can perceptually process some things better than the left can. As can be seen in Figure 4.30, both the left and right

FIGURE 4.30 The human right hemisphere can process some things better than the left.
While either hemisphere can decide whether the illusory shapes in the left column are "fat" or "thin," if outlines are added then only the right hemisphere can still tell the difference. The right hemisphere is able to perceive the whole when only a part is visible, known as amodal completion.

hemispheres perceived a fat shape in the top left figure and a skinny shape in the lower left figure, but only the right hemisphere could perceive the same shapes in the figures of amodal completion on the right side. Corballis termed this ability by the right hemisphere as the "right hemisphere interpreter."

The unique specialization of the left hemisphere—the interpreter—allows our mind to seek explanations for internal and external events in order to produce appropriate response behaviors. It is a powerful mechanism that, once glimpsed, makes investigators wonder how often our brains make spurious correlations. As we noted earlier and will see in Chapter 9, the interpreter also attempts to explain our emotional states and moods. Finally, as we discuss at the end of the chapter, this specialization offers us unique insight into the nature of our conscious awareness.

Evidence From Patients With Unilateral Cortical Lesions

Research on hemispheric specialization has not been limited to split-brain studies. Many researchers have examined the performance of patients with unilateral, focal brain lesions, which we present in this section. We then close this portion of the chapter with some clever experimental designs that test the differential processing of the two hemispheres in people with intact brains.

When testing patients having unilateral brain lesions, the basic idea has been to compare the performance of patients with right-hemisphere lesions against those with left-hemisphere lesions. An appealing feature of this approach is that there is no need to lateralize the stimuli to one side or the other. Laterality effects are assumed to arise because of the unilateral lesions. If lesions to the left hemisphere result in more disruption in reading tasks, for example, then the deficit is attributed to the hemisphere's specialization in reading processes. To properly interpret these types of studies, it is necessary to carry out double dissociations (see Chapter 3) to determine whether similar lesions to the opposite hemisphere produce a similar deficit. For instance, it has been demonstrated consistently that lesions in the left hemisphere can produce deficits in language functions (such as speaking and reading) that are not seen in patients with comparable lesions to the right hemisphere. Similarly, lesions to the right hemisphere can disrupt spatial orientation, such as the ability to accurately locate visually presented items. Comparable lesions to the left hemisphere do not cause corresponding spatial deficits.

Because information can travel along multiple pathways through the brain, it is important to study lateralization by comparing results of experiments using a number of independent methods. Are interhemispheric connections between the two halves of the cerebral cortex always *necessary* for spatial processing? Carol Colby and her colleagues at the University of Pittsburgh (Berman et al., 2005) used a clever method to ask if updating of spatial information can occur without a corpus callosum. They based their experiment on the understanding that our brain constructs a dynamic map of space as our eyes move about collecting visual information. Further, this information—stored as retinotopic coordinates—can be updated as we "scan" our memory to reconstruct where something was previously located. First, split-brain monkeys (including the anterior commissure), while focusing on a fixation point (FP in Figure 4.31), were shown two targets in succession: T1 remained on the screen, and T2 was rapidly extinguished. Next, the monkeys had to turn their gaze to T1 (first eye movement) and then, from memory, they were to look toward the location of T2 (second eye movement). Neurophysiological studies have shown that when the eyes move to the first target, the retinotopic coordinates of the second target are updated in our memory. Interestingly, when T2 was located between FP and T1, the memory trace of T2's location shifts between the monkey's hemispheres (see the left-hand panel in Figure 4.31a). This happens because T2 was seen in the right visual field when the monkey was staring at FP; but when its gaze shifts to T1, then the relative position of T2 is now left of the location of T1, so it is now considered to be in the left visual field, which is mapped onto the right hemisphere. (Recall that our visual system is highly contralateralized.) If this shift requires the corpus callosum, animals that have undergone the callosotomy procedure should fail miserably. And they do, for a while. Surprisingly, though, the animals quickly mastered the task (blue curve in Figure 4.31b). One hypothesis is that, in the absence of transcallosal connections, subcortical pathways may be sufficient to support the transfer of visuospatial information.

In extreme cases in humans, however, the hemispheric biases for one level of representation can completely override other levels. In the case study at the beginning of this chapter, W.J. was unable to manipulate blocks into their global configuration when he was restricted to using his right hand. Similar dramatic things happen with stroke victims. Figure 4.32 displays drawings made by patients who recently had a stroke in either the right or the left hemisphere. They were shown a hierarchical stimulus and asked to reproduce it from memory. Drawings from patients with left-hemisphere lesions faithfully followed the contour, but without any hint of local elements. In contrast, patients with right-hemisphere lesions produced only local elements. Note that this pattern was consistent whether the stimuli were

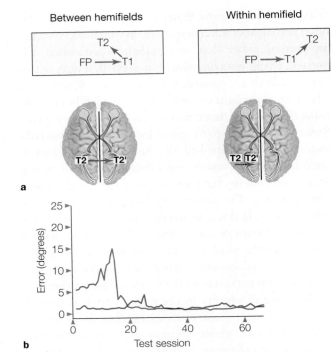

FIGURE 4.31 Interhemispheric communication in split-brain monkeys.

(a) Experimental setup; details are in the text. **(b)** Spatial error was measured by the difference between the end of the second eye movement and the target location. Accuracy was near perfect when the second eye movement was in the same direction as the first (red curve). During the initial test sessions, the monkey failed to move its eyes to the second location in the across-hemifield condition (blue curve) and generally moved its eyes straight above the end of the first eye movement. The increase in error starting around the fifth session occurred when the animal generated large eye movements in attempting to locate the second target. With subsequent sessions, performance quickly improved, and eventually the monkey was equally accurate in both conditions, suggesting that interhemispheric transfer could be accomplished by intact subcortical pathways.

linguistic or nonlinguistic; hence, the representational deficits were not restricted to certain stimuli. Note also that, because of the plasticity of the brain, such stark differences might dissipate and not be seen months after the stroke.

Evidence From the Normal Brain

Researchers have also designed clever experiments to test the differential processing of the two hemispheres in people with intact brains. In the visual domain, comparisons are made between presentations of stimuli to the left or right visual field. Although this procedure ensures that information will be projected initially to the contralateral hemisphere, the potential for rapid transcortical transfer is high. Even so, consistent differences are

Linguistic stimulus

| Target stimulus | Lesion in right-hemisphere | Lesion in left-hemisphere |

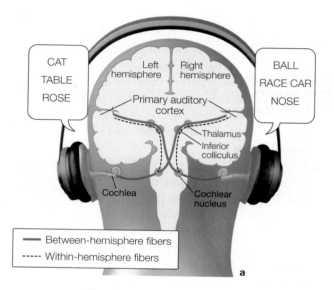

a

Nonlinguistic stimulus

| Target stimulus | Lesion in right-hemisphere | Lesion in left-hemisphere |

b

FIGURE 4.32 Extreme failures of hierarchical processing following brain damage.
Two patients were asked to draw the two figures shown in the left column of each panel. The patient with right-hemisphere damage was quite accurate in producing the local element—the Z in (a) or the square in (b)—but failed to arrange these elements into the correct global configuration. The patient with left-hemisphere damage drew the overall shapes but left out all of the local elements. Note that for each patient, the drawings were quite consistent for both the linguistic (a) and the nonlinguistic (b) stimuli, suggesting a task-independent representational deficit.

observed depending on which visual hemifield is stimulated. For example, participants are more adept at recognizing whether a briefly presented string of letters forms a word when the stimulus is shown in the right visual field than they are when it is presented in the left visual field. Such results led to the hypotheses that transfer of information between the hemispheres is of limited functional utility, or that the information becomes degraded during transfer. Thus, we conclude that performance is dominated by the contralateral hemisphere with peripheral visual input.

Studies of auditory perception similarly attempt to isolate the input to one hemisphere. As in vision work, the stimuli can be presented monaurally—that is, restricted to one ear. Because auditory pathways are not as strictly lateralized as visual pathways (see Figure 5.3 on p. 168), however, an alternative methodology for isolating the input is the **dichotic listening task** shown in Figure 4.33a. In this task, introduced in the early 1970s by Doreen Kimura (1973), two competing messages are presented

simultaneously, one to each ear, and the subject tries to report both messages. The ipsilateral projections from each ear presumably are suppressed when a message comes over the contralateral pathway from the other ear.

In a typical study, participants heard a series of dichotically presented words. When asked to repeat as many words as possible, participants consistently produced words that had been presented to the right ear—an effect dubbed the *right-ear advantage* (Figure 4.33b). Results like these mesh well with expectations that the left hemisphere is dominant for language.

b

FIGURE 4.33 The dichotic listening task is used to compare hemispheric specialization in auditory perception.
(a) Competing messages are presented, one to the left ear and one to the right ear. Auditory information is projected bilaterally. Although most of the ascending fibers from the cochlear nucleus project to the contralateral thalamus, some fibers ascend on the ipsilateral side. (b) Participants are asked either to report the stimuli or to judge whether a probe stimulus was part of the dichotic message. Comparisons focus on whether they heard the reported information in the right or left ear, with the assumption that the predominant processing occurred in the contralateral hemisphere. With linguistic stimuli, participants are more accurate in reporting the information presented to the right ear.

The demonstration of visual and auditory performance asymmetries with lateralized stimuli generated great excitement among psychologists. Here at last were simple methods for learning about hemispheric specialization in neurologically healthy people. It is not surprising that thousands of laterality studies on healthy participants have been conducted using almost every imaginable stimulus manipulation.

The limitations of this kind of laterality research should be kept in mind (Efron, 1990), however.

- The effects are small and inconsistent, perhaps because healthy people have two functioning hemispheres connected by an intact corpus callosum that transfers information quite rapidly.
- There is a bias in the scientific review process to publish papers that find significant differences over papers that report no differences. It is much more exciting to report asymmetries in the way we remember lateralized pictures of faces than to report that effects are similar for right- and left-visual-field presentations.
- Interpretation is problematic. What can be inferred from an observed asymmetry in performance with lateralized stimuli? In the preceding examples, the advantages of the right visual field and the right ear were assumed to reflect that these inputs had better access to the language processes of the left hemisphere. Perhaps, however, people are just better at identifying information in the right visual field or in the right ear.

To rule out this last possibility, investigators must identify tasks that produce an advantage for the left ear or left visual field. For example, shortly after Kimura's initial work, scientists discovered that people are better at recognizing the left-ear member of dichotic melody pairs; indeed, a double dissociation happens when participants are presented with dichotic pairs of sung melodies (Bartholomeus, 1974). We find a right-ear advantage for the song's words but a left-ear advantage for its melodies (Figure 4.34).

TAKE-HOME MESSAGES

- The left hemisphere is dominant for language, speech, and major problem solving; the right hemisphere appears specialized for visuospatial tasks such as drawing cubes and other three-dimensional patterns. Thus, split-brain patients cannot name or describe visual and tactile stimuli presented to the right hemisphere, because the sensory information is disconnected from the dominant left (speech) hemisphere.
- There may be two lexicons (associations of words with specific meanings), one in each hemisphere. The right

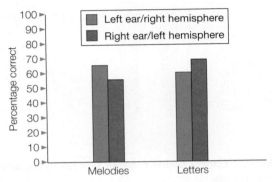

FIGURE 4.34 A right-ear advantage is not found on all tasks. Participants listened to a dichotic message in which each ear was presented with a series of letters sung to short melodies. When given a recognition memory test, participants were more accurate on the letters task for stimuli heard in the right ear. In contrast, a left-ear advantage was observed when the participants were tested on the melodies.

hemisphere's lexicon seems organized differently from the left hemisphere's lexicon, and these lexicons are accessed in different ways.
- The right hemisphere has been linked to one aspect of speech perception, prosody, which is the connotative aspect of oral language—the way we vary articulation to convey affect or intonation.
- Some studies show that the right hemisphere is specialized for visuospatial processing.
- The right hemisphere has special processes devoted to the efficient detection of upright faces. The left hemisphere outperforms the right hemisphere when the faces are dissimilar, and the right hemisphere outperforms the left when the faces are similar.
- Although touching any part of the body is noted by either hemisphere, patterned somatosensory information is lateralized. Thus, a split-brain patient who is holding an object in the left hand is unable to find an identical object with the right hand.
- Surprisingly, split-brain patients can use either hemisphere to direct attention to positions in either the left or the right visual field.

- The right hemisphere appears to be specialized for causal perception (the ability to detect that one object is influencing another object in both time and space), and the left hemisphere is more capable with tasks that require causal inference.
- Using Navon's stimuli, investigators showed that patients with left-sided lesions were slow to identify local targets, and patients with right-sided lesions were slow with global targets, thus demonstrating that the left hemisphere is more adept at representing local information and the right hemisphere is better with global information.
- The left hemisphere contains what Michael Gazzaniga and Joseph LeDoux have called the interpreter, a system that seeks explanations for internal and external events in order to produce appropriate response behaviors.

The Evolutionary Basis of Hemispheric Specialization

So far in this chapter, we have reviewed general principles of hemispheric specialization in humans. Humans, of course, have evolutionary ancestors, so we might expect to find evidence of lateralized functions in other animals. Indeed, this is the case.

Hemispheric Specialization in Nonhumans

Due to the central role of language in hemispheric specialization, laterality research has focused primarily on humans. But the evolutionary pressures that underlie hemispheric specialization—the need for unified action, rapid communication, and reduced costs associated with interhemispheric processing—would also be potentially advantageous to other species. It is now clear that hemispheric specialization is not a uniquely human feature (Bradshaw & Rogers, 1993).

In birds, almost all of the optic fibers cross at the optic chiasm, ensuring that all of the visual input from each eye projects solely to the contralateral hemisphere. The lack of crossed and uncrossed fibers probably reflects the fact that there is little overlap in the visual fields of birds, owing to the lateral placement of the eyes (Figure 4.35). Moreover, birds lack a corpus callosum, so communication between the visual systems within each hemisphere is limited, and functional asymmetries might result. Several asymmetries are known in birds. Chickens and pigeons are better at categorizing stimuli viewed by the right eye and left hemisphere than by the left eye and right hemisphere. You may wonder what is meant when

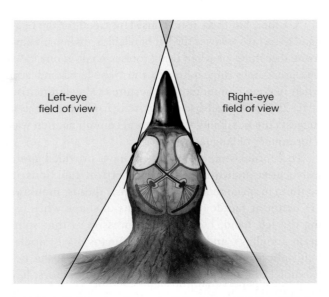

FIGURE 4.35 Visual pathways in birds are completely crossed. This organization indicates that there is little overlap in the regions of space seen by each eye, and thus the visual input to the left hemisphere is independent of the visual input to the right hemisphere. This anatomical segregation would be expected to favor the emergence of hemispheric asymmetries.

a chicken categorizes stimuli. Here is one such category: Edible or not? Chickens are more proficient in discriminating food from nonfood items when stimuli are presented to the right eye, whereas the right hemisphere (left eye) is more adept when they are trained to respond to unique properties like color, size, and shape, or when the task requires them to learn the exact location of a food source.

Almost all birds have a communication system: They caw, tweet, and chirp to scare away enemies, mark territory, and lure mates. In many species, the mechanisms of song production depend on structures in the left hemisphere. Fernando Nottebohm of Rockefeller University discovered that sectioning the canary's hypoglossal nerve in its left hemisphere severely disrupted song production (Nottebohm, 1980). In contrast, right-hemisphere lesions had little effect. A similar effect can be found in other bird species, although in some species lesions to either hemisphere can interfere with song production.

Nonhuman primates also show differences in hemispheric structure and perhaps function. Old World monkeys and apes have lateral fissures that slope upward in the right hemisphere, similar to the asymmetry found in humans. Whether these anatomical asymmetries are associated with behavioral specializations remains unclear. Unlike humans, however, nonhuman primates do not commonly show a predominance of right-handedness. Individual animals may show a preference for one hand or the other, but there is no consistent trend for the right hand to be favored over the left hand, either when making manual gestures or when using tools, except in one case. The great apes appear to use the right hand and arm when making communicative gestures (Meguerditchian et al., 2010). We will discuss this more in Chapter 11, as it suggests the possibility that gestural communication was a forerunner of language.

Perceptual studies, however, have provided more provocative indications of asymmetrical functions in nonhuman primates. Like humans, rhesus monkeys are better at tactile discriminations of shape when using the left hand. Even more impressive is that split-brain monkeys and split-brain humans have similar hemispheric interactions in visual perception tasks. For example, in a face recognition task, the monkeys, like humans, have a right-hemisphere advantage; in a line orientation task, the monkeys share a left-hemisphere advantage. The visual system of monkeys, however, transfers visual information across an intact anterior commissure, but there is no transfer of visual information across the human anterior commissure. In addition, left-hemisphere lesions in the Japanese macaque can impair the animal's ability to comprehend the vocalizations of conspecifics. Unlike the effects on some aphasic patients, however, this deficit is mild and transient. There is also evidence from split-brain monkeys that unlike humans, their left brain is better at spatial judgments. This observation is tantalizing, because it is consistent with the idea that the evolution of language in the left hemisphere has resulted in the loss of some visuospatial abilities.

In summary, like humans, nonhuman species exhibit differences in the function of the two hemispheres. The question remains, how should we interpret these findings? Does the left hemisphere, which specializes in birdsong and human language, reflect a common evolutionary antecedent? If so, this adaptation has an ancient history, because humans and birds have not shared a common ancestor since before the dinosaurs. The hemispheric specialization that occurs in many species may instead reflect a general design principle of the brain.

Modularity

In this chapter, we have reviewed general principles of hemispheric specialization in humans. A first step in understanding why these specializations exist is to look at what is known about the structure of the brain and its organizing principles. In Chapter 2 (see the box "How the Brain Works: Billions and Billions"), we briefly touched on the idea that certain "wiring laws" apply to the evolutionary development of the large human brain

(Striedter, 2005). We saw that as the brain grew larger, the proportional connectivity decreases, thus changing the internal structure and resulting in a decrease in overall connectivity.

The wiring plan that evolved, which has a high degree of local efficiency and fast communication with the global network, is known as "small-world" architecture (Watts & Strogatz, 1998). This structure is common to many complex systems, that is, systems whose overall behavior can be characterized as more than the sum of their parts. This mode of organization is characterized by many short connections between components, resulting in faster signaling and lower energy requirements. It also has a high level of clustering, which gives the overall system greater tolerance to the failure of individual components or connections. The local networks in the brain are made up of elements (neurons) that are more highly connected to one another than to elements in other networks. This division of circuits into numerous networks both reduces the interdependence of networks and increases their robustness. What's more, it facilitates behavioral adaptation (Kirschner & Gerhart, 1998), because each network can both function and change its function without affecting the rest of the system. These local specialized networks, which can perform unique functions and can adapt or evolve to external demands, are known as **modules**. The general concept of modularity is that the components of a system can be categorized according to their functions (Bassett & Gazzaniga, 2011).

By reducing constraints on change, the principle of modularity forms the structural basis on which subsystems can evolve and adapt (Wagner et al., 2007) in a highly variable environment. Hemispheric specialization takes that idea a step further and says that cerebral asymmetries in this modular organization must also have adaptive value. Therefore, cerebral asymmetries should not be proposed lightly, and investigators must be sure they are real. For instance, during the 1990s, a popular model of the organization of memory in the brain based on early neuroimaging studies suggested that episodic encoding was predominantly a left hemisphere function and that episodic retrieval was predominantly a right hemisphere function (the model was called HERA, for hemispheric encoding/retrieval asymmetry). When this model was tested directly with split-brain patients, however, it turned out that each hemisphere was equally efficient at encoding and retrieval (M. Miller et al., 2002). This study showed that apparent asymmetries in memory encoding could be produced by varying the stimuli being encoded. Verbal material was preferentially processed in the participants' left hemisphere, and facial material was preferentially processed in the right—a pattern somewhat reminiscent of the chicken's and pigeon's lateralized object discrimination.

Hemispheric Specialization: A Dichotomy in Function or Stylishly Different?

Laterality researchers continually grapple with appropriate ways to describe asymmetries in the function of the two hemispheres (Allen, 1983; Bradshaw & Nettleton, 1981; Bryden, 1982). While early hypotheses fixed on the stimuli's properties and the tasks employed, a more recent approach is to look for differences in *processing style*. This concept suggests that the two hemispheres process information in complementary ways, dividing the workload of processing a stimulus by tackling it differently. From this perspective, the left hemisphere has been described as analytic and sequential, and the right hemisphere is viewed as holistic and parallel.

Hemispheric specializations may emerge because certain tasks benefit from one processing style or another. Language, for example, is seen as sequential: We hear speech as a continuous stream that requires rapid dissection and analysis of its component parts. Spatial representations, in contrast, call for not just perceiving the component parts, but seeing them as a coherent whole. The finding that the right hemisphere is more efficient at global processing is consistent with this idea.

Although this analytic–holistic dichotomy has intuitive appeal, it is difficult to know whether a particular cognitive task would benefit more from analytic or holistic processing. In many cases, the theoretical interpretation disintegrates into a circular re-description of results. For example, a right-ear advantage exists in the perception of consonants, but no asymmetry is found for vowels; consonants require the sequential, analytic processors of the left hemisphere, and vowel perception entails a more holistic form of processing. Here we have redefined the requirements of processing vowels and consonants according to our theoretical framework, rather than using the data to establish and modify that theoretical framework.

With verbal–spatial and analytic–holistic hypotheses, we assume that a single fundamental dichotomy can characterize the differences in function between the two hemispheres. The appeal of "dichotomania" is one of parsimony: The simplest account of hemispheric specialization rests on a single difference. Current dichotomies, however, all have their limitations.

It is also reasonable to suppose that a fundamental dichotomy between the two hemispheres is a fiction. Hemispheric asymmetries have been observed in many task domains: language, motor control, attention, and object recognition. Perhaps specializations are specific to particular task domains and are the consequences of more primitive hemispheric specializations. There need not be a causal connection between hemispheric specialization in motor control (e.g., why people are right- or left-handed) and hemispheric differences in representing language or visuospatial information. Maybe the commonality across task domains is their evolution: As the two hemispheres became segregated, they shared an impetus for the evolution of systems that were non-identical.

Asymmetry in how information is processed, represented, and used may be a more efficient and flexible design principle than redundancy across the hemispheres. With a growing demand for cortical space, perhaps the forces of natural selection began to modify one hemisphere but not the other. Because the corpus callosum exchanges information between the hemispheres, mutational events could occur in one lateralized cortical area while leaving the contralateral hemisphere intact, thus continuing to provide the previous cortical function to the entire cognitive system. In short, asymmetrical development allowed for no-cost extensions; cortical capacity could expand by reducing redundancy and extending its space for new cortical zones. Support for this idea is provided by the fascinating work of Galuske and colleagues, which has revealed that differences in the neuronal organization of the left and right Brodmann area 22 are related to the processing of auditory signals associated with human speech (Galuske et al., 2000; Gazzaniga, 2000). The left is specialized for word detection and generation; the right is specialized for melody, pitch, and intensity, which are properties of all auditory communication from bird tweets to monkey calls.

The idea of asymmetrical processing also underscores an important point in modern conceptualizations of hemispheric specialization—namely, that the two hemispheres may work in concert to perform a task, even though their contributions may vary widely. There is no need to suppose that some sort of master director decides which hemisphere is needed for a task. While language is predominantly the domain of the left hemisphere, the right hemisphere also might contribute, although the types of representations it derives may not be efficient or capable of certain tasks. In addition, the left hemisphere does not defer to the right hemisphere on visuospatial tasks, but processes this information in a different way. By seeing the brain organized in this way, we begin to realize that much of what we learn from clinical tests of hemispheric specialization tells us more about our tasks rather than the computations performed by each hemisphere. This point is also evident in split-brain research. With the notable exception of speech production, each hemisphere has some competence in every cognitive domain.

Is There a Connection Between Handedness and Left-Hemisphere Language Dominance?

With all this talk of laterality, your left hemisphere no doubt is searching for a causal relationship between the predominance of right-handedness and the left hemisphere's specialization for language. Join the club. Many researchers have tried to establish a causal relationship between the two by pointing out that the dominant role of the left hemisphere in language strongly correlates with **handedness**. About 96% of right-handers are left-hemisphere dominant for speech. Most left-handers (60%), however, are also left-hemisphere dominant for speech (Risse et al., 1997). Because left-handers constitute only 7% to 8% of the total population, this means that 96% of humans, regardless of which hand is dominant, have a left-hemisphere specialization for language.

Some theorists point to the need for a single motor center as the critical factor. Although there may be benefits to perceiving information in parallel, that is, it is okay for the input to be asymmetric, our response to these stimuli—the output—must be unified. Imagine what it would be like if your left hemisphere could choose one course of action while your right hemisphere opted for another. What happens when one hemisphere is commanding half your body to sit, and the other hemisphere is telling the other half to vacuum? Our brains may have two halves, but we have only one body. By localizing action planning in a single hemisphere, the brain achieves unification.

One hypothesis is that the left hemisphere is specialized for the planning and production of sequential movements. Speech certainly depends on such movements. Our ability to produce speech is the result of many evolutionary changes that include the shape of the vocal tract and articulatory apparatus. These adaptations make it possible for us to communicate, and to do so at phenomenally high rates (think of auctioneers); the official record is 637 words per minute, set on the late-1980s British television show *Motormouth*. Such competence requires exquisite control of the sequential gestures of the vocal cords, jaw, tongue, and other articulators.

The left hemisphere has also been linked to sequential movements in domains that are not involved with speech. For example, left-hemisphere lesions are more likely to cause apraxia—a deficit in motor planning, in which the ability to produce coherent actions is lost, even though the muscles work properly and the person understands and wants to perform an action (see Chapter 8). In addition,

oral movements have left-hemisphere dominance, whether the movements create speech or nonverbal facial gestures. Evidence suggests that facial gestures are more pronounced on the right side of the face, and activation of the right facial muscles occurs more quickly than activation of the corresponding muscles on the left. Time-lapse photography reveals that smiles light up the right side of the face first. Hence, the left hemisphere may have a specialized role in the control of sequential actions, and this role may underlie hemispheric asymmetries in both language and motor functions.

Some have theorized that the recursive processing capabilities used by the speech center are available to other left-hemisphere functions, including control of the right hand. With bipedalism, the hands became free to operate independently. This ability is unlike that of our quadruped friends, whose forelimbs and hind limbs are used primarily for locomotion. Here, symmetry is vital for the animal to move in a linear trajectory. If the limbs on one side of the body were longer or stronger than the other, an animal would move in a circle. As our ancestors adopted an upright posture, however, they no longer had to use their hands to move symmetrically.

The generative and recursive aspects of an emerging communication system also could have been applied to the way hands manipulated objects, and the lateralization of these properties would have favored the right hand. The favoring of one hand over another would be most evident in tool use. Although nonhuman primates and birds can fashion primitive tools to gain access to foods that are out of reach or encased in hard shells, humans manufacture tools generatively: We design tools to solve an immediate problem, and we also can recombine the parts to create new tools. The wheel, an efficient component of devices for transportation, can be used to extract energy from a flowing river or record information in a compact, easily accessible format. Handedness, then, is most apparent in our use of tools. As an example, right-handers differ only slightly in their ability to use either hand to block balls thrown at them. But when they are asked to catch or throw the balls, the dominant hand has a clear advantage.

Or, the situation could have been reversed. The left hemisphere's dominance in language may be a consequence of an existing specialization in motor control. The asymmetrical use of hands to perform complex actions, including those associated with tool use, may have promoted the development of language. From comparative studies of language, we believe that most sentence forms convey actions; infants issue commands such as "come" or "eat" before they start using adjectives (e.g., "hungry"). If the right hand was being used for many of these actions, there may have been a selective pressure

HOW THE BRAIN WORKS
To Approach or Withdraw: The Cerebral Tug-of-War

It is Friday night, and you are heading to a party at the apartment of a friend of a friend. You arrive and look around: Loud music and swirling bodies move about the living room, and a throng has gathered in the kitchen around a counter laid out with chips and dips. Unfortunately, your friend is nowhere to be seen, and you have yet to recognize a single person among the crowd.

Your reaction will depend on a number of factors: how comfortable you feel mingling with strangers, how lively you are feeling tonight, whether a host approaches and introduces you to a few of the guests. Unless you have a flair for flamboyance, you are unlikely to head straight to the dance floor. A more likely response is that you will head for the kitchen and find yourself something to drink.

Richard Davidson (1995) of the University of Wisconsin proposed that the fundamental tension for any mobile organism is between approach and withdrawal. Is a stimulus a potential food source to be approached and gobbled up, or a potential predator that must be avoided? Even the most primitive organisms display at least a rudimentary distinction between approach and withdrawal behaviors. The evolution of more complex nervous systems has provided mechanisms to modulate the tension between these two behavioral poles: We might overcome our initial reaction to flee the party, knowing that if we stay we are likely to make a few new friends and have a few good laughs.

According to Davidson, this tension involves a delicate interplay between processing within the medial regions of the prefrontal cortex in the right and left cerebral hemispheres. The prefrontal cortex is a major point of convergence in the central nervous system, processing information not only from other cortical regions but also from subcortical regions, especially those involved in emotional processing (see Chapter 10). In Davidson's theory, these inputs are processed asymmetrically. Left-hemisphere processing is biased to promote approach behaviors; in contrast, right-hemisphere processing is biased to promote withdrawal behaviors.

This theory has provided an organizing principle to evaluate the changes in behavior that follow neurological damage. For example, damage to the left frontal lobe can result in severe depression, a state in which the primary symptom is withdrawal and inactivity. Although we might expect depression to be a normal response to brain injury, the opposite profile has been reported in patients with right frontal damage. These patients may appear manic. Damage to the right-hemisphere "withdrawal" system biases the patient to be socially engaging, even when such behaviors are no longer appropriate.

More compelling evidence comes from physiological studies that have looked at the brain's response to affective, or emotional, stimuli (Gur et al., 1994). By their very nature, positive stimuli are likely to elicit approach, and negative stimuli will elicit withdrawal or avoidance. Thus, depending on its valence, an affective stimulus is likely to engage the two hemispheres differentially.

Davidson (1995) tested this idea by taking electroencephalographic (EEG) measurements while participants viewed short video clips that were chosen to evoke either positive (e.g., a puppy playing with flowers) or negative (e.g., a leg being amputated) emotional reactions. The EEG activity during these stimuli was compared to that during a baseline condition in which the participants watched a neutral video segment. As predicted, more neural activity was observed over the left frontal lobe when the participants watched the positive videos in comparison to the negative videos. In contrast, a huge increase in activity over the right frontal lobe was recorded while participants viewed the disturbing video.

There are, of course, individual differences in this cerebral tug-of-war between approach and withdrawal. Depression has been linked to an abnormal imbalance favoring neural activity in the right hemisphere. Whether the imbalance preceded or followed the depression remains unclear. More provocative, EEG asymmetries in 3-year-old children are correlated with how well the kids tolerate being separated from their mothers. Children showing higher basal EEG activity in the right hemisphere are more inhibited, staying next to their mother even when surrounded by an array of new toys. Children with higher basal EEG activity in the left hemisphere are quite content to leave their mother to play with the toys.

The study of hemispheric asymmetries in emotion is in its infancy. Before the 1990s, physiological studies of emotion generally focused on interactions between the subcortical limbic system and the cortex. In developing his account of cortical differences, Davidson started from a consideration of a marked behavioral dichotomy. What remains to be explored are the computations that might lead to one type of behavior over another, and whether these computations are related to those uncovered in the study of hemispheric specialization in other cognitive domains.

In the interim, however, we might cull from this work one strategy to test the next time we find ourselves alone at a party: Start talking to someone, just to get the left hemisphere active. Perhaps the reason why the left hemisphere appears specialized to promote approach behavior is its dominance in language, that most social of all behaviors.

for the left hemisphere to be more proficient in establishing these symbolic representations.

But remember, correlation is not causation. It is also possible (and your left brain is just going to have to get over it) that the mechanisms producing hemispheric specialization in language and motor performance are unrelated. The correlation between these two cardinal signs of hemispheric asymmetry is not perfect. Not only do a small percentage of right-handers exhibit either right-hemisphere language or bilateral language, but in at least half of the left-handed population, the left hemisphere is dominant for language.

These differences may reflect the fact that handedness is affected at least partly by environmental factors. Children may be encouraged to use one hand over the other, perhaps owing to cultural biases or to parental pressure. Or handedness and language dominance may simply reflect different factors. Fred Previc (1991), a researcher with the U.S. Air Force, proposed an intriguing hypothesis along these lines. According to Previc, the left-hemisphere dominance for language is related primarily to a subtle asymmetry in the skull's structure. In most individuals, the orofacial bones on the left side of the face are slightly larger—an enlargement that encroaches on middle-ear function and could limit the sensitivity to certain sound frequencies. Previc maintained that this enlargement has a deleterious effect on the projection of auditory information to the right hemisphere, especially in the frequency region that carries most of the critical information for speech. As such, the left hemisphere is favored for phonemic analysis and develops a specialization for language.

In contrast to this explanation of hemispheric specialization, Previc (1991) argued that handedness is determined by the position of the fetus during gestation (Figure 4.36). Two thirds of fetuses are oriented with the head downward and the right ear facing the mother's front. This orientation leads to greater in vitro stimulation of the left utricle, part of the vestibular apparatus in the inner ear that is critical for balance. This asymmetrical stimulation will lead to a more developed vestibular system in the right side of the brain, causing babies to be born with a bias to use the left side of the body for balance and the maintenance of posture. Thus the right side of the body is freed for more exploratory movement, resulting in right-handedness. This still leaves 33% with reversed symmetry, but only 7% to 8% of the population actually is reversed. So other factors, either environmental or biological, likely play a role. According to Previc's theories, different factors determine language asymmetries and handedness. Current data are too scant for evaluating either mechanism, but they do raise the interesting possibility that many

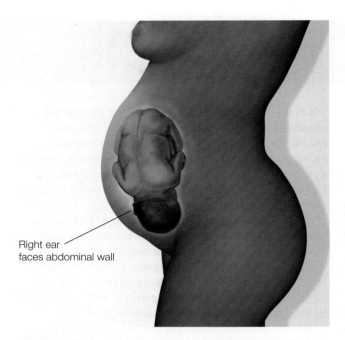

Right ear faces abdominal wall

FIGURE 4.36 The womb may affect postnatal manual coordination. According to Fred Previc, functional asymmetries in manual coordination are sometimes attributed to the prenatal environment of the fetus. The position of the fetus in the uterus is thought to influence prenatal vestibular experience. Most fetuses are oriented with the right ear facing outward, resulting in a larger vestibular signal in the right hemisphere. At birth, the left side of the body is more stable, freeing the right hand for exploration.

unrelated factors determine patterns of hemispheric specialization.

Several genetic models attempt to explain the distribution of handedness among humans. One model states that one gene has two alleles: The *D* (as in the Latin *dextro*) allele specifies right-handedness, and the *C* allele leaves the handedness to chance. In this model, 100% of *DD* individuals are right-handed, 75% of the heterozygotes (*CD*) are right-handed, and 50% of *CC* individuals are right-handed (McManus, 1999). Marian Annett proposed a different model that could also fit with Previc's theory, in which handedness exists on a spectrum and the alleles are for cerebral dominance rather than for handedness (Annett, 2002). In her model, right-handedness implies left-hemisphere dominance. Her two alleles are the "right shift" allele (RS^+) and an ambivalent allele that has no directional shift (RS^-). Homozygous individuals, designated RS^{++}, would be strongly right-handed; heterozygous individuals (RS^{+-}) would be less strongly right-handed; and the handedness of homozygous (RS^{--}) individuals would be up to chance, but still on a spectrum from right- to left-handed, where some would be ambidextrous. Although genes may play a role in handedness or other asymmetries, no genes for handedness have been identified.

Split-Brain Research as a Window into Conscious Experience

As we mentioned at the beginning of the chapter, the fundamental mystery presented by split-brain patients remains unsolved; that is, these patients feel no difference in their conscious experience before and after surgery that disconnects their two hemispheres. This essential finding, along with the discovery of the interpreter, specialized to the left hemisphere, may provide a unique window into the true nature of our conscious experience.

One astonishing quality of split-brain patients is that they are utterly unaware of their special status. Although they have lost the ability to transfer most information between their cerebral hemispheres, it has no impact on their overall psychological state. For example, it doesn't bother them that following the callosotomy, they have lost the ability to verbalize what is in their left visual field. It is not because they have been warned that it will occur; they do not even comment that it is occurring. The left hemisphere in these patients doesn't seem to miss the right hemisphere at all. More than that, the left brain acts as if the right brain had never been there. This finding has major implications for understanding the role of the brain in conscious experience.

Perhaps consciousness is not a single, generalized process. Rather, consciousness may be an emergent property, arising out of hundreds or thousands of specialized systems—that is, modules (Gazzaniga, 2011). These specialized neural circuits enable the processing and mental representation of specific aspects of conscious experience. Many of these modules may be connected to some of the other modules, but not to most of them. And these components compete for attention. For instance, the neural circuits responsible for the itch on your back, the memory of Friday night's date, the rumblings of your stomach, the feeling of the sun on your cheek, and the paper that you are working on are fighting for attention. From moment to moment, different modules win the competition, and its neural representation is what you are conscious of in that moment. *This dynamic, moment-to-moment cacophony of systems comprises our consciousness.* Yet, the weird thing is that we don't experience the chatter going on up there as the battle rages. What emerges is a unified experience in which our consciousness flows smoothly from one thought to the next, comprising a single unified narrative. The interpreter is crafting this narrative. This specialized neural system continually interprets and rationalizes our behavior, emotions, and thoughts after they occur.

Remarkably, this view of consciousness is completely dependent on the existence of the specialized modules. If a particular module is impaired or loses its inputs, it alerts the whole system that something is wrong. For example, if the optic nerve is severed, the patient immediately notices that he is blinded. But if the module itself is removed, as in the case of cortical blindness (see Chapter 5), then no warning signal is sent and the specific information processed by that specialized system is no longer acknowledged (out of sight, out of mind—so to speak).

This view explains the phenomenon known as anosognosia, in which patients with certain brain lesions are unaware of and deny that they have clearly observable deficits. For instance, one whole side of their body may be paralyzed, yet they deny they have any problems.

This model of the physical basis of conscious experience can also explain the behavior of split-brain patients. When the left hemisphere's interpreter does not receive input from any of the right hemisphere's modules, then the right hemisphere and any knowledge of the right hemisphere cease to consciously exist. Thus, the split-brain patient's speaking left brain never complains about the shortcomings it may be experiencing due to its disconnection from the right brain. It doesn't know there are any. Some may argue that this is because the right hemisphere contributes little to cognition, but we have seen in this chapter that the right brain is clearly superior at a number of tasks, including part–whole relations, spatial relationships, spatial matching, veridical memory recollections, amodal completion, causal perception, and processing faces. The right hemisphere must contribute to conscious experience when the corpus callosum is intact; yet when severed, the right hemisphere is not missed. This observation is in synch with the idea that our entire conscious experience arises out of the moment-to-moment tussle as an untold number of specialized modules in the brain are vying for attention, while the left hemisphere's interpreter strings them together in a coherent narrative.

Summary

Research on laterality has provided extensive insights into the organization of the human brain. Surgical disconnection of the cerebral hemispheres has produced an extraordinary opportunity to study how perceptual and cognitive processes are distributed and coordinated within the cerebral cortex. We have seen how visual perceptual information, for example, remains strictly lateralized to one hemisphere following callosal section. Tactile-patterned information also remains lateralized, but attentional mechanisms are not divided by separation of the two hemispheres. Taken together, cortical disconnection produces two independent sensory information-processing systems that call upon a common attentional resource system in the carrying out of perceptual tasks.

Split-brain studies also have revealed the complex mosaic of mental processes that contribute to human cognition. The two hemispheres do not represent information in an identical manner, as evidenced by the fact that each hemisphere has developed its own set of specialized capacities. In the vast majority of individuals, the left hemisphere is clearly dominant for language and speech and seems to possess a uniquely human capacity to interpret behavior and to construct theories about the relationship between perceived events and feelings. Right-hemisphere superiority, on the other hand, can be seen in tasks such as facial recognition and attentional monitoring. Both hemispheres are likely to be involved in the performance of any complex task, but each contributes in its specialized manner.

Complementary studies on patients with focal brain lesions and on normal participants tested with lateralized stimuli have underscored not only the presence, but the importance, of lateralized processes for cognitive and perceptual tasks. Recent work has moved laterality research toward a more computational account of hemispheric specialization, seeking to explicate the mechanisms underlying many lateralized perceptual phenomena. These theoretical advances have moved the field away from the popular interpretations of cognitive style and have refocused researchers on understanding the computational differences and specializations of cortical regions in the two hemispheres.

Key Terms

amobarbital (p. 125)
anterior commissure (p. 128)
cerebral specialization (p. 132)
corpus callosum (p. 128)
dichotic listening task (p. 151)
functional asymmetry (p. 126)

handedness (p. 156)
heterotopic areas (p. 128)
hierarchical structure (p. 144)
homotopic areas (p. 126)
interpreter (p. 146)
module (p. 154)

planum temporale (p. 126)
posterior commissure (p. 128)
splenium (p. 128)
split-brain research (p. 123)
Sylvian fissure (p. 125)
transcortical (p. 134)
Wada test (p. 125)

Thought Questions

1. What have we learned from over 50 years of split-brain research? What are some of the questions that remain to be answered?

2. What are the strengths of testing patients who have suffered brain lesions? Are there any shortcomings to this research approach? If so, what are they? What are some of the ethical considerations?

3. Why are double dissociations diagnostic of cerebral specializations? What pitfalls exist if a conclusion is based on a single dissociation?

4. Why do you think the human brain evolved cognitive systems that are represented asymmetrically between the cerebral hemispheres? What are the advantages of asymmetrical processing? What are some possible disadvantages?

Suggested Reading

Brown, H., & Kosslyn, S. (1993). Cerebral lateralization. *Current Opinion in Neurobiology, 3*, 183–186.

Gazzaniga, M. S. (2000). Cerebral specialization and inter-hemispheric communication: Does the corpus callosum enable the human condition? *Brain, 123*, 1293–1326.

Gazzaniga, M. S. (2005). Forty-five years of split brain research and still going strong. *Nature Reviews Neuroscience, 6*, 653–659.

Gazzaniga, M. S. (2011). *Who's in charge: Free will and the science of the brain.* New York: (Ecco) Harper Row.

Hellige, J. B. (1993). *Hemispheric asymmetry: What's right and what's left.* Cambridge, MA: Harvard University Press.

Hutsler, J., & Galuske, R. A. (2003). Hemispheric asymmetries in cerebral cortical networks. *Trends in Neuroscience, 26*, 429–435.

Monet is only an eye, but my God, what an eye!

Paul Cezanne

Sensation and Perception

IN HOSPITALS ACROSS THE COUNTRY, Neurology Grand Rounds is a weekly event. There, staff neurologists, internists, and residents gather to review the most puzzling and unusual cases being treated on the ward. In Portland, Oregon, the head of neurology presented such a case. He was not puzzled about what had caused his patient's problem. That was clear. The patient, P.T., had suffered a cerebral vascular accident, commonly known as a stroke. In fact, he had sustained two strokes. The first, suffered 6 years previously, had been a left-hemisphere stroke. The patient had shown a nearly complete recovery from that stroke. P.T. had suffered a second stroke a few months before, however, and the CT scan showed that the damage was in the right hemisphere. This finding was consistent with the patient's experience of left-sided weakness, although the weakness had mostly subsided after a month.

The unusual aspect of P.T.'s case was the collection of symptoms he continued to experience 4 months later. As he tried to resume the daily routines required on his small family farm, P.T. had particular difficulty recognizing familiar places and objects. While working on a stretch of fence, for example, he might look out over the hills and suddenly realize that he did not know the landscape. It was hard for him to pick out individual dairy cows—a matter of concern lest he attempt to milk a bull! Disturbing as this was, it was not the worst of his problems. Most troubling of all, he no longer recognized the people around him, including his wife. He had no trouble seeing her and could accurately describe her actions, but when it came to identifying her, he was at a complete loss. She was completely unrecognizable to him! He knew that her parts—body, legs, arms, and head—formed a person, but P.T. failed to see these parts as belonging to a specific individual. This deficit was not limited to P.T.'s wife; he had the same problem with other members of his family and friends from his small town, a place he had lived for 66 years.

A striking feature of P.T.'s impairment was that his inability to recognize objects and people was limited to the visual modality. As soon as his wife spoke, he immediately recognized her voice. Indeed, he claimed that, on hearing her voice, the visual percept of her would "fall into place." The shape in front of him would suddenly morph into his wife. In a similar fashion, he could recognize specific objects by touching, smelling, or tasting them.

Senses, Sensation, and Perception

The overarching reason why you are sitting here reading this book today is that you had ancestors who successfully survived their environment and reproduced. One reason they were able to do this was their ability to sense and perceive things that could be threatening to their survival and then act on those perceptions. Pretty obvious, right? Less obvious is that most of these perceptions and behavioral responses never even reach people's conscious awareness, and what does reach our awareness is not an exact replica of the stimulus. This latter phenomenon becomes more evident when we are presented with optical illusions (as we see later in the chapter). *Perception* begins with a stimulus from the environment, such as sound or light, which stimulates one of the sense organs such as the ear or eye. The input from the sound or light wave is transduced into neural activity by the sense organ and sent to the brain for processing. *Sensation* refers to the early processing that goes on. The mental representation of that original stimulus, which results from the various processing events, whether it accurately reflects the stimulus or not, is called a percept. Thus, perception is the process of constructing the percept.

Our *senses* are our physiological capacities to provide input from the environment to our neurological system. Hence, our sense of sight is our capacity to capture light waves on the retina, convert them into electrical signals, and ship them on for further processing. We tend to give most of the credit for our survival to our sense of sight, but it does not operate alone. For instance, the classic "we don't have eyes in the back of our head" problem means we can't see the bear sneaking up behind us. Instead, the rustling of branches or the snap of a twig warns us. We do not see particularly well in the dark either, as many people know after stubbing a toe when groping about to find the light switch. And though the milk may look fine, one sniff tells you to dump it down the drain. Although these examples illustrate the interplay of senses on the conscious level, neuroimaging studies have helped to reveal that extensive interaction takes place between the sensory modalities much earlier in the processing pathways than was previously imagined.

In normal perception, all of the senses are critical. Effectively and safely driving a car down a busy highway requires the successful integration of seeing, touch, hearing, and perhaps even smell (warning, for example, that you have been riding the brakes down a hill). Enjoying a meal also involves the interplay of the senses. We cannot enjoy food intensely without smelling its fragrance. The sense of touch is an essential part of our gastronomic experience also, even if we don't think much about it. It gives us an appreciation for the texture of the food: the creamy smoothness of whipped cream or the satisfying crunch of an apple. Even visual cues enhance our gustatory experience—a salad of green, red, and orange hues is much more enticing than one that is brown and black.

In this chapter, we begin with an overview of sensation and perception and then turn to a description of what is known about the anatomy and function of the individual senses. Next we tackle the issue of how information from our different sensory systems is integrated to produce a coherent representation of the world. We end by discussing the interesting phenomenon of synesthesia—what happens when sensory information is more integrated than is usual.

Sensation: Early Perceptual Processing

Shared Processing From Acquisition to Anatomy

Before dealing with each sense individually, let's look at the anatomical and processing features that the sensory systems have in common. Each system begins with some sort of anatomical structure for collecting, filtering, and amplifying information from the environment. For instance, the outer ear, the ear canal, and inner ear concentrate and amplify sound. In vision, the muscles of the eye direct the gaze, the pupil size is adjusted to filter the amount of light, and the cornea and lens refract light to focus it on the retina. Each system has specialized receptor cells that transduce the environmental stimulus, such as sound waves or light waves or chemicals, into neural signals. These neural signals are passed along their specific sensory nerve pathways: the olfactory signals via the olfactory nerve (first cranial nerve); visual signals via the optic nerve (second cranial nerve); auditory signals via the cochlear nerve (also called the auditory nerve, which joins with the vestibular nerve to form the eighth cranial nerve); taste via the facial and glossopharyngeal nerves (seventh and ninth cranial nerves); facial sensation via the trigeminal nerve (fifth cranial nerve); and sensation for the rest of the body via the sensory nerves that synapse in the dorsal roots of the spinal cord.

The sensory nerves from the body travel up the spinal cord and enter the brain through the medulla, where the glossopharyngeal and vestibulocochlear nerves also enter. The facial nerve enters the brainstem at the pontomedullary junction. The trigeminal nerve enters at the level of the pons. These nerves all terminate in different parts of the thalamus (Figure 5.1). The optic nerve travels from the eye socket to the optic chiasm, where fibers from the nasal visual fields cross to the opposite side of the brain, and most (not all) of

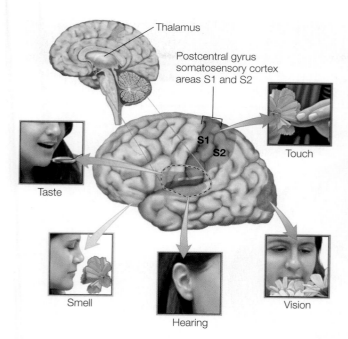

FIGURE 5.1 Major sensory regions of the cerebral cortex.

the newly combined fibers terminate in the thalamus. From the thalamus, neural connections from each of these pathways travel first to what are known as primary sensory cortex, and then to secondary sensory cortex (Figure 5.1). The olfactory nerve is a bit of a rogue. It is the shortest cranial nerve and follows a different course. It terminates in the olfactory bulb, and axons extending from here course directly to the primary and secondary olfactory cortices without going through the brainstem or the thalamus.

Receptors Share Responses to Stimuli

Across the senses, receptor cells share a few general properties. Receptor cells are limited in the range of stimuli that they respond to, and as part of this limitation, their capability to transmit information has only a certain degree of precision. Receptor cells do not become active until the stimulus exceeds some minimum intensity level. They are not fixed entities, but rather adapt as the environment changes.

Range Each sensory modality responds to a limited range of stimuli. Most people's impression is that human color vision is unlimited. However, there are many colors, or parts of the electromagnetic spectrum, that we cannot see (Figure 5.2). Our vision is limited to a small region of this spectrum, wavelengths of light in the range of 400 to 700 nanometers (nm). Individual receptor cells respond to just a portion of this range. This range is not the same for all species. For example, birds and insects have receptors that are sensitive to shorter wavelengths

and thus, can see ultraviolet light (Figure 5.2b, right). Some bird species actually exhibit sexual dichromatism (the male and female have different coloration) that is not visible to humans. Similar range differences are found in audition. We are reminded of this when we blow a dog whistle (invented by Francis Galton, Charles Darwin's cousin). We immediately have the dog's attention, but we cannot hear the high-pitched sound ourselves. Dogs can hear sound-wave frequencies of up to about 60 kilohertz (kHz), but we hear only sounds below about 20 kHz. Although a dog has better night vision than we do, we see more colors. Dogs cannot see the red–green spectrum. As limited as our receptor cells may be, we do respond to a wide range of stimulus intensities. The threshold stimulus value is the minimum stimulus that will activate a percept.

Adaptation Adaptation refers to how sensory systems stay fine-tuned. It is the adjusting of the sensitivity of the sensory system to the current environment and to important changes in the environment. You will come to see that perception is mainly concerned with changes in sensation. This makes good survival sense. Adaptation happens quickly in the olfactory system. You smell the baking bread when you

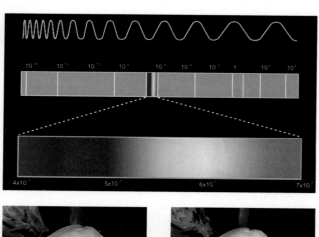

FIGURE 5.2 Vision and light.
(a) The electromagnetic spectrum. The small, colored section in the center indicates the part of the spectrum that is visible to the human eye. (b) The visible region of the electromagnetic spectrum varies across species. An evening primrose as seen by humans (left) and bees (right). Bees perceive the ultraviolet part of the spectrum.

ANATOMICAL ORIENTATION

Anatomy of the senses

Sensory inputs about taste, touch, smell, hearing, and seeing travel to specific regions of the brain for initial processing.

walk into the bakery, but the fragrance seems to evaporate quickly. Our auditory system also adapts rather quickly. When we first turn the key to start a car, the sound waves from the motor hit our ears, activating sensory neurons. But this activity soon stops, even though the stimulus continues as we drive along the highway. Some neurons continue to fire as long as the stimulus continues, but their rate of firing slows down: the longer the stimulus continues, the less frequent the action potentials are. The noise of the computer drops into the background, and we have "adapted" to it.

Visual system adaptation also occurs for changes in the light intensity in the environment. We frequently move between areas with different light intensities, for instance, when walking from a shaded area into the bright sunlight. It takes some time for the eyes to reset to the ambient light conditions, especially when going from bright light into darkness. When you go camping for the first time with veteran campers, one of the first things you are going to be told is not to shine your flashlight into someone's eyes. It would take about 20–30 minutes for that person to regain her "night vision," that is, to regain sensitivity to the low level of ambient light after being exposed to the bright light. We discuss how this works later, in the Vision section.

Acuity Our sensory systems are tuned to respond to different sources of information in the environment. Light activates receptors in the retina, pressure waves produce mechanical and electrical changes in the eardrum, and odor molecules are absorbed by receptors in the nose. How good we are at distinguishing among stimuli within a sensory modality, or what we would call *acuity*, depends on a couple of factors. One is simply the design of the stimulus collection system. Dogs can adjust the position of their two ears independently to better capture sound waves. This design contributes to their ability to hear sounds that are up to four times farther away than humans are capable of hearing. Another factor is the number and distribution of the receptors. For instance, for touch, we have many more receptors on our fingers than we do on our back; thus, we can discern stimuli better with our fingers. Our visual acuity is better than that of most animals, but not better than an eagle. Our acuity is best in the center of our visual field, because the central region of the retina, the *fovea*, is packed with photoreceptors. The farther away from the fovea, the fewer the receptors. The same is true for the eagle, but he has two foveas.

In general, if a sensory system devotes more receptors to certain types of information (e.g., as in the sensory receptors of the hands), there is a corresponding increase in cortical representation of that information (see, for example, Figure 5.16). This finding is interesting, because many creatures carry out exquisite perception without a cortex. So what is our cortex doing with all of the sensory information? The expanded sensory capabilities in humans, and mammals in general, are probably not for better sensation per se; rather, they allow that information to support flexible behavior, due to greatly increased memory capacity and pathways linking that information to our action and attention systems.

Sensory Stimuli Share an Uncertain Fate The physical stimulus is transduced into neural activity (i.e., electrochemical signals) by the receptors and sent through subcortical and cortical regions of the brain to be processed. Sometimes a stimulus may produce subjective sensory awareness. When that happens, the stimulus is not the only factor contributing to the end product. Each level of processing—including attention, memory, and emotional systems—contributes as well. Even with all of this activity going on, most of the sensory stimulation never reaches the level of consciousness. No doubt if you close your eyes right now, you will not be able to describe

everything that is in front of you, although it has all been recorded on your retina.

Connective Similarities Most people typically think of sensory processing as working in one direction; that is, information moves from the sensor organs to the brain. Neural activity, however, is really a two-way street. At all levels of the sensory pathways, neural connections are going in both directions. This feature is especially pronounced at the interface between the subcortex and cortex. Sensory signals from the visual, auditory, somatosensory, and gustatory (taste) systems all synapse within the thalamus before projecting onto specific regions within the cortex. The visual pathway passes through the lateral geniculate nucleus (LGN) of the thalamus, the auditory system through the **medial geniculate nucleus (MGN)**, the somatic pathway through the ventral posterior nuclear complex and the gustatory pathway through the ventral posteromedial nucleus. Just exactly what is going on in the thalamus is unclear. It appears to be more than just a relay station. Not only are there projections from these nuclei to the cortex, but the thalamic nuclei are interconnected, providing an opportunity for **multisensory integration**, an issue we turn to later in the chapter. The thalamus also receives descending, or feedback, connections from primary sensory regions of the cortex as well as other areas of the cortex, such as the frontal lobe. These connections appear to provide a way for the cortex to control, to some degree, the flow of information from the sensory systems (see Chapter 7).

Now that we have a general idea of what is similar about the anatomy of the various sensory systems and processing of sensory stimuli, let's take a closer look at the individual sensory systems.

Audition

Imagine you are out walking to your car late at night, and you hear a rustling sound. Your ears (and heart!) are working on overdrive, trying to determine what is making the sound (or more troubling, who) and where the sound is coming from. Is it merely a tree branch blowing in the breeze, or is someone sneaking up behind you? The sense of hearing, or audition, plays an important role in our daily lives. Sounds can be essential for survival—we want to avoid possible attacks and injury—but audition also is fundamental for communication. How does the brain process sound? What happens as sound waves enter the ear? And how does our brain interpret these signals? More specifically, how does the nervous system figure out the *what* and the *where* of sound sources?

Neural Pathways of Audition

Figure 5.3 presents an overview of the auditory pathways. The complex structures of the inner ear provide the mechanisms for transforming sounds (variations in sound pressure) into neural signals. This is how hearing works: Sound waves arriving at the ear enter the *auditory canal*. Within the canal, the sound waves are amplified, similar to what happens when you honk your car's horn in a tunnel. The waves travel to the far end of the canal, where they hit the *tympanic membrane*, or *eardrum*, and make it vibrate. These low-pressure vibrations then travel through the air-filled middle ear and rattle three tiny bones, the *malleus*, *incus*, and *stapes*, which cause a second membrane, the oval window, to vibrate.

The oval window is the "door" to the fluid-filled *cochlea*, the critical auditory structure of the inner ear. Within the cochlea are tiny *hair cells* located along the inner surface of the *basilar membrane*. The hair cells are the sensory receptors of the auditory system. Hair cells are composed of up to 200 tiny filaments known as *stereocilia* that float in the fluid. The vibrations at the oval window produce tiny waves in the fluid that move the basilar membrane, deflecting the stereocilia. The location of a hair cell on the basilar membrane determines its *frequency tuning*, the sound frequency that it responds to. This is because the thickness (and thus, the stiffness) of the basilar membrane varies along its length from the oval window to the apex of the cochlea. The thickness constrains how the membrane will move in response to the fluid waves. Near the oval window, the membrane is thick and stiff. Hair cells attached here can respond to high-frequency vibrations in the waves. At the other end, the apex of the cochlea, the membrane is thinner and less stiff. Hair cells attached here will respond only to low frequencies. This spatial arrangement of the sound receptors is known as *tonotopy*, and the arrangement of the hair cells along the cochlear canal form a tonotopic map. Thus, even at this early stage of the auditory system, information about the sound source can be discerned.

The hair cells act as *mechanoreceptors*. When deflected by the membrane, mechanically gated ion channels open in the hair cells, allowing positively charged ions of potassium and calcium to flow into the cell. If the cell is sufficiently depolarized, it will release transmitter into a synapse between the base of the hair cell and an afferent nerve fiber. In this way, a mechanical event, the deflections of the hair cells, is converted into a neural signal (Figure 5.4).

Natural sounds like music or speech are made up of complex frequencies. Thus, a natural sound will activate a broad range of hair cells. Although we can hear sounds up to 20,000 hertz (Hz), our auditory system is most sensitive to sounds in the range of 1000 to 4000 Hz, a range that carries much of the information critical for human communication, such as speech or the cries of a hungry infant. Other species have sensitivity to very different frequencies. Elephants can hear very low-frequency sounds, allowing them to communicate

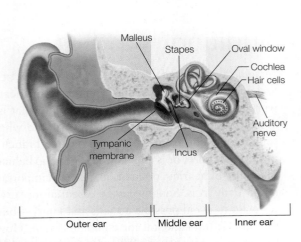

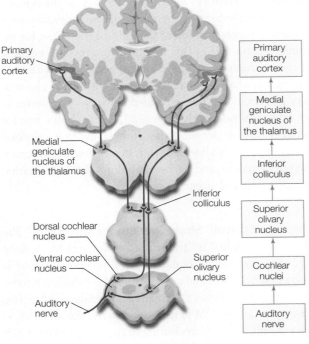

FIGURE 5.3 Overview of the auditory pathway.
The hair cells of the cochlea are the primary receptors. The output from the auditory nerve projects to the cochlear nuclei in the brainstem. Ascending fibers reach the auditory cortex following synapses in the inferior colliculus and medial geniculate nucleus.

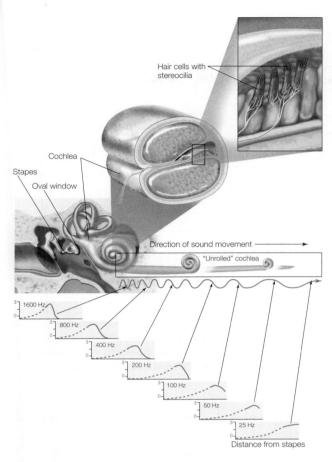

FIGURE 5.4 Transduction of sound waves along the cochlea. The cochlea is unrolled to show how the sensitivity to different frequencies varies with distance from the stapes.

over long distances (since such sounds are only slowly distorted by distance); mice communicate at frequencies well outside our hearing system. These species-specific differences likely reflect evolutionary pressures that arose from the capabilities of different animals to produce sounds. Our speech apparatus has evolved to produce changes in sound frequencies in the range of our highest sensitivity.

The auditory system contains several synapses between the hair cells and the cortex. The cochlear nerve, also called the auditory nerve, projects to the cochlear nucleus in the medulla. Axons from this nucleus travel up to the pons and split to innervate the left and right olivary nucleus, providing the first point within the auditory pathways where information is shared from both ears. Axons from the cochlear and olivary nuclei project to the **inferior colliculus**, higher up in the midbrain. At this stage, the auditory signals can access motor structures; for example, motor neurons in the colliculus can orient the head toward a sound. Some of the axons coursing through the pons branch off to the *nucleus of the lateral lemniscus* in the midbrain, where another important

characteristic of sound, timing, is processed. From the midbrain, auditory information ascends to the MGN in the thalamus, which in turn projects to the **primary auditory cortex (A1)** in the superior part of the temporal lobe.

Neurons throughout the auditory pathway continue to have *frequency tuning* and maintain their tonotopic arrangement as they travel up to the cortex. As described in Chapter 2 (p. 56), the primary auditory cortex contains a tonotopic map, an orderly correspondence between the location of the neurons and their specific frequency tuning. Cells in the rostral part of A1 tend to be responsive to low-frequency sounds; cells in the caudal part of A1 are more responsive to high-frequency sounds. The tonotopic organization is evident in studies using single-cell recording methods, and thanks to the resolution provided by fMRI, it can also be seen in humans (Figure 5.5). Tonotopic maps are also found in secondary auditory areas of the cortex.

As Figure 5.6 shows, the tuning curves for auditory cells can be quite broad. The finding that individual cells do not give precise frequency information but provide only coarse coding may seem puzzling, because animals can differentiate between very small differences in sound frequencies. Interestingly, the tuning of individual neurons becomes sharper as we move through the auditory system. A neuron in the cat's cochlear nucleus that responds maximally to a pure tone of 5000 Hz may also respond to tones ranging from 2000 to 10,000 Hz. A comparable neuron in the cat auditory cortex responds to a much narrower range of frequencies. The same principle is observed in humans. In one study, electrodes were placed in the auditory cortex of epileptic patients to monitor for seizure activity (Bitterman et al., 2008). Individual cells were exquisitely tuned, showing a strong response to, say, a tone at 1010 Hz but no response, or even a slight inhibition to tones just 20 Hz different. This fine resolution is essential for making the precise discriminations for perceiving sounds, including speech. Indeed, it appears that human auditory tuning is sharper than that of all other species except for the bat.

While A1 is, at a gross level, tonotopically organized, more recent studies using high-resolution imaging methods in the mouse suggest that, at a finer level of resolution, organization may be much more messy. At this level, adjacent cells frequently show very different tuning. Thus, there is a large-scale tonotopic organization but with considerable heterogeneity at the local level (Bandyopadhyay et al., 2010; Rothchild et al., 2010). This mixture may reflect the fact that natural sounds contain information across a broad range of frequencies and that the local organization arises from experience with these sounds.

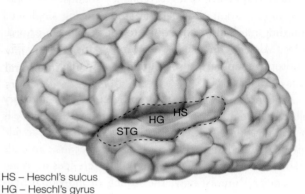

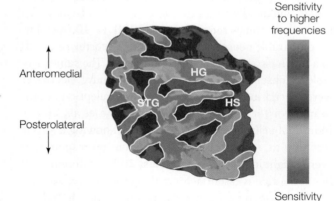

HS – Heschl's sulcus
HG – Heschl's gyrus
a STG – Superior temporal gyrus

Sensitivity to higher frequencies

Anteromedial

Posterolateral

Sensitivity to lower frequencies

b

FIGURE 5.5 The auditory cortex and tonotopic maps.
(a) The primary auditory cortex is located in the superior portion of the temporal lobe (left and right hemispheres), with the majority of the region buried in the lateral sulcus on the transverse temporal gyrus and extending onto the superior temporal gyrus. **(b)** A flat map representation of primary and secondary auditory regions. Multiple tonotopic maps are evident, with the clearest organization evident in primary auditory cortex.

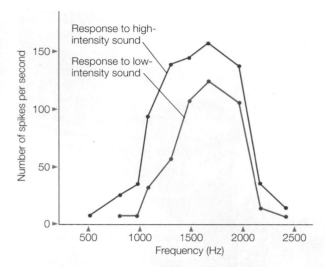

FIGURE 5.6 Frequency-dependent receptive fields for a cell in the auditory nerve of the squirrel monkey.
This cell is maximally sensitive to a sound of 1600 Hz, and the firing rate falls off rapidly for either lower- or higher-frequency sounds. The cell is also sensitive to intensity differences, with stronger responses to louder sounds. Other cells in the auditory nerve would show tuning for different frequencies.

Computational Goals in Audition

Frequency data are essential for deciphering a sound. Sound-producing objects have unique resonant properties that provide a characteristic signature. The same note played on a clarinet and a trumpet will sound differently, because the *resonant properties* of each instrument will produce considerable differences in the note's harmonic structure. Yet, we are able to identify a "G" from different instruments as the same note. This is because the notes share the same base frequency. In a similar way, we produce our range of speech sounds by varying the resonant properties of the vocal tract. Movements of our lips, tongue, and jaw change the frequency content of the acoustic stream produced during speech. Frequency variation is essential for a listener to identify words or music.

Auditory perception does not merely identify the content of an acoustic stimulus. A second important function of audition is to localize sounds in space. Consider the bat, which hunts by echolocation. High-pitched sounds are emitted by the bat and bounce back, as echoes from the environment. From these echoes, the bat's brain creates an auditory image of the environment and the objects within it—preferably a tasty moth. But knowing that a moth ("what") is present will not lead to a successful hunt. The bat also has to determine the moth's precise location ("where"). Some very elegant work in the neuroscience of audition has focused on the "where" problem. In solving the "where" problem, the auditory system relies on integrating information from the two ears.

In developing animal models to study auditory perception, neuroscientists select animals with well-developed hearing. A favorite species for this work has been the barn owl, a nocturnal creature. Barn owls have excellent *scotopia* (night vision), which guides them to their prey. Barn owls, however, also must use an exquisitely tuned sense of hearing to locate food, because visual information can be unreliable at night. The low levels of illumination provided by the moon and stars fluctuate with the lunar cycle and clouds. Sound, such as the patter of a mouse scurrying across a field, offers a more reliable stimulus. Indeed, barn owls have little trouble finding prey in a completely dark laboratory.

Barn owls rely on two cues to localize sounds: the difference in when a sound reaches each of the two ears, the **interaural time**, and the difference in the sound's *intensity* at the two ears. Both cues exist because the sound reaching two ears is not identical. Unless the sound source is directly parallel to the head's orientation, the sound will reach one ear before the other. Moreover, because the intensity of a sound wave becomes attenuated over time, the magnitude of the signal at the two ears will not be identical. The time and intensity differences are minuscule. For example, if the stimulus is located at a 45° angle to the line of sight, the interaural time difference will be approximately 1/10,000 of a second. The intensity differences resulting from sound attenuation are even smaller—indistinguishable from variations due to "noise." However, these small differences are amplified by a unique asymmetry of owl anatomy: The left ear is higher than eye level and points downward, and the right ear is lower than eye level and points upward. Because of this asymmetry, sounds coming from below are louder in the left ear than the right. Humans do not have this asymmetry, but the complex structure of the human outer ear, or *pinna*, amplifies the intensity difference between a sound heard at the two ears (Figure 5.7).

Interaural time and intensity differences provide independent cues for sound localization. To show this, researchers use little owl headphones. Stimuli are presented over headphones, and the owl is trained to turn its head in the perceived direction of the sound. The headphones allow the experimenter to manipulate each cue separately. When amplitude is held constant, asynchronies in presentation times prompt the owl to shift its head in the horizontal plane. Variations in amplitude produce vertical head movements. Combining the two cues by fusing the inputs from the two ears provides the owl with a complete representation of three-dimensional space. If one ear is plugged, the owl's response indicates that a sound has been detected, but it cannot localize the source.

Mark Konishi of the California Institute of Technology has provided a well-specified neural model of how neurons in the brainstem of the owl code interaural time differences by operating as coincidence detectors (M. Konishi, 1993). To be activated, these neurons must simultaneously receive input from each ear. In computer science terms, these neurons act as AND operators. An input from either ear alone or in succession is not sufficient; the neurons will fire only if an input arrives at the same time from both ears.

To see how this model works, look at Figure 5.8. In Figure 5.8a, the sound source is directly in front of the animal. In this situation the coincidence detector in the middle is activated, because the stimulus arrives at each ear at the same time. In Figure 5.8b, the sound source is to the animal's left. This gives the axon from the left ear a slight head start. Simultaneous activation now occurs in a coincidence detector to the left of center. This simple arrangement provides the owl with a complete representation of the horizontal position of the sound source.

  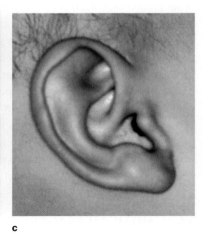

a
b
c

FIGURE 5.7 Variation in pinnae.
The shape of the pinnae help filter sounds and can amplify differences in the stimulus at the two ears. Considerable variation is seen across species. **(a)** Great Horned Owl, **(b)** Fennec Fox, and **(c)** human.

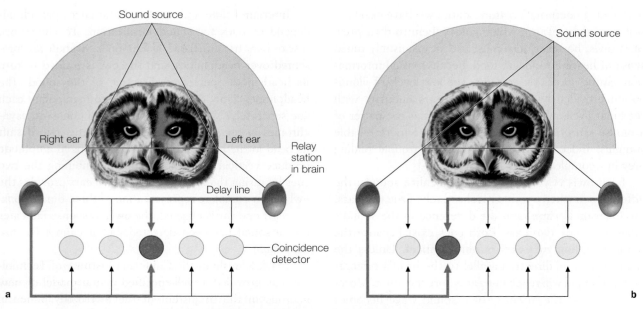

FIGURE 5.8 Slight asymmetries in the arrival times at the two ears can be used to locate the lateral position of a stimulus.
(a) When the sound source is directly in front of the owl, the stimulus will reach the two ears at the same time. As activation is transmitted across the delay lines, the coincidence detector representing the central location will be activated simultaneously from both ears. **(b)** When the sound source is located to the left, the sound reaches the left ear first. Now a coincidence detector offset to the opposite side receives simultaneous activation from the two ears.

A different coding scheme represents interaural intensities. For this stimulus dimension, the neural code is based on the input's firing rate. The stronger the input signal, the more strongly the cell fires. Neurons sum the combined intensity signals from both ears to pinpoint the vertical position of the source.

In Konishi's model, the problem of sound localization by the barn owl is solved at the level of the brainstem. To date, this theory has not explained higher stages of processing, such as in the auditory cortex. Perhaps cortical processing is essential for converting location information into action. The owl does not want to attack every sound it hears; it must decide if the sound is generated by potential prey. Another way of thinking about this is to reconsider the issues surrounding the computational goals of audition. Konishi's brainstem system provides the owl with a way to solve "where" problems but has not addressed the "what" question. The owl needs a more detailed analysis of the sound frequencies to determine whether a stimulus results from the movement of a mouse or a deer.

TAKE-HOME MESSAGES

- Signal transduction from sound wave to neuronal signal begins at the eardrums. Sound waves disturb the hair cells. This mechanical input is transformed into a neural

output at the cochlea. Signals are processed in the hair cells and basilar membrane of the cochlea. The cochlea sends its information in the form of neuronal signals to the inferior colliculus and the cochlear nucleus. Information then travels to the medial geniculate nucleus of the thalamus and on to the primary auditory cortex.
- Neurons throughout the auditory pathway maintain their tonotopic arrangement as they travel up to the cortex, but the tight organization is less apparent in the auditory cortices A1 and A2 when viewed with high-resolution methods.
- Sound localization is aided by the processing of differences in interaural time and interaural sound intensity, which are each coded separately in the brain.

Olfaction

We have the greatest awareness of our senses of sight, sound, taste, and touch. Yet the more primitive sense of smell is, in many ways, equally essential for our survival. Although the baleen whale probably does not smell the tons of plankton it ingests, the sense of smell *is* essential for terrestrial mammals, helping them to recognize foods that are nutritious and safe. Olfaction may have evolved primarily as a mechanism for evaluating whether a potential food is edible, but it serves other important roles as well—for instance, in avoiding hazards, such as fire or airborne toxins. Olfaction also plays an important role in social communication. Pheromones are excreted or secreted chemicals perceived by the olfactory system that trigger a social response in another individual of the same species. Pheromones are well documented in some insects, reptiles, and mammals. It also appears that they play an important role in human social interactions. Odors generated by women appear to vary across the menstrual cycle, and we are all familiar with the strong smells generated by people coming back from a long run. The physiological responses to such smells may be triggered by pheromones. To date, however, no compounds or receptors have been identified in humans. Before discussing the functions of *olfaction*, let's review the neural pathways of the brain that respond to odors.

Neural Pathways of Olfaction

Smell is the sensory experience that results from the transduction of neural signals triggered by odor molecules, or **odorants**. These molecules enter the nasal cavity, either during the course of normal breathing or when we sniff. They will also flow into the nose passively, because air pressure in the nasal cavity is typically lower than in the outside environment, creating a pressure gradient. Odorants can also enter the system through the mouth, traveling back up into the nasal cavity (e.g., during consumption of food).

How olfactory receptors actually "read" odor molecules is unknown. One popular hypothesis is that odorants attach to odor receptors, which are embedded in the mucous membrane of the roof of the nasal cavity, called the *olfactory epithelium*. There are over 1,000 types of receptors, and most of these respond to only a limited number of odorants, though a single odorant can bind to more than one type of receptor. Another hypothesis is that the molecular vibrations of groups of odorant molecules contribute to odor recognition (Franco et al., 2011; Turin, 1996). This model predicts that odorants with similar vibrational spectra should elicit similar olfactory responses, and it explains why similarly shaped molecules, but with dissimilar vibrations, have very different fragrances. For example, alcohols and thiols have almost exactly the same structure, but alcohols have a fragrance of, well, alcohol, and thiols smell like rotten eggs.

Figure 5.9 details the olfactory pathway. The olfactory receptor is called a *bipolar neuron* because appendages extend from opposite sides of its cell body. When an odorant triggers the neuron, whether by shape or vibration, a signal is sent to the neurons in the *olfactory bulbs*, called the **glomeruli**. Tremendous convergence and divergence take place in the olfactory bulb. One bipolar neuron may activate over 8,000 glomeruli, and each glomerulus, in turn, receives input from up to 750 receptors. The axons from the glomeruli then exit laterally from the olfactory bulb, forming the olfactory nerve. Their destination is the **primary olfactory cortex**, or *pyriform cortex*, located at the ventral junction of the frontal and temporal cortices. The olfactory pathway to the brain is unique in two ways. First, most of the axons of the olfactory nerve project to the ipsilateral cortex. Only a small number cross over to

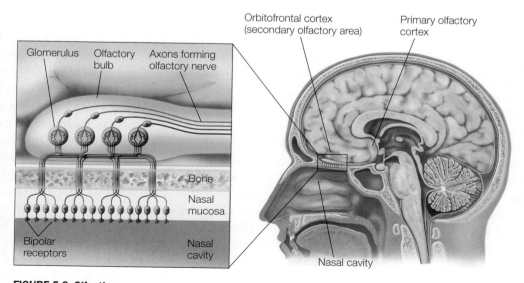

FIGURE 5.9 Olfaction.
The olfactory receptors lie within the nasal cavity, where they interact directly with odorants. The receptors then send information to the glomeruli in the olfactory bulb, the axons of which form the olfactory nerve that relays information to the primary olfactory cortex. The orbitofrontal cortex is a secondary olfactory processing area.

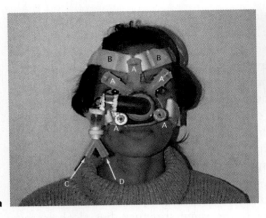
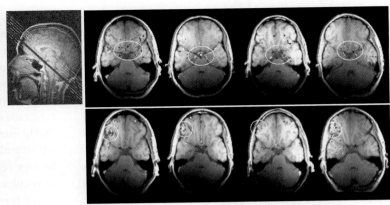

FIGURE 5.10 Sniffing and smelling.
(a) This special device was constructed to deliver controlled odors during fMRI scanning. **(b, top)** Regions activated during sniffing. The circled region includes the primary olfactory cortex and a posteromedial region of the orbitofrontal cortex. **(b, bottom)** Regions more active during sniffing when an odor was present compared to when the odor was absent.

innervate the contralateral hemisphere. Second, unlike the other sensory nerves, the olfactory nerve arrives at the primary olfactory cortex without going through the thalamus. The primary olfactory cortex projects to a secondary olfactory area within the *orbitofrontal cortex*, as well as making connections with other brain regions including the thalamus, hypothalamus, hippocampus, and amygdala. With these wide-ranging connections, it appears that odor cues influence autonomic behavior, attention, memory, and emotions—something that we all know from experience.

The Role of Sniffing in Olfactory Perception

Olfaction has gotten short shrift from cognitive neuroscientists. This neglect reflects, in part, our failure to appreciate the importance of olfaction in people's lives: We have handed the sniffing crown over to bloodhounds and their ilk. In addition, some thorny technical challenges must be overcome to apply tools such as fMRI to study the human olfactory system. First is the problem of delivering odors to a participant in a controlled manner (Figure 5.10a). Nonmagnetic systems must be constructed to allow the odorized air to be directed at the participant's nostrils while he is in the fMRI magnet. Second, it is hard to determine when an odor is no longer present. The chemicals that carry the odor can linger in the air for a long time. Third, although some odors overwhelm our senses, most are quite subtle, requiring exploration through the act of sniffing to detect and identify. Whereas it is almost impossible to ignore a sound, we can exert considerable control over the intensity of our olfactory experience.

Noam Sobel of the Weizmann Institute in Israel developed methods to overcome these challenges, conducting neuroimaging studies of olfaction that have revealed an intimate relationship between smelling and sniffing (Mainland & Sobel, 2006; Sobel et al., 1998). Participants were scanned while being exposed to either nonodorized, clean air or one of two chemicals: vanillin or decanoic acid. The former has a fragrance like vanilla, the latter, like crayons. The odor-absent and odor-present conditions alternated every 40 seconds. Throughout the scanning session, the instruction, "Sniff and respond, is there an odor?" was presented every 8 seconds. In this manner, the researchers sought to identify areas in which brain activity was correlated with sniffing versus smelling (Figure 5.10b).

Surprisingly, smelling failed to produce consistent activation in the primary olfactory cortex. Instead, the presence of the odor produced a consistent increase in the fMRI response in lateral parts of the orbitofrontal cortex, a region typically thought to be a secondary olfactory area. Activity in the primary olfactory cortex was closely linked to the rate of sniffing. Each time the person took a sniff, the fMRI signal increased regardless of whether the odor was present. These results seemed quite puzzling and suggested that the primary olfactory cortex might be more a part of the motor system for olfaction.

Upon further study, however, the lack of activation in the primary olfactory cortex became clear. Neurophysiological studies of the primary olfactory cortex in the rat had shown that these neurons habituate (adapt) quickly. It was suggested that perhaps the primary olfactory cortex lacks a smell-related response because the hemodynamic response measured by fMRI exhibits a similar habituation. To test this idea, Sobel's group modeled the fMRI signal by assuming a sharp increase followed by an extended drop after the presentation of an odor—an elegant example of how single-cell results can be used to interpret imaging data. When analyzed in this manner, the hemodynamic response in the primary olfactory cortex was found to be related to smell as well as to sniffing. These results suggest that the role of the primary olfactory cortex might be essential for detecting a change in the external odor and that the secondary olfactory cortex plays a critical role in identifying the odor itself. Each sniff represents an active sampling of the olfactory environment, and the primary olfactory cortex plays a critical role in determining if a new odor is present.

One Nose, Two Odors

The importance of sniffing for olfactory perception is underscored by the fact that our ability to smell is continually being modulated by changes in the size of the nasal passages. In fact, the two nostrils appear to switch back and forth—one is larger than the other for a number of hours, and then the reverse. These changes have a profound effect on how smell is processed (Figure 5.11). Why might the nose behave this way?

The olfactory percept depends not only on how intense the odor is but also on how efficiently we sample it (Mozell et al., 1991). The presence of two nostrils of slightly different sizes provides the brain with slightly different images of the olfactory environment. To test the importance of this asymmetry, Sobel monitored which nostril was allowing high airflow and which nostril was allowing low airflow, while presenting odors with both high and low absorption rates to each nostril. As predicted (see Figure 5.11), when sniffed through the high-airflow nostril, the odorant with a high absorption rate was judged to be more intense compared to when the same odorant was presented to the low-airflow nostril. The opposite was true for the odorant with a low absorption rate; here, the odor with a low rate of absorption was judged to be more intense when sniffed through the low-airflow nostril. Some of the participants were monitored when the flow rate of their nostrils reversed. The perception of the odorant presented to the same nostril reversed with the change in airflow.

As we saw in Chapter 4, asymmetrical representations are the rule in human cognition, perhaps providing

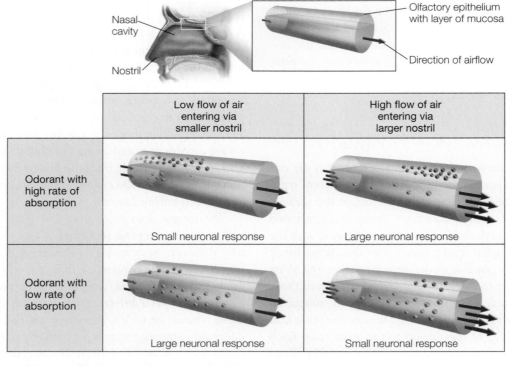

FIGURE 5.11 Human nostrils have asymmetric flow rates.
Although the same odorants enter each nostril, the response across the epithelium will be different for the two nostrils because of variation in flow rates. One nostril always has a greater input airflow than the other, and the nostrils switch between the two rates every few hours. This system of having one low-flow and one high-flow nostril has evolved to give the nose optimal accuracy in perceiving odorants that have both high and low rates of absorption.

a more efficient manner of processing complex information. With the ancient sense of olfaction, this asymmetry appears to be introduced at the peripheral level by modulation of the rate of airflow through the nostrils.

TAKE-HOME MESSAGES

- Signal transduction from odorant to neuronal signal begins when the odorant attaches to an odor receptor in the olfactory epithelium. The signal is then sent to the olfactory bulb through the olfactory nerve, which projects to the primary olfactory cortex. Signals are also relayed to the orbitofrontal cortex, a secondary olfactory processing area.
- The primary olfactory cortex is important for detecting a change in external odor, and the secondary olfactory cortex is important for identifying the smell itself.
- Similar to the importance of sampling sound from two ears, we use our two nostrils to obtain different olfactory samples, varying the rate of airflow through each nostril and thus altering the rate of absorption.
- The olfactory pathway is the only sensory pathway that does not send information to the thalamus.

Gustation

The sense of taste depends greatly on the sense of smell. Indeed, the two senses are often grouped together because they both begin with a chemical stimulus. Because these two senses interpret the environment by discriminating between different chemicals, they are referred to as the **chemical senses**.

Neural Pathways of Gustation

Gustation begins with the tongue. Strewn across the surface of the tongue in specific locations are different types of *papillae*, the little bumps you can feel on the surface. Papillae serve multiple functions. Some are concerned with gustation, others with sensation, and some with the secretion of lingual lipase, an enzyme that helps break down fats. The papillae in the anterior region and along the sides of the tongue contains several *taste buds*; those types found predominantly in the center of the tongue do not have taste buds. *Taste pores* are the conduits that lead from the surface of the tongue to the taste buds. Each taste bud contains many *taste cells* (Figure 5.12). Taste buds are also found in the cheeks and parts of the roof of the mouth. There are five basic tastes: salty, sour, bitter, sweet, and umami. *Umami* is the savory taste you experience when you eat steak or other protein-rich substances.

Sensory transduction in the gustatory system begins when a food molecule, or **tastant**, stimulates a receptor in a taste cell *and* causes the receptor to depolarize (Figure 5.12). Each of the basic taste sensations has a different form of chemical signal transduction. For example, the experience of a salty taste begins when the salt molecule (NaCl) breaks down into Na^+ and Cl^-, and the Na^+ ion is absorbed by a taste receptor, leading the cell to depolarize. Other taste transduction pathways, such as sweet carbohydrate tastants, are more complex, involving receptor binding that does not lead directly to depolarization. Rather, the presence of certain tastants will initiate a cascade of chemical "messengers" that eventually leads to cellular depolarization. Synapsing with the taste cells in the taste buds are bipolar neurons. Their axons form the chorda tympani nerve.

The chorda tympani nerve joins other fibers to form the facial nerve (the 7th cranial nerve). This nerve projects to the gustatory nucleus, located in the *rostral* region of the *nucleus of the solitary tract* in the brainstem. Meanwhile, the *caudal* region of the solitary nucleus receives sensory neurons from the gastrointestinal tract. The integration of information at this level can provide a rapid reaction. For example, you might gag if you taste something that is "off," a strong signal that the food should be avoided.

The next synapse in the gustatory system is on the *ventral posterior medial nucleus* (VPM) of the thalamus. Axons from the VPM synapse in the **primary gustatory cortex**. This is a region in the *insula* and *operculum*, structures at the intersection of the temporal and frontal lobes (Figure 5.12). Primary gustatory cortex is connected to secondary processing areas of the *orbitofrontal cortex*, providing an anatomical basis for the integration of tastes and smells. While there are only five types of taste cells, we are capable of experiencing a complex range of tastes. This ability must result from the integration of information conveyed from the taste cells and processed in areas like the orbitofrontal cortex.

The tongue does more than just taste. Some papillae contain nociceptive receptors, a type of pain receptor. These are activated by irritants such as capsaicin (contained in chili peppers), carbon dioxide (carbonated drinks), and acetic acid (vinegar). The output from these receptors follows a different path, forming the trigeminal nerve (cranial nerve V). This nerve not only carries pain information but also signals position and temperature information. You are well aware of the reflex response to activation by these irritants if you have ever eaten a hot chili: salivation, tearing, vasodilation (the red face), nasal secretion, bronchospasm (coughing), and decreased respiration. All these are meant to dilute that irritant and get it out of your system as quickly as possible.

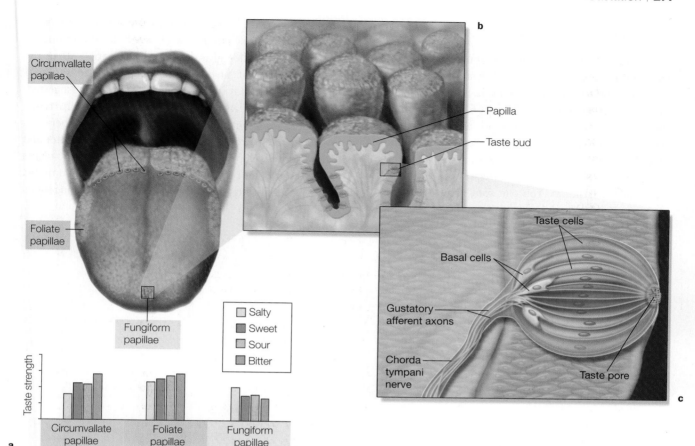

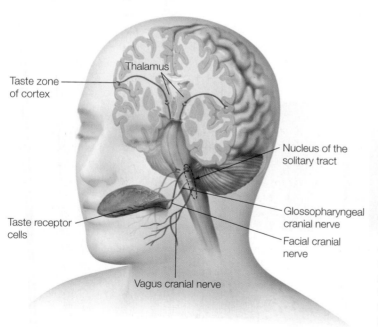

FIGURE 5.12 The gustatory transduction pathway.
(a) Three different types of taste papillae span the surface of the tongue. Each cell is sensitive to one of five basic tastes: salty, sweet, sour, bitter, and umami. The bar graph shows how sensitivity for four taste sensations varies between the three papillae. (b) The papillae contain the taste buds. (c) Taste pores on the surface of the tongue open into the taste bud, which contains taste cells. (d) The chorda tympani nerve, formed by the axons from the taste cells, joins with the facial nerve to synapse in the nucleus of the solitary tract in the brain stem, as do the sensory nerves from the GI tract via the vagus nerve. The taste pathway projects to the ventral posterior medial nucleus of the thalamus and information is then relayed to the gustatory cortex in the insula.

Gustatory Processing

Taste perception varies from person to person because the number and types of papillae and taste buds vary considerably between individuals. In humans, the number of taste buds varies from 120 to 668 per cm². Interestingly, women generally have more taste buds than men (Bartoshuk et al., 1994). People with large numbers of taste buds are known as supertasters. They taste things more intensely, especially bitterness, and feel more pain from tongue irritants. You can spot the two ends of the tasting spectrum at the table. One is pouring on the salsa or drinking grapefruit juice while the other is cringing.

The basic tastes give the brain information about the types of food that have been consumed. The sensation of umami tells the body that protein-rich food is being ingested, sweet tastes indicate carbohydrate intake, and salty tastes give us information that is important for the balance between minerals or electrolytes and water. The tastes of bitter and sour likely developed as warning signals. Many toxic plants taste bitter, and a strong bitter taste can induce vomiting. Other evidence suggesting that bitterness is a warning signal

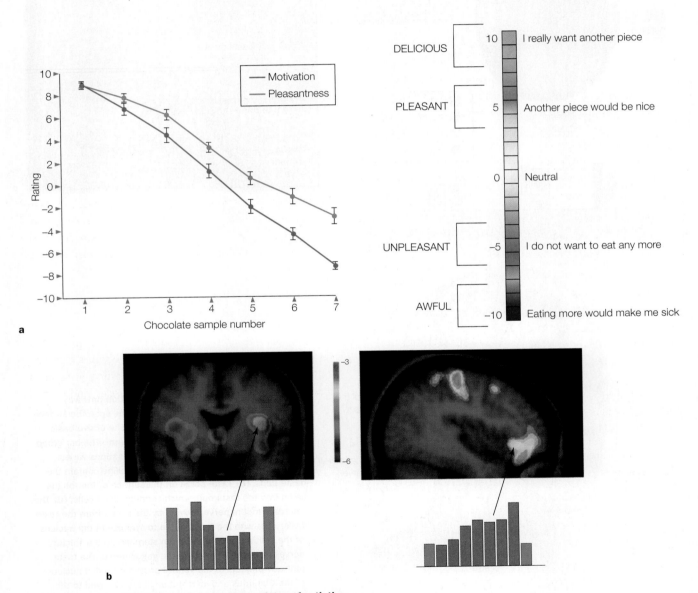

FIGURE 5.13 The neural correlates of satiation.
(a) Participants use a 10-point scale to rate the motivation and pleasantness of chocolate when offered a morsel seven times during the PET session. Desire and enjoyment declined over time. **(b)** Activation as measured during PET scanning during repeated presentations of chocolate (red). Water was presented during the first and last scans (blue). Across presentations, activity dropped in primary gustatory cortex (left) and increased in orbitofrontal cortex (right). The former could indicate an attenuated response to the chocolate sensation as the person habituates to the taste. The latter might correspond to a change in the participants' desire (or aversion) to chocolate.

is the fact that we can detect bitter substances 1,000 times better than, say, salty substances. Therefore, a significantly smaller amount of bitter tastant will yield a taste response, allowing toxic bitter substances to be avoided quickly. No wonder supertasters are especially sensitive to bitter tastes. Similarly, but to a lesser extent, sour indicates spoiled food (e.g., "sour milk") or unripe fruits.

Humans can readily learn to discriminate similar tastes. Richard Frackowiak and his colleagues at University College London (Castriota-Scanderberg et al., 2005) studied wine connoisseurs (sommeliers), asking how their brain response compared to that of nonexperts when tasting wines that varied in quite subtle ways. In primary gustatory areas, the two groups showed a very similar response. The sommeliers, however, exhibited increased activation in the insula cortex and parts of the orbitofrontal cortex in the left hemisphere, as well as greater activity bilaterally in dorsolateral prefrontal cortex. This region is thought to be important for high-level cognitive processes such as decision making and response selection (see Chapter 12).

The orbitofrontal cortex also appears to play an important role in processing the pleasantness and reward value of eating food. Dana Small and her colleagues (2001) at Northwestern University used positron emission tomography (PET) to scan the brains of people as they ate chocolate (Figure 5.13). During testing, the participants rated the pleasantness of the chocolate and their desire to eat more chocolate. Initially, the chocolate was rated as very pleasant and the participants expressed a desire to eat more. But as the participants became satiated, their desire for more chocolate dropped. Moreover, although the chocolate was still perceived as pleasant, the intensity of their pleasure ratings decreased.

By comparing the neural activation in the beginning trials with the trials at the end of the study, the researchers were able to determine which areas of the brain participated in processing the reward value of the chocolate (the pleasantness) and the motivation to eat (the desire to have more chocolate). The posteromedial portion of the orbitofrontal cortex was activated when the chocolate was highly rewarding and the motivation to eat more was strong. In contrast, the posterolateral portion of the orbitofrontal cortex was activated during the satiated state, when the chocolate was unrewarding and the motivation to eat more was low. Thus, the orbitofrontal cortex appears to be a highly specialized taste-processing region containing distinct areas able to process opposite ends of the reward value spectrum associated with eating.

TAKE-HOME MESSAGES

- Gustation and olfaction are known together as the chemical senses because the initial response is to molecules (chemicals) in the environment.

- The five basic tastes are salty, sour, bitter, sweet, and umami. The perception of more complex tastes arises from the complex cortical processing of these individual tastes in areas of the brain such as the secondary gustatory cortex in the orbitofrontal region.

- Signal transduction is initiated when a taste cell in the mouth responds to a tastant by depolarizing and sends a signal to the gustatory nucleus in the dorsal medulla. From there, a signal zips to the ventral posterior medial (VPM) nucleus of the thalamus. The VPM synapses with the primary gustatory cortex found in the operculum and insula. The primary gustatory cortex connects with the secondary processing areas found in the orbitofrontal cortex.

- The orbitofrontal cortex is also involved in processing the reward value of food and the resulting motivation to eat food.

Somatosensation

Somatosensory perception is the perception of all mechanical stimuli that affect the body. This includes interpretation of signals that indicate the position of our limbs and the position of our head, as well as our sense of temperature, pressure, and pain. Perhaps to a greater degree than with our other sensory systems, the somatosensory system includes an intricate array of specialized receptors and vast projections to many regions of the central nervous system.

Neural Pathways of Somatosensation

Somatosensory receptors lie under the skin (Figure 5.14) and at the musculoskeletal junctions. Touch is signaled by specialized receptors in the skin, including *Meissner's* **corpuscles**, *Merkel's cells*, *Pacinian corpuscles*, and *Ruffini corpuscles*. These receptors differ in how quickly they adapt and in their sensitivity to various types of touch, such as deep pressure or vibration. Pain is signaled by **nociceptors**, the least differentiated of the skin's sensory receptors. Nociceptors come in three flavors: thermal receptors that respond to heat or cold, mechanical receptors that respond to heavy mechanical stimulation, and polymodal receptors that respond to a wide range of noxious stimuli including heat, mechanical insults, and chemicals. The experience of pain is often the result of chemicals, such as histamine, that the body releases in response to injury. Nociceptors are located on the skin, below the skin, and in muscles and joints. Afferent pain neurons may be either myelinated or unmyelinated. The myelinated fibers quickly conduct information about pain. Activation of these cells usually produces immediate action. For example, when you touch a hot stove, the myelinated nociceptors can trigger a response that will cause you to quickly

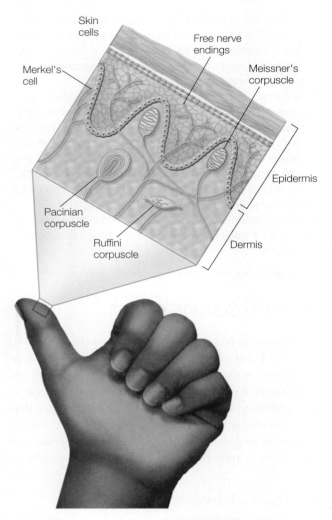

FIGURE 5.14 Somatosensory receptors underneath the skin. Merkel's cells detect regular touch; Meissner's corpuscles, light touch; Pacinian corpuscles, deep pressure; Ruffini corpuscles, temperature. Nociceptors (also known as free nerve endings), detect pain.

lift your hand, possibly even before you are aware of the temperature. The unmyelinated fibers are responsible for the duller, longer-lasting pain that follows the initial burn and reminds you to care for the damaged skin.

Specialized nerve cells provide information about the body's position, or what is called **proprioception** (*proprius*: Latin for "own," –*ception*: "receptor"; thus, a receptor for the self). Proprioception allows the sensory and motor systems to represent information about the state of the muscles and limbs. Proprioceptive cues, for example, signal when a muscle is stretched and can be used to monitor if that movement is due to an external force or from our own actions (see Chapter 8).

Somatosensory receptors have their cell bodies in the dorsal-root ganglia (or equivalent cranial nerve ganglia).

The somatosensory receptors enter the spinal cord via the dorsal root (Figure 5.15). Some synapse on motor neurons in the spinal cord to form reflex arcs. Other axons synapse on neurons that send axons up the dorsal column of the spinal cord to the medulla. From here, information crosses over to the ventral posterior nucleus of the thalamus and then on to the cerebral cortex. As in vision (which is covered later in the chapter) and audition, the primary peripheral projections to the brain are crosswired; that is, information from one side of the body is represented primarily in the opposite, or contralateral, hemisphere. In addition to the cortical projections, proprioceptive and somatosensory information is projected to many subcortical structures, such as the cerebellum.

Somatosensory Processing

The initial cortical receiving area is called **primary somatosensory cortex** or **S1** (Figure 5.16a), which includes Brodmann areas 1, 2, and 3. S1 contains a somatotopic representation of the body, called the *sensory homunculus* (Figure 5.16b). Recall from Chapter 2 that the relative amount of cortical representation in the sensory homunculus corresponds to the relative importance of somatosensory information for that part of the body. For example, the hands cover a much larger portion of the cortex than the trunk does. The larger representation of the hands is essential given the great precision we need in using our fingers to manipulate objects and explore surfaces. When blindfolded, we can readily identify an object placed in our hand, but we would have great difficulty in identifying an object rolled across our back.

Somatotopic maps show considerable variation across species. In each species, the body parts that are the most important for sensing the outside world through touch are the ones that have the largest cortical representation. A great deal of the spider monkey's cortex is devoted to its tail, which it uses to explore objects that might be edible foods or for grabbing onto tree limbs. The rat, on the other hand, uses its whiskers to explore the world; so a vast portion of the rat somatosensory cortex is devoted to representing information obtained from the whiskers (Figure 5.17).

Secondary somatosensory cortex (S2) builds more complex representations. From touch, for example, S2 neurons may code information about object texture and size. Interestingly, because of projections across the corpus callosum, S2 in each hemisphere receives information from both the left and the right sides of the body. Thus, when we manipulate an object with both hands, an integrated representation of the somatosensory information can be built up in S2.

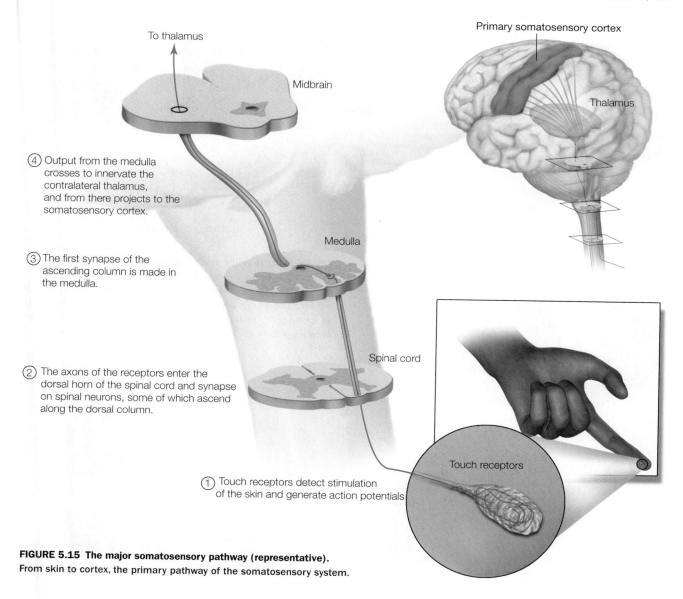

To thalamus

Midbrain

Primary somatosensory cortex

Thalamus

④ Output from the medulla crosses to innervate the contralateral thalamus, and from there projects to the somatosensory cortex.

③ The first synapse of the ascending column is made in the medulla.

Medulla

② The axons of the receptors enter the dorsal horn of the spinal cord and synapse on spinal neurons, some of which ascend along the dorsal column.

Spinal cord

Touch receptors

① Touch receptors detect stimulation of the skin and generate action potentials.

FIGURE 5.15 The major somatosensory pathway (representative).
From skin to cortex, the primary pathway of the somatosensory system.

Plasticity in the Somatosensory Cortex

Looking at the somatotopic maps may make you wonder just how much of that map is set in stone. What if you worked at the post office for many years sorting mail. Would you see changes in parts of the visual cortex that discriminate numbers? Or if you were a professional violinist, would your motor cortex be any bigger than that of the person who has never picked up a bow? Would anything happen to the part of your brain that represents your finger if you lost it in an accident? Would that part atrophy, or does the neighboring finger expand its representation and become more sensitive?

In 1949, Donald Hebb bucked the assumption that the brain was set in stone after the early formative years. He suggested a theoretical framework for how

functional reorganization, or what neuroscientists refer to as *cortical plasticity*, might occur in the brain through the remodeling of neuronal connections. Since then, more people have been looking for and observing brain plasticity in action. Michael Merzenich (Merzenich & Jenkins, 1995; Merzenich et al., 1988) at the University of California, San Francisco, and Jon Kaas (1995) at Vanderbilt University discovered that in adult monkeys, the size and shape of the cortical sensory and motor maps can be altered by experience. For example, when the nerve fibers from a finger to the spinal cord are severed (deafferented), the relevant part of the cortex no longer responds to the touch of that finger (Figure 5.18). Although this is no big surprise, the strange part is that the area of the cortex that formerly represented the denervated finger soon becomes active again. It begins to

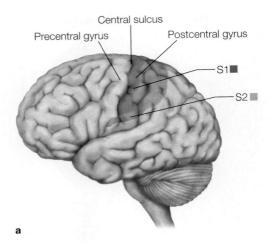

a

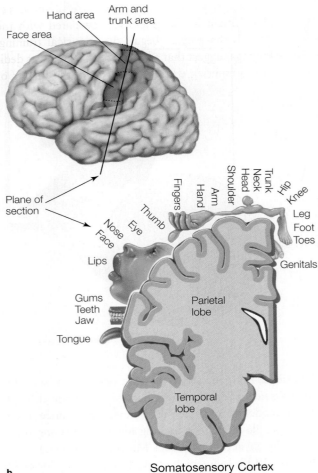

b

Somatosensory Cortex

FIGURE 5.16 **(a)** Somatosensory cortex (S1) lies in the postcentral gyrus, the most anterior portion of the parietal lobe. The secondary somatosensory cortex (S2) is ventral to S1. **(b)** The somatosensory homunculus as seen along the lateral surface and in greater detail in the coronal section. Note that the body parts with the larger cortical representations are most sensitive to touch.

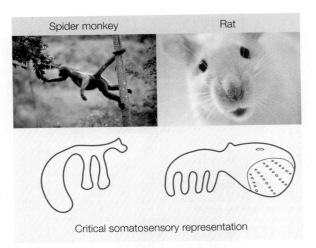

Critical somatosensory representation

FIGURE 5.17 Variation in the organization of somatosensory cortex reflects behavioral differences across species.
The cortical area representing the tail of the spider monkey is large because this animal uses its tail to explore the environment as well as for support. The rat explores the world with its whiskers; clusters of neurons form whisker barrels in the rat somatosensory cortex.

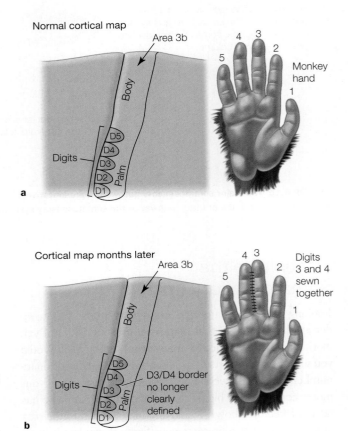

FIGURE 5.18 Reorganization of sensory maps in the primate cortex.
(a) In a mapping of the somatosensory hand area in normal monkey cortex, the individual digit representations can be revealed by single-unit recording. **(b)** If two fingers of one hand are sewn together, months later the cortical maps change such that the sharp border once present between the sewn fingers is now blurred.

respond to stimulation from the finger adjacent to the amputated finger. The surrounding cortical area fills in and takes over the silent area. Similar changes are found when a particular finger is given extended sensory stimulation: It gains a little more acreage on the cortical map. This functional plasticity suggests that the adult cortex is a dynamic place where changes can still happen, and it demonstrates a remarkable plasticity.

Extending these findings to humans, Vilayanur Ramachandran at the University of California, San Diego, studied the cortical mapping of human amputees. Look again at the human cortical somatosensory map in Figure 5.16b. What body part is represented next to the fingers and hand? Ramachandran reasoned that a cortical rearrangement ought to take place if an arm is amputated, just as had been found for the amputation of a digit in monkeys. Such a rearrangement might be expected to create bizarre patterns of perception, since the face area is next to the hand and arm area. Indeed, in one case study, Ramachandran examined a young man whose arm had been amputated just above the elbow a month earlier (1993). When a cotton swab was brushed lightly against his face, he reported feeling his amputated hand being touched! Feelings of sensation in missing limbs are the well-known phenomenon of *phantom limb sensation*. The sensation in the missing limb is produced by touching a body part that has appropriated the missing limb's old acreage in the cortex. In this case, the sensation was introduced by stimulating the face. Indeed, with careful examination, a map of the young man's hand could be demonstrated on his face (Figure 5.19).

These examples of plasticity led researchers to wonder if changes in experience within the normal range—say, due to training and practice—also result in changes in the organization of the adult human brain. Thomas Elbert and his colleagues at the University of Konstanz used magnetoencephalography (MEG) to investigate the somatosensory representations of the hand area in violin players (Elbert et al., 1995). They found that the responses in the musicians' right hemisphere, which controls the left-hand fingers that manipulate the violin strings, were stronger than those observed in nonmusicians (Figure 5.20). What's more, they observed that the size of the effect (the enhancement in the response) correlated with the age at which the players began their musical training. These findings suggest that a larger cortical area was dedicated to representing the sensations from the fingers of the musicians, owing to their altered but otherwise normal sensory experience. Another study used a complex visual motor task: juggling. After 3 months of training, the

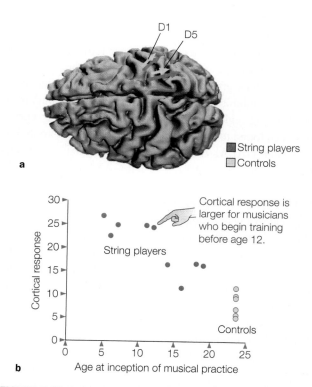

FIGURE 5.20 Increase in cortical representation of the fingers in musicians who play string instruments.
(a) Source of MEG activity for controls (yellow) and musicians (red) following stimulation of the thumb (D1) and fifth finger (D5). The length of the arrows indicates the extent of the responsive region. **(b)** The size of the cortical response, plotted as a function of the age at which the musicians begin training. Responses were larger for those who began training before the age of 12 years; controls are shown at the lower right of the graph.

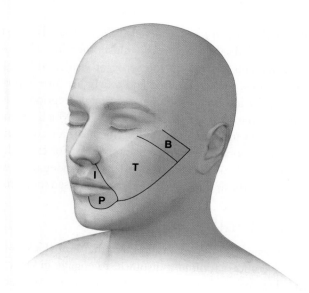

FIGURE 5.19 Perceived sensation of a phantom, amputated hand following stimulation of the face.
A Q-tip was used to lightly brush different parts of the face. The letters indicate the patient's perceptual experience. The region labeled T indicates the patient experienced touch on his phantom thumb. P is from the pinkie, I, the index finger, and B the ball of the thumb.

new jugglers had increased gray matter in the extrastri-ate motion-specific area in their visual cortex and in the left parietal sulcus, an area that is important in spatial judgments. (Draganski et al., 2004). Indeed, there is evidence that cortical reorganization can occur after just 15 to 30 minutes of practice (Classen et al., 1998).

The kicker is, however, that when the jugglers stopped practicing, these areas of their brain returned to their pretraining size, demonstrating something that we all know from experience: Use it or lose it. The realization that plasticity is alive and well in the brain has fueled hopes that stroke victims who have damaged cortex with resultant loss of limb function may be able to structurally reorganize their cortex and regain function. How this process might be encouraged is actively being pursued. One approach is to better understand the mechanisms involved.

Mechanisms of Cortical Plasticity

Most of the evidence for the mechanisms of cortical plasticity comes from animal studies. The results suggest a cascade of effects, operating across different timescales. Rapid changes probably reflect the unveiling of weak connections that already exist in the cortex. Longer-term plasticity may result from the growth of new synapses and/or axons.

Immediate effects are likely to be due to a sudden reduction in inhibition that normally suppresses inputs from neighboring regions. Reorganization in the motor cortex has been found to depend on the level of gamma-aminobutyric acid (GABA), the principal inhibitory neurotransmitter (Ziemann et al., 2001). When GABA levels are high, activity in individual cortical neurons is relatively stable. If GABA levels are lower, however, then the neurons may respond to a wider range of stimuli. For example, a neuron that responds to the touch of one finger will respond to the touch of other fingers if GABA is blocked. Interestingly, temporary deafferentation of the hand (by blocking blood flow to the hand) leads to a lowering of GABA levels in the brain. These data suggest that short-term plasticity may be controlled by a release of tonic inhibition on synaptic input (thalamic or intracortical) from remote sources.

Changes in cortical mapping over a period of days probably involve changes in the efficacy of existing circuitry. After loss of normal sensory input (e.g., through amputation or peripheral nerve section), cortical neurons that previously responded to that input might undergo "denervation hypersensitivity." That is, the strength of the responses to any remaining weak excitatory input is upregulated: Remapping might well depend on such modulations of *synaptic efficacy*. Strengthening of synapses is enhanced in the motor cortex by the neurotransmitters

norepinephrine, dopamine, and acetylcholine; it is decreased in the presence of drugs that block the receptors for these transmitters (Meintzschel & Ziemann, 2005). These changes are similar to the forms of long-term potentiation and depression in the hippocampus that are thought to underlie the formation of spatial and episodic memories that we will discuss in Chapter 9.

Finally, some evidence in animals suggests that the growth of intracortical axonal connections and even sprouting of new axons might contribute to very slow changes in cortical plasticity.

TAKE-HOME MESSAGES

- Corpuscles located in the skin respond to somatosensory touch information.
- Nociceptors (free nerve endings) respond to pain and temperature information.
- Nerve cells at the junctions of muscles and tendons provide proprioceptive information.
- Primary somatosensory cortex (S1) contains a homunculus of the body, wherein the more sensitive regions encompass relatively larger areas of cortex.
- Somatosensory representations exhibit plasticity, showing variation in extent and organization as a function of individual experience.

Vision

Now let's turn to a more detailed analysis of the most widely studied sense: vision. Like most other diurnal creatures, humans depend on the sense of vision. Although other senses, such as hearing and touch, are also important, visual information dominates our perceptions and appears even to frame the way we think. Much of our language, even when used to describe abstract concepts with metaphors, makes reference to vision. For example, we say "I see" to indicate that something is understood, or "Your hypothesis is murky" to indicate confused thoughts.

Neural Pathways of Vision

One reason vision is so important is that it enables us to perceive information at a distance, to engage in what is called *remote sensing* or *exteroceptive perception*. We need not be in immediate contact with a stimulus to process it. Contrast this ability with the sense of touch. For touch, we must be in direct contact with the stimulus. The advantages of remote sensing are obvious. An organism surely can avoid a predator better when it can detect the predator at a distance. It is probably too late to flee once a shark has sunk its teeth into you, no matter how fast your neural response is to the pain.

The Receptors Visual information is contained in the light reflected from objects. To perceive objects, we need sensory detectors that respond to the reflected light. As light passes through the lens of the eye, the image is inverted and focused to project on the back surface of the eye (Figure 5.21), the **retina**. The retina is only about 0.5 mm thick, but it is made up of 10 densely packed layers of neurons. The deepest layers are composed of millions of **photoreceptors**, the *rods* and *cones*. These contain *photopigments*, protein molecules that are sensitive to light. When exposed to light, the photopigments become unstable and split apart. Unlike most neurons, rods and cones do not fire action potentials. The decomposition of the photopigments alters the membrane potential of the photoreceptors and triggers action potentials in downstream neurons. Thus, photoreceptors provide for translation of the external stimulus of light into an internal neural signal that the brain can interpret.

The rods contain the pigment *rhodopsin*, which is destabilized by low levels of light. Rods are most useful at night when light energy is reduced. Rods also respond to bright light, but the pigment quickly becomes depleted and the rods cease to function until it is replenished. Because this takes several minutes, they are of little use during the day. Cones contain a different type of photopigment, called a *photopsin*. Cones require more intense levels of light but can replenish their photopigments rapidly. Thus, cones are most active during daytime vision. There are three types of cones, defined by their sensitivity to different regions of the visible spectrum: (a) a cone that responds to short wavelengths, the blue part of the spectrum; (b) one that responds to medium wavelengths, the greenish region; and (c) one that responds to the long "reddish" wavelengths (Figure 5.22). The activity of these three different receptors ultimately leads to our ability to see color.

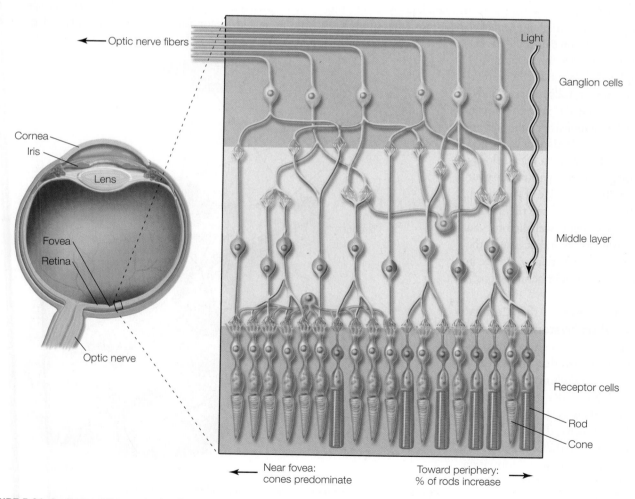

FIGURE 5.21 Anatomy of the eye and retina.
Light enters through the cornea and activates the receptor cells of the retina located along the rear surface. There are two types of receptor cells: rods and cones. The output of the receptor cells is processed in the middle layer of the retina and then relayed to the central nervous system via the optic nerve, the axons of the ganglion cells.

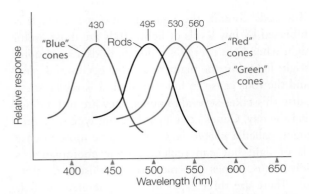

FIGURE 5.22 Spectral sensitivity functions for rods and the three types of cones.
The short-wavelength ("blue") cones are maximally responsive to light with a wavelength of 430 nm. The peak sensitivities of the medium-wavelength ("green") and long-wavelength ("red") cones are shifted to longer wavelengths. White light, such as daylight, activates all three receptors because it contains all wavelengths.

Rods and cones are not distributed equally across the retina. Cones are densely packed near the center of the retina, in a region called the **fovea**. Few cones are in the more peripheral regions of the retina. In contrast, rods are distributed throughout the retina. You can easily demonstrate the differential distribution of rods and cones by having a friend slowly bring a colored marker into your view from one side of your head. Notice that you see the marker and its shape well before you identify its color, because of the sparse distribution of cones in the retina's peripheral regions.

The Retina to the Central Nervous System
The rods and cones are connected to bipolar neurons that then synapse with the **ganglion cells**, the output layer of the retina. The axons of these cells form a bundle, the *optic nerve*, that transmits information to the central nervous system. Before any information is shipped down the optic nerve, however, extensive processing occurs within the retina, an elaborate convergence of information. Indeed, though humans have an estimated 260 million

photoreceptors, we have only 2 million ganglion cells to telegraph information from the retina. Many rods feed into a single ganglion cell. By summing their outputs, the rods can activate a ganglion cell even in low light situations. For cones, however, the story is different: Each ganglion cell is innervated by only a few cones. Thus, they carry much more specific information from only a few receptors, ultimately providing a sharper image. The compression of information, as with the auditory system, suggests that higher-level visual centers should be efficient processors to unravel this information and recover the details of the visual world.

Figure 5.23 diagrams how visual information is conveyed from the eyes to the central nervous system. As we discussed in the last chapter, before entering the brain, each optic nerve splits into two parts. The temporal (lateral) branch continues to traverse along the ipsilateral side. The nasal (medial) branch crosses over to project to the contralateral side; this crossover place is called the *optic chiasm*. Given the eye's optics, the crossover of nasal fibers ensures that visual information from each side of external space will be projected to contralateral brain structures. Because of

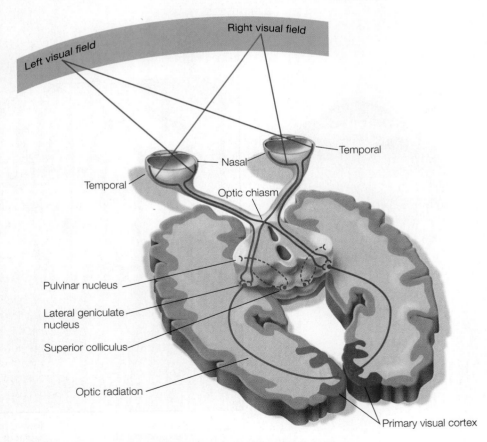

FIGURE 5.23 The primary projection pathways of the visual system.
The optic fibers from the temporal half of the retina project ipsilaterally, and the nasal fibers cross over at the optic chiasm. In this way, the input from each visual field is projected to the primary visual cortex in the contralateral hemisphere after the fibers synapse in the lateral geniculate nucleus (geniculocortical pathway). A small percentage of visual fibers of the optic nerve terminate in the superior colliculus and pulvinar nucleus.

the retina's curvature, the temporal half of the right retina is stimulated by objects in the left visual field. In the same fashion, the nasal hemiretina of the left eye is stimulated by this same region of external space. Because fibers from each nasal hemiretina cross, all information from the left visual field is projected to the right hemisphere, and information from the right visual field is projected to the left hemisphere.

Each optic nerve divides into several pathways that differ with respect to where they terminate in the subcortex. Figure 5.23 focuses on the pathway that contains more than 90% of the axons in the optic nerve, the *retinogeniculate pathway*, the projection from the retina to the **lateral geniculate nucleus (LGN)** of the thalamus. The LGN is made up of six layers. One type of ganglion cell, the M cell, sends output to the bottom two layers. Another type of ganglion cell the P cell, projects to the top four layers. The remaining 10% of the optic nerve fibers innervate other subcortical structures, including the *pulvinar nucleus* of the thalamus and the **superior colliculus** of the midbrain. Even though these other receiving nuclei are innervated by only 10% of the fibers, these pathways are still important. The human optic nerve is so large that 10% of it constitutes more fibers than are found in the entire auditory pathway. The superior colliculus and pulvinar nucleus play a large role in visual attention.

The final projection to the visual cortex is via the *geniculocortical pathway*. This bundle of axons exits the LGN and ascends to the cortex, and almost all of the fibers terminate in the **primary visual cortex (V1)** of the occipital lobe. Thus visual information reaching the cortex has been processed by at least four distinct neurons: photoreceptors, bipolar cells, ganglion cells, and LGN cells. Visual information continues to be processed as it passes through higher order visual areas in the cortex.

There are diseases and accidents that damage the eyes' photoreceptors, but otherwise leave the visual pathway intact. Until recently, people in this situation would go blind. But things are looking brighter for these patients thanks to microelectronics (see "How the Brain Works: When the Receptors No Longer Function").

TAKE-HOME MESSAGES

- Light activates the photoreceptors, the rods and cones, on the retina.
- The optic nerve is formed from the axons of the ganglion cells, some of which decussate at the optic chiasm.
- Axons in the optic nerve synapse on the LGN, and from the LGN become the optic radiations that are sent to V1.
- Ten percent of the fibers from the retina innervate non-LGN subcortical structures, including the pulvinar and superior colliculus.

Keeping the Picture Straight: Retinotopic Maps

Due to the optics of the eye, light reflecting off of objects in the environment strikes the eye in an orderly manner. Light reflected off of an object located to the right of someone's gaze will activate photoreceptors on the medial, or nasal, side of the right retina and lateral or temporal side of the left retina. As this information is projected upstream via the optic nerve, however, the direct link between neural activity and space is lost. Nonetheless, neurons in the visual system represent space. This is shown by the fact that most visual neurons only respond when a stimulus is presented in a specific region of space, or what is defined as the **receptive field** of the neuron. For example, a cell in the right visual cortex may respond to a bar of light, but only if that bar is presented in a specific region of space (e.g., the upper left visual field; see Figure 3.19). Moreover, there is an orderly relationship between the receptive fields of neighboring cells. Thus, external space is represented continuously within neural regions such as the LGN or V1. As with the somatosensory and auditory systems, the receptive fields of visual cells form an orderly mapping between an external dimension (in this case, spatial location) and the neural representation of that dimension. In vision, these topographic representations are referred to as **retinotopic maps**. A full retinotopic map contains a representation of the entire contralateral hemifield (e.g., left hemisphere V1 will have a full representation of the right side of space).

Receptive fields range in size, becoming larger across the visual system (Figure 5.24). LGN cells have receptive fields responding only if the stimulus falls within a very limited region of space, about one degree of visual angle. Cells in V1 have slightly larger receptive fields, and this magnification process continues through the visual system: Cells in the temporal lobe have receptive fields that may encompass an entire hemifield.

TAKE-HOME MESSAGES

- Visual neurons respond only to a stimulus that is presented in a specific region of space. This property is known as the receptive field of the cell.
- Visual cells form an orderly mapping between spatial location and the neural representation of that dimension. In vision, these topographic representations are referred to as retinotopic maps.

Cortical Visual Areas

A primary physiological method for establishing visual areas is to measure how spatial information is represented across a region of cortex. Figure 5.24 shows a map of the

HOW THE BRAIN WORKS
When the Receptors No Longer Function: The Retinal Implant

After being blind for 5 years, a patient sits at a table and is able to identify not only where a mug and various cutlery are placed, but can also tell that his name, spelled out in large letters, has been spelled incorrectly. He is one of three patients who have had an electronic chip implanted behind the retina (Zrenner et al., 2011). This chip is designed for patients who are suffering from blindness caused by degenerative diseases that affect photoreceptors and result in progressive vision loss. In the first few years of blindness the other cells of the retina remain intact—a situation this particular retinal implant uses to its advantage.

The tiny implant chip, measuring 3 mm by 3.1 mm, contains 1,500 light-sensitive microphotodiodes (Figure 1). Light enters the eye through the lens, passes through the transparent retina, and hits the chip. The image is simultaneously captured several times per minute by all of the photodiodes, each of which controls a tiny amplifier connected to an electrode, together known as an element (pixel). Each element generates a voltage at its electrode, the strength of which depends on the intensity of light hitting the photodiode. The voltage then passes to the adjacent bipolar neurons in the retina, and the signal proceeds through the rest of the visual pathway. One question facing those designing retinal implants is, how many photodiodes are needed to gain an acceptable image? When you consider that the eye contains millions of photoreceptors, 1,500 seems like a drop in the bucket. Indeed, this number produces only crude images. This system is in its infancy, but it allows a blind person to navigate and make simple discriminations. The chip is powered by an implanted cable that runs from the eye under the temporalis muscle and out from behind the ear, where it is attached to a wirelessly operated power control unit that the patient wears around his neck. This implant was placed temporarily, for just a few weeks, to test the concept. The next-generation system, currently being tested, is not cable bound. Instead, an encapsulated coil is implanted behind the ear and connected to a transmitter that magnetically attaches to an outside power coil.

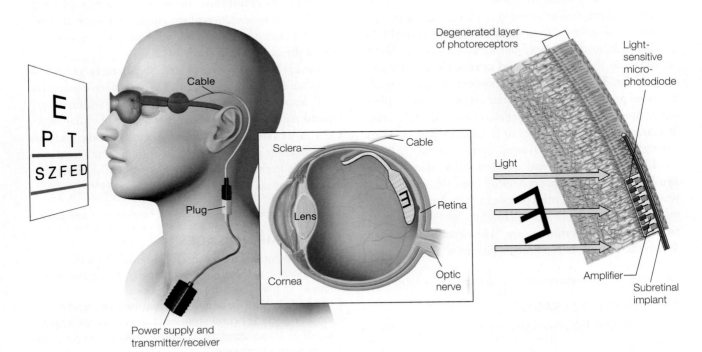

FIGURE 1 Retinal implant device.

visual areas of the cortex as defined by their physiology. Each box in the figure stands for a distinct region of visual processing, defined because the region contains its own retinotopic map. Thus, the boundaries between anatomically adjacent visual areas are marked by topographic discontinuities (Figure 5.25). As one area projects to another, topography and precise spatial information is preserved by these multiple retinotopic maps, at least in early visual areas. Over 30 distinct **cortical visual areas** have been identified in the monkey, and the evidence indicates that humans have even more.

Note that the names for the areas shown in Figure 5.24 primarily draw on the nomenclature developed by physiologists (see Chapter 2). Striate cortex, or V1, is the initial projection region of geniculate axons. Although other areas have names such as V2, V3, and V4, this numbering scheme *should not be taken to mean that the synapses proceed sequentially from one area to the next.* The lines connecting these **extrastriate visual areas** demonstrate extensive convergence and divergence across visual areas. In addition, connections between many areas are reciprocal; areas frequently receive input from an area to which they project.

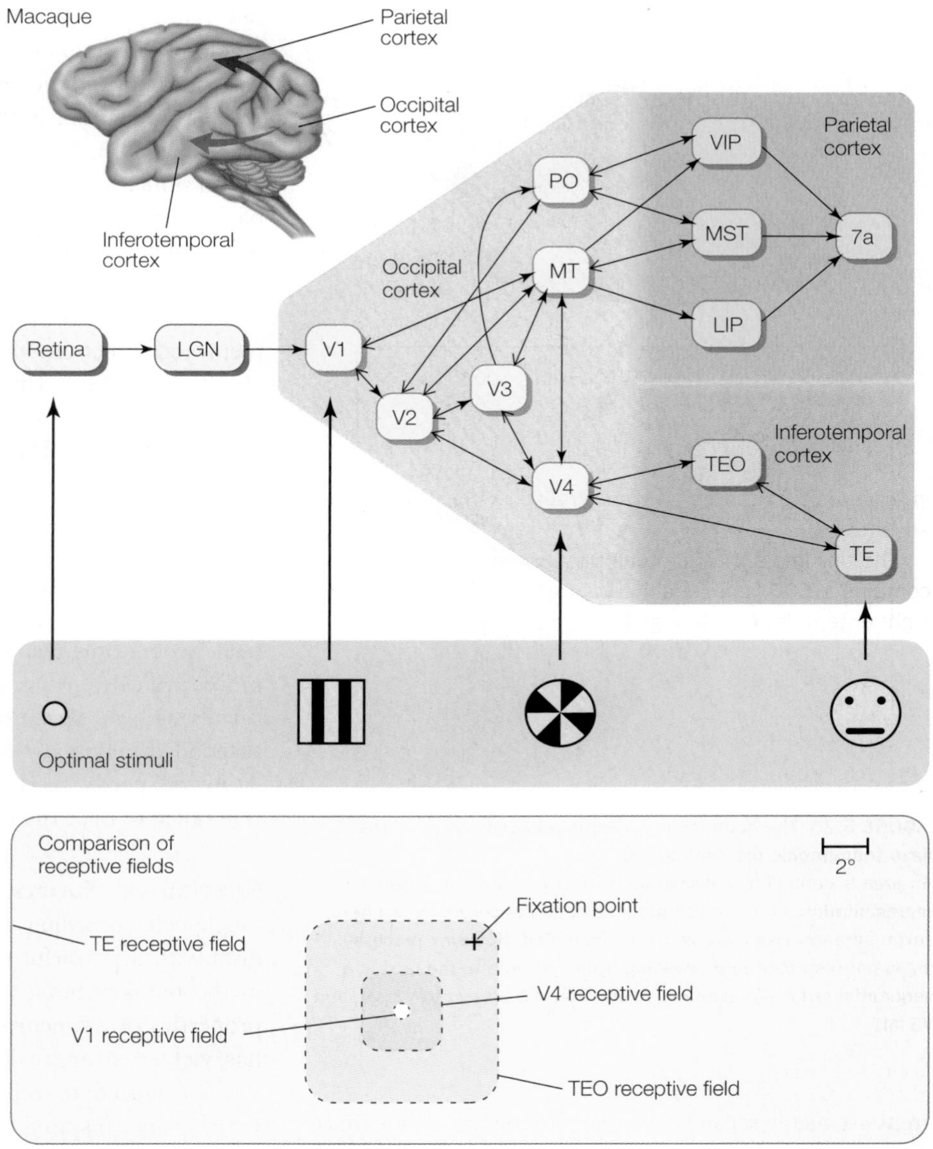

FIGURE 5.24 **Prominent cortical visual areas and the pattern of connectivity in the macaque brain.** Whereas all cortical processing begins in V1, the projections form two major processing streams, one along a dorsal pathway and the other along a ventral pathway (see Chapter 6). The stimulus required to produce optimal activation of a cell becomes more complex along the ventral stream. In addition, the size of the receptive fields increases, ranging from the 0.5° span of a V1 cell to the 40° span of a cell in area TE. The labels for the areas reflect a combination of physiological (e.g., V1) and anatomical (e.g., LIP) terms.

Cellular Properties Vary Across Cortical Visual Areas Why would it be useful for the primate brain to have evolved so many visual areas? One possibility is that visual processing is *hierarchical.* Each area, representing the stimulus in a unique way, successively elaborates on the representation derived by processing in earlier areas. The simple cells of the primary visual cortex calculate edges. Complex cells in secondary visual areas use the information from many simple cells to represent corners and edge terminations. In turn, higher order visual neurons integrate information from complex cells to

represent shapes. Successive elaboration culminates in formatting the representation of the stimulus so that it matches (or doesn't match) information in memory. An interesting idea, but there is a problem. As Figure 5.24 shows, there is no simple hierarchy; rather, extensive patterns of convergence and divergence result in multiple pathways.

An alternative hypothesis is based on the idea that visual perception is an *analytic process.* Although each visual area provides a map of external space, the maps represent different *types* of information. For instance, neurons in some

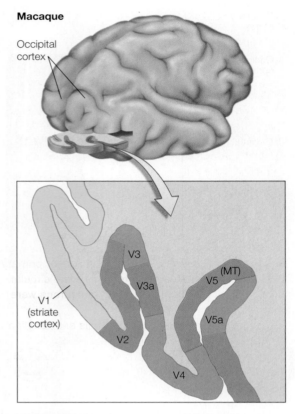

Macaque

Occipital cortex

V3
V3a
V5 (MT)
V1 (striate cortex)
V5a
V2
V4

FIGURE 5.25 The boundaries between adjacent visual areas have topographic discontinuities.
An area is defined by a discontinuity or reversal in the retinotopic representation. Along the continuous ribbon of cortex shown here, seven different visual areas can be identified. However, processing is not restricted to proceeding from one area to the next in a sequential order. For example, axons from V2 project to V3, V4, and V5/MT.

areas are highly sensitive to color variation. In other areas, they are sensitive to movement but not to color.

Based on this hypothesis, neurons within an area not only code where an object is located in visual space but also provide information about the object's attributes. By this perspective, visual perception can be considered to entail a divide-and-conquer strategy. Rather than all attributes of an object being represented by all visual areas, each visual area provides its own limited analysis. Processing is distributed and specialized. As signals advance through the visual system, different areas elaborate on the initial information in V1 and begin to integrate this information across dimensions to form recognizable percepts. Early work on these ideas is presented in "Milestones in Cognitive Neuroscience: Pioneers in the Visual Cortex."

Specialized Function of Visual Areas in Monkeys

Extensive physiological evidence supports the specialization hypothesis. Consider cells in **area MT** (sometimes

referred to as V5), so named because it lies in the *middle temporal* lobe region of the macaque monkey, a species used in many physiology studies. Single-cell recordings reveal that neurons in this region do not show specificity regarding the color of the stimulus. These cells will respond similarly to either a green or a red circle on a white background. Even more striking, these neurons respond weakly when presented with an alternating pattern of red and green stripes whose colors are equally bright.

In contrast, MT neurons are quite sensitive to movement and direction, as Figure 5.26 shows (Maunsell & Van Essen, 1983). The stimulus, a rectangular bar, was passed through the receptive field of a specific MT cell in varying directions. The cell's response was greatest when the stimulus was moved downward and left. In contrast, this cell was essentially silent when the stimulus was moved upward or to the right. Thus the cell's activity correlates with two attributes of the stimulus. First, the cell is active only when the stimulus falls within its receptive field. Second, the response is greatest when the stimulus moves in a certain direction. Activity in MT cells also correlates with the speed of motion. The cell in Figure 5.26 responded maximally when the bar was moved rapidly. At lower speeds, the bar's movement in the same direction failed to raise the response rate above baseline.

Specialized Function of Human Visual Areas

Single-cell recording studies have provided physiologists with a powerful tool for mapping the visual areas in the monkey brain and characterizing the functional properties of the neurons within these areas. This work has yielded strong evidence that different visual areas are specialized to represent distinct attributes of the visual scene. Inspired by these results, researchers have employed neuroimaging techniques to describe the functional architecture of the human brain.

In a pioneering study, Semir Zeki (1993) of University College London and his colleagues at London's Hammersmith Hospital used positron emission tomography (PET) to explore similar principles in the human visual system, starting with the goal of identifying areas that were involved in processing color or motion information. They used subtractive logic by factoring out the activation in a control condition from the activation in an experimental condition.

Let's check out the color experiment to see how this works. For the control condition, participants passively viewed a collage of achromatic rectangles. Various shades of gray, spanning a wide range of luminances, were chosen. The control stimulus was expected to activate neural regions with cells that are contrast sensitive (e.g., sensitive to differences in luminance).

For the experimental condition, the gray patches were replaced by a variety of colors (Figure 5.27a). Each

Like the voyages of 15th-century European explorers, initial investigations into the neurophysiology of the cerebral cortex required a willingness to sail in uncharted waters. The two admirals in this enterprise were David Hubel and Torsten Wiesel. Hubel and Wiesel arrived at Johns Hopkins University in the late 1950s, hoping to extend the pioneering work of Steve Kuffler (1953). Kuffler's research had elegantly described the receptive-field organization of ganglion cells in the cat retina, laying out the mechanisms that allowed cells to detect the edges that define objects in the visual world. Rather than focusing on the lateral geniculate nucleus (LGN), the next relay in the system, Hubel and Wiesel (1977) set their sights on the primary visual cortex. Vernon Mountcastle, another Hopkins researcher, was just completing his seminal work, in which he laid out the complex topographic organization of the somatosensory cortex (Mountcastle, 1976). Hubel and Wiesel were inspired to look for similar principles in vision.

During the first few weeks of their recordings, Hubel and Wiesel were puzzled by what they observed. Although they had little difficulty identifying individual cortical cells, the cells failed to respond to the kinds of stimuli that had proved so effective in Kuffler's studies: small spots of light positioned within a cell's receptive fields. Indeed, the lack of consistent responses made it difficult to determine where the receptive field was situated. Hubel and Wiesel had a breakthrough, though, when they switched to dark spots, which they created by placing an opaque disk on a glass slide. Although the cell did not respond to the dark spot, Hubel and Wiesel noticed a burst in activity as the edge of the glass moved across part of the retina. After hours of play with this stimulus, the first organizational principle of primary visual cortex neurons became clear: Unlike the circular receptive fields of ganglion cells, cortical neurons were responsive to edges.

Subsequent work revealed that LGN cells and ganglion cells behave similarly: Both are maximally excited by small spots of light. Such cells are best characterized as exhibiting a concentric center–surround organization. Figure 1 shows the receptive field of an LGN cell. When a spot of

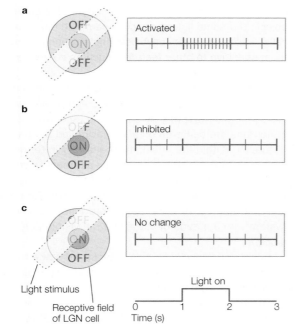

Light stimulus

Receptive field of LGN cell

Light on

Time (s)

FIGURE 1 Characteristic response of a lateral geniculate nucleus (LGN) cell.
Cells in the LGN have concentric receptive fields with either an on-center, off-surround organization or an off-center, on-surround organization. The on-center, off-surround cell shown here fires rapidly when the light encompasses the center region (**a**) and is inhibited when the light is positioned over the surround (**b**). A stimulus that spans both the center and the surround produces little change in activity (**c**). Thus, LGN cells are ideal for signaling changes in illumination, such as those that arise from stimulus edges.

192 | CHAPTER 5 Sensation and Perception

MILESTONES IN COGNITIVE NEUROSCIENCE
Pioneers in the Visual Cortex (*continued*)

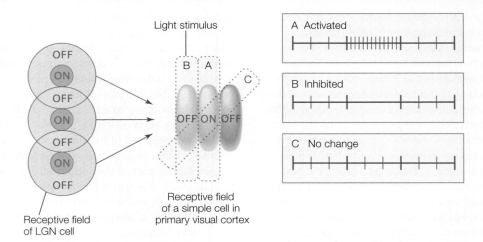

FIGURE 2 Simple cells in the primary visual cortex can be formed by the linking of outputs from concentric lateral geniculate nucleus (LGN) cells with adjacent receptive fields. In addition to signaling the presence of an edge, simple cells are selective for orientation. The simple cell illustrated here is either excited or inhibited by an edge that follows its preferred orientation. It shows no change in activity if the edge is at a perpendicular orientation.

light falls within the excitatory center region, the cell is activated. If the same spot is moved into the surrounding region, the activity is inhibited. A stimulus that encompasses both the center and the surrounding region will fail to activate the cell, because the activity from the excitatory and inhibitory regions will cancel each other out. This observation clarifies a fundamental principle of perception: *The nervous system is most interested in change.* We recognize an elephant not by the homogeneous gray surface of its body, but by the contrast of the gray edge of its shape against the background.

In Figure 2, outputs from three LGN cells with receptive fields centered at slightly different positions are linked to a single cortical neuron. This cortical neuron would continue to have a center–surround organization, but for this cell the optimal stimulus would have to be an edge. In addition, the cell would be selective for edges in a certain orientation. As the same stimulus was rotated within the receptive field, the cell would cease to respond, because the edge would now span excitatory and inhibitory regions of the cell. Hubel and Wiesel called these cells *simple cells*, because their simple organization would extract a

fundamental feature for shape perception: the border of an object. The same linking principle can yield more complex cells—cells with a receptive-field organization that makes them sensitive to other features, such as corners or edge terminations.

Orientation selectivity has proved to be a hallmark of neurons in the primary visual cortex. Across a chunk of cortex measuring 2 mm by 2 mm, the receptive fields of neurons are centered on a similar region of space (Figure 3). Within the chunk, the cells vary in terms of their preferred orientation, and they alternate between columns that are responsive to inputs from the right and left eyes. A series of such chunks allows for the full representation of external space, providing the visual system with a means of extracting the visible edges in a scene.

Hubel and Wiesel's studies established how a few organizational principles can serve as building blocks of perception derived from simple sensory neurons. The importance of their pioneering studies was acknowledged in 1981, when they shared the Nobel Prize in Physiology or Medicine.

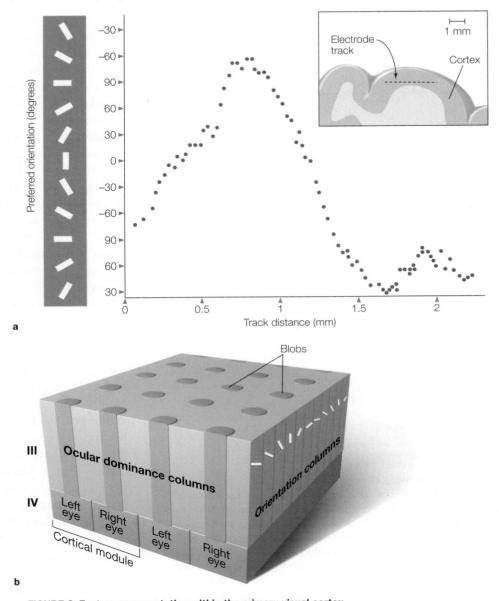

a

b

FIGURE 3 Feature representation within the primary visual cortex.
(a) As the recording electrode is moved along the cortex, the preferred orientation of the cells
continuously varies. The preferred orientation is plotted as a function of the location of the electrode.
(b) The orientation columns are crossed with ocular dominance columns to form a cortical module.
Within a module, the cells have similar receptive fields (location sensitivity), but they vary based on
input source (left or right eye) and sensitivity to orientation, color, and size. For example, the so-called
blobs contain cells that are sensitive to color and finer details in the visual input. This organization is
repeated for each module.

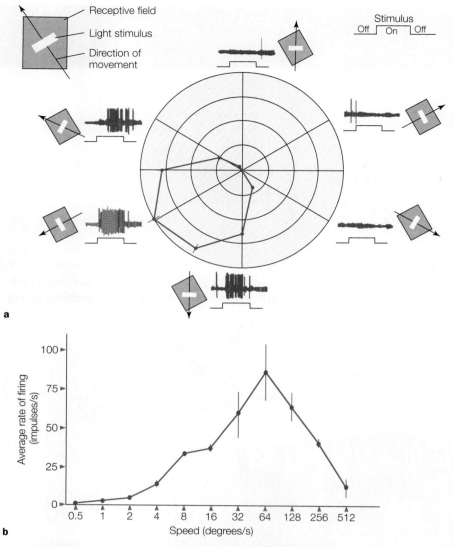

FIGURE 5.26 Direction and speed tuning of a neuron from area MT.
(a) A rectangle was moved through the receptive field of this cell in various directions. The red traces beside the stimulus cartoons indicate the responses of the cell to these stimuli. In the polar graph, the firing rates are plotted; the angular direction of each point indicates the stimulus direction, and the distance from the center indicates the firing rate as a percentage of the maximum firing rate. The polygon formed when the points are connected indicates that the cell was maximally responsive to stimuli moved down and to the left; the cell responded minimally when the stimulus moved in the opposite direction. **(b)** This graph shows speed tuning for a cell in MT. In all conditions, the motion was in the optimal direction. This cell responded most vigorously when the stimulus moved at 64°/s.

color patch was matched in luminance to its corresponding gray patch. With this setup, neurons sensitive to luminance information should be equally activated in control and experimental conditions. The colored stimulus, however, should produce more activity in neural regions sensitive to chromatic information. These regions should be detected if the metabolic activity recorded when participants viewed the gray stimulus is subtracted from the activity recorded when participants viewed the color stimulus.

The same logic was used to design the motion experiment. For this study, the control stimulus consisted of a complex black-and-white collage of squares (Figure 5.27b). The same stimulus was used in the experimental condition, except that the squares were set in motion. They would move in one direction for 5 seconds and then in the reverse direction for the next 5 seconds.

The results of the two studies provided clear evidence that the two tasks activated distinct brain regions (Figure 5.28). After subtracting activation during viewing of the achromatic collage, investigators found numerous residual foci of activation when participants viewed the colored collage. These foci were bilateral and located in the most anterior and inferior regions of the occipital lobe (Figure 5.28a). Although the spatial resolution of PET is coarse, these areas were determined to be in front of the striate (V1) and prestriate (V2) cortex. In contrast, after the appropriate subtraction in the motion experiment, the residual foci were bilateral but near the junction of the temporal, parietal, and occipital cortices (Figure 5.28b). These foci were more superior and much more lateral than the color foci.

Zeki and his colleagues were so taken with this dissociation that they proposed applying the nomenclature developed by primate researchers here. They labeled the area activated in the color foci as **area V4** and the area activated in the motion task as V5. Note that researchers frequently refer to area V5 as *human* area MT, even though the area is not in the temporal lobe in the human brain. Of course, with PET data we cannot be sure that the foci of activation really consist of just one visual area.

A comparison of Figures 5.25 and 5.28 reveals striking between-species differences in the relative position of the color and motion areas. For example, human MT is on the lateral surface of the brain, whereas the monkey MT is more medial. Such differences probably exist be-

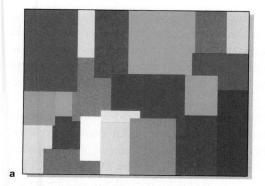

FIGURE 5.27 Stimuli used in a PET experiment to identify regions involved in color and motion perception.
(a) For the color experiment, the stimuli were composed of an arrangement of rectangles that were either shades of gray (control) or various colors (experimental). **(b)** For the motion experiment, a random pattern of black and white regions was either stationary (control) or moving (experimental).

problem, vision scientists prefer to work with flat maps of the brain. High-resolution anatomical MRI scans are obtained, and computer algorithms transform the folded, cortical surface into a two-dimensional map by tracing the gray matter. The activation signals from the fMRI study are then plotted on the flattened surface, and areas that were activated at similar times are color-coded.

Researchers have used this procedure to reveal the organization of the human visual system in exquisite detail. Activation maps, plotted on both a normal brain and as flattened maps, are shown in Figure 5.30. In the flat maps, primary visual cortex (V1) lies along the calcarine sulcus. As in all physiological studies, the physical world is inverted. Except for the most anterior aspects of visual cortex, areas above the sulcus are active when the rotating stimulus is in the lower quadrant; the reverse is true when the stimulus is in the upper quadrant. Moreover, the activation patterns show a series of repetitions across

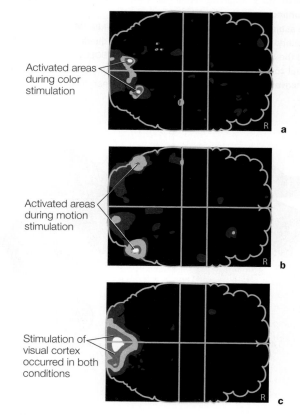

FIGURE 5.28 Regions of activation when the control conditions were subtracted from the experimental conditions in the experiment illustrated in Figure 5.27. (a) In the color condition, the prominent activation was medial, in areas corresponding to human V4. **(b)** In the motion condition, the activation was more lateral, in areas corresponding to human MT. The foci also differed along the dorsoventral axis: The slice showing MT is superior to that showing V4. **(c)** Both stimuli produced significant activation in primary visual cortex, when compared to a control condition in which there was no visual stimulation.

cause the surface area of the human brain is substantially larger, and this expansion required additional folding of the continuous cortical sheet.

The activation maps in Zeki's PET study are rather crude. Vision scientists now employ sophisticated fMRI techniques to study the organization of human visual cortex. In these studies, a stimulus is systematically moved across the visual field (Figure 5.29). For example, a semicircular checkerboard pattern is slowly rotated about the center of view. In this way, the blood oxygen level–dependent (BOLD) response for areas representing the superior quadrant will be activated at a different time than areas representing the inferior quadrant—and in fact, the representation of the entire visual field can be continuously tracked. To compare areas that respond to foveal stimulation and those that respond to peripheral stimulation, researchers use a dilating and contracting ring stimulus. By combining these different stimuli, they can measure the cortical representation of external space.

Due to the convoluted nature of the human visual cortex, the results from such an experiment would be difficult to decipher if we were to plot the data on the anatomical maps found in a brain atlas. To avoid this

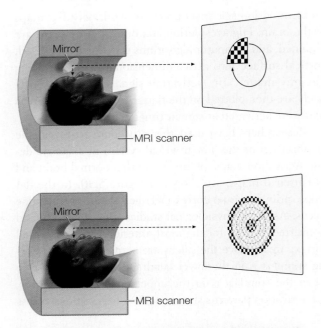

the visual cortex indicating distinct topographic maps. Following the conventions adopted in the single-cell studies in monkeys, the visual areas are numbered in increasing order, where primary visual cortex (V1) is most posterior and secondary visual areas (V2, V3/VP, V4) more anterior.

Functional MRI mapping procedures can reveal multiple visual areas and can be used for comparison with the data obtained in work with monkeys. Within lateral occipital cortex (LOC), two subareas, LO1 and LO2, are evident. These regions had not been identified in previous studies of the monkey, and they provide further evidence of the expansion of visual cortex in humans (Figure 5.30). Interestingly, although activity in these areas is not modulated by motion per se, the regions do show an increase in the BOLD response when motion signals define object boundaries (e.g., a moving stimulus occludes the background) as well as when viewing displays of objects compared to scrambled images.

Figure 5.30b also shows how *eccentricity*, the distance away from the fixation point, is also represented in these visual areas. Eccentricity refers to the radial distance from the center of vision (the foveal region) to the periphery. The cortical representation of the fovea, the regions shown in purple, pink, and red, is quite large. Visual acuity is much

FIGURE 5.29 Mapping visual fields with functional magnetic resonance imaging (fMRI).
The subject views a rotating circular wedge while fMRI scans are obtained. The wedge passes from one visual quadrant to the next, and the blood oxygenation level–dependent (BOLD) response in visual cortex is measured continuously to map out how the regions of activation change in a corresponding manner.

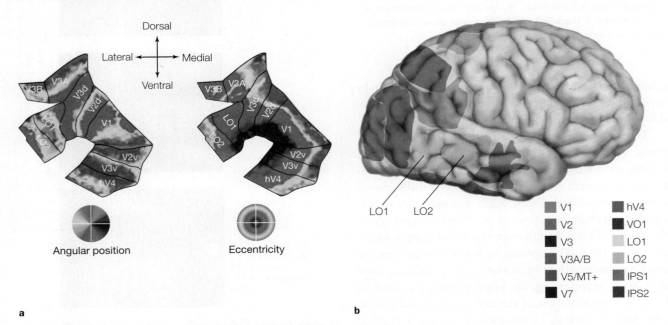

a

b

FIGURE 5.30 Two retinotopic areas in human lateral occipital cortex (LOC).
(a) The circular displays at the bottom represent the display on which a stimulus was projected, with the person instructed to fixate at the center of the crosshair. Across the scanning run, the position of the stimulus spans visual space. Left side shows color coding of activation patterns on flat map of visual cortex when the angular position of a stimulus was varied. For example, areas responding when the stimulus was presented below fixation are coded as red. Multiple retinotopic maps are evident in dorsal and ventral regions. Right side shows color coding of activation patterns when the eccentricity of the stimulus was varied (e.g., dark purple indicates activation areas when stimulus was at center of fixation).
(b) Position of visual areas shown in (a) on an inflated brain. The size and location can only be approximated in a lateral view of the 3-d image.

greater at the fovea due to the disproportionate amount of cortex that encodes information from this part of space.

As we discussed in Chapter 3, technology marches on, and even more powerful tools are constantly being developed to provide better images of brain function. In the MRI world, stronger magnets improve the resolution of the fMRI signal. A 7-tesla (T) fMRI system is capable of providing detailed pictures of organizational principles within a visual area (Yacoub, 2008). Within V1, a 7-T magnet can reveal ocular dominance columns whose areas have similar retinotopic tuning, thus showing a preference for input from either the right or left eye. A shift across voxels in terms of orientation tuning is also visible. Such specificity is striking when we keep in mind that the activation within a voxel reflects the contribution of millions of neurons. Orientation tuning does not mean that all of these neurons have similar orientation preferences. Rather, it means that the relative contribution of orientation-selective neurons varies across voxels. Some voxels have a stronger contribution from vertically oriented cells; others, a stronger contribution from horizontally oriented cells (Figure 5.31).

TAKE-HOME MESSAGES

- The visual cortex is made up of many distinct regions. These regions are defined by their distinct, retinotopic maps. The visual areas have functional differences that reflect the types of computations performed by cells within the areas. For instance, cells in area V4 are sensitive to color information, and cells in V5 are sensitive to motion information.
- Humans also have visual areas that do not correspond to any region in our close primate relatives.

From Sensation to Perception

In Chapter 6, we will explore the question of how our sensory experiences are turned into percepts—how we take the information from our sensory systems and use it to recognize objects and scenes. Here we briefly discuss the relationship between sensation and perception, describing experiments that ask how activation in early sensory areas relates to our perceptual experience. For example, is activation in early visual cortex sufficient to support perception? Or does that information have to be relayed to higher visual areas in order for us to recognize the presence of a stimulus?

We have seen in the previous section that certain elementary features are represented in early sensory areas, usually with some form of topographic organization. Cells

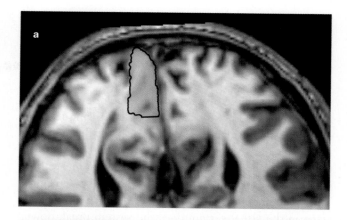

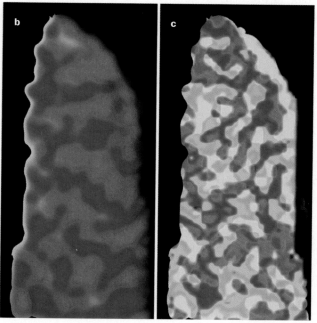

FIGURE 5.31 High field resolution of human visual cortex.
(a) Selected region of interest (ROI) in primary visual cortex targeted with a 7T MRI scanner. **(b)** At this resolution, it is possible to image ocular dominance columns, with red indicating areas that were active when the stimulus was presented to the right eye and blue areas that were active when the stimulus was presented to the left eye. **(c)** Orientation map in the ROI. Colors indicate preference for bars presented at different angles.

in auditory cortex are tuned to specific frequency bands; cells in visual cortex represent properties such as orientation, color, and motion. The information represented in primary sensory areas is refined and integrated as we move into secondary sensory areas. An important question is: At what stage of processing does this sensory stimulation become a percept, something we experience phenomenally?

Where Are Percepts Formed?

One way to study this question is to "trick" our sensory processing systems with stimuli that cause us to form percepts that do not correspond to the true stimuli in the environment. In other words, what we perceive is an illusion. By following the processing of such stimuli using fMRI, we can attempt to determine where in the processing stream the signals become derailed. For instance, if we look at a colored disc that changes color every second from red to green, we have no problem seeing the two colors in succession. If the same display flips between the two colors 25 times per second (or 25 Hz), however, then the percept is of a fused color—a constant, yellowish white disc (the additive effects of red and green light). This phenomenon is known as flicker fusion. At what stage in the visual system does the system break down, failing to keep up with the flickering stimulus? Does it occur early in processing within the subcortical structures, or is it later, in one of the cortical visual areas?

Using a flickering stimulus, Sheng He and colleagues tested participants while observing the changes in visual cortex (Jiang et al., 2007). In Figure 5.32, compare the fMRI BOLD responses for visual areas V1, V4, and VO during a 5-Hz full-contrast flicker condition (perceptually two colors), a 30-Hz full-contrast flicker condition (perceptually one fused color), and a control condition, which was a 5-Hz subthreshold contrast condition (perceptually indistinguishable from the 30-Hz flicker). Subcortical processing and several of the lower cortical processing areas, V1 and V4, were able to distinguish between the 5-Hz flicker, the 30-Hz flicker, and the 5-Hz nonflickering control. In contrast, the BOLD response within a visual area just adjacent to V4, VO, did not differentiate between the high-flicker stimulus and the static control stimulus (Figure 5.32). We can conclude that the illusion—a yellowish object that is not flickering—is formed in this higher visual area (known variously as either VO or V8), indicating that although the information is sensed accurately at earlier stages within the visual stream, conscious perception, at least of color, is more closely linked to higher-area activity.

In a related study, John-Dylan Haynes and Geraint Rees at the University College London asked if fMRI could be used to detect the neural fingerprints of unconscious "perception" (Haynes & Rees, 2005). Participants were asked to decide which of two ways a stimulus was oriented (Figure 5.33). When shown the stimulus for just a 20th of a second, people can identify its orientation with a high degree of accuracy. If, however, the stimulus is presented even faster—say, for just a 30th of a second—and it is preceded and followed by a mask of crosshatched lines, performance drops to chance levels. Nonetheless, by using a sophisticated pattern recognition algorithm on the fMRI data, the researchers were able to show that activity in V1 could distinguish which stimulus had been presented—an effect that was lost in V2 and V3.

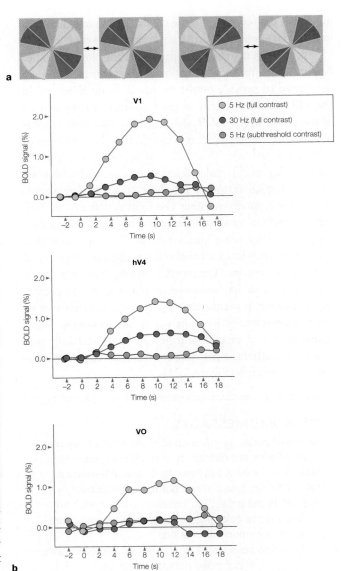

FIGURE 5.32 Imaging the neural correlates of perception.
(a) Flickering pinwheel stimulus for studying limits of temporal resolution. The left and right stimuli alternated at different rates or contrast. **(b)** BOLD response to the flickering stimuli in three visual areas, V1, hV4, and VO. The activation profile in VO matches the participants' perceptual experience since the color changes in the stimulus were invisible at the high 30 Hz rate or when the contrast was below threshold. In contrast, the activation profile in V1 and hV4 is correlated with the actual stimulus when the contrast was above threshold.

As the preceding examples indicate, our primary sensory regions provide a representation that is closely linked to the physical stimulus, and our perceptual experience is more dependent on activity in secondary and association sensory regions. Note, though, that the examples base this argument on the fact that the absence of a perceptual experience was matched by the absence of detectable activity in secondary regions. We can also consider the flip side of the coin, by asking what brain regions show

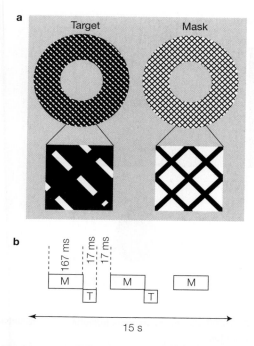

FIGURE 5.33 Activity in V1 can predict orientation of an invisible stimulus.
(a) Participants viewed an annulus in which the lines were either oriented in only one direction (target) or both directions (mask).
(b) In some trials, the target was presented for only 17 ms and was preceded by the mask. On these trials, the target was not visible to the participant. A pattern classifier was used to predict from the fMRI data if the target was oriented to the left or right. When the stimulus was visible, the classifier was very accurate when using data from V1, V2, or V3. When the stimulus was invisible due to the mask, the classifier only achieved above chance performance for the data from V1.

activation patterns that are correlated with illusory percepts. Stare at the Enigma pattern in Figure 5.34. After a few seconds, you should begin to see scintillating motion within the blue circles—an illusion created by their opposed orientation to the radial black and white lines. What are the neural correlates of this illusion? We know that moving patterns produce a strong hemodynamic response in V5. Is this same area also activated during illusory motion? Both PET and fMRI have been used to show that viewing displays like the Enigma pattern does indeed lead to pronounced activity in V5. This activation is selective: Activity in V1 does not increase during illusory motion.

An even stronger case for the hypothesis that perception is more closely linked to secondary sensory areas would require evidence showing that activity in these areas can be sufficient, and even predictive of perception. This idea was tested in a remarkable study performed by Michael Shadlen and his colleagues at the University of Washington (Ditterich et al., 2003). They used a reverse engineering strategy to manipulate activation patterns in sensory cortex. As we noted earlier, physiologists usually eavesdrop on

neurons in sensory cortex using electrodes that probe how cells respond to information in the environment. The same electrodes can also be used to activate cells. When a current passes through the electrode, neurons near the tip of the electrode are activated. In the Shadlen study, researchers used this method to measure motion perception. Monkeys were trained to make an eye movement, indicating the perceived direction of a patch of moving dots (Figure 5.35). To make the task challenging, only a small percentage of the dots moved in a common direction; the rest moved in random directions. The researchers then recorded from a cell in area MT. After determining the directional tuning of that cell, they passed a current through the electrode while the stimulus was present. This manipulation increased the probability that the monkey would report that the stimulus was moving in the cell's preferred direction (Figure 5.35). Note that the electrical current, at least with this method, will likely induce activity in many neurons. Nonetheless, the finding that the animal's percept was altered suggests that neighboring cells have similar direction-tuning properties, consistent with a topographic representation of motion direction in MT.

Of course, with the monkeys, we can only infer their perception from behavior; it is problematic to infer that these percepts correspond to conscious experience. Similar stimulation methods have been used on rare occasions in humans during intraoperative surgical procedures. In one such procedure, electrodes were positioned along the ventral regions of visual cortex (Murphey et al., 2008). This region includes at least two areas that are known to be involved with color processing: the posterior center in the lingual gyrus of the occipital lobe (V4) and

FIGURE 5.34 The Enigma pattern: a visual illusion.
When viewing the Enigma pattern, we perceive illusory motion. Viewing the pattern is accompanied by activation in area MT.

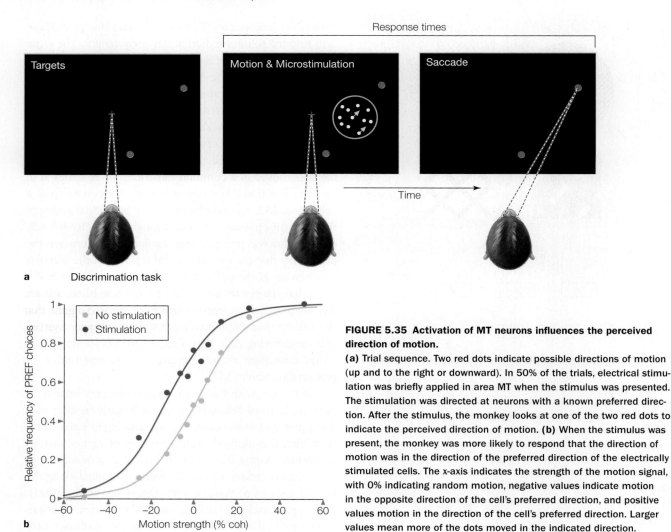

a Discrimination task

b

FIGURE 5.35 Activation of MT neurons influences the perceived direction of motion.
(a) Trial sequence. Two red dots indicate possible directions of motion (up and to the right or downward). In 50% of the trials, electrical stimulation was briefly applied in area MT when the stimulus was presented. The stimulation was directed at neurons with a known preferred direction. After the stimulus, the monkey looks at one of the two red dots to indicate the perceived direction of motion. **(b)** When the stimulus was present, the monkey was more likely to respond that the direction of motion was in the direction of the preferred direction of the electrically stimulated cells. The x-axis indicates the strength of the motion signal, with 0% indicating random motion, negative values indicate motion in the opposite direction of the cell's preferred direction, and positive values motion in the direction of the cell's preferred direction. Larger values mean more of the dots moved in the indicated direction.

the anterior center in the medial fusiform gyrus of the temporal lobe, which has been labeled V4α. When used as recording devices, electrodes in either area responded in a selective manner to chromatic stimuli. For example, the activity at one location was stronger to one color as compared to another. Even more interesting was what happened when the electrodes were used as stimulating devices. In the anterior color region, stimulation led to the patient reporting seeing a colored, amorphous shape. Moreover, the color of the illusion was similar to the preferred color for that site. Thus, in this higher visual area, there was a close correspondence between the perception of a color when it was elicited by a visual stimulus and when the cortex was electrically stimulated.

Individual Differences in Perception

Occasionally, when viewing illusions with a friend, you will find that the two of you don't have the same reaction. You might be saying, "This is crazy!" Mean-

while, your friend is shrugging her shoulders, wondering what you are seeing. Although we commonly accept the idea that people have different emotional reactions to similar situations, we tend to assume that everyone perceives the same things. In this example, we might assume your friend just doesn't know how to "look" at the display in the right way. To test this assumption, researchers sought to identify neural biomarkers that might account for individual differences in perception (Schwarzkopf et al., 2011).

Figure 5.36 shows one of the classic illusions in visual perception: the Ebbinghaus illusion, devised by Hermann Ebbinghaus (1850–1909), a German pioneer in experimental psychology. Compare the size of the two circles in the middle of the displays on the left and right. Does one look larger than the other? By how much? Everyone sees the middle circle on the right as larger than the one on the left, but people vary considerably regarding how much larger they think the circle is. Some individuals see the right inner circle as larger by only about 10%. For others, the illusion is close to 50%. These differences

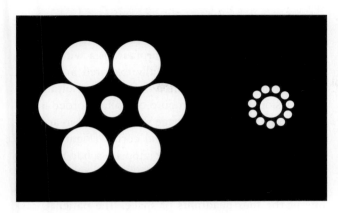

FIGURE 5.36 Strength of a visual size illusion is correlated with size of V1.
Compare the size of the center circle in the two images. People see the one on the right as larger, an illusion first described by Ebbinghaus. Across individuals, the strength of the illusion is correlated with the size of V1.

are quite reliable and can be observed across a range of size illusions, leading the research team to wonder about their underlying cause. They used fMRI to identify retinotopic areas and then measured the size of the functionally defined area. Remarkably, they observed a negative correlation between the size of the illusion and the size of V1. The smaller the area of V1, the larger the perceived illusion. This correlation was not found with V2 or V3.

Why might people with a larger V1 show a smaller illusion? One hypothesis is that with a large visual cortex, each region of space has a better representation. A corollary of this is that each region of space is less likely to be influenced from neighboring regions of space. Hence, in the Ebbinghaus illusion, the neighboring circles have less influence on the central circle when a larger V1 provides a higher-resolution representation of space. Perception, then, is in the brain anatomy of the beholder.

To try out more fascinating illusions, go to http://www.michaelbach.de/ot/.

TAKE-HOME MESSAGES

- Our percepts are more closely related to activity in higher visual areas than to activity in primary visual cortex.
- Anatomical differences among people in the size of V1 affect the extent of visual illusion.

Deficits in Visual Perception

Before the advent of neuroimaging, much of what we learned about visual processing in the human brain came from lesion studies. In 1888, Louis Verrey (cited in Zeki, 1993), described a patient who, after suffering a stroke, had lost the ability to perceive colors in her right visual field. Verrey reported that while the patient had problems with acuity within restricted portions of this right visual field, the color deficit was uniform and complete. After his patient's death, Verrey performed an autopsy. What he found led him to conclude there was a "centre for the chromatic sense" (Zeki, 1993) in the human brain, which he located in the lingual and fusiform gyri. We can guess that this patient's world looked similar to the drawing in Figure 5.37: On one side of space, the world was multicolored; on the other, it was a montage of grays.

Deficits in Color Perception: Achromatopsia

When we speak of someone who is color-blind, we are usually describing a person who has inherited a gene that produces an abnormality in the photoreceptor system. *Dichromats*, people with only two photopigments, can be classified as red–green color-blind if they are missing the photopigment sensitive to either medium or long wavelengths, or blue–yellow color-blind if they are missing the short-wavelength photopigment. *Anomalous trichromats*, in contrast, have all three photopigments, but one of the pigments exhibits abnormal sensitivity. The incidence of these genetic disorders is high in males: about 8% of the population. The incidence in females is less than 1%.

Much rarer are disorders of color perception that arise from disturbances of the central nervous system. These disorders are called **achromatopsia** (from the prefix *a–*, "without," and the stem *chroma*, "hue"). J. C. Meadows (1974)

FIGURE 5.37 People with achromatopsia see the world as devoid of color.
Because color differences are usually correlated with brightness differences, the objects in a scene might be distinguishable and appear as different shades of gray. This figure shows how the world might look to a person with hemiachromatopsia. Most of the people who are affected have some residual color perception, although they cannot distinguish between subtle color variations.

of the National Hospital for Neurology and Neurosurgery in London described one such patient as follows:

> Everything looked black or grey [Figure 5.37]. He had difficulty distinguishing British postage stamps of different value, which look alike, but are of different colors. He was a keen gardener, but found that he pruned live rather than dead vines. He had difficulty distinguishing certain foods on his plate where color was the distinguishing mark. (p. 629)

Patients with achromatopsia often report that colors have become a bland palette of "dirty shades of gray." The shading reflects variations in brightness rather than hue. Other aspects of vision, such as depth and texture perception, remain intact, enabling someone with achromatopsia to see and recognize objects in the world. Indeed, color is not a necessary cue for shape perception. The subtlety of color perception is underscored when we consider that people often do not notice the change from black and white to color when Dorothy lands in Oz in the movie *The Wizard of Oz.* Nonetheless, when lost forever, this subtlety is sorely missed.

Achromatopsia has consistently been associated with lesions that encompass V4 and the region anterior to V4. The lesions, however, typically extend to neighboring regions of the visual cortex. Color-sensitive neurons are also orientation selective; as such, many achromatic patients have difficulty with form perception.

The hypothesis linking achromatopsia with deficits in form perception was carefully explored in the case study of a patient who suffered a stroke resulting in a small lesion near the temporo-occipital border in the *right* hemisphere. The damage was centered in area V4 and anterior parts of the visual cortex (Figure 5.38a). To assess the patient's achromatopsia, a hue-matching experiment was performed in which a sample color was presented at the fovea, followed by a test color in one of the four quadrants of space. The patient's task was to judge if the two colors were the same. The difference between the sample and test color was adjusted until the patient was performing correctly on 80% of the trials, and this difference was measured separately for each quadrant. Regardless of the sample hue, the patient was severely impaired on the hue-matching task when the test color was presented in the *upper left* visual field (Figure 5.38b). The fact that the deficit was found only in the upper *contralesional* visual field is consistent with previous reports of achromatopsia.

The next order of business was to examine shape perception. Would the patient show similar deficits in shape perception in this quadrant? If so, what types of shape perception tasks would reveal the impairment? To

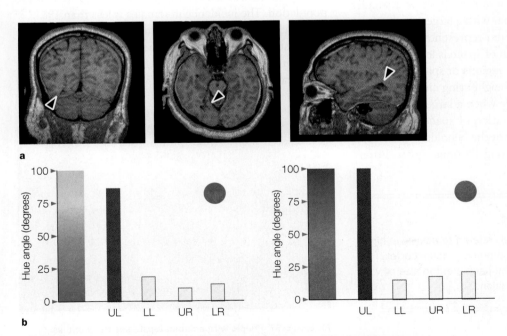

FIGURE 5.38 Color and shape perception in a patient with a unilateral lesion of V4.
(a) MRI scans showing a small lesion encompassing V4 in the right hemisphere.
(b) Color perception thresholds in each visual quadrant. The patient was severely impaired on the hue-matching task when the test color was presented to the upper left visual field. The y-axis indicates the color required to detect a difference between a patch shown in each visual quadrant (UL = upper left, LL = lower left, UR = upper right, LR = lower right) and the target color shown at the fovea. The target color was red for the results shown in the top panel and green for the results shown in the bottom panel.

answer these questions, a variety of tasks were administered. The stimuli are shown in Figure 5.39. On the basic visual discriminations of contrast, orientation, and motion, the patient's performance was similar for all four quadrants and comparable to the performance of control participants. He showed impairment on tests of higher order shape perception, however; and again, this impairment was restricted to the upper left quadrant. For these tasks, shape information requires combining information from neurons that might detect simple properties such as line orientation. For example, the orientation of the line separating the two semicircles (Figure 5.39d) is defined only by the combination of the lengths of the individual stripes and their offset.

Characterizing area V4 as a "color" area is too simplistic. This area is part of secondary visual areas devoted to shape perception. Color can provide an important cue about an object's shape. V4 may be invaluable for using color information as one cue to define the boundaries that separate the objects that form our visual environment.

Revisiting patient P.T. Let's return to patient P.T., who we met at the beginning of the chapter. Recall that he had difficulty recognizing familiar places and objects follow-

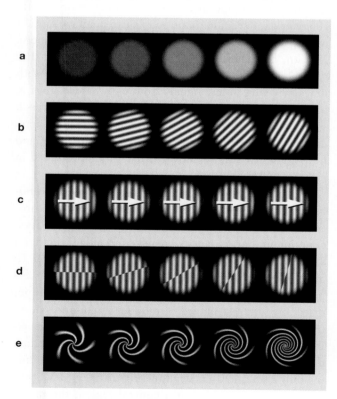

FIGURE 5.39 Tests of form perception.
Stimuli used to assess form perception in the patient with damage to area V4 illustrated in Figure 5.38. On basic tests of luminance (a), orientation (b), and motion (c), the patient's perceptual threshold was similar in all four quadrants. Thresholds for illusory contours (d) and complex shapes (e) were elevated in the upper left quadrant.

ing a stroke to his right hemisphere. Further examination revealed some puzzling features of his perceptual deficits.

P.T. was shown two paintings: one by Monet, depicting a subdued 19th-century countryman dressed in his Sunday suit; the other by Picasso, of a woman with a terrified expression (Figure 5.40). P.T. was asked to describe what he saw in each painting. When shown the Monet, he looked puzzled. He saw no definable forms, just an abstract blend of colors and shapes. His problem in interpreting the painting was consonant with the deficits he experienced at home. Yet he readily identified the figure in Picasso's painting and pointed out that it was a woman, or perhaps a young girl. This dissociation is compelling, for most would readily agree that the Monet is more realistic. Picasso painted the parts of his work as separate units. He used sharp contrasts in brightness and vivid colors to highlight facial regions. Monet opted for a softer approach, in which parts are best seen in a continuous whole, with gradual changes in contrast and color. Can any of these factors account for P.T.'s performance in identifying the figures in Picasso and Monet?

The neurologist evaluating P.T. emphasized that the primary problem stemmed from a deficit in color perception. This hypothesis is in accord with one of the primary differences between the Monet and the Picasso. In the Monet painting, the boundaries between the face and the background are blended: Gradual variations in color demarcate the facial regions and separate them from the background landscape. A deficit in color perception provided a parsimonious account of the patient's problems in recognizing faces and landscapes. The rolling green hills of an Oregon farm can blur into a homogeneous mass if a person cannot discern fine variations in color. In a similar way, each face has its characteristic coloration.

It seems equally plausible, however, that the problem stemmed from a deficit in contrast or contour perception. These features are salient in the Picasso and absent in the Monet. Indeed, we know from our recent discussion of V4 that color and shape perception are often conflated. It is clear that the patient's stroke affected primarily the cortical projections of the pathways essential for color and form perception. In contrast, the cortical projections of the pathway involved in motion were intact. The patient had no trouble recognizing his wife as she moved from the stove to the kitchen table; indeed, P.T. commented that her idiosyncratic movement enabled him to recognize her.

Deficits in Motion Perception: Akinetopsia

In 1983, researchers at the Max Planck Institute in Munich reported a striking case of a woman who had incurred

a   b

FIGURE 5.40 Two portraits.
(a) Detail from *Luncheon on the Grass*, painted in the 1860s by the French Impressionist Claude Monet. **(b)** Pablo Picasso's *Weeping Woman*, painted in 1937 during his Cubist period. © 2008 Estate of Pablo Picasso/Artists Right Society (ARS), New York.

a selective loss of motion perception, or **akinetopsia** (Zihl et al., 1983). For this woman, whom we call M.P., perception was akin to viewing the world as a series of snapshots. Rather than seeing things move continuously in space, she saw moving objects appear in one position and then another. When pouring a cup of tea, M.P. would see the liquid frozen in air, like a glacier. She would fail to notice the tea rising in her cup and would be surprised when the cup overflowed. The loss of motion perception also made M.P. hesitant about crossing the street. As she noted, "When I'm looking at the car first, it seems far away. But then, when I want to cross the road, suddenly the car is very near" (Zihl et al., 1983, p. 315).

Examination revealed M.P.'s color and form perception to be intact. Her ability to perceive briefly presented objects and letters, for example, was within the normal range. Nonetheless, her ability to judge the direction and speed of moving objects was severely impaired. This deficit was most apparent with stimuli moving at high speeds. At speeds faster than 20°/s, M.P. never reported detecting the motion. She could see that a dot's position had changed and hence could infer motion. But her percept was of two static images; there was no continuity from one image to the other. Even when presented with stimuli moving more slowly, M.P. was hesitant to report a clear impression of motion.

CT scans of M.P. revealed large, bilateral lesions involving the temporoparietal cortices. On each side, the lesions included posterior and lateral portions of the middle temporal gyrus. These lesions roughly corresponded to areas that participate in motion perception. Furthermore, the lesions were lateral and superior to human V4, including the area identified as V5, the human equivalent of area MT (Figure 5.41).

Although the case of M.P. has been cited widely for many years, the fact that similar patients have not been identified suggests that severe forms of akinetopsia result only from bilateral lesions. With unilateral lesions, the motion perception deficits are much more subtle (Plant et al., 1993). Perhaps people can perceive motion as long as human V5 is intact in at least one hemisphere. Motion, by definition, is a dynamic percept, one that typically unfolds over an extended period of time. With longer viewing times, signals from early visual areas in the impaired hemisphere have an opportunity to reach secondary visual areas in the unimpaired hemisphere. The receptive fields in primate area V5 are huge and have cells that can be activated by stimuli presented in either visual field.

Still, the application of transcranial magnetic stimulation (TMS; see Chapter 3) over human V5 can produce transient deficits in motion perception. In one such experiment, participants were asked to judge whether a stimulus moved up or down (Stevens et al., 2009). To make the task demanding, the displays consisted of a patch of dots, only some of which moved in the target direction; the rest moved in random directions. Moreover, the target was preceded and followed by "masking" stimuli in which all of the dots moved in random directions. Thus, the stimulus direction was visible during only a brief 100-ms window (Figure 5.42). TMS was applied over either V5 or a control region, the motor cortex. Performance of the motion task was disrupted by stimulation over V5, creating a transient form of akinetopsia.

One feature of TMS that makes it such an excellent research tool is that investigators can vary the timing of

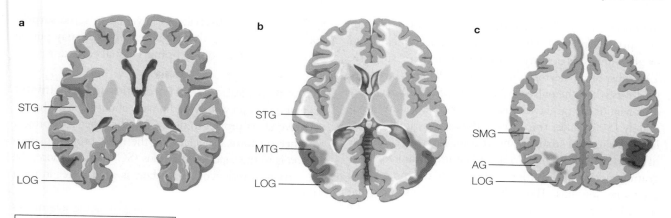

STG	Superior temporal gyrus
MTG	Medial temporal gyrus
LOG	Lateral occipital gyri
AG	Angular gyrus
SMG	Supramarginal gyrus

FIGURE 5.41 Reconstruction of a lesion producing severe akinetopsia.
Three horizontal sections showing the patient's bilateral lesions in the left and right hemispheres. Note that the lesions encompass area MTG in both hemispheres.

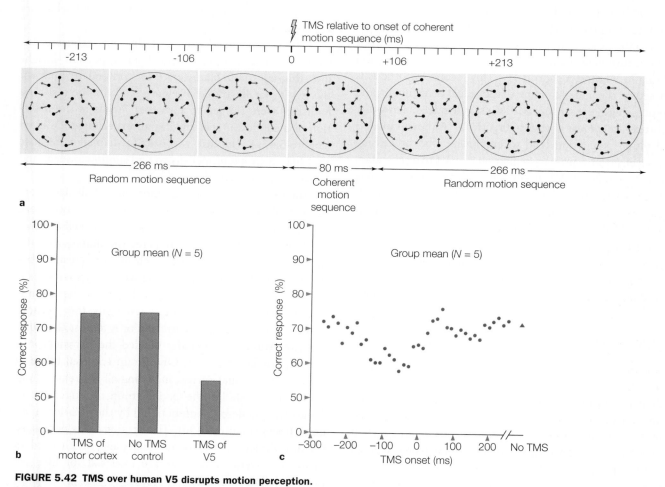

FIGURE 5.42 TMS over human V5 disrupts motion perception.
(a) The stimulus was an 80 ms display of moving dots in which a small percentage of the dots moved in the same direction. This display was preceded and followed by displays in which the direction of motion for all of the dots was random. (b) Performance was impaired when the TMS was applied over V5, relative to two control conditions (TMS over motor cortex or no TMS). (c) When the timing of the TMS pulse was varied to either come before the stimulus (negative values) or after the stimulus (positive values), two epochs of disruption were identified.

the magnetic pulses to determine the time of maximum disruption. Knowing when a disruption occurs can help locate where it is occurring. To the researchers' surprise, TMS disrupted performance at two distinct intervals. One was when the pulse was applied about 100 ms *before* the onset of the target stimulus. The second was approximately 150 ms after the onset of the target stimulus. This latter timing isn't so surprising. It coincides with estimates of when activity within V5 would be important for integrating motion information to determine the direction of a moving stimulus. Thus, the researchers assumed that the pulses applied at this point in time added noise to the representations in V5.

What was that first disruption, when the TMS pulse was delivered before the onset of the target stimulus? The phenomenon was puzzling. The deficit here is unlikely to be the direct result of a perturbation of V5 neurons, because if that were true, we should not see performance improve before falling off again. Two other hypotheses should be considered. First, TMS at this point might disrupt the observer's *attentional* focus, making it hard to orient to the target stimulus. Second, TMS over V5 may not only cause neurons in V5 to fire but also trigger neural firing in V1 after a short delay. This second hypothesis is based on the understanding that cortical connectivity and processing along sensory pathways, and indeed, across the cortex, are almost always bidirectional. Although models of visual perception tend to emphasize that processing proceeds from a primary region such as V1 to a secondary visual area such as V5, prominent pathways also are going in the reverse direction. Based on the second hypothesis, the first dip in performance is due to the indirect effect of the TMS pulse on V1 activity, and the second dip in performance is due to the direct effect of the TMS pulse on V5 activity. This observation is roughly consistent with the temporal pattern of activity observed in single-cell recordings in these two areas in response to moving stimuli.

Perception Without a Visual Cortex

Almost all of the ascending axons from the LGN terminate in the primary visual cortex. An individual with damaged primary visual cortex is expected to be blind; and indeed, this is what is observed. The blindness may be incomplete, however. If the lesion is restricted to one half of the visual field, the loss of perception will be restricted to the contralateral side of space; such a deficit is referred to as **hemianopia**. Smaller lesions may produce more discrete regions of blindness, or **scotomas**. Patients with primary visual cortex lesions are unable to report seeing anything presented within a scotoma. As anatomists have shown, however, the cortex includes not only multiple visual pathways but also prominent subcortical visual

pathways. These observations have led to some surprising findings showing that visual capabilities may persist even in the absence of the primary visual cortex.

Cortical and Subcortical Perception in the Hamster

As mentioned previously, in humans about 90% of the optic nerve fibers project to the LGN. The other 10% project to other subcortical nuclei, and the most prominent projection is to the superior colliculus (SC). What's more, the proportion of retinocollicular fibers is even larger in most other species.

The SC plays a critical role in producing eye movements. If this midbrain structure becomes atrophied, as in a degenerative disorder such as supranuclear palsy, eye movements become paralyzed. Stimulation of neurons in the SC can also trigger eye movements; the direction of movement depends on the stimulation site. Observations like this emphasize an important motor role for the SC, but it is also interesting to ask about the representation of the visual world in the SC. What kinds of visual behaviors are possible from this system?

Gerald Schneider (1969), at the Massachusetts Institute of Technology, provided an important insight into this question. Hamsters were trained to perform the two tasks illustrated in Figure 5.43. In one task, the hamsters were trained to turn their heads in the direction of a sunflower seed held in an experimenter's hand (Figure 5.43a). The task was easy for hamsters because they have a strong propensity to find sunflower seeds and put them in their cheeks.

The second task presented more of a challenge. Here the animals were trained to run down a two-armed maze and enter the door behind which a sunflower seed was hidden (Figure 5.43b). The task required the animals to make simple visual discriminations, such as distinguishing between black and white doors or between doors with vertical or horizontal stripes. For normal hamsters, the discriminations are not taxing. Within a few trials, they became proficient in selecting the correct door in almost all trials.

After training, Schneider divided the hamsters into two experimental groups. One group received bilateral lesions of the visual cortex, including all of areas 17 and 18 (Figure 5.43c). For the second group, the superior colliculus was rendered nonfunctional by the ablation of its input fibers (Figure 5.43d). This strategy was necessary because direct lesions to the colliculus, which borders many brainstem nuclei that are essential for life, are likely to kill the animals.

The two lesions yielded a double dissociation. Cortical lesions severely impaired the animals' performance on the visual identification tasks. The animals could run down the maze and had sufficient motor capabilities to enter one of the doors, but they could not discriminate black from white or horizontal from vertical stripes. In contrast, the animals with collicular lesions demonstrated no impairment on this task.

On the sunflower seed localization task, the deficits were reversed. Animals with cortical lesions were perfect at this task once they had recovered from the surgery. Yet animals with collicular lesions acted as though they were blind. They made no attempt to orient toward the seeds—and not because they were unmotivated or had a motor problem. If the seed brushed against a whisker, the animal rapidly turned toward it and gobbled it up.

These data provide compelling evidence for dissociable functions of the hamsters' superior colliculus and visual cortex. The collicular lesions impaired their ability to orient toward the position of a stimulus, and the cortical lesions disrupted visual acuity. For the hamster, this double dissociation might be thought of as reflecting two systems: one devoted to spatial orientation, the other devoted to object identification. As we will see in the next chapter, the idea that the representation of the properties of a stimulus and its location may entail different neural pathways is also an important idea for understanding visual processing within the cortex. We will return to the issue of residual perception following damage to the primary visual cortex in Chapter 14 when we turn to the question of consciousness.

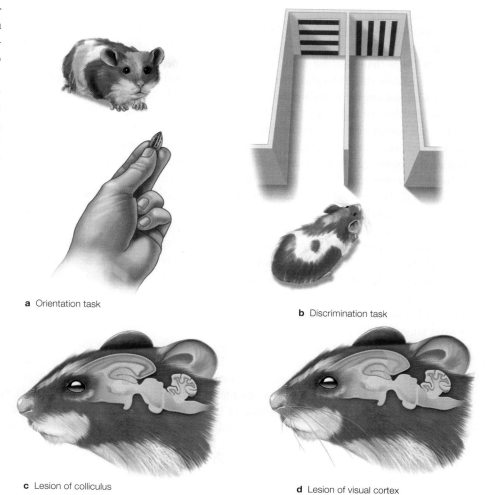

a Orientation task

b Discrimination task

c Lesion of colliculus

d Lesion of visual cortex

FIGURE 5.43 Double dissociation between lesions of the superior colliculus and visual cortex. **(a)** In the orientation task, hamsters were trained to collect sunflower seeds that were held at various positions in space. **(b)** In the discrimination task, hamsters were trained to run down one of two alleys toward a door that had either horizontal or vertical stripes. **(c)** Lesions of the colliculus disrupted performance on the localization task. **(d)** Lesions of the visual cortex selectively impaired performance on the discrimination task.

- These regions do not just represent color, however; they are also important for shape perception. Color is one attribute that facilitates the perception of shape.
- Akinetopsia, the inability to process motion, results from lesions to area V5 (human MT).
- As with many neurological conditions, the deficit can be quite subtle for unilateral lesions.

TAKE-HOME MESSAGES

- Superior colliculus lesions impair the ability of an animal to orient toward the position of a stimulus (which is important for spatial orientation); visual cortex lesions impair visual acuity (which is important for object identification).
- Achromatopsia, the inability to perceive color, results from lesions to areas in and around human V4.

Multimodal Perception: I See What You're Sayin'

Each of our senses gives us unique information about the world we live in. Color is a visual experience; pitch is uniquely auditory. Even though the information provided by each sense is distinct, the resulting representation of the surrounding world is not one of disjointed sensations, but of a unified multisensory experience. A meal in a restaurant is more than just the taste of the food. Restaurant owners know that the visual presentation of the food and the surroundings, the background noise or the lack of it, the comfort of the chairs, the fragrances from the kitchen, the interaction with the server, all contribute to how you will rate the restaurant's cooking—that is, the combined experience of all the senses affects the taste of the food. How much of that experience happens because it is expected? If all else is perfect, you may rate the food better than it actually is because you expect it to be in line with your other sensations. Or, in contrast, even if you are served the most delicious fettuccine in the world, if the restaurant has the fragrance of cabbage, a 4-year-old is screaming and kicking in the booth behind you, and a rude server delivers your meal on a greasy plate, you most likely will not judge the pasta to be so great. Much of what we experience is what we expect to experience. At a Washington, D.C., metro station, most people don't expect to hear a virtuoso. When the virtuoso Joshua Bell, clad in jeans and a T-shirt, propped open his violin case for change and played six classical masterpieces on one of the finest-sounding violins ever made—a 1713 creation by Antonio Stradivari—only a handful of the hundreds of commuters passing by stopped to listen. A few nights earlier, they would have had to pay over $100 to hear Mr. Bell perform at a nearby concert hall. With our eyes closed and nose pinched, if we are asked to bite into an "apple" and guess whether it is a Fuji or a Golden Delicious, most of us will say one or the other. We wouldn't be able to tell, at least in the first bite, that we have been tricked into biting an onion.

When you sit enthralled in a movie theater, staring up at the screen, you have the perception that the voices are coming from the actors. Nevertheless, the sounds are actually coming from the speakers located at the sides of the screen. How about the puppet sitting on the lap of the ventriloquist? We know that the ventriloquist is doing the talking, but we see the puppet moving his lips: We have the perception that it is the puppet who is talking. In both cases, the location of the auditory cue is "captured" by the location of the visual cue. We can study our sensory systems in isolation, but perception is really a synthetic process, one in which the organism uses all available information to converge on a coherent representation of the world.

A particularly powerful demonstration of the multimodal nature of perception comes from the world of speech perception. Most people think of speech as an inherently auditory process—we decipher the sounds of language to identify phonemes, combining these into words, sentences, and phrases (see Chapter 11). Speech perception can certainly occur if the input is limited to audition: We can readily understand a friend over the phone, and people who are congenitally blind learn to speak with minimal difficulty. If you are learning a new language, however, then that phone conversation is notoriously more difficult than if the conversation is face-to-face: The sounds we hear can be influenced by visual cues. This principle has been shown in what has come to be called the McGurk effect, in which the perception of speech—what you believe that you "hear"—is influenced by the lip movements that your eyes see. Examples of this compelling visual-auditory illusion can be found at www.youtube.com/watch?v=G-lN8vWm3m0.

Cross-modal capture effects aren't limited to interactions between vision and audition. We can even be fooled into misidentifying an inanimate object as part of our body. In the rubber hand illusion, a rubber left hand is placed in a biologically plausible position on a table in full view of the subject, while her real left arm and hand are blocked from her view by a screen (see http://www.youtube.com/watch?v=TCQbygjG0RU). The researcher then runs a brush over the person's hand (still blocked from her view) while performing the same action with a different brush in the corresponding direction over the rubber hand that the subject sees. After a couple of minutes, she will "feel" that the rubber hand is her own. If blindfolded and asked to point to her hand, she will point to the rubber hand rather than her own. Even more dramatic, if the experimenter suddenly reaches out and hits the rubber hand with a hammer, she is likely to scream.

These illusions work because they take advantage of correlations that are generally present between the senses in day-to-day life. The gestures of a speaker's lips normally conform to the sounds we hear; when we see something close to our hand and feel something touching our hand, we correctly assume they are one and the same. It is only through the illusion that the processing can be teased apart and we realize that information from different sensory systems have been integrated in our brain.

Multimodal Processing in the Brain

How Does It Happen? How does the brain integrate information from the different senses to form a coherent percept? An older view was that some senses dominated others. In particular, vision was thought to dominate over all of the other senses, as in the examples given earlier. A more recent alternative is that the brain combines the input from multiple sensory systems about a particular external property (e.g., the location of a sound or touch), weighs the reliability of each sense, and makes

FIGURE 5.44 The McGurk effect.

an estimate, a decision, from this information about the external property in question. In this view, visual capture occurs because the brain judges visual information in most circumstances to be the most reliable and thus, gives it the most weight. The system is flexible, however, and the context can lead to a change in how information is weighed. When walking in the woods at dusk, we give more emphasis to somatosensory information as we step gingerly to avoid roots or listen carefully for breaking twigs that might signal that we've wandered off the path. It appears that other considerations are factored in and tip the weighting of information scales; in this case, the ambient light, or lack of it, favors the other senses.

So, sometimes the visual system can be overruled. A compelling demonstration of this is shown by the finding that when a flash of light is paired with two beeps, participants perceive the light as having flashed twice (Shams, 2000). This illusion, known as *auditory driving*, differs some from our previous examples. Instead of all of the modalities passing on information about one external property (the puppet or the rubber hand), here the stimulation of one sense (the ear) appears to affect the judgment about a property typically associated with a different sense. Specifically, the auditory beeps create a context of two events, a feature that the brain then applies to the light, creating a coherent percept.

How sensory processing is integrated between modalities is currently a hot topic. It includes the usual cast of questions: Where is information from different sensory systems integrated in the brain? Is it early or late in processing? What are the pathways that are involved?

Where Does It Happen? Brain regions containing neurons that respond to more than one sense are described as multisensory. Multisensory integration (Holmes & Spence, 2005) occurs at many different regions in the brain, both subcortically and cortically. Let's look at some of the studies that have been exploring this question.

In animal studies, neurophysiological methods have been especially useful: Once an electrode has been placed in a targeted brain region, the animal can be presented with a range of stimuli to see if, and by what, the region is activated. For instance, when exploring visual responses, the researcher might vary the position of the stimulus, or its color or movement. To evaluate multisensory processing, the researcher can present stimuli along different sensory channels, asking not only if the cell responds to more than one sense but also about the relationship between the responses to stimuli from different senses.

Subcortical: Superior Colliculus. One well-studied multimodal site is the superior colliculus, the subcortical midbrain region that we discussed earlier in regard to eye movements. The superior colliculus contains orderly topographic maps of the environment in visual, auditory, and even tactile domains (Figure 5.45). Many cells in the superior colliculus show multisensory properties, being activated by inputs from more than one sensory modality. These neurons combine information from different sensory channels and integrate that information. In fact, the response of the cell is stronger when there are inputs from multiple senses compared to when the input is from a single modality (Stein, 2004). Such enhanced responses are most effective when a unimodal stimulus fails to produce a response on its own. In this way the combination of weak, even subthreshold, unimodal signals can be detected and cause participants to orient toward the stimulus. Multisensory signals are also treated

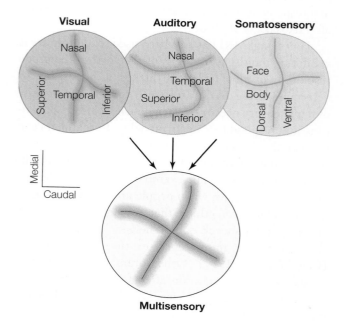

FIGURE 5.45 The interaction of visual, auditory, and somatosensory spatial maps in the superior colliculus provides a representation of multisensory space.

by the brain as more reliable than signals from a single sensory channel. A rustling sound in the grass could indicate the presence of a snake, or just the rising evening breeze. But if that sound is combined with a glimmer of something slithering along, you can bet the brain will generate a fast-response eye movement to verify the presence of a snake.

Integration effects require that *the different stimuli be coincident in both space and time.* For example, if a visual event is spatially and temporally synchronous with a loud noise, as in the auditory driving example described earlier, the resulting multisensory response will be enhanced. If, however, the sound originates from a different location than the light, or is not temporally synchronized with the light, the response of the collicular cell will be lower than if either stimulus were presented alone. Such effects again demonstrate how the brain weights information in terms of its reliability. In the natural world, we have learned that visual and auditory cues are usually closely synchronized; we can learn that a distant visual event such as a flash of lightning will be followed by a crack of thunder. Because they are not coincident in time and space, however, our orienting system here will be driven by just one or the other, especially since these signals can be quite intense.

Cortical Processing. Multisensory activity is also observed in many cortical regions. The superior temporal sulcus (STS) is known to have connections both coming from and going to the various sensory cortices. Neurophysiologists have identified cells in the STS of monkeys that respond to visual, auditory, and somatosensory stimuli (Hikosaka et al., 1988).

Functional MRI has also been used to identify areas exhibiting multisensory areas of the cortex. The crude resolution of this technique makes it impossible to determine if the BOLD response reflects the activity of multisensory neurons or neighboring clusters of neurons that respond to a single modality. Researchers can build on the ideas of multisensory integration, however, to ask if the activation reflects the combination of different sensory cues. For example, the STS in the left hemisphere is active when people are actively engaged in lip-reading (something that we unconsciously use during normal speech comprehension), but not when the sounds are mismatched to the lip movements (Calvert et al., 1997). Other brain regions showing similar sensory integration effects include various regions of the parietal and frontal lobes, as well as the hippocampus (Figure 5.46).

With careful study, we can actually see multisensory effects even in areas that are traditionally thought to be sensory specific. For instance, in one fMRI study, activation in

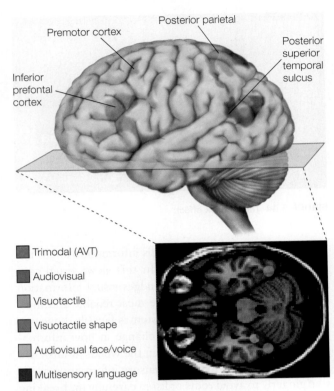

Trimodal (AVT)
Audiovisual
Visuotactile
Visuotactile shape
Audiovisual face/voice
Multisensory language

FIGURE 5.46 Multisensory regions of the cerebral cortex. Areas of the left hemisphere that show increased BOLD response when comparing responses to unisensory and multisensory stimulation. A similar picture is evident in the right hemisphere.

auditory cortex was greater when the sounds were accompanied by simultaneous visual stimulation (Kayser et al., 2007). Given the slow rise time of the BOLD response, this increase may have been more of a preparatory response that treated the visual signals as a cue for sounds. Event-related potential (ERP) studies have found, however, that the very early visual component of the ERP wave is enhanced when the visual stimulus is presented close in space to a corresponding tactile stimulus (Kennett et al., 2001).

Vincenzo Romei (2007) and his colleagues at the University of Geneva have sought to understand how early sensory areas might interact to support multisensory integration. Participants in one of their studies were required to press a button as soon as they detected a stimulus. The stimulus could be a light, a sound, or both. To disrupt visual processing, the researchers applied a TMS pulse over the visual cortex just after the stimulus onset. As expected, the response time (RT) to the visual stimulus was slower on trials in which the TMS pulse was applied compared to trials without TMS. But surprisingly, the RT to the auditory stimulus was faster after TMS over the visual cortex.

Why might disruption of the visual cortex improve a person's ability to detect a sound? One possibility is that the two sensory systems are in competition with one another. Thus, TMS of the visual cortex handicaps a competitor of auditory cortex. Alternatively, neurons in visual cortex that are activated by the TMS pulse might produce signals that are sent to auditory cortex (as part of a multisensory processing pathway), and in this way enhance auditory cortex activity and produce faster RTs to the sounds (Figure 5.47).

Romei came up with a clever way to evaluate these two hypotheses by looking at the reverse situation, asking if an auditory stimulus could enhance visual perception. When TMS is applied over visual cortex, people report seeing phosphenes—an illusory flash of light. Phosphenes can also be produced mechanically by rubbing the eye. (The next time you go to the Louvre in Paris and stand in front of the huge epic painting of the *Raft of the Medusa* by Géricault, you can wow your neuroscientist friends with this bit of trivia: The word *phosphene* was coined by J. B. H. Savigny, the ship surgeon of the *Méduse*.) Romei first determined the intensity level of TMS required to produce phosphenes for each person. He then randomly stimulated the participants at a level that was a bit below the threshold in one of two conditions: alone or concurrently with an auditory stimulus. At this subthreshold level, the participants perceived phosphenes when the auditory stimulus was present, but not when the TMS pulse was presented alone. This finding supports the hypothesis that auditory and visual stimuli can enhance perception in the other sensory modality.

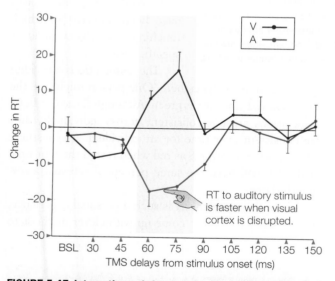

FIGURE 5.47 Interactions of visual and auditory information. RT to auditory stimulus is faster when visual cortex is disrupted. Participants responded as quickly as possible to a visual (V) or auditory (A) stimulus. A single TMS pulse was applied over the occipital lobe at varying delays after stimulus onset (x-axis). The y-axis shows the change in RT for the different conditions. RTs to the visual stimulus were slower (positive numbers) in the shaded area, presumably because the TMS pulse made it harder to perceive the stimulus. Interestingly, RTs to auditory stimuli were faster (negative numbers) during this same epoch.

What are the Pathways? All the hubbub about multisensory processing has spawned several hypotheses about the pathways and connections between the processing areas and the resulting way that the processing occurs. The most radical suggestion is that the entire neocortex is in some sense multisensory, and the initial integration has occurred subcortically (Figure 5.48a). We do know from neuroanatomy that there is multisensory input to the cortex from the thalamus, but it would be an exaggeration to think that the entire cortex is multisensory. A lesion of primary visual cortex produces a profound and permanent blindness with no real effect on the other senses (or, if anything, some enhanced sensitivity in the other senses). The primary sensory cortical regions, and even secondary sensory regions, are clearly dedicated to a single modality. A less radical version is that the cortex has specific sensory areas, but they contain some multisensory interneurons (Figure 5.48b).

Alternatively, multisensory integration may involve projections originating in modality-specific cortical areas. These projections could go from one sensory region to another, allowing for fast modulation within primary and secondary sensory regions (Figure 5.48c). Or, the projections could be to multisensory convergence zones in the cortex, which in more traditional models of sensory function were referred to as association sensory areas. In these models, cross-modal influences on early sensory signals occur via feedback connections from the convergence zones to sensory-specific areas of the cortex (Figure 5.48d).

All of these ideas likely contain some degree of truth. As we have pointed out repeatedly, the sensory systems of the brain have evolved to reconstruct the external environment. This process is surely facilitated by exploiting all of the available information.

TAKE-HOME MESSAGES

- Some areas of the brain, such as the superior colliculus and superior temporal sulci, process information from more than one sensory modality, integrating the multimodal information to increase the sensitivity and accuracy of perception.
- When multisensory information is presented coincidently in time and space, the multisensory neural response is enhanced. The reverse is also true; when multisensory information is not presented coincidently in time and space, the multisensory neural response is depressed.

Errors in Multimodal Processing: Synesthesia

J.W. experiences the world differently from most people. He tastes words. The word *exactly*, for example,

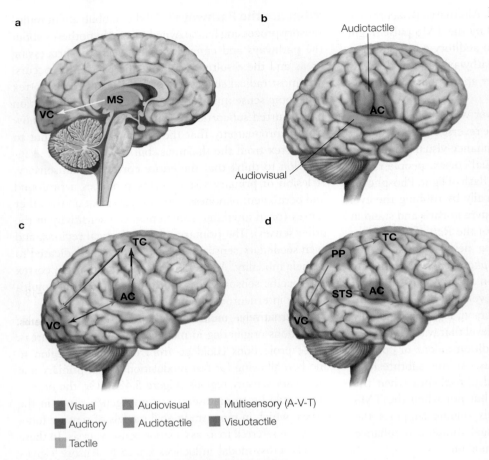

FIGURE 5.48 Various schemes of multisensory interaction.
(a) Multisensory integration occurs subcortically (e.g., thalamus). Input to cortical areas is already influenced by information from other sensory modalities. **(b)** Modality specific regions are surrounded by multisensory regions that receive input from other modalities. **(c)** Multisensory interactions occur through communication between modality specific regions. **(d)** Certain cortical areas are specialized for multisensory processing. PP = posterior parietal cortex; STS = superior temporal sulcus.

have a genetic basis (Baron-Cohen et al., 1996; Smilek et al., 2005). If you think that you may experience some form of synesthesia, you can find out by taking the tests at this website: http://synesthete.org/.

Colored-grapheme synesthesia, in which black or white letters or digits are perceived in assorted colors, is the best-studied form of synesthesia. A synesthete might report "seeing" the letter *A* as red, the letter *B* as yellow, and so forth for the entire set of characters, as in the example shown in Figure 5.49. The appearance of color is a feature of many forms of synesthesia. In colored hearing, colors are experienced for spoken words or for sounds like musical notes. Colored touch and colored smell have also been reported. Much less common are synesthetic experiences that involve other senses. J.W. experiences taste with words; other rare cases have been reported in which touching an object induces specific tastes.

The associations are idiosyncratic for each synesthete. One person might see the letter *B* as red, another as green. Although the synesthetic associations are not consistent across individuals, they are consistent over time for an individual. A synesthete who reports the letter *B* as red when tested the first time in the lab will have the same percept if retested a few months later.

Given that synesthesia is such a personal experience, researchers have had to come up with clever methods to

tastes like yogurt, and the word *accept* tastes like eggs. Most conversations are pleasant tasting; but when J.W. is tending bar, he cringes whenever Derek, a frequent customer, shows up. For J.W., the word *Derek* tastes of earwax!

This phenomenon, in which the senses are mixed, is known as **synesthesia**, from the Greek *syn–* ("union" or "together") and *aesthesis* ("sensation"). Synesthesia is characterized by an idiosyncratic union between (or within) sensory modalities. Tasting words is an extremely rare form of synesthesia. More common are synesthesias in which people hear words or music as colors, or see achromatic lettering (as in books or newspapers) as colored.

The frequency of synesthesia is hard to know, given that many individuals are unaware that their multisensory percepts are odd: Estimates range from as rare as one in 2,000 to as high as one in 200. Synesthesia tends to recur in families, indicating that at least some forms

FIGURE 5.49 Artistic rendition of the color–letter and color–number associations for one individual with synesthesia.

verify and explore this unique phenomenon. One approach with colored-grapheme synesthesia is to create modified versions of the Stroop task. As described in Chapter 3 (page 78), the Stroop task requires a person to name the color of written words. For instance, if the word *green* is written in red ink, the subject is supposed to say "red." In the synesthetic variant of the Stroop task with a colored-grapheme synesthete, the stimuli are letters, and the key manipulation is whether the colors of the letters are congruent or incongruent to the individual's synesthetic palette. For the example in Figure 5.49, when the letter *A* is presented in red, the physical color and synesthetic color are congruent. However, if the *A* is presented in green, the physical and concurrent colors are incongruent. Synesthetes are faster to name the colors of the letters when the physical color matches the concurrent colors for the particular letter (Mattingley et al., 2001). People without synesthesia, of course, do not show this effect. To them, any color–letter pairing is equally acceptable.

Brain-imaging studies indicate that the multisensory experience of synesthesia arises and is manifest at various stages along the visual pathway. Jeffrey Gray at King's College in London performed an fMRI study with a group of individuals who had colored-hearing synesthesia (Nunn et al., 2002). When listening to words, these individuals reported seeing specific colors; when listening to tones, they had no visual experience. Compared to control participants, the synesthetes showed increased activation in V4, similar to what we have seen in other studies of illusory color perception, and in the STS, one of the brain regions associated with multimodal perception. Other studies have shown recruitment of the left medial lingual gyrus (a higher-order color processing area previously implicated in color knowledge) in synesthetes during the perception of colored-grapheme synesthesia (Rich et al., 2006).

A different approach is to ask if synesthesia is the result of abnormal anatomical connections. For example, do synesthetes have more connectivity between sensory regions than non-synesthetes? Using diffusion tensor imaging (DTI), Steven Scholte (2007) and his colleagues at the University of Amsterdam showed that grapheme–color synesthetes had greater anisotropic diffusion, a marker of larger white matter tracts, in the right inferior temporal cortex, the left parietal cortex, and bilaterally in the frontal cortex (green lines in Figure 5.50). Moreover, the researchers found that individual differences in the amount of connectivity in the inferior temporal cortex differentiated between subtypes of synesthetes. Participants who saw color in the outside world (known as "projectors") had greater connectivity in the inferior temporal cortex compared with those who saw color in their "mind's eye" only (known as "associators").

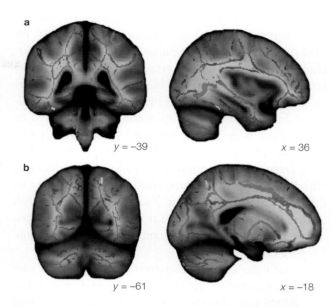

FIGURE 5.50 Stronger white matter connectivity in synesthetes. Green indicates white matter tracts identified with DTI in all participants. Yellow region in right inferior temporal cortex **(a)** and left parietal **(b)** show areas where the FA value is higher in synesthetes compared to controls.

TAKE-HOME MESSAGES

- People with synesthesia experience a mixing of the senses, for example, colored hearing, colored graphemes, or colored taste.
- Synthesia is associated with both abnormal activation patterns in functional imaging studies and abnormal patterns of connectivity in structural imaging studies.

Perceptual Reorganization

As we have just seen, people with synesthesia provide a dramatic example of how the brain is able to link information between distinct sensory systems. The extent of the connectivity between sensory systems is also revealed by studies on people who are deprived of input from one of their senses. When a person is blind, what happens to those regions of the brain that are usually used for visual perception? Might this unused neural tissue be able to reorganize to process other information, as it does on the somatosensory cortex (see Figure 5.16)? Is the situation for individuals who have been blind since birth different from that of individuals who became blind after having had vision?

The results of one PET study suggest that a remarkable degree of functional reorganization goes on (Sadato et al., 1996). The participants in this study included people with normal vision and people who were congenitally blind—that is, blind from birth. The participants were scanned under two experimental conditions. In one condition, they were simply required to sweep their fingers back and forth over a rough surface covered with dots. In the second condition, they were given tactile discrimination tasks such as deciding whether two grooves in the surface were the same or different. Blood flow in the visual cortex during each of these tasks was compared to that during a rest condition in which the participants were scanned while keeping their hands still.

Amazingly, changes in activation in the visual cortex were in opposite directions for the two groups. For the sighted participants, a significant *drop* in activation was found in the primary visual cortex during the tactile

discrimination tasks. Analogous decreases in the auditory or somatosensory cortex occurred during visual tasks. Therefore, as attention was directed to one modality, activation (as measured by blood flow) decreased in other sensory systems. In blind participants, however, the activation in the primary visual cortex *increased* during discrimination tasks, but only when they were actively using the tactile information. Interestingly, a second group of participants, who had become blind early in childhood (before their fifth year), also showed the same recruitment of visual cortex when performing the tactile discrimination task.

A second experiment explored the same issue but used a task that is of great practical value to the blind: reading Braille (Sadato et al., 1998). Here, the participants explored strings of eight Braille letters and had to decide whether the strings formed a word. In accord with the results of the first study, activation of the primary and secondary visual cortex increased during Braille reading

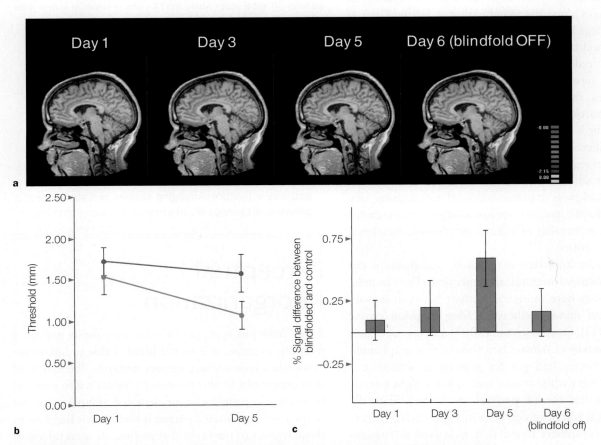

FIGURE 5.51 Perceptual and neural changes resulting from extended visual deprivation in sighted individuals.
(a) fMRI activation during tactile exploration. By Day 5, the blindfolded group showed greater activation than the controls in the occipital cortex. This effect disappeared after the blindfold was removed.
(b) Performance on tactile acuity after one or five days of practice. Lower values correspond to greater sensitivity. (Green: blindfolded participants; Red: Controls.) **(c)** Difference in occipital activation between blindfolded and control participants across days.

in comparison with the resting state, but only in the blind participants.

Of course the term *visual cortex* is a misnomer when applied to blind individuals. The results of the studies just described indicate that tissue, which during normal development will become sensitive to visual inputs, can be exploited in a radically different manner when the environmental context is changed—for example, when all visual input is lost. Currently, it is unclear how tactile information ends up activating neurons in the visual cortex of blind people. One possibility is that somatosensory projections to thalamic relays spread into the nearby lateral geniculate nucleus, exploiting the geniculostriate pathway. This hypothesis is unlikely, since the activation changes in the blind participants' visual cortices were bilateral. Somatosensory inputs to the thalamus are strictly lateralized. Because they performed the tactile tasks with the right hand, the blood-flow changes should have been restricted to the left hemisphere. A more viable hypothesis is that a massive reorganization of corticocortical connections follows peripheral blindness. The sensory-deprived visual cortex is taken over, perhaps through back-projections originating in polymodal association cortical areas.

Alvaro Pascual-Leone and his colleagues at Harvard Medical School (Merabet et al., 2008) have studied cortical plasticity effects that occur when *sighted* volunteers are deprived of visual information for an extended period. These participants were blindfolded for 5 days and received intensive Braille training (Figure 5.51). A matched control group was given the same training, but they were not blindfolded. At the end of training, the blindfolded participants could discriminate Braille letters better than the nonblindfolded participants did; those who wore blindfolds were also better at other tactile discrimination tasks. Furthermore, fMRI tests of these participants revealed *activation in the visual cortex during tactile stimulation* of the right or left fingertips, even with

stimuli that would not be expected to generate visual images. Interestingly, just 20 hours after the blindfold was removed (on day 6), the activation in visual cortex during tactile stimulation disappeared (Figure 5.51a, c). These data argue that, when deprived of normal input, the adult visual system rapidly reorganizes to become more proficient in processing information from the other senses.

Although these studies are a dramatic demonstration of cortical plasticity, the results also suggest a neurobiological mechanism for the greater nonvisual perceptual acuity exhibited by blind people. Indeed, Louis Braille's motivation to develop his tactile reading system was spurred by his belief that vision loss was offset by heightened sensitivity in the fingertips. One account of this compensation focuses on nonperceptual mechanisms. Though the sensory representation of somatosensory information is similar for blind and sighted participants, the former group is not distracted by vision (or visual imagery). If the focus of attention is narrowed, somatosensory information can be used more efficiently. The imaging results reviewed here, though, suggest a more perceptual account: Sensitivity increases because more cortical tissue is devoted to representing nonvisual information.

TAKE-HOME MESSAGES

- Following sensory deprivation, the function of sensory regions of the cortex may become reorganized, or exhibit what is called plasticity.
- For instance, in blind individuals, areas of the brain that are usually involved in visual function may become part of the somatosensory cortex.
- Plasticity can also be observed in healthy individuals if they are deprived of information from one sensory modality for even relatively short periods of time.

Summary

The five basic sensory systems of audition, olfaction, gustation, somatosensation, and vision allow us to interpret the environment. Each sense involves unique pathways and processes to translate external stimuli into neural signals that are interpreted by the brain. Within each sense, specialized sensory mechanisms have evolved to solve computational problems to facilitate and enhance our perceptual capabilities. As shown in neuroimaging and neuropsychological studies, specialization is found across the sensory cortices of the brain; thus, people may retain the ability to see, even in the absence of cortical mechanisms for color or motion perception. In extreme situations of sensory deprivation, the cortical systems for perception may become radically reorganized. Even in people with intact sensory systems, the five senses do not work in isolation, but rather work in concert to construct a rich interpretation of the world. It is this integration that underlies much of human cognition and allows us to survive, and indeed thrive, in a multisensory world.

Key Terms

achromatopsia (p. 201)
akinetopsia (p. 204)
area MT (p. 190)
area V4 (p. 194)
chemical senses (p. 176)
corpuscle (p. 179)
cortical visual area (p. 189)
extrastriate visual area (p. 189)
fovea (p. 186)
ganglion cells (p. 186)
glomerulus (p.173)
hemianopia (p. 206)
inferior colliculus (p. 169)

interaural time (p. 171)
lateral geniculate nucleus (LGN) (p. 187)
medial geniculate nucleus (MGN) (p. 167)
multisensory integration (p. 167)
nociceptor (p. 179)
odorant (p. 173)
photoreceptor (p. 185)
primary auditory cortex (A1) (p. 169)
primary gustatory cortex (p. 176)
primary olfactory cortex (p. 173)

primary somatosensory cortex (S1) (p. 180)
primary visual cortex (V1) (p. 187)
proprioception (p. 180)
receptive field (p. 187)
retina (p. 185)
retinotopic map (p. 187)
scotoma (p. 206)
secondary somatosensory cortex (S2) (p. 180)
superior colliculus (p. 187)
synesthesia (p. 212)
tastant (p. 176)

Thought Questions

1. Compare and contrast the functional organization of the visual and auditory systems. What computational problems must each system solve, and how are these solutions achieved in the nervous system?

2. A person arrives at the hospital in a confused state and appears to have some impairment in visual perception. As the attending neurologist, you suspect that the person has had a stroke. How would you go about examining the patient to determine at which level in the visual pathways the damage has occurred? Emphasize the behavioral tests you would administer, but feel free to make predictions about what you expect to see on MRI scans.

3. Define the physiological concepts of *receptive field* and *visual area*. How is the receptive field of a cell established? How are the boundaries between visual areas identified by researchers using either single-cell recording methods or fMRI?

4. This chapter has focused mainly on salient visual properties such as color, shape, and motion. In looking around the environment, do you think these properties seem to reflect the most important cues for a highly skilled visual creature? What other sources of information might an adaptive visual system exploit?

5. How might abnormalities in multisensory processing (e.g., synesthesia) be important for understanding how and why information becomes integrated across different sensory channels? Similarly, given the plasticity of the brain, does it even make sense to talk about a "visual system" or an "auditory system"?

FIGURE 6.1 Our view of the world depends on our vantage point. These two photographs are taken of the same scene, but from two different positions and under two different conditions. Each vantage point reveals new views of the scene, including objects that were obscured from the other vantage point. Moreover, the colors change, depending on the time of day and weather. Despite this variability, we easily recognize that both photographs are of the Golden Gate Bridge, with San Francisco in the distance.

different angle and still recognize it. Somehow, no matter if the inputs are partial, upside down, full face, or sideways, hitting varying amounts of the retina or all of it, the brain interprets it all as the same object and identifies it: "That, my friend, is San Francisco!" We take this constancy for granted, but it is truly amazing when we consider how the sensory signals are radically different with each viewing position. (Curiously, this stability varies for different classes of objects. If, while upside down, we catch sight of a group of people walking toward us, then we will not recognize a friend quite as readily as when seeing her face in the normal, upright position. As we shall see, face perception has some unique properties.)

Fourth, *the product of perception is also intimately interwoven with memory.* Object recognition is more than

linking features to form a coherent whole; that whole triggers memories. Those of us who have spent many hours roaming the hills around San Francisco Bay recognize that the pictures in Figure 6.1 were taken from the Marin headlands just north of the city. Even if you have never been to San Francisco, when you look at these pictures, there is interplay between perception and memory. For the traveler arriving from Australia, the first view of San Francisco is likely to evoke comparisons to Sydney; for the first-time tourist from Kansas, the vista may be so unusual that she recognizes it as such: a place unlike any other that she has seen.

In the previous chapter, we saw how objects and scenes from the external world are disassembled and input into the visual system in the form of lines, shapes, and colors. In this chapter, we explore how the brain processes those low-level inputs into the high-level, coherent, memory-invoking percepts of everyday life. We begin with a discussion of the cortical real estate that is involved in object recognition. Then, we look at some of the computational problems that the object recognition system has to solve. After that, we turn to patients with object recognition deficits and consider what their deficits tell us about perception. Next, we delve into the fascinating world of category-specific recognition problems and their implications for processing. Along the way, it will be useful to keep in mind the four concepts introduced earlier: Perception and recognition are two different animals; we perceive objects as unified wholes, and do so in a manner that is highly flexible; and our perception and memory are tightly bound. We close the chapter with a look at how researchers are putting theories of object recognition to the test by trying to predict what a person is viewing simply by looking at his fMRI scans—the 21st-century version of mind reading.

TAKE-HOME MESSAGES

- Sensation, perception, and recognition refer to distinct phenomena.
- People perceive an object as a unified whole, not as an entity separated by its color, shape, and details.
- Although our visual perspective changes, our ability to recognize objects remains robust.
- Memory and perception are tightly linked.
- Patients with visual agnosia are unable to recognize common objects presented to them visually. This deficit is modality specific. Patients can recognize an object when they touch, smell, taste, or hear it.

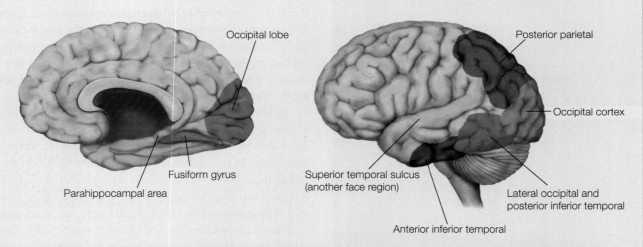

ANATOMICAL ORIENTATION

The anatomy of object recognition

Specific regions of the brain are used for distinct types of object recognition. The parahippocampal area and posterior parietal cortex process information about places and scenes. Multiple regions are involved in face recognition, including fusiform gyrus and superior temporal sulcus, while other body parts are recognized using areas within the lateral occipital and posterior inferior temporal cortex.

Multiple Pathways for Visual Perception

The pathways carrying visual information from the retina to the first few synapses in the cortex clearly segregate into multiple processing streams. Much of the information goes to the primary visual cortex (also called V1 or striate cortex; see Chapter 5 and Figures 5.23 and 5.24), located in the occipital lobe. Output from V1 is contained primarily in two major fiber bundles, or *fasciculi*. Figure 6.2 shows that the *superior longitudinal fasciculus* takes a dorsal path from the striate cortex and

other visual areas, terminating mostly in the posterior regions of the parietal lobe. The *inferior longitudinal fasciculus* follows a ventral route from the occipital striate cortex into the temporal lobe. These two pathways are referred to as the **ventral (occipitotemporal) stream** and the **dorsal (occipitoparietal) stream**. This anatomical separation of information-carrying fibers from the visual cortex to two separate regions of the brain raises some questions. What are the different properties of processing within the ventral and dorsal streams? How do they differ in their representation of the visual input? How does processing within these two streams interact to support object perception?

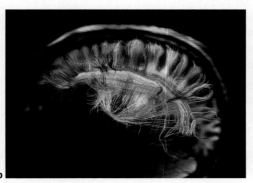
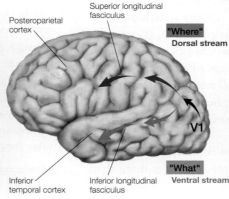

FIGURE 6.2 The major object recognition pathways.
(a) The longitudinal fasciculus, shown here in shades of purple.
(b) The ventral "what" pathway terminates in the inferotemporal cortex, and the dorsal "where" pathway terminates in the posteroparietal cortex.

Gaze at the picture in Figure 1 for a couple of minutes. If you are like most people, you initially saw a vase. But surprise! After a while the vase changed to a picture of two human profiles staring at each other. With continued viewing, your perception changes back and forth, satisfied with one interpretation until suddenly the other asserts itself and refuses to yield the floor. This is an example of *multistable perception*.

How are multistable percepts resolved in the brain? The stimulus information does not change at the points of transition. Rather, the interpretation of the pictorial cues changes. When staring at the white region, you see the vase. If you shift attention to the black regions, you see the profiles. But here we run into a chicken-and-egg question. Did the representation of individual features change first and thus cause the percept to change? Or did the percept change and lead to a reinterpretation of the features?

To explore these questions, Nikos Logothetis of the Max Planck Institute in Tübingen, Germany, turned to a different form of multistable perception: binocular rivalry (Sheinberg & Logothetis, 1997). The exquisite focusing capability of our eyes (perhaps assisted by an optometrist) makes us forget that they provide two separate snapshots of the world. These snapshots are only slightly different, and they provide important cues for depth perception. With some technological tricks, however, it is possible to present radically different inputs to the two eyes. To accomplish this, researchers employ special glasses that have a shutter which alternately blocks the input to one eye and then the other at very rapid rates. Varying the stimulus in synchrony with the shutter allows a different stimulus to be presented to each eye.

Do we see two things simultaneously at the same location? The answer is no. As with the ambiguous vase–face profiles picture, only one object or the other is seen at any single point in time, although at transitions there is sometimes a period of fuzziness in which neither object is clearly perceived. Logothetis trained his monkeys to press one of two levers to indicate which object was being perceived. To make sure the animals were not responding randomly, he included nonrivalrous trials in which only one of the objects was presented. He then recorded from single cells in various areas of the visual cortex. Within each area he selected two objects, only one of which was effective in driving the cell. In this way he could correlate the activity of the cell with the animal's perceptual experience.

As his recordings moved up the ventral pathway, Logothetis found an increase in the percentage of active cells, with activity mirroring the animals' perception rather than the stimulus conditions. In V1, the responses of less than 20% of the cells fluctuated as a function of whether the animal perceived the effective or ineffective stimulus. In V4, this percentage increased to over 33%. In contrast, the activity of all the cells in the visual areas of the temporal lobe was tightly correlated with the animal's perception. Here the cells would respond only when the effective stimulus, the monkey face, was perceived (Figure 2). When the animal pressed the lever indicating that it perceived the ineffective stimulus (the starburst) under rivalrous conditions, the cells were essentially silent. In both V4 and the temporal lobe, the cell activity changed in advance of the animal's response, indicating that the percept had changed. Thus, even when the stimulus did not change, an increase in activity was observed prior to the transition from a perception of the ineffective stimulus to a perception of the effective stimulus.

These results suggest a competition during the early stages of cortical processing between the two possible percepts. The activity of the cells in V1 and in V4 can be thought of as perceptual hypotheses, with the patterns across an ensemble of cells reflecting the strength of the different hypotheses. Interactions between these cells ensure that, by the time the information reaches the inferotemporal lobe, one of these hypotheses has coalesced into a stable percept. Reflecting the properties of the real world, the brain is not fooled into believing that two objects exist at the same place at the same time.

FIGURE 1 Does your perception change over time as you continue to stare at this drawing?

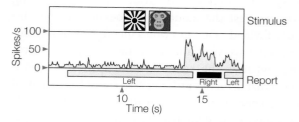

FIGURE 2 When the starburst or monkey face is presented alone, the cell in the temporal cortex responds vigorously to the monkey face but not to the starburst.
In the rivalrous condition, the two stimuli are presented simultaneously, one to the left eye and one to the right eye. The bottom bar shows the monkey's perception, indicated by a lever press. About 1 s after the onset of the rivalrous stimulus, the animal perceives the starburst; the cell is silent during this period. About 7 s later, the cell shows a large increase in activity and, correspondingly, indicates that its perception has changed to the monkey face shortly thereafter. Then, 2 s later, the percept flips back to the starburst and the cell's activity is again reduced.

The *What* and *Where* Pathways

To address the first of these questions, Leslie Ungerleider and Mortimer Mishkin, at the National Institutes of Health, proposed that processing along these two pathways is designed to extract fundamentally different types of information (Ungerleider & Mishkin, 1982). They hypothesized that the *ventral stream* is specialized for *object perception and recognition*—for determining *what* we're looking at. The *dorsal stream* is specialized for *spatial perception*—for determining *where* an object is—and for analyzing the spatial configuration between different objects in a scene. "What" and "where" are the two basic questions to be answered in visual perception. To respond appropriately, we must (a) recognize what we're looking at and (b) know where it is.

The initial data for the what–where dissociation of the ventral and dorsal streams came from lesion studies with monkeys. Animals with *bilateral lesions to the temporal lobe* that disrupted the ventral stream had great difficulty discriminating between different shapes—a "what" discrimination (Pohl, 1973). For example, they made many errors while learning that one object, such as a cylinder, was associated with a food reward when paired with another object (e.g., a cube). Interestingly, these same animals had no trouble determining where an object was in relation to other objects; this second ability depends on a "where" computation. The opposite was true for animals with parietal lobe lesions that disrupted the dorsal stream. These animals had trouble discriminating where an object was in relation to other objects ("where") but had no problem discriminating between two similar objects ("what").

More recent evidence indicates that the separation of what and where pathways is not limited to the visual system. Studies with various species, including humans, suggest that auditory processing regions are similarly divided. The anterior aspects of primary auditory cortex are specialized for auditory-pattern processing (what is the sound?), and posterior regions are specialized for identifying the spatial location of a sound (where is it coming from?). One particularly clever experiment demonstrated this functional specialization by asking cats to identify the where and what of an auditory stimulus (Lomber & Malhotra, 2008). The cats were trained to perform two different tasks: one task required the animal to locate a sound, and a second task required making discriminations between different sound patterns. The researchers then placed thin tubes over the anterior auditory region; through these tubes, a cold liquid could be passed to cool the underlying neural tissue. This procedure temporarily inactivates the targeted tissue, providing a transient lesion (akin to the logic of TMS studies conducted with people). Cooling resulted in selective deficits in the pattern discrimination task, but not in the localization task. In a second phase of the study, the tubes were repositioned over the posterior auditory region. This time there was a deficit in the localization task, but not in the pattern discrimination one—a neat double dissociation in the same animal.

Representational Differences Between the Dorsal and Ventral Streams

Neurons in both the temporal and parietal lobes have large receptive fields, but the physiological properties of the neurons within each lobe are quite distinct. Neurons in the parietal lobe may respond similarly to many different stimuli (Robinson et al., 1978). For example, a parietal neuron recorded in a fully conscious monkey might be activated when a stimulus such as a spot of light is restricted to a small region of space or when the stimulus is a large object that encompasses much of the hemifield. In addition, many parietal neurons are responsive to stimuli presented in the more eccentric parts of the visual field. Although 40% of these neurons have receptive fields near the central region of vision (the fovea), the remaining cells have receptive fields that exclude the foveal region. These eccentrically tuned cells are ideally suited for detecting the presence and location of a stimulus, especially one that has just entered the field of view. Remember in Chapter 5 that, when examining subcortical visual processing, we suggested a similar role for the superior colliculus, which also plays an important role in visual attention (discussed in Chapter 7).

The response of neurons in the ventral stream of the temporal lobe is quite different (Ito et al., 1995). The receptive fields for these neurons *always encompass the fovea*, and most of these neurons can be activated by a stimulus that falls within either the left or the right visual field. The disproportionate representation of central vision appears to be ideal for a system devoted to object recognition. We usually look directly at things we wish to identify, thereby taking advantage of the greater acuity of foveal vision.

Cells within the visual areas of the temporal lobe have a diverse pattern of selectivity (Desimone, 1991). In the posterior region, earlier in processing, cells show a preference for relatively simple features such as edges. Others, farther along in the processing stream, have a preference for much more complex features such as human body parts, apples, flowers, or snakes. Recordings from one such cell, located in the inferotemporal cortex, are shown in Figure 6.3. This cell is most highly activated by the human hand. The first five images in the figure show the response of the cell to various views of a hand. Activity is high regardless of the hand's orientation and is only slightly reduced when the hand is considerably

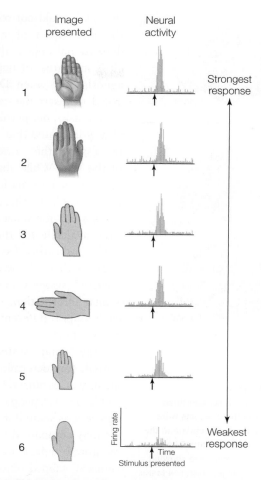

Image presented | Neural activity

1 — Strongest response

2

3

4

5

6 — Weakest response

Firing rate / Time / Stimulus presented

FIGURE 6.3 Single-cell recordings from a neuron in the inferior temporal cortex.
Neurons in the inferior temporal cortex rarely respond to simple stimuli such as lines or spots of light. Rather, they respond to more complex objects such as hands. This cell responded weakly when the image did not include the defining fingers (6).

smaller. The sixth image, of a mitten, shows that the response diminishes if the same shape lacks defining fingers.

Neuroimaging studies with human participants have provided further evidence that the dorsal and ventral streams are activated differentially by "where" and "what" tasks. In one elegant study using positron emission tomography (S. Kohler et al., 1995), trials consisted of pairs of displays containing three objects each (Figure 6.4a). In the *position* task, the participants had to determine if the objects were presented at the same locations in the two displays. In the *object* task, they had to determine if the objects remained the same across the two displays. The irrelevant factor could remain the same or change: The objects might change on the position task, even though the locations remained the same; similarly, the same objects might be presented at new locations in the object task. Thus, the stimulus displays were identical for the two conditions; the only difference was the task instruction.

The PET data for the two tasks were compared directly to identify neural regions that were selectively activated by one task or the other. In this way, areas that were engaged similarly for both tasks—because of similar perception, decision, or response requirements—were masked. During the position task, regional cerebral blood flow was higher in the parietal lobe in the right hemisphere (Figure 6.4b, left panel). In contrast, the object task led to increased regional cerebral blood flow bilaterally at the junction of the occipital and temporal lobes (Figure 6.4b, right panel).

Perception for Identification Versus Perception for Action

Patient studies offer more support for a dissociation of "what" and "where" processing. As we shall see in Chapter 7, the parietal cortex is central to spatial attention. Lesions of this lobe can also produce severe disturbances in the ability to represent the world's spatial layout and the spatial relations of objects within it.

More revealing have been functional dissociations in the performance of patients with visual agnosia. Mel Goodale and David Milner (1992) at the University of Western Ontario described a 34-year-old woman, D.F., who suffered carbon monoxide intoxication because of a leaky propane gas heater. For D.F., the event caused a severe object recognition disorder. When asked to name household items, she made errors such as labeling a cup an "ashtray" or a fork a "knife." She usually gave crude descriptions of a displayed object; for example, a screwdriver was "long, black, and thin." Picture recognition was even more disrupted. When shown drawings of common objects, D.F. could not identify a single one. Her deficit could not be attributed to *anomia*, a problem with naming objects, because whenever an object was placed in her hand, she identified it. Sensory testing indicated that D.F.'s agnosia could not be attributed to a loss of visual acuity. She could detect small gray targets displayed against a black background. Although her ability to discriminate small differences in hue was abnormal, she correctly identified primary colors.

Most relevant to our discussion is the dissociation of D.F.'s performance on two tasks, both designed to assess her ability to perceive the orientation of a three-dimensional object. For these tasks, D.F. was asked to view a circular block into which a slot had been cut. The orientation of the slot could be varied by rotating the block. In the explicit matching task, D.F. was given a card and asked to orient her hand so that the card would fit into the slot. D.F. failed miserably, orienting the card vertically even when the slot was horizontal (Figure 6.5a). When asked to insert the card into the slot, however, D.F. quickly reached forward and inserted the card (Figure 6.5b). Her performance on this

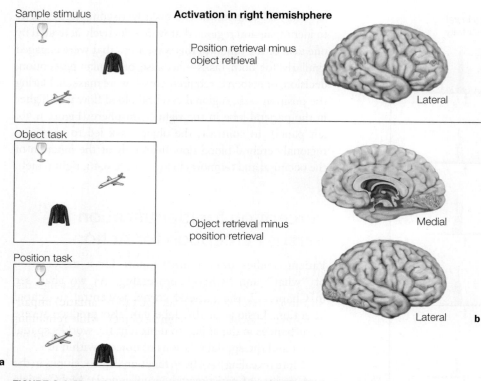

Sample stimulus

Activation in right hemishphere

Position retrieval minus object retrieval

Lateral

Object task

Object retrieval minus position retrieval

Medial

Position task

Lateral **b**

a

FIGURE 6.4 Matching task used to contrast position and object discrimination.
(a) Object and position matching to sample task. The Study and Test displays each contain three objects in three positions. On object retrieval trials, the participant judges if the three objects were the same or different. On position retrieval trials, the participant judges if the three objects are in the same or different locations. In the examples depicted, the correct response would be "same" for the object task trial and "different" for the position task trial. **(b)** Views of the right hemisphere showing cortical regions that showed differential pattern of activation in the position and object retrieval tasks.

visuomotor task did not depend on tactile feedback that would result when the card contacted the slot; her hand was properly oriented even before she reached the block.

D.F.'s performance showed that the two processing systems make use of perceptual information from different sources. The explicit matching task showed that D.F. could not recognize the orientation of a three-dimensional object; this deficit is indicative of her severe agnosia. Yet when D.F. was asked to insert the card (the action task), her performance clearly indicated that she had processed the orientation of the slot. While shape and orientation information were not available to the processing system for objects, they were available for the visuomotor task. This dissociation suggests that the "what" and "where" systems may carry similar information, but they each support different aspects of cognition.

The "what" system is essential for determining the identity of an object. If the object is familiar, people will recognize it as such; if it is novel, we may compare the percept to stored representations of similarly shaped objects. The "where" system appears to be essential for more than determining the locations of different objects; it is also critical for *guiding interactions with these objects*. D.F.'s performance is an example of how information accessible to action systems can be dissociated from information accessible to knowledge and consciousness. Indeed, Goodale and Milner argued that the dichotomy should be

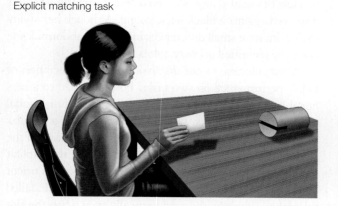

Explicit matching task

Action task

a **b**

FIGURE 6.5 Dissociation between perception linked to awareness and perception linked to action.
(a) The patient performed poorly in the explicit matching task when asked to match the orientation of the card to that of the slot. **(b)** In the action task, the patient was instructed to insert the card in the slot. Here, she produced the correct action without hesitation.

between "what" and "how," to emphasize that the dorsal visual system provides a strong input to motor systems to compute how a movement should be produced. Consider what happens when you grab a glass of water to drink. Your visual system has factored in where the glass is in relation to your eyes, your head, the table, and the path required to move the water glass directly to your mouth.

Goodale, Milner, and their colleagues have subsequently tested D.F. in many studies to explore the neural correlates of this striking dissociation between vision for recognition and vision for action (Goodale & Milner, 2004). Structural MRI scans showed that D.F. has widespread cortical atrophy with concentrated bilateral lesions in the ventral stream that encompass **lateral occipital cortex (LOC)** (Figure 6.6; T. James et al., 2003). Functional MRI scans show that D.F. does have some ventral activation in spared tissue when she was attempting to recognize objects, but it was more widespread than is normally seen in controls. In contrast, when asked to grasp objects, D.F. showed robust activity in anterior regions of the inferior parietal lobe. This activity is similar to what is observed in neurologically healthy individuals (Culham et al., 2003).

Patients who suffer from carbon monoxide intoxication typically have diffuse damage, so it is difficult to pinpoint the source of the behavioral deficits. Therefore, cognitive neuroscientists tend to focus their studies on patients with more focal lesions, such as those that result from stroke. One recent case study describes a patient, J.S., with an intriguing form of visual agnosia (Karnath et al., 2009). J.S. complained that he was unable to see objects, watch TV, or read. He could dress himself, but only if he knew beforehand exactly where his clothes were located. What's more, he was unable to recognize familiar people by their faces, even though he could identify them by their voices. Oddly enough, however, he was able to walk around the neighborhood without a problem. He could easily grab objects presented to him at different locations, even though he could not identify the objects.

J.S. was examined using tests similar to those used in the studies with D.F. (see Figure 6.5). When shown an object, he performed poorly in describing its size; but he could readily pick it up, adjusting his grip size to match the object's size. Or, if shown two flat and irregular shapes, J.S. found it very challenging to say if they were the same or different, yet could easily modify his hand shape to pick up each object. As with D.F., J.S. displays a compelling dissociation in his abilities for object identification, even though his actions indicate that he has "perceived" in exquisite detail the shape and orientation of the objects. MRIs of J.S.'s brain revealed damage limited to the medial aspect of the ventral occipitotemporal cortex (OTC). Note that J.S.'s lesions are primarily in the medial aspect of the OTC, but D.F.'s lesions were primarily in lateral occipital cortex. Possibly both the lateral and medial parts of the ventral stream are needed for object recognition, or perhaps the diffuse pathology associated with carbon monoxide poisoning in D.F. has affected function within the medial OTC as well.

Patients like D.F. and J.S. offer examples of single dissociations. Each shows a selective (and dramatic) impairment in using vision to recognize objects while remaining proficient in using vision to perform actions. The opposite dissociation can also be found in the clinical literature: Patients with **optic ataxia** can recognize objects, yet cannot use visual information to guide their actions. For instance, when someone with optic ataxia reaches for an object, she doesn't move directly toward it; rather,

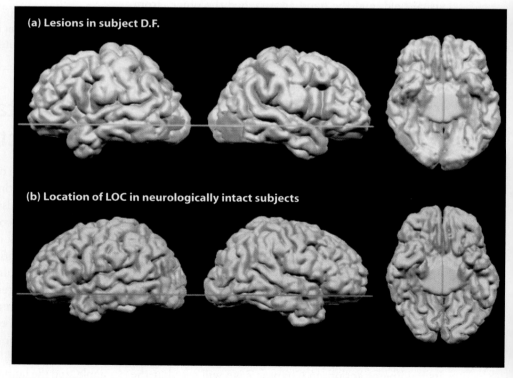

(a) Lesions in subject D.F.

(b) Location of LOC in neurologically intact subjects

FIGURE 6.6 Ventral-stream lesions in patient D.F. shown in comparison with the functionally-defined lateral occipital complex (LOC) in healthy participants.
(a) Reconstruction of D.F.'s brain lesion. Lateral views of the left and right hemispheres are shown, as is a ventral view of the underside of the brain. (b) The highlighted regions indicate activation in the lateral occipital cortex of neurologically healthy individuals when they are recognizing objects.

she gropes about like a person trying to find a light switch in the dark. Although D.F. had no problem avoiding obstacles when reaching for an object, patients with optic ataxia fail to take obstacles into account as they reach for something (Schindler et al., 2004). Their eye movements present a similar loss of spatial knowledge. *Saccades*, or directed eye movements, may be directed inappropriately and fail to bring the object within the fovea. When tested on the slot task used with D.F. (see Figure 6.5), these patients can report the orientation of a visual slot, even though they cannot use this information when inserting an object in the slot. In accord with what researchers expect on the basis of dorsal–ventral dichotomy, optic ataxia is associated with lesions of the parietal cortex.

Although these examples are dramatic demonstrations of functional separation of "what" and "where" processing, do not forget that this evidence comes from the study of patients with rare disorders. It is also important to see if similar principles hold in healthy brains. Lior Shmuelof and Ehud Zohary designed a study to compare activity patterns in the dorsal and ventral streams in normal subjects (Shmuelof & Zohary, 2005). The participants viewed video clips of various objects that were being manipulated by a hand. The objects were presented in either the left or right visual field, and the hand approached the object from the opposite visual field (Figure 6.7a). Activation of the dorsal parietal region was driven by the position of the hand (Figure 6.7b). For example, when viewing a right hand reaching for an object in the left visual field, the activation was stronger in the left parietal region. In contrast, activation in ventral occipitotemporal cortex was correlated with the position of the object. In a second experiment, the participants were asked either to identify the object or judge how many fingers were used to grasp the object. Here again, ventral activation was stronger for the object identification task, but dorsal activation was stronger for the finger judgment task (Figure 6.7c).

In sum, the what–where or what–how dichotomy offers a functional account of two computational goals of higher visual processing. This distinction is best viewed as heuristic rather than absolute. The dorsal and ventral streams are not isolated from one another, but rather communicate extensively. Processing within the parietal lobe, the termination of the "where" pathway, serves many purposes. We have focused here on its guiding of action; in Chapter 7 we will see that the parietal lobe also plays a critical role in *selective attention*, the enhancement of processing at some locations instead of others. Moreover, spatial information can be useful for solving "what" problems. For example,

depth cues help segregate a complex scene into its component objects. The rest of this chapter concentrates on object recognition—in particular, the visual system's assortment of strategies that make use of both dorsal and ventral stream processing for perceiving and recognizing the world.

TAKE-HOME MESSAGES

- The ventral stream, or occipitotemporal pathway, is specialized for object perception and recognition. This is often referred to as the "what" pathway. It focuses on "vision for recognition."

- The dorsal stream, or occipitoparietal pathway, is specialized for spatial perception and is often referred to as the "where" or "how" pathway. It focuses on "vision for action."

- Neurons in the parietal lobe have large, nonselective receptive fields that include cells representing both the fovea and the periphery. Neurons in the temporal lobe have large receptive fields that are much more selective and always represent foveal information.

- Patients with selective lesions of the ventral pathway may have severe problems in consciously identifying objects, yet they can use the visual information to guide coordinated movement. Thus we see that visual information is used for a variety of purposes.

- Patients with optic ataxia can recognize objects but cannot use visual information to guide action. Optic ataxia is associated with lesions of the parietal cortex.

Computational Problems in Object Recognition

Object perception depends primarily on an analysis of the shape of a visual stimulus. Cues such as color, texture, and motion certainly also contribute to normal perception. For example, when people look at the surf breaking on the shore, their acuity is not sufficient to see grains of sand, and water is essentially amorphous, lacking any definable shape. Yet the textures of the sand's surface and the water's edge, and their differences in color, enable us to distinguish between the two regions. The water's motion is important too. Nevertheless, even if surface features like texture and color are absent or applied inappropriately, recognition is minimally affected: We can readily identify an elephant, an apple, and the human form in Figure 6.8, even though they are shown as pink, plaid, and wooden, respectively. Here object recognition is derived from a perceptual ability to match an analysis of shape and form to an object, regardless of color, texture, or motion cues.

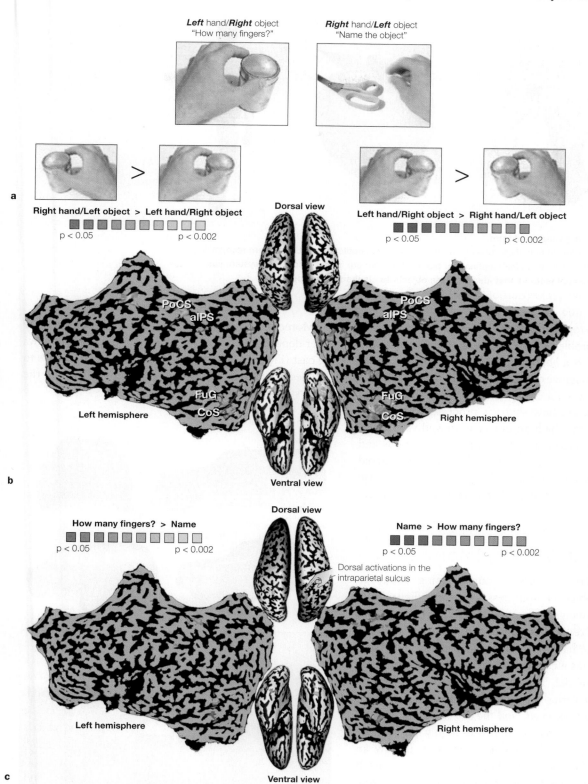

FIGURE 6.7 Hemispheric asymmetries depend on location of object and hand used to reach the object.
(a) Video clips showed a left or right hand, being used to reach for an object on the left or right side of space. In the "Action" condition, **participants** judged the number of fingers used to contact the object. In the "Recognition" condition, participants named the object. **(b)** Laterality pattern in dorsal and ventral regions reveal preference for either the hand or object. Dorsal activation is related to the position of the hand, being greater in the hemisphere contralateral to the hand grasping the object. Ventral activation is related to the position of the object, being greater in the hemisphere contralateral to the object being grasped. **(c)** Combining across right hand and left hand pictures, dorsal activation in the intraparietal sulcus (orange) was stronger when judging how many fingers would be required to grasp the object, whereas ventral activation in occipitotemporal cortex (blue) was greater when naming the object.

FIGURE 6.8 Analyzing shape and form.
Despite the irregularities in how these objects are depicted, most people have little problem recognizing them. We may never have seen pink elephants or plaid apples, but our object recognition system can still discern the essential features that identify these objects as elephants and apples.

To account for shape-based recognition, we need to consider two problems. The first has to do with shape encoding. How is a shape represented internally? What enables us to recognize differences between a triangle and a square or between a chimp and a person? The second problem centers on how shape is processed, given that the position from which an object is viewed varies. We recognize shapes from an infinite array of positions and orientations, and our recognition system is not hampered by scale changes in the retinal image as we move close to or away from an object. Let's start with the latter problem.

Variability in Sensory Information

Object constancy refers to our amazing ability to recognize an object in countless situations. Figure 6.9a shows four drawings of an automobile that have little in common with respect to sensory information reaching the eye. Yet we have no problem identifying the object in each picture as a car, and discerning that all four cars are the same model. The visual information emanating from an object varies for several reasons: *viewing position, how it is illuminated, and the object's surroundings.* First, sensory information depends highly on viewing position. Viewpoint changes not only as you view an object from different angles, but when the object itself moves and thus changes its orientation relative to you. When a dog rolls over, or you walk around the room gazing at him, your interpretation of the object (the dog) remains the same despite the changes in how the image hits the retina and the retinal projection of shape. The human perceptual system is adept at separating changes caused by shifts in viewpoint from changes intrinsic to an object itself.

Moreover, while the visible parts of an object may differ depending on how light hits it and where shadows are cast (Figure 6.9b), recognition is largely insensitive to changes in illumination. A dog in the sun and dog in the shade still register as a dog.

a

b

FIGURE 6.9 Object constancy.
(a) The image on the retina is vastly different for these four drawings of a car. **(b)** Other sources of variation in the sensory input include shadows and occlusion (where one object is in front of another). Despite this sensory variability, we rapidly recognize the objects and can judge if they depict the same object or different objects.

Lastly, objects are rarely seen in isolation. People see objects surrounded by other objects and against varied backgrounds. Yet, we have no trouble separating a dog from other objects on a crowded city street, even when the dog is partially obstructed by pedestrians, trees, and hydrants. Our perceptual system quickly partitions the scene into components.

Object recognition must overcome these three sources of variability. But it also has to recognize that changes in perceived shape can actually reflect changes in the object. Object recognition must be general enough to support object constancy, and it must also be specific enough to pick out slight differences between members of a category or class.

View-Dependent Versus View-Invariant Recognition

A central debate in object recognition has to do with defining the frame of reference in which recognition occurs (D. Perrett et al., 1994). For example, when we look at a bicycle, we easily recognize it from its most typical view, from the side; but we also recognize it when looking down upon it or straight on. Somehow, we can take two-dimensional information from the retina and recognize a three-dimensional object from any angle. Various theories have been proposed to explain how we solve the problem of viewing position. These theories can be grouped into two categories: recognition is *dependent* on the frame of reference; or, recognition is *independent* of the frame of reference.

Theories with a **view-dependent frame of reference** posit that people have a cornucopia of specific representations in memory; we simply need to match a stimulus to a stored representation. The key idea is that the stored representation for recognizing a bicycle from the side is different from the one for recognizing a bicycle viewed from above (Figure 6.10). Hence, our ability to recognize that two stimuli are depicting the same object is assumed to arise at a later stage of processing.

One shortcoming with view-dependent theories is that they seem to place a heavy burden on perceptual memory. Each object requires multiple representations in memory, each associated with a different vantage point. This problem is less daunting, however, if we assume that recognition processes are able to match the input to stored representations through an interpolation process. We recognize an object seen from a novel viewpoint by comparing the stimulus information to the stored representations and choosing the best match. When our viewing position of a bicycle is at a 41° angle, relative to vertical, a stored representation of a bicycle viewed at 45° is likely good enough to allow us to recognize the

FIGURE 6.10 View-dependent object recognition. View-dependent theories of object recognition posit that recognition processes depend on the vantage point. Recognizing that all four of these drawings depict a bicycle—one from a side view, one from an aerial view, and two viewed at an angle—requires matching the distinct sensory inputs to view-dependent representations.

object. This idea is supported by experiments using novel objects—an approach that minimizes the contribution of the participants' experience and the possibility of verbal strategies. The time needed to decide if two objects are the same or different increases as the viewpoints diverge, even when each member of the object set contains a unique feature (Tarr et al., 1997).

An alternative scheme proposes that recognition occurs in a **view-invariant frame of reference**. Recognition does not happen by simple analysis of the stimulus information. Rather, the perceptual system extracts structural information about the components of an object and the relationship between these components. In this scheme, the key to successful recognition is that critical properties remain independent of viewpoint (Marr, 1982). To stay with the bicycle example, the properties might be features such as an elongated shape running along the long axis, combined with a shorter, stick-like shape coming off of one end. Throw in two circular-shaped parts, and we could recognize the object as a bicycle from just about any position.

As the saying goes, there's more than one way to skin a cat. In fact, the brain may use both view-dependent and view-invariant operations to support object recognition. Patrick Vuilleumier and his colleagues at University College London explored this hypothesis in an fMRI study (Vuilleumier et al., 2002). The study was motivated by the finding from various imaging studies that, when a stimulus is repeated, the blood oxygen level–dependent (BOLD) response is lower in the second presentation compared to the first. This **repetition suppression effect** is hypothesized to indicate increased neural efficiency: The neural response to the stimulus is more efficient and perhaps faster when the pattern has been recently activated. To ask about view dependency, study participants were shown pictures of objects, and each picture was repeated over the course of the scanning session. The second presentation was either in the same orientation or from a different viewpoint.

Experimenters observed a repetition suppression effect in left ventral occipital cortex, regardless of whether the object was shown from the same or a different viewpoint (Figure 6.11a), consistent with a view-invariant representation. In contrast, activation in right ventral occipital cortex decreased only when the second presentation was from the original viewpoint (Figure 6.11b), consistent with a view-dependent representation. When the object was shown from a new viewpoint, the BOLD response was similar to that observed for the object in the initial presentation. Thus the two hemispheres may process information in different ways, providing two snapshots of the world (this idea is discussed in more detail in Chapter 4).

Shape Encoding

Now let's consider how shape is encoded. In the last chapter, we introduced the idea that recognition may involve hierarchical representations in which each successive stage adds complexity. Simple features such as lines can be combined into edges, corners, and intersections, which—as processing continues up the hierarchy—are grouped into parts, and the parts grouped into objects.

People recognize a pentagon because it contains five line segments of equal length, joined together to form five corners that define an enclosed region (Figure 6.12). The same five line segments can define other objects, such as a pyramid. With the pyramid, however, there are only four points of intersection, not five; and the lines define a more complicated shape that implies it is three-dimensional. The pentagon and the pyramid might activate similar representations at the lowest levels of the hierarchy, yet the combinations of these features into a shape produces distinct representations at higher levels of the processing hierarchy.

One way to investigate how we encode shapes is to identify areas of the brain that are active when comparing contours that form a recognizable shape versus contours that are just squiggles. How do activity patterns in the brain change when a shape is familiar? This question emphasizes the idea that perception involves a connection between sensation and memory (recall our four guiding principles of object recognition). Researchers explored this question in a PET study designed to isolate the specific mental operations used when people viewed familiar shapes, novel shapes, or stimuli formed by scrambling the shapes to form random drawings (Kanwisher et al., 1997a). All three types of stimuli

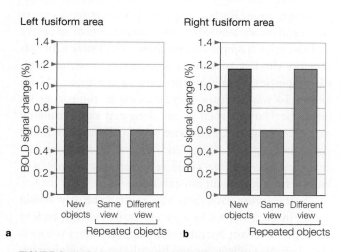

a

FIGURE 6.11 Asymmetry between left and right fusiform activation to repetition effects.
(a) A repetition suppression effect is observed in left ventral occipital cortex regardless of whether an object is shown from the same or a different viewpoint, consistent with a view-invariant representation. **(b)** In contrast, activation in the right ventral occipital cortex decreased relative to activity during the presentation of novel stimuli only when the second object was presented in the original viewpoint, consistent with a view-dependent representation.

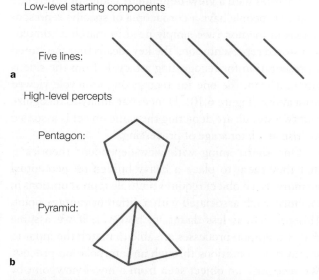

b

FIGURE 6.12 Basic elements and the different objects they can form.
The same basic components (five lines) can form different items (e.g., a pentagon or a pyramid) depending on their arrangement. Although the low-level components **(a)** are the same, the high-level percepts **(b)** are distinct.

Sample stimuli				Feature extraction	Shape description	Memory matching
Familiar				✓	✓	✓
Novel				✓	✓	
Scrambled				✓		

a
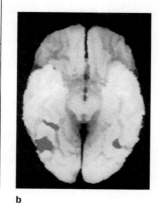
b

FIGURE 6.13 Component analysis of object recognition.
(a) Stimuli for the three conditions and the mental operations required in each condition. Novel objects are hypothesized to engage processes involved in perception even when verbal labels do not exist.
(b) Activation was greater for the familiar and novel objects compared to the scrambled images along the ventral surface of the occipitotemporal cortex.

should engage the early stages of visual perception, or what is called *feature extraction* (Figure 6.13a). To identify areas involved in object perception, a comparison can be made between responses to novel objects and responses to scrambled stimuli—as well as responses between familiar objects and scrambled stimuli—under the assumption that scrambled stimuli do not define objects per se. The memory retrieval contribution should be most evident when viewing novel or familiar objects. In the PET study, both novel and familiar stimuli led to increases in regional cerebral blood flow bilaterally in lateral occipital cortex (LOC, sometimes referred to as lateral occipital complex; Figure 6.13b). Since this study, many others have shown that the LOC is critical for shape and object recognition. Interestingly, no differences were found between the novel and familiar stimuli in these posterior cortical regions. At least within these areas, recognizing that something is unfamiliar may be as taxing as recognizing that something is familiar.

When we view an object such as a dog, it may be a real dog, a drawing of a dog, a statue of a dog, or an outline of a dog made of flashing lights. Still, we recognize each one as a dog. This insensitivity to the specific visual cues that define an object is known as *cue invariance.* Research has shown that, for the LOC, shape seems to be the most salient property of the stimulus. In one fMRI study, participants viewed stimuli in which shapes were defined by either lines (our normal percepts) or the coherent motion of dots. When compared to

control stimuli with similar sensory properties, the LOC response was similar to the two types of object depictions (Grill-Spector et al., 2001; Figure 6.14). Thus the LOC can support the perception of the pink elephant or the plaid apple.

Grandmother Cells and Ensemble Coding

An object is more than just a shape, though. Somehow we also know that one dog shape is a real dog, and the other is a marble statue. How do people recognize specific objects? Some researchers have attempted to answer this question at the level of neurons by asking whether there are individual cells that respond only to specific integrated percepts. Furthermore, do these cells code for the individual parts that define the object? When you recognize an object as a tiger, does this happen because a neuron sitting at the top of the perceptual hierarchy, having combined all of the information that suggests a tiger, then becomes active? If the object had been a lion, would the same cell have been silent, despite the similarities in shape (and other properties) between a tiger and lion? Alternatively, does perception of an object depend on the firing of a collection of cells? In this case, when you see a tiger, a group of neurons that code for different features of the tiger might become active, but only some of them are also active when you see a lion.

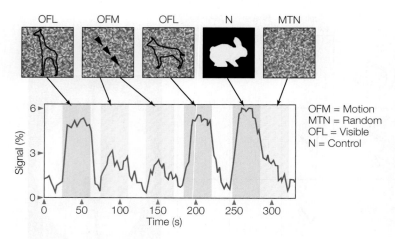

OFM = Motion
MTN = Random
OFL = Visible
N = Control

FIGURE 6.14 BOLD response in lateral occipital cortex is responsive to shape, even if the boundaries of the objects are never physically presented.
The BOLD response is high when an object is perceived, either defined by luminance or a correlated pattern of moving dots. The response is low when the dots move in a coherent direction or at random.

Earlier in this chapter, we touched on the finding that cells in the inferotemporal lobe selectively respond to complex stimuli (e.g., objects, places, body parts, or faces; see Figure 6.3). This observation is consistent with hierarchical theories of object perception. According to these theories, cells in the initial areas of the visual cortex code elementary features such as line orientation and color. The outputs from these cells are combined to form detectors sensitive to higher order features such as corners or intersections—an idea consistent with the findings of Hubel and Wiesel (see Milestones in Cognitive Science: Pioneers in the Visual Cortex in Chapter 5). The process continues as each successive stage codes more complex combinations (Figure 6.15). The type of neuron that can recognize a complex object has been called a **gnostic unit** (from the Greek *gnostikos*, meaning "of knowledge"), referring to the idea that the cell (or cells) signals the presence of a known stimulus—an object, a place, or an animal that has been encountered in the past.

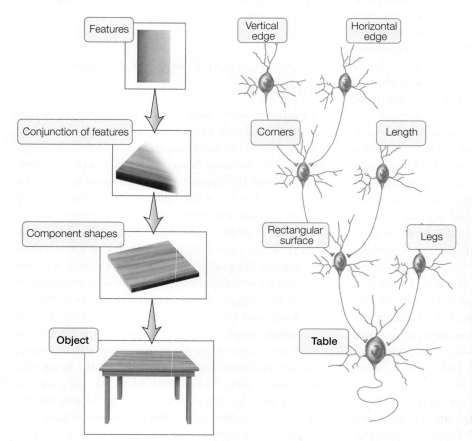

FIGURE 6.15 The hierarchical coding hypothesis.
Elementary features are combined to create objects that can be recognized by gnostic units. At the lowest level of the hierarchy are edge detectors, which operate similarly to the simple cells discussed in Chapter 5. These feature units combine to form corner detectors, which in turn combine to form cells that respond to even more complex stimuli, such as surfaces. The left-hand panel shows hypothesized computational stages for hierarchical coding. The right-hand panel is a cartoon of neural implementation of the computational stages illustrated in the left-hand panel.

It is tempting to conclude that the cell represented by the recordings in Figure 6.3 signals the presence of a hand, independent of viewpoint. Other cells in the inferior temporal cortex respond preferentially to complex stimuli such as jagged contours or fuzzy textures. The latter might be useful for a monkey, in order to identify that an object has a fur-covered surface and therefore, might be the backside of another member of its group. Even more intriguing, researchers have discovered cells in the inferotemporal gyrus and the floor of the superior temporal sulcus that are selectively activated by faces. In a tongue-in-cheek manner, they coined the term *grandmother cell* to convey the notion that people's brains might have a gnostic unit that becomes excited only when their grandmother comes into view. Other gnostic units would be specialized to recognize, for example, a blue Volkswagen or the Golden Gate Bridge.

Itzhak Fried and his colleagues at the University of California, Los Angeles, explored this question by making single-cell recordings in human participants (Quiroga et al., 2005). The participants in their study all had epilepsy; and, in preparation for a surgical procedure to alleviate their symptoms, they each had electrodes surgically implanted in their temporal lobe. In the study, participants were shown a wide range of pictures including animals, objects, landmarks, and individuals. The investigators' first observation was that, in general, it was difficult to make these cells respond. Even when the stimuli were individually tailored to each participant based on an interview to determine that person's visual history, the temporal lobe cells were generally inactive. Nonetheless, there were exceptions. Most notable, these exceptions revealed an extraordinary degree of stimulus specificity. Recall Figure 3.21, which shows the response of one temporal lobe neuron that was selectively activated in response to photographs of the actress Halle Berry. Ms. Berry could be wearing sunglasses, sporting dramatically different haircuts, or even be in costume as Catwoman from one of her movie roles—but in all cases, this particular neuron was activated. Other actresses or famous people failed to activate the neuron.

Let's briefly return to the debate between grandmother-cell coding versus ensemble coding. Although you might be tempted to conclude that cells like these are gnostic units, it is important to keep in mind the limitations of such experiments. First, aside from the infinite number of possible stimuli, the recordings are performed on only a small subset of neurons. As such, this cell potentially could be activated by a broader set of stimuli, and many other neurons might respond in a similar manner. Second, the results also suggest that these gnostic-like units are not really "perceptual." The same cell was also activated when the words *Halle Berry* were presented. This observation takes the wind out of the argument that this is a grandmother cell, at least in the original sense of the idea. Rather, the cell may represent the concept of "Halle Berry," or even represent the name Halle Berry, a name that is likely recalled from memory for any of the stimuli relevant to Halle Berry.

Studies like this pose three problems for the traditional grandmother-cell hypothesis:

1. The idea of grandmother cells rests on the assumption that the final percept of an object is coded by a single cell. Because cells are constantly firing and refractory, a coding scheme of this nature would be highly susceptible to error. If a gnostic unit were to die, we would expect to experience a sudden loss for an object. You would pass grandma (or Halle Berry) on the street without a second thought.
2. The grandmother-cell hypothesis cannot adequately account for how it is possible to perceive novel objects.
3. Third, the gnostic theory does not account for how the grandmother cell would have to adapt as grandmother changed over time. Granny may have had a face-lift, dumped her glasses after corrective eye surgery, dyed her hair, and lost 30 pounds on a low-carb diet. Actually. . . in that case, you might have a problem recognizing her.

One alternative to the grandmother-cell hypothesis is that object recognition results from activation across complex feature detectors (Figure 6.16). Granny, then, is recognized when some of these higher order neurons are activated. Some of the cells may respond to her shape, others to the color of her hair, and still others to the features of her face. According to this ensemble hypothesis, recognition is not due to one unit but to the collective activation of many units. Ensemble theories readily account for why we can recognize similarities between objects (say, the tiger and lion) and may confuse one visually similar object with another: Both objects activate many of the same neurons. Losing some units might degrade our ability to recognize an object, but the remaining units might suffice. Ensemble theories also account for our ability to recognize novel objects. Novel objects bear a similarity to familiar things, and our percept results from activating units that represent their features.

The results of single-cell studies of temporal lobe neurons are in accord with ensemble theories of object recognition. Although it is striking that some cells are selective for complex objects, the selectivity is almost always relative, not absolute. The cells in the inferotemporal cortex prefer certain stimuli to others, but they are also activated by visually similar stimuli. The cell represented in Figure 6.3, for instance, increases its activity when presented with a mitten-like stimulus. No cells respond to a particular individual's hand; the hand-selective cell responds equally to just about any hand. In contrast, as people's perceptual abilities demonstrate, we make much finer discriminations.

Summary of Computational Problems

We have considered several computational problems that must be solved by an object recognition system. Information is represented on multiple scales. Although early visual input can specify simple features, object perception involves intermediate stages of representation in which features are assembled into parts. Objects are not determined solely by their parts, though; they also are defined by the relationship between the parts. An arrow and the letter *Y* contain the same parts but differ in their arrangement. For object recognition to be flexible and robust, the perceived spatial relations among parts should not vary across viewing conditions.

TAKE-HOME MESSAGES

- Object constancy refers to the ability to recognize objects in countless situations, despite variation in the physical stimulus.
- Object perception may occur in a view-dependent frame of reference or a view-invariant frame of reference. In view-dependent theories, perception is assumed to be specific to a particular viewpoint. View-invariant theories posit that recognition occurs at a level that is not linked to specific stimulus information.

- The lateral occipital cortex is critical for the recognition of the shape of an object.
- The term *grandmother cell* has been coined to convey the notion that recognition arises from the activation of neurons that are finely tuned to specific stimuli.
- Ensemble theories, on the other hand, hypothesize that recognition is the result of the collective activation of many neurons.

Failures in Object Recognition: The Big Picture

Now that we have some understanding of how the brain processes visual stimuli in order to recognize objects, let's return to our discussion of agnosia. Many people who have suffered a traumatic neurological insult, or who have a degenerative disease such as Alzheimer's, may experience problems recognizing things. This is not necessarily a problem of the visual system. It could be the result of the effects of the disease or injury on attention, memory, and language. Unlike someone with visual agnosia, for a person with Alzheimer's disease, recognition failures persist even when an object is placed in their hands or if it is verbally described to them. As noted earlier, people with visual agnosia have difficulty recognizing objects that are presented visually or require the use of visually based representations. The key word is *visual*—these patients' deficit is restricted to the visual domain. Recognition through other sensory modalities, such as touch or audition, is typically just fine.

Like patient G.S., who was introduced at the beginning of this chapter, visual agnostics can look at a fork yet fail to recognize it as a fork. When the object is placed in their hands, however, they will immediately recognize it (Figure 6.17a). Indeed, after touching the object, an agnosia patient may actually report seeing the object clearly. Because the patient can recognize the object through other modalities, and through vision with supplementary support, we know that the problem does not reflect a general

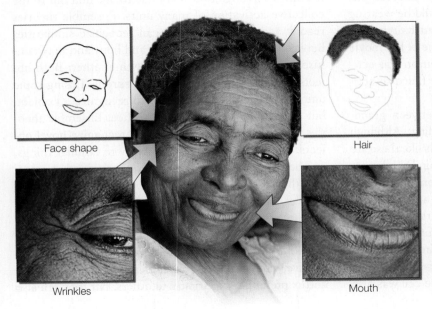

Face shape

Hair

Wrinkles

Mouth

FIGURE 6.16 The ensemble coding hypothesis. Objects are defined by the simultaneous activation of a set of defining properties. "Granny" is recognized here by the co-occurrence of her wrinkles, face shape, hair color, and so on.

Agnosia

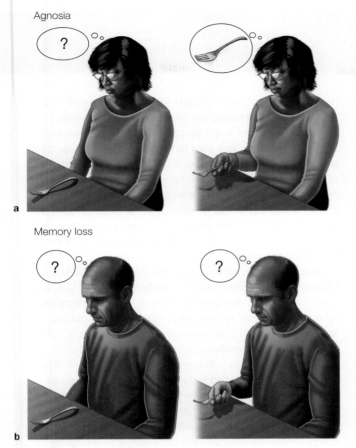

Memory loss

FIGURE 6.17 Agnosia versus memory loss.
To diagnose an agnosic disorder, it is essential to rule out general memory problems. **(a)** The patient with visual agnosia is unable to recognize a fork by vision alone but immediately recognizes it when she picks it up. **(b)** The patient with a memory disorder is unable to recognize the fork even when he picks it up.

loss of knowledge. Nor does it represent a loss of vision, for they can describe the object's physical characteristics such as color and shape. Thus, their deficit reflects either a loss of knowledge limited to the visual system or a disruption in the connections between the visual system and modality-independent stores of knowledge. So, we can say that the label *visual agnosia* is restricted to individuals who demonstrate object recognition problems even though visual information continues to be registered at the cortical level.

The 19th-century German neurologist Heinrich Lissauer was the first to suggest that there were distinct subtypes of visual object recognition deficits. He distinguished between recognition deficits that were sensory based and those that reflected an inability to access visually directed memory—a disorder that he melodramatically referred to as *Seelenblindheit*, or "soul blindness" (Lissauer, 1890). We now know that classifying agnosia as sensory based is not quite correct, at least not if we limit "sensory" to processes such as

the detection of shape, features, color, motion, and so on. The current literature broadly distinguishes between three major subtypes of agnosia: apperceptive agnosia, integrative agnosia, and associative agnosia, roughly reflecting the idea that object recognition problems can arise at different levels of processing. Keep in mind, though, that specifying subtypes can be a messy business, because the pathology is frequently extensive and because a complex process such as object recognition, by its nature, involves a number of interacting component processes. Diagnostic categories are useful for clinical purposes, but generally have limited utility when these neurological disorders are used to build models of brain function. With that caveat in mind, we can now look at each of these forms of agnosia in turn.

Apperceptive Agnosia

Apperceptive agnosia can be a rather puzzling disorder. A standard clinical evaluation of visual acuity may fail to reveal any marked problems. The patient may perform normally on shape discrimination tasks and even have little difficulty recognizing objects, at least when presented from perspectives that make salient the most important features. The object recognition problems become evident when the patient is asked to identify objects based on limited stimulus information, either because the object is shown as a line drawing or seen from an unusual perspective.

Beginning in the late 1960s, Elizabeth Warrington embarked on a series of investigations of perceptual disabilities in patients possessing unilateral cerebral lesions caused by a stroke or tumor (Warrington & Rabin, 1970; Warrington, 1985). Warrington devised a series of tests to look at object recognition capabilities in one group of approximately 70 patients (all of whom were right-handed and had normal visual acuity). In a simple perceptual matching test, participants had to determine if two stimuli, such as a pattern of dots or lines, were the same or different. Patients with right-sided parietal lesions showed poorer performance than did either control subjects or patients with lesions of the left hemisphere. Left-sided damage had little effect on performance. This result led Warrington to propose that the core problem for patients with right-sided lesions involved the integration of spatial information (see Chapter 4).

To test this idea, Warrington devised the Unusual Views Object Test. Participants were shown photographs of 20 objects, each from two distinct views (Figure 6.18a). In one photograph, the object was oriented in a standard or prototypical view; for example, a cat was photographed with its head facing forward. The other photograph depicted an unusual or atypical view; for example, the cat was photographed from behind, without its face or feet in

HOW THE BRAIN WORKS
Auditory Agnosia

Other sensory modalities besides visual perception surely contribute to object recognition. Distinctive odors in a grocery store enable us to determine which bunch of greens is thyme and which is basil. Using touch, we can differentiate between cheap polyester and a fine silk garment. We depend on sounds, both natural and human-made, to cue our actions. A siren prompts us to search for a nearby police car or ambulance, or anxious parents immediately recognize the cries of their infant and rush to the baby's aid. Indeed, we often overlook our exquisite auditory capabilities for object recognition. Have a friend rap on a wooden tabletop, or metal filing cabinet, or glass window. You will easily distinguish between these objects.

Numerous studies have documented failures of object recognition in other sensory modalities. As with visual agnosia, a patient has to meet two criteria to be labeled *agnosic*. First, a deficit in object recognition cannot be secondary to a problem with perceptual processes. For example, to be classified as having auditory agnosia, patients must perform within normal limits on tests of tone detection; that is, the loudness of a sound that's required for the person to detect it must fall within a normal range. Second, the deficit in recognizing objects must be restricted to a single modality. For example, a patient who cannot identify environmental sounds such as the ones made by flowing water or jet engines must be able to recognize a picture of a waterfall or an airplane.

Consider a patient, C.N., reported by Isabelle Peretz and her colleagues (1994) at the University of Montreal. A 35-year-old nurse, C.N. had suffered a ruptured aneurysm in the right middle cerebral artery, which was repaired. Three months later, she was diagnosed with a second aneurysm, in the left middle cerebral artery which also required surgery. Postoperatively, C.N.'s abilities to detect tones and to comprehend and produce speech were not impaired. But she immediately complained that her perception of music was deranged. Her *amusia*, or impairment in music abilities, was verified by tests. For example, she could not recognize melodies taken from her personal record collection, nor could she recall the names of 140 popular tunes, including the Canadian national anthem.

C.N.'s deficit could not be attributed to a problem with long-term memory. She also failed when asked to decide if two melodies were the same or different. Evidence that the problem was selective to auditory perception was provided by her excellent ability to identify these same songs when shown the lyrics. Similarly, when given the title of a musical piece such as *The Four Seasons*, C.N. responded that the composer was Vivaldi and could even recall when she had first heard the piece.

Just as interesting as C.N.'s amusia was her absence of problems with other auditory recognition tests. C.N. understood speech, and she was able to identify environmental sounds such as animal cries, transportation noises, and human voices. Even within the musical domain, C.N. did not have a generalized problem with all aspects of music comprehension. She performed as well as normal participants when asked to judge if two-tone sequences had the same rhythm. Her performance fell to a level of near chance, however, when she had to decide if the two sequences were the same melody. This dissociation makes it less surprising that, despite her inability to recognize songs, she still enjoyed dancing!

Other cases of domain-specific auditory agnosia have been reported. Many patients have an impaired ability to recognize environmental sounds, and, as with amusia, this deficit is independent of language comprehension problems. In contrast, patients with pure word deafness cannot recognize oral speech, even though they exhibit normal auditory perception for other types of sounds and have normal reading abilities. Such category specificity suggests that auditory object recognition involves several distinct processing systems. Whether the operation of these processes should be defined by content (e.g., verbal versus nonverbal input) or by computations (e.g., words and melodies may vary with regard to the need for part-versus-whole analysis) remains to be seen . . . or rather heard.

---

the picture. Participants were asked to name the objects shown. Although normal participants made few, if any, errors, patients with right posterior lesions had difficulty identifying objects that had been photographed from unusual orientations. They could name the objects photographed in the prototypical orientation, which confirmed that their problem was not due to lost visual knowledge.

This impairment can be understood by going back to our earlier discussion of object constancy. A hallmark of human perceptual systems is that from an infinite set of percepts, we readily extract critical features that allow us to identify objects. Certain vantage points are better than others, but the brain is designed to overcome variability in the sensory input to recognize both similarities and differences between different inputs. The ability to achieve object constancy is compromised in patients with apperceptive agnosia. Although these patients can recognize objects, this ability diminishes when the perceptual input is limited (as with

FIGURE 6.18 Tests used to identify apperceptive agnosia.
(a) In the unusual-views test, participants must judge whether two images seen from different vantage points show the same object.
(b) In the shadows test, participants must identify the object(s) when seen under normal or shadowed illumination. In both tests, patients with right-hemisphere lesions, especially in the posterior area, performed much worse than did control participants (not shown) or patients with left-hemisphere lesions.

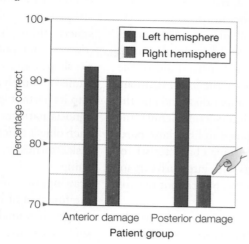

a

Unusual-views test

Patients with right-hemisphere lesions, especially in the posterior area, performed much worse than patients with left-hemisphere lesions.

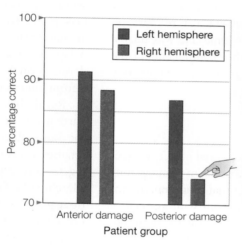

b

Shadows test

Patients with right-hemisphere lesions, especially in the posterior area, performed much worse than patients with left-hemisphere lesions.

shadows; Figure 6.18b) or does not include the most salient features (as with atypical views). The finding that this type of disorder is more common in patients with right-hemisphere lesions suggests that this hemisphere is essential for the operations required to achieve object constancy.

Integrative Agnosia

People with **integrative agnosia** are unable to integrate features into parts, or parts of an object into a coherent whole. This classification of agnosia was first suggested by Jane Riddoch and Glyn Humphreys following an intensive case study of one patient, H.J.A. The patient had no problem doing shape-matching tasks and, unlike with apperceptive agnosia, was successful in matching photographs of objects seen from unusual views. His object recognition problem, however, became apparent when he was asked to identify objects that overlapped one another (Humphreys & Riddoch, 1987; Humphreys et al., 1994). He was either at a loss to describe what he saw, or would build a percept only step-by-step. Rather than perceive an object at a glance, H.J.A. relied on recognizing salient features or parts. To recognize a dog, he would perceive each of the legs, the characteristic shape of the body and head, and then use these part representations to identify the whole object. Such a strategy runs into problems when objects overlap, because the observer must not only identify the parts but also correctly assign parts to objects.

A telling example of this deficit is provided by the drawings of another patient with integrative agnosia— C.K., a young man who suffered a head injury in an automobile accident (Behrmann et al., 1994). C.K. was shown a picture consisting of two diamonds and one circle in a particular spatial arrangement and asked to reproduce the drawing (Figure 6.19). Glance at the

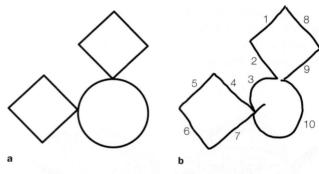

a   b

FIGURE 6.19 Patients with integrative agnosia do not see objects holistically.
Patient C.K. was asked to copy the figure shown in **(a)**. His overall performance **(b)** was quite good; the two diamonds and the circle can be readily identified. However, as noted in the text, the numbers indicate the order he used to produce the segments.

drawing in Figure 6.19b—not bad, right? But now look at the numbers, indicating the order in which C.K. drew the segments to form the overall picture. After starting with the left-hand segments of the upper diamond, C.K. proceeded to draw the upper left-hand arc of the circle and then branched off to draw the lower diamond before returning to complete the upper diamond and the rest of the circle. For C.K., each intersection defined the segments of different parts. He failed to link these parts into recognizable wholes—the defining characteristic of integrative agnosia. Other patients with integrative agnosia are able to copy images perfectly, but cannot tell you what they are.

Object recognition typically requires that parts be integrated into whole objects. The patient described at the beginning of this chapter, G.S., exhibited some features of integrative agnosia. He was fixated on the belief that the combination lock was a telephone because of the circular array of numbers, a salient feature (part) on the standard rotary phones of his time. He was unable to integrate this part with the other components of the combination lock. In object recognition, the whole truly is greater than the sum of its parts.

Associative Agnosia

Associative agnosia is a failure of visual object recognition that cannot be attributed to a problem of integrating parts to form a whole, or to a perceptual limitation, such as a failure of object constancy. A patient with associative agnosia can perceive objects with his visual system, but cannot understand or assign meaning to the objects. Associative agnosia rarely exists in a pure form; patients often perform abnormally on tests of basic perceptual abilities, likely because their lesions are not highly localized. Their perceptual deficiencies, however, are not proportional to their object recognition problem.

For instance, one patient, F.R.A., awoke one morning and discovered that he could not read his newspaper—a condition known as **alexia**, or *acquired alexia* (R. McCarthy & Warrington, 1986). A CT scan revealed an infarct of the left posterior cerebral artery. The lesioned area was primarily in the occipital region of the left hemisphere, although the damage probably extended into the posterior temporal cortex. F.R.A. could copy geometric shapes and could point to objects when they were named. Notably, he could segment a complex drawing into its parts (Figure 6.20). Apperceptive and integrative agnosia patients fail miserably when instructed to color each object differently. In contrast, F.R.A. performed the task effortlessly. Despite this ability, though, he could not name the objects that he had colored. When shown line drawings of common objects, he could name or describe the function of only half of them. When presented with images of animals that were depicted to be the same size, such as a mouse and a dog, and asked to point to the larger one, his performance was barely above chance. Nonetheless, his knowledge of such properties was intact. If the two animal names were said aloud, F.R.A. could do the task perfectly. Thus his recognition problems reflected an inability to access that knowledge from the visual modality. Associative agnosia is reserved for patients who derive normal visual representations but cannot use this information to recognize things.

Recall that in the Unusual Views Object Test, study participants are required to judge if two pictures depict the same object from different orientations. This task requires participants to categorize information according to perceptual qualities. In an alternative task, the Matching-by-Function Test, participants are shown three pictures and asked to point to the two that are functionally similar. In Figure 6.21, the correct response in the top panel is to match the closed umbrella to the open umbrella, even though the former is physically more similar to the cane. In the bottom panel, the director's chair should be matched with the beach chair, not the more similar looking wheelchair. The Matching-by-Function Test requires participants to understand the meaning of the object, regardless of its appearance.

Patients with posterior lesions in either the right or the left hemisphere are impaired on this task. When considered in conjunction with other tasks used by Warrington, it

FIGURE 6.20 Alexia patient F.R.A.'s drawings.
Despite his inability to name visually presented objects, F.R.A. was quite successful in coloring in the components of these complex drawings. He had clearly succeeded in parsing the stimuli but still was unable to identify the objects.

FIGURE 6.21 Matching-by-Function Test.
Participants are asked to choose the two objects that are most similar in function.

tional connection between the two visual percepts. They lack access to the conceptual representations needed to link the functional association between the open and closed umbrellas. This is associative agnosia.

TAKE-HOME MESSAGES

- Apperceptive agnosia can be considered a problem in achieving object constancy. The patient with apperceptive agnosia may recognize an object from a typical viewpoint, but performance deteriorates when asked to name an object that is seen from an unusual viewpoint or is occluded by shadows.
- Integrative agnosia is a deficit that arises from the inability to integrate features into parts, or parts of an object into a coherent whole.
- Associative agnosia describes patients who are unable to access conceptual knowledge from visual input. Their perceptual abilities may be (relatively) intact, but they fail to link that representation to knowledge about the object is used for, where it might be found, and so on.

Category Specificity in Agnosia: The Devil Is in the Details

Categorizing agnosia into apperceptive, associative, and integrative is helpful for understanding the processes involved with object recognition. Further insight has come from seemingly bizarre cases of agnosia in which the patients exhibit object recognition deficits that are selective for specific categories of objects. These cases have shown that there is more to visual agnosia than meets the eye.

Animate Versus Inanimate?

We have learned that associative agnosia results from the loss of semantic knowledge regarding the visual structures or properties of objects. Early perceptual analyses proceed normally, but the long-term knowledge of visual information is either lost or can't be accessed; thus, the object cannot be recognized. Consider, however, the case of patient J.B.R.

J.B.R. was diagnosed with herpes simplex encephalitis. His illness left him with a complicated array of deficits, including profound amnesia and word-finding difficulties. His performance on tests of apperceptive agnosia was normal, but he had a severe associative agnosia. Most notably, his agnosia was disproportionately

appears that the problems in the two groups happen for different reasons. Patients with right-sided lesions cannot do the task because they *fail to recognize many objects*, especially those depicted in an unconventional manner such as the closed umbrella. This is apperceptive agnosia. Patients with left-sided lesions *cannot make the func-*

Stop reading for a minute and imagine yourself walking along the beach at sunset. Got it? Most likely your image is of a specific place where you once enjoyed an ocean sunset. Some details may be quite salient and others may require further reflection. Were any boats passing by on the horizon in the image? Was the surf calm or rough; were the gulls squawking; was it cloudy? When we imagine our beachside sunset, are we activating the same neural pathways and performing the same internal operations as when we gaze upon such a scene with our eyes? Probably.

Neuropsychological research provides compelling evidence of shared processing for imagery and perception. Patients with perceptual deficits have also been shown to have corresponding deficits in imagery (Farah, 1988). Strokes may isolate visual information from areas that represent more abstract knowledge, causing difficulty in both perception and imagery tasks. For example, one patient was able to sort objects according to color, but when asked to name a color or point to a named color, her performance was impaired. With imagery tasks, the patient also could not answer questions about the colors of objects. She could say that a banana is a fruit that grows in southern climates but could not name its color. Even more surprising, the patient answered metaphorical questions about colors. For example, she could answer the question "What is the color of envy?" by responding, "Green." Questions like these cannot be answered through imagery.

Patients with higher order visual deficits have related deficits in visual imagery. For instance, one patient with occipitotemporal lesions had difficulty imagining faces or animals, but he could readily draw a floor plan of his house and locate major cities on a map of the United States. In contrast, another patient with damage to the parietal-occipital pathways produced vivid descriptions when he was asked to imagine objects, but he failed spatial imagery tasks. Together, these patients provide evidence of dissociation in imagery of what–where processing that closely parallels the dissociation observed in perception.

The evidence provides a compelling case that mental imagery uses many of the same processes that are critical for perception. The sights in an image are likely to activate visual areas of the brain; the sounds, auditory areas; and the smells, olfactory areas. Indeed, in one fMRI study, approximately 90% of the voxels showed correlated activation patterns during perception and imagery, even if the magnitude of the signal was larger during perception (Ganis et al., 2005). Despite the similarities between perception and imagery, the two are not identical. We know when we are imagining the Spanish Steps in Rome that we are not really there. The inability to distinguish between real and imagined states of mind has been hypothesized to underlie certain psychiatric conditions such as schizophrenia.

One provocative issue that has received relatively little attention is how visual memory changes over time following damage to systems involved in visual perception. If we are deprived of consistent input, then it seems reasonable to expect that our knowledge base will be reorganized. In his essay "The Case of the Colorblind Painter," Oliver Sacks (1995) described Mr. I, a successful artist who suffered complete achromatopsia (loss of color vision) following a car accident. A lover of color, he was horrified upon returning to his studio to discover that all of his vividly colored abstract paintings now appeared a morass of grays, blacks, and whites. Food was no longer appetizing given that the colors of tomatoes, carrots, and broccoli all were varying shades of gray. Even sex became repugnant after he viewed his wife's flesh, and indeed his own flesh, as a "rat-colored" gray. No doubt most of us would agree with Mr. I's initial description of his visual world: "awful, disgusting."

Interestingly, his shock underscores the fact that his color knowledge was still intact. Mr. I could remember with great detail the colors he expected to see in his paintings. It was the mismatch between his expectation and what he saw that was so depressing. He shunned museums because the familiar pictures just looked wrong.

During the subsequent year, however, a transition occurred. Mr. I's memory for colors started to slip away. He no longer despaired when gazing at a tomato devoid of red or a sunset drained of color. He knew that something wasn't quite right, but his sense of the missing colors was much vaguer. Indeed, he began to appreciate the subtleties of a black-and-white world. Overwhelmed by the brightness of the day, Mr. I became a night owl, appreciating forms in purity, "uncluttered by color." This change can be seen in his art (Figure 1). Prior to the accident, Mr. I relied on color to create subtle boundaries, to evoke movement across the canvas. In his black-and-white world, geometric patterns delineated sharp boundaries.

FIGURE 1 An abstract painting by Mr. I, produced 2 years after his accident.
Mr. I was experimenting with colors at this time, although he was unable to see them.

worse for living objects than for inanimate ones. When he was shown drawings of common objects, such as scissors, clocks, and chairs, and asked to identify them, his success rate was about 90 %. Show him a picture of a tiger or a blue jay, however, and he was at a loss. He could correctly identify only 6% of the pictures of living things. Other patients with agnosia have reported a similar dissociation for living and nonliving things (Satori & Job, 1988).

Organizational Theories of Category Specificity

How are we to interpret such puzzling deficits? If we assume that associative agnosia represents a loss of knowledge about visual properties, we might suppose that a category-specific disorder results from the selective loss within, or a disconnection from, this knowledge system. We recognize that birds, dogs, and dinosaurs are animals because they share common features. In a similar way, scissors, saws, and knives share characteristics. Some might be physical (e.g., they all have an elongated shape) and others functional (e.g., they all are used for cutting). Brain injuries that produce agnosia in humans do not completely destroy the connections to semantic knowledge. Even the most severely affected patient will recognize some objects. Because the damage is not total, it seems reasonable that circumscribed lesions might destroy tissue devoted to processing similar types of information. Patients with **category-specific deficits** support this form of organization.

J.B.R.'s lesion appeared to affect regions associated with processing information about living things. If this interpretation is valid, we should expect to find patients whose recognition of nonliving things is disproportionately impaired. Reports of agnosia patients exhibiting this pattern, however, are much rarer. There could be an anatomical reason for the discrepancy. For instance, regions of the brain that predominantly process or store information about animate objects could be more susceptible to injury or stroke. Alternatively, the dissociation could be due to differences in how we perceive animate and inanimate objects.

One hypothesis is that many nonliving things evoke representations not elicited by living things (A. Damasio, 1990). In particular, manufactured objects can be manipulated. As such, they are associated with kinesthetic and motoric representations. When viewing an inanimate object, we can activate a sense of how it feels or of the actions required to manipulate it (Figure 6.22). Corresponding representations may not exist for living objects. Although we may have a kinesthetic sense

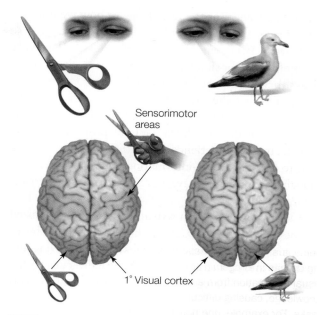

FIGURE 6.22 Sensorimotor areas assist in object recognition. Our visual knowledge of many inanimate objects is supplemented by kinesthetic codes developed through our interactions with these objects. When a picture of scissors is presented to a patient with an object-specific deficit, the visual code may not be sufficient for recognition. When the picture is supplemented with priming of kinesthetic codes, however, the person is able to name the object. Kinesthetic codes are unlikely to exist for most living things.

of how a cat's fur feels, few of us have ever stroked or manipulated an elephant. We certainly have no sense of what it feels like to pounce like a cat or fly like a bird.

According to this hypothesis, manufactured objects are easier to recognize because they activate additional forms of representation. Although brain injury can produce a common processing deficit for all categories of stimuli, these extra representations may be sufficient to allow someone to recognize nonliving objects. This hypothesis is supported by patient G.S.'s behavior. Remember that when G.S. was shown the picture of the combination lock, his first response was to call it a telephone. Even when he was verbalizing "telephone," however, his hands began to move as if they were opening a combination lock. Indeed, he was able to name the object after he looked at his hands and realized what they were trying to tell him.

Neuroimaging studies in healthy participants provide converging support for this hypothesis. When people view pictures of manufactured objects such as tools, the left ventral premotor cortex, a region associated with action planning, is activated. Moreover, this region is activated when the stimuli are pictures of natural objects that can be grasped and manipulated, such as a rock (Gerlach et al., 2002; Kellenbach et al., 2003). These results suggest that this area of the brain responds preferentially to action knowledge, or the knowledge of how we interact with objects.

Martha Farah and Jay McClelland (1991) used a series of computer simulations to integrate some of these ideas. Their study was designed to contrast two ways of conceptualizing the organization of semantic memory of objects. *Semantic memory* refers to our conceptual knowledge of the world, the facts or propositions that arise from our experience (e.g., that a steamroller is used to flatten roads—information you may have, even though you probably have never driven a steamroller; Figure 6.23a).

One hypothesis is that semantic memory is organized by *category membership*. According to this hypothesis, there are distinct representational systems for living and nonliving things, and perhaps further subdivisions within these two broad categories. An alternative hypothesis is

that semantic memory reflects an organization based on *object properties*. The idea that nonliving things are more likely to entail kinesthetic and motor representations is one variant of this view. The computer simulations were designed to demonstrate that category-specific deficits, such as animate and inanimate, could result from lesions to a semantic memory system organized by object properties. In particular, the simulations focused on the fact that living things are distinguished by their visual appearance, whereas nonliving things are also distinguished by their functional attributes.

The architecture of Farah and McClelland's model involved a simple *neural network*, a computer model in which information is distributed across a number of processing units (Figure 6.23b). One set of units corresponded to peripheral input systems, divided into a verbal and a visual system. Each of these was composed of 24 input units. The visual representation of an object involved a unique pattern of activation across the 24 visual units. Similarly, the name of an object involved a unique pattern of activation across the 24 verbal units.

Each object was also linked to a unique pattern of activation across the second type of unit in the model: the semantic memory. Within the semantic system were two types of units: visual and functional (see Figure 6.23b). Although these units did not correspond to specific types of information (e.g., colors or shapes), the idea here is that semantic knowledge consists of at least two types of information. One type of semantic knowledge is visually based; for example, a tiger has stripes or a chair has legs. The other type of semantic memory corresponds to people's functional knowledge of objects. For example, functional semantics would include our knowledge that tigers are dangerous or that a chair is a type of furniture.

To capture psychological differences in how visual and functional information might be stored, the researchers imposed two constraints on semantic memory: The first constraint was that, of the 80 semantic units, 60 were visual and 20 were functional. This 3:1 ratio was based on a preliminary study in which human participants were asked to read the dictionary definitions of living and nonliving objects and indicate whether a descriptor was visual or functional. On average, three times as many descriptors were classified as visual. Second, the preliminary study indicated that the ratio of visual to functional descriptors differed for the two classes of objects. For living objects the ratio was 7.7:1, but for nonliving objects this ratio dropped to 1.4:1. Thus, as discussed previously, our knowledge of living objects is much more dependent on visual information than is our knowledge of nonliving objects. In

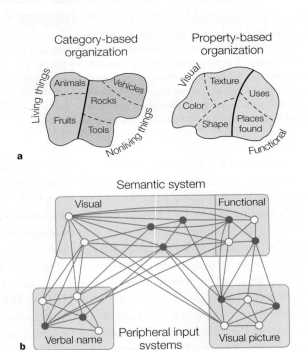

FIGURE 6.23 Two hypotheses about the organization of semantic knowledge.
(a) A category-based hypothesis (*left*) proposes that semantic knowledge is organized according to our categories of the world. For example, one prominent division would put living things in one group and nonliving things in another. A property-based hypothesis (*right*) proposes that semantic knowledge is organized according to the properties of objects. These properties may be visual or functional. **(b)** The architecture of Farah and McClelland's connectionist model of a property-based semantic system. The initial activation for each object is represented by a unique pattern of activation in two input systems and the semantic system. In this example, the darkened units would correspond to the pattern for one object. The final activation would be determined by the initial pattern and the connection weights between the units. There are no connections between the two input systems. The names and pictures are linked through the semantic system.

the model, this constraint dictated the number of visual and functional semantic units used for the living and nonliving objects being varied.

The model was trained to link the verbal and visual representations of a set of 20 objects, half of them living and the other half nonliving. Note that the verbal and visual units were not directly linked, but could interact only through their connections with the semantic system. The strength of these connections was adjusted in a training procedure. This procedure was not intended to simulate how people acquire semantic knowledge. Rather, the experimenters set all of the units—both input and semantic—to their values for a particular object and then allowed the activation of each unit to change

depending on both its initial activation and the input it received from other units. Then, to minimize the difference between the resulting pattern and the original pattern, the experimenters adjusted the connection weights. The model's object recognition capabilities could be tested by measuring the probability of correctly associating the names and pictures.

This model proved extremely adept. After 40 training trials, it was perfect when tested with stimuli from either category: living or nonliving. The key question centered on how well the model did after receiving "lesions" to its semantic memory—lesions assumed to correspond to what happens in patients with visual associative agnosia. Lesions in a model consist of the deactivation of a certain percentage of the semantic units. As Figure 6.24 shows, selective lesions in either the visual (a) or the functional (b) semantic system produced category-specific deficits. When the damage was restricted to visual semantic memory, the model had great difficulty associating the names and pictures correctly for living objects. In contrast, when the damage was restricted to functional semantic memory, failures were limited to nonliving objects. Moreover, the "deficits" are much more dramatic in the former simulation, consistent with the observation that patients are more likely to have selective deficits in recognizing living things compared to selective deficits in recognizing non-living things.

This result meshes nicely with reports in the neuropsychological literature that there are many more instances of patients with a category-specific agnosia for living things. Even when functional semantic memory was damaged, the model remained proficient in identifying nonliving objects, presumably because knowledge of these objects was distributed across both the visual and the functional memory units.

These simulations demonstrate how category-specific deficits might reflect the organization of semantic memory knowledge. The modeling work makes an important point: We need not postulate that our knowledge of objects is organized along categories such as living and nonliving. The double dissociation between living and nonliving things has been taken to suggest that humans have specialized systems sensitive to these categorical distinctions. Although this organization is possible, the Farah and McClelland model shows that the living–nonliving dissociation can occur even when a single system is used to recognize both living and nonliving things. Rather than assuming a partitioning of representational systems based on the type of object, Farah and McClelland proposed that semantic memory is organized according to the properties that define the objects. We will return to this question a bit later in the chapter.

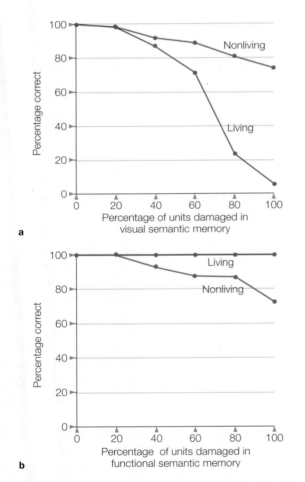

FIGURE 6.24 Measuring category-specific deficits in a neural network.
Lesions in the semantic units resulted in a double dissociation between the recognition of living and nonliving objects. After a percentage of the semantic units were eliminated, two measurements were made. **(a)** When the lesion was restricted to the visual semantic memory units, the model showed a marked impairment in correctly identifying living things. **(b)** When the lesion was restricted to the functional semantic memory units, the impairment was much milder and limited to nonliving things.

Prosopagnosia Is a Failure to Recognize Faces

It's hard to deny—one of the most important objects that people recognize, living or otherwise, is faces. Though we may have characteristic physiques and mannerisms, facial features provide the strongest distinction between people. The importance of face perception is reflected in our extraordinary ability to remember faces. When we browse through old photos, we readily recognize the faces of people we have not seen for many years. Unfortunately, our other memory abilities are not as keen. Although we may recall that the person in a photograph was in our third-grade class, her name may remain elusive. Of course, it does not take years to experience this frustration; fairly often, we run into an acquaintance whose face is familiar but are unable to remember her name or where and when we previously met.

Prosopagnosia is the term used to describe an impairment in face recognition. Given the importance of face recognition, prosopagnosia is one of the most fascinating and disturbing disorders of object recognition. As with all other visual agnosias, prosopagnosia requires that the deficit be specific to the visual modality. Like patient P.T., described at the beginning of the last chapter, patients with prosopagnosia are able to recognize a person upon hearing that person's voice.

One prosopagnosic patient with bilateral occipital lesions failed to identify not only his wife but also an even more familiar person—himself (Pallis, 1955). As he reported, "At the club I saw someone strange staring at me, and asked the steward who it was. You'll laugh at me. I'd been looking at myself in the mirror" (Farah, 2004, p. 93). Not surprisingly, this patient was also unable to recognize pictures of famous individuals of his time, including Churchill, Hitler, Stalin, Marilyn Monroe, and Groucho Marx. This deficit was particularly striking because in other ways the patient had an excellent memory, recognized common objects without hesitation, and could read and recognize line drawings—all tests that agnosia patients often fail.

The study of prosopagnosia has been driven primarily by the study of patients with brain lesions. These cases provide striking examples of the abrupt loss of an essential perceptual ability. More recently, researchers have been interested in learning if this condition is also evident in individuals with no history of neurological disturbance. The inspiration here comes from the observation that people show large individual differences in their ability to recognize faces. Recent studies suggest that some individuals can be considered to have congenital prosopagnosia, that is, a lifetime problem with face perception.

A familial component has been identified in congenital prosopagnosia. Monozygotic twins (same DNA) are more similar than dizygotic twins (share only 50% of the same DNA) in their ability to perceive faces. Moreover, this ability is unrelated to general measures of intelligence or attention (Zhu et al., 2009). Genetic analyses suggest that congenital prosopagnosia may involve a gene mutation with autosomal dominant inheritance. One hypothesis is that during a critical period of development, this gene is abnormally expressed, resulting in a disruption in the development of white matter tracts in the ventral visual pathway (see How the Brain Works: Autism and Face Perception).

Processing Faces: Are Faces Special?

Face perception may not use the same processing mechanisms as those used in object recognition—a somewhat counterintuitive hypothesis. It seems more reasonable and certainly more parsimonious to assume that brains have a single, general-purpose system for recognizing all sorts of visual inputs. Why should faces be treated differently from other objects?

When we meet someone, we usually look at his face to identify him. In no cultures do individuals look at thumbs or knees or other body parts to recognize one another. The tendency to focus on faces reflects behavior that is deeply embedded in our evolutionary history. Faces offer a wealth of information. They tell us about age, health, and gender. Across cultures, facial expressions also give people the most salient cues regarding emotional states, which helps us discriminate between pleasure and displeasure, friendship and antagonism, agreement and confusion. The face, and particularly the eyes, of another person can provide significant clues about what is important in the environment. Looking at someone's lips when she is speaking helps us to understand words more than we may realize.

Although these evolutionary arguments can aid in developing a hypothesis about face recognition, it is essential to develop empirical tests to either support or refute the hypothesis. A lot of data has been amassed on this problem; investigators draw evidence from studies of people with prosopagnosia, electrophysiological studies of primates, and fMRI and EEG imaging studies of healthy humans. This work is relevant not only for the question of how faces are perceived. More generally, the notion that the brain may have category-specific mechanisms is important for thinking about how it is organized. Is the brain organized as a system of specialized modules,

Autism is defined by the presentation of a constellation of unusual symptoms in the first few years of life. Autistic children fail to have normal social interactions or even an interest in such interactions. Both verbal and nonverbal language are delayed. Autistic children may exhibit repetitive and stereotyped patterns of behavior, interests, and activities. The pattern, though, is diverse from one child to the next. This heterogeneity has made it difficult for researchers to specify the underlying psychological mechanisms, and hampered efforts to identify the cause or causes of autism.

Given the emphasis on problems in social interactions, there has been concerted study of face perception in people with autism. fMRI studies have revealed that these individuals show hypoactivity in the FFA and other face processing regions (Corbett et al., 2008; Humphreys et al., 2008; Figure 1a). Postmortem examinations of autistic brains reveal fewer neurons and less neuronal density in the layers of the fusiform gyrus compared to the brains of non-autistic individuals (Figure 1b). These differences were not seen in the primary visual cortex or in the cerebral cortex as a whole (van Kooten et al., 2008). While this kind of microscopic analysis has been performed only in a few brains, these results suggest a cellular basis for the abnormalities in face perception found in autism.

We must be careful, however, when ascribing cause and effect with these data. Do autistic people have poor face perception because they have fewer cells in fusiform cortex, or abnormal patterns of activity in these cells? Or are there fewer cells and reduced activity because they don't look at faces?

In a recent study, postmortem examination of brains found developmental changes in autistic brains that appeared to be the result of altered production, migration, and growth of neurons in multiple regions across the brain (Weigel et al., 2010). These widespread developmental changes may help explain the heterogeneity of the clinical autistic phenotype. It also supports the notion that poor face perception is the result of fewer cells, caused by abnormal development of neurons during gestation.

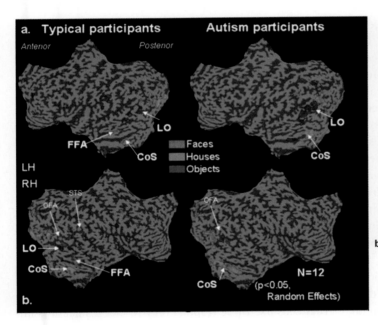

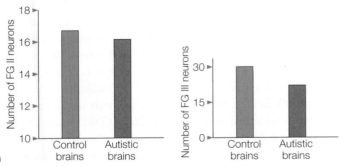

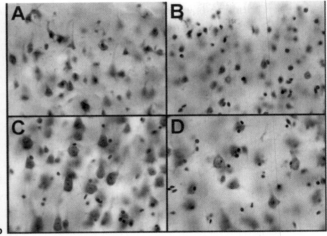

FIGURE 1 Functional and structural neural correlates of autism.
(a) Flattened cortical maps showing activation in response to faces, houses, and objects from typical developing individuals (left) and individuals with autism (right). The autistic individuals show a marked reduction in areas that are most activated by face stimuli. **(b)** Photomicrographs of 200 μm thick sections showing labeled neurons in cortical layers II (A, B) and III (C, D) of the fusiform gyrus. A control brain sample is on the left (A,C) and an autistic brain on the right (B,D). There is a reduction in the number of neurons in the autistic sample in Layer III.

or is it best viewed as a general processor in which particular tasks (such as face perception) draw on machinery that can solve a range of problems?

To investigate whether face recognition and other forms of object perception use distinct processing systems, three criteria are useful.

1. Does face perception involve physically distinct mechanisms? That is, are there particular regions of the brain or specialized cells that respond to faces?
2. Are the systems functionally and operationally independent? The logic of this criterion is essentially the same as that underlying the idea of double dissociations (see Chapter 3).
3. Do the two systems process information differently?

Let's see what evidence we have to answer these questions.

Regions of the Brain Involved in Face Recognition

Do the processes of face recognition and non-facial object recognition involve physically distinct mechanisms? Although some patients show impairment only on face perception tests, more often, a patient's performance on other object recognition tasks is also below normal. This result is, in itself, inconclusive regarding the existence of specialized brain mechanisms for face perception. Don't forget that brain injury in humans is an uncontrolled experiment, in which multiple regions can be affected. With this caveat in mind, we can still evaluate whether patients with prosopagnosia have a common focus of lesions. In her classic book, Martha Farah performed a meta-analysis of the clinical and experimental literature on prosopagnosia (Farah, 2004). Table 6.1 summarizes the general location of the pathology in 71 cases where there was sufficient information about the location of the patients' pathology. The most notable information is that the lesions were bilateral in 46 patients (65%). For the remaining 25 patients (35%) with unilateral lesions, the incidence was *much higher for right-sided lesions* than for left-sided lesions. For both bilateral and unilateral cases, the lesions generally involved occipital and temporal cortices.

Given the messiness of human neuropsychology, it is important to look for converging evidence using the physiological tools of cognitive neuroscience. Neurophysiologists have recorded from the temporal lobes of primates to see if cells in this region respond specifically to faces. In one study (Baylis et al., 1985), recordings were made from cells in the superior temporal sulcus while presenting a monkey with stimuli like those at the top of Figure 6.25. Five of these stimuli (A–E) were faces: four of other monkeys, and one of an experimenter. The

Table 6.1 Summary of Lesion Foci in Patients with Prosopagnosia

Location of Lesion	Percentage of Total[a]
Bilateral (n = 46)	**65**
Temporal	61
Parietal	9
Occipital	91
Left only (n = 4)	**6**
Temporal	75
Parietal	25
Occipital	50
Right only (n = 21)	**29**
Temporal	67
Parietal	28
Occipital	95

[a]Within each subcategory, the percentages indicate how the lesions were distributed across the temporal, parietal, and occipital lobes. The sum of these percentages is greater than 100% because many of the lesions spanned more than one lobe. Most of the patients had bilateral lesions.

other five stimuli (F–J) ranged in complexity but included the most prominent features in the facial stimuli. For example, the grating (image G) reflected the symmetry of faces, and the circle (image I) was similar to eyes. The results revealed that some cells were highly selective, responding only to the clear frontal profile of another monkey. Other cells raised their firing rate for all facial stimuli. Non-facial stimuli hardly activated the superior temporal sulcus cells. In fact, compared to spontaneous firing rates, activity decreased for some non-facial stimuli. The behavior of these cells closely resembles what would be expected of a grandmother cell.

Research over the past two decades has confirmed that cells in at least two distinct regions of the temporal lobe are preferentially activated by faces: One region is in the superior temporal sulcus, the other is in the inferotemporal gyrus (Rolls, 1992). We cannot conclude that cells like these respond only to faces, since it is impossible to test all stimuli. Still, the degree of specificity is quite striking, as shown by a study that combined two neurophysiological methods in a novel manner. Monkeys were placed in an fMRI scanner and shown pictures of faces or objects. As expected, sectors of the superior temporal sulcus showed greater activation to the face stimuli; in fact, three distinct subregions in the superior temporal sulcus responded to faces (Tsao et al., 2006; Figure 6.26a).

The researchers went on to record from individual neurons, using the imaging results to position the electrodes within one of the face-sensitive subregions of the superior

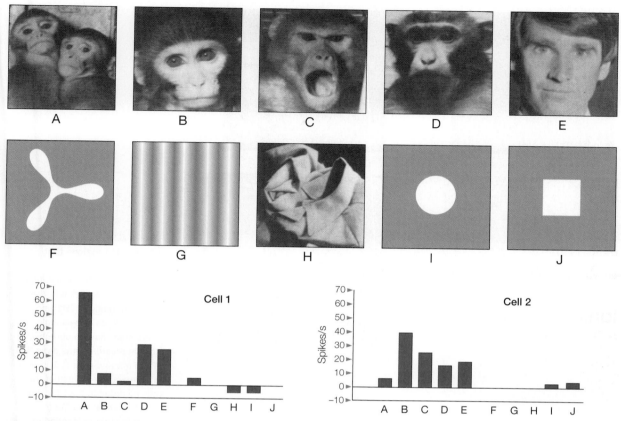

FIGURE 6.25 Identifying face cells in the superior temporal sulcus of the macaque monkey.
The graphs (*bottom row*) show the responses of two cells to the 10 stimuli (labeled A–J). Both cells responded vigorously to many of the facial stimuli. Either there was no change in activity when the animal looked at the objects, or, in some cases, the cells were actually inhibited relative to baseline. The firing-rate data are plotted as a change from baseline activity for that cell when no stimulus was presented.

temporal sulcus. In that subregion, 97% of the neurons exhibited a strong preference for faces, showing strong responses to any face-containing stimulus and minimal responses to a wide range of other stimuli, such as body parts, food, or objects (Figure 6.26b, c). These data provide one of the most striking examples of stimulus specificity within a restricted part of the visual system.

Various ideas have been considered to account for face selectivity. For example, facial stimuli might evoke emotional responses, and this property causes a cell to respond strongly to a face and not to other equally complex stimuli. The same cells, however, are not activated by other types of stimuli that produce a fear response in monkeys.

A vigorous debate now taking place in the human fMRI literature concerns a dedicated face-perception area in the brain. Functional MRI is well suited to investigate this problem, because its spatial resolution can yield a much more precise image of face-specific areas than can be deduced from lesion studies. As in the monkey study just described, we can ask two questions by comparing conditions in which human participants

view different classes of stimuli. First, what neural regions show differential activation patterns when the participant is shown faces compared to the other stimulus conditions? Second, do these "face" regions also respond when the non-facial stimuli are presented?

In one such study (G. McCarthy et al., 1997), participants were presented with pictures of faces together with pictures of either inanimate objects or random patterns (Figure 6.27). Compared to the BOLD response when viewing the random patterns, faces led to a stronger BOLD response along the ventral surface of the temporal lobe in the **fusiform gyrus**. When faces were alternated with inanimate objects, the response to faces in the fusiform gyrus of the right hemisphere remained significant. Many subsequent studies have shown that, relative to other classes of stimuli, faces produce activation in this region of the brain. Indeed, the consistency of this observation has led researchers to refer to this region as the **fusiform face area**, or **FFA**, a term that combines anatomy and function.

The FFA is not the only region that shows a strong BOLD response to faces relative to other visual stimuli.

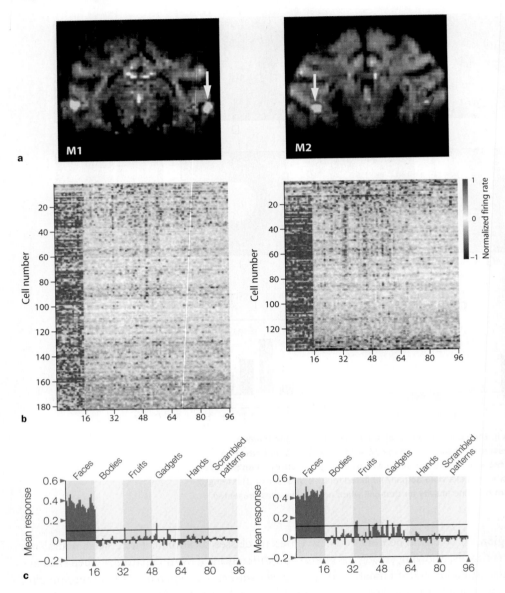

FIGURE 6.26 Superior temporal sulcus (STS) regions that respond to faces.
(a) Functional MRI activations during face perception in two macaque monkeys (M1 and M2). The white arrows indicate where subsequent neurophysiological recording was done (left STS in M1 and right STS in M2). (b) The activity of each of the cells recorded in the STS of M1 (left; 182 cells) and M2 (right; 138 cells) that responded to visual stimuli (face, bodies, fruits, gadgets, hands, or scrambled patterns). In these graphs, each row corresponds to a different cell, and each column corresponds to a different image category. (c) The average response size for each of the image categories across all cells. These cells were highly selective for face stimuli.

Consistent with primate studies (discussed earlier), face regions have been identified in other parts of the temporal lobe, including the superior temporal sulcus. One hypothesis is that these different regions may show further specializations for processing certain types of information from faces. As noted earlier, people use face perception to identify individuals and to extract information about emotion and level of attention. Identifying people is best accomplished by using invariant features of facial structure (e.g., are the eyes broadly spaced?), and emotion identification requires processing dynamic features (e.g., is the mouth smiling?). One hypothesis is that the FFA is important for processing invariant facial properties, whereas the superior temporal sulcus is important for processing more dynamic features (Haxby et al., 2000). Indeed, the superior temporal

sulcus not only is responsive to facial expressions but also is activated during lip reading or when monitoring eye gaze. This distinction can be observed even in the BOLD response, when the faces are presented so quickly that people fail to perceive them consciously (Jiang & He, 2006). In that study, FFA was activated in response to all faces, independent of whether the faces depicted strong emotional expressions. The superior temporal sulcus, in contrast, responded only to the emotive faces (Figure 6.28).

Electrophysiological methods also reveal a neural signature of face perception. Faces elicit a large negative evoked response in the EEG signal approximately 170 ms after stimulus onset. This response is known as the N170 response. A similar negative deflection is found for other classes of objects, such as cars, birds,

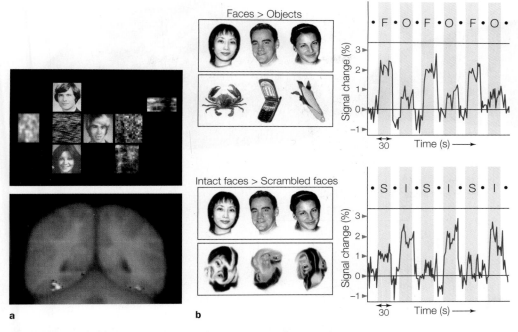

FIGURE 6.27 Isolating neural regions during face perception.
(a) Bilateral activation in the fusiform gyrus was observed with fMRI when participants viewed collages of faces and random patterns compared with collages of only random patterns. Note that, following neuroradiological conventions, the right hemisphere is on the left. **(b)** In another fMRI study, participants viewed alternating blocks of stimuli. In one scanning run, the stimuli alternated between faces and objects; in another run, they alternated between intact and scrambled faces. The right-hand column shows the BOLD signal in the fusiform face area during the scanning run for the various stimuli. In each interval, the stimuli were drawn from the different sets—faces (F), objects (O), scrambled faces (S), or intact faces (I)—and these intervals were separated by short intervals of fixation only. The BOLD signal is much larger during intervals in which faces were presented.

and furniture, but the magnitude of the response is much larger for human faces (Carmel & Bentin, 2002; Figure 6.29). Interestingly, the stimuli need not be pictures of real human faces. The N170 response is also elicited when people view faces of apes or if the facial stimuli are crude, schematic line drawings (Sagiv & Bentin, 2001).

Recording methods, either by single-cell physiology in the monkey or by fMRI and EEG recordings in people, are correlational in nature. Tests of causality generally require that the system be perturbed. For example, strokes can be considered a dramatic perturbation of normal brain function. More subtle methods involve transient perturbations. To this end, Hossein Esteky and colleagues at the Shaheed Beheshti University in Tehran used microstimulation in monkeys to test the causal contribution of inferior temporal cortex to face perception (Afraz et al., 2006). They used a set of fuzzy images that combined pictures of either flowers or faces, embedded in a backdrop of noise (i.e., random dots). A stimulus was shown on each trial, and the monkey had to judge if the stimulus contained a picture of a face or flower. Once the

animals had mastered the task, the team applied an electrical current, targeting a region within inferior temporal cortex that contained clusters of face-selective neurons. When presented with ambiguous stimuli, the monkeys showed a bias to report seeing a face (Figure 6.30). This effect was not seen when the microstimulation was targeted at nearby regions of the cortex.

Although face stimuli are very good at producing activation in FFA, a rather heated debate has emerged in the literature on the question of whether the FFA is selectively activated for faces. An alternative hypothesis is that this region is recruited when people have to make fine perceptual discriminations among highly familiar stimuli. Advocates of this hypothesis point out that imaging studies comparing face and object recognition usually entail an important, if underemphasized, confound: *the level of expertise.*

Consider the comparison of faces and flowers. Although neurologically healthy individuals are all experts in perceiving faces, the same is not true when it comes to perceiving flowers. Unless you are a botanist, you are unlikely to be an expert in recognizing flowers. In

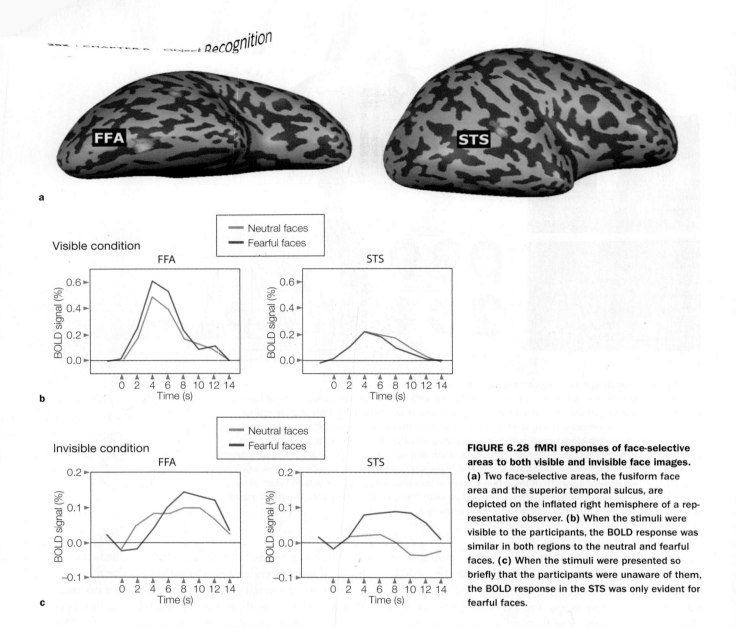

a

Visible condition

Neutral faces
Fearful faces

FFA

STS

FIGURE 6.28 fMRI responses of face-selective areas to both visible and invisible face images. **(a)** Two face-selective areas, the fusiform face area and the superior temporal sulcus, are depicted on the inflated right hemisphere of a representative observer. **(b)** When the stimuli were visible to the participants, the BOLD response was similar in both regions to the neutral and fearful faces. **(c)** When the stimuli were presented so briefly that the participants were unaware of them, the BOLD response in the STS was only evident for fearful faces.

b

Invisible condition

Neutral faces
Fearful faces

FFA

STS

c

addition, faces and flowers differ in terms of their social relevance: Face perception is essential to our social interactions. Whether or not we set out to remember someone's face, we readily encode the features that distinguish one face from another. The same is probably not true for other classes of objects. Most of us are happy to recognize that a particular picture is of a pretty flower, perhaps even to note that it is a rose. But unless you are a rose enthusiast, you are not likely to recognize or encode the difference between a Dazzler and a Garibaldi, nor will you be able to recognize a particular individual rose that you have already seen.

To address this confound, researchers have used imaging studies to determine if the FFA is activated in people who are experts at discriminating within specific classes of objects, such as cars or birds (Gauthier et al., 2000). The results are somewhat mixed. Activation in fusiform cortex, which is made up of more than just the FFA, is in fact greater when people view objects for which they have some expertise. For example, car aficionados will respond more to cars than to birds. What's more, if participants are trained to make fine discriminations between novel objects, the fusiform response increases as expertise develops (Gauthier et al., 1999). The categorization of objects by experts, however, activates a much broader region of ventral occipitotemporal cortex, extending beyond the FFA (Grill-Spector et al., 2004; Rhodes et al., 2004; Figure 6.31).

Thus, it appears that both the face-specific and expertise hypotheses may hold some elements of truth. The ventral occipitotemporal cortex is involved in object recognition, and the engagement of this region, including FFA, increases with expertise (as measured by BOLD).

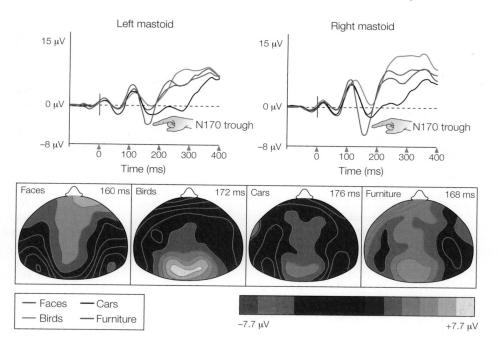

FIGURE 6.29 Electrophysiological response to faces: the N170 response.
Participants viewed pictures of faces, birds, furniture, and cars and were instructed to press a button whenever they saw a picture of a car. The event-related potentials shown in the graphs are from the area surrounding the back of the skull at about the level of the ears (called the *left* and *right mastoid*). Note that the negative-going deflection in the waveform around 170 ms is much larger for the face stimuli compared to the other categories.

Nonetheless, within FFA, the brain shows a strong preference for face stimuli.

Parts and Wholes in Visual Perception

Are the processes of face recognition and non-facial object recognition functionally and operationally independent? Face perception appears to use distinct physical processing systems. Can face and object perception be completely dissociated? Can a person have one without the other? As we have discovered, many case reports describe patients who have a selective disorder in face perception; they cannot recognize faces, but they have little problem recognizing other objects. Even so, this evidence does not mandate a specialized processor for faces. Perhaps the tests that assess face perception are more sensitive to the effects of brain damage than are the tests that evaluate object recognition.

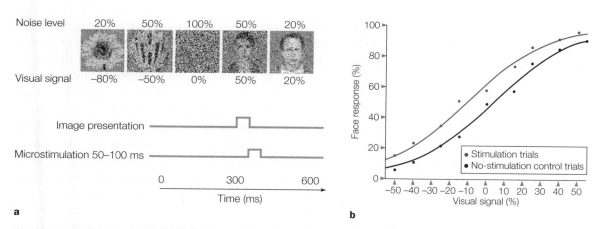

FIGURE 6.30 Effect of microstimulation of a face-selective region within inferior temporal cortex of a macaque monkey.
(a) Random dots were added to make it hard to differentiate between a flower (−100% image) and a face (+100% image). The 0% stimulus is only random dots. The image was presented for 50 ms. On experimental trials, microstimulation started at the end of the stimulus interval and lasted for 50 ms. The monkey was very accurate whenever the image contained at least 50% of either the flower or face stimuli so testing was limited to stimuli between −50% and +50%. **(b)** Percentage of trials in which the monkey made an eye movement to indicate that the stimulus contained a face and not a flower. "Face" responses were more likely to occur on experimental trials compared to control trials.

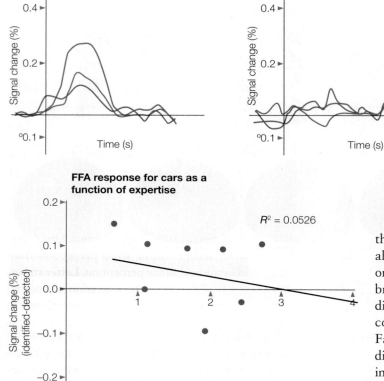

Faces

Signal change (%)

Time (s)

Cars

Signal change (%)

Time (s)

FFA response for cars as a function of expertise

Signal change (%) (identified-detected)

$R^2 = 0.0526$

FIGURE 6.31 FFA activity is related to stimulus class and not expertise.
A group of car aficionados viewed pictures of faces and cars that were presented very briefly (less than 50 ms). The stimuli were grouped based on whether the participant identified the specific face or car (green), correctly identified the category but failed to identify the person or car model (blue), or failed to identify the category (red). BOLD response in FFA varied with performance for the faces, with strongest response to stimuli correctly identified. The BOLD response was weak and unrelated to performance to the cars, even for these experts.

Striking cases have emerged, however, of the reverse situation—patients with severe object recognition problems but no evidence of prosopagnosia. Work with C.K., the patient described earlier in the section on integrative agnosia (see Figure 6.19), provides a particularly striking example. Take a look at Figure 6.32, a still life produced by the quirky 16th-century Italian painter Giuseppe Arcimboldo. When shown this picture, C.K was stumped. He reported a mishmash of colors and shapes, failing to recognize either the individual vegetables or the bowl. But when the painting was turned upside down, C.K. immediately perceived the face. When compared to patients with prosopagnosia, individuals like C.K. provide a double dissociation in support of the hypothesis that the brain has functionally different systems for face and object recognition.

A different concern arises, however, when we consider the kinds of tasks typically used to assess face and object perception. In one important respect, face perception tests are qualitatively different from tests that evaluate the recognition of common objects. The stimuli for assessing face perception are all from the same category: faces. Study participants may be asked to decide whether two faces are the same or different, or

they may be asked to identify specific individuals. When patients with visual agnosia are tested on object perception, the stimuli cover a much broader range. Here participants are asked to discriminate chairs from tables, or to identify common objects such as clocks and telephones. Face perception tasks involve within-category discriminations; object perception tasks typically involve between-category discriminations. Perhaps the deficits seen in prosopagnosia patients reflect a more general problem in perceiving the subtle differences that distinguish the members of a common category.

The patient literature fails to support this hypothesis, however. For example, a man who became a sheep farmer (W.J.) after developing prosopagnosia was tested on a set of within-category identification tasks: one involving people, the other involving sheep (McNeil & Warrington, 1993). In a test involving the faces of people familiar to him, W.J. performed at the level of chance. In a test involving the faces of sheep familiar to him, by contrast, W.J. was able to pick out photographs of sheep from his own flock. In a second experiment, W.J.'s recognition memory was tested. After viewing a set of pictures of sheep or human faces, W.J. was shown these same stimuli mixed with new photographs. W.J.'s performance in recognizing the sheep faces was higher than that of other control participants, including other sheep farmers. For human faces, though, W.J.'s performance was at the level of chance, whereas the control participants' performances were close to perfect. This result suggests that for recognizing human faces, we use a particular mental pattern or set of cues. W.J. was no longer able to use the pattern, but that didn't matter when it came to sheep faces. Perhaps he was superior at recognizing sheep faces because he did not have such a pattern interfering with his processing of sheep faces. We will return to this idea in a bit.

FIGURE 6.32 What is this a painting of?
The Arcimboldo painting that stumped C.K. when he viewed it right side up but became immediately recognizable as a different form when he turned it upside down. To see what C.K. saw, keep an eye on the turnip when you turn the image upside down.

Faces Are Processed in a Holistic Manner

Do the mechanisms of face recognition and non-facial object recognition process information differently? To address this question, let's contrast prosopagnosia with another subtype of visual agnosia—acquired alexia. Patients with acquired alexia following a stroke or head trauma have reading problems. Although they understand spoken speech and can speak normally, reading is painstakingly difficult. Errors usually reflect visual confusions. The word *ball* may be misread as *doll*, or *bail* as *talk*. Like prosopagnosia, alexia is a within-category deficit; that is, the affected person fails to discriminate between items that are very similar.

In healthy individuals, fMRI scans reveal very different patterns of activation during word perception from those observed in studies of face perception. Letter strings do not activate the FFA; rather, the activation is centered more dorsally (Figure 6.33) and is most prominent in the left hemisphere, independent of whether the words are presented in the left or right visual field (L. Cohen et al., 2000). Moreover, the magnitude of the activation increases when the letters form familiar words (L. Cohen et al., 2002). Though this area may be thought of as specialized for reading, an evolutionary argument akin to what has been offered for face perception does not seem tenable. Learning to read is a challenging process that is part of our recent cultural history. Even so, computations performed by this region of the brain appear to be well suited for developing the representations required for reading.

Prosopagnosia and alexia rarely occur in isolation. Put another way, both types of patients usually have problems with other types of object recognition. Importantly, the dissociation between prosopagnosia and acquired alexia becomes evident when we consider the patterns of correlation among three types of agnosia: for faces, for objects, and for words. Table 6.2 lists the pattern of co-occurrence from one meta-analysis of visual associative agnosia (Farah, 1990). Patients who are impaired in recognizing all three types of

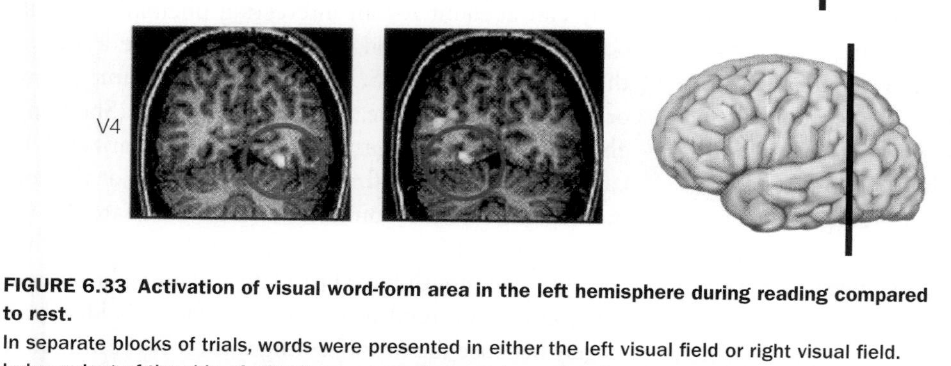

Stimulated hemifield

Left   Right

Left fusiform gyrus

V4

FIGURE 6.33 Activation of visual word-form area in the left hemisphere during reading compared to rest.
In separate blocks of trials, words were presented in either the left visual field or right visual field. Independent of the side of stimulus presentation, words produced an increase in the BOLD response in the left fusiform gyrus (green circled region in top row), an area referred to as the visual word form. In contrast, activation in V4 (blue and red circles in bottom row) was always contralateral to the side of stimulation. The black bars on the lateral views of the brain indicate the anterior-posterior position of the coronal slices shown on the left. V4 is more posterior to the visual word form area.

Table 6.2 Patterns of Co-occurrence of Prosopagnosia, Object Agnosia, and Alexia

Pattern	Number of Patients
Deficits in all three	21
Selective deficits	
Face and objects	14
Words and objects	15
Faces and words	1 (possibly)
Faces alone	35
Words alone	Many described in literature
Objects only	1 (possibly)

materials likely have extensive lesions that affect multiple processes. The more interesting cases are the patients with impairments limited to just two of the three categories. A patient could be prosopagnosic and object agnosic without being alexic. Or a patient could be object agnosic and alexic without being prosopagnosic. But only one patient was reported to have prosopagnosia and alexia with normal object perception, and even in this case, the report was unclear.

Another way to view these results is to consider that agnosia for objects never occurs alone; it is always accompanied by a deficit in either word or face perception, or both. Because patients with deficits in object perception also have a problem with one of the other types of stimuli, it might be tempting to conclude that object recognition involves two independent processes. It would not be parsimonious to postulate three processing subsystems. If that were the case, we would expect to find three sets of patients: those with word perception deficits, those with face perception deficits, and those with object perception deficits.

Given that the neuropsychological dissociations suggest two systems for object recognition, we can now examine the third criterion for evaluating whether face perception depends on a processing system distinct from the one for other forms of object perception: Do we process information in a unique way when attempting to recognize faces? That is, are there differences in how information is represented when we recognize faces in comparison to when we recognize common objects and words? To answer these questions, we need to return to the computational issues surrounding the perception of facial and non-facial stimuli.

Face perception appears to be unique in one special way—whereas object recognition decomposes a stimulus into its parts, face perception is more holistic. We recognize an individual according to the facial configuration, the sum of the parts, not by his or her idiosyncratic nose or eyes or chin structure. By this hypothesis, if patients with prosopagnosia show a selective deficit in one class of stimuli—faces—it is because they are unable to form the holistic representation necessary for face perception.

Research with healthy people reinforces the notion that face perception requires a representation that is not simply a concatenation of individual parts. In one study, participants were asked to recognize line drawings of faces and houses (Tanaka & Farah, 1993). Each stimulus was constructed of limited parts. For faces, the parts were eyes, nose, and mouth; for houses, the parts were doors, living room windows, and bedroom windows. In a study phase, participants saw a name and either a face or a house (Figure 6.34a, upper panel). For the face, participants were instructed to associate the name with the face; for example, "Larry had hooded eyes, a large nose, and full lips." For the house, they were instructed to learn the name of the person who lived in the house; for example, "Larry lived in a house with an arched door, a red brick chimney, and an upstairs bedroom window."

After this learning period, participants were given a recognition memory test (Figure 6.34a, lower panel). The critical manipulation was whether the probe item was presented in isolation or in context, embedded in the whole object. For example, when asked whether the stimulus matched Larry's nose, the nose was presented either by itself or in the context of Larry's eyes and mouth. As predicted, house perception did not depend on whether the test items were presented in isolation or as an entire object, but face perception did (Figure 6.34b). Participants were much better at identifying an individual facial feature of a person when that feature was shown in conjunction with other parts of the person's face.

The idea that faces are generally processed holistically can account for an interesting phenomenon that occurs when looking at inverted faces. Take a look at the faces in Figure 6.35. Who is it? Is it the same person or not? Now turn the book upside down. Shocking, eh? One of the images has been "Thatcherized," so called because it was first done to an image of the former English prime minister, Margaret Thatcher (P. Thompson, 1980). For this face, we fail to note that the eyes and mouth have been left in their right-side-up orientation. We tend to see the two faces as identical, largely because the overall configuration of the stimuli is so similar. Rhesus monkeys show the same reaction as humans to distorted, inverted faces. They don't notice the change in features until they are presented right side up (Adachi et al., 2009). This evidence suggests that

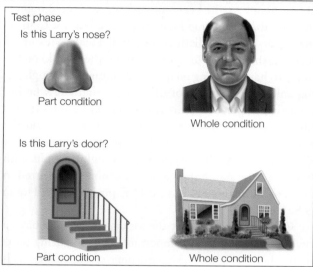

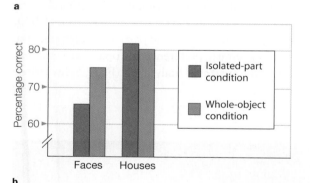

a

FIGURE 6.35 Who is this person?
Is there anything unusual about the picture? Recognition can be quite difficult when faces are viewed upside down. Even more surprising, we fail to note a severe distortion in the upper image created by inversion of the eyes and mouth—something that is immediately apparent when the image is viewed right side up. The person is Margaret Thatcher.

b

FIGURE 6.34 Facial features are poorly recognized in isolation.
(a) In the study phase, participants learned the names that correspond with a set of faces and houses. During the recognition test, participants were presented with a face, a house, or a single feature from the face or house. They were asked if a particular feature belonged to an individual. **(b)** When presented with the entire face, participants were much better at identifying the facial features. Recognition of the house features was the same in both conditions.

a face perception mechanism may have evolved in an ancestor common to humans and rhesus monkeys more than 30 million years ago.

When viewed in this way, the question of whether face perception is special changes in a subtle yet important way. Farah's model emphasizes that higher-level perception reflects the operation of two distinct representational systems. The relative contribution of the analysis-by-parts and holistic systems will depend on the task (Figure 6.36). Face perception is at one extreme. Here, the critical information requires a holistic representation to capture the configuration of the defining parts. For these stimuli, discerning the parts is of little importance. Consider how hard it is to notice that a casual acquaintance has shaved his mustache. Rather, recognition requires that we perceive a familiar arrangement of the parts. Faces are special, in the sense that the representation derived from an analysis by parts is not sufficient.

Words represent another special class of objects, but at the other extreme. Reading requires that the letter strings be successfully decomposed into their constituent parts. We benefit little from noting general features

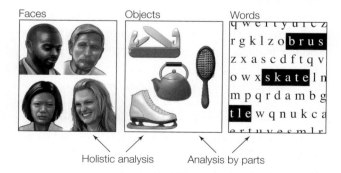

FIGURE 6.36 Farah's two-process model for object recognition.
Recognition can be based on two forms of analysis: holistic analysis and analysis by parts. The contributions of these two systems vary for different classes of stimuli. Analysis by parts is essential for reading and is central for recognizing objects. A unique aspect of face recognition is its dependence on holistic analysis. Holistic analysis also contributes to object recognition.

such as word length or handwriting. To differentiate one word from another, we have to recognize the individual letters.

In terms of recognition, objects fall somewhere between the two extremes of words and faces. Defining features such as the number pad and receiver can identify a telephone, but recognition is also possible when we perceive the overall shape of this familiar object. If either the analytic or the holistic system is damaged, object recognition may still be possible through operation of the intact system. But performance is likely to be suboptimal. Thus, agnosia for objects can occur with either alexia or prosopagnosia.

In normal perception, both holistic and part-based systems are operating to produce fast, reliable recognition. These two processing systems converge on a common percept, although how efficiently they do so will vary for different classes of stimuli. Face perception is primarily based on a holistic analysis of the stimulus. Nonetheless, we are often able to recognize someone by his distinctive nose or eyes. Similarly, with expertise, we may recognize words in a holistic manner, with little evidence of a detailed analysis of the parts. The distinction between **analytic processing** and **holistic processing** has also been important in theories of hemispheric specialization; the core idea is that the left hemisphere is more efficient at analytic processing and the right hemisphere is more efficient at holistic processing (see Chapter 4). For our present purposes, it is useful to note that alexia and prosopagnosia are in accord with this lateralization hypothesis: lesions to the right hemisphere are associated with prosopagnosia and those to the left with alexia. As we saw in Chapter 4, an important principle in cognitive neuroscience is that parallel systems (e.g., the two hemispheres) may afford different snapshots of the world, and the end result is an efficient way to represent different types of information. A holistic system supports and may even have evolved for efficient face perception; an analytic system allows us to acquire fine perceptual skills like reading.

Does the Visual System Contain Other Category-Specific Systems?

If we accept that evolutionary pressures have led to the development of a specialized system for face perception, a natural question is whether additional specialized systems exist for other biologically important classes of stimuli. In their investigations of the FFA, Russell Epstein and Nancy Kanwisher (1998) used a large set of control stimuli that were not faces. When they analyzed the results, they were struck by a serendipitous finding. One region of the ventral pathway, the parahippocampus, was consistently engaged when the control stimuli contained pictures of scenes such as landscapes. This region was not activated by face stimuli or by pictures of individual objects. Subsequent experiments confirmed this pattern, leading to the name **parahippocampal place area**, or **PPA**. The BOLD response in this region was especially pronounced when people were required to make judgments about spatial properties or relations, such as, is an image of an outdoor or indoor scene? or, is the house at the base of the mountain?

Reasonable evolutionary arguments can be made concerning why the brain might have dedicated regions devoted to recognizing faces or places, but not to making other types of distinctions. Individuals who could distinguish one type of apple from another would be unlikely to have a strong adaptive advantage (although being able to perceive color differences that cue whether a particular piece of fruit is ripe would be important). Our ancestors who could remember where to find the ripe fruit, however, would have a great advantage over their more forgetful peers. Interestingly, people with lesions to the parahippocampus become disoriented in new environments (Aguirre & D'Esposito, 1999; Habib & Sirigu, 1987).

Other studies suggest the visual cortex may have a region that is especially important for recognizing parts of the body (Figure 6.37; Downing et al., 2001). This area, at the border of the occipital and temporal cortices, is referred to as the **extrastriate body area (EBA)**. Another region, adjacent to and partially overlapping the FFA, shows a similar preference for body parts and has been called the **fusiform body area** (**FBA**; Schwarzlose et al., 2005).

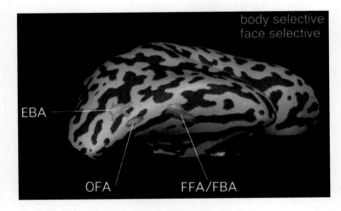

FIGURE 6.37 Locations of the EBA and FBA.
Right-hemisphere cortical surface of an "inflated brain" in one individual identifying the EBA, FBA, and face-sensitive regions. Regions responded selectively to bodies or faces versus tools. Note that two regions respond to faces, the OFA and FFA. (EBA = extrastriate body area; OFA = occipital face area; FFA = fusiform face area; FBA = fusiform body area.)

Functional MRI has proven to be a powerful tool for exploring category-specific preferences across the visual cortex. Some regions, such as FFA, PPA, and EBA, show strong preferences for particular categories. Other areas respond similarly to many different categories of visual stimuli. As we've already seen, functional hypotheses have been proposed to explain why some degree of specialization may exist, at least for stimuli of long-standing biological importance. Still, it is necessary to confirm that these regions are, in fact, important for specific types of perceptual judgments. Brad Duchaine and his colleagues used transcranial magnetic stimulation (TMS) to provide one such test by seeking to disrupt activity in three different regions that had been shown to exhibit category specificity (Pitcher et al.,

2009). The study participants performed a series of discrimination tasks that involved judgments about faces, bodies, and objects.

In separate blocks of trials, the TMS coil was positioned over the right occipital face area (rOFA), the right extrastriate body area (rEBA), and the right lateral occipital area (rLO; Figure 6.38a). (The FFA was not used because, given its medial position, it is inaccessible to TMS.) The results showed a neat triple dissociation (Figure 6.38b–d). When TMS was applied over the rOFA, participants had problems discriminating faces, but not objects or bodies. When it was applied over the rEBA, the result was impaired discrimination of bodies, but not faces or objects. Finally, as you have probably guessed, when TMS was

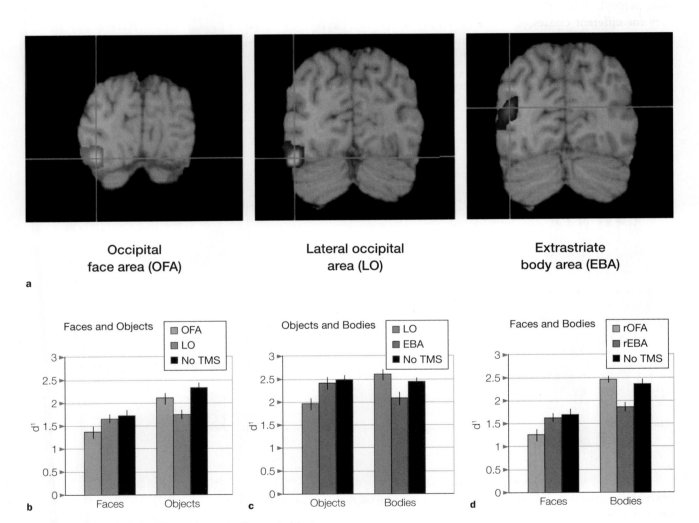

FIGURE 6.38 Triple dissociation of faces, bodies, and objects.
(a) TMS target sites based on fMRI studies identifying regions in the right hemisphere sensitive to faces (OFA), objects (LO), and bodies (EBA). **(b–d)** In each panel, performance on two tasks was compared when TMS was applied in separate blocks to two of the stimulation sites, as well as in a control condition (no TMS). The dependent variable in each graph is d', a measure of perceptual performance (high values = better performance). Face performance was disrupted by TMS over OFA. Object perception was disrupted by TMS over LO. Body perception was disrupted by TMS over EBA.

applied over the rLO, the participants had difficulty picking out objects, but not faces or bodies (Pitcher et al., 2009). The latter result is especially interesting because the perception of faces and bodies was not disrupted. Regions that are involved in category-independent object recognition processes must be downstream from rLO.

The question remains, what are the causes of such category specificity within the organization of the visual system? Has it been shaped by visual experience, or are we born with it? Put another way, do category preferences depend on visual experience that defines dimensions of similarity, or by dimensions of similarity that cannot be reduced to visual experience? This issue was addressed in our discussion of the computational model proposed by Farah and McClelland to account for the difference between living and nonliving objects. That model emphasized functional differences between these two categories, but the fMRI data has also shown some degree of anatomical segregation. Inanimate

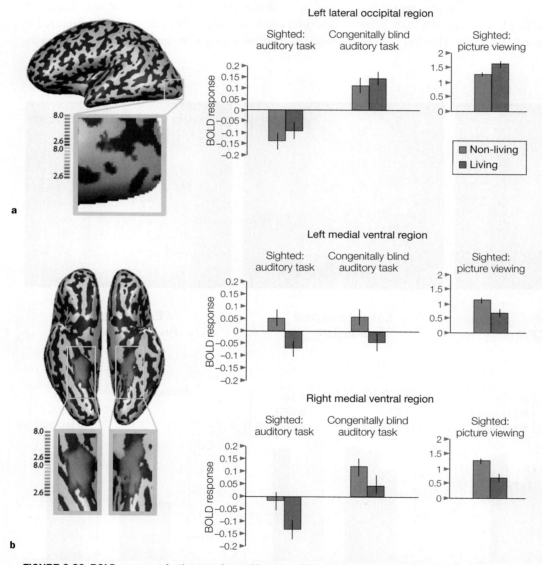

FIGURE 6.39 BOLD response in three regions of interest (ROIs) defined in scans from sighted individuals.
Sighted participants viewed the stimuli or listened to words naming the stimuli. Congenitally blind participants listened to the words. **(a)** The blind participants show stronger response to animals compared to objects in left lateral occipital ROI, similar to that observed in sighted individuals when viewing the pictures. **(b)** Medial ventral ROIs show preference for the objects in both groups. Note that all three ROIs are deactivated when sighted participants listened to the words.

objects produce stronger activation in the medial regions of the ventral stream (the medial fusiform gyrus, lingual gyrus, and parahippocampal cortex), whereas animate objects produce stronger activation in more lateral regions (the lateral fusiform gyrus and the inferior temporal gyrus).

Brian Mahon and his colleagues (2009) investigated whether congenitally blind adults, who obviously have had no visual experience, would show a similar categorical organization in their visual areas. "Visual cortex" in the congenitally blind is recruited during verbal processing (e.g., Amedi et al., 2004). Based on this knowledge, Mahon asked if a medial–lateral distinction would be apparent when blind participants had to make judgments about the sizes of objects that were presented to them auditorily. In each trial, the participants heard a word, such as "squirrel." Then they were presented with five additional words of the same conceptual category, for instance, *piglet, rabbit, skunk, cat,* and *moose* (all animals), and asked to indicate if any of the items were of a vastly different size (in this example, the moose). The point of the judgment task was to ensure that the participants had to think about each stimulus. Sighted participants performed the same task and were also tested with visual images. As it turns out, the regions that exhibited category preferences during the auditory task were the same in both the sighted and nonsighted groups (Figure 6.39). Moreover, these regions showed a similar difference to animate and inanimate objects when the sighted participants repeated the task, but this time with pictures. Thus, visual experience is not necessary for category specificity to develop within the organization of the ventral stream. The difference between animate and inanimate objects must reflect something more fundamental than what can be provided by visual experience.

TAKE-HOME MESSAGES

- Category-specific deficits are deficits of object recognition that are restricted to certain classes of objects.
- Prosopagnosia is an inability to recognize faces that cannot be attributed to deterioration in intellectual function.
- Acquired alexia is characterized by reading problems that occur after a patient has a stroke or head trauma.
- Neurons in various areas of the monkey brain show selectivity for face stimuli.
- Similarly, specificity is observed in fMRI studies, including an area in the fusiform gyrus of the temporal lobe, the fusiform face area, or FFA.

- Analytic processing is a form of perceptual analysis that emphasizes the component parts of an object, a mode of processing that is important for reading.
- Holistic processing is a form of perceptual analysis that emphasizes the overall shape of an object, a mode of processing that is important for face perception.
- Just as the FFA is specialized for processing faces, the parahippocampal place area (PPA) is specialized for processing information about spatial relations or for classifying objects based on spatial properties (e.g., an indoor vs. outdoor scene).
- Likewise, the extrastriate body area (EBA) and the fusiform body area (FBA) have been identified as more active when body parts are viewed.

Mind Reading

We have seen various ways in which scientists have explored specialization within the visual cortex. In Chapter 5, emphasis was on how basic sensory properties such as shape, color, and motion are processed. In this chapter, we have looked at more complex properties such as animacy, faces, places, and body parts. The basic research strategy has been to manipulate the input and then measure the response to the different types of inputs. For example, FFA is more responsive to face stimuli than non-face stimuli.

These observations have led scientists to realize that it should, at least in principle, be possible to analyze the system in the opposite direction (Figure 6.40). That is, we should be able to look at someone's brain activity and infer what the person is currently seeing (or has recently seen, assuming our measurements are delayed), a form of mind reading. This idea is referred to as **decoding**.

Encoding and Decoding Brain Signals

As the name implies, decoding is like breaking a secret code. The brain activity, or whatever measurement we are using, provides the coded message, and the challenge is to decipher that message and infer what is being represented. In other words, we could read a person's mind, making inferences about what they are currently seeing or thinking, even if we don't have direct access to that input.

All this may sound like science fiction, but as we'll see, over the past decade scientists have made tremendous advances in mind reading. While consid-

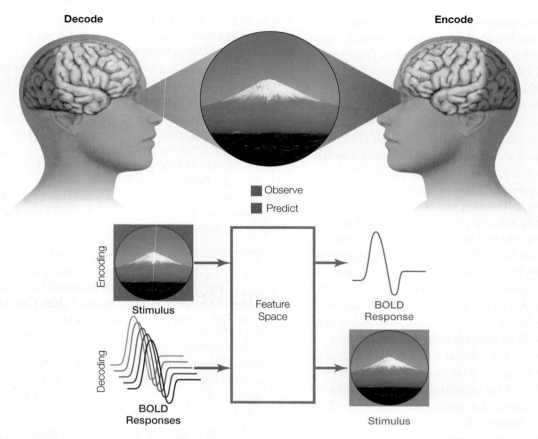

Decode

Encode

■ Observe
■ Predict

Encoding

Stimulus

Feature Space

BOLD Response

Decoding

BOLD Responses

Stimulus

FIGURE 6.40 Encoding and decoding neural activity.
Encoding refers to the problem of how stimulus features are represented in neural activity. The image is processed by the sensory system and the scientist wants to predict the resulting BOLD activity. Decoding (or mind reading) refers to the problem of predicting the stimulus that is being viewed when a particular brain state is observed. In fMRI decoding, the BOLD activity is used to predict the stimulus being observed by the participant. Successful encoding and decoding require having an accurate hypothesis of how information is represented in the brain (feature space).

ering the computational challenges involved, we must keep two key issues in mind. First, our ability to decode will be limited by the resolution of our measurement system. Single-cell neurophysiology, if we have identified the "right" cell, might be useful for telling us if the person is looking at Halle Berry. In fact, we might even be able to detect when the person is daydreaming about Halle Berry if our cell were as selective as suggested in Figure 3.21. Currently, decoding methods allow us to sample only a small number of cells. Nonetheless, in some future time, scientists may develop methods that allow the simultaneous measurement of thousands, or even millions, of cells; perhaps the entire ventral pathway. Until then, we have to rely on much cruder tools such as EEG and fMRI. EEG is rapid, so it provides excellent temporal resolution. But the number of recording channels is limited (current systems generally have a maximum of 256 channels), and each channel integrates information over large regions of the cortex, and thus, limits spatial resolution. Although fMRI is slow

and provides only an indirect measure of neural activity, it provides much better spatial resolution than EEG does. With fMRI, we can image the whole brain and simultaneously take measurements in hundreds of thousands of voxels. Using more focused scanning protocols can reduce the size of the voxels, thus providing better spatial resolution. Of course, mind reading is not going to be all that useful if the person has to maintain the same thought for, say, 10 or 20 seconds before we get a good read on their thoughts. Perception is a rapid, fluid process. A good mind-reading system should be able to operate at similar speeds.

The second issue is that our ability to decode mental states is limited by our models of how the brain encodes information. Developing good hypotheses about the types of information that are represented in different cortical areas will help us make inferences when we attempt to build a brain decoder. To take an extreme example, if we didn't know that the occipital lobe was responsive to visual input, it would be very hard to look at the activity in the occipital lobe and make inferences about what the person was currently doing. Similarly, having a good model of what different regions represent—for example, that a high level of activity in V5 is correlated with motion perception—can be a powerful constraint on the predictions we make of what the person is seeing.

Early efforts at mind reading were inspired by the discovery of category-specific visual areas. We saw in the previous section that the BOLD signals in FFA and PPA vary as a function of whether the person is looking at faces or places. This information provides a simple **encoding model**. Kathleen O'Craven and Nancy Kanwisher at MIT found that this distinction could be used to constrain a decoding model (O'Craven & Kanwisher, 2000). People were placed in an fMRI scanner and asked to imagine either a famous face or a familiar place. Using just the resulting BOLD activity measured in FFA and PPA, it was possible to predict if the person was looking at a face or place on about 85% of the trials (Figure 6.41). What's impressive about this result is that even though the BOLD signal in each area is very small for a single event, especially when there is no overt visual stimulus, the observer, who had to choose either "face" or "place," almost always got the right answer.

Could this analysis be done by a machine and in a much shorter amount of time? Geraint Rees and his colleagues at University College London reasoned that more parts of the brain than just the PPA and FFA likely contributed to the mental event. Thus, they constructed a decoder that took the full spatial pattern of brain activity into account by simultaneously measuring many locations within the brain, including the early visual areas (Haynes & Rees, 2006). Using a single brain image and data collected from the participant over just 2 seconds, their pattern-based decoder extracted considerably more information and had a prediction accuracy of 80%.

Statistical Pattern Recognition

Impressive, yes; but also rather crude. After all, the decoder wasn't presented with a very challenging mind-reading problem. It only had to decide between two very different categories. What's more, the predictor was given the two categories to choose from. That binary decision process is nothing like how random thoughts flit in and out of our minds. Moreover, discrimination was only at the categorical level. A much more challenging problem would be to make distinctions within a category. There is a big difference between Santa Claus and Marilyn Monroe or Sioux City and Tahiti. Can we do better, even given the limitations of fMRI?

We can. To do it, we need a much more sophisticated encoding model. We need one that gives us more than just a description of how information is represented across relatively large areas of cortex such as FFA. We need an encoding model that can characterize representations within individual voxels. If we have an encoding model that takes a stimulus and predicts the BOLD signal in each voxel, then we can turn this design around and develop a decoding model that uses the BOLD signal as input to predict the stimulus.

How do we build a complex encoding model that operates at the level of the voxel? You have to start with an educated guess. For the visual system, you could start by characterizing voxels in early visual processing areas that have tuning properties similar to what is seen with

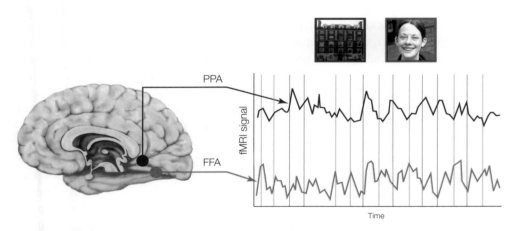

FIGURE 6.41 Decoding visual object perception from fMRI responses.
During periods of face imagery (red lines), signals are elevated in the FFA whereas during the imagery of buildings (blue lines), signals are elevated in PPA. Using just the data from the FFA and PPA of a single participant, it was possible to estimate with 85% accuracy whether the person was imagining a face or place.

individual neurons—things like edges, orientation, and size. Keep in mind that each voxel contains hundreds of thousands, if not millions, of neurons, and the neurons within one voxel will have different tuning profiles (e.g., for line orientation, some will be tuned for horizontal, vertical, or at some angle). Fortunately, having the same tuning profiles isn't essential. The essential thing is for there to be some detectable difference between voxels in their aggregate response along these dimensions. That is, one voxel might contain more neurons that are tuned to horizontal lines, while another voxel has more neurons tuned to vertical lines.

Jack Gallant and his colleagues at UC Berkeley set out to build an encoding model based on these ideas (Kay et al., 2008). Recognizing the challenge of characterizing individual voxels, they opted against the standard experimental procedure of testing 15–20 naive participants for an hour each. Instead, they took two highly motivated people (that is, two of the authors of the paper) and had them lie in the MRI scanner for many hours, looking repeatedly at a set of 1,750 natural images. To further improve the spatial resolution, the BOLD response was recorded only in areas V1, V2, and V3. From this large data set, the researchers constructed the "receptive field" of each voxel (Figure 6.42).

They were then ready for the critical test. The participants were shown a set of 120 new images, ones that had not been used to construct the encoding model. The BOLD response in each voxel was measured for each of the 120 images. From these hemodynamic signals, the decoder was asked to reconstruct the image. To test the accuracy of the decoded prediction, the team compared the predicted image to the actual image. They also quantified the results by determining the best match between the predicted image and the full set of 120 novel images. The results were stunning (Figure 6.43). For one of the participants, the decoding model was accurate in picking the exact match for 92% of the stimuli. For the other, the decoder was accurate for 72% of the stimuli. Remember that if the decoder were acting randomly, an exact match would be expected for only 8% of the stimuli. As the Gallant research team likes to say, the experiment was similar to a magician performing a card trick: "Pick a card (or picture) from the deck, show me the BOLD response to that picture, and I'll tell you what picture you are looking at." No sleight of hand involved here; just good clean fMRI data.

As impressive as this preliminary study might be, we should remain skeptical that it constitutes real mind reading. The stimulation conditions were still highly artificial, owing to the successive presentation of a set of static images. Moreover, the encoding model was quite limited, restricted to representations of relatively simple visual features. An alternative coding scheme should build on our knowledge of how information is represented in higher order visual areas, areas that are sensitive to more complex properties such as places and faces. The encoding model here could be based on more than the physical properties of a stimulus. It could also incorporate semantic properties, such as, "does the stimulus contain a fruit?" or "is a person present?"

To build a more comprehensive model, Gallant's lab combined two representational schemes. For early visual areas like V1, the model was based on the receptive field properties (as in Figure 6.42a). For higher visual field areas, each voxel was modeled in terms of semantic properties whereby the BOLD response was based on the presence or absence of different features (Figure 6.44). In this way, the team sought to develop a general model that could be tested with an infinite set of stimuli, akin to the task our visual system faces. To develop the model, the stimuli could be drawn from 6 million natural images, randomly selected from the Internet. This hybrid decoder was accurate in providing appropriate matches (Figure 6.45), and also proved informative in revealing the limitations of models that use only physical properties or only semantic properties (Huth, 2012). For example, when the physical model is used exclusively, it does well with information from the early visual areas but poorly with information from the higher order visual areas. On the other hand, when the semantic model is used alone, it does well with the higher order information but not as well with information from the early visual areas. When both models are combined, the reconstructions, although not completely accurate, reveal the essence of the image and are more accurate than either model alone.

The next step in this research was to add action to the encoding model. After all, the world and our visual experience are full of things that move. Because action is fast and the fMRI is slow, the researchers had to give their encoding model the feature of motion, which is central to many regions of the brain. The test participants returned to the MRI scanner, this time to watch movie clips (Nishimoto et al., 2011). Reams of data were collected and used to build an elaborate encoding model. Then it was time for the decoding test. The participants watched new movies, and the decoder was used to generate continuous predictions. You can see the results at www.youtube.com/user/gallantlabucb. While it is mind-boggling to see the match between the actual, fast-paced movie and the predicted movie, based solely on the (sluggish) fMRI data, it is also informative to consider the obvious mismatches between the two. These mismatches will help guide researchers as they construct the next generation of encode–decode models.

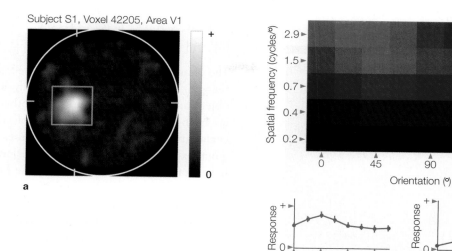

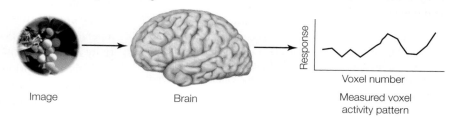

FIGURE 6.42 Using an encoding model to decode brain activity to natural images.
(a) Receptive field encoding model of voxels in human V1. After recording the BOLD response to thousands of images, the receptive field of each voxel in V1 can be characterized by three dimensions, location, orientation, and size, similar to the way neurophysiologists characterize visual neurons in primate visual areas. Note that each voxel reflects the activity of millions of neurons, but over the population, there remains some tuning for these dimensions. The heat map on the right side shows the relative response strength for one voxel to stimuli of different sizes (or technically, spatial frequency) and orientations. The resulting tuning functions are shown on the bottom. This process is repeated for each voxel to create the full encoding model.
(b) Mind reading by decoding fMRI activity to visual images.
1. An image is presented to the participant and the BOLD response is measured at each voxel. 2. The predicted BOLD response across the set of voxels is calculated for each image in the set. 3. The observed BOLD response from 1) is compared to all of the predicted BOLD responses and the image with the best match is identified. If the match involves the same stimulus as the one shown, then the encoder is successful on that trial (as shown here).

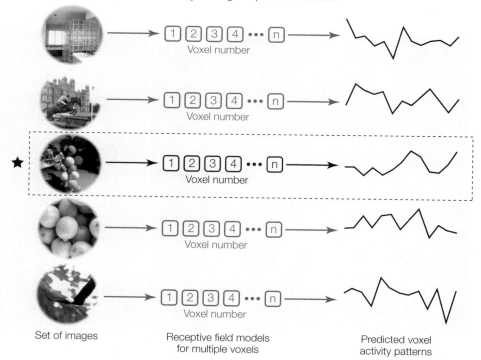

1. Measure brain activity for an image.

Image   Brain   Measured voxel activity pattern

2. Predict brain activity for a set of images using receptive field models.

Voxel number

Set of images   Receptive field models for multiple voxels   Predicted voxel activity patterns

3. Select the image (★) whose predicted brain activity is most similar to the measured brain activity.

b

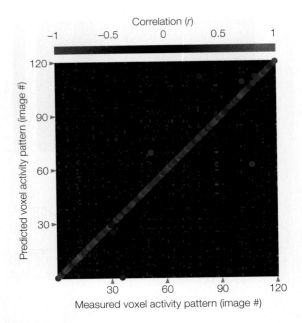

FIGURE 6.43

Accuracy of the brain decoder. Rather than just choose the best match, the correlation coefficient can be calculated between the measured BOLD response for each image and the predicted BOLD response. For the 120 images, the best predictors almost always matched the actual stimulus, indicated by the bright colors along the major diagonal).

A Look Into the Future of Mind Reading

The mind reading we have discussed so far involves recognizing patterns of brain activity associated with object and face recognition. Many other imaging studies have probed the processing involved in developing social attitudes, making moral judgments, having religious experiences, and making decisions. Studies also have examined the differences in the brains of violent people and psychopaths, and the genetic differences and variability in brain development. From these studies, brain maps have been constructed for moral reasoning, judgment, deception, and emotions. It is possible that, with sophisticated models, the pattern of activity across these maps may reveal a person's preferences, attitudes, or thoughts. Mind reading with these goals sounds like the plot for a bad movie—and certainly these ideas, if realized, are brimming with ethical issues. At the core of these ethical issues is the assumption that a person's thoughts can be determined by examining activity in that person's brain in response to various stimuli. This assumption is not at all certain (Illes & Racine, 2005): The validity and predictive value of brain maps for actual human behavior has not been ascertained.

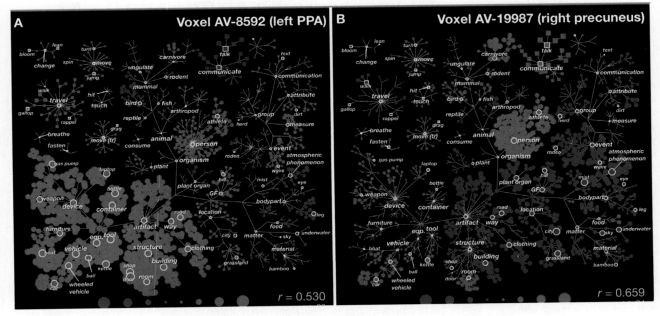

FIGURE 6.44 Semantic representation of two voxels, one in FFA and the other in PPA.

Rather than use basic features such as size and orientation, the encoding model for voxels in FFA and PPA incorporates semantic properties. The colors indicate the contribution of each feature to the BOLD response: Red indicates that the feature produced a greater-than average BOLD response and blue indicates that the feature produced a less-than-average BOLD response. The size of each circle indicates the strength of that effect. This FFA voxel is most activated to stimuli containing communicative carnivores.

Original Image

Reconstruction

FIGURE 6.45 visual images using a hybrid encoding model.
The top row shows representative natural images (out of a nearly infinite set) that are presented to the model. The bottom row shows the predicted image, based on a hybrid model of multivoxel responses across multiple visual areas. The model was developed by measuring the BOLD response to a limited set of stimuli.

Thus, there is the concern that any conclusions about a person's thoughts based on measuring brain activity may be faulty—no matter how it is used. Assuming, however, that such determinations could be made and were accurate, the issue remains that people believe that their thoughts are private and confidential. So what do we need to consider if it becomes possible to decode people's thoughts without their consent or against their will? Are there circumstances in which private thoughts should be made public? For example, should a person's thoughts be admissible in court, just as DNA evidence now can be? Should a jury have access to the thoughts of a child molester, murder defendant, or terrorist—or even a witness—to determine if they are telling the truth? Should interviewers have access to the thoughts of applicants for jobs that involve children or for police or other security work? And who should have access to this information?

Right now, however, people who work in the field of mind reading have other goals, beginning with the reconstruction of imagined visual images, like those in dreams. It is notable that fMRI activation *patterns* are similar whether people perceive objects or imagine them, even if the *level* of activity is much stronger in the former condition (e.g., Reddy et al., 2010). As such, we could imagine using mind-reading techniques as a new way to interpret dreams. There are also pressing clinical applications. For example, mind reading has the potential to provide a new method of communication for people who have severe neurological conditions.

Consider the case of R.H., an engineering student who had remained unresponsive for 23 years after a car accident. Based on their clinical tests, his team of physicians considered R.H. to be in a vegetative state, a state of consciousness where the patient can exhibit signs of wakefulness, but no signs of awareness. His family had faithfully visited on a regular basis, hoping to prod him out of his coma. Sadly, R.H. had shown no real signs of recovery, failing to respond to even the simplest commands.

Recently, neurologists and neuroscientists have become concerned that some patients thought to be in a vegetative state may actually have locked-in syndrome. Patients with locked-in syndrome may be cognizant of their surroundings, understanding what is spoken to them, but they are unable to make any voluntary movements. Some very primitive movements may persist—for example, the patient may be able to blink her eyes, but communication is either extremely limited or completely absent. Imagine how terrifying this must be. Studies in the United States, England, and Belgium have found that about 40% of people diagnosed to be in a vegetative state are actually in what is termed a minimally conscious state, a state that is more like locked-in syndrome. They are capable of some limited form of inconsistent but reproducible goal-directed behaviors (Andrews et al., 1996; Childs et al., 1993; Schnakers et al., 2009).

With the advent of new technologies, scientists are recognizing the potential to use neuroimaging techniques with individuals such as R.H. to help with diagnosis and treatment. Although the social reasons for why it is important to differentiate between the two states may be obvious, it is also important in terms of the patients' medical management. Patients in a minimally conscious state show the same brain activations to painful stimuli as do normal controls (Boly et al., 2008), whereas those in a vegetative state do not show the same widespread activations (Laureys et al., 2002).

Another reason is that future technology may allow such patients to communicate by thinking in creative ways. Encoding methods can be used to gain insight into the level of a patient's understanding. Consider the case of one 23-year-old woman, who had been unresponsive for 5 months, meeting all of the criteria consistent with a diagnosis of vegetative state. Adrian Owen and his team at Cambridge University attempted a novel approach. They put the patient in the scanner and asked her, in separate epochs of 30 seconds, either to imagine playing tennis or to imagine walking about her house (Figure 6.46). The results were amazing (Owen et al., 2006). The BOLD activity was nearly indistinguishable from that of normal, healthy volunteers performing the same imagery tasks. When the woman played tennis in her mind, a prominent BOLD response was evident in the supplementary motor area; when she imagined walking about the house, the response shifted to the parahippocampal gyrus, the posterior parietal lobe, and the lateral premotor cortex. The especially striking part of this experiment is that the patient seems to have been responding in a volitional manner. If the researchers merely had shown pictures of faces and observed a response in FFA, it might be speculated that this was the result of some form of automatic priming, arising because of the woman's extensive pre-injury experience in perceiving faces. The BOLD response to these two imagery tasks, however, was sustained for long periods of time.

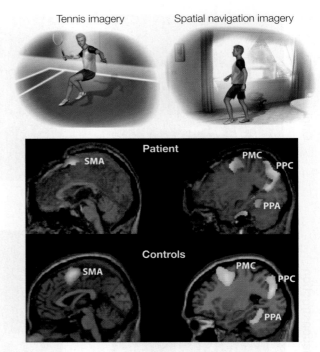

FIGURE 6.46 Comprehension in a patient thought to be in a vegetative state.
While in the MRI scanner, the patient and control participants were given various imagery instructions. The patient exhibits similar BOLD activity as observed in the controls, with increased activation in the supplementary motor area (SMA) when told to imagine playing tennis and increased activation in parahippocampal place area (PPA), posteroparietal cortex (PPC), and lateral premotor cortex (PMC) activity when told to imagine walking around a house.

Results like these indicate that our current guidelines for diagnosing vegetative state need to be reconsidered. These results also make scientists wonder whether these individuals could modulate their brain activity in order to communicate with the outside world. Can we build decoders to provide that link? A complex decoder would be needed to interpret what the patient is thinking about. A much simpler decoder could suffice to allow the patient to respond "yes" or "no" to questions. They could tell us when they are hungry or uncomfortable or tired.

Laureys, Owen, and their colleagues studied 54 patients with severe brain injuries who were either in a minimally conscious state or a vegetative state. Five of these patients were able to modulate their brain activity in the same way that normal controls did when they imagined a skilled behavior like playing tennis, or a spatial task such as walking about their home. One of these five underwent additional testing. He was asked a series of questions and was instructed to imagine the skilled action if the answer were yes, and the spatial task if the answer were no. While the patient was unable to make any overt responses to the questions, his answers from mind reading were similar to that observed in control participants (Monti et al., 2010). For such patients, even this simple type of mind reading gives them a means of communication.

Other applications for mind reading are also being developed. Decoders could enable soldiers to talk with each other in the field without speaking. As we will see in Chapter 8, decoders can also be used to control machines, via so-called brain–machine interfaces. There is undoubtedly potential for abuse and many ethical issues that need to be addressed in developing this kind of technology. Questions like, "Should people accused of murder or child molestation be required to undergo mind reading?" are only the tip of the iceberg.

TAKE-HOME MESSAGES

- Encoding models are used to predict the physiological response, such as the BOLD response to a stimulus.
- Decoding models are used in the reverse manner, predicting the stimulus (or mental state) based on a physiological response such as the BOLD activity across a set of voxels.
- Mind reading may one day be used to communicate with people who are currently unable to speak.

Summary

This chapter provided an overview of the higher-level processes involved in visual perception and object recognition. Like most other mammals, people are visual creatures: Most of us rely on our eyes to identify not only *what* we are looking at, but also *where* to look, to guide our actions. These processes are surely interactive. To accomplish a skilled behavior, such as catching a thrown object, we have to determine the object's size and shape and track its path through space so that we can anticipate where to place our hands.

Object recognition can be achieved in a multiplicity of ways and involves many levels of representation. It begins with the two-dimensional information that the retina provides. Our visual system must overcome the variability inherent in the sensory input by extracting the critical information that distinguishes one shape from another. Only part of the recognition problem is solved by this perceptual categorization. For this information to be useful, the contents of current processing must be connected to our stored knowledge about visual objects. We do not see a meaningless array of shapes and forms. Rather, visual perception is an efficient avenue for recognizing and interacting with the world (e.g., determining what path to take across a cluttered room or which tools make our actions more efficient).

Moreover, vision provides a salient means for one of the most essential goals of perception: recognizing members of our own species. Evolutionary theory suggests that the importance of face perception may have led to the evolution of an alternative form of representation, one that quickly analyzes the global configuration of a stimulus rather than its parts. On the other hand, multiple forms of representation may have evolved, and face perception may be relatively unique in that it is highly dependent on the holistic form of representation.

Our knowledge of how object information is encoded has led to the development of amazing techniques that allow scientists to infer the contents of the mind from the observation of physiological signals, such as the BOLD response. This form of mind reading, or decoding, makes it possible to form inferences about general categories of viewed or imagined objects (e.g., faces vs. places). It also can be used to make reasonable estimates of specific images. Brain decoding may offer new avenues for human communication. No doubt the first person who picked up an object and flipped it over, wondering, "How does my visual system figure out what this is?" would be impressed to see the progress achieved by those who took up that challenge and have now reached the point where they are able to use this information to read minds.

Key Terms

agnosia (p. 220)
alexia (p. 240)
analytic processing (p. 258)
apperceptive agnosia (p. 237)
associative agnosia (p. 240)
category-specific deficits (p. 243)
decoding (p. 261)
dorsal (occipitoparietal) stream (p. 222)
encoding model (p. 263)
extrastriate body area (EBA) (p. 258)
fusiform body area (FBA) (p. 258)

fusiform face area (FFA) (p. 249)
fusiform gyrus (p. 249)
gnostic unit (p. 234)
holistic processing (p. 258)
integrative agnosia (p. 239)
lateral occipital complex (or cortex) (LOC) (p. 227)
object constancy (p. 230)
optic ataxia (p. 227)
parahippocampal place area (PPA) (p. 258)
prosopagnosia (p. 246)

repetition suppression effect (p. 231)
ventral (occipitotemporal) stream (p. 222)
view-dependent frame of reference (p. 231)
view-invariant frame of reference (p. 231)
visual agnosia (p. 220)

Thought Questions

1. What are some of the differences between processing in the dorsal and ventral visual pathways? In what ways are these differences useful? In what ways is it misleading to imply a functional dichotomy of two distinct visual pathways?

2. Mrs. S. recently suffered a brain injury. She claims to have difficulty in "seeing" as a result of her injury. Her neurologist has made a preliminary diagnosis of agnosia, but nothing more specific is noted. To determine the nature of her perceptual problems, a cognitive neuroscientist is called in. What behavioral and neuroimaging tests should be used to analyze and make a more specific diagnosis? What results would support possible diagnoses? Remember that it is also important to conduct tests to determine if Mrs. S's deficit reflects a more general problem in visual perception or memory.

3. Review different hypotheses concerning why brain injury may produce the puzzling symptom of disproportionate impairment in recognizing living things. What sorts of evidence would support one hypothesis over another?

4. As a member of a debating team, you are assigned the task of defending the hypothesis that the brain has evolved a specialized system for perceiving faces. What arguments will you use to make your case? Now change sides. Defend the argument that face perception reflects the operation of a highly experienced system that is good at making fine discriminations.

5. EEG is an appealing alternative to fMRI for mind reading because a patient does not have to be in a scanner for the system to work. Describe what kinds of problems you anticipate for using EEG for mind reading and suggest possible solutions that will allow some degree of communication.

Suggested Reading

Desimone, R. (1991). Face-selective cells in the temporal cortex of monkeys. *Journal of Cognitive Neuroscience, 3,* 1–8.

Farah, M. J. (2004). *Visual agnosia* (2nd ed.). Cambridge, MA: MIT Press.

Goodale, M. A., & Milner, A. D. (2004). *Sight unseen: An exploration of conscious and unconscious vision.* New York: Oxford University Press.

Mahon, B. Z., & Caramazza, A. (2011). What drives the organization of object knowledge in the brain? *Trends in Cognitive Sciences, 15,* 97–103.

Naselaris, T., Kay, K. N., Nishimoto, S., & Gallant J. L. (2011). Encoding and decoding in fMRI. *Neuroimage, 56*(2), 400–410.

Riddoch, M. J., & Humphreys, G. W. (2001). Object recognition. In B. Repp (Ed.), *The handbook of cognitive neuropsychology: What deficits reveal about the human mind* (pp. 45–74). Philadelphia: Psychology Press.

Any man who can drive safely while kissing a pretty girl
is simply not giving the kiss the attention it deserves.

Albert Einstein

Attention

A PATIENT, WHO HAD a severe stroke several weeks earlier, sits with his wife as she talks with his neurologist. Although at first it seemed that the stroke had left him totally blind, his wife states that he can sometimes see things. They are hoping his vision will improve. The neurologist soon realizes that her patient's wife is correct. The man does have serious visual problems, but he is not completely blind. Taking a comb from her pocket, the doctor holds it in front of her patient and asks him, "What do you see?" (Figure 7.1a).

"Well, I'm not sure," he replies, "but . . . oh . . . it's a comb, a pocket comb."

"Good," says the doctor. Next she holds up a spoon and asks the same question (Figure 7.1b).

After a moment the patient replies, "I see a spoon."

The doctor nods and then holds up the spoon and the comb together. "What do you see now?" she asks.

He hesitantly replies, "I guess . . . I see a spoon."

"Okay . . . ," she says as she overlaps the spoon and comb in a crossed fashion so they are both visible in the same location. "What do you see now?" (Figure 7.1c). Oddly enough, he sees only the comb. "What about a spoon?" she asks.

"Nope, no spoon," he says, but then suddenly blurts out, "Yes, there it is, I see the spoon now."

"Anything else?"

Shaking his head, the patient replies, "Nope."

Shaking the spoon and the comb vigorously in front of her patient's face, the doctor persists, "You don't see anything else, nothing at all?"

He stares straight ahead, looking intently, and finally says, "Yes . . . yes, I see them now . . . I see some numbers."

"What?" says the puzzled doctor. "Numbers?"

"Yes," he squints and appears to strain his vision, moving his head ever so slightly, and replies, "I see numbers." The doctor then notices that the man's gaze is directed to a point beyond her and not toward the objects she is holding. Turning to glance over her own shoulder, she spots a large clock on the wall behind her!

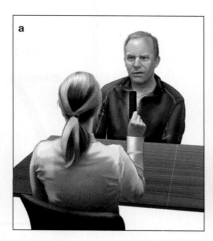
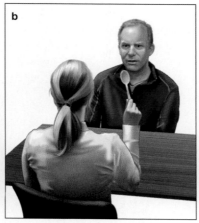
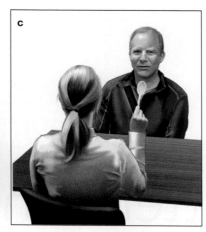

FIGURE 7.1 Examination of a patient recovering from a cortical stroke.
(a) The doctor holds up a pocket comb and asks the patient what he sees. The patient reports seeing the comb. **(b)** The doctor then holds up a spoon, and the patient reports seeing the spoon too. **(c)** But when the doctor holds up both the spoon and the comb at the same time, the patient says he can see only one object at a time. The patient has Bálint's syndrome.

Even though the doctor is holding both objects in one hand directly in front of her patient, overlapping them in space and in good lighting, he sees only one item at a time. That one item may even be a different item altogether: one that is merely in the direction of his gaze, such as the clock on the wall. The neurologist diagnoses the patient: He has **Bálint's syndrome**, first described in the late 19th century by the Hungarian neurologist and psychiatrist Rezső Bálint. It is a severe disturbance of visual attention and awareness, caused by bilateral damage to regions of the posterior parietal and occipital cortex. The result of this attention disturbance is that only one or a small subset of available objects are perceived at any one time and are mislocalized in space. The patient can "see" each of the objects presented by the doctor—the comb, the spoon, and even the numbers on the clock. He fails, however, to see them all together and cannot accurately describe their locations with respect to each other or to himself.

Bálint's syndrome is an extreme pathological instance of what we all experience daily: We are consciously aware of only a small bit of the vast amount of information available to our sensory systems from moment to moment. By looking closely at patients with Bálint's syndrome and the lesions that cause it, we have come to learn more about how, and upon what, our brain focuses attention. The central problem in the study of attention is how the brain is able to select some information at the expense of other information.

Robert Louis Stevenson wrote, "The world is full of a number of things, I'm sure we should all be as happy as kings." Although those things may make us happy, the sheer number of them presents a problem to our perception system: information overload. We know from experience that we are surrounded by more information than we can handle and comprehend at any given time. The nervous system, therefore, has to make "decisions" about what to process. Our survival may depend on which stimuli are selected and in what order they are prioritized for processing. **Selective attention** is the ability to prioritize and attend to some things while ignoring others. What determines the priority? Many things. For instance, an optimal strategy in many situations is to attend to stimuli that are relevant to current behavior and goals. For example, to survive this class, you need to attend to this chapter rather than your Facebook page. This is goal-driven control (also called top-down control) driven by an individual's current behavioral goals and shaped by learned priorities based on personal experience and evolutionary adaptations. Still, if you hear a loud bang, even while dutifully attending this book, you reflexively pop up your head and check it out. That is good survival behavior because a loud noise may presage danger. Your reaction was stimulus driven and is therefore termed stimulus-driven control (also known as bottom-up or reflexive control), which is much less dependent on current behavioral goals.

Attention grabbed the attention of William James (Figure 7.2). At the end of the 19th century, this great American psychologist made an astute observation:

> Everyone knows what attention is. It is the taking possession by the mind, in clear and vivid form, of one out of what seem several simultaneously possible objects or trains of thought. Focalization, concentration of consciousness are of its essence. It implies withdrawal from some things in order to deal effectively with others, and is a condition which has a real opposite in the confused, dazed, scatterbrain state. (James, 1890)

FIGURE 7.2
William James (1842–1910), the great American psychologist.

In this insightful quote, James has captured key characteristics of attentional phenomena that are under investigation today. For example, his statement "it is the taking possession by the mind" suggests that we can choose the focus of attention; that is, it can be voluntary. His mention of "one out of what seem several simultaneously possible objects or trains of thought" refers to the inability to attend to many things at once, and hence the *selective* aspects of attention. James raises the idea of *limited capacity* in attention, by noting that "it implies withdrawal from some things in order to deal effectively with others."

As clear and articulate as James's writings were, little was known about the behavioral, computational, or neural mechanisms of attention during his lifetime. Since then, knowledge about attention has blossomed, and researchers have identified multiple types and levels of attentive behavior. First, let's distinguish selective attention from arousal. *Arousal* refers to the global physiological and psychological state of the organism. Our *level of arousal* is the point where we fall on the continuum from being hyper-aroused (such as during periods of intense fear) to moderately aroused (which must describe your current state as you start to read about the intriguing subject of attention) to groggy (when you first got up this morning) to lightly sleeping to deeply asleep.

Selective attention, on the other hand, is not a global brain state. Instead, it is how—at any level of arousal—attention is allocated among relevant inputs, thoughts, and actions while simultaneously ignoring irrelevant or distracting ones. As shorthand, we will use the term *attention* when referring to the more specific concept of selective attention. Attention influences how people code sensory inputs, store that information in memory, process it semantically, and act on it to survive in a challenging world. This chapter focuses on the mechanisms of selective attention and its role in perception and awareness.

Mechanisms that determine where and on what our attention is focused are referred to as *attentional control mechanisms*. They involve widespread, but highly specific, brain networks. These attentional control mechanisms influence specific stages of information processing, where it is said that "selection" of inputs (or outputs) takes place—hence the term *selective* attention. In this chapter, we first review the anatomical structures involved in attention. Then, we consider how damage to the

brain changes human attention and gives us insights into how attention is organized in the brain. Next, we discuss how attention influences sensation and perception. We conclude with a discussion of the brain networks used for attentional control.

TAKE-HOME MESSAGES

- Attention is the ability to focus awareness on one stimulus, thought, or action while ignoring other irrelevant stimuli, thoughts, and actions.
- Arousal is a global physiological and psychological brain state, whereas selective attention describes what we attend and ignore within any specific level (high vs. low) of arousal.
- Attention influences how we process sensory inputs, store that information in memory, process it semantically, and act on it.

The Anatomy of Attention

Our attention system uses subcortical and cortical networks within the brain that interact to enable us to selectively process information in the brain.

Several subcortical structures are relevant to both attentional control and selection. The superior colliculus in the midbrain and the pulvinar are involved in aspects of the control of attention. We know that damage to these structures can lead to deficits in the ability to orient overt (i.e., eye gaze) and covert (i.e., attention directed without changes in eyes, head, or body orientation) attention. Within the cortex are several areas that are important in attention—portions of the frontal cortex, posterior parietal cortex, and posterior superior temporal cortex as well as more medial brain structures including the anterior cingulate cortex, the posterior cingulate cortex, and insula. Cortical and subcortical areas involved in controlling attention are shown in the Anatomical Orientation box. As we will learn, cortical sensory regions are also involved, because attention affects how sensory information is processed in the brain.

The Neuropsychology of Attention

Much of what neuroscientists know about brain attention systems has been gathered by examining patients who have brain damage that influences attentional behavior.

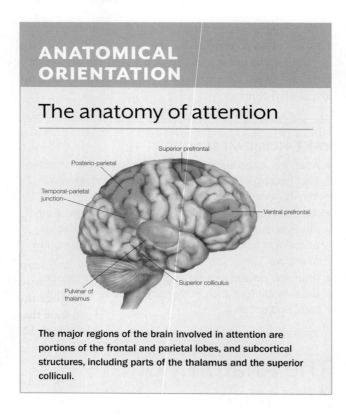

ANATOMICAL ORIENTATION

The anatomy of attention

Superior prefrontal
Posterio-parietal
Temporal-parietal junction
Ventral prefrontal
Pulvinar of thalamus
Superior colliculus

The major regions of the brain involved in attention are portions of the frontal and parietal lobes, and subcortical structures, including parts of the thalamus and the superior colliculi.

Many disorders result in deficits in attention, but only a few provide clues to which brain systems are being affected. Some of the best-known disorders of attention (e.g., attention deficit/hyperactivity disorder, or ADHD) are the result of disturbances in neural processing within brain attention systems. The portions of the brain's attention networks affected by ADHD have only recently begun to be identified.

In contrast, important information has been derived about attentional mechanisms and the underlying neuroanatomical systems supporting attention, by investigating classic syndromes like "unilateral spatial neglect" (described next) and Bálint's syndrome. These disorders are the result of focal brain damage (e.g., stroke) that can be mapped in postmortem analyses and with brain imaging in the living human. Let's consider how brain damage has helped us understand brain attention mechanisms.

Neglect

Unilateral spatial neglect, or simply **neglect**, results when the brain's attention network is damaged in only one hemisphere. The damage typically occurs from a stroke and, unfortunately, is quite common. Although either hemisphere could be affected, the more severe and persistent effects occur when the right hemisphere

is damaged. Depending on the severity of the damage, its location, and how much time has passed since the damage occurred, patients may have reduced arousal and processing speeds, as well as an attention bias in the direction of their lesion (ipsilesional). For example, a right-hemisphere lesion would bias attention toward the right, resulting in a neglect of what is going on in the left visual field. Careful testing can show that these symptoms are not the result of partial blindness, as we will describe later. A patient's awareness of his lesion and deficit can be severely limited or lacking altogether. For instance, patients with right-hemisphere lesions may behave as though the left regions of space and the left parts of objects simply do not exist. If you were to visit a neglect patient and enter the room from the left, he might not notice you. He may have groomed only the right side of his body, leaving half his face unshaved and half his hair uncombed. If you were to serve him dinner, he may eat only what is on the right side of his plate; when handed a book, he may read only the right-hand page. What's more, he may deny having any problems. Such patients are said to "neglect" the information.

A graphic example of neglect is seen in paintings by the late German artist Anton Raederscheidt. At age 67, Raederscheidt suffered a stroke in the right hemisphere, which left him with neglect. The pictures in Figure 7.3 are self-portraits that he painted at different times after the stroke occurred and during his partial recovery. The paintings show his failure to represent portions of contralateral space—including, remarkably, portions of his own face. Notice in the first painting (Figure 7.3a), done shortly after his stroke, that almost the entire left half of the canvas is untouched. The image he paints of himself, in addition to being poorly formed, is missing the left half. The subject has one eye, part of a nose, and one ear; toward the left, the painting fades away. In each of the next three paintings (Figure 7.3b–d), made over the following several weeks and months, Raederscheidt uses more and more of the canvas and includes more and more of his face, until in Figure 7.3d, he uses most of the canvas. He now has a bilaterally symmetrical face, although some minor asymmetries persist in his painting.

Typically, patients show only a subset of these extreme signs of neglect, and indeed, neglect can manifest itself in different ways. The common thread is that, despite normal vision, neglect involves deficits in attending to and acting in the direction that is opposite the side of the unilateral brain damage. One way to observe this phenomenon is to look at the patterns of eye movements in patients with neglect. Figure 7.4 (top) shows eye movement patterns in a patient with

a   b

c   d

FIGURE 7.3 Recovering from a stroke.
Self-portraits by the late German artist Anton Raederscheidt,
painted at different times following a severe right-hemisphere
stroke, which left him with neglect to contralesional space. © 2013
Artists Rights Society (ARS), New York/VG Bild-Kunst, Bonn.

in the middle by drawing a vertical line. Patients
with lesions of the right hemisphere and neglect
tend to bisect the lines to the right of the midline. They may also completely miss lines on the
left side of the paper (Figure 7.5). In this example, the pattern of line cancellation is evidence
of neglect at the level of object representations
(each line) as well as visual space (the visual
scene represented by the test paper).

A related test is copying objects or scenes.
When asked to copy a simple line drawing, such
as a flower or clock face, patients with neglect
have difficulty. Figure 7.6 shows an example
from a patient with a right-hemisphere stroke
who was asked to copy a clock. Like the artist
Raederscheidt, the patient shows an inability to
draw the entire object and tends to neglect the
left side. Even when they know and can state that
clocks are round and include numbers 1 to 12,
they cannot properly copy the image or draw it
from memory.

So far, we have considered neglect for items
that are actually present in the visual world.
But neglect can also affect the imagination and
memory. Eduardo Bisiach and Claudio Luzzatti
(1978) studied patients with neglect caused by
unilateral damage to their right hemisphere. They
asked their patients, who were from Milan, Italy, to imagine themselves standing on the steps
of the Milan Cathedral (the Duomo di Milano)

a right hemisphere lesion and neglect during rest and
when searching a bilateral visual array for a target letter.
The patient's eye movements are compared to those of
patients with right hemisphere strokes who showed no
signs of neglect (Figure 7.4, bottom). The neglect patient shows a pattern of eye movements that are biased
in the direction of the right visual field, while those
without neglect search the entire array, moving their
eyes equally to the left and right.

Neuropsychological Tests of Neglect

To diagnose neglect of contralesional space, neuropsychological tests are used. In the line cancellation test,
patients are given a sheet of paper containing many horizontal lines and are asked to bisect the lines precisely

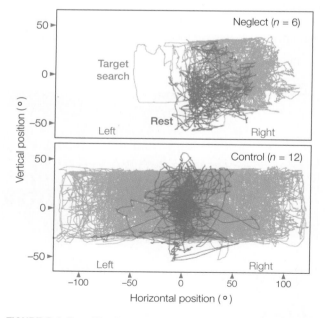

FIGURE 7.4 Gaze bias in neglect patients.
Neglect patients **(top)** show an ipsilesional gaze bias while searching for a target letter in a letter array (blue traces) and at rest
(green traces). Non-neglect patients **(bottom)** showed no bias.

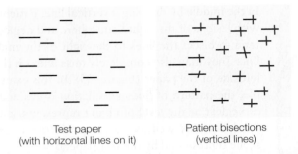

Test paper
(with horizontal lines on it)

Patient bisections
(vertical lines)

FIGURE 7.5 Patients with neglect are biased in the cancellation tasks.
Patients suffering from neglect are given a sheet of paper containing many horizontal lines and asked under free-viewing conditions to bisect the lines precisely in the middle with a vertical line. They tend to bisect the lines to the right (for a right-hemisphere lesion) of the midline of each page and/or each line, owing to neglect for contralesional space and the contralesional side of individual objects.

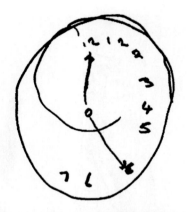

FIGURE 7.6 Image drawn by a right-hemisphere stroke patient who has neglect.
See text for details.

and to describe from memory the piazza (church square) from that viewpoint. Amazingly, the patients neglected things on the side of the piazza contralateral to their lesion, just as if they were actually standing there looking at it. When the researchers next asked the patients to imagine themselves standing across the piazza, facing *toward* the Duomo, they reported items from visual memory that they had previously neglected, and neglected the side of the piazza that they had just described (Figure 7.7).

Thus, neglect is found for items in visual memory during remembrance of a scene as well as for items in the external sensory world. The key point in the Bisiach and Luzzatti experiment is that the patients' neglect could not be attributed to lacking memories but rather indicated that *attention to parts of the recalled images was biased.*

Extinction

How do we distinguish neglect from blindness in the contralateral visual hemifields? Well, visual field testing can show that neglect patients detect stimuli normally when those stimuli are salient and presented in isolation. For example, when simple flashes of light or the wiggling fingers of a neurologist are shown at different single locations within the visual field of a neglect patient, he can see all the stimuli, even those that are in the contralateral (neglected) hemifield. This result tells us that the patient does not have a primary visual deficit. The patient's neglect becomes obvious when he is presented simultaneously with two stimuli, one in each hemifield. In that case, the patient fails to perceive or act on the contralesional stimulus. This result is known as **extinction**, because the presence of the competing stimulus in the

View from the cathedral

View toward the cathedral

FIGURE 7.7 Visual recollections of two ends of an Italian piazza by a neglect patient.
The neglected side in visual memory (shaded gray) was contralateral to the side with cortical damage.
The actual study was performed using the famous Piazza del Duomo in Milan.

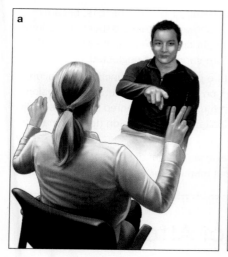  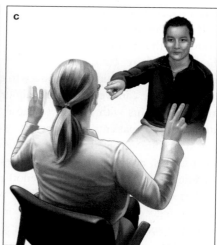

FIGURE 7.8 Test of neglect and extinction.
To a patient with a right-hemisphere lesion from a stroke, a neurologist presented a visual stimulus (raised fingers) first in the left hemifield **(a)** and then in the right hemifield **(b)**. The patient correctly detected and responded (by pointing) to the stimuli if presented one at a time, demonstrating an ability to see both stimuli and therefore no major visual field defects. When the stimuli were presented simultaneously in the left and right visual fields **(c)**, however, the patient reported seeing only the one in the right visual field. This effect is called *extinction* because the simultaneous presence of the stimulus in the patient's right field leads to the stimulus on the left of the patient being extinguished from awareness.

ipsilateral hemifield prevents the patient from detecting the contralesional stimulus. With careful testing, doctors often can see residual signs of extinction, even after the most obvious signs of neglect have remitted as a patient recovers. Figure 7.8 shows a neurologist testing a patient with right parietal damage in order to investigate his vision, and to reveal his neglect by showing extinction.

It's important to realize that these biases against the contralesional sides of space and objects can be overcome if the patient's attention is directed to the neglected locations of items. This is one reason the condition is described as a bias, rather than a loss of the ability to focus attention contralesionally.

One patient's comments help us understand how these deficits might feel subjectively: "It doesn't seem right to me that the word neglect should be used to describe it. I think concentrating is a better word than neglect. It's definitely concentration. If I am walking anywhere and there's something in my way, if I'm concentrating on what I'm doing, I will see it and avoid it. The slightest distraction and I won't see it" (Halligan & Marshall, 1998).

Comparing Neglect and Bálint's Syndrome

Let's compare the pattern of deficits in neglect with those of the patient with Bálint's syndrome, described at the beginning of this chapter. In contrast to the patient with

neglect, a Bálint's patient demonstrates three main deficits that are characteristic of the disorder: simultanagnosia, ocular apraxia, and optic ataxia.

Simultanagnosia is difficulty perceiving the visual field as a whole scene, such as when the patient saw only the comb or the spoon, but not both at the same time. *Ocular apraxia* is a deficit in making eye movements (saccades) to scan the visual field, resulting in the inability to guide eye movements voluntarily. When the physician overlapped the spoon and comb in space (see Figure 7.1), the Bálint's patient should have been able, given his direction of gaze, to see both objects, but he could not. Lastly, Bálint's patients also suffer from *optic ataxia*, a problem in making visually guided hand movements. If the doctor had asked the Bálint's patient to reach out and grasp the comb, he would have had a difficult time reaching through space to grasp the object.

Both neglect and Bálint's syndrome include severe disturbances in perception. The patterns of perceptual deficits are quite different, however, because different brain areas are damaged in each disorder. Neglect is the result of unilateral lesions of the parietal, posterior temporal, and frontal cortex. Neglect also can be due to damage in subcortical areas including the basal ganglia, thalamus, and midbrain. Bálint's patients suffer from bilateral occipitoparietal lesions. Thus, researchers obtain clues about the organization of the brain's attention system by considering the location of the lesions that cause these disorders and the differing perceptual and behavioral results. Neglect shows us that a network of cortical and subcortical areas, especially in the right hemisphere, result in disturbances of spatial attention. Bálint's syndrome shows us that posterior parietal and occipital damage to both hemispheres leads to an inability to perceive multiple objects in space, which is necessary to create a scene.

What else can we understand about attention by contrasting patients with neglect to those with Bálint's syndrome? From patients with neglect, we understand that the symptoms involve biases in attention based on spatial coordinates, and that these coordinates can be described in different reference frames. Put another way, neglect can be based on spatial coordinates either with respect to the patient (egocentric reference frame) or with respect to an object in space (allocentric reference frame). This finding tells us that attention can be directed within space and also within objects. Most likely these two types of neglect are guided by different processes. Indeed, the brain mechanisms involved with attending objects can be affected even when no spatial biases are seen. This phenomenon is seen in patients with Bálint's syndrome, who have relatively normal visual fields but cannot attend to more than one or a few objects at a time, even when the objects overlap in space.

The phenomenon of extinction in neglect patients suggests that sensory inputs are competitive, because when two stimuli presented simultaneously compete for attention, the one in the ipsilesional hemifield will win the competition and reach awareness. Extinction also demonstrates that after brain damage, patients experience reduced attentional capacity: When two competing stimuli are presented at once, the neglect patient is aware of only one of them.

It is important to note that none of these attentional deficits are the result of damage to the visual system *per se*, because the patient is not simply blind. These observations from brain damage and resultant attentional problems set the stage for us to consider several questions:

- How does attention influence perception?
- Where in the perceptual system does attention influence perception?
- How is attention allocated in space versus to stimulus features and objects?
- What neural mechanisms control attention?

To answer these questions, let's look next at the cognitive and neural mechanisms of attention.

TAKE-HOME MESSAGES

- Unilateral spatial neglect may result from damage to the right parietal, temporal, and/or frontal cortices, as well as subcortical structures. This kind of damage leads to reduced attention to and processing of the left-hand side of scenes and objects.

- Neglect is not the result of sensory deficits, because visual field testing shows that these patients have intact vision. Under the right circumstances, they can easily see objects that are sometimes neglected.

- A prominent feature of neglect is extinction, the failure to perceive or act on stimuli contralateral to the lesion (contralesional stimuli) when presented simultaneously with a stimulus ipsilateral to the lesion (ipsilesional stimulus).

- Neglect affects external personal hemispace and objects as well as internal memory for objects arrayed in space.

Models of Attention

When people turn their attention to something, the process is called orienting. The concept of orienting our selective attention can be divided into two categories: voluntary attention and reflexive attention. **Voluntary attention** is our ability to intentionally attend to something, such as this book. It is a goal-driven process, meaning that goals, knowledge, or expectations are used to guide information processing. **Reflexive attention** is a bottom-up, stimulus-driven process in which a sensory event—maybe a loud bang, the sting of a mosquito, a whiff of garlic, a flash of light or motion—captures our attention. As we will see later in this chapter, these two forms of attention differ in their properties and perhaps partly in their neural mechanisms.

Attentional orienting also can be either overt or covert. We all know what **overt attention** is—when you turn your head to orient toward a stimulus, whether it is for your eyes to get a better look, your ears to pick up a whisper, or your nose to sniff the frying bacon—you are exhibiting overt attention. You could appear to be reading this book, however, while actually paying attention to the two students whispering at the table behind you. This behavior is **covert attention**.

Hermann von Helmholtz and Covert Attention

In 1894, Hermann von Helmholtz (Figure 7.9a) performed a fascinating experiment in visual perception. He constructed a screen on which letters were painted at various distances from the center (Figure 7.9b). He hung the screen at one end of his lab and then turned off all the lights to create a completely dark environment. Helmholtz then used an electric spark to make a flash of light that briefly illuminated the screen. His goal was to investigate aspects of visual processing when stimuli were briefly perceived. As often happens in science, however, he stumbled on an interesting phenomenon.

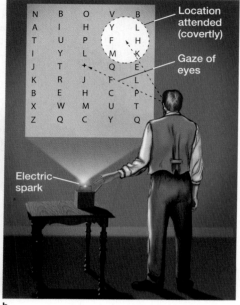

FIGURE 7.9 Helmholtz's visual attention experiment.
(a) Hermann von Helmholtz (1821–1894).
(b) Experimental setup by Helmholtz to study visual attention. Helmholtz observed that, while keeping his eyes fixated in the center of the screen during a very brief illumination of the screen, he could covertly attend to any location on the screen and perceive the letters located within this region but had difficulty perceiving the letters at other locations. He attributed this phenomenon to attention and speculated on the possible mechanisms underlying this ability.

Helmholtz noted that the screen was too large to view in its entirety without moving his eyes. Nonetheless, even when he kept his eyes fixed right at the center of the screen, he could decide in advance where he would pay attention: He made use of his covert attention. As we noted in the introduction to this section, *covert* means that the location he directed his attention toward could be different from the location toward which he was looking. Through these covert shifts of attention, Helmholtz observed that during the brief period of illumination, he could perceive letters located within the focus of his attention better than letters that fell outside the focus of his attention, even when his eyes remained directed toward the center of the screen.

Try this yourself using Figure 7.9. Hold the textbook 12 inches in front of you and stare at the plus sign in the center of Helmholtz's array of letters. Now, without moving your eyes from the plus sign, read out loud the letters closest to the plus sign in a clockwise order. You have covertly focused on the letters around the plus sign. As Helmholtz wrote in his *Treatise on Physiological Optics* (translated into English in 1924), "These experiments demonstrated, so it seems to me, that by a voluntary kind of intention, even without eye movements, and without changes of accommodation, one can concentrate attention on the sensation from a particular part of our peripheral nervous system and at the same time exclude attention from all other parts."

In the mid 20th century, experimental psychologists began to develop methods for quantifying the influence of attention on perception and awareness. Models of how the brain's attention system might work were built from these data and from observations like those of Helmholtz—and from everyday experiences, such as attending a Super Bowl party.

The Cocktail Party Effect

Imagine yourself at a Super Bowl party having a conversation with a friend. How can you focus on this single conversation while the TV is blasting and boisterous conversations are going on around you? British psychologist E. C. Cherry (1953) wondered the same thing while attending cocktail parties. His curiosity and subsequent research helped to found the modern era of attention studies, with what was dubbed the *cocktail party effect*.

Selective auditory attention allows you to participate in a conversation at a busy bar or party while ignoring the rest of the sounds around you. By selectively attending, you can perceive the signal of interest amid the other noises. If, however, the person you are conversing with is boring, then you can give covert attention to a conversation going on behind you while still seeming to focus on the conversation in front of you (Figure 7.10).

Cherry investigated this ability by designing a cocktail party in the lab: Normal participants, wearing headphones, listened to competing speech inputs to the two ears—this setup is referred to as **dichotic listening**. Cherry then asked the participants to attend to and verbally "shadow" the speech (immediately repeat each word) coming into one ear, while simultaneously ignoring the input to the other ear. Cherry discovered that under such conditions, participants could not (mostly) report any details of the speech in the unattended ear

FIGURE 7.10 Auditory selective attention in a noisy environment. The cocktail party effect of Cherry (1953), illustrating how, in the noisy, confusing environment of a cocktail party, people are able to focus attention on a single conversation, and, as the man in the middle right of the cartoon illustrates, to covertly shift attention to listen to a more interesting conversation than the one in which they continue to pretend to be engaged.

(Figure 7.11). In fact, all they could reliably report from the unattended ear was whether the speaker was male or female. *Attention, in this case voluntary attention, affected what was processed.* This finding led Cherry and others to propose that attention to one ear results in better encoding of the inputs to the attended ear and loss or degradation of the unattended inputs to the other ear. You experience

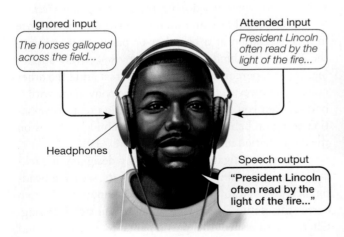

FIGURE 7.11 Dichotic listening study setup. Different auditory information (stories) are presented to each ear of a participant. The participant is asked to "shadow" (immediately repeat) the auditory stimuli from one ear's input (e.g., shadow the left-ear story and ignore the right-ear input).

this type of thing when the person sitting next to you in lecture whispers a juicy tidbit in your ear. A moment later, you realize that you just missed what the lecturer said, although you could just as well have heard him with your other ear. As foreshadowed by William James, information processing **bottlenecks** seem to occur at stages of perceptual analysis that have a **limited capacity**. What is processed are the high-priority inputs that you selected. Many processing stages take place between the time information enters the eardrum and you become aware of speech. At what stages do these bottlenecks exist such that attention is necessary to favor the attended over the unattended signals?

This question has been difficult to answer. It has led to one of the most debated issues in psychology over the past five decades. Are the effects of selective attention evident *early* in sensory processing or only later, after sensory and perceptual processing are complete? Think about this question differently: Does the brain faithfully process all incoming sensory inputs to create a representation of the external world, or can processes like attention influence sensory processing? Is what you perceive a combination of what is in the external world and what is going on inside your brain? By "going on inside your brain," we mean what your current goals may be, and what knowledge is stored in your brain. Consider the example in Figure 7.12. The first time you look at this image, you won't see the Dalmatian dog in the black-and-white scene; you cannot perceive it easily. Once it is pointed out to you, however, you perceive the dog whenever you are shown the picture. Something has changed in your brain, and it is not simply knowledge that it is a photo of dog—the dog jumps out at you, even when you forget having seen the photo before. This is an example of the knowledge stored in your brain influencing your perception. Perhaps it is not either-or; it may be that attention affects processing at many steps along the way from sensory transduction to awareness.

FIGURE 7.12
Dalmatian illusion.

Early Versus Late Selection Models

Cambridge University psychologist Donald Broadbent (1958) elaborated on the idea that the *information processing system* has a limited-capacity stage or stages through which only a certain amount of information can pass (Figure 7.13)—that is, a bottleneck, as hinted at by the writings of James and the experiments of Cherry. In Broadbent's model, the sensory inputs that can enter higher levels of the brain for processing are screened so that only the "most important," or attended, events pass through. Broadbent described this mechanism as a gate that could be opened for attended information and closed for ignored information. Broadbent argued for information selection early in the information processing stream. **Early selection**, then, is the idea that a stimulus can be selected for further processing, or it can be tossed out as irrelevant before perceptual analysis of the stimulus is complete.

In contrast, models of **late selection** hypothesize that all inputs are processed equally by the perceptual system. Selection follows to determine what will undergo additional processing, and perhaps what will be represented in awareness. The late-selection model implies that attentional processes cannot affect our perceptual analysis of stimuli. Instead, selection takes place at higher stages of information processing that involve internal decisions about whether the stimuli should gain complete access to awareness, be encoded in memory, or initiate a response. (The term *decisions* in this context refers to nonconscious processes, not conscious decisions made by the observer.) Figure 7.14 illustrates the differential stages of early versus late selection.

The original "all or none" early selection models, exemplified by gating models, quickly ran into a problem. Cherry observed in his cocktail party experiments that sometimes salient information from the *unattended ear* was consciously perceived, for example, when the listener's own name or something very interesting was included in a nearby conversation. The idea of a simple gating mechanism, which assumed that ignored information was completely lost, could not explain this experimental finding. Anne Treisman (1969), now at Princeton University, proposed that unattended channel

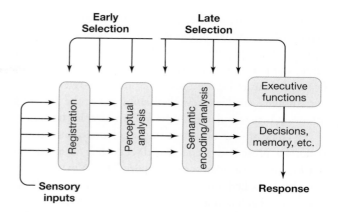

FIGURE 7.14 Early versus late selection of information processing.
This conceptualization is concerned with the extent of processing that an input signal might attain before it can be selected or rejected by internal attentional mechanisms. Early-selection mechanisms of attention would influence the processing of sensory inputs before the completion of perceptual analyses. In contrast, late-selection mechanisms of attention would act only after the complete perceptual processing of the sensory inputs, at stages where the information had been recoded as a semantic or categorical representation (e.g., "chair").

information was not completely blocked from higher analysis but was degraded or attenuated instead—a point Broadbent agreed with. Thus, early-selection versus late-selection models were modified to make room for the possibility that information in the unattended channel could reach higher stages of analysis, but with greatly reduced signal strength. To test these competing models of attention, researchers employed increasingly sensitive methods for quantifying the effects of attention. Their methods included chronometric analysis—the analysis of the time course of information processing on a millisecond-to-millisecond level of resolution, as described next.

Quantifying the Role of Attention in Perception

One way of measuring the effect of attention on information processing is to examine how participants respond to target stimuli under differing conditions of attention.

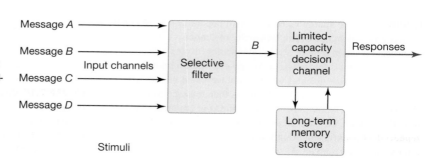

FIGURE 7.13 Broadbent's model of selective attention.
In this model, a gating mechanism determines what limited information is passed on for higher level analysis. The gating mechanism shown here takes the form of descending influences on early perceptual processing, under the control of higher order executive processes. The gating mechanism is needed at stages where processing has limited capacity.

Various experimental designs have been used for these explorations, and we describe some of them later in this chapter. One popular method is to provide cues that direct the participant's attention to a particular location or target feature before presenting the task-relevant target stimulus. In these so-called *cuing tasks*, the focus of attention is manipulated by the information in the cue.

In cuing studies of voluntary spatial attention, participants are presented a cue that directs their attention to one location on a video screen (Figure 7.15). Next, a target stimulus is flashed onto the screen at either the cued location or another location. Participants may be asked to press a button as fast as they can following the presentation of a target stimulus to indicate that it occurred; or they may be asked to respond to something about the stimulus, such as, "was it red or blue?" Such designs can provide information on how long it takes to perform the task (reaction time or response time), how accurately the participant performs the task, or both. In one version of this experiment, participants are instructed that although the cue, such as an arrow, will indicate the most likely location of the upcoming stimulus, they are to respond to the target wherever it appears. The cue, therefore, predicts the location of the target on most trials (a trial is one presentation of the cue and subsequent target, along with the required response). This form of cuing is known as **endogenous cuing**. Here, the

orienting of attention to the cue is driven by the participant's voluntary compliance with the instructions and the meaning of the cue, rather than merely by the cue's physical features (see Reflexive Attention, later in this chapter, for a contrasting mechanism).

When a cue correctly predicts the location of the subsequent target, we say we have a *valid trial* (Figure 7.15a). If the relation between cue and target is strong—that is, the cue usually predicts the target location (say, 90% of the time)—then participants learn to use the cue to predict the next target's location. Sometimes, though, because the target may be presented at a location not indicated by the cue, the participant is misled, and we call this an *invalid trial* (Figure 7.15b). Finally, the researcher may include some cues that give no information about the most likely location of the impending target; we call this situation a *neutral trial* (Figure 7.15c).

In cuing studies of voluntary attention, the time between the presentation of the attention-directing cue and the presentation of the subsequent target might be very brief or last up to a second or more. When participants are not permitted to move their eyes to the cued spot, but the cue correctly predicts the target's location, participants respond faster than when neutral cues are given (Figure 7.16). This faster response demonstrates the *benefits* of attention. In contrast, reaction times are slower when the stimulus appears at an unexpected location, revealing the *costs* of attention. If the participants

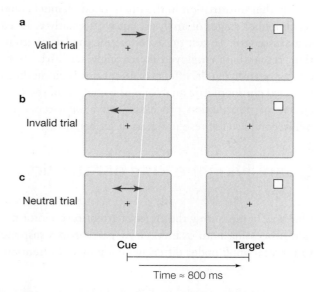

FIGURE 7.15 The spatial cuing paradigm popularized by Michael Posner and colleagues at the University of Oregon.
A participant sits in front of a computer screen, fixates on the central cross, and is told never to deviate eye fixation from the cross. An arrow cue indicates which visual hemifield the participant should covertly attend to. The cue is then followed by a target (the white box) in either the correctly cued **(a)** or the incorrectly cued **(b)** location. On other trials **(c)**, the cue (e.g., double-headed arrow) tells the participant that it is equally likely that the target will appear in the right or left location.

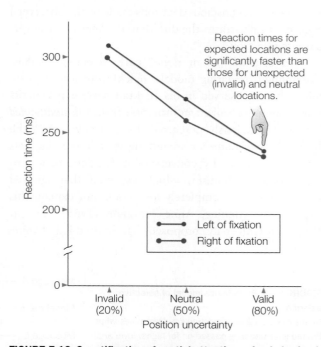

FIGURE 7.16 Quantification of spatial attention using behavioral measures.
Results of the study by Posner and colleagues illustrated in Figure 7.15, as shown by reaction times to unexpected, neutral, and expected location targets for the right and left visual hemifields.

are asked to discriminate some feature of the target, then benefits and costs of attention can be expressed in terms of accuracy instead of, or in addition to, reaction time measures.

Benefits and costs of attention have been attributed to the influence of covert attention on the efficiency of information processing. According to some theories, such effects result when the predictiveness of the cue induces the participants to direct their covert attention internally—a sort of mental "spotlight" of attention—to the cued visual field location. The spotlight is a metaphor to describe how the brain may attend *to a spatial location*. Because participants are typically required to keep their eyes on a central fixation spot on the viewing screen, internal or covert mechanisms must be at work.

Among others, University of Oregon professor Michael Posner and his colleagues (1980) have suggested that this attentional spotlight affected reaction times by influencing sensory and perceptual processing: Thus the stimuli that appeared in an attended location were processed faster than the stimuli that appeared in the unattended location. This enhancement of attended stimuli, a type of early selection, suggests that *changes in perceptual processing* can happen when the participant is attending a stimulus location. Now you might be thinking, "Ahhh, wait a minute there, fellas . . . responding more quickly to a target appearing at an attended location does not imply that the target was more efficiently processed in our visual cortex (early selection). These measures of reaction time—or behavioral measures more generally—are not measures of specific stages of neural processing. They provide only indirect measures. These time effects could solely reflect events going on in the motor system." Exactly. Can we be sure that the perceptual system actually is responsible? In order to determine if changes in attention truly affected perceptual processing, researchers turned to some cognitive neuroscience methods in combination with the voluntary cuing paradigm.

TAKE-HOME MESSAGES

- Attention involves both top-down (voluntary), goal-directed processes and bottom-up (reflexive), stimulus-driven mechanisms.
- Attention can be either overt or covert.
- According to early-selection models, a stimulus need not be completely perceptually analyzed before it can be selected for further processing or rejected as irrelevant. Broadbent proposed such a model of attention.
- Late-selection models hypothesize that attended and ignored inputs are processed equivalently by the perceptual system, reaching a stage of semantic (meaning) encoding and analysis where selection may occur.

- Our perceptual system contains stages at which it can process only a certain amount of information at any given time, what are called limited-capacity stages which result in *processing bottlenecks*. Attention limits the information to only the most relevant, thereby preventing overload of the limited-capacity stages.
- Cuing tasks, where the focus of attention is manipulated by the information in the cue, are often used to study the effect of attention on information processing.
- Spatial attention is often thought of metaphorically as a "spotlight" of attention that can move around as the person consciously desires, or that can be reflexively attracted by salient sensory events.

Neural Mechanisms of Attention and Perceptual Selection

Although most of the experiments discussed in this chapter focus on the visual system and, hence, on visual attention, this should not be taken to suggest that attention is only a visual phenomenon. Selective attention operates in all sensory modalities. In fact, it was investigations of the auditory system, spurred on by curiosity about the cocktail party effect, that led to the first round of cognitive neuroscience studies looking at the affect of attention on perceptual selection. These early studies made it clear that attention did affect early processing of perceptual stimuli, but not without some bumps in the road. Take a look at the How the Brain Works: Attention, Arousal, and Experimental Design box before we proceed to the land of visual attention.

After these early auditory ERP studies were conducted (heeding Näätänen's precautions discussed in the box), vision researchers became interested in studying the effects of attention on their favorite sense. They wanted to know if attention affected visual processing, and if so, when and where during processing it occurred. We begin with research of voluntary visual-spatial attention. Visual spatial attention involves selecting a stimulus on the basis of its spatial location. It can be voluntary, such a when you look at this page, or it can be reflexive, when you might glance up having been diverted by a motion or flash of light.

Voluntary Spatial Attention

Cortical Attention Effects Neural mechanisms of visual selective attention have been investigated using cuing paradigm methods, which we have just described. In a typical experiment, participants are given instructions to covertly (without diverting gaze from a central fixation spot) attend to stimuli presented at one

HOW THE BRAIN WORKS
Attention, Arousal, and Experimental Design

Since the turn of the 19th century, scientists have known that the ascending auditory pathway carries two-way traffic. Each neural relay sends axons to the auditory cortex and also sends return axons back to the preceding processing stage, even out to the cochlea via the olivocochlear bundle (OCB). Because this appears to be a sign of top-down communication in the auditory system, researchers have investigated whether the behavioral effects of attention, like those revealed in dichotic listening studies, might be the result of gating that occurs very early in auditory processing, such as in the thalamus, brainstem, or even all the way back to the cochlea.

The esteemed Mexican neurophysiologist Raul Hernández-Peón and his colleagues (1956) attempted to determine whether phenomena like the cocktail party effect might result from a gating of auditory inputs in the ascending auditory pathways. They recorded the activity in neurons within the subcortical auditory pathway of a cat while it was passively listening to the sound from a speaker (Figure 1a). They compared those results with recordings from the same cat when it was ignoring the sound coming from the speaker. How did they know the cat was ignoring the sounds? They showed mice to the cat, thereby attracting its visual attention (Figure 1b). They found that the amplitude of activity of neurons in the cochlear nucleus was reduced when the animal attended to the mice—apparently strong evidence for early-selection theories of attention.

Unfortunately, these particular experiments suffered fatal flaws that could affect attention. The cat—being a cat—was more aroused once it spotted a mouse, and because a speaker was used to present the stimuli instead of little cat headphones, movements of the ears led to changes in the amplitudes of the signals between conditions. Hernández-Peón and his colleagues had failed to control for the differences either in the state of arousal or in the amplitude of the sound at the cat's ears.

These problems have two solutions, and both are necessary. One solution is to introduce experimental controls that match arousal between conditions of attention. The other is to carefully control the stimulus properties by rigorously monitoring ear, head, and eye positions.

In 1969, a Finnish psychologist, Risto Näätänen, laid out the theoretical issues that have to be addressed to permit a valid neurophysiological test of selective attention. Among the issues he noted were that the experimental design had to be able to distinguish between simple behavioral arousal (low state of arousal vs. high state of arousal) and truly selective attention (e.g., attending one source of relevant sensory input while simultaneously ignoring distracting events).

Indeed, when Hernández-Peón's students repeated the 1956 experiment and carefully avoided changes in the sound amplitude at the ear, no differences were found subcortically between the neural response to attended and ignored sound.

The first physiological studies to control for both adjustments of peripheral sensory organs and nonspecific effects of behavioral arousal were conducted on humans by Steven Hillyard and his colleagues (1973) at the University

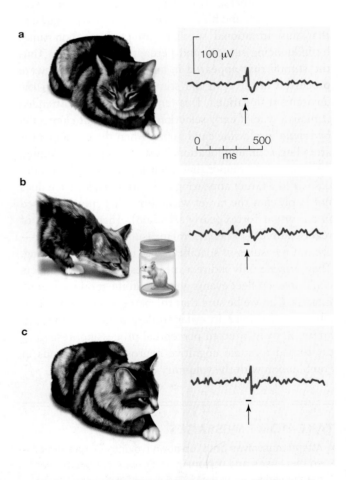

FIGURE 1 Early study of the neurophysiology of attention. A sound was played to a cat through a loudspeaker under three conditions while recordings from the cochlear nucleus in the brainstem were obtained. **(a)** While the animal sits passively in the cage listening to sounds, the evoked response from the cochlear nucleus is robust. **(b)** The animal's attention is attracted away from the sounds that it is hearing to visual objects of interest (a mouse in a jar). **(c)** The animal is once again resting and passively hearing sounds. The arrows indicate the responses of interest, and the horizontal lines indicate the onsets and offsets of the sounds from the loudspeaker.

of California, San Diego. ERPs were recorded because they provide a *precise temporal record* of underlying neural activity, and the ERP waves are related to different aspects of sensory, cognitive, and motor processing. Hillyard presented streams of sounds into headphones being worn by volunteers. Ten percent of the sounds were a deviant tone that differed in pitch. During one condition, participants were asked to attend to and count the number of higher pitched tones in one ear while ignoring those in the other (e.g., attend to right-ear sounds and ignore left-ear sounds). In a second condition, they were asked to pay attention to the stimuli in the other ear (e.g., attend to left-ear sounds and ignore right-ear sounds). In this way the researchers separately obtained auditory ERPs to stimuli entering one ear when input to that ear was attended and when it was ignored (while attending the other ear). The significant design feature of the experiment was that, during the two conditions of attention, the participants were always engaged in a difficult attention task, thus controlling for differing arousal states. All that varied was the direction of covert attention—to which ear the participants directed their attention. Figure 2 shows that the auditory sensory ERPs had a larger amplitude for attended stimuli, providing evidence that sensory processes were directed by attention. This result supported early-selection models

and gives us a physiological basis for the cocktail party effect. Note that the subject also heard the sound through headphones to avoid the problem of differing sound strength at the ear drum, as occurred in the cat studies of Hernández-Peón.

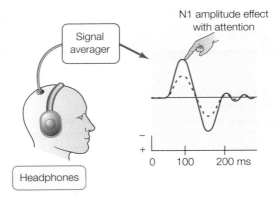

FIGURE 2 Event-related potentials in a dichotic listening task. The solid line represents the idealized average voltage response to an attended input over time; the dashed line, the response to an unattended input. Hillyard and colleagues found that the amplitude of the N1 component was enhanced when attending to the stimulus compared to ignoring the stimulus.

location (e.g., right field) and ignore those presented at another (e.g., left field) while event-related potential (ERP) recordings are made (see Chapter 3, page 100).

Looking at a typical ERP recording from a stimulus in one visual field (Figure 7.17), the first big ERP wave is a positive one that begins at 60–70 ms and peaks at about 100 ms (P1; first trough in Figure 7.17b) over the contralateral occipital cortex. It is followed by a negative wave that peaks at 180 ms (N1; Figure 7.17b). Modulations in the visual ERPs due to attention begin as early as 70–90 ms after stimulus onset, and thus, affect the P1 wave (Eason et al., 1969; Van Voorhis & Hillyard, 1977). When a visual stimulus appears at a location to which a subject is attending, the P1 is larger in amplitude than when the same stimulus appears at the same location but attention is focused elsewhere (Figure 7.17b). This is consistent with the attention affects observed in studies of auditory and tactile selective attention, which also modulates sensory responses.

This effect of visual attention primarily occurs with manipulations of *spatial attention* and not when attention is focused selectively on the features (e.g., one color vs. another) or object properties (e.g., car keys vs.

wallet) of stimuli alone. Attention effects for the more complex tasks of feature attention or object attention are observed later in the ERPs (greater than 120-ms latency—but see Figure 7.38 and related text). We describe these effects later in the chapter when we discuss attention to stimulus features. Thus, it seems that spatial attention has the earliest effect on stimulus processing. This early influence of spatial attention may be possible because retinotopic mapping of the visual system means that the brain encodes space very early—as early as at the retina—and space is a strong defining feature of relevant versus irrelevant environmental events.

Where, within the visual sensory hierarchy, are these earliest effects of selective visuospatial attention taking place and what do they represent? The P1 attention effect has a latency of about 70 ms from stimulus onset, and it is sensitive to changes in physical stimulus parameters, such as location in the visual field and stimulus luminance. We've learned from intracranial recordings that the first volleys of afferent inputs into striate cortex (V1) take place with a latency longer than 35 ms, and that early visual cortical responses are in the same latency range as

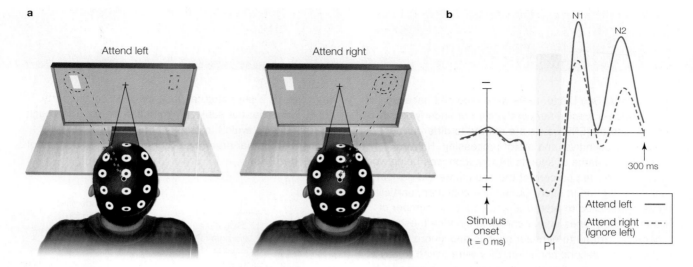

FIGURE 7.17 Stimulus display used to reveal physiological effects of sustained, spatial selective attention.
(a) The participant fixates the eyes on the central crosshairs while stimuli are flashed to the left (shown in figure) and right fields. **(left panel)** The participant is instructed to covertly attend to the left stimuli, and ignore those on the right. **(right panel)** The participant is instructed to ignore the left stimuli and attend to the right stimuli. Then the responses to the same physical stimuli, such as the white rectangle being flashed to left visual hemifield in the figure, are compared when they are attended and ignored. **(b)** Sensory ERPs recorded from a single right occipital scalp electrode in response to the left field stimulus. The waveform shows a series of characteristic positive and negative voltage deflections over time, called ERP components. Notice that the positive voltage is plotted downward. Their names reflect their voltage (P = positive; N = negative) and their order of appearance (e.g., 1 = first deflection). Attended stimuli (red trace) elicit ERPs with greater amplitude than do unattended stimuli (dashed blue trace).

the P1 response. Taken together, these clues suggest that the P1 wave is a sensory wave generated by neural activity in the visual cortex, and therefore, *its sensitivity to spatial attention supports early selection models of attention.* We know from Chapter 3, however, that ERPs represent the summed electrical responses of tens of thousands of neurons, not single neurons. This combined response produces a large enough signal to propagate through the skull to be recorded on the human scalp. Can the effect of attention be detected in the response of single visual neurons in the cortex? For example, let's say your attention wanders from the book and you look out your window to see if it is still cloudy and WHAT??? You jerk your head to the right to get a double take. A brand new red Maserati Spyder convertible is sitting in your driveway. As a good neuroscientist, you immediately think, "I wonder how my spatial attention, focused on this Maserati, is affecting my neurons in my visual cortex right now?" rather than "What the heck is a Maserati doing in my driveway?"

Jeff Moran and Robert Desimone (1985) revealed the answer to this question (the former, not the latter). The scientists investigated how visuospatial selective attention affected the firing rates of individual neurons in the visual cortex of monkeys. Using single-cell recording, they first recorded and characterized the responses of

single neurons in extrastriate visual area V4 (ventral stream area) to figure out what regions of the visual field they coded (receptive field location) and which specific stimulus features the neurons responded to most vigorously. The team found, for example, that neurons in V4 fired robustly in response to a single-colored, oriented bar stimulus (e.g., a red horizontal bar) more than another (e.g., a green vertical bar). Next, they simultaneously presented the preferred (red horizontal) and non-preferred (green vertical) stimuli near each other in space, so that both stimuli were within the region of the visual field that defined the neuron's receptive field. Over a period of several months, the researchers had previously trained the monkeys to fixate on a central spot on a monitor, to covertly attend to the stimulus at one location in the visual field, and to perform a task related to it while ignoring the other stimulus. Responses of single neurons were recorded and compared under two conditions: when the monkey *attended* the preferred (red horizontal bar) stimulus, and when it instead attended the non-preferred (green vertical bar) stimulus that was located a short distance away. Because the two stimuli (attended and ignored) were positioned in different locations, the task can be characterized as a spatial attention task. How did attention affect the firing rate of the neurons?

When the red stimulus was attended, it elicited a stronger response (more action potentials fired per second) in the corresponding V4 neuron that preferred red horizontal bars than when the red stimulus was ignored while attending the green vertical bar positioned at another location. Thus, spatial selective attention affected the firing rates of V4 neurons (Figure 7.18). As with the ERPs in humans, the activity of single visual cortical neurons are found to be modulated by spatial attention.

Several studies have replicated the attention effects observed by Moran and Desimone in V4 and have extended this finding to other visual areas, including later stages of the ventral pathway in the inferotemporal region. In addition, work in dorsal-stream visual areas has demonstrated effects of attention in the motion processing areas MT and MST of the monkey. Researchers also investigated whether attention affected even earlier steps in visual processing—in primary visual cortex (V1), for example.

Carrie McAdams and Clay Reid (2005), at Harvard Medical School, carried out experiments to determine which level of processing within V1 was influenced by attention. Recall from Chapter 6 that many stages of neural processing take place within a visual area, and in V1 different neurons display characteristic receptive-field properties—some are called *simple cells*, others

complex cells, and so on. Simple cells exhibit orientation tuning and respond to contrast borders (like those found along the edge of an object). Simple cells are also relatively early in the hierarchy of neural processing in V1—so, if attention were to affect them, this would be further evidence of how early in processing, and by what mechanism, spatial attention acts within V1.

McAdams and Reid trained monkeys to fixate on a central point and covertly attend a black-and-white flickering noise pattern in order to detect a small, colored pixel that could appear anywhere within the pattern (Figure 7.19a). When the monkeys detected the color, they were to signal this by making a rapid eye movement (a saccade) from fixation to the location on the screen that contained that color. The attended location would be positioned either over the receptive field of the V1 neuron they were recording or in the opposite visual field. Thus, the researchers could evaluate responses of the neuron when that region of space was attended and when it was ignored (in different blocks). They also could use the flickering noise pattern to create a spatiotemporal receptive-field map (Figure 7.19b) showing regions of the receptive field that were either excited or inhibited by light. In this way, the researchers could first determine whether the neuron had the properties of simple cells.

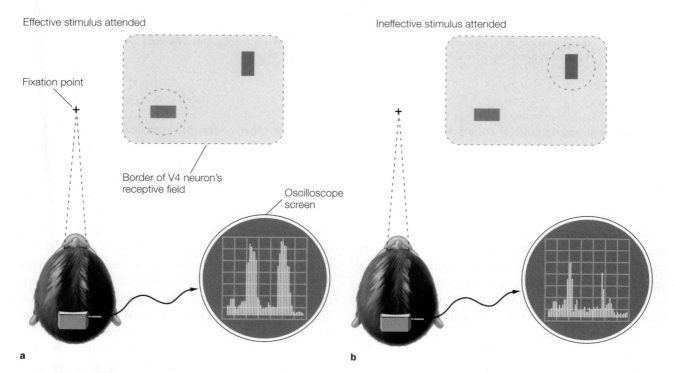

FIGURE 7.18 Spatial attention modulates activity of V4 neurons.
The areas circled by dashed lines indicate the attended locations for each trial. A red bar is an effective sensory stimulus, and a green bar is an ineffective sensory stimulus for this neuron. The neuronal firing rates are shown to the right of each monkey head. The first burst of activity is to the cue, and the second burst in each image is to the target array. **(a)** When the animal attended to the red bar, the V4 neuron gave a good response. **(b)** When the animal attended to the green bar, a poor response was generated.

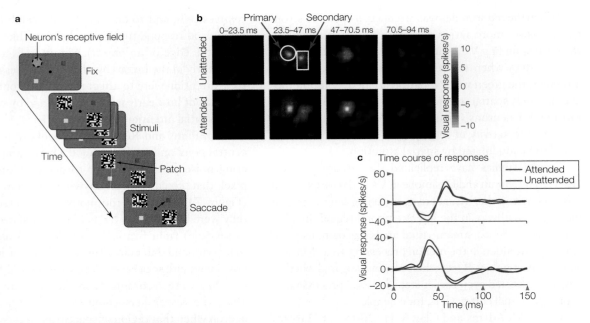

FIGURE 7.19 Attention effects in V1 simple cells.
(a) The stimulus sequence began with a fixation point and two color locations that would serve as saccade targets. Then two flickering black-and-white patches appeared, one over the neuron's receptive field and the other in the opposite visual field. Before the onset of the stimuli, the monkey was instructed which of the two patches to attend. The monkey had been trained to covertly attend the indicated patch to detect a small color pixel that would signal where a subsequent saccade of the eyes was to be made (to the matching color) for a reward. **(b)** The spatiotemporal receptive field of the neuron when unattended (attend opposite visual field patch) and when attended. Each of the eight panels corresponds to the same spatial location as that of the black-and-white stimulus over the neuron's receptive field. The excitatory (red) and inhibitory (blue) regions of the receptive field are evident; they are largest from 23.5 to 70 ms after stimulus onset **(middle two panels)**. Note that the amplitudes of the responses were larger when attended than when unattended. This difference can be seen in these receptive-field maps and is summarized as plots in **(c)**.

They could also see whether attention affected the firing pattern and receptive-field organization. What did they come up with? They found that *spatial attention enhanced the responses of the simple cells* but did not affect the spatial or temporal organization of their receptive fields (Figure 7.19c).

Does the same happen in humans? Yes, but different methods have to be used, since intracranial recordings are rarely done in humans. Neuroimaging studies of spatial attention show results consistent with those from cellular recordings in monkeys. Whole brain imaging studies have the advantage that one may investigate attention effects in multiple brain regions all in one experiment. Such studies have shown that spatial attention modulates the activity in multiple cortical visual areas. Hans-Jochen Heinze and his colleagues (1994) directly related ERP findings to functional brain neuroanatomy by combining positron emission tomography (PET) imaging with ERP recordings. They demonstrated that *visuospatial attention results in modulation of blood flow* (related to neuronal

activity) *in visual cortex.* Subsequent studies using fMRI have permitted a more fine-grained analysis of the effects of spatial attention in humans.

For example, Joseph Hopfinger and his colleagues (2000) used a modified version of a spatial cuing task combined with event-related fMRI. On each trial, an arrow cue was presented at the center of the display and indicated the side to which participants should direct their attention. Eight seconds later, the bilateral target display (flickering black-and-white checkerboards) appeared for 500 ms. The participants' task was to press a button if some of the checks were gray rather than white, but only if this target appeared on the cued side. The 8-s gap between the arrow and the target display allowed the slow hemodynamic responses (see Chapter 3) linked to the attention-directing cues to be analyzed separately from the hemodynamic responses linked to the detection of and response to the target displays. The results are shown in Figure 7.20 in coronal sections through the visual cortex of a single participant in the Hopfinger study.

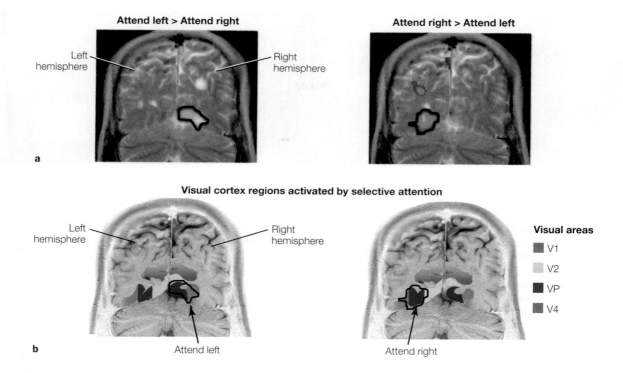

FIGURE 7.20 Selective attention activates specific regions of the visual cortex, as demonstrated by event-related fMRI.

(a) Areas of activation in a single participant were overlaid onto a coronal section through the visual cortex obtained by structural MRI. The statistical contrasts reveal where attention to the left hemifield produced more activity than attention to the right (reddish to yellow colors, **left**) and the reverse, where attention to the right hemifield elicited more activity than did attention to the left (bluish colors, **right**). As demonstrated in prior studies, the effects of spatial attention were activations in the visual cortex contralateral to the attended hemifield. **(b)** The regions activated by attention (shown in black outline) were found to cross multiple early visual areas (shown as colored regions—refer to key).

As you can see in this figure, attention to one visual hemifield activated multiple regions of visual cortex in the contralateral hemisphere.

Roger Tootell and Anders Dale at Massachusetts General Hospital (R. Tootell et al., 1998) investigated how all of the attention-related activations in visual cortex related to the multiple visual cortical areas in humans using retinotopic mapping. That is, they wanted to differentiate and identify one activated visual area from another on the scans. They combined high-resolution mapping of the borders of early visual cortical areas (retinotopic mapping; see Chapter 3) with a spatial attention task. Participants were required to selectively attend to stimuli located in one visual field quadrant while ignoring those in the other quadrants; different quadrants were attended to in different conditions while the participants' brains were scanned with fMRI methods. This permitted the researchers to map the attentional activations onto the flattened computer maps of the visual cortex, thus permitting the attention effects to be related directly to the multiple visual areas of human visual cortex.

They found that spatial attention produced robust modulations of activity in multiple extrastriate visual areas, as well as a smaller modulation of striate cortex (V1; Figure 7.21). This work provides a high-resolution view of the functional anatomy of multiple areas of extrastriate and striate cortex during sustained spatial attention in human visual cortex.

Now we know that spatial attention does influence the processing of visual inputs. Attended stimuli produce greater neural responses than do ignored stimuli, and this difference is observed in multiple visual cortical areas. Is the effect of spatial attention different in the different visual areas? It seems so. The Tootell fMRI work hints at this possibility, because attention-related modulation of activity in V1 appeared to be less robust than that in extrastriate cortex; also, work by Motter (1993) suggested a similar pattern in the visual cortex of monkeys. If so, what mechanisms might explain a hierarchical organization of attention effects as you move up the visual hierarchy from V1 through extrastriate cortical areas?

Robert Desimone and John Duncan (1995) proposed a *biased competition model* for selective attention.

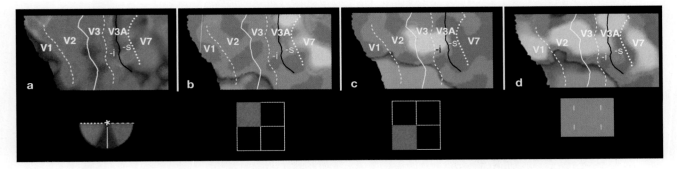

FIGURE 7.21 Spatial attention produced robust modulation of activity in multiple extrastriate visual areas, as demonstrated by fMRI.
Panel **a** shows the retinotopic mappings of the left visual field for each participant, corresponding to the polar angles shown at right (which represents the left visual field). Panel **b** shows the attention-related modulations (attended versus unattended) of sensory responses to a target in the upper left quadrant (the quadrant to which attention was directed is shown at right in red). Panel **c** shows the same for stimuli in the lower left quadrant. In b and c, the yellow to red colors indicate areas where activity was greater when the stimulus was attended to than when ignored; the bluish colors represent the opposite, where the activity was greater when the stimulus was ignored than when attended. The attention effects in b and c can be compared to the pure sensory responses to the target bars when passively viewed (**d**).

Their model may help explain two questions. First, why are the effects of attention larger when multiple competing stimuli fall within a neuron's receptive field? And second, how does attention operate at different levels of the visual hierarchy as neuronal receptive fields change their properties? In the biased competition model, when different stimuli in a visual scene fall within the receptive field of a visual neuron, the bottom-up signals from the two stimuli *compete* like two snarling dogs to control the neuron's firing. The model suggests that attention can help resolve this competition in favor of the attended stimulus. Given that the sizes of neuronal receptive fields increase as you go higher in the visual hierarchy, there is a greater chance for competition between different stimuli within a neuron's receptive field, and therefore, a greater need for attention to help resolve the competition (to read more about receptive fields, see Chapter 3).

Sabine Kastner and her colleagues (1998) used fMRI to investigate the biased competition model during spatial attention in humans (Figure 7.22). To do this, they first asked whether, in the *absence* of focused spatial attention, nearby stimuli could interfere with one another. The answer was yes. They found that when they presented two nearby stimuli simultaneously, the stimuli interfered with each other and the neural response evoked by each stimulus was reduced compared to when one stimulus was presented alone. If attention is introduced and directed to one stimulus in the display, however, then simultaneous presentation of the competing stimulus no longer interferes (Figure 7.23), and this effect tended to be larger in area V4 than in V1. The attention focused on one stimulus attenuates the influence of the competing stimulus. To return to our analogy, one of the snarling dogs (the competing stimulus) is muzzled.

It appears to be the case that, for a given stimulus, spatial attention operates differently at early (V1) versus later (e.g., V4) stages of the visual cortex. Why? Perhaps because the neuronal receptive fields differ in size from one

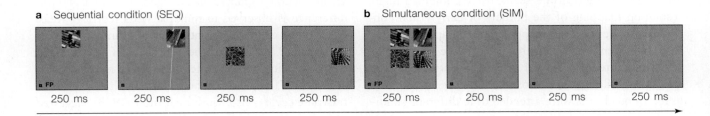

a Sequential condition (SEQ)   **b** Simultaneous condition (SIM)

250 ms   250 ms   250 ms   250 ms   250 ms   250 ms   250 ms   250 ms

Time

FIGURE 7.22 Design of the task for attention to competing stimuli used to test the biased competition model.
Competing stimuli were presented either sequentially (**a**) or simultaneously (**b**). During the attention condition, covert attention was directed to the stimulus closest to the point of fixation (FP), and the other stimuli were merely distracters.

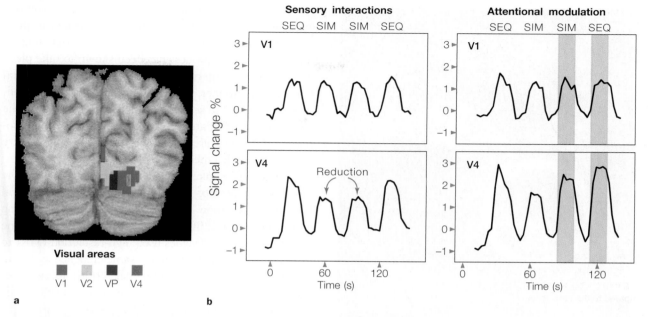

FIGURE 7.23 Functional MRI signals in the study investigating the biased competition model of attention.

(a) Coronal MRI section in one participant, where the pure sensory responses in multiple visual areas are mapped with meridian mapping (similar to that used in Figure 7.20). **(b)** The percentage of signal changes over time in areas V1 and V4 as a function of whether the stimuli were presented in the sequential (SEQ) or simultaneous (SIM) condition, and as a function of whether they were unattended **(left)** or whether attention was directed to the target stimulus (**right**, shaded blue). In V4 especially, the amplitudes during the SEQ and SIM conditions were more similar when attention was directed to the target stimulus (shaded blue areas at right) than when it was not (unshaded areas).

visual cortical area to the next. Thus, although smaller stimuli might fall within a receptive field of a single V1 neuron, larger stimuli would not; but these larger stimuli would fall within the larger receptive field of a V4 neuron. In addition, exactly the same stimulus can occupy different spatial scales depending on its distance from the observer. For example, look at the flowers in Figure 7.24. When viewed at a greater distance (panel b), the same flowers occupy less of the visual field (compare what you see in the yellow circles). All of the flowers actually could fall into the receptive field of a single neuron at an earlier stage of the visual hierarchy. This observation suggests that attention operates at different stages of vision, depending on the spatial scale of the attended and ignored stimuli. Does it? How would you design a study to answer this question?

Max Hopf and colleagues (2006) combined recordings of ERPs, magnetoencephalography (MEG; see Chapter 3), and fMRI. The simple stimuli they used are shown in Figure 7.25a–c. In each trial, the target appeared as either a square or a group of squares, small or large, red or green, and shifted either up or down in the visual field. Participants were to attend to the targets of one color as instructed and to push one of two buttons depending on whether the targets were shifted up or down. The study revealed that attention acted at earlier

levels of the visual system for the smaller targets than it did for the large targets (Figure 7.25d). So, although attention does act at multiple levels of the visual hierarchy, it also optimizes its action to match the spatial scale of the visual task.

Now that we have seen the effects of attention on the cortical stages of the visual hierarchy, have you started to wonder if attention might also cause changes in processing at the level of the subcortical visual relays? Well, others have also been curious, and this curiosity stretches back for more than 100 years. Recall the reflections of Helmholtz that we described earlier about the possible mechanisms of covert spatial attention? (See also How The Brain Works: Attention, Arousal, and Experimental Design.) Contemporary researchers have been able to shed light on this question of whether attention might influence subcortical processing.

Subcortical Attention Effects Could attentional filtering or selection occur even earlier along the visual processing pathways—in the thalamus or in the retina? Unlike the cochlea, the human retina contains no descending neural projections that could be used to modulate retinal activity by attention. But massive neuronal projections do extend from the visual cortex (layer 6 neurons) back to

FIGURE 7.24 Competition varies between objects depending on their scale.
The same stimulus can occupy a different sized region of visual space depending on its distance from the observer. **(a)** Viewed from up close, a single flower may occupy all of the receptive field of a V4 neuron (yellow circles), whereas multiple flowers fit within the larger receptive field of high-order inferotemporal (IT) neurons (blue circles). **(b)** Viewed from greater distance, multiple flowers are present within the smaller V4 receptive field and the larger IT receptive field.

the thalamus. These projections synapse on neurons in what is known as the **thalamic reticular nucleus (TRN;** also known as the *perigeniculate nucleus*), which is the portion of the reticular nucleus that surrounds the lateral geniculate nucleus (LGN) (Figure 7.26).

These neurons maintain complex interconnections with neurons in the thalamic relays and could, in principle, modulate information flow from the thalamus to the cortex. Such a process has been shown to take place in cats during intermodal (visual–auditory) attention (Yingling & Skinner, 1976). The TRN was also implicated in a model to select the visual field location for the current spotlight of attention in perception—an idea proposed by Nobel laureate Francis Crick (1992). Is there support for such a mechanism?

Studies on monkeys in which attention affected the metabolic activity of the LGN neurons provided initial hints that attention might influence LGN processing (Vanduffel et al., 2000). Subsequent studies by Sabine Kastner and her colleagues used high-resolution fMRI to assess whether attention had the same influence in the human LGN (reviewed in Kastner et al., 2006). Researchers presented participants with a bilateral array of flickering checkerboard stimuli (Figure 7.27a), which activated the LGN and multiple visual cortical areas (Figure 7.27b). Participants were cued to attend to either the left or right half of the array. The results (Figure 7.27c) showed that the amplitude of the activation was greater in the LGN and visual cortex that were contralateral to the attended array compared to the activity in response to the unattended array. So, *highly focused* visuospatial attention can modulate activity in the thalamus. Since fMRI studies do not provide timing information, however, it is hard to know what such effects indicate. Do they reflect attentional gating of the afferent LGN neurons heading to V1? Or instead, do they reflect reafferent feedback to the thalamus from the cortex that is not the incoming afferent volley of information?

McAlonan, Cavanaugh, and Wurtz (2008), at the National Eye Institute, recorded from LGN relay neurons and the surrounding TRN neurons of monkeys that had been trained to attend covertly to a target at one location while ignoring other targets. When the monkeys' attention was directed to the location of the stimulus within the LGN neuron's receptive field, the firing rate of the neuron increased (Figure 7.28a). In addition, however, the firing rate decreased in the surrounding TRN neurons (which, as you will recall, are not relay neurons, but instead are interneurons that receive input from the visual cortex; Figure 7.28b). Why is that? Well, we know from other work that the TRN neurons synapse onto the LGN neurons with *inhibitory* signals.

We can now explain the entire circuit. Attention involves either activating or inhibiting signal transmission from the LGN to visual cortex via the TRN circuitry. Either a descending neural signal from the cortex, or a separate signal from subcortical inputs travels to the TRN neurons. These inputs to the TRN can either excite the TRN neurons, thereby inhibiting information

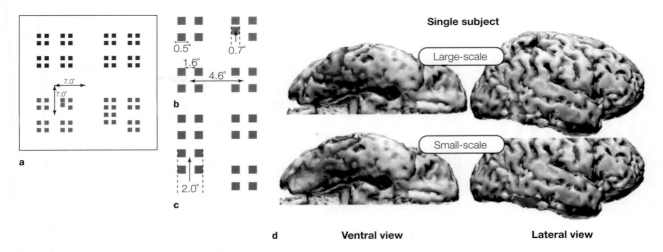

FIGURE 7.25 Study of effects of attention for different stimulus spatial scales.
(a) Example of an entire stimulus array from the spatial scale experiment. **(b–c)** Examples of the stimuli within a single quadrant of the array with the target at small **(b)** and large **(c)** scales. **(d)** MEG measures for the N2pc effect (an ERP reflecting focused attention) from 250 to 300 ms after the onset of the array, from a single volunteer. Large-scale trials **(top rows)** and small-scale trials **(bottom rows)** are shown on a ventral view (left panel images) and a left lateral view (right panel images) of the right hemisphere. One can see that for the small-scale trials, the activity in the brain is more posterior, reflecting neural responses from earlier stages of the visual system.

transmission from LGN to visual cortex, or the inputs can suppress the TRN neurons. Thus, transmission from LGN to visual cortex increases. The latter mechanism is consistent with the increased neuronal responses observed for the neurons in LGN and V1 when coding the location of an attended stimulus.

These studies demonstrate that *highly* focused spatial attention can modulate activity early in the visual system in the subcortical relay nuclei in the thalamus. This finding provides strong support for the early-selection models of attention. As you know, however, our attention is not always highly focused. In fact, yours may not be right now. You may have had to read the last couple of sentences over again. By passing these modulations along passively to higher visual areas, do these early modulations form the basis for all spatial attention effects in the visual system? Alternatively, can spatial attention act independently at multiple stages of visual processing (i.e., LGN, V1, and extrastriate cortical areas)? To learn more about this question, see How the Brain Works: Shocking Studies of Attention.

Reflexive Spatial Attention

So far in our discussion on spatial attention, we have considered voluntary attention. We can voluntarily direct our attention to the words on this page or to remembering what we had for breakfast. Oftentimes, however, things in the environment attract our attention without our cooperation. This is known as reflexive attention, *and it is activated by stimuli that are conspicuous in some way.*

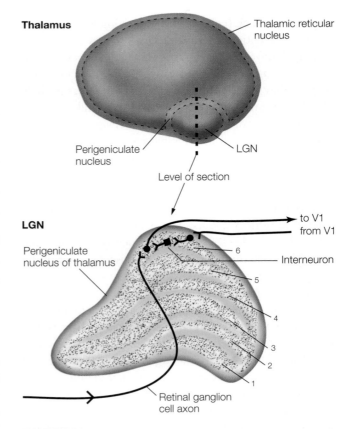

FIGURE 7.26
The thalamus, its perigeniculate nucleus, and projections to and from the thalamus and visual cortex.

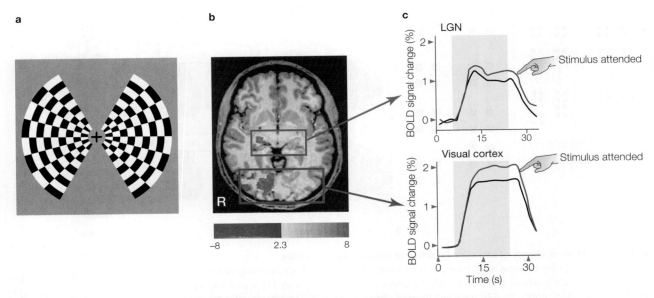

FIGURE 7.27 Functional MRI study of spatial attention effects in the lateral geniculate nucleus (LGN).
(a) Before stimulus onset, an arrow cue at fixation instructed the participants which hemifield to attend.
Next, a checkerboard stimuli presented bilaterally for 18 s (shown as blue shaded area in **c**). The task
was to detect randomly occurring luminance changes in the flickering checks in the cued hemifield.
(b) Functional MRI activations (increased BOLD responses) were observed in the LGN (red box) and in
multiple visual cortical areas (green box). **(c)** Increased activations were seen when the stimulus in the
hemifield contralateral to the brain region being measured was attended. The effect was observed both
in the LGN **(top)** and in multiple visual cortical areas **(bottom)**.

The more salient (conspicuous) the stimulus, the more easily our attention is captured: Think of how we respond to a rapid movement at the corner of our eye (eek! a rat!), the shattering of glass in a restaurant, or someone whistling as they walk by the open door of the lecture hall. Heads turn toward the sounds and sights and then wag back a moment or two later, unless the event is behaviorally relevant. This head wagging may happen before we can prevent it, because our reflexive attention may lead to overt orientation to the sensory stimulus—*overt* because heads and eyes turn toward the event. Even without overt signs of orientation, however, covert attention can be attracted to sensory events. This leads to a question: Are reflexive and voluntary attention processed in the same way? To tackle this question, we can use a variant of the cuing method (see Figure 7.15) to demonstrate this phenomenon experimentally.

The effects of reflexive attention can be demonstrated by examining how a task-*irrelevant* flash of light somewhere in the visual field affects the speed of responses to subsequent task-*relevant* target stimuli. This method is referred to as **reflexive cuing** or **exogenous cuing**, because attention is controlled by low-level features of an external stimuli, not by internal voluntary control. Although the light flash "cues" do not predict the location of subsequent targets, responses are faster to targets that appear in the vicinity of the light flash—*but only for*

a short time after the flash, about 50–200 ms. These types of effects tend to be spatially specific. That is, they influence processing in and around the *location* of the reflexive cue only. Therefore, they can also be described by the spotlight metaphor introduced earlier in this chapter. In this case, however, the spotlight is reflexively attracted to a location and is short-lived.

The interesting thing is that when more than about 300 ms passes between the task-irrelevant light flash and the target, the pattern of effects on reaction time is reversed. Participants respond more slowly to stimuli that appear in the vicinity of where the flash had been. This phenomenon is called the *inhibitory aftereffect* or, more commonly, **inhibition of return** (**IOR**). Why would reflexive attentional orienting have profound variations in its effect over time following a sensory event? Consider the advantages of this kind of system. If sensory events in the environment caused reflexive orienting that lasted for many seconds, people would be continually distracted by things happening around them and would be unable to attend to a goal. Our ancestors might never have made it to reproductive age and thus, we wouldn't be here reading this book. They would have been watching for a lion or looking for food, but then been distracted and entranced by a bird's song—whoops, missed the lion! Or whoops, no meal, again! In today's world, imagine the consequences if a driver's attention became reflexively focused on a

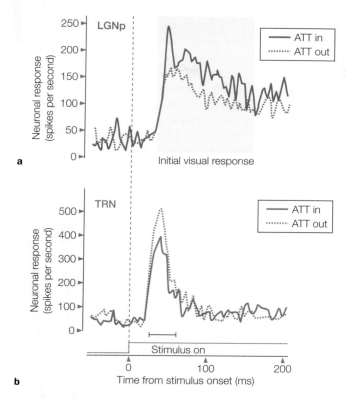

FIGURE 7.28 Effects of spatial attention on neuronal firing rates in the thalamus.

The solid lines show the amplitude of the neuronal response (spikes per second) when a light bar was flashed within the neuron's RF and attention was directed there (ATT in = attend in the receptive field). Dashed traces are also responses to a light bar being flashed within the neuron's receptive field, but under the condition where attention was directed elsewhere (ATT out = attend outside the receptive field). The dashed vertical line is the stimulus onset. **(a)** Responses of a parvocellular lateral geniculate nucleus neuron (LGNp), which is a thalamic relay neuron projecting to V1. **(b)** Responses of a sample thalamic reticular nucleus (TRN) neuron, which is not a relay neuron from retina to cortex, but instead receives descending neuronal inputs from cortex, and can inhibit the LGN relays neuron via an interneuron (see Figure 7.26).

distraction off to the side of the road and then remained focused on that event for more than an instant. Our automatic orienting system has built-in mechanisms to prevent reflexively directed attention from becoming stuck at a location for more than a couple of hundred milliseconds. The reflexive capturing of attention subsides, and the likelihood that our attention will be drawn back to that location is reduced slightly. Does this mean that things that attract our attention reflexively cannot be attended for longer than a couple of hundred milliseconds? No, we know from experience that isn't true. If the event is important and salient, we can rapidly invoke our voluntary mechanisms to sustain attention longer, thereby overriding the inhibition of return. Thus, the nervous system has evolved clever, complementary mechanisms to control attention so that we can function in a cluttered, rapidly changing sensory world.

It may seem that there is not much difference between the responses to an endogenous cue and an exogenous cue. Both result in *attention shifts that enhance the processing of attended sensory stimuli and decrease that of the unattended.* In the case of reflexive attention, however, the cuing effect is quick and short-lived, and processing of stimuli in the neighborhood of the cue is enhanced. With voluntary attention cuing, however, the effect is slower and more sustained. Do these differences in processing represent different neural mechanisms?

We have learned that voluntarily focusing attention at a location in response to verbal instructions or instructive visual pre-cues will enhance the visual responses to stimuli occurring at that location. Do these same changes occur when our attention is reflexively attracted to a location in the visual field by a sensory event? Joseph Hopfinger and colleagues (1998, 2001) answered yes to this question. They recorded ERPs in response to target stimuli in a reflexive cuing task like the one described earlier (Figure 7.29a). They found that the early occipital P1 wave is larger for targets that quickly follow a sensory cue at the same location versus trials in which the sensory cue and target occur at different locations. As the time after cuing grows longer, however, this effect reverses and the P1 response diminishes—and may even be inhibited—just as in measurements of reaction time (Figure 7.29b). Therefore, these data indicate that both reflexive (stimulus driven) and voluntary (goal directed) shifts in spatial attention induce similar physiological modulations in early visual processing. Presumably, the neural networks implementing these attentional modulations of sensory analysis are different, reflecting the differing ways in which attentional control is triggered for the two forms of attention.

Visual Search

In everyday perception, voluntary attention (driven by our goals) and reflexive attention (driven by stimuli in the world) interact in a push-pull fashion, struggling to control the focus of our attention. For example, we frequently search about for a specific item in a cluttered scene. Perhaps we watch for a friend coming out of the building after class, or we look for our suitcase on the baggage claim carousel of a busy airport. If the suitcase is red and covered with flowered stickers, the search is quite easy. If the suitcase is a medium-sized black bag with rollers, the task can be quite challenging. As you cast your gaze around for that friend or suitcase, you don't keep going back to places that you have just scanned. Instead, you are biased, moving your eyes to new objects in new locations. The last time you stood in baggage claim, you probably didn't wonder what role attentional processes play in this visual search

It is clear that effects of visual attention, particularly spatial attention, can be detected at multiple stages of visual information processing. The effects begin as early as the LGN of the thalamus, and they include early and later stages of visual cortical processing. It is also clear that information processing in visual cortex is influenced by top-down attentional control systems that bias the activity of visual neurons. One question that remains unclear is whether attention can influence visual information processing at multiple loci along the ascending visual pathways, or if instead, attentional filtering takes place by influencing a single early stage of processing, such as the subcortical relays, and then passively transmits the effects of attention to later stages of visual analysis.

Functional imaging studies demonstrate that, when participants prepare for a target in one location in the visual field while ignoring other locations, the background (pre-target) activity in multiple loci in the ascending visual pathways increases, suggesting that attention does act simultaneously at multiple stages. But this evidence is somewhat indirect.

Bestmann and colleagues (2007) attained more direct evidence with transcranial magnetic stimulation (TMS) to demonstrate that spatial attention can act directly on sites in the cortex. Using TMS in human volunteers, they induced phosphenes (see Chapter 5, page 211) by the direct stimulation of visual cortex and were able to demonstrate that visual percepts were influenced by attention.

They conducted this study as follows (Figure 1). Attention was covertly (without displacement of gaze) directed toward a particular location (left or right) during a task involving real visual stimuli. In two different conditions, attention was either cued with a predictive arrow cue or directed to the left or right in a sustained manner throughout a block consisting of many trials (essentially versions of the designs discussed previously in this chapter). The trick here was that, on some trials, instead of a real visual stimulus, TMS was applied to produce a phosphene, either at the attended location or in the opposite (unattended) hemifield. Thus, by measuring the phosphene threshold (PT), which is the amplitude of the TMS pulse needed to create a phosphene for the observer, the researchers could determine whether perception of the TMS-induced phosphenes was influenced by spatial attention.

Bestmann and colleagues found that PTs were lowered for trials in which the TMS pulse was delivered to the visual cortex that corresponded to the attended (contralateral) visual hemifield: This meant that spatial attention was modulating the TMS-induced phosphenes. Because these "signals" in visual cortex did not pass through the thalamic relays to reach visual cortex, this evidence suggests that attention can act directly within the sensory cortex and does not rely on the modulation of visual inputs in the LGN. That is, the direct activation of visual cortex using transcranial magnetic stimulation in humans provides converging evidence that attentional control is not limited to gating subcortical inputs to cortex. This statement does not, of course, imply that attention does not influence processing in the LGN (in this chapter, we have reviewed evidence that this influence does occur). Rather, the TMS study demonstrates that attention can act directly on cortical processing, independently of its actions in subcortical structures.

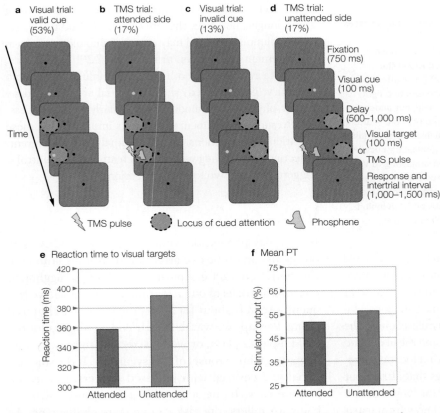

FIGURE 1 Attentional modulations of phosphenes induced by transcranial magnetic stimulation (TMS) in humans.

(a–d) Stimuli and task sequence in the spatial cuing design. Participants were shown an arrow cuing them to the left or right visual field. After a delay of 500 to 1,000 ms, they were shown either a target **(a)** or TMS-induced phosphenes **(b)** at the attended location, or a target **(c)** or TMS-induced phosphenes **(d)** at the unattended location. **(e)** Cuing produced the well-known reaction time benefits on target processing: Targets at the attended location were detected faster. **(f)** Similarly, the phosphene threshold (PT) was lower for TMS-induced phosphenes at the attended location.

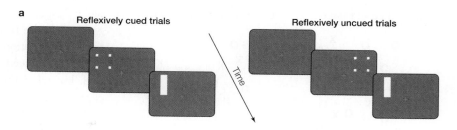

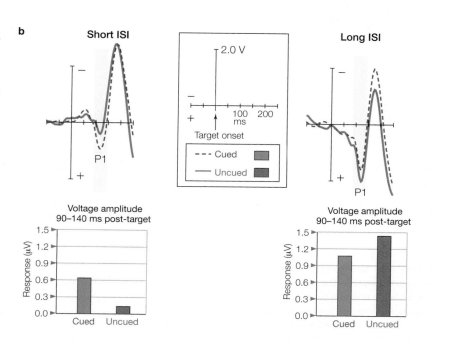

FIGURE 7.29 Event-related potential (ERP) waveforms from persons performing a reflexive cuing task.
(a) When attention is reflexively attracted to a location by an irrelevant abrupt onset of a visual stimulus, reaction times to subsequent targets presented to that same location are facilitated for short periods of time, as described in the text. **(b)** When ERPs are measured to these targets, the same cortical response (P1 wave—see yellow shaded time period) that is affected by voluntary spatial attention is enhanced by reflexive attention (dotted versus solid lines at left) for short cue-to-target interstimulus intervals (ISIs). The time course of this reflexive attention effect is not the same as that for voluntary cuing, but it is similar to the pattern observed in reaction times during reflexive cuing. The enhanced response is replaced within a few hundred milliseconds by a relative inhibition of the P1 response **(right)**.

process. Are you getting curious now? How are voluntary and reflexive spatial attention mechanisms related to visual search?

While we don't know if Anne Treisman (Princeton University) had suitcase issues at the airport, we do know that she and her colleagues have long been curious about the mechanisms of visual search. In one set of experiments, they observed that targets are located more quickly among a field of distracters if the target can be identified by a single stimulus feature, such as color (e.g., a red *O* among green *X*s and *O*s). It doesn't matter how many distracters appear in the array. We can demonstrate this relation by plotting participants' reaction times as a function of the number of distracter items in the display (search function), as shown in Figure 7.30. When the target can be identified by a single feature, such as the red *O* in Figure 7.30a (or one red suitcase in a sea of black suitcases), the resulting search function is flat (Figure 7.30c, blue line). We refer to this phenomenon as *pop-out* because the red *O* literally appears to pop out of the array of green letters based on its color alone. If the target shares features with the distracters, however, so that it cannot be distinguished by a single feature (e.g., a red *O* among green *X*s and *O*s and red *X*s,

as in Figure 7.30b, or a medium-sized red suitcase among medium-sized black suitcases and large red and black suitcases), then the time it takes to determine whether the target is present or absent in the array increases with the number of distracters in the array. The resulting search function is a sloped line (Figure 7.30c, red line). This type of search is known as a *conjunction search* because the target is defined by the conjunction of two or more features (e.g., the color red and the letter's identity as an *O*, or the color and size of the suitcase).

To explain why conjunction targets take longer to find, Treisman and Gelade (1980) proposed that while elementary stimulus features such as color, motion, shape, and spatial frequency can be analyzed preattentively and in parallel within multiple specialized feature maps (located within visual cortical areas), spatial attention is more complicated. Spatial attention must be directed to relevant stimuli in order to integrate the features into the perceived object, and it must be deployed in a sequential manner for each item in the array. This condition is necessary to link the information (in this case, color and letter identity, or suitcase color and size) in the different feature maps so that the target can be analyzed and identified.

a   Pop-out search   b   Conjunction search

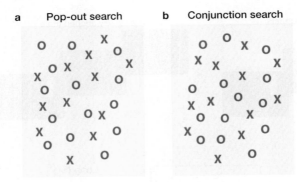

c

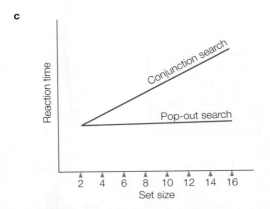

FIGURE 7.30 Searching for targets among distracters.
(a) A search array with a pop-out target (red O). Stimuli are said to pop out when they can be identified from among distracter stimuli by a simple single feature and the observer can find the target without searching the entire array. **(b)** A search array in which the target (red O) is defined by a conjunction of features shared with the distracters. **(c)** Idealized plot of reaction times as a function of set size (the number of items in the array) during visual search for pop-out stimuli versus feature conjunction stimuli. In pop-out searches, where an item can be distinguished from distracters by a single feature, the participants' reaction times do not increase as much because of set size as they do in conjunction searches.

This concept is called the **feature integration theory of attention**. Returning to the spotlight analogy, the idea here is that a spotlight of attention must move *sequentially* from one item in the array to another. Does this theory relate to the metaphorical spotlight of attention we introduced during our discussion of voluntary and reflexive spatial attention? Some evidence suggests that it does indeed.

To test this idea, Jeremy Wolfe and his colleagues (2000) at Harvard University asked: How does voluntary spatial attention modulate visual search? They employed a visual search task in which two conditions were compared. In one condition, participants knew in advance where to focus their attention, but in the other, the participants were not instructed where to focus their attention. Under the former condition—in which participants knew in advance where the target might be—the participants could use voluntary attention to perform the task. They found that people took longer to find their targets

when deliberate movements of attention were required in a visual search task compared to when deliberate movements of attention were not required and search was permitted to proceed automatically. These results may seem odd, but what they tell us is that visual search is most rapid when you permit the focus of attention to be driven by the visual sensory information in the array, rather than by executing a slow, voluntarily controlled search of the items. In other words, the brain automatically scans the visual world with a fast, automatic spotlight of attention. You will find that red suitcase faster if you allow your attention to wander randomly rather than directing your search from one suitcase to the next in an orderly way. We still don't know, however, how that automatic spotlight moves. Wolfe and colleagues conjectured that it also moved sequentially from item to item, but there is another possibility.

In most models, this automatic process involves low-level feature maps (maps about such things as borders, line orientation, color, etc.) of the visual world that provide information about the salience of objects. Based on feature information, spatial attention is reflexively biased toward the locations of the most salient objects. Then, the spotlight of attention can be focused on the location of interest, linking the features of the item, and enabling discrimination and identification in order to determine if it is the item of interest (There's my suitcase!). This model suggests that the spotlight of attention in visual search might be similar to the spotlight of attention observed in cuing paradigms. Is there any way to determine if there is a relationship between the spotlight of attention demonstrated in physiological studies (e.g., see Figure 7.17) and the findings from visual search studies?

Steven Luck and his colleagues (1993) hypothesized that if a probe stimulus were to appear at a location where spatial attention is focused during visual search, then it would elicit larger visual ERPs than when a probe appeared at locations where attention was not focused. To test this hypothesis, participants were presented with arrays that contained a field of upright and inverted blue, green, and red "t" shapes. In each trial, the target they were to look for was a "t" of a particular color (blue or green), of which there would be only one that varied in location from trial to trial—a pop-out (see Figure 7.31a). At brief time intervals after the search array was presented, a solitary ERP-eliciting probe stimulus was flashed either at the location of the pop-out target item (to the "t" where attention had been drawn) or at the location of a distracter item on the opposite side of the array. The probe stimulus was the white outline of a square, which appeared around either the blue "t" or the green "t," but never around a red "t."

The probe elicited larger early visual responses (P1) at the location of the designated conjunction target (where their attention was focused) as compared to regions where only distracters were present, thus supporting Luck's hypothesis. Perhaps a similar neural mechanism is at work for the early selection of visual information during visual search, as well as during voluntary attention in cuing and sustained attention paradigms. Of course, the difference is that, during visual search, the location of the target is not known until the search concludes. In the cuing paradigms or the sustained attention paradigms, however, attention is directed to a known location based on the information in the cue or in the verbal instructions given to the participant. Surprisingly, this difference doesn't seem to matter. In both cases, spatial attention changes early processing in the visual cortex through neural mechanisms that appear to be quite similar.

Despite knowing that spatial attention affects early processing in visual search, we still haven't answered the question about how spatial attention arrived at the location of the conjunction target. Was spatial attention automatically moving freely from item to item until the target was located, as suggested by the work of Jeremy Wolfe and colleagues? Or was visual information in the array helping to guide the movements of spatial attention among the array items, as other models have proposed? That is, does spatial attention have to precede feature or object attention in a hierarchical fashion? Or can object features (e.g., shape and color) be identified and selected, at least to some extent, independently of spatial attention, as suggested in Treisman's feature integration theory? Perhaps feature attention provides a signal that enables spatial attention to be directed to the location of a stimulus containing a relevant feature, whereupon more detailed analysis within the focus of spatial attention can take place. The neurophysiological evidence described next supports the latter schema, which has been predicted in numerous models (e.g., see A. Cohen & Ivry, 1989).

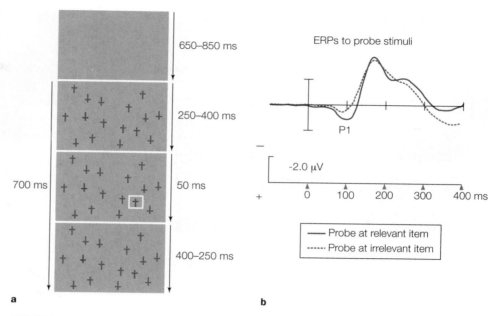

FIGURE 7.31

(a) Stimuli were shown to participants, who were told to search for either a blue or green "t" on each trial, and to indicate with a button push whether that item was upright or inverted. The red "t's" were always irrelevant distracters. An irrelevant white outlined square was flashed (50 ms duration) as a probe stimulus either around the blue or green "t." Moreover, the white probe could be flashed around the blue or green item when the colored item was the target, or when it was merely an irrelevant distracter. In this way, the amplitude of the probe ERP could be taken as an index of the location and strength of spatial attention just after the onset of the search array, at the point where participants would have located the target and discriminated its form (upright or inverted). The white probe was flashed either 250 ms or 400 ms after the onset search array. The search array remained on the screen for 700 ms. **(b)** The irrelevant white probe elicited a larger sensory-evoked occipital P1 wave when it occurred at the location of a relevant target (e.g., blue "t") compared to the irrelevant target (e.g., green "t"). These findings support the idea that focal spatial attention is directed to the location of the target in the array during visual search, and show that this corresponds to amplitude modulations in early visual cortex, just as in spatial cuing paradigms.

Feature Attention

So far, we have focused on visual *spatial* attention, the ability to direct our attention to some locations at the expense of others in the environment. Although we have been concentrating on visual attention, for completeness we will add that spatial attention also influences auditory and somatosensory information processing. As our own experience tells us, we have learned that selectively attending to spatial locations, either voluntarily or reflexively, leads to changes in our ability to detect and respond to stimuli in the sensory world. As Robert Louis Stevenson pointed out, however, the world is full of objects of interest, some more interesting than others. For instance, when you gaze across the expanse of Monument Valley (Figure 7.32), your attention is not drawn to some random bush, but to the mesas. Why does that happen?

Objects are defined by their collection of elementary features, as we discussed in Chapters 5 and 6. We will

FIGURE 7.32 Photo of Monument Valley in northern Arizona. How is your attention attracted when you view this picture? What are the salient objects that jump out to you?

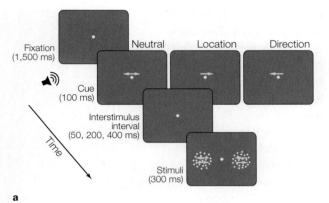

a

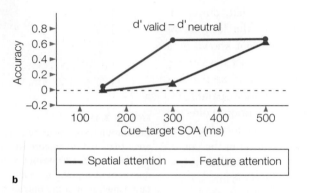

b

FIGURE 7.33 Precuing attention to visual features improved performance.
(a) Each trial began with a warning tone that was followed by one of three types of cues. The cues indicated either the location or the direction of motion of the subsequent target if present, and the double-headed arrow indicated that the location or direction of motion was equiprobably left or right. **(b)** The difference in accuracy of detection (valid vs. neutral cue) of the moving dots is plotted here as a function of cue-to-target stimulus onset asynchrony (**SOA**) in milliseconds, for both the spatial attention and feature attention conditions. (SOA is the amount of time between the start of one stimulus and the start of another stimulus.) Note that in both cases, the selective attention effects build up over time, such that at longer SOAs, the effects are larger, with the spatial attention effects appearing more rapidly in this study.

now revisit these concepts with selective attention in mind.

How does selectively attending to a stimulus feature (e.g., motion, color, shape) or object properties (e.g., a face vs. a house) influence information processing? For instance, if cued to expect that an upcoming stimulus is moving, are we better able to discriminate the target stimulus if indeed it is moving than if it is unexpectedly not moving? If your friend says she will pick you up at the airport and will drive around the airport terminals until you spot her, will it take you longer to spot her if she is parked at the curb instead? And, of course, we still want to know how feature and spatial attention interact, given that the world is full of features and objects located in specific locations.

Marissa Carrasco and her colleagues at New York University performed a set of experiments to address these questions. They compared *spatial attention* and *feature attention* in a voluntary cuing paradigm. The dependent measure of attention was detection accuracy (Liu et al., 2007). In one condition (using spatial attention), arrow cues were used to indicate the location where attention should be directed. In the other condition (the feature attention condition), arrows indicated the direction of motion of the upcoming target (Figure 7.33a). The researchers found that prior knowledge from the cue produced the typical voluntary cuing effect for spatial attention: Participants were more accurate at detecting the presence of the target (a change in the velocity of moving dots) at the cued location compared to when the cue (a double-headed arrow) did not signal one location over another (Figure 7.33b, red line). In a similar vein, they found that, during the feature attention condition, cuing the direction of motion of the target also enhanced accuracy independently of whether it appeared in the left

or right visual field array (Figure 7.33b, blue line). Thus, pre-cuing attention to a visual feature (motion direction in this case) improved performance. This finding tells us that attention can be directed in advance to spatial locations as well as to nonspatial features of the target stimuli. Now let's ferret out the neural bases of selective attention to features and objects, and contrast these mechanisms with those of spatial attention.

In the early 1980s, Thomas Münte, a German neurologist working in Steve Hillyard's lab developed a clever experimental paradigm (Hillyard & Münte, 1984). Using ERPs, they isolated the brain responses that are related to selectively attending the color of a stimulus from those related to attending stimulus location. Rather than cuing participants to different stimulus features, they presented participants with blocks of many trials where small red and blue vertical rectangles were flashed in a random sequence in the left and right visual fields (the rectangles could be tall or short). Each block of trials lasted a minute or so. Participants fixated on the central crosshairs on the screen while covertly attending to one color at the attended location. They ignored the other color at the attended location, as well as ignoring both colors at the unattended location.

For example, participants were told, "For the next minute, attend and push the button to the shorter red bars on the right only." On the next block, they were told, "For the next minute, attend and push the button to the shorter blue bars on the right only." In other blocks of trials, they were also told the same for the bars on the left. Thus, there were four different attention conditions, and the investigators could compare the ERPs generated under the four conditions. In this ingenious setup, the comparisons independently revealed the processing for spatial attention and feature attention. For example, spatial attention to a left–red stimulus (attend left vs. attend right) could be experimentally uncoupled from feature attention (attend red vs. attend blue). The brain responses for each of these conditions are shown in Figure 7.34. In

Figure 7.34a, the ERPs show the typical spatial attention effects shown earlier in Figure 7.17 (solid vs. dotted ERP trace). Figure 7.34b shows the ERPs showing the color attention ERPs. Note the very different patterns that spatial and color attention produced in the ERPs, which are especially obvious in the ERP attention difference waves (Figure 7.34c vs. d). The early P1 wave that indexes spatial attention (top row) is absent for color attention (bottom row), which shows only longer latency changes in the waveform. Also of interest from this work is that effects of color attention were largely absent at the unattended location (lower right traces solid vs. dotted). This research indicates that both spatial and feature attention can produce selective processing of visual stimuli, and that the mechanisms for spatial and feature attention differ. Good to know, but exactly where do these feature attention effects take place in the brain?

Well, it depends. Maurizio Corbetta and his colleagues at Washington University investigated what neural systems are involved in feature discrimination under two different conditions: divided attention and selective attention (Corbetta et al., 1991). In one of the first neuroimaging studies of selective attention, the researchers

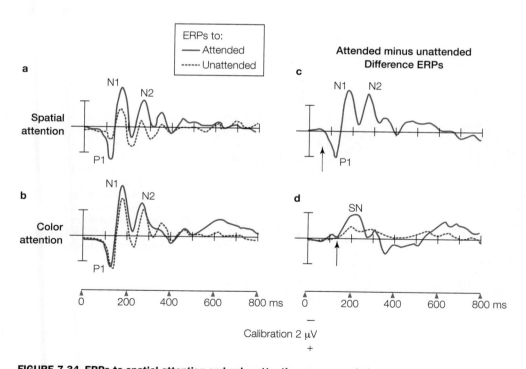

FIGURE 7.34 ERPs to spatial attention and color attention are uncoupled.
(a) ERPs recorded to right visual field stimuli when subjects covertly attended right (solid line) and when subjects attended left (dotted line) independently of stimulus color or which color was attended. **(b)** ERPs to right visual field stimuli when attending right and the color of the evoking stimulus was attended (solid line) versus when attending right but the unattended color was presented there (dotted line). **(c)** Difference ERPs associated with attended versus unattended spatial locations. **(d)** Difference ERPs associated with stimuli of attended versus unattended color at the attended location (solid line) and the unattended location (dotted line). The arrows in the right panels indicate the onset of the attention effects, which was later in this experiment for color attention. Positive voltage is plotted downward.

used PET to identify changes that occur in extrastriate cortex and elsewhere, when people selectively attend to a single stimulus feature such as color, shape, or motion versus when their attention was divided among all three features (as a comparison condition). Radioactive water was used as a tracer to monitor blood flow in the brain, as volunteers were shown pairs of visual displays containing arrays of stimulus elements. The first display of each trial was a reference stimulus, such as a red square; the second was a test stimulus, perhaps a green circle. The participants' task during the selective attention condition was to compare the two arrays to determine whether a change had occurred to a *pre-specified* stimulus dimension (color, shape, or motion). During the divided attention condition, participants were instructed to detect a change in *any of the three* stimulus dimensions. This experimental design permitted the investigators to contrast brain activity under conditions in which the participants selectively attended a particular stimulus dimension (e.g., only color) with the condition in which they divided their attention among all stimulus dimensions. As you might expect, behavioral sensitivity for discriminating slight changes in a stimulus was higher when judging only one feature (selective attention) rather than multiple features (divided attention).

Selective attention to one feature activated distinct, largely nonoverlapping regions of extrastriate cortex (Figure 7.35) in comparison to divided attention. Extrastriate cortical regions specialized for the perceptual processing of color, form, or motion were modulated only during visual attention to the corresponding stimulus features. These findings provide additional support for the idea that *selective attention*, in modality-specific cortical areas, alters the perceptual processing of inputs *before the completion of feature analysis*. Subsequent fMRI studies have identified specialized areas of human visual cortex that process features, such as stimulus motion or color. Corresponding areas had been found previously in monkey visual cortex. These specialized feature analysis regions are modulated by selective visual attention, as suggested by the earlier work of Corbetta and colleagues.

When do these various attention effects occur during processing? To address this question, one study combined MEG and fMRI in order to provide temporal and spatial information (Schoenfeld et al., 2007). Participants were cued to attend selectively to either changes in color or changes in motion that could occur in an upcoming display (Figure 7.36a). The stimulus sequence randomly presented motion and color changes, permitting the measurement of brain activity in response to

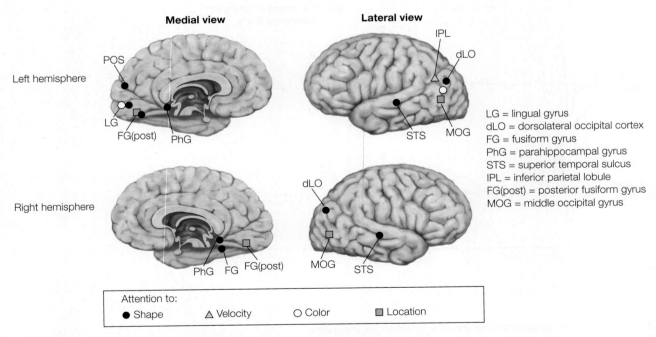

FIGURE 7.35 Summary of early neuroimaging attention studies using position emission tomography (PET).
PET studies by Corbetta and colleagues (1991), Heinze and colleagues (1994), and Mangun and colleagues (1997) revealed regions of extrastriate cortex specialized for the processing of color, shape, or motion (from the work of Corbetta) that are selectively modulated during visual attention to these stimulus features (feature selective attention). As described earlier, we now know that spatial attention influences processing in multiple visual cortical areas (see Figure 7.21) and in subcortical structures (see Figures 7.27 and 7.28).

a

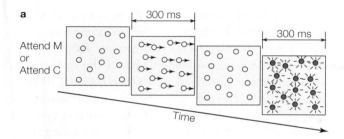

Attend M
or
Attend C

300 ms

300 ms

Time

b Motion attention

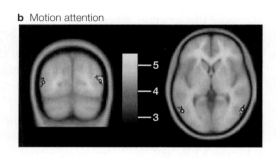

c Color attention

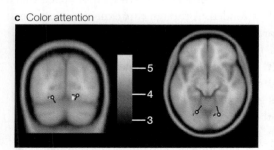

d

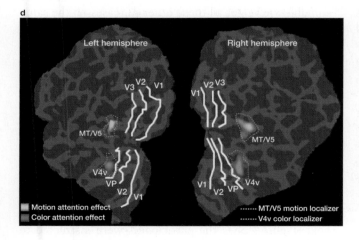

Left hemisphere

Right hemisphere

V3 V2 V1

V2 V3

V1

MT/V5

MT/V5

V4v

VP

V4v

V2 V1

V1 VP

V2

■ Motion attention effect
■ Color attention effect

······ MT/V5 motion localizer
······ V4v color localizer

FIGURE 7.36 Attention modulates activity in feature-specific visual cortex.
(a) Blocks began with a letter cue (*M* or *C*) indicating that participants should attend to either motion (fast versus slow) or color (red versus orange), respectively, and press a button representing the indicated feature. Dots would appear, and they randomly would either move or change color. In this way, responses to changes in motion (or color) could be contrasted when motion was attended versus when color was attended. **(b)** When motion was attended, activity in lateral occipitotemporal regions (human MT/V5) was modulated. **(c)** When color was attended, ventral area V4 (V4v in the posterior fusiform gyrus) was modulated. This relation was found for fMRI BOLD responses (shown as the reddish yellow blobs on the MRI) and for MEG measures taken in a separate session (shown as circles with arrows in **(b)** and **(c)**, overlapping regions of significant BOLD signal change). The high temporal resolution of the MEG measures indicated that the latency of the attention effect after the onset of the moving or color arrays was about 100 ms. **(d)** Retinotopic mapping on a single participant verifies the extrastriate region associated with the motion and color attention effects on flattened cortical representations.

changes in either feature as a function of attention to motion or color. By using fMRI to localize brain regions sensitive to selective attention to color or motion, the investigators found (as expected) that attending to motion modulated activity in the visual cortical motion processing area MT/V5 (in the dorsal stream). Similarly, attending to color led to modulations in ventral visual cortex area V4 (in the ventral stream; Figure 7.36b–d). Importantly, the team's related MEG recordings demonstrated that attention-related activity in these areas appeared with a latency of 100 ms or less after onset of the change in the stimulus—much sooner than previous studies had reported.

Thus, feature-based selective attention acts at relatively early stages of visual cortical processing with relatively short latencies after stimulus onset. Spatial attention, however, still beats the clock and has an earlier effect. We see, once again, that the effects of feature attention occur with longer latencies (100 ms vs. 70

ms after stimulus onset) and at later stages of the visual hierarchy (extrastriate cortex rather than striate cortex or the subcortical visual relays in the thalamus).

Interplay Between Spatial and Feature Attention

Are features selected before spatial attention is focused on a target location or after? Max Hopf and his colleagues (Hopf et al., 2004) used a visual search task while they recorded ERPs of participants to address this question. Before looking at this study, we need to talk about ERPs. Early P1 attention effects are followed in time by other ERPs that index nonspatial, feature-based attention, collectively referred to as *feature selection ERPs* (see Figure 7.34). Steve Luck and Steve Hillyard (1994) identified a human brain wave they called N2pc, where *N2* refers to the second negative deflection, and *pc* refers to *p*osterior electrode site *c*ontralateral to the attended stimulus, the location where the component appears. Experimental work has established that the N2pc component of a spatial selection ERP is a sign of the covert focusing of visual spatial attention during visual search. It represents a stage of processing that occurs before object recognition is completed.

In the study by Hopf and colleagues, the team investigated mechanisms of visual search by using feature selection ERPs and the N2pc as indices of feature and spatial attention, respectively. In the visual search task, the spatial distribution of distracters (variously colored and oriented C-shaped items) was varied independently of the location of the target. Participants could locate the target item by relying solely on its unique color (pop-out). The distracting features provided no information about the target's location or identity. By using simultaneous ERP and MEG recordings, the researchers found that, 140 ms after onset of the search array, a feature selection ERP was generated in ventral occipito-temporal cortex (blue and red dots in Figure 7.37). This feature attention effect was quickly followed (about 30 ms later) by an N2pc response generated in more anterior regions of the occipitotemporal cortex, indicating that the participants were focusing spatial attention on the target.

These findings clearly demonstrate that feature selective attention may *precede* visuospatial attention *when the location of the target is* not *known in advance* (as is always the case in visual search paradigms). These intriguing results suggest that feature selection may

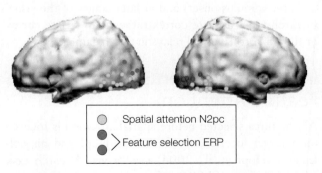

FIGURE 7.37 Feature and spatial attention mechanisms in visual search.
Lateral views of left **(a)** and right **(b)** hemispheres rendered from MRI scans showing the locations of feature (red and blue circles) and spatial (yellow circles) attention effects. Feature selection ERPs occurred earlier (onset of 140 ms) over more posterior regions of occipitotemporal cortex; subsequent spatial attention ERPs (N2pc) were slightly later in time (onset 170 ms) and were localized by means of MEG to slightly more anterior locations in occipitotemporal cortex.

guide subsequent shifts of attention to the locations of those features so that higher resolution mechanisms can process and identify conjunction targets. This concept would be consistent with the tenets of the feature integration theory, described earlier (see Figure 7.30 and associated text). If it is true that feature attention is separate from and does not depend on spatial attention, then we might expect to see effects of attending to a feature, such as color, outside the region of space that is currently attended. Although this expectation makes sense, it presents a quandary. Previous studies that investigated feature attention (color) at attended versus unattended locations found no evidence for feature attention outside the attended location (see Figure 7.34). What was going on?

Weiwei Zhang and Steve Luck (2009) reasoned that these previous studies had neglected to consider that attention selection is dependent on competition. After all, visual search involves multiple competitive stimuli—we've got all those other suitcases on the same baggage carousel where our suitcase should be. The researchers hypothesized that under such conditions, if attention to features can affect sensory processing outside the attended region of space, then when attending a feature, such as the color red because our suitcase is red, a task-irrelevant red item (a heart-shaped box of Valentine candy) presented in an unattended location (sitting in someone's baggage cart) might elicit a larger response in visual cortex than a green item, which, in this case, is an irrelevant color. How did they test this hypothesis? They asked participants to view a monitor that displayed a continuous stream of red and green dots in one visual field (Figure 7.38). The participants were instructed to attend to the red dots but ignore the green dots. Sometimes the streams of red and green colored dots were presented simultaneously, and at other times the red and green streams of dots were presented sequentially. The participants' task was to push a button when the brightness of the attended color stimuli decreased momentarily. Occasionally, as shown in the figure, a display of colored dots (probe stimulus) in either the attended or unattended color was flashed briefly to the opposite (unattended) side of the visual field. These stimuli were task-irrelevant, and to be ignored. Then, using recordings of ERPs from scalp electrodes, the researchers measured the activity in visual cortex to the probe, which was either the same color as the participant was attending, or a different color. They did these measurements in the two conditions of simultaneous and sequential presentation of the task-relevant red and green colored arrays. What did the scientists find?

When the attended array contained both the attended (red) and unattended (green) dots at the same time—

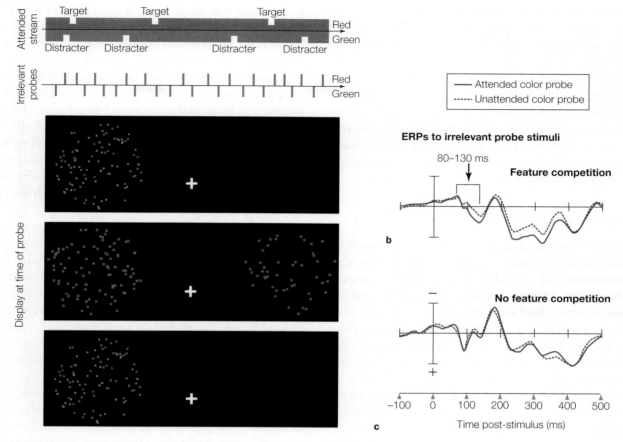

FIGURE 7.38 Feature attention mechanisms with and without feature competition.
(a) In the condition where there was feature competition, red and green dots were intermingled as streams of stimuli during each 15 second trial. The participants' task was to covertly attend to and detect a decrement in luminance of the to-be-attended color, while ignoring the intermingled dots of the other color. Task-irrelevant probe stimuli, either all-green or all-red occasionally flashed in the opposite visual hemifield. Thus, the probe stimuli could share the feature color with the attended stimuli or not. In a different condition where there was no feature competition (not shown), the task–relevant stimulus streams of red and green were presented separately in alternating sequence (i.e., all red or all green) with the task being the same one of detecting luminance decrements in one color while ignore the other. Once again in this condition, irrelevant probes of all red or all green dots were flashed in the unattended hemifield. **(b)** ERPs to the probe stimuli during feature competition. The ERPs showed a significant increase in amplitude to the irrelevant probe of the attended color compared to the irrelevant probe of the unattended color in the latency range of 80–130 msec over contralateral occipital scalp (characteristic of the P1 component). **(c)** ERPs to the probe stimuli when there was no feature competition (the red and green streams of dots were not present simultaneously). During the same short-latency time period (80–130 ms), there were no significant differences in the waveforms evoked by the irrelevant probes when they shared versus did not share the color of the attended targets in the streams. Feature attention, therefore, may only result in facilitation of relevant feature information outside the focus of spatial attention when there is competition between relevant and irrelevant features.

that is, *when there was some stimulus competition*—then the ERPs elicited by the probe were greater in amplitude for the attended color (Figure 7.38b). This was true even though the probe was flashed at an unattended location. Thus, attending to a color (red) in one stimulus location facilitated processing of stimuli in that same color (red) located at another location in the visual field that was outside the focus of spatial attention. Not only that, but the effect could occur at short latencies in the brain

response—as short as attention effects for spatial attention are often observed (by 80–100 msec after probe onset). As we described earlier, spatial attention effects are typically found to precede nonspatial (feature and object) effects of attention (see Figure 7.34 for comparison), but not in the face of feature competition.

Importantly, the researchers found this effect only when the attended array contained both the attended (red) and unattended (green) color dots intermingled at the same time, not when they were presented sequentially (Figure 7.38c). Once again, we see how the degree of competition among stimuli can influence attention. This study provides evidence that attention to color may activate color-sensitive neurons across the visual field, and it can explain how searching for a red stimulus (or a red suitcase) may guide the focusing of spatial attention. That is, if the color red, for example, is the relevant feature, and it evokes a larger sensory response wherever in space it is located, this signal might summon spatial attention to that location.

Object Attention

We have now described the effects of spatial-based attention and feature-based attention in visual cortex. Can attention also act on higher order stimulus representations, namely, objects? When searching for a friend in a crowd, we don't merely search *where* we think our friend will be, especially if we haven't agreed on a place to meet. We also don't search for our friend only by hair color (unless it is highly salient, like fluorescent pink). Rather, we look for the conjunction of features that define the person. For lack of a better word, we can refer to this quality as *object properties*—the collection of elementary stimulus features that, when combined in a particular way, yield an identifiable object or person. Behavioral work has demonstrated evidence for *object-based attention* mechanisms.

In a seminal study, John Duncan (1984) contrasted attention to location (spatial attention) with attention to objects (object-based attention). Holding spatial distance constant, he discovered that two perceptual judgments concerning the same object can be made simultaneously without loss of accuracy, whereas the same two judgments about different objects cannot. For instance, in a split second you can process that a dog is big and brown; but when two dogs are present, processing that one is big and the other is brown takes longer. This processing limitation in attending to two objects implicates an object-based attention system in addition to a space-based system. In line with this view, the behavioral reaction time *costs* (slowing) and *benefits* (speeding) of the spatial cues of attention are greater *between* two objects as compared to within one object (Egly et al., 1994). This result suggests that the spread of attention is facilitated within the confines of an object, or that there is an additional cost to move attention between objects, or both.

Notger Mueller and Andreas Kleinschmidt (2003) designed an fMRI study to determine what effect objects had on spatial attention. They wondered if attending to an object had any impact on processing in the early visual processing areas, and if so, what? They cued participants on a trial-by-trial basis to expect a target at one location in the visual field (e.g., upper left quadrant) and then presented targets there on most trials (valid trials). In a minority of trials, they presented them to uncued locations (invalid trials). Following the design of Egly et al. (1994), Mueller and Kleinschmidt included objects on the screen so that the uncued target could fall within the same object that was cued (but at another location in the object), or at another location that was not within the bounds of that object. To get a better idea of their design, look at Figure 7.39a.

The displayed objects were wrench-like figures, and these figures could be oriented horizontally on the screen or vertically. For example, when the wrenches were oriented horizontally and the upper left quadrant location was cued, the upper right quadrant location would be spatially uncued (unattended) but be within the *same* object. When the wrenches were vertically oriented, however, that location would be spatially uncued and within a *different* object. Mueller and Kleinschmidt replicated the behavioral reaction time effects of Egly and colleagues (Figure 7.39b). What's more, they found that in visual cortical areas V1 through V4, *increased activity* occurred in uncued locations that were located on the same object (the wrench) as the cued location compared to when the uncued location was not on the same object that was cued (Figure 7.39c–d).

This result is evidence that the presence of objects influences the way spatial attention is allocated in space: In essence, attention spreads within the object, thereby leading to some activity for uncued locations on the object as well. An effect of spatial attention also remains, because within the object, the cued location still shows greater activity than do uncued locations. Thus, object representations can modulate spatial attention. Can attention to objects also operate independently of spatial attention?

An ingenious fMRI study was done (O'Craven et al., 1999) to address this question. It made use of the knowledge that (a) faces activate the fusiform face area (FFA; see Chapter 6), which is less active in response to images of other objects, such as houses; and (b) a region of parahippocampal cortex is more active in response to images of houses than faces (the so-called parahippocampal place area, or PPA). What was so clever about this study?

First, the researchers presented superimposed, transparent images of faces and houses so that they occupied the same region of space yet could be seen at the same time (Figure 7.40). Then, they designed the display so

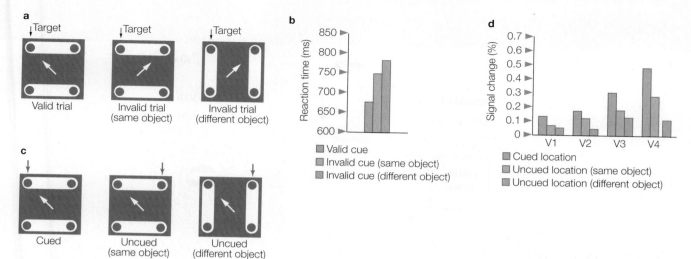

FIGURE 7.39 Object representations can modulate spatial attention.
(a) Wrench-like objects were continually presented on the screen and were oriented horizontally **(left and middle)** or vertically **(right)**. On each trial, a centrally located cue (white arrow) indicated the most likely location of subsequent targets that required a fast response whether at the cued location (frequent) or elsewhere (infrequent). **(b)** Reaction times to targets were fastest when the cues validly predicted the target location, were slowest to invalid cue trials when the target appeared on a different object, and were intermediate in speed for invalid trials where the target appeared on the same object. **(c)** Stimulus display for the fMRI experiment, where the upper left location was always cued and where the target appeared on most trials. Uncued locations in the upper right quadrant (for example) could be either on the same object as the cued location **(middle)** or on a different object **(right)**. The red arrows above each panel indicate the visual field locations corresponding to regions of interest in the visual cortex from which hemodynamic responses were extracted. **(d)** Hemodynamic responses (percentage signal change) are shown as bar graphs from regions of interest in visual cortical areas V1 to V4. In each area, the largest response is in the cued location, and smaller responses are obtained from uncued locations (the main effect of spatial attention). Importantly, when the uncued location was on the same object as the cued location, the fMRI activation was larger, demonstrating the effect of object attention.

that one of the objects moved back and forth while the other was stationary. The motion of the moving stimulus activated cortical motion area MT/V5. Which image moved and which was stationary varied in different blocks. In these different blocks, participants were told to attend selectively to the face, to the house, or to the motion. The activity in the FFA, the PPA, or MT/V5 provided relatively pure measures of the responses to each of these three stimulus dimensions. When participants attended to faces, activity in the FFA increased but activity in the PPA did not; when the participants attended to houses, the opposite pattern of activity was observed. Interestingly, when participants selectively attended to the motion, activity in the MT/MST increased, as did activity in the region (FFA or PPA) corresponding to the object that was moving (face or house, respectively).

The results from the house-face study demonstrate how attention acts on object representations: Attention facilitates processing of all the features of the attended

object. For example, face processing was facilitated when the attended moving stimulus was a face, even though the task did not require identification or attention to the face itself. Importantly, these findings show that, when spatial attention is not involved, *object representations can be the level of perceptual analysis affected by goal-directed attentional control.*

Review of Attention and Perceptual Selection Mechanisms

While we most likely have realized from experience that attention affects the processing of perceptual stimuli, we are not conscious of when, where, and to what extent in the chain of processing that attention exerts its effects. The studies presented in this portion of the chapter are beginning to reveal how and where attention affects processing of perceptual stimuli. We now know that visual spatial

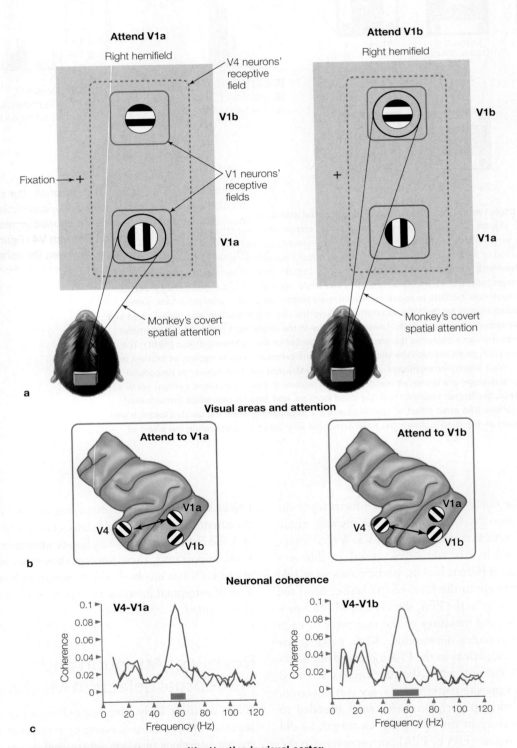

FIGURE 1 Neuronal coherence with attention in visual cortex.
(a) Stimuli consisted of grating stimuli that were in the same V4 receptive field (larger dashed green box) but were in different receptive fields in area V1 (smaller red and blue boxes). (b) Diagram of the left visual cortex of the macaque monkey, showing two regions in V1 (V1a and V1b) that mapped the stimuli shown in (a), as well as how these stimuli were represented in higher order visual area V4. The arrows indicate hypothesized coherences in attention. (c) Neuronal coherence is shown between regions of V1 and V4, depending on which stimulus is attended (see text for more details).

When attention is focused on a stimulus, something happens to the neurons in the visual system that causes the higher visual areas to represent primarily the attended stimulus. Neurons might be modulated by various hypothetical mechanisms, and although we remain uncertain about the precise mechanisms, some interesting models are being tested. One such model suggests that at different stages of visual analysis (e.g., V1 and V4), neurons that code the receptive field location of an attended stimulus show increased synchrony in their activity.

Pascal Fries and his colleagues (Bosman et al., 2012) used cortical surface grids of more than 250 electrodes in the monkey to test this model. They presented monkeys with two drifting gratings separated in visual space, and they trained the monkeys to keep their eyes fixed on a central crosshair but covertly attend one of the drifting gratings at a time to detect when the shape of the gratings changed slightly (Figure 1a). Given the retinotopic organization and small receptive field sizes (~1 degree of visual angle) in V1, stimuli separated by several degrees stimulate different populations of neurons in V1. In higher order visual areas like V4, which have much larger receptive fields (several degrees of visual angle), however, the same stimuli fall within the receptive field of the same V4 neuron (Figure 1a).

The researchers hypothesized that if spatial attention can alter the flow of information from early stages of the visual hierarchy (V1) to later stages (V4) in a spatially specific manner, then this effect might be subserved by selective synchronization of local field potentials (LFPs) between these early and later stages of visual processing (Figure 1b). That is precisely what they observed. They measured the cortical surface LFPs oscillating in the gamma-band frequency (60–80 Hz) and found that coherence increased with spatial attention between the site in V1 coding the attended stimulus location (e.g., location V1a in the figure) and the V4 site coding the stimulus location. So, if the monkey attended location V1a, it showed increased synchronization in gamma-bond LFPs with V4 (Figure 1c, left panel, red). At the same time, however, the coherence remained low between the other V1 location which coded the ignored location (e.g., location V1b in the figure) and V4 (shown in Figure 1c, left panel, blue). Interestingly enough, though, when the animal was cued to switch attention to the other stimulus location (i.e., V1b in the figure), then the V1–V4 coherence went up for that V1 site and V4, and coherence at the first location dropped (shown in Figure 1c, right panel, blue vs. red). These studies suggest that attention alters the effective connectivity between neurons by altering the inter-areal pattern of rhythmic synchronization.

attention can affect the processing of a stimulus very early in the ascending sensory pathway, and we know where in the cortex this happens. In this section, we also have seen that attention enhances the processing of features of a stimulus. Attention can also be directed at objects. As we have seen, attention mechanisms involve the neuronal machinery specific to processing a particular feature or object. The effects of attention go beyond simple space and feature processing. We have just learned that attention can speed the processing of all the features within an object.

TAKE-HOME MESSAGES

- Spatial attention influences the processing of visual inputs: Attended stimuli produce greater neural responses than do ignored stimuli, and this process takes place in multiple visual cortical areas.
- Highly focused spatial attention can also modulate activity in the visual system in the subcortical relay nuclei in the thalamus, thereby providing strong evidence for early-selection models of attention.

- Reflexive attention is automatic and is activated by stimuli that are conspicuous in some way. Reflexive attention also results in changes in early sensory processing, although only transiently.
- A hallmark of reflexive attention is inhibition of return—the phenomenon in which the recently reflexively attended location becomes inhibited over time such that responses to stimuli occurring there are slowed.
- Extrastriate cortical regions specialized for the perceptual processing of color, form, or motion can be modulated during visual attention to the individual stimulus features.
- Selective attention can be directed at spatial locations, at object features, or at an entire object.

Attentional Control Networks

Thus far, we have been considering the influence of attention on sensory processing; we have been looking at the *sites of influence of attention*. This is only part of the

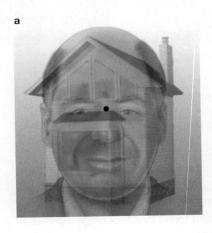

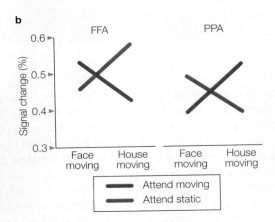

FIGURE 7.40 **Attention modulates object representations in the brain.** **(a)** Houses and faces were superimposed transparently to create stimuli that participants could not attend to using spatial mechanisms. **(b)** Functional MRI signal intensity for the different conditions of attention from regions of interest in the fusiform face area (FFA) and the parahippocampal place area (PPA).

attention story. For the rest of the chapter, we turn to how the focus of attention is controlled.

Control of attention can be both goal directed (top-down) and stimulus directed (bottom-up). Right now, you are using goal-directed attention to focus on this book. But if the fire alarm goes off, your attention will be grabbed by the stimulus, a bottom-up intrusion. Spatial attention is controlled by a mixture of stimulus-driven and goal-directed mechanisms. In goal-directed attention, neuronal projections from executive attentional control systems (with inputs about goals, emotional states, personal experiences, etc.) contact neurons in sensory-specific cortical areas to alter their excitability. As a result, the response in the sensory areas to a stimulus may be enhanced if the stimulus is given high priority, or attenuated if it is irrelevant to the current goal. In contrast, in stimulus-driven attention, the stimulus itself—or some salient features of the stimulus—captures attention, so presumably this process involves circuits from the sensory system interacting with those that orient and engage attention. Selective attention may mediate cortical excitability in the visual cortex through a network that includes at least the posterior parietal cortex, the dorsolateral and superior prefrontal cortex, and the pulvinar nucleus of the thalamus (Figure 7.41). More generally, though, attentional control systems are involved in modulating thoughts and actions, as well as sensory processes.

Studies of patients with either unilateral neglect or Bálint's syndrome have provided us clues about the control of attention. As noted earlier in this chapter, bilateral lesions to portions of the posterior parietal and occipital cortex result in Bálint's syndrome, and unilateral lesions of the parietal, temporal, and frontal cortex, especially in the right hemisphere, are implicated in neglect. Neglect may also result from damage to subcortical structures like the superior colliculus and parts of the thalamus. Neurologists, including M. Marcel Mesulam and his colleagues, have described how damage in a variety of these brain

areas results in symptoms of neglect (Mesulam, 1981). Mesulam suggested that the disorder of neglect was the result of damage to the brain's attention network, not the result of damage to a specific brain area (e.g., parietal cortex). What structures constitute the brain's attentional control network? Does a single network control attention, or are multiple networks involved?

Current models of attentional control suggest that two separate frontoparietal cortical systems are at play in directing different attentional operations during selective attention: a *dorsal attention system*, primarily concerned with spatial attention, and a *ventral attention system*, concerned with the nonspatial aspects of attention (Corbetta & Shulman, 2011). It appears that the two control systems interact and cooperate to produce normal behavior. These interactions are disrupted in patients with neglect. These models are based on behavioral studies in healthy persons or in patients with brain lesions, as well as the results of neuroimaging and electrophysiology experiments.

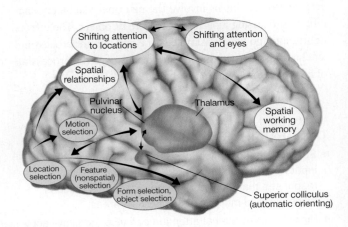

FIGURE 7.41 **Sources and sites of attention.** Model of executive control systems, showing how visual cortex processing is affected by the goal-directed control of a network of brain areas.

Dorsal Attention Network: Frontoparietal Attention System

Joseph Hopfinger and his colleagues (2000) and Maurizio Corbetta and his coworkers (2000) both employed event-related fMRI to study attentional control. We reviewed some of the findings from Hopfinger's study earlier in this chapter, focusing on how spatial attention involves selective processing in visual cortex (the site of attention). Now, we return to this research to see what they learned about the brain regions that control attention.

Finding the Sources of Attentional Control Over Spatial Attention

Recall that Hopfinger used a modified spatial cuing paradigm, as shown in Figure 7.15. The participants were presented a cue and were required on some trials to orient attention to one half of the visual field and ignore the other. Then, 8 seconds later, stimuli were presented on both sides of space simultaneously, and the participant was to discriminate target features and make a response. Thus, a goal-directed attentional control network could be identified that was engaged by the appearance of the cue and that was active prior to the appearance of the target stimuli. Such activity can be ascribed to goal-directed attentional control.

What did the researchers find? When the participant attended and responded to the stimulus, a network of dorsal cortical regions showed increased activity. These regions together are called the *dorsal frontoparietal attention network*. None of the regions in this network were primarily involved in sensory processing of the visual features of the cue, which took place in the visual cortex. We now understand that this dorsal frontoparietal network reflects the *sources* of attention signals in the *goal-directed* control of attention. Why did the researchers conclude that these regions are involved in attentional control? First, the identified brain regions were found to be active only when the subjects were instructed (cued) to covertly attend either right or left locations. Second, when the targets appeared after the cue, a different pattern of activity was observed. Third, when participants only *passively* viewed the presented cues—and didn't attend to them or act on them—then these frontal-parietal brain regions that were active in the former condition were not activated during passive viewing, even though the visual cortex was engaged in processing the visual features of the passively viewed cues.

The key cortical nodes involved in the frontoparietal network include the frontal eye fields (FEF), located at the junction of the precentral and superior frontal sulcus in each hemisphere, and the supplementary eye fields (SEF) in the frontal cortex; the intraparietal sulcus

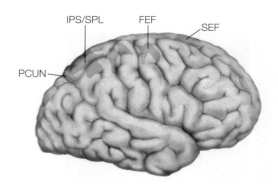

FIGURE 7.42 Cortical regions involved in attentional control. Diagrammatic representation of cortical activity seen during attentional control. In blue are the regions of the dorsal attention network, which includes the intraparietal sulcus (IPS), the superior parietal lobule (SPL), and the frontal eye fields (FEF).

(IPS); the superior parietal lobule (SPL) and precuneus (PC) in the posterior parietal lobe; and related regions (Figure 7.42). From studies like those from Hopfinger or Corbetta, we know that the dorsal frontoparietal network is active when voluntary attention is engaged. How does this network function to modulate sensory processing?

Linking the Control Network for Spatial Attention to Attentional Changes

First, let's look at the evidence that activity in the frontoparietal attention network is actually linked to attention-related changes in sensory processing. We'll take another look at Hopfinger's study (2000). After the cue was presented, but *before the target displays appeared*, activations were observed in visual cortical regions that would later process the incoming target (Figure 7.43). What caused the visual cortex to be activated even before any stimuli were presented? These activations in visual cortex were spatially specific—they were dependent on the direction of spatial attention. This attentional "priming" of the sensory cortex to a particular location may provide preferential processing to some target inputs (those in that location) over others, a result similar to what has been observed in neurophysiological studies in monkeys (Luck et al., 1997). This priming could be accomplished if neurons in the frontoparietal network send signals either directly or indirectly to the visual cortex, which produce selective changes in visual processing in those visual neurons (e.g., biasing inputs in favor of one location vs. another). Does any data support this biasing effect on the visual cortex?

Frontal Cortex and Attention Control

Indirect evidence comes from patients with prefrontal cortical lesions. Neurologist Robert T. Knight and his colleagues (Barceló et al., 2000) found that patients with

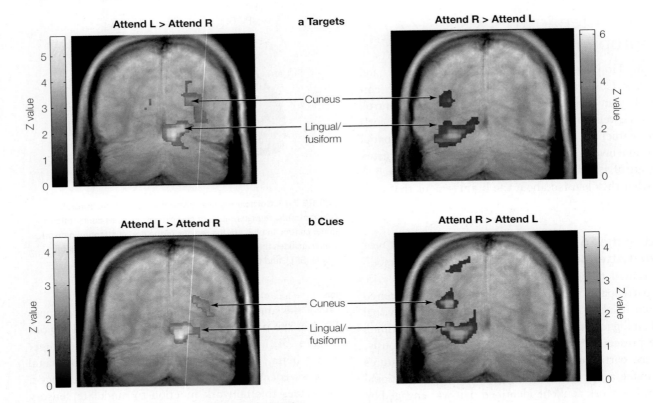

FIGURE 7.43 Priming of visual cortex by spatial attention.

(a) The same visual cortical activation is seen (attended vs. unattended) as in Figure 7.20a, but collapsed over a group of six participants (from Hopfinger et al., 2000). **(b)** When these same regions of visual cortex were investigated before the targets actually appeared but after the cue was presented, a preparatory priming of these areas can be observed as increased activity. These regions of increased activity closely overlap with the regions that will later receive the target stimuli shown in **(a)**, but the amplitude of the effects is smaller.

frontal cortex damage due to stroke had "decreased" visually evoked responses in ERP recordings over visual cortex. This evidence suggests that the frontal cortex (source) has a modulatory influence on the visual cortex (site). More direct evidence comes from intracranial studies in monkeys. As mentioned earlier, a key component of the frontoparietal attention network is the frontal eye fields (FEFs). The FEFs are located bilaterally in the dorsal–lateral–posterior portions of the prefrontal cortex (see Figure 7.42). They coordinate eye movement and gaze shifts, which are important for orienting and attention. Stimulation of FEF neurons produces topographically mapped saccadic eye movements (see Chapter 5). Tirin Moore and his colleagues (Moore & Fallah, 2001) at Stanford University investigated reports suggesting that brain mechanisms for planning eye movements and directing visuospatial attention overlapped. If this is so, then if they altered oculomotor signals within the brain by stimulating them with electrodes, would spatial attention be affected? Using intracortical electrical stimulation and recording techniques in monkeys, they stimulated FEF neurons

with very low currents that did not evoke saccadic eye movements. Was there any effect on attention? Yes! While the monkey was performing a spatial attention task (Figure 7.44), the weak stimulations resulted in enhanced performance in the attention task. These effects were spatially specific. That is, attention was enhanced to attended targets only if the targets were at a specific spot. That spot was the location in space where the saccadic eye movements would have been had the stimulation to the FEF been strong enough to generate them: Stimulation of the FEF with currents that do not evoke saccades does bias the selection of targets for eye movements. We now have more evidence that components of the dorsal attention system, in this case the FEF, exerts control over attention.

This finding led the researchers to hypothesize that if FEF microstimulation initiates both saccade preparation and visual selection, then stimulating it also could induce a spatial-attention-like modulation of the visual cortex (Moore & Armstrong, 2003). Again, they placed a stimulating electrode in FEF that could deliver very weak electrical stimulation. This time, they also recorded from

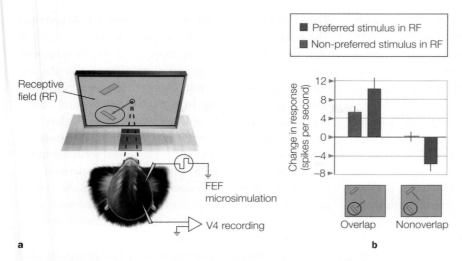

a

b

FIGURE 7.44 FEF stimulation participates in attentional control of visual cortex.
(a) Diagram of stimulus display, and recording and stimulating procedure. The monkey fixated on a central point while stimuli flashed within the receptive field (circled region in the figure) of the recorded V4 neuron, or outside the receptive field. Subthreshold stimulation of the FEF was performed for neurons whose saccade vector (indicated by red arrow) was toward to the neuron's receptive field or for neurons whose vector was away, toward the other stimulus. **(b)** Under the "overlap condition," when the receptive field and saccade vector overlapped, the responses of the V4 neuron were increased in comparison to the nonoverlap condition. The difference was greater when the flashed stimulus was one that elicited large responses from the neuron (preferred stimulus) as compared to when the stimulus did not (non-preferred stimulus). FEF stimulation mimics the effects of visual attention on V4 activity.

V4 neurons whose receptive fields were located in the visual field where stimulation of the FEF would direct a saccade (Figure 7.44a). First they presented a stimulus to the receptive field of the V4 neuron. The stimulus was one of two types: either preferred or non-preferred for that particular neuron. The neuron's elicited response was always weaker in the case of the non-preferred stimulus. Then stimulation was applied to the FEF site 200–500 ms after the appearance of the visual stimulus. This delay allowed the investigators to examine the effects of FEF stimulation on the activity in V4 that was evoked by the visual stimulus, as opposed to any changes in V4 activity that might have been the direct result of FEF stimulation alone. The FEF stimulation could have had one of three results. It could have amplified the V4 activity, interfered with it, or had no effect on it. What happened? While the monkey was fixating on a central point on the screen, weak stimulation of the FEF-enhanced stimulus evoked V4 activity (i.e., it increased the number of spikes per second) for the preferred over the non-preferred stimulus (Figure 7.44b). If the V4 neuron was not activated by the visual stimulus, then stimulation of the FEF did not affect the activity of the V4 cell. This result mimics the ones observed when monkeys attend and ignore stimuli in V4 (see Figure 7.18). FEF signals appear to participate in goal-directed attentional control over V4 activity.

We have just seen that microstimulation of the FEF in monkeys modulated the neural responses in the posterior visual fields. This is evidence that goal-directed signals from the frontal cortex cause modulations of neural activity. What is the nature of these signals? Are they task specific? For instance, if your task is to identify a face, will goal-directed signals alert only the fusiform face area? Or are signals more broadly transmitted, so that the motion area would also be alerted? Yosuke Morishima and his colleagues (2009) set their sights on answering these questions.

They designed an attention task in which human participants were cued on a trial-by-trial basis to perform a visual discrimination task for either motion direction or face gender. The cue was followed by either a short interval of 150 ms or a long interval of 1,500 ms before the stimulus was presented. The stimulus was a vertical grating that moved to the right or the left, superimposed on an image of a male or female face. In half of the trials, 134 ms after the cue, the FEF was stimulated using transcranial magnetic stimulation.

Recall from Chapter 3 that TMS is a method that uses bursts of focused magnetic fields at the scalp to stimulate neurons in the human brain. Depending on how the magnetic fields are applied, TMS either disrupts or enhances neuronal activity.

Morishima and coworkers used TMS at low enough levels that task performance was unaffected. Thus, TMS did not modify processing in FEF neurons *per se*, instead it generated a signal in regions of the visual cortex that were functionally interconnected with FEF. Changes in visual cortex activity with TMS were measured by recording ERPs generated by activity of the human motion processing area MT/V5 (MT+) and face processing area (the fusiform face area, FFA). The effect of FEF stimulation on these two brain regions during task performance was evaluated. The results revealed that when participants were cued to discriminate the motion stimulus, the TMS-induced activity in MT/V5 was increased; but when they were cued to discriminate the gender of the face, the same TMS was found to induce increased activity in the face processing region, the FFA (Figure 7.45a). Thus, impulses from the FEF actually coded information about the task that is to be performed, indicating that the dorsal system is involved in generating task-specific, goal-directed attentional control signals.

This study neatly demonstrates that the FEF, a component of the dorsal attention control network, has an influence on visual cortex. This goal-directed influence is task specific, such that the functional connectivity between FEF and specific visual areas is increased as a function of the specific state of attention (i.e., attend face vs. attend motion).

The Parietal Cortex and Control of Attention

The posterior parietal lobe is the other major cortical region that is part of the frontoparietal attention system. The parietal cortex occupies a special place in the annals of attention research, owing to the long history of observing that damage to the posterior parietal cortex is related to disorders of attention, such as neglect. We have distinguished between two regions of the posterior parietal lobe (see Figure 7.42). The dorsal areas along the intraparietal sulcus (IPS) and the superior parietal lobule (SPL) belong to the dorsal network, and the ventral areas, which make up part of the temporoparietal junction (TPJ), are a part of the ventral attention network (Corbetta & Shulman, 2002).

The parietal lobe has extensive connections with subcortical areas like the pulvinar and the frontal cortex, as well as other parts of the visual pathways. The parietal lobe contains multiple representations of space. What is the role of the parietal cortex in attention? Numerous physiological studies in monkeys have addressed this question. Attentional shifts are correlated with significant changes in the activity of parietal neurons. Whenever attention is directed to a stimulus, the firing rates of primate parietal neurons increase (Mountcastle, 1976), both when using the stimulus as a target for a saccade or a reaching movement, as well as when covertly discriminating its features (Wurtz et al., 1982). When a monkey

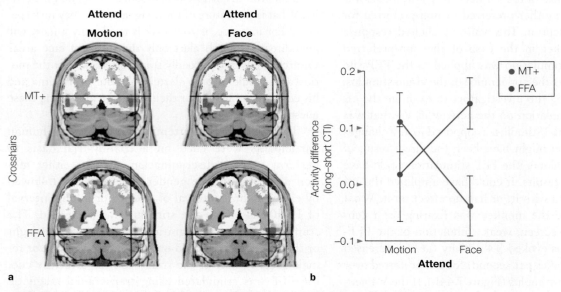

FIGURE 7.45 Impulses from the FEF code information about the task that is to be performed.
(a) Coronal sections through a template brain, showing the activations in posterior brain regions (in red) coding motion (MT+; **top row at crosshairs**) and faces (FFA; **bottom row at crosshairs**) that were induced by TMS to FEF when participants were attending motion **(left)** and attending faces **(right)**. The maximum activations, are seen in MT+ when attending motion **(top left)** and in the FFA when attending faces **(bottom right)**. **(b)** Graph of the differential activity evoked in MT+ (green) and FFA (red) when attending motion **(left)** and faces **(right)**.

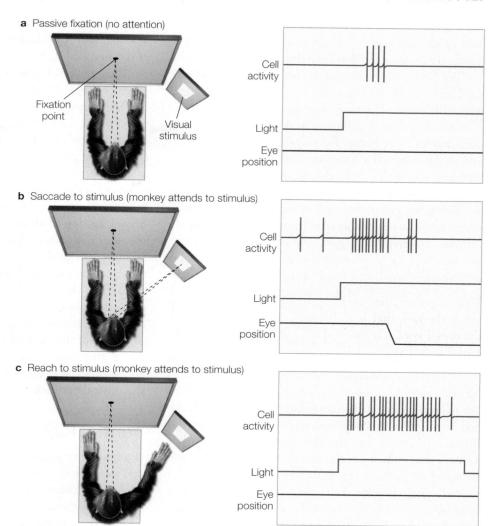

a Passive fixation (no attention)

Fixation point

Visual stimulus

Cell activity

Light

Eye position

b Saccade to stimulus (monkey attends to stimulus)

Cell activity

Light

Eye position

c Reach to stimulus (monkey attends to stimulus)

Cell activity

Light

Eye position

FIGURE 7.46 Properties of parietal neurons in visual attention. **(a)** The monkey passively fixates while a lateral-field stimulus is presented, generating some action potentials from the neuron **(right)**. **(b)** When the monkey has the task of making a saccadic eye movement to the target when it appears the neurons showed increased firing to the stimulus. **(c)** When the animal must keep its eyes fixated straight ahead, but is required to reach to the target, the neuron increases its firing rate to targets that are presented and covertly attended. Thus, the neuron is spatially selective—a sign of covert attention.

is merely waiting for the next trial in a sequence of trials, however, the parietal neurons do not usually show an enhanced response to visual stimuli in their receptive fields (Figure 7.46).

Most studies of attention using single-neuron recording and functional imaging have focused on the intraparietal area, especially the intraparietal sulcus (IPS) and a subregion within the IPS, known in monkeys as the lateral intraparietal (LIP) area (Figure 7.47). This region is involved in the saccadic eye movements mentioned earlier and in visuospatial attention. It is part of the dorsal frontoparietal attention network.

To investigate what role LIP neurons play in visuospatial attention, James Bisley and Mickey Goldberg (2006) collected intracranial recordings of LIP neurons from monkeys as they performed a discrimination task. The monkeys were to detect the properties of a stimulus at a covertly attended location to determine whether to execute a planned saccade to that attended location. While the animal was covertly attending the cued location, occasional distracter stimuli appeared elsewhere. The LIP neuronal activity

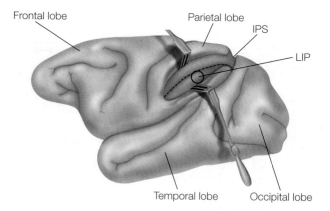

Frontal lobe

Parietal lobe

IPS

LIP

Temporal lobe

Occipital lobe

FIGURE 7.47 Location of the intraparietal area involved in visuospatial attention.
The intraparietal sulcus (IPS) in the parietal lobe is shown retracted to reveal the depths of the sulcus, which contains several distinct areas. One of these distinct areas is the lateral intraparietal area (LIP). Neurons in the LIP receive inputs from and project to neurons in the frontal eye field and the superior colliculus. In humans, functional imaging data suggest that the functional equivalent of the monkey LIP is also located in the IPS, but along its medial aspect. This is a left lateral view of a macaque brain.

when there was and was not a distraction was compared. This result was also compared to the monkey's performance (i.e., its contrast detection threshold) (Figure 7.48).

The best performance was observed when the target feature to be discriminated occurred in the location where LIP neuronal activity was higher. Put another way, if neuronal activity was highest at the attended location, performance was better for targets presented to that attended location. If a distracter had been presented, and neuronal activity had temporarily switched to be higher at another region of the LIP (corresponding to where the distracter was presented), however, then target discrimination was better at that (supposedly unattended) location. For example, Figure 7.48 plots the results from one monkey. Right after the distracter appeared, probe performance was better (*panel a, red curve below the blue curve*) at the location of the distracter. But around 400 ms (*yellow shading*) the curves cross. For the remainder of the plot the performance is better at the saccade target location (*panel a, blue curve is now below the red curve*). This tells us that the distracter briefly captured attention to its location (see Figure 7.29), but then attention returned to the location of the saccade goal. What were the neurons doing at the same time? In Figure 7.48b the red curve plots the neuronal responses evoked by the distracter stimulus and the blue curve shows the earlier saccade goal stimulus at the attended location. When the neuronal response to the distracter is larger than to the saccade goal stimulus, behavioral performance (shown in panel a) is better for the probe at the distracter location. But when the neuronal response to the distracter

drops below that for the saccade goal stimulus at around 400 ms, that is when performance crosses back in favor of the attended location for probe discrimination.

Thus, by looking at the pattern of activity over the extent of the LIP, the researchers could actually predict the monkey's performance. By inference, they also could predict the momentary locus of the animal's visual attention. Bisley and Goldberg (2006) interpreted this finding as evidence that activity in LIP provides a salience or priority map. A saliency map pools the different individual feature maps (color, orientation, movement, etc.) of a stimulus onto a topographical map, resulting in an overall map that shows how conspicuous a stimulus is from those surrounding it (Koch & Ullman, 1985). This map is used by the oculomotor system as a saccade goal when a saccade is appropriate (i.e., when the stimulus is highly salient). At the same time, the visual system uses this map to determine the locus of attention. Thus, it appears that the LIP, which is an area of the parietal cortex and a component of the dorsal attention system, is concerned with the location and saliency of objects. Let's now turn our attention to the ventral network.

Ventral Right Attention Network

If a fire alarm goes off while you are reading this chapter, most likely your attention will shift. According to Maurizio Corbetta and his colleagues, this reaction is due to your ventral frontoparietal attention network, which exerts stimulus-driven control. While your dorsal

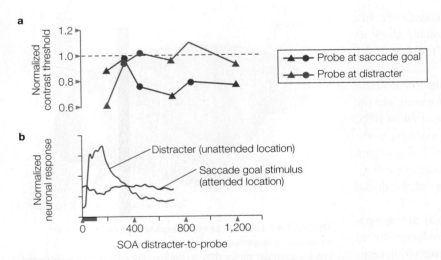

FIGURE 7.48 Behavior and neuronal attention effects in monkey parietal cortex during visuospatial attention.
(a) Behavioral performance from one monkey is plotted. Smaller values on the y-axis indicate better performance because this means the monkey could detect the probe orientation at a lower stimulus contrast. (*red curve*) Probe appeared at the unattended location where the distracter had appeared. (*blue curve*) Probe appeared at the attended location, i.e., the saccade target. **(b)** Neuronal responses from the same monkey are plotted. See the text for details.

network keeps you focused on the book, the ventral network is standing guard, vigilant for any significant stimuli, at any location in all sensory modalities. This ventral network is *strongly lateralized to the right hemisphere*. It includes the temporoparietal junction (TPJ) in the posterior parietal cortex, located at the juncture of the posterior temporal lobe and the inferior parietal lobe (Figure 7.49a). The ventral network also includes the ventral frontal cortex (VFC), made up of the inferior and middle frontal gyri.

Corbetta's group (2002) observed that when a person is selectively attending a region of space, if a relevant stimulus appears somewhere else (from out of the blue, so to speak), a more ventral set of brain areas becomes engaged. In studies that used cues to predict the subsequent target location and cues that did not, the response to stimuli that appeared in unexpected locations activated the TPJ. This region was not engaged during the generation or maintenance of attention, nor with visual searching which engages the dorsal attention network (Figure 7.49b). What did engage the TPJ strongly though was *target detection*, especially when something occurred in an unexpected location. Interestingly, when this happened, the activity was much greater in the right TPJ. The right TPJ, in fact, responds equally to novel stimuli in both the right and left visual fields (Corbetta et al., 2000).

Similar regions are also engaged by infrequent changes in a stimulus feature, independent of the modality of the change, and by detection of novel stimuli at an expected location. Thus, it seems to be engaged by stimuli that are unexpected, or stimuli that change unexpectedly, what we could call warning stimuli. These are the regions that activate when the birds suddenly stop chirping, or a mouse darts across your room. The TPJ appears to provide an alert that acts like a circuit breaker, interrupting the current attentional focus that is established by the goal-directed dorsal network. Indeed, lesions to the TPJ result in deficits in disengaging spatial attention. Of course, the dorsal and ventral networks are interconnected. Corbetta and colleagues suggest that the dorsal network, specifically the intraparietal sulcus (IPS), provides the TPJ with behaviorally relevant information about stimuli, that is, their salience.

The ventral system is involved with stimulus-driven attention, the detection of salient targets (especially when they appear in unexpected locations), and the reorientation of attention. It is not concerned with spatial attention, *per se*. Consistent with this lack of concern for space, so far, no topographic maps have been found in the ventral regions.

The regions of the lesioned brain most associated with neglect overlap this ventral attention network (Figure 7.49c). So the dorsal and ventral networks work together. They direct attention to relevant locations and potential targets (frontoparietal system), and they interrupt this attentional state when a novel target appears elsewhere (TPJ and ventrolateral frontal cortex), enabling us to reorient the focus of our attention.

We know something is going on subcortically during stimulus processing, in addition to the activity in the cortex. What is happening there that contributes to attentional control?

Subcortical Components of Attention Control Networks

Superior Colliculi Changing your focus of attention often involves eye movements, for instance, when you look up from this book to gaze out the window.

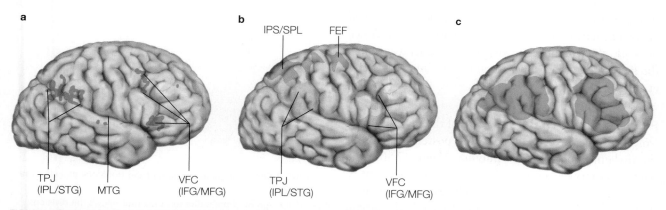

FIGURE 7.49 Brain regions involved in detection of novelty and attentional reorienting.
(a) This view of the right hemisphere shows regions of temporoparietal junction (TPJ), middle temporal gyrus (MTG), middle frontal gyrus (MFG), and inferior frontal gyrus (IFG) that were activated when participants received an invalid trial in which a cue incorrectly predicted the target location. These activations are more ventral than those observed to the preceding cue that reflect attentional control (shown in blue in b). **(c)** Regions of cortex known from neuropsychological studies to result in neglect when lesioned.

The **superior colliculi**, midbrain structures, are involved in this process. They are made up of many layers of neurons that receive inputs from many sources, including the retina, other sensory systems, the basal ganglia, and the cerebral cortex. The superior colliculi project multiple outputs to the thalamus and the motor system that, among other things, control eye movements. Input from the frontal eye fields helps generate intentional saccades, and input from the parietal eye fields aids in triggering reflexive saccades.

In the early 1970s, Robert Wurtz and his colleagues discovered visually responsive neurons in the superior colliculus that were activated based on *how* monkeys responded to stimuli. Activation required the animal to attend to the location of the stimulus (as is true for cortical neurons) and also to prepare to move its eyes to the target (not necessarily true for cortical neurons). These superior colliculus neurons do not participate in voluntary visual selective attention *per se*, but are part of an eye movement system and appear to have a role in overt rather than covert aspects of attention. They are sensitive to the saliency of a stimulus (Shipp, 2004), and because of this, they not only detect salient items, but guide eye movements toward them.

Patients with degeneration of the superior colliculus and parts of the basal ganglia, a disease called progressive supranuclear palsy (PSP), have difficulty *shifting* their attention and are slow to respond to cued targets.

The superior colliculi also appear to be involved with visual search. This was demonstrated by a patient with a rare injury, who, due to bleeding in one hemisphere, damaged only one of the superior colliculi (Sapir et al., 1999). Recall that inhibition of return (IOR) is a bias against reorienting attention to a previously cued location in visual search. This patient had a reduced IOR for inputs to the lesioned colliculus. In the case of reduced IOR, the superior colliculus, in turn, appears to depend on being activated by input from parts of the dorsal network, the frontal eye fields, and the parietal cortex in the hemisphere that is ipsilateral to the site of IOR (Ro et al., 2003).

Pulvinar of the Thalamus One of the many outputs from the superior colliculi goes to a posterior region of the thalamus known as the **pulvinar** (Figure 7.50). The pulvinar is actually a group of nuclei with connections to many parts of the brain. It has visually responsive neurons that exhibit selectivity for color, motion, and orientation. In addition, it has areas containing retinotopic maps of the visual world and interconnections with frontal, parietal, occipital, and temporal cortical areas. Pulvinar neurons show enhanced activity when a stimulus is the target of a saccadic eye movement or when a stimulus is

attended without eye movements to the target. Thus, this structure may be involved in both voluntary and reflexive attention.

To figure out how the pulvinar functions in attention control, Steve Petersen, David Lee Robinson, and their colleagues (Petersen et al., 1987, 1992) chemically deactivated it in monkeys and then observed how their attention changed (Figure 7.51). They injected the drug muscimol, a GABA agonist that inhibits neuronal activity and temporarily deactivates neurons, into the dorsomedial region of the pulvinar. Following the injection, the monkeys had difficulty orienting attention covertly to targets in the contralateral visual field. They also had difficulty filtering distracting information. When competing distracters were present in the visual

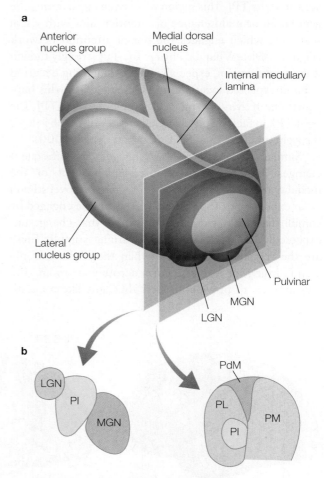

FIGURE 7.50 Anatomical diagram of the thalamus showing the pulvinar.
(a) This diagram of the entire left thalamus shows the divisions of the major groups of nuclei, and the relationships between the visual lateral geniculate (LGN) and auditory medial geniculate (MGN) nuclei, and the pulvinar nucleus. **(b)** These cross sections through the pulvinar at anterior levels show the LGN and MGN, and at more posterior levels, the lateral (PL), dorsomedial (PdM), medial (PM), and inferior (PI) subdivisions of the pulvinar.

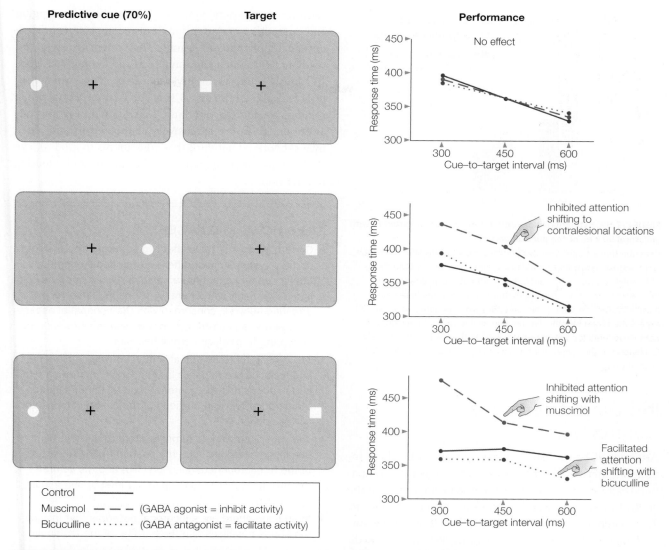

FIGURE 7.51 Effects on behavior when the left dorsal medial region of the pulvinar is injected with GABA agonists and antagonists.
The trial types—predictive peripheral cue (**left column**) and target (**middle column**)—correspond to the data presented on the **right**. The measure is reaction time to target detection as a function of cue-to-target interval (ms). When animals had to direct attention in the direction ipsilesional to the injected pulvinar (top panels), the drugs had no effect. But when directing attention contralaterally (middle panels), then deactivation of pulvinar with muscimol resulted in poorer (slower) behavioral responses. Finally, facilitation of neuronal activity with bicuculine resulted in improved (faster) behavioral responses in the case where attention had to be reoriented into the contralateral hemifield following an invalid cue (bottom panels).

field, the subjects had difficulty discriminating color or form. Other studies have shown that as the number of distracting stimuli increases, the activity of a normally functioning pulvinar increases (LaBerge, 1990; Buchsbaum et al., 2006). Petersen and colleagues also showed that when bicuculline, a GABA antagonist, was administered, the monkeys readily directed their attention covertly to contralesional targets. Hence, the pulvinar is central to covert spatial attention and filtering of stimuli.

Patients with pulvinar lesions have deficits in attentional orienting. They have a problem *engaging attention* at a *cued* location. Compared with normal participants, their reaction times are increased for both validly cued and invalidly cued targets that appear in the contralesional space. This condition is in contrast to patients with cortical lesions of the inferior parietal and temporoparietal junction. Their main deficit was greatly increased reaction times to invalid targets in the contralesional space but not to valid targets (Figure 7.52).

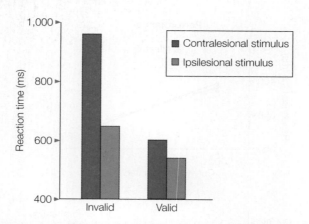

FIGURE 7.52 Extinction-like reaction time pattern in patients with unilateral lesions of the parietal cortex.
Reaction times to pre-cued (valid) targets contralateral to the lesion were almost "normal": Although reactions were slower than those of healthy control participants, they were not much slower than the patients' reactions to targets that occurred in the ipsilesional hemifield when that field was cued. But when patients were cued to expect the target stimulus in the field ipsilateral to the lesion (e.g., right visual field for a right parietal lesion), they were unusually slow to respond to the target when it occurred in the opposite (left) field (invalid trials).

Review of Attentional Control Networks

Attention is controlled by what appears to be three interacting networks. The goal-directed dorsal (frontoparietal) attention network is concerned primarily with the control of spatial attention and the saliency of objects. This system enables us to maintain attention on the current goal. It also receives inputs from systems that mediate emotion, memory, and planning. The stimulus-driven ventral frontoparietal system is essential for disengaging and reorienting our attention. It also detects unexpected, infrequent, or changing stimuli. This system stands guard, ready to shift your attentional focus, if a stimulus is conspicuously different in any way. These two systems interact to allow humans to stay focused on a goal while remaining alert to anything that should warrant our attention. Both are extensively connected to and aided by a subcortical network that contributes to arousal, eye movements, filtering input, and the shifting and orienting of attention.

TAKE-HOME MESSAGES

- Current models suggest that two separate frontoparietal cortical systems direct different attentional operations during sensory orienting: *a dorsal attention network*, concerned primarily with orienting attention, and *a ventral attention network*, concerned with the nonspatial aspects of attention and alerting. The two systems interact and cooperate to produce normal behavior.

- The dorsal frontoparietal attention network is bilateral and includes the superior frontal cortex, inferior parietal cortex (located in the posterior parietal lobe), superior temporal cortex, and portions of the posterior cingulate cortex and insula.

- The ventral network is strongly lateralized to the right hemisphere and includes the posterior parietal cortex of the temporoparietal junction (TPJ) and the ventral frontal cortex (VFC) made up of the inferior and middle frontal gyri.

- In addition, there are subcortical networks that include the superior colliculi and the pulvinar of the thalamus.

Summary

If William James and Hermann von Helmholtz were alive today, they would marvel at how much behavioral and physiological data we can provide to answer their questions about attention and awareness. Although in this chapter we did not address all the current information about attention, we did look at key aspects of attentional mechanisms and examined the goal-directed executive systems, and bottom-up stimulus-driven mechanisms, that engender orienting and selection within the sensory pathways.

The picture we find is of distributed but highly specific brain systems participating in attentional control. The roles and limits of these systems in attention are becoming more clearly defined as we combine attentional theory, experimental and cognitive psychological findings, and neurophysiological approaches in healthy participants and patients with brain damage. Systems for controlling attention include portions of the parietal lobe, temporal cortex, frontal cortex, and subcortical structures; these comprise the *sources* of attentional control. The result in visual processing—which has been our example system—is that, in the sensory pathways, we observe modulations in the activity of neurons as they analyze and encode perceptual information as a function of their relevance. These areas affected by attention are the *sites* of attentional selection.

We no longer wonder whether early or late selection is the mechanism for selective attention, because we now know that attention can operate at multiple stages of processing, including subcortical stages of the sensory pathways. The fascinating fact is that physical stimuli that impinge on our sensory receptors may not be expressed in our awareness, either at the time they occur or later via our recollections. The interaction of stimulus salience and goal-directed attention determine which inputs reach awareness and which do not.

Attentional phenomena are diverse and entail many brain computations and mechanisms. When these are compromised by damage or disease, the results can be devastating for the individual. Cognitive neuroscience is vigorously carving away at the physiological and computational underpinnings of these phenomena, with the dual goals of providing a complete account of the functioning of the healthy brain, and shedding light on how to ameliorate attentional deficits in all their forms.

Key Terms

Bálint's syndrome (p. 274)
bottleneck (p. 282)
covert attention (p. 280)
dichotic listening (p. 281)
early selection (p. 283)
endogenous cuing (p. 284)
exogenous cuing (p. 296)
extinction (p. 278)

feature integration theory of
 attention (p. 300)
inhibition of return (IOR) (p. 296)
late selection (p. 283)
limited capacity (p. 282)
neglect (p. 276)
overt attention (p. 280)
pulvinar (p. 320)

reflexive attention (p. 280)
reflexive cuing (p. 296)
selective attention (p. 274)
superior colliculus (p. 320)
thalamic reticular nucleus
 (TRN) (p. 294)
unilateral spatial neglect (p. 276)
voluntary attention (p. 280)

Thought Questions

1. Do we perceive everything that strikes the retina? What might be the fate of stimuli that we do not perceive but that nonetheless stimulate our sensory receptors?

2. Are the same brain mechanisms involved when we focus our intention voluntarily as when our attention is captured by a sensory event, such as a flash of light?

3. Does attention act on inputs from locations, from object representations, or both? If both, how are the two levels of representation related during selective attention?

4. Is neglect following brain damage a deficit in perception, attention, or awareness?

5. Compare and contrast the way attention is reflected in the activity of single neurons in visual cortex versus parietal cortex. Can these differences be mapped onto the distinction between attentional control and attentional selection?

Suggested Reading

Briggs, F., Mangun, G. R., and Usrey, W. M. (2013). Attention enhances synaptic efficacy and signal-to-noise in neural circuits. *Nature, Advanced Online Publication,* doi:10.1038/nature12276.

Corbetta, M., & Shulman, G. (2011). Spatial neglect and attention networks. *Annual Review of Neuroscience, 34,* 569–99.

Hillis, A. E. (2006). Neurobiology of unilateral spatial neglect. *Neuroscientist, 12,* 153–163.

Luck, S. J., Woodman, G. F., & Vogel, E. K. (2000). Event-related potential studies of attention. *Trends in Cognitive Sciences, 4,* 432–440.

Mangun, G. R. (Ed.). (2012). *The neuroscience of attention: Attentional control and selection.* New York: Oxford University Press.

Moore, T. (2006). The neurobiology of visual attention: Finding sources. *Current Opinion in Neurobiology, 16,* 1–7.

Posner, M. (2011). *Attention in a social world.* New York: Oxford University Press.

Posner, M. (2012). *Cognitive neuroscience of attention* (2nd ed.). New York: Guilford.

Rees, G., Kreiman, G., & Koch, C. (2002). Neural correlates of consciousness in humans. *Nature Reviews Neuroscience, 3,* 261–270.

Wolfe, J. M., & Horowitz, T. S. (2004). What attributes guide the deployment of visual attention and how do they do it? *Nature Reviews Neuroscience, 5,* 495–501.

him at http://www.ted.com/talks/daniel_wolpert_the_real_reason_for_brains.html). According to these claims, well over 100% of our brain acreage would be spoken for without even considering the other sensory systems or functions such as memory and language. Of course, as we will soon learn, an area can be involved in both vision and motor control. It might be easier to learn about brain systems by dividing chapters into simple headings like memory, perception, and action; but in reality, each of these divisions, both functionally and on a neural level, are integrated and not physically divisible. Just as Shakespeare spoke of one man playing many parts, one brain region can affect many functions. By focusing on the kinds of computations performed by different neural regions and systems, we come to see that perception and action are intimately interwoven, a theme that recurs in this chapter.

You might expect that our understanding of the motor system is very advanced. Unlike an internal process such as perception or memory, the output of the motor system can be directly observed from our actions. Nonetheless, many aspects of motor function remain elusive. Even a clear understanding of what the motor cortex encodes and how that code produces movement remains the subject of considerable debate.

We begin this chapter with a look at the anatomy and organization of the motor system. Following this, we develop a more detailed picture from a cognitive neuroscience perspective, focusing on the computational problems faced by the motor system: What are motor neurons encoding? How are motor goals represented? How are actions planned and selected? The chapter is peppered with discussions of movement disorders to illustrate what happens when particular regions of the brain no longer function properly; also included is an overview of exciting new treatment methods for some of these disorders. We close this chapter with a look at motor learning and expertise.

The Anatomy and Control of Motor Structures

The motor system is organized in a hierarchical structure with multiple levels of control that span the spinal cord, the subcortex, and the cerebral cortex (Scott, 2004). As Figure 8.2 illustrates, the lowest level of the hierarchy contains local circuits made up of motor neurons and interneurons in the

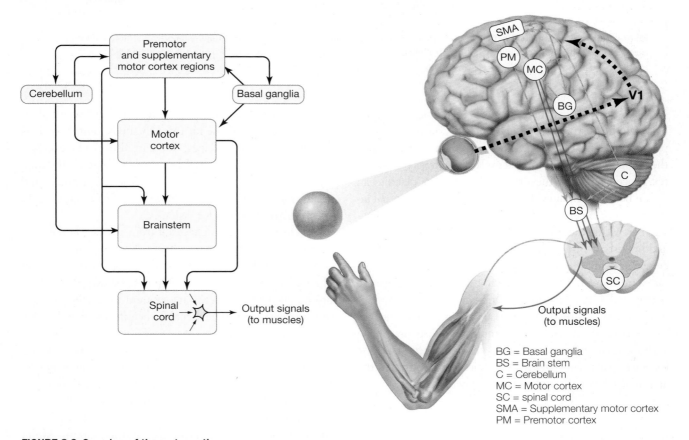

FIGURE 8.2 Overview of the motor pathways.
All connections to the arms and legs originate in the spinal cord. The spinal signals are influenced by inputs from the brainstem and various cortical regions, whose activity in turn is modulated by the cerebellum and basal ganglia. Thus control is distributed across various levels of a control hierarchy. Sensory information from the muscles is transmitted back to the brainstem, cerebellum, and cortex (not shown).

ANATOMICAL ORIENTATION

Anatomy of action

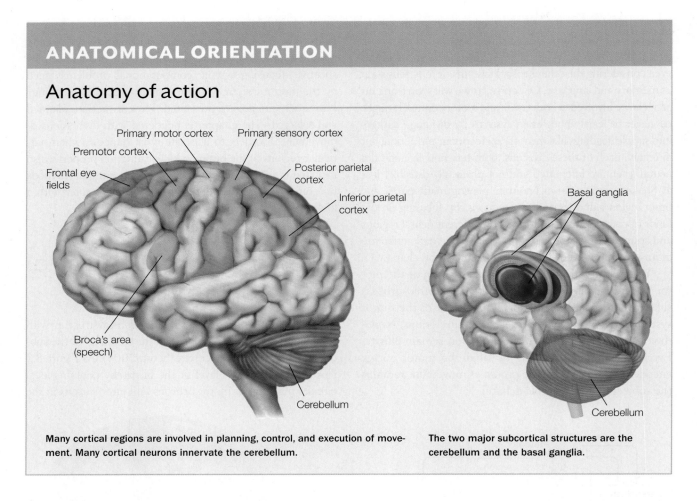

Many cortical regions are involved in planning, control, and execution of movement. Many cortical neurons innervate the cerebellum.

The two major subcortical structures are the cerebellum and the basal ganglia.

spinal cord. The spinal mechanisms are the point of contact between the nervous system and muscles. They are also capable of producing simple reflexive movements. At the top of the hierarchy are premotor and association areas of the cortex. Processing within these regions is critical for planning an action based on an individual's current goals, perceptual input, and past experience. Between the premotor and association areas and the spinal cord sit the primary motor cortex and brainstem structures, which with the assistance of the cerebellum and the basal ganglia, translate this action goal into a movement. These cortical and subcortical regions are highlighted in the Anatomical Orientation box. Because of this hierarchical structure, lesions at various levels of the motor system affect movement differently. In this section, along with the anatomy, we also discuss the deficits produced by lesions to particular regions. We begin at the bottom of the anatomical hierarchy and make our way to the top.

Muscles, Motor Neurons, and the Spinal Cord

Action, or motor movement, is generated by stimulating skeletal muscle fibers of an effector. An **effector** is a part

of the body that can move. For most actions, we think of distal effectors—those far from the body center, such as the arms, hands, and legs. We can also produce movements with more proximal or centrally located effectors, such as the waist, neck, and head. The jaw, tongue, and vocal tract are essential effectors for producing speech; the eyes are effectors for vision.

All forms of movement result from changes in the state of muscles that control an effector or group of effectors. Muscles are composed of elastic fibers, tissue that can change length and tension. As Figure 8.3 shows, these fibers are attached to the skeleton at joints and are usually arranged in antagonist pairs, which enable the effector to either flex or extend. For example, the biceps and triceps form an antagonist pair that regulates the position of the forearm. Contracting or shortening the biceps muscle causes flexion about the elbow. If the biceps muscle is relaxed, or if the triceps muscle is contracted, the forearm is extended.

Muscles are activated by motor neurons, which are the final neural elements of the motor system. **Alpha motor neurons** innervate muscle fibers and produce contractions of the fibers. *Gamma motor neurons* are part of the proprioceptive system, important for sensing and regulating the length of muscle fibers. Motor neurons

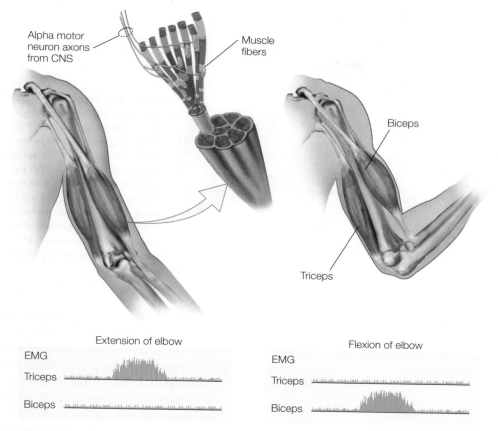

Extension of elbow

EMG

Triceps

Biceps

Flexion of elbow

EMG

Triceps

Biceps

FIGURE 8.3 Muscles are activated by the alpha motor neurons.
An electromyogram (EMG) is recorded from electrodes placed on the skin over the muscle to measure electrical activity produced by the firing of alpha motor neurons. The input from the alpha motor neurons causes the muscle fibers to contract. Antagonist pairs of muscles span many of our joints. Activation of the triceps produces extension of the elbow; activation of the biceps produces flexion of the elbow.

originate in the spinal cord, exit through the ventral root, and terminate in the muscle fibers. As with other neurons, an action potential in a motor neuron releases a neurotransmitter; for alpha motor neurons, the transmitter is acetylcholine. The release of transmitter does not modify downstream neurons, however. Instead, it makes the muscle fibers contract. The number and frequency of the action potentials and the number of muscle fibers in a muscle determine the force the muscle can generate. Thus, alpha motor neurons provide a physical basis for translating nerve signals into mechanical actions, changing the length and tension of muscles.

Input to the alpha motor neurons comes from a variety of sources. Alpha motor neurons receive peripheral input from *muscle spindles*, sensory receptors embedded in the muscles that provide information about how much the muscle is stretched. The axons of the spindles form an afferent nerve that enters the dorsal root of the spinal cord and synapses directly on corresponding efferent alpha motor neurons. If the stretch is unexpected, the alpha motor neuron is activated, causing the muscle to return to its original length, or what is called the stretch

reflex (Figure 8.4). Reflexes allow postural stability to be maintained without any help from the cortex. They also serve protective functions; for example, reflexes can contract a muscle to avoid a painful stimulus well before you consciously feel the pain.

Motor neurons are also innervated by **spinal interneurons**, which lie within the spinal cord. The interneurons are innervated both by afferent sensory nerves from the skin, muscles, and joints and by descending motor fibers (upper motor neurons) that originate in several subcortical and motor cortical structures. Thus, the signals to the muscles involve continual integration of sensory feedback with the motor commands from higher centers. This integration results in voluntary movement. The descending signals can be either excitatory or inhibitory. For example, descending commands that activate the biceps muscle produce flexion of the elbow. Because of this flexion, the triceps stretches. If unchecked, the stretch reflex would lead to excitation of the triceps and move the limb toward its original position. Thus, to produce movement (and demonstrate the size of your biceps), excitatory signals to one muscle, the agonist,

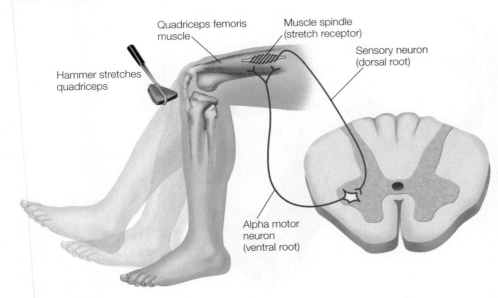

Quadriceps femoris muscle

Muscle spindle (stretch receptor)

Sensory neuron (dorsal root)

Hammer stretches quadriceps

Alpha motor neuron (ventral root)

FIGURE 8.4 The stretch reflex. When the doctor raps your knee, the quadriceps is stretched. This stretch triggers receptors in the muscle spindle to fire. The sensory signal is transmitted through the dorsal root of the spinal cord and directly activates an alpha motor neuron to contract the quadriceps. In this manner, the stretch reflex helps maintain the stability of the limb following an unexpected perturbation.

are accompanied by inhibitory signals to the antagonist muscle via interneurons. In this way, the stretch reflex that efficiently stabilizes unexpected perturbations can be overcome to permit volitional movement.

Subcortical Motor Structures

Moving up the hierarchy, we encounter many neural structures of the motor system located in the brainstem. The 12 cranial nerves, essential for critical reflexes associated with breathing, eating, eye movements, and facial expressions, originate in the brainstem. Many nuclei within the brainstem, including the vestibular nuclei, the reticular formation nuclei, and the substantia nigra, send direct projections down the spinal cord. These motor pathways are referred to collectively as the **extrapyramidal tracts**, meaning they are not part of the pyramidal tracts, the axons that travel directly from the cortex to the spinal segments (Figure 8.5). Extrapyramidal tracts are a primary source of indirect control over spinal activity modulating posture, muscle tone, and movement speed; they receive input from subcortical and cortical structures.

Cerebellum Figure 8.6 shows the location of two prominent subcortical structures that play a key role in motor control: the cerebellum and the basal ganglia. The **cerebellum** is a massive, densely packed structure containing more neurons than the rest of the central nervous system combined. Most of these neurons are contained in the layers of the cerebellar cortex. Inputs to the cerebellum primarily project to the cerebellar cortex. The output from the cerebellum originates in the deep cerebellar nuclei, projecting to brainstem nuclei and the cerebral cortex via the thalamus. An unusual feature of the cerebellum is that because the input from and output to

the cortex both cross over to the contralateral side, the net effect is that the cerebellum has an ipsilateral organization: The right side of the cerebellum is associated with movements on the right side of the body, and the left side is associated with movements on the left side of the body.

The cerebellum is made up of three regions, which appear to have followed different paths in phylogeny (Figure 8.7). Each region has unique anatomical inputs and outputs, and when lesioned, results in distinct clinical symptoms. The smallest and oldest region, the *vestibulocerebellum*, works with the brainstem vestibular nuclei to control balance and coordinate eye movements with body movements. For example, the vestibulo-ocular reflex (VOR) ensures that the eyes remain fixed on an object despite movements of the head or body. If the eyes were displaced with each movement, it would be difficult to monitor another organism or keep track of the location of a stimulus.

The medial region, the *spinocerebellum*, receives sensory information from the visual and auditory systems as well as proprioceptive information from the spinocerebellar tract. The output from the spinocerebellum innervates the spinal cord and nuclei of the extrapyramidal system. Lesions of the spinocerebellum can result in an unsteady gait and disturbances of balance. Cells in this region are especially sensitive to the effects of alcohol. Chronic alcohol abuse can cause persistent problems with balance. Even with acute alcohol use, cerebellar symptoms can be observed: Tests used by police on suspected drunk drivers are essentially assessing cerebellar function.

The lateral zones of the cerebellar hemispheres constitute the newest region, the *neocerebellum*. This area is heavily innervated by descending fibers originating from many regions within the parietal and frontal lobes. Output from the neocerebellum projects back to the

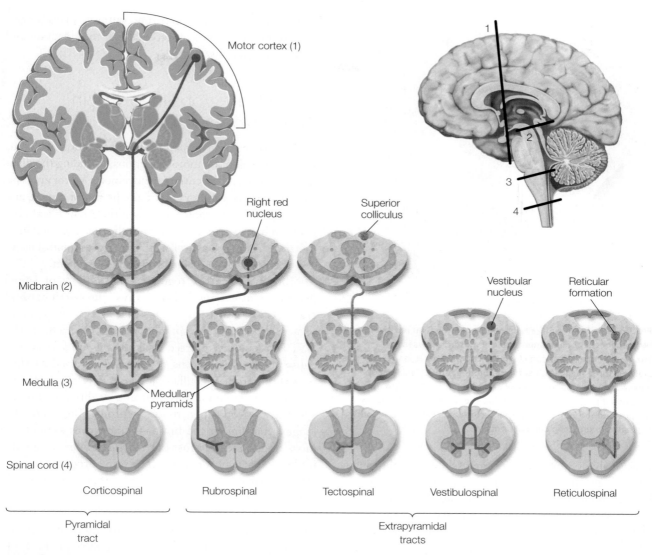

FIGURE 8.5 The brain innervates the spinal cord via the pyramidal and extrapyramidal tracts.
The pyramidal (corticospinal) tract originates in the cortex and terminates in the spinal cord. Almost
all of these fibers cross over to the contralateral side at the pyramids. The extrapyramidal tracts
originate in various subcortical nuclei and terminate in both contralateral and ipsilateral regions of
the spinal cord.

cortex via the thalamus, and the thalamic projections terminate in the primary motor, lateral premotor, and prefrontal cortices. Lesions to the neocerebellum produce **ataxia**, problems with sensory coordination of the distal limb movements, thus disrupting fine coordination. The classic test for this type of ataxia is touching the nose with a finger, which reveals the wavering, jerky movements of an *intention tremor* that occur while performing an intentional act (in contrast to *resting tremors*). Lesions to the most inferior regions of the neocerebellum produce subtler problems that may affect a range of more cognitive functions. These observations underscore the functional diversity of the cerebellum, inspiring current research efforts that challenge our traditional conceptions of the cerebellum as purely a

"motor structure." Using a range of cognitive neuroscience tools, evidence over the past twenty-five years has pointed to a role for the cerebellum in attention, language processing, planning, and more (Stoodley, 2012; Strick et al., 2009).

Basal Ganglia The other major subcortical motor structure is the **basal ganglia**, a collection of five nuclei: the caudate nucleus and the putamen (referred to together as the striatum), the globus pallidus, the subthalamic nucleus, and the substantia nigra (see Figure 8.6). The organization of the basal ganglia bears some similarity to that of the cerebellum: Input is restricted mainly to the two nuclei forming the striatum, and output is almost

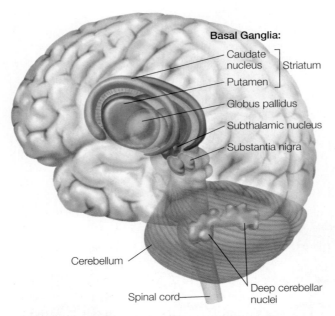

FIGURE 8.6 The basal ganglia and the cerebellum are two prominent subcortical components of the motor pathways.
The basal ganglia proper include the caudate, putamen, and globus pallidus, three nuclei that surround the thalamus. Functionally, however, the subthalamic nuclei and substantia nigra also are considered part of the basal ganglia. The cerebellum sits below the posterior portion of the cerebral cortex. All cerebellar output originates in the deep cerebellar nuclei.

exclusively by way of the internal segment of the globus pallidus and part of the substantia nigra. The remaining components (the rest of the substantia nigra, the subthalamic nucleus, and the external segment of the globus pallidus) modulate activity within the basal ganglia. Axons of the globus pallidus terminate in the thalamus, which in turn projects to motor and frontal regions of the cerebral cortex. Later we will see that the basal ganglia, with all of its inputs and outputs, plays a critical role in motor control, especially in the selection and initiation of actions.

Cortical Regions Involved in Motor Control

We will use the term *motor areas* to refer to cortical regions involved in voluntary motor functions, including the planning, control, and execution of movement. Motor areas include the primary motor cortex, the premotor cortex, and the supplementary motor area (see the Anatomical Orientation box). Other areas such as the posterior and inferior parietal cortex, as well as the primary somatosensory cortex, are also essential in producing movement.

The motor cortex regulates the activity of spinal neurons in direct and indirect ways. The **corticospinal tract (CST)** consists of axons that exit the cortex and project directly to the spinal cord (see Figure 8.5). The CST is frequently referred to as the *pyramidal tract* because the mass of axons resemble a pyramid as they pass through the medulla oblongata. CST axons terminate either on spinal interneurons or directly (monosynaptically) on alpha motor neurons. These are the longest neurons in the brain—some axons extend for more than 1 meter. Most corticospinal fibers originate in the primary motor cortex, but some originate in premotor cortex, supplemental motor area, and even somatosensory cortex.

As with the sensory systems, each cerebral hemisphere is devoted primarily to controlling movement on the opposite side of the body. About 80% of the CST axons cross, or *decussate*, at the junction of the medulla and the spinal cord; another 10% cross when they exit

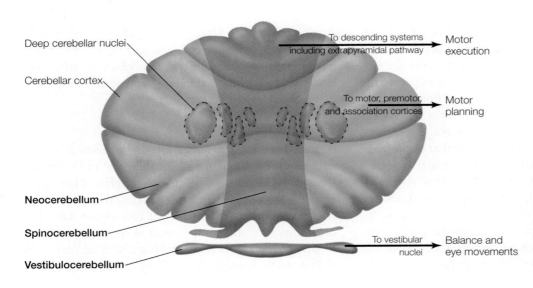

FIGURE 8.7 The three divisions of the cerebellum.
These regions of the cerebellum are shown diagrammatically along with their anatomical projections to the deep cerebellar nuclei and extracerebellar target regions.

the spinal cord. Most extrapyramidal fibers also decussate. As we have already seen, the one exception to this crossed arrangement is the cerebellum.

Primary motor cortex The **primary motor cortex (M1)**, or Brodmann area 4 (Figure 8.8), is located in the most posterior portion of the frontal lobe, spanning the anterior wall of the central sulcus and extending onto the precentral gyrus. M1 receives input from almost all cortical areas implicated in motor control. These areas include the parietal, premotor, supplementary motor, and frontal cortices as well as subcortical structures such as the basal ganglia and cerebellum. In turn, the output of the primary motor cortex constitutes the largest signal in the corticospinal tract.

M1 includes two anatomical subdivisions, an evolutionarily older rostral region and a more recently evolved

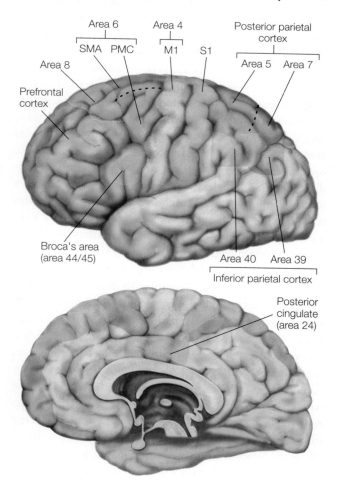

FIGURE 8.8 Motor areas of the cerebral cortex.
Brodmann area 4 is the primary motor cortex (M1). Area 6 encompasses the supplementary motor area (SMA) on the medial surface and premotor cortex (PMC) on the lateral surface. Area 8 includes the frontal eye fields. Inferior frontal regions (area 44) are involved in speech. Regions of parietal cortex associated with the planning and control of coordinated movement include S1, the primary somatosensory cortex, secondary somatosensory areas, and posterior and inferior parietal regions.

caudal region (Rathelot & Strick, 2009). The rostral part appears to be homologous across many species, but the more caudal part is thought to have evolved in a few species of Old World monkeys. It is present only in humans and some of our primate cousins. Unlike rostral corticospinal neurons that terminate on spinal interneurons, corticospinal neurons originating in the caudal region may terminate directly on alpha motor neurons. Interestingly, these motor neurons project to muscles of the upper limb. Functionally, this relatively recent adaptation is thought to provide more direct control of effectors essential for volitional movement. It allows greater dexterity as well as the ability to produce novel patterns of motor output.

M1 contains a crude somatotopic representation: Different regions represent different body parts. For example, an electrical stimulus applied directly to the medial wall of the precentral gyrus creates movement in the foot; the same stimulus applied at a ventrolateral site elicits tongue movement. It is possible to map this somatotopy non-invasively with transcranial magnetic stimulation (TMS), simply by moving the position of the coil over the motor cortex. Placing the coil a few centimeters off the midline will elicit jerky movements of the upper arm. As the coil is shifted laterally, the twitches shift to the wrist and then to hand movements.

Given the relatively crude spatial resolution of TMS (approximately 1 cm of surface area), the elicited movements are not limited to single muscles. Even with more precise stimulation methods, however, it is apparent that the somatotopic organization in M1 is not nearly as distinct as that seen in the somatosensory cortex. It is as if the map within M1 for a specific effector, such as the arm, were chopped up and thrown back onto the cortex in a mosaic pattern. Moreover, the representation of the effectors does not correspond to their actual size but reflects the importance of that effector for movement and the level of control required for manipulating it. Thus, despite their small size, the fingers span a large portion of the human motor cortex, thanks to their essential role in manual dexterity.

The preeminent status of the primary motor cortex for movement control is underscored by the knowledge that lesions to this area, or to the corticospinal tract, will produce a devastating loss of motor control. Lesions of the primary motor cortex usually result in **hemiplegia**, the loss of voluntary movements on the contralateral side of the body. Hemiplegia most frequently results from a hemorrhage in the middle cerebral artery; perhaps the most telling symptom of a stroke, it leaves the patient unable to move the affected limb. The problem is not a matter of will or awareness; the hemiplegic patient may exert great effort, but the limb will not move. Hemiplegia usually affects the most distal effectors, such as the fingers or hand.

Reflexes are absent immediately after a stroke that produces hemiplegia. Within a couple of weeks, though, the reflexes return and may become hyperactive and even spastic (resistant to stretch), reflecting a change in muscle tone. These changes result from a shift in control. Voluntary movement requires the inhibition of reflexive mechanisms. Without this, the stretch reflex would counteract the gesture. When the cortical influence is removed, primitive reflexive mechanisms take over.

Unfortunately, recovery from hemiplegia is minimal. Patients rarely regain significant control over the limbs of the contralateral side when the motor cortex has been damaged.

Nonetheless, scientists are using the tools and results from cognitive nueroscience to develop new treatment inventions to restore motor function. One approach is to look for ways that would promote neural recovery in the damaged hemisphere. For example, repetitive TMS over the lesioned cortex may stimulate neural plasticity (Kleim et al., 2006).

Other methods take a more behavioral approach, based on the idea that the brain may favor short-term solutions over long-term gains. Consider a patient with a hemiplegic right arm who has an itchy leg. The patient can scratch it quickly by using her left arm; to use the right would require considerable effort, even if the patient had recovered some ability to use this limb. Indeed, the situation may present a self-fulfilling prophecy: The advantage in using the left hand becomes more pronounced upon repeated use. This condition, in which the patient fails to use an affected limb even after significant recovery, is called learned disuse. To counteract this tendency, rehabilitation specialists use constraint-induced movement therapy (CIMT), a method that restrains patients from using their unaffected limb. For example, they might be required to wear a thick mitt on the unaffected limb, forcing them to use the affected limb if they need to grasp something. Two weeks of intensive CIMT has been found to produce substantial improvement in both strength and function of the paretic upper extremities, and the improvements are still evident 2 years later (Wolf et al., 2008).

Later in this chapter, we will review a more radical treatment approach for hemiplegia and paralysis, one that uses the neural signals of the patient's cortex to directly control prosthetic devices.

Secondary Motor Areas Brodmann area 6, located just anterior to the primary motor cortex, contains the secondary motor areas (see Figure 8.8). Multiple somatotopic maps are found within the secondary motor areas (Dum & Strick, 2002)—although, as with M1, the maps are not clearly delineated and may not contain a full body representation. The lateral and medial aspects of area 6 are referred to as **premotor cortex** and **supplementary motor area (SMA)**, respectively. Within premotor cortex, physiologists distinguish between ventral premotor cortex (PMv) and dorsal premotor cortex (PMd).

Secondary motor areas are involved with the planning and control of movement. One functional distinction between premotor cortex and SMA is whether the action is externally or internally guided. Premotor cortex has strong reciprocal connections with the parietal lobe, providing the anatomical substrate for external sensory-guided actions, such as grabbing a cup of coffee or catching a ball (see Chapter 6). SMA, in contrast, has stronger connections with medial frontal cortex, areas that we will see in Chapter 12 are associated with internally guided personal preferences and goals. For example, SMA might help decide which object to choose (e.g., coffee or soda), or with the planning of a sequence of learned actions (e.g., playing the piano).

Lesions to the secondary motor areas do not result in hemiparesis or hemiplegia. Because these regions are involved with the planning and guiding of movement, however, patients with lesions to these regions have problems in performing purposeful and coordinated movements. This disorder, known as **apraxia**—a loss of "praxis," or skilled action—is a condition that affects motor planning. Patients with apraxia have no motor or sensory impairment. They have normal muscle strength and tone, and they do not exhibit movement disorders such as tremors. The patients can produce simple gestures, like opening and closing their fist or moving each finger individually. Nonetheless, they cannot link these gestures into meaningful actions, such as sequencing an arm and wrist gesture to salute. Apraxia is most commonly a result of left-sided lesions, yet the problems may be evident in gestures produced by either limb.

The symptoms and deficits seen in apraxia depend on the location of the lesion. Neurologists distinguish between two general subtypes of apraxia: ideomotor and ideational. In **ideomotor apraxia,** the patient appears to have a rough sense of the desired action but has problems executing it properly. If asked to pantomime how to comb his hair, the patient might knock his fist against his head repeatedly. **Ideational apraxia** is much more severe. Here, the patient's knowledge about the intent of an action is disrupted. He may no longer comprehend the appropriate use for a tool. For example, one patient used a comb to brush his teeth, demonstrating by the action that he could make the proper gesture, but used the wrong object to do it.

Association Motor Areas As we saw in Chapter 6, the parietal cortex is a critical region for the representation of space. This representation is not limited to the external environment; somatosensory cortex provides a representation of the body and how it is situated in space. This information is critical to a person's ability to move effectively. Think about a skill such as hitting a tennis ball. You need to track a moving object effectively; position your body so that you can swing the racquet to intersect the ball at the appropriate time and place; and, if you're skilled, keep an eye on your opponent to attempt to place your shot out of her reach. Along the intraparietal sulcus in monkeys, neurophysiologists have identified distinct regions associated with eye movements, arm movements, and hand movements (Andersen & Buneo, 2002). Homologous regions have been observed in human imaging studies, leading to a functionally defined mosaic of motor areas within parietal cortex. Of course a skilled action, like playing tennis, will entail coordinated activity across all these effectors.

Given the importance of the parietal lobe in sensory integration, it should not be surprising that lesions there can also produce apraxia. Indeed, ideational apraxia is more often associated with parietal damage than with damage to secondary motor areas. What's more, parietal damage may disrupt the ability to produce movement and lead to impairments in the recognition of actions produced by others, even if the patient's sensory capabilities appear to be intact.

Harking back to our motor chauvinists, many other association areas of the cortex are implicated in motor function. Broca's area, located within the posterior aspect of the inferior frontal gyrus in the left hemisphere (Hillis et al., 2004), and the insular cortex (medial to Broca's area) are involved in the production of speech movements. Area 8 includes the frontal eye fields, a region (as the name implies) that contributes to the control of eye movements. The anterior cingulate cortex is also implicated in the selection and control of actions, evaluating the effort or costs required to produce a movement (see Chapter 12).

In summary, the motor cortex has direct access to spinal mechanisms via the corticospinal tract. Movement can also be influenced through many other connections. First, the primary motor cortex and premotor areas receive input from many regions of the cortex by way of corticocortical connections. Second, some cortical axons terminate on brainstem nuclei, thus providing a cortical influence on the extrapyramidal tracts. Third, the cortex sends massive projections to the basal ganglia and cerebellum. Fourth, the *corticobulbar tract* is composed of cortical fibers that terminate on the cranial nerves.

TAKE-HOME MESSAGES

- A part of the body that can move is referred to as an *effector*.
- Alpha motor neurons provide the point of translation between the nervous system and the muscular system, originating in the spinal cord and terminating on muscle fibers. Action potentials in alpha motor neurons cause the muscle fibers to contract.

- *Extrapyramidal tracts* are neural pathways that project from the subcortex to the spinal cord.
- The corticospinal or pyramidal tract is made up of descending fibers that originate in the cortex and project monosynaptically to the spinal cord.
- Two prominent subcortical structures involved in motor control are the cerebellum and basal ganglia.
- The primary motor cortex (Brodmann area 4) spans the anterior bank of the central sulcus and the posterior part of the central gyrus. It is the source of most of the corticospinal tract.
- Hemiplegia is a loss of the ability to produce voluntary movement. It results from damage to the primary motor cortex or the corticospinal tract, and the deficits are present in effectors contralateral to the lesion.
- Brodmann area 6 includes secondary motor areas. The lateral aspect is referred to as premotor cortex, and the medial aspect as supplementary motor area.
- The primary and secondary motor cortices contain somatotopic representations, although the maps are not as well defined as is seen in sensory cortices.

Computational Issues in Motor Control

We have seen the panoramic view of the motor system: how muscles are activated and which spinal, subcortical, and cortical areas shape this activity. Though we have identified the major anatomical components, we have only touched on their function. We now turn to some core computational issues that must be addressed when constructing theories about how the brain choreographs the many signals required to produce actions.

Central Pattern Generators

As described earlier, the spinal cord is capable of producing orderly movement. The stretch reflex provides an elegant mechanism to maintain postural stability even in the absence of higher-level processing. Are these spinal mechanisms a simple means for assembling and generating simple movements into more complicated actions?

In the late 1800s, Sherrington developed a procedure in which he severed the spinal cord in cats to disconnect the spinal apparatus from the cortex and subcortex (Sherrington, 1947). This procedure allowed Sherrington to observe the kinds of movements that could be produced in the absence of descending commands. As expected, stretch reflexes remained intact; in fact, these reflexes were exaggerated because inhibitory influences were removed from the brain. More surprisingly, Sherrington observed that these animals could alternate

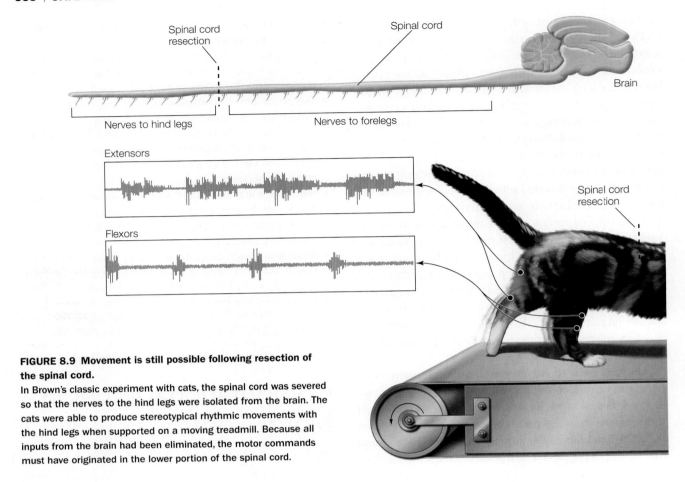

FIGURE 8.9 Movement is still possible following resection of the spinal cord.
In Brown's classic experiment with cats, the spinal cord was severed so that the nerves to the hind legs were isolated from the brain. The cats were able to produce stereotypical rhythmic movements with the hind legs when supported on a moving treadmill. Because all inputs from the brain had been eliminated, the motor commands must have originated in the lower portion of the spinal cord.

the movements of their hind limbs. With the appropriate stimulus, one leg flexed while the other extended; then the first leg extended while the other flexed. In other words, without any signals from the brain, the animal displayed movements that resembled walking. While such elementary movement capabilities are also present in people with spinal cord injuries, these individuals are unable to maintain their posture without descending control signals from the cortex and subcortex.

One of Sherrington's students, Thomas Graham Brown, went on to show that such movements did not even require any sensory feedback. Brown sectioned the spinal cord and then went a step further: He also cut the dorsal root fibers in the spinal cord, removing all feedback information from the effector. Even under these extreme conditions, the cat was able to generate rhythmic walking movements when put on a kitty treadmill (Figure 8.9). Thus, neurons in the spinal cord could produce an entire sequence of actions without any descending commands or external feedback signals.

These neurons have come to be called **central pattern generators**. They offer a powerful mechanism for the hierarchical control of movement. Consider, for instance, how the nervous system might initiate walking. Brain structures would not have to specify patterns of muscle activity. Rather, they would simply activate the appropriate pattern generators in the spinal cord, which in turn would trigger muscle commands. The system is truly hierarchical, because the highest levels are concerned only with issuing commands to achieve an action, whereas lower-level mechanisms translate the commands into a specific neuromuscular pattern to produce the desired movement. Central pattern generators most likely evolved to trigger actions essential for survival, such as locomotion. The production of other movements may have evolved using these mechanisms as a foundation. When we reach to pick up an object, for example, low-level mechanisms could automatically make the necessary postural adjustments to keep the body from tipping over as the center of gravity shifts.

Central Representation of Movement Plans

What exactly are cortical neurons coding, if not specific patterns of motor commands? To answer this question, we have to consider how actions are represented

HOW THE BRAIN WORKS
Where Is It? Assessing Location Through Perception and Action

To demonstrate that spatial information can be represented differently in systems involved in conscious perception and those associated with guiding action, try the experiment outlined in Figure 1. While standing in an open area,

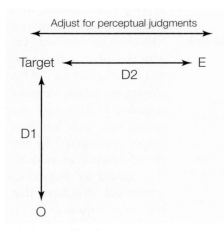

Adjust for perceptual judgments

Target ← D2 → E

D1

O

FIGURE 1 Perceptual judgment of distance.
Two people are needed for this demonstration. The observer, O, stands at a fixed location in an open area. The experimenter, E, places a target at some point in the area. E walks along the perpendicular direction away from the target and stops when O judges that they are equidistant to the target D1 = D2). The results will be quite striking. When compared to the condition in which O is asked to walk to the target with the eyes closed.

have a friend place an object 6 to 12 m from you. Then have your friend move along the perpendicular direction and stop him or her when you perceive that you are both equidistant from the object. Measure your accuracy. Now have your friend place the object in a new location, again 6 to 12 m away. When ready, close your eyes and walk forward, attempting to stop right over the object. Measure your accuracy.

Assuming that your performance matches that of the average person, you will notice a striking dissociation (Loomis et al., 1992). You will probably be quite inaccurate on the first task, underestimating the distance from you to the object. Yet on the second task, you should be very accurate. These results reveal a dissociation between two forms of judgment: one perceptual, the other motoric. In both situations the results suggest that separate representational systems underlie judgments of location and distance. Although location judgments are accurate, the representation of distance is subject to perceptual distortions. Our perception of distance is highly compressed: Things almost always are farther away than they appear. (Could this be a "safety" mechanism to ensure that we ready ourselves for an approaching predator?) As this experiment demonstrates, however, our action systems are not similarly fooled. Little, if any, compression of distance occurs when we move to a target location.

(Keele, 1986). Consider this scenario: You are busily typing at the computer and decide to pause and take a sip of coffee. To accomplish this goal, you must move your hand from the keyboard to the coffee cup. So how is this action coded in your brain? Well, it could be represented in at least two ways. First, by comparing the positions of your hand and the cup, you could plan the required movement trajectory—the path that would transport your hand from the keyboard to the cup. Alternatively, the action plan might simply specify the location of the cup (on the desk) and specify the motor commands that correspond to the limb being at that position (extended arm at 75 degrees), not how to get there. Of course, both forms of representations—trajectory based and location based—might exist in motor areas of the cortex and subcortex (see How the Brain Works: Where Is It? Assessing Location Through Perception and Action).

In an early study attempting to understand the neural code for movements, Emilio Bizzi and his colleagues (1984) at the Massachusetts Institute of Technology

performed an experiment to test whether trajectory and/or location were being coded. The experiments involved monkeys who had, through a surgical procedure, been deprived of all somatosensory, or *afferent*, signals from the limbs. These de-afferented monkeys were trained in a simple pointing experiment. On each trial, a light appeared at one of several locations. After the light was turned off, the animal was required to rotate its elbow to bring its arm to the target location—the point where the light had been.

The critical manipulation included trials in which an opposing torque force was applied just when movement started. These forces were designed to keep the limb at the starting position for a short time. Because the room was dark and the animals were de-afferented, they were unaware that their movements were counteracted by an opposing force. The crucial question was, where would the movement end once the torque force was removed? If the animal had learned that a muscular burst would transport its limb a certain distance, applying an opposing

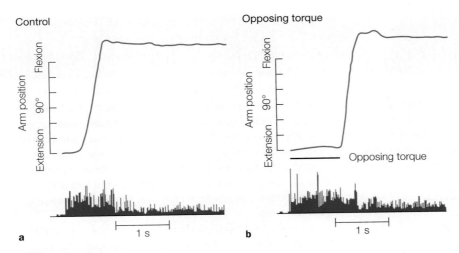

FIGURE 8.10 Endpoint control.
De-afferented monkeys were trained to point in the dark to a target indicated by the brief illumination of a light. The top traces (red) show the position of the arm as it goes from an initial position to the target location. The bottom traces (blue) show the EMG activity in the biceps. **(a)** In the control condition, the animals were able to make the pointing movements accurately, despite the absence of all sources of feedback. **(b)** In the experimental condition, an opposing force was applied at the onset of the movement, preventing the arm from moving (bar under the arm position trace). Once this force was removed, the limb rapidly moved to the correct target location. Because the animal could not sense the opposing force, it must have generated a motor command corresponding to the target location.

force should have resulted in a movement trajectory that fell short of the target. If, however, the animal generated a motor command specifying the desired position, it should have achieved this goal once the opposing force was removed. As Figure 8.10 shows, the results clearly favor the latter location hypothesis. When the torque motor was on, the limb stayed at the starting location. As soon as it was turned off, the limb rapidly moved to the correct location. This experiment provided dramatic evidence showing that central representations can be based on a location code.

Although this experiment provides impressive evidence of location planning, it doesn't mean that location is the only thing that is being coded. It just means that it is one of the things being coded. We know that you can also control the form with which a movement is executed. For example, in reaching for your coffee cup, you could choose simply to extend your arm. Alternatively, you might rotate your body, reducing the distance the arm has to move. If the coffee cup were tucked behind a book, you could readily adjust the reach to avoid a spill. Indeed, for many tasks, such as dodging a predator or being in a tango competition, the trajectory and type of movement are as important as the final goal. So although **endpoint control** reveals a fundamental capability of the motor control system, distance and trajectory planning demonstrate additional flexibility in the control processes.

Hierarchical Representation of Action Sequences

We must also take into account that most of our actions are more complex than simply reaching to a location in space. More commonly, an action requires a sequential set of simple movements. In serving a tennis ball, we have to toss the ball with one hand and swing the racquet with the other so that it strikes the ball just after the apex of rotation. In playing the piano, we must strike a sequence of keys with appropriate timing and force. Are these actions simply constructed by the linking of independent movements, or are they guided by hierarchical representational structures that govern the entire sequence? The answer is that they are guided. Hierarchical representational structures organize movement elements into integrated chunks. Researchers originally developed the idea of chunking when studying memory capacity, but it has also proven relevant to the representation of action.

Donald MacKay (1987) of the University of California, Los Angeles, developed a behavioral model to illustrate how hierarchical ideas could prove insightful for understanding skilled action. At the top of the hierarchy is the *conceptual level* (Figure 8.11), corresponding to a representation of the goal of the action. In this example, the man's intention (goal) is to accept the woman's invitation to dance. At the next *level*, this goal must be translated into an effector system. He could make a physical gesture or offer a verbal response. Embedded within each of those options are more options. He can nod his head or extend his hand, or if he has the gift of gab, he can select one sentence from a large repertoire of potential responses: "I was hoping you would ask"; or "You will have to be careful, I have two left feet." Lower levels of the hierarchy then translate these movement plans into patterns of muscular activation. For example, a verbal response entails a pattern of activity across the speech articulators, and extension of the hand requires movements of the arm and fingers.

The hierarchical properties of this model are explicit. Each level corresponds to a different form for representing the action. Actions can be described in relation to the goals to be achieved (accepting the invitation), and this

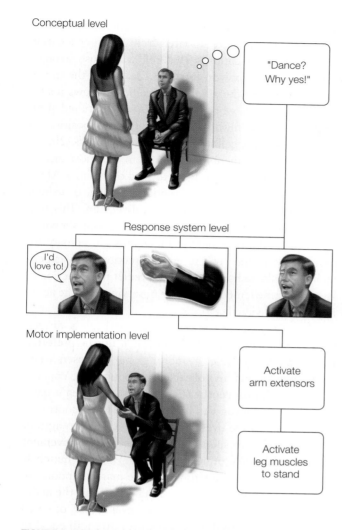

Conceptual level

"Dance? Why yes!"

Response system level

I'd love to!

Motor implementation level

Activate arm extensors

Activate leg muscles to stand

FIGURE 8.11 Hierarchical control of action.
Motor planning and learning can occur at multiple levels. At the lowest level are the actual commands to implement a particular action. At the highest level are abstract representations of the goal for the action. Multiple actions can usually achieve the same goal.

level need not be tied to a specific form of implementation (nodding or verbalizing). The two forms of responding, however, share a level of representation. In a similar fashion, when we convey a linguistic message by speaking or by writing, a common level of representation is on both the conceptual and the lexical levels. Higher levels in the hierarchy need not represent all of the information.

Viewing the motor system as a hierarchy enables us to recognize that motor control is a distributed process. Just like in a large corporation where the chief executive, sitting at the top of the organizational hierarchy, is unconcerned with what is going on in the shipping department, the highest levels of the motor hierarchy might not be concerned with the details of a movement.

Hierarchical organization also can be viewed from a phylogenetic perspective. Unlike humans, many animals

without a cerebral cortex are capable of complex actions: The fly can land with near-perfect precision; the lizard can flick its tongue at the precise moment to snare its evening meal. We might consider the cortex as an additional piece of neural machinery superimposed on a more elementary control system. Movement in organisms with primitive motor structures is based primarily on simple reflexive actions. A blast of water against the abdominal cavity of the sea slug automatically elicits a withdrawal response. More highly evolved motor systems, however, have additional layers of control that can shape and control these reflexes. For example, brainstem nuclei can inhibit spinal neurons so that a change in a muscle length does not automatically trigger a stretch reflex.

In a similar way, the cortex can provide additional means for regulating the actions of the lower levels of the motor hierarchy, offering an organism even greater flexibility in its actions. We can generate any number of movements in response to a sensory signal. As a ball comes whizzing toward him, a tennis player can choose to hit a crosscourt forehand, go for a drop shot, or pop a defensive lob. Cortical mechanisms also enable us to generate actions that are minimally dependent on external cues. We can sing aloud, wave our hands, or pantomime a gesture. Reflecting this greater flexibility, it is no surprise that the corticospinal tract is one of the latest evolutionary adaptations, appearing only in mammals. It affords a new pathway that the cerebral hemispheres can take to activate ancient motor structures.

Theories about how the motor system functions need to incorporate two observations: Pattern generators produce fixed action patterns but don't require cortical input; nonetheless, movements are flexible and not mechanical. Somehow those fixed action patterns are modified into more complex, goal-oriented movements by inputs from multiple areas of the motor cortex and brainstem. At higher levels, central representations are concerned with spatial goals and planning the more abstract components of the movement. They are not concerned with the detailed pattern of muscular contractions.

TAKE-HOME MESSAGES

- Neurons within the spinal cord can generate an entire sequence of actions without any external feedback signal. These circuits are called central pattern generators.
- Descending motor signals modulate the spinal mechanism to produce voluntary movements.
- The motor system is hierarchically organized. Subcortical and cortical areas represent movement goals at various levels of abstraction.

Physiological Analysis of Motor Pathways

So far in this chapter, we have stressed two critical points on movement: First, as with all complex domains, motor control depends on several distributed anatomical structures. Second, these distributed structures operate in a hierarchical fashion. We have seen that the concept of hierarchical organization also applies at the behavioral level of analysis. The highest levels of planning are best described by how an action achieves an objective; the lower levels of the motor hierarchy are dedicated to translating a goal into a movement. We now turn to the problem of relating structure to behavior: What are the functional roles of the different components of the motor system? In this section, we take a closer look at the neurophysiology of motor control to better understand how the brain produces actions.

Neural Coding of Movement

Neurophysiologists have long puzzled over how best to describe cellular activity in the motor structures of the CNS. Stimulation of the primary motor cortex, either during neurosurgery or via TMS, can produce discrete movements about single joints, providing a picture of the somatotopic organization of the motor cortex. This method, however, does not provide insight into the activity of single neurons, nor can it be used to study how and when cells become active during volitional movement. To address these issues, we have to record the activity of single cells and ask what parameters of movement are coded by such cellular activity. For example, is cellular activity correlated with parameters of muscle activity such as force, or with more abstract entities such as movement direction or desired final location?

In a classic series of experiments, Apostolos Georgopoulos (1995) and his colleagues studied this question by recording from cells in various motor areas of rhesus monkeys. The monkeys were trained with the apparatus shown in Figure 8.12 on what has come to be called the *center-out task*. The animal initiates the trial by moving the lever to the center of the table. After a brief hold period, a light illuminates one of eight surrounding target positions, and the animal moves the lever to this position to obtain a food reward. This movement is similar to a reaching action and usually involves rotating two joints, the shoulder and the elbow.

The results of these studies convincingly demonstrate that the activity of the cells in the primary motor cortex correlates much better with *movement direction* than with

target location. Figure 8.12a shows a neuron's activity when movements were initiated from a center location to eight radial locations. This cell was most strongly activated (red arrows in Figure 8.12a) when the movement was toward the animal. Figure 8.12b shows results from the same cell when movements were initiated at radial locations and always ended at the center position. In this condition, the cell was most active (Figure 8.12b, red arrows) for movements initiated from the most distant position; movement was again toward the animal. Many cells in motor areas show directional tuning, or exhibit what is referred to as a **preferred direction**. This tuning is relatively broad. For example, the cell shown in Figure 8.12 shows a significant increase in activity for movements in four of the eight directions. An experimenter would be hard-pressed to predict the direction of an ongoing movement if he were observing only the activity of this individual cell.

We can assume, however, that activity is distributed across many cells, each with their unique preferred direction. To provide a more global representation, Georgopoulos and his colleagues introduced the concept of the **population vector** (Figure 8.13). The idea is quite simple: Each neuron can be considered to be contributing a "vote" to the overall activity level. The strength of the vote will correspond to how closely the movement matches the cell's preferred direction: If the match is close, the cell will fire strongly; if the match is poor, the cell will fire weakly or even be inhibited. Thus, the activity of each neuron can be described as a vector, oriented to the cell's preferred direction with a strength equal to its firing rate. The population vector is the sum of all the individual vectors.

The population vector has proved to be a powerful tool in motor neurophysiology. With relatively small numbers of neurons (e.g., 30–50), the population vector provides an excellent predictor of movement direction. The population vector is not limited to simple 2-D movements; it also has proven effective at representing movements in 3-D space. Interestingly, neural activity in many motor areas appears to be correlated with movement direction.

It is important to keep in mind that the physiological method is inherently correlational. Directional tuning is prevalent in motor areas, but this does not mean that direction is the key variable represented in the brain. Note that the experiment outlined in Figure 8.12 contains a critical confound. We can describe the data in terms of movement direction, interpreting the results to show that the cell is active for movements toward the animal. To move in this direction, the animal activates the biceps muscle to produce flexion about the elbow. From these data, we do not know if the cell is coding direction, or the

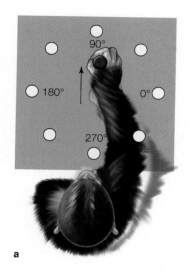
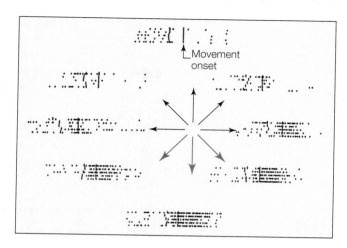

a

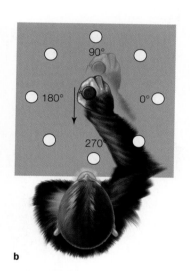
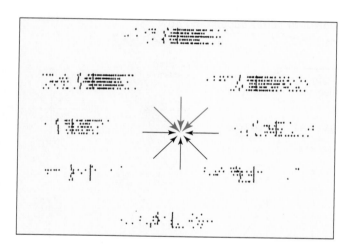

b

FIGURE 8.12 Motor cortex activity is correlated with movement direction.
(a) The animal was trained to move a lever from the center location to one of eight surrounding locations. The activity of a motor cortex neuron is plotted next to each target location. Each row represents a single movement, and the dots correspond to action potentials. The data are aligned by movement (vertical bar). **(b)** Here, movements originated at the eight peripheral locations and always terminated at the center location. The activity for the neuron is now plotted next to the starting locations. The neuron is most active (i.e., greatest density of dots) for movements in the downward direction (red arrows), regardless of starting and final locations.

level of biceps activation when the elbow is being flexed, or some other parameter correlated with these variables. Subsequent experiments have addressed this problem. The results are, as so often happens when looking at the brain, complex. Within any given area, a mixture of representations is found. The activity of some cells is best correlated with external movement direction, and the activity of other cells with parameters more closely linked to muscular activation patterns (Kakei et al., 1999).

Alternative Perspectives on Neural Representation of Movement

The population vector is dynamic and can be calculated continuously over time. Indeed, after defining the preferred direction of a set of neurons, we can calculate the population vector from the activation of that set of neurons even before the animal starts to move. To do this, and provide a way to dissociate planning- and movement-related

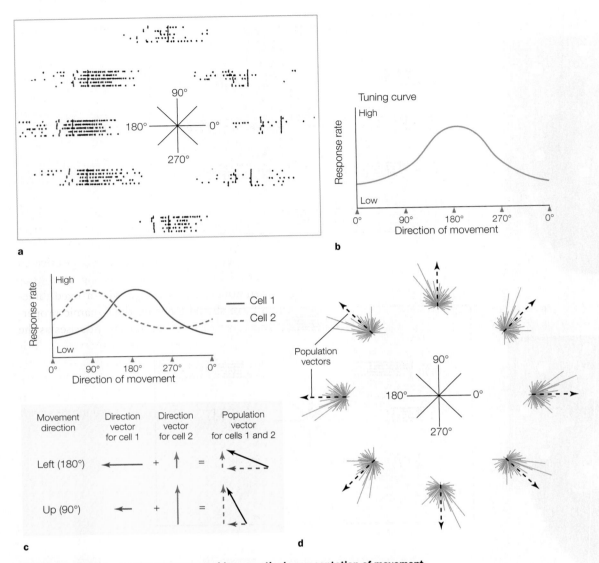

FIGURE 8.13 The population vector provides a cortical representation of movement.
The activity of a single neuron in the motor cortex is measured for each of the eight movements **(a)** and plotted as a tuning profile **(b)**. The preferred direction for this neuron is 180°, the leftward movement. **(c)** Each neuron's contribution to a particular movement can be plotted as a vector. The direction of the vector is always plotted as the neuron's preferred direction, and the length corresponds to its firing rate for the target direction. The population vector (dashed line) is the sum of the individual vectors. **(d)** For each direction, the solid lines are the individual vectors for each of 241 motor cortex neurons; the dotted line is the population vector calculated over the entire set of neurons. Although many neurons are active during each movement, the summed activity closely corresponds to the actual movements.

activity, experimenters frequently impose a delay period. The animal is first given a cue indicating the direction of a forthcoming movement and then required to wait for a "go" signal before initiating the movement (Figure 8.14). This procedure reveals that the population vector shifts in the direction of the upcoming movement well *before the movement is produced*, suggesting that at least some of the cells are involved in planning the movement and not simply recruited once the movement is being executed. In fact, by looking at the population vector, which was recorded more than 300 ms *before* the movement, the direction of

the forthcoming movement can be precisely predicted. This result may not sound like that big of a deal to you, but it put motor researchers into a frenzy—although not until about 10 years after Georgopolous's initial studies on the population vector. With hindsight, can you see why? As a hint, consider how this finding might be used to help people with spinal cord injuries. We will explore this a bit later in the section called "The Brain–Machine Interface."

Even though directional tuning and population vectors have become cornerstone concepts in motor neurophysiology, it is also important to consider that many cells do

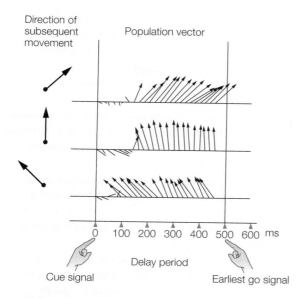

FIGURE 8.14 The direction of the population vector predicts the direction of a forthcoming movement.
At the cue, one of the eight targets is illuminated, indicating the direction for a subsequent movement. The animal must refrain from moving until the go signal (500 ms later in this example). The population vector was calculated every 20 milliseconds. The population vector is oriented in the direction for the planned movement, even though EMG activity is silent in the muscles during the delay period.

not show strong directional tuning. Even more puzzling, the tuning may be inconsistent: The tuning exhibited by a cell before movement begins may shift during the actual movement (Figure 8.15a). What's more, many cells that exhibit an increase of activity during the delay phase show a brief drop in activity just before movement begins (Figure 8.15b), or a different firing pattern in preparation and execution of a movement (Figure 8.15c). This result is at odds with the assumption that the planning phase is just a weaker, or subthreshold version of the cell's activity during the movement phase.

What are we to make of these unexpected findings, in which the tuning properties change over the course of an action? Mark Churchland and his colleagues (2012) suggest that we need a radically different perspective on motor neurophysiology. Rather than viewing neurons as static representational devices (e.g., with a fixed directional tuning), we should focus on the dynamic properties of neurons, recognizing that movement arises as the set of neurons move from one state to another. By this view, we might see that neurons wear many hats, coding different features depending on time and context. There need not be a simple mapping from behavior to neural activity. Indeed, given the challenge of using limbs with

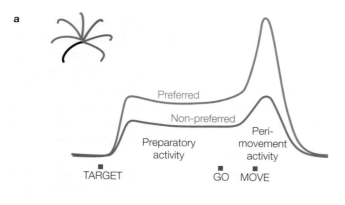

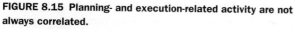

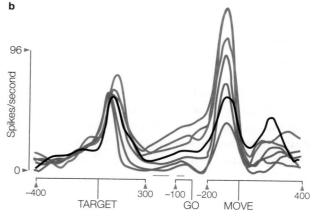

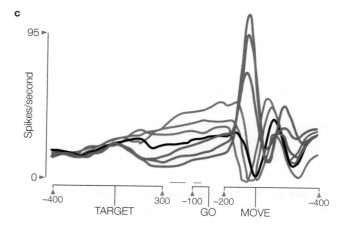

FIGURE 8.15 Planning- and execution-related activity are not always correlated.
(a) Schematic of what would be expected if neural activation during movement execution was an amplified version of that observed during movement planning. This neuron is more active when planning movements toward the upper left region of the workspace (red) compared to when the movement will be to the right (green). This planning-related difference is maintained after the "Go" signal when the animal executes the movement. **(b)** A neuron in motor cortex showing a firing pattern similar to the idealized neuron. **(c)** A different neuron in motor cortex that shows a different preferred direction during the planning phase compared to the execution phase (reversal or red-green pattern right around the time of movement onset).

complex biomechanics to interact with a wide range of objects and environments, we might expect the nervous system to have evolved such that information is represented in a multidimensional format, coding a wide range of variables such as force, velocity, and context. This form of representation may be harder for the experimenter to decode, but it is likely an important adaptation that gives the motor system maximum flexibility (not to mention job stability for neurophysiologists).

Although scientists refer to one part of the brain as motor cortex and another region as sensory cortex, we know that these areas are closely entwined with one another. People produce movements in anticipation of their sensory consequences: We increase the force used to grip and lift a full cup of coffee in anticipation of the weight we expect to experience. Similarly, we use sensory information to adjust our actions. If the cup is empty, we quickly reduce the grip force to avoid moving the cup upward too quickly. Physiologists observe this interdependency and have recognized for some time that the motor cortex isn't just "motor," and the sensory cortex isn't just "sensory." For example, in rats, the neurons that control whisker movements are predominantly in somatosensory cortex.

In monkeys, sensory inputs rapidly reshape motor activity (reviewed in Hatsopoulos & Suminski, 2011). In fact, some evidence suggests that the directional tuning of some motor cortex neurons is more about "sensory" tuning. Consider the same shoulder movement induced by two different sensory events. One is caused by a nudge to the elbow and the other following a nudge to the shoulder. As early as 50 ms, well before the sensory signals in sensory cortex would have been processed and sent to the motor system, M1 neurons show differential responses to the two types of nudges. It appears that the sensory information was processed within M1 directly, allowing for fast, nearly real-time feedback (Pruszynski et al., 2011a, b).

Taken together, the neurophysiological evidence points to a more nuanced picture than we might have anticipated from our hierarchical control model. Rather than a linkage of different neural regions with specific levels in a processing hierarchy, one that moves from abstract to more concrete representations, the picture reveals an interactive network of motor areas that represent multiple features. This complexity becomes even more apparent in the next section, when we turn our attention to motor planning.

TAKE-HOME MESSAGES

- Motor neurophysiologists correlate cellular activity in motor cortex with the animal's behavior.
- A common observation is that neurons in motor areas exhibit a preferred direction, in which the firing rate is strongest for movements in a limited set of directions.
- The population vector is a representation based on combining the activity of many neurons.
- Population vectors that provide a close match to behavior can be constructed from many motor areas, although this does not mean that all of these cells represent movement direction.
- Before movement even begins, the population vector is a reliable signal of the direction of a forthcoming movement. This finding indicates that some cells are involved in planning movements as well as executing movement.
- Neurons have dynamic properties, coding different features depending on time and context. There need not be a simple mapping from behavior to neural activity.
- The heterogeneity of responses exhibited by neurons in M1 includes both motor and sensory information.

Goal Selection and Action Planning

We now understand that the neural codes found in motor areas can be abstract, more related to the *goals* of an action than to the specific muscle patterns required to produce the movement needed to achieve that goal. Using the current context, including sensory information and feedback, the motor cortex may have more than one option for achieving that goal. In this section, we will look at how we select goals and plan motor movements to achieve them.

Consider again the situation where you are at your computer, working on a paper, with a steaming cup of coffee on your desk. You may not realize it, but you are faced with a problem that confronts all animals in their environment: deciding what to do and how to do it. Should you continue typing or sip your coffee? If you choose the coffee, then some intermediate goals must be attained—for example, reaching for the cup, grasping the cup, and bringing it to your mouth—to achieve the overarching goal of a swig of coffee. Each step requires a set of gestures, but in each case there is more than one way to perform them. For example, the cup is closer to your left hand, but your right hand is more trustworthy; which to use? Decisions must be made at multiple levels. We have to choose a goal, choose an option for achieving the goal, and choose how to perform each intermediate step.

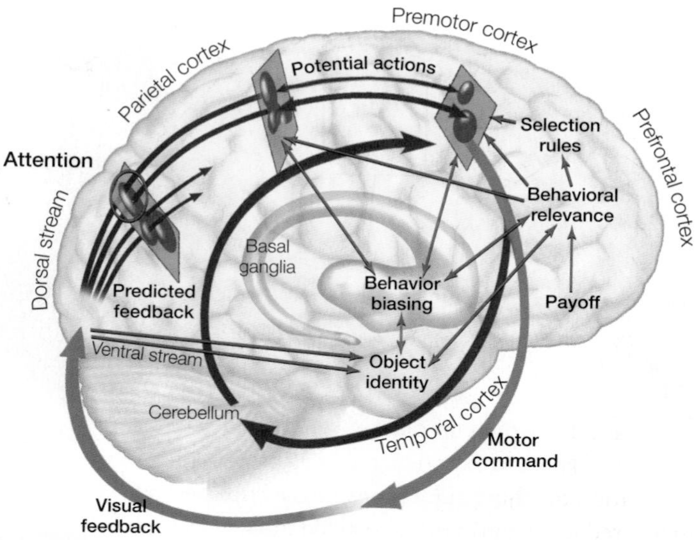

FIGURE 8.16 Sketch of the affordance competition hypothesis in the context of visually guided movement. Schematic of the processes and pathways when choosing to reach for one object among a display of many objects. The multiple pathways from visual cortex across the dorsal stream correspond to action plans for reaching to the different objects. The thickness of the arrows and circles indicate the strength for each competing plan. Selection is influenced by many sources (red arrows). The movement (green arrow) results in visual feedback of the action and results in the competition starting anew, but now in a different context.

Action Goals and Movement Plans

Paul Cisek of the University of Montreal (2007) offers one hypothesis for how we set goals and plan actions. It incorporates many of the ideas and findings that we are going to look at, providing a general framework for action selection. His *affordance competition hypothesis* is rooted in an evolutionary perspective. This hypothesis considers that the brain's functional architecture has evolved to mediate real-time interactions with the world. *Affordances* are the opportunities for action defined by the environment (Gibson, 1979). Our ancestors, driven by internal needs such as hunger and thirst, evolved in a world where they engaged in interactions with a changing, and sometimes hostile, environment that held a variety of opportunities and demands for action. To survive and reproduce, early humans had to be ever ready, anticipating the next predator or properly positioning themselves to snag available prey or ripe fruit. Many interactions don't allow time for carefully evaluating goals, considering options, and then planning the movements—what's known as serial processing.

A better survival strategy is to develop multiple plans in parallel. Cisek's affordance competition hypothesis proposes that the processes of action selection (what to do) and specification (how to do it) occur simultaneously within an interactive neural network, and they evolve continuously. Even when performing one action, we are preparing for the next. The brain uses the constant stream of sensory information arriving from the environment through sensorimotor feedback loops to continuously specify and update potential actions and how to carry them out. That's the affordance part. This sensory information is constrained by our internal drive states, longer-range goals, expected rewards, and anticipated costs, and we use all this information to assess the utility of the different actions. This is the competition part. At some point, one option wins out over the other competitors. An action is selected and executed.

This selection process involves many parts of the motor pathway, where interactions within frontoparietal circuits have a prominent role (see Figure 8.16). This schema implies that decision-making processes are embedded in the neural systems associated with motor control, not carried out by some sort of detached central control center. Is there any evidence supporting this? Let's start with the notion that an action has multiple goals, and each goal is linked with the plan to accomplish it.

Cisek (2005) developed his model based on evidence obtained in single-cell recordings from the premotor cortex of monkeys. In each trial of his study, the animal was presented with two targets, either of which it could reach with its right arm. After a delay period, a cue indicated the target location for the current trial. During this delay period, neural signatures for both movements could be observed in the activity of premotor neurons, even though the animal had yet to receive a cue for the required action. These signatures can be viewed as potential action plans. With the onset of the cue, the decision scales were tipped. Activity associated with movement to that target became stronger, and activity associated with the other movement became suppressed. Thus, following the cue, the initial dual representation consolidated into a single movement (Figure 8.17). In a variant of this task, only one target is presented. Even here, though, researchers

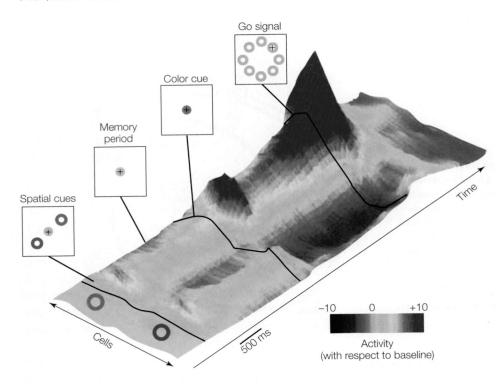

Go signal

Color cue

Memory period

Spatial cues

Cells

Time

500 ms

−10   0   +10

Activity
(with respect to baseline)

FIGURE 8.17 3-D representation of activity in a population of neurons in the dorsal premotor cortex.
Preferred direction of the cells is represented along the bottom left of the figure and time along the bottom right. When the two cues appear, the firing rate increases in neurons tuned to either target. When the color cue appears, indicating the target, activity increases for cells tuned to this direction and decrease for cells tuned to the other direction.

can observe the simultaneous specifications of multiple potential actions in the anterior intraparietal area. In this case, the multiple representations are for different ways the goal could be reached (Baumann et al., 2009). So it also appears that goals can have more than one plan, and the plans to attain them are coupled.

Representational Variation Across Motor Areas of the Cortex

Other cells in premotor cortex have been shown to represent action goals more abstractly. For example, some neurons discharge whenever the monkey grasps an object, regardless of the effector used. It could be the right hand, the left hand, the mouth, or both hand and mouth. Giacomo Rizzolatti of the University of Parma, Italy, proposed that these neurons form a basic vocabulary of motor acts (Rizzolatti et al., 2000). Some cells are preferentially activated when the animal *reaches* for an object with its hand; others become active when the animal makes the same gesture to *hold* the object; and still others, when the animal attempts to *tear* the object—a behavior that might find its roots in the wild, where monkeys break off tree leaves. Therefore, cellular activity in this area might reflect not only the trajectory of a movement, but also basic gestural classes of actions such as reaching, holding, and tearing.

As described earlier, Brodmann area 6 includes premotor cortex on the lateral surface and supplementary motor area on the medial surface. We noted that one distinction between these two secondary regions was in terms of their integration of external and internal information. Lateral premotor is more heavily connected with parietal cortex, and this finding is consistent with a role for this region in sensory-guided action. The supplementary motor area (SMA), with its strong connections to medial frontal cortex, is likely biased to influence action selection and planning based on internal goals and personal experience (see Chapter 12).

The SMA has also been hypothesized to play an important role in more complex actions such as those involving sequential movements or those requiring coordinated movements of the two limbs. Usually, skilled behavior requires a precise interplay of both hands. The two hands may work in a similar fashion, as when we push a heavy object or row a boat. In other tasks, however, the two hands take on different, complementary roles, as when we open a jar or tie our shoes. Damage to the SMA, in both monkeys and humans, can lead to impaired performance on tasks that require integrated use of the two hands, even though the individual gestures performed by either hand alone are unaffected (Wiesendanger et al., 1996). If a person is asked to pantomime opening a drawer with one hand and to retrieve an object with the other, both hands may mime the opening gesture. Again, this deficit fits with the idea of a competitive process in which an abstract goal—to retrieve an object from the drawer—is activated and a competition ensues to determine how the required movements are assigned to each hand. When the SMA is damaged, the assignment process is disrupted and execution fails, even though the person is still able to express the general goal.

Lesions of the SMA can also result in *alien hand syndrome*, a condition in which one limb produces a seemingly meaningful action but the person denies responsibility for the action. For example, the person may reach out and grab an object and then be surprised to find the object in her hand. In more bizarre cases, the two hands may work in opposition to one another, a condition that is especially prevalent after lesions or resection of the corpus callosum. One patient described how her left hand would attempt to unbutton her blouse as soon as she finished getting dressed. When she was asked to give the experimenter a favorite book, her left hand reached out and snagged the closest book, whereupon she exclaimed with surprise, "Oh, that's not the one!" These behaviors provide further evidence of motor planning as a competitive process, one that can entail a competition not just between potential targets of an action (e.g., the coffee cup or the computer keyboard) but also between the two limbs (see How the Brain Works: Patting Your Head While Rubbing Your Stomach).

As we might expect, given its role in spatial representation, planning-related activity is also evident in the parietal lobe. When a spatial target is presented to a monkey, neurons begin to discharge in at least two regions within posterior parietal cortex (PPC), the lateral intraparietal (LIP) area, and the medial intraparietal (MIP) area (Calton et al., 2002; Cui & Andersen, 2007). When an arm movement is used to point to the target, the activity becomes stronger in MIP than LIP. If, however, the animal simply looks at the target, activity becomes stronger in LIP than MIP. Besides demonstrating effector specificity within the PPC, these findings also emphasize that plans for both reaching and eye movements are simultaneously prepared, consistent with the affordance competition hypothesis. Effector specificity within the parietal lobe has also been identified in humans with the aid of fMRI, which shows that different regions of the intraparietal sulcus are activated for eye and arm movements (Tosoni et al., 2008).

Together, these results help reveal how action selection and movement planning evolve within parietofrontal pathways. In general, we see many similarities between posterior parietal cortex and premotor regions. For example, cells in both regions exhibit directional tuning, and population vectors derived from either area provide an excellent match to behavior.

These areas, however, also have some interesting differences. One difference is seen in the *reference frame* for movement. To take our coffee cup example, we need to recognize that reaching requires a transformation from vision-centered coordinates to hand-centered coordinates. Our eyes can inform us of where objects lie in space. To reach that object with the hand, however, we need to define the position of the object with respect to the hand, not the eyes. Moreover, to sense hand position, we don't have to look at our hands. Somatosensory information is sufficient. You can prove this to yourself by trying to reach for something with the starting position of your hand either visible or occluded. Your accuracy is just as good either way. Physiological studies suggest that representations within parietal cortex tend to be in an eye-centered reference frame, whereas those in premotor cortex are more hand-centered (Batista et al., 1999). Thus parietofrontal processing involves a reference frame transformation.

Another intriguing difference between parietal and premotor motor areas comes from a fascinating study that attempted to identify where intentions are formed and how we become aware of them (Desmurget et al., 2009). The study employed direct brain stimulation during neurosurgery. When the stimulation was over posterior parietal cortex, the patients reported that they experienced the intention or desire to move, making comments such as "I felt a desire to lick my lips." In fact, if the stimulation level was increased, the intention was replaced with the perception that they had actually performed the movement. This experience, however, was illusory. The patients did not produce any overt movement, and even careful observation of the muscles showed no activity. In contrast, stimulation of the dorsal premotor cortex triggered complex multi-joint movements such as arm rotation or wrist flexion, but here the patients had no conscious awareness of the action and no sense of movement intention. It is unclear what to make of this striking dissociation. These researchers suggested that the posterior parietal cortex is more strongly linked to motor intention, the movement goals, and premotor cortex to movement execution. The signal we are aware of when making a movement does not emerge from the movement itself but rather from the prior conscious intention and predictions we make about the movement in advance of action.

This idea is further supported by an fMRI study conducted by Scott Grafton and colleagues at the

Patting Your Head While Rubbing Your Stomach

Recall the childhood challenge to pat your head while rubbing your stomach? Then you already know this apparently simple task is not so easy. It's nearly impossible to generate the conflicting spatial trajectories—moving one hand up and down while using the other to make a circular movement. The two movements compete. We fail to map one direction for one hand and the other direction for the opposite hand. Eventually one of the movements dominates, and we end up rubbing both the head and the stomach or patting both of them. Based on the selection hypothesis outlined in this chapter, we can think of this bimanual conflict as competition between two movement goals. Each task activates both hemispheres, and we cannot keep the crosstalk created by these activation patterns from interfering with the movements.

If this hypothesis is correct, spatial interference should be eliminated when each movement goal is restricted to a single hemisphere and the pathways connecting the two hemispheres are severed. To test this idea, Elizabeth Franz and her colleagues (1996) at the University of California, Berkeley, tested a patient whose corpus callosum had been resected. The stimuli for this bimanual movement study were a pair of three-sided figures whose sides followed either a common axis or perpendicular axes. The stimuli were projected briefly—one stimulus appeared in the left visual field, the other in the right visual field. After viewing the stimuli, the participants were instructed to produce the two patterns simultaneously, using the left hand for the pattern projected in the left visual field and the right hand for the pattern in the right visual field. The brief presentation was used to ensure that each stimulus was isolated to a single hemisphere in the split-brain patient. In control participants, rapid transfer of information via the corpus callosum was expected.

As Figure 1, top shows, control participants had little difficulty producing bilateral movements when the segments of the squares followed a common axis of movement (upper left). When the segments required movements along perpendicular axes, however (lower left), their performance deteriorated dramatically. Long pauses occurred before each segment, and trajectories frequently deviated from the target—something you can demonstrate to yourself by trying this task.

In contrast, the split-brain patient's performance (right column) did not differ significantly between the two movements. He initiated and completed movements in the two conditions with comparable speed, and the movements were accurate in both. Indeed, in a second experiment, this patient simultaneously drew a square with the left hand and a circle with the right hand. Each hemisphere produced

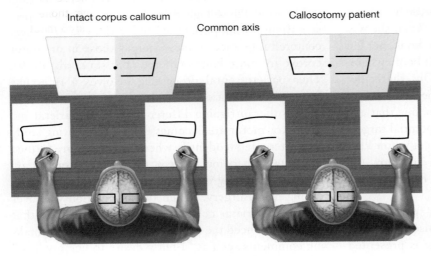

Intact corpus callosum   Callosotomy patient

Common axis

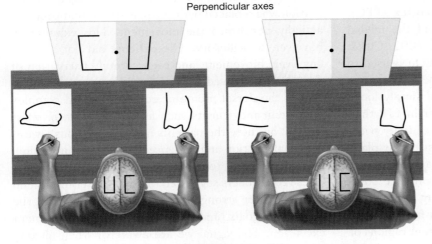

Perpendicular axes

FIGURE 1 Bimanual movements following resection of the corpus callosum. While looking at a central fixation point, participants were briefly shown the two patterns. They were instructed to simultaneously draw the pattern on the left with the left hand and the one on the right with the right hand. Normal participants **(left column)** were able to draw the patterns that shared a common axis but had severe difficulty when the orientation of the two figures differed by 90°. The split-brain patient **(right column)** performed equally well in both conditions.

the pattern with no signs of interference from demands presented to the opposite hemisphere.

These results indicate that the callosotomy procedure yields a spatial uncoupling in bimanual movements. Another striking observation was that, even for the split-brain patient, the actions of the two hands were not independent of one another. As with the control participants, the two hands moved in synchrony. They initiated and terminated the segments of the squares at approximately the same time. This temporal coupling was seen more clearly when participants were asked to produce oscillatory movements in which each hand moved along a single axis. Regardless of whether the two hands followed a common axis (e.g., both horizontal or both vertical) or perpendicular axes (e.g., one horizontal and the other vertical), the two hands reversed direction at the same time.

This study provided valuable insights into the neural structures underlying bimanual coordination. First, the spatial goals for bimanual movements are coordinated via processing across the corpus callosum. When a task requires conflicting directions of movement, interference is extensive as long as the callosal connections are intact.

Second, these connections are not necessary for the temporal coupling of movement. Perhaps the initiation of movement is regulated either by a single hemisphere or by subcortical mechanisms. Third, the dissociation of spatial and temporal coupling emphasizes a distributed view of how the motor system's neural structures contribute to coordination. The neural structures that represent the spatial goals are separate from those involved in initiating the movements selected to meet these goals.

University of California, Santa Barbara (Hamilton & Grafton, 2007). They questioned whether motor representations in parietal regions correspond to the nuts and bolts of the movements per se, or the grander intentions concerned with the goals and outcome of the action. This study took advantage of the widely studied *repetition suppression (RS) effect*. RS was first described in studies of visual perception: When a stimulus is repeated, the blood oxygen level–dependent (BOLD) response to the second presentation of the stimulus is lower than that to the initial presentation. In applying this fMRI method to action perception, the researchers asked whether the RS effect was linked to the goal of an action, the specific movement, or a combination of these factors (Figure 8.18). To test this, participants were shown videos of short action clips. The videos showed a box that could be opened by sliding the cover forward or backward. In this way, the researchers could present pairs of video clips in which either the same goal was achieved (e.g., closing the cover) by two different actions, in which one clip showed sliding forward and the other backward; or the same movement was made, but resulted in two different goals, one resulting in an open box and the other a closed box. The results showed that RS in the right inferior parietal cortex was related to the action goal, whereas RS in left frontal cortex was related to the

movement (Figure 8.19), providing a slick demonstration of goal-based processing in parietal cortex and movement-based processing in frontal cortex.

TAKE-HOME MESSAGES

- The affordance competition hypothesis proposes that the processes of action selection (what to do) and specification (how to do it) occur simultaneously within an interactive neural network that continuously evolves from planning to execution.

- Action selection involves a competitive process.

- Rather than view selection and planning as serial processes, neural activity reveals that there is parallel activation of multiple goals and movement plans.

- Supplementary motor area is important for coordinating motor behavior in time (sequential movements) and between limbs (bimanual coordination).

- Parietal motor areas also show topography: Different regions of the intraparietal cortex are associated with hand, arm, and eye movements.

- Parietal motor representations are more goal oriented, whereas premotor-motor representations are more closely linked to the movement itself.

- Conscious awareness of movement appears to be related to the neural processing of action intention rather than the movement itself.

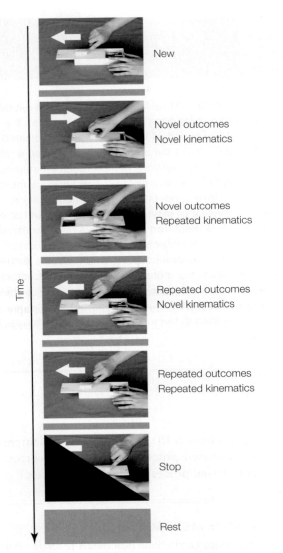

FIGURE 8.18 A set of stimuli for inducing repetition suppression. Participants watched a series of movie clips of a hand opening or closing a box. In this example, the initial clip shows the hand moving forward to open the box. In subsequent clips, the outcome was either repeated or novel, and the kinematics (direction of motion) was either repeated or novel relative to the previous clip. Repetition suppression effects were measured by comparing the BOLD response over successive clips.

The Brain–Machine Interface

Can neural signals be used to control a movement directly with the brain, bypassing the intermediate stage of muscles? For instance, could you plan an action in your motor cortex (e.g., let's fold the laundry), somehow connect those motor cortex neurons to a computer, and send the planned action to a robot, which would fold the laundry? Sounds extraordinary? Yet it is happening. The process is called a **brain–machine interface (BMI)**. It uses decoding principles (see

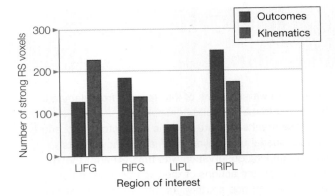

FIGURE 8.19 Brain regions showing repetition suppression effects for repeated outcomes and movements. Voxels showing RS in inferior frontal gyrus (IFG) and inferior parietal lobe (IPL) in the right and left hemispheres. RS was strongest in left IFG when the movement was repeated and strongest in right IPL when the outcome was repeated.

Chapter 6) to control brain–machine interface systems, which have incredible potential to improve the lives of people with spinal cord injuries, amputations, and other diseases that have affected their ability to move at will.

Early Work on Brain–Machine Interface Systems

John Chapin of the State University of New York (Chapin et al., 1999) provided one of the first demonstrations of the viability of a BMI by using a simple motor task in a highly motivated population: thirsty rats. He first trained the rats to press a button that caused a lever arm to rotate. The lever was connected to a computer, which measured the pressure on the button and used this signal to adjust the position of a robot arm. One end of the lever contained a small well; if positioned properly, a few drops of water would fill the well. Thus, by learning to vary the pressure of the button press, the rat controlled the lever arm and could replenish the water and then spin the lever to take a drink (Figure 8.20). Chapin recorded from neurons in the motor cortex during this task, measuring the correlation between each neuron and the force output the rat used to adjust and move the lever. Once the rat's behavior had stabilized, Chapin could construct an online population vector, one that matched the animal's force output rather than movement direction. With as few as 30 or so neurons, the match between the population vector and behavior was excellent.

Here is where things get interesting. Chapin then disconnected the input of the button to the computer and instead used the output of the time-varying population vector as input to the computer to control the position of the lever arm. The rats still pushed the button, but that no longer controlled the lever; it was now controlled by their brain activity. If the

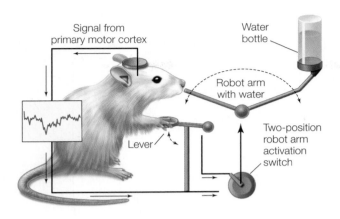

FIGURE 8.20 Rats can be trained to use a lever to control a robot arm that delivers them drops of water.
Neurons in the rat's primary motor cortex are recorded while the animal presses the lever. A population vector is constructed, representing the force exerted by the animal. A switch is then activated so that the position of the lever is now based on the population vector. The rat soon learns that he does not have to press the lever to retrieve the water.

activity level in the vector was high, the arm swiveled in one direction; if low, it swiveled in the other direction, or even stopped the lever arm entirely. Amazingly, population vectors generated from as few as 25 neurons proved sufficient for the rats to successfully control the robot arm to obtain water.

As impressive as this result was, Chapin could not, of course, tell the animals about the shift from arm control to brain control. Unaware of the switch to BMI, the rats continued to press and release the button. Over time, though, the animals became sensitive to the lack of a precise correlation between their arm movements and the lever position (the correlation was not perfect). Amazingly, they continued to generate the cortical signals necessary to control the lever, but they also stopped moving their limb. They learned they could kick back, relax, and simply think about pushing the button with the precision required to satiate their thirst.

Over the past 20 years, research on brain–machine interface (BMI) systems has skyrocketed. Three elements are required: microelectrode arrays implanted on the cortex to record neural activity, a computer with decoding algorithms, and a prosthetic effector. In the first primate studies, monkeys were trained to control the two-dimensional position of a computer cursor. With more sophisticated algorithms, these animals have learned to use BMI systems that control a robotic arm with multiple joints, moving the prosthetic limb through three-dimensional space to grasp food and bring it to their mouth (Velliste et al., 2008). Videos are available at http://motorlab.neurobio.pitt.edu/multimedia.php. Besides controlling BMI with output from primary motor cortex, BMI also works with cells in premotor, supplementary motor, and parietal cortex (Carmena et al., 2003). The control algorithms have also

become more advanced, adopting ideas from work on computer learning. Rather than use a serial process in which the directional tuning of the neurons is fixed during the initial free-movement stage, researchers now use computer algorithms that allow the tuning to be updated by real-time visual feedback as the animal learns to control the BMI device (D. Taylor et al., 2002).

Making Brain–Machine Interface Systems Stable

One major challenge facing BMI researchers is how to establish a stable control system, one that can last for years. In a typical experiment, the animal starts each daily session by performing real movements to allow the researcher to construct the tuning profiles of each neuron. The process is rather like a daily recalibration. Once the neuron profiles are established, the BMI system is implemented. This approach, though, is not practical for BMI use as a clinical treatment. First, it is very difficult to record a fixed set of neurons over a long period of time. Moreover, construction of neuron profiles using real movements won't be possible for BMI to be useful for paralyzed individuals or people who have lost a limb.

To address this issue, researchers have looked at both the stability and flexibility of neural representations. Karunesh Ganguly and Jose Carmena (2009) at the University of California, Berkeley, implanted a grid of 128 microelectrodes in the motor cortex of a monkey. This device allowed them to make continuous daily recordings. Although the signal from some electrodes would change from day to day, a substantial number of neurons remained stable for days (Figure 8.21). Using the output from this stable set, a BMI system successfully performed center-out reaching movements over a 3-week period. The animals achieved close to 100% accuracy in reaching the targets, and the time required to complete each movement became much shorter over the 3-week period. This result suggested that with a stable decoder, the motor cortex neurons used a remarkably stable activation pattern for prosthetic control.

The shocker came in the next experiment. Using these well-trained animals, researchers randomly shuffled the decoder. For example, if a neuron had a preferred direction of 90 degrees, the algorithm was altered so that the output of this neuron was now treated as if it had a preferred direction of 130 degrees. This new "stable" decoder, of course, played havoc with BMI performance. The monkey would think "move up," and the cursor would move sideways. Over a few days of practice, however, the monkey was able to adapt to the new decoder, again reaching near-perfect performance (Figure 8.21c). With visual feedback, the animal could learn to use a decoder unrelated to arm movements. As long as the algorithm remained stable, it could actually reshape the decoder. Even more impressive,

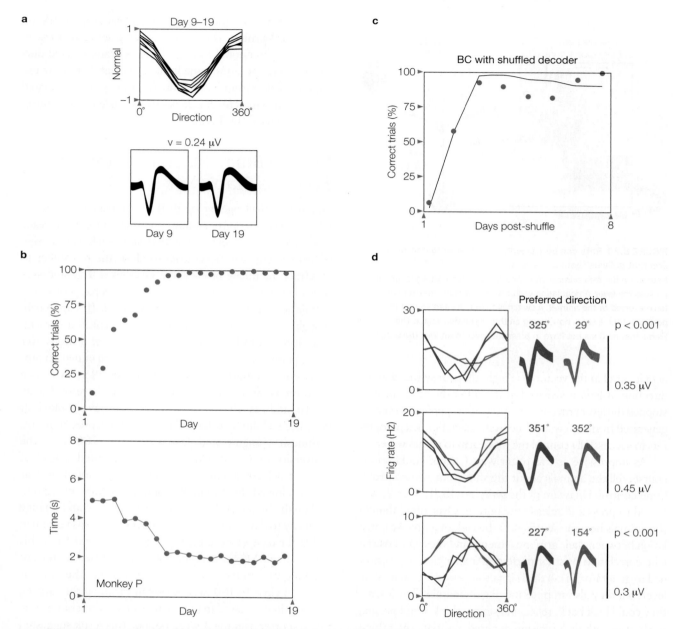

FIGURE 8.21 Stability and flexibility of performance and neutral activity during BMI control.
(a) Recordings were made for 19 consecutive days from an ensemble of neurons in motor cortex. Directional tuning for two neurons show remarkable stability across Sessions 9–19. **(b)** Using a fixed decoder based on the output of the neural ensemble, the monkey learns to successfully move a cursor under BMI control in the center-out task. Accuracy becomes near perfect within a few days and the time required on each trial becomes much faster. **(c)** Performance with a shuffled decoder. The input to the BMI algorithm was randomly shuffled in Session 20 and the animal failed to reach any targets. With continued use of the shuffled decoder, however, the animal quickly became proficient at reaching the target. **(d)** Tuning functions for three neurons when used in original decoder (blue) or shuffled decoder (red). Tuning functions for some neurons shifted dramatically for the two contexts. With practice, the animal could successfully control the cursor with either decoder.

when the original decoder was reinstated, the animal again quickly adapted. Interestingly, with this adaptive system, the tuning functions of each neuron varied from one context to the next and even deviated from their shape during natural movement (Figure 8.21d). It appears, then, that long-term neuroprosthetic control leads to the

formation of a remarkably stable cortical map that is readily recalled and resistant to the storage of a second map.

These results hold great promise for the translation of BMI research into the clinic. They demonstrate that the representation of individual neurons can be highly flexible, adapting to the current context. Such flexibility is essential for ensuring that the system will remain stable over time, and it is also essential for using a single BMI system to control a host of devices such as computer cursors or eating utensils. It is reasonable to assume that a single set of neurons can learn to incorporate the different challenges presented by devices that have no friction or mass (the position of a mouse on a computer screen) to ones with large mass and complicated moving parts (a prosthetic arm or a robot).

There is great urgency to get BMI ideas into clinical practice. The numbers of patients who would benefit from such systems are huge. In the United States alone, over 5.5 million people suffer some form of paralysis, either from injury or disease, and 1.7 million have limb loss. This need has motivated some scientists to move toward clinical trials in humans. John Donoghue and his colleagues at Brown University presented the first such trial, working with a patient, M.N., who became quadriplegic following a stab wound that severed his spinal cord. The researchers implanted an array of microchips in the patient's motor cortex (Hochberg et al., 2006). Despite 3 years of paralysis, the cells were quite active. Moreover, the firing level of the neurons varied as M.N. imagined different types of movements. Some units were active when he imagined making movements that involved the shoulder, others while imagining moving his hand. The researchers were also able to determine the directional tuning profiles of each neuron, asking M.N. to imagine movements over a range of directions.

From this data, they created population vectors and used them as control signals for BMI interface devices. Using the output of approximately 100 neurons, M.N. was able to move a cursor around a computer screen (Figure 8.22).

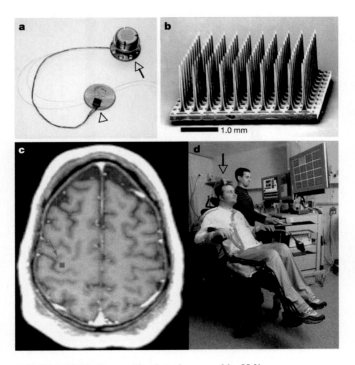

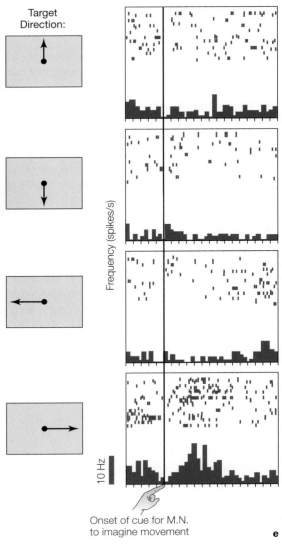

FIGURE 8.22 Brain–machine interface used by M.N.
(a) The size of the implanted electrode device in relation to a U.S. penny. (b) A magnified image of the recording electrode array. (c) The location in the precentral gyrus where the electrode array was implanted. (d) The subject M.N. with the implanted device. He is controlling a cursor on the computer screen with his neural activity. (e) The firing of one cell during four different conditions in which M.N. was cued to imagine moving his hand up, down, left, or right. The cell shown here fired best when M.N. imagined moving his hand to the right; other cells fired selectively when M.N. imagined moving his hand left, up, or down. When information from all of the cells recorded from the implanted electrode was combined, the desired direction of movement could be predicted. Once the BMI device learned how the pattern of M.N.'s activity correlated with the desire to move in these directions, M.N. could begin to use his intentions to move a cursor wherever he chose. Using this technology, M.N. was also able to open simulated e-mails, operate a television, open and close a prosthetic hand, and move a robotic arm. Such technology holds great promise for people like M.N., who cannot otherwise physically interact with their environment.

His responses were relatively slow and the path of the cursor somewhat erratic. Nonetheless, M.N. could control the cursor to open his e-mail, use software programs to make drawings, or play computer games such as PONG. When connected to a prosthetic limb, M.N. could control the opening and closing of the hand, a first step to performing much more complicated tasks. Another patient has learned, after months of training, to use a BMI system to control a robotic arm to reach and grasp objects (Hochberg et al., 2012). (Video clips of people using BMI systems can be seen at http://www.nature.com/nature/journal/v442/n7099/suppinfo/nature04970.html and http://www.nature.com/nature/journal/v485/n7398/full/nature11076.html#/supplementary-information.)

BMI research is still in its infancy. This work, though, provides a compelling example of how basic findings in neuroscience—the coding of movement direction and population vector representations—can be combined with principles from bioengineering to develop vital clinical therapies.

TAKE-HOME MESSAGES

- Brain–machine interface systems use neural signals to directly control robotic devices such as a computer cursor or a prosthetic device.

- BMIs offer a promising avenue for rehabilitation of people with severe movement disorders such as those resulting from spinal cord injury.

- Early BMI systems required two phases. In the first phase, neural activity was recorded while the animal produced movement and the tuning properties (such as preferred direction) were recorded. In the second phase, the output from these neurons was used to control an interface device.

- Current studies are exploring how decoders can be adapted through experience in BMI control and are looking at the stability of such systems over extended periods of time. Advances on these problems are essential for building BMI systems that will be useful in clinical settings.

Movement Initiation and the Basal Ganglia

With multiple action plans dueling it out in the cortex, how do we decide on which movement to execute? We can't use our right arm to simultaneously type on the computer keyboard and reach for a cup of coffee. Parallel processing works fine for planning, but at some point, the system must commit to a particular action.

The basal ganglia appear to play a critical role in movement initiation. To understand this, it is important to examine the neuroanatomical wiring of this subcortical structure which is diagrammed in Figure 8.23. Almost all of the afferent fibers to the basal ganglia terminate in two of the nuclei, the caudate and putamen, or what are collectively referred to as the *striatum*. These input fibers originate across much of the cerebral cortex, including sensory, motor, and association cortices. The basal ganglia have two output pathways, which originate in the internal segment of the globus pallidus (GP$_i$) and the pars reticularis of the substantia nigra (SN$_r$).

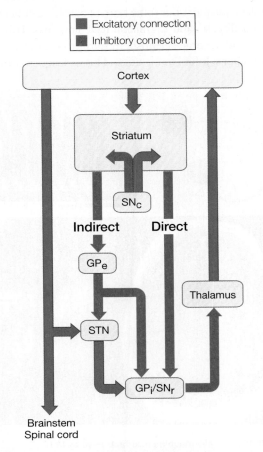

FIGURE 8.23 Wiring of the direct and indirect pathways in the basal ganglia.
Green links indicate excitatory projections, and red links indicate inhibitory projections. Inputs from the cortex project primarily to the striatum. From here, processing flows along two pathways. The direct pathway goes to the output nuclei: the internal segment of the globus pallidus (GP$_i$) and the pars reticularis of the substantia nigra (SN$_r$). The indirect pathway includes a circuit through the external segment of the globus pallidus (GP$_e$) and the subthalamic nucleus (STN) and then to the output nuclei. The output projections to the thalamus are relayed to the cortex, frequently terminating close to the initial source of input. The dopaminergic projections of the pars compacta of the substantia nigra (SN$_c$) modulate striatal activity by facilitating the direct pathway via the D$_1$ receptors and inhibiting the indirect pathway via the D$_2$ receptors. The output of the basal ganglia also inhibits other subcortical structures such as the superior colliculus (not shown).

SN$_r$ axons project to and terminate primarily in the superior colliculus and provide a crucial signal for the initiation of eye movements. GP$_i$ axons, on the other hand, terminate in thalamic nuclei, which in turn project to the motor cortex, supplementary motor area, and prefrontal cortex.

Processing within the basal ganglia takes place along two pathways (DeLong, 1990). The *direct pathway* involves fast, direct, inhibitory connections from the striatum to the GP$_i$ and SN$_r$. The *indirect pathway* takes a slower, roundabout route to the GP$_i$ and SN$_r$. Striatal axons inhibit the external segment of the globus pallidus (GP$_e$), which in turn inhibits the subthalamic nucleus and GP$_i$. The output from the basal ganglia via the GP$_i$ and SN$_r$ is also inhibitory. Indeed, these nuclei have high baseline firing rates, producing strong tonic inhibition of the motor system via their inhibitory projection to the thalamus or the superior colliculi, a region important for eye movements.

The final internal pathway of note is the projection from the pars compacta of the substantia nigra (SN$_c$) to the striatum, known as the *dopamine pathway*. Interestingly, this pathway has opposite effects on the direct and indirect pathways, despite having a common transmitter, dopamine. The substantia nigra excites the direct pathway by acting on one type of dopamine receptor (D$_1$) and inhibits the indirect pathway by acting on a different type of dopamine receptor (D$_2$).

The Basal Ganglia as a Gatekeeper

Tracing what happens when cortical fibers activate the striatum can help us understand basal ganglia function. Via the direct pathway, target neurons in the output nuclei (GP$_i$

and SN$_r$) of the basal ganglia are inhibited, thus encumbering the connection to the thalamus. This results in excitation of the thalamus and cortical motor areas. On the other hand, striatal activation along the indirect pathway results in increased excitation of the output nuclei, leading to increased inhibition of the cortex. It appears, then, that the direct and indirect pathways are at odds with one another. If processing along the indirect pathway is slower, however, the basal ganglia can act as a gatekeeper of cortical activity; less inhibition from the direct pathway is followed by more inhibition from the indirect pathway. The nigrostriatal fibers of the dopamine pathway enhance the direct pathway while reducing the effects of the indirect pathway.

Seen in this light, the basal ganglia can be hypothesized to play a critical role in the initiation of actions (Figure 8.24). As we argued earlier in this chapter, processing in the cortical motor areas can be viewed as a competitive process in which candidate actions compete for control of the motor apparatus. The basal ganglia are positioned to help resolve the competition. The strong inhibitory baseline activity keeps the motor system in check, allowing cortical representations of possible movements to become activated without triggering movement. As a specific motor plan gains strength, the inhibitory signal is decreased for selected neurons. This movement representation breaches the gate, thus winning the competition.

Interestingly, computational analyses demonstrate that the physiology of the direct pathway in the basal ganglia is ideally designed to function as a winner-take-all system—a method for committing to one action plan from among the various alternatives. Greg Berns and Terry Sejnowski (1996) of the Salk Institute in La Jolla,

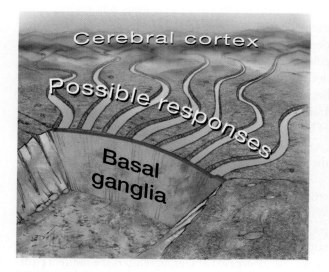

FIGURE 8.24 Computational model of the basal ganglia's role in movement initiation.
The inhibitory output of the basal ganglia keeps potential responses in check until activation for one of the options reaches a threshold, resulting in the initiation of that movement. By this model, "selection" occurs even though the basal ganglia need not evaluate the possible choices, but rather, only monitors their activation level.

California, evaluated the functional consequences of all possible pair-wise connections of two synapses, either of which could be excitatory or inhibitory. By their analysis, a series of two successive inhibitory links is the most efficient way to make a selected pattern stand out from the background. With this circuit, the disinhibited signal stands out from a quiet background. In contrast, with a pair of excitatory connections the selected pattern has to raise its signal above a loud background. Similarly, a combination of inhibitory and excitatory synapses in either order is not efficient in making the selected pattern distinct from the background. Berns and Sejnowski noted that the double inhibition of the direct pathway is relatively unique to the basal ganglia. This arrangement is particularly useful for selecting a response in a competitive system. For example, consider if you were at the beach, searching for a friend's kayak on the horizon. If the ocean is filled with all sorts of sailing vessels, your task is challenging. But if the waters are empty that afternoon, it will be easy to detect the kayak as it comes around the point. Similarly, a new input pattern from the striatum will stand out much more clearly when the background activity is inhibited.

As mentioned earlier, dopamine has opposite effects on the direct and indirect pathway. Dopamine has long been known to be a critical neurotransmitter in signaling reward. Dopamine receptors are found in many brain regions, but they are especially prevalent in the striatum (see Chapter 12 for a detailed discussion of dopamine and reward). The direct pathway has D_1 receptors, which are excitatory and produce excitatory postsynaptic potentials (EPSPs); the indirect pathway has D_2 receptors, which are inhibitory and produce IPSPs. The net result is that dopamine release has the effect of promoting selected actions represented in the direct pathway and discouraging nonselected actions via the indirect pathway. Thus, rewarded actions are more likely to occur in the future, providing a link between movement initiation, reward, and motor learning (see "Contributions of the Basal Ganglia to Learning and Cognition").

Disorders of the Basal Ganglia

Looking at the basal ganglia circuits in Figure 8.23 makes it clear that lesions in any part of the basal ganglia interfere with coordinated movement, but the form of the problem would vary considerably depending on the location of the lesion. For instance, **Huntington's disease** is a hereditary neurodegenerative disorder that appears during the fourth or fifth decade of life. The onset is subtle, usually a gradual change in mental attitude in which the patient is irritable, absentminded, and loses interest in normal activities. Within a year, movement abnormalities are noticed: clumsiness, balance problems, and a general restlessness. Involuntary writhing movements, or *chorea*, gradually dominate normal motor

function. The patient may adopt contorted postures, and his arms, legs, trunk, and head may be in constant motion.

We can understand the excessive movements, or hyperkinesia, seen with Huntington's disease by considering how the pathology affects information flow through the basal ganglia. The striatal changes occur primarily in inhibitory neurons forming the indirect pathway. As shown in Figure 8.25a, these changes lead to a reduced output from the basal ganglia, and thus greater excitation of thalamic neurons, which in turn excite the motor cortex. Later in the disease, many regions of the brain area are affected. But atrophy is most prominent in the basal ganglia, where the cell death rate is ultimately as high as 90% in the striatum.

The genetic origin of Huntington's disease is briefly reviewed in Chapter 3. This fatal disease has no cure, and patients usually die within 12 years of onset. At autopsy, the brain of a Huntington's disease patient typically reveals widespread pathology in cortical and subcortical areas. These changes are also evident from imaging studies performed as the disease unfolds.

Parkinson's disease, the most common and well-known disorder affecting the basal ganglia, is the result of the loss of dopaminergic neurons in the substantia nigra pars compacta (SN_c; Figure 8.26). As with most brain tissue, dopaminergic neurons in the substantia nigra (SN_c) atrophy with age. Parkinsonian symptoms become manifest when too many of these neurons are lost (Figure 8.26b).

Symptoms of Parkinson's disease related to the basal ganglia include disorders of posture and locomotion, **hypokinesia**, and **bradykinesia**. *Hypokinesia* refers to an absence of or reduction in voluntary movement. Parkinson's patients act as if they are stuck in a posture and cannot change it. This problem, which we might think of as a stuck or blocked gate, is especially evident when the patients try to initiate a new movement. Many patients develop small tricks to help them overcome the hypokinesia. For example, one patient walked with a cane, not because he needed help maintaining his balance, but because it was a visual target that helped him to get a jump start. When he wanted to walk, he placed the cane in front of his right foot and kicked it—which caused him to overcome inertia and commence his walking. Once started, the movements are frequently slow, or *bradykinetic*.

Look at Figure 8.25b. Parkinson's disease primarily reduces the inhibitory activity along the direct pathway. With no excitatory SN_c input into the striatum, the output along the direct pathway decreases and the inhibitory output from the GP_i to the thalamus increases. At the same time, decreased SN_c input inhibits the indirect pathway. The net physiological effect is increased thalamic inhibition, either because GP_e produces less inhibition of GP_i or because the subthalamic nucleus (STN) increases its excitation of the GP_i. The net result of all these effects

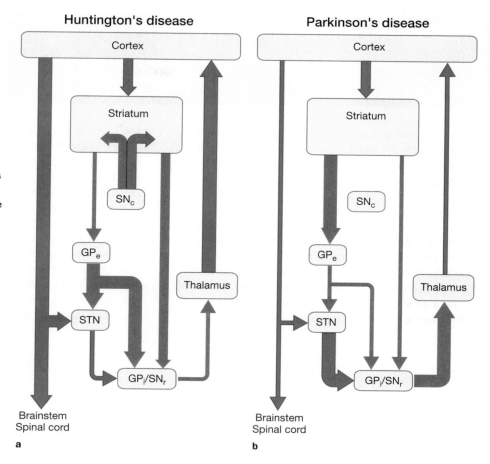

FIGURE 8.25 Differential neuro-chemical alterations in Huntington's and Parkinson's diseases.
As in Figure 8.23, green links indicate excitatory projections, and red links indicate inhibitory projections. **(a)** In Huntington's disease, the inhibitory projection along the indirect pathway from the striatum to the external segment of the globus pallidus (GP$_e$) is reduced. The net consequence is reduced inhibitory output from the internal segment of the globus pallidus (GP$_i$) and thus an increase in cortical excitation and movement. **(b)** Parkinson's disease primarily reduces the inhibitory activity along the direct pathway, resulting in increased inhibition from the GP$_i$ to the thalamus and thus a reduction in cortical activity and movement.

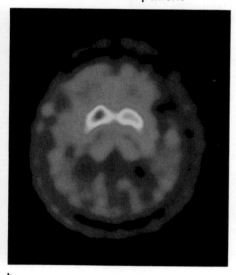

FIGURE 8.26 Radioactive tracers to label the distribution of specific neurotransmitters with PET.
Healthy individuals and Parkinson's disease patients were injected with a radioactive tracer, fluorodopa (seen as yellow, red, and orange). This agent is visible in the striatum, reflecting the dopaminergic projections to this structure from the substantia nigra. Compare the greater uptake in the scan from a healthy person **(a)** to the uptake in a patient's scan **(b)**.

Contributions of the Basal Ganglia to Learning and Cognition

Parkinson's patients get stuck in one position or posture and have difficulty shifting to a new one. After a number of years, they also show cognitive problems, performing below normal on various tests of neuropsychological function. This may be either secondary to effects of chronic L-DOPA therapy or the result of reduced dopaminergic input to the cerebral cortex. Their cognitive deficits, however, could be at the heart of both the motor and cognitive problems of these patients. Perhaps the basal ganglia perform an operation that is critical for shifting from one movement to another as well as from one idea (mental set) to another.

To test this idea, Steven Keele and his colleagues at the University of Oregon (Hayes et al., 1998) developed

two tasks: one required a motor shifting operation (Figure 1) and the other a cognitive shift. For the motor task, patients were taught two sequences of three key presses (1-2-3 and 1-3-2). After this training phase, the patients were required to produce a six-element sequence composed of either the two sequences in succession or two repetitions of one of the sequences. As predicted, in the shifting sequence condition (from the 1-2-3 to 1-3-2), the responses for the Parkinson's patients were especially slow at the switching point, the transition from the third to the fourth element. Note that, in both the repetition and the shifting condition, the fourth element requires exactly the same response: a finger press with the index finger.

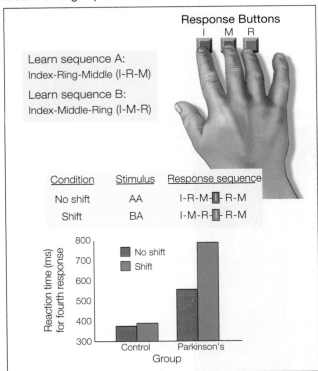

Motor shifting experiment

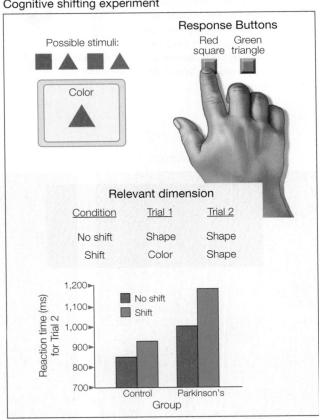

Cognitive shifting experiment

a

b

FIGURE 1 Motor and cognitive tests of set shifting.
(a) In the motor task, participants performed two successive sequences that were either identical or different. Although the movement at the transition point was the same in both the no-shift and the shift conditions, Parkinson's patients were much slower in the latter condition. **(b)** In the cognitive task, participants had to respond to either the color or the shape of a stimulus. Trials were paired such that the second response was either the same dimension (no shift) or the other dimension (shift). As in the motor task, Parkinson's patients were especially slow when they had to shift.

In the shifting condition, however, this response is part of a different sub-sequence.

For the cognitive task, patients were trained on reaction time tasks involving either color or shape discrimination. After training on each dimension, pairs of trials were introduced in which the two responses were either along the same dimension (e.g., color–color for both trials) or required a shift from one dimension to the other (e.g., shape on one trial switching to color on the next). As in the motor task, the Parkinson's patients were significantly slower when they had to shift dimensional sets. This problem cannot be attributed to a motor deficit, because the motor responses (pressing a key) on the second trial were identical in all conditions.

The shifting hypothesis offers a unified framework for understanding basal ganglia function in both action and cognition. Located in a position to monitor activation across wide regions of the cortex, the basal ganglia are able to orchestrate a shift between different actions or between different mental sets. The shifting hypothesis is also relevant when thinking about the more general role of the basal ganglia and dopamine in reinforcement learning.

Behaviors have consequences, and when consequences affect the probability that a behavior will or will not be repeated, we call that a *reinforcement contingency*. We know that when a consequence is rewarding, we alter our behavior to repeat the reward, just like a dog does when he is rewarded with a treat. Dopamine neurons encode both present rewards and the prediction of future rewards (Chapter 12). Thus, a rewarding consequence, such as a winning crosscourt forehand in tennis, will result in the release of dopamine in the striatum. It can be hypothesized that dopamine modifies the input–output channels in the basal ganglia, biasing the system to produce certain responses over others. This makes it more likely that the same response will be initiated when the rewarded input pattern is reactivated in the future (Figure 2). In fact,

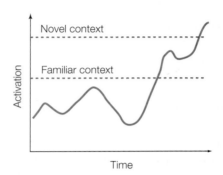

FIGURE 2

corticostriatal synaptic plasticity is strongly modulated by dopamine (Reynolds & Wickens, 2000). The next time the tennis ball whizzes by from the same direction, your arm powers back in the previously successful pattern. Thus, by biasing behavior and making it more likely that an animal will shift to the newly rewarded action when it runs across the same circumstances again, the dopamine neurons of the basal ganglia facilitate reinforcement learning.

The ability to alter responses according to probable outcomes is essential for producing novel behavior or for combining patterns of behavior into novel sequences. We can now see a link between basal ganglia dysfunction and psychiatric disorders characterized by the repetitive production of stereotyped movement patterns. Examples are Tourette's syndrome, where a simple tic or a hand brushing across the face may be seen, and obsessive-compulsive disorder, where an entire behavioral sequence, such as hand washing, can be performed over and over. A failure to shift may result in the repeated production of a single pattern—or in an absence of movement, the problem of the patient with Parkinson's disease. In either case, basal ganglia dysfunction makes it difficult to select new actions that arise when sensory input or internal goals change.

is reduced excitation of the cortex due to the excessive thalamic inhibition. The cortex may continue to plan movements, but without normal functioning basal ganglia, the ability to quickly initiate a movement is compromised. Once movement is initiated, it is frequently slow.

One of the great breakthroughs in neurology occurred in the 1950s with the development of L-DOPA, a synthetic precursor of dopamine. L-DOPA can cross the blood–brain barrier and be metabolized to create dopamine, providing a replacement therapy for the loss of endogenous dopamine. This therapy provided a tremendous benefit to people with Parkinson's disease and, in fact, continues to do so today. Almost all people who are diagnosed with Parkinson's are put on some form of L-DOPA therapy, providing a simple medication protocol that considerably improves their motor problems. Over time, however, the efficacy of the drug may change. Many patients develop drug-induced movement disorders, or hyperkinesias—

excessive, involuntary movements that are as debilitating as the symptoms of the disease. Moreover, the medication does not prevent the loss of dopamine-producing neurons, so the disease continues to progress until at some point patients may no longer be responsive to L-DOPA therapy.

Due to the limitations of drug therapy, clinicians have sought to develop alternative or supplemental treatments for Parkinson's disease. For instance, neurosurgeons have devised interventions that seek to restore the balance of inhibitory and excitatory circuits between the basal ganglia and the cortex. The hyperactivity of the globus pallidus that occurs when inhibitory striatal signals are attenuated by the disease can be reduced by pallidotomy, a procedure in which small lesions are made in the globus pallidus. This procedure has proven effective in many patients. The pallidus, however, is quite large, and identifying the best location for the lesions is problematic. What's more, significant risks are associated with the procedure (de Bie et al., 2002).

An alternative approach that has gained widespread acceptance over the past decade involves another surgical method, **deep-brain stimulation** (**DBS**; Figure 8.27). DBS consists of implanting an electrode into a targeted neural region; for Parkinson's disease, this is usually the STN, although some patients receive implants in the globus pallidus and others in the thalamus. A current is then passed through the electrode at high frequencies. This stimulation alters activity in the targeted region and throughout the circuit.

Why DBS works on Parkinson's disease remains a mystery (Gradinaru et al., 2009). It is unclear which circuit elements are responsible for the therapeutic effects. The stimulation level is usually quite high, also creating unnatural activity levels in the nearby basal ganglia circuitry. As can be seen in Figure 8.23, stimulation of the STN should increase excitation of the globus pallidus and result in increased inhibition of the thalamus. Thus, DBS might have been expected to exacerbate parkinsonian symptoms. The mystery is that it doesn't. One hypothesis is that the periodic output of the DBS stimulator provides a mechanism to normalize neural oscillations between the basal ganglia and cortex. By this view, it is not the overall level of activity that is important, but the pattern of activity.

Whatever the actual mechanism, it is now clear that DBS can be a very effective treatment for people with advanced Parkinson's disease and for some individuals who do not respond to drug therapy. Indeed, the effects can be dramatic. With the stimulator off, the patient may be frozen in place, only able to initiate locomotion with great effort—and even then, taking tiny, shuffling steps. Turn on the device, wait 10 minutes, and the person is sprinting down the hallway. DBS has proven extremely popular: In its first decade of use, the procedure was performed on over 75,000 patients.

DBS is now used to treat a host of movement disorders such as tremor and dystonia (involuntary muscle spasms and twisting of the limbs). Clinical trials are now under way for many other uses, including chronic headache, Alzheimer's disease, and even drug addiction (Lyons, 2011). Much of the focus here is on comparing the efficacy of different implant locations in the treatment of these disorders. As with Parkinson's disease, we lack a clear understanding of why the treatment works in many of these cases (nor do we have enough data to verify the long-term benefit). But the demand for effective treatments is great. Sometimes it is beneficial to test new procedures once they have been deemed safe, even if we are unsure of their clinical efficacy.

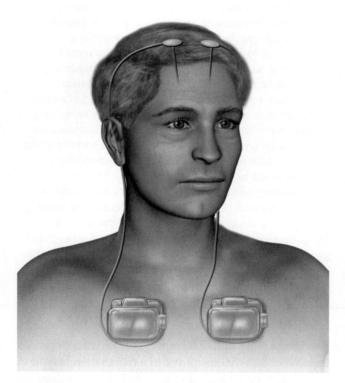

FIGURE 8.27 Deep-brain stimulation for Parkinson's disease is achieved by implanting electrodes in the subthalamic nucleus of the basal ganglia.
A pacemaker-like device is connected to the electrodes and implanted subcutaneously. The electrodes can then be stimulated by the pacemaker at regular intervals, leading to improvement in many of the symptoms of Parkinson's disease.

TAKE-HOME MESSAGES

- The output from the basal ganglia, via thalamic projections, influences activity in the cortex, including the motor cortex.
- All of the output signals from the basal ganglia are inhibitory. Thus, in the tonic state, the basal ganglia dampen cortical activity.
- Movement initiation requires disinhibition: The striatal projection to the GP$_i$ inhibits an inhibitory signal, resulting in excitation at the cortex.

- Striatal neurons influence the output nuclei of the basal ganglia via the direct pathway and the indirect pathway.
- Dopamine is produced in the substantia nigra pars compacta, a brainstem nucleus that projects to the striatum. It has an excitatory effect on the direct pathway and an inhibitory effect on the indirect pathway.
- Parkinson's disease results from cell death in dopamine-producing cells in the substantia nigra.
- Parkinson's disease includes disorders of posture and locomotion, hypokinesia (the absence or reduction of voluntary movement), and bradykinesia (slowness in initiating and executing movement).
- The drug L-DOPA is used in treating Parkinson's disease because it can compensate for the loss of endogenous dopamine.
- Deep-brain stimulation is a surgical technique in which electrodes are implanted in the brain. This procedure has become a novel treatment for Parkinson's disease. Implants usually are placed in the subthalamic nucleus.
- The basal ganglia may play a general function in state changes. For the motor system, a state change would correspond to the initiation of a new movement. In the cognitive system, a state change could be a change in mental set, such as when we change from one goal to another. Dopamine acts as a reinforcement signal to bias some states over others.

Action Understanding and Mirror Neurons

Defining where perception ends in the brain and action starts may be an impossible task. Perceptual systems have evolved to support action; likewise, actions are produced in anticipation of sensory consequences. For a monkey in the wild, seeing a ripe banana on a tree engages the action systems required to retrieve the food—movements that allow the animal to climb skillfully among the branches and that result in the satisfying taste of the fruit.

A serendipitous observation in the laboratory of Giacomo Rizzolatti provided some of the most compelling evidence of the links between perception, action, and cognition, helping to launch one of the most exciting areas of research in the cognition of action. This research group was conducting a study of premotor cortex, recording from neurons that were involved in the control of hand and mouth actions. The story goes that a graduate student walked into the lab holding a cone of gelato. As he moved the cone to his mouth to lick it, a surge in cellular activity was observed in the monkey's neuron that would be activated were the monkey to grasp and move something to his mouth, even though, in this instance, the animal was not moving. In fact, the animal seemed distracted, having shifted its focus to the grad student.

Rizzolatti and his colleagues had previously demonstrated that premotor cells show an increase in activity when the monkey performs goal-based actions, such as grasping or tearing an object, independent of the specific context for that action. As for the gelato incident, years later Rizzolatti commented, "It took us several years to believe what we were seeing" (Blakeslee, 2006). What they were seeing was that simply observing or imagining the action was all it took to activate some of the same premotor cells. For instance, they had monkeys view different objects. On some trials, the monkey produced an action such as reaching for or grasping the object (e.g., a peanut). On other trials, the monkey observed the experimenter performing similar actions. Although some premotor neurons were active only during production trials, other neurons were *also* active during action perception. Exactly the same neuron fired when an individual monkey observed the action of reaching for a peanut and when it performed the same action itself (Figure 8.28a–c). Perception and action were linked. These latter neurons were appropriately named **mirror neurons**.

You might suppose that the activity in mirror neurons reflects the similar visual properties of the action and perception conditions. A hand moving toward a peanut looks much the same whether it is your hand or someone else's. Additional experiments, however, ruled out this hypothesis. First, the same mirror neuron is activated by the sound of a peanut being cracked (Figure 8.28d). Second, mirror neurons are also active when a monkey watches someone reach behind a screen for a peanut but cannot see the grasping of the peanut. In fact, there doesn't even need to be a peanut behind the screen, as long as the monkey thinks that there is. If the monkey *knows* that there is no hidden peanut behind the screen, however, the mirror neurons remain silent (Umilta et al., 2001). Thus, the activity of the mirror cell is correlated with a goal-oriented action—retrieving a peanut—independent of how this information is received—by the monkey's own action, by viewing another person's action, by hearing another person's action, or by viewing only a portion of another person's action but believing that the action is taking place.

The intimate link between perception and action is underscored by the finding that our comprehension of the actions of others appears to depend on the activation of the neural structures that would be engaged if we were to produce the action ourselves. In recognition of this codependency, neuroscientists speak of a **mirror system** to describe a distributed network of neural regions involved in action production and comprehension. The term *mirror* here is intended to capture the idea that understanding the actions of another person involves referring to our knowledge of how that action would be produced. The perceptual

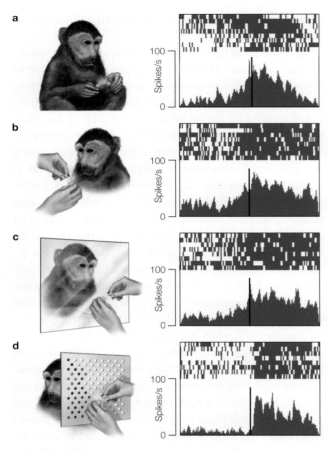

FIGURE 8.28 Identification of a mirror neuron.
Responses of a single neuron in a monkey's ventral premotor cortex during the performance or perception of different actions: **(a)** when the monkey itself breaks a peanut and views and hears the breaking of the peanut, **(b)** when the monkey watches someone else breaking a peanut and views and hears the breaking of the peanut, **(c)** when the monkey sees someone else breaking a peanut but cannot hear the peanut breaking, and **(d)** when the monkey hears but does not see someone else breaking a peanut. This neuron is considered a mirror neuron because it responds to actions that are undertaken by the monkey, as well as to actions that are viewed or heard by the monkey.

system is not divorced from the action system. The brain does not form abstract representations of visual patterns that conform to actions such as grasping, throwing, or dancing. Rather, our comprehension of such actions involves referring to our own ability to grasp an object or to

dance with another individual. This notion of self-reference is sometimes referred to as *embodied cognition*: Our conceptual knowledge is grounded in our body knowledge.

Mirror neurons are not limited to the premotor cortex. Neurons in parietal and temporal lobes also show similar activity patterns during action production and comprehension, suggesting a distributed mirror system rather than a dedicated local region for linking perception and action. This point is supported by many neuroimaging studies in humans. In Chapter 6, we saw that the dorsal pathway, including parietal lobe and premotor cortex, was activated when people were asked to make judgments about the use of an object. These regions are also activated during movement execution. Interestingly, the extent and intensity of the activation pattern reflect the individual's own particular motor repertoire. Skilled dancers show stronger activation in the mirror network when watching videos of familiar dance routines as compared to unfamiliar dances (Figure 8.29).

Imaging studies fail to show activation of the *primary motor cortex* during the observation of action. Even so, the excitability of neurons in motor cortex is modulated when people observe actions produced by another individual. Indeed, this modulation shows a high degree of effector specificity. When motor evoked potentials (MEPs) were recorded from muscles following transcranial stimulation of the motor cortex, their amplitude correlated with motor excitability. For example, TMS-elicited MEPs in hand muscles are larger when people observe video clips of gestures being made with the same hand as compared to videos of the same gestures by the opposite hand. Similar effects are elicited with relatively abstract presentations of the actions, such as the sounds of hands clapping.

The excitability changes within motor cortex also reflect the participants' expertise. One study of action comprehension compared three groups of people: elite basketball players, sports journalists (selected because they watched basketball 7–8 hours a week), and a control group who knew nothing about basketball (Aglioti et al., 2008). The participants were shown short video clips, either of a person about to shoot a basketball free throw or initiate a free kick in soccer (Figure 8.30). The basket-

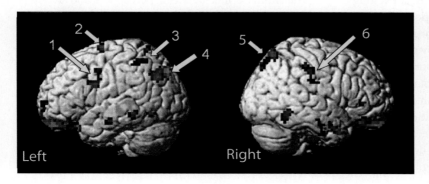

Left   Right

FIGURE 8.29 Activation of mirror neurons is affected by level of expertise.
When skilled dancers observe a dance they are experts in (versus a dance they have no expertise in), an increase in the BOLD response is observed in the premotor cortex (1, 2), intraparietal sulcus (3, 6), posterior superior temporal sulcus (4), and superior parietal lobe (5). These areas make up the neural network of action observation and include regions that are also activated when the person produces skilled movements, constituting what is considered the human mirror neuron system.

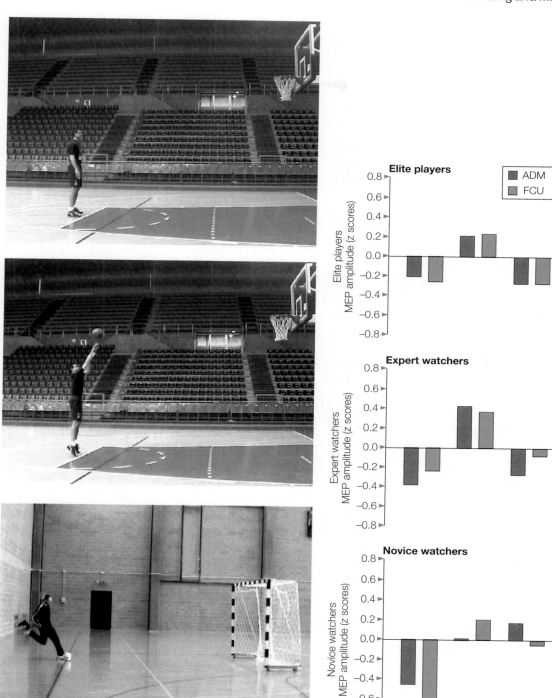

FIGURE 8.30 Increased excitation of motor cortex during action observation by skilled performers.
Examples of photographs shown to elite basketball players, expert observers and novices while MEPs
were recorded from hand muscles (ADM=abductor digiti minimi; red) and forearm (FCU=flexor carpi
ulnaris; green) muscles. Relative to the static condition (top photo), the basketball players and expert
observers showed an increase in hand and arm muscle MEPs when observing the player shooting a
basketball, but not when shooting a soccer ball. The novices show a more inconsistent pattern, with an
increase in excitability in one of the muscles when viewing the active images.

ball players and the journalists both showed an increase in motor cortex excitability while watching the basketball shots, but not while watching soccer kicks. In contrast, the novices showed a nonspecific effect—an increase in hand MEPs for both basketball and soccer videos. Even more interesting, only the skilled players showed a differential response to whether the video clip depicted a free throw that was either going to be successful or inaccurate even before the outcome was known. This response suggests that, with expertise, the motor system has a fine sensitivity to discriminate good and poor performance during action observation, a form of action comprehension. It also suggests that the well-practiced motor system is anticipatory in nature, giving it the ability to predict others' actions in the arena of their expertise.

Mirror systems have been implicated in more than motor action understanding. Many neuroscientists argue that they are important for imitation and learning new skills and for simulating the actions of others, leading to understanding their intentions. What's more, by simulating the emotions of others, mirror systems provide the neural basis for empathy. We will discuss these ideas in Chapter 13.

Is the activation that is seen in motor areas during observation of action essential for comprehending action? Does the modulation of excitability in motor cortex indicate that understanding the actions of another requires representations in motor cortex? Or are these activation patterns some sort of priming effect, reflecting the subtle and automatic planning of the action when presented with a familiar stimulus? These are difficult questions to answer (see Hickok, 2009). Nonetheless, fMRI and TMS studies are important in demonstrating the degree of overlap between neural systems involved in perception and action. They remind us that dividing the brain into perception and motor regions may be useful for pedagogical reasons (say, for defining chapters in a textbook), but that the brain does not honor such divisions.

TAKE-HOME MESSAGES

- Mirror neurons are neurons in premotor cortex and other areas (like the parietal lobe) that respond to an action, both when that action is produced by an animal and when the animal observes a similar action produced by another animal.
- The mirror system has been hypothesized to be essential for comprehending the actions produced by other individuals.
- The engagement of the mirror system is modulated by motor expertise.

Learning and Performing New Skills

Dick Fosbury was a revolutionary figure in the world of sports. In high school, he was a very good high jumper, though not quite good enough to get the scholarship he desired to go to college and study engineering. One day, however, he had an idea. His school had recently replaced the woodchip landing pad in the high-jump pit with soft foam rubber. Fosbury realized that he no longer had to land on his feet to avoid injury. Instead of taking off on the inside foot and "scissoring" his legs over the bar, he could rotate his body to go over the bar backward, raising his feet toward the sky, and then land on his back. With this conceptual breakthrough, Fosbury went on to reach new heights, culminating in the gold medal at the 1968 Olympics in Mexico City. High jumpers all over the world adopted the "Fosbury flop." And yes, Fosbury did get his scholarship and became an engineer.

Shift in Cortical Control with Learning

People frequently attribute motor learning to low levels of the hierarchy. We speak of "muscle memory," or our muscles having learned how to respond—for example, how to maintain balance on a bike, or how our fingers type away at the keyboard. The fact that we have great difficulty verbalizing how to perform these skills reinforces the notion that the learning is noncognitive. The Olympic gymnast Peter Vidman expressed this sentiment when he said, "As I approach the apparatus . . . the only thing I am thinking about is . . . the first trick. . . . Then, my body takes over and hopefully everything becomes automatic" (Schmidt, 1987, p. 85).

On closer study, however, we find that some aspects of motor learning are independent of the muscular system used to perform the actions. Demonstrate this independence to yourself by taking a piece of paper and signing your name. Having done this, repeat the action but use your nondominant hand. Now do it again, holding the pen between your teeth. If you feel especially adventurous, you can take off your shoes and socks and hold the pen between your toes.

Although the atypical productions will not be as smooth as your standard signature, the more dramatic result of this demonstration is the high degree of similarity across all of the productions. Figure 8.31 shows the results of one such demonstration. This high-level representation of the action is independent of any particular muscle group. The differences in the final product

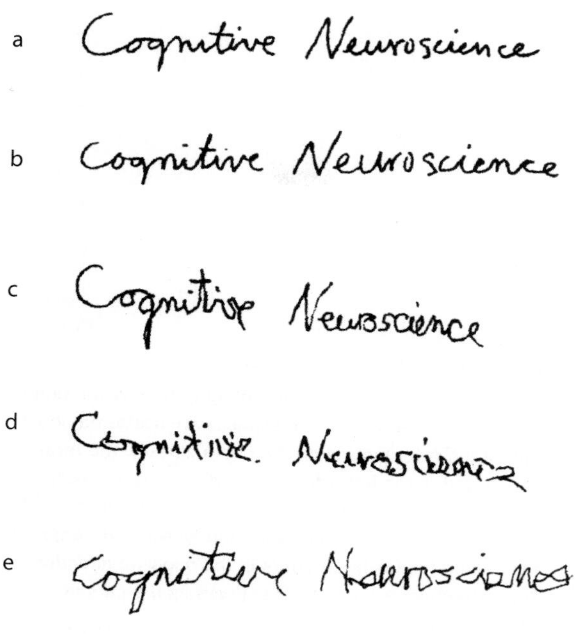

a *Cognitive Neuroscience*

b *Cognitive Neuroscience*

c *Cognitive Neuroscience*

d *Cognitive Neuroscience*

e *Cognitive Neuroscience*

FIGURE 8.31 Motor representations are not linked to particular effector systems.
These five productions of the words *Cognitive Neuroscience* were produced by the same person moving a pen with the right hand (**a**), the right wrist (**b**), the left hand (**c**), the mouth (**d**), and the right foot (**e**). The productions show a degree of similarity, despite the vast differences in practice writing with these five body parts.

show that some muscle groups simply have more experience in translating an abstract representation into a concrete action.

When people are acquiring a new action, the first effects of learning likely will be at a more abstract level. Fosbury's learning started in the abstract realm with a simple insight: The new landing material could allow for a different landing. From this point, he was able to adopt a radically new style of jumping. As Fosbury describes it, "I adapted an antiquated style and modernized it to something that was efficient" (Zarkos, 2004). These cognitive abilities no doubt apply to all types of learning, not just learning motor skills. For instance, the same abilities would contribute to the makings of a great jazz improvisationist. She is great not because of the technical motor expertise of her fingers (though that is important), but because she sees new possibilities for a riff, a new pattern.

Once Fosbury had settled on what to do, he had to learn to do it. Our motor system has some basic movement patterns down. Learning to perform a new action builds on these basic patterns. Learning the skill takes practice—what we typically mean when we talk about motor learning. Motor learning can involve linking a series of gestures in a completely new way. Or it may involve a more subtle retuning, repeating a learned sequence over and over to get the coordination pattern

exactly right. The latter is frequently referred to as motor adaptation. Gradually the motor system learns to execute the movement in what feels like an automatic manner, requiring little conscious thought.

Learning how to produce the action in an optimal manner—becoming an expert—takes us to a different level of skill. Becoming an expert fine-tunes the system to make the movement in the *most* efficient and skillful manner. This result requires other cognitive abilities, such as persistence, attention, and self-control. Motor skill also involves honing perceptual skills. LeBron James's skill on the basketball court is due not only to his extraordinary motor skills but also to his ability to rapidly recognize the position of his teammates and opponents. His pattern recognition abilities allow him to quickly determine if he should drive to the basket or pull up and pass to one of his open teammates. Becoming skillful at any task can be acquired only through practice, and a lot of it. In fact, the rule of thumb is that expertise in any domain requires at least 10,000 hours of practice. Ready to become an expert at something? Got 3 hours a day to devote to that activity for the next 10 years? That's what you'll need.

Adaptive Learning Through Sensory Feedback

Imagine climbing aboard a boat that is rocking in the waves. At first you feel clumsy, unwilling to let go of the gunwales, but soon you adapt, learning to remain steady despite the roll of the boat. Next, you're even willing to venture a few steps across the deck. After a few hours at sea, you're an old salt, not giving a thought to the pitch and roll of the boat. When you come back to shore, you are surprised to find your first few steps are wobbly again. It takes a moment or two to become acclimated to the stability of the dock, and to abandon your rolling gait.

This example is a form of **sensorimotor adaptation**. Researchers have devised all sorts of novel environments to challenge the motor system and explore the neural mechanisms essential for this form of motor learning. One of the first and most radical tests was performed by George Stratton, the founder of the psychology department at the University of California, Berkeley. He devised a set of eyeglasses that inverted the visual input. After initially donning his new spectacles, Stratton was at a loss, afraid to take a step for fear he would fall over. Reaching was impossible. He would reach for a glass and observe his arm moving in the wrong direction. But with time, Stratton's motor system adapted (just as the monkeys in BMI studies did when the decoder algorithm was shuffled). By the fourth day, he was walking about at a nearly normal speed and his movements were coordinated. With time, observers were hard-pressed

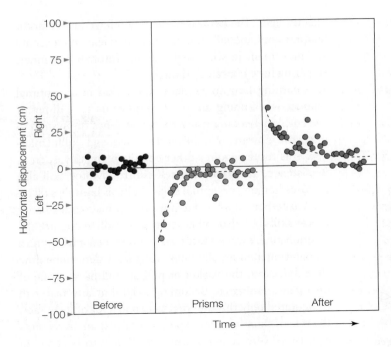

FIGURE 8.32 Prism adaptation.
Participants throw a ball, attempting to hit a visual target. At baseline ("Before"), the responses are scattered about the target. After putting on the prism glasses, the throws are shifted to the left. After about 20 throws, the person becomes adapted to the glasses and is again successful in landing near the target. When the glasses are removed, the person makes large errors in the opposite direction. This aftereffect eventually disappears as the person "de-adapts."

to realize from watching Stratton that his world was topsy-turvy. His sensorimotor system had adapted to the new environment.

More modern studies of sensorimotor adaption use less dramatic environmental distortions. In some, visuomotor rotations are imposed when people perform the center-out task such that the visual feedback of the limb is displaced by 30 degrees, introducing a mismatch between the visual and proprioceptive (felt position of the limb) information (Figure 8.32). In others, force fields are imposed that displace the moving limb to the side when a person attempts to reach directly to a target. The motor system is amazingly adept at modifying itself in response to these perturbations. Within a hundred movements or so, people have modified their behavior and make straight movements to the targets. Although they were aware that the environment had been altered with the introduction of the perturbation, the system quickly adapts, and the person is soon unaware of the change. This becomes obvious when the perturbation is removed, and the person has to repeat the adaptation process (or what is called de-adaptation, just as when you step from a boat back onto the dock). We cannot simply "switch back" to the normal state, but rather must re-learn how to control our limbs in the absence of a visual or force distortion.

Neural Mechanisms of Adaptation

Cognitive neuroscientists have employed many tools to explore the neural systems of **sensorimotor learning**. Imaging studies show that with the introduction of a

perturbation, such as a visuomotor rotation, there is a large increase in activity in many cortical areas, including prefrontal, premotor, and motor cortex in the frontal lobes, as well as changes in parietal, temporal, and even visual cortex (Seidler, 2006). Increases are also seen subcortically in the cerebellum and basal ganglia. With practice, the activation in these areas is reduced, returning back toward that observed when you move without a perturbation.

Knowing exactly how to interpret these activation patterns is difficult: Do they reflect the formation and storage of new motor patterns? Or are the activations indicative of other processes that are engaged when a perturbation is introduced? For example, a visuomotor rotation introduces a violation of a visual expectancy—you expect the cursor to move up, but it moves to the side: the activations could be the result of this prediction error, or they may reflect the increased attention needed to adjust to the visual feedback (see Chapter 7). Motor cortex changes could be the result of adaptation, or they could result because people tend to make corrective movements when the feedback indicates an error. Other activations may be triggered by the participants' awareness that the environment has been distorted.

To gain more insight into the functional contribution of the different areas identified in the imaging studies, researchers have conducted neuropsychological and brain stimulation studies. For instance, patients who have cerebellar damage due to either degenerative processes or stroke have severe impairments in learning to move in novel environments, such as when a visuomotor perturbation is introduced (Figure 8.33; T. Martin et al., 1996).

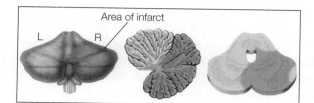

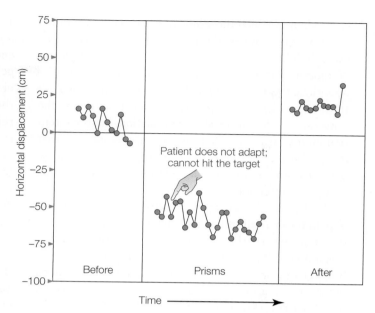

FIGURE 8.33 Impaired prism adaptation in a patient with a large cerebellar lesion.
The shaded regions in the top figures show the extent of damage in the inferior cerebellum. The damage is mostly in the right cerebellum, although it extends across the midline. There is no evidence of adaptation when wearing the prism glasses. The patient shows a bias to throw the ball slightly to the right before and after adaptation.

Similar problems can be observed in patients with prefrontal or parietal lesions.

Can we identify differential contributions of these neural regions? Joseph Galea and his colleagues (2011) applied transcranial direct current stimulation (tDCS) during a **visuomotor adaptation** task, targeting either primary motor cortex or the cerebellum. As discussed in Chapter 3, this procedure is thought to increase the excitability of the area under the anodal electrode. Assuming that more excitable neurons are also better for learning (e.g., more "plastic" as described in Chapter 9), the researchers considered two hypotheses. First, if an area is involved in using the error information to modify the sensorimotor system, then learning

to compensate for the visuomotor perturbation should occur more quickly. Second, if an area is involved in retaining the new behavior, the effects of learning should persist for a longer period of time, even when the perturbation is removed. To look at retention in this study, the feedback was removed and the experimenters measured how long it took for the person to show normal reaching movements.

The results point to a striking functional dissociation between the cerebellum and motor cortex (Figure 8.34). Cerebellar tDCS led to faster learning. Participants receiving stimulation over this region learned to compensate for the visuomotor perturbation faster than those receiving tDCS over M1 or sham stimulation over the

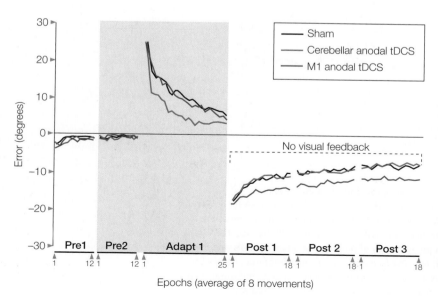

FIGURE 8.34 Double dissociation in sensorimotor adaptation following tDCS of the cerebellum and motor cortex.
Anodal tDCS was applied during a baseline phase (Pre2) and throughout the adaptation phase in which the visual feedback was rotated. Learning was faster when the tDCS was applied over the cerebellum, compared to the sham and M1 conditions, although all three groups eventually reached comparable levels of adaptation. When the rotation was removed, the aftereffect persisted for a longer time when tDCS was applied over M1, suggesting stronger consolidation in this condition.

cerebellum in which the stimulator is turned on for only a few seconds. When the rotation was removed, however, the effects of learning decayed (or were implicitly "forgotten") at the same rate as for the sham group. The opposite pattern was observed for the group receiving M1 tDCS. For these participants, learning occurred at the same rate as those given sham stimulation, but the retention interval was extended. In sum, results indicate that the cerebellum is essential for learning the new mapping, but M1 is important for consolidating the new mapping (long-term retention).

Earlier in the chapter, we discussed the role of dopamine in reinforcement learning, focusing on the projections from the substantia nigra to the striatum. Dopamine terminals are also scattered across the cerebral cortex, including in M1. The origin of these fibers, however, is not in the SN_r; it is in a different brainstem nucleus, the ventral tegmental area (VTA; Chapter 12).

To determine if these dopamine neurons are important for motor learning, one study placed rats into a specialized apparatus in which they could retrieve food pellets by making a reaching movement with their forelimb (Hosp et al., 2011). This task was challenging for the rats—reaching is not a typical part of their motor repertoire. They typically use their forelimbs for locomotion (being quadrupeds) or to hold pellets of food. Nonetheless, when motivated by extra tasty food pellets, the animals were able to maneuver their forelimbs to grasp a pellet and bring the morsel to their mouth. Animals with lesions of the VTA were unable to learn the task. If L-DOPA was then directly applied to M1, however, the animals recovered their ability to learn the novel reaching movements (Figure 8.35). Thus, the dopaminergic pathway from the VTA to M1 is necessary for acquiring a novel motor skill through repeated training.

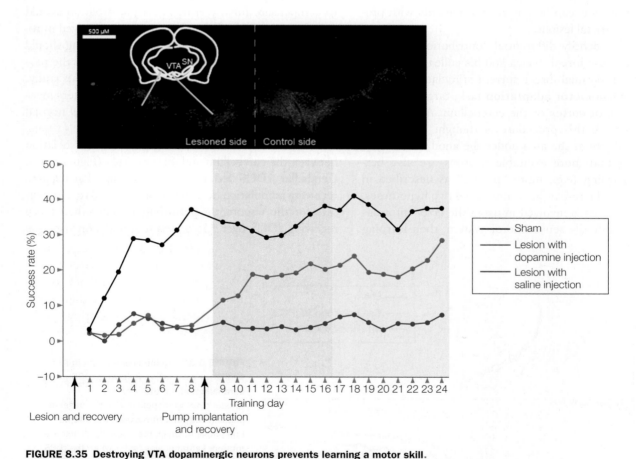

FIGURE 8.35 Destroying VTA dopaminergic neurons prevents learning a motor skill.
Rats were trained to retrieve a food reward by reaching with their forepaws, a difficult task for a rodent. Two groups of animals received lesions of the VTA, eliminating a primary source of dopamine to the motor cortex. Whereas animals with sham lesions became relatively proficient with practice, the VTA-lesioned animals failed to improve. Starting with the ninth day of training, the sham animals and one of the lesioned group received L-dopa injections into M1. The lesioned animals now improved, consistent with the idea that dopamine release in the cortex is important for motor skill learning. Performance in lesioned animals remained stable when the injections were discontinued (blue background).

Forward Models: Using Sensorimotor Predictions for Motor Control and Learning

You may have had the experience of walking down a set of stairs in the complete dark and thinking that you had stepped off the last stair when, in fact, there was another to go. Your body already had automatically adjusted its balance in preparation for stepping across level ground, but lo and behold, you sank another 8 inches. If you were fortunate, you quickly adjusted your balance and corrected your movement. If not so fortunate, you ended up falling or twisting an ankle. This example captures how the brain operates in a predictive mode: Your motor system is issuing commands for movement, and it is also generating predictions of the anticipated sensory consequences of those movements. Errors occur when the actual feedback doesn't match this prediction. The brain uses this information to make adjustments to an ongoing movement as well as for learning.

Prediction is especially important because the brain is working with a system in which the motor commands to the muscles and sensory signals from the limbs take time to travel back and forth. It can take 50 to 150 ms for a motor command to be generated in the cortex and for the sensory consequences of that action to return to the cortex. By then, things in the periphery will have changed, especially if the signals involve moving parts. For skilled motor behavior, that time lag is enough to throw off smooth, coordinated movement. To compensate for these delays, we have a system that generates an expectancy of the sensory consequences of our action, or what is referred to as a **forward model**.

The cerebellum is a key part of the neural network for the generation of forward models (Wolpert et al., 1998). It receives a copy of motor signals being sent to the muscles from the cortex, information that can be used to generate sensory predictions. It also receives massive input from the various receptors of the somatosensory system. By comparing these sources of information, the cerebellum can help ensure that an ongoing movement is produced in a coordinated manner. It can also use a mismatch to aid in sensorimotor learning. For example, when we put on prism glasses, the visual information is shifted to one side. If we reach to a target, a mismatch will occur between where the hand was directed and our visual (and tactile) feedback of the outcome of the movement. Given sufficient time, we use that error to correct the movement to reach the target. The error is also used to correct future predictions, thus, adapting learning such that we make more predictions that are suited for this novel environment. Consider again the tDCS results discussed in the previous section. Cerebellar stimulation led to faster learning, presumably because the error signals were amplified. Imaging studies of motor learning support a similar conclusion. In general, activation in the cerebellum decreases with practice, a finding interpreted as reflecting a reduction in error as skill improves.

As noted earlier, forward models are also important for online control of movements. People with ataxia are capable of making movements; they can select the right muscles and activate them in the right sequence. Their movements are far from smooth, however. The concept of the forward model can be useful for understanding this loss of coordination. Consider what would happen if motor commands were based on outdated sensory signals; say, for example, the system had to work with the actual sensory signals instead of the expected sensory signals. If you were to reach rapidly for a target, you would overshoot the goal because you failed to slow your hand in an anticipatory manner. Damage to the spinocerebellum frequently results in *hypermetric* movements, those that extend beyond the intended target or that oscillate around the target location (Hore et al., 1991). Prediction is especially important when producing complex actions that require coordination across multiple joints. Ataxia is especially pronounced in such situations, underscoring why this deficit is frequently described as a loss of skilled movement.

Chris Miall and his colleagues (2007) provided an elegant demonstration of the role of the cerebellum in the utilization of a forward model. They designed a task in which participants were shown a visual target located in front of them. Each participant was then required to move her right arm to the side until she heard a tone. The tone signaled that she should now move as quickly as possible to the target. To accomplish this task, the participant's motor system must anticipate that, due to momentum, her arm actually would be displaced a bit farther sideways before she initiated the forward reach. In short, she has to predict where her arm actually will be when she hears the reach command. In a normal context, the participants had no difficulty reaching the target, even when visual feedback of the reach was eliminated. When transcranial magnetic stimulation (TMS) was applied over the cerebellum, however, the participants' reaches missed the target. Their hands landed at a location that indicated they were using outdated sensory information to plan the movement (Figure 8.36). In combination with the work on motor learning, we now see how the cerebellum uses forward models for coordinating ongoing movements as well as for motor learning.

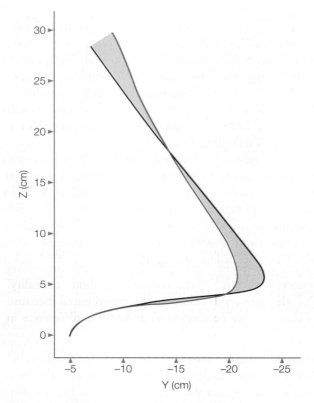

FIGURE 8.36 Predictive function of the cerebellum.
Participants performed a two-step task, first moving their arm laterally (y-direction) and following the onset of a tone, to reach towards
an unseen target positioned in front of them (z-direction). Because
the arm is moving, the participant must estimate where the arm
will be at the start of the forward component of the movement.
On control trials (blue), the final position of the hand was slightly
displaced to the right of the target. This error was much larger
when TMS was applied over the lateral cerebellum, suggesting that
the participants failed to fully anticipate the lateral displacement
of their arm.

Prediction is a feature of all brain areas (everything
is doing pattern matching of some sort). In addition, it
has also been hypothesized that the cerebellum is also
critical for sensorimotor learning, because it generates
predictions that are *temporally* precise. We need to know
more than what is coming in the future; we also need to
predict exactly when it is coming. When going down the
stairs, we anticipate the contact of our foot with a surface at a specific moment in time. Though cortical areas
primarily select the effectors needed to perform a task,
the cerebellum supplies the precise timing needed for
activating these effectors.

The timing hypothesis offers another way to think
about the role of the cerebellum in motor learning.
Cerebellar lesions are most disruptive to highly practiced
movements, which present the greatest need for precise

timing. The novice tennis player may be pleased if he can
simply get the ball over the net, but the expert requires
exquisite timing to make the perfect shot.

This point is highlighted in an experiment involving
a simple model of motor learning: eyeblink conditioning. When a puff of air is directed at the eye, a reflexive
blink is produced—an evolved response to minimize
potential eye damage. If a neutral stimulus, such as a
tone, is presented in advance of the air puff on a consistently timed basis, the animal learns to blink in response to the tone (Figure 8.37). What's more, the

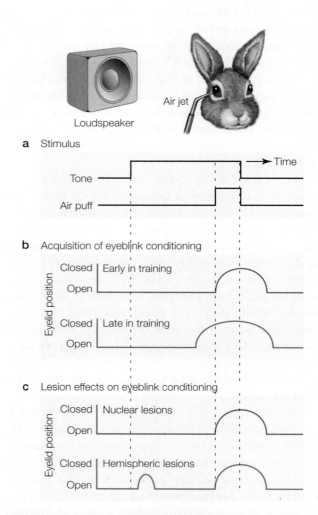

**FIGURE 8.37 Lesions of the cerebellum disrupt the learned
response in eyeblink conditioning.**
(a) A neutral tone precedes and co-terminates with an aversive
air puff to the eye. **(b)** Early in training, the air puff causes the
animal to blink. Late in training, the animal blinks in response
to the tone, thus reducing the impact of the air puff. **(c)** Lesions
of the deep cerebellar nuclei abolish the learned response. The
animal continues to blink reflexively in response to the air puff; this
behavior indicates that the lesion has produced a learning deficit
and not a motor deficit. The anticipatory, learned responses are still
present following lesions of the cerebellar cortex. However, they are
timed inappropriately and thus are no longer adaptive.

timing of the acquired response is perfectly adaptive: The eye closure reaches the highest amplitude exactly at the onset of the air puff. As Figure 8.37c shows, rabbits with cerebellar lesions have no motor problem and continue to blink to the tone, but the response is no longer appropriately timed: The eye is exposed at the time of the air puff and, thus, the blink is no longer adaptive in avoiding the air puff (S. Perrett et al., 1993). At a computational level, the timing hypothesis helps specify how the cerebellum contributes to motor learning. It is important for the animal to learn that the tone and air puff co-occur, but the response is adaptive only if the animal learns that the tone predicts exactly when the air puff will occur. The animal must be able to represent the temporal relationship between the two stimuli.

Experts

How do experts differ from nonexperts (Figure 8.38)? The multitalented Francis Galton, Charles Darwin's cousin, opined that it required innate ability, zeal, and laborious work (remember the 10,000 hours of practice?) to become eminent in a field (see Ericsson et al., 1993). Do experts have brains that differ in both structure and function? Are these differences innate, the result of extensive practice, or some combination of nature and nurture?

Neuroanatomists have identified some realms of skilled performance that are associated with structural differences. Studies using diffusion-weighted MRI have found evidence that the connectivity in a specific region of the corpus callosum between the left and right supplementary motor areas varies between individuals. The degree of bimanual coordination that a person exhibits correlates positively with the connectivity between the two regions (Figure 8.39; Johansen-Berg et al., 2007). Certainly an interesting observation, but it tells us nothing about causality. Did the person become more coordinated because of the stronger connectivity, or has this difference in connectivity emerged because she engages in more bimanual activities, perhaps because she finds them more rewarding?

FIGURE 8.38 Humans show an extraordinary ability to develop motor skills.

FIGURE 8.39 Relating motor skill to brain anatomy.
Participants performed a bimanual coordination task, producing alternating taps with the two fingers. The tapping rate was varied such that, at high frequencies, the participants had trouble maintaining the pattern. Measures of FA in voxels from the body of the corpus callosum (left) correlated with bimanual coordination (high ratio indicates better performance). Red circles indicate female participants and the blue circles are male.

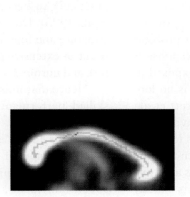

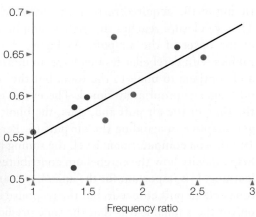

To get at causality, researchers have looked at changes that occur in the brain after extensive practice. Consider juggling, a skill that requires the coordination of the two hands, not to mention the ability to integrate complex spatial patterns created by the motions of the hands and balls. To the novice, juggling may seem impossible; but with just a modest amount of daily practice, most people can become quite skilled after a few months. This level of practice in one sample was sufficient to produce measurable increases in gray matter in areas V5 and IP—temporal and parietal regions associated with motion processing and movement planning and control (Draganski et al., 2004). When the jugglers stopped practicing, the gray matter volume in these regions of interest shrank, although it remained above the baseline level. Findings like these indicate that practice can readily shape the macroscopic landscape of the brain.

Our parents and teachers may often remind us that practice makes perfect, but it is also hard not to argue that other factors are at play in determining expertise. Some individuals just seem to be more adept at certain skills. Some differences may reflect genetic differences, or gene–environment interactions. Genetic polymorphisms have been associated with physiological differences that affect oxygen uptake and consumption, cardiac output, and muscle type and strength. How much these factors contribute to an individual becoming an elite athlete is yet to be determined, but it looks like Galton's intuition was on the right track.

One factor we tend to ignore when thinking about skilled performance is the importance of motivation. We consider how genetics might influence muscle size (and height if we are thinking about a sport like basketball), but there are also large individual differences in motivation: Some people are more willing to put in hours of practice than others. Although Galton defined motivation as "zeal," a more modern notion is that motivation is about the importance we place on action outcomes and their utilities (Niv, 2007). In other words, is it worth the effort? How much do we value the goal and its predicted reward relative to the cost we have to expend? Worth is subjective and has many variables, and in Chapter 12 we will consider this issue in detail. An interesting study of musical performers revealed that the most elite performers actually found practice less pleasurable than nonelite, but skilled, performers (Ericsson et al., 1993). One inference drawn from this work is that expertise requires not just hours of practice, but effortful practice in which the performer is constantly pushing him or herself to explore new methods or endlessly repeating the selected routine.

It is clear that experts, amateurs, and novices have different brains. Researchers find it easier to identify structural differences in experts in a physical activity—compared to, say, experts in theoretical physics—perhaps because we have a good idea of where we might expect to observe such differences. We can look in the hand area of the right motor cortex to see structural differences between violin players and musicians who play instruments that do not place such emphasis on left-hand fingering skills. Even so, we should be cautious in assuming such differences are at the heart of expertise. Across domains as diverse as motor skills, mathematics, and the arts, many commonalities are found among the most elite performers. A good explanation of the neural correlates of these commonalities has yet to be articulated.

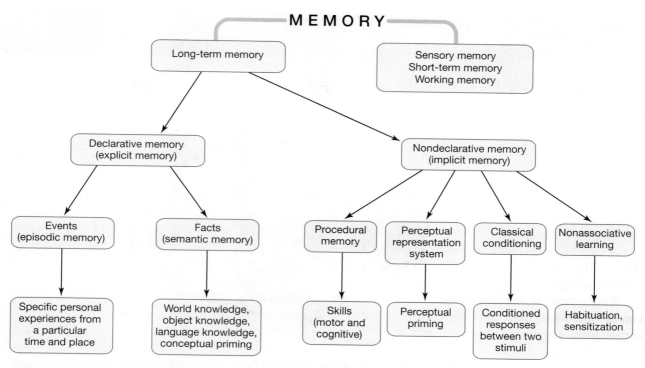

FIGURE 9.2 The hypothesized structure of human memory, diagramming the relationships among different forms of memory.

Researchers divide learning and memory into three major processing stages:

1. **Encoding** is the processing of incoming information that creates *memory traces* to be stored. It has two separate steps, the first is **acquisition**. Sensory systems are constantly being bombarded by tons of stimuli. Most only produce a very brief transient sensory response that fades quickly (about 1000 ms after presentation) without ever reaching short term memory. During this period, however, the stimuli are available for processing. This state is known as a *sensory buffer*. Only some of these stimuli are sustained and make the cut into short term memory, the acquisition. The second step is **consolidation**, in which changes in the brain stabilize a memory over time resulting in a long term memory. This can occur over days to months, even years, and creates a stronger representation over time. There are many theories as to what is occurring when a memory is consolidated, which we discuss later in the chapter.
2. **Storage** is the result of acquisition and consolidation and represents the permanent record of the information.
3. **Retrieval** involves accessing stored information and using it to create a conscious representation or to execute a learned behavior, such as a motor act.

In this chapter, we explore what is known about the neuroscience of learning and memory, starting with a tour of the brain regions involved in memory encoding, storage, and retrieval. We also look at what we have learned about memory and learning from patients with amnesia. Then we look at how memory has been categorized and discuss the current thinking about what memory systems exist and how they work. At the end of the chapter, we discuss the cellular mechanisms that are thought to mediate memory formation.

The Anatomy of Memory

The brain has the ability to change through experience—in other words, to learn. At the neural level, this means that changes occur in the synaptic connections between neurons. It also implies that learning can occur in multiple regions of the brain. Learning can be accomplished in a number of ways, and it appears that different parts of the brain are specialized for different types of learning. For instance, in the last chapter we discussed the role of the basal ganglia in reinforcement learning and the involvement of the cerebellum in trial-and-error learning based on prediction error signals. The amygdala is involved with fear learning, which we will read more about in the next chapter.

As can be seen in the Anatomical Orientation box, many regions of the brain are also involved in one or more aspects of memory. What has come to be called the medial temporal lobe memory system, first described after H.M.'s surgery, is made up of the hippocampus, an infolding of the medial temporal cortex that is shaped like a sea horse (*Hippocampus* is the genus name for the

ANATOMICAL ORIENTATION

The anatomy of memory

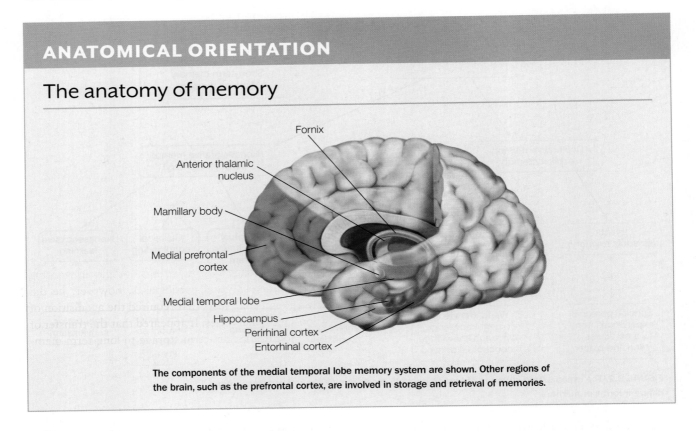

The components of the medial temporal lobe memory system are shown. Other regions of the brain, such as the prefrontal cortex, are involved in storage and retrieval of memories.

marine fish known as a sea horse), and the various structures interconnected with the hippocampus. These include the surrounding entorhinal cortex, perirhinal cortex and parahippocampal cortex within the temporal lobe, and subcortical structures including the mammillary bodies and anterior thalamic nuclei. The hippocampus is reciprocally connected with wide regions of the cortex via the entorhinal cortex and the output projection pathway of the fimbria and fornix to the subcortical portions of the system, which themselves project to the prefrontal cortex. Although the amygdala, also located in the temporal lobe, is primarily involved in affective processing, which can have an influence on learning and memory as we will see later in the chapter, it is not involved with memory in general.

TAKE-HOME MESSAGES

- Learning is the process of acquiring new information, the outcome of which is memory.
- Learning and memory have many stages, including encoding (acquisition and consolidation), storage, and retrieval.
- What is known as the medial temporal lobe memory system is made up of the hippocampus and the surrounding rhinal and parahippocampal cortices.
- Other areas involved with memory include the prefrontal cortex, the parietal cortex, and subcortical structures.

Memory Deficits: Amnesia

Memory deficits and loss can result from brain damage caused by surgery, disease, or physical or psychological trauma, and are known collectively as **amnesia**. Amnesia is a form of memory impairment that affects all of the senses. Typically, amnesiacs display deficits in specific types of memory or in aspects of memory processing. Each type of functional deficit is associated with a lesion in a different brain region. For instance, left hemisphere damage can result in selective impairment in verbal memory, whereas right hemisphere damage may result in nonverbal memory impairment.

The loss of memory for events that occur after a lesion is known as **anterograde amnesia.** It results from the inability to learn new things. A loss of memory for events and knowledge that occurred before a lesion is called **retrograde amnesia.** Sometimes retrograde amnesia is **temporally limited**, extending back only a few minutes or hours. In other severe cases, it is extensive, sometimes encompassing almost the entire previous life span. Retrograde amnesia tends to be greatest for the most recent events. This effect, known as a **temporal gradient** or **Ribot's Law,** was first postulated by Théodule Ribot, a 19th-century French psychologist. Amnesia can differentially affect short-term memory, working memory, or long-term memory abilities.

Because the extent and locations of lesions are known after surgery, a lot of the information about the organization of human memory was first derived from patients left accidentally amnesic after surgical treatments. We return now to the story of H.M., one of a series of patients who had surgery in the late 1940s and early 1950s to treat neurological and psychiatric disease. Elsewhere in the chapter, we will look at other patients with amnesia resulting from other types of lesions.

Brain Surgery and Memory Loss

In a 1954 report on the bilateral removal of the medial temporal lobe in H.M. and several schizophrenic patients, Scoville wrote:

> Bilateral resection of the uncus [anterior aspect of the hippocampal gyrus], and amygdalum alone, or in conjunction with the entire pyriform amygdaloid hippocampal complex, has resulted in no marked physiologic or behavioral changes with the one exception of a very grave, recent memory loss, so severe as to prevent the patient from remembering the locations of the rooms in which he lives, the names of his close associates, or even the way to the toilet. (Scoville, 1954)

To better understand the deficits of his post-surgical patients with medial temporal lobe resections, Scoville teamed up with psychologist Brenda Milner (Chapter 1). Through neuropsychological examinations, Milner found that the extent of the memory deficit depended on how much of the medial temporal lobe had been removed. The more posterior along the medial temporal lobe the resection was made, the worse the amnesia was (Scoville & Milner, 1957). Strikingly, however, only *bilateral* resection of the hippocampus resulted in severe amnesia. By comparison, in one patient whose entire right medial temporal lobe (hippocampus and hippocampal gyrus) was removed, no residual memory deficit was reported by Scoville and Milner (although today's more sensitive tests would reveal some memory deficits).

The most interesting and famous of these patients was H.M.—Henry Molaison, whose name was revealed after his death in 2008 at the age of 82. Over the years, he unstintingly allowed himself to be tested by over 100 researchers. His case holds a prominent position in the history of memory research for several reasons. One was that although he had a memory deficit, he had no other cognitive deficits. His problem was purely a memory problem: He was of normal intelligence, had normal perceptions, except for some olfactory deficits due to surgery, and had no psychological or mental illness. Also, because his memory loss was the result of surgery, the exact

regions of the brain that were affected were thought to be known (Scoville & Milner, 1957; Milner et al., 1968). As we will see later in the chapter, this last point was not quite true.

After the surgery, H.M. knew the autobiographical details of his life and all the other things he had learned in his life up to the 2 years immediately before his surgery. For those 2 years before surgery, however, he could not remember anything. He also showed selective memory loss for *events* as far back as a decade before the surgery. H.M. had normal short-term memory (sensory registers and working memory) and procedural memory (like riding a bicycle). Like many other amnesics (Figure 9.3), H.M. had normal *digit span* abilities (how many numbers a person can hold in memory over a short period of time) and did well at holding strings of digits in working memory. Unlike normal participants, however, he did poorly on digit span tests that required the acquisition of new long-term memories. It appeared that the transfer of information from short-term storage to long-term memory was disrupted. H.M. had anterograde amnesia, and could form no new long-term memories. Interestingly, even though he could not consciously remember new experiences, his behavior would be affected by them. The researchers were surprised when they discovered that H.M. could learn some things: tasks that involved motor skills, perceptual skills, or procedures became easier over time, though he could not remember practicing the new skill or being asked to learn it. There was a dissociation between remembering the experience of learning and the actual learned information.

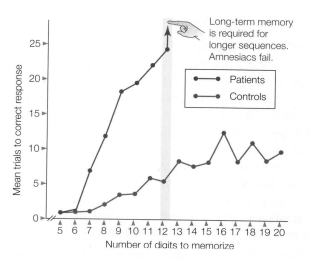

FIGURE 9.3 Digit span for amnesic patients and control participants.
A sequence of five digits was read to the participants, who were then asked to repeat the digits to the experimenter. If the digits were repeated correctly, one more digit was added to the next sequence presented. If the digits in a sequence were reported incorrectly, that sequence was repeated until the participant reported it correctly.

Recent Studies on Memory Loss

Studies of H.M. changed how people thought about the brain's memory processes. Previously, it was thought that memory could not be separated from perceptual and intellectual functions. These latter functions, however, remained intact in H.M., implying that memory was to some degree distinct from these processes. From H.M., researchers also learned that the medial temporal lobes are necessary for forming long-term memory and for transferring information about events and facts from short-term memory into long-term memory. Studies of H.M. also suggest that the medial temporal lobes are not necessary for the formation and retrieval of short-term memories or for learning new long-term memory that involves learning procedures or motor skills. Thus, the medial temporal lobe memory system is involved in certain memory functions, but not others, and is not critical for general intelligence, cognitive control, language, perception, or motor functions.

Studies in H.M. and other patients with amnesia have also shown that they can learn some forms of new information in addition to procedures, motor skills, and perceptual skills. They can also learn new concepts and world knowledge (semantic memory). But the amnesic patients, nonetheless, do not remember the *episodes* during which they learned or observed the information previously. The growing evidence from cases of amnesia suggests that long-term memories for events, facts, and procedures can be partially dissociated from one another, as expressed in their differential sensitivity to brain damage. Throughout this chapter, we explore additional studies that used patients with amnesia as participants.

TAKE-HOME MESSAGES

- Anterograde amnesia is the loss of the ability to form new memories, as in the case of H.M.
- Patient H.M. developed amnesia after bilateral removal of his medial temporal lobes to treat epilepsy.
- Retrograde amnesia is the loss of memory for events that happened in the past.
- Retrograde amnesia tends to be greatest for the most recent events, an effect known as a temporal gradient or Ribot's Law.
- Patients with retrogade amnesia may have normal short-term memory as shown by digit span tests.

Mechanisms of Memory

Although patients with memory deficits have revealed many key aspects of human memory, models of memory continue to evolve, and different models emphasize different factors in the organization of learning and memory. Many different memory models have been proposed, including, for example, those based on how long memories persist, the type of information that is retained, whether memories are conscious or unconscious, and the time it takes to acquire them (see Figure 9.2 for a summary of the essential relations among different forms of long-term and short-term memory). In the next few sections, we discuss different forms of memory, and describe some of the evidence supporting theoretical distinctions among them.

Short-Term Forms of Memory

As mentioned earlier, short-term memory is memory that persists for milliseconds, seconds, or minutes. Short-term memories include the transient retention of sensory information in sensory structures (sensory memory), short-term stores for information about the world (short-term memory), and working memory. We discuss these three forms of memory in turn.

Sensory Memory Imagine that you are watching the final game of the World Cup. The score is tied and there are only seconds to go when your mother enters the room. She begins a soliloquy, but you're not really paying attention. Suddenly you detect an increase in the volume of her voice and hear the words, "You haven't heard a word I said!" Wisely, your response is not to admit it. Instead, and in the nick of time to avoid repercussions, you metaphorically reach back and retrieve the most recent sentence accurately enough to say, "Sure I did; you said that the neighbor's goat is in our yard again eating the lettuce, and you want me to get it out."

Almost everyone you ask about this phenomenon knows what you mean. The auditory verbal information just presented to you seems to persist as a sort of echo in your head, even when you are not really paying attention to it. If you try to retrieve it quickly enough, you find it is still there, and you can repeat it out loud to assuage your interrogator. We refer to this type of memory as *sensory memory*, which, for hearing, we call *echoic memory*. For vision, we say *iconic memory*.

The persistence of the auditory sensory memory trace in humans has been measured in different ways, including physiological recordings. An event-related potential (ERP) known as the electrical *mismatch negativity* (*MMN*), or its magnetic counterpart, the *mismatch field* (*MMF*), has proven highly informative about the duration of echoic memory. The MMN brain response is elicited by the presentation of a deviant stimulus, such as a high-frequency tone presented

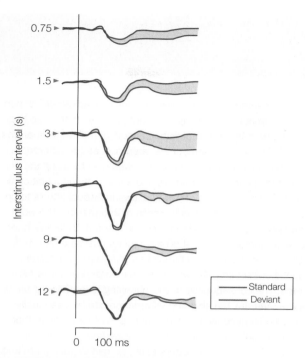

FIGURE 9.4 The mismatch field response.
The magnetic brain response known as the *mismatch field (MMF)* elicited by deviant tones (blue trace) in comparison to the magnetic responses elicited by standard tones (red traces). The amplitude of the MMF (indicated by the shaded difference between the blue and red traces) declines as the time between the preceding standard tone and the deviant tone increases to 12 s. This result can be interpreted as evidence for an automatic process in auditory sensory (echoic) memory that has a time course on the order of approximately 10 s.

within a sequence of identical standard low tones. These mismatch responses are interpreted as representing sensory memory processes that hold recent auditory experience in echoic memory for comparison to new inputs: When the inputs differ, the MMN and MMF are generated. Hence, the amplitudes of these brain responses at different time intervals between the deviant and standard tones could be used to index how long the echoic memory trace persists.

Mikko Sams, Ritta Hari, and their colleagues (1993) at the Helsinki University of Technology in Finland did precisely that. They varied the interstimulus intervals between standard and deviant tones and found that the MMF could still be elicited by the deviant tone at interstimulus intervals of 9 to 10 s (Figure 9.4). After about 10 s, the amplitude of the MMF declined to the point where it could no longer be distinguished reliably from noise. Because the MMF is generated in the auditory cortex, these physiological studies also provide information about where sensory memories are stored: in sensory structures as a short-lived neural trace.

What about the time course of the neural trace for a visual sensory memory? Does it also last several seconds? No, and you know this is true because when you look at a painting and then turn away, the image does not persist very long. Most estimates of the time course of visual sensory memory suggest that the neural trace for a visual stimulus lasts only 300 to 500 ms. Both echoic and iconic sensory memory, however, have a relatively high capacity: These forms of memory can, in principle, retain a lot of information, but only for a very short period of time.

Short-Term Memory In contrast to sensory memory, *short-term memory* has a longer time course—seconds to minutes—and a more limited capacity. Early data on short-term memory led to the development of some influential models that proposed discrete stages of information processing during learning and memory. The *modal model*, developed by Richard Atkinson and Richard Shiffrin (1968), proposes that information is first stored in sensory memory (Figure 9.5). From there, items selected by attentional processes (see Chapter 7) can move into short-term storage. Once in short-term memory, if the item is rehearsed, it can be moved into long-term memory. The modal model suggests that, at each stage, information can be lost by *decay* (information degrades and is lost over time), *interference* (new information displaces old information), or a combination of the two. This model formalized the idea that discrete stages of memory exist and that they have different characteristics. In addition, this model has a strong serial structure: Information coming into sensory memory can be passed to short-term memory and only then into long-term memory.

The ensuing decades have seen intense debate over this model from the standpoint of the psychology of

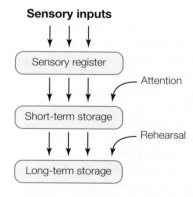

FIGURE 9.5 The Atkinson and Shiffrin modal model of memory. Sensory information enters the information-processing system and is first stored in a sensory register. Items that are selected via attentional processes are then moved into short-term storage. With rehearsal, the item can move from short-term to long-term storage.

HOW THE BRAIN WORKS
Short-Term Memory Capacity

Short-term memory is limited, but how limited? Precisely how much information a healthy person can retain in short-term memory varies among individuals. Experiments have demonstrated an interesting characteristic of human memory. In the 1950s, George Miller (G. Miller, 1956; see Figure 1.20 in Chapter 1) investigated how much information individuals can process. Although the initial work centered on perception, the research has been extended to memory for the retention of items.

Volunteers were presented with items to be remembered, in groups of varying size. The results were amazing: Regardless of the content of the items (e.g., digits, letters, or words), the number of items that were retained typically proved to be about seven. When more than seven items were presented, volunteers were less successful at recalling all of them. Miller referred to this characteristic feature of human memory as the *span of immediate memory*, or, in the terminology we have been using up to now, the *span of short-term memory*. When digits are used, this feature is referred to as *digit span*, and it is commonly measured in neuropsychological tests.

The memory limits discovered in these studies are defined by the number of items, not the content of each item, so they tell us about the way information is coded in short-term stores. This distinction has sometimes been cast as the difference between a *bit* of information and a *chunk*—a *bit* being the elementary piece of information, and a *chunk* being a unit composed of bits. The use of words allows individual letters to be chunked into one meaningful piece of information. The word *cerebellum* is either 10 letters or one word. If 10 letters have to be remembered, the short-term memory system is taxed; but if the letters can be chunked as one word (*cerebellum*), then about seven of these chunks (or words) can be remembered. The consequence of this chunking is that, during recall of the material, the chunked information can be essentially unpacked (unchunked) to yield more bits of information than normally could be retained. That is, if we can retain in our memory 7 words of 10 letters each, we can unpack them into 70 bits of information by using knowledge about word spelling. This evidence points to the ability of humans to recode information in manageable packets, packets that can be handled within the constraints of short-term memory.

---

memory as well as the neuroscience of memory. Data has been presented to support, challenge, and extend the model. A key question is whether memories have to be encoded in short-term memory before being stored in long-term memory. Another way to look at this question is to ask whether the brain systems that retain information over the short term are the same or different from those that store information over the long term. Atkinson and Shiffrin pondered this issue themselves, writing in 1971:

> Our account of short-term and long-term storage does not require that the two stores necessarily be in different parts of the brain or involve different physiological structures. One might consider the short-term store simply as being a temporary activation of some portion of the long-term store. (p. 89)

Studies of patients with brain damage permit a test of the hierarchically structured modal model of memory. In 1969, neuropsychologists Tim Shallice and Elizabeth Warrington at University College London reported that a patient (K.F.) with damage to the left perisylvian cortex (the region around the Sylvian fissure) displayed reduced digit span ability (about 2 items, as opposed to 5 to 9 items

for healthy persons). The test involves first reading lists of digits for the participants to remember and then, after a delay of only a few seconds, having participants repeat those digits. The lists can be from two to five or more digits long, and the maximum number that a person can recall and report is known as his digit span ability (see Figure 9.3).

Remarkably, however, in a long-term memory test of associate learning that pairs words, K.F. retained the ability to form certain types of new long-term memories that could last much longer than a few seconds. Therefore, it seemed that the patient displayed an interesting dissociation between short-term and long-term memory. If this interpretation of the finding is true, it has important implications for models of memory: Short-term memory might not be required in order to form long-term memory. This conclusion is in contrast to how the information flows in the modal model (Figure 9.5), which requires serial processing. One issue with this view is that the two tests presented to K.F. were different (digit span and word association), and it's hard to pinpoint whether the dissociation is one of memory processes or actually due to the different tasks.

A more recent example of a similar patient comes from the work of Hans Markowitsch and colleagues

(1999) at Bielefeld University in Germany. Their patient, E.E., had a tumor centered in the left angular gyrus. The tumor affected the inferior parietal cortex and posterior superior temporal cortex (Figure 9.6), regions similar to but slightly different from those affected in patient K.F. After undergoing surgery to remove the tumor, E.E. showed below-normal short-term memory ability but preserved long-term memory—a pattern similar to K.F.'s. E.E. showed normal speech production and comprehension, and normal reading comprehension. He had poor short-term memory for abstract verbal material, however, as well as deficits in transposing numbers from numerical to verbal, and vice versa, even though he could calculate normally. Interestingly, on tests of his visuospatial short-term memory and both verbal and nonverbal long-term memory, E.E. performed normally.

The pattern of behavior displayed by these patients demonstrates a deficit of short-term memory abilities but a preservation of long-term memory. This pattern suggests that short-term memory is not the gateway to long-term memory in the manner laid out in the modal model. Perhaps information from sensory memory registers can be encoded directly into long-term memory.

The data from patients like K.F. and E.E. demonstrate a dissociation between long-term memory ability and short-term retention of information. In contrast, patients like H.M. have preserved short-term memory but deficits in the ability to form new long-term memories. Together, these two different patterns of memory deficit present an apparent double dissociation for short- and long-term retention of information, specifically in relation to both the memory processes and the underlying neuroanatomy (i.e., left perisylvian cortex vs. the medial temporal lobes).

As described in Chapter 3, a double dissociation is the strongest pattern of effects that can be obtained in attempts to identify and distinguish two mental processes. Investigators disagree, however, on whether these in-

teresting patient case studies demonstrate a true double dissociation. Some have argued that the evidence from these patient cases does not support a strong double dissociation of short- and long-term memory. Because the short-term memory tests are testing for the retention of overlearned materials such as digits and words, such tests may not be effective for learning about short-term memory. In fact, when novel materials are used to test short-term memory retention, patients with medial temporal lobe lesions sometimes fail.

Working Memory The concept of working memory was developed to extend the concept of short-term memory and to elaborate the kinds of mental processes that are involved when information is retained over a period of seconds to minutes. *Working memory* represents a limited-capacity store for retaining information over the short term (*maintenance*) and for performing mental operations on the contents of this store (*manipulation*). For example, we can remember a list of numbers, and we can also add (manipulate) them in our head by using working memory. The contents of working memory could originate from sensory inputs (as in the modal model), such as when someone asks you to multiply 55 times 3, or it could be retrieved from long-term memory, such as when you visit the carpet store and recall the dimensions of your living room and multiply them to figure out its square feet. In each case, working memory contains information that can be acted on and processed, not merely maintained by rehearsal, although such maintenance is one aspect of working memory.

Psychologists Alan Baddeley and Graham Hitch (1974) at the University of York argued that the idea of a unitary short-term memory was insufficient to explain the maintenance and processing of information over short periods. They proposed a three-part working memory system consisting of a central executive mechanism for controlling two subordinate systems involved in rehearsal of different types of information: phonological and visuospatial (Figure 9.7).

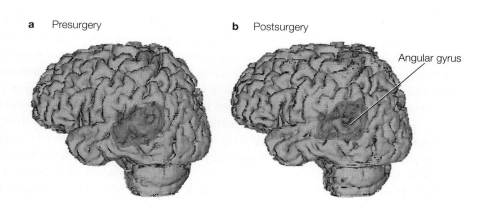

FIGURE 9.6 MRI scans reconstructed to provide a three-dimensional rendering of patient E.E.'s left hemisphere. E.E. had selective deficits in short-term memory. **(a)** The reconstructed scan taken before surgery; **(b)** the scan taken after surgery. The area of the tumor is indicated by shading. The physicians used positron emission tomography (PET) with a radiolabeled methionine tracer to identify the tumor according to its increased metabolic profile (red).

a Presurgery

b Postsurgery

Angular gyrus

The proposed *central executive mechanism* is a cognitive system, a command-and-control center that presides over and coordinates the interactions between two subordinate systems that are short-term memory stores (the phonological "loop" and the visuospatial "sketch pad") and long-term memory.

The *phonological loop* is a hypothesized mechanism for acoustically coding information in working memory (thus, it is modality specific). The evidence for modality specificity first came from studies that asked participants to recall strings of consonants. The letters were presented visually, but the pattern of recall errors indicated that perhaps the letters were not coded visually over the short term. The participants were apparently using an acoustic code, because during recall they were more likely to replace a presented letter with an erroneous letter having a similar sound (e.g., *T* for *G*) rather than one with a similar shape (e.g., *Q* for *G*). This was the first insight suggesting that an acoustic code might play a part in rehearsal.

In line with this idea is evidence that immediate recall of lists of words is poorer when many words on the list sound similar than when they sound dissimilar, even when the dissimilar words are semantically related. This finding indicates that an acoustic code rather than a semantic code is used in working memory, because words that sound similar interfere with one another, whereas words related by meaning do not. The phonological loop might have two parts: a short-lived acoustic store for sound inputs and an articulatory component that plays a part in the subvocal rehearsal of visually presented items to be remembered over the short term.

The *visuospatial sketch pad* is a short-term memory store that parallels the phonological loop and permits information storage in either purely visual or visuospatial codes. Evidence for this system came from studies of participants who were instructed to remember a list of words using either a verbal strategy such as rote rehearsal or a visuospatial strategy based on an imagery mnemonic. Under control conditions in which the memory rehearsal was the only task, participants were better on the memory test when they used the visuospatial strategy. The verbal strategy, however, proved better when the participants were required to concurrently track a moving stimulus by operating a stylus during the retention interval. In contrast, people are impaired on verbal memory tasks (but not nonverbal memory tasks) when they are required to repeat nonsense syllables during the retention interval, presumably because the phonological loop is disrupted. Dissociations like these cannot be explained by assuming that there is a unitary memory system.

Deficits in short-term memory abilities, such as remembering items on a digit span test, can be correlated

FIGURE 9.7 Simplified representation of the working memory model proposed by Baddeley and Hitch. This three-part working memory system has a *central executive* that controls two subordinate systems: the *phonological loop*, which encodes information phonologically (acoustically) in working memory; and the *visuospatial sketch pad*, which encodes information visually in working memory.

with damage to the subcomponents of the working memory system. Evidence about the distinct nature of these subsystems and their anatomical substrates in the human brain first came from studies of patients with specific brain lesions. In fact, each system can be damaged selectively by different brain lesions.

One expectation is that the phonological loop and the visuospatial sketch pad might correspond to working memory functions of the left and right hemispheres, respectively—an idea consistent with the general picture of hemispheric specialization (see Chapter 4). Indeed, patients with lesions of the left supramarginal gyrus (Brodmann area 40) have deficits in phonological working memory (Figure 9.8; see also Figure 9.6) resulting in reduced auditory–verbal memory spans: They cannot hold strings of words in working memory. The rehearsal process of the phonological loop involves a region in the left premotor region (area 44). Thus, a left-hemisphere network consisting of the lateral frontal and inferior parietal lobes is involved in phonological working memory. These deficits in working memory for auditory–verbal material (digits, letters, words) have not been found to be associated with deficits in speech perception or production. This distinction between aphasia—language deficits following brain damage (see Chapter 11)—and deficits in

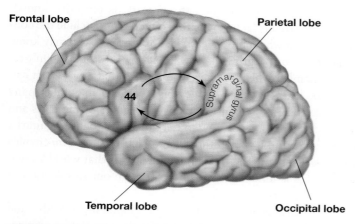

FIGURE 9.8 Lateral view of the left hemisphere, indicating that there is an information loop involved in phonological working memory flowing between BA44 and the supramarginal gyrus (BA40).

auditory–verbal short-term memory is important to keep in mind.

The visuospatial sketch pad is compromised by damage to the parieto-occipital region of either hemisphere, but damage to the right hemisphere produces more severe deficits in visuospatial short-term memory. Patients with lesions in the right parieto-occipital region have difficulty with nonverbal visuospatial working memory tasks like retaining and repeating the sequence of blocks *touched* by another person. For example, if an investigator touches blocks on a table in sequences that the patient must repeat, and gradually increases the number of blocks touched, patients with parieto-occipital lesions show below-normal performance, even when their vision is otherwise normal. Similar lesions in the left hemisphere can lead to impairments in short-term memory for visually presented *linguistic* material.

Early neuroimaging studies have helped to support this distinction. Using PET imaging in healthy volunteers, Edward Smith and his colleagues (1996) at Columbia University provided evidence for dissociations in the brain regions activated while performing spatial versus verbal working memory tasks. Participants were presented with either an array of locations marked on a computer screen or an array of letters, and were asked to remember the locations or the letters during a delay period of 3 s. Next, they presented a location marker for the spatial memory task or a letter at fixation for the verbal memory task and asked participants whether the location or letter had been in the original array. For verbal working memory tasks, they found activation (increasing blood flow coupled to increased neural activity) in left-hemisphere sites in inferolateral frontal cortex, but for the spatial working memory task, activation was primarily in right-hemisphere regions (inferior frontal, posterior parietal, and extrastriate cortex in the occipital lobe; Figure 9.9).

Several years later, Smith and colleagues compiled a meta-analysis of 60 PET and fMRI studies (Wager & Smith, 2003). Although their analysis confirmed that activation is found during working memory tasks with verbal stimuli in the left ventrolateral prefrontal cortex, the evidence for spatial working memory showed activation to be more bilateral in the brain. Why is there a behavior difference in visuospatial tasks with right-sided lesions, but activity with these tasks is also seen on the left side on fMRI? The left-hemisphere activity during spatial working memory may reflect, at least in some studies, a verbal recoding of the nonverbal stimuli. For example, when asked to remember the locations of a set of stimuli, we might think "upper left" and "lower right." We will return to further discussion of working memory in Chapter 12.

Long-Term Forms of Memory

Information retained for a significant time (days, months or years) is referred to as *long-term memory*. Theorists have tended to split long-term memory into two major divisions, taking into account the observable fact that not all stored knowledge is the same. The key distinction is between declarative and nondeclarative memories.

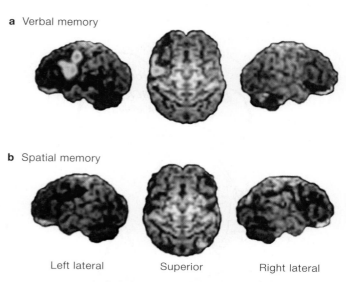

a Verbal memory

b Spatial memory

Left lateral   Superior   Right lateral

FIGURE 9.9 Changes in local cerebral blood flow, measured with positron emission tomography.
Verbal (a) and spatial (b) working memory tasks were tested in healthy volunteers. In each case, the views of the cortical surface show the left hemisphere (**left**); superior (dorsal) surface of both hemispheres, with the frontal lobe at the top (**middle**); and right hemisphere (**right**). See text for details.

Declarative Memory **Declarative memory** is defined as memory for events and for facts, both personal and general, that we have conscious access to and that can be verbally reported. This form of memory is sometimes referred to as *explicit memory*. Declarative memory is the type of memory that is impaired in H.M. and, thus, it is dependent on the medial temporal lobe. In the 1970s, psychologist Endel Tulving introduced the idea that declarative memory can be further broken down into **episodic memory** and **semantic memory**. Episodic memories are memories of personal experiences that we recall about our own lives and what, where, when, and with whom they happened. They are our own personal, autobiographical memories. They differ from personal knowledge (Figure 9.10). For instance, you have personal knowledge of what day you were born, but you do not remember the experience. Episodic memories always include the self as the agent or recipient of some action. For example, the memory of falling off your new red bicycle (what) on Christmas day (when), badly skinning your elbow on the asphalt driveway (where), and your mother (who) running over to comfort you is an episodic memory. Episodic memory is the result of rapid associative learning in that the what, where, when, and who of a single episode, its context, become associated and bound together and can be retrieved from memory after a single episode. More recently, evidence has been unearthed that not all memory of experiences is conscious. We will discuss this research later in the chapter, when we examine *relational memory*.

FIGURE 9.10 Tulving and his cat.
According to Tulving, animals like his cat have no episodic memory, although they have knowledge of many things. Tulving argues that they therefore do not remember their experiences the same way we do; they can merely know about such experiences.

Semantic memory, in contrast, is objective knowledge that is factual in nature but does not include the context in which it was learned. For instance, you may know that corn is grown in Iowa, but you most likely don't remember when or where you learned that fact. A fact can be learned after a single episode, but it may take many exposures. Semantic memory reflects knowing facts and concepts such as how to tell time, who the lead guitarist is for the Rolling Stones, and what quantum mechanics is all about. The take-home message is that world knowledge is fundamentally different from our recollection of events in our own lives.

Interestingly, in human development, episodic and semantic memory appear at different ages. Babies who are 2 years old have been able to demonstrate recall of things they had witnessed at age 13 months (Bauer & Wewerka, 1995). It isn't until children are at least 18 months, however, that they actually seem to include themselves as part of the memory, although this ability tends to be more reliably present in 3- to 4-year-olds (Perner & Ruffman, 1995; M. Wheeler et al., 1997).

When Tulving introduced the idea of episodic versus semantic memory decades ago, the dominant thinking was that there was a unitary memory system. If Tulving is right, however, then perhaps different underlying brain systems support these two different flavors of declarative long-term memory.

Nondeclarative Memory **Nondeclarative memory** is so named because it cannot be "declared," that is, verbally reported. It is also known as *implicit memory*, knowledge that we have no conscious access to. Several types of memory fall under this category: priming, simple learned behaviors that derive from conditioning, habituation, sensitization, and procedural memory, such as learning a motor or cognitive skill. This form of memory is revealed when previous experiences facilitate performance on a task that does not require intentional recollection of the experiences. This type of memory was unimpaired in H.M. because nondeclarative memory is not dependent on the medial temporal lobe. It involves other brain structures, including the basal ganglia, the cerebellum, the amygdala, and the neocortex.

Procedural Memory **Procedural memory** is one form of nondeclarative memory that depends on extensive and repeated experience. Tasks that require us to use procedural memory include learning motor skills like how to ride a bike, type, or swim, and learning cognitive skills such as how to read. Studies of amnesia have revealed some fundamental distinctions between long-term memory for events in your life, such as seeing your first bike under the Christmas tree, and procedural memory, such as riding a bicycle.

One test of procedural learning is the *serial reaction time task*. In one experimental setup, participants sit at a console having four buttons. Placing the fingers of one hand over the buttons, participants would press buttons that correspond to locations of stimuli in front of them. Each button corresponds to one of four lights—the mapping between button and light can simply be their spatial relationships (i.e., the left light maps to the left button). The task would be to press the button with the finger that corresponds to the light that is illuminated (Figure 9.11a). The lights can be flashed in different sequences: A totally random sequence can be flashed; or a pseudorandom sequence might be presented, in which the participant thinks the lights are flashing randomly when in reality they are flashing in a complex, repetitive sequence.

Over time, normal participants respond faster to the repeating sequence than they do to a totally random sequence (Figure 9.11b). Thus, their improved performance indicates that they have learned the sequence. When asked whether the sequences were random, however, participants report that the sequences were completely random. They do not seem to know that any pattern existed, yet they learned the skill. Such behavior is typical of procedural learning, which requires no explicit knowledge about what was learned. This kind of evidence has been used to argue for the distinction between declarative and procedural knowledge, because participants appear to acquire one (procedural knowledge) in the absence of the other (declarative knowledge).

Some have challenged the idea that normal participants learn without having any explicit knowledge of what was learned. For example, sometimes the investigators ask normal volunteers about the sequences and find that they can in fact explicitly describe the learned material. Perhaps those who deny any such knowledge have less confidence in their knowledge and hence deny it. Given this possibility in normal participants, if we do not find evidence for explicit knowledge during skill acquisition, how can we be sure it is not there? Perhaps the person merely failed to demonstrate it.

An answer comes from procedural learning studies in persons with anterograde amnesia, like H.M.. These people cannot form new declarative (or at least episodic) memories. When tasks like the one in Figure 9.11a were presented to amnesic patients, it was found that those with dense anterograde amnesia (with loss of episodic learning) improved their performance for repeated sequences (compared to random ones) over a series of days; their improvement was shown as a speeding up of reaction time (as in Figure 9.11b). Even though they state they have never performed the task before, these amnesic participants have learned the procedure. Therefore, procedural learning can proceed independently of the brain systems required for episodic memory.

What brain systems support procedural memory? Learning motor skills may involve the basal ganglia. Patients with disorders of the basal ganglia or inputs to these subcortical structures show poor performance on a variety of procedural learning tasks. As we learned in the previous chapter, these individuals include patients with Parkinson's disease, in which cell death in the substantia nigra disrupts dopaminergic projections into the basal ganglia, and patients with Huntington's disease, who have degeneration of neurons in the basal ganglia. These patients, who are not amnesic *per se*, have impairments in acquisition and retention of motor skills as assessed by a variety of tests involving motor skill learning.

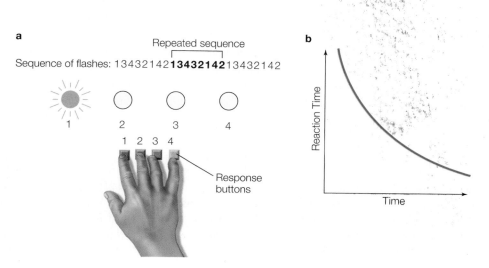

FIGURE 9.11 Procedural learning of sequences in the serial reaction-time task.
(a) Using their fingers, participants are asked to push buttons corresponding to flashes of lights in a complex sequence that is repeated but not obvious. (b) Over time, participants reaction time to the repeating sequence becomes faster as compared to a sequence that is totally random, although they apparently do not know that any pattern exists.

Priming Another form of nondeclarative memory is priming. **Priming** refers to a change in the response to a stimulus, or in the ability to identify a stimulus, following prior exposure to that stimulus. For instance, if you were to see a picture of bicycle handlebars from an odd angle, you would recognize them as part of a bike faster if you had just seen a typical picture of a bike. If you had not, you would find them more difficult to identify. Priming can be perceptual, conceptual, or semantic.

Perceptual priming acts within the **perceptual representation system** (**PRS**). In the PRS, the structure and form of objects and words can be primed by prior experience, and the effects persist for months. For example, participants can be presented with lists of words, and their memory of the lists can be evaluated using a word-fragment completion task. In such a task, during the later test phase, participants are shown only some letters from real words; for example, t_ou_h_s for "thoughts." These fragments can be from either new words (not present in the original list) or old words (present in the original list). The participants are simply asked to complete the fragments. Participants are significantly better and faster at correctly completing fragments for words presented in the initial list—they show priming. The important idea is that participants benefit from having seen the words before, even if they are not told and do not realize that the words were in the previous list. This priming for fragment completion does not lessen over time, and it is specific for the sensory modality of the learning and test phases. To put this another way, if the word lists are presented auditorily and the word-fragment completion is done visually, then the priming is reduced, suggesting that priming reflects a PRS that subserves structural, visual, and auditory representations of word form. Lastly, perceptual priming can also be seen with non-word stimuli, such as pictures, shapes, and faces. In summary, the PRS mediates word and non-word forms of priming. Moreover, it is not based on conceptual systems, but rather is perceptual in nature. Interestingly, this type of priming is also found in amnesia patients like H.M. H.M. would show evidence of priming even when he could not remember ever having seen the word list or ever having done a fragment-complete task before. This behavior tells us that the PRS system does not rely on the medial temporal lobe, because both of H.M.'s were removed surgically. But this is merely a single dissociation. Is there any evidence that brain lesions can affect the PRS system while leaving long-term memory intact?

There is: John Gabrieli and his colleagues (1995) at Stanford University tested a patient, M.S., a man who had a right occipital lobe lesion. M.S. had experienced intractable epileptic seizures and at age 14 underwent surgery to treat them. The surgery removed most of Brodmann areas 17, 18, and 19 of his right occipital lobe, leaving him blind in the left visual field. He has above average intelligence and memory. Explicit tests of memory (recognition and cued recall) and implicit memory (perceptual priming) were administered to M.S., and his performance was compared to amnesiacs similar to H.M., who had anterograde amnesia for episodic memory. The test materials were words briefly presented visually and then read aloud by the subjects. During the *implicit* memory test, the words were presented and then masked with rows of *X*'s. The duration of presentation increased from 16 ms to a time when the participant could read the word. If less time was required to read the word after it had been seen previously, then there would be evidence for implicit perceptual priming. In a separate *explicit* recognition test, participants saw old and new words and had to judge whether they had seen them before.

The amnesic patients displayed the expected impairments of explicit word recognition, but they did not show impairment in the implicit perceptual priming test. In contrast, M.S. had normal performance on explicit recognition, but impairment in the implicit perceptual priming test. This deficit was not due to his partial blindness, because his explicit memory for word recognition and recall indicated that he perceived them normally by using the intact portions of his visual field. M.S. showed a pattern opposite to that typical of amnesiacs like H.M. These data show that perceptual priming can be damaged even when explicit memory is not impaired, thereby completing a double dissociation for declarative and nondeclarative memory systems. The anatomical data indicate that perceptual priming depends on the perceptual system, because M.S. had lesions to the visual cortex leading to deficits in perceptual priming.

Priming also occurs for *conceptual features* rather than perceptual features, though it doesn't last nearly as long. Here, participants are quicker at answering general knowledge questions if the concept had been presented earlier. For example, if we had been talking about pasta and its different shapes, and then you were asked to name an Italian food, most likely you would say pasta, rather than pizza or veal parmigiana. Conceptual priming is also not affected by lesions to the medial temporal lobe, but rather by lesions to the lateral temporal and prefrontal regions.

Another form of priming is *semantic priming*, in which the prime and target are words that are different but related semantically. For instance, the prime may be the word *hammer*, but the target word is *wrench*. Semantic priming is brief, lasting only a few seconds.

Classical Conditioning and Nonassociative Learning Two other domains of nondeclarative memory include *classical conditioning*, a type of associative learning, and *nonassociative learning*. In classical conditioning, sometimes referred to as *Pavlovian conditioning*, a conditioned stimulus (CS; an otherwise neutral stimulus to the organism) is paired with an unconditioned stimulus (US; one that elicits an established response from the organism) and becomes associated with it. The conditioned stimulus will then evoke a conditioned response (CR) similar to that typically evoked by the unconditioned stimulus (the unconditioned response, UR). Russian Ivan Pavlov (1849–1936) received a Nobel Prize after first demonstrating this type of learning with his dogs, which started to salivate at the sound of a bell that Pavlov rang before he gave them food (Figure 9.12). Before conditioning, the bell was not associated with food and did not cause salivation. After conditioning, in which the bell and the food were paired, the bell (CS) caused salivation even in the absence of the food (US). We will discuss more about conditioning in Chapters 10 and 12. Classical conditioning comes in two flavors: *delay* and *trace conditioning*. In delay conditioning, the US begins while the CS is still present; but in trace conditioning, there is a time gap, and thus a memory trace

is necessary for an association to be made between the CS and US. Studies with normal participants and those with amnesia resulting from hippocampal damage have found that damage to the hippocampus does not impair delay conditioning, but does impair trace conditioning (R. Clark & Squire, 1998). Thus, some types of associative learning depend on the hippocampus, and others do not.

Nonassociative learning, as its name implies, does not involve the association of two stimuli to elicit a behavioral change. Rather, it consists of forms of simple learning such as *habituation*, where the response to an unchanging stimulus decreases over time. For instance, the first time you use an electric toothbrush, your entire mouth tingles; but after a few uses, you no longer feel a response. Another type of nonassociative learning is *sensitization*, in which a response increases with repeated presentations of the stimulus. The classic example is rubbing your arm. At first it merely creates a feeling of warmth. If you continue, however, it starts to hurt. This is an adaptive response that warns you to stop the rubbing because it may cause injury. Nonassociative learning primarily involves sensory and sensory motor (reflex) pathways. We do not consider classical conditioning, nonassociative learning, or nonassociative memory further in this chapter. Instead, we focus on the neural substrates of declarative (episodic and semantic memory) and nondeclarative memory (procedural memory and the perceptual representation system).

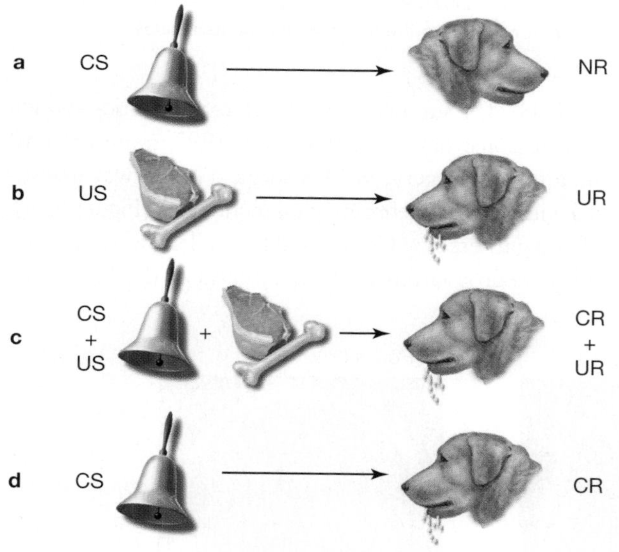

FIGURE 9.12 Classical (Pavlovian) conditioning.
When a stimulus is presented that has no meaning to an animal, such as the sound of a bell (CS), there is no response (NR) **(a)**. In contrast, presentation of a meaningful stimulus like food (US) generates an unconditioned response (UR) **(b)**. When the sound is paired with the food, however, the animal learns the association **(c)**; and later the newly conditioned stimulus (CS) alone can elicit the response, which is now called a conditioned response (CR) **(d)**.

TAKE-HOME MESSAGES

- Traditional memory theories include two main distinctions about how we learn and retain knowledge: by how long the information is retained and by what type of information the knowledge contains.

- Memory classified by duration includes sensory memory, lasting only seconds at most; short-term memory, lasting from seconds to minutes; and long-term memory, lasting from days to years.

- Echoic memory is sensory memory for audition; iconic memory is sensory memory for vision.

- Working memory extends the concept of short-term memory: It contains information that can be acted on and processed, not merely maintained by rehearsal.

- Long-term memory is split into two divisions defined by content: declarative and nondeclarative. Declarative memory is knowledge that we can consciously access, including personal and world knowledge. Nondeclarative memory is knowledge that we cannot consciously access, such as motor and cognitive skills, and other behaviors derived from conditioning, habituation, or sensitization.

- Declarative memory can be further broken down into episodic and semantic memory. Episodic memory involves conscious awareness of past events; it is our personal, autobiographical memory. Semantic memory is the world knowledge that we remember even without recollecting the specific circumstances surrounding its learning.

- Procedural memory is a form of nondeclarative memory that involves the learning of various motor and cognitive skills. Other forms of nondeclarative memory include perceptual priming, conditioned responses, and non-associative learning.

- Different types of information may be retained in partially or wholly distinct memory systems.

The Medial Temporal Lobe Memory System

So far, we have learned from H.M. that the brain's ability to acquire new declarative memories (episodic and semantic memory) depends on the medial temporal lobe, whereas short-term and nondeclarative memories are supported more directly by brain mechanisms outside the medial temporal lobe system. We now explore how the medial temporal lobe affects long-term memory by looking first at patients with memory deficits, then lesion studies in animals, and finally imaging evidence from humans.

Evidence From Amnesia

As we have learned, the medial temporal lobe includes the amygdala, the hippocampus, and the surrounding parahippocampal, entorhinal, and perirhinal cortical areas. We also know that memory mechanisms have been divided into acquisition, consolidation, storage, and retrieval. Let's look first at those functions lost in amnesic patients like H.M., and ask: What neural mechanisms and brain structures enable us to acquire new long-term memories?

H.M.'s original surgical reports indicated that his hippocampi were completely removed bilaterally (Figure 9.13). Decades later, Suzanne Corkin of the Massachusetts Institute of Technology and journalist-author Philip Hilts (1995) discovered through some detective work that the clips

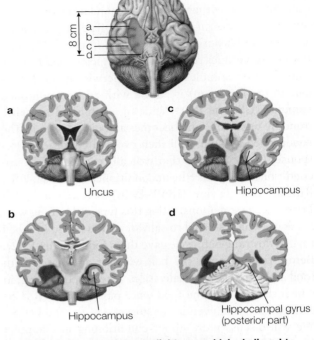

FIGURE 9.13 Region of the medial temporal lobe believed to have been removed from H.M.
As reported by his surgeon, the areas of H.M.'s brain that were removed are shown in red. (The resection is shown here on the left side only, for comparison of the resected region with an intact brain, on the right side, at the same level. H.M.'s actual lesion was bilateral.) At the top is a ventral view of the brain, showing both hemispheres and the details of the right medial temporal area (at left). The four anterior-to-posterior levels (a–d) shown in this ventral view correspond to the four coronal sections below.

used in H.M.'s surgery were not ferromagnetic—which meant he could have an MRI. So in 1997, more than 40 years after his surgery, H.M.'s surgical lesion was investigated with modern neuroimaging techniques (Figure 9.14).

Data gathered by Corkin and her colleagues were analyzed by neuroanatomist David Amaral of the University

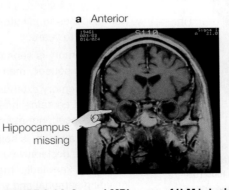
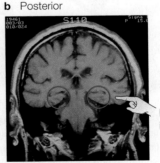

FIGURE 9.14 Coronal MRI scans of H.M.'s brain.
(a) In this anterior slice, the hand points to where the hippocampus has been removed bilaterally. (b) In this more posterior slice, however, the hand points to where the hippocampus is still intact in both hemispheres! This finding is in marked contrast to the belief that H.M. has no hippocampus—a view, based on the surgeon's report, that the scientific community held for 40 years.

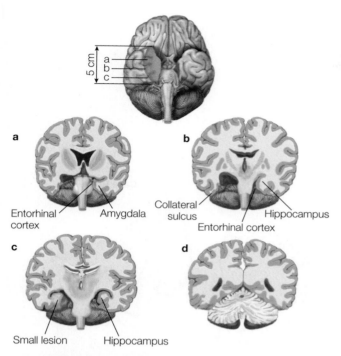

a

Entorhinal cortex   Amygdala

b

Collateral sulcus   Hippocampus

Entorhinal cortex

c

Small lesion   Hippocampus

d

FIGURE 9.15 Region of the medial temporal lobe actually removed from H.M.
Modern reconstruction by Amaral and colleagues, showing that portions of H.M.'s posterior hippocampus were not removed during surgery. This tissue, however, shows signs of atrophy and may no longer be functioning normally. Red areas indicate where portions were removed. Compare with Figure 9.13.

of California, Davis (Corkin et al., 1997). This analysis revealed (Figure 9.15) that H.M.'s lesion was smaller than originally reported. Contrary to Scoville's reports, approximately half of the posterior region of H.M.'s hippocampus was intact, and only 5 cm (not 8 cm) of the medial temporal lobe had been removed. Thus, the posterior parahippocampal gyrus was mostly spared; but the anterior portion, the perirhinal and entorhinal cortices, was removed. The remaining portions of H.M.'s hippocampi, however, were atrophied, probably due to the loss of inputs from the surrounding perihippocampal cortex that had been removed in the 1953 surgery. Thus, despite the original error in our knowledge about H.M.'s lesion, it may be that no functional hippocampal tissue remained. Consequently, H.M.'s lesions cannot help us determine the role of the hippocampus versus parahippocampal cortex in memory.

Consider another remarkable patient story, that of R.B. In 1978, R.B. lost his memory after an ischemic episode (reduction of blood to the brain) during heart bypass surgery. Changes in his memory performance were studied in detail by Stuart Zola, Larry Squire, and David Amaral at the University of California, San Diego. R.B. developed dense anterograde amnesia similar to H.M.'s: He could not form new long-term memories. He also had a mild temporal retrograde amnesia that went back

about 1 or 2 years, so R.B.'s amnesia was slightly less severe than H.M.'s retrograde loss. After his death, an autopsy revealed that R.B.'s lesions were restricted to a particular region of his hippocampus only. Although on gross examination his hippocampus appeared to be intact (Figure 9.16a), histological analysis revealed that, within each hippocampus, he had sustained a specific lesion restricted to the CA1 pyramidal cells (Figure 9.16b). Compare his hippocampus (Figure 9.16c) with that of a normal person after death (Figure 9.16b).

These findings of specific hippocampal damage in patient R.B. support the idea that the hippocampus is crucial for the formation of new long-term memories. R.B.'s case also supports the distinction between areas that store long-term memories and the role of the hippocampus in forming new memories. Even though retrograde amnesia is associated with damage to the medial temporal lobe, it is temporally limited and does not affect long-term memories of events that happened more than a few years prior to the amnesia-inducing event. Subsequently, several patients with similar medial temporal lobe lesions also have been identified and studied, and they show highly similar patterns of memory loss.

Further evidence that the hippocampus is involved in long-term memory comes from patients with **transient global amnesia** (**TGA**). This syndrome is triggered by a number of causes, but most commonly by physical exertion in men and emotional stress in women over 50. In this situation, the normal blood flow is disrupted in the brain. In particular, the vertebral-basilar artery system, which supplies blood to the medial temporal lobe and the diencephalon has been implicated as a critical site. The result is a transient ischemia that later returns to normal. High-resolution imaging data now suggest that the lesions caused by such an event are located within the CA1 subfield of the hippocampus and that these neurons are selectively vulnerable to metabolic stress (see Bartsch & Deuschl, 2010). This disruption of blood flow results in a sudden transient anterograde amnesia, and retrograde amnesia spanning weeks, months, and sometimes even years. In a typical scenario, a person may wind up in the hospital but not be sure about where he is, or why, or how he got there. He knows his name, birth date, job, and perhaps address; but if he has moved recently, he will supply his past address and circumstances. He performs normally on most neuropsychological tests, except for those that call for memory. He has normal short-term memory, and thus, can repeat lists of words told to him. When asked to remember a list of words, however, he forgets it within a couple of minutes if he is prevented from rehearsing it. He continually asks who the physician is and why he is there. He does show an awareness that he *should* know the

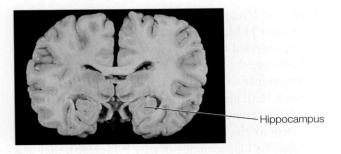

a

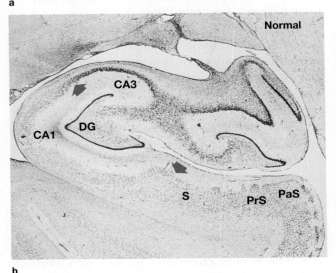

b

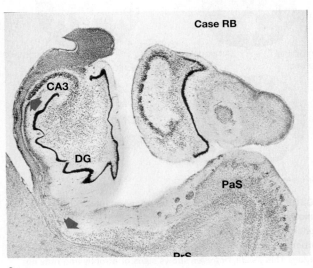

c

FIGURE 9.16 Comparison of R.B.'s brain with that of a normal participant.
(a) This section is from R.B.'s brain following his death. In contrast to the MRI sections from H.M. in
Figure 9.15, which show an absence of the anterior and middle portions of the hippocampus, R.B.'s
medial temporal lobe appeared intact on gross examination. **(b)** Compare normal histology here with
R.B.'s in **(c)**. This histological section from the brain of a normal participant shows an intact CA1 region
(labeled "CA1" and delimited as the region between the arrows). **(c)** Careful histological examination
of R.B.'s temporal lobe revealed that cells in the CA1 region of the hippocampus were absent (see
the region between the arrows). The absence of cells was the result of an ischemic episode following
surgery. Cells of the CA1 region are particularly sensitive to transient ischemia (temporary loss of blood
supply to a brain region).

answer to some questions, which worries him. He manifests a loss of time sense, and so he responds incorrectly to questions asking how long he has been in the hospital. During the hours following the amnesia-inducing event, distant memories return, and his anterograde memory deficit is resolved. Within 24 to 48 hours, he is essentially back to normal, although mild deficits may persist for days or weeks.

As you may have noticed, the patients with transient global amnesia have symptoms similar to those of people with permanent damage to the medial temporal lobe, such as H.M. So far, we do not know whether these patients have normal implicit learning or memory, in part because their impairment does not last long enough for researchers to adequately index things like procedural learning. The answer to this question would improve our

understanding of human memory and of a form of amnesia that any of us could experience later in life.

Converging evidence for the role of the hippocampus in forming long-term memory also comes from patients with amnesia caused by lesions in regions connected to, but outside of, the medial temporal lobes (e.g., damage to the diencephalon). Damage to these midline subcortical regions can be caused by stroke, tumors, trauma, and metabolic problems like those brought on by chronic alcoholism, such as Korsakoff's syndrome. Because patients with Korsakoff's syndrome initially have no damage to the medial temporal lobe, it is likely that connections between the anterior and dorso-medial diencephalon and medial temporal lobe are disrupted, giving rise to the deficit by compromising the circuitry that involves the hippocampus.

Further evidence comes from patients with Alzheimer's disease (AD). This disease causes widespread neuronal deterioration, including severe disruptions in the parietal lobe structures of the retrosplenial cortex, posterior cingulate, precuneus, and angular gyrus. But neuroscientists now widely believe that the hippocampus also deteriorates more rapidly in patients with AD than in people undergoing the normal aging process. The amyloid plaques (clumps of insoluble protein between neurons) and neurofibrillary tangles (tangles of protein fibers within cortical neurons) that are characteristic of AD congregate in this medial temporal area (Figure 9.17). MRI measurements of brain volumes have shown that the size of the hippocampus changes with the progression of AD: People with thicker hippocampi develop dementia to a lesser extent (Jobst et al., 1994; Jack et al., 2002).

Morris Moscovitch and colleagues at the Rotman Research Institute and the University of Toronto, Canada, have demonstrated that the extent of atrophy in the medial temporal lobe in Alzheimer's patients is most closely related to their deficits in episodic memory (Gilboa et al., 2005). In addition, there is a large loss of acetylcholine cells that connect to the hippocampus and prefrontal cortex in Alzheimer's disease. This dysfunctional connectivity between the hippocampus and prefrontal cortex due to the loss of acetylcholine appears to play a role in the progressive loss of ability to form new episodic memories in Alzheimer's patients.

Evidence From Animals With Medial Temporal Lobe Lesions

Studies in animals with lesions to the hippocampus and surrounding cortex have been invaluable to improving our understanding about the contributions of the medial temporal lobe to memory. This immense field of study includes investigations in invertebrates as well as studies in various mammalian species, including nonhuman primates. A comprehensive review of this field of work is beyond the scope of this textbook, but a few of the most important findings from animal studies are essential for understanding memory mechanisms. A key question in memory research has been how much does the hippocampus alone, as compared with surrounding structures in the medial temporal lobe, participate in the memory deficits of patients like H.M.? In other words, what structures of the medial temporal lobe system are involved in episodic memory? For example, does the amygdala influence memory deficits in amnesiacs (Figure 9.18)? Data from amnesic patients indicate that the amygdala is not part of the brain's episodic memory system, although—as we will learn in Chapter 10—it has a role in emotion and emotional memories. Another question is, what kind of memory and learning is impaired with various temporal lobe lesions?

Nonhuman Primate Studies To test whether the amygdala is essential in memory formation, surgical lesions were created in the medial temporal lobe and amygdala of monkeys. In classic work on monkeys conducted by Mortimer Mishkin (1978) at the National Institute of Mental Health, either the hippocampus, the

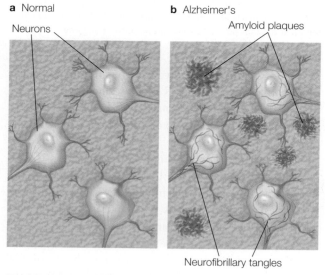

FIGURE 9.17 Comparison of cortex in Alzheimer's patients and normal participants.
These diagrams depict a normal section of cortex with cortical neurons (a) and a section of cortex in an Alzheimer's patient containing amyloid plaques between neurons and neurofibrillary tangles within neurons (b).

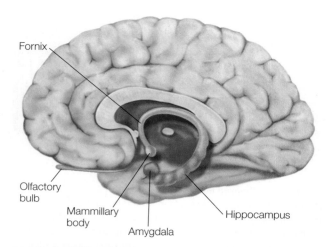

FIGURE 9.18 The amygdala.
The medial temporal lobe structures are shown in a medial view of the right hemisphere.

amygdala, or both were removed surgically. Mishkin found that the resulting amount of impairment varied according to what had been lesioned.

The brain-lesioned monkeys were tested with a popular behavioral task that Mishkin developed, known as the *delayed nonmatch-to-sample task*. A monkey is placed in a box with a retractable door in the front (Figure 9.19). When the door is closed so the monkey cannot see out, a food reward is placed under an object (Figure 9.19a). The door is opened, and the monkey is allowed to pick up the object to get the food (Figure 9.19b). The door is closed again, and the same object plus a new object are put in position (Figure 9.19c). The new object now covers the food reward, and after a delay that can be varied, the door is reopened and the monkey must pick up the new object to get the food reward. If the monkey picks up the old object, as in Figure 9.19d, there is no reward. With training, the monkey picks the new, or nonmatching, object; hence, learning and memory are measured by observing the monkey's performance.

In his early work, Mishkin found that, in the monkey, memory was impaired only if the lesion included both the hippocampus and the amygdala. This finding led to the (incorrect) idea that the amygdala is a key structure

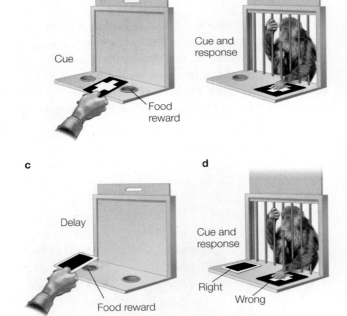

FIGURE 9.19 Delayed nonmatch-to-sample task.
(a) The correct response has a food reward located under it.
(b) The monkey is shown the correct response, which will yield a reward for the monkey. **(c)** The door is closed, and the reward is placed under a second response option. **(d)** The monkey is then shown two options and must pick the correct response (the one that *does not* match the original sample item) to get the reward. Here the monkey is shown making an error.

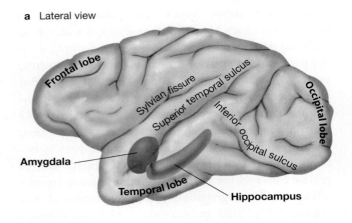

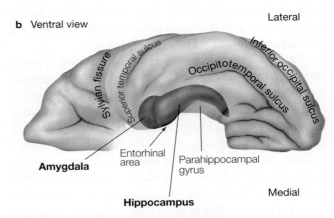

FIGURE 9.20 Gross anatomy of the medial temporal lobe.
(a) This lateral, see-through view of the left hemisphere shows the amygdala (red) and hippocampus (purple) within the temporal lobe. **(b)** This view from the ventral surface of the same hemisphere shows the amygdala and hippocampus, and indicates the locations of the parahippocampal gyrus and the entorhinal area (consisting of Brodmann areas 28 and typically also 34, which are located in the most anterior portion of the parahippocampal gyrus).

in memory. That idea, however, does not fit well with data from amnesiacs like R.B. (described earlier), who had anterograde amnesia caused by a lesion restricted to CA1 neurons of the hippocampus and no damage to the amygdala.

Stuart Zola, Larry Squire, and colleagues (Zola-Morgan et al., 1993) at the University of California, San Diego, investigated this dilemma. They created more selective lesions of the brains of monkeys by distinguishing between the amygdala and the hippocampus as well as the surrounding cortex near each structure. They surgically created lesions of the amygdala, the entorhinal cortex (Brodmann areas 28 and 34; Figure 9.20), or the surrounding neocortex of the parahippocampal gyrus and the perirhinal cortex (Brodmann areas 35 and 36). They wanted to extend Mishkin's work, which always involved lesions of the neocortex surrounding the amygdala or hippocampus owing to the way the surgery was performed.

The results indicated that lesions of the hippocampus and amygdala produced the most severe memory deficits only when the cortex surrounding these regions was also lesioned. When lesions of the hippocampus and amygdala were made but the surrounding cortex was spared, the presence or absence of the amygdala lesion did not affect the monkey's memory. The amygdala, then, could not be part of the system that supported the acquisition of long-term memory.

In subsequent investigations, Zola and his colleagues selectively created lesions of the surrounding cortex in the perirhinal, entorhinal, and parahippocampal regions. The parahippocampal and perirhinal areas receive information from the visual, auditory, and somatosensory association cortex and send these inputs to the hippocampus (Figure 9.21) and from there to other cortical regions. These selective lesions worsened memory performance in delayed nonmatch-to-sample tests (Figure 9.22). Follow-up work showed that lesions of only the parahippocampal and perirhinal cortices also produced significant memory deficits.

How do we reconcile these results with R.B.'s profound anterograde amnesia, caused by damage limited to the hippocampus and not involving the surrounding parahippocampal or perirhinal cortex? The answer is that the hippocampus cannot function properly if these vital connections are damaged. But more than this, we now know that these regions are involved in a great deal of processing themselves, and hence lesions restricted to the hippocampus do not produce as severe a form of amnesia as do lesions that include surrounding cortex.

In summary, the data from animals are highly consistent with evidence from amnesic patients such as R.B. and H.M. implicating *both* the hippocampal system in the medial temporal lobe and the associated cortex as

critical for forming long-term memories. Lesions that damage the hippocampus directly, or damage the input–output relations of the hippocampus with the neocortex (Figure 9.23), produce severe memory impairments. The amygdala is not a crucial part of the system for episodic memory, but it is important for emotional memory (see Chapter 10).

Moreover, the animal data corroborates the data from amnesic patients with regard to the preservation of short-term memory processes after the medial temporal lobe has been damaged. That is, monkeys' memory deficits in the delayed nonmatch-to-sample task became more pronounced as the interval between the sample and the test increased. The medial temporal lobe, then, is not essential for short-term or working memory processes. As we noted earlier, the medial temporal lobe is most likely not the locus of long-term storage, because retrograde amnesia is not total after damage to this area. Rather, the medial temporal lobe is a key component in organizing and consolidating long-term memory that is permanently stored in a distributed fashion in the neocortex.

Rodent Studies Another key question that animal researchers have addressed involves the kind of memory and learning that is impaired with lesions to the hippocampus. Early studies in rodents found that hippocampal lesions did not disrupt stimulus–response learning, yet the lesioned rats did exhibit a bewildering variety of abnormal behaviors. These observations led to the suggestion that the hippocampus was involved with the storage and retrieval of one specific type of memory: contextual memory (Hirsh, 1974).

For instance, when electrodes were implanted in the rat hippocampus, certain cells, later known as *place cells*, fired only when the rat was situated in a particular location and facing a particular direction (O'Keefe & Dostrovsky, 1971). A particular place cell may become silent when the animal moves to a different environment, but then assume a location-specific firing in that new area. As the animal moves about an environment, the activity of specific CA1 and CA3 hippocampal neurons correlates with specific locations. This study led to the idea that the hippocampus represented spatial contexts (O'Keefe & Nadel, 1978), the *where* in context memory. It was soon found to be involved in spatial navigational learning.

In rats, spatial navigational learning is tested using the Morris water maze (R. Morris, 1981). This apparatus is a circular tank filled with opaque water. Above the water are different identifiable visual cues, such as windows and doors, and somewhere below the surface of the water is an invisible platform. Rats are dropped into the tank at different points on different trials. The time

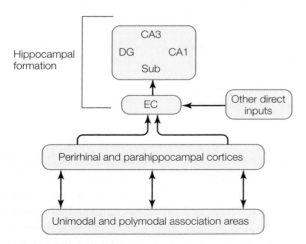

FIGURE 9.21 Flow of information between the neocortex and the hippocampal system.
CA = cornu ammonis neuronal fields (CA1–CA3); DG = dentate gyrus; EC = entorhinal cortex; Sub = subiculum.

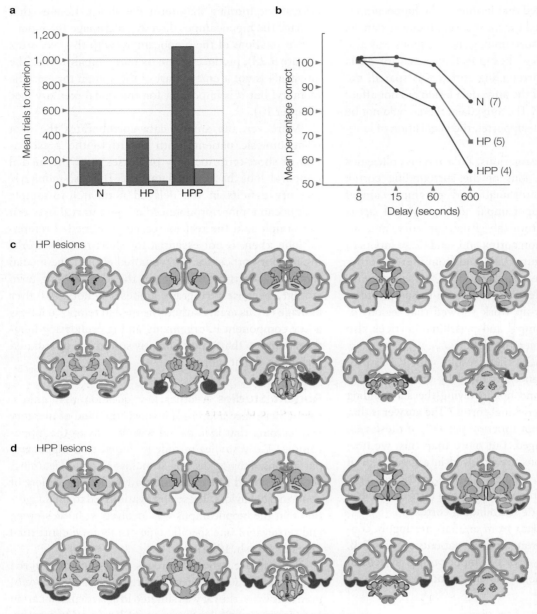

FIGURE 9.22 Selective lesions around the hippocampus worsen memory.
Performance on the delayed nonmatch-to-sample task on two different occasions for normal monkeys
(N); monkeys with lesions of the hippocampal formation and the parahippocampal cortex (HP); and
monkeys with lesions of the hippocampal formation, parahippocampal cortex, and perirhinal cortex
(HPP). **(a)** Initial learning of the task with a delay of 8 s. Red bars = first test; blue bars = second test.
(b) Performance across delays for the same groups. Lesions (red) in HP **(c)** and HPP monkeys **(d)** are
shown in coronal sections.

it takes for them to reach the platform becomes shorter over time, indicating that they have learned where the platform is in relation to the visual cues above the water. Rats with hippocampal lesions do not learn to associate the visual cues with the platform's location when dropped from different spots, but swim randomly about on every trial looking for the platform (Schenk & Morris, 1985). If they are always dropped into the water from exactly the same spot, however, they do learn where the

platform is located (Eichenbaum et al., 1990). Thus, with hippocampal lesions they can learn a repeated, practiced task (a stimulus–response task) but are unable to relate space information with different contextual information.

Context is not just about space. Some rat hippocampal neurons have been found to fire for specific odors and for specific combinations of odors and locations (Wood et al., 1999), some for visual or auditory stimuli or a combination of both (Sakurai, 1996), and some for

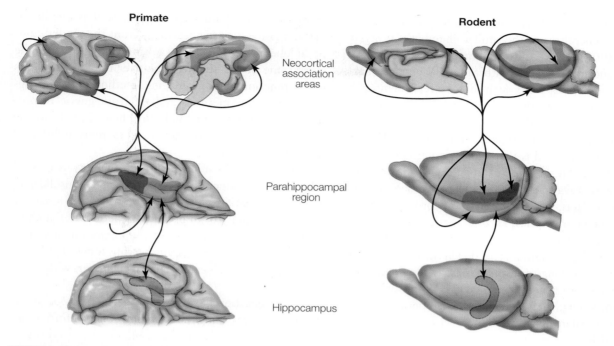

FIGURE 9.23 Anatomy of the hippocampal memory system in monkeys and rats.
Most areas of cortex send information to the hippocampus. Different neocortical zones (blue) project to one or more subdivisions of the parahippocampal region. These subdivisions are the perirhinal cortex (light purple), the parahippocampal cortex (dark purple), and the entorhinal cortex (pink). These latter areas are interconnected and project to different regions of the hippocampus (green), including the dentate gyrus, the CA3 and CA1 fields of the hippocampus, and the subiculum. As a result, various cortical inputs converge within the parahippocampal region. In addition, the parahippocampal region passes this information from the cortex to the hippocampus. Following processing in the hippocampus, information can be fed back via the parahippocampal region to the same areas of the cortex that the original inputs came from.

many other nonspatial features, including behavior (see Eichenbaum et al., 1999). These findings have led to the suggestion that the function of the hippocampus may be to bind together different contextual information to form a complex contextual memory.

Although initial work in both animals (see Squire, 1992) and humans suggested that the hippocampus was not involved in the retrieval of long-term distant memories and had only a temporary involvement with forming and retrieving new contextual memories, more recent work has suggested otherwise. For instance, in spatial navigation tasks, both recent and remote memories are equally disrupted after hippocampal lesions (S. Martin et al., 2005).

The retrieval of contextual memory in rats is often studied using *contextual fear learning*, where rats are placed in a small chamber with specific visual features and a foot shock is delivered. The rats then show a variety of conditioned responses, such as freezing, when placed back into the same visually identifiable chamber. The retention of fear conditioning is evaluated by the amount of freezing the rats show. In one study, after experiencing a single shock episode, some rats underwent sham (control) surgery. Other rats had their hippocampus

partially or fully destroyed either 1 week, 2 months, or 6 months later. None of the rats had been put back into the shock chamber in the interval between the shock and the surgery. Two weeks after surgery, all of these groups were tested for fear retention. The control rats froze when put back in the chamber, though the response lessened with longer retention intervals. The rats with a completely destroyed hippocampus did not freeze no matter what the interval, while the rats with partial damage showed some, but less freezing than controls, especially at longer intervals. The severity of retrograde amnesia for the contextual fear was related to the extent of hippocampal damage, but amnesia existed for even remote retrograde contextual memory (Lehmann et al., 2007).

Such studies suggest that the hippocampus has a more extensive role in long-term contextual (and episodic) memory retrieval than was originally postulated after early studies of H.M. There is yet another variable to be considered: memory detail and its accuracy. For example, mice are initially able to distinguish between a fear conditioning chamber and slightly different chambers: They freeze only in the specific chamber where they were first shocked. Over time, however, they no longer distinguish between the similar chambers, and their fear generalizes to the similar chambers (Wiltgen & Silva, 2007). Thus, contextual memories become less detailed and more general with time, allowing the animal to be more adaptable, such that the fear memory is activated in novel, but similar, contexts. It has been proposed that *memory quality* may be a critical factor that determines whether the hippocampus is essential for retrieval. The proposal is that it plays a permanent role in retrieving detailed contextual memory, but is not necessary for retrieval once detail is lost and memory has generalized. Thus, if testing conditions promote retention of detailed memories, such as spatial navigation in water mazes where the exact location of a platform is required, the hippocampus is needed in their retrieval for both short- and long-term memories. If the conditions result in memory generalization across time, such as in fear conditioning, they will lead to a temporal gradient of hippocampal involvement in memory retrieval, as was seen in the last experiment.

Interestingly, if the fear memory was reactivated 45 days after it was formed (when it no longer requires the hippocampus for expression) and then a hippocampal lesion was made, the rats no longer showed fear when placed back in the chamber (Debiec et al., 2002). It seems that *retrieval* and *reactivation* of a hippocampal-independent memory made that memory hippocampal-dependent again and susceptible to hippocampal damage. In the next sections, we see how some of these findings have been mirrored in humans.

TAKE-HOME MESSAGES

- The hippocampus is critical for the formation of long-term memory.
- Cortex surrounding the hippocampus is critical for normal hippocampal function in memory.
- The delayed non-match to sample task is used to assess memory in non-human primates.
- The amygdala is not a crucial part of the system for episodic memory, but it is important for emotional memory.
- Neurons that activate when rats are in a particular place and facing a particular direction have been identified in the hippocampus and are called place cells. They provide evidence that the hippocampus has cells that encode contextual information.

Imaging Human Memory

The work described so far has dealt primarily with evidence from humans and animals with brain damage. It suggests a degree of independence of procedural memory and perceptual priming (as well as conditioning and nonassociative learning) from the medial temporal lobe memory system. Let's now integrate into the story some of the studies done over the past 15 years using functional brain-imaging methods (both magnetic resonance methods and electromagnetic recording methods). These methods have helped to clarify the role of various brain structures and systems in different memory processes.

As mentioned earlier, long-term memory is created when new information is encoded and consolidated; stored information can then be retrieved to create a conscious memory or to produce an action. Researchers have eagerly tested the role of the hippocampal system in creating long-term memories using functional brain-imaging methods in healthy human volunteers with intact memory ability.

A key question has been whether the hippocampus becomes active during the encoding of new information, during the retrieval of information, or both. In this section, we review evidence demonstrating that the hippocampus is involved in both, which is in agreement with the animal studies discussed earlier. We also see that different types of memory rely on different subregions of the medial temporal lobe during encoding and retrieval and that during retrieval, the medial temporal lobe memory systems reactivate cortical regions that were important during the original encoding of the information. We end this section with a discussion of the role of the frontal cortex in long-term memory encoding and retrieval.

Encoding and the Hippocampus

Functional MRI studies have shown that the human hippocampus is active when new information is encoded. This kind of work typically involves the *subsequent-memory paradigm*, where participants are presented with items that they are asked to remember. Their brain activity is measured with fMRI or ERPs while they are encoding the information. Later, their memory for the items is assessed. This can be done in different ways. One is to ask them whether they have seen the item previously when it is embedded in lists containing new items. Using event-related methods, it is then possible to sort and analyze the original data gathered during encoding as a function of whether the items were later correctly remembered or forgotten.

One study that demonstrates the involvement of the hippocampus in encoding (among other findings that we will return to) was done by Charan Ranganath and his colleagues (2003). They combined fMRI with the subsequent-memory paradigm, as shown in

Figure 9.24. Healthy volunteers were presented with words on a screen at a rate of about one word every 2 seconds. The words (360 in total), printed in either red or green, were of either animate or inanimate items that were either large or small. Depending on the color, the participants were required to make either an animacy judgment or a size judgment for each item. While the participants viewed the words and made their decisions (the encoding phase of the experiment), they were scanned using fMRI. Later, outside of the scanner, they were tested on their memory for the items that they had been shown by being presented with the 360 "old" items that were mixed with 360 "new" items. Participants were asked to rate each item (which were shown in black) on a scale of 1 to 6 to indicate how confident they were that they had seen the word before. They also were asked to specify whether the item had been presented in green or red (a source memory judgment, where the source was the context in which the item had been previously viewed). Researchers had to sort and separately analyze the old items as a function of whether they were properly recollected, and whether the source was correctly identified. What brain regions were active at *encoding* for correctly

a Experimental design

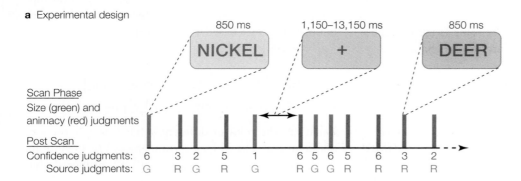

b Behavioral results

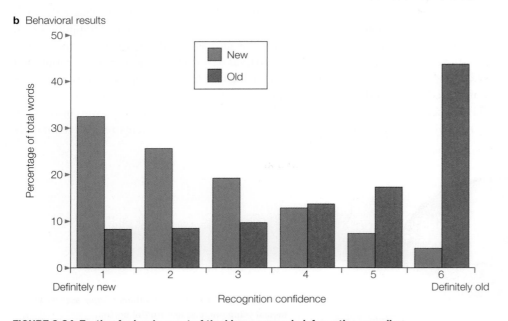

FIGURE 9.24 Testing for involvement of the hippocampus in information encoding.
(a) The sequence of events in one scanning run. At encoding, participants viewed a series of words and made either an animacy (animate versus not animate) or size (large versus small) judgment for each word, depending on the color of that word (e.g., green font meant, perform an animacy judgment, so for the word *NICKEL* in green ink, the correct response would be "inanimate"). Later, in a test at retrieval after the scan session, participants made two decisions about the items presented, which included the old items and new items never seen before. First, participants were asked to indicate whether and how well (how confidently) they recognized the items (e.g., on a scale of 1 to 6, from definitely new to definitely old). Second, for each word they had to make a source memory judgment (had it previously been presented in red or in green?). **(b)** Mean proportions of studied ("old") and unstudied ("new") items endorsed at each confidence level. Performance on the source memory judgment (red or green) is not shown.

recollected items (those that the participant had seen, reported having seen before, and correctly indicated the color of their presentation)? Correctly recollected words activated regions of both the hippocampus and the posterior parahippocampal cortex (Figure 9.25a) during *encoding*. This evidence that the medial temporal lobe, including the hippocampus proper, was activated during encoding fits well with evidence from studies in animals and patients with amnesia. Those studies suggested that the hippocampus is important for the formation of new long-term memories. Thus, one problem with hippocampal damage may be an inability to encode the information properly in the first place. Ranganath and colleagues also observed that regions of the frontal cortex were activated during encoding (Figure 9.25b), a topic that we will return to later in the chapter.

Retrieval and the Hippocampus

The hippocampus is also involved in the retrieval of information from long-term memory. In one study, similar to that described in the preceding section, event-related fMRI methods were used to reveal that the hippocampus is activated when information is correctly recollected (Eldridge et al., 2000). Participants in this task memorized a list of words. No other task was involved at the encoding stage, and no memory strategy was suggested. Twenty minutes later, in a retrieval task, participants were presented with a new list consisting of previously studied (old) and unstudied (new) words and were asked, one by one, if they had seen the word before. If they answered yes, then they were asked to make a decision about whether they actually remembered (recollected) seeing it before (an episodic

memory with a spatial and temporal context) or whether the item merely seemed familiar to them.

The interesting part of this study was that neuroimaging data were collected during the retrieval phase of the study, and brain responses measured with fMRI could be sorted according to whether the participants actually recollected the item, were only familiar with the item, were sure they had not seen the word before, or were mistaken about whether they had seen the word. The neuroimaging results were clear: During retrieval, the hippocampus was selectively active *only* for items that were actually *correctly recollected* (Figure 9.26), thus indicating an episodic memory. This finding strongly suggests that the hippocampus is involved in retrieval for episodic memories but not memories based on familiarity.

Recollection, Familiarity, and the Medial Temporal Lobe

What are the roles of different subdivisions of the medial temporal lobe in long-term memory? In 1999, John Aggleton and Malcolm Brown (1999) proposed that encoding processes that merely identify an item as being *familiar*, and encoding processes that correctly identify the item as having been seen before (recollection), each depend on different regions of the medial temporal lobes. Support for this idea soon followed. For example, in the study of retrieval described in the previous section and illustrated in Figure 9.26, the hippocampus was activated only for episodic recollections. It was not activated for memory that did not contain awareness of the prior event—that is, when the items recollected merely

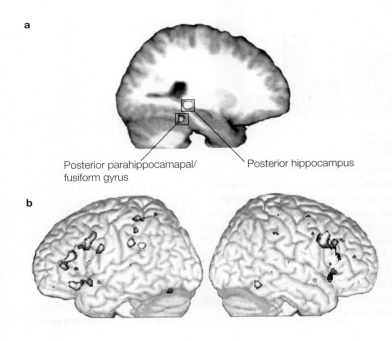

Posterior parahippocampal/
fusiform gyrus

Posterior hippocampus

FIGURE 9.25 Correct recollections trigger activity in medial temporal lobe and frontal cortex.
Subsequent-memory effects: activity at encoding that correlates with better recollection of words at testing—that is, those for which the source memory judgment of red or green (see Figure 9.24) was correct. **(a)** Sagittal section through the right medial temporal lobe. Two regions in the medial temporal lobe that exhibited subsequent recollection effects were the posterior hippocampus and the posterior parahippocampal cortex. **(b)** Surface renderings of the left and right hemispheres show additional regions of cortical activation at encoding for items recollected correctly later.

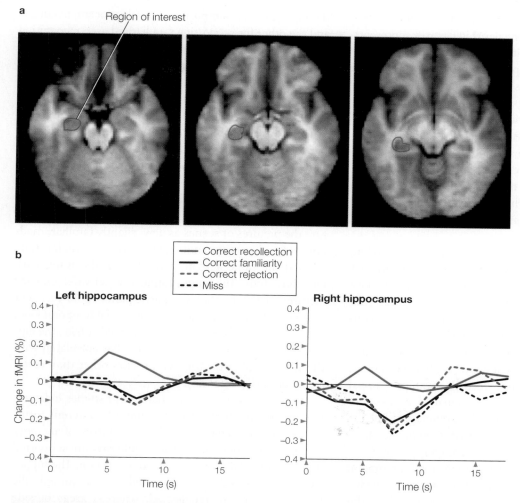

a

Region of interest

b

Correct recollection
Correct familiarity
Correct rejection
Miss

Left hippocampus

Change in fMRI (%)

Right hippocampus

Time (s)

Time (s)

FIGURE 9.26 Retrieval in the hippocampus.
(a) Horizontal sections through the brain at the level of the inferior (left panel), middle (center panel), and superior (right panel) hippocampus. The red outline of the region of interest in the left hippocampus is based on anatomical landmarks. **(b)** Hemodynamic responses from event-related fMRI measures taken during the retrieval of previously studied words (see text for paradigm). The hippocampus was activated by correctly recollected words (solid red line) but not by words that the participants had previously seen but could not recollect, indicating that the words merely seemed familiar (solid black line). No hippocampal activity occurred for words that were correctly identified as new (not seen previously; dashed red line) nor for errors in which the participant did not remember the words (dashed black line) despite having seen them previously.

seemed familiar to the participants and were recognized by their *familiarity* alone. Such data raised the question of what brain regions are involved in episodic versus nonepisodic (familiarity-based) memory encoding and retrieval.

The process of encoding episodic memory involves encoding an event and binding it to a time and place, as we hinted at in the rodent studies. When you recall the first rock concert that you ever attended, you may recall who you saw, where you saw them, and with whom you went. This memory may be distinguished from memories of other rock concerts, other events held at the same place, and other places you have been with the same friend. How does our brain accomplish this?

Anatomy offers some clues: Different types of information from all over the cortex converge on the medial temporal lobe regions surrounding the hippocampus, but not all types pass through the same structures. Information about the features of items ("what" an item is) coming from unimodal sensory regions of neocortex passes through the anterior parts of the parahippocampal region known as *perirhinal cortex (PRC)*. In contrast, information from polymodal neocortical areas about "where" something is located passes through the more posterior parts of the parahippocampal cortex. Both information types project into the entorhinal cortex but do not converge until they are within the hippocampus (Eichenbaum et al.,

2007). A model known as the *binding of items and contexts (BIC) model* proposes that the perirhinal cortex represents information about specific items (e.g., who and what), the parahippocampal cortex represents information about the context in which these items were encountered (e.g., where and when), and processing in the hippocampus binds the representations of items with their context (Diana et al., 2007; Ranganath, 2010). As a result, the hippocampus is able to relate the two types of information about something that the individual encounters. This form of memory is referred to as **relational memory**. So, to recognize that something is familiar, perirhinal cortex is sufficient; but to remember the full episode and everything related to it, the hippocampus is necessary.

For support of this theory we return to the encoding study of Ranganath and his colleagues (2003). In that study, participants were required to make source memory judgments related to episodic memory (see Figures 9.25 and 9.26). Study participants also had to rate their confidence about whether they had seen the item before—a measure of **familiarity**. Figure 9.27 presents the neuroimaging results from this analysis of confidence ratings. Regions of the left anterior medial parahippocampal gyrus—in and around the perirhinal cortex—were activated during recognition based on familiarity, but the hippocampus itself was not activated. Combining these results with those in the previous paragraph, this work demonstrates a double dissociation in the medial temporal lobe for *encoding* different forms of memory: one medial temporal lobe mechanism for recognition based on the recollection of episodic (source) information involving the hippocampus and posterior parahippocampal cortex, and the other for supporting familiarity-based recognition memory in the perirhinal cortex.

A similar distinction has also been found between the recollection and familiarity components of *retrieval* of long-term memories. One study that nicely makes this point is the work of Daniela Montaldi and her colleagues at the University of Oxford (2006). They showed study participants pictures of scenes during an encoding session. Two days later, researchers tested the participants' recognition with a mixed batch of new and old scenes while monitoring their brain activity with fMRI.

Montaldi and colleagues asked the participants to rate the pictures of scenes as new, slightly familiar, moderately familiar, very familiar, or recollected. Their results showed the same activity pattern as in the Ranganath encoding study. The hippocampus was activated only for pictures of scenes that the participants could recollect having seen before. Regions of the medial temporal lobe, like the perirhinal cortex, that are located outside the hippocampus showed activity patterns that correlated with the strength of familiarity with scenes other than recollected ones (Figure 9.28).

In sum, evidence from a number of studies indicates that the medial temporal lobe supports different forms of memory and that these different forms of memory (recollective experience versus familiarity) are supported by different subdivisions of this brain region. The hippocampus is involved in encoding and retrieval for episodic memories that are recollected, whereas areas outside the hippocampus, especially the perirhinal cortex, sup-

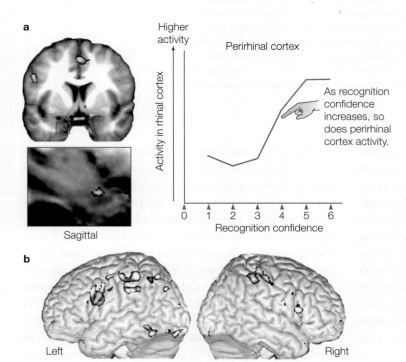

FIGURE 9.27 Familiarity-based recognition memory. Brain activity during encoding correlates with the confidence of recognizing that an item has been seen before. **(a)** Coronal section through the brain at the level of the anterior medial temporal lobe. Functional MRI activations that correlated with confidence ratings can be seen in the entorhinal cortex (red box and in an expanded view below the coronal section). The graph shows that as recognition confidence increases, activity in the perirhinal cortex also increases. **(b)** Images of the left and right hemispheres show additional regions of cortical activation.

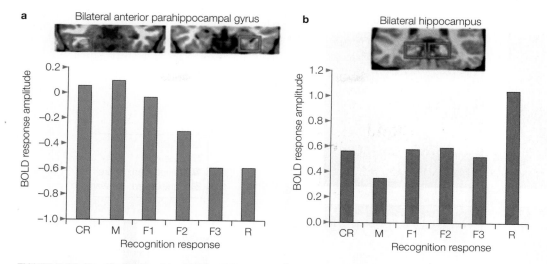

FIGURE 9.28 Recollection and familiarity during retrieval.
Participants studied scenes and were scanned during recognition testing. The partial images of the brain are coronal sections through the hippocampus. **(a)** Activation in bilateral anterior parahippocampal regions decreased with increasing confidence. **(b)** In contrast, activations in bilateral hippocampal regions increased for recollected items only, as compared with nonrecollected items. CR = correct rejection (an item that was correctly identified as new); M = miss (an item that was seen before but the participant reported as not having seen previously); F1 = weak familiarity, F2 = moderate familiarity, F3 = strong familiarity; R = recollected.

port recognition based on familiarity. These findings also suggest that the nature of the representations should be considered in distinguishing between memory systems (Nadel & Hardt, 2011).

Relational Memory What we have been referring to as *episodic information* that leads to recollective experiences is relational memory, so called because we can indicate that something has been encountered previously. Moreover, we can retrieve the relational context (the sources) in which it was previously encountered and know that it is different from the present encounter. For instance, if you live in Los Angeles, you may see Tom Hanks drive past in a Porsche and know that you've seen him before—not in a Porsche, but in a movie. Neal Cohen and his colleagues (Ryan et al., 2000) at the University of Illinois have investigated relational memory using measures of eye fixation as study participants watched complex scenes where the object and spatial relationships were experimentally manipulated. They found that healthy participants were sensitive to changing relationships in the scenes, even when they were unaware of them, as demonstrated by their altered patterns of eye movements (Figure 9.29). In contrast, patients with amnesia as a result of hippocampal damage were insensitive to the changes (Figure 9.29b). These researchers have argued, therefore, that medial temporal amnesia is a disorder of relational memory and is distinct from episodic memory, which requires conscious awareness. Cohen and colleagues amassed additional evidence to support their argument in a study on amnesic patients with damage limited to the

hippocampus (Konkel, 2007). The researchers evaluated memory performance for three different types of relational tasks: spatial, associative, and sequential. They also compared single-item recollection by the amnesiacs to that by normal participants and patients with more extensive medial temporal lobe damage. Those with hippocampal-only damage were impaired on all of the relational tasks, but not on the single-item recollection task. Patients with more extensive medial temporal lobe damage were impaired on both types of tests. Multiple neuroimaging studies show increased hippocampal activation when the relationship between items is being evaluated; in contrast, when an item is being individually encoded, activity is not observed in the hippocampus but is seen in other medial temporal lobe cortical regions, especially in the perirhinal cortex (Davachi & Wagner, 2002; Davachi et al., 2003).

Retrieval and Reactivation in Long-Term Memory Where in the brain is the what and where information stored? The projections of "what" and "where" information from the neocortex into the hippocampus described in the previous section are matched by a similar outflow from the hippocampus that travels back to the entorhinal cortex, then to the perirhinal and parahippocampal cortex, and then to the neocortical areas that provided the inputs to the neocortex in the first place. You may already have guessed the role of this feedback system in memory storage and retrieval, and some findings from neuroimaging studies during retrieval may back up your guess.

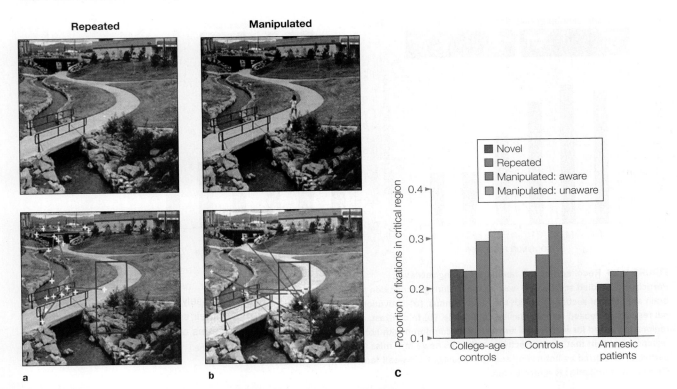

Repeated   **Manipulated**

a   b   c

FIGURE 9.29 Scenes with changing relational information used to test for relational memory.
(a,b) Eye movements were recorded from healthy participants as they viewed scenes at two time points. Eye movements (red lines) and fixations (white crosses) are shown superimposed on the same scene (bottom panels) under two conditions. **(a)** The scene the participants viewed did not change (top vs. bottom panels). **(b)** The scene changed. At first viewing, it contained two people in a critical region (top panel), while in the second it did not (bottom panel). The critical region where the people were located is outlined by the blue rectangle (the box was not on the screen; it was placed in the figure to indicate the region of interest in this test). **(a)** When nothing changed in the critical area, the critical area did not attract eye fixations (bottom panel). **(b)** When the scene was viewed as a manipulated scene (the people present during the first viewing were removed in the second viewing), many eye fixations focused on the critical region that had contained the people. Some participants were aware of the change, while others were not. **(c)** Quantification of proportions of fixations in the critical area of **a** and **b** for healthy young controls, age-, education- and intelligence-matched controls, and six patients with amnesia. Both control groups showed more fixations in the critical region when the scene changed, as in **b**, than when it did not change, as in **a**. The amnesic patients failed to show this effect of relational memory.

Mark Wheeler and his colleagues at Washington University in St. Louis (2000) investigated brain regions involved in the retrieval of different types of information. They asked participants to learn a set of sounds (auditory stimuli) or pictures (visual stimuli) during a 2-day encoding period. Each sound or picture was paired with a written label describing the item (e.g., the word *BELL*, followed by the sound of a bell). On the third day the participants were given perceptual and memory tests while in an fMRI scanner. In the perceptual test, stimuli (label plus sound or picture) were presented and brain activity was measured to identify brain regions involved in the perceptual processing of items. In the memory retrieval test, only the word label was presented and the participant pressed a button to indicate whether the item was associated with a sound or a picture.

Wheeler and coworkers found that during retrieval of pictures, regions of neocortex that had been activated during perception of the pictures were reactivated. Similarly, during retrieval of sounds, different areas of the neocortex that had been activated during the perception of sounds were reactivated. In each case, during memory retrieval the modality-specific regions of activity in the neocortex were subsets of the areas activated by presentation of the perceptual information alone, when no memory task was required (Figure 9.30). The activated areas of sensory-specific neocortex were not lower-level sensory cortical regions; they were later stages of visual and auditory association cortex, where incoming signals would have been perceptually well processed (e.g., to the point where identity was coded).

These results suggest that the specific relational information for items stored in long-term memory may be coded during retrieval by *reactivation* of the original neocortical areas that provide input to the hippocampus during the original encoding. In subsequent work, Wheeler and colleagues (M. Wheeler et al., 2006) showed that visual processing regions in inferotemporal cortex were

HOW THE BRAIN WORKS
False Memories and the Medial Temporal Lobes

When our memory fails, we usually forget events that happened in the past. Sometimes, however, something more surprising occurs: We remember events that never happened. Whereas forgetting has been a topic of research for more than a century, memory researchers did not have a good method to investigate false memories in the laboratory until Henry Roediger and Kathleen McDermott at Washington University rediscovered an old technique in 1995. In this technique participants are presented with a list of words (e.g., *thread, pin, eye, sewing, sharp, point, haystack, pain, injection,* etc.) in which all the words are highly associated to a word that is not presented (in this case, *needle*; did you have to go back and recheck the list?). When participants are asked subsequently to recall or recognize the words in the list, they show a strong tendency to falsely remember the associated word that was not presented. The memory illusion is so powerful that participants are willing to claim that they vividly remember seeing the nonpresented critical word in the study list.

When participants are interrogated carefully about the conscious experience associated with remembering items from the list (true items) and the critical nonpresented words (false items), however, they tend to rate true items higher than false items in terms of sensory details (Mather et al., 1997; K. Norman & Schacter, 1997). This finding introduced a conundrum in false-memory research: How can human participants believe in their illusory recollections, and at the same time be able to differentiate them from genuine recollections in terms of sensory detail?

Roberto Cabeza at Duke University and collaborators (2001) provided a possible answer to this conundrum. In their study, participants watched a videotape segment in which two speakers alternatively presented lists of associated words. The participants then were required to perform an old/new recognition test that included true items, closely related false items, and unrelated new words (new items) while their brains were scanned with functional MRI. Changes in blood flow in the brain that indicated changing patterns of neural activity were measured separately for each kind of item. Memory performance showed the same pattern as in previous studies: Participants were able to reject new items but showed a strong tendency to falsely recognize closely related false items.

The researchers found a dissociation between two medial temporal lobe regions (Figure 1). In the hippocampus bilaterally, false items elicited more neural activity than did new items, and as much activity as true items. But in the left parahippocampal gyrus, a region surrounding the hippocampus, closely related false items elicited about the same amount of activity as new items and significantly less activity than true items. In other words, the hippocampus responded similarly to true and false items, and the parahippocampal gyrus responded more strongly to true than to false items.

Because true and closely related false items were similar in their semantic content but differed in sensory content, these results suggest that the hippocampus is involved in the retrieval of semantic information, whereas the parahippocampal gyrus is involved in the retrieval of sensory information.

This dissociation provides a possible solution for the aforementioned conundrum: The memory system in the medial temporal lobes can generate two different types of messages when information is presented. Whereas anterior hippocampal activity suggests that closely related false items are like true items, posterior parahippocampal activity suggests that they are like new items. These two messages are not contradictory. Closely related false items are like true items in terms of their semantic properties, but they are like new items in terms of their sensory properties.

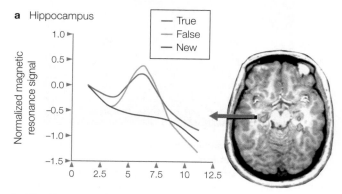

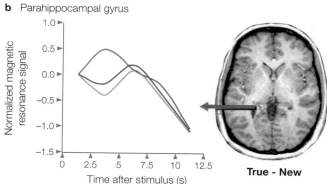

FIGURE 1 Significant increases in blood flow in regions of the medial temporal lobes (right side of figure), and their corresponding hemodynamic response functions (left side of figure). (a) Bilateral hippocampal regions were more activated for true and closely related false items than for new items. There was no difference between activations for true and false items. **(b)** A left posterior parahippocampal region was more activated for true items than for closely related false and new items. There was no difference between activations for false and new items. The hemodynamic response functions at left were taken from the regions of interest defined by the statistical contrast of true activations minus new activations, which is shown at right in the brain sections.

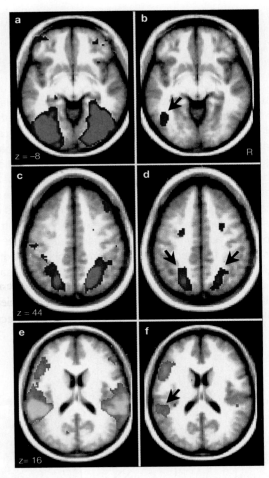

FIGURE 9.30 Reactivation of modality-specific cortex during long-term memory retrieval.
Areas activated by viewing pictures (**a, c**) and hearing sounds (**e**). Areas activated during the retrieval of pictures (**b, d**) or sounds (**f**) from memory. Arrows indicate regions of overlap between memory and perceptual activations. The right hemisphere of the brain is on the right of each image.

involved in the preparation to retrieve visual information, whereas the more dorsal parietal and superior occipital activity was related to the process of searching memory for the relevant item. These findings help refine the role of different brain regions in reactivation during long-term memory retrieval.

Encoding, Retrieval, and the Frontal Cortex

Neuroimaging research and studies of amnesic patients have consistently found that the frontal cortex is involved in both short-term and long-term memory processes. Its role in the encoding and retrieval of long-term memory, however, has been a key point of debate. A meta-analysis of the literature (Nyberg et al., 1996) found that the left frontal cortex is often involved in *encoding* of episodic information, whereas the right frontal cortex is often found to be activated in episodic *retrieval* (Figure 9.31). These findings led Roberto Cabeza and colleagues to develop a model proposing that contributions to episodic encoding (left frontal) and retrieval (right frontal) were lateralized within frontal cortex. Figure 9.31 also shows, however, that both semantic *encoding* and *retrieval* involve the left frontal cortex, including Broca's area (Brodmann area 44 extending into area 46) and the ventral lateral region (Brodmann areas 44 and 45). This lateralization to the left hemisphere for semantic information remains regardless of whether the memories being retrieved are of objects or of words.

Others, including William Kelley at Dartmouth College and his colleagues, have argued that lateralization of frontal cortex activity during long-term memory retrieval is related more to the nature of the material to be processed than to a distinction between encoding and retrieval (Buckner et al., 1999). They believe that the left hemisphere is more involved in processes coded by linguistic representations, whereas the right frontal cortex is more involved in object and spatial memory information (Figure 9.32). Much work remains to be done to establish the roles of the frontal cortex in memory processing. For now, various competing models remain viable explanations of the patterns of deficits seen in amnesia and the activations in functional imaging that have been reported.

Retrieval and the Parietal Cortex

Over the past half century, memory researchers have largely ignored the parietal lobe, partially because parietal lobe

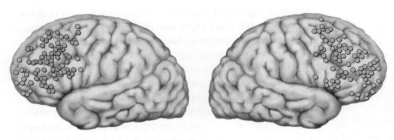

Episodic encoding and semantic retrieval

Episodic retrieval

FIGURE 9.31 Summary of regions in the prefrontal cortex that show activation for episodic encoding and semantic retrieval or episodic retrieval.
The data are from many studies, reported in Nyberg, Cabeza, and Tulving (1996, 1998) and Tulving et al. (1994).

FIGURE 9.32 Material-specific frontal cortex activation during memory encoding.
(a) Words activate left frontal cortex during encoding. **(b)** Nameable objects activate both left and right frontal cortex during encoding. **(c)** Encoding of faces activates primarily right frontal cortex.

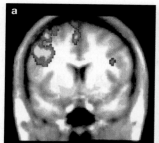 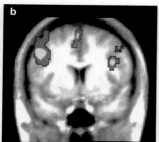 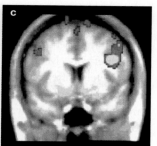

lesions are not generally associated with memory loss. There is, however, a notable exception: Retrosplenial lesions can produce both retrograde and anterograde amnesia. A finding dubbed the old/new effect, which was first identified in ERP studies, stimulated memory research that focused on the parietal cortex. The findings showed that the parietal cortex displays different responses when an individual correctly recognizes a previously encountered item (termed a hit) as compared to correctly identifying that a new item was not previously encountered (a correct rejection). Event-related fMRI studies have revealed greater activation during hits than during correct rejections in posterior parietal cortex (PPC), including inferior and superior parietal lobules as well as medial structures that extend from precuneus into posterior cingulate cortex (PCC) and retrosplenial cortex (RSC).

The past few years have witnessed an explosion of functional neuroimaging studies, which have revealed that successful *memory retrieval*, especially for contextual information, is consistently associated with activity in lateral PPC, including the RSC. During encoding, however, these areas are usually less active than baseline levels (Figure 9.33; Daselaar et al., 2009), unless the items are encoded in a self-relevant manner (Leshikar & Duarte, 2012), or are likely to evoke self-referential (V. C. Martin et al., 2011) or emotional processing (Ritchey et al., 2011). This encoding preference for self-referential items suggests that the RSC is more attuned to internal information sources. Interestingly, these same parietal regions are active during conscious rest when a highly interconnected network of cortical association areas

is activated; this is the so-called default mode network which we discuss in Chapter 13. The salient point for this discussion is that the default network is active whenever an individual's mind turns to thinking about self-related past and future scenarios.

The anatomical connections of the parietal cortex are also suggestive of its involvement in memory. The lateral parietal, retrosplenial, and posterior cingulate cortices are connected to the medial temporal lobe, both directly and indirectly. Notably, the retrosplenial cortex is extensively interconnected

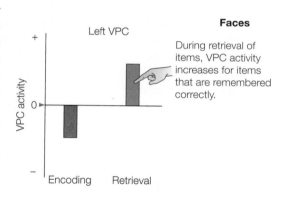 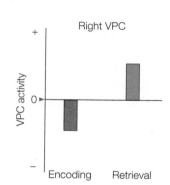

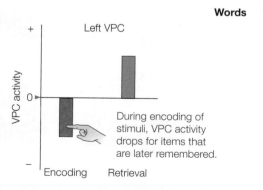 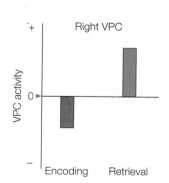

FIGURE 9.33 Encoding and retrieval flip in ventral parietal cortex.
While encoding different types of stimuli (faces or words), fMRI revealed lower activity (red bars) in both left and right ventral parietal cortex for a stimulus that was successfully encoded (i.e., later remembered, referred to as Encoding Hits) than for one that was not encoded (i.e., later forgotten; Encoding Misses). During retrieval, the opposite was found. Activity was greater (blue bars) for remembered items (called Retrieval Hits) than for items remembered incorrectly (called Retrieval Misses).

with the parahippocampal cortex (PHC), and both interface with similar regions in the posterior hippocampus, subiculum, mammillary bodies, and anterior thalamus as well as the default network. Meanwhile, the perirhinal cortex displays a completely different connectivity pattern, not with the posterior hippocampus but with the anterior hippocampus, amygdala, ventral temporopolar cortex (VTPC), and lateral orbitofrontal cortex (Suzuki & Amaral, 1994).

Building on this anatomy and on the binding of items and contexts model, Charan Ranganath and Maureen Ritchey (2012) have proposed a memory model made up of two systems: the anterior temporal (AT) system, which includes the perirhinal cortex and its above-mentioned connections; and the posterior medial (PM) system, which is composed of the core components of the PHC and RSC, the mammillary bodies, anterior thalamic nuclei, subiculum, and default mode network (Figure 9.34). Ranganath and Richey propose that these two systems support different forms of memory-guided behavior. Thus, they are involved not only in memory, as in traditional medial temporal lobe models, but also in other aspects of cognition (Figure 9.35). The PRC in the anterior system supports memory for items, and it is involved in familiarity-based recognition, associating features of objects, and making fine-grained perceptual or semantic discriminations. Ranganath and Richey suggest that the overall cognitive job of the anterior system (in collaboration with the amygdala, VTPC, and lateral orbital frontal cortex) may be to assess the significance of entities. The PHC and RSC, which are not traditionally included in medial temporal lobe systems, support recollection-based memories, such

as memory for scenes, spatial layouts, and contexts. These researchers also propose that this system, together with the other posterior medial system structures, may construct mental representations of the relationships between entities, actions, and outcomes. Some support for this theory comes from neurological patients. Recall that along with hippocampal damage, Alzheimer's disease, with its episodic memory impairment, is associated with severe disruptions in the retrosplenial cortex, posterior cingulate, precuneus, and angular gyrus, which together are the proposed posterior medial system. In contrast, patients with semantic dementia, which is characterized by a loss of knowledge about objects, have extensive damage to the anterior temporal lobes.

In closing, while the parietal cortex is well known for its role in attention (see Chapter 7), it also appears to have a greater role in memory than had been considered previously. What is that role? Although the answers are not known, several hypotheses have been suggested. The working memory maintenance hypothesis (Wagner et al., 2005) says that activation of the parietal cortex is related to the maintenance of information in working memory. The multimodal integration hypothesis (Vilberg et al., 2008; Shimamura, 2011) suggests that parietal activations indicate integration of multiple types of information. The bottom-up attention hypothesis (Cabeza, 2008) proposes that the activity reflects the capture of bottom-up attention by information entering working memory either from the senses or from long-term memory.

Finally, keep in mind that the studies presented so far implicate specific brain regions in distinct forms of memory impairment. For individuals to learn and retain new

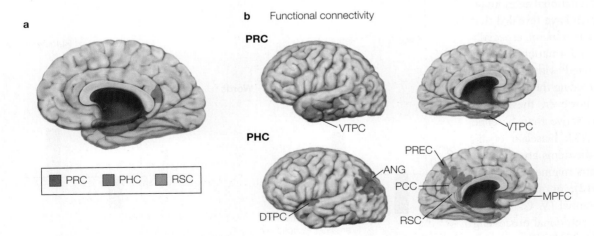

FIGURE 9.34 Anatomy of the perirhinal, parahippocampal, and retrosplenial cortices.
(a) The perirhinal cortex (PRC), parahippocampal cortex (PHC), and retrosplenial cortex (RSC) regions are shown. **(b)** Functional connectivity profiles of the PRC (top) and PHC (bottom) showing regions that were significantly correlated with the PRC and PHC during resting-state scans. Resting state fMRI scans evaluate covariations in spontaneous fluctuations in the BOLD signal across the brain while the participant performs no task, and are taken as evidence of intrinsic functional connectivity between brain regions that covary. PRC was found to be functionally connected to ventral temporopolar cortex (VTPC) where higher-order visual areas are located. In contrast, PHC is functionally connected to the dorsal temporopolar cortex (DTPC), the retrosplenial cortex (RSC), the posterior cingulate cortex (PCC), the precuneus (PREC), the medial prefrontal cortex (MPFC), and the angular gyrus (ANG).

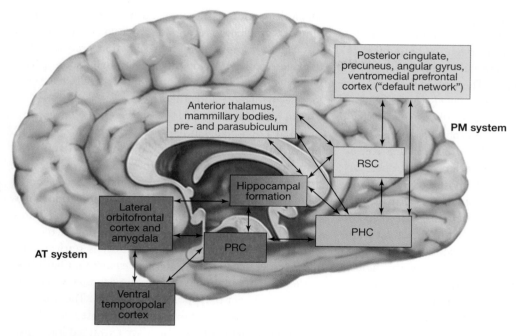

FIGURE 9.35 Model of two neocortical systems for memory-guided behavior.
The components of the anterior temporal (AT) system are shown in red. The posterior medial (PM)
system is shown in blue. Regions with strong anatomical connections are indicated with arrows.

information about their autobiographical history (episodic memory), they must have an intact medial temporal lobe (primarily hippocampus) and related structures, such as the midline diencephalon and the retrosplenial cortex in the parietal lobe. Damage to these areas impedes the formation of *new* declarative memories (anterograde amnesia) and leads to difficulties in remembering events in the years immediately before the injury (time-limited retrograde amnesia). It leaves intact, however, most previous episodic and semantic memories acquired during life. Therefore, these structures are not likely to be the storage sites of information in long-term memory, but they appear to be essential for consolidating new information in long-term stores. In contrast, damage to regions of the temporal lobe outside the hippocampus can produce dense retrograde amnesia, an apparent loss of episodic memories, even though the ability to acquire new memories may be intact.

TAKE-HOME MESSAGES

- Functional MRI evidence suggests that the hippocampus is involved in encoding and retrieval for episodic memories that are recollected. Areas outside the hippocampus, especially the entorhinal cortex, support recognition based on familiarity.
- Neuroimaging has confirmed the neural basis of memory demonstrated by animal and lesion studies and has provided some notable new findings—including, for example, evidence that the hippocampus and surrounding parahippocampal and perirhinal cortices may play different roles in memory, supporting different forms of recognition memory.

- The retrosplenial cortex in the parietal lobe appears also to be crucial for memory.
- The PHC and RSC have anatomical and functional connectivity patterns that are similar to each other and are very different from the PRC.

Memory Consolidation

Consolidation is an old concept, first proposed by Marcus Fabius Quintilianus, a first-century Roman teacher of rhetoric, who stated:

> [It] is a curious fact, of which the reason is not obvious, that the interval of a single night will greatly increase the strength of the memory. . . . Whatever the cause, things which could not be recalled on the spot are easily coordinated the next day, and time itself, which is generally accounted one of the causes of forgetfulness, actually serves to strengthen the memory. (as quoted in Walker, 2009)

The Hippocampus and Consolidation

Consolidation is the process that stabilizes a memory over time after it is first acquired. In most current models, consolidation consists of an initial rapid consolidation process, followed by a slower permanent consolidation process. One line of evidence for temporal consolidation comes from patients who have undergone electroconvulsive therapy (ECT) to treat psychological disorders. In ECT, an electrical current is passed through the brain by electrodes placed on the scalp—a useful treatment for conditions such as severe depression. This procedure can result in a retrograde amnesia that is more likely to affect items that were learned close to the time of the treatment (Figure 9.36). A similar phenomenon is observed with severe head trauma that results in a closed head injury. Retrograde amnesia is more likely for recent events, and even as the amnesia fades over time, the most recent events are affected for the longest time—sometimes permanently. The items that are lost appear to be those that have undergone initial rapid consolidation but have not yet completed the slower permanent consolidation process.

The medial temporal lobes, particularly the hippocampi, are essential for the rapid consolidation and initial storage of information for episodic and semantic memories. The mechanisms of the slow consolidation process, however, remain more controversial. There are two main theories. The *standard consolidation theory*, proposed by Larry Squire and his colleagues, considers the neocortex to be crucial for the storage of fully consolidated long-term memories, whereas the hippocampus plays only a temporary role. In this view, the representations of an event that are distributed throughout the cortex come together in the medial temporal lobe where the hippocampus binds them. Then, through some sort of interaction between the medial temporal lobe and the neocortex, the bound information is slowly transferred and replaced by a permanent memory trace in the neocortex. Consolidation occurs after repeated reactivation of the memory creates direct connections within the cortex between the various representations. This process takes place when an individual is either conscious or asleep, and it eventually makes the memory independent of the hippocampus. This model proposes the same process for both episodic and

semantic memories. Although it can explain why there is a temporal gradient to retrograde amnesia (some memories just hadn't completed the consolidation process before damage occurred), it doesn't explain why some people who have amnesia due to hippocampal damage have good long-term memory and others have severe loss.

An alternative model, the *multiple trace theory*, proposed by Lynn Nadel in Arizona and Morris Moscovitch in Toronto, suggests that only the long-term stores for semantic information rely on the neocortex while some aspects of episodic memory, consolidated or not, continue to rely on the hippocampus. In this formulation, a new memory trace, composed of a combination of attributes, is set down in the hippocampus every time a memory is retrieved: The more times a memory is retrieved, the more traces are set down. Remote events that have been retrieved more often have more hippocampal traces and become resistant to hippocampal damage. The traces are not exactly alike, but may differ in attributes. Slowly, the common elements of the traces are extracted into "gist" information and then stored as semantic memory elsewhere in the cortex. This theory suggests that episodic memories degrade over time and are slowly converted to semantic memory. It predicts that partial hippocampal damage would partially affect episodic memory, but complete damage would completely destroy it. Although a more detailed discussion of these models is beyond the scope of this chapter, both models agree on one point: Memory consolidation via the hippocampus is rapid.

The Lateral Anterior Temporal Lobe and Consolidation

The temporal neocortex outside the medial temporal lobe is important for the permanent consolidation of semantic information. Lesions that damage the lateral cortex of the anterior temporal lobe near the anterior pole, such as those associated with semantic dementia and herpes simplex encephalitis, can lead to severe retrograde amnesia, which may extend back many decades or may encompass the patient's entire life. In severe cases of semantic dementia, perirhinal atrophy is also observed (Davies et al., 2004). Some patients with anterior temporal lobe damage and the consequent dense retrograde amnesia can still form new long-term episodic memories. This condition is known as isolated retrograde amnesia. For instance, patients with semantic dementia have progressive loss of previously established semantic knowledge (non-context-specific fact, word, and object knowledge), yet their episodic memory is intact and they are still able to learn new episodic information (Hodges et al., 1992). Thus, these portions of the temporal lobe are not essential for acquiring new episodic information. What role do they play?

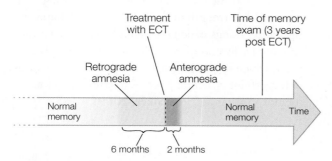

FIGURE 9.36 Effects of electroconvulsive therapy (ECT) on memory performance.
After electroconvulsive therapy, patients show a temporally graded retrograde memory loss. This tells us that memory apparently changes for a long time after initial learning. Some material is forgotten, and the material that remains becomes more resistant to disruption.

HOW THE BRAIN WORKS
Stress and Memory

Stress, both physical and psychological, triggers the release of cortisol. This hormone is produced by the adrenal cortex in the adrenal glands, which are located above the kidneys. In small quantities, cortisol can aid learning and increase attentiveness. Chronic high stress, however, has detrimental effects on cognitive functions, including memory. The receptors in the brain that are activated by cortisol are called *glucocorticoid receptors* and are found at concentrated levels in the hippocampus (especially in the dentate gyrus and CA1 region; see Figure 9.16b).

The CA1 region of the hippocampus is the origin of connections from the hippocampus to the neocortex that are important in consolidation of episodic memory. The functions of this circuitry can be disrupted by high levels of cortisol, perhaps by impairment of long-term potentiation (LTP; see the last section of this chapter for a discussion of LTP). Researchers have discovered that episodic memory (but not procedural memory) is impaired by high levels of cortisol. Clemens Kirschbaum at the Technical University of Dresden in Germany and his colleagues (1996) showed that a single dose of hydrocortisone (10 mg) had a detrimental effect on verbal episodic memory. Participants were given a list of words to study, after which they received either a dose of hydrocortisone or a placebo. In a cued recall test given an hour after administration of the dosages, participants who received the hydrocortisone recalled significantly fewer words than did the control participants who received a placebo.

Clinical evidence from all disorders characterized by high levels of cortisol—including Cushing's syndrome, major depression, and asthma treated with the glucocorticoid prednisone—show impaired memory function (Payne & Nadel, 2004). Furthermore, Sonia Lupien of McGill University, and her colleagues (2005) found that elderly individuals, who have experienced chronic stress and have prolonged high levels of cortisol, have a 14% reduction in hippocampal volume as compared to age-matched individuals without chronic stress and with normal levels of cortisol, indicating a long-term deleterious effect of cortisol on the hippocampus. These individuals also show marked impairment of episodic memory.

Interestingly, cortisol levels normally rise gradually during the night as we sleep, from low levels at the beginning of sleep to the highest levels before awaking. In concert with this knowledge is the finding that dreams rich in episodic material are concentrated at the beginning of sleep, and episodic memory consolidation is most likely to occur early in the sleep process. Jessica Payne and Lynn Nadel (2004) at the University of Arizona propose that "variations in cortisol . . . determine the functional status of hippocampal/neocortical circuits, thereby influencing the memory consolidation processes that transpire during sleep" (p. 671). Sleep research is a hot topic in neuroscience (see How the Brain Works: Sleep and Memory Consolidation), and new studies should elucidate whether Payne and Nadel's appealing theory is correct.

One possibility is that these lateral and anterior regions of the temporal lobe are sites where long-term semantic memories are stored. Another view is that these regions may be important for the retrieval of information from long-term stores. This latter hypothesis is supported by neuroimaging studies suggesting that memories are stored as **distributed representations** throughout the neocortex, involving the regions that originally encoded the perceptual information along with the regions representing information that was associated with this incoming information. As noted already in this chapter, the medial temporal lobe may coordinate the consolidation of this information over time.

TAKE-HOME MESSAGES

- Two prominent theories of long-term memory consolidation are the standard consolidation theory and the multiple trace theory.

- Hippocampal memory consolidation is quick.
- Lesions to the anterior temporal cortex can cause severe retrograde amnesia.
- Damage to the temporal lobe outside of the hippocampus can produce the loss of semantic memory even while the ability to acquire new episodic memories remains intact.

Cellular Basis of Learning and Memory

Most models of the cellular bases of memory hold that memory is the result of changes in the strength of synaptic interactions among neurons in neural networks. How would synaptic strength be altered to enable learning and memory? Hebb (1949) proposed one possibility: Hebb's law states that, if a synapse is active when

HOW THE BRAIN WORKS
Sleep and Memory Consolidation

Recent evidence suggests that sleep plays a crucial role in memory consolidation after learning. Matt Wilson and his colleagues at the Massachusetts Institute of Technology have studied the relationship between sleep and memory in the rat. They used multi-electrode methods to record from ensembles of neurons in the rat hippocampus that fire when an animal is in a specific place in its environment (in relation to a landmark cue). These cells are called *place cells*. In the initial study, Matt Wilson and Bruce McNaughton (1994) of the University of Arizona found that the place cells that fired together during the learning of spatial behavioral tasks were more likely to fire together during postlearning sleep than they had been before the task was learned, indicating that the neurons might be "replaying" the learned tasks during sleep.

Further studies of a similar nature have shown that hippocampal cells tended to replay not only with spatial coordination but also in the same temporal sequence of neuronal firing in which they were learned. Activities (and resulting neuronal firing patterns) that took place over minutes were replayed during sleep in a sequential pattern corresponding to that of the awake activity. These studies implicate the hippocampus in the consolidation of memory via "replaying" of the neuronal firing of spatial and temporal patterns that were first activated during awake learning. Replay of this type is not limited to sleep.

Foster and Wilson (2006) recently reported that sequential replay also takes place in the rat hippocampus when the animal is awake, in the period just after the rat experiences a pattern of spatial activity. Interestingly, replay during waking has the unusual property of taking place in the reverse temporal order of the original experience (e.g., running in a maze). One hypothesis is that this sort of waking replay of neural activity represents a basic mechanism for learning and memory.

Thus two mechanisms are involved in replaying an activity: the reverse waking replay of neural activity, and the sleep-related replay, in which activity is replayed in the same temporal order as it was experienced. Something about the sleep-related forward replay is apparently related to memory consolidation. But the reverse waking replay must be doing something different. Foster and Wilson propose that it reflects a mechanism that permits recently experienced events to be compared to their "memory trace" and may, potentially, reinforce learning.

---

a postsynaptic neuron is active, the synapse will be strengthened; this phenomenon is known as **Hebbian learning**.

Long-Term Potentiation and the Hippocampus

Due to the role of the hippocampal formation in memory, it has long been hypothesized that neurons in the hippocampus must be plastic—meaning able to change their synaptic interactions. Although it is now clear that storage itself is not in the hippocampus, this fact does not invalidate the hippocampal models that we will examine, because the same cellular mechanisms can operate in various cortical and subcortical areas.

First, let's review the major excitatory neural components of the hippocampus (Figure 9.37): Neocortical association areas project to the entorhinal cortex via the parahippocampal cortex or perirhinal cortex. The entorhinal cortex projects via the *perforant pathway* onto the granule cells of the dentate gyrus with excitatory inputs. Distinctive unmyelinated axons, known as *mossy fibers* because of their appearance, connect the granule cells of the dentate gyrus to the dendritic spines of the hippocampal CA3 pyramidal cells. The *Schaffer collaterals* connect the CA3 pyramidal cells to the CA1 pyramidal cells. This system is used to examine synaptic plasticity as the mechanism of learning at the cellular level.

In studies by Bliss and Lømo (1973), stimulation of axons of the perforant pathway of the rabbit resulted in a long-term increase in the magnitude of excitatory postsynaptic potentials (EPSPs). That is, stimulation led to greater synaptic strength in the perforant pathway so that when stimulated again later, larger postsynaptic responses resulted in the granule cells of the dentate gyrus. This phenomenon, named *long-term potentiation (LTP)* (*potentiate* means "to strengthen or make more potent"), later was also found to occur in the other two excitatory projection pathways of the hippocampus. The changes could last for hours in isolated slices of hippocampal tissue placed in dishes, where recording was easier. LTP can even last days or weeks in living animals. It has since been found that the LTP in the three pathways varies and also takes

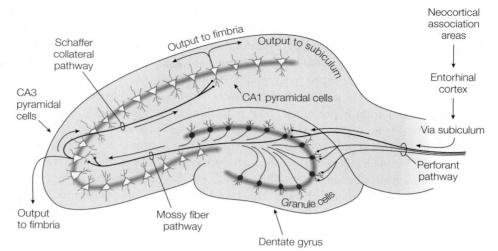

FIGURE 9.37 Synaptic organization of the rat hippocampus.
See text for description of the major projection pathways.

place in other brain regions, including the amygdala, basal ganglia, cerebellum, and cortex (all involved with learning).

Hebb's law was confirmed physiologically by the discovery of LTP. LTP can be recorded by placing stimulating electrodes on the perforant pathway and a recording electrode in a granule cell of the dentate gyrus (Figure 9.38). A single pulse is presented, and the resulting EPSP is measured. The size of this first recording is the strength of the connection before the LTP is induced. Then the perforant pathway is stimulated with a burst of pulses; early studies used approximately 100 pulses/s, but more recent studies have used as few as 5 pulses/s. After LTP is induced, a single pulse is sent again, and the magnitude of the EPSP in the postsynaptic cell is measured. The magnitude of the EPSP increases after LTP is induced, signaling the greater strength of the synaptic effect (Figure 9.38, red curve). A fascinating finding is that, when the pulses are presented slowly (as low-frequency pulses), the opposite effect—long-term depression (LTD)—develops (Figure 9.38, blue curve).

Hebbian Learning *Associative LTP* is an extension of Hebb's law. It asserts that, if a neuron is simultaneously activated by a pathway with a weak input and another pathway with a strong input, both pathways show LTP and the weak synapse becomes stronger. This association has been tested directly by manipulating LTP in the CA1 neurons of the hippocampus. When two weak inputs (W1 and W2) and one strong input (S1) are given to the same cell, and when W1 and S1 are active together, W1 is strengthened but W2 is not. Subsequently, if W2 and S1 are active together, W1 is not affected by the LTP induced from W2 and S1. From this finding, three rules for associative LTP have been drawn:

1. *Cooperativity.* More than one input must be active at the same time.
2. *Associativity.* Weak inputs are potentiated when co-occurring with stronger inputs.
3. *Specificity.* Only the stimulated synapse shows potentiation.

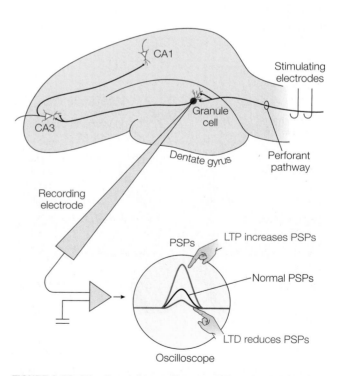

FIGURE 9.38 Stimulus and recording setup for the study of long-term potentiation (LTP) in perforant pathways.
The pattern of responses (in millivolts) before and after the induction of LTP is shown as the red curve. The pattern of responses in long-term depression (LTD) is shown as the blue curve. PSPs = postsynaptic potentials.

For LTP to be produced, in addition to receiving excitatory inputs, the postsynaptic cells must be depolarized; in fact, LTP is reduced by inhibitory inputs to postsynaptic cells. This is what happens when habituation occurs. Moreover, when postsynaptic cells are hyperpolarized, LTP is prevented. Conversely, when postsynaptic inhibition is prevented, LTP is facilitated. If an input that is normally not strong enough to induce LTP is paired with a depolarizing current to the postsynaptic cell, LTP can be induced. Thus, through associative LTP, weak pathways become strengthened and specifically associated with other pathways. This process supports learning in the way that Hebb proposed.

The NMDA Receptor The molecular mechanism that mediates LTP is fascinating. It is dependent on the neurotransmitter glutamate, the major excitatory transmitter in the hippocampus. Glutamate binds to two types of glutamate receptors. Normal synaptic transmissions are mediated by the AMPA (α-amino-3-hydroxyl-5-methyl-4-isoxazole propionate) receptor. LTP is initially mediated by the NMDA (N-methyl-D-aspartate) receptors (Figure 9.39), which are located on the dendritic spines of postsynaptic neurons. When the NMDA receptors of CA1 neurons are blocked with the chemical AP5 (2-amino-5-phosphonopentanoate), then LTP induction is prevented. Once LTP is established in these cells, however, AP5 treatment has no effect. Therefore, NMDA receptors are central to producing LTP, but not maintaining it. Maintenance of LTP probably depends on the AMPA receptors, although the mechanisms are not fully understood.

NMDA receptors are also blocked by magnesium ions (Mg^{2+}), which prevent other ions from entering the postsynaptic cell. The Mg^{2+} ions can be ejected from the NMDA receptors only when the cell is depolarized. Thus, the ion channel opens only when two conditions are met: (1) when the neurotransmitter glutamate binds to the receptors, and (2) when the membrane is depolarized. These two conditions are another way of saying that the NMDA receptors are transmitter- and voltage-dependent (also called gated; Figure 9.40).

The open ion channel allows Ca^{2+} ions to enter the postsynaptic cell. The effect of Ca^{2+} influx via the NMDA receptor is critical in the formation of LTP. The Ca^{2+} acts as an intracellular messenger conveying the signal, which changes enzyme activities that influence synaptic strength. Despite rapid advances in understanding the mechanisms of LTP at physiological and biochemical levels, the molecular mechanisms of synaptic strengthening in LTP are still the subject of extensive debate.

The synaptic changes that create a stronger synapse after LTP induction likely include presynaptic and postsynaptic mechanisms. One hypothesis is that LTP raises the sensitivity of postsynaptic AMPA glutamate receptors and prompts more glutamate to be released presynaptically. Or perhaps changes in the physical characteristics of the dendritic spines transmit EPSPs more effectively to the dendrites. Finally, via a message from the postsynaptic cell to the presynaptic cell, the efficiency of presynaptic neurotransmitter release is increased.

Long-Term Potentiation and Memory Performance

With a candidate cellular mechanism for long-term plastic changes in synaptic strength identified, it should be possible to produce deficits in learning and memory, which can be demonstrated behaviorally, by eliminating LTP. Chemically blocking LTP in the hippocampus of normal mice impairs their ability to demonstrate normal place learning; thus, blocking LTP prevents normal spatial memory. In a similar way, genetic manipulations that block the cascade of molecular triggers for LTP also impair spatial learning. These experiments provide strong evidence that blocking NMDA receptors and preventing LTP impairs spatial learning.

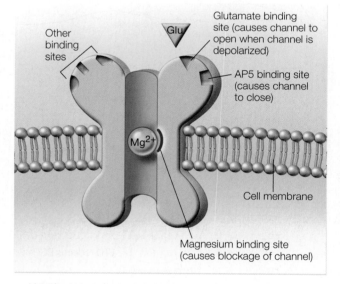

Other binding sites

Glu

Glutamate binding site (causes channel to open when channel is depolarized)

AP5 binding site (causes channel to close)

Mg^{2+}

Cell membrane

Magnesium binding site (causes blockage of channel)

FIGURE 9.39 The NMDA receptor.
As this simplified cross-sectional schematic shows, the NMDA receptor is naturally blocked by Mg^{2+} ions. Unblocking (channel opening) occurs when the proteins that form the channel shift following the binding of glutamate to the glutamate binding site.

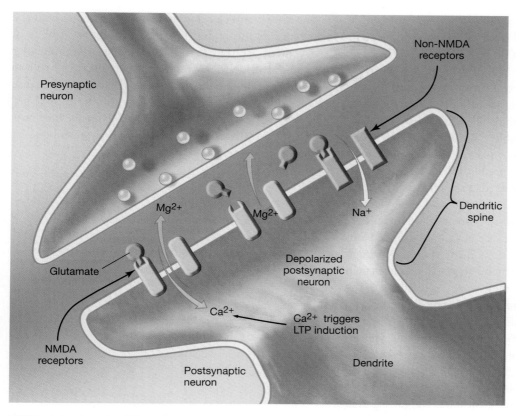

FIGURE 9.40 The role of Mg²⁺ and Ca²⁺ in the functioning of the NMDA receptor. See text for details.

NMDA receptors in the CA1 region of the hippocampus are necessary for most forms of synaptic plasticity, and their activation is required for spatial and contextual learning. Once learning has occurred, however, new memories can be formed without their activation. This surprising finding came from two classic water-maze studies (Bannerman et al., 1995; Saucier & Cain, 1995). Both experiments found that pharmacological NMDA receptor blockers did not stop rodents that had been pretrained to navigate in one maze from learning how to navigate in a second water maze; the animals were able to develop a new spatial map even when LTP was prevented. The conclusion is that NMDA receptors may be needed to learn a spatial strategy but not to encode a new map.

In another experiment, when mice were pretrained with a nonspatial task, spatial memory was not interrupted by the introduction of an NMDA antagonist. The conclusion is that the pretraining merely allowed the motor-related side effects of NMDA receptor blockage to be avoided. Although neither study has excluded the possibility that new spatial learning involves NMDA receptors, they do point to the possibility that at least two memory systems could use NMDA receptors. These systems participate in the water-maze task, but they might be consolidated by pretraining.

On the cellular and behavioral levels, the role of LTP in memory is still being unraveled. Whether the maintenance of LTP is located presynaptically or postsynaptically, and even whether LTP is necessary for spatial memory, is the subject of much debate. Daniel Zamanillo and his colleagues (1999) at the Max Planck Institute in Heidelberg, Germany, used gene knockout protocols to study mice that could not produce LTP in the synapses of neurons between the CA3 and CA1 regions of the hippocampus. Behaviorally, however, these mice could learn spatial tasks just as easily as normal control mice.

Bannerman and his colleagues (2012) found that genetically modified mice, which lacked NMDA receptor function in hippocampal CA1 and dentate gyrus granule cells, could not produce LTP in the neurons in these two regions. These mice performed as well as controls in a water-maze learning and memory task. Where the mice did show impairment was in the radial arm maze. The radial arm maze is a circular arena, rather like the hub of a wagon wheel, with six identical arms radiating from it. Like the water maze, there are physical identifiers in the larger environment in which the maze sits. Food rewards are put at the end of three of the corridors. In this type of maze, the NMDA knockout mice showed little improvement in identifying the corridors with the food. By contrast, controls were able to learn to pick the right corridor and rarely erred. Why the difference in learning success? These researchers suggested that the problem lies in picking between ambiguous local cues—that is, the six identical corridors—versus more distant predictive cues.

To test this idea, they used a modified water maze that added ambiguous local cues. A small local cue was put above the platform and the same cue, a faux cue, at the opposite end of the tank. The mice were dropped into the water at different positions in the maze. Although both the controls and the genetically modified mice could find the platform, when they were dropped near the faux cue, the knockout mice were more likely to swim to the faux cue. The control mice (using their spatial memory) were not influenced by the faux cue, and instead swam to the platform. It appears then, that the mice lacking the NMDA receptor function are able to form spatial memories, but they don't use them when confronted with ambiguous local cues, suggesting that the NMDA receptor function is more subtle than previously thought (Maford, 2012). Martine Migaud and colleagues (1998) at the University of Edinburgh studied mice with enhanced LTP and found that they exhibited severe impairments in spatial learning.

Although much remains to be understood about the cellular and molecular basis of learning, two points of agreement are that (a) LTP does exist at the cellular level, and (b) NMDA receptors play a crucial role in LTP induction in many pathways of the brain. Because LTP is also in brain areas outside of the hippocampal system, the possibility that LTP forms the basis for long-term modification within synaptic networks remains promising.

TAKE-HOME MESSAGES

- In Hebbian learning, if a synapse is active when a postsynaptic neuron is active, the synapse will be strengthened. Long-term potentiation is the long-term strengthening of a synapse.
- NMDA receptors are central to producing LTP but not to maintaining it.

What can be surmised about the amygdala and emotional processing from S.M.?

1. First, the amygdala must play a critical role in the identification of facial expressions of fear.
2. Second, although S.M. fails to experience the emotion of fear, she has little impairment in her comprehension of other emotions.
3. Third, her inability to feel a particular emotion, fear, seems to have contributed to her inability to avoid dangerous situations.

It is difficult to understand who we are or how we interact with the world without considering our emotional lives. Under the umbrella of cognitive neuroscience, the study of emotion was slow to emerge because, for a number of reasons, emotion is difficult to study systematically. For a long time, emotion was considered to be subjective to the individual and thus, not amenable to empirical analysis. Researchers eventually realized that conscious emotions arise from unconscious processes that can be studied using the tools of psychology and cognitive neuroscience (see a review of the problem in LeDoux, 2000). It has become apparent that emotion is involved with much of cognitive processing. Its involvement ranges from influencing what we remember (Chapter 9), to where we direct our attention (Chapter 7), to the decisions that we make (Chapter 12). Our emotions modulate and bias our own behavior and actions. Underlying all emotion research is a question: Is there a neural system dedicated to emotions or are they just another form of cognition that is only phenomenologically different (S. Duncan & Barrett, 2007)? The study of emotion is emerging as a critical and exciting research topic.

We begin this chapter with some attempts to define emotion. Next, we review the areas of the brain that are thought to mediate emotion processing. We also survey the theories about emotions and how they are generated. Much of the research on emotion has concentrated on the workings of the amygdala, so we examine this part of the brain in some detail. We also look at the progress made in answering the questions that face emotion researchers:

- What is an emotion?
- Are some emotions basic to everyone?
- How are emotions generated?
- Is emotion processing localized, generalized, or a combination of the two?
- What effect does emotion have on the cognitive processes of perception, attention, learning, memory, and decision making and on our behavior?

- Do these cognitive processes exert any control over our emotions?

We close the chapter with a look at several (especially) complex emotions, including happiness and love.

What Is an Emotion?

People have been struggling with this question for at least several thousand years. Even today, the answer remains unsettled. In the current *Handbook of Emotions* (3rd ed.), the late philosopher Robert Soloman (2008) devotes an entire chapter to discussing the lack of a good definition of emotion and looking at why it is so difficult to define. How would you define emotion?

Maybe your definition starts with "An emotion is a feeling you get when. . . ." And we already have a problem, because many researchers claim that a **feeling** is the subjective experience of the emotion, but not the emotion itself. These two events are dissociable and, as we see later in this chapter, they use separate neural systems. Perhaps evolutionary principles can help us with a general definition. Emotions are neurological processes that have evolved, which guide behavior in such a manner as to increase survival and reproduction. How's that for vague? Here is a definition from Kevin Ochsner and James Gross (2005), two researchers whose work we look at in this chapter:

Current models posit that **emotions** are valenced responses to external stimuli and/or internal mental representations that

- involve changes across multiple response systems (e.g., experiential, behavioral, peripheral, physiological),
- are distinct from moods, in that they often have identifiable objects or triggers,
- can be either unlearned responses to stimuli with intrinsic affective properties (e.g., pulling your hand away when you burn it) or learned responses to stimuli with acquired emotional value (e.g., fear when you see a dog that previously bit you),
- can involve multiple types of appraisal processes that assess the significance of stimuli to current goals, that
- depend upon different neural systems.

Most psychologists agree that emotion consists of three components:

1. A physiological reaction to a stimulus,
2. a behavioral response, and
3. a feeling.

Neural Systems Involved in Emotion Processing

Many parts of the nervous system are involved in our emotions. When emotions are triggered by an external event or stimulus (as they often are), our sensory systems play a major role. Sometimes emotions are triggered by an episodic memory, in which case our memory systems are involved (see Chapter 9). The physiologic components of emotion (that shiver up the spine, or the racing heart and dry mouth people experience with fear) involve the autonomic nervous system (ANS), a division of the peripheral nervous system. Recall from Chapter 2 that the ANS is made up of the sympathetic and the parasympathetic nervous systems (see Figure 2.17), and its motor and sensory neurons extend to the heart, lungs, gut, bladder, and sexual organs. The two systems work in combination to achieve homeostasis. As a rule of thumb, the sympathetic system promotes "fight or flight" arousal, and the parasympathetic promotes "rest and digest." The ANS is regulated by the hypothalamus. The hypothalamus also controls the release of hormones from the pituitary gland. Of course, the fight-or-flight response uses the motor system. Arousal is a critical part of many theories on emotion. The arousal system is regulated by the reticular activating system, which is composed of sets of neurons running from the brainstem to the cortex via the rostral intralaminar and thalamic nuclei.

All of the neural systems mentioned so far are important in triggering an emotion or in generating physiological and behavioral responses. Yet where do emotions reside? We turn to that question next.

Early Concepts: The Limbic System as the Emotional Brain

The notion that emotion is separate from cognition and has its own network of brain structures underlying emotional behavior is not new. As we mentioned in Chapter 2, James Papez (pronounced "payps") proposed a circuit theory of the brain and emotion in 1937, suggesting that emotional responses involve a network of brain regions made up of the hypothalamus, anterior thalamus, cingulate gyrus, and hippocampus. Paul MacLean (1949, 1952) later named these structures the *Papez circuit*. He then extended this emotional network to include what he called the visceral brain, adding Broca's limbic lobe and some subcortical nuclei and portions of the basal ganglia. Later, MacLean included the amygdala and the orbitofrontal cortex. He called this extended neural circuit of emotion the limbic system, from the Latin

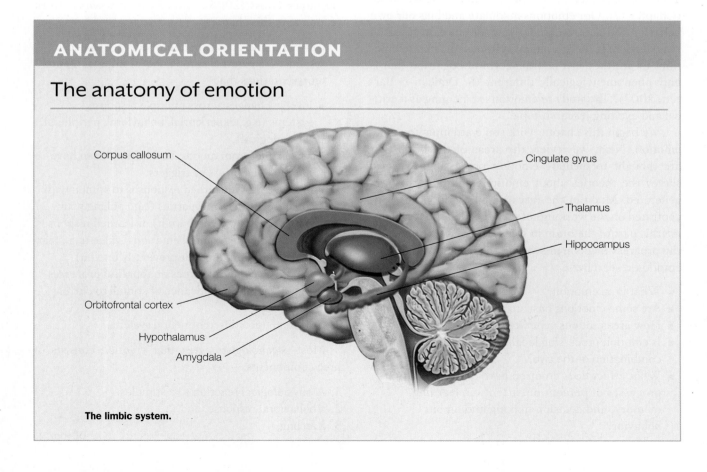

ANATOMICAL ORIENTATION

The anatomy of emotion

Corpus callosum

Cingulate gyrus

Thalamus

Hippocampus

Orbitofrontal cortex

Hypothalamus

Amygdala

The limbic system.

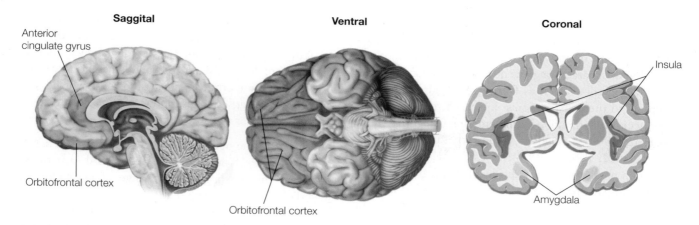

FIGURE 10.3 Specific brain regions are hypothesized to be associated with specific emotions.
The rust colored orbitofrontal cortex is associated with anger, the anterior cingulate gyrus in purple with sadness, the blue insula with disgust, and the green amygdala with fear.

limbus, meaning "rim." The structures of the limbic system roughly form a rim around the corpus callosum (Anatomical Orientation figure; also see Figure 2.26).

MacLean's early work identifying the limbic system as the "emotional" brain was influential. To this day, studies on the neural basis of emotion include references to the "limbic system" or "limbic" structures. The continued popularity of the term *limbic system* in more recent work is due primarily to the inclusion of the orbitofrontal cortex and amygdala in that system. As we shall see, these two areas have been the focus of investigation into the neural basis of emotion (Figure 10.3; Damasio, 1994; LeDoux, 1992). The limbic system concept as strictly outlined by MacLean, however, has not been supported over the years (Brodal, 1982; Kotter & Meyer, 1992; LeDoux, 1991; Swanson, 1983). We now know that many brainstem nuclei that are connected to the hypothalamus are not part of the limbic system. Similarly, many brainstem nuclei that are involved in autonomic reactions important to MacLean's idea of a visceral brain are not part of the limbic system. Although several limbic structures are known to play a role in emotion, it has been impossible to establish criteria for defining which structures and pathways should be included in the limbic system. At the same time, classic limbic areas such as the hippocampus have been shown to be more important for other, nonemotional processes, such as memory (see Chapter 9). With no clear understanding as to why some brain regions and not others are part of the limbic system, MacLean's concept has proven to be more descriptive and historical than functional in our current understanding of the neural basis of emotion.

Early attempts to identify neural circuits of emotion viewed emotion as a unitary concept that could be localized to one specific circuit, such as the limbic system. Viewing the "emotional brain" as separate from the rest

of the brain spawned a locationist view of emotions. The locationist account hypothesizes that all mental states belonging to the same emotion category are produced by activity that is recurrently associated with a specific region in the brain (Figure 10.3). Also, this association is an inherited trait, and homologies are seen in other mammalian species (Panksepp, 1998; for a contrary view, see Lindquist et al., 2012).

Emerging Concepts of Emotional Networks

Over the last several decades, scientific investigations of emotion have become more detailed and complex. By measuring brain responses to emotionally salient stimuli, researchers have revealed a complex interconnected network involved in the *analysis* of emotional stimuli. This network includes the thalamus, the somatosensory cortex, higher order sensory cortices, the amygdala, the insular cortex (also called the insula), and the medial prefrontal cortex, including the orbitofrontal cortex, ventral striatum, and anterior cingulate cortex (ACC).

Those who study emotion now acknowledge that it is a multifaceted behavior that may vary along a spectrum from basic to more complex: It isn't captured by one definition or contained within a single neural circuit. Indeed, S.M.'s isolated emotional deficit in fear recognition following bilateral amygdala damage supports the idea that there is no single emotional circuit. Emotion research now focuses on specific types of emotional tasks and on identifying the neural systems underlying specific emotional behaviors. Depending on the emotional task or situation, we can expect different neural systems to be involved. The question remains, however, whether discrete neural mechanisms and circuits underlie the different emotion categories, or if emotions emerge out of basic operations that are not specific to emotion (*psychological constructionist* approach), or if a combination exists whereby some brain systems are common to all emotions allied with separable regions dedicated to processing individual emotions such as fear, anger, and disgust. According to the constructionist approach, the brain does not necessarily function within emotion categories (L. F. Barrett, 2009; S. Duncan & Barrett, 2007; Lindquist et al., 2012; Pessoa, 2008). Instead, the psychological function mediated by an individual brain region is determined, in part, by the network of brain regions it is firing with (A. R. McIntosh, 2004). In this view, each brain network might involve some brain regions that are more or less specialized for emotional processing, along with others that serve many functions, depending on what role a particular emotion plays. For instance, the dorsomedial prefrontal areas that represent self and others are active across all emotions (Northoff et al., 2005), while brain regions that support attentional vigilance are recruited to detect threat signals; the brain regions that represent the consequence that a stimulus will have for the body are activated for disgust, but not only for disgust. So, just as a definition for emotion is in flux, so too are the anatomical correlates of emotional processing.

TAKE-HOME MESSAGES

- The Papez circuit describes the brain areas that James Papez believed were involved in emotion. They include the hypothalamus, anterior thalamus, cingulate gyrus, and hippocampus. The limbic system includes these structures and the amygdala, orbitofrontal cortex, and portions of the basal ganglia.

- Investigators no longer think there is only one neural circuit of emotion. Rather, depending on the emotional task or situation, we can expect different neural systems to be involved.

Categorizing Emotions

At the core of emotion research is the issue of whether emotions are "psychic entities" that are specific, biologically fundamental, and hardwired with dedicated brain mechanisms (as Darwin supposed). Or, are emotions states of mind that are assembled from more basic, general causes, as William James suggested?

> The trouble with the emotions in psychology is that they are regarded too much as absolutely individual things. So long as they are set down as so many eternal and sacred psychic entities, like the old immutable species in natural history, all that can be done with them is reverently to catalogue their separate

characters, points, and effects. But if we regard them as products of more general causes (as "species" are now regarded as products of heredity and variation), the mere distinguishing and cataloguing becomes of subsidiary importance. Having the goose which lays the golden eggs, the description of each egg already laid is a minor matter. (James, 1890, p. 449)

James was of the opinion that emotions were not basic, nor were they found in dedicated neural structures, but were the melding of a mélange of psychological ingredients honed by evolution.

As we noted earlier in this chapter, most emotion researchers agree that the response to emotional stimuli is adaptive, comprised of three psychological states: *a peripheral physiological response* (e.g., heart racing), *a behavioral response*, and *the subjective experience* (i.e., feelings). What they don't agree on are the underlying mechanisms. The crux of the disagreement among the different theories of **emotion generation** involves the timing of these three components and whether cognition plays a role. An **emotional stimulus** is a stimulus that is highly relevant for the well-being and survival of the observer. Some stimuli, such as predators or dangerous situations, may be threats; others may offer opportunities for betterment, such as food or potential mates. How the status of a stimulus is determined is another issue, as is whether the perception of the emotional stimulus leads to quick automatic processing and stereotyped emotional responses or if the response is modified by cognition. Next, we discuss the basic versus dimensional categorization of emotion and then look at representatives of the various theories of emotion generation.

Fearful, sad, anxious, elated, disappointed, angry, shameful, disgusted, happy, pleased, excited, and *infatuated* are some of the terms we use to describe our emotional lives. Unfortunately, our rich language of emotion is difficult to translate into discrete states and variables that can be studied in the laboratory. In an effort to apply some order and uniformity to our definition of emotion, researchers have focused on three primary categories of emotion:

1. **Basic emotions** comprise a closed set of emotions, each with unique characteristics, carved by evolution, and reflected through facial expressions.
2. **Complex emotions** are combinations of basic emotions, some of which may be socially or culturally learned, that can be identified as evolved, long-lasting feelings.
3. **Dimensions of emotion** describe emotions that are fundamentally the same but that differ along one or more dimensions, such as valence (pleasant or unpleasant, positive or negative) and arousal (very pleasant to very unpleasant), in reaction to events or stimuli.

Basic Emotions

We may use *delighted, joyful,* and *gleeful* to describe how we feel, but most people would agree that all of these words represent a variation of feeling happy. Central to the hypothesis that basic emotions exist is the idea that emotions reflect an inborn instinct. If a relevant stimulus is present, it *will* trigger an evolved brain mechanism in the same way, every time. Thus, we often describe basic emotions as being innate and similar in all humans and many animals. As such, basic emotions exist as entities independent of our perception of them. In this view, each emotion produces predictable changes in sensory, perceptual, motor, and physiological functions that can be measured and thus provide evidence that the emotion exists.

Facial Expressions and Basic Emotions For the past 150 years, many investigators have considered **facial expressions** to be one of those predictable changes. Accordingly, it is believed that research on facial expressions opens an extraordinary window into these basic emotions. This belief is based on the assumption that facial expressions are observable, automatic manifestations that correspond to a person's inner feelings. Duchenne de Boulogne carried out some of the earliest research on facial expressions. One of his patients was an elderly man who suffered from near-total facial anesthesia. Duchenne developed a technique to electrically stimulate the man's facial muscles and methodically trigger muscle contractions, and he recorded the results with the newly invented camera (Figure 10.4). He published his findings in *The Mechanism of Human Facial Expression* (1862). Duchenne believed that facial expressions revealed underlying emotions. Duchenne's studies influenced Darwin's work on the evolutionary basis of human emotional behavior, outlined in *The Expression of the Emotions in Man and Animals* (1873). Darwin had questioned people familiar with different cultures about the emotional lives of these varied cultures. From these discussions, Darwin determined that humans have evolved to have a finite set of basic emotional states, and each state is unique in its adaptive significance and physiological expression. The idea that humans have a finite set of universal, basic emotions was born, and this was the idea that William James protested.

The study of facial expressions was not taken up again until the 1960s, when Paul Ekman sought evidence for his hypothesis that (a) emotions varied only along a pleasant to unpleasant scale; (b) the relationship between a facial expression and what it signified was learned socially; and (c) the meaning of a particular facial expression varied among cultures. He studied cultures from around the world and discovered that, counter to

FIGURE 10.4 Duchenne triggering muscle contractions in his patient, who had facial anesthesia.

his early hypothesis, the facial expressions humans use to convey emotion do not vary much from culture to culture. Whether people are from the Bronx, Beijing, or Papua New Guinea, the facial expressions we use to show that we are happy, sad, fearful, disgusted, angry, or surprised are pretty much the same (Ekman & Friesen, 1971; Figure 10.5). From this work, Ekman and others suggested that *anger, fear, disgust, sadness, happiness,* and *surprise* are the six basic human facial expressions and that each expression represents a basic emotional state (Table 10.1). Since then, other emotions have been added as potential candidate basic emotions.

Jessica Tracy and David Matsumoto (2008) have provided evidence that might change the rank of pride and shame to that of true basic emotions. They looked at the nonverbal expressions of pride or shame in reaction to winning or losing a judo match at the 2004 Olympic and Paralympic Games in contestants from 37 nations. Among the contestants, some were congenitally blind. Thus, the researchers assumed that in congenitally blind participants, the body language of their behavioral response was not learned culturally. All of the contestants

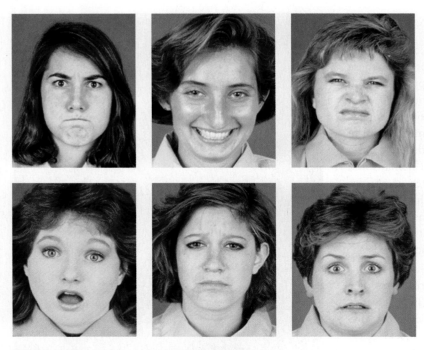

FIGURE 10.5 The universal emotional expressions.
The meaning of these facial expressions is similar across all cultures. Can you match the faces to the emotional states of anger, disgust, fear, happiness, sadness, and surprise?

displayed prototypical expressions of pride upon winning (Figure 10.6). Most cultures displayed behaviors associated with shame upon losing, though the response was less pronounced in athletes from highly individualistic cultures. This finding suggested to these researchers that behavior associated with pride and shame is innate and that these two emotions are basic.

Although considerable debate continues as to whether any single list is adequate to capture the full range of

TABLE 10.1 The Well-Established and Possible Basic Emotions According to Ekman (1999)

Well-established basic emotions	Candidate basic emotions
Anger	Contempt
Fear	Shame
Sadness	Guilt
Enjoyment	Embarrassment
Disgust	Awe
Surprise	Amusement
	Excitement
	Pride in achievement
	Relief
	Satisfaction
	Sensory pleasure
	Enjoyment

emotional experiences, most scientists accept the idea that all basic emotions share three main characteristics. They are all innate, universal, and short-lasting human emotions. Table 10.2 is a set of criteria that some emotion researchers, such as Ekman, believe are common to all basic emotions.

Some basic emotions such as fear and anger have been confirmed in animals, which show dedicated subcortical circuitry for such emotions. Ekman also found that humans have specific physiological reactions for anger, fear, and disgust (see Ekman, 1992, for a review). Consequently, many researchers start with the assumption that everyone, including animals, has a set of basic emotions.

Complex Emotions

Even if we accept that basic emotions exist, we are still faced with identifying which emotions are basic and which are complex (Ekman, 1992; Ortigue et al., 2010a). Some commonly recognized emotions, such as jealousy and parental love, are absent from Ekman's list (see Table 10.1; Ortigue et al., 2010a; Ortigue & Bianchi-Demicheli, 2011). Ekman did not exclude these intense feelings from his list of emotions, but called them "emotion complexes" (see Darwin et al., 1998). He differentiated them from basic emotions as follows: "Parental love, romantic love, envy, or jealousy last for much longer periods—months, years, a lifetime for love and at least hours or days for envy or jealousy" (Darwin et al., 1998, p. 83). Jealousy is one of the most interesting of the complex emotions (Ortigue & Bianchi-Demicheli, 2011). A review of the clinical literature of patients who experienced delusional jealousy following a brain infarct or a traumatic brain injury revealed that delusional jealousy is mediated by more than just the limbic system. A broad network of regions within the brain, including higher order cortical areas involved with social cognition (Chapter 13), theory of mind (Chapter 13), and interpretation of actions performed by others (Chapter 8) are involved (Ortigue & Bianchi-Demicheli, 2011). Clearly, jealousy is a complex emotion.

Similarly, romantic love is far more complicated than researchers initially thought (Ortigue et al., 2010a). (We do have to wonder who ever thought love was not complicated.) Ekman differentiates love from the basic emotions because no universal facial expressions exist for romantic love (see Table 10.1; Sabini & Silver, 2005). As Charles Darwin mentioned, "Although the emotion of love, for instance that of a mother for her infant, is

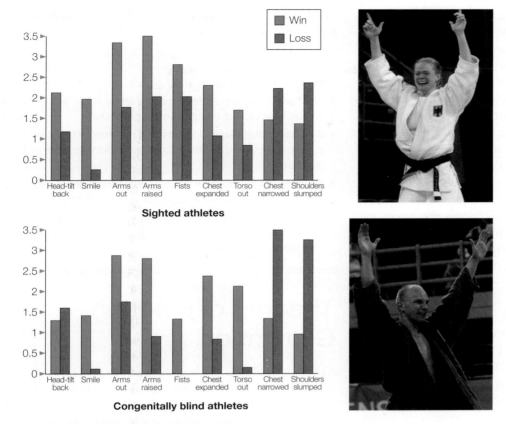

FIGURE 10.6 Athletes from 37 countries exhibit spontaneous pride and shame behaviors.
The graphs compare the mean levels of nonverbal behaviors spontaneously displayed in response to wins and losses by sighted athletes on the top and congenitally blind athletes on the bottom.

one of the strongest of which the mind is capable, it can hardly be said to have any proper or peculiar means of expression" (Darwin, 1873, p. 215). Indeed, with love we can feel intense feelings and inner thoughts that facial expressions cannot reflect. Love may be described as invisible—though some signs of love, such as kissing and hand-holding, are explicit and obvious (Bianchi-Demicheli et al., 2006, 2010b). The visible manifestations of love, however, are not love per se (Ortigue et al., 2008, 2010b). The recent localization of love in the hu-

man brain—within subcortical reward, motivation, and emotion systems as well as higher order cortical brain networks involved in complex cognitive functions and social cognition—reinforces the assumption that love is a complex, goal-directed emotion rather than a basic one (Ortigue et al., 2010a; Bianchi-Demicheli et al., 2006). Complex emotions, such as love and jealousy, are considered to be refined, long-lasting cognitive versions of basic emotions that are culturally specific or individual.

Dimensions of Emotion

Another way of categorizing emotions is to describe them as reactions that vary along a continuum of events in the world, rather than as discrete states. That is, some people hypothesize that emotions are better understood by how arousing or pleasant they may be or by how motivated they make a person feel about approaching or withdrawing from an emotional stimulus.

Valence and Arousal Most researchers agree that emotional reactions to stimuli and events can be characterized by two factors: *valence* (pleasant–unpleasant

TABLE 10.2 Criteria of the Basic Emotions According to Ekman (1994)

- Distinctive universal signals
- Presence in other primates
- Distinctive physiology
- Distinctive universals in antecedent events
- Rapid onset
- Brief duration
- Automatic appraisal
- Unbidden occurrence

NOTE: In 1999, Ekman developed three additional criteria: (1) distinctive appearance developmentally; (2) distinctive thoughts, memories, images; and (3) distinctive subjective experience.

or good–bad) and *arousal* (the intensity of the internal emotional response, high–low; Osgood et al., 1957; Russell, 1979). For instance, most of us would agree that being happy is a pleasant feeling (positive valence) and being angry is an unpleasant feeling (negative valence). If we find a quarter on the sidewalk, however, we would be happy but not really all that aroused. If we were to win $10 million in a lottery, we would be intensely happy (ecstatic) and intensely aroused. Although in both situations we experience something that is pleasant, the intensity of that feeling is certainly different. By using this dimensional approach—tracking valence and arousal—researchers can more concretely assess the emotional reactions elicited by stimuli. Instead of looking for neural correlates of specific emotions, these researchers look for the neural correlates of the dimensions—arousal and valence.

Approach or Withdraw A second dimensional approach characterizes emotions by the actions and goals that they motivate. Richard Davidson and colleagues (1990) at the University of Wisconsin–Madison suggested that different emotional reactions or states can motivate us to either approach or withdraw from a situation. For example, the positive emotion of happiness may excite a tendency to *approach* or engage in the eliciting situations, whereas the negative emotions of fear and disgust may motivate us to *withdraw* from the eliciting situations. Motivation, however, involves more than just valence. Anger, a negative emotion, can motivate approach. Sometimes the motivating stimuli can excite both approach and withdrawal: It is 110 degrees, and for hours you have been traveling across the Australian outback on a bus with no air conditioning. You are hot, sweaty, dirty, and your only desire is to jump into the river you've been slowly approaching all day. You are finally dropped off at your campground by the Katherine River, where you see a rope swing dangling invitingly next to the water. You drop your pack and trot to the river, which is stimulating you to approach. As you get closer, you catch a glimpse of a typically Australian sign next to the river's edge: "Watch out for crocs." Hmm . . . the river is no longer as approachable. You want to go in, and yet. . . .

Categorizing emotions as basic, complex, and dimensional does not adequately capture all of our emotional experiences. Think of these categories instead as a framework that we can use in our scientific investigations of emotion. No single approach is correct all of the time, so we must not get drawn into an either-or debate. It is essential, though, to understand how *emotion* is defined, so that as we analyze specific examples of emotion research, meaningful consensus can emerge from a range of results. Next we examine some of the many theories of how emotions are generated.

TAKE-HOME MESSAGES

- Emotions have been categorized as either basic or complex, or varying along dimensional lines.
- Six basic human facial expressions represent emotional states: anger, fear, disgust, happiness, sadness, and surprise.
- Complex emotions (such as love) may vary conceptually as a function of culture and personal experiences.
- The dimensional approach, instead of describing discrete states of emotion, describes emotions as reactions that vary along a continuum.

Theories of Emotion Generation

As we outlined near the beginning of this chapter, every emotion, following the perception of an emotion-provoking stimulus, has three components. There is a physiological response, a behavioral response, and a feeling. The crux of every theory of emotion generation involves the timing of the physiological reaction (for instance, the racing heart), the behavior reaction (such as the fight-or-flight response), and the experiential feeling (I'm scared!).

James–Lange Theory

William James proposed that the emotions were the perceptual results of somatovisceral feedback from bodily responses to an emotion-provoking stimulus. He used the example of fear associated with spotting a bear.

> Our natural way of thinking about these standard emotions is that the mental perception of some fact excites the mental affection called the emotion, and that this latter state of mind gives rise to the bodily expression. My thesis on the contrary is that *the bodily changes follow directly the* PERCEPTION *of the exciting fact, and that our feeling of the same changes as they occur* IS *the emotion.* Common sense says, . . . we meet a bear, are frightened and run; . . . The hypothesis here to be defended says that this order of sequence is incorrect, that the one mental state is not immediately induced by the other, that the bodily manifestations must first be interposed between, and that the more rational statement is that we feel . . . afraid because we tremble, and not that we . . . tremble, because we are . . . fearful, as the case may be. Without the bodily

states following on the perception, the latter would be purely cognitive in form, pale, colourless, destitute of emotional warmth. We might then see the bear, and judge it best to run . . . but we could not actually *feel* afraid. (James, 1884, p.189)

Thus, in James's view, you don't run because you are afraid, you are afraid because you become aware of your bodily change when you run. A similar proposition was suggested by a contemporary of James, Carl Lange, and the theory was dubbed the James–Lange theory.

So Lange and James theorize that

> The bear (perception of stimulus) → physiologic re-action (adrenaline released causing increased heart and respiratory rates, sweating, and fight-or-flight response) → automatic, *nonconscious* interpretation of the physiological response (my heart is beating fast, I am running; I must be afraid) = subjective emotional feeling (scared!).

Thus James and Lange believed that with emotion there is a specific physiological reaction and that people could not feel an emotion without first having a bodily reaction.

Cannon–Bard Theory

James's proposal caused quite an uproar. A counter-proposal was offered several years later by a pair of physiologists from Harvard, Walter Cannon and Philip Bard. They thought that physiological responses were not distinct enough to distinguish among fear, anger, and sexual attraction, for example. Cannon and Bard also believed that the neuronal and hormonal feed-back processes are too slow to precede and account for the emotions. Cannon (who was the first person to describe the fight-or-flight response) thought that the sympathetic nervous system coordinated the reaction while the cortex *simultaneously* generated the emotional feeling. Cannon found that when he severed the cortex from the brainstem above the hypothalamus and thala-mus, cats still had an *emotional reaction* when provoked. They would growl, bare their teeth, and their hair would stand on end. They had the emotional reaction without cognition. These researchers proposed that an emotion-al stimulus was processed by the thalamus and sent si-multaneously to the neocortex and to the hypothalamus that produced the peripheral response. Thus the neocor-tex generated the emotional feeling while the periphery carried out the slower emotional reaction. Returning to the bear-in-the-woods scenario, the Cannon–Bard theory is

> fast
> cortex (interpretation: → → → scared dangerous situation)
>
> ↑
> The bear → thalamus
> ↓
>
> slower
> hypothalamus   →   emotional reaction
> (sympathetic nervous system)   (fight or flight)

Subsequent research, however, refuted some of Can-non's and Bard's ideas. For instance, Paul Ekman showed that at least some emotional responses (anger, fear, and disgust) can be differentiated by autonomic activity. The Cannon–Bard theory remains important, however, because it introduced into emotion research the model of parallel processing.

Appraisal Theory

Appraisal theory is a group of theories in which emotional processing is dependent on an interaction between the stimulus properties and their interpretation. The theo-ries differ about what is appraised and the criteria used for this appraisal. Since appraisal is a subjective step, it can account for the differences in how people react. Richard Lazarus proposed a version of appraisal theory in which emotions are a response to the reckoning of the ratio of harm versus benefit in a person's encounter with something. In this appraisal step, each of us considers personal and environmental variables when deciding the significance of the stimulus for our well-being. Thus, the cause of the emotion is both the stimulus and its significance. The cognitive appraisal comes before the emotional response or feeling. This appraisal step may be automatic and unconscious.

> He sees the bear → cognition (A quick risk–benefit appraisal is made: A dangerous wild animal is lumbering toward me, and he is showing his teeth → risk/benefit = high risk/no foreseeable benefit → I am in danger!) → Feels the emotion (he's scared!) → response (fight or flight).

Singer–Schachter Theory: Cognitive Interpretation of Arousal

You may have read about the experiment in which in-vestigators gave two different groups of participants an injection of adrenaline (Schachter & Singer, 1962). The control group was told that they would experience the symptoms associated with adrenaline, such as a racing heart. The other group was told they had been injected with vitamins and should not experience any side effects. Each of the participants was then placed with a confederate, who was acting in either a euphoric or an angry manner. When later asked how they felt and why, the participants who knowingly received an adrenaline injection attributed their physiological responses to the drug, and those who did not know they had been given adrenaline attributed their symptoms to the environment (the happy or angry confederate) and interpreted their emotion accordingly. The Singer–Schachter theory of emotion generation is based on these findings. The theory is a blend of the James–Lange and appraisal theories. Singer and Schachter proposed that emotional arousal and then reasoning is required to appraise a stimulus before the emotion can be identified.

So they see the bear → physiological reaction (arousal: heart races, ready to run) → cognition (What's going on? Yikes! We are between a mother and her cub!) = feel the emotion (they're scared!).

Constructivist Theories

Constructivist theories suggest that emotion emerges from cognition as molded by our culture and language. A recent and influential constructivist theory is the conceptual act model, proposed by Lisa Barrett. In this theory, emotions are human-made concepts that emerge as we make meaning out of sensory input from the body and from the world. First we form a mental representation of the bodily changes that have been called **core affect** (Russell, 2003). This representation is then classified according to language-based emotion categories. Barrett suggests that these categories vary with a person's experience and culture, so there are no empirical criteria for judging an emotion (Barrett, 2006b).

Sensory input (she sees the bear) → physiologic response (her heart races, she feels aroused in a negative way) → her brain calculates all previous bear encounters, episodes of racing heart, degree of arousal, valence, and you name it → categorizes the current reaction in reference to all the past ones and ones suggested by her culture and language → ah, this is an emotion, and I call it fear.

Evolutionary Psychology Approach

Evolutionary psychologists Leda Cosmides and John Tooby proposed that emotions are conductors of an orchestra of cognitive programs that need to be coordinated to produce successful behavior (Cosmides & Tooby, 2000). They suggest that the emotions are an overarching program that directs the cognitive subprograms and their interactions.

From this viewpoint, an emotion is not reducible to any one category of effects, such as effects on physiology, behavioral inclinations, cognitive appraisals, or feeling states, because it involves coordinated, evolved *instructions for all of them together*. An emotion also involves instructions for other mechanisms distributed throughout the human mental and physical architecture.

They see the bear → possible stalking and ambush situation is detected (a common scenario of evolutionary significance) and automatically activates a hardwired program (that has evolved thanks to being successful in these types of situations) that directs all of the subprograms.

Response: Perception and attention shift automatically; goal and motivations change from a picnic in the woods to stayin' alive; information-gathering mechanisms are redirected and a change in concepts takes place: looking for the tree as shade for a picnic becomes looking for a tall tree for escape; memory comes on board; communication changes; interpretive systems are activated (did the bear see us? If the answer is no, the people automatically adopt freeze behavior; if it is yes, they scamper); learning systems go on (they may develop a conditioned response to this trail in the future); physiology changes; behavior decision rules are activated (which may be automatic or involuntary) → they run for the tree (whew).

LeDoux's High Road and Low Road

Joseph LeDoux of New York University has proposed that humans have two emotion systems operating in parallel. One is a neural system for our emotional responses that is separate from a system that generates the conscious feeling of emotion. This emotion-response system is hardwired by evolution to produce fast responses that increase our chances of survival and reproduction. Conscious feelings are irrelevant to these responses and are not hardwired, but learned by experience.

fast hardwired fight-or-flight response

LeDoux sees the bear: ⟶ ↑↓

slow cognition (whoa, that looks suspiciously like an *Ursus arctos horribilis*, good thing I've been keeping in shape) → emotion (feels scared)

LeDoux was one of the first cognitive neuroscientists to study emotions. His research on the role of the amygdala in fear has shown that the amygdala plays a major role in emotional processing in general, not just fear. Researchers know more about the role of the amygdala in emotion than they do about the role of other regions of the brain in emotion.

TAKE-HOME MESSAGES

■ Emotions are made up of three psychological components—a physiological response, a behavioral response, and a subjective feeling—that have evolved to allow humans to respond to significant stimuli. The underlying mechanisms and timing of the components are disputed.

■ Researchers do not agree on how emotions are generated, and many theories exist.

The Amygdala

The **amygdalae** (singular: **amygdala**) are small, almond-shaped structures in the medial temporal lobe adjacent to the anterior portion of the hippocampus (Figure 10.7a). Each amygdala is an intriguing and complex structure that in primates is a collection of 13 nuclei. There has been some controversy about the concept of "the amygdala" as a single entity, and some neurobiologists consider the amygdala to be neither a structural nor a functional unit (Swanson & Petrovich, 1998). The nuclei can be grouped into three main amygdaloid complexes (Figure 10.7b).

1. The largest area is the basolateral nuclear complex, consisting of the *lateral*, *basal*, and *accessory basal nuclei*. The *basal nucleus* is the gatekeeper of the amygdala input, receiving inputs from all the sensory systems. The multifaceted basal nucleus is important for mediating instrumental behavior, such as running from bears.

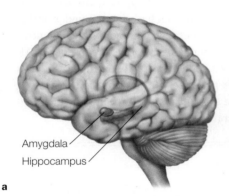

Amygdala
Hippocampus

a

FIGURE 10.7 Location and circuitry of the amygdala.
(a) The left hemisphere amygdala is shown here in its relative position to the lateral brain aspect. It lies deep within the medial temporal lobe adjacent to the anterior aspect of the hippocampus. **(b)** Inputs and outputs to some of the lateral (La), basal (B), and central nuclei (Ce) of the amygdala. Note that the lateral nucleus is the major site receiving sensory inputs and the central nucleus is thought to be the major output region for the expression of innate emotional responses and the physiological responses associated with them. Output connections of the basal nucleus connect with striatal areas involved in the control of instrumental behaviors.

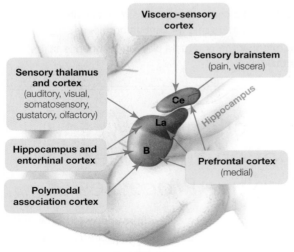

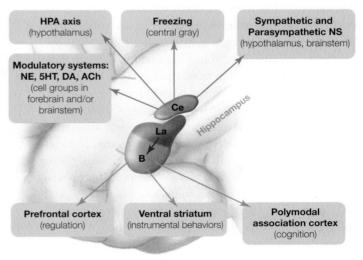

b　　　　　　　Inputs　　　　　　　　　　　　　　　　　Outputs

2. The centromedial complex consists of the *central nucleus* and the *medial nucleus*. The latter is the output region for innate emotional responses including behavioral, autonomic, and endocrine responses. Figure 10.7b depicts some of the inputs and outputs of the lateral (La), basal (B), and central nuclei (Ce).

3. The smallest complex is the *cortical nucleus*, which is also known as the "olfactory part of the amygdala" because its primary input comes from the olfactory bulb and olfactory cortex.

Structures in the medial temporal lobe were first proposed to be important for emotion in the early 20th century, when Heinrich Klüver and Paul Bucy at the University of Chicago (1939) documented unusual emotional responses in monkeys following damage to this region. One of the prominent characteristics, of what later came to be known as *Klüver–Bucy syndrome* (Weiskrantz, 1956), was a lack of fear manifested by a tendency to approach objects that would normally elicit a fear response. The observed deficit was called *psychic blindness* because of an inability to recognize the emotional importance of events or objects. In the 1950s, the amygdala was identified as the primary structure underlying these fear-related deficits. When the amygdala of monkeys was lesioned more selectively, monkeys manifested a normal disproportionate impairment in cautiousness and distrust: They approached novel or frightening objects or potential predators, such as snakes or human strangers. Not just once, they did it again and again, even if they had a bad experience. Once bitten, they were not twice shy. Although humans with amygdala damage do not show all of the classic signs of Klüver–Bucy syndrome, they do exhibit deficits in fear processing, as S.M. demonstrated. She exhibited a lack of cautiousness and distrust (Feinstein et al., 2011), and she too did not learn to avoid what others would term fearful experiences.

While studying the amygdala's role in fear processing, investigators came to realize that it was important for emotional processing in general, because of its vast connections to many other brain regions. In fact, the amygdala is the veritable Godfather of the forebrain and is its most connected structure. The extensive connections to and from the amygdala reflect its critical roles in learning, memory, and attention in response to emotionally significant stimuli. The amygdala contains receptors for the neurotransmitters glutamate, dopamine, norepinephrine, serotonin, and acetylcholine. It also contains hormone receptors for glucocorticoids and estrogen, and peptide receptors for opioids, oxytocin, vasopressin, corticotropin-releasing factor, and neuropeptide Y. There are many ideas concerning what role the amygdala plays. Luiz Pessoa (2011) boils down the amygdala's job description by suggesting that it is involved in determining *what a stimulus is* and *what is to be done about it*; thus, it is involved in attention, perception, value

representation, and decision making. In this vein, Karen Lindquist and colleagues (2012) have proposed that the amygdala is active when the rest of the brain cannot easily predict what sensations mean, what to do about them, or what value they hold in a given context. The amygdala signals other parts of the brain to keep working until these issues have been figured out (Whalen, 2007). Lindquist's proposal has been questioned, however, by people who have extensively studied patient S.M. (Feinstein et al., 2011), the woman we met at the beginning of this chapter. S.M. appears to have no deficit in any emotion other than fear. Even without her amygdala, she correctly understands the salience of emotional stimuli, but she has a specific impairment in the induction and experience of fear across a wide range of situations. People who have studied S.M. suggest that the amygdala is a critical brain region for triggering a state of fear in response to encounters with threatening stimuli in the external environment. They hypothesize that the amygdala furnishes connections between sensory and association cortex that are required to represent external stimuli, as well as connections between the brainstem and hypothalamic circuitry, which are necessary for orchestrating the action program of fear. As we'll see later in this chapter, damage to the lateral amygdala prevents fear conditioning. Without the amygdala, the evolutionary value of fear is lost. For much of the remainder of this chapter, we look at the interplay of emotions and cognitive processes, such as learning, attention, and perception. Although we cannot yet settle the debate on the amygdala's precise role, we will get a feel for how emotion is involved in various cognitive domains as we learn about the amygdala's role in emotion processing.

TAKE-HOME MESSAGES

- The amygdala is the most connected structure in the forebrain.
- The amygdala contains receptors for many different neurotransmitters and for various hormones.
- The role that the amygdala plays in emotion is still controversial.

Interactions Between Emotion and Other Cognitive Processes

In previous chapters, we have not addressed how emotion affects the various cognitive processes that have been discussed. We all know from personal experience, however, that this happens. For instance, if we are angry about something, we may find it hard to concentrate on reading a homework assignment. If we are really enjoying what we are doing, we may not notice we are tired or hungry. When we are sad, we may find it difficult to make decisions or carry out any physical activities. In this section, we look at how emotions modulate the information processing involved in cognitive functions such as learning, attention, and decision making.

The Influence of Emotion on Learning

One day, early in the 20th century, Swiss neurologist and psychologist Édouard Claparède greeted his patient and introduced himself. She introduced herself and shook his hand. Not such a great story, until you know that he had done the same thing every day for the previous five years and his patient never remembered him. She had Korsakoff's syndrome (Chapter 9), characterized by an absence of any short-term memory. One day Claparède concealed a pin in

his palm that pricked his patient when they shook hands. The next day, once again, she did not remember him; but when he extended his hand to greet her, she hesitated for the first time. Claparède was the first to provide evidence that two types of learning, implicit and explicit, apparently are associated with two different pathways (Kihlstrom, 1995).

Implicit Emotional Learning

As first noted by Claparède, implicit learning is a type of Pavlovian learning in which a neutral stimulus (the handshake) acquires aversive properties when paired with an aversive event (the pin prick). This process is a classic example of **fear conditioning**. It is a primary paradigm used to investigate the amygdala's role in emotional learning. Fear conditioning is a form of classical conditioning in which the unconditioned stimulus is aversive. One advantage of using the fear-conditioning paradigm to investigate emotional learning is that it works essentially in the same way across a wide range of species, from fruit flies to humans. One laboratory version of fear conditioning is illustrated in Figure 10.8.

Before training

Light alone (CS): no response

Foot shock alone (US₁): normal startle (UR)

Loud noise alone (US₂): normal startle (UR)

a

During training **After training**

Light and foot shock: normal startle (UR)

Light alone: normal startle (CR)

Light and sound but no foot shock: potentiated startle (potentiated CR)

b **c**

FIGURE 10.8 Fear conditioning.
(a) Before training, three different stimuli—light (CS), foot shock (US₁), and loud noise (US₂)—are presented alone, and both the foot shock and the noise elicit a normal startle response in rats. **(b)** During training, light (CS) and foot shock (US₁) are paired to elicit a normal startle response (UR). **(c)** In tests following training, presentation of light alone now elicits a response (CR), and presentation of the light together with a loud noise but no foot shock elicits a potentiated startle (potentiated CR) because the rat is startled by the loud noise and has associated the light (CS) with the startling foot shock (US).

The light is the *conditioned stimulus* (*CS*). In this example, we are going to condition the rat to associate this neutral stimulus with an aversive stimulus. Before training (Figure 10.8a), however, the light is solely a neutral stimulus and does not evoke a response from the rat. In this pretraining stage, the rat will respond with a normal startle response to any innately aversive *unconditioned stimulus* (*US*)—for example, a foot shock or a loud noise—that invokes an innate fear response. During training (Figure 10.8b), the light is paired with a shock that is delivered immediately before the light is turned off. The rat has a natural fear response to the shock (usually startle or jump), called the *unconditioned response* (*UR*). This stage is referred to as *acquisition*. After a few pairings of the light (CS) and the shock (US), the rat learns that the light predicts the shock, and eventually the rat exhibits a fear response to the light alone (Figure 10.8c). This anticipatory fear response is the *conditioned response* (*CR*).

The CR can be enhanced in the presence of another fearful stimulus or an anxious state, as is illustrated by the potentiated startle reflex exhibited by a rat when it sees the light (the CS) at the same time that it experiences a loud noise (a different US). The CS and resulting CR can become unpaired again if the light (CS) is presented alone, without the shock, for many trials. This phenomenon is called *extinction* because at this point the CR is considered extinguished (and the rat will again display the same response to light as in Figure 10.8a).

Many responses can be assessed as the CR in this type of fear-learning paradigm, but regardless of the stimulus used or the response evoked, one consistent finding has emerged in rats (and we will soon see that this also holds true in humans): Damage to the amygdala impairs conditioned fear responses. Amygdala lesions block the ability to acquire and express a CR to the neutral CS that is paired with the aversive US.

Two Pathways: The High and Low Roads Using the fear-conditioning paradigm, researchers such as Joseph LeDoux (1996), Mike Davis (1992) of Emory University, and Bruce Kapp and his colleagues (1984) of the University of Vermont have mapped out the neural circuits of fear learning, from stimulus perception to emotional response. As Figure 10.9 shows, the lateral nucleus of the amygdala serves as a region of convergence for information from multiple brain regions, allowing for the formation of associations that underlie fear conditioning. Based on results from single-unit recording studies, it is widely accepted that cells in the superior dorsal lateral amygdala have the ability to rapidly undergo changes that pair the CS to the US. After several trials, however, these cells reset to their starting point; but by then, cells in the inferior dorsal lateral region have undergone a change that maintains the adverse association. This result may be why fear that has seemingly been eliminated can return under stress—because it is retained in the memory of these cells (LeDoux, 2007). The lateral nucleus is connected to the central nucleus of the amygdala. These projections to the central nucleus initiate an emotional

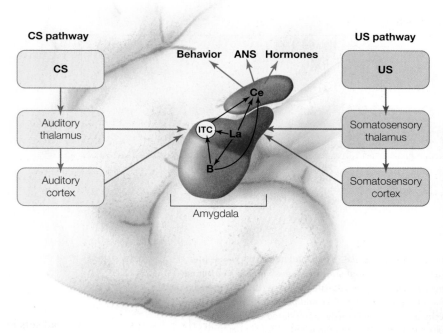

FIGURE 10.9 Amygdala pathways and fear conditioning.
Both the CS and US sensory information enter the amygdala through cortical sensory inputs and thalamic inputs to the lateral nucleus. The convergence of this information in the lateral nucleus induces synaptic plasticity, such that after conditioning, the CS information flows through the lateral nucleus and intra-amygdalar connections to the central nucleus just as the US information does. ITC are intercalated cells, which connect the lateral and basal nuclei with the central nucleus.

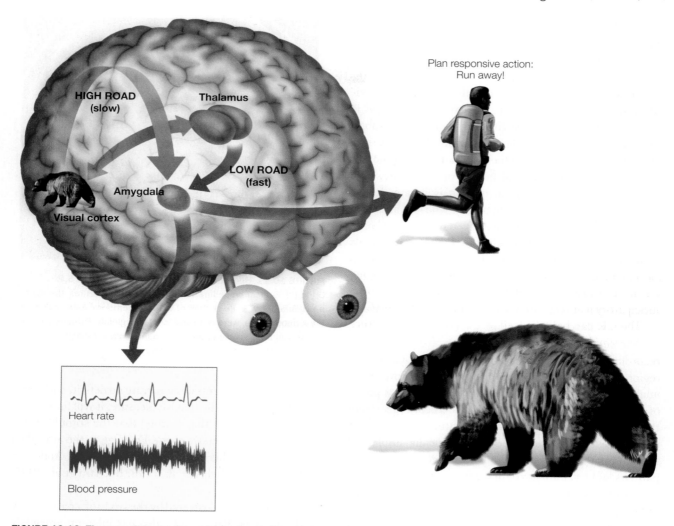

FIGURE 10.10 The amygdala receives sensory input along two pathways.
When a hiker chances upon a bear, the sensory input activates affective memories through the cortical "high road" and subcortical "low road" projections to the amygdala. Even before these memories reach consciousness, however, they produce autonomic changes, such as an increased heart rate, blood pressure, and a startled response such as jumping back. These memories also can influence subsequent actions through the projections to the frontal cortex. The hiker will use this emotion-laden information in choosing his next action: Turn and run, slowly back up, or shout at the bear?

response if a stimulus, after being analyzed and placed in the appropriate context, is determined to represent something threatening or potentially dangerous.

An important aspect of this fear-conditioning circuitry is that information about the fear-inducing stimulus reaches the amygdala through *two separate but simultaneous pathways* (Figure 10.10; LeDoux, 1996). One goes directly from the thalamus to the amygdala without being filtered by conscious control. Signals sent by this pathway, sometimes called the *low road*, reach the amygdala rapidly (15 ms in a rat), although the information this pathway sends is crude. At the same time, sensory information about the stimulus is being projected to the amygdala via another cortical pathway, sometimes referred to as the *high road*. The high road is slower,

taking 300 ms in a rat, but the analysis of the stimulus is more thorough and complete. In this pathway, the sensory information projects to the thalamus; then the thalamus sends this information to the sensory cortex for a finer analysis. The sensory cortex projects the results of this analysis to the amygdala. The low road allows for the amygdala to receive information quickly in order to prime, or ready, the amygdala for a rapid response if the information from the high road confirms that the sensory stimulus is the CS. Although it may seem redundant to have two pathways to send information to the amygdala, when it comes to responding to a threatening stimulus, it is adaptive to be both fast and sure. Now we see the basis of LeDoux's theory of emotion generation (see p. 436). After seeing the bear, the person's faster low road sets in motion the fight-or-flight response, while the slower high road through the cortex provides the learned account of the bear and his foibles.

Is the amygdala particularly sensitive to certain categories of stimuli such as animals? Two lines of evidence suggest that it is. The first has to do with what is called *biological motion*. The visual system extracts subtle movement information from a stimulus that it uses to categorize the stimulus as either animate (having motion characteristic of a biological entity) or inanimate. This ability to recognize biological motion is innate. It has been demonstrated in newborn babies, who will attend to biological motion within the first few days of life (Simion et al., 2008), and it has been identified in other mammals (Blake, 1993). This preferential attention to biological motion is adaptive, alerting us to the presence of other living things. Interestingly, PET studies have shown that the right amygdala is activated when an individual perceives a stimulus exhibiting biological motion (Bonda et al., 1996).

The second line of evidence comes from single-cell recordings from the right amygdala. Neurons in this region have been found to respond preferentially to images of animals. This effect was shown by a group of researchers who did single-cell recordings from the amygdala, hippocampus, and entorhinal cortex in patients who had had electrodes surgically implanted to monitor their epilepsy. The recordings were made as patients looked at images of persons, animals, landmarks, or objects. Neurons in the right amygdala, but not the left, responded preferentially to pictures of animals rather than to pictures of other stimulus categories. There was no difference in the amygdala's response to threatening or cute animals. This categorical selectivity provides evidence of a domain-specific mechanism for processing this biologically important class of stimuli that includes predators or prey (Mormann et al., 2011).

Amygdala's Effect on Implicit Learning The role of the amygdala in learning to respond to stimuli that have come to represent aversive events through fear conditioning is said to be *implicit*. This term is used because the *learning is expressed indirectly* through a behavioral or physiological response, such as autonomic nervous system arousal or potentiated startle. When studying nonhuman animals, we can assess the CR only through indirect, or implicit, means of expression. The rat is startled when the light goes on. In humans, however, we can also assess the response directly, by asking the participants to report if they know that the CS represents a potential aversive consequence (the US). Patients with amygdala damage fail to demonstrate an indirect CR—for instance, they would not shirk Claparède's handshake. When asked to report the parameters of fear conditioning explicitly or consciously,

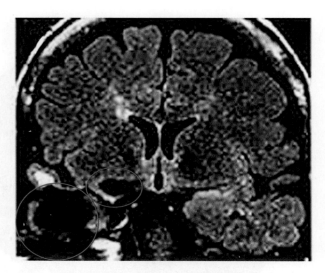

FIGURE 10.11 Bilateral amygdala lesions in patient S.P. During a surgical procedure to reduce epileptic seizures, the right amygdala and a large section of the right temporal lobe, including the hippocampus, were removed (circled regions). Pathology in the left amygdala is visible in the white band, indicating regions where cells were damaged by neural disease.

however, these patients demonstrate no deficit, and might respond with "Oh, the handshake, sure, it will hurt a bit." Thus, we know that they learned that the stimulus is associated with an aversive event. Damage to the amygdala appears to leave this latter ability intact (A. K. Anderson & Phelps, 2001; Phelps et al., 1998; Bechara et al., 1995; LaBar et al., 1995).

This concept is illustrated by the study of a patient very much like S.M. Patient S.P. also has bilateral amygdala damage (Figure 10.11). To relieve epilepsy, at age 48 S.P. underwent a lobectomy that removed her right amygdala. MRI at that time revealed that her left amygdala was already damaged, most likely from mesial temporal sclerosis, a syndrome that causes neuronal loss in the medial temporal regions of the brain (A. K. Anderson & Phelps, 2001; Phelps et al., 1998). Like S.M., S.P. is unable to recognize fear in the faces of others (Adolphs et al., 1999).

In a study on the role of the amygdala in human fear conditioning, S.P. was shown a picture of a blue square (the CS), which the experimenters periodically presented for 10 s. During the acquisition phase, S.P. was given a mild electrical shock to the wrist (the US) at the end of the 10-s presentation of the blue square (the CS). In measures of skin conductance response (Figure 10.12), S.P.'s performance was as predicted: She showed a normal fear response to the shock (the UR), but no change in response when the blue square (the CS) was presented, even after several acquisition trials. This lack of change in the skin conductance response to the blue square demonstrates that she failed to acquire a CR.

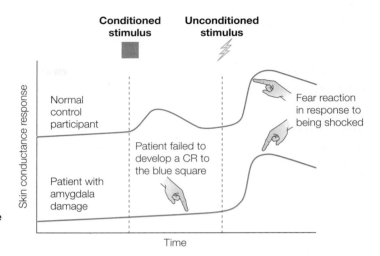

FIGURE 10.12 S.P. showed no skin conductance response to conditioned stimuli.

Unlike control participants, S.P. (red line) showed no response to the blue square (CS) after training but did respond to the shock (the US).

Following the experiment, S.P. was shown her data and that of a control participant, as illustrated in Figure 10.12, and she was asked what she thought. She was somewhat surprised that she showed no change in skin conductance response (the CR) to the blue square (the CS). She reported that she knew after the very first acquisition trial that she was going to get a shock to the wrist when the blue square was presented. She claimed to have figured this out early on and expected the shock whenever she saw the blue square. She was not sure what to make of the fact that her skin conductance response did not reflect what she consciously knew to be true. This dissociation between intact explicit knowledge of the events that occurred during fear conditioning and impaired conditioned responses has been observed in other patients with amygdala damage (Bechara et al., 1995; LaBar et al., 1995).

As discussed in Chapter 9, explicit or declarative memory for events depends on another medial temporal lobe structure: the hippocampus, which, when damaged, impairs the ability to explicitly report memory for an event. When the conditioning paradigm that we described for S.P. was conducted with patients who had bilateral damage to the hippocampus but an intact amygdala, the opposite pattern of performance emerged. These patients showed a normal skin conductance response to the blue square (the CS), indicating acquisition of the conditioned response. When asked what had occurred during conditioning, however, they were unable to report that the presentations of the blue square were paired with the shock, or even that a blue square was presented at all—just like Claparède's patient.

This double dissociation between patients who have amygdala lesions and patients with hippocampal lesions is evidence that the amygdala is necessary for the implicit expression of emotional learning, but not for all forms of emotional learning and memory. The hippocampus is necessary for the acquisition of explicit or declarative knowledge of the emotional properties of a stimulus, whereas the amygdala is critical for the acquisition and expression of an implicitly conditioned fear response.

Explicit Emotional Learning

The double dissociation just described clearly indicates that the amygdala is necessary for implicit emotional learning, but not for explicit emotional learning. This does not mean that the amygdala is uninvolved with explicit learning and memory. How do we know? Let's look at an example of explicit emotional learning.

Liz is walking down the street in her neighborhood and sees a neighbor's dog, Fang, on the sidewalk. Even though she is a dog owner herself and likes dogs in general, Fang scares her. When she encounters him, she becomes nervous and fearful, so she decides to walk on the other side of the street. Why might Liz, who likes dogs, be afraid of this particular dog? There are a few possible reasons: For example, perhaps Fang bit her once. In this case, her fear response to Fang was acquired through fear conditioning. Fang (the CS) was paired with the dog bite (the US), resulting in pain and fear (the UR) and an acquired fear response to Fang in particular (the CR).

Liz may fear Fang for another reason, however. She has heard from her neighbor that this is a mean dog that *might* bite her. In this case she has no aversive experience linked to this particular dog. Instead, she learned about the aversive properties of the dog explicitly. Her ability to learn and remember this type of information depends on her hippocampal memory system. She likely did not experience a fear response when she learned this information during a conversation with her neighbor. She did not experience a fear response until she actually encountered Fang. Thus, her reaction is not based on actual experience with the dog, but rather is anticipatory and based on her explicit knowledge of the potential aversive properties of this dog. This type of learning, in which we learn to fear or avoid a stimulus because of what we are told (as opposed to actually having the experience), is a common example of emotional learning in humans.

The Amygdala Effect on Explicit Learning The question is this: Does the amygdala play a role in the indirect expression of the fear response in *instructed* fear? From what we know about patient S.M., what would you guess? Elizabeth Phelps of New York University and her colleagues (Funayama et al., 2001; Phelps et al., 2001) addressed this question using an *instructed fear paradigm*, in which the participant was told that a blue square may be paired with a shock. They found that, even though explicit learning of the emotional properties of the blue square depends on the hippocampal memory system, the amygdala is critical for the expression of some fear responses to the blue square (Figure 10.13a). During the instructed-fear paradigm, patients with amygdala damage *were able to learn and explicitly report* that some presentations of the blue square might be paired with a shock to the wrist. In truth, though, none of the participants ever received a shock. Unlike normal control participants, however, patients with amygdala damage *did not show a potentiated startle response when the blue square was presented.* They knew consciously that they would receive a shock, but had no emotional response. Normal control participants showed an increase in skin conductance response to the blue square that was correlated with amygdala activity

(Figure 10.13b). These results suggest that, in humans, the amygdala is sometimes critical for the indirect expression of a fear response when the emotional learning occurs explicitly. Similar deficits have been observed when patients with amygdala lesions respond to emotional scenes (Angrilli et al., 1996; Funayama et al., 2001).

Although animal models of emotional learning highlight the role of the amygdala in fear conditioning and the indirect expression of the conditioned fear response, human emotional learning can be much more complex. We can learn that stimuli in the world are linked to potentially aversive consequences in a variety of ways, including instruction, observation, and experience. In whatever way we learn the aversive or threatening nature of stimuli—whether explicit and declarative, implicit, or both—the amygdala may play a role in the indirect expression of the fear response to those stimuli.

Amygdala, Arousal, and Modulation of Memory The instructed-fear studies indicate that when an individual is taught that a stimulus is dangerous, amygdala activity can be influenced by a hippocampal-dependent declarative representation about the emotional properties of stimuli (in short, the memory that someone told you the dog was mean). The amygdala activity subsequently modulates some indirect emotional responses. But is it possible for the reverse to occur? Can the amygdala modulate the activity of the hippocampus? Put another way, can the amygdala influence what you learn and remember about an emotional event?

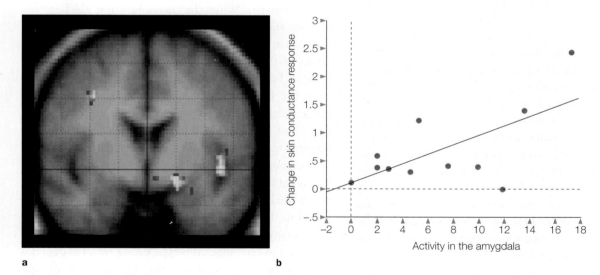

a   b

FIGURE 10.13 Responses to instructed fear.
(a) While performing a task in the instructed fear protocol, participants showed an arousal response (measured by skin conductance response) consistent with fear to the blue square, which they were told might be linked to a shock. The presentation of the blue square also led to amygadal activation.
(b) There is a correlation between the strength of the skin conductance response indicating arousal and the activation of the amygdala.

The types of things we recollect every day are things like where we left the keys, what we said to a friend the night before, or whether we turned the iron off before leaving the house. When we look back on our lives, however, we do not remember these mundane events. We remember a first kiss, being teased by a friend in school, opening our college acceptance letter, or hearing about a horrible accident. The memories that last over time are those of emotional (not just fearful) or important (i.e., arousing) events. These memories seem to have a persistent vividness that other memories lack.

James McGaugh and his colleagues (1992, 1996; Ferry & McGaugh, 2000) at the University of California, Irvine, investigated whether this persistence of emotional memories is related to the action of the amygdala during emotional arousal. An arousal response can influence people's ability to store declarative or explicit memories. For example, investigators frequently use the Morris water maze task (see Chapter 9) to test a rat's spatial abilities and memory. McGaugh found that a lesion to the amygdala does not impair the rats' ability to learn this task under ordinary circumstances. If a rat with a normal amygdala is aroused immediately after training, by either a physical stressor or the administration of drugs that mimic an arousal response, then the rat will show improved retention of this task. The memory is *enhanced* by arousal. In rats with a lesion to the amygdala, however, this arousal-induced enhancement of memory, rather than memory acquisition itself, is blocked (McGaugh et al., 1996). Using pharmacological lesions to temporarily disable the amygdala immediately after learning also eliminates any arousal-enhanced memory effect (Teather et al., 1998).

Two important aspects of this work help us understand the mechanism underlying the role of the amygdala in enhancing declarative memory that has been observed with arousal. *The first is that the amygdala's role is modulatory.* The tasks used in these studies depend on the hippocampus for acquisition. In other words, the amygdala is not necessary for learning this hippocampal-dependent task, but it is necessary for the arousal-dependent modulation of memory for this task.

The second important facet of this work is that this effect of modulation with arousal can occur *after* initial encoding of the task, *during the retention interval.* All of these studies point to the conclusion that the amygdala modulates hippocampal, declarative memory by *enhancing retention*, rather than by altering the initial encoding of the stimulus. Because this effect occurs during retention, the amygdala is thought to enhance hippocampal consolidation. As described in Chapter 9, *consolidation* occurs over time, after initial encoding, and leads to memories becoming more or less stable. Thus,

when there is an arousal response, the amygdala alters hippocampal processing by strengthening the consolidation of memories. McGaugh and colleagues (1996) showed that the basolateral nucleus of the amygdala is important for this effect. Additional evidence, however, also suggests that the amygdala can interact directly with the hippocampus during the *initial* encoding phase (not just the consolidation phase) of an experience, which in turn also positively affects the long-term consolidation (Dolcos et al., 2004). Thus, the amygdala can modulate hippocampal-dependent declarative memory at multiple stages, leading to a net effect of enhanced retention.

This role for the amygdala in enhancing emotional, declarative memory has also been demonstrated in humans. Various studies over the years have indicated that a mild arousal response can enhance declarative memory for emotional events (e.g., see Christianson, 1992). This effect of arousal on declarative memory is blocked in patients with bilateral amygdala damage (Cahill et al., 1995). Interestingly, studies on patients with unilateral amygdala damage reveal that the right, and not the left, amygdala is most important for the retrieval of autobiographical emotional memories relating to negative valence and high arousal (Buchanan et al., 2006). In addition, functional neuroimaging studies have shown that activity observed in the human amygdala during the presentation of emotional stimuli is correlated with the arousal-enhanced recollection of these stimuli (Cahill et al., 1996; Hamann et al., 1999). The more active the amygdala, the stronger the memory. There is also increased effective connectivity bidirectionally between the amygdala and hippocampus during recall of emotional information that is relative to current behavior (A.P.R. Smith et al., 2006). These studies indicate that normal amygdala function plays a role in the enhanced declarative memory observed with arousal in humans.

The mechanism for this effect of arousal appears to be related to the amygdala's role in modifying the rate of forgetting for arousing stimuli. In other words, *arousal may alter how quickly we forget.* This is consistent with the notion of a post-encoding effect on memory, such as enhancing hippocampal storage or consolidation. Although the ability to recollect arousing and nonarousing events may be similar immediately after they occur, arousing events are not forgotten as quickly as nonarousing events are (Kleinsmith & Kaplan, 1963). Unlike normal control participants, who show less forgetting over time for arousing compared to nonarousing stimuli, patients with amygdala lesions forget arousing and nonarousing stimuli at the same rate (LaBar & Phelps, 1998).

Studies on both animal models and human populations converge on the conclusion that the amygdala acts to *modulate hippocampal consolidation* for arousing events. This mechanism, however, does not underlie all the effects of emotion on human declarative memory. Emotional events are more distinctive and unusual than are everyday life events. They also form a specific class of events. These and other factors may enhance declarative or explicit memory for emotional events in ways that do not depend on the amygdala (Phelps et al., 1998).

Stress and Memory It appears that acute stress can facilitate memory. Kevin LaBar and his colleagues at Duke University (Zorawski et al., 2006) have found that the amount of endogenous stress hormone (cortisol) released during the acquisition of a conditioned fear accurately predicts how well fear memories are retained one day later in humans. Robert Sapolsky of Stanford University (1992) and his colleagues demonstrated, however, that extreme arousal or chronic stress may actually *impair* performance of the hippocampal memory system. This memory impairment is due to the effect of excessive stress hormones, such as glucocorticoids, on the hippocampus. The precise role of the amygdala in this impairment of hippocampal memory during chronic or excessive stress is not fully understood.

The amygdala's interactions with the hippocampal memory system and explicit memory are specific and complex. The amygdala acts to modulate the storage of arousing events, thus ensuring that they will not be forgotten over time. And luckily, we can learn explicitly that stimuli in the environment are linked to potential aversive consequences, without having to experience these consequences ourselves (Listen to Mom!). This explicit, hippocampal-dependent representation of the emotional properties of events can affect amygdala activity and certain indirect fear responses. The interactions of the amygdala and hippocampus help ensure that we remember important and emotionally charged information and events for a long time. These memories ultimately ensure that our bodily response to threatening events is appropriate and adaptive.

The Influence of Emotion on Perception and Attention

No doubt you have had the experience of being in the midst of a conversation and hearing your name mentioned behind you—and you immediately turn to see who said it. We exhibit an increased awareness for and pay attention to emotionally salient stimuli. Attention researchers often use the *attentional blink paradigm*, in which stimuli are presented so quickly in succession that an individual stimulus is difficult to identify. When participants are told that they can ignore most of the stimuli—say, all the

words printed in green and attend only to the few targets printed in blue—then participants are able to identify the targets. This ability, however, is limited by the amount of time between the target (blue) stimuli. If a second target stimulus is presented immediately after the first, in what is known as the early lag period, participants will often miss this second target. This impaired perceptual report reflects the temporal limitations of attention and is known as the **attentional blink**. If, however, that second word is emotionally significant, then people notice it (Anderson, 2005). An emotionally significant word is distinctive, arousing (energizing), and has either a positive or negative valence. In this experiment, arousal value (how reactive the participant is to a stimulus), not the valence of the word or its distinctiveness, overcame the attentional blink. Studies have shown that when the left amygdala is damaged, then patients don't recognize the second target even if it is an arousing word (Anderson & Phelps, 2001). So it appears that when attentional resources are limited, it is the arousing emotional stimuli that reach awareness, and the amygdala again plays a critical role in enhancing our attention when emotional stimuli are present.

There are two theories about how this happens. One is that emotional learning involves an enduring change in sensory cortical tuning, and the other is that it produces a more transient change.

The first theory arose out of fear conditioning studies done on rats (Weinberger, 1995). It was found that the auditory cortex became especially sensitive to the stimuli used for the conditioned stimulus. Classical conditioning and fear conditioning (Bakin et al., 1996) shift the tuning frequency of the cortical neurons to the frequency of the conditioned stimulus. This cortical plasticity of the receptor field is associative and highly specific. It happens quickly and is retained indefinitely. The idea is that changes that occur in perceptual processing for stimuli with emotional properties (acquired through learning) are long lasting. Although this mechanism has not been explicitly demonstrated in humans, hints of it have been observed. In imaging studies, in which fear conditioning occurred using subliminally exposed face stimuli as the CS, with an aversive loud noise as the US, an *increasing* responsiveness to the CS was seen in both the amygdala and in the visual cortex over a series of trials (J. S. Morris et al., 2001). The presence of a learning response occurring in parallel in the amygdala and the visual cortex supports the idea that feedback efferents from the amygdala to the visual cortex act to modulate visual processing of emotionally salient stimuli.

The second theory proposes a mechanism that produces a more transient change in attentional thresholds. Recall that the amygdala has reciprocal connections with the sensory cortical processing regions and that it receives inputs of emotional significance before awareness takes place. Studies have indicated that attention and awareness don't have much impact on the amygdala's response to fearful stimuli (A. K. Anderson et al., 2003; Vuilleumier et al., 2001), which is consistent with the finding that the emotional qualities of stimuli are processed automatically (Zajonc, 1984). Thus, although you may be thinking about your lunch while hiking up the trail, you will still be startled at movement in the grass. You have just experienced a rapid and automatic transient change in attention spurred by emotional stimuli. The proposed mechanism for this attentional change is that early in the perceptual processing of the stimulus, the amygdala receives input about its emotional significance and, through projections to sensory cortical regions, modulates the attentional and perceptual processes (A.K. Anderson & Phelps, 2001; Vuilleumier et al., 2004). This idea is based first on the finding that there is enhanced activation of visual cortical regions to novel emotional stimuli (Kosslyn et al., 1996), combined with imaging studies that showed a correlation between visual cortex activation and amygdala activation in response to these same stimuli (Morris et al., 1998). Some evidence suggests that *novelty* is a characteristic of a stimulus that engages the amygdala independently of other affective properties such as valence and arousal. A recent fMRI study that examined valence, arousal, and novelty of emotional photo images found that the amygdala had higher peak responses and was activated longer for novel stimuli versus familiar stimuli, and the effect was independent of both valence and arousal (Weierich et al., 2010). The investigators also observed increased activity in early visual areas V1 and V2 when participants viewed novel emotional stimuli. This activation was different from the activation seen in later visual areas that occurred for valence and arousal.

What's more, fMRI studies show that patients with damage to the amygdala do not show significant activation for fearful versus neutral faces in the visual cortex, whereas controls and patients with hippocampal damage do. Taken together, it seems that when emotional stimuli are present, the amygdala has a leading role in mediating the transient changes in visual cortical processing.

Clearly, the amygdala is critical in getting an unattended but emotional stimulus into the realm of conscious awareness by providing some feedback to the primary sensory cortices, thus affecting perceptual processing. This function was demonstrated by Phelps and her colleagues (2006). They examined the effect of fearful face cues on contrast sensitivity—an aspect of visual processing that occurs early in the primary visual cortex and is enhanced by covert attention. They found that when a face cue directed covert attention, contrast sensitivity was enhanced. This was an expected result. The

interesting finding was that a fearful face enhanced contrast sensitivity, whether covert attention was directed to the face or not. So the emotion-laden stimulus enhanced perception without the aid of attention. The team also found that if the fearful face did cue attention, contrast sensitivity was enhanced even more than would have been predicted for the independent effects of a fearful face and covert attention. Thus emotion-laden stimuli receive greater attention and priority perceptual processing.

Emotion and Decision Making

Let's say you have a big decision to make, and it has an uncertain outcome. You are considering elective knee surgery. You don't need the surgery to survive; you get around OK, and you have no trouble boogie boarding. The problem is, you can't do your favorite sport, snowboarding. You anticipate that you will be able to snowboard again if you have surgery. There is a drawback to this plan, however. What if you have the surgery and it doesn't go so well? You could end up worse off than you are now (it happened to a friend of yours), and you would regret having had it done. What will you decide, and exactly what is going on in your brain as you go through this decision-making process?

Many decision models are based on mathematic and economic principles, and we will talk more about decision making in Chapters 12 and 13. Although these models are built on the logical principles of cost–benefit analysis, they fail to describe how people actually act. In constructing these models, it became obvious some factor in decision making was not being taken into account. In the early 1990s, Antonio Damasio and his colleagues at the University of Iowa made a surprising discovery while working with patient E.V.R., who had orbitofrontal cortex (OFC) damage. When faced with social reasoning tasks, E.V.R. could generate solutions to problems, but he could not prioritize his solutions based on their ability to solve the problem. In the real world, he made poor decisions about his professional and social life (Saver & Damasio, 1991). The researchers, studying a group of patients with similar lesions, found that the patients had difficulty anticipating the consequences of their actions and did not learn from their mistakes (Bechara et al., 1994). This discovery was surprising because at that time, researchers believed the orbitofrontal cortex handled emotional functions. Their belief was based on the many connections of the OFC to the insular cortex and the cingulate cortex, the amygdala, and the hypothalamus—all areas involved with emotion processing. Because emotion was considered a disruptive force in decision making, it was surprising that impairing a region involved in emotion would result in impaired decision making. Seemingly, an individual's decision-making ability should have improved with such a lesion. Damasio wondered whether damage to the orbito-frontal cortex impaired decision making because emotion was actually needed to optimize it. At the time, this was a shocking suggestion. To test this idea, Damasio and his colleagues devised the Iowa Gambling Task. In the Iowa Gambling Task, skin conductance response (SCR) is measured while participants continually draw cards from their choice of four decks. The cards indicate monetary amounts resulting in either gain or loss. What participants don't know is that two of the decks are associated with net winnings; although they have low payoffs, they have even lower losses. The other two decks are associated with net losses because, although they have high payoffs, they have even larger losses. Participants must figure out that they can earn the most money by choosing the decks associated with net winnings yet low payoffs.

Healthy adults and patients with damage outside the orbitofrontal cortex gamble in a manner that maximizes winnings. In contrast, patients with orbitofrontal damage fail to favor the decks that result in net winnings. Based on these results, Damasio proposed the somatic marker hypothesis, which states that emotional information, in the form of physiological arousal, is needed to guide decision making. When presented with a situation that requires us to make a decision, we may react emotionally to the situation around us. This emotional reaction is manifest in our bodies as **somatic markers**—changes in physiological arousal. It is theorized that orbitofrontal structures support learning the associations between a complex situation and the somatic changes (i.e., emotional state) usually associated with that particular situation. The orbitofrontal cortex and other brain regions together consider previous situations that elicited similar patterns of somatic change. Once these situations have been identified, the orbitofrontal cortex can use these experiences to rapidly evaluate possible behavioral responses and their likelihood for reward. Decision making can then selectively focus on option–outcome pairings that are potentially rewarding.

Based on our current understanding, three types of emotions influence decision making.

1. Your current emotional state.
2. Your anticipatory emotions; the ones that occur before you make your decision.
3. Based on personal experience, the emotion that you expect to feel after you have made the decision.

Although acquisition of fear conditioning requires the amygdala, normal *extinction* of a conditioned response (that is, learning that there has been a change and the stimulus is no longer associated with a punishment) involves interactions of the amygdala and the prefrontal

cortex (Morgan & LeDoux, 1999). It has been suggested that the Iowa Gambling Task may be challenging for patients with orbitofrontal damage because it requires them to change their initial perceptions of the potential for rewards in the risky decks (Fellows & Farah, 2005). The decks with the net losses are very appealing at the beginning of the task because the rewards are so large. As participants continue to draw cards from those decks, however, the monumental losses begin to appear. These researchers found that if the task is modified so that the card order in the decks makes it clear earlier in the task that there are large wins but even larger losses, then patients with orbitofrontal damage perform this task as well as do healthy control participants. Thus, it appears that OFC damage results in the *inability to respond to changing patterns of reward and punishment.* Reversal learning does not take place, and these patients don't learn from experience. This finding is consistent with research in monkeys, where investigators found that orbitofrontal damage makes it difficult to reverse an association once it has been learned (Jones & Mishkin, 1972). Single-cell recordings in monkeys have identified specific neurons in the OFC that respond only when reinforcement contingencies change (i.e., how closely an action or stimulus is linked to a reward or punishment; Rolls et al., 1996).

Edmund Rolls and his colleagues believe that emotion is the motivator for seeking reward and avoiding punishment. They investigated whether the OFC was activated by abstract rewards and punishment, such as winning or losing money. If so, they wondered if the neural representations were distinct or overlapping, and if there were any correlation to activation and amounts of reward or punishments. Using an event-related fMRI study, they determined that the OFC has distinct regions for reward and punishment. The lateral OFC is activated following a punishing outcome, and the medial OFC for a rewarding one. The amount of activation correlated positively with the magnitude of the reward or punishment (O'Doherty et al., 2001). The medial region that showed increased activation to reward also exhibited a decreased BOLD signal when punishment was meted out. Similarly, the lateral orbitofrontal cortex region that was activated when the outcome was punishment showed a decreased BOLD signal when the outcome was a reward. Thus an inability to represent the magnitude of rewards and punishments (i.e., the cost–benefit ratio) would obviously lead to poor decision making. We see that the OFC is selectively active for the magnitude of reward and punishment and for their changing patterns.

Regret is the feeling you get when you compare the voluntary choice you made with rejected alternatives that might have turned out better. You feel regret because you are able to think counterfactually. You can say, "If I had done this instead of that, then things would have been better." We dislike feeling regret, and so we learn from our experience and take steps to minimize feeling regret by making choices to avoid it. In contrast, disappointment is an emotion related to an unexpected negative outcome without the sense of personal responsibility. "I won teacher of the year, but because I was the last one hired, I was the first one fired." People with OFC lesions have normal emotional reactions to their wins and losses, but they do not feel regret. They also do not learn from regret-inducing decisions or anticipate negative consequences of their choices (Camille et al., 2004).

To study the brain activity associated with regret, Georgio Coricelli and his colleagues (2005) induced regret in healthy participants by having them make a gambling choice and then telling them the better outcome of the unchosen gamble. Using fMRI, the researchers found that enhanced activity in the medial OFC, the anterior cingulate cortex, and the anterior hippocampus correlated with increasing regret. The more the choice was regretted, the greater the activity of the medial OFC. They also found that after multiple trials, their participants became risk averse, a behavior reflected in enhanced activity within the medial OFC and the amygdala. This same pattern of activation was also exhibited just before making a choice. This intriguing result suggests *that the same circuit mediates both the experience and the anticipation of the emotion of regret.* The team also observed different patterns of neural activation when participants were experiencing regret (medial OFC), when they were simply evaluating results (processed in the ventral striatum), and when they were experiencing disappointment for an outcome that was less than expected (middle temporal gyrus and brainstem). The researchers found that the feeling of regret strongly influences decision choice, leading to more risk-aversive choices over time.

The emotion that you are feeling can influence your decision. For example, say you are leafing through the paper that your professor just returned. You spent your entire three-day weekend working very hard on that paper. As you flip it over to see your grade, a friend comes up and asks you to head up the fund drive for your soccer club. What you see on that paper will produce an emotion in you—elation, frustration, satisfaction—that may affect the response you give to your friend.

What function is served by having emotions play such a role in decision making? Ellen Peters (2006) and her colleagues suggest that experienced feelings about a stimulus and feelings that are independent of the stimulus, such as mood states, have four roles in decision making.

1. They can act as information.
2. They can act as "common currency" between disparate inputs and options (you can feel slightly aroused by a book and very aroused by a swimming pool).
3. They can focus attention on new information, which can then guide the decision.
4. They can motivate approach or avoid behavior decisions.

Hans-Rüdiger Pfister and Gisela Böhm (2008) suggest four different categories in which emotions have a role in decision making: to provide information about pleasure and pain to build preferences, to enable rapid choices under time pressure, to focus attention on relevant aspects of a decision problem, and to generate commitment concerning morally and socially significant decisions.

Emotion and Social Stimuli

Chapter 13 covers the topic of social cognition, which involves how we recognize emotions in others. Here in Chapter 10, we introduce some aspects of social cognition as they relate to emotional processing.

Facial Expressions Studies have shown that there is a dissociation between identifying an individual's face and identifying the emotional expression on that face. Our patient S.M. had no trouble identifying faces; she just couldn't recognize the expression of fear on a face. People with amygdalar damage do not have a problem recognizing nonemotional facial features. In addition, they are able to recognize the similarity between facial expressions whose emotional content they label incorrectly. What's more, their deficit appears to be restricted to the *recognition* of facial expressions. Some of them are able to generate and communicate a full range of facial expressions themselves (A. K. Anderson & Phelps, 2000). Depending on the specific facial expression, it appears that different neural mechanisms and regions of the brain are at work, not for processing specific facial expressions per se, but more generally for processing different emotions.

Evidence for this idea comes from studies in which investigators presented different facial expressions to participants while they were undergoing PET scans. The scans were then analyzed to identify areas of the brain that were uniquely activated for the emotions they saw (Figure 10.14). James Blair and colleagues (1999) applied this strategy in a landmark study of the neural basis of anger. They used a computer program to manipulate a neutral facial expression into one that looked increasingly angry (Figure 10.14a) and searched for brain activation associated with the gradient of expression intensity. They found that the right **orbitofrontal cortex** (**OFC**; see Figure 10.3b) was increasingly active when participants viewed increasingly expressive angry faces

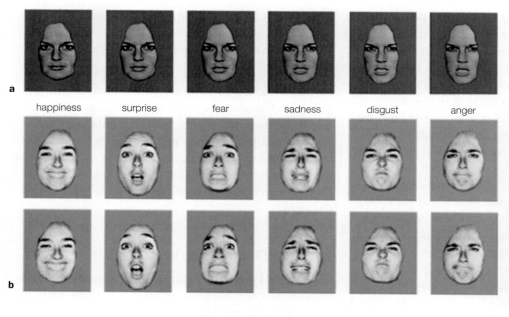

FIGURE 10.14 Examples of morphed facial expressions. (a) Transition from a neutral expression (far left) to an angry expression (far right) in increments of 20% increased intensity. (b) Exaggeration of various facial expressions from 100% (top row) to 150% (bottom row). Facial expressions produced by morphing software have proven to be useful stimuli for investigating the neural correlates of facial expression identification.

(Figure 10.15). This region was not active when participants viewed sad faces. These results suggest a role for the OFC in explicit emotional labeling of angry faces.

Neuroimaging experiments in normal participants and patients with anxiety disorders have reported increased amygdala activation in response to brief presentations of faces with fearful expressions compared to faces with neutral expressions (Breiter et al., 1996; Cahill et al., 1996; Irwin et al., 1996; Morris et al., 1998). Although the amygdala is activated in response to other emotional expressions, such as happy or angry, the activation response to fear is significantly greater. One interesting aspect of the amygdala's response to fearful facial expressions is that the participant does not have to be aware of seeing the fearful face for the amygdala to respond. When fearful facial expressions are presented subliminally and then masked with neutral expressions, the amygdala is activated as strongly as when the participant is aware of seeing the faces (Whalen et al., 1998).

This critical role for the amygdala in explicitly evaluating fearful faces also extends to other social judgments about faces, such as indicating from a picture of a face whether the person appears trustworthy or approachable (Adolphs et al., 2000; Said et al., 2010). Once again, this observation is consistent with the behavior of patients with amygdala damage, who rated pictures of individuals whose faces were deemed untrustworthy by normal controls as both more trustworthy and more approachable (Adolphs et al., 1998).

After nearly a decade of testing S.M., Ralph Adolphs and his colleagues (Adolphs et al., 2005; Kennedy and Adolphs, 2010) discovered an explanation for her inability to recognize fearful faces. Using computer software that exposed only parts of either a fearful or happy facial expression, the researchers were able to figure out what regions of the face participants relied on to discriminate between expressions. They found that control participants consistently relied on eyes to make decisions about expression. S.M., on the other hand, did not derive information from the eyes. Indeed, a subsequent experiment using eye-tracking technology confirmed that she did not even look at the eyes of *any* face, regardless of the emotion it conveyed (Figure 10.16a). So if, unlike controls, S.M. did not automatically use eyes to derive information from faces, why did she only have trouble with identifying fear?

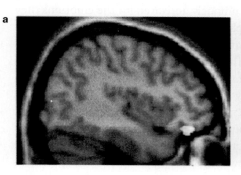
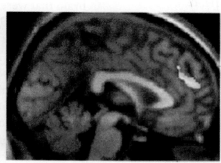

FIGURE 10.15 Neural correlates of the perception of anger. Activity in the (a) right orbitofrontal cortex and (b) anterior cingulate increased as the intensity of an angry facial expression increased.

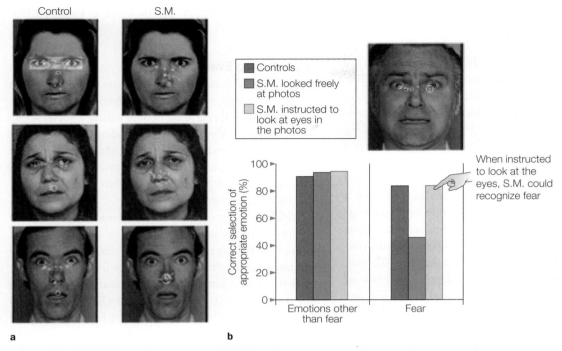

Control   S.M.

■ Controls
■ S.M. looked freely at photos
□ S.M. instructed to look at eyes in the photos

When instructed to look at the eyes, S.M. could recognize fear

Correct selection of appropriate emotion (%)

Emotions other than fear   Fear

a   b

FIGURE 10.16 Abnormal eye movement patterns during face perception following amygdala lesions.
(a) Unlike control participants, S.M.'s eye movements do not target the eyes of other faces. **(b)** When instructed to focus on the eyes, however, S.M. is able to identify fearful expressions as well as controls can. The top panel shows that, when instructed, S.M. is able to look at the eyes. Red lines indicate eye movements and white circles indicate points of fixation.

Most expressions contain other cues that can be used for identification. For instance, an expression of happiness reliably contains a smile, and disgust a snarl of sorts. The identifying feature of a fearful expression, however, is the increase in size of the white region (sclera) of the eyes (Figure 10.17). This prominent characteristic is captured by the frequently used phrase, "I could see the fear in his eyes." More empirically, one study found that viewing sclera from a fearful face without any other accompanying facial information is sufficient to increase amygdala activity in normal participants (relative to sclera from facial expressions of happiness; Whalen et al., 2004).

In another study, investigators masked expressions of happiness or sadness in order to find brain areas associated with automatic, implicit analysis of emotion (Killgore & Yurgelun-Todd, 2004). These investigators found amygdala activity associated with analysis of happy but not sad faces. Although a smile is part of a happy expression, a smile can be faked. First observed by Duchenne and known as the Duchenne smile, the telling part of a truly happy facial expression is the contraction of the orbicularis oculi muscle, which cannot be done voluntarily by most people (Ekman, 2003). This causes the lateral eye margins to crinkle, the cheeks to be pulled up, and the lateral portion of the brow to drop. Perhaps amygdala activation when looking at happy faces is due to our attention being drawn to the eyes and identifying this aspect of the happy facial expression.

FIGURE 10.17 Size of eye whites alone is sufficient to induce differential amygdala response to fearful expressions.
(a) Volume of eye whites is greater in fearful expressions than in happy expressions. **(b)** Activity in the left ventral amygdala in response to eye whites and eye blacks relative to fixation demonstrate that fearful eye whites alone induce increased response above baseline. Eye blacks were control stimuli, which were identical in shape to the stimuli in **(a)** but had inverted colors, such that the eye whites were actually black on a white screen.

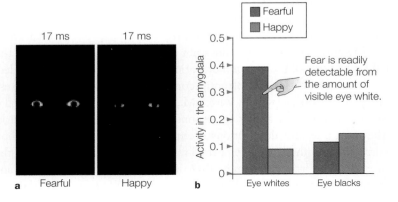

■ Fearful
■ Happy

17 ms   17 ms

Activity in the amygdala

Fear is readily detectable from the amount of visible eye white.

a   Fearful   Happy   b   Eye whites   Eye blacks

Stunningly, the investigators could induce S.M. to overcome her deficit by providing her with a simple instruction: "Focus on the eyes." If told to do so, she no longer had any difficulty identifying fearful faces (see Figure 10.16b). She would focus on the eyes only when reminded, however. Consequently, the amygdala appears to be an integral part of a system that automatically directs visual attention to the eyes when encountering any facial expressions. Impaired eye gaze is also a main characteristic of several psychiatric illnesses and social disorders in which the amygdala may be dysfunctional (e.g., autism spectrum disorder). Adolphs and colleague's findings that looking at the eyes are important to recognizing facial expressions and experimental manipulations that promote eye gaze may hold promise for interventions in such populations (D. P. Kennedy & Adolphs, 2010; Gamer & Buchel, 2009). This novel function of the amygdala is still not fully understood and is just one example of the diverse topics on the frontier of emotion research. Recent studies performed at the California Institute for Telecommunication and Information Technology extend these findings by identifying all the physical characteristics (e.g., eyebrow angle, pupil dilation, etc.) that make facial expressions of fear and the other basic emotions unique. They have developed a robot, Einstein, that can identify and then imitate facial expressions of others. You can watch Einstein at http://www.youtube.com/watch?v=pkpWCu1k0ZI.

Beyond the Face You may be familiar with the study in which participants were shown a film of various geometric shapes moving around a box. The movement was such that the participants described the shapes as if they were animate, with personalities and motives, moving about in a complex social situation—that is, participants anthropomorphized the shapes (Heider & Simmel, 1944). Patients with either amygdala damage or autism do not do this. They describe the shapes as geometric figures, and their description of the movement is devoid of social or emotional aspirations (Heberlein & Adolphs, 2004). Thus, the amygdala seems to have a role in perceiving and interpreting emotion and sociability in a wide range of stimuli, even inanimate objects. It may play a role in our ability to anthropomorphize.

The amygdala, however, does not appear to be critical for all types of social communication. Unlike patients with damage to the orbitofrontal cortex, patients with amygdala lesions, as we saw with S.M., do not show gross impairment in their ability to respond to social stimuli. They can interpret descriptions of emotional situations correctly, and they can give normal ratings to emotional prosody (the speech sounds that indicate emotion), even when a person is speaking in a fearful tone of voice

(Adolphs et al., 1999; A. K. Anderson & Phelps, 1998; S. K. Scott et al., 1997).

Social Group Evaluation The amygdala also appears to be activated during the categorization of people into groups. Although such implicit behavior might sometimes be helpful (separating people within a social group from people outside of the group or identifying the trustworthiness of a person), it can also lead to behaviors such as racial stereotyping. A variety of research has looked at racial stereotyping from both a behavioral and a functional imaging perspective.

Behavioral research has gone beyond simple, explicit measures of racial bias, as obtained through self-reporting, to implicit measures that examine indirect behavioral responses demonstrating a preference for one group over another. One common indirect measure for examining bias is the Implicit Association Test (IAT). Devised by Greenwald and colleagues (1998), the IAT measures the degree to which social groups (black versus white, old versus young, etc.) are automatically associated with positive and negative evaluations (see https://implicit.harvard.edu/implicit to take the test yourself). Participants are asked to categorize faces from each group while simultaneously categorizing words as either good or bad. For example, for one set of trials the participant responds to "good" words and black faces with one hand, and to "bad" words and white faces with the other hand. In another set of trials, the pairings are switched. The measure of bias is computed by the difference in the response latency between the black-and-good/white-and-bad trials versus the black-and-bad/white-and-good trials.

To study the neural basis of this racial bias, Elizabeth Phelps and her colleagues (2000) used functional MRI to examine amygdala activation in white participants viewing black and white faces. They found that the amygdala was activated when white Americans viewed unfamiliar black faces (but not faces of familiar, positively regarded blacks like Michael Jordan, Will Smith, and Martin Luther King Jr.). More important, the magnitude of the amygdala activation was significantly correlated with indirect measures of racial bias as determined by the IAT. Participants who showed more racial bias as measured by the IAT showed greater amygdala activity during the presentation of black faces. The researchers concluded that the amygdala responses and behavioral responses to black versus white faces in white participants reflected cultural evaluations of social groups as modified by experience. But is this really what was happening?

Although the amygdala does appear to be activated during these tasks, is it necessary for such evaluation? Phelps and colleagues (2003) compared the performance of the patient S.P., who had bilateral amygdala damage, to the performance of control participants on explicit and implicit measures of racial bias. They found no significant differences between the patient and controls on either measure and were forced to conclude that the amygdala is not a critical structure for the indirect evaluation of race, suggesting instead that it might be important for differences in the perceptual processing of "same" versus "other" race faces.

More recent studies have expanded our understanding of the role that the amygdala plays in social group evaluations. William Cunningham and colleagues (2004) compared areas of brain activation in white participants using fMRI for brief and more prolonged presentation of faces of black males and white males. Their findings led them to propose two separate systems for social evaluation processing (Figure 10.18). For brief presentations, where the evaluation must be made quickly and automatically, the amygdala is activated, and the activation is greater for black faces than

for white faces. With longer presentations, when controlled processing can take place, amygdala activation is not significantly different between races. Instead, significantly more activity occurred in the right ventrolateral prefrontal cortex during viewing of black faces than of white faces. Cunningham's team proposed that there are distinct neural differences between automatic and more controlled processing of social groups and that the controlled processing may modulate the automatic evaluation.

We must be careful in drawing sweeping conclusions about racial stereotypes from this data. It may appear that certain processes in the brain make it likely that people will categorize others on the basis of race, but is that what they actually do? This suggestion does not make sense to evolutionary psychologists. They point out that our human ancestors did not travel over very great distances. It would have been highly unusual for them to come across humans of other races, so it makes no sense

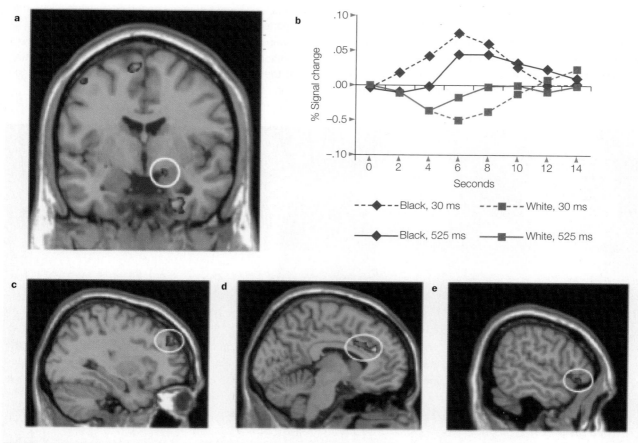

FIGURE 10.18 Differential neural response in white participants to masked and unmasked black and white faces.
Black and white faces were presented for either 30 ms (masked) or for 525 ms (unmasked). **(a)** The right amygdala is more active for black versus white faces when faces are presented for 30 ms. **(b)** The pattern of amygdala activity is similar at 525 ms, though the effect is attenuated. Also during the longer stimulus presentation, activity in the **(c)** dorsolateral prefrontal cortex, **(d)** anterior cingulate cortex, and **(e)** ventrolateral prefrontal cortex was greater for black faces relative to white faces. Activity in one or more of these areas may be responsible for the attenuation of amygdala activity at 525 ms.

that humans should have evolved a neural process to categorize race. It would make sense, however, to be able to recognize whether other humans belonged to one's own social or family group or not, and hence whether they could be trusted or not. Guided by this evolutionary perspective, Kurzban and colleagues (2001) found that when categorization cues stronger than race are present (e.g., one's group is a team wearing green shirts and the opposing group wears red shirts), the categorization based on race nearly disappears.

A recent study may help explain what is going on here. Researchers compared the amygdala response to a set of faces that varied along two dimensions centered on an average face (Figure 10.19). The faces differed in social content along one dimension (trustworthiness) and were socially neutral along the other dimension. In both the amygdala and much of the posterior face network, a similar response to both dimensions was seen, and responses were stronger the farther the face was along the dimension from an average face. These findings suggest that what may be activating these regions is the degree of difference from a categorically average face (Said et al., 2010). If you are from an Asian culture, your average face would be Asian, and thus, your amygdala would be activated for any non-Asian face. This response is not the same thing as determining whether someone is a racist. The ability to use such a categorization strategy may lead to racism, but it does not do so necessarily.

TAKE-HOME MESSAGES

- Fear conditioning is a form of classical conditioning in which the unconditioned stimulus is aversive. It is a form of implicit learning.

- The amygdala is heavily involved in fear conditioning (a form of implicit memory).

- The conditioned stimulus is a neutral stimulus that, through classical conditioning, will eventually evoke a response. The unconditioned stimulus is the stimulus that, even without training, evokes a response.

- The unconditioned response is the response naturally elicited (without training) by the unconditioned stimulus. The conditioned response is the response that is elicited (with training) by the conditioned stimulus. Usually the unconditioned response and the conditioned response are the same (e.g., the startle response in the rat), but they have different names depending on what elicits the response.

- Patients with bilateral amygdala damage fail to acquire a conditioned response during fear conditioning, indicating that the amygdala is necessary for such conditioning to occur.

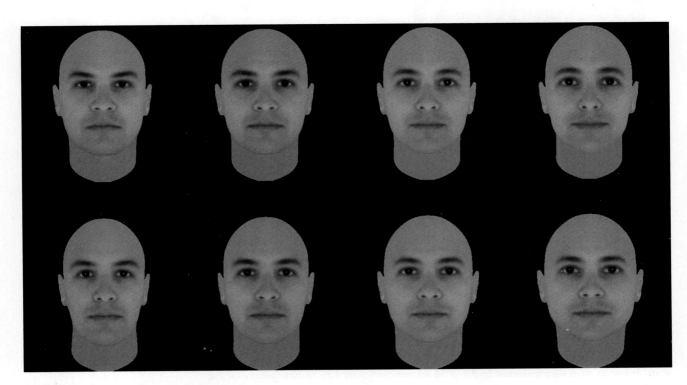

FIGURE 10.19 Faces used in the fMRI experiment.
The faces in the top row varied along the valence dimension ranging from −3, −1, 1, and 3 standard deviations away from the average face. Trustworthy judgments are highly correlated with valence. The socially neutral faces used in the control condition are on the bottom row. Their shape varies from values of −5, −1.67, 1.67, and 5 standard deviations away from the average face.

- Information can reach the amygdala via two separate pathways: The "low road" goes directly from the thalamus to the amygdala; the "high road" goes from the cortex to the amygdala.

- The amygdala is also important for explicit memory of emotional events. First, the amygdala is necessary for normal indirect emotional responses to stimuli whose emotional properties are learned explicitly, by means other than fear conditioning. Second, the amygdala can enhance the strength of explicit (or declarative) memories for emotional events by modulating the storage of these memories.

- The amygdala appears to be necessary for automatically deriving information from the eyes of others when identifying emotional facial expressions. This ability is especially critical for the proper identification of fear, because the defining characteristic of fear is an increase in the volume of the eye whites.

- When looking at faces, the activity of the amygdala increases with the degree of difference from a categorically average face.

- The amygdala is activated by novel stimuli independent of valence and arousal.

- Attention, perception, and decision making are all affected by emotion.

Get a Grip! Cognitive Control of Emotion

The offensive lineman who yells at the referee for a holding penalty may be considered a "bad sport." But what is really happening? The player is not controlling his negative emotional response to having his goal—blocking the tackle—thwarted. In contrast, the wife who smiles at her husband as he goes off on a dangerous endeavor "so that he will remember me with a smile on my face and not crying" is consciously controlling her sad emotional response. **Emotion regulation** refers to the processes that influence the type of emotions we have, when we have them, and how we express and experience them. Recall that emotions arise from brain systems that appraise the significance of a stimulus with respect to our goals

and needs. That appra... evaluation processes, a... to regulate emotion ca... ways (Figure 10.20). Th... can intervene at multip... tion process, some early... are conscious and contro... and some are unconsciou...

Typically, research in... ried out by changing the... or the output (the emoti... ...... The former can be done by avoiding the stimulus altogether, changing the attention paid to it (for instance, by being distracted), or altering the emotional impact of the stimulus by reappraisal. Changing the output can be accomplished by intensifying, diminishing, prolonging, or curtailing the emotional experience, expression, or physiologic response (Gross, 1998b).

We are all well aware that peoples' emotional reactions and their ability to control them are notoriously variable. Sometimes this variation is due to an increased ability to consciously control emotion and sometimes from an increased ability to automatically control emotion. Characteristic patterns in neural activity in the prefrontal and emotional appraisal systems have been found, both at rest and when emotionally stimulated, that correlate with regulatory ability and with gender, personality, and negative affect (see The Cognitive Neuroscientist's Toolkit: Dimensions of Emotional Style).

For instance, one of the differences in emotion regulation appears to be related to differences in the resting activity of the right and left frontal lobes. Daren Jackson and his colleagues found that people who had more left-sided frontal activation at rest (seen on EEG) than right frontal activation were better able to voluntarily suppress negative emotion (Jackson et al., 2000). Based on this finding, the team predicted that these same types of people also would automatically suppress an emotion more readily. They demonstrated this behavior by measuring decreased EEG responses to unpleasant pictures following, but not during, picture presentation. That is, the study participant's negative emotion was

FIGURE 10.20 Diagram of the processing steps proposed by Ochsner and his colleagues for generating an emotion and how the emotional outcome might be regulated by cognitive control processes (blue box).
The arrows pointing down from the cognitive control processes indicate the effects of different emotion regulation strategies and which emotion generation stage they influence.

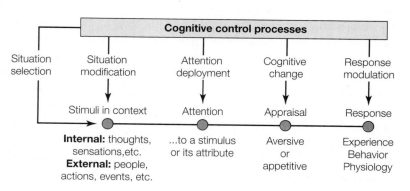

For several decades, Richard Davidson (2012) has studied the different ways in which people respond to emotional events. He has formulated what he calls the six dimensions of emotional style, each grounded in a particular pattern of brain activity. Every person lands somewhere on each dimension, and taken together the six dimensions describe our emotional style. Davidson sees these styles as partly genetic and, to some degree, plastic. The six dimensions and their specific pattern of activity are as follows.

1. **Resilience: The rate at which we recover from setbacks or losses.** People with more left prefrontal cortex activation in a resting state are higher on the resilience scale than people with more right prefrontal activation. In addition, for people in the former category, the duration of their amygdalar activation is shorter after a negative emotional experience. Combining MRI imaging and tests of emotional resilience shows a positive relationship between the amount of white matter (axonal connections) that people have running between their prefrontal cortex and the amygdala and their degree of resilience.

2. **Outlook: The capacity to sustain positive emotion over time.** The nucleus accumbens, located in the ventral striatum (the ventral part of the basal ganglia), is packed with neurons that either release or capture dopamine and endogenous opiates. The nucleus accumbens is activated when people anticipate a reward or something pleasurable. This activity is sustained by signals from the prefrontal cortex. People who are closer to the positive end of the outlook dimension exhibit greater activity in both the nucleus accumbens and the associated prefrontal cortex.

3. **Social intuition: Sensitivity to the emotional states of others.** People who are highly intuitive have high levels of activity in the fusiform gyrus and low levels of amygdala activity. Those who are puzzled by other people's emotional states have an opposite pattern of activation. Shyness and sociability are related to where you stand on this scale.

4. **Self-awareness: Awareness of our own physiologic and emotional cues.** The larger and more active our insula is, the more self-aware we are.

5. **Sensitivity to context: Awareness of the social environment and sensitivity to the rules of social engagement.** Our capacity to appropriately regulate our emotions and behavior is based on our social awareness and sensitivity. Unusually low activity in the hippocampus coupled with fewer connections between the hippocampus and other brain regions correlates with people who are not in tune with their environment. Hyperactivity in the hippocampus and strong connections can cause excessive focus on context at the opposite end of the range of this dimension. Adaptability reflects sensitivity to context.

6. **Attention: The ability to focus attention and screen out emotional distractions.** The more focused we are, the more the prefrontal cortex exhibits a phase-locking response to external stimuli. Also, focused attention is associated with moderate activation of the P300 signal during an emotional attentional blink test. Impulsivity exhibits an inverse relationship to the attention scale. The more unfocused we are, the more impulsive we tend to be.

generated by the stimulus, but it would be suppressed more quickly in those who had more left-sided activation at rest (Jackson et al., 2003). After obtaining a resting EEG, researchers showed participants images on a computer screen that were either pleasant, unpleasant, or neutral. They were to watch the picture the entire time it was on the screen and not look away or close their eyes. Meanwhile, their eyeblink startle magnitude was measured (with EMG) at intervals both during and after the presentation. The eyeblink startle reflex has been found to index the duration of the emotional response following emotional provocation—the smaller the magnitude, the less the emotional response (Davidson, 1998). Participants with greater left anterior EEG activation at rest had attenuated startle magnitude following the negative stimuli. In contrast, these EEG asymmetries did not predict negative reactivity during picture presentation. The study results suggest that the initial reaction to an emotional picture and the response that persists following the picture are mediated by dissociable mechanisms. This relation between resting frontal activation and emotional recovery following an aversive event supports the idea of a frontally mediated mechanism involved in one form of automatic emotion regulation. The relatively fast recovery following a negative-affect elicitor is one index of individual differences in automatic emotion regulation—regulation that occurs in the absence of specific intentions to suppress negative emotion.

The capacity to control emotions is important for functioning in the world, especially the social world. We are so adept at controlling our emotions that we tend to notice only when someone does not: the angry customer yelling at the cashier, the giggler during the wedding ceremony, or a depressed friend overwhelmed with sadness. Indeed, disruptions in emotion regulation are thought to underlie mood and anxiety disorders.

Research into emotion regulation over the past couple of decades has concentrated on *how* and *when* regulation takes place. In 1998, James Gross at Stanford University proposed the model in Figure 10.21 to account for seemingly divergent ideas between the psychological and physical literature on emotion regulation. The psychological literature indicated that it was healthier to control and regulate your emotions, while the literature on physical health advanced the idea that chronically suppressing emotions such as anger resulted in hypertension and other physical ailments. Gross hypothesized that "shutting down" an emotion at different points in the process of emotion generation would have different consequences and thus, could explain the divergent conclusions. To test his theory, he compared **reappraisal**, a form of antecedent-focused emotion regulation, with emotion **suppression**, a response-focused form. Reappraisal is a cognitive-linguistic strategy that reinterprets an emotion-laden stimulus in nonemotional terms. For instance, a woman wiping the tears from her eyes could be crying because she is sad; or, on reappraisal, she may simply have something in her eye she is trying to remove. Suppression is a strategy in which we inhibit an emotion-expressive behavior during an emotionally arousing situation (for instance, smiling when you are upset). In the experiment, Gross showed participants a disgust-eliciting film under one of three conditions. In the reappraisal condition, they were to adopt a detached and unemotional attitude; in the suppression condition, they were to behave such that an observer could not tell they were feeling disgusted; in the third condition, they were simply asked

to watch the film. While watching the film, participants were videotaped and their physiological responses were monitored. Afterward, they completed an emotion rating form. Whereas both reappraisal and suppression reduced emotion-expressive behavior, only reappraisal actually reduced the disgust experience. But suppression actually increased sympathetic activation, causing participants to be more aroused, and this increased sympathetic activity lasted for a while after the film ended (Gross, 1998b). Continued research on emotion regulation has provided fMRI data that support Gross's hypothesis about the timing of reappraisal and suppression strategies (Goldin et al., 2008).

How does this behavior apply in the real world? Suppose you come home to find that your friend has dropped in and cleaned your house, and you start thinking, "How dare she! She should have asked," and you feel yourself getting madder than a hornet. You now have three choices. You could wallow in your anger; you could suppress it by putting on a false front; or you could reappraise the situation. In the latter case you think, "Yeah, well, I hate cleaning. Now it looks spotless! This is great." You start to feel good, and a smile lights up your face. You have just done a little cognitive reappraising and reduced your physiological arousal. This approach is good for your overall health.

Conscious reappraisal reduces the emotional experience; this finding supports the idea that emotions, to some extent, are subject to conscious cognitive control. In an initial fMRI study to investigate the cognitive control of emotion, Kevin Ochsner and his colleagues (2002) found that using reappraisal to decrease a negative emotion increased prefrontal cortex (PFC) activity (implicated in cognitive control; see Chapter 12) and decreased amygdala activity, suggesting that the PFC modulates emotional activity in subcortical structures such as the amygdala. Reappraisal can mentally make a bad situation better, but it can also mentally make a bad situation worse (or a good situation mentally bad). Would the same neural system also be at work if a person enhanced an emotion, or would altering the strategy alter the system that mediates regulation? Ochsner and his colleagues (2004) hypothesized that cognitive control regions mediating reappraisal (the PFC) would modulate regions involved in appraising the emotional qualities of a stimulus (amygdala). Thus, cognitive upregulation would be associated with greater activation of the amygdala and downregulation would be associated with less. They did an fMRI study of reappraisal that looked at both making a bad situation better (downregulating negative emotions) and making a bad situation worse (upregulating negative emotions).

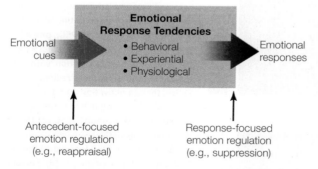

FIGURE 10.21 James Gross's proposed model of emotion. Gross proposed a model in which emotions may be regulated either by manipulating the input to the system (*antecedent-focused* emotion regulation) or by manipulating its output (*response-focused* emotion regulation).

Participants in this study looked at negative images. They were divided into two groups, a self-focused group or a situation-focused group. In the self-focused group, participants were instructed to imagine themselves or a loved one in the negative scene (increasing negative emotion); to view the pictures in a detached way (decreasing negative emotion); or, in the control condition, simply to look at the image. In the situation-focused group, they were told to increase emotion by imagining that the situation was becoming worse, or to decrease emotion by imagining it was getting better, or again just to look at the image. Each participant then had to report how effective and effortful the reappraisal was. All participants reported success in increasing and decreasing their emotions, but indicated that downregulation took more effort.

Which regions of the brain were involved with the cognitive control of emotions brought about by reappraisal? The team found that whether negative emotions were enhanced or reduced, regions of the left lateral PFC that are involved with working memory and cognitive control (Chapter 12) and dorsal anterior cingulate cortex (dACC) implicated in the online monitoring of performance were activated, suggesting that these regions were involved with evaluating and "deciding" the cognitive strategy (Figure 10.22). They also observed regions of the PFC that were uniquely active. The dorsal medial PFC, implicated in self-monitoring and self-evaluation (Chapter 13), was active in both cases of self-focused reappraisal; but when downregulation was externally focused on the situation, it was the lateral PFC that turned on. During upregulation, the left rostromedial PFC and the PCC (implicated in the retrieval of emotion knowledge) were active, but downregulation activated a different region associated with behavioral inhibition—the right lateral and orbital PFC. It appears,

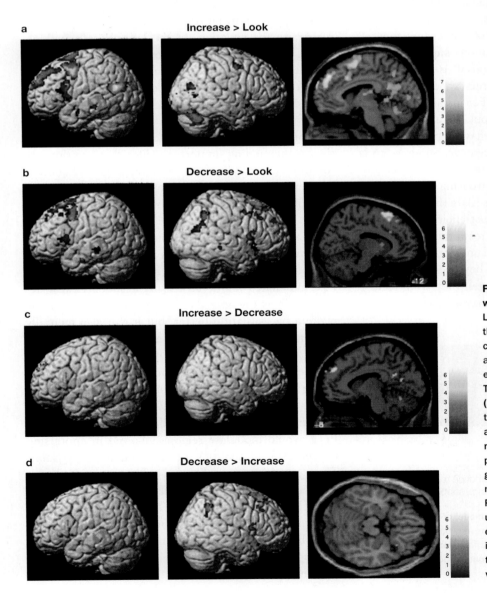

FIGURE 10.22 Unique regions activate when increasing or decreasing emotion. Left and right lateral views are seen in the left and center panels. **(a)** When increasing negative emotions, activations are generally left sided in the dorsolateral prefrontal cortex (DLPFC), and ACC. The right panel shows left medial view. **(b)** When decreasing emotion, some of the same left hemisphere regions are active, though activations tend to be more bilateral or right sided. The right panel is the right medial view. **(c)** Regions uniquely activated when increasing negative emotion: the left rostral medial PFC and posterior cingulate. **(d)** Regions uniquely activated when decreasing emotion. The right lateral PFC is seen in the center view and right lateral orbitofrontal activation is seen in the axial view on the far right.

then, that different cognitive reappraisal goals and strategies activate some of the same PFC regions as well as some regions that are different.

What about the amygdala? Amygdala activation was modulated either up or down depending on the regulatory goal: Activity increased when the goal was to enhance negative emotion and decreased when the goal was to reduce it. The apparent modulation of the amygdala by prefrontal activity suggests that its activity will be increased if the current processing goals fit with the evaluative aspects of stimuli (in this case, to make a negative stimulus more negative), not the actual valence (positive or negative) of the emotion.

Does cognitive control via reappraisal depend on interactions between the PFC regions that support cognitive control processes and subcortical networks that generate emotional responses, as we have been assuming? Today, a decade after this idea was presented, over 50 imaging studies support this hypothesis (Ochsner et al., 2012).

Although early research suggested that the amygdala was involved exclusively in automatic processing of negative information, Ochsner's study and more recent research suggest otherwise. The amygdala appears to have a more flexible role in processing the relevance of various stimuli depending on a person's current goals and motivation (Cunningham et al., 2005; 2008). This trait is known as **affective flexibility**. For instance, if you go to Las Vegas with the idea that you don't want to lose any money, your amygdala will be more active when you are losing money. But if you go with the idea of winning money, your amygdala will be more active when you are winning. Amygdala processing, however, appears to be constrained by a negativity bias (Cunningham et al., 2008). Amygdala modulation is more pronounced for positive than for negative information, so it processes negative information less flexibly. PFC modulation can't completely eradicate the negative stimuli, but—for survival and your wallet—this is a good thing.

Emotion regulation research is in its adolescence. While much remains to be understood, the use of functional imaging coupled with behavioral studies has been fruitful. Much of the research so far has centered on the two cognitive strategies that we have discussed, reappraisal and suppression. Areas of research that need to be addressed are on the deployment of attention (such as ignoring a stimulus or being distracted from it), alternative forms of regulation, such as situation selection (avoiding or seeking certain types of stimuli), and situation modification. Research is also needed to understand the processes behind the range of differences in people's emotional responses to situations and their ability to regulate their emotions. Achieving a better understanding of emotion regulation

will aid in clinical interventions in cases of impaired emotion regulation, which has been implicated in many psychiatric conditions, including depression, borderline personality disorder, social anxiety disorder, and substance abuse disorders (e.g., Denny et al., 2009).

TAKE-HOME MESSAGES

- Emotion regulation is complex and involves many processes.
- Emotion regulation is dependent on the interaction of frontal cortical structures and subcortical brain regions.
- Different emotion regulation strategies have different physiological effects.

Other Areas, Other Emotions

We have seen that the amygdala is involved in a variety of emotional tasks, ranging from fear conditioning to social responses. But the amygdala is not the only area of the brain necessary for emotions. We consider these other areas next.

The Insular Cortex

The insular cortex (or **insula**) is tucked between the frontal and temporal lobes in the Sylvan fissure (Figure 10.23). The insula has extensive reciprocal connections with limbic forebrain areas, such as the amygdala, medial prefrontal cortex, and anterior cingulate gyrus (Augustine, 1996; Craig, 2009). It also has

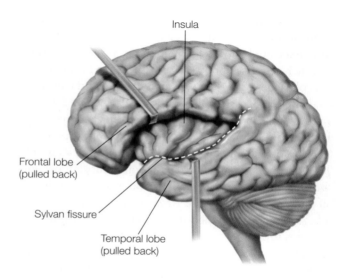

FIGURE 10.23 The insula.

reciprocal connections with frontal, parietal, and temporal cortical areas involved with attention, memory, and cognition (Augustine, 1996).

There is a significant correlation between insular activity and the perception of internal bodily states (Critchley, 2009; Pollatos, et al., 2007); this function is known as **interoception**. Various interoceptive stimuli that activate the anterior insula include thirst, sensual touch, itch, distention of the bladder and intestinal tract, exercise, and heartbeat. The connections and activation profile of the insula suggest that it integrates all of the visceral and somatic input and forms a representation of the state of the body (Craig, 2009; Saper, 2002). Interestingly, people with a bigger right insula are better at detecting their heartbeats than are people with a smaller right insula (Critchley et al., 2004), and those same types of people are also more aware of their emotions (L. Barrett et al., 2004).

Several models of emotion speculate that direct access to bodily states is necessary to experience emotion. It may be that the insula plays a key role in this process. Suggestively, fMRI studies show that the anterior insula and anterior cingulate cortex are jointly active in participants experiencing emotional feelings including maternal and romantic love, anger, fear, sadness, happiness, disgust, and trust. It appears, then, that the insula is active with all feelings, both physical (body states) and emotional, suggesting that it may be the junction where cognitive and emotional information are integrated. The role of the insula as "body information central" is also indicated by its connections to networks across the cortex and to the amygdala with its role in evaluating emotional stimuli (Craig, 2009; Critchley, 2009).

Insular activity also has been reported to be associated with evaluative processing, for instance, when people make risk-adverse decisions. The riskier the decision, the more active is the insula (Xue et al., 2010). Its activity is also associated with the perception of positive emotions in other people (Jabbi et al., 2007). Gary Berntson and his colleagues (2011) investigated the role of the insula in evaluative processing by examining valence and arousal ratings in response to picture stimuli. They compared the behavioral performance of three groups of participants: a group of patients with lesions of the insula, a control-lesion group, and an amygdala-lesion group. All patients were asked to rate the positivity and negativity (valence) of each presented picture (from *very unpleasant* to *very pleasant*) and how emotionally arousing they found the pictures to be.

The study results showed that patients with insular lesions (compared with patients in the control-lesion group) reported both *reduced arousal* (to both unpleasant and pleasant stimuli) and *reduced valence* ratings. In contrast, the *arousal* ratings of patients with amygdala lesions were selectively attenuated for unpleasant stimuli, but they had the same positive and negative valence ratings as the control-lesion group. These findings are in line with an earlier study (Berntson et al., 2007), which found that patients with amygdala damage showed a complete *lack of an arousal gradient across negative stimuli*, although they displayed a *typical arousal gradient to positive stimuli*. These results were not attributable to the inability of amygdala patients to process the hostile nature of the stimuli, because the patients with amygdala damage accurately recognized and categorized both positive and negative features of the stimuli. Taken together, these results support the view that the insula may play a broad role in integrating affective and cognitive processes, whereas the amygdala may have a more selective role in affective arousal, especially for negative stimuli (Berntson et al., 2011).

Casting the amygdala as a vigilant watchdog looking out for motivationally relevant stimuli (A. K. Anderson & Phelps, 2001; Whalen, 1998) may prove true, but just what is it watching out for? The answer to that question still eludes investigators. Another fMRI study found that the amygdala is more sensitive to valence than to arousal (Anders et al., 2008). A study mentioned previously reported that novel stimuli generated higher peak responses in the amygdala and activated it for longer than did familiar stimuli (Weierich et al., 2010). Obviously, the amygdala remains enigmatic.

Disgust

Disgust is one emotion that has been linked directly to the insula. This finding should be no surprise, given the insula's role as the great perceiver of bodily states. Based on imaging studies, many cognitive neuroscientists agree that the anterior insula is essential for detecting and experiencing disgust (Phillips et al., 1997, 1998). This conclusion is consistent with a report of a patient who had insula damage and was unable to detect disgust conveyed in various modalities (Calder et al., 2000).

A study done by Giacomo Rizzolatti (see mirror neurons in Chapter 8) and colleagues (Wicker et al., 2003) confirmed these findings and went a step further. These investigators analyzed the neural response during observation of others experiencing disgust while having firsthand experience of disgust. They observed that the same portion of the anterior insula was activated both when participants viewed expressions of disgust in others and when they smelled unpleasant odors (a firsthand experience of disgust). These results are significant for two reasons. First, they suggest that understanding the emotions of others may require simulating, and thus mildly experiencing, these emotions ourselves (Craig, 2009). This line of thought implies a role for emotion in empathy and theory of mind (discussed in Chapter 13). Second, the results provide additional evidence that the insula is a neural correlate of disgust identification in others and of experiencing disgust directly.

Some have taken all of this evidence to mean that the anterior insula is the region of the brain that is essential for disgust. A large meta-analysis of fMRI studies done by Katherine Vytal and Stephan Hamann (2010) found that disgust consistently activated the inferior frontal gyrus and the anterior insula, and these regions reliably differentiated disgust from all other emotion states. In fact, these researchers' analysis found locationist evidence for anger, fear, sadness, and happiness. In contrast, Kristen Lindquist and her colleagues (2012), in another large meta-analysis of multiple fMRI studies analyzed by a different method, did not find the insula to be consistently and specifically activated for the emotion of disgust. They found that although the anterior insula is more active during instances of disgust perception, anterior insula activation is observed in a number of tasks that involve awareness of body states, such as gastric distention, body movement, and orgasm. They also found that activation of the left anterior insula was more likely during incidents of anger than of any other emotion. Lindquist and colleagues suggest that the anterior insula plays a key but more general role in representing core affective feelings in awareness. They also found no evidence for a locationist view for the other brain regions. The debate continues.

Happiness

Over the last several years, a small but growing body of research has reported on the neural bases of happiness. It's not easy to define what makes us happy, so it is a challenging emotion to study. Experimental methods used to study happiness have participants view happy faces, watch films, or try to induce a happy mood by various methods, but they have not been consistently reliable, valid, or comparable across studies. Because of these difficulties, only a few neuroimaging studies have focused on happiness (Habel et al., 2005). One group contrasted participants' brain activity in response to smiling faces versus sad faces (Lane et al., 1997). In a separate fMRI study, 26 healthy male participants were scanned during sad and happy mood induction as well as while performing a cognitive task that functioned as the experimental control (Habel et al., 2005). Sad and happy moods produced similar activations in the amygdala–hippocampal area extending into the parahippocampal gyrus, prefrontal and temporal cortex, anterior cingulate, and the precuneus. Happiness produced stronger activations in the dorsolateral prefrontal cortex, the cingulate gyrus, the inferior temporal gyrus, and the cerebellum (Figure 10.24). These results reinforce the role of the limbic system and its connections in the processing and expression of positive emotions. Nonetheless, the study of happiness remains extremely challenging. For example, happiness is not necessarily the opposite of sadness. What's more, happiness is not automatically induced by looking at smiling faces.

Freud equated happiness with pleasure, but others have suggested that it also requires achievement, whether cognitive, aesthetic, or moral. Psychologist Mihaly Csikszentmihalyi suggests that people are really happy when totally immersed in a challenging task that closely matches their abilities (Csikszentmihalyi, 1990). Csikszentmihalyi came to this conclusion following an experiment in which he had participants carry beepers that randomly beeped several times a day. On that signal, they would whisk a notebook from their pockets and jot down what they were doing and how much they were enjoying it. He found that there were two types of pleasure: bodily pleasures such as eating and sex, and, even more enjoyable, the state of being "in the zone," what Csikszentmihalyi calls **flow**. Csikszentmihalyi describes flow as the process of having an optimal experience. Flow occurs when you are so into what you are doing that you forget about everything else. It could be riding the top of a wave, working out a theorem, or doing a tango across the dance floor. It involves a challenge that you are equal to, that fully engages your attention, and offers immediate feedback at each step that you are on the right track and pulling it off. When both challenges and skills are high, the person is not only enjoying the moment but also stretching his or her capabilities. This improves the likelihood of learning new skills, and increasing both self-esteem and personal complexity (Csikszentmihalyi & LeFevre, 1989). The concept of flow and what it means suggests that the circuits involved in pleasure, reward, and motivation are essential in the emotion of happiness.

Love

Unlike the studies of happiness, love experiments cannot use facial expressions as either a stimulus or a variable of interest. Indeed, as we noted previously, love is not characterized by any specific facial expressions. Thus the "facial feedback hypothesis" suggesting that facial expressions produce emotional expressions as

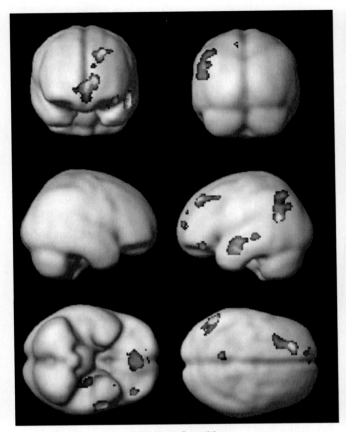

Sadness–Cognition   Happiness–Cognition

FIGURE 10.24 Common and different brain regions are activated with sadness and happiness.
Sad and happy moods produced similar activations but differences emerged. In the sadness condition,
there was greater activation in the left transverse temporal gyrus and bilaterally in ventrolateral PFC,
the left ACC and the superior temporal gyrus. In the happiness condition, higher activation was seen
in the right DLPFC, the left medial and posterior cingulate gyrus, and the right inferior temporal gyrus.
It appears that negative and positive moods have distinct activations within a common network.

well as reflect it (Darwin, 1873; Ekman 1992) cannot be applied to the study of love. Love scientists use stimuli that evoke the concept of emotion rather than its visual expression, such as names of loved ones. Subjective feelings of love that participants have for their beloved are usually evaluated with standard self-report questionnaires, such as the Passionate Love Scale (Hatfield & Rapson, 1987).

Stephanie Cacioppo (née Ortigue) and her colleagues (2010a) recently reviewed the fMRI studies of love to identify which brain network(s) is commonly activated when participants watch love-related stimuli, independent of whether the love being felt is maternal, passionate, or unconditional (Figure 10.25).

Overall, love recruits a distributed subcortico-cortical reward, motivational, emotional, and cognitive system that includes dopamine-rich brain areas such as the insula, the caudate nucleus and the putamen, the ventral tegmental area, anterior cingulated cortex, bilateral posterior hippocampus, left inferior frontal gyrus, left middle temporal gyrus, and parietal lobe. This finding reinforces the assumption that love is more complex than a basic emotion. No activation of the amygdala has been reported in fMRI studies of love.

Interestingly, each type of love recruits a different specific brain network. For instance, passionate love is mediated by a specific network localized within the limbic system and also within higher order brain areas sustaining cognitive functions, such as self-representation, attention, and social cognition (Figure 10.26). Interestingly, the reported length of time in love correlates with the cerebral activation in particular regions: the right insular cortex, right anterior cingulated cortex, bilateral posterior cingulated cortices, left inferior frontal gyrus, left ventral putamen/pallidum, left middle temporal gyrus, and right parietal lobe (Aron et al., 2005).

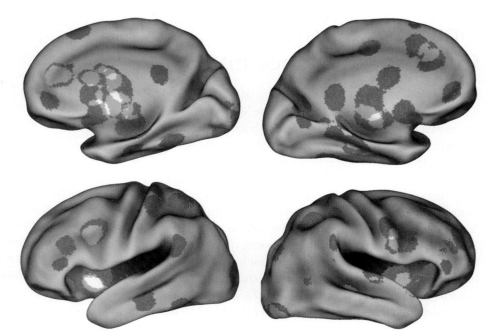

FIGURE 10.25 Love activations encompass multiple brain regions. Composite meta-analysis map of fMRI studies related to love (including passionate love, maternal love, and unconditional love). The top panels are the left and right medial views and the bottom panels are left and right lateral views of an average human cortical surface model with the activation results superimposed.

On the other hand, while the maternal love circuit also involves cortical and subcortical structures that overlap the area of activity observed with passionate love, there is one activation that is not shared with passionate love: the subcortical periaqueductal (central) gray matter (PAG). As far as love goes, activations in this region were mostly observed in maternal love, suggesting that PAG activation might be specific to maternal love. This conclusion would make sense, because PAG receives direct connections from the limbic emotional system and contains a high density of vasopressin receptors, which are important in maternal bonding (Ortigue et al., 2010a). Love is a complicated business, and it appears to light up much of the brain—but you didn't need an fMRI study to tell you that.

TAKE-HOME MESSAGES

- Different brain areas are associated with the processing of different emotions. The orbitofrontal cortex is activated when identifying angry facial expressions and hearing angry prosody, and the anterior insula is linked to identification and experience of disgust.

- The insula appears to play a broad role in integrating affective and cognitive processes.

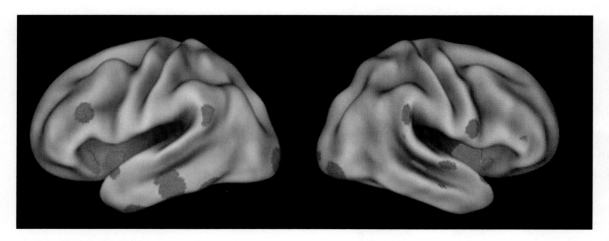

FIGURE 10.26 Passionate love network.
Superimposed on lateral views of an average human cortical surface model are cortical networks specifically related to passionate love. Brain areas recruited are known to mediate emotion, motivation, reward, social cognition, attention, and self-representation.

Unique Systems, Common Components

It may be an oversimplification to associate each of the emotions we have addressed with a single brain structure. By revealing the various locations in the brain with which different emotions are associated, however, we have made it clear that no single brain area is responsible for all emotions (Figure 10.27). For instance, in a recent meta-analysis including 105 fMRI studies and 1,785 brain coordinates that yielded an overall sample of 1,600 healthy participants, Paulo Fusar-Poli and his colleagues (2009) demonstrated that the processing of emotional faces was associated with increased activation in a variety of visual, limbic, temporoparietal, and prefrontal brain areas. For instance, happy, fearful, and sad faces specifically activate the amygdala, whereas angry or disgusted faces had no clear effect on this brain region. Furthermore, in line with the clinical literature, amygdala sensitivity was greater for fearful than for happy or sad faces.

These results have been reinforced by the previously mentioned fMRI meta-analysis performed by Lindquist and her colleagues (2012). They delineated a so-called neural reference space for emotion (see Figure 10.28). A neural reference space is a region made up of sets of neurons that are probabilistically involved in realizing a class of mental events, in this case, emotion. In these researchers' view, a set of neurons in this space is not specific to any emotion category, but is somewhat like an ingredient that may or may not be used in a recipe. Lindquist and colleagues concluded that their results do not support a locationist hypothesis of amygdala

function. They suggested that the amygdala is part of the distributed network that helps realize core affect because it is involved in signaling salient stimuli (Adolphs, 2008, 2009; Whalen, 1998, 2007). This conclusion is also consistent with a large body of evidence reporting that the amygdala is constantly implicated in orienting responses to motivationally relevant stimuli (Holland & Gallagher, 1999), novel stimuli (e.g., Blackford et al., 2010; Breiter et al., 1996; Moriguchi et al., 2010; Wright et al., 2008), and unusual stimuli (e.g., Blackford et al., 2010). Similarly, when compared to participants with intact amygdalae, individuals with amygdala lesions do not automatically allocate attention to aversive stimuli (A. K. Anderson & Phelps, 2001) and socially relevant stimuli (D. P. Kennedy & Adolphs, 2010).

Although our earlier discussion of the amygdala focused on how this structure operates in isolation, this growing body of evidence suggests that much of the exciting research in the cognitive neuroscience of emotion is outlining how the amygdala works with other brain areas to produce normal emotional responses. For example, as we mentioned earlier, although acquisition of fear conditioning requires the amygdala, normal extinction of a conditioned response involves interactions of the amygdala and the prefrontal cortex (Morgan & LeDoux, 1999). These two structures may also be the culprits in studies examining the ability to associate a reward with a stimulus (Baxter et al., 2000; Hampton et al., 2007). A neuroanatomical model of depression suggests that a circuit comprised of the amygdala, orbitofrontal cortex, and thalamus is overactive in depressed patients, and that the structures in this circuit, working in concert, lead to some of the symptoms of depression (Drevets,

Emotion	Associated brain area	Functional role
Fear	Amygdala	Learning, avoidance
Anger	Orbitofrontal cortex, anterior cingulate cortex	Indicate social violations
Sadness	Amygdala, right temporal pole	Withdraw
Disgust	Anterior insula, anterior cingulate cortex	Avoidance

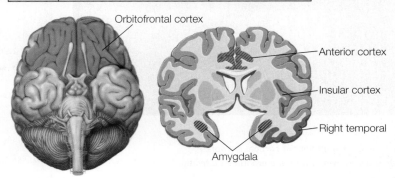

FIGURE 10.27 Brain areas associated with various emotions.
Ventral view of brain on left and coronal view through the insula and amygdala on the right.

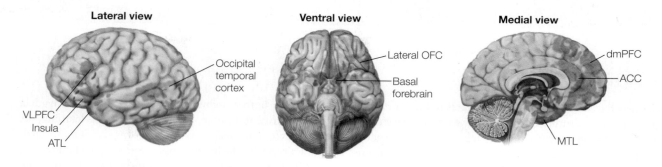

FIGURE 10.28 The neural reference space for discrete emotions.
These are regions seen to be active consistently across studies of emotion experience or perception.

1998). Finally, Damasio's somatic marker hypothesis proposes that the amygdala and orbitofrontal cortex interact and make unique contributions to emotional decision making.

Together these findings clearly suggest that emotion research has shifted from identifying areas that specialize in a specific emotion to characterizing how these areas interact and determining if there are any interactions common to different types of emotional experience. To this end, some promising evidence suggests that the anterior cingulate cortex (ACC) could be essential for generalized emotional processing. One study found that emotional arousal while watching films and recalling various emotional experiences was associated with increased activity in the ACC (Lane et al., 1997). Furthermore, the ACC is known to receive projections from the amygdala, the OFC, and the anterior insula (Devinsky et al., 1995), thus making it plausible that the ACC is an essential

component of common emotional circuitry. The ACC was also activated during recognition of facial expressions of disgust (Wicker et al., 2003), anger (Blair et al., 1999), happiness (Lane et al., 1997; Habel et al., 2005), and love (Ortigue et al., 2010a).

These observations are suggestive but are far from conclusive. As the study of emotion progresses, it will be essential to develop an understanding of how distant areas of the brain interact to facilitate the detection and experience of emotion.

TAKE-HOME MESSAGE

- Ultimately, understanding how we perceive and experience emotion will require studying the interactions of a diverse set of neural structures.

Summary

Scientists have attributed emotional states to brain processing for almost a century. Recently, however, in case studies on intriguing impairments following bilateral amygdala damage, as well as functional imaging studies that indicate how and where emotions are processed in the brain, we have made great strides toward characterizing the functional neuroanatomy of emotion.

Scientists face many challenges in studying emotion, a behavior that is often difficult to define and therefore difficult to manipulate and study scientifically. One challenge has been establishing a proper place for studies of emotion in cognitive neuroscience. Earlier research and theories tended to view emotion as separate from cognition, implying that they could be studied and understood separately. As research in the neuroscience of emotion proceeded, however, it became clear that emotion could not be considered independently from other, more "cognitive" abilities, or vice versa. The neural systems of emotion and other cognitive functions are interdependent. Although emotion, like all other behaviors, has unique and defining characteristics, current research strongly argues against a concrete emotion–cognition dichotomy.

Studies in the cognitive neuroscience of emotion have tended to emphasize the importance of the amygdala. Our understanding of the role of the amygdala in emotion has been influenced significantly by research with nonhuman animals. In both humans and other species, the amygdala plays a critical role in implicit emotional learning, as demonstrated by fear conditioning. In addition, through interactions with the hippocampus, the amygdala is involved in explicit emotional learning and memory. We have seen that the amygdala is also involved with decision making, attention, and perception. It is also prominently involved in social interactions, enabling us to automatically derive information from the eyes of other people when assessing facial expressions and facilitating categorization of other individuals.

The amygdala is no longer the sole focus of research seeking to characterize the neural correlates of emotion. Different emotions are associated with other neural structures, including the orbitofrontal cortex (anger), the angular gyrus (passionate love), and the insula (disgust). Despite the success of relating these structures to various emotions, an emerging shift in our approach to studying the cognitive neuroscience of emotion is transferring the emphasis from the study of isolated neural structures to the investigation of neural systems. Certainly the amygdala, orbitofrontal cortex, and insula are critical for different forms of emotional processing. But it is now clear that to understand how the brain produces normal and adaptive emotional responses, we need to understand how these structures interact with each other and with other brain regions.

Key Terms

affective flexibility (p. 459)
amygdala (p. 437)
attentional blink (p. 446)
basic emotion (p. 430)
complex emotion (p. 430)
core affect (p. 436)
dimensions of emotion (p. 430)

emotion (p. 427)
emotion generation (p. 430)
emotion regulation (p. 455)
emotional stimulus (p. 430)
facial expression (p. 431)
fear conditioning (p. 439)
feeling (p. 427)

flow (p. 461)
insula (p. 459)
interoception (p. 460)
orbitofrontal cortex (OFC) (p. 449)
reappraisal (p. 457)
somatic marker (p. 448)
suppression (p. 457)

ANATOMICAL ORIENTATION

The anatomy of language

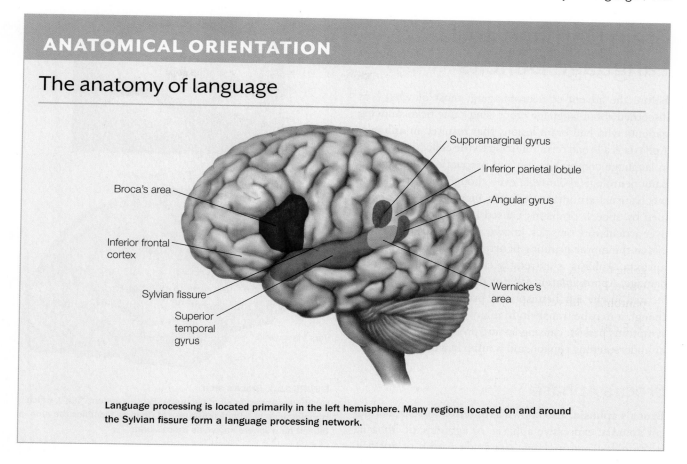

Language processing is located primarily in the left hemisphere. Many regions located on and around the Sylvian fissure form a language processing network.

The Anatomy of Language

Split-brain patients as well as patients with lateralized, focal brain lesions have taught us that a great deal of language processing is lateralized to the left-hemisphere regions surrounding the **Sylvian fissure**. Neuroimaging data, cortical stimulation mapping, and electrical and magnetic brain recording methods are revealing the details of the neuroanatomy of language. Language areas include the left temporal cortex, which includes **Wernicke's area** in the posterior superior temporal gyrus, portions of the left anterior temporal cortex, the inferior parietal lobe (which include the supramarginal gyrus and the angular gyrus), the left inferior frontal cortex, which includes **Broca's area**, and the left insular cortex (see the Anatomical Orientation box). Collectively, these brain areas, and their interconnections, form the *left perisylvian language network* of the human brain (they surround the Sylvian fissure; Hagoort, 2013).

The left hemisphere may do the lion's share of language processing, but the right hemisphere does make some contributions. The right superior temporal sulcus plays a role in processing the rhythm of language (prosody), and the right prefrontal cortex, middle temporal gyrus, and posterior cingulate activate when sentences have metaphorical meaning.

Language production, perception (think lip reading and sign language), and comprehension also involve both motor movement and timing. Thus, all the cortical (premotor cortex, motor cortex, and supplementary motor area—SMA) and subcortical (thalamus, basal ganglia, and cerebellum) structures involved with motor movement and timing that we discussed in Chapter 8, make key contributions to our ability to communicate (Kotz & Schwartze, 2010).

TAKE-HOME MESSAGES

- Anomia is the inability to find the words to label things in the world. It is not a deficit of knowledge.
- A left-hemisphere network involving the frontal, parietal, and temporal lobes is especially critical for language production and comprehension.
- The right hemisphere does have roles in language, especially in processing the prosody of language.

Brain Damage and Language Deficits

Before the advent of neuroimaging, most of what was discerned about language processing came from studying patients who had brain lesions that resulted in **aphasia**. Aphasia is a broad term referring to the collective deficits in language comprehension and production that accompany neurological damage, even though the articulatory mechanisms are intact. Aphasia *may* also be accompanied by speech problems caused by the loss of control over articulatory muscles, known as **dysarthria,** and deficits in the motor planning of articulations, called speech **apraxia**. Aphasia is extremely common following brain damage. Approximately 40% of all strokes (usually those located in the left hemisphere) produce some aphasia, though it may be transient. In many patients, the aphasic symptoms persist, causing lasting problems in producing or understanding spoken and written language.

Broca's Aphasia

Broca's aphasia, also known as anterior aphasia, nonfluent aphasia, expressive aphasia, or agrammatic aphasia, is the oldest and perhaps best-studied form of aphasia. It was first clearly described by Parisian physician Paul Broca in the 19th century. He performed an autopsy on a patient who for several years before his death could speak only a single word, "tan." Broca observed that the patient had a brain lesion in the posterior portion of the left inferior frontal gyrus, which is made up of the pars triangularis and pars opercularis, now referred to as Broca's area (Figure 11.1). After studying many patients with language problems, Broca also concluded that brain areas that produce speech were localized in the left hemisphere.

In the most severe forms of Broca's aphasia, single-utterance patterns of speech, such as that of Broca's original patient, are often observed. The variability is large, however, and may include unintelligible mutterings, single syllables or words, short simple phrases, sentences that mostly lack function words or grammatical markers, or idioms such as "Barking up the wrong tree." Sometimes the ability to sing normally is undisturbed, as might be the ability to recite phrases and prose, or to count. The speech of Broca's aphasics is often telegraphic, coming in uneven bursts, and very effortful (Figure 11.2a). Finding the appropriate word or combination of words and then executing the pronunciation is compromised. This condition is often accompanied by apraxia of speech (Figure 11.2b). Broca's aphasics are aware of their errors and have a low tolerance for frustration.

Broca's notion that these aphasics had only a disorder in speech production, however, is not correct. They can

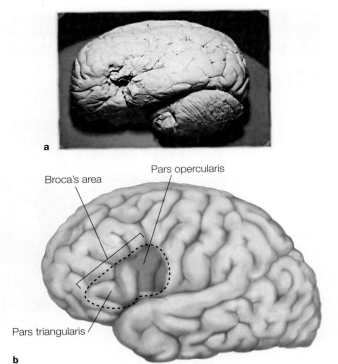

FIGURE 11.1 Broca's area.
(a) The preserved brain of Leborgne (Broca's patient "Tan"), which is maintained in a Paris museum. **(b)** Shading identifies the area in the left hemisphere known as Broca's area.

also have comprehension deficits related to **syntax** (rules governing how words are put together in a sentence). Often only the most basic and overlearned grammatical forms are produced and comprehended, a deficit known as **agrammatic aphasia**. For example, consider the following sentences: "The boy kicked the girl" and "The boy was kicked by the girl." The first sentence can be understood from word order, and Broca's aphasics understand such sentences fairly well. But the second sentence has a more complicated grammar, and in such cases Broca's aphasics would misunderstand who kicked whom (Figure 11.2c).

When Broca first described this disorder, he related it to damage to the cortical region now known as Broca's area (see Figure 11.1b). Challenges to the idea that Broca's area was responsible for speech deficits seen in aphasia have been raised since Broca's time. For example, aphasiologist Nina Dronkers (1996) at the University of California, Davis, reported 22 patients with lesions in Broca's area, as defined by neuroimaging, but only 10 of these patients had Broca's aphasia.

Broca never dissected the brain of his original patient, Leborgne, and could therefore not determine whether there was damage to structures in the brain that could not be seen on the surface of the brain. Leborgne's brain was preserved and is now housed in Musée Dupuytren in Paris (as is Broca's brain). Recent high-resolution MRI

a **Spontaneously speaking**

"Son ... university ... smart ... boy ... good ... ... good ..."

b **Repeating**

"Chrysanthemum"

"Chrysa... ...mum... mum..."

c **Listening for comprehension**

"The boy was hit by the girl. Who hit whom?"

"Boy hit girl"

FIGURE 11.2 Speech problems in Broca's aphasia.
Broca's aphasics can have various problems when they speak or when they try to comprehend or repeat the linguistic input provided by the clinician. **(a)** The speech output of this patient is slow and effortful, and it lacks function words. It resembles a telegram. **(b)** Broca's aphasics also may have accompanying problems with speech articulation because of deficits in regulation of the articulatory apparatus (e.g., muscles of the tongue). **(c)** Finally, these patients sometimes have a hard time understanding reversible sentences, where a full understanding of the sentence depends on correct syntactic assignment of the thematic roles (e.g., who hit whom?).

scans showed that Leborgne's lesions extended into regions underlying the superficial cortical zone of Broca's area, and included the insular cortex and portions of the basal ganglia (Dronkers et al., 2007). This finding suggested that damage to the classic regions of the frontal cortex known as Broca's area may not be solely responsible for the speech production deficits of Broca's aphasics.

Wernicke's Aphasia

Wernicke's aphasia, also known as posterior aphasia or receptive aphasia, was first described fully by the German physician Carl Wernicke, and is a disorder primarily of language comprehension. Patients with this syndrome

have difficulty understanding spoken or written language and sometimes cannot understand language at all. Although their speech is fluent with normal prosody and grammar, what they say is nonsensical.

In performing autopsies on his patients who showed language comprehension problems, Wernicke discovered damage in the posterior regions of the superior temporal gyrus, which has since become known as Wernicke's area (Figure 11.3). Because auditory processing occurs nearby (anteriorly) in the superior temporal cortex within Heschl's gyri, Wernicke deduced that this more posterior region participated in the auditory storage of words—as an auditory memory area for words. This view is not commonly proposed today. As with Broca's aphasia and Broca's area, inconsistencies are seen in the relationship between brain lesion and language deficit in Wernicke's aphasia. Lesions that spare Wernicke's area can also lead to comprehension deficits.

More recent studies have revealed that dense and persistent Wernicke's aphasia is ensured only if there is damage in Wernicke's area *and* in the surrounding cortex of the posterior temporal lobe, or damage to the underlying white matter that connects temporal lobe language areas to other brain regions. Thus, although Wernicke's area remains in the center of a posterior region of the brain whose functioning is required for normal comprehension, lesions confined to Wernicke's area produce only temporary Wernicke's aphasia. It appears that damage to this area does not actually cause the syndrome. Instead, secondary damage due to tissue swelling in surrounding regions contributes to the most severe problems. When swelling around the lesioned cortex goes away, comprehension improves.

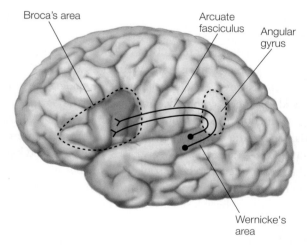

FIGURE 11.3 Lateral view of the left hemisphere language areas and dorsal connections.
Wernicke's area is shown shaded in red. The arcuate fasciculus is the bundle of axons that connects Wernicke's and Broca's areas. It originates in Wernicke's area, goes through the angular gyrus, and terminates on neurons in Broca's area.

Conduction Aphasia

In the 1880s, Ludwig Lichtheim introduced the idea of a third region that stored conceptual information about words, not word storage per se. Once a word was retrieved from word storage, he proposed that the word information was sent to the concept area, which supplied all that was associated with the word. Lichtheim first described the classical localizationist model (Figure 11.4), where linguistic information, word storage (A = Wernicke's area), speech planning (M = Broca's area), and conceptual information stores (B) are located in separate brain regions interconnected by white matter tracts. The white matter tract that flows from Wernicke's area to Broca's area is the **arcuate fasciculus**. Wernicke predicted that a certain type of aphasia should result from damage to its fibers. It was not until the late 1950s, when neurologist Norman Geschwind became interested in aphasia and the neurological basis of language, that Wernicke's connection idea resurfaced and was later revived (Geschwind, 1967). Disconnection syndromes, such as **conduction aphasia**, have been observed with damage to the arcuate fasciculus (see Figure 11.3).

Conduction aphasics can understand words that they hear or see and can hear their own speech errors, but they cannot repair them. They have problems producing spontaneous speech as well as repeating speech, and sometimes they use words incorrectly. Recall that H.W. was impaired in word-repetition tasks. Similar symptoms, however, are also evident with lesions to the insula and portions of the auditory cortex. One explanation for this similarity may be that damage to other nerve fibers is not detected, or that connections between Wernicke's area and Broca's area are not as strong as connections between the more widely spread anterior and posterior language areas outside these regions. Indeed, we now realize that the emphasis should not really be on Broca's and Wernicke's areas, but on the brain regions currently understood to be better correlated with the syndromes of Broca's aphasia and Wernicke's aphasia. Considered in this way, a lesion to the area surrounding the insula could disconnect comprehension from production areas.

We could predict from the model in Figure 11.4 that damage to the connections between conceptual representation areas (area B) and Wernicke's area (A) would harm the ability to comprehend spoken inputs but not the ability to repeat what was heard (this is known as transcortical sensory aphasia). Such problems exist as the result of lesions in the supramarginal and angular gyri regions of patients. These patients have the unique ability to repeat what they have heard and to correct grammatical errors when they repeat it, but they are unable to understand the meaning. These findings have been interpreted as evidence that this aphasia may come from losing the ability to access semantic (the meaning of a word) information, without

losing syntactic (grammatical) or phonological abilities. A third disconnection syndrome, transcortical motor aphasia, results from a disconnection between the concept centers (B) and Broca's area (M) while the pathway between Wernicke's area and Broca's area remains intact. This condition produces symptoms similar to Broca's aphasia, yet with the preserved ability to repeat heard phrases. Indeed, these patients may compulsively repeat phrases, a behavior known as echolalia. Finally, **global aphasia** is a devastating syndrome that results in the inability to both produce and comprehend language. Typically, this type of aphasia is associated with extensive left-hemisphere damage, including Broca's area, Wernicke's area, and regions between them.

Although the classical localizationist model could account for many findings, it could not explain all of the neurological observations, nor can it explain current neuroimaging findings. Studies in patients with specific aphasic syndromes have revealed that the classical model's assumption that only Broca's and Wernicke's areas are associated with Broca's aphasia and Wernicke's aphasia, respectively, is incorrect. Part of the problem is that the original lesion localizations were not very sophisticated. Another part of the problem lies in the classification of the syndromes themselves: Both Broca's and Wernicke's aphasias are associated with a mixed bag of symptoms and do not present with purely production and comprehension deficits, respectively. As we have seen, Broca's aphasics may have apraxia of speech *and* problems with comprehension, which are

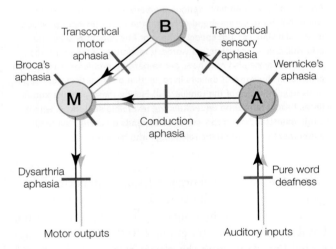

FIGURE 11.4 Lichtheim's classical model of language processing. The area that stores permanent information about word sounds is represented by A. The speech planning and programming area is represented by M. Conceptual information is stored in area B. The arrows indicate the direction of information flow. This model formed the basis of predictions that lesions in the three main areas, or in the connections between the areas, or the inputs to or outputs from these areas, could account for seven main aphasic syndromes. The locations of possible lesions are indicated by the red line segments. A = Wernicke's area. B = conceptual information stores. M=Broca's area.

different linguistic processes. It is not at all surprising that this variety of language functions is supported by more than Broca's area. The tide has turned away from a purely locationist view, and scientists have begun to assume that language emerges from a network of brain regions and their connections. You also may have noticed that the original models of language were mostly concerned with the recognition and production of individual words and, as we discuss later in the chapter, language entails much more than that.

Information about language deficits following brain damage and studies in split-brain patients (see Chapter 4) have provided a wealth of information about the organization of human language in the brain, specifically identifying a left-hemisphere language system. Language, however, is a vastly complicated cognitive system. To understand it, we need to know much more than merely the gross functional anatomy of language. We need to learn a bit about language itself.

TAKE-HOME MESSAGES

- Language disorders, generally called aphasia, can include deficits in comprehension or production of language resulting from neurological damage.
- Patients with Broca's aphasia have problems with speech production, syntax, and grammar, but otherwise comprehend what is said or written fairly well.
- The lesions that produce Broca's aphasia may not be limited to the classically defined Broca's area in the left inferior frontal cortex.
- People with Wernicke's aphasia have severe comprehension deficits but can produce relatively fluid speech; it is, however, rather meaningless. Originally linked to damage solely in Wernicke's area (the posterior superior temporal gyrus), today Wernicke's aphasia is also linked to damage outside the classic Wernicke's area.
- Aphasia can also result from damage to the connection between Wernicke's and Broca's areas (the arcuate fasciculus). Conduction aphasia is the disorder that results from such damage, and people with this type of aphasia have problems producing spontaneous speech as well as repeating speech.

The Fundamentals of Language in the Human Brain

Words and the Representation of Their Meaning

Let's begin with some simple questions. How does the brain cope with spoken, signed, and written input to derive

meaning? And, how does the brain produce spoken, signed, and written output to communicate meaning to others? We can tackle these questions by laying out the aspects of language we need to consider in this chapter. First, the brain must store words and concepts. One of the central concepts in word (lexical) representation is the **mental lexicon**—a mental store of information about words that includes semantic information (the words' meanings), syntactic information (how the words are combined to form sentences), and the details of word forms (their spellings and sound patterns). Most theories agree on the central role for a mental lexicon in language. Some theories, however, propose one mental lexicon for both language comprehension and production, whereas other models distinguish between input and output lexica. In addition, the representation of orthographic (vision-based) and phonological (sound-based) forms must be considered in any model. The principal concept, though, is that a store (or stores) of information about words exists in the brain. Words we hear, or see signed or written must first, of course, be analyzed perceptually.

Once words are perceptually analyzed, three general functions are hypothesized: lexical access, lexical selection, and lexical integration. **Lexical access** refers to the stage(s) of processing in which the output of perceptual analysis activates word-form representations in the mental lexicon, including their semantic and syntactic attributes. **Lexical selection** is the next stage, where the lexical representation in the mental lexicon that best matches the input can be identified (selected). Finally, to understand the whole message, **lexical integration** integrates words into the full sentence, discourse, or larger context. Grammar and syntax are the rules by which lexical items are organized in a particular language to produce the intended meaning. We must also consider not only how we comprehend language but also how we produce it as utterances, signs, and in its written forms. First things first, though: We begin by considering the mental lexicon, the brain's store of words and concepts, and ask how it might be organized, and how it might be represented in the brain.

A normal adult speaker has passive knowledge of about 50,000 words and yet can easily recognize and produce about three words per second. Given this speed and the size of the database, the mental lexicon must be organized in a highly efficient manner. It cannot be merely the equivalent of a dictionary. If, for example, the mental lexicon were organized in simple alphabetical order, it might take longer to find words in the middle of the alphabet, such as the ones starting with *K*, *L*, *O*, or *U*, than to find a word starting with an *A* or a *Z*. Fortunately, this is not the case.

Instead, the mental lexicon has other organizational principles that help us quickly get from the spoken or written input to the representations of words. First is the representational unit in the mental lexicon, called the **morpheme**, which is the smallest meaningful unit in a language. As an example consider the words *frost*, <u>de</u>*frost*, and *defroster*. The root of these words, *frost*, forms one morpheme; the prefix "de" in *defrost* changes the meaning of the word *frost* and is a morpheme as well; and finally the word *defroster* consists of three morphemes (adding the morpheme "er"). An example of a word with a lot of morphemes comes from a 2007 *New York Times* article on language by William Safire; he used the word *editorializing*. Can you figure out how many morphemes are in this word? A second organizational principle is that more frequently used words are accessed more quickly than less frequently used words; for instance, the word *people* is more readily available than the word *fledgling*.

A third organizing principle is the lexical neighborhood, which consists of those words that differ from any single word by only one phoneme or one letter (e.g., bat, cat, hat, sat). A **phoneme** is the smallest unit of *sound* that makes a difference to meaning. In English, the sounds for the letters *L* and *R* are two phonemes (the words *late* and *rate* mean different things), but in the Japanese language, no meaningful distinction is made between *L* and *R*, so they are represented by only one phoneme. Behavioral studies have shown that words having more neighbors are identified more slowly during language comprehension than words with few neighbors (e.g., *bat* has many neighbors, but *sword* does not). The idea is that there may be competition between the brain representations of different words during word recognition—and this phenomenon tells us something about the organization of our mental lexicon. Specifically, words with many overlapping phonemes or letters must be organized together in the brain, such that when incoming words access one word representation, others are also initially accessed, and selection among candidate words must occur, which takes time.

A fourth organizing factor for the mental lexicon is the **semantic** (meaning) relationships between words. Support for the idea that representations in the mental lexicon are organized according to meaningful relationships between words comes from semantic priming studies that use a lexical (word) decision task. In a semantic priming study, participants are presented with pairs of words. The first member of the word pair, the *prime*, is a word; the second member, the *target*, can be a real word (*truck*), a nonword (like *rtukc*), or a pseudoword (a word that follows the phonological rules of a language but is not a real word, like *trulk*). If the target is a real word, it can be related or unrelated in meaning to the prime. For the task, the participants must decide as quickly and accurately as possible whether the target is a word (i.e., make a lexical decision), pressing a button indicating their decision. Participants are faster and more accurate at making the lexical decision when the target is preceded by a related prime (e.g., the prime *car* for the

target *truck*) than an unrelated prime (e.g., the prime *sunny* for the target *truck*). Related patterns are found when the participant is asked to simply read the target out loud and there are only real words presented. Here, naming latencies are faster for words related to the prime word than for unrelated ones. What does this pattern of facilitated response speed tell us about the organization of the mental lexicon? It reveals that words related in meaning must somehow be organized together in the brain, such that activation of the representation of one word also activates words that are related in meaning. This makes words easier to recognize when they follow a related word that primes their meaning.

Models of the Mental Lexicon

Several models have been proposed to explain the effects of semantic priming during word recognition. In an influential model proposed by Collins and Loftus (1975), word meanings are represented in a semantic network in which words, represented by conceptual nodes, are connected with each other. Figure 11.5 shows an example of a semantic network. The strength of the connection and the distance between the nodes are determined by the semantic relations or associative relations between the words. For example, the node that represents the word *car* will be close to and have a strong connection with the node that represents the word *truck*.

A major component of this model is the assumption that activation spreads from one conceptual node to others, and nodes that are closer together will benefit more from this spreading activation than will distant nodes. If we hear "car," the node that represents the word *car* in the semantic network will be activated. In addition, words like *truck* and *bus* that are closely related to the meaning of *car*, and are therefore nearby and well connected in the semantic network, will also receive a considerable amount of activation. In contrast, a word like *rose* most likely will receive no activation at all when we hear "car." This model predicts that hearing "car" should facilitate recognition of the word *truck* but not *rose*, which is true.

Although the semantic-network model that Collins and Loftus proposed has been extremely influential, the way that word meanings are organized is still a matter of dispute and investigation. There are many other models and ideas of how conceptual knowledge is represented. Some models propose that words that co-occur in our language prime each other (e.g., *cottage* and *cheese*), and others suggest that concepts are represented by their semantic features or semantic properties. For example, the word *dog* has several semantic features, such as "is animate," "has four legs," and "barks," and these features are assumed to be represented in the conceptual network. Such models are confronted with the problem of activation: How many features have to be activated for a person to recognize a dog?

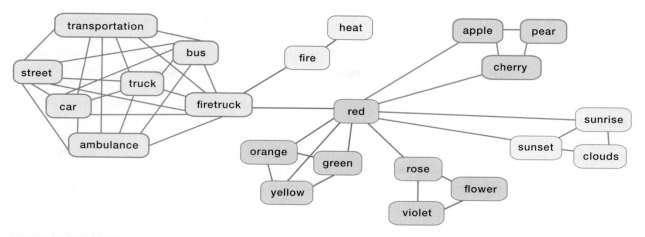

FIGURE 11.5 Semantic network.
Words that have strong associative or semantic relations are closer together in the network (e.g., *car* and *truck*) than are words that have no such relation (e.g., *car* and *clouds*). Semantically related words are colored similarly in the figure, and associatively related words (e.g., *firetruck–fire*) are closely connected.

For example, it is possible to train dogs not to bark, yet we can recognize a dog even when it does not bark, and we can identify a barking dog that we cannot see. Furthermore, it is not exactly clear how many features would have to be stored. For example, a table could be made of wood or glass, and in both cases we would recognize it as a table. Does this mean that we have to store the features "is of wood/glass" with the table concept? In addition, some words are more "prototypical" examples of a semantic category than others, as reflected in our recognition and production of these words. When we are asked to generate bird names, for example, the word *robin* comes to mind as one of the first examples; but a word like *ostrich* might not come up at all, depending on where we grew up or have lived.

In sum, it remains a matter of intense investigation how word meanings are represented. No matter how, though, everyone agrees that a mental store of word meanings is crucial to normal language comprehension and production. Evidence from patients with brain damage and from functional brain-imaging studies is revealing how the mental lexicon and conceptual knowledge may be organized.

Neural Substrates of the Mental Lexicon

Through observations of deficits in patients' language abilities, we can infer a number of things about the functional organization of the mental lexicon. Different types of neurological problems create deficits in understanding and producing the appropriate meaning of a word or concept, as we described earlier. Patients with Wernicke's aphasia make errors in speech production that are known as **semantic paraphasias**. For example, they might use the word *horse* when they mean *cow*. Patients with *deep*

dyslexia make similar errors in reading: They might read the word *horse* where *cow* is written.

Patients with *progressive semantic dementia* initially show impairments in the conceptual system, but other mental and language abilities are spared. For example, these patients can still understand and produce the syntactic structure of sentences. This impairment has been associated with progressive damage to the temporal lobes, mostly on the left side of the brain. But the superior regions of the temporal lobe that are important for hearing and speech processing are spared (these areas are discussed later, in the subsection on spoken input). Patients with semantic dementia have difficulty assigning objects to a semantic category. In addition, they often name a category when asked to name a picture; when viewing a picture of a horse, they will say "animal," and a picture of a robin will produce "bird." Neurological evidence from a variety of disorders provides support for the semantic-network idea because related meanings are substituted, confused, or lumped together, as we would predict from the degrading of a system of interconnected nodes that specifies meaning relation.

In the 1970s and early 1980s, Elizabeth Warrington and her colleagues performed groundbreaking studies on the organization of conceptual knowledge in the brain, originating with her studies involving perceptual disabilities in patients possessing unilateral cerebral lesions. We have discussed these studies in some detail in Chapter 6, so we will only summarize them here. In Chapter 6 we discussed category-specific agnosias and how they might reflect the organization of semantic memory (conceptual) knowledge. Warrington and her colleagues found that semantic memory problems fell into semantic categories. They suggested that the patients' problems were reflections of the types of information stored with different words in the semantic network. Whereas the biological categories rely more on physical properties or visual features, man-made objects are identified by their functional properties. Some of these studies were done on patients who would now be classified as suffering from semantic dementia.

Since these original observations by Warrington, many cases of patients with category-specific deficits have been reported, and there appears to be a striking correspondence between the sites of lesions and the type of semantic deficit. The patients whose impairment involved living things had lesions that included the inferior and medial temporal cortex, and often these lesions were located anteriorly. The anterior inferotemporal cortex is located close to areas of the brain that are crucial for visual object perception, and the medial temporal lobe contains important relay projections from association cortex to the hippocampus, a structure that, as you might remember from Chapter 9, has an important function in the encoding of information in long-term memory. Furthermore, the inferotemporal lobe is the end station for "what" information, or the object recognition stream, in vision (see Chapter 6).

Less is known about the localization of lesions in patients who show greater impairment for human-made things, simply because fewer of these patients have been identified and studied. But left frontal and parietal areas appear to be involved in this kind of semantic deficit. These areas are close to or overlap with areas of the brain that are important for sensorimotor functions, and so they are likely to be involved in the representation of actions that can be undertaken when human-made artifacts such as tools are being used.

Correlations between the type of semantic deficit and the area of brain lesion are consistent with a hypothesis by Warrington and her colleagues about the organization of semantic information. They have suggested that the patients' problems are reflections of the types of information stored with different words in the semantic network. Whereas the biological categories (fruits, foods, animals) rely more on physical properties or visual features (e.g., what is the color of an apple?), human-made objects are identified by their functional properties (e.g., how do we use a hammer?).

This hypothesis by Warrington and colleagues has been both supported and challenged. The computational model by Martha Farah and James McClelland (1991), which has been discussed in Chapter 6, supported Warrington's model. A challenge to Warrington's proposal comes from observations by Alfonso Caramazza and others (e.g., Caramazza & Shelton, 1998) that the studies in patients did not always use well-controlled linguistic materials. For example, when comparing living things versus human-made things, some studies did not control the stimulus materials to ensure that the objects tested in each category were matched on things like visual complexity, visual similarity

across objects, frequency of use, and the familiarity of objects. If these variables differ widely between the categories, then clear-cut conclusions about differences in their representation in a semantic network cannot be drawn. Caramazza has proposed an alternative theory in which the semantic network is organized along lines of the conceptual categories of animacy and inanimacy. He argues that the selective damage that has been observed in brain-damaged patients, as in the studies of Warrington and others, genuinely reflects "evolutionarily adapted domain-specific knowledge systems that are subserved by distinct neural mechanisms" (Caramazza & Shelton, 1998, p. 1).

In the 1990s, studies using imaging techniques in neurologically unimpaired human participants looked further into the organization of semantic representations. Alex Martin and his colleagues (1996) at the National Institute of Mental Health (NIMH) conducted studies using PET imaging and functional magnetic resonance imaging (fMRI). Their findings reveal how the intriguing dissociations in neurological patients that we just described can be identified in neurologically normal brains. When participants read the names of or answered questions about animals, or when they named pictures of animals, the more lateral aspects of the fusiform gyrus (on the brain's ventral surface) and the superior temporal sulcus were activated. But naming animals also activated a brain area associated with the early stages of visual processing—namely, the left medial occipital lobe. In contrast, identifying and naming tools were associated with activation in the more medial aspect of the fusiform gyrus, the left middle temporal gyrus, and the left premotor area, a region that is also activated by imagining hand movements. These findings are consistent with the idea that in our brains, conceptual representations of living things versus human-made tools rely on separable neuronal circuits engaged in processing of perceptual versus functional information.

More recently, studies of the representation of conceptual information indicate that there is a network that connects the posterior fusiform gyrus in the inferior temporal lobe to the left anterior temporal lobes. Lorraine Tyler and her colleagues (Taylor et al., 2011) at the University of Cambridge have studied the representation and processing of concepts of living and nonliving things in patients with brain lesions to the anterior temporal lobes and in unimpaired participants using fMRI, EEG, and MEG measures. In these studies, participants are typically asked to name pictures of living (e.g., tiger) and nonliving (e.g., knife) things. Further, the level at which these objects should be named was varied. Participants were asked to name the pictures at the specific level (e.g., tiger or knife), or they were asked to name the pictures at the domain general level (e.g., living or nonliving).

Tyler and colleagues suggest that naming at the specific level requires retrieval and integration of more detailed semantic information than at the domain general level. For example, whereas naming a picture at a domain general level requires activation of only a subset of features (e.g., for animals: has-legs, has-fur, has-eyes, etc.), naming at the specific level requires retrieval and integration of additional and more precise features (e.g., to distinguish a tiger from a panther, features such as "has-stripes" have to be retrieved and integrated as well). Interestingly, as can be seen in Figure 11.6, whereas nonliving things can be represented by only a few features (e.g., knife), living things are represented by many features (e.g., tiger). Thus, it may be more difficult to select the feature that distinguishes living things from each other (e.g., a tiger from a panther; has-stripes vs. has-spots) than it is to distinguish nonliving things (e.g., a knife from a spoon; cuts vs. scoops; Figure 11.6b). This model suggests that the dissociation between naming of nonliving

and living things in patients with category-specific deficits may also be due to the complexity of the features that help distinguish one thing from another.

Tyler and colleagues observed that patients with lesions to the anterior temporal lobes cannot reliably name living things at the specific level, indicating that the retrieval and integration of more detailed semantic information is impaired. Functional MRI studies in unimpaired participants showed greater activation in the anterior temporal lobe with specific-level naming of living things than with domain-level naming (Figure 11.7).

Finally, studies with MEG and EEG have revealed interesting details about the timing of the activation of conceptual knowledge. Activation of the perceptual features occurs in primary cortices within the first 100 ms after a picture is presented; activation of more detailed semantic representations occurs in the posterior and anterior

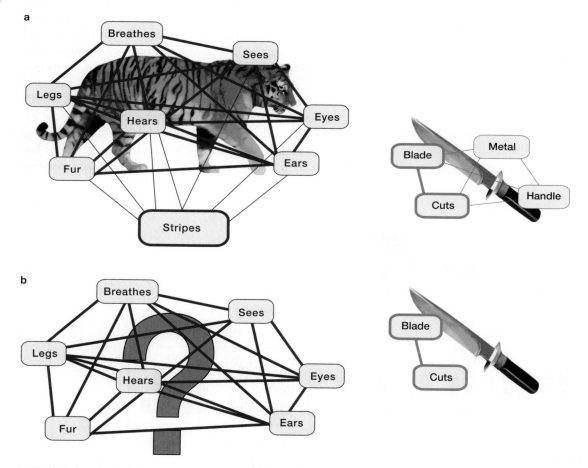

FIGURE 11.6 Hypothetical conceptual structures for tiger and knife.
(a) One model suggests that living things are represented by many features that are not distinct whereas nonliving things can be represented by only a few features that are distinct. In this hypothetical concept structure, the thickness of the straight lines correlates with the strength of the features, and the thickness of the boxes' border correlates with the distinctness of the features. Although the tiger has many features, it has fewer features that distinguish it from other living things, whereas the knife has more distinct features that separate it from other possible objects. **(b)** Following brain damage resulting in aphasia, patients find it harder to identify the distinctive feature(s) for living things (lower left panel) than for non-living objects.

ventral–lateral cortex between 150 and 250 ms; and starting around 300 ms, participants are able to name the specific object that is depicted in the picture, which requires the retrieval and integration of detailed semantic information that is unique to the specific object.

TAKE-HOME MESSAGES

- The mental lexicon is the brain's store of words and concepts.
- A morpheme is the smallest unit of language that has meaning.
- A phoneme is the smallest unit of sound that makes a difference to meaning.
- Semantic (meaning) relationships between words are an organizational principle of the mental lexicon.
- Syntax refers to the way in which words in a particular language are organized into grammatically permitted sentences.
- Grammar refers to the structural rules that govern the composition of words, phrases, and sentences in a particular natural language.
- Patients with neurological damage may name an item with an incorrect but semantically-related word (e.g., "animal" for "horse"), which supports the idea that the mental lexicon contains semantic networks of related meanings clustered together.

Language Comprehension

Perceptual Analyses of the Linguistic Input

In understanding spoken language and understanding written language, the brain uses some of the same processes; but there are also some striking differences in how spoken and written inputs are analyzed. When attempting to understand spoken words (Figure 11.8), the listener has to decode the acoustic input. The result of this acoustic analysis is translated into a phonological code because, as discussed above, that is how the lexical representations of auditory word forms are stored in the mental lexicon. After the acoustic input has been translated into a phonological format, the lexical representations in the mental lexicon that match the auditory input can be accessed (lexical access), and the best match can then be selected (lexical selection). The selected word includes grammatical and semantic information stored with it in the mental lexicon. This information helps to specify how the word can be used in the given language. Finally, the word's meaning (store of the lexical-semantic information) results in activation of the conceptual information.

The process of reading words shares at least the last two steps of linguistic analysis (i.e., lexical and meaning

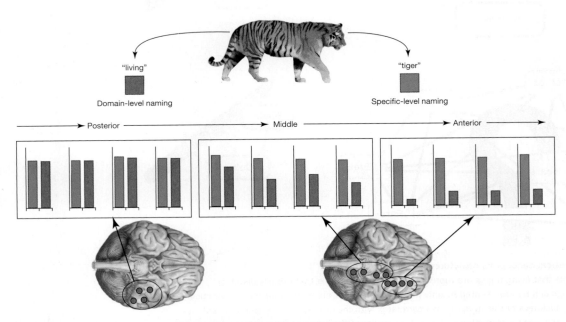

FIGURE 11.7 The anterior temporal lobes are involved in naming living things.
When identifying the tiger at the less complex domain level (living things), activity was restricted to more posterior occipitotemporal sites (red bars). Naming the same object stimulus at the specific-level (blue bars) was associated with activity in both posterior occipitotemporal and anteromedial temporal lobes.

activation) with auditory comprehension, but, due to the different input modality, it differs at the earlier processing steps, as illustrated in Figure 11.8. Given that the perceptual input is different, what are these earlier stages in reading? The first analysis step requires that the reader identify orthographic units (written symbols that represent the sounds or words of a language) from the visual input. These orthographic units may then be directly mapped onto orthographic (vision-based) word forms in the mental lexicon, or alternatively, the identified orthographic units might be translated into phonological units, which in turn activate the phonological word form in the mental lexicon as described for auditory comprehension.

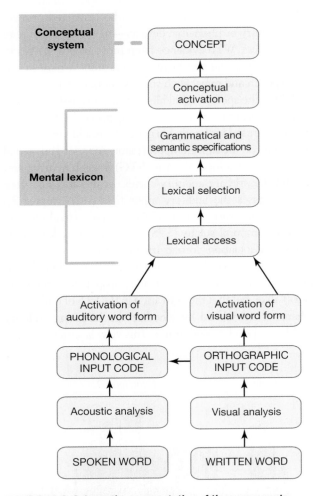

FIGURE 11.8 Schematic representation of the components involved in spoken and written language comprehension. Inputs can enter via either auditory (spoken word) or visual (written word) modalities. Notice that the information flows from the bottom up in this figure, from perceptual identification to "higher level" word and meaning activation. So-called interactive models of language understanding would predict top-down influences to play a role as well. For example, activation at the word-form level would influence earlier perceptual processes. We could introduce this type of feedback into this schematic representation by making the arrows bidirectional (see "How the Brain Works: Modularity Versus Interactivity").

In the next few sections, we delve into the processes involved in the understanding of spoken and written inputs of words. Then we consider the understanding of sentences. We begin with auditory processing and then turn to the different steps involved in the comprehension of reading, also known as visual language input.

Spoken Input: Understanding Speech

The input signal in spoken language is very different from that in written language. Whereas for a reader it is immediately clear that the letters on a page are the physical signals of importance, a listener is confronted with a variety of sounds in the environment and has to identify and distinguish the relevant speech signals from other "noise."

As introduced earlier, important building blocks of spoken language are phonemes. These are the smallest units of sound that make a difference to meaning; for example, in the words *cap* and *tap* the only difference is the first phoneme (/c/ versus /t/). The English language uses 40 phonemes; other languages may use more or less. Perception of phonemes is different for speakers of different languages. As we mentioned earlier in this chapter, for example, in English, the sounds for the letters *L* and *R* are two phonemes (the words *late* and *rate* mean different things, and we easily hear that difference). But in the Japanese language, *L* and *R* cannot be distinguished by adult native speakers, so these sounds are represented by only one phoneme.

Interestingly, infants have the perceptual ability to distinguish between *any* possible phonemes during their first year of life. Patricia Kuhl and her colleagues at the University of Washington found that, initially, infants could distinguish between any phonemes presented to them; but during the first year of life, their perceptual sensitivities became tuned to the phonemes of the language they experienced (Kuhl et al., 1992). So, for example, Japanese infants can distinguish *L* from *R* sounds, but then lose that ability over time. American infants, on the other hand, do not lose that ability, but do lose the ability to distinguish phonemes that are not part of the English language. The babbling and crying sounds that infants articulate from ages 6–12 months grow more and more similar to the phonemes that they most frequently hear. By the time babies are one year old, they no longer produce (nor perceive) nonnative phonemes. Learning another language often involves phonemes that don't occur in a person's native language, such as the guttural sounds of Dutch or the rolling *R* of Spanish. Such nonnative sounds can be difficult to learn, especially when we are older and our native phonemes have become automatic, and make it challenging or impossible to lose our native accent. Perhaps that was Mark Twain's problem when he quipped, "In Paris they just simply opened their eyes and stared when we spoke to them in French! We never did succeed in making those idiots understand their own language" (from *The Innocents Abroad*).

Recognizing that phonemes are important building blocks of spoken language and that we all become experts in the phonemes of our native tongue does not eliminate all challenges for the listener. The listener's brain must resolve a number of additional difficulties with the speech signal; some of these challenges have to do with (a) the variability of the signal (e.g., male vs. female speakers), and (b) the fact that phonemes often do not appear as separate little chunks of information. Unlike the case for written words, auditory speech signals are not clearly segmented, and it can be difficult to discern where one word begins and another word ends. When we speak, we usually spew out about 15 phonemes per second, which adds up to about 180 words a minute. The puzzling thing is that we say these phonemes with no gaps or breaks: that is, there are no pauses between words. Thus, the input signal in spoken language is very different from that in written language, where the letters and phonemes are neatly separated into word chunks. Two or more spoken words can be slurred together or, in other words, speech sounds are often *coarticulated*. There can also be silences within words as well. The question of how we differentiate auditory sounds into separate words is known as the *segmentation problem*. This is illustrated in Figure 11.9, which shows the speech signal of the sentence, "What do you mean?"

How do we identify the spoken input, given this variability and the segmentation problem? Fortunately, other clues help us divide the speech stream into meaningful segments. One important clue is the *prosodic* information, which is what the listener derives from the speech rhythm and the pitch of the speaker's voice. The speech rhythm comes from variation in the duration of words and the placement of pauses between them. Prosody is apparent in all spoken utterances, but it is perhaps most clearly illustrated when a speaker asks a question or emphasizes something. When asking a question, a speaker raises the frequency of the voice toward the end of the question; and when emphasizing a part of speech, a speaker raises the loudness of the voice and includes a pause after the critical part of the sentence.

In their research, Anne Cutler and colleagues (Tyler and Cutler, 2009) at the Max Planck Institute for Psycholinguistics in the Netherlands have revealed other clues that can be used to segment the continuous speech stream. These researchers showed that English listeners use syllables that carry an accent or stress (strong syllables) to establish word boundaries. For example, a word like *lettuce*, with stress on the first syllable, is usually heard as a single word and not as two words ("let us"). In contrast, words such as *invests*, with stress on the last syllable, are usually heard as two words ("in vests") and not as one word.

Neural Substrates of Spoken-Word Processing

Now we turn to the questions of where in the brain the processes of understanding speech signals may take place and what neural circuits and systems support them. From animal studies, studies in patients with brain lesions, and imaging and recording (EEG and MEG) studies in humans, we know that the superior temporal cortex is important to sound perception. At the beginning of the 20th century, it was already well understood that patients with bilateral lesions restricted to the superior parts of the temporal lobe had the syndrome of "pure word deafness." Although they could process other sounds relatively normally, these patients had specific difficulties recognizing speech sounds. Because there was no difficulty in other aspects of language processing, the problem seemed to be restricted primarily to auditory or phonemic deficits—hence the term *pure word deafness*. With evidence from more recent studies in hand, however, we can begin to determine where in the brain speech and nonspeech sounds are first distinguished.

When the speech signal hits the ear, it is first processed by pathways in the brain that are not specialized for speech but that are used for hearing in general. Heschl's gyri, which are located on the supratemporal plane, superior and medial to the superior temporal gyrus (STG) in each hemisphere, contain the primary auditory cortex, or the area of cortex that processes the auditory input first (see Chapter 2). The areas that surround Heschl's gyri and extend into the superior temporal sulcus (STS) are collectively known as auditory association cortex. Imaging and recording studies in humans have shown that Heschl's gyri of both hemispheres are activated by speech and nonspeech sounds (e.g., tones) alike, but that the activation in the STS of both hemispheres is modulated by whether the incoming auditory signal is a speech sound or not. This view is summarized in

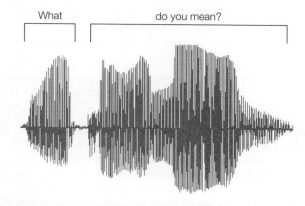

FIGURE 11.9 Speech waveform for the question, "What do you mean?"
Note that the words *do you mean* are not physically separated. Even though the physical signal provides few cues to where the spoken words begin and end, the language system is able to parse them into the individual words for comprehension.

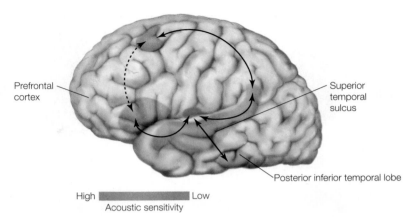

FIGURE 11.10 Brain areas important to speech perception and language comprehension.
Acoustic sensitivity decreases moving anteriorly and posteriorly away from primary auditory cortex, while speech sensitivity increases. Anterior and posterior regions of the superior temporal sulcus are increasingly speech specific. Posterior inferior temporal lobe and prefrontal regions are also important during speech processing. Heschl's gyrus (primary auditory cortex; red spot) is not speech specific, but is instead activated by all auditory inputs.

Figure 11.10 showing that there is a hierarchy in the sensitivity to speech in our brain (Peelle et al., 2010; Poeppel et al., 2012). As we move farther away from Heschl's gyrus toward anterior and posterior portions of the STS, the brain becomes less sensitive to changes in nonspeech sounds but more sensitive to speech sounds. Although more left lateralized, the posterior portions of the STS of both hemispheres seem especially relevant to processing of phonological information. It is clear from many studies, however, that the speech perception network expands beyond the STS.

As described earlier, Wernicke found that patients with lesions in the left temporoparietal region that included the STG (Wernicke's area) had difficulty understanding spoken and written language. This observation led to the now-century-old notion that this area is crucial to word comprehension. Even in Wernicke's original observations, however, the lesions were not restricted to the STG. We can now conclude that the STG alone is probably not the seat of word comprehension.

One study that has contributed to our new understanding of speech perception is an fMRI study done by Jeffrey Binder and colleagues (2000) at the Medical College of Wisconsin. Participants in the study listened to different types of sounds, both speech and nonspeech. The sounds were of several types: white noise without systematic frequency or amplitude modulations; tones that were frequency modulated between 50 and 2,400 Hz; reversed speech, which was real words played backward; pseudowords, which were pronounceable strings of nonreal words that contain the same letters as the real word—for example, *sked* from *desk*; and real words.

Figure 11.11 shows the results of the Binder study. Relative to noise, the frequency-modulated tones activated posterior portions of the STG bilaterally. Areas that were more sensitive to the speech sounds than to tones were more ventrolateral, in or near the superior temporal sulcus, and lateralized to the left hemisphere. In the same study, Binder and colleagues showed that these areas are most likely not involved in lexical-semantic aspects

of word processing (i.e., the processing of word forms and word meaning), because they were equally activated for words, pseudowords, and reversed speech.

Based on their fMRI findings and the findings of other groups identifying brain regions that become activated in relation to subcomponents of speech processing, Binder and colleagues (2000) proposed a hierarchical model of word recognition (Figure 11.12). In this model, processing proceeds anteriorly in the STG. First, the stream of auditory information proceeds from auditory cortex in Heschl's gyri to the superior temporal gyrus. In these parts of the brain, no distinction is made between speech and nonspeech sounds, as noted earlier. The first evidence of such a distinction is in the adjacent mid-portion of the superior temporal sulcus, but still, no lexical-semantic information is processed in this area.

Neurophysiological studies now indicate that recognizing whether a speech sound is a word or a pseudoword happens in the first 50–80 ms (MacGregor et al., 2012). This processing tends to be lateralized more to the left hemisphere, where the combinations of the different features of speech sounds are analyzed (pattern recognition). From the superior temporal sulcus, the information proceeds to the final processing stage of word recognition in the middle temporal gyrus and the inferior temporal gyrus, and finally to the angular gyrus, posterior to the temporal areas just described (see Chapter 2), and in more anterior regions in the temporal pole (Figure 11.10).

Over the course of the decade following the Binder study, multiple studies were done in an attempt to localize speech recognition processes. In reviewing 100 fMRI studies, Iain DeWitt and Josef Rauschecker (2012) of Georgetown University Medical Center confirmed the findings that the left mid-anterior STG responds preferentially to phonetic sounds of speech. Researchers also have tried to identify areas in the brain that are particularly important for the processing of phonemes. Recent fMRI studies from the lab of Sheila Blumstein at Brown University suggest a network of areas involved in phonological processing

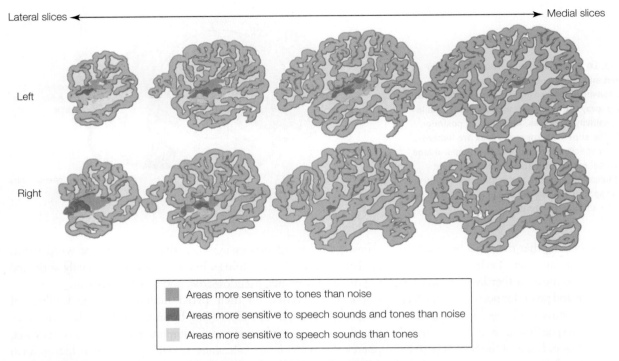

Lateral slices ←——————————————————————————————————→ Medial slices

Left

Right

Areas more sensitive to tones than noise

Areas more sensitive to speech sounds and tones than noise

Areas more sensitive to speech sounds than tones

FIGURE 11.11 Superior temporal cortex activations to speech and nonspeech sounds.
Four sagittal slices are shown for each hemisphere. The posterior areas of the superior temporal gyrus are more active bilaterally for frequency-modulated tones than for simple noise (in blue). Areas that are more active for speech sounds and tones than for noise are indicated in red. Areas that are more sensitive to speech sounds (i.e., reversed words, pseudo words, and words) are located ventrolaterally to this area (in yellow), in or near the superior temporal sulcus. This latter activation is somewhat lateralized to the left hemisphere (top row).

during speech perception and production, including the left posterior superior temporal gyrus (activation), the supramarginal gyrus (selection), inferior frontal gyrus (phonological planning), and precentral gyrus (generating motor plans for production; Peramunage et al., 2011).

TAKE-HOME MESSAGES

- There are no pauses between phonemes in speech that correspond to words.

- The prosody of speech is the rhythm and the pitch of the speaker's voice.

- Sound comprehension involves the superior temporal cortex. People with damage to this area have pure word deafness.

- Distinguishing speech from nonspeech sounds occurs in the mid-portion of the superior temporal sulcus (STS), but no lexical-semantic information is processed in this area.

- Spoken-word recognition processing proceeds anteriorly in the superior temporal gyrus (STG): Phoneme processing appears localized to the left mid-STG, integration of phonemes into words appears localized to the left anterior STG, and processing short phrases appears to be carried out in the most anterior locations of STS.

Written Input: Reading Words

Reading is the perception and comprehension of written language. For written input, readers must recognize a visual pattern. Our brain is very good at pattern recognition, but reading is a quite recent invention (about 5,500 years old). Although speech comprehension develops without explicit training, reading requires instruction. Specifically, learning to read requires linking arbitrary visual symbols into meaningful words. The visual symbols that are used vary across different writing systems. Words can be symbolized in writing in three different ways: alphabetic, syllabic, and logographic. For example, many Western languages use the alphabetic system, Japanese uses the syllabic system, and Chinese uses the logographic system.

Regardless of the writing system used, readers must be able to analyze the primitive features, or the shapes of the symbols. In the alphabetic system—our focus here—this process involves the visual analysis of horizontal lines, vertical lines, closed curves, open curves, intersections, and other elementary shapes.

In a 1959 paper that was a landmark contribution to the emerging science of artificial intelligence (i.e., machine learning), Oliver Selfridge proposed a collection of small components or *demons* (a term he used to refer to a discrete

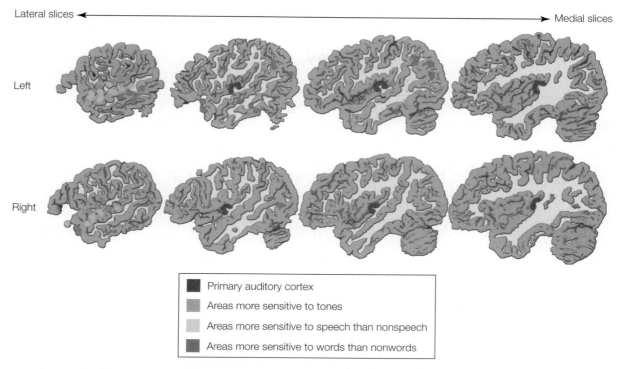

Lateral slices ←——————————————————————————————→ Medial slices

Left

Right

- ■ Primary auditory cortex
- ■ Areas more sensitive to tones
- □ Areas more sensitive to speech than nonspeech
- ■ Areas more sensitive to words than nonwords

FIGURE 11.12 Regions involved in a hierarchical processing stream for speech processing (see text for explanation).
Heschl's gyri, which contain the primary auditory cortex, are in purple. Shown in blue are areas of the dorsal superior temporal gyri that are activated more by frequency-modulated tones than by random noise. Yellow areas are clustered in the superior temporal sulcus and are speech-sound specific; they show more activation for speech sounds (words, pseudowords, or reversed speech) than for nonspeech sounds. Green areas include regions of the middle temporal gyrus, inferior temporal gyrus, angular gyrus, and temporal pole and are more active for words than for pseudowords or nonwords. Critically, these "word" areas are lateralized mostly to the left hemisphere.

stage or substage of information processing) that together would allow machines to recognize patterns. Demons record events as they occur, recognize patterns in those events, and may trigger subsequent events according to patterns they recognize. In his model, known as the pandemonium model, the sensory input (R) is temporarily stored as an iconic memory by the so-called *image demon*. Then 28 *feature demons* each sensitive to a particular feature like curves, horizontal lines, and so forth start to decode features in the iconic representation of the sensory input (Figure 11.13). In the next step, all representations of letters with these features are activated by *cognitive demons*. Finally, the representation that best matches the input is selected by the *decision demon*. The pandemonium model has been criticized because it consists solely of stimulus-driven (bottom-up) processing and does not allow for feedback (top-down) processing, such as in the word superiority effect (see Chapter 3). Humans are better at processing letters found in words than letters found in nonsense words or even single letters.

In 1981, James McClelland and David Rumelhart proposed a computational model that has been important for visual letter recognition. This model assumes three levels of representation: (a) a layer for the features of the letters of words, (b) a layer for letters, and (c) a layer for the representation of words. An important characteristic of this model is that it permits top-down information (i.e., information from the higher cognitive levels, such as the word layer) to influence earlier processes that happen at lower levels of representation (the letter layer and/or the feature layer).

This model contrasts sharply with Selfridge's model, where the flow of information is strictly bottom up (from the image demon to the feature demons to the cognitive demons and finally to the decision demon). Another important difference between the two models is that, in the McClelland and Rumelhart model, processes can take place in parallel such that several letters can be processed at the same time, whereas in Selfridge's model, one letter is processed at a time in a serial manner. As Figure 11.14 shows, the model of McClelland and Rumelhart permits both excitatory and inhibitory links between all the layers.

The empirical validity of a model can be tested on real-life behavioral phenomena or against physiological data. McClelland and Rumelhart's connectionist model does an excellent job of mimicking reality for the word

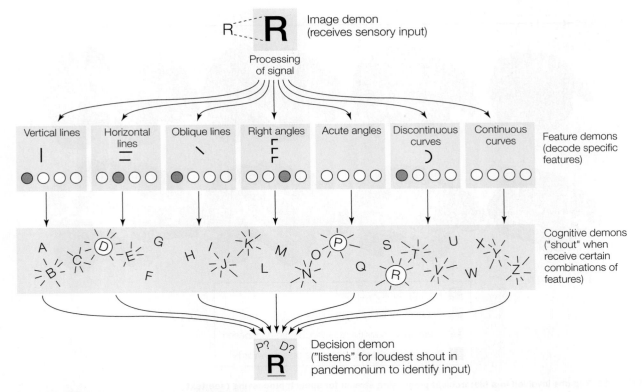

FIGURE 11.13 Selfridge's (1959) pandemonium model of letter recognition.
For written input, the reader must recognize a pattern that starts with the analysis of the sensory input. The sensory input is stored temporarily in iconic memory by the image demon, and a set of 28 feature demons decodes the iconic representations. The cognitive demons are activated by the representations of letters with these features, and the representation that best matches the input is then selected by the decision demon.

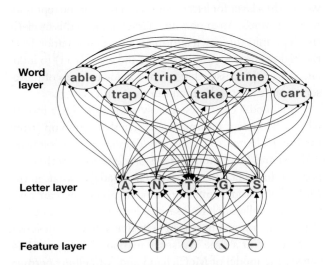

FIGURE 11.14 Fragment of a connectionist network for letter recognition.
Nodes at three different layers represent letter features, letters, and words. Nodes in each layer can influence the activational status of the nodes in the other layers by excitatory (arrows) or inhibitory (lines) connections.

superiority effect. This remarkable result indicates that words are probably not perceived on a letter-by-letter basis. The word superiority effect can be explained in terms of the McClelland and Rumelhart model, because the model proposes that top-down information of the words can either activate or inhibit letter activations, thereby helping the recognition of letters.

We learned in Chapters 5 and 6 that single-cell recording techniques have enlightened us about the basics of visual feature analysis and how the brain analyzes edges, curves, and so on. Unresolved questions remain, however, because letter and word recognition are not really understood at the cellular level, and recordings in monkeys are not likely to enlighten us about letter and word recognition in humans. Recent studies using PET and fMRI have started to shed some light on where letters are processed in the human brain.

Neural Substrates of Written-Word Processing
The actual identification of orthographic units may take place in occipitotemporal regions of the left hemisphere. It has been known for over 100 years that lesions in this area can give rise to pure **alexia,** a condition in which patients

cannot read words, even though other aspects of language are normal. In early PET imaging studies, Steven Petersen and his colleagues (1990) contrasted words with non-words and found regions of occipital cortex that preferred word strings. They named these regions the visual word form area. In later studies using fMRI in normal participants, Gregory McCarthy at Yale University and his colleagues (Puce et al., 1996) contrasted brain activation in response to letters with activation in response to faces and visual textures. They found that regions of the occipitotemporal cortex were activated preferentially in response to unpronounceable letter strings (Figure 11.15). Interestingly, this finding confirmed results from an earlier study by the same group (Nobre et al., 1994), in which intracranial electrical recordings were made from this brain region in patients who later underwent surgery for intractable epilepsy. In this study, the researchers found a large negative polarity potential at about 200 ms in occipitotemporal regions, in response to the visual presentation of letter strings. This area was not sensitive to other visual stimuli, such as faces, and importantly, it also appeared to be insensitive to lexical or semantic features of words.

In a combined ERP and fMRI study that included healthy persons and patients with callosal lesions, Laurent Cohen, Stanislas Dehaene, and their colleagues (2000) investigated the visual word form area. While the participants fixated on a central crosshair, a word or a non-word was flashed to either their right or left visual field. Non-words were consonant strings incompatible with French orthographic principles and were impossible to translate into **phonology**. When a word flashed on the screen, they were to repeat it out loud, and if a non-word flashed, they were to think "rien" (which means nothing; this was a French study after all).

The event-related potentials (ERPs) indicated that initial processing was confined to early visual areas contralateral to the stimulated visual hemifield. Activations then revealed a common processing stage, which was associated with the activation of a precise, reproducible site in the left occipitotemporal sulcus (anterior and lateral to area V4), part of the visual word form area, which coincides with the lesion site that causes pure alexia (Cohen et al., 2000). This and later studies showed that this activation was visually elicited (Dehaene et al., 2002) only for prelexical forms (before the word form was associated with a meaning), yet was invariant for the location of the stimulus (right or left visual field) and the case of the word stimulus (Dehaene et al., 2001). These findings were also in agreement with Nobre's findings. Finally, the researchers found that the processing beyond this point was the same for all word stimuli from either visual field—a result that corresponds to the standard model of word reading. Activation of the visual word form area is reproducible across cultures that use different types of symbols, such as Japanese kana (syllabic) and kanji (logographic;

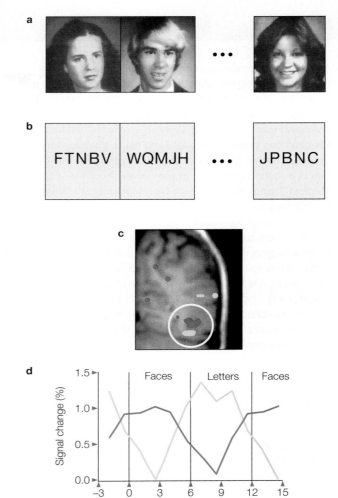

FIGURE 11.15 Regions in occipitotemporal cortex were preferentially activated in response to letter strings.
Stimuli were faces **(a)** or letter strings **(b)**. **(c)** Left hemisphere coronal slice at the level of the anterior occipital cortex. Faces activated a region of the lateral fusiform gyrus (yellow); letter strings activated a region of the occipitotemporal sulcus (red). **(d)** Graph shows the corresponding time course of fMRI activations averaged over all alternation cycles for faces (yellow line) and letter strings (pink line).

Bolger et al., 2005). This convergent neurological and neuroimaging evidence gives us clues as to how the human brain solves the perceptual problems of letter recognition.

TAKE-HOME MESSAGES

- Written-word processing takes place in occipitotemporal regions of the left hemisphere. Damage to this area can cause pure alexia, a condition in which patients cannot read words, even though other aspects of language are normal.

- Occipitotemporal regions of the left hemisphere may be specialized for the identification of orthographic units.

Awake, a young man lies on his side on a table, draped with clean, light-green sheets. His head is partially covered by a sheet of cloth, so we can see his face if we wish. On the other side of the cloth is a man wearing a surgical gown and mask. One is a patient; the other is his surgeon. His skull has been cut through, and his left hemisphere is exposed. Rather than being a scene from a sci-fi thriller, this is a routine procedure at the University of Washington Medical School, where George Ojemann and his colleagues (1989) have been using direct cortical stimulation to map the brain's language areas.

The patient suffers from epilepsy and is about to undergo a surgical procedure to remove the epileptic tissue. Because this epileptic focus is in the left, language-dominant hemisphere, it is first essential to determine where language processes are localized in the patient's brain. Such localization can be done by electrical stimulation mapping. Electrodes are used to pass a small electrical current through the cortex, momentarily disrupting activity; thus, electrical stimulation can probe where a language process is localized. The patient has to be awake for this test. Language-related areas vary among patients, so these areas must be mapped carefully. During surgery, it is essential to leave the critical language areas intact.

One benefit of this work is that we can learn more about the organization of the human language system (Figure 1). Patients are shown line drawings of everyday objects and are asked to name those objects. During naming, regions of the left perisylvian cortex are stimulated with low amounts of electricity. When the patient makes an error in naming or is unable to name the object, the deficit is correlated with the region being stimulated during that trial, so that area of cortex is assumed to be critical for language production and comprehension.

Stimulation of between 100 and 200 patients revealed that aspects of language representation in the brain are organized in mosaic-like areas of 1 to 2 cm^2. These mosaics usually include regions in the frontal cortex and posterior temporal cortex. In some patients, however, only frontal or posterior temporal areas were observed. The correlation between these effects in either Broca's area or Wernicke's area was weak; some patients had naming disruption in the classic areas, and others did not. Perhaps the single most intriguing fact is how much the anatomical localizations vary across patients. This finding has implications for how across-subject averaging methods, such as PET activation studies, reveal significant effects.

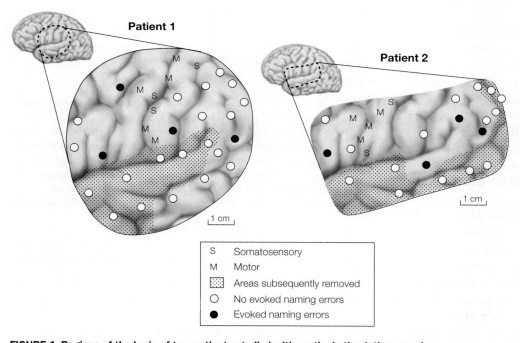

Patient 1

Patient 2

S	Somatosensory
M	Motor
▦	Areas subsequently removed
○	No evoked naming errors
●	Evoked naming errors

FIGURE 1 Regions of the brain of two patients studied with cortical stimulation mapping.
During surgery, with the patient awake and lightly anesthetized, the surgeon maps the somatosensory and motor areas by stimulating the cortex and observing the responses. The patient also is shown pictures and asked to verbally name them. Discrete regions of the cortex are stimulated with electrical current during the task. Areas that induce errors in naming when they are stimulated are mapped, and those regions are implicated as being involved in language. The surgeon uses this mapping to avoid removing any brain tissue associated with language. The procedure thus treats brain tumors or epilepsy as well as enlightens us about the cortical organization of language functions.

The Role of Context in Word Recognition

We come now to the point in word comprehension where auditory and visual word comprehension share processing components. Once a phonological or visual representation is identified as a word, then for it to gain any meaning, semantic and syntactic information must be retrieved. Usually words are not processed in isolation, but in the context of other words (sentences, stories, etc.). To understand words in their context, we have to integrate syntactic and semantic properties of the recognized word into a representation of the whole utterance.

At what point during language comprehension do linguistic and nonlinguistic context (e.g., information seen in pictures) influence word processing? Is it possible to retrieve word meanings before words are heard or seen when the word meanings are highly predictable in the context? More specifically, does context influence word processing before or after lexical access and lexical selection are complete?

Consider the following sentence, which ends with a word that has more than one meaning. "The tall man planted a tree on the bank." *Bank* can mean both "financial institution" and "side of the river." Semantic integration of the meaning of the final word *bank* into the context of the sentence allows us to interpret *bank* as the "side of the river" and not as a "financial institution." The relevant question is, when does the sentence's context influence the activation of the multiple meanings of the word *bank*? Do both the contextually appropriate meaning of *bank* (in this case "side of the river") and the contextually inappropriate meaning (in this case "financial institution") become briefly activated regardless of the context of the sentence? Or does the sentence context immediately constrain the activation to the contextually appropriate meaning of the word *bank*?

From this example, we can already see that two types of representations play a role in word processing in the context of other words: lower-level representations, those constructed from sensory input (in our example, the word *bank* itself); and higher-level representations, those constructed from the context preceding the word to be processed (in our example, the sentence preceding the word *bank*). Contextual representations are crucial to determine in what sense or what grammatical form a word should be used. Without sensory analysis, however, no message representation can take place. The information has to interact at some point. The point where this interaction occurs differs in competing models.

In general, three classes of models attempt to explain word comprehension. *Modular models* (also called autonomous models) claim that normal language comprehension is executed within separate and independent modules. Thus, higher-level representations cannot influence lower-level ones, and therefore, the flow is strictly data driven, or bottom up. In contrast, *interactive models* maintain that all types of information can participate in word recognition. In these models, context can have its influence even before the sensory information is available, by changing the activational status of the word-form representations in the mental lexicon. McClelland and colleagues (1989) have proposed this type of interactivity model, as noted earlier. Between these two extreme views is the notion that lexical access is autonomous and not influenced by higher-level information, but that lexical selection can be influenced by sensory and higher-level contextual information. In these *hybrid models*, information is provided about word forms that are possible given the preceding context, thereby reducing the number of activated candidates.

An elegant study by Pienie Zwitserlood (1989), involving a lexical decision task, addressed the question of modularity versus interactivity in word processing. She asked participants to listen to short texts such as: "With dampened spirits the men stood around the grave. They mourned the loss of their *captain*." At different points during the auditory presentation of the word *captain* (e.g., when only /c/ or only /ca/ or only /cap/, etc., could be heard), a visual target stimulus was presented. This target stimulus could be related to the actual word *captain*, or to an auditory competitor—for example, *capital*. In this example, target words could be words like *ship* (related to *captain*) or *money* (unrelated to *captain*, but related to *capital*). In other cases, a pseudoword would be presented. The task was to decide whether the target stimulus was a word or not (lexical decision task).

The results of this study showed that participants were faster to decide that *ship* was a word in the context of the story about the men mourning their captain, and slower to decide that *money* was a word, even when only partial sensory information of the stimulus word *captain* was available (i.e., before the whole word was spoken). Apparently, the lexical selection process was influenced by the contextual information that was available from the text that the participants had heard before the whole word *captain* was spoken.

This finding is consistent with the idea that lexical selection can be influenced by sentence context. We do not know for certain which type of model best fits word comprehension, but growing evidence from studies like that of Zwitserlood and others suggests that at least lexical selection is influenced by higher-level contextual information. More recently, William Marslen-Wilson and colleagues (Zhuang et al., 2011) have performed fMRI studies of word recognition and shown that the processes of lexical access and lexical selection involve a network that includes the middle temporal gyrus (MTG), superior temporal gyrus (STG), and the ventral inferior and bilateral dorsal inferior frontal gyri (IFG). They showed that MTG and STG are important for the translation of speech sounds to word meanings. They also showed that the frontal cortex regions were important in the selection process and that greater involvement of dorsal IFG occurred when selection required choosing the actual word from among many lexical candidates (lexical competition).

Integration of Words in Sentences

Normal language comprehension requires more than just recognizing individual words. To understand the message conveyed by a speaker or a writer, we have to integrate the syntactic and semantic properties of the recognized word into a representation of the whole sentence, utterance, or signed message. Let's consider again the sentence, "The tall man planted a tree on the bank." Why do we read *bank* to mean "side of the river" instead of "financial institution"? We do so because the rest of the sentence has created a context that is compatible with one meaning and not the other. This integration process has to be executed quickly, in real time—as soon as we are confronted with the linguistic input. If we come upon a word like *bank* in a sentence, usually we are not aware that this word has an alternative meaning, because the appropriate meaning of this word has been rapidly integrated into the sentence context.

Higher order semantic processing is important to determine the right sense or meaning of words in the context of a sentence, as with ambiguous words such as *bank*, which have the same form but more than one meaning. Semantic information in words alone, however, is not enough to understand the message, as made clear in the sentence, "The little old lady bites the gigantic dog." Syntactic analysis of this sentence reveals its structure: who was the actor, what was the theme or action, and what was the subject. The syntax of the sentence demands that we imagine an implausible situation in which an old lady is biting and not being bitten. Syntactic analysis goes on even in the absence of real meaning. In various studies, normal participants can detect a target word in a sentence when it makes no sense but is grammatically correct faster than they can do so when the grammar is locally disrupted. An example from the famous linguist Noam Chomsky illustrates this. The sentence "Colorless green ideas sleep furiously" is easier to process than "Furiously sleep ideas green colorless." This is because the first sentence, even though meaningless, still has an intact syntactic structure, but the second sentence lacks both meaning and structure.

How do we process the structure of sentences? As we have learned, when we hear or read sentences, we activate word forms that in turn activate the grammatical and semantic information in the mental lexicon. Unlike the representation of words and their syntactic properties that are stored in a mental lexicon, however, representations of whole sentences are not stored in the brain. It is just not feasible for the brain to store the incredible number of different sentences that can be written and produced. Instead, the brain has to assign a syntactic structure to words in sentences. This is called **syntactic parsing**. Syntactic parsing is, therefore, a building process that does not, and cannot, rely on the retrieval of representations of sentences. To investigate the neural bases of semantic and syntactic analyses in sentence processing, researchers have used cognitive neuroscience tools, such as electrophysiological methods. We review these briefly in the next sections.

Semantic Processing and the N400 Wave

After pulling the fragrant loaf from the oven, he cut a slice and spread the warm bread with socks. What? You may not realize it, but you just had a large N400 response in your brain. Marta Kutas and Steven Hillyard (1980) at the University of California, San Diego, first described the **N400 response**, an ERP component related to linguistic processes. The name *N400* indicates that it is a negative-polarity voltage peak in brain waves that usually reaches maximum amplitude about 400 ms after the onset of a word stimulus that has evoked it. This brain wave is especially sensitive to semantic aspects of linguistic input. They discovered the wave when they were comparing the processing of the last word of sentences in three conditions:

1. Normal sentences that ended with a word congruent with the preceding context, such as "It was his first day at work."
2. Sentences that ended with a word anomalous to the preceding context, such as "He spread the warm bread with socks."
3. Sentences that ended with a word semantically congruent with the preceding context but physically deviant, such as "She put on her high-heeled SHOES."

The sentences were presented on a computer screen, one word at a time. Participants were asked to read the sentences attentively, knowing that questions about the sentences would be asked at the end of the experiment. The electroencephalograms (EEGs) were averaged for the sentences in each condition, and the ERPs were extracted by averaging data for the last word of the sentences separately for each sentence type.

When anomalous words ended the sentence, the amplitude of N400 was greater than the amplitude of N400 when the participants read congruent words (see Figure 11.16). This amplitude difference is called the

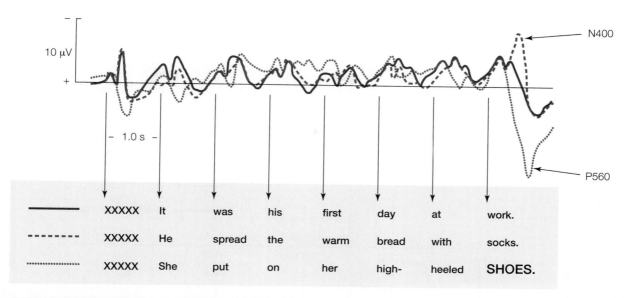

FIGURE 11.16 ERPs reflecting semantic aspects of language.
ERP waveforms differentiate between congruent words at the end of sentences (*work* in the first sentence) and anomalous last words that do not fit the semantic specifications of the preceding context (*socks* in the second sentence). The anomalous words elicit a large negative deflection (plotted upward) in the ERP called the *N400*. Words that fit into the context but are printed with a larger font (*SHOES* in the third sentence) elicit a positive wave (P560) and not the N400, indicating that the N400 is not generated simply by surprises at the end of the sentence.

N400 effect. In contrast, words that were semantically congruent with the sentence but were merely physically deviant (e.g., having larger letters) elicited a positive potential rather than an N400. Subsequent experiments showed that nonsemantic deviations like musical or grammatical violations also failed to elicit the N400. Thus, the N400 effect is specific to semantic analysis.

The N400 response is also sensitive to comprehension of language that goes beyond single sentences. In a series of studies, Jos van Berkum and colleagues (1999, 2008) found an N400 response to words that were inconsistent with the meaning of an entire story. In these studies, participants listened to or read short stories. In the last sentence of these stories, words could be included that were inconsistent with the meaning of the story. For example, in a story about a man who had become a vegetarian, the last sentence could be: "He went to a restaurant and ate a steak that was prepared well." Although the word *steak* is fine when this sentence is read by itself, it is inconsistent within the context of the story. The researchers found that participants who read this sentence in this story exhibited an N400 effect.

Syntactic Processing and the P600 Wave

The **P600 response**, also known as the *syntactic positive shift* (SPS), was first reported by Lee Osterhout at Washington University and Phil Holcomb (1992) at Tufts, and Peter

Hagoort, Colin Brown, and their colleagues (1993) in the Netherlands. Osterhout and Holcomb observed it at about 600 ms after the onset of words that were incongruous with the expected syntactic structure. It is evoked by the type of phrase that headline writers love: *Drunk gets nine months in violin case* or *Enraged cow injures farmer with ax*. Known as garden path phrases or sentences, they are temporarily ambiguous because they contain a word group which appears to be compatible with more than one structural analysis: We are "led down the garden path," so to speak.

Peter Hagoort, Colin Brown, and their colleagues asked participants to silently read sentences that were presented one word at a time on a video monitor. Brain responses to normal sentences were compared with responses to sentences containing a grammatical violation. Figure 11.17 shows the results: There is a large positive shift to the syntactic violation in the sentence, and the onset of this effect is approximately 600 ms after the violating word (*throw* in the example). The P600 shows up in response to a number of other syntactic violations as well, and it occurs both when participants have to read sentences and when they have to listen to them. As with the N400, the P600 response has now been reported for several different languages.

Finally, Gina Kuperberg and colleagues (2003, 2007) demonstrated that the P600 response is also evoked by a semantic violation in the absence of any syntactic violation. For instance, when there is a semantic violation between a verb and its subject but the syntax is correct, such

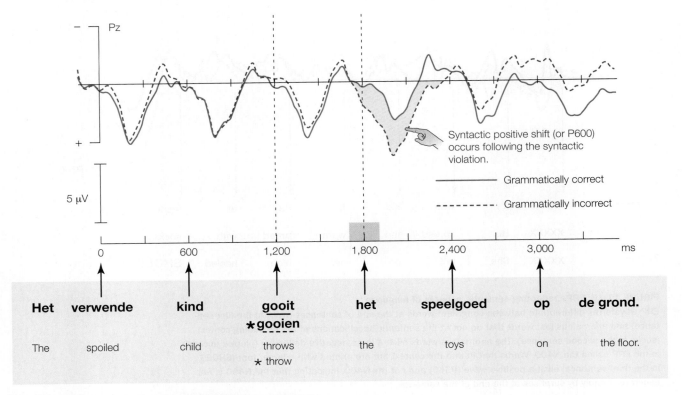

FIGURE 11.17 ERPs reflecting grammatical aspects of language.
ERPs from a parietal (Pz) scalp recording site elicited in response to each word of sentences that are
syntactically anomalous (dashed waveform) versus those that are syntactically correct (solid waveform).
In the violated sentence, a positive shift emerges in the ERP waveform at about 600 ms after the
syntactic violation (shaded). It is called the syntactic positive shift (SPS), or P600.

as: "The eggs would eat toast with jam at breakfast." This sentence is grammatically correct and not ambiguous, but it contains a so-called thematic violation (eggs cannot eat). Eggs and eating often occur in the same scenario, however, and are semantically related to each other. The P600 response in these types of sentences is elicited because the syntactic-based analysis of a sentence structure (e.g., subject-verb-object) is challenged by strong semantic relations of the words in a sentence.

Syntactic processing is reflected in other types of brain waves as well. Cognitive neuroscientists Thomas Münte and colleagues (1993) and Angela Friederici and colleagues (1993), described a negative wave over the left frontal areas of the brain. This brain wave has been labeled the left anterior negativity (LAN) and has been observed when words violate the required word category in a sentence (e.g., as in "the red eats," where noun instead of verb information is required), or when morphosyntactic features are violated (e.g., as in "he mow"). The LAN has about the same latency as the N400 but a different voltage distribution over the scalp, as Figure 11.18 illustrates.

What do we know about the brain circuitry involved in syntactic processing? Some brain-damaged patients have severe difficulty producing sentences and understanding complex sentences. These deficits are apparent in patients with agrammatic aphasia, who generally produce two- or three-word sentences consisting exclusively of content words and hardly any function words (*and*, *then*, *the*, *a*, etc.). They also have difficulty understanding complex syntactic structures. So when they hear the sentence "The gigantic dog was bitten by the little old lady," they will most likely understand it to mean that the lady was bitten by the dog. This problem in assigning syntactic structures to sentences traditionally has been associated with lesions that include Broca's area in the left hemisphere. But not all agrammatic aphasic patients have lesions in Broca's area. So, we do not want to assign syntactic processing to a specific structure like Broca's area. Instead, the evidence suggests that the left inferior frontal cortex (in and around classical Broca's area) has some involvement in syntactic processing.

Neuroimaging evidence from studies by David Caplan and colleagues (2000) at Harvard Medical School provides some additional clues about syntactic processing in the brain. In these studies, PET scans were made while participants read sentences varying in syntactic complexity. Caplan and colleagues found increased activation in the left inferior frontal cortex for the more complex syntactic structures (Figure 11.19).

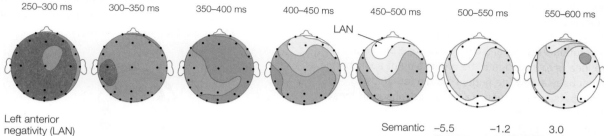

a Semantic N400

250–300 ms | 300–350 ms | 350–400 ms | 400–450 ms | 450–500 ms | 500–550 ms | 550–600 ms

N400

b Left anterior negativity (LAN)

LAN

Semantic −5.5   −1.2   3.0

μV

Syntactic −3.1   −0.4   2.3

FIGURE 11.18 ERPs related to semantic and syntactic processing.
The voltage recorded at multiple locations on the scalp at specific time periods can be displayed
as a topographic voltage map. These maps show views of the topographies of **(a)** the N400 to
semantic violations (see Figure 11.16 for equivalent waveforms) and **(b)** a left anterior negativity
(LAN) to syntactic violations. The maps are read in a manner similar to the way elevation maps of
mountain ranges are read, except here the topography shows "mountains" and "valleys" of voltage.
The N400 and LAN have different scalp topographies, implying that they are generated in different
neural structures in the brain.

In other studies, sentence complexity manipulations led to activation of more than just the left inferior frontal cortex. For example, Marcel Just and colleagues (1996) reported activation in Broca's and Wernicke's areas and in the homologous areas in the right hemisphere. PET studies have identified portions of the anterior superior temporal gyrus, in the vicinity of area 22 (Figure 11.20a) as another candidate for syntactic processing. Nina Dronkers at the University of California, Davis, and colleagues (1994) also implicated this area in aphasics' syntactic processing deficits (Figure 11.20b).

Thus, a more contemporary view is emerging: Syntactic processing takes place in a network of left inferior frontal and superior temporal brain regions that are activated during language processing.

TAKE-HOME MESSAGES

- Three classes of models attempt to explain word comprehension: *Modular models, interactive models* and *hybrid models.*
- Lexical selection can be influenced by sentence context.
- Lexical access and selection involve a network that includes the middle temporal gyrus (MTG), superior temporal gyrus (STG), and the ventral inferior and bilateral dorsal inferior frontal gyri (IFG) of the left hemisphere.

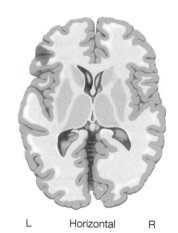
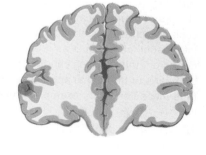

L   Horizontal   R   L   Coronal   R

FIGURE 11.19 Increase in blood flow in left inferior prefrontal cortex (red spots) when participants are processing complex syntactic structures relative to simple ones. See text for further explanation. The change in blood flow was measured using PET imaging.

Do aphasic symptoms reflect processing losses, representational losses, or some combination of the two? One way of tackling this question is to analyze online measures of language processing. Such measures include the event-related potentials (ERPs) elicited by language processing. The idea is to investigate the processing of spoken language, observe how the patient's brain responds to linguistic inputs, and to compare these responses to those in healthy control participants. One study used the N400 component of the ERP to investigate spoken-sentence understanding in Broca's and Wernicke's aphasics. Tamara Swaab (now at the University of California, Davis), Colin Brown, and Peter Hagoort at the Max Planck Institute for Psycholinguistics in the Netherlands (1997) tried to determine whether spoken-sentence comprehension might be hampered by a deficit in the online integration of lexical information.

Patients listened to sentences spoken at a normal rate (Figure 1). In half of the sentences, the meaning of the final word of the sentence matched the semantic meaning building up from the sentence context. In the other half of the sentences, the final word was anomalous with respect to the preceding context. As in Kutas and Hillyard's (1980) study, the amplitude of the N400 wave should be larger in response to the anomalous final words than it is in response to the congruent final words. This result was obtained for normal age-matched control participants. Non-aphasic brain-damaged patients (controls with right-hemisphere damage) and aphasic patients with a light comprehension deficit (high comprehenders) had an N400 effect comparable to that of neurologically unimpaired participants. In aphasics with moderate to severe comprehension deficits (low comprehenders), the N400 effect was reduced and delayed.

The results are compatible with the idea that aphasics with moderate to severe comprehension problems have an impaired ability to integrate lexical information into a higher order representation of the sentence context, because the N400 component indexes the process of lexical integration. By incorporating electrical recordings into studies of neurological patients with behavioral deficits such as aphasia, scientists can track the processing of information in real time as it occurs in the brain. Observations from this tracking can be combined with analysis by means of traditional approaches such as reaction time measures in, for example, lexical decision tasks.

Significantly, ERPs can also provide measures of processing in patients whose neurobehavioral deficit is too severe to use behavior alone because their comprehension is too low to understand the task instructions.

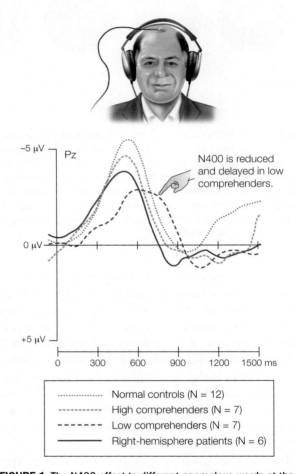

FIGURE 1 The N400 effect to different anomalous words at the end of a sentence in different groups of patients and healthy control participants. The recording is from a single electrode located at the midline parietal scalp site, Pz, in elderly healthy control participants, aphasics with high comprehension scores, aphasics with low comprehension scores, and patients with right-hemisphere lesions (control patients). The waveform for the low comprehenders is clearly delayed and somewhat reduced compared to that for the other groups. The waveforms for the normal control participants, the high comprehenders, and the patients with right-hemisphere lesions are comparable in size and do not differ in latency. This pattern implies a delay in time course of language processing in the patients with low comprehension.

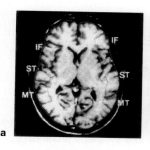
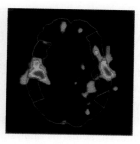

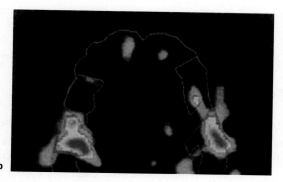

FIGURE 11.20 Localization of syntactic processing in the brain. **(a)** PET activations in the anterior portion of the superior temporal gyrus related to syntactic processing. IF = inferior frontal; MT = middle temporal; ST = superior temporal. **(b)** Summary of lesions in the anterior superior temporal cortex that lead to deficits in syntactic processing.

- Left MTG and STG are important for the translation of speech sounds to word meanings.
- Syntactic parsing is the process in which the brain assigns a syntactic structure to words in sentences.
- In the ERP method, the N400 is a negative-polarity brain wave related to semantic processes in language, and the P600/SPS is a large positive component elicited after a syntactic and some semantic violations.
- Syntactic processing takes place in a network of left inferior frontal and superior temporal brain regions that are activated during language processing.

Neural Models of Language Comprehension

Many new neural models of language have emerged that are different from the classical model initiated by the work of Paul Broca, Carl Wernicke, and others. In the contemporary models, these classical language areas are no longer always considered language specific, nor are their roles in language processing limited to those proposed in the classical model. Moreover, additional areas

in the brain have been found to be part of the circuitry that is used for normal language processing.

One recent neural model of language that combines work in brain and language analysis has been proposed by Peter Hagoort (2005). His model divides language processing into three functional components—memory, integration, and control—and identifies their possible representation in the brain (Figure 11.21):

1. *Memory.* Storage and retrieval from the mental lexicon or the long-term memory store for word information, as defined earlier in this chapter.
2. *Unification.* Integration of lexically retrieved phonological, semantic, and syntactic information into an overall representation of the whole utterance. In language comprehension, the unification processes for phonological, semantic, and syntactic information can operate in parallel (or at the same time); and interaction between these different types of information is possible. Unification makes Hagoort's model a constraint-based interactive model, as discussed earlier.
3. *Control.* Relating language to action (e.g., in bilingualism and turn taking).

As Figure 11.21 shows, the temporal lobes are especially important for the storage and retrieval of word representations. Phonological and phonetic properties of words are stored in the central to posterior superior temporal gyrus (STG, which includes Wernicke's area) extending into the superior temporal sulcus (STS), and semantic information is distributed over different parts of the left, middle, and inferior temporal gyri. This part of the model is very similar to what we have seen before in Binder's neural model of spoken-word comprehension (see Figure 11.11).

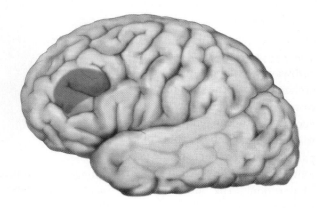

FIGURE 11.21 Memory–unification–control model. The three components of the model are shown in colors overlaid onto a drawing of the left hemisphere: the memory component (yellow) in the left temporal lobe, the unification component (blue) in the left inferior frontal gyrus, and the control component (purple) in the lateral frontal cortex.

The processes that combine and integrate (unify) phonological, lexical-semantic, and syntactic information recruit frontal areas of the brain, including our old friend Broca's area or the left inferior frontal gyrus (LIFG). LIFG now appears to be involved in all three unification processes: semantic unification in Brodmann's area 47 and BA45, syntactic unification in BA45 and BA44, and phonological unification in BA44 and parts of BA6.

The control component of the model becomes important when people are actually involved in communication—for example, when they have to take turns during a conversation. Cognitive control in language comprehension has not been studied very much, but areas that are involved in cognitive control during other tasks, such as the anterior cingulate cortex (ACC) and the dorsolateral prefrontal cortex (DLPC, BA46/9), also play a role during cognitive control in language comprehension.

Networks of the Left-Hemisphere Language System

We have reviewed a lot of studies focusing on brain regions in the left hemisphere that are involved in various language functions. How are these brain regions organized to create a language network in the brain? From recent studies that have considered the functional and structural connectivity in a language network, several pathways have been identified that connect the representations of words in the temporal lobes to the unification areas in the frontal lobes. For spoken sentence comprehension, Angela Friederici has elaborated a model of the language network that includes the connecting pathways (Figure 11.22). In this model, four pathways are distinguished. Two ventral pathways connect the posterior temporal lobes with the anterior temporal lobe and the frontal operculum. These ventral pathways are important for comprehension of the meanings of words. Two dorsal pathways connect the posterior temporal lobes to the frontal lobes. The dorsal pathway that connects to the premotor cortex is involved in speech preparation. The other dorsal pathway connects Broca's area (specifically BA44) with the superior temporal gyrus and superior temporal sulcus. This pathway is important for aspects of syntactic processing.

TAKE-HOME MESSAGES

- Models of language involve unifying information from linguistic inputs or from retrieved linguistic representations with stored knowledge.
- White matter tracks in the left hemisphere connect frontal and temporal lobes to create specific circuits for speech, semantic analysis, and syntactic processing.

Neural Models of Speech Production

So far we have focused mainly on language comprehension. Now we turn our attention to language production. To provide a framework for this discussion, we will concentrate mostly on one influential cognitive model for language production, proposed by Willem Levelt (1989) of the Max Planck Institute for Psycholinguistics in the Netherlands. Figure 11.23 illustrates this model.

A seemingly trivial but nonetheless important difference between comprehension and production is our starting point. Whereas language comprehension starts with spoken or written input that has to be transformed into a concept, language production starts with a concept for which we have to find the appropriate words.

The first step in speech production is to prepare the message. Levelt maintains that there are two crucial aspects to message preparation: macroplanning and

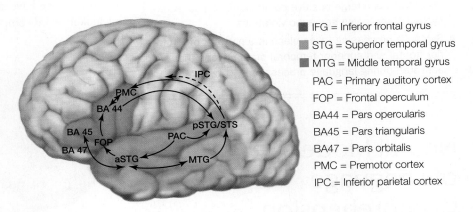

IFG = Inferior frontal gyrus
STG = Superior temporal gyrus
MTG = Middle temporal gyrus
PAC = Primary auditory cortex
FOP = Frontal operculum
BA44 = Pars opercularis
BA45 = Pars triangularis
BA47 = Pars orbitalis
PMC = Premotor cortex
IPC = Inferior parietal cortex

FIGURE 11.22 Cortical language circuit proposed by Angela Friederici, consisting of two ventral and two dorsal pathways.
The black lines indicate direct pathways and direction of information flow between language-related regions. The broken line suggests an indirect connection between the pSTG/STS and the MTG via the inferior parietal cortex. The ventral pathways are important for comprehension of the meanings of words. The dorsal pathway that connects to the premotor cortex is involved in speech preparation. The other dorsal pathway connects Broca's area (specifically BA44) with the superior temporal gyrus and superior temporal sulcus and is involved in syntactic processing.

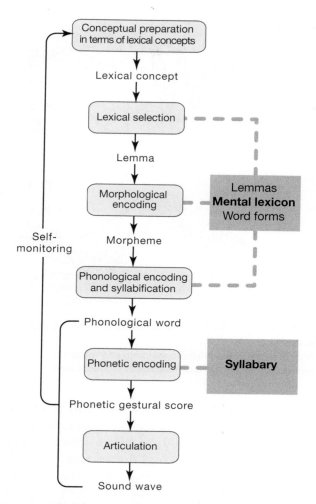

FIGURE 11.23 Outline of the theory of speech production developed by Willem Levelt.
The processing components in language production are displayed schematically. Word production proceeds through stages of conceptual preparation, lexical selection, morphological and phonological encoding, phonetic encoding, and articulation. Speakers monitor their own speech by making use of their comprehension system.

microplanning. The speaker must determine what she wants to express in her message to the listener.

A message directing someone to our home will be formulated differently from a message instructing someone to close the door. The intention of the communication is represented by goals and subgoals, which are expressed in an order that best serves the communicative plan. This aspect of message planning is macroplanning.

Microplanning, in contrast, proposes how the information is expressed, which means adopting a perspective. If we describe a scene in which a house and a park are situated side by side, we must decide whether to say, "The park is next to the house" or "The house is next to the park." The microplan determines word choice and the grammatical roles that the words play (e.g., subject, object).

The output of the macroplanning and microplanning is a conceptual message that constitutes the input for the hypothetical *formulator*, which puts the message in a grammatically and phonologically correct form. During grammatical encoding, a message's surface structure is computed. The surface structure is a message's syntactic representation, including information such as "is subject of," "is object of," the grammatically correct word order, and so on. The lowest-level elements of surface structure (known as lemmas) are about a word's syntactic properties (e.g., whether the word is a noun or a verb, gender information, and other grammatical features) and its semantic specifications, and/or the conceptual conditions where it is appropriate to use a certain word. These types of information in the mental lexicon are organized in a network that links lemmas by meaning.

Levelt's model predicts the following result when someone is presented with a picture of a flock of goats and is asked to name them. First the concept that represents a goat is activated, but concepts related to the meaning of goat are also activated—for example, *sheep*, *cheese*, *farm*. Activated concepts, in turn, activate representations in the mental lexicon, starting with "nodes" at the lemma level to access syntactic information such as word class (in our example, *goat* is a noun, not a verb). At this point, lexical selection occurs when the syntactical properties of the word appropriate to the presented picture must be retrieved. The selected information (in our example, *goat*) activates the word form. Next it undergoes morphological encoding when the suffix is added: goats. The newly formed morpheme contains both phonological information and *metrical information*, which is information about the number of syllables in the word and the stress pattern (in our example, *goats* consists of one syllable that is stressed). The process of phonological encoding ensures that the phonological information is mapped onto the metrical information. Sometimes we cannot activate the sound form of a word, because there is a rift between the syntax and the phonology; this is known as the tip of the tongue (TOT) state. You most likely have experienced a TOT state—you know a lot about the thing (i.e., a goat) that you are trying to name: You can say that it has four legs and white curly hair, you can visualize it in your mind, you can also reject words that do not match the concept (e.g., horse), and if someone tells you the word's first letter (*g*), you probably will say, "Oh yes, goats."

In addition to mentally blocking on a word, speech errors might happen during production. Sometimes we mix up speech sounds or exchange words in a sentence. Usually all goes well, though. The appropriate word form is selected, and phonetic and articulatory programs are matched. In the last phase of speech production, we plan our articulation: The word's syllables are mapped onto motor patterns that move the tongue, mouth, and vocal apparatus to generate the word. At this stage, we can repair any errors in our speech, for example, by saying "um," which gives us more time to generate the appropriate term.

Brain damage can affect each of these processing stages. Some anomic patients (impaired in naming), like H.W. at the beginning of the chapter, are afflicted with an extreme TOT state. When asked to name a picture, they can give a fairly accurate description—even naming the gender of the word they are looking for if the language requires one—but they cannot name the word. Their problem is not one of articulation, because they can readily repeat the word aloud. Their problems are on the word-form level. Patients with Wernicke's aphasia produce semantic paraphasias, generating words related in meaning to the intended word. This can be due to inappropriate selection of concepts or lemmas or lexemes (units of lexical meaning). These patients might also make errors at the phoneme level by incorrectly substituting one sound for another. Finally, as mentioned earlier, Broca's aphasia is often accompanied by dysarthria, which hinders articulation and results in effortful speech, because the muscles that articulate the utterance cannot be properly controlled.

In contrast to the modular view in Levelt's model, interactive models such as the one proposed by Gary Dell (1986) at the University of Illinois suggest that phonological activation begins shortly after the semantic and syntactic information of words has been activated. Unlike modular models, interactive models permit feedback from the phonological activation to the semantic and syntactic properties of the word, thereby enhancing the activation of certain syntactic and semantic information.

Ned Sahin and his colleagues (2009) had the rare opportunity to shed some light on this question of how different forms of linguistic information are combined during speech production. They recorded electrical responses from multiple electrodes implanted in and around Broca's area during presurgical screening of three epilepsy patients. To investigate word production in the brain, patients were engaged in a task involving three conditions that distinguished lexical, grammatical, and phonological linguistic processes. Most of the electrodes in Broca's area yielded strong triphasic electrical responses (Figure 11.24). The responses (waves) correlated with distinct linguistic processing stages (Figure 11.25). The first wave, at about 200 ms, appeared to reflect lexical identification. The second wave occurred at about 320 ms (Figure 11.25b) and was modulated by inflectional demands. It was not, however, modulated by phonological programming. This was seen in the third wave (Figure 11.25c) that appeared at about 450 ms and reflected phonological encoding.

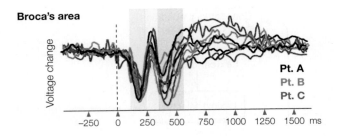

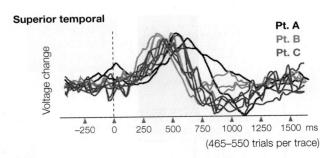

FIGURE 11.24 Cortical evoked potentials from three epilepsy patients.
In all three patients, a triphasic waveform was specific to recordings from cortical depth electrodes in Broca's area.

In naming tasks, speech typically occurs at 600 ms. Sahin and coworkers could also see that motor neuron commands occur 50–100 ms before speech, putting them just after the phonological wave (Figure 11.25d). These apparent processing steps were separated not only temporally but also spatially, but only by a few millimeters (below the resolution of standard fMRI), and all were located in Broca's area. These findings provide support for serial processing, at least initially during speech production. Inflectional processing did not occur before the word was identified, and phonological processing did not occur until inflected phonemes were selected. The results are also consistent with the idea that Broca's area has distinct circuits that process lexical, grammatical, and phonological information.

Imaging studies of the brain during picture naming and word generation found activation in the inferior temporal regions of the left hemisphere and in the left frontal operculum (Broca's area). The activation in the frontal operculum might be specific to phonological encoding in speech production. The articulation of words likely involves the posterior parts of Broca's area (BA44), but in addition, studies showed bilateral activation of motor cortex, the supplementary motor area (SMA), and the insula. PET and fMRI studies of the motor aspect of speech have shown that they involve the SMA, the opercular parts of the precentral gyrus, the posterior parts of the inferior frontal gyrus (Broca's area), the insula, the mouth region of the primary sensory motor cortex, the basal ganglia, thalamus, and cerebellum (reviewed in Ackermann

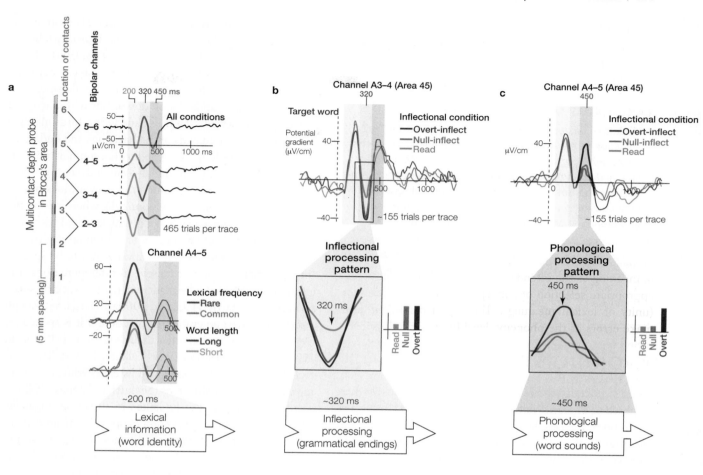

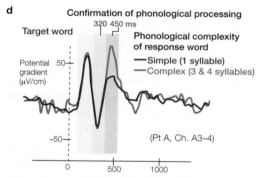

FIGURE 11.25 Lexical, grammatical, and phonological information is processed sequentially in overlapping circuits.

Results from one of several depth probes placed in Broca's area while people read words verbatim or grammatically inflected them. The shaded areas indicate the three separate wave components. **(a, top)** Recorded from several channels in Broca's area BA45, the task consistently evoked three local field potential (LFP) components (~200, ~320, and ~450 ms). **(a, bottom)** The first component that occurred at ~200 ms was sensitive to word frequency but not word length. Thus, it is not merely reflecting perception, but suggests that it indexes a lexical identification process. **(b)** The second LFP pattern at ~320 ms suggests inflectional processing. **(c)** The third LFP pattern at ~450 ms suggests phonological processing. **(d)** The waveform component occurring at ~450 ms, which is sensitive to phonological differences among inflectional conditions, is also sensitive to phonological complexity (the more syllables, the greater the peak) of the target word.

& Riecker, 2010). It is clear that a widespread network of brain regions, predominantly in the left hemisphere in most people, are involved in producing speech.

TAKE-HOME MESSAGES

- Models of language production must account for the selection of the information to be contained in the message; retrieving words from the lexicon; sentence planning and grammatical encoding using semantic and syntactic properties of the word; using morphological and phonological properties for syllabification and prosody; and preparing articulatory gestures for each syllable.

- Each stage in Levelt's model for language production occurs serially, and its output representation is used for input to the next stage. It avoids feedback, loops, parallel processing, and cascades, and it fits well with the findings of ERPs recorded intracranially.

Evolution of Language

Young children acquire language easily and quickly when exposed to it. This behavior led Charles Darwin to suggest in his book *The Descent of Man, and Selection in Relation to Sex* that humans have a biological predisposition toward language. The evolutionary origins of language remain unknown, though there is no shortage of theories. Indeed, Noam Chomsky took the view in 1975 that language was so different from the communication systems used by other animals that it could not be explained in terms of natural selection. Stephen Pinker and Paul Bloom suggested in an article in 1990 that only natural selection could have produced the complex structures of language. There are divergent views as to when language emerged, whether the question trying to be explained is an underlying cognitive mechanism specific to language or a cooperative social behavior, and what crucial evolutionary problems had to be solved before language could emerge (Sterelny, 2012).

Shared Intentionality

Communication is the transfer of information by speech, signals, writing, or behavior. The function of human language is to influence the behavior of others by changing what they know, think, believe, or desire (Grice, 1957), and we tend to think communication is intentional. When we are looking for the origins of language, however, we cannot assume that communication sprang up in this form. Animal communication is more specifically defined as any behavior by one animal that affects the current or future behavior of another animal, intentional or otherwise.

A well-known series of studies in animal communication were done by Robert Seyfarth and Dorothy Cheney on vervet monkeys in Kenya (Seyfarth et al., 1980). These monkeys have different alarm calls for snakes, leopards, and predatory birds. Monkeys that hear an alarm call for a snake will stand up and look down. But with a leopard call, they scamper into the trees; and with a bird call, they run from the exposed ends of the branches and huddle by the trunk. Formerly it was thought that animal vocalizations were exclusively emotional—and indeed, they most likely originated as such. A vervet, however, does not always make an alarm call, seldom calls when it is alone, and is more likely to call when it is with kin than with non-kin. The calls are not an automatic emotional reaction.

If a call is to provide information, it has to be specific (the same call can't be used for several different reasons) and informative—it has to be made whenever a specific situation arises (Seyfarth & Cheney, 2003a). Thus, even though a scream may be an emotional reaction, if it is specific, it can convey information other than the emotion (Premack, 1972). Natural selection favors callers who vocalize to affect the behavior of listeners and listeners who acquire information from vocalizations (Seyfarth & Cheney, 2003b). The two do not need to be linked by intention originally, and indeed, vervet monkeys don't appear to attribute mental states to others (Seyfarth & Cheney, 1986). Most animal studies suggest that although animal vocalizations may result in a change of another's behavior, this outcome is unintentional (see Seyfarth & Cheney, 2003a).

Alarm calls have since been found in many other monkey species and non-primate species. For instance, they have been observed with meerkats (Manser et al., 2001) and chickadees (Templeton et al., 2005) among others. The Diana monkeys of West Africa comprehend the alarm calls of another species that resides in the area, the Campbell monkey (Zuberbühler, 2001). They also understand that if the alarm call is preceded by a "boom" call, the threat is not as urgent. Thus, it appears calls are strung together to enable a simple grammar, indicating that the communications include syntax and semantics (meaning). The communication skills of these monkeys are impressive, but it remains clear that such communication is quite different from human language.

Studying vocalization, however, may not be the best place to look for the precursors of human language. Michael Tomasello, a researcher at the Max Planck Institute for Evolutionary Anthropology, points out that among primates, especially the great apes, the *function* of communication differs depending on whether it is vocal or gestural (Tomasello, 2007). In general, vocal calls in primates tend to be involuntary signals, associated with a specific emotional state, produced in response to specific stimuli, and broadcast to the surrounding group. They are inflexible. By contrast, gestures are flexible, they are used in non-urgent contexts to initiate such things as playing and grooming with a specific individual, and some are learned socially by gorillas (Pika et al., 2003), chimps (Liebal et al., 2004), and bonobos (Pika et al., 2005). Tomasello emphasizes that unlike vocalizations, using gestures requires knowing the attentional state of the communicating partner. No good making a gesture if no one is paying attention to you. He concludes that primate gestures, which are flexible, socially learned, and require shared attention, are more like human language than primate vocalizations, which typically are inflexible, automatic, and independent from shared attention. Tomasello suggests that language evolved from gestural communication.

Interestingly, nonhuman primates have little cortical control over vocalization but have excellent cortical control over the hands and arms (Ploog, 2002). From these findings and what we know about primate anatomy, it is not surprising that attempts to teach nonhuman primates to speak have failed. Teaching them to communicate manually has been more successful. For instance, Washoe, a chimp, learned a form of manual sign language (Gardener & Gardener, 1969); and Kanzi, a bonobo, learned to point to abstract visual symbols (lexigrams) on a keyboard (Savage-Rumbaugh & Lewin, 1994).

Kanzi is able to match pictures, objects, lexigrams, and spoken words. He freely uses the keyboard to ask for objects he wants. He can indicate a place with a lexigram and then go there. He can generalize a specific reference; for instance, he uses the lexigram for *bread* to mean all breads including tacos. He can listen to an informational statement and adjust what he is doing using the new information. Thus, Kanzi is able to understand signs in a symbolic way.

According to Chomsky, language cannot be explained in terms of learned sequences, but depends on rules; and its most distinct feature is that it is generative, meaning that it allows us to create and understand an endless variety of novel sequences. The arrangement of the words and the meaning of the sequence depend on the conventional rules of the grammar.

Now consider that Kanzi understands the difference between "Make the doggie bite the snake" and "Make the snake bite the doggie," and he demonstrates his understanding by using stuffed animals. Seventy percent of the time, he will respond correctly to spoken sentences (from a concealed instructor) that he has never heard before, such as "Squeeze the hot dog." He is the first nonhuman to demonstrate either of these abilities. Kanzi uses both the keyboard and gesture, sometimes combining the two in an arbitrary rule (syntax) that he has developed. For instance, to specify an action, he will use a lexigram first and then a pointing gesture to specify the agent, always in that order, even if he has to walk across the room to point to the lexigram first and then return to indicate the agent. Not too surprising, since primates use combinations of gestures, vocalizations, and facial expressions.

Michael Corballis has also reached the conclusion that language began with gestures. He has proposed that generative language evolved, perhaps from *Homo habilis* on, as a system of manual gestures, but switched to a predominantly vocal system with *H. sapiens sapiens* (1991; 2009). Giacomo Rizzolatti and Michael Arbib (1998) suggest that language arose from a combination of gesture and facial movements, speculating that mirror neurons are a piece of the language puzzle. Mirror neurons, you recall, were first discovered in area F5 in the monkey. The dorsal portion of F5 is involved with hand movements and the ventral portion with movement of the mouth and larynx. Tantalizingly, area F5 is the homolog for Brodmann's area (BA) 44, a portion of Broca's area in the human. BA44 is involved not only in speech production and larynx control but also in complex hand movements as well as in sensorimotor learning and integration (Binkofski & Buccino, 2004).

Many studies in humans show how hand gestures and language are connected. For example, one study found that both congenitally blind speakers and sighted speakers gestured as they spoke at the same rate and used the same range of gesture forms. The blind speakers gestured even while they spoke to another blind person, which suggests that gestures are tightly coupled to the act of speaking (Iverson & Goldin-Meadow, 1998). Another study followed the progress of congenitally deaf Nicaraguan children who had had no previous contact with each other and were brought together in a school. Although the school was geared to teaching them to speak orally, the children, on their own, gradually developed their own fully communicative hand gesture language, complete with syntax (Senghas, 1995).

Initially this close association of hand and mouth may have been related to eating, but later could have expanded to gesture and vocal language. There is some evidence for this proposal. In macaque monkeys, neurons in the lateral part of F5 have been found to activate with conditioned vocalizations, that is, voluntary coo-calls the monkeys were trained to make (Coudé et al., 2011). We know that the left hemisphere controls the motor movements of the right side of the body, both in humans and the great apes. Chimpanzees exhibit preferential use of the right hand in gestural communication both with other chimps and with humans (Meguerditchian et al., 2010), but not when making noncommunicative gestures. This behavior is also seen in captive baboons (Meguerditchian

& Vauclair, 2006; Meguerditchian et al., 2010), suggesting that the emergence of language and its typical left lateralization may have arisen from a left lateralized gestural communication system in the common ancestor of baboons, chimps, and humans.

Indeed, the cortical location of signing ability in humans has been studied in the few congenitally deaf "signers" who have had right- or left-hemisphere lesions. Interestingly, patients with left-hemisphere lesions that involved the language areas of the temporal and frontal lobes were "aphasic," or impaired in sign production and comprehension, whereas those with right hemisphere lesions in similar areas were not. They, however, were impaired in emotional processing and expression, as might be expected with impaired prosody (for a full review of the brain organization in deaf signers, see Bellugi et al., 2010).

A few brain imaging studies provide support for the theory that gestures and language are connected. In the macaque monkey, the rostral part of the inferior parietal lobule, an area involved with control of hand and orofacial action (homologous to the human supramarginal gyrus) is linked via a distinct branch of the superior longitudinal fasciculus with area 44 (homologous with part of Broca's area) and the ventral part of the premotor cortex, which controls the orofacial musculature (Petrides & Pandya, 2009). This may be analogous to the dorsal stream in humans (see Chapter 6), involved with mapping of sound to motor articulation. These monkeys also recognize the correspondence of an auditory "coo" and "threat" call with the facial expression that coincides with it.

In addition, a PET study on chimps found that when they made a communicative gesture or an atypical novel sound when begging for food, the left inferior frontal gyrus was activated, a region considered to be homologous to Broca's area (Taglialatela et al., 2008). What is an atypical sound? First described in 1991 (Marshall et al., 1991), atypical sounds are produced only by some captive chimps. Three have been identified: a "raspberry," an "extended grunt," and a "kiss." The sounds have been observed to be socially learned and selectively produced

to gain the attention of an inattentive human (Hopkins et al., 2007). This behavior suggests that chimps have some voluntary control over some of their vocalizations and facial expressions and a link between sensory perception and motor action. These sounds are unlike the species-typical vocalizations that are related to a specific emotional state (Goodall, 1986) and context (Polick & DeWaal, 2007).

The left-hemisphere dominance for language may also be present in the chimpanzee. In humans, the left lateralization of speech is actually visible: The right side of the mouth opens first and wider. In contrast, the left side gears up first with emotional expressions. In two large colonies of captive chimps, the same thing was found: A left-hemispheric dominance for the production of learned attention-getting sounds, and right-hemispheric dominance for the production of species-typical vocalizations (Losin et al., 2008; Wallex et al., 2011). These studies all suggest that the left hemisphere's voluntary control of hand gestures (area F5) and vocalizations may have combined into an integrative system.

Chomsky was on the mark when he observed that human language is very different from the communications of other animals. That it is spontaneously generated, however, has not proven to be the case. Rudimentary roots of human language have been observed in our primate relatives in both their behavior and brain structures.

TAKE-HOME MESSAGES

- Animal calls can carry meaning and show evidence of rudimentary syntax. In general, however, animal calls tend to be inflexible, associated with a specific emotional state, and linked to a specific stimulus.
- Many researchers suggest that language evolved from hand gestures, or a combination of hand gestures and facial movement.
- Areas that control hand movement and vocalizations are closely located in homologous structures in monkeys and humans.

HOW THE BRAIN WORKS
Genetic Components of Language

In 1990, a report was published about the KE family in England. Half the family members, spanning three generations, suffered a severe speech and language disorder (Hurst et al., 1990). Their verbal and oral dyspraxia closely resembled that seen in Broca's aphasia. Since that time, the family has been studied extensively (i.e., Vargha-Khadem et al., 1995). In a direct comparison with patients with aphasia, they were found to be equally impaired on tests of grammar competence, manipulating *inflectional morphology* (i.e., distinctions between the same lexeme, such as the verb endings to *paints, painting, painted*), and *derivational morphology* (i.e., distinctions between different lexemes that are related, such as *paintings* and *painting*). There were differences too. In tests of word and non-word repetition, the aphasics could repeat the words but not the non-words, but the affected KE family members could do neither, suggesting that the aphasics had learned the articulation patterns of real words before the onset of their aphasia. When it came to semantic, phonemic, and written fluency, the KE family members were less impaired (Vargha-Khadem et al., 2005). Extensive behavioral testing suggested at least one core deficit: orofacial dyspraxia. Whether the semantic and other cognitive impairments were secondary to this deficit or were also core deficits remains undetermined.

The neural basis of the abnormalities was sought using structural and functional imaging. Bilateral abnormalities were seen in several motor-related regions. For instance, affected family members had a 25% reduction in the volume of the caudate nucleus. Abnormally low levels of gray matter were also found in other motor areas including the inferior frontal gyrus (Broca's area), precentral gyrus, frontal pole, and cerebellum. Meanwhile, abnormally high levels were seen in the superior temporal gyrus (Wernicke's area), angular gyrus, and putamen. Functional MRI studies using silent verb generation, spoken verb generation, and word repetition tasks revealed that the affected members had posterior and bilateral activations in regions not generally used for language functions for both tasks (reviewed in Vargha-Khadem et al., 2005).

By looking at the family tree, researchers found that the disorder was inherited in a simple fashion: The disorder in the KE family resulted from a defect in a single autosomal dominant gene (Hurst et al., 1990). The person with the mutation has a 50% chance of passing it to his or her offspring.

The hunt for the gene commenced at the Wellcome Trust Centre for Human Genetics at the University of Oxford. Researchers found a single base-pair mutation in the *FOXP2* gene sequence (adenine for guanine) in the affected members of the KE family (Lai et al., 2001). This mutation caused the amino acid histidine to be substituted for arginine in the FOXP2 protein. The *FOX* genes are a large family of genes, and this particular arginine is invariant among all of them, suggesting that it has a crucial functional role.

How can one little change do so much damage? *FOX* genes code for proteins that are transcription factors, which act as switches that turn gene expression on or off. Mutations in *FOX* genes may cause phenotypes as varied as cancer, glaucoma or, as we see here in the case of the *FOXP2* gene, language disorders.

If the *FOXP2* gene is so important in the development of language, is it unique to humans? This question is complicated, and its complexity speaks to huge differences between talking about genes and talking about the expression of genes. The *FOXP2* gene is present in a broad range of animals. The protein encoded for by the *FOXP2* gene differs at five amino acids between humans and birds, three amino acids between mouse and man, and only two between humans and chimpanzees or gorillas. The sequencing of Neandertal DNA revealed that they had the same *FOXP2* gene that we have (Krause et al., 2007). These researchers also found that the gene changes lie on the common modern human haplotype (DNA sequences that are next to each other on a chromosome that are transmitted together), which was shown earlier to have been subject to a selective sweep (Enard et al., 2002; Zhang et al., 2002). A selective sweep means what it sounds like. This gene was a hot item that produced a characteristic that gave its owners an obvious competitive advantage. Whoever had it had more offspring, and it became the dominant gene. These findings support the idea that these genetic changes and the selective sweep predate the common ancestor of modern human and Neandertal populations, which existed about 300,000–400,000 years ago. Thus humans do have a unique version of the *FOXP2* gene that produces unique FOXP2 proteins.

Is this the gene that codes for speech and language? Not necessarily. What we have is a uniquely human modification of a gene that seems to influence human brain phenotype (Preuss, 2012). Many questions remain. For instance, what genes are regulated by *FOXP2*? A lot. Genes involved with morphogenesis, intracellular signaling, cation homeostasis, neuron outgrowth, axonal morphology, dendritic branching, calcium mobilization and concentration, and learning have been identified. Although this gene has been extensively studied, there is still no direct connection to human speech or language. The neuroscientist Todd Preuss at Yerkes National Primate Research Center observes that the problem with tying *FOXP2* to language is that we are trying to relate a gene that has many functions to a complex, high-level phenotype. This effort is probably not realistic, because most phenotypes arise through the interactions of multiple genes, and most genes influence multiple phenotypes—lessons learned from population genetics (Preuss, 2012). Most likely the evolution of the *FOXP2* gene is one of many changes on the pathway to language function.

Summary

Language is unique among mental functions in that only humans possess a true language system. How is language organized in the human brain, and what can this functional and anatomical organization tell us about the cognitive architecture of the language system? We have known for more than a century that regions around the Sylvian fissure of the dominant left hemisphere participate in language comprehension and production. Classical models, however, are insufficient for understanding the computations that support language. Newer formulations based on detailed analysis of the effects of neurological lesions (supported by improvements in structural imaging), functional neuroimaging, human electrophysiology, transcranial magnetic stimulation (TMS), and computational modeling now provide some surprising modifications of older models. The human language system is complex, and much remains to be learned about how the biology of the brain enables the rich speech and language comprehension that characterize our daily lives. The future of language research is promising as psycholinguistic models combine with neuroscience to elucidate the neural code for this uniquely human mental faculty.

Key Terms

agrammatic aphasia (p. 472)

alexia (p. 486)

anomia (p. 469)

aphasia (p. 472)

apraxia (p. 472)

arcuate fasciculus (p. 474)

Broca's aphasia (p. 472)

Broca's area (p. 471)

conduction aphasia (p. 474)

dysarthria (p. 472)

global aphasia (p. 474)

lexical access (p. 475)

lexical integration (p. 475)

lexical selection (p. 475)

mental lexicon (p. 475)

morpheme (p. 476)

N400 response (p. 490)

P600 response (p. 491)

phoneme (p. 476)

phonology (p. 487)

semantic (p. 476)

semantic paraphasia (p. 477)

Sylvian fissure (p. 471)

syntactic parsing (p. 490)

syntax (p. 472)

Wernicke's aphasia (p. 473)

Wernicke's area (p. 471)

Thought Questions

1. How might the mental lexicon be organized in the brain? Would we expect to find it localized in a particular spot in cortex? If not, why not?

2. At what stage of input processing are the comprehension of spoken and of written language the same, and where must they be different? Are there any exceptions to this rule?

3. Describe the route that an auditory speech signal might take in the cortex, from perceptual analysis to comprehension.

4. What evidence exists for the role of the right hemisphere in language processing? If the right hemisphere has a role in language, what might that role be?

5. Can knowledge of the world around you affect the way you process and understand words?

6. Describe the anatomy and circuitry on the left perisylvian language system.

Anatomy of cognitive control

The prefrontal cortex includes all of the areas in front of the primary and secondary motor areas. The four subdivisions of prefrontal cortex are the lateral prefrontal cortex, ventromedial prefrontal cortex, frontal pole, and medial frontal cortex. The most ventral part of the ventromedial prefrontal cortex is frequently referred to as the orbitofrontal cortex, referring to the cortex which lies above the bony orbits of the eyes.

The Anatomy Behind Cognitive Control

As might be suspected of any complex process, cognitive control requires the integrated function of many different parts of the brain. This chapter highlights the frontal lobes, and in particular, prefrontal cortex. The discussion, however, also requires references to other cortical and subcortical areas that are massively interconnected with the frontal cortex, forming the networks that enable goal-oriented behavior. This network includes the parietal lobe and the basal ganglia, regions that were discussed in previous chapters when we considered the neural mechanisms for attention and action selection.

Subdivisions of the Frontal Lobes

The frontal lobes comprise about a third of the cerebral cortex in humans. The posterior border with the parietal lobe is marked by the *central sulcus*. The frontal and temporal lobes are separated by the lateral fissure.

As we learned in Chapter 8, the most posterior part of the frontal lobe is the *primary motor cortex*, encompassing the gyrus in front of the central sulcus and extending into the central sulcus itself. Anterior and ventral to the motor cortex are the *secondary motor areas*, including the *lateral premotor cortex* and the *supplementary motor area*. The remainder of the frontal lobe is termed the **prefrontal cortex (PFC)**. The prefrontal cortex includes half of the entire frontal lobe in humans. The ratio is considerably smaller for non-primate species (Figure 12.1). We will refer to four regions of prefrontal cortex in this chapter: the **lateral prefrontal cortex (LPFC)**, the **frontal polar region (FP)**, the **orbitofrontal cortex (OFC**, or sometimes referred to as ventromedial zone), and the **medial frontal cortex (MFC)**.

The frontal cortex is present in all mammalian species. In human evolution, however, it has expanded tremendously, especially in the more anterior aspects of prefrontal cortex. Interestingly, when compared to other primate species, the expansion of prefrontal cortex in the human brain is more pronounced in the white matter (the axonal tracts) than in the gray matter (the cell bodies; Schoenemann et al., 2005). This finding suggests that the cognitive capabilities that are uniquely human may be more a result of how our brains are connected rather than due to an increase in the number of neurons.

Because the development of functional capabilities parallels phylogenetic trends, the frontal lobe's expansion is related to the emergence of the complex cognitive capabilities that are especially pronounced in humans. What's more, as investigators frequently note, "Ontogeny recapitulates phylogeny." Compared to the rest of the brain, prefrontal cortex matures late in terms of the development of neural density patterns and white matter tracts. Correspondingly, cognitive control processes appear relatively late in development, as evident in the "me-oriented" behavior of the infant and the rebellious teenager.

Networks Underlying Cognitive Control

The prefrontal cortex coordinates processing across wide regions of the central nervous system (CNS). It contains a massively connected network that links the brain's motor, perceptual, and limbic regions (Goldman-Rakic,

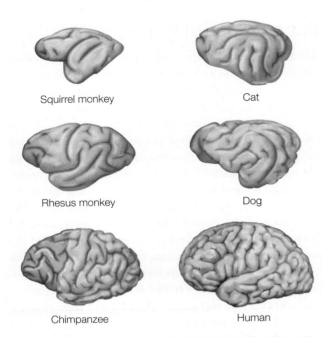

Squirrel monkey

Cat

Rhesus monkey

Dog

Chimpanzee

Human

FIGURE 12.1 A comparison of prefronal cortex in different species. The purple region indicates prefrontal cortex in six mammalian species. Although the brains are not drawn to scale, the figure makes clear that the PFC spans a much larger percentage of the overall cortex in the chimpanzee and human.

1995; Passingham, 1993). Extensive projections connect the prefrontal cortex to almost all regions of the parietal and temporal cortex, and even prestriate regions of the occipital cortex. The largest input comes from the *thalamus*, which connects the prefrontal cortex with subcortical structures including the *basal ganglia*, *cerebellum*, and various brainstem nuclei. Indeed, almost all cortical and subcortical areas influence the prefrontal cortex either through direct projections or indirectly via a few synapses. The prefrontal cortex also sends reciprocal connections to most areas that project to it, and to premotor and motor areas. It also has many projections to the contralateral hemisphere—projections to homologous prefrontal areas via the corpus callosum as well as bilateral projections to premotor and subcortical regions.

When we arrive at the discussion on decision making, which plays a prominent role in this chapter, we consider a finer-grained analysis of the **dopamine** system. This system includes the **ventral tegmental area**, a brainstem nucleus, the basal ganglia, and the dorsal and ventral striata (singular: **striatum**).

Cognitive Control Deficits

Patients with frontal lobe lesions like W.R., the wayward lawyer, present a paradox. From a superficial look at their everyday behavior, it is frequently difficult to detect a neurological disorder. They seem fine: They do not display obvious disorders in any of their perceptual abilities, they can execute motor actions, and their speech is fluent and coherent. These patients are unimpaired on conventional neuropsychological tests of intelligence and knowledge. They generally score within the normal range on IQ tests. Their memory for previously learned facts is fine, and they do well on most tests of long-term memory. With more sensitive and specific tests, however, it becomes clear that frontal lesions can disrupt different aspects of normal cognition and memory, producing an array of problems. Such patients may persist in a response even after being told that it is incorrect; this behavior is known as **perseveration**. These patients may be apathetic, distractible, or impulsive. They may be unable to make decisions, unable to plan actions, unable to understand the consequences of their actions, impaired in their ability to organize and segregate the timing of events in memory, unable to remember the source of their memories, and unable to follow rules—including a disregard of social conventions (discussed in the next chapter). Because the deficits seem to vary with the location of the patient's lesion, it suggests that the neural substrates within the prefrontal cortex subserve different processes. As we'll see, those processes are involved with cognitive control.

Ironically, patients with frontal lobe lesions are aware of their deteriorating social situation, have the intellectual capabilities to generate ideas that may alleviate their problems, and may be able to tell you the pros and cons of each idea. Yet their efforts to prioritize and organize these ideas into a plan and put them into play are haphazard at best. Similarly, though they are not amnesic, they are able to tell you a list of rules from memory, but may not be able to follow them.

A demonstration of how these problems are manifest in everyday behavior was given by Tim Shallice (Shallice & Burgess, 1991). He asked three patients with frontal lesions from head trauma to go to the local shopping center to make a few purchases (e.g., a loaf of bread), keep an appointment, or collect information such as the exchange rate of the rupee. These chores presented a real problem for the patients. For instance, one patient failed to purchase soap because the store she visited did not carry her favorite brand; another wandered outside the designated shopping center in pursuit of an item that could easily be found within the designated region. All became embroiled in social complications. One succeeded in obtaining the newspaper but was pursued by the merchant for failing to pay! In a related experiment, patients were asked to work on three tasks for 15 minutes. Whereas control participants successfully juggled their schedule to ensure that they made enough progress on each task, the patients got bogged down on one or two tasks.

Lesion studies in animals have revealed a similar paradox. Unilateral lesions of prefrontal cortex also tend to produce relatively mild deficits. When the lesions are bilateral, however, dramatic changes can be observed. Consider the observations of Leonardo Bianchi (1922), an Italian psychiatrist of the early 20th century:

> The monkey which used to jump on to the window-ledge, to call out to his companions, after the operation jumps to the ledge again, but does not call out. The sight of the window determines the reflex of the jump, but the purpose is now lacking, for it is no longer represented in the focal point of consciousness. . . . Another monkey sees the handle of the door and grasps it, but the mental process stops at the sight of the bright colour of the handle. The animal does not attempt to turn it so as to open the door. . . . Evidently there are lacking all those other images that are necessary for the determination of a series of movements coordinated towards one end.

As with W.R., the monkeys demonstrate a loss of goal-oriented behavior.

The behavior of these monkeys underscores an important aspect of goal-oriented behavior. *Following the lesions, the behavior is stimulus driven.* The animal sees the ledge and jumps up; another sees the door and grasps the handle, but that is the end of it. They no longer appear to have a purpose for their actions. The sight of the door is no longer a sufficient cue to remind the animal of the food and other animals that can be found beyond it. The question is, what is the deficit? Is it a problem with motivation, attention, memory, or something else? Insightfully, Bianchi thought it was a problem with lack of representation in the "focal point of consciousness," what we now think of as working memory.

A classic demonstration of this tendency for stimulus-driven behavior among humans with frontal lobe injuries is evident from the clinical observations of Francois Lhermitte of the Hôpital de la Salpêtrière in Paris (Lhermitte, 1983; Lhermitte et al., 1986). Lhermitte invited a patient to meet him in his office. At the entrance to the room, he had placed a hammer, a nail, and a picture. Upon entering the room and seeing these objects, the patient spontaneously used the hammer and nail to hang the picture on the wall. In a more extreme example, Lhermitte put a hypodermic needle on his desk, dropped his trousers, and turned his back to his patient. Whereas most people in this situation would consider filing ethical charges, the frontal lobe patient was unfazed. He simply picked up the needle and gave his doctor a healthy jab in the buttocks! Lhermitte coined the term **utilization behavior** to characterize this extreme dependency on prototypical responses for guiding behavior. The patients with frontal lobe damage retained knowledge about prototypical uses of objects such as a hammer or needle,

saw the stimulus, and responded. They were not able to inhibit their response or flexibly change it according to the context in which they found themselves. Their cognitive control mechanisms were out of whack.

TAKE-HOME MESSAGES

- Cognitive control refers to mental abilities that involve planning, controlling, and regulating the flow of information processing.
- Prefrontal cortex includes four major components: lateral prefrontal cortex, frontal pole, medial frontal cortex, and ventromedial prefrontal cortex. All are associated with cognitive control.
- The ability to make goal-directed decisions is impaired in patients with frontal cortex lesions, even if their general intellectual capabilities remain unaffected.

Goal-Oriented Behavior

Our actions are not aimless, nor are they entirely automatic—dictated by events and stimuli immediately at hand. We choose to act because we want to accomplish a goal or gratify a personal need.

Researchers distinguish between two fundamental types of actions. **Goal-oriented actions** are based on the assessment of an expected reward or value and the knowledge that there is a causal relationship between the action and the reward (**action–outcome**). Most of our actions are of this type. We turn on the radio when getting into the car so that we can catch the news on the drive home. We put money into the soda machine to purchase a favorite beverage. We resist going out to the movies the night before an exam to get in some extra studying, with the hope that this effort will lead to the desired grade.

In contrast to goal-oriented actions stand habitual actions. A **habit** is defined as an action that is no longer under the control of a reward, but is stimulus driven; as such, we can consider it automatic. The habitual commuter might find herself flipping on the car radio without even thinking about the expected outcome. The action is triggered simply by the context. It becomes obvious that this is a habit when our commuter reaches to switch on the radio, even though she knows it is broken. Habit-driven actions occur in the presence of certain stimuli that trigger the retrieval of well-learned associations. These associations can be useful, allowing us to rapidly select a response (Bunge, 2004), such as stopping quickly at a red light. They can also develop into persistent bad habits, however, such as eating junk food when bored or lighting up a cigarette when anxious. Habitual responses make addictions difficult to break.

The distinction between goal-oriented behavior and habits is graded. Though the current context is likely to dictate our choice of actions and may even be sufficient to trigger a habitual-like response, we are also capable of being flexible. The soda machine might beckon invitingly, but if we are on a health kick, we might walk on past or choose to purchase a bottle of water. These are situations in which cognitive control comes into play.

Cognitive control provides the interface through which goals influence behavior. Goal-oriented behaviors require processes that enable us to maintain our goal, focus on the information that is relevant to achieving that goal, ignore or inhibit irrelevant information, monitor our progress toward the goal, and shift flexibly from one sub-goal to another in a coordinated way.

Cognitive Control Requires Working Memory

As we learned in Chapter 9, **working memory**, a type of short-term memory, is the transient representation of task-relevant information—what Patricia Goldman-Rakic has called the "blackboard of the mind." These representations may be from the distant past, or they may be closely related to something that is currently in the environment, or has been experienced recently. Working memory refers to the temporary maintenance of this information, providing an interface between perception, long-term memory, and action and thus, enabling goal-oriented behavior and decision making.

Working memory is critical for animals whose behavior is not exclusively stimulus driven. What is immediately in front of us surely influences our behavior, but we are not automatons. We can (usually) hold off eating until all the guests sitting around the table have been served. This capacity demonstrates that we can represent information that is not immediately evident, in this case social rules, in addition to reacting to stimuli that currently dominate our perceptual pathways (the fragrant food and conversation). We can mind our dinner manners (stored knowledge) by choosing to respond to some stimuli (the conversation) while ignoring other stimuli (the food). This process requires integrating current perceptual information with stored knowledge from long-term memory.

Prefrontal Cortex Is Necessary for Working Memory but Not Associative Memory

The lateral prefrontal cortex appears to be an important interface between current perceptual information and stored knowledge, and thus, constitutes a major component of the working memory system. Prefrontal cortex is necessary for cognitive control. Its importance in working memory was first demonstrated in animal studies using a variety of **delayed-response tasks**. In the simplest version, sketched in Figure 12.2, a monkey is situated within reach of two food wells. At the start of a trial, the monkey observes the experimenter placing a food morsel in one of the two wells (perception). Then the two wells are covered, and a curtain is lowered to prevent the monkey from reaching toward either well. After a delay period, the curtain is raised and the monkey is allowed to choose one of the two wells and recover the food. Although this appears to be a simple task, it demands one critical cognitive capability: The animal must continue to represent the location of the unseen food during the delay period (working memory). Monkeys with lesions of the lateral prefrontal cortex do poorly on the task.

The problem for these animals does not reflect a general deficit in forming associations. In an experiment to test associative memory, the food wells are covered with distinctive visual cues: The well with the food has a plus sign, and the empty well has a negative sign. In this condition, the researcher may shift the food morsel's location during the delay period, but the associated visual cue—the food cover—will be relocated with the food. Prefrontal lesions do not disrupt performance in this task.

These two tasks clarify the concept of working memory (Goldman-Rakic, 1992). In the delayed-response task (see Figure 12.2a), the animal must remember the currently baited location during the delay period. In contrast, in the associative learning condition (see Figure 12.2b), it is only necessary for the visual cue to reactivate a long-term association of which cue is associated with the reward. The reappearance of the two visual cues can trigger recall and guide the animal's performance.

Studies of patients with prefrontal lesions have also emphasized the role of this region in working memory. One example comes from studies of **recency memory**, the ability to organize and segregate the timing or order of events in memory (Milner, 1995). In a recency discrimination task, participants are presented with a series of study cards and every so often are asked which of two pictures was seen most recently. For example, one of the pictures might have been on a study card presented 4 trials previously, and the other, on a study card shown 32 trials back. For a control task, the procedure is modified: The test card contains two pictures, but only one of the two pictures was presented earlier. Following the same instructions, the participant should choose that picture because, by definition, it is the one seen most recently. Note, though, that the task is really one of *recognition memory*. There is no need to evaluate the temporal position of the two choices.

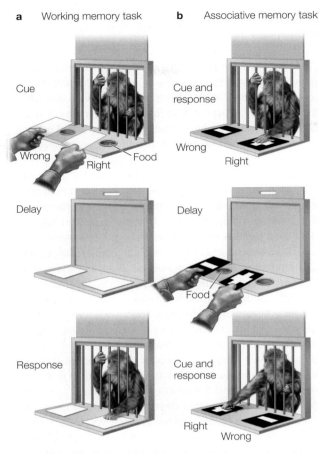

a Working memory task

Cue

Wrong   Right   Food

Delay

Response

b Associative memory task

Cue and response

Wrong   Right

Delay

Food

Cue and response

Right   Wrong

FIGURE 12.2 Prefrontal lesions impair working memory performance.
(a) In the working memory task, the monkey observes one well being baited with food. After a delay period, the animal retrieves the food. The location of the food is determined randomly. (b) In the associative memory task, the food reward is always associated with one of the two visual cues. The location of the cues (and food) is determined randomly. Working memory is required in the first task because, at the time the animal responds, no external cues indicate the location of the food. Long-term memory is required in the second task because the animal must remember which visual cue is associated with the reward.

Patients with frontal lobe lesions perform as well as control participants on the recognition memory task, but they have a selective deficit in recency judgments. The memory task can be performed by evaluating if one of the stimuli was recently presented—or perhaps more relevant, if one of the stimuli is novel. The recency task, though, requires working memory in the sense that the patient must also keep track of the relationship between recently presented stimuli. This is not to suggest that the person could construct a full timeline of all of the stimuli—this would certainly exceed the capacity of working memory. But to compare the relative timing of two items, the frontal lobes are required to maintain the representations of those items at the time of the probe. When frontal lobes are damaged, this temporal structure is lost.

A breakdown in the temporal structure of working memory may account for more bizarre aspects of frontal lobe syndrome. For example, Wilder Penfield described a patient who was troubled by her inability to prepare her family's evening meal. She could remember the ingredients for dishes and perform all of the actions to make the dish, but unless someone was there to tell her the proper sequence step by step, she could not organize her actions into a proper temporal sequence and could not prepare a meal (Jasper, 1995).

Another, albeit indirect, demonstration of the importance of prefrontal cortex in working memory comes from developmental studies. Adele Diamond of the University of Pennsylvania (1990) pointed out that a common marker of conceptual intelligence, Piaget's Object Permanence Test, is logically similar to the delayed-response task. In this task, a child observes the experimenter hiding a reward in one of two locations. After a delay of a few seconds, the child is encouraged to find the reward. Children younger than 1 year are unable to accomplish this task. At this age, the frontal lobes are still maturing. Diamond maintained that the ability to succeed in tasks such as the Object Permanence Test parallels the development of the frontal lobes. Before this development takes place, the child acts as though the object is "out of sight, out of mind." As the frontal lobes mature, the child can be guided by representations of objects and no longer requires their presence.

It seems likely that many species must have some ability to recognize object permanence. A species would not have survived for long if its members did not understand that a predator that had stepped behind a particular bush was still there. The difference between species may be in the capacity of the working memory, how long information can be maintained in working memory, and the ability to maintain attention (see the box How the Brain Works: Working Memory, Learning, and Intelligence).

Physiological Correlates of Working Memory

A working memory system requires a mechanism to access stored information and a way to keep it active. The prefrontal cortex can perform both operations. In the delayed-response studies described earlier, single-cell recordings from the prefrontal cortex of monkeys (see Figure 12.3) showed that these neurons become active during the delayed-response task and show sustained activity throughout the delay period (Fuster, 1989). For some cells, activation doesn't commence until after the delay begins and can be maintained up to 1 minute. These cells provide a neural correlate for keeping a representation active after the triggering stimulus is no longer

Humans are obsessed with identifying why people differ in what we call "intelligence." We have looked at anatomical measures such as brain size, prefrontal cortex size, amount of grey matter, and amount of white matter (connectivity). These measures have all been shown to account for some of the variation observed on tests of intelligence. Another approach is to consider differences among types of intelligence. For example, we can compare *crystallized intelligence* and *fluid intelligence*. Crystallized intelligence refers to our knowledge, things like vocabulary and experience. Fluid intelligence refers to the ability to engage in creative abstract thinking, to recognize patterns, and to solve problems.

Fluid intelligence is closely linked to working memory. A child's working memory at 5 years old turns out to be a better predictor of academic success than is IQ (Alloway & Alloway, 2010). Observations like these have inspired research on the neural mechanisms that are behind the differences in fluid intelligence. One study (Burgess et al., 2011) investigated whether the relationship between fluid intelligence and working memory is mediated by *interference control*, the ability to suppress irrelevant information. The researchers used fMRI while participants performed a classic working memory *n*-back task. Participants were presented with either word or face stimuli, and they were to respond when a stimulus matched one presented three items back. The researchers were curious about the neural response to "lures," a stimulus that was recently presented but not 3-back (e.g., 2-back or 4-back). They assumed that the participants would show a tendency to respond to the lures and would need to exhibit interference control to suppress these responses. Indeed, an impressive positive correlation was found between the magnitude of the BOLD response to the lures in PFC (and parietal cortex) and fluid intelligence (Figure 1). They concluded that a key component of fluid intelligence is the ability to maintain focus on task-relevant information in working memory.

As we shall see in this chapter, the neurotransmitter dopamine plays an important role in learning. Dopamine receptors are abundant in PFC and thought to serve a modulatory function, sharpening the response of PFC neurons. It might be hypothesized that having more dopamine would predict better learning performance. Unlike fun, however, you can have too much dopamine. Various studies have shown that the efficacy of dopamine follows an inverted U-shaped function when performance is plotted as a function of dopamine levels. As dopamine levels increase, learning performance improves—but only to a point. At some level, increasing dopamine levels results in a reduction in performance.

The inverted U-shaped function can help explain some of the paradoxical effects of L-dopa therapy in Parkinson's disease. In these patients, the reduction in dopamine levels is most pronounced in dorsal (motor) striatum, at least in the early stages of the disease; dopamine levels in ventral striatum and the cerebral cortex are less affected. L-dopa treatment boosts dopamine levels back to normal in the dorsal striatum and thus improves motor function. The same treatment, however, produces an overdose effect in the ventral striatum and frontal lobe. This can result in impaired performance on tasks that depend on ventral striato-frontal circuitry such as reversal learning, where you have to change your behavior to gain a reward (Graef & Heekeren, 2010).

Genetic data shows that different alleles can affect dopamine levels, which in turn have an effect on PFC function. The catecholamine-O-methyltransferase (COMT) gene is associated with the production of an enzyme that breaks down dopamine. There are different alleles of COMT, resulting in different levels of the enzyme. People with the allele that lowers the rate of dopamine breakdown have higher dopamine levels, especially in the PFC. Interestingly, this allele has been implicated in an increased risk for schizophrenia and other neuropsychiatric phenotypes.

FIGURE 1 Correlation of control network activity and measures of fluid intelligence.
Participants performed a working memory task. Trials were divided into those with lures where a mismatch was a stimulus that had been previously seen (and thus had potential for a false alarm) and trials without lures where the stimulus had not been seen. **(a)** Regions in prefrontal and parietal cortex that had increased BOLD response on lure trials compared to no-lure trials. **(b)** Correlation between individual scores on the Lure activity factor (Lure–No Lure) and measures of fluid intelligence (left) or a measure of working memory span from a different task (right).

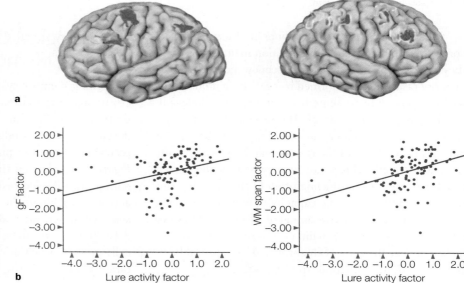

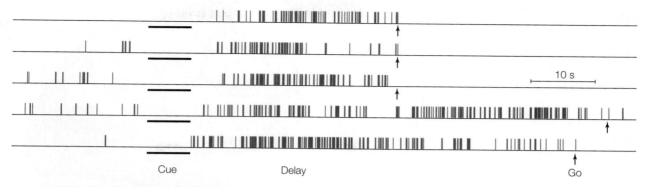

Cue   Delay   Go

FIGURE 12.3 Prefrontal neurons can show sustained activity during delayed-response tasks.
Each row represents a single trial. The cue indicated the location for a forthcoming response. The monkey was trained to withhold the response until a "Go" signal (arrows) appeared. Each vertical tick represents an action potential. This cell did not respond during the cue interval. Rather, its activity increased when the cue was turned off, and activity persisted until the response.

visible. The cells provide a continuous record of the response required for the animal to obtain the reward.

Lateral prefrontal cortex (LPFC) cells simply could be providing a generic signal that supports representations in other cortical areas. Alternatively, they could

be coding specific stimulus features. To differentiate between these possibilities, Earl Miller and his colleagues (Rao et al., 1997) trained monkeys on a working memory task that required successive coding of two stimulus attributes: identity and location. Figure 12.4a depicts the

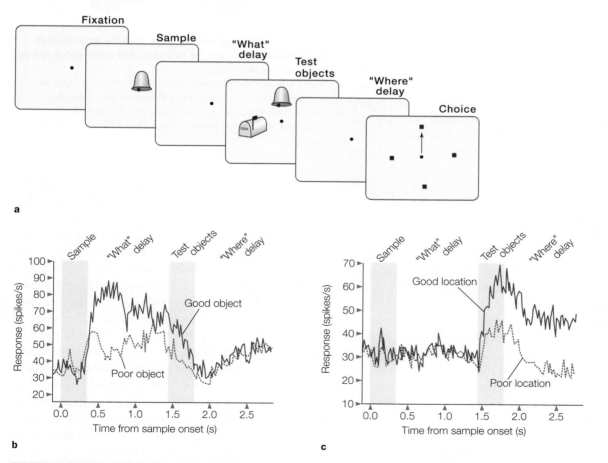

FIGURE 12.4 Coding of "what" and "where" information in single neurons of the prefrontal cortex in the macaque.
(a) Sequence of events in a single trial. See text for details. **(b)** Firing profile of a neuron that shows a preference for one object over another during the "what" delay. The neural activity is low once the response location is cued. **(c)** Firing profile of a neuron that shows a preference for one location. This neuron was not activated during the "what" delay.

sequence of events in each trial. A sample stimulus is presented, and the animal must remember the identity of this object for a 1-s delay period in which the screen is blank. Then two objects are shown, one of which matches the sample. The position of the matching stimulus indicates the target location for a forthcoming response. The response, however, must be withheld until the end of a second delay. Within the lateral prefrontal cortex, cells characterized as "what," "where," and "what–where" were observed (Figure 12.4). For example, "what" cells responded to specific objects, and this response was sustained over the delay period. "Where" cells showed selectivity to certain locations. In addition, about half of the cells were "what–where" cells, responding to specific combinations of "what" and "where" information. A cell of this type exhibited an increase in firing rate during the first delay period when the target was the preferred stimulus. Moreover, the same cell continued to fire during the second delay period if the response was directed to a specific location.

These results indicate that, in terms of stimulus attributes, cells in the prefrontal cortex exhibit task-specific selectivity. What's more, the activity of these PFC cells is dependent on the monkey using that information to obtain a response. That is, the activity of the PFC cells is task-dependent. If the animal only has to passively view the stimuli, then the response of these cells is minimal right after the stimulus is presented and entirely absent during the delay period. Moreover, the response of these cells is malleable. If the task conditions change, the same cells become responsive to a new set of stimuli (Freedman et al., 2001).

These cellular responses by themselves do not tell us what is represented by this protracted activity. It could be that long-term representations are stored in the prefrontal cortex, and the activity reflects the need to keep these representations active during the delay. Patients with frontal lobe lesions do not have deficits in long-term memory, however, so this hypothesis is unlikely. An alternative hypothesis is that prefrontal activation reflects a representation of the task goal, and as such, serves as an interface with task-relevant long-term representations in other neural regions (Figure 12.5). This latter hypothesis jibes nicely with the fact that the prefrontal cortex is extensively connected with postsensory regions of the temporal and parietal cortex. When a stimulus is perceived, a representation can be sustained through the interactions between prefrontal cortex and posterior brain regions, one that can facilitate goal-oriented behavior.

This alternative hypothesis has been examined in many functional imaging studies. In one representative study, researchers used a variant of a delayed-response task (Figure 12.6a). On each trial, four stimuli were presented

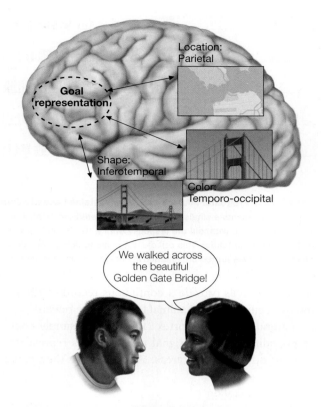

FIGURE 12.5 Working memory arises from the interaction of goal representations and the activation and maintenance of long-term knowledge.
In this example, the woman's goal is to tell her friend about the highlights of her recent trip to San Francisco. Her knowledge of the Golden Gate Bridge requires activation of a distributed network of cortical regions that underlie the representation of long-term memory.

successively for 1 s each during an encoding interval. The stimuli were either intact faces or scrambled faces. The participants were instructed to remember only the faces. Thus, by varying the number of intact faces presented during the encoding interval, the processing demands on working memory were manipulated. After an 8-s delay, a face stimulus—the probe—was presented, and the participant had to decide if the probe matched one of the faces presented during the encoding period. The BOLD response in the lateral prefrontal cortex bilaterally began to rise with the onset of the encoding period, and this response was maintained across the delay period even though the screen was blank (Figure 12.6b). This prefrontal response was sensitive to the demands on working memory. The sustained response during the delay period was greater when the participant had to remember three or four intact faces as compared to just one or two intact faces.

By using faces, the experimenters could also compare activation in the prefrontal cortex with that observed in the fusiform face area, the inferior temporal (also called the inferotemporal) lobe region that was discussed in

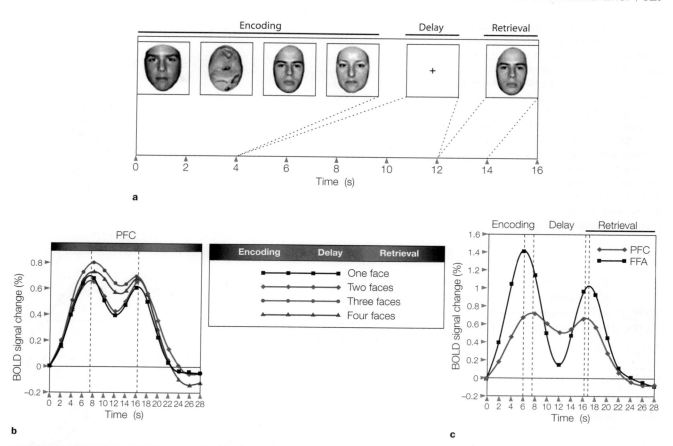

FIGURE 12.6 Functional MRI study of working memory.
(a) In a delayed-response task, a set of intact faces or scrambled faces is presented during an encoding period. After a delay period, a probe stimulus is presented and the participant indicates if that face was part of the memory set. (b) The BOLD response in lateral prefrontal cortex (PFC) rises during the encoding phase and remains high during the delay period. The magnitude of this effect is related to the number of faces that must be maintained in working memory. (c) The BOLD response in the lateral prefrontal cortex and the fusiform face area (FFA) rises during the encoding and retrieval periods. The black dotted and red dotted lines indicate the peak of activation in the FFA and PFC. During encoding, the peak is earlier in the FFA; during retrieval, the peak is earlier in the PFC.

Chapter 6. The BOLD responses for these two regions are shown in Figure 12.6c, where the data are combined over the different memory loads. When the stimuli were presented, either during the encoding phase or for the memory probe, the BOLD response was much stronger in the FFA than in the prefrontal cortex. During the delay period, as noted already, the prefrontal response remains high. Note, however, that although a substantial drop in the FFA BOLD response occurs during the delay period, the response does not drop to baseline, thus suggesting that this area continues to be active during the delay period. In fact, the BOLD response in other perceptual areas of the inferior temporal cortex actually goes below baseline—the so-called rebound effect. Thus, although the sustained response is small in the FFA, it is considerably higher than what would be observed with nonfacial stimuli.

The timing of the peak activation in the prefrontal cortex and the FFA is also intriguing. During encoding, the peak response is slightly earlier in the FFA as compared to the prefrontal cortex. In contrast, during memory retrieval the peak response is slightly earlier in the prefrontal cortex. Although this study does not allow us to make causal inferences, the results are consistent with the general tenets of the model sketched in Figure 12.5. Lateral prefrontal cortex is critical for working memory by sustaining a representation of the task goal (to remember faces) and working in concert with inferotemporal cortex to sustain information across the delay period that is relevant for achieving that goal.

Processing Differences Across Prefrontal Cortex

Working memory is necessary for keeping task-relevant information active as well as manipulating that information to accomplish behavioral goals. Think about what

FIGURE 12.7 Subregions of the prefrontal cortex are sensitive to either contents or processing requirements of working memory. **(a)** An instruction cue indicates the task required for the forthcoming trial. Following a delay period, a series of pictures containing letters and squares at various locations is presented. The participant must remember the order of the instruction-relevant stimuli to respond after the memory probe is presented. **(b)** Ventrolateral PFC is activated in a consistent fashion for all four tasks. Dorsolateral prefrontal cortex is more active when the stimuli must be remembered in reverse order, independent of whether the set is composed of locations or letters.

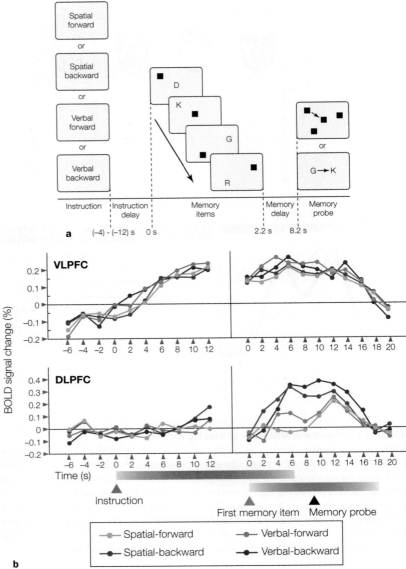

happens when you reach for your wallet to pay a bill after dinner at a restaurant. Besides the listed price, you have to remember to add a tip, drawing on your long-term knowledge of the appropriate behavior in restaurants. With this goal in mind, you then do some fancy mental arithmetic (if your cell phone calculator isn't handy). Michael Petrides (2000) suggests a model of working memory, in which information held in the posterior cortex is activated, retrieved, and maintained by the ventrolateral PFC (e.g., the standard percentage for a tip) and then manipulated with the relevant information (e.g., the price of the dinner) in more dorsal regions of lateral PFC, enabling successful attainment of the goal.

Let's consider the experimental setup shown in Figure 12.7a. Memory was probed in two different ways. When the judgment required that the items be remembered in the forward direction, study participants had to internally maintain a representation of the stimuli using a natural scheme in which the items could be rehearsed in the order presented. The backward conditions were more challenging, because the representations of the items had to be remembered and manipulated. As Figure 12.7b shows, the BOLD response was similar in ventral prefrontal region (ventrolateral PFC) for all conditions. In contrast, the response in dorsolateral PFC was higher for the two backward conditions.

A similar pattern is observed in many imaging studies, indicating that dorsolateral prefrontal cortex is critical when the contents of working memory must be manipulated. One favorite testing variant for studying manipulations in working memory is the *n*-back task (Figure 12.8). Here the display consists of a continuous

stream of stimuli. Participants are instructed to push a button when they detect a repeated stimulus. In the simplest version (*n* = 1), responses are made when the same stimulus is presented on two successive trials. In more complicated versions, *n* can equal 2 or more. With *n*-back tasks, it is not sufficient simply to maintain a representation of recently presented items; the working memory buffer must be updated continually to keep track of what the current stimulus must be compared to. Tasks such as *n*-back tasks require both the maintenance and the manipulation of information in working memory. Activation in the lateral prefrontal cortex increases as *n*-back task difficulty is increased, a response consistent with the idea that this region is critical for the manipulation operation.

The *n*-back tasks capture an essential aspect of prefrontal function, emphasizing the active part of working memory. The recency task that patients with frontal lobe

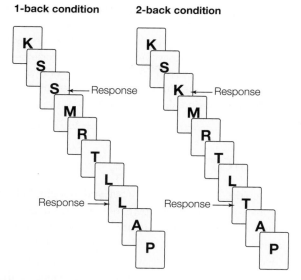

1-back condition   **2-back condition**

FIGURE 12.8 *n*-back tasks.
In *n*-back tasks, responses are required only when a stimulus matches one shown n trials earlier. The contents of working memory must be manipulated constantly in this task because the target is updated on each trial.

lesions fail also reflects the updating aspect of working memory. That task requires the participants to remember whether something is familiar as well as the context in which the stimulus was previously encountered.

Hierarchical Organization of Prefrontal Cortex

The maintain-manipulate distinction offers a processing-based account of difference in PFC function along a ventral-dorsal gradient. This idea was primarily based on activation differences in more posterior regions of PFC. But what about the most anterior region, the frontal pole? The study comparing verbal and spatial working memory provides one hint. The frontal pole was the one region that was recruited upon presentation of the instruction cue in all four conditions (shown in Figure 12.7) and that maintained a high level of activity throughout the trial. It has been proposed that the frontal pole is essential for integrating the specific contents of mental activity into a general framework. Consider that the participants in the scanner had to remember to study the test items and other details, such as staying awake, not moving, and responding quickly. They also had to remember the big picture, the context of the test: They had volunteered to participate in an fMRI study with hopes of doing well so that they could volunteer to work in the lab and run their own cool experiments in the future.

Work focused on the anterior–posterior gradient across the PFC suggests that activation patterns follow

a crude hierarchy: For the simplest of working memory tasks, the activation may be limited to more posterior prefrontal regions or even secondary motor areas. For example, if the task requires the participant to press one key upon seeing a flower and another upon seeing an automobile, then these relatively simple stimulus–response rules can be sustained by the ventral prefrontal cortex and lateral premotor cortex. If the stimulus–response rule, however, is defined not by the objects themselves but by a color surrounding the object, then the frontal pole is also recruited (Bunge, 2004). When such contingencies are made even more challenging by changing the rules from one block of trials to the next, activation extends even farther in the anterior direction (Figure 12.9). These complex experiments demonstrate how goal-oriented behavior can require the integration of multiple pieces of information.

As a heuristic, we can think of PFC function as organized along three separate axes (see O'Reilly, 2010):

1. A ventral–dorsal gradient organized in terms of maintenance and manipulation as well as in a manner that reflects general organizational principles observed in more posterior cortex, such as the ventral and dorsal visual pathways for "what" versus "how."

2. An anterior–posterior gradient that varies in abstraction, where the more abstract representations engage the most anterior regions (e.g., frontal pole) and the least abstract engage more posterior regions of the frontal lobes. In the extreme, we might think of the most posterior part of the frontal lobe, the primary motor cortex, as the point where abstract intentions are translated into concrete movement.

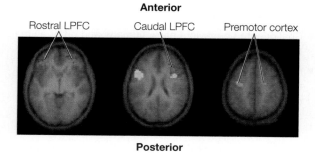

FIGURE 12.9 Hierarchical organization of the prefrontal cortex. Prefrontal activation in an fMRI study increased along a posterior-anterior gradient as the experimental task became more complex. Activation in the premotor cortex shown in green was related to the number of stimulus–response mappings that had to be maintained. Activation in caudal LPFC shown in yellow was related to the contextual demands of the task. For example, a response to a letter might be made if the color of the letter was green, but not if it was white. Activation in rostral LPFC shown in red was related to variation in the instructions from one scanning run to the next. For example, the rules in one run might be reversed in the next run.

3. A lateral–medial gradient related to the degree to which working memory is influenced by information in the environment (more lateral) or information related to personal history and emotional states (more medial). In this view, lateral regions of PFC integrate external information that is relevant for current goal-oriented behavior, whereas more medial regions allow information related to motivation and potential reward to influence goal-oriented behavior.

For example, suppose it is the hottest day of summer and you are at the lake. You think, "It would be great to have a frosty, cold drink." This idea starts off as an abstract desire, but then is transformed into a concrete idea as you remember root beer floats from summer days past. This transformation entails a spread in activation from the most anterior regions of PFC to medial regions as orbitofrontal cortex helps with the recall of the high value you associate with your previous encounters with root beer floats. More posterior regions become active as you begin to develop an action plan. You become committed to the root beer float, and that goal becomes the center of working memory and thus engages lateral prefrontal cortex. You think about how good these drinks are at A&W restaurants, drawing on links from more ventral regions of PFC to long-term memories associated with their floats. You also draw on dorsal regions that will be essential for forming a plan of action to drive to the A&W. It's a complicated plan, one that no other species would come close to accomplishing. Luckily for you, however, your PFC network is buzzing along now, highly motivated, with the ability to establish the sequence of actions required to accomplish your goal. Reward is just down the road.

TAKE-HOME MESSAGES

- Goal-oriented behaviors allow humans and other animals to interact in the world in a purposeful way.
- A goal-oriented action is based on the assessment of an expected reward and the knowledge that there is a causal relationship between the action and the reward. Goal-oriented behavior requires the retrieval, selection, and manipulation of task-relevant information.
- A habit is a response to a stimulus that is no longer based on a reward.
- Working memory consists of transient representations of task-relevant information. The prefrontal cortex (especially the lateral prefrontal cortex) is a key component in a working memory network.
- Physiological studies in primates show that cells in the prefrontal cortex remain active even when the stimulus is no longer present in delayed-response tasks. A similar picture is observed in functional imaging studies with humans. These studies also demonstrate that working memory requires the interaction of the prefrontal cortex with other brain regions.
- Various frameworks have been proposed to understand functional specialization within the prefrontal cortex. Three gradients have been described to account for processing differences in prefrontal cortex: anterior–posterior, ventral–dorsal, and lateral–medial.

Decision Making

Go back to the hot summer day when you thought, "Hmm … that frosty, cold drink is worth looking for. I'm going to get one." That type of goal-oriented behavior begins with a decision to pursue the goal. We might think of the brain as a decision-making device whose perceptual, memory, and motor capabilities evolved to support decisions that determine actions. Our brains start making decisions as soon as our eyes flutter open in the morning: Do I get up now, or stay cozy and warm for another hour? Should I surf my email or look over my homework before class? Do I skip class to take off for a weekend ski trip? Though humans tend to focus on complex decisions such as who gets their vote in the next election, all animals need to make decisions. Even an earthworm decides when to leave a patch of lawn and move on to greener pastures.

Rational observers, such as economists and mathematicians, tend to be puzzled when they consider human behavior. To them, our behavior frequently appears inconsistent or irrational, not based on what seems to be a sensible evaluation of the circumstances and options. For instance, why would someone who is concerned about eating healthy food eat a jelly doughnut? Why would someone who is paying so much money for tuition skip classes?—a question that your non-economist parents might even ask. And why are people willing to spend large sums of money to insure themselves against low-risk events (e.g., buying fire insurance even though the odds are overwhelmingly small that they will ever use it), yet are willing to engage in high-risk behaviors (e.g., driving after consuming alcohol)?

The field of neuroeconomics has emerged as an interdisciplinary enterprise with the goal of explaining the neural mechanisms underlying decision making. Economists want to understand how and why we make the choices we do. Many of their ideas can be tested both with behavioral studies and, as in all of cognitive neuroscience, with data from cellular activity, neuroimaging, or lesion studies. This work also helps us understand the functional organization of the brain.

Theories about our decision-making processes are either normative or descriptive. **Normative decision theories** define how people *ought* to make decisions that yield the optimal choice. Very often, however, such theories fail to

distributed picture of value representation, and the latter emphasize specialization within components of a decision-making network. The discrepancy, though, is likely due to the differential sensitivity of the two methods. The fine-grained spatial resolution of neurophysiology allows us to ask if individual cells are sensitive to particular dimensions. In contrast, fMRI studies generally provide relative answers, asking if an area is more responsive to variation in one dimension compared to another dimension.

More Than One Type of Decision System?

The laboratory is an artificial environment. Many of the experimental paradigms used to study decision making involve conditions in which the participant has ready access to the different choices and at least some information about the potential rewards and costs. Thus, participants are in a position where they can calculate and compare values. In the natural environment, especially the one our ancestors roamed about in, this situation is the exception and not the norm. Rather, we frequently face situations where we must choose between an option with a known value and one or more options of unknown value (Rushworth et al., 2012). The classic example here is foraging: Animals have to make decisions about where to seek food and water, precious commodities that tend to occur in restricted locations and for only a short time. Foraging requires decisions such as, "Do I keep eating/hunting/fishing here or move on to (what may or may not be) greener pastures, birdier bushes, or fishier water holes?" In other words, do I continue to *exploit* the resources at hand or set out to *explore* in hopes of finding a richer niche? Here the animal must calculate the value of the current option, richness of the overall environment, and the costs of exploration.

Worms, bees, wasps, spiders, fish, birds, seals, monkeys, and human subsistence foragers all obey a basic principle in their foraging behavior. This principle is referred to as the *marginal value theorem* (Charnov, 1974). The animal exploits a foraging patch until its intake rate falls below the average intake rate for the overall environment. At that point, the animal becomes exploratory. Because this behavior is so consistent across so many species, scientists have hypothesized that this tendency may be deeply encoded in our genes. Indeed, biologists have identified a specific set of genes that influence how worms decide when it is time to start looking for "greener lawns" (Bendesky et al., 2011).

Benjamin Hayden (2011) and his colleagues investigated the neural mechanisms that might be involved in foraging-like decisions. They hypothesized that such decisions require a *decision variable*, a representation that specifies the current value of leaving a patch, even if the alternative choice is relatively unknown. When this variable

reaches a threshold, a signal is generated indicating that it is time to look for greener pastures. A number of factors influence how soon this threshold is reached: the current expected payoff, the expected benefits and costs for traveling to a new patch, and the uncertainty of obtaining reward at the next location. For instance, in our fishing example, if it takes two hours instead of one to go around the lake to a better fishing spot, you are less likely to move.

Hayden recorded from cells in the ACC of monkeys, choosing this region because it has been linked to the monitoring of actions and their outcomes (which we discuss later in the chapter). The animals were presented with a virtual foraging task in which they chose one of two targets. One stimulus was followed by a reward after a short delay, but the amount decreased with each successive trial (equivalent to remaining in a patch and reducing the food supply by eating it). The other stimulus allowed the animals to change the outcome contingencies. They received no reward on that trial, but after waiting for a variable period of time (the cost of exploration), the choices were presented again and the payoff for the rewarded stimulus was reset to its original value (a greener patch). Consistent with the marginal value theorem, they were less likely to choose the rewarded stimulus as the waiting time increased or the amount of reward decreased. What's more, the cellular activity in ACC was highly predictive of the amount of time the animal would continue to "forage" by choosing the rewarding stimulus. Most interesting, the cells showed the property of a threshold: When the firing rate was greater than 20 spikes per second, the animal left the patch (Figure 12.13).

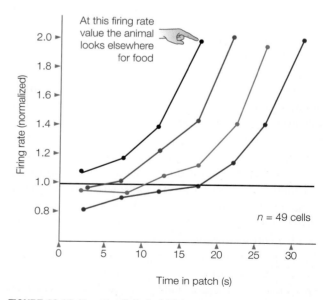

FIGURE 12.13 Neural activity in ACC is correlated with decision by monkeys to change to a new "patch" in a sequential foraging task. Data were sorted according to the amount of time the animal stayed in one patch (from shortest to longest: black, red, blue, purple). For each duration, the animal switched to a new patch when the firing rate of the ACC neurons was double the normal level of activity.

The hypothesis that the ACC plays a critical role in foraging-like decisions is further supported by fMRI studies with humans (Kolling et al., 2012). When the person is making choices about where to sample in a virtual world, the BOLD response in ACC correlates positively with search value (explore) and negatively with the encounter value (exploit) regardless of which choice participants made. In this condition, ventromedial regions of the PFC did not signal overall value. If, however, experimenters modified the task so that the participants were engaged in a comparison decision, activation in VMPFC reflected the chosen option value. Taken together, these studies suggest that ACC signals exert a type of control by promoting a particular behavior: exploring the environment for better alternatives compared to the current course of action (Rushworth et al., 2012).

Dopamine Activity and Reward Processing

We have seen that rewards, especially those associated with primary reinforcers like food and sex, are fundamental to the behavior of all animals. It follows that we might expect the processing of such signals to involve phylogenetically older neural structures. Indeed, converging lines of evidence indicate that many subcortical areas represent reward information, including the dorsal and ventral striatum, hypothalamus, amygdala, and lateral habenula (for a review, see Hikosaka et al., 2008). Much of the work on reward has focused on the neurotransmitter dopamine. We should keep in mind, however, that reinforcement likely involves the interplay of many transmitters. For instance, evidence suggests that serotonin is important for temporal discounting of reward value (Tanaka et al., 2007).

Dopaminergic cells are scattered throughout the midbrain, sending axonal projections to many cortical and subcortical areas. Two of the primary loci of dopaminergic neurons are two brainstem nuclei, the substantia nigra pars compacta (SN_c) and ventral tegmental area (VTA). As discussed in Chapter 8, the dopaminergic neurons from the substantia nigra project to the dorsal striatum, the major input nucleus of the basal ganglia. Loss of these neurons is related to the movement initiation problems observed in patients with Parkinson's disease. Dopaminergic neurons that originate in the VTA project through two pathways. The mesolimbic pathway travels to structures important to emotional processing, including the **nucleus accumbens** (ventral striatum) of the basal ganglia, the amygdala, the hippocampus, and the anterior cingulate cortex. The VTA also has dopaminergic projections that travel through the **mesocortical pathway** to the neocortex, particularly to the medial portions of the frontal lobe.

The link between dopamine and reward began with the classic work of James Olds and Peter Milner in the early 1950s (Olds, 1958; Olds & Milner, 1954). They implanted electrodes into the brains of rats and then gave the rats the opportunity to control the electrodes. When the rat pushed a lever, the electrode became activated. Some of the rats rarely pressed the lever. Others pressed the lever like crazy. The difference turned out to be the location of the electrodes. The rats who couldn't stop self-stimulating were the ones whose electrodes were activating dopaminergic pathways. These observations led to the idea that dopamine was the neural correlate of reward.

In the modern version of this study, researchers have used more refined techniques, such as optogenetics, to stimulate dopaminergic receptors in the striatum. In one study, mice were placed in a box with levers that could be activated by a nose poke (Kravitz et al., 2012). Touching one lever would turn on the laser and activate the cells. Touching the other did nothing. When the genetic label was targeted at dopaminergic receptors that were excitatory (D_1 receptors of the direct, "go" pathway; see Chapter 8), the animals were much more likely to poke the lever (Figure 12.14). When the genetic label was targeted at dopamine receptors that were inhibitory (D_2 receptor of the indirect, "no-go" pathway), the animals steered away from the lever.

Originally, neuroscientists thought that the stimulation caused a release of dopamine (or, in the optogenetic study, simulated the effects of dopamine release), and this event resulted in a pleasurable sensation. This

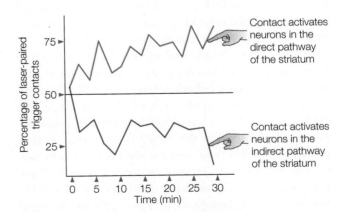

FIGURE 12.14 Optogenetic control of self-stimulation behavior in the mouse.
Mice were placed in a box with two levers. Contact with one lever resulted in optogenetically-triggered activation of dopamine receptors (active), whereas contact with the other level resulted in no stimulation (inactive). Over time, the mice were more likely to contact the active lever when the stimulation was of the D1 receptors in the direct pathway. In contrast, the mice learned to avoid the active lever when the stimulation was targeted at the D2 receptors of the indirect pathway.

hypothesis, however, turns out to be too simplistic, and understanding the effects of dopamine has become a major focus of interest in the neurosciences. A key challenge to the reward hypothesis came about when investigators recognized that the activation of dopaminergic neurons was not tied to the size of the reward per se, but was more closely related to the *expectancy* of reward (for a review, see Shultz, 1998). Dopaminergic neurons were especially active when a reward was unexpected. This observation led to a new view of the role of dopamine in reinforcement and decision making.

Dopamine and Prediction Error We know from experience that the value of an item can change. Your favorite fishing hole may no longer be a favorite with the fish. After a couple of unsuccessful visits, you update your value (now that spot is not your favorite, either) and look for a new fishing hole. How do we learn and update the values associated with different stimuli and actions? An updating process is essential, because the environment may change. Updating is also essential because our own preferences change over time. Think about that root beer float. Would you be so eager to drink one if you had just downed a couple of ice cream cones?

Wolfram Shultz and his colleagues at Cambridge University have conducted a series of revealing experiments using a simple Pavlovian conditioning task with monkeys (Chapter 9). The animals were trained such that a light, the conditioned stimulus (CS), was followed after a few seconds by an unconditioned stimulus (US), a sip of juice (Figure 12.15). To study the role of dopamine, Schultz recorded from dopaminergic cells in the ventral tegmental area (VTA). As expected, when the training procedure started, the cells showed a large burst of activity after the US was presented. Such a response could be viewed as representing the reward. When the CS-US events were repeatedly presented, however, two interesting things occurred. First, the dopamine response to the juice, the US, decreased over time. Second, the cells started to fire when the light, the CS, was presented. That is, the dopamine response gradually shifted from the US to the CS.

A reinforcement account of the reduced response to the US might emphasize that the value of the reward drops over time as the animal feels less hungry. Still, this hypothesis could not account for why the CS now triggers a dopamine response. It seems that the response here suggests that the CS has now become rewarding.

Schultz proposed a new hypothesis to account for the role of dopamine in reward-based learning. Rather than think of dopamine as representing the reward, he suggested that it should be viewed as a **prediction error (PE)**, a signal that represents the difference between the obtained reward and the expected reward. First, consider

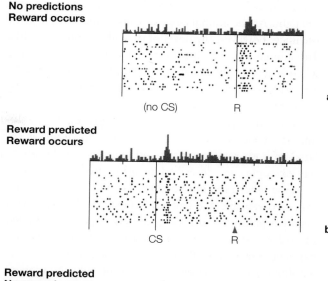

No predictions
Reward occurs

(no CS)   R   **a**

Reward predicted
Reward occurs

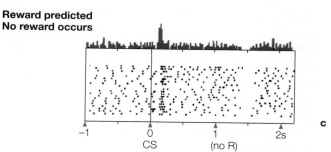

CS   R   **b**

Reward predicted
No reward occurs

−1   0   1   2s   **c**
CS   (no R)

FIGURE 12.15 Dopamine neurons respond to an error in prediction. The raster plots show spikes in a midbrain dopamine neuron on single trials, with the data across trials summarized in the histograms at the top of each panel. **(a)** When a drop of juice (R) is given in absence of a conditioned stimulus (CS), the DA neuron shows a burst of activity. **(b)** When the CS is repeatedly paired with R, the DA neuron shows a temporal shift, now firing when the CS is presented since this is the unexpected, positive event. **(c)** On trials in which the R is not given, the neuron shows a positive prediction error after the CS (as in b) and a negative prediction error around the time of expected reward.

the *reduction* in the dopaminergic response to the juice. On the first trial, the animal has not learned that the light is always followed by the juice. Thus, the animal does not expect to receive a reward following the light, but a reward is given. This event results in a positive prediction error (PPE), because the obtained reward is greater than the expected reward. With repeated presentation of the light–juice pairing, however, the animal comes to expect a reward when the light is presented. As the expected and obtained values become more similar, the size of the PPE is reduced, and thus, the dopaminergic response becomes attenuated.

Now, consider the *increase* in the dopaminergic response to the light. When the animal is sitting in the test apparatus between trials, it has no expectancy of reward. Initially, the animal does not associate the light with a reward. Thus, when it flashes, there is no PE: Expectancy is low, and the reward is associated with the juice, not the light. As the animal begins to associate the light with the juice, however, the onset of the light results in a PPE. The animal has no expectation (it is just hanging out), when it gets a stimulus associated with reward (yippee!). This PPE is represented by the dopaminergic response to the light.

The prediction error model has proven to be an important idea for thinking about how dopamine is related to both reinforcement and learning. In the previous example, we described positive prediction errors, the case where the obtained reward is greater than the expected reward. We can also consider situations with negative prediction errors, cases in which the obtained reward is less than the expected reward. This situation happens during a trial when the experimenter meanly withholds the juice after presenting the light. Now there is a dip in the response of the DA neuron around the time when the juice was expected (Figure 12.15C). This negative prediction error occurs because the animal is expecting the juice, but none is obtained. If the juice is repeatedly withheld, the size of both the increase in the dopaminergic response to the light and the decrease in the dopaminergic response to the absence of the juice are reduced. This situation corresponds to the phenomenon of extinction, where a response previously associated with a stimulus is no longer produced. With enough trials, the dopaminergic neurons show no change in baseline firing rates. The light is no longer reinforcing (so the PPE to the light is extinguished), and the absence of the juice is no longer a violation of an expectancy (so the negative prediction error, or NPE, when the juice was anticipated is also abolished).

As we have seen in this example, the dopaminergic response changes with learning. Indeed, scientists have recognized that the prediction error signal itself can be useful for reinforcement learning, serving as a teaching signal. As discussed earlier, models of decision making assume that events in the world (or internal states) have associated values. Juice is a valued commodity, especially to a thirsty monkey. Over time, the light also becomes a valued stimulus, signaling the upcoming reward. The PE signal can be used to update representations of value. Computationally, this process can be described as taking the current value representation and multiplying it by some weighted factor (gain) of the PE (Dayan & Niv, 2008). If the PE is positive, the net result is an increase in value. If the PE is negative, the net result is a decrease in value.

This elegant, yet simple model not only predicts how values are updated but also accounts for changes in the amount that is learned from one trial to the next. Early in training, the value of the light is low. The large PE that occurs when it is followed by the juice will lead to an increase in the value associated with the light. With repeated trials, though, the size of the PE decreases, so subsequent changes in the value of the light also will increase more slowly. This process, in which learning is initially rapid and then occurs in much smaller increments over time, is characteristic of almost all learning functions. Although this effect might occur for many reasons (e.g., the benefits of practice diminish over time), the impressive thing is that it is predicted by a simple model in which value representations are updated by a simple mechanism based on the difference between the predicted and obtained reward.

As we saw previously, many factors influence value, including magnitude, probability, and timing. Experiments have shown that the magnitude of a dopaminergic response varies with these factors and that this variation can be accounted for by the prediction error model. For example, the dopamine response to the US decreases when a CS more reliably predicts the reward (Fiorillo et al., 2003: Figure 12.16a), and it scales in the expected direction when the amount of reward is altered (Tobler et al., 2005). Another way to vary the PE is by lengthening the time between the CS and US. To take an extreme example, suppose that the CS occurs an hour before the US. Because of the long delay, it would be hard for an animal to learn the predictive value of CS, even if the US always followed. As shown in Figure 12.16b, the dopaminergic response to the CS is strongest at short delays and falls off with increasing delay (S. Kobayashi & Schultz, 2008). The opposite happens to the US with longer delays: The dopaminergic response to the US increases, indicating that the reward is more unexpected the further away in time it appears from the CS. Interestingly, these dopamine responses seem to mirror behavioral preferences: Large, probable, immediate rewards are preferred to smaller, less likely, and distant ones.

Reward and Punishment Not all options are rewarding: just consider your dog's response after he has tried to nudge a porcupine out of a rotting tree. Talk about prediction error and learning by experience! Are positive and negative reinforcers treated by the same or different systems? Although it may seem like it, punishment is not the withholding of a reward. Whereas the absence of an expected reward is coded by negative prediction errors, punishment involves the experience of something aversive, like getting a shock or a nose full of porcupine quills. Aversive events are the opposite of rewarding events in that they are unpleasant, should be avoided, and have opposite motivational values.

In one important respect, however, reinforcement and punishment are similar. They are both motivationally

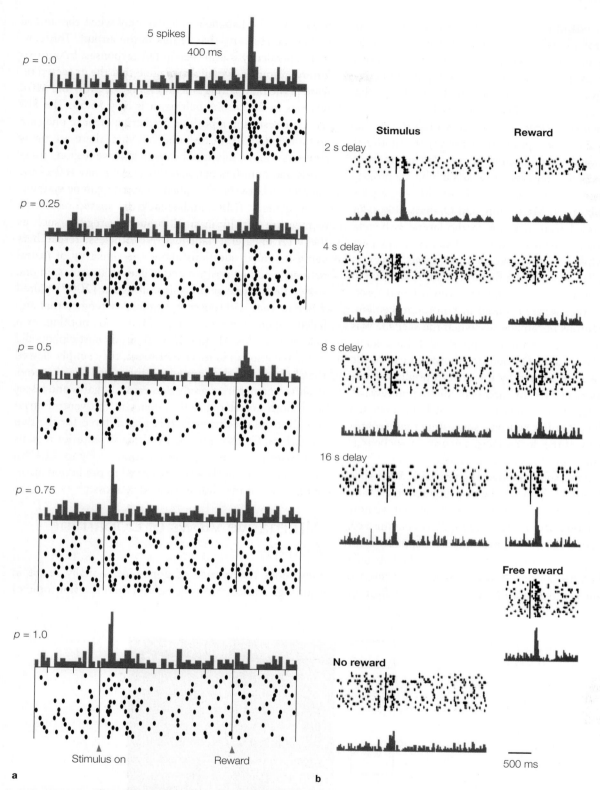

FIGURE 12.16 Dopamine neuron activity is modulated by reward probability and reward delay.
(a) The DA burst increases to the CS and decreases to the US as the CS-US reward probability increases. In the top row, the occurrence of the reward is independent of the timing of the CS. In the other rows, the R follows the CS with varying probabilities. **(b)** The DA burst to the CS decreases as the interval between the CS and R increases, even if probability remains constant.

salient, the kinds of events that draw our attention and engage control processes to influence behavior. The role of dopamine in aversive events has been difficult to pin down: Some studies show increases in dopamine activity, others find decreases, and some find both within the same study. Can these findings be reconciled?

The *habenula*, a structure located within the dorsal thalamus, is in a good position to represent emotional and motivational events because it receives inputs from the forebrain limbic regions and sends inhibitory projections to dopamine neurons in the substantia nigra pars compacta. Masayuki Matsumoto and Okihide Hikosaka (2007) recorded from neurons in the lateral habenula and dopaminergic neurons in the substantia nigra pars compacta while monkeys saccaded to a target that was either to the left or right of a fixation point. A saccade to one target was associated with a juice reward, and a saccade to the other target resulted in non-reinforcement. Habenula neurons became active when the saccade was to the *no* reward side and were suppressed if the saccade was to the reward side. DA neurons showed the opposite profile: They were excited by the reward-predicting targets and suppressed by the targets predicting no reward. Even weak electrical stimulation of the habenula elicited strong inhibition in DA neurons, suggesting that reward-related activity of the dopaminergic neurons may be regulated by input from the lateral habenula.

Value is in one sense relative. If given a 50–50 chance to win $100 or $10, we would be disappointed to get only $10. If the game were changed, however, so that we now stand to win either $10 or $1, we're thrilled to get the $10. Habenula neurons show a similar context dependency. If two actions result in either juice or nothing, the habenula is active when the nothing choice is made. But if the two actions result in either nothing or an aversive puff of air

to the eye, the habenula is active only when the animal makes the response that results in the airpuff. This context dependency is also seen in DA responses. In our two lottery examples, we might imagine that the expected reward in the first pairing is $55 (average of $100 and $10), whereas in the second pairing, it is only $5.50. The $10 outcome results in a positive prediction error in one case and a negative PE in the other. In sum, there are many computational similarities between how we respond to rewards and punishments, and this finding may reflect the interaction between the habenula and dopamine system.

In general, fMRI studies lack the spatial resolution to measure activity in small brainstem regions such as the VTA or lateral habenula. Nonetheless, researchers can ask similar questions about the similarity of neural regions in coding positive and negative outcomes. In one study, Ben Seymour and his colleagues (2007) paired different cues with possible financial outcomes that signaled a gain versus nothing, a loss versus nothing, or a gain versus a loss (Figure 12.17a). Study participants did not make choices in this experiment; they simply viewed the choices, and the computer determined the outcome. Positive and negative prediction errors of gains and losses were both correlated with activity in the ventral striatum, but the specific striatal region differed for the two conditions. Gains were encoded in more anterior regions and losses in the more posterior regions (Figure 12.17b). A region in the insula also responded to prediction error, but only when the choice resulted in a loss.

Alternative Views of Dopamine Activity

How does the release of dopamine actually result in learning? Although this question remains a hot topic of

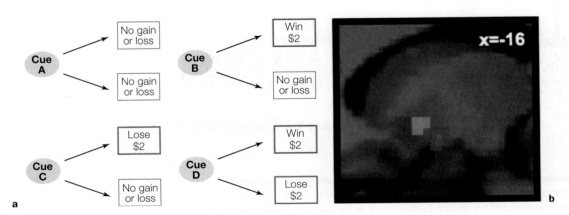

FIGURE 12.17 Coding of gain and loss in the ventral striatum with fMRI.
(a) People were presented with one of four cues. Over time, they learned that each cue was associated with one of two possible outcomes (or for Cue A, the same neutral outcome). **(b)** Prediction errors reliably predicted the BOLD response in the ventral striatum, with the center of the positive prediction error response (green) slightly anterior to the center of the negative prediction error response (red).

research, computational models have focused on how the PE signal might influence neural plasticity. One hypothesis is based on the idea of Hebbian learning (see Chapter 1) with a twist: "Neurons that fire together wire together, as long as they get a burst of dopamine." Figure 12.18 illustrates a model of how positive and negative PE are thought to influence synapses in the striatum.

The PE story elegantly accounts for the role of dopaminergic cells in reinforcement and learning, but there remain viable alternative hypotheses. Kent Berridge (2007) argues that dopamine release is the result, not the cause, of learning. He points out a couple of problems with the notion that dopamine acts as a learning signal. First, mice that are genetically unable to synthesize dopamine can still learn (Cannon & Bseikri, 2004; Cannon & Palmiter, 2003). Second, genetically mutant mice with high dopamine levels do not learn any faster, nor do they maintain habits longer, than mice with normal levels of dopamine. Given these puzzles, Berridge suggests that dopamine neurons do not cause learning by encoding PE. Instead, they code the informational consequence of prediction and learning (generated elsewhere in the brain) and then do something with the information. He proposes that dopamine activity is indicative of the salience of a stimulus or an event.

Berridge describes a reward as made up of three dissociable components: wanting, learning, and liking. His view is that dopamine mediates only the "wanting" component. Dopamine activity indicates that something is worth paying attention to, and when these things are associated with reward, the dopamine activity reflects how desirable the object is. The distinction between wanting and liking may seem subtle, but it can have serious implications when we consider things like drug abuse. In one experiment, cocaine users were given a drug that lowered their dopamine levels (Leyton et al., 2005). In the lowered dopamine state, cues indicating the availability of the drug were rated as less desirable. When given the drug, however, the users' feelings of euphoria and the rate of self-administration were unaffected. That is, with reduced dopamine, study participants still liked the drug in the same way (reinforcement was unchanged), even though they didn't particularly want it.

It is, of course, reasonable to suppose that dopamine serves multiple functions. Indeed, neurophysiologists have described two classes of responses when recording from DA neurons in the brainstem (Matsumoto & Hikosaka, 2009b). One subset of dopamine neurons responded in terms of *valence*. These cells increase their firing rate to stimuli that are predictive of reward and decrease their firing rate to aversive stimuli (Figure 12.19a). A greater number of dopamine neurons, however, were excited by the increased likelihood of *any* reinforcement, independent of whether it was a reward or a punishment, and especially when it was unpredictable (Figure 12.19b). The first response class is similar to what would be expected of neurons coding prediction errors, the second to what would be expected of neurons coding salience or signaling things that require attention. Interestingly,

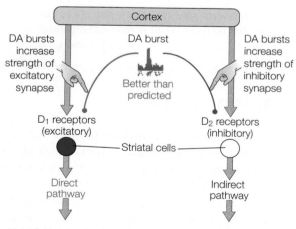

Net effect promotes future occurrence of the selected action

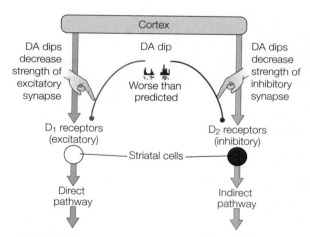

Net effect reduces future occurrence of the selected action

FIGURE 12.18 Dopamine activity modulates synapse strength in direct and indirect pathways to promote learning.
For positive prediction errors (red), the excitatory D1 receptor will strengthen corticostriatal synapses in the direct pathway while the inhibitory D2 receptor will weaken the corticostriatal synapses in the indirect pathway. The net effect is to promote the rewarded action. For negative prediction errors (blue), the opposite occurs. The reduction in the activity in the dopamine neuron will weaken synapses in the direct pathway and strengthen synapses in the indirect pathway (by removing an inhibitory input). The net effect is to reduce the likelihood of the response that failed to produce an expected reward.

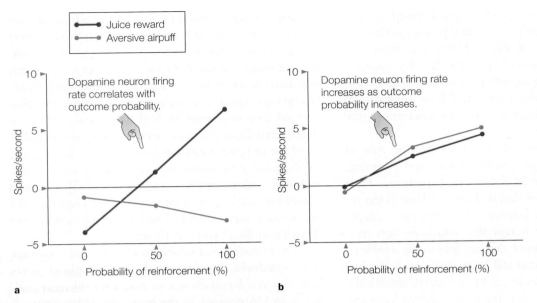

FIGURE 12.19 Two classes of dopamine neurons.
(a) Response profile of dopamine neurons that code valence. These neurons increase their firing rate as the probability of a positive outcome increases and decrease their firing rate as the probability of a negative outcome increases. **(b)** Response profile of dopamine neurons coding salience. These neurons increase their firing rate as reinforcement probability increases, independent of whether the reinforcement is positive or negative, signaling that the stimulus is important (or predictive).

the reward neurons were located more ventromedially in the substantia nigra and VTA, areas that project to the ventral striatum and are part of a network involving orbitofrontal cortex. In contrast, the neurons excited by salience were located more dorsolaterally in the substantia nigra, regions with projections to the dorsal striatum and a network of cortical areas associated with the control of action and orientation. We can see that when damage occurs within the dopamine system, or when downstream structures in the cortex are compromised, control problems are going to be reflected in behavioral changes related to motivation, learning, reward valuation, and emotion. These observations bring us back to how frontal lobe control systems are at work in both decision-making and goal-oriented behavior.

TAKE-HOME MESSAGES

- A decision is the selection of one option among others based on the predicted value of the consequences (reward).
- Some rewards are primary reinforcers, such as food, water and sex; others are secondary reinforcers, such as money and status.
- The subjective value of an item is made up of multiple variables that include payoff amount, context, probability, effort/cost, temporal discounting, novelty, and preference.
- Single-cell recordings in monkeys and fMRI studies in humans have implicated frontal regions, including orbitofrontal cortex, in value representation.

- Prediction error (PE) is the difference between the expected reward and what was actually obtained. The firing rate of dopamine neurons is correlated with prediction error.
- Prediction error is used to update value information and learning.
- All dopaminergic neurons appear to give alerting signals, but some are activated by reward value while others are activated by reward salience, which may act to control motivated behavior. Their anatomical organization appears to reflect their functional organization.

Goal Planning

Once humans choose a goal, we have to figure out how to accomplish it. We usually make a plan in which we organize and prioritize our actions. Patients with prefrontal lesions, like W.R., often exhibit poor planning and prioritizing skills. Three components are essential for successfully developing and executing an action plan (Duncan, 1995). First, the person must identify the goal and develop subgoals. For instance, in preparing for an exam, a conscientious student develops an action plan like the one in Figure 12.20. This plan can be represented as a hierarchy of subgoals, each requiring actions to achieve the goal: Reading must be completed, lecture notes reviewed, and material integrated to identify themes and facts. Second, in choosing among goals and subgoals, consequences

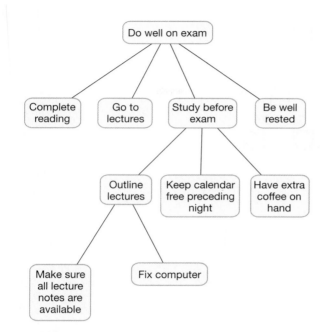

FIGURE 12.20 Action hierarchy.
Successfully achieving a complex goal such as doing well on an exam requires planning and organization at multiple levels of behavior.

must be anticipated. Would the information be remembered better if the student sets aside 1 hour a day to study during the week preceding the exam, or would it be better to cram intensively the night before? Third, the student must determine what is required to achieve the subgoals. A place must be identified for study. The coffee supply must be adequately stocked. It is easy to see that these components are not entirely separate. Purchasing coffee, for example, can be an action and a goal.

When an action plan is viewed as a hierarchical representation, it is easy to see that failure to achieve a goal can happen in many ways. In the example illustrated in Figure 12.20, if reading is not completed, the student may lack knowledge essential for an exam. If a friend arrives unannounced the weekend before the exam, critical study time can be lost. Likewise, the failures of goal-oriented behavior in patients with prefrontal lesions can be traced to many potential sources. Problems can arise because of deficits in filtering irrelevant information, making it difficult to keep the eyes on the prize. Or the challenge may come in prioritizing information to help select the best way to achieve a particular goal or subgoal.

As discussed earlier, processing differences along the anterior–posterior gradient of PFC can be described in terms of the level of abstraction of action goals. As a clear demonstration of this hierarchy, consider an fMRI study in which participants completed a series of nested tasks (Badre & D'Esposito, 2007). The simplest task manipulated *response competition* by varying the number of possible finger responses to a series of colored squares

presented one at a time (Figure 12.21a). In the color task, the response was based on the color of the square. The feature task added another layer of complexity because the response was based on texture and the colors indicated which response was associated with which texture. The third and fourth tasks added additional levels of complexity: The former required participants to use the color to determine the relevant dimension, and the fourth involved the manipulation of the stimulus–response mapping. Consistent with the hierarchical gradient hypothesis, more anterior regions of PFC were recruited as the task became more complex (Figure 12.21b). For the simplest task, varying response complexity activated premotor cortex. When the participant had to use color to select the appropriate dimension for the response, activation was also observed in more prefrontal cortex and extended into polar frontal cortex for the most complex task.

It might be supposed that, rather than reflect a hierarchy, the different activation patterns show that different subregions of PFC are required for things like response selection or rule specification. A key idea of hierarchy, however, is that processing deficits will be asymmetric. Individuals who fail at operations required for performance at the lower levels of a hierarchy will also fail when given more challenging tasks. In contrast, individuals who fail at tasks that require the highest levels should still be able to perform tasks that are dependent only on lower levels. This behavior is indeed what is observed in patients with PFC damage (Badre et al., 2009). If the lesions were restricted to the most anterior regions, the patients performed similar to controls on the first and second task conditions. Patients with more posterior lesions, those centered in premotor cortex, were impaired at all of the tasks.

A clever demonstration of the importance of the frontal lobes in this hierarchical evaluation process captured the real-world problems faced by patients with penetrating head injuries (Goel et al., 1997). The patients were asked to help plan the family budget of a couple who were having trouble living within their means. The patients understood the overriding need to identify places where savings could be achieved, and they could appreciate the need to budget. Their solutions did not always seem reasonable, however. For instance, instead of eliminating optional expenditures, one patient focused on the family's rent. Noting that the $10,800 yearly expense for rent was by far the biggest expense in the family budget, he proposed that it be eliminated. When the experimenter pointed out that the family would need a place to live, the patient didn't waver from his assessment and was quick with an answer: "Yes. Course I know a place that sells tents cheap. You can buy one of those."

Response experiment

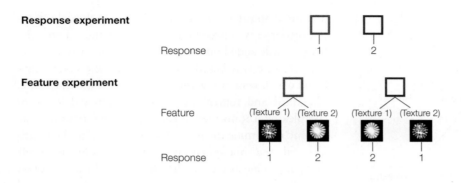

Feature experiment

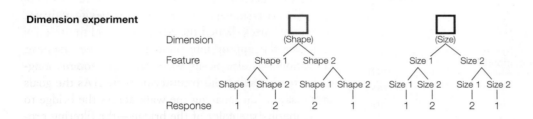

Dimension experiment

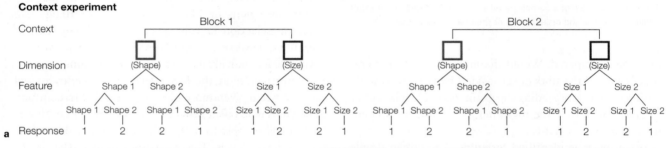

Context experiment

a

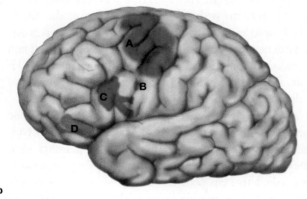

b

FIGURE 12.21 Goal representation becomes more abstract as you move forward along the anterior-posterior gradient of the frontal lobe.
(a) Experimental design. Top row shows representative stimuli. A colored square containing texture objects of varying size was presented on each trial. There were four different tasks. In the response task, the response was based on stimulus color. In the feature task, the response was based on the texture, and the mapping of texture to finger varied for the two colors. In the dimension task, one color indicated that the response was based on shape, and the other color indicated that the response was based on size. The mapping of shape/size to finger varied as a function of color. The context task was the same as the dimension task except that the mappings changed from one block to the next. **(b)** Frontal regions showing a change in the BOLD response as a function of the four tasks. Anterior regions show more specific activation patterns, consistent with idea that these areas are recruited as the task requires more embedded goals. A: Premotor cortex was sensitive to all four tasks. B: Anterior premotor cortex was sensitive the feature, dimension, and context tasks. C: Inferior frontal sulcus was sensitive to the dimension and context tasks. D: Frontopolar cortex was only sensitive to the context task.

Cognitive Control Is Necessary for Planning and Staying on Goal

By focusing on the housing costs, the patient is perseverating, demonstrating inflexibility in his decision. The large price tag assigned to rent was a particularly salient piece of information, and the patient's budgeting efforts were focused on the potential savings to be found here. From a strictly monetary perspective, this decision makes sense. But at a practical level, we realize the inappropriateness of this choice. Making wise decisions with complex matters, such as long-term financial goals, requires keeping an eye on the overall picture and not losing track of the forest because of the trees. To succeed in this kind of activity, we must monitor and evaluate the different subgoals. An essential feature of cognitive control is the ability to shift our focus from one subgoal to another. Complex actions require that we maintain our current goal, focusing on the information that is relevant to achieving that goal, ignore irrelevant information, and, when appropriate, shift from one subgoal to another in a coordinated manner.

Retrieval and Selection of Task-Relevant Information

Goal-oriented behavior requires people to select task-relevant information and filter out task-irrelevant information. Here selection refers to the ability to focus attention on perceptual features or information in memory. This selection process is a cardinal feature of tasks associated with the lateral prefrontal cortex, highlighting its role in working memory and attention.

Suppose that you are telling a friend about walking across the Golden Gate Bridge during a recent trip to San Francisco (Figure 12.22). The conversation will

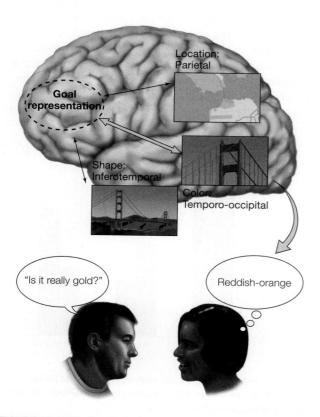

FIGURE 12.22 Prefrontal cortex as a filtering mechanism in the retrieval and maintenance of task-relevant information.
When the person is asked about the color the Golden Gate Bridge (the task goal), links to memory of the color of the bridge is amplified while links to memory of the location and shape of the bridge are inhibited.

have activated semantic information from your long-term memory about the location, shape, and color of the bridge, as well as episodic information related to your trip. These representations constitute the contents of working memory. If your friend then asks you about the color of the bridge, you must be able to focus on your memory of the color of the bridge. This example demonstrates that working memory is more than the passive sustaining of representations. It also requires an attentional component in which the participant's goals modify the salience of different sources of information. To capture this idea, the PFC has been conceptualized as a **dynamic filtering** mechanism (Shimamura, 2000). Reciprocal projections between PFC and posterior cortex provide a way for goals, represented in PFC, to maintain task-relevant information that requires long-term knowledge stored in posterior cortex. As the goals shift—say, from recalling the walk across the bridge to remembering the color of the bridge—the filtering process will make salient links to representations associated with the color.

The filtering hypothesis offers a way to appreciate the role of the frontal lobe in tasks where memory demands are minimal. Frontal lobe patients display heightened interference on the Stroop task, in which participants are shown a list of colored words and the words spell color names such as *red*, *green*, or *blue*. In the congruent condition, the colors of the words correspond to their names; in the incongruent condition, the word names and colors do not correspond (see Figure 3.5). With years of reading experience, we have a strong urge to read words even when the task requires us to ignore them in favor of color. Thus everyone is slower in responding to incongruent stimuli in comparison with congruent stimuli. This difference is even greater in patients with frontal lobe lesions.

The contribution of prefrontal cortex to selection is evident in a series of elegant experiments conducted by Sharon Thompson-Schill (Thompson-Schill et al., 1997, 1998). In early PET studies on language, experimenters found that when participants were given a noun and had to generate a semantically associated word, a prominent increase in activation was observed in the inferior frontal gyrus of the left hemisphere. Thompson-Schill hypothesized that this prefrontal activation reflected filtering of the transient representations (the semantic associates of the target item) as they were being retrieved from long-term memory in the posterior cortex. To test this hypothesis, the researchers conducted an fMRI study in which they varied the demands on a filtering process during a verb generation task (Figure 12.23). In the low-filtering condition, each noun was associated with a single verb. For example, when asked to name the action that goes with scissors, almost everyone will respond

HOW THE BRAIN WORKS
Thinking Outside the (Match)Box

Consider the following puzzle: Your task is to fix a candle to the wall of a room and light it. You have been supplied with a candle, a box of matches, and some thumbtacks. Are you up for the challenge? Go.

You probably solved this rather quickly. Simply take a thumbtack, stick it through the candle and into the wall, and then light the candle. Not so fast. We forgot to tell you that the diameter of the candle is much thicker than the length of the thumbtack. Take another shot.

Stumped? Don't be discouraged—thousands of students have been mystified by this brainteaser since Rainer Dunker introduced it in his monograph on problem solving in 1945 (cited in Wickelgren, 1974). Here's a hint: Suppose that there is only one match, and it sits on the table outside the matchbox. Now give it another go.

When the problem is presented in this format, many people experience an "aha" moment. They suddenly realize that the matchbox can serve more than one purpose. In addition to providing a striker for the matches, it could be used as a crude candlestick. Tack the box to the wall with the thumbtacks, light the candle and let it drip into the box, and then set the candle in the goo so that when the drippings cool, the candle will be secure in an upright position.

These problems are challenging because stimuli trigger the retrieval of associations that we have made previously. Thus, in developing an action plan, we tend to think narrowly about the possible uses of an object—a phenomenon that psychologists refer to as *functional fixedness*. Functional fixedness might be seen as an undesired consequence of having evolved the kind of rapid-response selection ability associated with the prefrontal cortex. As we have seen in the work on semantic generation, the lateral prefrontal cortex facilitates the selection of viable responses from a set of automatically activated long-term representations. With the matchbox, we immediately think of its common use—to light matches—and then mull over how those thumbtacks can be applied to the candle. By emptying the box of matches, we might realize new possibilities; but even here, many people continue to be unable to see novel uses because of the strong association between the stimulus and an action. Chris Frith (2000) has referred to the selection process of lateral prefrontal cortex as "sculpting the response space."

Ready for your next brainteaser? Here is a false arithmetic statement in Roman numerals, represented by match*sticks:*

Problem 1: VI = VII + I

Provide a correct solution by moving only one stick. Not too hard. Moving one of the Is from the VII to the VI renders the correct statement, VII = VI + I.

Now try a problem that, with the one-move rule, is much more difficult:

Problem 2: VI = VI + VI

Stuck again? Moving a matchstick from one of the *VI*s on the right side of the equation to the left won't do it. Nor will turning a VI into a IV. The answer here requires an unusual transformation of one of the operators and a kind of arithmetic statement that we rarely encounter: VI = VI = VI.

On the basis of the selection hypothesis, Carlo Reverberi and his colleagues at the University of Milan (2005) made an unusual prediction. They proposed that patients with lateral prefrontal cortex lesions would actually do better on Problem 2 than would healthy control participants. This prediction was based on the idea that an impaired selection process would make it easier for the patients to represent atypical actions. Indeed, this is exactly what they found. The superior performance of the patients was especially striking, given that these individuals were worse than the controls when presented with equations like those in Problem 1 or equations that required standard operator transformations (e.g., V = III − II, in which the equal and minus signs are swapped by the movement of one matchstick). Here the patients' impairment became greater as the number of possible moves increased, consistent with the idea that the lateral prefrontal cortex is especially critical when the response space must be narrowed. But for equations like Problem 2, the "sculpting" process of prefrontal cortex led

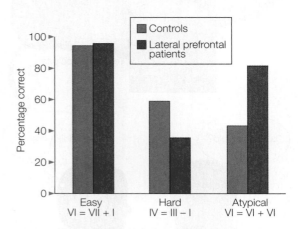

FIGURE 1 Patients with lateral prefrontal lesions do better than healthy control participants on a problem-solving task that requires unusual solutions.
For the easy and hard conditions, the solution requires moving a matchstick from one side of the equation to the other to transform a numeral or the operators. For the atypical condition, the solution requires rotating a matchstick to create a three-part equality.

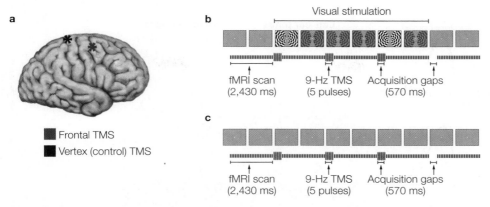

FIGURE 12.25 Combined use of TMS and fMRI to study top-down prefrontal control of visual cortex.
(a) TMS was targeted to disrupt activity in the frontal eye fields (red) or a control site (blue). **(b, c)**
A series of five TMS pulses were applied during a 570-ms interval that separated phases during which
fMRI data were collected while participants viewed either visual stimuli **(b)** or a blank screen **(c)**. By
comparing these conditions, the experimenters could assess whether the retinotopic maps in visual
cortex were altered when top-down signals from the frontal cortex were disrupted.

locations. Similarly, when multiple sources of information come from the same location, we might selectively enhance the task-relevant information (color in the Stroop test) or inhibit the irrelevant information (the word in the Stroop test). In behavioral tasks, it is often difficult to distinguish between facilitatory and inhibitory modes of control. Moreover, as seen in times of budgetary crises, the hypotheses are not mutually exclusive. If we have fixed resources, allocating resources to one thing places a limit on what is available for others; thus, the form of goal-based control may vary as a function of task demands.

Evidence for a loss of **inhibitory control** with frontal lobe dysfunction comes from electrophysiological studies. Robert Knight and Marcia Grabowecky (1995) recorded the evoked potentials in groups of patients with localized neurological disorders. In the simplest experiment, participants were presented with tones, and no response was required. As might be expected, the evoked responses were attenuated in patients with lesions in the temporoparietal cortex in comparison to control participants. This difference was apparent about 30 ms after stimulus onset, the time when stimuli would be expected to reach the primary auditory cortex. The attenuation presumably reflects tissue loss in the region that generates the evoked signal. A more curious aspect is shown in Figure 12.26. Patients with frontal lobe lesions have *enhanced* evoked responses. This enhancement was not seen in the evoked responses at subcortical levels. The effect did not reflect a generalized increase in sensory responsiveness, but was limited to the cortex.

The failure to inhibit irrelevant information was more apparent when participants in this study were instructed to attend to auditory signals in one ear and ignore similar sounds in the opposite ear, when signals in the attended ear varied between blocks (see Figure 12.26b). In this way, an assessment can be made of the evoked response to identical stimuli under different attentional sets (e.g., response to left-ear sounds when they are attended or ignored). With healthy participants, these responses diverge at about 100 ms; the evoked response to the attended signal becomes greater. This difference is *absent* in patients with prefrontal lesions, especially for stimuli presented to the ear contralateral to the lesion (e.g., left ear for a patient with a lesion in right hemisphere prefrontal cortex). What happens is that the unattended stimulus produces a heightened response. This result is consistent with the hypothesis that the frontal lobes modulate the salience of perceptual signals by inhibiting unattended information.

In the study just described, we can see inhibition operating to minimize the impact of irrelevant perceptual information. This same mechanism can be applied to memory tasks for which information must be internally maintained. Consider the monkey attempting to perform a delayed-response task (see Figure 12.2). The monkey views the target being placed in one of the food wells and then the blind is closed during the delay period. The monkey's mind does not just shut down; the animal sees and hears the blind being drawn, looks about the room during the delay interval, and perhaps contemplates its hunger. All such intervening events can distract the animal and cause it to lose track of which location is baited. To succeed in finding the food, it must ignore the distractions and sustain the representation of its forthcoming response. We have all experienced failures in similar situations. A friend gives us her telephone number, but we forget it. The problem is not a failure to encode the number. Something else captures our attention, and we

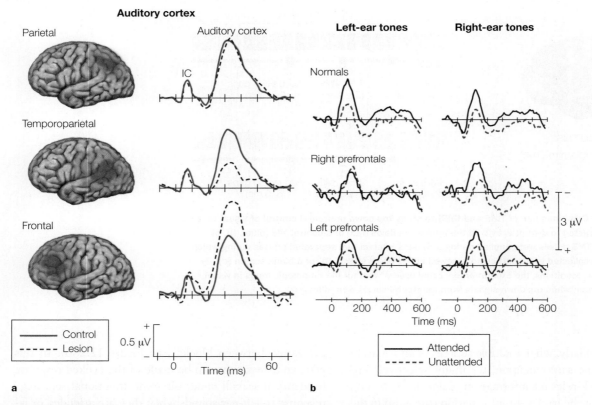

a   **b**

FIGURE 12.26 Evoked potentials reveal filtering deficits in patients with lesions in the lateral prefrontal cortex.
(a) Evoked responses to auditory clicks in three groups of neurological patients. The participants were not required to respond to the clicks. Note that in these ERPs, the positive voltage is above the x-axis. The first positive peak occurs at about 8 ms and reflects neural activity in the inferior colliculus (IC). The second positive peak occurs at about 30 ms (the P30), reflecting neural responses in the primary auditory cortex. Both responses are normal in patients with parietal damage (top). The second peak is reduced in patients with temporoparietal damage (middle), reflecting the loss of neurons in the primary auditory cortex. The auditory cortex response is amplified in patients with frontal damage (bottom), suggesting a loss of inhibition from frontal lobe to temporal lobe. Note that the evoked response for control participants is repeated in each panel. (b) Difference waves for attended and unattended auditory signals. Participants were instructed to monitor tones in either the left or the right ear. The evoked response to the unattended tones is subtracted from the evoked response to the attended tones. In healthy individuals, the effects of attention are seen at approximately 100 ms, marked by a larger negativity (N100). Patients with right prefrontal lesions show no attention effect for contralesional tones presented in the left ear but show a normal effect for ipsilesional tones. Patients with left prefrontal lesions show reduced attention effects for both contralateral and ipsilateral tones.

fail to block out the distraction. This point is underscored by the finding that primates with prefrontal lesions perform better on delayed-response tasks when the room is darkened during the delay (Malmo, 1942) or when they are given drugs that decrease distractibility.

The preceding discussion emphasizes how goal-based control might be achieved by the inhibition of task-irrelevant information. Mark D'Esposito and his colleagues (Druzgal & D'Esposito, 2003) used fMRI to further explore interactions between prefrontal cortex and posterior cortex. In a series of experiments, they exploited the fact that regions in the inferior temporal lobe are preferentially activated by face and place stimuli—the so-called FFA

(fusiform face area) and PPA (parahippocampal place area), respectively (Chapter 6). The researchers asked whether activation in these regions is modulated when people are given the task goal to remember either faces or places for a subsequent memory test (Figure 12.27). At the start of each trial, an instruction cue indicated the current task. Then a set of four pictures was presented; it included two faces and two scenes. As expected, a subsequent memory test verified that the participants selectively attended to the relevant dimension.

More interesting was the finding that activation in the FFA and PPA was modulated in different ways by the instruction cues (Figure 12.27b), showing both enhancement

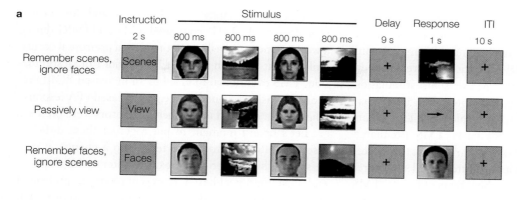

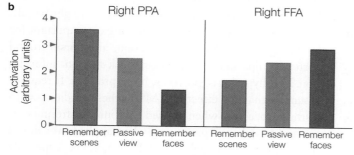

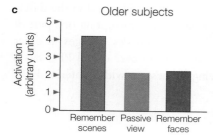

FIGURE 12.27 Modulation in posterior cortex as a function of task goals.
(a) In a delayed-response task, participants had to remember either faces or scenes. **(b)** Compared to a passive viewing control condition, activation in the parahippocampal place area (PPA) was greater when participants attended to scenes and reduced when participants attended to faces. The reverse effect was observed in the fusiform face area (FFA). **(c)** Within the PPA region of interest, older participants also showed an increase in the BOLD response when attending to scenes. This response was not suppressed in the attend faces condition, however, suggesting a selective age-related decline in inhibition.

and suppression effects. Compared to the passive viewing condition (control), the response in the FFA of the right hemisphere was greater when the participants were instructed to remember the faces and lower when the participants were instructed to remember the scenes. The reverse pattern was evident in the PPA, and here the effect was seen in both hemispheres. This study reveals that the task goal, specified by the instruction, can modulate perceptual processing by either amplifying task-relevant information or inhibiting task-irrelevant information.

In an interesting extension, the experiment was repeated, but this time the participants were older, neurologically healthy individuals (Gazzaley et al., 2005b). Unlike college-age participants, the older participants showed only an enhancement effect; they did not show the suppression effect in either FFA or PPA when results were compared to the passive viewing condition (Figure 12.27c). These findings are intriguing for two reasons. First, they suggest that enhancement (i.e., amplification) and suppression (i.e., inhibition) involve different neural mechanisms and that inhibition is more sensitive to the effects of aging. Second, given that aging is thought to disproportionately

affect prefrontal function, perhaps inhibitory goal-based control is more dependent on prefrontal cortex than are the attentional mechanisms that underlie the amplification of task-relevant information.

Prefrontal Cortex and Modulation of Processing

The work described in the previous section reveals that the task goal, specified by the instruction, can modulate perceptual processing by either amplifying task-relevant information or inhibiting task-irrelevant information. The data do not reveal, however, if this modulation is the result of prefrontal activation. To explore this question, researchers have applied TMS over prefrontal cortex and then asked how this perturbation affects processing in posterior perceptual areas. In one study, TMS was applied over inferior frontal cortex while participants were instructed to attend to either the color or motion of a visual stimulus (Zanto et al., 2011). Not only was performance poorer after TMS, but the difference between the

P100 to the attended and ignored stimuli was reduced (Figure 12.28). This reduction occurred because after TMS, the P100 was larger for the ignored stimuli. In another study (Higo et al., 2011), participants received either low-frequency repetitive TMS or sham stimulation over prefrontal cortex. They next entered an fMRI machine where measurements were taken while they attended to places, faces, or body parts. TMS attenuated the modulation of category-specific responses in posterior cortex due to the participants' attentional set. Moreover, the results indicated that the effects of frontal TMS primarily disrupted the participants' ability to ignore irrelevant stimuli but had little effect on their ability to attend to relevant stimuli, a dissociation similar to that described above for older participants.

In a related study, Eva Feredoes and Jon Driver (Feredoes et al., 2011) combined TMS and fMRI during a working memory task, targeting dorsal prefrontal cortex. Unlike what has been reported for inferior frontal stimulation, TMS over dorsal PFC led to an increased BOLD response in task-relevant areas (e.g., increased FFA response when responding to faces) when distractors were present.

Let's take a moment to put together these different results. TMS over frontal cortex led to a change in processing within posterior cortex, consistent with the general idea that goal-based representations in prefrontal cortex are used to modulate how perceptual information is selectively filtered. Moreover, the results might be taken to suggest that inferior frontal cortex is important for inhibiting task-irrelevant information, and dorsal frontal cortex is important for enhancing task-relevant information. This hypothesis, however, has a problem: It requires assuming that the effect of TMS in these studies was to disrupt processing when applied over inferior frontal cortex and to enhance processing when applied over dorsal frontal cortex. Although this effect is possible, especially since the TMS protocols were not identical in the different studies, it is also possible that disrupting one part of prefrontal cortex with TMS produces changes in other prefrontal regions. Perhaps TMS over dorsal PFC has a side effect of improving processing within inferior PFC.

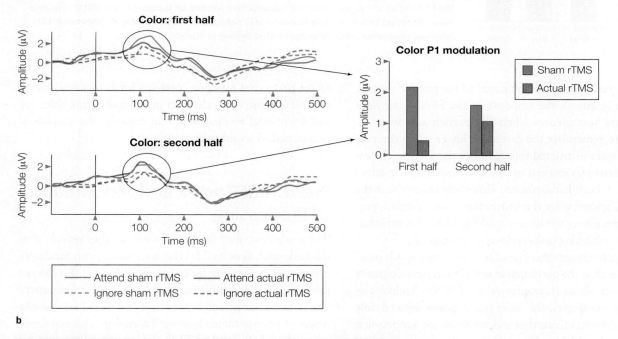

FIGURE 12.28 **rTMS of prefrontal cortex disrupts early ERP response to attended stimuli.**
Participants viewed visual stimuli, attending to either the color or direction of motion. rTMS was applied over inferior frontal cortex prior to the start of experiment. **(a)** Accuracy on the color task was disrupted by rTMS over PFC compared to sham TMS. This effect only lasted for the first half of the experiment. **(b)** ERPs from posterior electrodes. The P100 amplitude was larger when attending to color (solid) compared to when attending to motion (dotted). Bar graph on right shows the difference in amplitude between the Attend Color and Attend Motion P100 response. This difference was reduced after rTMS in the first half.

alleviate the motor symptoms of Parkinson's disease, it comes at the cost of being too impulsive.

TAKE-HOME MESSAGES

- In goal-directed control, information processing is influenced by goals and the allocation of attentional resources.
- Goal-oriented behavior involves the amplification of task-relevant information and the inhibition of task-irrelevant information. Amplification and inhibition may entail separate processes given that aging selectively affects the ability to inhibit task-irrelevant information.
- Patients with prefrontal cortex damage lose inhibitory control. For example, they cannot inhibit task-irrelevant information.
- A network spanning prefrontal cortex and posterior cortex provides the neural substrates for interactions between goal representations and perceptual information. This dynamic process is revealed in studies that combine different cognitive neuroscience methods to show that, as task goals are modified, activation in perceptual areas is either increased or decreased compared to baseline conditions.
- The inhibition of action constitutes another form of cognitive control. In the stop-signal task, participants attempt to abort a planned response. The right inferior frontal gyrus and the subthalamic nucleus are important for this form of control.

Ensuring That Goal-Oriented Behaviors Succeed

Tim Shallice and Donald Norman developed the psychological model in Figure 12.31 to account for goal-oriented behavior. Like the concepts developed in Chapter 8, this model conceptualizes the selection of an action as a competitive process. At the heart of the model is the notion of *schema control units*, or *representations of responses* (a term used in a generic sense here). These schemas can correspond to explicit movements or to the activation of long-term representations that lead to purposeful behaviors. They are activated by either perceptual stimuli or another recently activated schema. For example, hearing your phone ring may activate the motor schema to answer it, or seeing a word printed on paper can activate a schema for an articulatory gesture. The activated schema of reading the word may in turn activate the semantic meaning and associated representations.

Schema control units receive input from many sources. Norman and Shallice emphasized perceptual inputs and

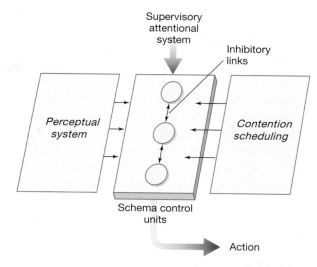

FIGURE 12.31 Norman and Shallice's model of response selection. Actions are linked to schema control units. The perceptual system produces input to these control units. Selection of these units can be biased, however, by the contention scheduling units and the supervisory attentional system (SAS). The SAS provides flexibility in the response selection system.

their link to these control units, but it is the strength of the connections between the two that reflects the effects of learning. If we have had experience in restaurant dining, walking into a restaurant will activate behaviors associated with waiting for the hostess or looking at the menu. As we review the menu, decision-making processes come into play: We may place a high "payoff" on a preferred dish such as baked stuffed lobster, but also consider the fresh sole when we see it is half the price and also won't require wearing a lobster bib in front of our new date.

External inputs can be all it takes to trigger schema control units. For example, it is hard not to move your eyes when tracking a moving object. But in most situations, our actions are not dictated by the input alone; many schema control units can be activated at the same time, and so we need a control process to ensure that the appropriate control units are selected. Norman and Shallice postulated two types of selection processes. One is *contention scheduling*, which manages schemas for automatic or familiar actions. This process is fast, but passive. Although schemas are driven by perceptual inputs, they also compete with one another, especially when two control units are mutually exclusive. Contention scheduling, through its inhibitory connections between schemas, prevents competing actions and ensures that we act coherently. This is why we cannot look at two places at the same time, or move the same hand to pick up a glass and a fork simultaneously. Only one schema (or nonoverlapping schemas) can win the competition. If competition does not resolve the conflict, none of the schemas are activated enough to trigger a response, and the result is no action.

The second means of selection in this model comes by way of the **supervisory attentional system (SAS)**, which can supersede contention scheduling. The SAS is essential for ensuring that behavior is flexible by allowing us to override automatic behavior. It is a mechanism for favoring certain schema control units to reflect the demands of the situation or to emphasize some goals over others.

The SAS is a psychological model of cognitive control. It specifies some of the key situations when control operations would be useful. We introduced these situations near the beginning of this chapter. Selection might benefit from the SAS in situations when

- planning or decision making is required;
- responses are novel or not well learned;
- the required response competes with a strong, habitual response;
- error correction or troubleshooting is required; or
- the situation is difficult or dangerous.

Although the SAS in this model (Figure 12.31) is sketched as a single entity, research over the past 30 years suggests that multiple neural structures are involved in all of these operations. The functions embodied in the SAS are part of a distributed network, a set of neural regions that, as a group, come into play in the situations we have described here.

The last four situations just listed share one aspect of cognitive control that has not been discussed in detail to this point. For a person engaged in goal-oriented behavior, especially a behavior that includes subgoals, it is important to have a way to monitor moment-to-moment progress. If this is a well-learned process, there should be a means for signaling deviations from the expected course of events.

The Medial Frontal Cortex as a Monitoring System

One might expect the task of a **monitoring** system to be like that of a supervisor, keeping an eye on the overall flow of activity and being ready to step in whenever a problem arises. The head chef must attend to the actions of her staff to ensure the team's activities are coordinated to produce the perfect meal. If the salad course is delayed because the prep cook has taken an extended break, the entire production can collapse. By monitoring the various components of the operation, the chef can make online adjustments, texting the prep chef to get back from his break or alerting the sous-chef to step in as the problem develops. For a neural monitoring system, however, there is a problem with this analogy: It has the feel of a homunculus. The head chef, or supervisor, has to have knowledge of the entire process and understand how the parts work together. A goal for any physiological model of cognitive control is, in one sense, the opposite: How can the

kinds of simple operations that characterize neurons lead to cognitive control operations such as monitoring?

The last 30 years have witnessed burgeoning interest in the *medial frontal cortex* (MFC), especially the **anterior cingulate cortex**, as a critical component of a monitoring system. Moreover, the evolution of theoretical accounts of the MFC provides an especially interesting story within the history of cognitive neuroscience. Buried in the depths of the frontal lobes and characterized by a primitive cytoarchitecture, the cingulate cortex was assumed to be a component of the limbic system, helping to modulate autonomic responses during painful or threatening situations. The functional roles ascribed to most cortical regions have been inspired by behavioral problems associated with neurological disorders. Interest in the anterior cingulate, however, was sparked when serendipitous activations were seen in this region during some of the first neuroimaging studies.

Subsequent studies have revealed that the medial frontal cortex is consistently engaged whenever a task becomes more difficult, the type of situation in which monitoring demands are likely to be high. One meta-analysis highlighted the center of activation in 38 fMRI studies that included conditions in which monitoring demands were high. The activations were clustered in the anterior cingulate regions (areas 24 and 32) but also extended into areas 8 and 6; thus, we refer to this entire region as medial frontal cortex.

How Does Medial Frontal Cortex Monitor Processing in Cognitive Control Networks?

As with much of the frontal cortex, the medial frontal cortex exhibits extensive connectivity with much of the brain. For example, DTI studies suggest that there are at least 11 subregions just within the ACC (Figure 12.32). These subregions are defined by their distinct patterns of white matter connectivity with other brain regions. One region shows strong connectivity with OFC, another with ventral striatum, another with premotor cortex, and so on. This anatomy is consistent with the hypothesis that the medial frontal cortex is in a key position to influence decision making, goal-oriented behavior, and motor control. Making sense of the functional role of this region has proven to be an area of ongoing and lively debate. We now turn to some hypotheses that have been proposed to account for the functional role of the medial frontal cortex.

Attentional Hierarchy Hypothesis An early hypothesis centered on the idea that the medial frontal cortex should be conceptualized as part of an attentional

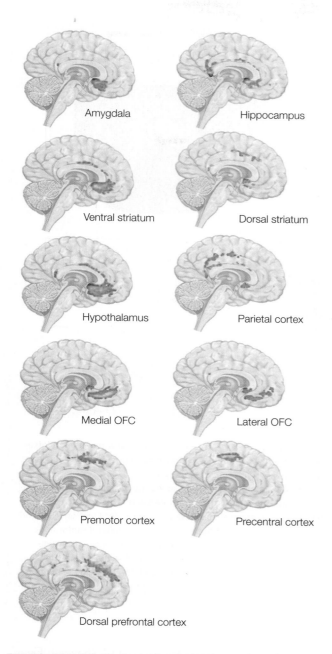

FIGURE 12.32 Diffusion tensor imaging (DTI) to identify anatomical connections between cingulate cortex and other brain regions. Highlighted regions indicate cingulate voxels that showed significant connectivity with eleven different brain regions.

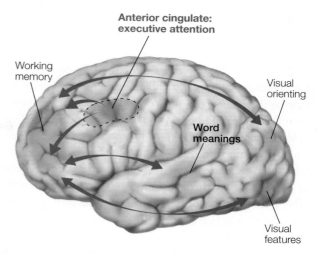

FIGURE 12.33 The anterior cingulate has been hypothesized to operate as an executive attention system.
This system ensures that processing in other brain regions is most efficient, given the current task demands. Interactions with the prefrontal cortex may select working memory buffers; interactions with the posterior cortex can amplify activity in one perceptual module over others. The interactions with the posterior cortex may be direct, or they may be mediated by connections with the prefrontal cortex.

conditions were associated with enhanced activity in feature-specific regions of visual association areas. For example, attending to motion was correlated with greater blood flow in the lateral prestriate cortex, whereas attending to color stimulated blood flow in more medial regions. During the divided-attention task, however, the most prominent activation was in the anterior cingulate cortex. These findings suggest that selective attention causes local changes in regions specialized to process certain features. The divided-attention condition, in contrast, requires a higher-level attentional system—one that simultaneously monitors information across these specialized modules.

An association between the medial frontal cortex and attention is further shown by how activation in this region changes as attentional demands decrease. If the verb generation task (see Figure 12.23) is repeated over successive blocks, the primary activation shifts from the cingulate and prefrontal regions to the insular cortex of the temporal lobe (Raichle et al., 1994). This shift indicates that the task has changed. In the initial trial, participants have to choose between alternative semantic associates. If the target noun is *apple*, then possible responses are "peel," "eat," "throw," or "juggle," and the participant must select between these alternatives. On subsequent trials, however, the task demands change from semantic generation to memory retrieval. The same semantic associate is almost always reported. Thus, if a participant reports "peel" on the first trial, invariably he will make the same choice on subsequent trials.

hierarchy. In this view, the medial frontal cortex occupies an upper rung on the hierarchy, playing a critical role in coordinating activity across attentional systems (Figure 12.33). Consider a PET study of visual attention in which participants must selectively attend to a single visual dimension (color, motion, shape) or monitor changes in all three dimensions simultaneously. In the latter condition, attentional resources must be divided (Corbetta et al., 1991). Compared to control conditions in which stimuli were viewed passively, the selective-attention

Activation of the anterior cingulate during the first trial can be related to two of the functions of a supervisory attentional system (SAS): responding (a) under novel conditions and (b) with more difficult tasks. The generation condition is more difficult than the repeat condition because the response is not constrained. But over subsequent trials, the generation condition becomes easier (as evidenced by markedly reduced response times), and the items are no longer novel. Meanwhile, the elevated activation of the cingulate dissipates, reflecting a reduced need for the SAS. That this shift indicates the loss of novelty rather than a general decrease in the medial frontal cortex activity with practice is shown by the finding that, when a new list of nouns is used, the cingulate activation returns.

One concern with the hierarchy model is that it is descriptive rather than mechanistic. The model recognizes that the medial frontal cortex is recruited when attentional demands are high, but it does not specify how this recruitment occurs, nor does it specify the kinds of representations supported by the medial frontal cortex. We might suppose that the representation includes the current goal as well as all the suboperations required to achieve that goal. This type of representation, however, is quite complex. What's more, even if all of this information were represented in the medial frontal cortex, we would still not be able to explain how it uses this information to implement cognitive control. In a sense, the hierarchical attention model is reminiscent of the homunculus problem: To explain control, we postulate a controller without describing how the controller is controlled.

Error Detection Hypothesis Concern about the attentional hierarchy hypothesis has led researchers to consider other models of how medial frontal cortex might be involved in monitoring behavior. The starting point for one model comes from evidence implicating medial frontal cortex in the detection of errors. Evoked-potential studies have shown that the medial frontal cortex provides an electrophysiological signal correlated with the occurrence of errors. When people make an incorrect response, a large evoked response sweeps over the prefrontal cortex just after the movement is initiated (Figure 12.34). This signal, referred to as the **error-related negativity (ERN)** response, has been localized to the anterior cingulate (Dehaene et al., 1994). It might be supposed that a monitoring system would detect when an error has occurred and that this information would be used to increase cognitive control.

This hypothesis provides a different perspective on the co-occurrence of activation in medial and lateral prefrontal cortex—one that captures many of the functional benefits of an attentional system. Typically, we make errors when we are not paying much attention to the task at hand.

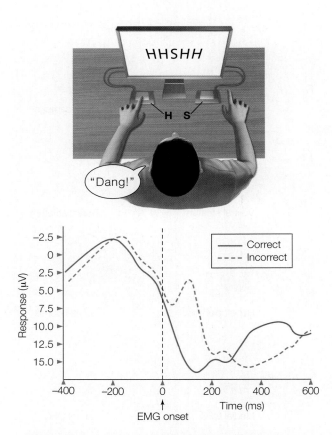

FIGURE 12.34 Participants were tested on a two-choice letter discrimination task in which they made accelerated responses with either the right or the left hand.
Participants made errors when speed was emphasized and when targets were flanked by irrelevant distracters. Evoked potentials for incorrect responses deviated from those obtained on trials with correct responses just after the onset of peripheral motor activity. This error detection signal is maximal over a central electrode positioned above the prefrontal cortex, and it has been hypothesized to originate in the anterior cingulate. The zero position on the x-axis indicates the onset of electromyographic (EMG) activity. Actual movement would be observed about 50 to 100 ms later.

Consider being asked to perform the task shown in Figure 12.34 for an hour, during which the stimulus appears only once every 6 seconds. Pretty boring, right? At some point, your mind will start to wander. You might think about your evening plans. This new goal begins to occupy working memory, displacing the experimentally defined (boring) goal to respond to the letter in the center and not the letters on the side. Oops—you suddenly find yourself pressing the wrong key. Physiological responses such as the ERN could be used to reactivate the experimental goal in working memory.

One group of researchers (Eichele et al., 2008) used fMRI to see if they could predict when people were likely to make an error. They looked at the event-related response over successive trials, asking how the signals changed in advance of an error. Two changes were especially notable. First, before an error was made, the researchers observed a steady decrease in activity within a network spanning medial frontal cortex and right inferior frontal cortex, a decrease that could be detected up to 30 s before the error (Figure 12.35). Second, activity increased over a similar time period in the precuneus and retrosplenial cortex. These two regions are key components of the default network, which is postulated to be associated with self-referential processing (e.g., when you start to think about something other than the task at hand; see Chapter 13). Thus, we can see a shift in activity from the monitoring system to the mind-wandering system, which builds until a person makes an error.

The ERN is an especially salient signal of a monitoring system. The engagement of medial frontal cortex, however, is not limited to conditions in which people make errors. Medial frontal cortex activation is also prominent in many tasks in which errors rarely occur. The Stroop task is one such example. The difficulty that people have when the words and colors are incongruent is typically detected in the reaction time data and only minimally, if at all, in measures of accuracy. That is, people take longer, but they don't make mistakes. Still, activation of the medial frontal cortex is much higher on incongruent trials compared to when the words and colors are congruent (Bush et al., 2000). Similarly, activation is higher when people are asked to generate the verbs associated with nouns compared to when they just repeat the nouns, even though errors rarely occur.

Response Conflict Hypothesis Jonathan Cohen and his colleagues (2000) at Princeton University have hypothesized that a key function of the medial frontal cortex is to evaluate **response conflict**. This hypothesis is intended to provide an umbrella account of the monitoring role of this region, encompassing earlier models that focused on attentional hierarchies or error detection. Difficult and novel situations should engender high response conflict. In the verb generation task, there is a conflict between acceptable alternative responses. Errors, by definition, are also situations in which conflict exists. Similarly, tasks such as the Stroop task entail conflict in that the required response is in conflict with a more habitual response. In Cohen's view, conflict monitoring is a computationally appealing way to allocate attentional resources. When the monitoring system detects that conflict is high, there is a need to increase attentional vigilance. Increases in anterior cingulate activity can then be used to modulate activity in other cortical areas.

Event-related fMRI has been used to pit the error detection hypothesis against the conflict-monitoring hypothesis. One study used the flanker task, similar to that shown in Figure 12.34, except that the letters were replaced by a row of five arrows (Botvinick et al., 1999). Participants responded to the direction of the central arrow, pressing a button on the right side if this arrow pointed to the right and pressing a button on the left side if this arrow pointed to the left. On compatible trials, the flanking

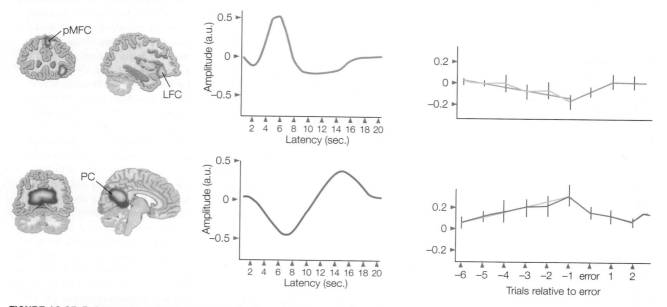

FIGURE 12.35 Balance of activity between monitoring and default networks correlates with likelihood of making an error.
Top row shows areas in medial and lateral frontal cortex that exhibit increased BOLD response after stimulus onset. Bottom row shows precuneus area, a part of the default network, in which BOLD response decreases after stimulus onset. Right side graphs indicate relative response in pMFC and precuneus across trials. Activation in pMFC is relatively low just before an error, whereas BOLD in precuneus is relatively high before an error. Note the dramatic change in relative activation in both areas right after an error occurs.

arrows pointed in the same direction; on incompatible trials, the flanking arrows pointed in opposite directions. Neural activity in the medial frontal cortex was higher on the incompatible trials compared to the compatible trials. Importantly, this increase was observed even when participants responded correctly. These results strongly suggest that the monitoring demands, and not the occurrence of an error, engage the medial frontal cortex.

Subsequent work has sought to clarify how a conflict-monitoring process might be part of a network for cognitive control. Consider a variant of the Stroop task in which a cue is presented at the beginning of each trial to indicate whether the participant should read the word or name the color. After a delay, the cue is replaced by a Stroop stimulus. By using a long delay between the cue and stimulus, researchers can separately examine the neural responses related to goal selection and the neural responses related to response conflict. Moreover, by using a cue, the design allows the experimenters to manipulate two factors: (a) goal difficulty, given the assumption that it is easier to read words than to name their ink color; and (b) color–word congruency.

The results showed distinct neural correlates of these two factors (Figure 12.36). The degree of difficulty for goal selection was evident in the activation of the lateral prefrontal cortex. When the task was made more difficult, the BOLD response in this region increased even before the actual stimulus was presented. In contrast, activation in the medial frontal cortex was sensitive to the degree of response conflict, being greater when the word and stimulus color were different. The picture here is similar to that observed in the ERN literature. The lateral prefrontal cortex represents the task goal, and the medial frontal cortex monitors whether that goal is being achieved. One difference from the error detection model, though, is that the medial monitoring process is recruited not just when errors occur. Rather, it is engaged whenever there is conflict—which we would expect to be quite high in novel contexts or with particularly demanding tasks.

Note that the preceding study shows only the distinct contributions of the lateral and medial frontal regions. A subsequent event-related fMRI study provided direct evidence that these two regions work in tandem to provide cognitive control. Activation in the lateral prefrontal cortex was highly correlated with activation in the medial frontal cortex on the *preceding* trial (Figure 12.36c). Thus a signal of high response conflict on an incongruent Stroop trial led to a stronger response in the lateral prefrontal cortex. As with the error model, the medial

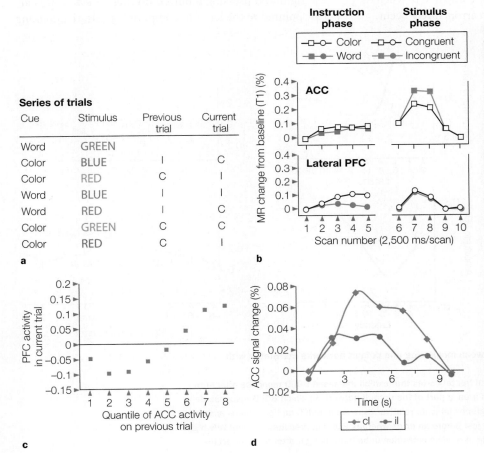

FIGURE 12.36 Interactions between the medial and lateral frontal cortex to facilitate goal-oriented behavior. **(a)** Participants performed a series of Stroop trials, responding to either the word or the color as indicated by a cue. C = congruent; I = incongruent. **(b)** Functional MRI showing double dissociation between the lateral prefrontal cortex (PFC) and the anterior cingulate cortex (ACC). PFC activation in the instruction phase differs between conditions in which the cue indicates that the task will be easy (word) or hard (color). ACC activation varies in the stimulus phase as a function of response conflict (incongruent is greater than congruent). **(c)** Correlation between ACC and PFC activation across successive trials. The PFC representation of the task goal is enhanced following the detection of a conflict by the ACC monitoring system. **(d)** The ACC signal is lower on incongruent trials preceded by an incongruent trial (iI) as compared to when the preceding trial was congruent (cI). This reduction is hypothesized to occur because the goal representation in PFC is stronger, and thus there is less conflict.

monitoring function can be used to modulate the activation of the goal in working memory. Difficult trials help remind the person to stay on task. We can hypothesize that the medial frontal activity modulates filtering operations of the prefrontal cortex, ensuring that the irrelevant word names are ignored. Interestingly, activation in the medial frontal cortex on incongruent trials was lower when the previous trial was also incongruent. Assuming that an incongruent trial leads to a stronger activation of the task goal in working memory and, as a result, there is better filtering of irrelevant information on the next trial, the degree of conflict generated on that trial will decrease.

ACC Function Is Still Up in the Air

The conflict-monitoring hypothesis remains a work in process, and the literature suggests some problems that need to be addressed. For example, activation in the anterior cingulate is more closely linked with the participant's anticipation of possible errors than with the degree of conflict (J. W. Brown & Braver, 2005). This result suggests that the medial frontal cortex may be doing more than simply monitoring the level of conflict presented by the current environment. It may also be anticipating the likelihood of conflict, suggesting a risk prediction and error avoidance role. As seen in our earlier discussion of decision making, the cingulate cortex has been linked to evaluating the effort associated with a behavioral choice, helping to perform a cost–benefit analysis. This hypothesis has led to a reinterpretation of the prevalent activation of medial frontal cortex observed on difficult tasks. Jack Grinband and his colleagues (2008) observed that the response times tend to be larger in such conditions. They suggested that the activation here may simply reflect the amount of time spent on the task, a variant of effort. To test this idea, they had participants view a checkerboard that flashed on and off for a variable duration of time, and simply press a button when the checkerboard disappeared. In this task, the stimulus is unambiguous, only one response is possible, and no choice decision is required. Thus, there were no errors, nor is there any conflict. Even so, medial frontal cortex activation was modulated by task duration and was similar to that observed when the participants performed a Stroop task. It is, of course, hard to make inferences about a null result (similar activation in these two tasks), but the results provide an alternative view on why activation of medial frontal cortex is correlated with task difficulty.

More perplexing are the results of studies involving patients with lesions of the medial frontal cortex. These patients show little evidence of impairment on various tasks that would appear to require cognitive control, one reason why the cingulate had not been identified as having a role until fMRI came along. For example, these patients are as sensitive to the effects of an error on the Stroop task as are control participants (Fellows & Farah, 2005). In fact, the patient data fail to confirm a number of behavioral predictions derived from models of how medial frontal function contributes to cognitive control. Although their cognitive performance appears to be relatively normal, these patients do exhibit a marked impairment: They fail to show normal changes in arousal when challenged either physically through exercise or mentally with math problems (Critchley et al., 2003). This finding suggests that medial frontal cortex may play a regulatory role in modulating autonomic activity in response to the current context, providing an interface between cognition and arousal. This modulation would be an indirect form of control, linked to regulatory mechanisms in the brainstem rather than through direct interactions with the cognitive representations of prefrontal cortex.

Importantly, the error detection and conflict-monitoring hypotheses suggest a way to achieve rather sophisticated control without resorting to homunculus-like notions. It is possible to envision a rather simple neural mechanism that assesses the degree to which multiple responses are concurrently active. Whether these ideas prove to have lasting value, they do offer an encouraging example of how even the most advanced of our cognitive competencies can be subject to rigorous experimental investigation, given the many tools of cognitive neuroscience.

TAKE-HOME MESSAGES

- The supervisory attentional system (SAS) is a psychological model to account for how goal-oriented behavior succeeds. It is proposed to describe cognitive control required for planning an action, performing in novel situations that do not involve well-learned responses, and when errors are likely to occur.
- The medial frontal cortex is thought to be a critical part of a monitoring system, identifying situations in which cognitive control is required.
- The error-related negativity (ERN) response is an event-related potential (ERP) component that occurs when an error is produced. This response is generated by the medial frontal cortex.
- The medial frontal cortex is engaged when response conflict is high. Through its interactions with lateral regions of the prefrontal cortex, a monitoring system can regulate the level of cognitive control.

Summary

The prefrontal cortex plays a crucial role in cognitive control functions that are critical for goal-oriented behavior and decision making. Cognitive control systems allow us to be flexible and not driven solely by automatic behavior. The prefrontal cortex contains a massively connected network linking the brain's motor, perceptual, and limbic regions and is in an excellent position to coordinate processing across wide regions of the central nervous system (CNS).

Goal-oriented behavior and decision making involve planning, evaluating options, and calculating the value of rewards and consequences. These behaviors require that we represent information that is not always immediately present in the environment. Working memory is essential for this function. It allows for the interaction of current goals with perceptual information and knowledge accumulated from personal experience. Not only must we be able to represent our goals, but these representations must persist for an extended period of time. Working memory must be dynamic. It requires the retrieval, amplification, and manipulation of representations that are useful for the task at hand as well as the ability to ignore potential distractions. Yet we must also be flexible. If our goals change, or if the context demands an alternative course of action, we must be able to switch from one plan to another. These operations require a system that can monitor ongoing behavior, signaling when we fail or when there are potential sources of conflict.

Two functional systems have been emphasized in this chapter: (a) The lateral prefrontal cortex and frontal pole support goal-oriented behavior, providing a working memory system that recruits and selects task-relevant information stored in the more posterior regions of the cortex. (b) The medial frontal cortex is hypothesized to work in tandem with the prefrontal cortex, monitoring ongoing activity so as to be able to modulate the degree of cognitive control. As we emphasized in this chapter and in Chapter 8, the control of action has a hierarchical nature. Just as control in the motor system is delegated across many functional systems, an analogous organization characterizes prefrontal function. With control distributed in this manner, the need for an all-powerful controller, a homunculus, is minimized.

The content of ongoing processing is embedded in a context that reflects the history and current goals of the actor. Up to now, we have focused on relatively impersonal goals: naming words, attending to colors, remembering locations. But most of our actions are socially oriented. They reflect our personal desires, both as individuals and as members of social groups. To gain a more complete appreciation of goal-oriented behavior, we must turn to the study of the social brain, asking how our behavior is influenced by our interactions with others. In Chapter 13 we will address this topic, with the spotlight focusing on the ventromedial prefrontal cortex. By recognizing the intimate connections between the regions of prefrontal cortex, we can start to appreciate how a mind emerges from the architecture of the human brain.

Key Terms

action–outcome (p. 511)
action–outcome decision (p. 521)
anterior cingulate cortex (p. 550)
cognitive control (p. 508)
delayed-response task (p. 512)
descriptive decision theory (p. 521)
dopamine (p. 510)
dynamic filtering (p. 535)
error-related negativity (ERN) (p. 552)
frontal pole (FP) (p. 509)
goal-oriented action (p. 511)
goal-oriented behavior (p. 508)

habit (p. 511)
inhibitory control (p. 541)
lateral prefrontal cortex (LPFC) (p. 509)
medial frontal cortex (MFC) (p. 509)
mesocortical pathway (p. 526)
monitoring (p. 550)
normative decision theory (p. 520)
nucleus accumbens (p. 526)
orbitofrontal cortex (OFC) (p. 509)
perseveration (p. 510)
prediction error (PE) (p. 527)
prefrontal cortex (PFC) (p. 509)

primary reinforcer (p. 522)
recency memory (p. 512)
response conflict (p. 553)
secondary reinforcer (p. 522)
striatum (p. 510)
stimulus–response decision (p. 521)
supervisory attentional system (SAS) (p. 550)
utilization behavior (p. 511)
value (p. 522)
ventral tegmental area (p. 510)
working memory (p. 512)

we turn to you—or rather, the sense of self and how you get to know yourself. Then we investigate how you get to know others. We consider whether learning about others and learning about ourselves are similar processes that involve the same neural substrates. Understanding ourselves and other people, however, is only part of successfully navigating our social worlds. We also need to learn social rules and use them to guide our behavior. How do we make decisions that are guided by social knowledge? What can the brain tell us about the psychological functions that might be involved in this process? The answers to these questions will give us insight into our everyday experiences. Note that social responses, including facial expressions, social group evaluation, and racial stereotyping—which are all considered to be social cognitive neuroscience topics—were covered in Chapter 10, which focused on emotion.

TAKE-HOME MESSAGES

- The damage that Phineas Gage suffered to the orbito-frontal cortex resulted in a change of his behavior and personality, such that, as one person commented, "Gage was no longer Gage."
- Social cognitive neuroscience research explores the neural mechanisms involved in human social interactions.

Anatomical Substrates of Social Cognition

Does the processing of information about others and about ourselves happen in separate brain regions, overlapping regions, or all in the same place? Welcome to an active debate! When identifying brain regions that are concerned with self-referential processing—such as when you think about your personal traits, beliefs and desires, your past, and so forth—we encounter an interesting problem. Even though philosophers, theologians, clergy, and scientists have batted about the concept of self for thousands of years, no all-encompassing definition of *self* exists. What's more, a lot of evidence suggests there is no single brain region we can point to and say, "This is where the self is located." Increasingly, it looks like the self is a pastiche: It is made up of separable processes, full of separable content from a vast supply of sources, both from within and without the brain and the body. Lose a process, and you lose a part of your old self and turn into a new one, who may be quite different. Phineas Gage's old friends may have considered him as no longer his old self, but he did have a self—just one that was different.

Regions of the prefrontal cortex (PFC) are a primary focus in this chapter. The PFC is the anterior aspect of

the frontal lobe (see the Anatomical Orientation box). The lateral aspect of the PFC is divided into the dorsolateral prefrontal cortex (DLPFC) and the ventrolateral prefrontal cortex (VLPFC). The medial regions that we are concerned with are the orbitofrontal cortex (OFC) and the ventromedial prefrontal cortex (VMPFC). The regions that have been implicated in self-referential processing are the DLPFC and VMPFC, posterior cingulate cortex (PCC), and the medial and lateral parietal cortex. Subjective feelings also contribute to our sense of self and are mediated by all those regions that we outlined in Chapter 10 (Emotion), including the OFC, anterior cingulate cortex (ACC), and insula, as well as areas not limited to the cortex, including the autonomic nervous system (ANS), hypothalamic-pituitary-adrenal axis (HPA), and endocrine systems that regulate bodily states, emotion, and reactivity. Because memory is also part of self-referential processing, the temporal lobe is involved. When we try to understand others, various brain networks are activated that, depending on the task, can include the amygdala and its interconnections with the superior temporal sulcus (STS), the medial prefrontal cortex and OFC, ACC, and fusiform face area (FFA), regions associated with mirror neuron systems, the temporal poles, temporoparietal junction (TPJ), and the medial parietal cortex.

Deficits

As we saw in the chapter opener, damage to the orbitofrontal cortex may result in socially inappropriate behavior. Some people, who are diagnosed with autism spectrum disorders (ASD), also exhibit social deficits. These are pervasive but highly varied developmental disorders associated with impaired social interaction, among other symptoms. They include **autism**, Asperger's syndrome, childhood disintegrative disorder, Rett syndrome, and pervasive developmental disorders not otherwise specified.

Individuals with autism tend to show little interest in other individuals or social interactions. Instead, they focus on their internal thoughts or on inanimate external stimuli. They may prefer routine activities and may become upset if these routines are interrupted. For example, seeing the table set in an unusual way, getting a new school bus driver, or having a change in plans can be upsetting. Instead of seeking out social interaction, people with autism may prefer to engage in repetitive behavior by themselves, such as repeatedly flicking a string back and forth. Rather than seeking out a hug, they may comfort themselves by rocking their bodies or twisting their hands and fingers. They may also be hypersensitive to sensory stimuli.

ANATOMICAL ORIENTATION

Anatomy of social cognition

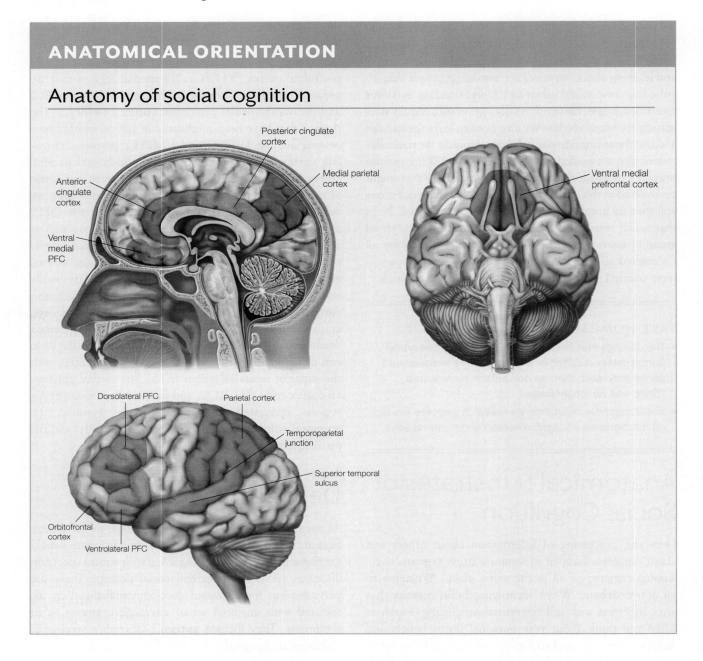

Simon Baron-Cohen of Cambridge University (Baron-Cohen et al., 1985) has proposed that individuals with autism direct their attention away from other people because of deficiencies in the ability to understand the mental states of others. Chapter 6 described people with prosopagnosia, patients who become "face-blind" because they cannot identify people on the basis of facial information. Drawing on this notion, Baron-Cohen coined the term *mindblindness* to reflect the inability of children with autism to properly represent the mental states of others (Baron-Cohen, 1995). The mindblindness associated with autism extends to impaired use of non-verbal cues (such as facial expressions) to reason about

another person's internal states. A large body of research shows that people with autism are impaired on a variety of tasks that require the use of facial perception for social judgments (e.g., Baron-Cohen, 1995; Klin et al., 1999; Weeks & Hobson, 1987).

People with autism have difficulty identifying emotion and mental states from facial expressions, and they do not use this information in the same way that healthy control participants do. When asked to sort a set of facial pictures, most children organize them according to the emotional expressions on the faces. In other words, they put pictures of people expressing happiness in one pile, pictures of people expressing sadness in another pile, and so on. In contrast, children with autism are more likely to sort these pictures on the basis of physical features such as clothing. Recall from Chapter 10 that Ralph Adolphs and his colleagues investigated the facial perception abilities of patients with amygdala lesions by using computer software that presented small pieces of facial expressions at a time. They also conducted a study in which people with autism performed these procedures and found that they do not attend to eye gaze as much as normally developing and developed controls do (Spezio et al., 2007).

For other disorders that affect a wide range of brain regions involved in social cognition, see "Milestones in Cognitive Neuroscience: Psychiatric Disorders and the Frontal Lobes."

TAKE-HOME MESSAGES

- Autism is a developmental disorder marked by abnormal social behavior. People with autism do not engage in normal social interactions. They frequently focus on self-stimulation and display little interest in the actions of other individuals.
- One hypothesis is that people with autism have deficiencies in the ability to understand the mental states of others. This condition is known as mindblindness.

Socrates' Imperative: Know Thyself

Socrates emphasized the importance of "knowing thyself." How exactly do we do that? We develop our self-knowledge (e.g., information about our characteristics, desires, and thoughts) through self-perception processes designed to gather information about the self. Because the self is simultaneously the perceiver and the perceived, self-perception is a unique social cognitive process. In other words, when we think about ourselves, the self is doing the thinking and the self is also the subject of our thoughts—the ultimate in subjective appraisals. Consider also that knowing oneself involves the physical you, your body as you (Is that my arm? Do I have blue eyes? Am I strong?), and the essence of you, which is more the story of your character, memories, experiences, and so forth (Am I loyal? Where was I born? Do I enjoy traveling?). In addition, we must distinguish ourselves from others: Our sense of self relies partially on seeing the difference between our self-knowledge and the knowledge we have about other people's characteristics, desires, and thoughts. For example, you might be one of those unusual individuals who prefers a snake for a pet, but you can readily acknowledge that most people would prefer a dog. Your individual preferences help define what makes you

unique from other people. When you wince as your friend twists her ankle, you may share her pain, but you know that she is the one feeling it and not you. The big questions in social cognitive neuroscience center on what neural and psychological mechanisms support the processing of information about the self and about other people, whether these mechanisms are the same or different, and how the brain differentiates between self and other.

In this section, we look at how people represent and gather information about themselves and what the brain can tell us about the nature of self-perception. For instance, do we really want to know all sides of ourselves, or just the good things? If we want to focus on the positive, how does the brain help us do that?

Self-Referential Processing

Where were you born? Where was Napoleon born? We all know that we remember some information better than other information. It is a safe bet that you know where you were born, but when it comes to Napoleon, perhaps not. If you have visited his birthplace in Ajaccio on the island of Corsica, you are more likely to remember that information than if you had never been there. According to Fergus Craik and Robert Lockhart's levels-of-processing model of memory (1972), the depth of processing profoundly affects the storage of information. Craik and Lockhart found that information processed in a more meaningful way is remembered better than information processed more superficially. For example, in tests they performed, participants were much more likely to remember a list of words when they considered their meaning rather than when they considered their font. A few years after Craik and Lockhart's study, other research groups extended these ideas about memory. Two labs discovered independently that people remember significantly more information when it is processed in relation to themselves than when they process it in other ways (Markus, 1977; T. B. Rogers et al., 1977). For example, people are more likely to remember the adjective *happy* if they have to judge how well it describes themselves than if they have to judge how well it describes the president of the United States (Figure 13.2). This is true even if they do not know that they will be asked to remember the adjectives when judging their descriptiveness. The enhanced memory for information processed in relation to the self is known as the **self-reference effect**.

Two hypotheses have been considered about why memory is better for information processed in relation to the self. One suggests that the self is a unique cognitive structure with unique mnemonic or organizational elements that promote processing in a way that is distinct from all other cognitive structures (T. B. Rogers et al., 1977). The other hypothesis bursts the bubble on a special

Psychiatric disorders such as schizophrenia and depression represent a widespread breakdown in mental function. Problems faced by patients suffering from these disorders affect almost all aspects of their behavior. Most likely their problems are not linked to a simple physiological mechanism. Rather, the disorders are thought to arise from a delicate interplay of physiological mechanisms that reflect endogenous dispositions and a person's idiosyncratic experiences.

One of the most promising aspects of cognitive neuroscience is that it may offer new insights concerning the functional deficits associated with severe psychiatric disorders. Simple neuropsychological descriptions do not adequately account for these disorders. Schizophrenia cannot be thought of as a temporal lobe or frontal lobe problem; it arises as a disturbance in cognitive systems that span cortical and subcortical systems. For example, some imaging studies (Figure 1) have shown that schizophrenics have an underactive frontal cortex, especially in lateral regions. Losing their working memory and inhibitory

capabilities renders them more reliant on activity in the posterior cortex. They may be easier to distract, and hence fail to inhibit irrelevant representations such as those related to persistent hallucinations.

Depressed patients, on the other hand, tend to exhibit a profile of overactivity in prefrontal regions associated with working memory and in areas linked to the generation of affective memories. For these people, representations persist for a long time and have more effect. A situation that a normal person might find neutral, or at most mildly aggravating, becomes amplified and often highly unpleasant. The depressed patient cannot let a situation go; the representation of a thought or obsession persists, sustained by input from inappropriate somatic markers.

From a cognitive neuroscience perspective, we can make sense of the outcome of one of the great debacles of neurosurgery: frontal lobotomies for treating psychiatric disorders (Valenstein, 1986). Before the use of drug therapies in the 1950s and 1960s, mental institutions were

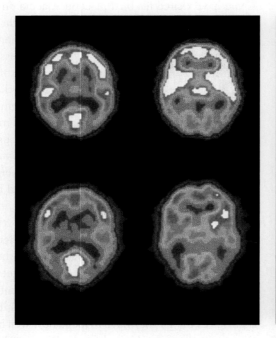
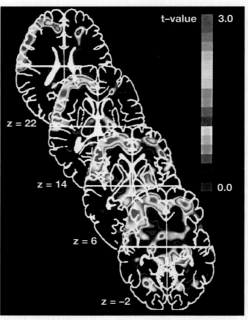

FIGURE 1 Positron emission tomography (PET) reveals abnormal patterns of blood flow in patients with psychiatric disorders.

(a) Schizophrenic patients show hypometabolism in the prefrontal cortex. This abnormality is especially marked during tasks that produce increased blood flow in this area in healthy participants. In this study, participants were involved in a continuous auditory discrimination task. Compared to the control participants **(top)**, uptake of the tracer is much lower in schizophrenic patients **(bottom)**. Metabolic rates are represented from low to high, respectively, by black, purple, blue, green, yellow, red, and white. The lower metabolic rates in the mid-prefrontal cortex (top of slice) of the schizophrenic patient are readily apparent. **(b)** Blood flow at rest was measured in control participants and patients with depression. Colored areas indicate regions of increased blood flow in the depressed patients. These areas are centered in the lateral prefrontal cortex in the left hemisphere.

overflowing with desperate patients and doctors, eager to try any procedure that promised relief. In the 1930s, Egas Moniz, a renowned Portuguese neurologist who had developed cerebral angiography in 1927, introduced a psychosurgical procedure for treating patients with severe schizophrenia and obsessive-compulsive disorder.

Moniz's inspiration came from an international scientific conference at which two American researchers had reported the effects of frontal lobectomy in chimpanzees. One animal appeared to have undergone a personality change. Before the operation, the chimp was uncooperative and threw temper tantrums. After removal of most of her frontal lobes, the animal was cheerful and participated in experimental tests without hesitation. Moniz reasoned that the procedure might bring relief to severely agitated patients—a well-intended thought, given the lack of alternatives.

Removing large amounts of tissue from the frontal lobes seemed excessive. Instead, Moniz decided to isolate the prefrontal cortex from the rest of the brain by severing the white matter's connecting fibers. In his early efforts, he applied toxic levels of alcohol through holes in the skull's lateral surface. Later, he switched to the procedure of lowering a leukotome (a plunger with an extractable blade) into the brain to sever fibers in targeted regions.

Walter Freeman at Georgetown University refined this procedure. He developed a simple technique that did not require a surgeon. The patient was first given an anesthetic consisting of a severe electrical shock. While the patient was unconscious, usually for 15 minutes, the surgeon performed the lobotomy by jabbing an ice pick through the bone above each eye and wiggling it back and forth. To promote the benefits of this miracle cure, Freeman set off on a barnstorming trip. He took with him a portable kit containing his electroshock apparatus, ice picks, and a small hammer (Figure 2). The public and scientific community were welcoming. Thousands of procedures were performed over the next few decades, and for his work, Moniz received the Nobel Prize in Physiology or Medicine in 1949.

Thanks to hindsight, we now recognize the abject failings of the lobotomy craze. The few outcome studies that were done revealed that the discharge rate from mental institutions was no greater for lobotomy patients than it was for control participants. Scant concern was given to the patients selected; the procedure had minimal effect on schizophrenics but drastically altered patients with affective disorders like depression or severe neurosis, who felt much less anxious, impulsive, and depressed. But these feelings brought new problems that rendered these patients incapable of functioning outside the institutional setting. They were now withdrawn and underactive, lacking in affect or responsiveness. The benefits, if any, were experienced by attendants, who rejoiced that the patients were docile and easy to manage. As with Phineas Gage, the patients' personalities had been transformed.

These differential outcomes make sense in light of metabolic studies. Lobotomies targeted the prefrontal cortex, a region already underactive in schizophrenia. Thus we might expect little effect on schizophrenics, or maybe new problems for those with overly dominant posterior brain function. For affective disorders, though, lobotomies isolated an overactive region. Moreover, the primary foci were medial regions, so the procedure may have eliminated behaviors associated with exaggerated emotionality but turned patients into unfeeling zombies.

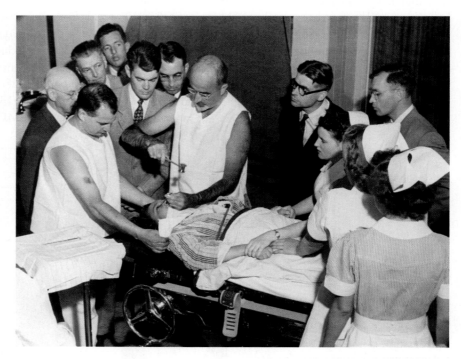

FIGURE 2 Walter Freeman, in 1949 at Western State Hospital, performing frontal lobotomy using the nonsurgical procedure he developed using an ice-pick-like instrument.

FIGURE 13.2 A typical self-referential processing experiment.
(a) Participants answer a series of questions about their own personality traits as well as the personality traits of someone else. **(b)** Then they are asked which of the trait words they can remember.

self and suggests that we simply have more knowledge about the self, and this encourages more elaborate coding of information that relates to the self (Klein & Kihlstrom, 1986). From this latter perspective, the greater depth of processing might result because participants have to consider the adjective in relation to the wealth of stored information about the self. In contrast, their more superficial judgment of whether the word *happy* has two syllables is considered only in relation to a single dimension that they may have stored about that word. While numerous behavioral studies have been conducted to examine these hypotheses, it was several imaging studies that revealed the neural systems that underlie the self-reference effect.

If the self is a special cognitive structure characterized by unique information processing, then distinct neural regions should be activated in relation to the self-reference effect. William Kelley and his colleagues (2002) at Dartmouth

College conducted one of the first fMRI studies to test this hypothesis. Participants judged personality adjectives in one of three experimental conditions: in relation to the self ("Does this trait describe you?"); in relation to another person ("Does this trait describe George Bush?"—the president at the time the study was conducted); or in relation to its printed format ("Is this word presented in uppercase letters?"). As found in numerous other studies of the self-reference effect, participants were most likely to remember words from the self condition and least likely to remember words from the printed-format condition.

Was there unique brain activity, then, when participants were making judgments in the self condition? The medial prefrontal cortex (MPFC) was differentially activated in the self condition compared to the other two conditions (Figure 13.3). Later studies found that the level of activity in the MPFC predicted which items would be

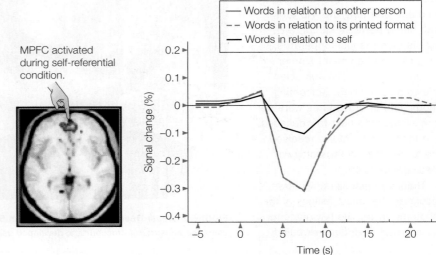

MPFC activated during self-referential condition.

FIGURE 13.3 Medial prefrontal cortex (MPFC) activity is associated with self-referential processing when compared to processing words in relation to another person ("other") or the printed format of the words.

— Words in relation to another person
--- Words in relation to its printed format
— Words in relation to self

Signal change (%)

Time (s)

remembered on the surprise memory test (Macrae et al., 2004). The relation between MPFC and self-reference also extends to instances where participants have to view themselves through another person's eyes. A similar region of MPFC is activated when people are asked to judge whether another individual would use particular adjectives to describe them (Ochsner et al., 2005).

Although much of this research has been conducted with functional MRI, event-related potential (ERP) studies provide convergent results. Self-referential processing produces positive-moving shifts in ERPs that emerge from a midline location consistent with the location of medial prefrontal cortex (Magno & Allan, 2007). These studies suggest that self-referential processing is more strongly associated with medial prefrontal cortex function than is the processing of information about people we do not know personally, such as the president of the United States.

Self-Descriptive Personality Traits

The self-reference effect on memory is just one example of the unique effect of the self on cognition. Another process that is unique to self-perception has to do with self-descriptive personality traits. For instance, when you are deciding about whether a trait is self-descriptive (Are you physically strong?), you use a different source of information compared to when you are deciding whether another person possesses that trait (Is Antonio strong?). In other words, people have a uniquely strong memory for traits that they judge in relation to themselves, and they also have a unique way of deciding whether the trait is self-descriptive. Specifically, when we decide whether an adjective is self-descriptive, we rely on self-perceptions that are summaries of our personality traits rather than considering various episodes in our lives. In contrast, when making judgments of other individuals, we often focus on specific instances in which the person might have exhibited behaviors associated with the adjective.

Stanley Klein and his colleagues at the University of California, Santa Barbara (1992), arrived at this finding when they asked whether self-description judgments rely on recall of specific autobiographical episodes. How did they figure this out? Participants were shown a personality adjective on a computer screen and either rated it for self-descriptiveness (e.g., "Are you generous?") or defined it ("What does *generous* mean?"). As a control, participants were shown a blank screen with no adjectives. After completing the initial task, participants were asked to describe a particular instance from their lives when they exhibited the personality characteristic. During this descriptive task, researchers recorded the time it took to perform the task. In the control condition, participants were asked to describe an episode when they exhibited a trait that they had not

been asked about, for example, "Give an example of when you were stubborn." If self-descriptions rely on looking through episodic memory for examples, participants should have been faster to recall an episode when they exhibited the personality characteristic that they had already been asked about, having just cruised through their episodic memory bank to make the self-descriptive judgment. What were the results? No differences were found between the self-judgment, definition, and control conditions. This result suggests that our judgments about self-characteristics are not linked to recall of specific past behaviors.

If this conclusion is correct, then we should be able to maintain a sense of self even if we are robbed of autobiographical memories across our lives. Can we do this? The ability to maintain a sense of self in the absence of specific autobiographical memories has been demonstrated in case studies of patients with dense amnesia (Klein et al., 2002; Tulving, 1993). Consider two patients who developed retrograde and anterograde amnesia (see Chapter 9). Patient D.B.'s memory problems developed after a heart attack as a result of the transient loss of oxygen to the brain—a condition known as *hypoxia*. Patient K.C. was in a motorcycle accident and sustained brain damage that resulted in amnesia. Neither of these patients could recall a single thing they had done or experienced in their entire life, yet both could accurately describe their own personality. For example, D.B. and K.C.'s personality judgments were consistent with judgments provided by their family members.

Possibly, however, this behavior reflects the preservation of more general social knowledge rather than the preservation of trait self-knowledge. This is seen in patients with Korsakoff's syndrome, who have a profound inability to recall events. In one study, such patients were shown two pictures of men and told a biographical story of each. One man's story was about a good guy; the other man's was about a bad guy. One month later, most of the patients preferred the picture of the man whose story revealed him to be a good guy, although they did not recall any of the biographical information about him (M. K. Johnson et al., 1985).

Klein and his colleagues made sure to address this question. They asked patient D.B. to rate his daughter's personality traits by using the same test that he so accurately completed about himself. His responses and those of his daughter varied wildly, while those of control patients and their children did not. Although D.B. was unable to retrieve accurate trait information about his daughter, he had no trouble recalling information about himself (Klein et al., 2002). These results provide additional support for the suggestion that semantic trait self-knowledge exists outside of general semantic knowledge. They also suggest that at least some of the mechanisms of self-referential processing rely on neural systems distinct from the neural systems used to process information about other people.

Indeed, Klein stumbled across something interesting when doing a review of research on self-based knowledge (Klein & Lax, 2010): Trait-based semantic knowledge about the self is remarkably robust against a host of neural insults and damage. In this regard it is unlike other types of semantic knowledge, even other types of semantic knowledge about the self (you may not know your birthday or recognize yourself in the mirror, but you still know that you are persistent). Klein's observation suggests that semantic trait knowledge about oneself is a special type of self-knowledge and that the self is not a single unified entity. The conclusion is that rather than being centered in one unique cognitive structure, the self is distributed across multiple systems. In fact, several different systems for self-knowledge have been identified, and they can be isolated functionally from each other. For example, there is a system for episodic memories of your own life (I had a great time hiking in South Dakota), another for semantic knowledge of the facts of your life (I am half Norwegian), one for a sense of personal agency (I am the agent that causes my arm to lift up), another for the ability to recognize your body in the mirror, in photos, and just looking down at your feet (That's me, alright!), and many more systems mediating other types of self-knowledge.

TAKE-HOME MESSAGES

- Knowledge of the self is strongly supported by the medial prefrontal cortex.
- The medial prefrontal cortex is associated with superior memory for information processed in relation to the self. This ability is known as the self-reference effect.
- Evidence suggests that our self-knowledge does not depend on reflecting on actual experiences to understand personality features, but rather is based on information abstracted from these experiences.
- It is possible to maintain a sense of self in the absence of specific autobiographical memories, because a distinct neural system supports the summaries of personality traits typically used to make self-descriptive judgments.

Self-Reference as a Baseline Mode of Brain Function

As we have seen in many previous chapters, during fMRI studies participants are given a task to perform. Between tasks, typically they are asked to rest. Imagine yourself lying in a "magnet" with nothing to do and being told to rest. Your mind does not turn off like a TV screen; you start thinking about the weekend, summer break, your friends, your dinner, the paper you have to write, something. And usually that something is all about you

or something or someone connected to you in some way. Can studying the brain tell us anything about why self-referential processing is so prevalent? Some research suggests that the medial prefrontal cortex, the region associated with self-referential processing, has unique physiological properties that may permit self-referential processing to occur even when we are not actively trying to think about ourselves. This notion emerged as it gradually dawned on researchers that although participants inside the MRI machine were supposedly at rest, activity in specific brain regions was noticeably increasing. In fact, this activity was as vigorous as activity in other regions when individuals were performing mental tasks, such as math problems. The brain at rest apparently was not "off." When participants were quizzed about what they were thinking during their "rest periods," the typical answer related to self-referential processing (Gusnard et al., 2001; Gusnard & Raichle, 2001).

Obviously, even when you are resting quietly and not thinking about something in particular, blood continues to circulate to your brain as it uses oxygen. In fact, a network of brain regions, including the MPFC, has metabolic rates that are higher "at rest." These circulatory and metabolic demands are costly because they take blood and oxygen away from other organs. Why would the brain consume so much of the body's energy when it is not engaged in a specific cognitive task? Raichle, Gusnard, and their colleagues argue that when we are at rest cognitively speaking, our brains continue to engage in a number of psychological processes that describe a default mode of brain function (Gusnard & Raichle, 2001). They have named the brain regions that support these processes the **default network** (Raichle et al., 2001). The default network consists of the MPFC, precuneus, TPJ, medial temporal lobe, lateral parietal cortex, and posterior cingulate cortex (Figure 13.4). The researchers hypothesized that the higher metabolic rate in the medial prefrontal cortex reflects self-referential processing, such as thinking about what we might be getting ready to do or evaluating our current condition. Thus, they concluded, the default network is there to ensure that we always have some idea of what is going on around us. This is called the *sentinel hypothesis*.

The default network is most active when tasks direct our attention away from external stimuli, and we are inwardly focused. This makes sense, because there are no primary sensory or motor regions connected to the default network. For instance, the default network is strongly active when we are engaged in self-reflective thought and judgment assessments that depend on social and emotional content. The default network is connected to the medial temporal lobe memory system, which explains why we often consider the past in these default ramblings. The default network is deactivated while

FIGURE 13.4 The Default Network.
Combined data from nine positron emission tomography (PET) studies showing the regions that were most active during passive tasks (in blue). The lateral (left) and medial (right) surfaces of the left hemisphere are shown.

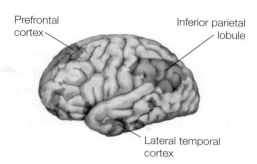

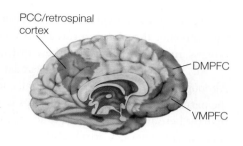

Prefrontal cortex

Inferior parietal lobule

PCC/retrospinal cortex

DMPFC

VMPFC

Lateral temporal cortex

performing active tasks. Thus, when you want to detach yourself from ruminating about your own plight, whether it is brought on by sadness, anger, or depression, you can do so by performing an active task, such as learning a new skill. The great Antarctic explorer Sir Ernest Shackleton knew this instinctively. In his book, *South*, he describes the ordeal that he and his men went through when their ship was sunk and they were stranded on the pack ice just off the Antarctic coast in 1915. At one point he relates,

> Then I took out to replace the cook [with] one of the men who had expressed a desire to lie down and die. The task of keeping the galley fire alight was both difficult and strenuous, and it took his thoughts away from the chances of immediate dissolution. In fact, I found him a little later gravely concerned over the drying of a naturally not over-clean pair of socks which were hung up in close proximity to our evening milk. Occupation had brough his thoughts back to the ordinary cares of life (Shackleton, 2004, p. 136).

Interestingly, however, while performing active tasks that involve self-referential judgments, the MPFC

deactivates less than it does for other types of tasks (Figure 13.5). Given that we generally think about ourselves when we are left to daydream, a self-referential task would not significantly change activation in the MPFC because it chronically engages in self-referential thinking, even during the rest or baseline condition. In the self-reference studies described earlier, the president and printed-format conditions direct cognitive resources away from self-referential thinking, and therefore the MPFC shows a strong deactivation relative to baseline.

Since the default network was first described, however, multiple studies have found that various tasks activate a set of regions remarkably similar to the default network. These include autobiographical memory tasks, tasks envisioning the self in the future or navigating to a different location, and tasks that evaluate personal moral dilemmas (e.g., would it be morally acceptable for you to push one person off a sinking boat to save five others?). Furthermore, similar regions of the brain are activated when we think about the beliefs and intentions of other people—that is, their mental states (known as theory of mind, which we discuss elsewhere in this chapter). Thus, the default network

FIGURE 13.5 Activity in the dorsal medial prefrontal cortex increases during tasks that involve self-referential mental activity or self-focused attention and decreases during tasks that involve externally focused attention. This finding is consistent with the observation that during goal-directed behaviors, self-focused attention decreases, and also indicates that at baseline, there should be some degree of self-referential mental activity engaging this region, a suggestion which has been supported by functional imaging data.

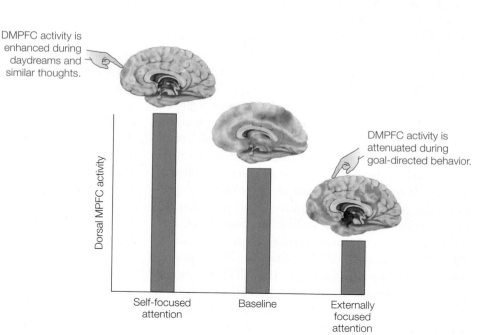

DMPFC activity is enhanced during daydreams and similar thoughts.

DMPFC activity is attenuated during goal-directed behavior.

Dorsal MPFC activity

Self-focused attention

Baseline

Externally focused attention

appears to do more than solely self-referential processing. Can you spot the common thread, or common cognitive process, running through all of these tasks?

All of these tasks have a similar core process. Although differing in content and goal, each task requires the participants to envision themselves in situations other than the here and now—that is, to adopt an alternative perspective (Buckner & Carroll, 2007; J. P. Mitchell, 2009). For example, imagine what you might think and feel if you had to change a flat tire in a rainstorm, without a raincoat, on the way to an important interview. Alternatively, how would you feel if you won a trip to Barcelona, or if you had to decide whether to push someone off a boat in order to save five other people? Each of these scenarios requires you to focus on thoughts that have no relation to the stimuli in your current environment. This type of cognitive process is exactly what we need to be able to infer the mental states of others, such as trying to imagine how your friend felt when he jumped up in the end zone and caught a seemingly impossible pass that won his team a ticket to the Orange Bowl. We need to step out of our shoes and into someone else's. As this account suggests, the processes that give rise to our understanding of other people's minds overlap with the processes that support speculations about our own activities. Jason Mitchell at Harvard University has suggested that the high resting activity measured in the default network may indicate that the human mind naturally prefers simulated realities over the immediate external environment (Tamir & Mitchell, 2011). Next time someone tells you to enjoy the moment instead of dreaming about the future, you can reply, "Dude, I'm high on my default network." Mitchell has proposed that the deactivation of such regions may indicate that these virtual scenarios have been set aside temporarily in order to orient to the actual, concrete world around us.

If the brain is already making a set of default psychological computations, then what are the implications for brain activation when we deviate from the default state and actively try to think about something else? Why do the brain regions that seem to be involved with social cognition "switch off" while other regions come online to perform nonsocial tasks? You might say, "Well, to cut your metabolic costs." This response seems logical, but in reality the task-related changes in local blood flow are insignificant. They are so small that during periods of transient task performance, metabolic rationing isn't worth the effort. In fact, deactivations can occur far from locations of increased metabolism or even in their absence (Gusnard & Raichle, 2001; Raichle et al., 2001). J. P. Mitchell (2011) has proposed that the elevated activity of MPFC, TPJ, and medial parietal cortex interferes with nonsocial forms of thought. If our default mode is always prepared for social interaction, and it doesn't quiet down when we engage in a task that involves objects governed by external forces, it could be rather incapacitating. Consider what it would be like if every time you popped a piece of bread into the toaster, you considered the feelings and thoughts of the bread (Does it want to be toasted?), or of the toaster (Would it rather be broiling than toasting?). What if your ancestors had gone into default mode while gazing at the rock they were poised to throw at the animal about to pounce on their toddler?

Mitchell suggests that the solution to this cognitive problem may require interrupting the spontaneous mental processes that otherwise induce a readiness for social thought. That is, we humans are naturally predisposed to think about mental states, but to interact appropriately with nonsocial aspects of our environment, we have to turn down those natural tendencies. We aren't always successful at doing this, for example, when we get mad at our disabled car and accuse it of intentionally ruining our interview. We are also notoriously poor at this shift when it comes to animate objects other than humans: We frequently project human thoughts and intentions onto various animals.

Self-Perception as a Motivated Process

The studies described in the preceding discussion examined a number of ways that we process information about the self. They do not, however, address the question of how accurately we process this information. Judgments about the self are somewhat unique because, although the richest possible database is available, this process is often inaccurate. A wide range of behavioral studies have shown that people often have unrealistically positive self-perceptions (S. E. Taylor & Brown, 1988). Among high school students, 70% rank themselves as above average in leadership ability, while 93% of college professors believe that they are above average at their work (reviewed in Gilovich, 1991). More than 50% of people believe they are above average in intelligence, physical attractiveness, and a host of other positive characteristics—as humorist Garrison Keillor's description of his fictitious hometown, Lake Wobegon, attests: "Where all the women are strong, all the men are good-looking, and all the children are above average." This view through rose-colored glasses extends to our expectations in life. People believe they are more likely than others to experience positive future events, such as winning the lottery, and less likely than others to experience negative future events, such as getting a divorce.

How does the brain allow us to maintain these positive illusions about ourselves? Chapter 6 described how optical illusions arise from higher order visual areas. Although research on self-perceptual biases is still unfolding, the results suggest that distinct higher order prefrontal regions allow people to focus selectively on positive aspects of themselves while preventing them from deviating too far from reality.

Two studies suggest that the most ventral portion of the anterior cingulate cortex is responsible for focusing attention on positive information about the self. An fMRI study conducted at Dartmouth College by Joseph Moran and his colleagues (2006) asked participants to make a series of self-descriptive judgments just like those in the self-reference studies. As expected from research on positive biases in self-perception, the participants tended to select more positive adjectives and fewer negative adjectives as self-descriptive. Differences in activity in the ventral anterior cingulate cortex were associated with making judgments about positive adjectives compared to negative adjectives, and this was particularly true for adjectives considered to be self-descriptive (Figure 13.6). Another fMRI study found that a similar region of anterior cingulate cortex was activated differentially when participants imagined experiencing a positive event in the future as compared to a negative event (Sharot et al., 2007). These studies suggest that the anterior cingulate cortex is important for distinguishing positive self-relevant information from negative self-relevant information. Marking information as positive versus negative may permit people to focus more on the positive.

Although self-perceptions are sometimes biased in a positive direction, on average, self-perceptions are not delusional or completely detached from reality. Accurate self-perception is essential for appropriate social behavior. For example, people must have some insight into their behavior to make sure they are following social norms and avoiding social mistakes. Patients with damage to the orbitofrontal cortex (like M.R. at the beginning of the chapter) tend to have unrealistically positive self-views along with inappropriate social behavior. Jennifer Beer wondered whether patients' behavior was inappropriate because they lacked insight into their own behavior or because they were unaware of the social norms. To explore this question, she videotaped healthy control participants, patients who had damage to the orbitofrontal cortex, and patients with lateral prefrontal cortex damage while they engaged in a structured social interaction with a stranger (Beer et al., 2006). In this interaction, the stranger made conversation with the participants by asking them a series of questions. Unlike the other two groups, patients with orbitofrontal damage tended to bring up impolite conversation topics. After the interview, the participants rated how appropriate their answers had been considering that they had been talking to a stranger. Patients with orbitofrontal damage believed they had performed very well on

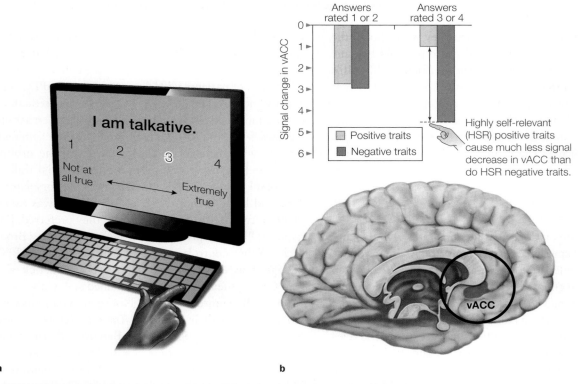

a　　　　　　　　　　　　　　　　　**b**

FIGURE 13.6 Neural activity in relation to judging positive information about the self.
(a) Participants rated the self-descriptiveness of a variety of personality traits. **(b)** Less deactivation in the anterior cingulate was associated with rating positive personality traits in comparison to negative personality traits. vACC is ventral anterior cingulate cortex.

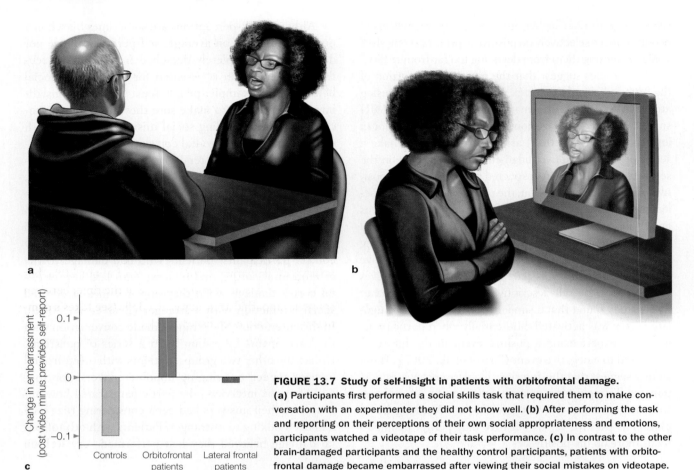

a

b

c

FIGURE 13.7 Study of self-insight in patients with orbitofrontal damage.
(a) Participants first performed a social skills task that required them to make conversation with an experimenter they did not know well. (b) After performing the task and reporting on their perceptions of their own social appropriateness and emotions, participants watched a videotape of their task performance. (c) In contrast to the other brain-damaged participants and the healthy control participants, patients with orbitofrontal damage became embarrassed after viewing their social mistakes on videotape.

the social interaction task. When they were shown the videotaped interview, however, these patients become embarrassed by their social mistakes (Figure 13.7). This study suggests that the orbitofrontal cortex is important for spontaneous, accurate self-perceptions, and that rather than being unaware of social norms, patients with orbitofrontal damage demonstrate lack of insight. We will return to the orbitofrontal cortex later in the chapter.

Predicting Our Future Mental State

How do we predict our own mental states? Do we consider actual experiences and predict from there, or do we use a set of rules that output a prediction? What if you were asked to choose between spending a year alone in a space station on Mars or alone in a submarine under the polar ice cap? This is a choice between scenarios that nobody has experienced, and thus, there are no general rules about how to choose. When participants had to make predictions about their mental states in novel scenarios, fMRI revealed that the ventral region of the MPFC was consistently engaged. It was also found that people's preferences for one novel situation over another are stable over time (reviewed in J. P. Mitchell, 2009). This insight

suggested to Mitchell that when we make these types of predictions, we begin by simulating the experience and then predicting which one we would like better.

Studies of patients with damage to the VMPFC support the notion that the VMPFC subserves predictions about an individual's own likes and dislikes. In one study (Fellows & Farah, 2007), three groups were examined: patients with damage principally involving the orbitofrontal and/or the ventral portion of the medial wall of the frontal lobe, patients with damage to the dorsolateral PFC, and healthy controls. Each participant was asked which of two actors, foods, or colors they preferred. For instance, "Do you prefer Ben Affleck or Matthew Broderick?" When controls or patients with dorsal lateral PFC damage chose Affleck over Broderick, but Broderick over Tom Cruise, their preferences remained stable; they said they liked Ben more than Tom. Not so with patients who had damage to their VMPFC. Their preferences were inconsistent—they might choose Ben over Matthew and Matthew over Tom, but then choose Tom over Ben.

If you were offered either $20 today or a guaranteed $23 next week, which would you pick? Oddly enough, most people pick the $20. In general, people tend to make shortsighted decisions, even when they can foresee the consequences and understand that they would be better off with a different choice. Why do we do this? Activity in brain regions associated with introspective self-reference (such as the VMPFC) are more engaged when predicting how much a person would enjoy an event in the present compared to when judging future events (J. P. Mitchell et al., 2011). Not only that, but by looking at the magnitude of VMPFC reduction, researchers could predict the extent to which participants would make shortsighted monetary decisions several weeks later. The more the VMPFC was activated when predicting future events, the less shortsighted decisions were made. If you happen to be one of the few people who can delay the payoff, most likely your VMPFC engages better than most when thinking about the future. Considering the previous finding that the VMPFC contributes to the ability to simulate future events from a first-person perspective, Mitchell proposes that an individual's shortsighted decisions may result in part from a failure to fully imagine the subjective experience of a future self.

TAKE-HOME MESSAGES

- The medial prefrontal cortex may promote chronic self-referential processing through its high baseline level of metabolism.

- We often view ourselves through rose-colored glasses. Regions within the frontal cortex may work together to permit a focus on positive aspects of the self without deviating too far from reality.

- The anterior cingulate cortex is important for selectively attending to positive information about the self, but orbitofrontal cortex function ensures that positively biased self-views do not deviate too far from reality.

- The VMPFC is key to predicting our state of mind: The more activated it is when we consider the future, the less shortsighted our decisions will be.

- Patients with orbitofrontal damage demonstrate many socially inappropriate behaviors. Although they understand social rules, they fail to recognize when they have broken these rules "in the moment."

Theory of Mind: Understanding the Mental States of Others

Although self-perception and awareness are important features of human cognition, we are also eager to interact with and understand the behavior of other individuals. In contrast to our self-perceptions, which have privileged access to our rich autobiographical memories, unexpressed mental states, and internal physiological signals, our perceptions of other people are made without direct access to their mental and physiological states. Instead, we have access only to the verbal and nonverbal cues they exhibit, and from those we infer what others are thinking and how they feel. Our inferences may not always be right, but we are pretty good at it. How good are we? William Ickes has made a study of this feature, and he concludes that we are as good as it is good for us to be. Evolutionary pressures have calibrated our accuracy to the level that is high enough to allow us to deal well with others, but not so high that we weigh everyone else's interest equal to our own, thus putting our genetic future at risk. **Empathic accuracy** refers to a perceiver's accuracy in inferring a target person's thoughts and feelings. Total strangers achieve an empathic accuracy score of about 20%, but among close friends it is about 30% of the time; between spouses, empathic accuracy is 30–35% (see Ickes's commentary in Zaki & Ochsner, 2011).

During our evolution as social animals, humans developed the ability to infer the current mental state of others—their intentions, thoughts, feelings, beliefs, and desires. Understanding the mental states of other people is critical for successful performance across a wide range of social activities, such as cooperating, empathizing, and accurately anticipating behavior. Most important, understanding the intentions of others is the basis of human cooperation (Moll & Tomasello, 2007).

This ability to infer the mental states of other people is known as **theory of mind**, a term coined by David Premack and Guy Woodruff of the University of Pennsylvania (1978). After working with chimpanzees for several years, they began to speculate about what might account for differences in cognition across species. They suggested that chimpanzees might be capable of inferring information about the mental states of other chimpanzees. This idea initiated an avalanche of research looking for evidence to support it. Although considerable debate continues on the competence of social cognition in nonhuman species (Call & Tomasello, 2008; Herrmann et al., 2007), the work of Premack and Woodruff sparked a deep interest in theory-of-mind research in humans. Theory of mind, also known as *mentalizing*, has received a considerable amount of attention in the developmental psychology literature and, more recently, in cognitive neuroscience studies.

Developmental Milestones

Curiosity about others appears at birth and is a primary source of motivation throughout life. For example, infants prefer to look at a human face rather than other objects. Research using ERP has found that even 4-month-old infants exhibit early evoked gamma activity at occipital channels and a late gamma burst over right prefrontal cortex channels in response to direct eye contact. These findings suggest that infants are quick to process information about faces and use neural structures similar to those found in adults (Grossmann et al., 2007). In adulthood, we continue to focus on the social aspects of our environment. Numerous studies have shown that humans spend on average 80% of their waking time in the company of others, and 80–90% of conversations are spent talking about ourselves and gossiping about other people (Emler, 1994).

Much of the behavioral work on theory of mind has examined how this ability develops over a person's life span. Many tasks have been created to understand how theory of mind works. For several years, the Sally–Anne False-Belief Task (which we describe a bit later in this chapter) was the essential test in determining the presence or absence of theory of mind. Children didn't reliably pass this test until they were about age 4. It eventually dawned on researchers, however, that this task was too difficult for young children and that it was more than just a false-belief task. It could be that later developing abilities, such as inhibition and problem solving, were confounding the results, whereas theory of mind could develop earlier than age 4 or even be innate. Changing the tasks revealed that infants younger than 4 years demonstrate the ability.

When an adult is looking for an object but doesn't know where it is, 12-month-old babies who know the object's location will point to where it is. When the adult does know the location, however, the babies do not point to it (Liszkowski et al., 2008), demonstrating that they understand the goals and intentions of the adult. Fifteen-month-old babies show "surprise" when someone searches in a container for a toy that had been placed there in their absence (Onishi & Baillargeon, 2005), suggesting that they understand that the person did not know the toy had been placed there. At 17 months, children understand that another person has a false belief (Southgate et al., 2010). At about age 3 or 4, children recognize that their physical vantage point gives them an individual perspective on the world that is different from the physical vantage point of other people. By 5 or 6 years of age, children appreciate that their mental states are distinct from the mental states of other people. Specifically, they are aware that two people can have different beliefs about the state of the world. At about 6 or 7 years of age, children can appreciate when the literal meanings of words communicate only part of the speaker's intention, or that the actual intention may be quite different from the literal meaning of what is said. For example, they can understand irony and differentiate between a joke and a lie. At about 9 to 11 years of age, children are able to simultaneously represent more than one person's mental state, and to discern when one person hurts another person's feelings. They are ready to be teenagers.

This is how things stood until recently, when Hungarian developmental psychologists Agnes Kovacs, Erno Teglas, and Ansgar Endress (2010) came up with a new task and a radical hypothesis. Dave Premack happily points out that "their ideas constitute the first significant novelty in ToM in at least ten years" (Premack, in press). The researchers propose that theory of mind is innate and automatic. They reasoned that if this is so, then computing the mental states of others should be spontaneous, and the mere presence of another should automatically trigger the computation of their beliefs, even when performing a task in which those beliefs are irrelevant. They designed a visual detection task to test this idea.

The participants in the study by Kovacs and colleagues were adults. They were shown several animated movie scenarios that started with an agent placing a ball on a table in front of an opaque screen. The ball then rolled behind the screen. Next, one of four possible scenarios occurred:

- The ball stays behind the screen while the agent is watching, and after the agent leaves, the ball stays put.
- The ball rolls out from behind the screen while the agent is watching, and after the agent leaves, the ball stays put.
- The ball stays behind the screen while the agent is watching, but after the agent leaves, the ball rolls away.
- The ball rolls out from behind the screen while the agent is watching, but after the agent leaves, the ball returns to its position behind the screen.

In the first two instances, when the agent returns, he will have a true belief about the location of the ball. In the latter two examples, when the agent returns, he will have a false belief about the ball's location. Participants, however, observed the ball in all four scenarios and know where it is. At the end of the film, the screen was lowered, and either the ball was there or it was not (independent of what the film had shown). The participants' task was to press a button as soon as they detected the ball. The time it took for them to push the button—their reaction time (RT)—was measured. Notice that the agent's beliefs were irrelevant to the task. The researchers predicted that reaction times should be faster when participants and agents thought the ball was behind the screen (and it was) compared to a baseline condition when neither the participant nor the agent thought the ball was there (but it was). The baseline scenario should produce the slowest RT.

Indeed, when the participants and the agents thought the ball was there, and it was, their RT was faster

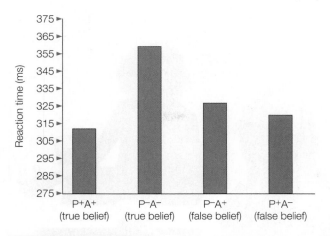

FIGURE 13.8 False-belief task.
Participant's reaction time is influenced by agent's belief, even though it is irrelevant. P = participant, A = agent.

compared to the baseline condition. It was also faster when the participant alone believed it was there. What do you think happened when the participant did not believe it was there but the agent did? Their RTs were also faster than the baseline condition. The agent's belief, though inconsistent with the participant's belief, influenced the participant's RT as much as his very own belief did (Figure 13.8). Thus it appears that adults track the beliefs of others automatically, but is this behavior acquired or innate? Do young infants also do this? The experiment was redesigned for 7-month-olds, this time using a violation of expectation task. The same results were found, suggesting that theory of mind is innate and that the mere presence of another automatically triggers belief computations. In addition, the researchers proposed that the mechanisms for computing someone else's beliefs might be part of a core human-specific "social sense" that was essential for the evolution of human societies. What are those mechanisms?

Mechanisms for Inferring Other People's Thoughts

Social cognitive neuroscientists are interested in how the brain supports our ability to make inferences about what other people are thinking, how we read their nonverbal cues, and how we understand the relation between the two. To infer the thoughts of others, the perceiver must translate what is observable (the behavior of another) into an inference about what is unobservable—his psychological state. Several theories have been proposed about how we accomplish this feat. One, known as **simulation theory**, or the more recently suggested term *experience sharing system* theory (ESS; see Zaki & Ochsner, 2011), proposes that we observe someone else's

behavior, imitate it, have a physiological response that we feel, and then infer that the other is feeling the same way. This process may occur unconsciously, involving a mirroring system similar to the mirror neuron systems involved with goal-directed actions and action understanding (discussed in Chapter 8). Alternatively, sometimes we can infer feelings by consciously "stepping into someone else's shoes." We often infer another person's mental state, however, even when we can't see them, or they are smiling on the outside but hurting on the inside, or they are saying one thing but intending another. That is, more than behavioral observation and imitation are at work here. **Theory theory**, or the newly suggested and perhaps clearer term, *mental state attribution system* theory (MSAS; Zaki & Ochsner, 2011), proposes that we may build a theory about the mental states of others from what we know about them. That knowledge involves memory about others, the situation they are in, their family, their culture, and so forth.

As is often true when hypothesizing about complex processes, the evidence suggests that both mechanisms, behavior reading and mind reading, are at work. And each behavior is associated with its own network of brain regions.

Simulation theory Recall that within the default network, MPFC activation is associated with the perception of both self and other people. Why would a common brain region be involved in both processes? One possibility is that a common brain region is recruited for both kinds of tasks, because a common psychological function can be used to perform both kinds of tasks. For example, people may draw on their self-representations to make inferences about another person. Simulation theory (or experience sharing) suggests that some aspects of inferring the thoughts of others, especially motor actions and emotions that can be mimicked, are based on an ability to put ourselves in the shoes of another person by using our own minds to simulate what might be going on in the mind of someone else (Harris, 1992; Figure 13.9). Such shared representations are considered by some to be the cornerstone of social cognition (Sebanz et al., 2006). How is the process of simulation reflected in brain activity?

Medial prefrontal cortex: Similar and close others. The theory of simulation suggests an intrinsic relation between the perception of self and the perception of others. Therefore, the reason for the MPFC's involvement in both types of perception may be that the perception of self is sometimes used to accomplish the perception of others. For example, in one fMRI study

FIGURE 13.9 Simulation theory.
People make inferences about the actions of others using their own expectations based on experiences from their own lives.

(J. P. Mitchell et al., 2006), scientists hypothesized that a similar region would be engaged when thinking about ourselves and a similar person, but it would not be activated when thinking about a person dissimilar to us. The researchers had participants read descriptions of two people: One person shared similar political views with the participants, and the other held the opposite political views. Next, the researchers measured the participants' brain activity while answering questions about their own preferences as well as when speculating about the preferences of the person with similar views and the one with dissimilar views. A ventral subregion of the MPFC was found to increase its activity for self-perceptions and perceptions of the similar person, whereas a different, more dorsal region of the MPFC was significantly activated for perceptions of the dissimilar person. These activation patterns in the MPFC have been held up as evidence that participants may have reasoned that their own preferences would predict the preferences of someone like them but would not be informative for speculating about the preferences of someone dissimilar to themselves. Other studies have since shown a variable pattern of activation between the ventral and dorsal regions: It is dependent not on similarity per se, but on the level of relatedness between the two people based on familiarity, closeness, emotional importance, warmth, competence and knowledge, and so forth.

For instance, Kevin Ochsner and Jennifer Beer showed that a similar region of the MPFC was activated for self-perception as well as perception of a current romantic partner (Ochsner et al., 2005). This effect was not driven by perceived similarities between the self and the romantic partner. The researchers suggest that this activation likely represents commonalities in the complexity or emotional nature of information stored about ourselves and romantic partners. Studies like this one suggest that the MPFC is important for thinking about the self and other people when a common psychological process underlies the thought processes. Sometimes we may use ourselves as a way of understanding someone we do not know well, but who appears to be related to us in some way. At other times, these processes may be linked because we create incredibly rich stores of information about ourselves as well as others we are close to.

Empathy Understanding the mental state of another involves more than understanding their beliefs, goals, and intentions. It also involves understanding their emotions. **Empathy**, our capacity to understand and respond to the unique experiences of another person (Decety & Jackson, 2004), epitomizes the strong relation between self-perception and the perception of others. To respond appropriately to another, we need the ability to accurately detect the emotional information being transmitted by that other person. Though the details regarding the process of empathy are debatable, it is generally agreed that the first step is to take the other person's perspective: We must momentarily create within ourselves the other person's internal state in our effort to understand it. What brain mechanisms permit us to share the experience of another person?

The perception–action model of empathy assumes that perceiving another person's state of mind automatically activates the same mental state in the observer, triggering somatic and autonomic responses. This model fits with the idea that we are able to understand a mental state by sharing it. Given the role of mirror neurons in imitation and action recognition (see Chapter 8), it has been proposed that mirror neurons may be a critical physiological mechanism that allows us to have the same representation of another's internal state within our own bodies. This mechanism is sometimes referred to as embodied simulation. For it to occur, some connection needs to be made with the structures for emotional processing. Evidence for such a connection was found in the primate brain, where the mirror neuron system and the limbic system are anatomically connected by the insula, suggesting that a large-scale network could be at the heart of the ability to empathize. As we mentioned in Chapter 10, a large body of research suggests that the brain regions supporting our emotional states are also activated when we perceive these emotional states in other people. For example, in humans, a series of experiments has found that the *experience* of disgust and the *perception* of facial expressions of disgust activate similar regions within the anterior insula. In fact, the magnitude of insula activation when observing facial expressions of disgust increases with the intensity of the other person's facial expression of disgust (Phillips et al., 1997; Figure 13.10). A subsequent fMRI study found that when people inhaled odorants that produce a feeling of disgust, the same sites in the anterior insula, and to a lesser extent the anterior cingulate cortex, were engaged as when they observed facial expressions of disgust (Wicker et al., 2003).

Consistent with these fMRI studies is one using depth electrodes that found some neurons in the anterior insula were fired when these patients viewed disgusted facial expressions (Krolak-Salmon et al., 2003). Finally, a single-patient case study of insula damage provides additional support for mirror neurons in the insula. After sustaining a lesion to the insula, this patient lost the ability to recognize disgust (Adolphs et al., 2003). Together, these studies suggest that the insula is important for experiencing disgust as well as for perceiving it in others.

In a pain study conducted by Tania Singer and her colleagues at University College London, fMRI revealed that the insula and anterior cingulate are activated when experiencing physical pain in oneself as well as when perceiving physical pain in others (T. Singer et al., 2004). The researchers examined brain activity when

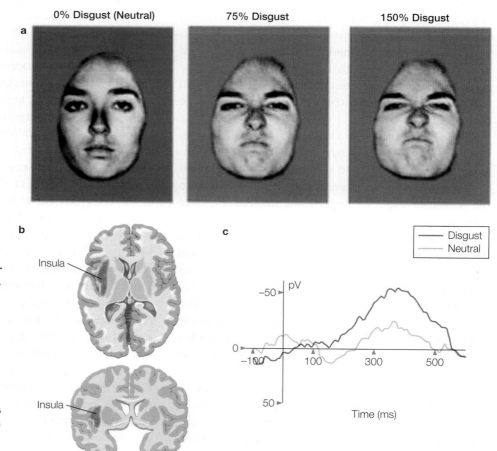

FIGURE 13.10 Exploring the neural regions responsive to disgust. (a) Computer morphing methods were used to generate a range of disgusted faces. A value of 100% (not shown) corresponds to a photo of someone showing actual disgust, 75% is a morphed version to show moderate disgust, and 150% is a morphed version showing extreme disgust. (b, c) As the expressions of disgust became more intense, the BOLD response in the insula increased.

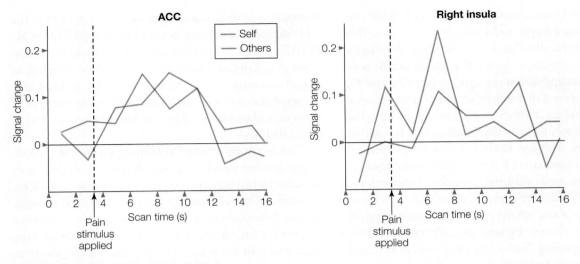

FIGURE 13.11 Study of empathy for pain.
Each participant watched as a partner's hand received a shock through a set of electrodes. Brain activity was very similar for one's own pain and the pain of the partner, and the degree of brain activation was correlated with empathy.

participants received painful stimulation through an electrode on their hand or saw the painful stimulation delivered through an electrode to a romantic partner's hand (Figure 13.11). Although the experience of pain activated a larger network of brain structures, both the experience of pain and the perception of a loved one's pain activated the anterior insula, adjacent frontal operculum, and anterior cingulate. Furthermore, participants who scored high on a questionnaire that measured their degree of empathy showed the greatest activation in the insula and anterior cingulate when perceiving pain in their romantic partners.

Additional evidence for shared activation comes from rare cases of patients who have had portions of their cingulate removed. Single-unit recordings have shown that the same neuron in the anterior cingulate fired both when the person was experiencing a painful stimulus and while anticipating or observing one (Hutchison et al., 1999).

The somatosensory cortex also appears to have a mirroring system. It is engaged when experiencing and observing painful touch (Avenanti et al., 2005) or nonpainful touch (Keysers et al., 2004, 2010). Consistent with these studies is an extensive study of lesion patients. Patients with damage to the somatosensory cortex were significantly impaired in their ability to identify another person's emotional state when compared to patients who had damage to other brain regions (Adolphs et al., 2000).

Together, these studies suggest that some regions of the brain become engaged when individuals experience an internal state and when they observe someone else experiencing that state. That sounds a lot like the kind of activity observed in mirror neurons.

How do we know who was feeling what? If the same brain regions are activated when we experience something or when we observe someone else having the same experience, how do we know who is feeling what? The answer is that we don't know, but a recent study has produced some interesting findings. Ryan Murray and his colleagues (2012) performed a meta-analysis of 23 fMRI and 2 PET studies that compared self-relevant processing against processing of close others and of public figures. The objective of the meta-analysis was to identify self-specific activations as well as activations that may permit differentiating between evaluation of close others and evaluation of people we have no connection with. Recall from Chapter 10 that the insula processes stimuli that arise from the body and mediates the conscious awareness of the physiological condition of the body (known as interoceptive awareness). The insula also performs other functions, such as affective evaluation (e.g., as in our previous discussion of disgust). Murray and colleagues found that the anterior insula is activated when appraising and processing information about the self as well as when appraising and processing close others, but not when appraising and processing public figures. Based on this finding, these researchers suggest that when we appraise ourselves and close others, we share a conscious mental representation that is internal, visceral, and actually felt physiologically. Known as embodied awareness, this mental representation affects each person's emotional perspective. This result would support the idea that we garner knowledge of close others based on our embodied experience of those people.

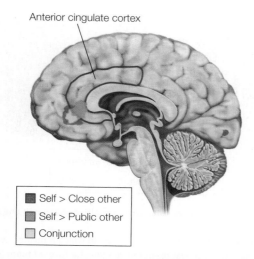

Anterior cingulate cortex

- ■ Self > Close other
- ■ Self > Public other
- □ Conjunction

FIGURE 13.12 Regions activated when performing a task relevant to public figures were more dorsal than, and significantly dissociated from, activations associated with tasks monitoring both close others and self. Activation for public figures was mostly in the left superior frontal gyrus, while activation for close other centered in the left VMPFC. Self activation was found in the right VMPFC.

Self-specific processing was found in regions of the vACC and dACC that were not active when appraising close others and public figures (Figure 13.12). The dACC has been described as an effortful, goal-directed mechanism for allocating and regulating attention; it also responds to self-related stimuli and engages in self-reflection and action monitoring (Schmitz & Johnson, 2007). Murray and his colleagues further suggest that, acting as an affective and cognitive evaluation and monitoring unit, certain regions of dACC and vACC specialize in self-specific processing by selecting representations and mental attributes that fit an individual's own personality. From these, representations which fit that person's self-concept are constructed.

They also found that within the MPFC were differential activations for self, close other, and public other. Activation for the self was clustered primarily in the right VMPFC; activation for close other was clustered primarily in the left VMPFC, including some shared activation differentially engaging the VMPFC according to the level of relatedness. Activation for public other was significantly dissociated from both these regions, demonstrating greater dorsal MPFC activation in the left superior frontal gyrus. Thus it appears that activations across different regions of the brain differentiate who is feeling what.

Modulation of empathic responses. After recognizing the distinction between ourselves and the other person, we somehow need to monitor our response. For instance, a doctor or dentist needs to understand that his patient is in pain, but neither he nor his patient wants him to be incapacitated by sharing it; the patient wants him to go about

the business of relieving it. Jean Decety (reviewed in Decety, 2011) and his colleagues have proposed a model that includes stimulus-driven processing of affective sharing (discussed earlier, in the section about inferring other people's thoughts) and goal-directed processing. In this model, the perceiver's motivation, intentions, and self-regulation influence the extent of an empathic experience, as well as the likelihood of behavior that benefits others.

One example of evidence for goal-directed regulation was an inventive experiment conducted by Decety and his colleagues in Taiwan. They hypothesized that regions typically associated with perceptions of physical pain would not be activated in acupuncturists, whose jobs require them to detach themselves from the painful aspect of administering acupuncture and instead focus on the long-term benefit to the patient (Cheng et al., 2007). To investigate this hypothesis, the researchers observed the brain activity of professional acupuncturists versus that of laypeople while they watched video clips depicting body parts receiving nonpainful stimulation (touch with cotton swab) or painful stimulation (acupuncture needles). Consistent with previous research, the study found that regions associated with the experience of pain, including the insula, anterior cingulate, and somatosensory cortex, were activated in nonexperts. In the acupuncturists, by contrast, these regions were not significantly activated— but regions associated with mental state attribution about others (discussed in the next section), such as the MPFC and rTPJ, were activated. Regions underpinning executive functions, self-regulation (dorsolateral and medial prefrontal cortex), and executive attention (precentral, superior parietal, and temporoparietal junction) also were activated. These findings suggest that activation of the mirror neuron system can be modulated by a goal-directed process that enhances flexible responses.

The researchers went on to study these acupuncturists by using ERPs (Decety et al., 2010), looking for the point when regulation of information processing occurs. Control participants had an early N100 differentiation between pain and no-pain conditions over the frontal area, and a late-positive potential around 300–800 ms over the centroparietal regions. Neither of these effects were detected in the physicians. It appears that in these physicians, emotional regulation occurs very early in the stimulus-driven processing of the perception of pain in others.

Tania Singer has studied whether fairness in social relations also affects empathy. That is, if you perceived someone as unfair, would you feel less empathy for them? For instance, would you feel the same when seeing a child trip and fall as when seeing the mugger who just grabbed your wallet trip and fall? In Singer's study (T. Singer et al., 2006), male and female participants played a card game (involving cash) with two confederates, one who cheated and the other who did not. Then she used fMRI to measure the participants' brain activity while they watched the confederates experiencing pain. Although both sexes had activation in the empathy-associated brain regions (frontoinsular and ACC) when watching the fair confederate receive pain, the empathy-induced activations in males were reduced significantly when seeing the cheater in pain. These reductions were actually accompanied by increased activation in the ventral striatum and nucleus accumbens, which are reward-associated areas. The males actually enjoyed seeing the cheater in pain. The degree of activation in the reward area correlated with an expressed desire for revenge, as indicated on a questionnaire that participants completed after the experiment. Singer points out that these findings suggest a neural foundation for social preferences: People value the gain positively if someone has gained something fairly, but not if it was gained unfairly. People (at least men) like cooperating with fair opponents, but they like punishing unfair ones.

What about sports rivalries? Mina Cikara wondered if the modulation of empathy seen on a personal level also applied at the group level (Cikara et al., 2011). For instance, when you watch a game between your favorite team (us) and a rival (them), what happens when you see your rivals fail? Do you feel good? How about when the opposing team scores? For her study, Cikara recruited avid fans of rival baseball teams: the Boston Red Sox and New York Yankees. While undergoing fMRI, participants viewed simulated figures representing the Red Sox or Yankees making baseball plays. In some plays the favored player was successful, and in others the rival was successful. Participants also viewed some control scenarios in which a player from a neutral team made plays against either the Red Sox or Yankees, or against another neutral team. After each play, participants rated the feelings of anger, pain, or pleasure they experienced while watching that play (Figure 13.13). Two weeks later,

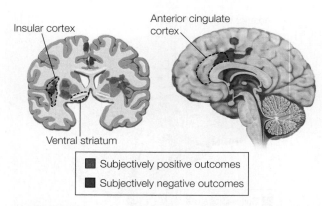

FIGURE 13.14 **Viewing subjectively positive outcomes engaged the ventral system.**
A subjectively positive outcome was one in which a favored team was successful or a rival team failed against a favored team. In this case, activations were seen in the ventral striatum, along with the left middle frontal and superior frontal gyrus, left insula, bilateral caudate, and SMA. A subjectively negative outcome was the opposite and activated the ACC, SMA, and the right insula.

the participants filled out a questionnaire that asked them to rate the likelihood that they would heckle, insult, throw food, threaten, shove, or hit a rival fan (i.e., either a Yankee or Red Sox fan) or hit an Orioles fan (the team that played in the control games).

Viewing subjectively positive plays (when the rival team failed) increased the response in the ventral striatum, whereas failure of the favored team and success of the rival team activated the ACC and insula (Figure 13.14) and correlated with the pain rating (Figure 13.15). Note that seeing an animated hypothetical baseball play elicited the same pain response in a diehard baseball fan as when participants (in previous studies) watched a close other undergo a painful experience! As in the Singer study discussed earlier, the ventral striatum reward effect correlated with the self-reported likelihood of aggression against the fan of the rival team. Thus, the response to a rival groups' misfortune is neural activation associated with pleasure (aka schadenfreude—enjoyment of others' troubles), which is correlated with endorsing harm against those groups.

Neural Correlates of Mental State Attribution

Sometimes mental states don't match their observable cues. Consider a situation in which you ask someone out on a date. She declines, smiles, and tells you that she has a prior engagement. Now what do you do? How do you know whether she truly has other plans, or whether she is just making a plausible excuse and smiling to be kind? Her true preference may be that she wants to go out, but

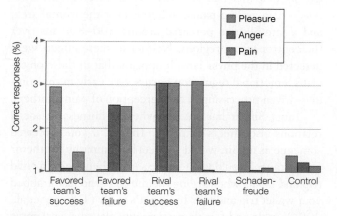

FIGURE 13.13 **The bars indicate the average ratings for pleasure, anger, and pain for the success or failure of favored or rival teams.**

as the fusiform face area (Chapter 6) and the role of the amygdala in using the face to make social judgments (Chapter 10). Research has also shown that attention to the direction of eye gaze is an important source of nonverbal information about another person's attentional state.

Within their first year of life, children develop **joint attention**, the ability to monitor another person's attention. One of the most typical ways that children monitor where other people are directing their attention is by noting the direction of their eye gaze. Humans are the only primates that follow eye gaze rather than the direction of where the head is pointing. We humans can tell where the eye is gazing because of the large "whites of our eyes" that no other primate possesses (Kobayashi & Kohshima, 2001). Michael Tomasello and his colleagues (2007) suggest that eyes evolved a new social function in human evolution: supporting cooperative (mutualistic) social interactions. Eye gaze may also be helpful for understanding when people's words may not match their mental states. For example, when your prospective date declines your invitation, does she make eye contact while turning you down? Or does she avoid your gaze so that you cannot see her true feelings? What neural systems support the ability to attend to another person's eye gaze and use this information to reason about their mental state?

One of the earliest lines of research examining this question comes from single-cell recording studies in monkeys. David Perrett of the University of St. Andrews in Scotland discovered that cells in the superior temporal sulcus (STS) are helpful for identifying head position and gaze direction. The STS lies below the superior temporal gyrus and above the middle temporal gyrus. Amazingly, some cells responded to head position while others responded to gaze direction. Although head position and direction of eye gaze are often consistent, the ability to distinguish head position from eye gaze opens the door for using these cues to make inferences about mental states. Individuals who turn their head in the same direction as their gaze may be thinking something very different from individuals who keep their head facing forward but direct their gaze in a different direction.

Converging evidence showing that the STS is important for interpreting eye gaze in relation to mental states comes from human neuroimaging studies. Kevin Pelphrey and his colleagues at Duke University examined whether activity in the STS depended on the mental states indicated by shifts of eye gaze in another person. Participants watched an animated woman, who directed her attention either toward or away from a checkerboard that appeared and flickered in her left or right visual field (Figure 13.19). Randomly, the figure took either 1 or

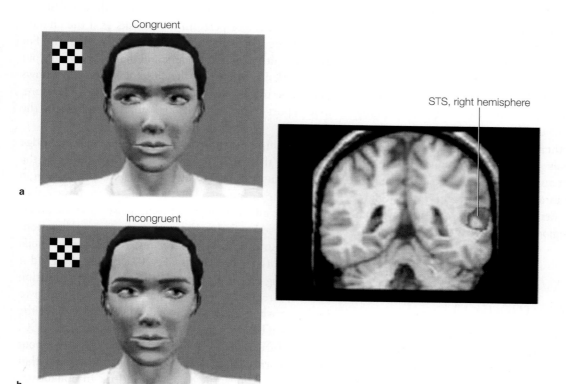

FIGURE 13.19 Participants viewed a virtual-reality character whose eye gaze moved either **(a)** in a congruent manner toward a flashing checkerboard or **(b)** in an incongruent manner away from a flashing checkerboard. The superior temporal sulcus tracked the intention behind shifts in eye gaze rather than all shifts in eye gaze.

3 seconds to shift her gaze. If the STS is involved solely in tracking shifts in eye gaze, then it would be activated to the same degree in relation to any shift in eye gaze. If, however, the STS is involved in integrating shifts in eye gaze with mental states, then activation of the STS should be related to where the character directs her attention, because eye gaze shifted toward the checkerboard and eye gaze shifted away from the checkerboard would indicate two different mental states.

Consistent with the latter prediction, activity in a posterior region of the STS varied in relation to shifts in eye gaze direction (Pelphrey et al., 2003). Gaze shifts to empty space evoked longer activation of the STS compared to when the gaze shifted to the checkerboard. The context of the gaze had an effect. The researchers conjectured that when the figure unexpectedly did not look at the target, observers were flummoxed and had to reformulate their expectation. This process takes longer, so STS activity was prolonged. The researchers found unexpectedly that STS activation was also related to the timing of the gaze. If the gaze shift occurred at 1 s after the checkerboard appeared, the context effect was seen; but if it took 3 s for the figure's gaze to shift, the effect was not seen. They proposed that when the time between the presentation of the checkerboard and the gaze shift was too long, the gaze shift was more ambiguous. The observer did not necessarily link it to the appearance of the checkerboard, and no expectations were violated when the gaze direction varied.

In a related study, a similar region in the STS was more strongly activated when a virtual-reality character made eye contact with the participant versus when the character averted his gaze from the participant (Pelphrey et al., 2004). Thus the STS appears to signal the focus of attention of another individual as well as provide important social signals: That individual may be trying to direct our attention away from a novel object or maybe wishing to engage in a social interaction. Interestingly, these studies also demonstrate that the activity in a visual processing region is sensitive to the context of the observed action.

Autism as a Window on the Role of Mental State Attribution

The study of autism provides a fascinating window into the important role of theory-of-mind abilities in navigating our social worlds. If theory-of-mind impairments are a central feature of autism, then we should see differences in many of the neural regions involved in person perception between autistic people and controls. Is this the case?

Anatomical studies suggest that a host of brain abnormalities are associated with autism. For example, Eric Courchesne and his colleagues at the University of San Diego have observed that infants with autism tend to have small head circumferences at birth, followed by an abrupt inflation of the head circumference in the first year of life (Courchesne & Pierce, 2005a). Brain abnormalities persist over the course of development, and studies suggest that autism is associated with reduced volume in a range of brain areas, including the frontal lobes, STS, amygdala, cerebellum, and hippocampus.

Changes in anatomy are accompanied by changes in connectivity. The researchers observed hyperconnectivity within the frontal lobe regions and decreased long-range connectivity and reciprocal interactions with other cortical regions (Courchesne & Pierce, 2005b). Aside from these anatomical changes, autism has been associated with abnormal function in a number of regions associated with person perception, including the MPFC, amygdala, FFA (discussed in Chapter 6), STS, anterior insula, and TPJ. It has become apparent that no single brain region, or even a single system, is responsible for the behaviors of autistic individuals. Although different brain regions support our ability to make sense of other people's minds and visible cues, the study of autism suggests that they function as a network.

False-belief tasks are particularly challenging for children with autism. Even when they are well past the age when most children are able to solve these problems, autistic individuals perform these tasks as if the characters have access to all of the information in the story. For example, although they understand that Sally initially put the marble in the basket, they also act as if Sally knows that Anne moved the marble to the drawer. Therefore, they report that Sally will look for the marble in the drawer.

Michael Lombardo and his colleagues at Cambridge looked for the specific neural systems responsible for the impairments in representing mental state information in autism. They examined whether deficits are observed in processing information about both the self and the other, and they tried to find out how, or if, the atypical functioning of these neural systems relates to variation in social impairment (Lombardo et al., 2011). They designed a mentalizing task—a task that elicited robust activation of all the regions within the standard circuit known to be active when a nonautistic individual thinks about the thoughts of both the self and others: the MPFC, the PCC, and the bilateral TPJ. In answering the question about which neural system was responsible, they found that the rTPJ functioned atypically in autism. In nonautistic individuals, the rTPJ was selectively more responsive to thinking about thoughts than physical judgments (both in the self and other conditions). But in autistic individuals, the rTPJ was less responsive, and specialization was completely absent. This lack of selectivity correlated with the degree of social impairment. Put another way, the less selective the rTPJ response, the more impaired that individual was in representing the mental states of others (i.e., mindblindness).

False-belief tasks often give participants information about other people's mental states; but as mentioned earlier, in real life we are often left to infer these states from nonverbal cues such as facial expression and eye gaze. People with autism, however, don't pay attention to eye gaze as much as nonautistic individuals do (Spezio et al., 2007). Why is that? Some researchers have suggested that people with autism may avoid the eye gaze of others because they find eye contact unpleasant (Dalton et al., 2005). A recent study from Finland (Kylliäinen et al., 2012) combined EEG with skin conductive responses to explore whether frontal EEG asymmetry, as a measure of approach–avoidance brain activity, could clarify whether another person's direct gaze is arousing or aversive to individuals with autism. These researchers found that a direct gaze with either normally open eyes or wide-open eyes (Figure 13.20) evoked neither avoidance-related brain responses nor approach responses in children with autism spectrum disorder (ASD). They did note, however, that autonomic arousal to faces increased as a function of the amount of sclera (white of the eye) visible in the direct gaze. This differed from the response of normally developing children for whom the normally open eyes evoked an approach response and wide-open eyes an avoidance response, but whose intensity of arousal was constant. This reaction is not so surprising when you look at the expressions (Figure 13.20) and recall that in facial expressions of fear, more of the sclera is visible (Chapter 10).

These findings do not support the suggestion that direct gaze is an aversive stimulus for children with autism (Kylliäinen et al., 2012). In fact, they support an alternate hypothesis proposed by Ami Klin and his colleagues at Yale University (2002b). Individuals with autism may fail to recognize the importance of eye gaze as a cue for understanding their social worlds. When watching the movie *Who's Afraid of Virginia Woolf?* (Figure 13.21), nonautistic individuals spent much of their viewing time paying attention to the characters' faces and eyes to gain understanding of their intentions and feelings. In contrast, autistic individuals fixated on mouths, bodies, and objects. Therefore, perhaps individuals with autism do not automatically distinguish eye gaze as an especially meaningful cue for perceiving other people.

Additional support for this explanation comes from several studies showing that autistic individuals exhibit significantly less activation in the STS when performing theory-of-mind tasks (see Frith, 2003, for a review). Instead, they exhibit activation in this region for a broader range of conditions. What happens when autistic individuals do the checkerboard task described in Figure 13.19? Not surprisingly, they show increased STS activation to *any* shift in eye gaze rather than specifically in response to eye gaze to unexpected locations.

The failure to pay attention to eye gaze can also be partially accounted for by the smaller amygdala size that is characteristic of autism. Recall from Chapter 10 that amygdala size correlates with attention to the eyes of other people. The smaller a person's amygdala is, the less likely that individual is to attend to the eyes of another person (Nacewicz et al., 2006).

Together, these studies suggest that in the brains of individuals with autism, the neural regions associated with person perception are not activated in the same way as in the brains of individuals without autism. It appears, then, that sometimes autism is associated with reduced function or volume in select brain regions, and sometimes

FIGURE 13.20 Three eye conditions: eyes closed, eyes opened normally, and widely opened eyes.

a

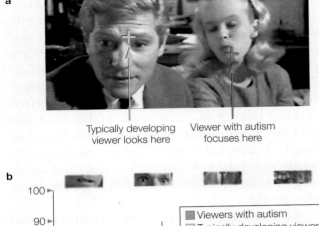

Typically developing   Viewer with autism
viewer looks here   focuses here

b

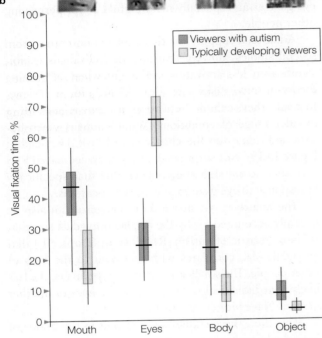

FIGURE 13.21 Study of eye gaze in healthy and autistic participants.
(a) The eye gaze of healthy participants is compared to that
of participants with autism while they are watching characters
in a film. (b) Healthy participants tend to focus on the eyes of
characters in a film. In comparison, participants with autism do
not show selective attention to the eyes in comparison to more
noninformative aspects of the face.

it is associated with more inclusive activation that is not
sensitive to subtle social cues (such as eye gaze specifically oriented toward an object of interest). Recently,
upon considering these various findings, researchers have
determined that ASD should be addressed by a systems-
level approach. With the realization that the brain is
made up of multiple, distinct, and interacting networks,
the complex symptomatology of ASD may become more
understandable.

It has been suggested that, on a systems level, autism
may affect the default brain network. As mentioned earlier in the chapter, the MPFC is part of a brain network
that has a higher level of metabolism at rest—and this

activity may reflect self-referential and social processing. The relation between autism and abnormalities in
MPFC function may also extend to this region's baseline
mode. When healthy participants engage in thinking
that takes their attention away from this self-referential
processing, they experience deactivation in the MPFC.
Participants with autism do not experience significantly
less activity in their MPFC when performing non-self-
referential tasks (D. P. Kennedy et al., 2006). That is,
no change in activation takes place between "resting"
and doing an active task. Is this because the default network is always on, or because it is always off? These researchers point out that PET studies are consistent with
the always-off conclusion. Interestingly, participants
with ASD report very different types of thoughts when
their mind is at rest: Two out of three reported seeing
only images but no internal speech, feelings, or bodily
sensations. None of them had ever even thought about
their inner experience. The third appeared to have no
inner thoughts at all, but merely described what his current actions were (Hurlburt et al., 1994). Kennedy and
his colleagues speculated that an absence of this resting
activity in autism may be directly related to their differences in internal thought.

These researchers have since found that in some
cases, the extent of these resting abnormalities correlates with the severity of autistic social impairments.
They propose that one cause of autism may be unusually low metabolic rates in medial frontal cortex (D. P.
Kennedy & Courchesne, 2008; Kennedy et al., 2006).
If this proposal were true, we could infer that the social
deficits seen in autistic individuals are partially due to
their brains not being constantly prepared for the type
of social thought that marks normal cognition. Some
evidence does support this notion. When given explicit
instructions to use a social process (e.g., pay attention
to the faces), specific brain regions were activated in
high-functioning autistic individuals. Unlike control
participants, people with ASD did not exhibit activation in the same regions when given vague instructions
in a social task (e.g., pay attention). Thus, people with
ASD may fail to engage instinctively in social processing, but they can when explicitly instructed to do so.
Possibly, they do not experience the constant impulse to
view most events through a social lens (D. P. Kennedy &
Courchesne, 2008; A. T. Wang et al., 2007).

Jason Mitchell (2011) has suggested that if autistic individuals truly are unencumbered by intensive
social processing, then they are freer to attend to objects and other nonsocial aspects of the environment.
Indeed, that is exactly where autistic individuals excel.
Many people with ASD are unusually adept in visuospatial and other nonsocial domains, such as exceptional

survived. The result, however, does not stop others from moralizing. Simon notes:

> Sometimes someone who thinks what I did was unacceptable will come up and verbally assault me. The rope between two climbers is symbolic of trust and to cut it is viewed as a selfish act. What's important is that Joe didn't think that, and the first thing he did when he crawled back into camp was to thank me for trying to get him down.

Although Joe wrote that Simon did what he would have done in the same situation, Yates was ostracized by much of the mountaineering community.

To save his own life, Simon broke the moral code of the mountaineering community. Do you think he was justified in further endangering someone else's life to save his own? Simon and Joe's story is certainly an extreme case, but it illustrates the reality that social behavior is shaped by multiple influences. To negotiate our social worlds successfully, we must not only understand the rules for appropriate behavior, but make choices consistent with those rules. In this section, we consider questions about social knowledge and its use in decision making. How do we know which aspects of knowledge to apply to a particular situation? If our own interests conflict with societal norms, deciding how to proceed can be difficult. What can the brain systems used to make these sorts of decisions tell us about this psychological process?

Representations of Social Knowledge

One of the most complicated aspects of social behavior is the lack of straightforward rules. The very same behavior that is appropriate in one context may be wildly inappropriate in another. For example, hugging a close friend is an act of affection, but hugging a stranger may be considered intrusive. And should you hug someone you are getting to know better but do not yet consider a close friend? Or how about that guy you have a crush on? When is it appropriate to greet a person with a hug? Social cognitive neuroscientists are just beginning to research the neural systems that help us make these decisions. Current research findings suggest that the frontal lobes are important for taking into account the particular situation in order to apply the appropriate rules.

Orbitofrontal cortex Patients with **orbitofrontal cortex (OFC)** damage have the most difficulty when they need to draw on their social knowledge to make sense of social interactions. In one fascinating line of work, Valerie Stone and her colleagues developed a social faux pas task that measures a person's ability to reason about the world. The task presents participants with a series of scenarios in which one of the characters commits a social faux pas by accidentally saying something impolite. One scenario tells the story of Jeannette and Anne. Anne receives a vase as a wedding gift from Jeannette. A year later, Anne has forgotten that the vase was from Jeannette. Jeannette accidentally breaks the vase while at Anne's house. Anne tells Jeannette not to worry because it was a wedding gift that she never liked anyway. The researchers then measure social reasoning by asking participants to identify whether someone in this scenario made a social mistake, and if so, why. Stone and her colleagues gave this test to patients with orbitofrontal damage, patients with lateral prefrontal cortex damage, and healthy control participants (Stone et al., 1998).

In comparison to all other participants, patients with orbitofrontal damage did not perform as well on the test, thus demonstrating a decreased ability to apply their social knowledge to the scenarios (Table 13.1). Patients with orbitofrontal damage understood that a character like Jeannette would feel bad about breaking the vase, but they did not understand that Anne's comment about

TABLE 13.1 Detection of Errors on Faux Pas Task

Group Tested	Detected Faux Pas (n = 10 problems)
DFC patients	
L.S.	10
R.T.	10
O.A.	10
W.E.	10
Mean	10
OFC patients	
D.H.	9
M.R.	6
R.V.	7
R.M.	8
R.B.	10
Mean	8
Anterior temporal control	
B.G.	10
Normal controls	
Mean	10

Source. From Stone et al., 1998.

not liking the vase actually was intended to reassure Jeannette. Instead, they often believed that Anne had intended to hurt Jeannette's feelings. The patients with orbitofrontal damage were not as able to take the context into account when reasoning about the social mistakes. These results suggest that orbitofrontal damage impairs the ability to use social knowledge to reason about social interactions.

A series of studies conducted by Jennifer Beer provides some important clues that orbitofrontal cortex supports appropriate social behavior (Beer et al., 2003, 2006). In her study reported earlier in the chapter, patients with orbitofrontal damage, patients with lateral prefrontal damage, and healthy controls took part in a structured conversation with a stranger. Compared to the other participants, patients with orbitofrontal damage were likely to introduce impolite conversation topics. Before beginning the social interaction task, however, all the participants reported that it was inappropriate to discuss emotional and personal information with strangers. The patients with orbitofrontal damage were unaware that their actual social behavior violated these social rules for conversations with a stranger.

This lack of awareness may be especially problematic because it makes it difficult for patients with orbitofrontal damage to feel embarrassment that might motivate them to behave differently in the future. In another study (Beer et al., 2003), patients with orbitofrontal damage and healthy control participants took part in a teasing task that required them to make up nicknames for an experimenter they did not know well. Healthy control participants were careful to come up with flattering nicknames and to apologize for having to tease someone they did not know well. In contrast, patients with orbitofrontal damage offered unflattering nicknames and were likely to announce them in a singsong voice more often used for teasing someone you know well. The orbitofrontal patients were not embarrassed by their inappropriate teasing; instead, they reported feeling especially proud of their social behavior.

Without awareness of their social mistakes, patients with orbitofrontal damage never generate the emotional feedback they need to change their future behavior. When we do something that makes us feel embarrassed, we don't like that feeling and are strongly motivated to avoid feeling that way again. When we do something that makes us feel proud, however, we are likely to repeat the action in order to continue the good feeling. These findings suggest that even though patients with orbitofrontal damage report an understanding of social rules, they do not apply this knowledge to their own social interactions (Figure 13.25). They are also unlikely to

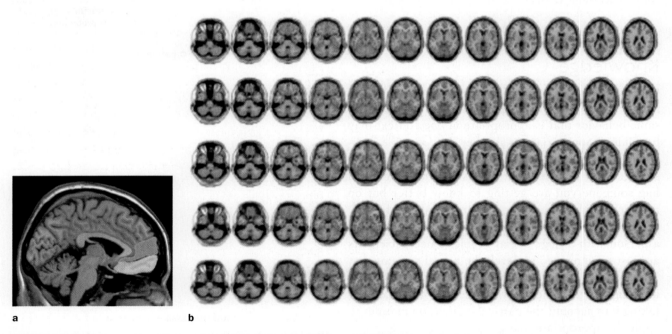

a b

FIGURE 13.25 Patients with orbitofrontal damage may lack insight into their behavior at a particular moment while maintaining accurate summaries of their traits. **(a)** The orbitofrontal cortex (yellow) lies just beneath the medial prefrontal cortex region (green) associated with the summaries of personality traits. **(b)** Typical orbitofrontal damage. Damage is indicated in red. Each row represents ascending brain slices beginning on the left, with the most superior slice to the far right, of a single patient. The bottom row is a composite of the findings from all the patients, indicating the extent of overlap in the location of lesions. Red indicates 75–100% overlap, green 50–75%, blue 25–50%, and pink 0–25%.

spontaneously recognize that their behavior is inappropriate, because they lack self-insight and do not generate the social emotions needed to correct their social mistakes in future social interactions.

Adult patients who have sustained orbitofrontal damage and behave inappropriately can retain intact social knowledge about what is proper—that is, social rules—but they appear to have trouble learning new social knowledge. This view is supported by case studies of orbitofrontal damage sustained in childhood. These patients also have inappropriate social behavior; but, in contrast to patients who receive this damage in adulthood, they do not understand social rules because they had not learned them before being injured (S. W. Anderson et al., 1999). This finding suggests that the orbitofrontal cortex is important for learning social knowledge as well as applying it to specific social interactions.

Using Social Knowledge to Make Decisions

The research described in the preceding discussion suggests that the orbitofrontal cortex is important for both learning social knowledge and using it in relevant situations. Even if we know the rules for a given social situation, we still have to decide what to do to ensure that we abide by the rules. Consider the following scenario. When you go to a friend's house for a party, you know that there are certain rules for being a polite guest. These rules may help you avoid inappropriate behavior, but they do not always point to one specific behavioral choice. For example, you can do a number of things and still be polite. Do you hug someone you are introduced to, or just shake their hand? Do you get something to eat now, or wait until later? Do you mention that you are a vegetarian, or just eat what you can without mentioning it? How do we make decisions about our social behavior? What are the brain mechanisms that support decision making using social knowledge?

Patients with ventromedial prefrontal cortex damage are notoriously poor at making social decisions. (Here the ventromedial prefrontal cortex includes the medial OFC.) Early research attempting to identify and understand the function of the brain regions involved with social decision making gave gambling tasks to VMPFC patients. These patients had a difficult time making decisions when the outcome was uncertain. Leslie Fellows and Martha Farah (2007) wondered, however, if this difficulty was specific to decisions involving uncertainty, or if it reflected a general difficulty in assessing the relative value of options. In the experiment discussed earlier, where the task was a simple preference judgment between two options of colors, actors, or food, we learned that the VMPFC

damage impairs value-based decision making even when no uncertainty exists.

In Chapter 10, we learned that people with OFC damage are unable to respond to changing patterns of reward and punishment. That is, they can learn that a stimuli is rewarding (its value), but when it becomes punishing (the value changes), they still choose it. Thus **reversal learning** does not take place, and individuals with OFC damage don't learn from a negative experience. To learn from experience, we must be able to change behavior as a result of unexpected negative feedback. Thus, in a social situation, sometimes hugging someone is appropriate and you get a hug back—positive feedback that your behavior was okay. Sometimes, however, the hug is not appropriate and the person stands frozen in your embrace. If your behavior unexpectedly receives the cold shoulder, you feel embarrassed, and you are guided by that negative feedback to change your behavior. When we consider that the VMPFC is involved in coding stimulus value, it seems odd that patients with VMPFC lesions can selectively learn a stimulus value initially, but not when the stimulus value is reversed. Geoffrey Schoenbaum and his colleagues found in rats that although the OFC may be critical in reversal learning, it is not because it flexibly represents positive and negative value. They found that the better the reversal learning, the less flexible the OFC value coding was. It appeared to them that the OFC does not code stimulus value, but signals the amygdala when the value expectation is violated (Schoenbaum et al., 2007).

Following this idea, Elizabeth Wheeler and Lesley Fellows (2008) investigated whether positive and negative feedback of stimulus value expectation influences behavior through separate and distinct neural mechanisms. The study participants were patients with damage to the ventromedial frontal lobe (VMF, a term the researchers used to refer to the region encompassing both medial OFC and adjacent ventral medial PFC), healthy controls, and patients with dorsolateral frontal (DLF) damage. The researchers asked the participants to do a probabilistic learning task with positive and negative feedback while undergoing fMRI. They found that VMF damage selectively disrupted the ability to learn from negative feedback, but not from positive feedback. The controls and patients with DLF damage performed equally and were able to learn from both positive and negative feedback: This evidence suggests two distinct neural mechanisms.

These researchers point out that these findings are consistent with much of the literature that implicates the VMF in reversal learning, extinction, fear conditioning, regret, and envy. The results, however, are hard to reconcile with the previous study by Fellows discussed

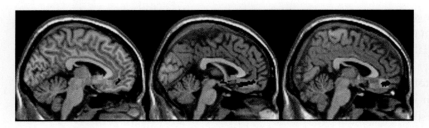

FIGURE 13.26 Cortical atrophy in frontotemporal lobar degeneration patients with social disorder (shown in blue) overlaps with brain regions that are seen to activate in fMRI studies of healthy adults undertaking judgments of negative social scenarios (shown in orange).

earlier (and findings in neuroeconomics that we discuss in the next section), suggesting that this region represents relative reward value and preferences. Perhaps, as the researchers propose, the VMF may carry representations of the expected (relative) reward value not to guide choice per se, but to serve as a benchmark to compare outcomes against. When the outcomes are negative and unexpectedly fail to match expectations, the VMF enables avoidance learning. Perhaps, as suggested by Geoffrey Schoenbaum and his colleagues (2007), this process takes place not directly, but indirectly by signaling to the amygdala and other regions to form new associative representations that may flexibly change their behavior. This proposal would suggest that in patients where the VMF is not functioning, no benchmark is provided, no outcomes are being compared, no negative feedback is generated, and no reversal learning can take place. A bad social experience has no effect. The positive feedback system is intact, however, and learning can take place through positive feedback.

Can we apply this finding to social judgments? For instance, when you expect a hug back and don't get one, is your OFC activated? Penn State researchers specifically addressed the role of VMPFC in the interpretation of negatively valenced feedback during social decision making (Grossman et al., 2010). They matched healthy controls with patients who had VMPFC degeneration due to frontotemporal lobar degeneration (FTLD). These patients make socially inappropriate comments, engage in socially unacceptable behavior, and often show little insight into the effects of these behaviors despite their social (and sometimes legal) consequences. The participants first judged 20 social situations (e.g., cutting into the ticket line at a movie theater) or minor infractions of the law (rolling through a red light at 2 a.m.) on a scale of 1 to 5 for social acceptability. These scenarios were then given contingencies that were either negatively biased (e.g., rolling through a red light at 2 a.m. *when a police car is at the intersection*) or positively biased (e.g., rolling through a red light at 2 a.m. *when rushing a sick child to the emergency room*). This time, participants were asked to judge according to two randomly presented instructions: "Should everyone

do this all of the time?" (rule-based condition) or "Is this generally okay?" (similarity-based condition). This manipulation was intended to ferret out differences that could be due to insensitivity to perceived legal and social rules. No differences were noted in the performance of the FTLD patients.

Although both the FTLD patients and the healthy adults rated the positively biased scenarios as equally acceptable, they rated the negatively biased scenarios differently. The FTLD patients judged negative scenarios to be more acceptable than the healthy adults judged them to be. When healthy adults judged these negative social scenarios, significantly greater activation occurred in their VMPFC than when they judged the positive social scenarios—the very region of cortical atrophy in FTLD patients (Figure 13.26). These studies support the hypothesis that VMPFC plays a crucial role in evaluating the negative consequences of social decision making.

As suggested in the previous section, the orbitofrontal cortex plays a strong role in applying social knowledge to our decisions in social settings. This region likely helps us choose the correct behaviors by supporting reversal learning through the evaluation of the negative consequences of social decisions. As the case of patient M.R. from the chapter opener suggests, the orbitofrontal cortex is helpful for recognizing when a hug is appropriate and when it is not.

Neuroeconomics

A recent perspective on the problem of how we make decisions using social knowledge comes from a new field called **neuroeconomics**. Neuroeconomics integrates psychology, neuroscience, economics, and computational models to yield an understanding of how people make value-based decisions (Rangel et al., 2008). Economic models of decision making assume that people should make rational decisions—those that maximize their rewards and minimize their losses. Specifically, rational decision making focuses on the choice that will reap the largest monetary outcomes. As we all know, however, people often don't make rational decisions, economic or otherwise. Recognizing that people do not always make decisions based on the greatest financial outcomes, these models have more recently begun to incorporate the role of emotional reactions that often arise in relation to concerns that are not financial. Some neuroeconomists propose that emotions may sometimes help people make optimal decisions by taking into account a wider range of consequences. These researchers are trying to create decision-making models that include cognitive and emotional variables driven by valuation of gains, losses, risks, and uncertainties.

Suppose you are given $50 and a chance to gamble with it. If you had either a guarantee of keeping $20 or a chance to gamble it all, which would you choose? What if you had a guarantee of losing $30 or a chance to gamble it all? Would you make a different choice then? Most people prefer to gamble when faced with a guaranteed loss, even when the monetary consequences of the guaranteed options are the same, as they are in the two bets outlined here (Figure 13.27). A guaranteed loss elicits a negative emotional response and makes people focus on any option that will help them avoid the guaranteed loss. Acting on emotion is detrimental, however,

because participants are not making decisions based on the actual monetary consequences. Benedetto De Martino and his colleagues at University College London (De Martino et al., 2006) conducted an fMRI study to understand the neural systems that underlie emotion-driven and rational decision making in this task. They found that participants who were misled by the loss frame tended to show activation in the amygdala. Orbitofrontal cortex activation was correlated with rational decision making. Specifically, participants who made decisions based on monetary principles had significantly more orbitofrontal cortex activation than did participants who based their decisions on emotion.

In the preceding example, emotion shaped participants' decision making in a detrimental manner. What about when we make financial decisions in the context of an interaction with another person? Some research suggests that emotions may lead to decision making that is financially irrational (because money will be lost) but beneficial for defending social reputation. One study examined decision making using the Ultimatum game (Sanfey et al., 2003). In the Ultimatum game, one player (P1) must split a sum of money with another player (P2).

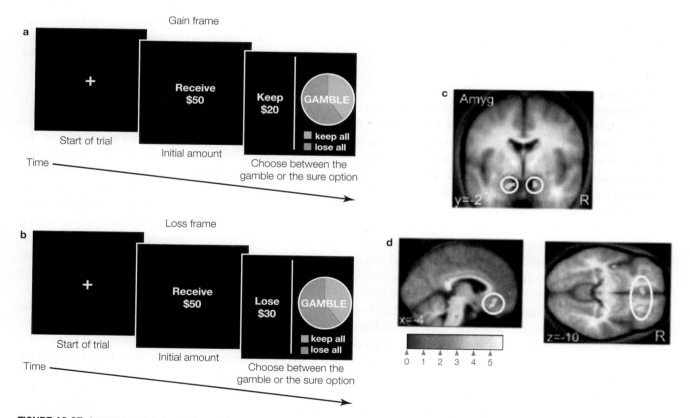

FIGURE 13.27 A gambling task in which participants can choose to gamble in the context of a guaranteed gain **(a)** or a guaranteed loss **(b)**. In both guaranteed cases, the outcome is the same; it is merely couched in different terms. **(c)** Participants who react to the condition of gain or loss rather than actual money amounts activate their amygdala when placing a bet. **(d)** Participants who bet on the basis of money amounts and are not swayed by a guaranteed gain versus loss activate their medial and lateral orbitofrontal cortex.

P1 offers a portion of the sum to P2 and P2 must decide to accept or reject the offer. The offers may be fair (e.g., very close to 50% for each person) or unfair (e.g., 80% for P1 and 20% for P2). If P2 rejects the offer, however, neither player gets any money.

In this study, the consideration of unfair offers was associated with dorsolateral prefrontal cortex and insula activity. Insula activity has often been associated with negative emotions such as disgust, anger, pain, and distress, suggesting that the participants experienced these emotions while considering the offer. What's more, increased insula activity during consideration of an unfair offer predicted a likelihood that the offer would be rejected. From a rational economic perspective, participants should not let their negative emotional reaction lead them to reject the unfair offer. Even if it is unfair, they can gain some money instead of no money. From a broader perspective, however, the negative emotional reaction leads participants to reject unfair offers that might otherwise compromise their social standing. If you continually accept less than your share, word may get around and people may begin to view you as deserving of less than an equal share. By rejecting the offer, you also punish the other player, who then also receives nothing. You may thus gain social standing by punishing unfair players.

In the Ultimatum game, P2 can only react to P1's offer. How does emotion help or hurt decision making when P2 has a more active role and has to speculate on the actions of P1? An fMRI study used the prisoner's dilemma game to test this question (Rilling et al., 2002). In the prisoner's dilemma game, participants again make decisions about how to divide a sum of money. Participants' winnings are determined by various combinations of their own decision to cooperate or betray their partners, and their partners' decisions to cooperate or betray them (e.g., combinations of whether each partner makes fair or unfair offers). The choice to cooperate is a double-edged sword; participants win the most if both players choose to cooperate, but lose the most if one player decides to cooperate and the other player decides to betray.

In this study, cooperation was related to areas associated with reward states, such as the nucleus accumbens, orbitofrontal cortex, anterior cingulate, and caudate nucleus. The authors suggest that this activation reflects a positive emotional experience that reinforces prosocial decision making.

It could be that being prosocial is its own reward, however. More recent investigations of the neural systems that underlie human prosociality consistently suggest that people experience prosocial acts as intrinsically rewarding. Help a stranger jump his car battery, and you get a little reward yourself and feel good. A rich and growing body of neuroscience research has reliably demonstrated that reward and subjective value rely on activity in mesolimbic dopaminergic targets—including the nucleus accumbens (NAcc) and OFC (Padoa-Schioppa & Assad, 2006; Rangel et al., 2008; Rolls, 2004; Tom et al., 2007). In humans and other animals, activity in these regions strongly correlates with the subjective value of a wide variety of reward types. These include primary rewards, such as food and juice, and secondary outcomes, such as monetary gains (Berns et al., 2001; Kable & Glimcher, 2007; Padoa-Schioppa & Assad, 2006; Schultz, 2002; Tom et al., 2007). (As described in Chapter 12, however, violations of expected value may be at the core of the brain activity, rather than value per se.) Surprisingly, even in the absence of direct, first-person rewards, these same regions are also activated by prosocial outcomes. For example, the NAcc responds robustly when a person is rewarded with money as well as when that person simply watches someone else win a cash reward he has gained fairly (Mobbs et al., 2009). This evidence suggests that perceivers experience positive outcomes for another person to be rewarding in their own right. Now you know why people like watching game shows. Along the same lines, similar patterns of neural response have been observed when one person agrees with others, suggesting that individuals experience interpersonal consensus as intrinsically rewarding (Klucharev et al., 2009). In both cases, these activations were observed even though participants received no immediate reward other than the prosocial outcomes associated with positive social events.

Moral Decisions

Neuroeconomics focuses on financial decisions, but the relative contributions of emotion and cognition have also been theorized to support other kinds of social decision making. How do we resolve moral dilemmas like the one that Simon Yates faced on the Siula Grande climb? What can the brain tell us about this process? Are we relying on emotion or on cognitive computations? For discussion of the implications of the relationships among brain function, moral judgment, and criminal behavior, see "The Cognitive Neuroscientist's Toolkit: Neuroethics."

Simon's dilemma is a real-life example of the classic trolley dilemma in philosophy. In this problem, a conductor loses control of his trolley car (Figure 13.28). As a witness to this event, you can see that, if nothing is done, five people are likely to be killed because they are directly in the path of the speeding trolley. You can throw a switch and divert the trolley onto another track. This option, however, comes at the cost of ensuring the death of a single construction worker who is on the alternate track. Do you throw the switch or not? Now consider the footbridge dilemma. This time you are standing next

a

b

FIGURE 13.28 The trolley and footbridge problems.
Would you be willing to sacrifice one life to save five lives? Would your decision be different if you had to **(a)** pull a switch to direct a trolley toward one person or **(b)** physically push a person off a footbridge into the path of a trolley car? Research suggests that the strong emotional response to actually pushing someone would make you decide differently in these two scenarios.

to a large stranger on a footbridge that crosses over the tracks. You see an out-of-control trolley car speeding toward five people. This time, the only way to stop the trolley car is to push the person next to you off the footbridge onto the tracks to impede the movement of the trolley car. Do you push the stranger onto the tracks in order to save the other five people?

Most people agree that is acceptable to throw the switch in the trolley dilemma, but they find it immoral to push the stranger in the footbridge dilemma. In both cases, one person's life is sacrificed to save five others, so why do we make such different choices? Simon's dilemma on Siula Grande draws on aspects of both the trolley car and the footbridge dilemmas. We know already that Simon could not simply walk away from Joe while he was alive. Thus he was willing to put his life at great risk to try to save Joe's. When Joe's life was again threatened, Simon made the opposite decision to save his own life and cut the rope, even though he could be sending Joe to his death. Do you think Simon would have cut the rope if he had been looking right at Joe? What would you have done if you were in Simon's position on Siula Grande?

Joshua Greene and his colleagues at Princeton University (2004) argue that we make different choices in the trolley and footbridge dilemmas because the level of personal involvement in causing the single death differentially engages emotional decision making. If you throw a switch, you still maintain some distance from the death of the construction worker. When you actually push the stranger, you perceive yourself as more directly causing the death. Greene and his colleagues conducted a series of fMRI studies that contrasted moral dilemmas

involving high levels of personal engagement with dilemmas involving low levels of personal engagement (Greene et al., 2001, 2004). As predicted, personal dilemmas and impersonal dilemmas were associated with distinct patterns of activation. Across the studies, impersonal decisions were associated with greater activation in the right lateral prefrontal cortex and bilateral parietal lobe, areas associated with working memory (Chapter 9). In contrast, when participants chose options that required more personal effort, regions such as the medial frontal cortex, the posterior cingulate gyrus, and the amygdala were significantly activated. These regions have been associated with emotional and social cognitive processes. Together, these studies suggest that the differences in our moral decisions are related to the extent that we permit emotions to influence our decisions about what is morally acceptable.

TAKE-HOME MESSAGES

- Current models of the role of the orbitofrontal cortex in social decision making propose that this region helps individuals identify which social rules are appropriate for a given situation so that they may flexibly change their behavior.

- The field of neuroeconomics integrates psychology, neuroscience, and economics to yield an understanding of how people make decisions.

- Decision making—whether about social behavior, money, or morality—may rely on a combination of emotional and cognitive systems.

On July 10, 2003, William Safire of the *New York Times* coined the term *neuroethics* to refer to "the field of philosophy that discusses the rights and wrongs of the treatment of, or enhancement of, the human brain." In the past few years, the term has come to encompass how society will "deal with social issues of disease, normality, morality, lifestyle and the philosophy of living" as informed by our understanding of the underlying brain mechanisms (Gazzaniga, 2005).

Antisocial personality disorder (APD) is a mental illness characterized by utter disregard for social rules and the rights of others. It is almost always accompanied by violence, aggression, deceitfulness, impulsivity, and lack of remorse. Genetic research on twins who were reared apart reveals some genetic influences on APD and aggressive behavior (Rowe, 2001). Genetic influences, however, are not always sufficient to produce the behaviors associated with APD. Such behaviors are most often expressed when environmental influences are also present.

Evidence for this observation comes from research on adopted children. In a study of Swedish male adoptees, researchers determined that, when both genetic factors for violence and environmental factors encouraging violence were present, 40% of adoptees had engaged in criminal behavior. When genetic factors were present in the absence of environmental factors encouraging violence, only 12% of adoptees had committed illegal acts. The percentages dropped to 7% of adoptees when genetic factors were absent and only environmental factors remained, and to just 3% when neither environmental nor genetic factors were present.

Based on this evidence, Adriane Raine of the University of Pennsylvania (2002) proposed a biosocial model for the development of violent behavior (Figure 1). The model outlines how genetic and environmental dispositions for violence, as well as genetic and environmental protective factors against violence, can influence the likelihood of violent behavior. In effect, this model demonstrates the subtle interplay between nature and nurture. Raine and his colleagues employed a variety of imaging techniques to assess this model. By using positron emission tomography, they found that individuals with violent and antisocial histories had reduced glucose metabolism in the orbitofrontal cortex. In terms of structural abnormalities, people with APD have reduced volume of prefrontal gray matter when compared to both a normal and a substance dependent control group (Figure 2). These findings suggest that a dysfunctional orbitofrontal cortex—resulting from environmental factors, genetic

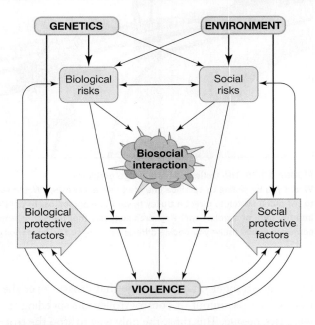

FIGURE 1 According to Adriane Raine's biosocial model of violence, both genetic and environmental factors are necessary for the behavioral result of violence.

factors, and the interaction of environmental and genetic factors—is associated with abnormal social behavior and violence.

The advances of neuroscience raise important ethical questions. APD is present in overwhelming proportions in the prison community (65%–80%). If such behavior has a neural correlate, then is the person at fault for committing

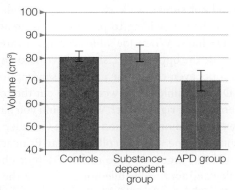

Prefrontal gray matter volume

FIGURE 2 In patients with antisocial personality disorder, the volume of cortex (gray matter) in the prefrontal region of the brain is significantly reduced from both a normal and a substance dependent control group.

ANATOMICAL ORIENTATION

The anatomy of consciousness

Cerebral cortex

Thalamus

Hypothalamus

Locus coeruleus

Pons

Reticular formation

Medulla oblongata

The cerebral cortex, the thalamus, the brainstem, and the hypothalamus are largely responsible for the conscious mind.

the sculptors of a civilized society? Do we ignore them to our peril? Is accountability what keeps us civilized, and should we be held accountable for our behavior? We close the chapter by looking at these questions.

Anatomical Orientation

The conscious mind primarily depends on three brain structures: the brainstem, including the hypothalamus; the thalamus; and the cerebral cortex (see the Anatomical Orientation box). When we look at the anatomical regions that contribute to consciousness, it is helpful to distinguish wakefulness from simple awareness and from more complex states. Neurologist Antonio Damasio has done this for us. First he makes the point that wakefulness is necessary for consciousness (except in dream sleep), but consciousness is not necessary for wakefulness. For example, patients in a vegetative state may be awake, but not conscious. Next he trims consciousness down to two categories: core consciousness and extended consciousness (Damasio, 1998). *Core consciousness* (or awareness)

is what goes on when the consciousness switch is flipped "on." The organism is alive, awake, alert, and aware of one moment: now, and in one place: here. It is not concerned with the future or the past. Core consciousness is the foundation for building increasingly complex levels of consciousness, which Damasio calls *extended consciousness*. Extended consciousness provides an organism with an elaborate sense of self. It places the self in individual historic time, includes thoughts of the past and future, and depends on the gradual buildup of an autobiographical self from memories and expected future experiences. Thus consciousness has nested layers of organizational complexity (Damasio & Meyer, 2008).

The Brainstem

The brain regions needed to modulate wakefulness, and to flip the consciousness "on" switch, are located in the evolutionarily oldest part of the brain, the brainstem. The primary job of brainstem nuclei is homeostatic regulation of the body and brain. This is performed mainly by nuclei in the *medulla oblongata* along with some input from the *pons.* Disconnect this portion of the brainstem, and the body dies (and the brain along with it). This is true for all mammals. Above the medulla are the nuclei of the pons and the mesencephalon. Within the pons is the *reticular formation* and the *locus coeruleus* (LC). The reticular formation is a heterogeneous collection of nuclei contributing to a number of neural circuits involved with motor control, cardiovascular control, pain modulation, and the filtering out of irrelevant sensory stimuli. Some nuclei influence the entire cortex via direct cortical connections, and some through neurons that comprise the neural circuits of the *reticular activating system* (RAS). The RAS has extensive connections to the cortex via two pathways. The dorsal pathway courses through the *intralaminar nucleus of the thalamus* to the cortex, and the ventral pathway zips through the *hypothalamus* and the *basal forebrain* and on to the cortex. The RAS is involved with arousal, regulating sleep–wake cycles, and mediating attention. Damage or disruption to the RAS can result in coma. Depending on the location, damage to the pons could result in locked-in syndrome, coma, a vegetative state, or death.

Arousal is also influenced by the outputs of the LC in the pons, which is the main site of norepinephrine production in the brain. The LC has extensive connections throughout the brain and, when active, prevents sleep by activating the cortex. With cell bodies located in the brainstem, it has projections that follow a route similar to that of the RAS up through the thalamus.

From the spinal cord, the brainstem receives afferent neurons involved with pain, interoception, somatosensory, and proprioceptive information as well as vestibular information from the ear and afferent signals from the thalamus, hypothalamus, amygdala, cingulate gyrus, insula, and prefrontal cortex. Thus, information about the state of the organism in its current milieu, along with ongoing changes in the organism's state as it interacts with objects and the environment, is all mediated via the brainstem.

The Thalamus

The neurons that connect the brainstem with the intralaminar nuclei (ILN) of the thalamus play a key role in core consciousness. The thalamus has two ILN, one on the right side and one on the left. Small and strategically placed bilateral lesions to the ILN in the thalamus turn core consciousness off forever, although a lesion in one alone will not. Likewise, if the neurons connecting the thalamic ILN and the brainstem are severed or blocked, so that the ILN do not receive input signals, core consciousness is lost.

We know from previous chapters that the thalamus is a well-connected structure. As a result, it has many roles

relating to consciousness. First, all sensory input, both about the body and the surrounding world (except smell, as we learned in Chapter 5), pass through the thalamus. This brain structure also is important to arousal, processing information from the RAS that arouses the cortex or contributes to sleep. The thalamus also has neuronal connections linking it to specific regions all over the cortex. Those regions send connections straight back to the thalamus, thus forming *connection loops*. These circuits contribute to consciousness by coordinating activity throughout the cortex. Lesions anywhere from the brainstem up to the cortex can disrupt core consciousness.

The Cerebral Cortex

In concert with the brainstem and thalamus, the cerebral cortex maintains wakefulness and contributes to selective attention. Extended consciousness begins with contributions from the cortex that help generate the core of self. These contributions are records from the memory bank of past activities, emotions, and experiences. Damage to the cortex may result in the loss of a specific ability, but not loss of consciousness itself. We have seen examples of these deficits in previous chapters. For instance, in Chapter 7, we came across patients with unilateral lesions to their parietal cortex: These people were not conscious of half of the space around them; that is, they suffered neglect.

===

TAKE-HOME MESSAGES

- The conscious mind primarily depends on three brain structures: the brainstem, including the hypothalamus; the thalamus; and the cerebral cortex.

- Core consciousness depends on the functions of the brainstem and thalamus. It occurs when an organism is alive, awake, alert, and solely aware of the current moment and place. It is the foundation for increasingly complex levels of consciousness.

- Extended consciousness depends on the cerebral cortex to provide an organism with an elaborate sense of self, to gradually build up from memories and expected future experiences, and to place the self in individual historic time.

===

Consciousness

The problem of consciousness, otherwise known as the mind–brain problem, was originally the realm of philosophers. The basic question is, how can a purely physical system (the body and brain) construct conscious intelligence (the mind)? In seemingly typical human fashion, philosophers have adopted dichotomous perspectives: **dualism** and **materialism**. Dualism, famously expounded by Descartes, states that mind and brain are two distinct and separate phenomena, and conscious experience is nonphysical and beyond the scope of the physical sciences. Materialism asserts that both mind and body are physical mediums and that by understanding the physical workings of the body and brain well enough, an understanding of the mind will follow. Within these philosophies, views differ on the specifics, but each side ignores an inconvenient problem. Dualism tends to ignore biological findings, and materialism overlooks the reality of subjective experience.

Notice that we have been throwing the word *consciousness* around without having defined it. Unfortunately, this has been a common problem and has led to much confusion in the literature. In both the 1986 and 1995 editions of the *International Dictionary of Psychology*, the psychologist Stuart Sutherland defined consciousness as follows:

Consciousness The having of perceptions, thoughts, and feelings; awareness. The term is impossible to define except in terms that are unintelligible without a grasp of what consciousness means. Many fall into the trap of equating consciousness with self-consciousness—to be conscious it is only necessary to be aware of the external world. Consciousness is a fascinating but elusive phenomenon: it is impossible to specify what it is, what it does, or why it evolved. Nothing worth reading has been written on it.

Harvard psychologist Steve Pinker also was confused by the different uses of the word: Some said that only man is conscious; others said that consciousness refers to the ability to recognize oneself in a mirror; some argued that consciousness is a recent invention by man or that it is learned from one's culture. All these viewpoints provoked him to make this observation:

Something about the topic of consciousness makes people, like the White Queen in *Through the Looking Glass*, believe six impossible things before breakfast. Could most animals really be unconscious—sleepwalkers, zombies, automata, out cold? Hath not a dog senses, affections, passions? If you prick them, do they not feel pain? And was Moses really unable to taste salt or see red or enjoy sex? Do children learn to become conscious in the same way that they learn to wear baseball caps turned around? People who write about consciousness are not crazy, so they must have something different in mind when they use the word. (Pinker, 1997, p. 133)

In reviewing the work of the linguist Ray Jackendoff of Brandeis University and the philosopher Ned Block

at New York University, Pinker pulled together a framework for thinking about the problem of consciousness in his book *How the Mind Works* (1997). The proposal for ending this consciousness confusion consists of breaking the problem of consciousness into three issues: self-knowledge, access to information, and sentience. Pinker summarized and embellished the three views as follows:

Self-knowledge: Among the long list of people and objects that an intelligent being can have accurate information about is the being itself. As Pinker said, "I cannot only feel pain and see red, but think to myself, 'Hey, here I am, Steve Pinker, feeling pain and seeing red!'" Pinker says that self-knowledge is no more mysterious than any other topic in perception or memory. He does not believe that "navel-gazing" has anything to do with consciousness in the sense of being alive, awake, and aware. It is, however, what most academic discussions have in mind when they banter about consciousness.

Access to information: Access awareness is the ability to report on the content of mental experience without the capacity to report on how the content was built up by all the neurons, neurotransmitters, and so forth, in the nervous system. The nervous system has two modes of information processing: conscious processing and unconscious processing. Conscious processing can be accessed by the systems underlying verbal reports, rational thought, and deliberate decision making and includes the product of vision and the contents of short-term memory. Unconscious processing, which cannot be accessed, includes autonomic (gut-level) responses, the internal operations of vision, language, motor control, and repressed desires or memories (if there are any).

Sentience: Pinker considers sentience to be the most interesting meaning of consciousness. It refers to subjective experience, *phenomenal awareness*, raw feelings, and the first person viewpoint—what it is like to be or do something. Sentient experiences are called **qualia** by philosophers and are the elephant in the room ignored by the materialists. For instance, philosophers are always wondering what another person's experience is like when they both look at the same color. In a paper spotlighting qualia, philosopher Thomas Nagel famously asked, "What is it like to be a bat?" (1974), which makes the point that if you have to ask, you will never know. Explaining sentience is known as the hard problem of consciousness. Some think it will never be explained.

By breaking the problem of consciousness into these three parts, cognitive neuroscience can be brought to bear on the topic of consciousness. Through the lens of cognitive neuroscience, much can be said about access

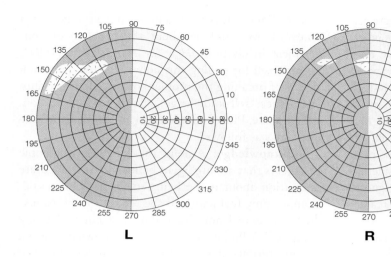

FIGURE 14.2 Blindsight.
Weiskrantz and colleagues reported the first case of blindsight in a patient with a lesion in the visual cortex. The hatched areas indicate preserved areas of vision for the left and right eyes for patient D.B.

to information and self-knowledge, but the topic of sentience remains elusive.

Conscious Versus Unconscious Processing and the Access of Information

We have seen throughout this book that the vast majority of mental processes that control and contribute to our conscious experience happen outside of our conscious awareness. An enormous amount of research in cognitive science clearly shows that we are conscious only of the content of our mental life, not what generates the content. For instance, we are aware of the products of mnemonic processing and the perceptual processing of imaging, not what produced the products. Thus, when considering conscious processes, it is also necessary to consider unconscious processes and how the two interact. A statement about conscious processing involves *conjunction*—putting together awareness of the stimulus with the identity, or the location, or the orientation, or some other feature of the stimulus. A statement about unconscious processing involves *disjunction*—separating awareness of the stimulus from the features of the stimulus such that even when unaware of the stimulus, participants can still respond to stimulus features at an above-chance level.

When Ned Block originally drew distinctions between sentience and access, he suggested that the phenomenon of blindsight provided an example where one existed without the other. **Blindsight**, a term coined by Larry Weiskrantz at Oxford University (1974; 1986), refers to the phenomenon that patients suffering a lesion in their visual cortex can respond to visual stimuli presented in the blind part of their visual field (Figure 14.2). Most interestingly, these activities happen outside the

realm of consciousness. Patients will deny that they can do a task, yet their performance is clearly above that of chance. Such patients have access to information but do not experience it.

Weiskrantz believed that subcortical and parallel pathways and centers could now be studied in the human brain. A vast primate literature had already developed on the subject. Monkeys with occipital lesions not only can localize objects in space but also can make color, luminance, orientation, and pattern discriminations. It hardly seemed surprising that humans could use visually presented information not accessible to consciousness. Subcortical networks with interhemispheric connections provided a plausible anatomy on which the behavioral results could rest.

Since blindsight demonstrates vision outside the realm of conscious awareness, this phenomenon has often been invoked as support for the view that perception happens in the absence of sensation, for sensations are presumed to be our experiences of impinging stimuli. Because the primary visual cortex processes sensory inputs, advocates of the secondary pathway view have found it useful to deny the involvement of the primary visual pathway in blindsight. Certainly, it would be easy to argue that perceptual decisions or cognitive activities routinely result from processes outside of conscious awareness. But it would be difficult to argue that such processes do not involve primary sensory systems.

Evidence supports the notion that the primary sensory systems are still involved. Involvement of the damaged primary pathway in blindsight has been demonstrated by Mark Wessinger and Robert Fendrich at Dartmouth College (Fendrich et al., 1992). They investigated this fascinating phenomenon using a dual Purkinje image eye tracker that was augmented with an image stabilizer, allowing for the sustained presentation of information in

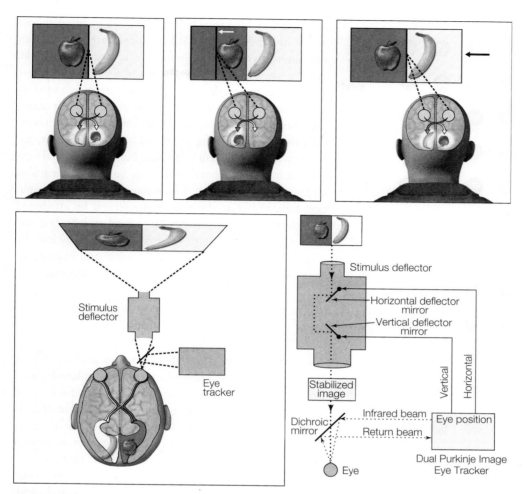

FIGURE 14.3 Schematic of the Purkinje image eye tracker.
The eye tracker compensates for a subject's eye movements by moving the image in the visual field in the same direction as the eyes, thus stabilizing the image on the retina.

discrete parts of the visual field (Figure 14.3). Armed with this piece of equipment and with the cooperation of C.L.T., a robust 55-year-old outdoorsman who had suffered a right occipital stroke 6 years before his examination, they began to tease apart the various explanations for blindsight.

Standard perimetry indicated that C.L.T. had a left homonymous hemianopia with lower-quadrant macular sparing. Yet the eye tracker found small regions of residual vision (Figure 14.4). C.L.T.'s scotoma was explored carefully, using high-contrast, retinally stabilized stimuli and an interval, two-alternative, forced-choice procedure. This procedure requires that a stimulus be presented on every trial and that the participant respond on every trial, even though he denies having seen a stimulus. Such a design is more sensitive to subtle influences of the stimulus on the participant's responses. C.L.T. also indicated his confidence on every trial. The investigators found regions of above-chance performance surrounded by regions of chance perfor-

mance within C.L.T.'s blind field. Simply stated, they found islands of blindsight.

Magnetic resonance imaging (MRI) reconstructions revealed a lesion that damaged the calcarine cortex, which is consistent with C.L.T.'s clinical blindness. But MRI also demonstrated some spared tissue in the region of the calcarine fissure. We assume that this tissue mediates C.L.T.'s central vision with awareness. Given this, it seems reasonable that similar tissue mediates C.L.T.'s islands of blindsight. More important, both positron emission tomography (PET) and functional magnetic resonance imaging (fMRI) conclusively demonstrated that these regions are metabolically active—these areas are alive and processing information! Thus, the most parsimonious explanation for C.L.T.'s blindsight is that it is directed by spared, albeit severely dysfunctional, remnants of the primary visual pathway rather than by a more general secondary visual system.

Before it can be asserted that blindsight is due to subcortical or extrastriate structures, we first must be

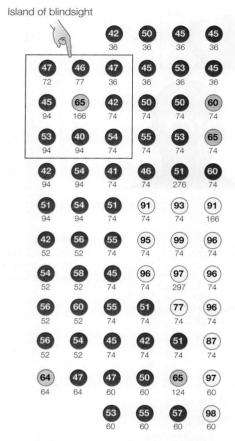

Island of blindsight

FIGURE 14.4 Results of stabilized image perimetry in left visual hemifield.
Results of stabilized image perimetry in C.L.T.'s left visual hemifield. Each test location is represented by a circle. The number in a circle represents the percentage of correct detections. The number under the circle indicates the number of trials at each location. White circles are unimpaired detection, green circles are impaired detection that was above the level of chance, and purple circles indicate detection that was no better than chance.

extremely careful to rule out the possibility of spared striate cortex. With careful perimetric mapping, it is possible to discover regions of vision within a scotoma that would go undetected with conventional perimetry. Through such discoveries, we can learn more about consciousness.

Similar reports of vision without awareness in other neurological populations can similarly inform us about consciousness. It is commonplace to design demanding perceptual tasks on which both neurological and nonneurological participants routinely report low confidence values but perform at a level above chance. Yet it is unnecessary to propose secondary visual systems to account for such reports, since the primary visual system is intact and fully functional. For example, patients with unilateral neglect (see Chapter 7) as a result of right-hemisphere damage are unable to name stimuli entering their left visual field. The conscious brain cannot access this information. When asked to judge whether two lateralized visual stimuli, one in each visual field, are the same or different (Figure 14.5), however, these same patients can do so. When they are questioned on the nature of the stimuli after a trial, they easily name the stimulus in the right visual field but deny having seen the stimulus in the neglected left field. In short, patients with parietal lobe damage, but spared visual cortex can make perceptual judgments outside of conscious awareness. Their failure to consciously access information for comparing the stimuli should not be attributed to processing within a secondary visual system, because their geniculostriate pathway is still intact. They lost the function of a chunk of parietal cortex, and because of that loss, they lost a chunk of conscious awareness.

The Extent of Subconscious Processing

A variety of reports extended these initial observations that information presented in the extinguished visual field can be used for decision making. In fact, quite complex information can be processed outside of conscious awareness (Figure 14.6). In one study of right-sided neglect patients, a picture of a fruit or an animal was quickly presented to the right visual field. Subsequently, a picture of the same item or of an item in the same category was presented to the left visual field. In another condition, the pictures presented in each field had nothing to do with each other (Volpe et al., 1979). All patients in the study denied that a stimulus had been presented in the left visual field. When the two pictures were related, however, patients responded faster than they did when the pictures were different. The reaction time to the unrelated pictures did not increase. In short, high-level information was being exchanged between processing systems, outside the realm of conscious awareness.

The vast staging for our mental activities happens largely without our monitoring. The stages of this production can be identified in many experimental venues. The study of blindsight and neglect yields important insights. First, it underlines a general feature of human cognition: Many perceptual and cognitive activities can and do go on outside the realm of conscious awareness. We can access information of which we are not sentient. Further, this feature does not necessarily depend on subcortical or secondary processing systems: More than likely, unconscious processes related to cognitive, perceptual, and sensory-motor activities happen at the level of the cortex. To help understand how consciousness and unconsciousness

FIGURE 14.5 The same–different paradigm presented to patients with neglect.
(a, b) The patient is presented with a single image, first to one hemifield, then to the other. The patient subsequently is asked to judge if the images are the same or different, a task that he is able to perform. **(c, d)** When the images are presented simultaneously to both hemifields, the patient with unilateral neglect is able to determine whether the images are the same or different, but cannot verbalize what image he saw in the extinguished hemifield that enabled him to make his correct comparison and decision.

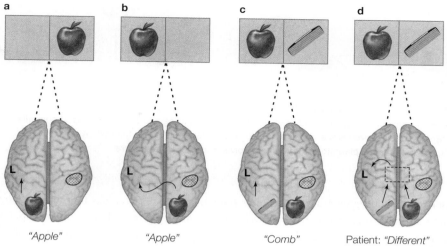

a
b
c
d

"Apple"

"Apple"

"Comb"

Patient: *"Different"*
Doctor: *"What exactly?"*
Patient: *"A comb and I don't know what the other was."*

interact within the cortex, it is necessary to investigate both conscious and unconscious processes in the intact, healthy brain.

Richard Nisbett and Lee Ross (1980) at the University of Michigan clearly made this point. In a clever experiment, using the tried-and-true technique of learning word pairs, they first exposed participants to word associations like *ocean–moon*. The idea is that participants might subsequently say "Tide" when asked to free-associate the word *detergent*. That is exactly what they do, but they do not know why. When asked, they might say, "Oh, my mother always used Tide to do the laundry." As we know from Chapter 4, that was their left brain interpreter system coming up with an answer from the information that was available to it.

Now, any student will commonly and quickly declare that he is fully aware of how he solves a problem even when he really does not know. Students solve the famous Tower of Hanoi (Figure 14.7) problem all the time. When researchers listen to the running discourse

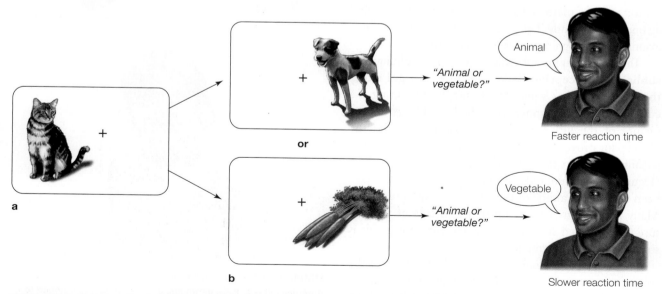

a

or

b

"Animal or vegetable?"

"Animal or vegetable?"

Animal

Vegetable

Faster reaction time

Slower reaction time

FIGURE 14.6 Category discrimination test presented to patients with right sided neglect.
(a) A picture of an item, such as a cat, was flashed to the left visual field. **(b)** A picture of the same item or a related item, such as a dog, was presented to the right visual field, and the participant was asked to discriminate the category that the second item belonged to. If the items were related by category, the time needed to categorize the second word was shorter.

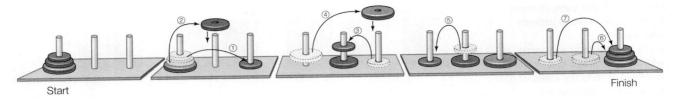

Start

Finish

FIGURE 14.7 The Tower of Hanoi problem.
The task is to rebuild the rings on another tower without ever putting a larger ring on top of a smaller ring. It can be done in seven steps, and after much practice, students learn the task. After they have solved it, however, their explanations for how they solved it can be quite bizarre.

of students articulating what they are doing and why they are doing it, the result can be used to write a computer program to solve the problem. The participant calls on facts known from short- and long-term memory. These events are accessible to consciousness and can be used to build a theory for their action. Yet no one is aware of how the events became established in short- or long-term memory. Problem solving is going on at two different levels, the conscious and the unconscious, but we are only aware of one.

Cognitive psychologists also have examined the extent and kind of information that can be processed unconsciously. Freud staked out the most complex range, where the unconscious was hot and wet. Deep emotional conflicts are fought, and their resolution slowly makes its way to conscious experience. Other psychologists placed more stringent constraints on what can be processed. Many researchers maintain that only low-level stimuli—like the lines forming the letter of a word, not the word itself—can be processed unconsciously. Over the last century, these matters have been examined time and again; only recently has unconscious processing been examined in a cognitive neuroscience setting.

The classic approach was to use the technique of **subliminal perception**. Here a picture of a girl either throwing a cake at someone, or simply presenting the cake in a friendly manner, is flashed quickly. A neutral picture of the girl is presented subsequently, and the participant proves to be biased in judging the girl's personality based on the subliminal exposures he received (Figure 14.8). Hundreds of such demonstrations have been recounted, although they are not easy to replicate. Many psychologists maintain that elements of the picture are captured subconsciously and that this result is sufficient to bias judgment.

Cognitive psychologists have sought to reaffirm the role of unconscious processing through various experimental paradigms. A leader in this effort has been Tony Marcel of Cambridge University (1983a, 1983b). Marcel used a masking paradigm in which the brief presentation of either a blank screen or a word was followed quickly by a masking stimulus of a crosshatch of letters. One of

two tasks followed presentation of the masking stimulus. In a detection task, participants merely had to choose whether a word had been presented. On this task, participants responded at a level of chance. They simply could not tell whether a word had been presented. If the

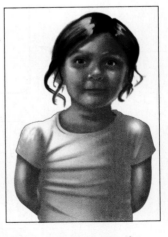

FIGURE 14.8 Testing subliminal perception.
A participant is quickly shown just one picture of a girl, similar to the images in the top row, in such a way that the participant is not consciously aware of the picture's content. The participant is then shown a neutral picture (**bottom row**) and is asked to describe the girl's character. Judgments of the girl's character have been found to be biased by the previous subthreshold presentation.

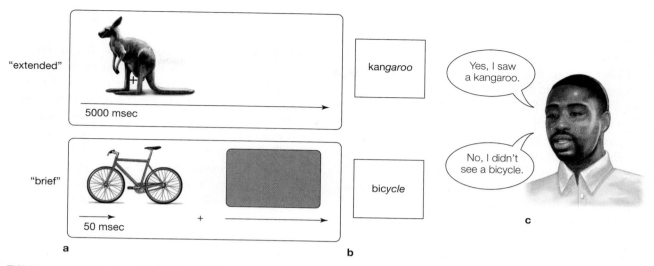

FIGURE 14.9 Picture-to-word priming paradigm.
(a) During the study, either extended and unmasked **(top)** or brief and masked **(bottom)** presentations were used. **(b)** During the test, participants were asked to complete word stems (kan and bic were the word stems presented in this example). Priming performance was identical between extended and brief presentations. **(c)** Afterward, participants were asked if they remembered seeing the words as pictures. Here performance differed—participants usually remembered seeing the extended presentations but regularly denied having seen the brief presentations.

task became a lexical decision task, however, the subliminally presented stimulus had effects. Here, following presentation of the masking stimulus, a string of letters was presented and participants had to specify whether the string formed a word. Marcel cleverly manipulated the subthreshold words in such a way that some were related to the word string and some were not. If there had been at least lexical processing of the subthreshold word, related words should elicit faster response times, and this is exactly what Marcel found.

Since then, investigations of conscious and unconscious processing of pictures and words have been combined successfully into a single cross-form priming paradigm. This paradigm involves presenting pictures for study and word stems for the test (Figure 14.9). Using both extended and brief periods of presentation, the investigators also showed that such picture-to-word priming can occur with or without awareness. In addition to psychophysically setting the brief presentation time at identification threshold, a pattern mask was used to halt conscious processing. Apparently not all processing was halted, however, because priming occurred equally well under both conditions. Given that participants denied seeing the briefly presented stimuli, unconscious processing must have allowed them to complete the word stems (primes). In other words, they were extracting conceptual information from the pictures, even without consciously seeing them. How often does this happen in everyday life? Considering the complexity of the visual world, and how rapidly our eyes look around, briefly fixating from object to object (about 100–200 ms), this situation probably happens quite often! These data

further underscore the need to consider both conscious and unconscious processes when developing a theory of consciousness.

Gaining Access to Consciousness

As cognitive neuroscientists make further attempts to understand the links between conscious and unconscious processing, it becomes clear that these phenomena remain elusive. We now know that obtaining evidence of subliminal perception depends on whether subjective or objective criteria set the threshold. When the criteria are subjective (i.e., introspective reports from each subject), priming effects are evident. When criteria are set objectively by requiring a forced choice as to whether a participant saw any visual information, no priming effects are seen. Among other things, these studies point out the gray area between conscious and unconscious. Thresholds clearly vary with the criteria.

Pinker (1997) presented an enticing analysis on how evolutionary pressures gave rise to access-consciousness. The general insight has to do with the idea that information has costs and benefits. He argued that at least three dimensions must be considered: cost of space to store and process it, cost of time to process and retrieve it, and cost of resources—energy in the form of glucose—to process it. The point is that any complex organism is made up of matter, which is subject to the laws of thermodynamics, and there are restrictions on the information it accesses. To operate optimally within these constraints, only information relevant to the problem at hand should be allowed into consciousness, which seems to be how the brain is organized.

Access-consciousness has four obvious features that Pinker recounted. It is brimming with sensations: the shocking pink sunset, the fragrance of jasmine, the stinging of a stubbed toe. Second, we are able to move information into and out of our awareness and into and out of short-term memory by turning our attentional spotlight on it. Third, this information always comes with salience, some kind of emotional coloring. Finally, there is the "I" that calls the shots on what to do with the information as it comes into the field of awareness.

Jackendoff (1987) argued that for perception, access is limited to the intermediate stages of information processing. Luckily, we do not ponder the elements that go into a percept, only the output. Consider the patient described in Chapter 6, who could not see objects but could see faces, thus indicating he was a face processor. When this patient was shown a picture that arranged pieces of vegetables in such a way as to make them look like a face, the patient immediately said he saw the face but was totally unable to state that the eyes were garlic cloves and the nose a turnip. He had access only to output of the module.

Concerning attention and its role in access, the work of Anne Treisman (1991) at Princeton University reveals that unconscious parallel processing can go only so far. Treisman proposed a candidate for the border between conscious and unconscious processes. In her famous pop-out experiments that we discussed in Chapter 7, a participant picks a prespecified object from a field of others. The notion is that each point in the visual field is processed for color, shape, and motion, outside of conscious awareness. The attention system then picks up elements and puts them together with other elements to make the desired percept. Treisman showed, for example, that when we are attending to a point in space and processing the color and form of that location, elements at unattended points seem to be floating. We can tell the color and shape, but we make mistakes about what color goes with what shape. Attention is needed to conjoin the results of the separate unconscious processes. The illusory conjunctions of stimulus features are first-glimpse evidence for how the attentional system combines elements into whole percepts.

We have discussed emotional salience in Chapter 10, and we will get to the "I" process in a bit. Before turning to such musings, let's consider an often overlooked aspect of consciousness: the ability to move from conscious, controlled processing to unconscious, automatic processing. Such "movement" from conscious to unconscious is necessary when we are learning complex motor tasks such as riding a bike or driving a car, as well as for complex cognitive tasks such as verb generation and reading.

At Washington University in St. Louis, Marcus Raichle and Steven Petersen, two pioneers in the brain imaging field, proposed a "scaffolding to storage" framework to account for this movement (Petersen et al., 1998). Initially, according to their framework, we must use conscious processing during practice while developing complex skills (or memories)—this activity can be considered the scaffolding process. During this time, the memory is being consolidated, or the skill is being developed and honed. Once the task is learned, brain activity and brain involvement change. This change can be likened to the removal of the scaffolding, or the disinvolvement of support structures and the involvement of more permanent structures as the tasks are "stored" for use.

Petersen and Raichle demonstrated this scaffolding to storage movement in the awake-behaving human brain. Using PET techniques participants either performed a verb generation task which was compared to simply reading verbs, or a maze tracing task, compared to tracing a square. They clearly demonstrated that early, unlearned, conscious processing uses a much different network of brain regions than does later, learned, unconscious processing (Figure 14.10). They hypothesized that during learning, a scaffolding set of regions is used to handle novel task demands. Following learning, a different set of regions is involved, perhaps regions specific to the storage or representation of the particular skill or memory. Further, once this movement from conscious to unconscious has occurred (once the scaffolding is removed), it is sometimes difficult to reinitiate conscious processing. A classic example is learning to drive with a clutch. Early on, you have to consciously practice the steps of releasing the gas pedal while depressing the clutch, moving the shift lever, and slowly releasing the clutch while applying pressure to the gas pedal again—all without stalling the car. After a few jerky attempts, you know the procedures well: The process has been stored, but it is rather difficult to separate the steps.

Similar processes occur in learning other complex skills. Chris Chabris, a cognitive psychologist at Harvard University, has studied chess players as they progress from the novice to the master level (Chabris & Hamilton, 1992). During lightning chess, masters play many games simultaneously and very fast. Seemingly, they play by intuition as they make move after move after move, and in essence they *are* playing by intuition—"learned intuition," that is. They intuitively know, without really knowing how they know, what the next best move is. For novices, such lightning play is not possible. They have to painstakingly examine the pieces and moves one by one (OK, if I move my knight over there, she

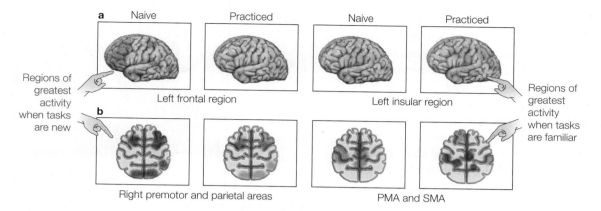

FIGURE 14.10 Activated areas of the brain change as tasks are practiced.
Based on positron emission tomography (PET) images, these eight panels show that practicing a task results in a shift in which regions of the brain are most active. **(a)** When confronted with a new verb generation task, areas in the left frontal region, such as the prefrontal cortex, are activated (green areas in leftmost panel). As the task is practiced, blood flow to these areas decreases (as depicted by the fainter color in the adjacent panel). In contrast, the insula is less active during naïve verb generation. With practice, however, activation in the insula increases, suggesting that with practice, activity in the insula replaces activity previously observed in the frontal regions. **(b)** An analogous shift in activity is observed elsewhere in the brain during a motor learning maze-tracing task. Activity in the premotor and parietal areas seen early in the maze task (red areas in leftmost panel) subsides with practice (fainter red in the adjacent panel) while increases in blood flow are then seen in the primary and supplementary motor areas as a result of practice.

will take my bishop; no, that won't work. Let's see, if I move the rook—no, then she will move her bishop and then I can take her knight . . . whoops, that will put me in check . . . hmmm). But after many hours of practice and hard work, as the novices develop into chess masters, they see and react to the chessboard differently. They now begin to view and play the board as a series of groups or clumps of pieces and moves, as opposed to separate pieces with serial moves. Chabris's research has shown that during early stages of learning, the talking, language-based, left brain is consciously controlling the game. With experience, however, as the different moves and possible groupings are learned, the perceptual, feature-based, right brain takes over.

For example, International Grandmaster chess player and two-time U.S. chess champion Patrick Wolff, who at age 20 defeated the world chess champion Gary Kasparov in 25 moves, was given 5 seconds to look at a picture of a chessboard with all the pieces set in a pattern that made chess sense. He was then asked to reproduce it, and he quickly and accurately did so, getting 25 out of 27 pieces in the correct position. Even a good player would place only about five pieces correctly. In a different trial, however, with the same board, the same number of pieces, but pieces in positions that didn't make chess sense, he got only a few pieces right, just like a person who doesn't play chess. Wolff's original accuracy was from his right brain automatically matching up patterns that it had learned from years of playing chess.

Although neuroscientists may know that Wolff's right-brain pattern perception mechanism is all coded, runs automatically, and is the source of this capacity, he did not. When he was asked about his ability, his left-brain interpreter struggled for an explanation: "You sort of get it by trying to, to understand what's going on quickly and of course you chunk things, right? . . . I mean obviously, these pawns, just, but, but it, I mean, you chunk things in a normal way, like I mean one person might think this is sort of a structure, but actually I would think this is more, all the pawns like this . . . ." When asked, the speaking left brain of the master chess player can assure us that it can explain how the moves are made, but it fails miserably to do so—as often happens when you try, for example, to explain how to use a clutch to someone who doesn't drive a car with a standard transmission.

The transition of controlled, conscious processing to automatic, unconscious processing is analogous to the implementation of a computer program. Early stages require multiple interactions among many brain processes, including consciousness, as the program is written, tested, and prepared for compilation. Once the process is well under way, the program is compiled, tested, recompiled, retested, and so on. Eventually, as the program begins to run and unconscious processing begins to take over, the scaffolding is removed, and the executable file is uploaded for general use.

This theory seems to imply that once conscious processing has effectively allowed us to move a task to the realm of the unconscious, we no longer need conscious processing. This transition would allow us to perform that task unconsciously and allow our limited conscious processing to turn to another task. We could unconsciously ride our bikes and talk at the same time.

One evolutionary goal of consciousness may be to improve the efficiency of unconscious processing. The ability to relegate learned tasks and memories to unconsciousness allows us to devote our limited consciousness resources to recognizing and adapting to changes and novel situations in the environment, thus increasing our chances of survival.

Sentience

Neurologist Antonio Damasio (2011) defines consciousness as a mind state in which the regular flow of mental images (defined as mental patterns in any of the sensory modalities) has been enriched by subjectivity, meaning mental images that represent body states. He suggests that various parts of the body continuously signal the brain and are signaled back by the brain in a perpetual resonant loop. Mental images about the self—that is, the body—are different from other mental images. They are connected to the body, and as such they are "felt." Because these images are felt, an organism is able to sense that the contents of its thoughts are its own: They are formulated in the perspective of the organism, and the organism can act on those thoughts. This form of self-awareness, however, is not meta self-awareness, or being aware that one is aware of oneself. Sentience does not imply that an organism knows it is sentient.

Neurons, Neuronal Groups, and Conscious Experience

Neuroscientists interested in higher cognitive functions have been extraordinarily innovative in analyzing how the nervous system enables perceptual activities. Recording from single neurons in the visual system, they have tracked the flow of visual information and how it becomes encoded and decoded during a perceptual activity. They have also directly manipulated the information and influenced an animal's decision processes. One of the leaders in this approach to understanding the mind is William Newsome at Stanford University.

Newsome has studied how neural events in area MT of the monkey cortex, which is actively involved in

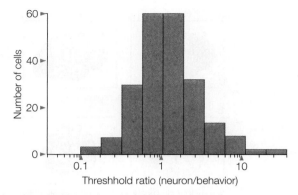

FIGURE 14.11 Motion discrimination can be predicted by a single-neuron response pattern.
Motion stimuli, with varying levels of coherent motion, were presented to rhesus monkeys trained in a task to discriminate the direction of motion. The monkey's decision regarding the direction of apparent motion and the responses of 60 single middle temporal visual area (MT) cells (which are selective for direction of motion) were recorded and compared to the stimulus coherence on each trial. On average, individual cells in MT were as sensitive as the entire monkey. In subsequent work, the firing rate of single cells predicted (albeit weakly) the monkey's choice on a trial-by-trial basis.

motion detection, correlate with the actual perceptual event (Newsome et al., 1989). One of his first findings was striking. The animal's psychophysical performance capacity to discriminate motion could be predicted by the neuronal response pattern of a single neuron (Figure 14.11). In other words, a single neuron in area MT was as sensitive to changes in the visual display as was the monkey.

This finding stirred the research community because it raised a fundamental question about how the brain does its job. Newsome's observation challenged the common view that the signal averaging that surely goes on in the nervous system eliminated the noise carried by individual neurons. From this view, the decision-making capacity of pooled neurons should be superior to the sensitivity of single neurons. Yet Newsome did not side with those who believe that a single neuron is the source for any one behavioral act. It is well known that killing a single neuron, or even hundreds of them, will not impair an animal's ability to perform a task, so a single neuron's behavior must be redundant.

An even more tantalizing finding, which is of particular interest to the study of conscious experience, is that altering the response rate of these same neurons by careful **microstimulation** can tilt the animal toward making the right decision on a perceptual task. Maximum effects are seen during the interval the animal is thinking about the task. Newsome and his colleagues (Salzman et al., 1990; Celebrini & Newsome, 1995), in effect, inserted an artificial signal into the monkey's nervous system and influenced how it thinks.

Based on this discovery, can the site of the micro-stimulation be considered as the place where the decision is made? Researchers are not convinced that this is the way to think about the problem. Instead, it's believed they have tapped into part of a neural loop involved with this particular perceptual discrimination. They argue that stimulation at different sites in the loop creates different perceptual subjective experiences. For example, let's say that the stimulus was moving upward and the response was as if the stimulus were moving downward. If this were your brain, you might think you saw downward motion if the stimulation occurred early in the loop. If, however, the stimulation occurred late in the loop and merely found you choosing the downward response instead of the upward one, your sensation would be quite different. Why, you might ask yourself, did I do that?

This question raises the issue of the timing of consciousness. When do we become conscious of our thoughts, intentions, and actions? Do we consciously choose to act, and then consciously initiate an act? Or is an act initiated unconsciously, and only afterward do we consciously think we initiated it?

Benjamin Libet (1996), an eminent neuroscientist-philosopher, researched this question for nearly 35 years. In a groundbreaking and often controversial series of experiments, he investigated the neural time factors in conscious and unconscious processing. These experiments are the basis for his **backward referral hypothesis**. Libet and colleagues (Libet et al., 1979) concluded that awareness of a neural event is delayed approximately 500 milliseconds after the onset of the stimulating event and, more important, this awareness is referred back in time to the onset of the stimulating event. To put it another way, you think that you were aware of the stimulus from the onset of the stimulus and are unaware of the time gap. Surprisingly, according to participant reports, brain activity related to an action increased as many as 300 ms *before* the *conscious intention* to act. Using more sophisticated fMRI techniques, John-Dylan Haynes (Soon et al., 2008) showed that the outcomes of a decision can be encoded in brain activity up to 10 seconds before it enters awareness.

Fortunately, backward referral of our consciousness is not so delayed that we act without thinking. Enough time elapses between the awareness of the intent to act and the actual beginning of the act than we can override inappropriately triggered behavior. This ability to detect and correct errors is what Libet believes is the basis for free will.

Whether or not error detection and correction are indeed experimental manifestations of free will, such

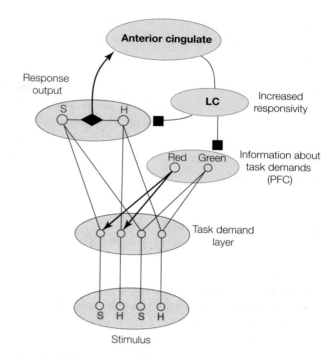

FIGURE 14.12 Model of the conflict monitoring system. Study participants were presented with two letters (*S* and/or *H*), one in red and the other in green. They were cued to respond to the red letter (dark black arrows) and asked whether it was an *S* or an *H*. Basic task-related components are in pink, and control-related components are in blue. The anterior cingulate cortex responds to conflict of response units. This directs the locus coeruleus (labeled LC) that leads to increases in responsivity of multiple processing units (via the *squares*). Specifically, selective attention is modulated via the prefrontal cortex (PFC), and motor preparation is modulated via the response units. Patients with damage to control-related components, particularly the PFC, have problems in recognizing and correcting their mistakes. The model was suggested by Gehring and Knight (2000).

abilities have been linked to brain regions (Figure 14.12). Not all people can detect and correct errors adequately. In a model piece of brain science linking event-related potentials (ERPs) and patient studies, Robert Knight at the University of California, Berkeley, and William Gehring at the University of Michigan, Ann Arbor, characterized the role of the frontal lobe in checking and correcting errors (Gehring & Knight, 2000). By comparing and contrasting the performance of patients and healthy volunteers on a letter discrimination task, they conclusively demonstrated that the lateral prefrontal cortex was essential for corrective behavior. The task was arranged such that flanking "distracters" often disrupted responses to "targets." Healthy volunteers showed the expected "corrective" neural activity in the anterior cingulate (see Chapter 12). Patients with lateral prefrontal damage also showed the corrective activity for errors. The patients, however, also showed the same sort of "corrective" activity for non-errors; that is, patients could not distinguish between errors and correct responses. It seems that patients with lateral prefrontal damage no longer have the ability to monitor and integrate their behavior across time. Perhaps they have even lost the ability to learn from their mistakes. It is as if they are trapped in the moment, unable to go back yet unable to decide to go forward. They seem to have lost a wonderful and perhaps uniquely human benefit of consciousness—the ability to escape from the here and now of linear time, or to "time-shift" away.

TAKE-HOME MESSAGES

- Most of the processing that goes on in the brain is considered to be unconscious.

- Subliminal processing is defined as brain activity evoked by a stimulus that is below the threshold for awareness. When processing is subliminal, the information is inaccessible to awareness.

- Preconscious processing is the brain state in which stimulus-driven activity is strong enough to generate significant sensory processing, but in the absence of top-down attention to amplify the signal, it does not reach the threshold for awareness.

- Conscious processing (awareness) occurs when stimulus salience is sufficiently strong and the signals are amplified by goal driven attention such that they exceed the threshold for awareness.

- According to Marcus Raichle and Steven Petersen, the ability to move from conscious, controlled processing to unconscious, automatic processing involves a "scaffolding to storage" framework. Unlearned, conscious processing uses a much different network of brain regions than does later, learned, unconscious processing.

- The ability to relegate learned tasks and memories to unconsciousness allows us to devote our limited consciousness resources to recognizing and adapting to changes and novel situations in the environment, thus increasing our chances of survival.

- Benjamin Libet and his colleagues observed increasing brain activity related to an action as many as 300 ms *before* the *conscious intention* to act.

The Emergence of the Brain Interpreter in the Human Species

The brain's modular organization has now been well established. The functioning modules do have some kind of physical instantiation, but brain scientists cannot yet specify the exact nature of the neural networks. It is clear that these networks operate mainly outside the realm of awareness, each providing specialized bits of information. Yet, even with the insight that many of our cognitive capacities appear to be automatic domain-specific operations, we feel that we are in control. Despite knowing that these modular systems are beyond our control and fully capable of producing behaviors, mood changes, and cognitive activity, we think we are a unified conscious agent—an "I" with a past, a present, and a future. With all of this apparent independent activity running in parallel, what allows for the sense of conscious unity we possess?

A private narrative appears to take place inside us all the time. It consists partly of the effort to tie together into a coherent whole the diverse activities of thousands of specialized systems that we have inherited through evolution to handle the challenges presented to us each day from both environmental and social situations. Years of research have confirmed that humans have a specialized process to carry out this interpretive synthesis, and, as we discussed in Chapter 4, it is located in the brain's left hemisphere. This system, called the **interpreter**, is most likely cortically based and works largely outside of conscious awareness. The interpreter makes sense of all the internal and external information that is bombarding the brain. Asking how one thing relates to another, looking for cause and effect, it offers up hypotheses, makes order out of the chaos of information, and creates a running narrative. The interpreter is the glue that binds together the thousands of bits of information from all over the cortex into a cause-and-effect, "makes sense" narrative: our personal story. It explains why we do the things we do, and why we feel the way we do. Our dispositions, emotional reactions, and past learned behavior are all fodder for the interpreter. If some action, thought, or emotion doesn't fit in with the rest of the story, the interpreter will rationalize it (I am a really cool, macho guy with tattoos and a Harley and I got a poodle because . . . ah, um . . . my great grandmother was French).

The interpreter, however, can use only the information that it receives. For example, a patient with *Capgras' syndrome* will recognize a familiar person but will insist that an identical double or an alien has replaced the person, and they are looking at an imposter. In this syndrome, it appears that the emotional feelings for the familiar person are disconnected from the representation of that person. A patient will be looking at her husband, but she feels no emotion when she sees him. The interpreter has to explain this phenomenon. It is receiving the information from the face identification module ("That's Jack, my husband"), but it is not receiving any emotional information. The interpreter, seeking cause and effect, comes up with a solution: "It must not really be Jack, because if it really were Jack I'd feel some emotion, so he is an imposter!"

actions. Sure, cheat on the test; it was preordained at the big bang about 13.7 billion years ago. So what if he raped and killed your daughter—his neurons, which he has no control over, made him do it. Forgive and forget about it. Many scientists and determinists think this is the way things are. The rest of us just don't believe it. If we were to be logical neuroscientists, however, shouldn't we?

Well, the physicists who got us into this mess are shaking their heads. In fact, most physicists have given up on determinism. What happened? The conception of the physical universe and the physicist's confidence in predicting its behavior changed dramatically in the early 1900s with the development of two new branches of physics: chaos theory and quantum mechanics.

Chaos

In 1889, French mathematician and physicist Jules Henri Poincaré gave the determinists pause when he made a major contribution to what had become known as "the three-body problem," or "n-body problem," that had been bothering mathematicians since Newton's time. Newton's laws, when applied to the motion of planets, were completely deterministic. The laws implied that if you knew the initial position and velocity of the planets, you could accurately determine their position and velocity in the future (or the past, for that matter). Although this proposal was true for simple astronomical systems with two bodies, it was not true for astronomical systems consisting of three or more orbiting astronomical bodies with interactions among all three. Everyone at the time realized that measurements weren't accurate, but it hadn't bothered them very much because they figured it was a measuring error: Improve the precision of the initial measurement, and the precision of the predicted answer would equally improve. All they needed was a better measuring device. Poincaré pointed out that no matter how carefully the initial measurement was done, it would never be infinitely precise. It would always contain a small degree of error, and even tiny differences in initial measurements would produce substantially different results, far out of proportion to what would be expected mathematically. In these types of systems, now known as **chaotic systems**, *extreme sensitivity to initial conditions* is called *dynamic instability* or *chaos*. Poincaré's findings were forgotten for about a half century. They didn't see the light of day until they were rediscovered by a mathematician-turned-meteorologist, Edward Lorenz.

Lorenz was developing *nonlinear models* (models where the components are not directly proportional to each other) to describe how an air current would rise and fall while being heated by the Sun. Having never heard of Poincaré's systems with extreme sensitivity to initial conditions, he thought that minute differences in input data were insignificant. He realized, however, that he was wrong. With only minute variations in his input data (initially he had rounded off the decimal 0.506127 to 0.506), his (deterministic) computer program produced wildly different results. Lorenz had rediscovered what is now known as chaos theory. In 1972, he gave a talk about how even tiny uncertainties would eventually overwhelm any calculations and defeat the accuracy of a long-term weather forecast. From this lecture, titled *Predictability: Does the Flap of a Butterfly's Wings in Brazil Set Off a Tornado in Texas?* came the term "butterfly effect" (O'Connor & Roberson, 2008). The problem with a chaotic system is that even though it is determined purely by mathematical laws, using the laws of physics to make precise long-term predictions is impossible, even in theory. Thus, for practical purposes, a deterministic process can be unpredictable. Chaotic behavior has been observed in many systems, including electrical circuits, population growth, and the dynamics of action potentials in neurons.

Quantum Theory

Why had Poincaré's work been lost from sight? At the time, most physicists' attention was not focused on the macro world of planets and hurricanes, but on the micro world of atoms and subatomic particles. Physicists were in a dither because they had found that atoms didn't obey the so-called universal laws of motion. How could Newton's laws be fundamental universal laws, if atoms—the stuff objects are made of—didn't obey the same laws as the objects themselves? As the brilliant and entertaining California Institute of Technology physicist Richard Feynman (1998) once pointed out, exceptions prove the rule . . . wrong. Newton's laws must not be universal.

Quantum theory was developed to explain why an electron stays in its orbit, which could not be explained by either Newton's laws or Maxwell's laws of classical electromagnetism. In quantum theory, the *Schrodinger equation* is the equivalent to Newton's laws (and it is time reversible). The Schrodinger equation has successfully described particles and atoms in molecules. Its insights have led to transistors and lasers. But here's the rub: The Schrodinger equation cannot predict with certainty where the electron is in its orbit at any one state in time; instead, that location is expressed as a probability. This is because certain pairs of physical properties are related in such a way that both properties cannot be known precisely at the same time. In the case of the electron in orbit, the paired properties are position and momentum.

The theoretical physicist Werner Heisenberg presented this as the *Uncertainty Principle.* Physicists with their deterministic views don't like uncertainty but have been forced into a different way of thinking. Niels Bohr (1937) wrote, "The renunciation of the ideal of causality in atomic physics . . . has been forced upon us." Systems theorist and emeritus professor at the State University of New York at Binghamton Howard Pattee (2001) describes the fundamental problem with causality: Because the microscopic equations of physics are time symmetric and therefore, reversible, they cannot support the irreversible concept of causation. Heisenberg went even further when he wrote, "I believe that indeterminism, that is, the nonvalidity of rigorous causality, is necessary" (quoted in Isaacson, 2007, p. 332). Quantum mechanics made it clear to physicists that when considering fundamental matter, they needed to shift their thinking from an inherently deterministic to an inherently nondeterministic worldview.

Physics had stumbled onto the fact that the physical world is organized on more than one level, and each level has its own set of laws. Although the Newtonian laws of classical mechanics were able to explain the behavior of macroscopic systems, such as baseballs and skyscrapers, they were unable to describe the behavior of microscopic systems like atoms and subatomic particles. It seems that when quantum matter aggregates into macroscopic objects, a new system emerges that follows new laws. Thus a nondeterministic process (quantum mechanics) can give rise to things that are predictable (Newtonian laws), which in the three-body problem become unpredictable in a new sense. This view suggests there are different levels of organization, and those different levels have their own laws that can be understood only at the level being examined. Or, is it even more complicated? Do the levels interact, giving rise to yet another abstraction? This brings us to the topic of emergence.

Emergence

A **complex system** is one composed of many interconnected parts, such that when they self-organize into a single system, the resulting system exhibits one or more properties not obvious from the properties of the individual parts. Examples of complex systems are ant colonies, plant communities such as the chaparral, the brain, the climate, and human social structures. One (the whole) is said to emerge from the other (the individual parts), and the behavior, function, and other properties of the new whole system are different from, or more than, the sum of the parts. **Emergence**, then, is the arising of a new structure (previously nonexistent), with a new level of organization and new properties, that occurs during the self-organization of a complex system (Goldstein, 1999). It is a phenomenon of collective organization. Thus Newton's laws are not fundamental, they are emergent; when quantum matter (which follows quantum laws) aggregates into macroscopic objects, a new level of organization emerges with its own set of laws, Newton's laws.

The key to understanding emergence is to understand that there are "layers" of organization. For example, consider traffic. One layer of organization is car parts, such as a brake pad and a fan belt, but traffic is another layer of organization, composed of a bunch of cars, human drivers, location, time, weather, and so forth. There are two schools of thought on emergence. The hard deterministic view is that there is only "weak emergence," where the new properties arise as a result of the interactions at an elemental level and the emergent property is reducible to its individual components. In short, you can predict one level to the next. From the viewpoint of weak emergence, Newton's laws could be predicted from the laws of quantum mechanics, and vice versa; it's just that we don't yet know enough to do so. Or, using our example of looking at car parts, we could predict that the Harbor Freeway in LA, between Wilshire and West 7th Street, on Friday, May 25, at 2:15 p.m., will be (or will not be) bumper to bumper; we just don't know how to do it yet. In "strong emergence," on the other hand, the new property is irreducible, is more than the sum of its parts, and the laws of one level cannot be predicted by an underlying fundamental theory or from an understanding of the laws of another level of organization. Thus, from this viewpoint, Newton's laws could not be predicted from quantum theory, nor could we predict the state of the 101 Freeway by looking at car parts. A new set of laws emerge that aren't predicted from the parts alone. The whole is more than the sum of its parts.

Physicists don't like the idea of unpredictable phenomena much, but many (not all) have come to accept that this is the way things are. That is, they accept "strong" emergence. One such physicist was Richard Feynman, who in his 1961 lectures to Caltech freshmen declared:

> Yes! Physics *has* given up. *We do not know how to predict what would happen in a given circumstance,* and we believe now that it is impossible, that the only thing that can be predicted is the probability of different events. It must be recognized that this is a retrenchment in our earlier ideal of understanding nature. It may be a backward step, but no one has seen a way to avoid it. . . . So at the present time we must limit ourselves to computing probabilities. We say "at the present time," but we suspect very

strongly that it is something that will be with us forever—that it is impossible to beat that puzzle—that this is the way nature really is. (Feynman et al., 1995, p. 135)

Whether or not nature will always remain unpredictable to us, and whether emergence is weak or strong, most physicists would agree that at different levels of structure, there are different types of organization with unique types of interactions governed by their own laws; and that one emerges from the other. This reality, however, introduces a complicating issue for neuroscience research. The differences in neuronal organization between the human brain and the brains of other animals may result in different emergent properties.

Emergence is a common phenomenon accepted by many in physics, biology, chemistry, sociology, and even art, but hard determinism reigns in neuroscience. Why? Because neuroscientists look at all the evidence which suggests that the brain functions automatically and that our conscious experience is an after-the-fact experience. From this they infer that neural processing produces mental states in a deterministic fashion. In their view, mental states, such as a belief, do not affect brain function or processing. Emergence is often seen as a way to sneak the mind in without having to explain how it works. In addition, emergence is inconsistent with experimental science explanations of the brain's machinations. Emergence is not a mystical ghost in the machine, however. It is a ubiquitous phenomenon in nature. The job of the neuroscientist is to understand the relationship between one level of organization and another, not to deny they exist. Viewing the organization of the brain as being multileveled, and those levels as having emergent properties, has far-reaching implications for our understanding of brain function. Describing a property as emergent, however, does not explain that property or how it came to be. Instead, it allows us to identify the appropriate level of inquiry. Indeed, the central focus of modern mind–brain research should be to understand how the levels interact.

Conscious thought may be an emergent property, and concentrating on the firing of neurons might not tell us all we need to know to understand that phenomenon. Neuroscience has assumed that we can derive the macro story from the micro story. Neural reductionists hold that every mental state has a one-to-one relationship with some as yet undiscovered neural state. Can we take from neurophysiology what we know about neurons and neurotransmitters and come up with a deterministic model to predict conscious thoughts or psychology? Brandeis University neuroscientist Eve Marder's work with spiny lobsters suggests this approach would not work (Prinz et al., 2004).

Multiple Realizability

The spiny lobster has a simple nervous system. Marder has been studying the neural underpinnings of the motility patterns of the lobster's gut (Figure 14.14). She has isolated the entire neural network and has mapped out every single neuron and synapse. She has modeled the synapse dynamics to the level of neurotransmitter effects. From a neural

FIGURE 14.14 The pyloric rhythm and pyloric circuit architecture of the spiny lobster.
(a) In the spiny lobster, the stomatogastric ganglion, which has a small number of neurons and a stereotyped motor pattern, produces the pyloric rhythm. The pyloric rhythm has a triphasic motor pattern with bursts occurring first from the anterior burster (AB) neuron electronically coupled to two pyloric dilator (PD) neurons. The next burst is from a lateral pyloric (LP) neuron, followed by a pyloric (PY) neuron. The recordings are done intracellularly from neurons in the stomatogastric ganglion. (b) A schematic representation of a simplified version of the underlying circuit. All synapses in the circuit are inhibitory. To generate the 20 million model circuits, the strengths of the seven synapses were varied and five or six different versions of the neurons in the circuit were used.

reductionist perspective, she should be able to piece together all her information and describe the exact neural pattern of synapses and neurotransmitters that results in the function of the lobster gut. Her laboratory simulated the more than 20 million possible network combinations of synapse strengths and neuron properties for this relatively simple gut nervous system. After modeling all those timing combinations, Marder found that about 1% to 2% of them could lead to the appropriate dynamics that would create the motility pattern observed in nature. Even though it is a small percentage, it still turns out that this very simple nervous system has 100,000 to 200,000 different tunings that will result in exactly the same gut behavior at any given moment. That is, normal pyloric rhythms were generated by networks with very different cellular and synaptic properties (Figure 14.15). The idea that there are many ways to implement a system to produce one behavior is known as **multiple realizability**. In a hugely complex system such as the human brain, how many possible tunings might there be for a single behavior? Can single-unit recordings and molecular approaches alone ever reveal what is going on to produce human behavior? This is a profound problem for the reductionist neuroscientist, because Marder's work shows that analyzing nerve circuits may be able to inform how the thing *could* work but not how it actually *does* work. Neuroscientists will have to figure out how, and at what level, to approach the nervous system to learn the deterministic rules for understanding it. It doesn't appear that investigating one level, however, will tell us all we need to know to predict how another level operates.

Nobel Prize–winning physicist Phillip Anderson (1972), in his seminal paper *More Is Different*, reiterated the idea that we can't get the macro story from the micro story:

> The main fallacy in this kind of thinking is that the reductionist hypothesis does not by any means imply a "constructionist" one: The ability to reduce everything to simple fundamental laws does not imply the ability to start from those laws and reconstruct the universe. In fact, the more the elementary particle physicists tell us about the nature of the fundamental laws, the less relevance they seem to have to the very real problems of the rest of science, much less to those of society.

He later admonishes biologists,

> The arrogance of the particle physicist and his intensive research may be behind us (the discoverer of the positron said "the rest is chemistry"), but we have yet to recover from that of some molecular biologists, who seem determined to try to reduce everything about the human organism to "only" chemistry, from the common cold and all mental disease to the religious instinct. Surely there are more levels of organization between human ethnology and DNA than there are between DNA and quantum electrodynamics, and each level can require a whole new conceptual structure.

Can Mental States Affect Brain Processing?

Let's pull back from all this theory for the moment and remember what the brain is for. The brain is a decision-making device, guided by experience, that gathers and computes information in real time to inform its decisions. If the brain is a decision-making device and gathers information to inform those decisions, then can a mental state such as a belief, which is the result of some experience or some social interaction, affect or constrain the brain, and by so doing, influence its future mental states and behaviors?

Kathleen Vohs, a psychology professor at the Carlson School of Management in Minnesota, and

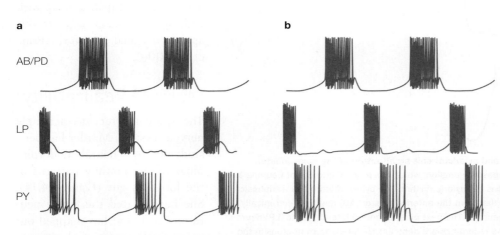

FIGURE 14.15 100,000 to 200,000 networks with very different cellular and synaptic properties generate the typical pyloric rhythm.
(a, b) Shown are the voltage traces from two model pyloric networks, which are very similar, even though they are produced by circuits with very different membranes and synaptic properties. The permeabilities and conductances for various ions differ among the circuits.

HOW THE BRAIN WORKS
Eyewitness Testimony

Every prosecutor in a criminal case knows that an eyewitness account is one of the most compelling types of evidence for establishing guilt. But is this type of testimony to be trusted? Elizabeth Loftus and her colleagues (Loftus & Greene, 1980; Loftus et al., 1978) illustrated the difficulty of relying on the recall of witnesses by showing participants color slides detailing an accident and, in a later test session, asking them what they saw. One of the slides showed a car at an intersection before it turned and hit a pedestrian. Half of the participants viewed a red stop sign; the other half, a red yield sign. Participants then answered questions about the slides: Half were presented with questions referring to the correct sign; the other half were asked questions referring to the incorrect sign. For example, a participant who was shown a yield sign might have been asked, "When the car came to the stop sign, did the driver stop?"

During subsequent recognition tests of whether a certain slide was what they had previously seen, 75% of the participants correctly recognized a previously seen slide if the correct sign had also been mentioned in the questioning session. But when participants previously had been questioned with the wrong sign being mentioned, only 41% correctly recognized the slides as previously seen or not seen. These findings indicate that recollections of an event can be influenced by misleading statements made during questioning.

Misinformation about things as obvious as hair color and the presence of a mustache can lead participants to wrongly identify people they have seen previously. What does this say about the suggestibility of witnesses and the influence of misinformation on recall? Do witnesses really know the correct information but later fail to distinguish between their own memories and information supplied by another person? One line of thinking is that perhaps the information was not encoded initially, and when forced to guess, the participant provides the information given by someone else.

Not just adults are eyewitnesses in court cases. Children often are asked to testify as witnesses. Given that adults with fully developed memories have difficulty recalling what they have seen, how do young children with potentially underdeveloped memory systems behave under the pressures of authorities and courtrooms? This is a controversial issue in situations such as child abuse or sexual abuse in which children are eyewitnesses to crimes against themselves, and may be the only witness.

The question of how well children remember and report things that they have experienced is of special concern when the event may be traumatic. One effective way to study such conditions is to use events that are traumatic for children involving contact with others that can be verified. Physicians sometimes must perform genital examinations on children, which may include painful medical procedures. The children's memories of these events can be examined systematically. In one study, half of 72 girls between the ages of 5 and 7 years were given a genital examination as part of necessary medical care, and half were not. Children who received the examination were unlikely to report having been touched in their genital region during free recall or when using anatomically detailed dolls. Only when asked leading questions did most of the girls reveal that they had been so examined. The control group made no false reports during free recall or with the dolls, but with leading questions, three children made false reports.

Psychologist Gail Goodman and her colleagues (1994) at the University of California, Davis, emphasized that one of the most important predictors of accurate memory performance is age. Memory performance for traumatic events is significantly worse in children 3 to 4 years old than in older children. Dr. Goodman also noted, however, that other factors influence memory accuracy in children. Such factors include how well the traumatic episode is actually understood, the degree of parental emotional support and communication, and the children's emotional (positive versus negative) feelings.

The goal of this research is to determine the validity of children's reports on events—including negative ones such as abuse—that may have happened to them, and how they might invent stories. Of special interest is whether leading questions can induce children to fabricate testimony. We need to know this when interpreting children's testimony that involves other persons, such as therapists or members of the legal system. From the cognitive neuroscience perspective, it is important to know whether the neural signature of real and false memories might be different (see How the Brain Works: False Memories and the Medial Temporal Lobes on p. 409).

Participant H.G.

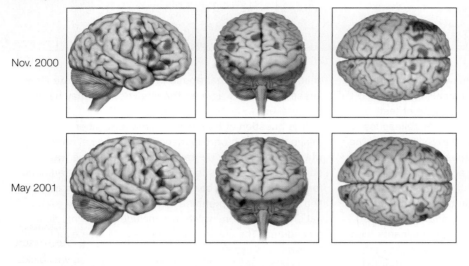

Participant K.B.

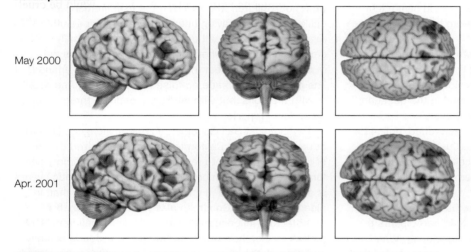

FIGURE 14.18 Regions of activation to an episodic retrieval task vary in the brain of the same individual tested at different times.
Each block contains the brain representation from an individual participant when performing the same word memory task on two separate occasions. The significant activations during the first session are compared to the significant activations for the same individual during the second session. The date when the session took place is noted on the left.

to a particular spot on a brain scan and state with 100% accuracy that a particular thought or behavior arises from activity in that area.

2. There are also variations in how our brains are connected and how they process information. For instance, when you are asked to name an object that is upside down, you use two processes: one process is present in the right hemisphere, which rotates an object in space; another process is in the left hemisphere, which names an object. So when viewing an upside-down boat, before you can name it, you first rotate it right-side-up in your right hemisphere. Next you send the rotated image to the left hemisphere, where the left hemisphere names the object, and then you say it ("Ah, boat"). Some people are fast at this and some are slow. The people who are fast use one part of their corpus callosum to transfer the information to their speech center, and the slow people use a totally different part. Using diffusion tensor imaging (DTI), researchers have found anatomical differences that could explain this phenomenon. It turns out that people vary tremendously in the number of fibers present in different parts of their callosum and in what routes are used to process this problem (Putnam et al., 2010). Capturing all this variation against or for a particular case in a legal setting may prove impossible.

3. The mind, emotions, and the way we think constantly change. What is measured in the brain at the time of scanning doesn't reflect what was happening at the time of a crime. For instance, when Miller and his colleagues brought the participants in the memory experiment back to repeat exactly the same tasks, their brain activity patterns differed (Figure 14.18).

4. Brains are sensitive to many factors that can alter scans: caffeine, tobacco, alcohol, drugs, fatigue, strategy, menstrual cycle, concomitant disease, nutritional state, and so forth.

5. Performance is not consistent. People do better or worse at any task from day to day.

6. Images of the brain are prejudicial. Studies (Weisberg et al., 2008) have shown that when adults read the explanations of psychological phenomena, the explanations are more positively evaluated and considered important if a brain scan is shown in

the material they read, even when the images have nothing to do with the explanations. In fact, bad explanations are more accepted with the presence of a brain scan.

Consider one case where brain scans were admitted as evidence. Simon Pirela had received two death sentences for two separate first-degree murder convictions in 1983. In 2004, twenty-one years later, brain scans were allowed as evidence and convinced one jury in a resentencing hearing that Pirela was not eligible for the death penalty, because he suffered from frontal lobe aberrations that diminished his capacity to function normally. In a separate appeal hearing to vacate the second death sentence, however, exactly the same scans were used to make a different claim. This time the scans were offered as evidence that Pirela was mentally retarded. Combined with testimony from a neuropsychologist, the scans were found "quite convincing" by the appellate judge. The same scans were accepted as evidence for two different diagnoses (Staff working paper, 2004).

When presented with the abnormal brain story, the law makes several false assumptions with no scientific basis. It assumes that an abnormal brain scan is an indicator of abnormal behavior. It does not follow that a person with an abnormal brain scan has abnormal behavior. This was a trap that orthopedic doctors fell into when MRI was first available to help diagnose back pain. It took them a while to realize that an abnormal disc shown on a lumbar MRI is not necessarily a problem. In fact, in a study of 98 participants with no history of back pain, 64% had abnormal disc protrusions on a lumbar MRI (Jensen et al., 1994). You can't look at an abnormal MRI scan of the lower back and predict whether the person has pain, just as you can't look at a brain scan and predict whether the person has abnormal behavior. Another erroneous assumption is that a person with an abnormal brain who does have abnormal behavior is automatically incapable of responsible behavior. Responsibility is not located in the brain. The brain has no area or network for responsibility. As previously noted, the way to think about responsibility is that it is an interaction between people, a social contract.

An abnormal brain does not mean that the person cannot follow rules, although with certain very specific lesions it may. An abnormal brain also does not necessarily mean that the person is more violent. People who have acquired left frontal lobe lesions may act oddly, but their violence rate only increases from the base rate of 3% to between 11% and 13%. A frontal lobe lesion in itself is not a predictor of violent behavior. In the case of an abnormal neurotransmitter disorder such as schizophrenia, there is a higher incidence of arrest for drug-related issues, but there is no higher incidence of violent behavior in people with schizophrenia while they are taking their medication and only a

very small increased incidence in those who are not. They still understand rules and obey them; for instance, they stop at traffic lights and pay cashiers. It is not true that just because you have schizophrenia, your base rate of violent behavior goes up and you are vastly more likely to commit a crime. If the court system concludes that having frontal lobe lesions or schizophrenia can exculpate a person for their behavior, that decision can result in two possible scenarios. Anyone with a frontal lobe lesion or schizophrenia has carte blanche for any behavior. Or, to take the opposite tack (which is based on the same reasoning that they cannot control their behavior), all people with frontal lobe lesions or schizophrenia should be locked up as a preventive measure. So in thinking about these things, we have to be careful that our best intentions aren't used inappropriately.

In the Simon Pirella case just discussed, the reason for seeking the diagnosis of mental retardation was based on a 2002 Supreme Court ruling, which declared that executing someone with mental retardation would be cruel and unusual punishment; as such, it was a violation of the 8th Amendment of the U.S. Constitution. Chief Justice Scalia summarized this case (*Atkins v. Virginia*):

After spending the day drinking alcohol and smoking marijuana, petitioner Daryl Renard Atkins and a partner in crime drove to a convenience store, intending to rob a customer. Their victim was Eric Nesbitt, an airman from Langley Air Force Base, whom they abducted, drove to a nearby automated teller machine, and forced to withdraw $200. They then drove him to a deserted area, ignoring his pleas to leave him unharmed. According to the co-conspirator, whose testimony the jury evidently credited, Atkins ordered Nesbitt out of the vehicle and, after he had taken only a few steps, shot him one, two, three, four, five, six, seven, eight times in the thorax, chest, abdomen, arms, and legs.

The jury convicted Atkins of capital murder. At resentencing . . . the jury heard extensive evidence of petitioner's alleged mental retardation. A psychologist testified that petitioner was mildly mentally retarded with an IQ of 59, that he was a "slow learne[r]," . . ., who showed a "lack of success in pretty much every domain of his life," . . ., and that he had an "impaired" capacity to appreciate the criminality of his conduct and to conform his conduct to the law, . . . Petitioner's family members offered additional evidence in support of his mental retardation claim. . . . The State contested the evidence of retardation and presented testimony of a psychologist who found "absolutely no evidence other than the IQ score . . . indicating that [petitioner] was in the least bit mentally retarded" and concluded that petitioner was "of average intelligence, at least." . . .

The jury also heard testimony about petitioner's 16 prior felony convictions for robbery, attempted robbery, abduction, use of a firearm, and maiming. . . . The victims of these offenses provided graphic depictions of petitioner's violent tendencies: He hit one over the head with a beer bottle. . .; he slapped a gun across another victim's face, clubbed her in the head with it, knocked her to the ground, and then helped her up, only to shoot her in the stomach, *id.,* . . . The jury sentenced petitioner to death. The Supreme Court of Virginia affirmed petitioner's sentence.

The three main justifications for capital punishment are deterrence, retribution, and incapacitation. Justice Stevens, writing for the majority of the Court, reasoned that two of the main justifications, deterrence and retribution, could not be appreciated by the defendant, who suffered mental retardation, and therefore, the sentence imposed cruel and unusual punishment. The legal decision was delivered in terms of existing *beliefs* about the purpose of punishment in the law. It was not based on the science of brain function—namely whether the defendant, because of his brain abnormality, could or could not form intentions, learn from experience, and the like. The decision also makes the assumption that anyone suffering any degree of "mental retardation" has no capacity for understanding the just deserts for a crime or what the society considers right or wrong. Was there any evidence on which to base this assumption? Not from the defendant's behavior.

In the case just described, the defendant was able to make a plan and take what was necessary to implement the plan. He was capable of learning and learned to drive a car following the rules of the road; understood that coercion was necessary to get money from a stranger and how to coerce; understood that shooting the victim was breaking a social rule and should not be done in public or within the public hearing; and was able to inhibit his actions until they were in an out-of-the-way location. His behavior more likely should have led to the assumption that he could follow rules, form intentions and plans, learn from experience, and inhibit his actions; further, he did have guilty intent, and did understand that there could be retributive consequences that he did not want to undergo, and hence tried to hide his actions. Whether he was retarded or not had no effect on these aspects of brain function.

Guilty—Now What?

However complicated the court system may be, proceedings that arrive at a verdict are the easy part. Most of the defendants who get to trial or plead guilty are the agents of the crime. After a defendant has been found guilty, next comes the sentencing. That is the hard part. What do you do with guilty people who have intentionally planned and committed known, morally wrong actions that harm others? The judge looks at all the mitigating and contributing factors (age, previous criminal record, severity of the crime, negligence versus intention, unforeseeable versus foreseeable harm, etc.), as well as the sentencing guidelines, and then makes a decision. Should the offender be punished? If so, should the goal of punishment be mindful of individual rights based on retribution, mindful of the good of society with reform and deterrence in mind, or mindful of the victim with compensation? This decision is affected by the judge's own beliefs of justice, which come in three forms: retributive justice, utilitarian justice, and restorative justice.

Retributive justice is geared toward punishing the individual criminal in proportion to the crime that was committed. Thus, its goal is extending just deserts to the criminal: an eye for an eye. The crucial variable is the degree of moral outrage the crime engenders, not the benefits to society resulting from the punishment. Therefore, a person does not get a life sentence for stealing a piece of pizza, nor does anyone get a month's probation for molesting a child. The punishment is focused solely on what the individual deserves for his crime, and nothing more or less. It appeals to the intuitive sense of fairness whereby every individual is equal and is punished equally. You cannot be punished for crimes you have not committed. No matter who you are, you should receive the same punishment for the same crime. You do not get a harsher sentence because you are or are not famous, because you are black or white or brown. The general welfare of society as a whole is not part of a calculation. *Retributive justice* is backward looking, and its only concern is to punish the criminal for a past action. It does not punish as a deterrent to others, nor to reform the offender, nor to compensate the victim. These outcomes may result as byproducts, but they are not the goal. It punishes to harm the offender, just as the victim was harmed. When Polly Klaas's father said, "Richard Allen Davis deserves to die for what he did to my child," he was speaking from the perspective of retributive justice.

Utilitarian justice (consequentialism), on the other hand, is forward looking. It is concerned about the greater future good for society that may result from punishing an individual offender. There are three types of utilitarian punishment. The first specifically *deters* the offender (or others who will learn by example) in the future, perhaps by fines, prison time, or community service. You speed past a school zone and get a ticket for $500. You might think twice about it next time and slow down. The second type of utilitarian justice *incapacitates* the offender. Incapacitation can be achieved geographically, such as when the British sent their debtors to Australia; by long prison sentences or banishment, which includes disbarment for lawyers and other such licensing losses; or by physical means, such as castration for rapists, capital punishment, severing the hands of thieves, and so forth. This is what Polly's father had in mind when he said, "It doesn't bring our daughter back into our lives, but it gets one monster off the streets." The third type of utilitarian justice is *rehabilitation* through treatment or education. The method chosen is decided by the probability of recidivism, degree of impulsiveness, criminal record, ethics (can treatment be forced on someone who is unwilling to undergo it?), and so forth, or by prescribed sentencing standards. This is another area where neuroscience will have something to contribute. Prediction of future criminal behavior is pertinent to utilitarian sentencing decisions, whether treatment, probation, involuntary commitment, or detention is chosen. Neural markers could be used to help identify an individual as a psychopath, sexual predator, impulsive, and so forth, in conjunction with other evidence to make predictions of future behavior. Obviously the reliability of such predictions is important, as is deciding what level of certainty about these determinations is acceptable. Because utilitarian justice punishes for uncommitted future crimes, its use can result in either decreasing or increasing harmful errors.

The goal of utilitarian justice (the greater good) may sound good on paper, but some of its aspects go against our sense of fairness. Utilitarian justice would permit harsher punishment for a famous person or the perpetrator of a highly publicized crime, because the publicity might deter many future crimes and thus benefit society. To increase the deterrence effect, harsh sentences for common, but minor, offenses are also allowed. For instance, some utilitarians advocate prison sentences (not just overnight in the local lockup) for first-time speeding and drunk driving offenses. No doubt you would think twice when you set your cruise control over the speed limit, if being caught resulted in a year in prison. This practice could save more innocent lives than punishing convicted murderers. The most common crime in the United States is shoplifting, which costs retailers about $13 billion to $35 billion a year. The crime has many hidden costs including higher prices for consumers, lost taxes to the community, and extra burden on police and courts. A harsh sentence for shoplifting could deter many who contemplate slipping a lipstick into their pocket and reduce the overall cost of goods for everyone. The extreme utilitarian case can be made that the punished need not even be guilty, just thought to be guilty by the public. This is why some people object to utilitarian justice: It can violate an individual's rights, and it may not seem "fair."

In British law, since the Norman invasion of England in 1066, crimes have been considered to be injuries against the state, rather than against an individual. American law has also taken this stance. The victim has no part in the justice system, thus ensuring neutrality in criminal proceedings and avoiding vengeful and unfair retaliation. **Restorative justice**, however, looks at crimes as having been committed against a person rather than against the state. Restorative justice holds the offender directly accountable to the victim and the affected community. It requires the offender to make things whole again to the extent possible, allows the victim a say in the corrections process, and encourages the community to hold offenders accountable, support victims, and provide opportunities for offenders to reintegrate themselves into the community. Victims of crimes are often enveloped in fear, which adversely affects the rest of their lives. For crimes of lesser magnitude, often a face-to-face, sincere apology and reparation are enough to relieve the victim's fear and anger. Restorative justice, however, may not be possible for more serious crimes. Would an apology be judged satisfactory by the parents of Polly Klaas or the voters who passed the three-strikes laws?

Born to Judge

When people are asked to label themselves as retributivists or deterrists, their answers vary widely. These individual differences seem to evaporate, however, when people are asked to assign hypothetical punishment for an offense. The vast majority, 97%, seek out information relevant to a retributive perspective and not to the utilitarian perspective (Carlsmith, 2006). They are highly sensitive to the severity of the offense and ignore the likelihood that the person would offend again. They punish for the harm done (retribution), not for the harm that might be done in the future (deterrence). When asked to punish only from the utilitarian perspective and to ignore retributive factors, people still used the severity of the crime to guide their judgments (Darley et al., 2000). Yet, when asked to allocate resources for catching offenders or preventing crime, they highly supported the utilitarian approach of preventing crime. So although people endorse the utilitarian theory of reducing crime, they don't want to do it through unjust punishment. They want to give a person what she deserves, but only after she deserves it. People want to be fair (Carlsmith & Darley, 2008).

Where does this retributive sense of fairness come from? We were born with it, along with a sense of reciprocity and punishment. When 2½-year-olds are asked to distribute treats to animated puppets, they will do so evenly (Sloane & Baillargeon, 2010). Even 16-month-old infants have a keen sense of fairness, exhibited by their preference for cartoon characters that divide prizes equally (Geraci & Surian, 2010). We also come wired for reciprocity, but only within our social group. Toddlers expect members of a group to play and share toys and are surprised when it doesn't happen. They are also surprised, however, when sharing happens between members of different groups. They are not surprised when it does not (He & Baillargeon, 2010). Toddlers recognize moral transgressors and react negatively to them. Children from 1½ to 2 years old help, comfort, and share with a victim of a moral transgression, even in the absence of overt emotional cues. Moral transgressors, on the other hand, incite the infants to protest vocally, and they are less inclined to help, comfort, or share with them (Vaish et al., 2010). Young children also understand intentionality and judge intentional violations of rules as "naughty," but they do not feel that way about accidental violations (Harris & Nunez, 1996). We feel these urges all the time, and we try to have big theories about them, but we are just born that way.

Knowing about these innate tendencies helps us to understand that although people say they endorse utilitarian policies in the abstract, they invoke retributivist ones in practice (Carlsmith, 2008). This lack of insight leads to fickle legislation. For instance, 72% of the voters of California enacted the three-strikes law that we spoke of at the beginning of the chapter, thus taking a utilitarian approach. A few years later, when they realized that this could mean an "unfair" life sentence for stealing a piece of pizza and sensed that the law was unfair from a retributivist perspective, voter support dropped to less than 50%. Because of this highly intuitive just-deserts impulse, it is doubtful that citizens will be willing to allow a purely restorative, no-punishment treatment for serious crimes.

We aren't the first to be wrestling with the ideas of retributive and utilitarian justice. Aristotle argued that justice based on fair treatment of the individual leads to a fair society. Plato, looking at the big picture, thought fairness to society was of primary importance and that individual cases should be judged in order to achieve that end. These two ways of thinking should remind you of the trolley problem in Chapter 13: the emotional situation and the more abstract situation. Facing the individual offender in a courtroom and deciding whether to punish is an emotional proposition, and it elicits an intuitive emotional reaction: "Throw the book at 'em!" or, "Poor guy, he didn't mean to do it, let him off easy!" How would you feel if you were sitting across the courtroom from the person who killed or molested your child? In an fMRI study done while participants were judging responsibility and assigning punishment in hypothetical cases, brain regions associated with emotion were activated during the punishment judgment—and the more activity these regions showed, the greater the punishment (Buckholtz et al., 2008). While participants were making third-party legal decisions, however, a region of the right dorsolateral prefrontal cortex was recruited, the same region that is recruited when judgments about punishments are made in the Ultimatum economic game. These researchers suggest that "our modern legal system may have evolved by building on preexisting cognitive mechanisms that support fairness-related behaviors in dyadic interactions." If an evolutionary link to relations between individuals in socially significant situations (for example, mates) is true, it makes sense that when faced with an individual, we resort to fairness judgments rather than utilitarian justice. Faced with the abstract questions of public policy, however, we leave the emotional reaction behind and can resort to the more abstract utilitarian thinking.

What's a Judge to Do?

If a judge believes that people are personally responsible for their behavior, then either retributive punishment or restorative justice makes sense. If the judge believes that deterrence is effective, or that punishment can change bad behavior into good, or that some people are irredeemable, then utilitarian punishment makes sense. If the judge has a determinist stance, there is still a retributist or utilitarian decision to be made. From the retributist perspective, his focus of concern may be (a) for *the offender's individual rights* and because the offender had no control over his determined behavior, he or she should not be punished (a retributist attitude) but perhaps should be treated (but not against their will?) if possible; or (b) for *the victim's rights* of restitution and any deterministic retributive feelings the victim might have; or the judge could go the utilitarian route and decide to sentence (c) for *the greater good of society* (it may not be the offenders' fault, but get 'em off the streets).

Boalt law professor Sanford Kadish (1987) sums up the stance taken by many hard-core determinists:

> To blame a person is to express moral criticism, and if the person's action does not deserve criticism, blaming him is a kind of falsehood, and is, to the extent the person is injured by being blamed, unjust to him.

In essence, he is saying that criminals are not responsible for the actions committed by their determinist brain; thus, they should not be blamed or punished. What do you do with them? Don't hold them accountable for their actions and turn them back out on the streets? Forgive and forget? Is forgiveness a viable concept? Is it possible to run a civilized society where forgiveness trumps accountability and punishment?

Crime and No Punishment?

Unlike any other species, we humans have evolved to co-operate on a massive scale with unrelated others. There are now 6.7 billion of us, more than twice the world population of 1950. The amazing thing is that we as a species are becoming less violent and get along rather well, contrary to what you may hear on the evening news (Pinker, 2011). The troublemakers, although still very much of a problem, are actually few and far between, perhaps 5% of the population. Where did this cooperation come from? Our relatives, the chimpanzees, are not known for their cooperation. They cooperate only in certain competitive situations and only with certain individuals. This behavior stands in marked contrast with humans, who are largely cooperative. Otherwise, how would an alphabet or a system of numbers have come about, or towns and cities been built? Brian Hare and Michael Tomasello have suggested that the social behavior of chimps is constrained by their temperament and that a different temperament was necessary for the development of more complex forms of social cognition. To develop the level of cooperation necessary to live in very large social groups, humans had to become less aggressive and less competitive than their ancestors. They had to evolve a different temperament. How did this come about?

Taming the Wild Beast

Hare and Tomasello hypothesize that humans may have undergone a self-domestication process in which overly aggressive or despotic others were either ostracized or killed by the group, eliminating them from the gene pool. The individuals who had systems that controlled emotional reactivity, such as aggression, were more successful and reproduced. "It is only after the human temperament evolved that variation in more complex forms of communicative and cooperative behaviors could have been shaped by evolution into the unique forms of cooperative cognition present in our species today" (Hare & Tomasello, 2005). This *emotional reactivity hypothesis* grew out of work done by a Russian geneticist, Dmitry Belyaev. In 1959, he began domesticating foxes at the Institute of Cytology and Genetics in Novosibirsk, Siberia, using only one criterion for his breeding selection process. He picked the young foxes that came the closest to his outstretched hand: Thus he was selecting for fearless and nonaggressive behavior toward humans (Figure 14.19).

After only a few years, the physiological, morphological, and behavioral by-products of this selection process were similar to what is seen in domestic dogs. The female foxes have higher serotonin levels (known to decrease some types of aggressive behavior) and an alteration

FIGURE 14.19 Aggressive and tame foxes.
(top) Fox displaying aggressive behavior. **(bottom)** Tame foxes.

in the levels of many of the chemicals in the brain that regulate stress and aggressive behavior (Belyaev, 1979). Some of the foxes have floppy ears, upturned tails, and piebald colorations like those seen in border collies (Figure 14.20). In fact, some of the same morphological changes have occurred in domesticated animals of many species (Figure 14.21). The domesticated foxes will also wag their tails and respond as well as domestic dogs to the human communicative gestures of pointing and gazing (Hare et al., 2005).

All these characteristics have been linked to the gene associated with fear inhibition. It seems that socio-cognitive evolution has occurred in the experimental foxes as a correlated by-product of selection on systems mediating fear and aggression. Dog domestication is thought to have occurred naturally by a similar process. Wild dogs that were less fearful of humans were the ones that approached their camps, scavenged food,

FIGURE 14.20 Morphological markers of domestication in foxes correlate with domesticated behaviors. Domesticated foxes show an unusually high incidence of floppy ears, shortened legs and tails, curled-up tails, and a star blaze. In Table 14.1, the rates of some common changes are compared. The increased incidence of the "star" depigmentation pattern and doglike tail characteristics was most marked.

stuck around, and reproduced. Hare and his colleagues (2012) suggest that a similar process has been at work on bonobos. Unlike their chimpanzee ancestors, bonobos will share food with unfamiliar conspecifics (Hare & Kwetuenda, 2010) and will spontaneously cooperate on a novel instrumental task (for a food reward). Like dogs but unlike chimps, bonobos are responsive to human gaze direction (Hermann et al., 2010). The researchers suggest that because of their geographical location, bonobos had less competition among themselves for

food than did chimpanzees and may have undergone a similar self-domestication process.

Henrike Moll and Michael Tomasello (2007) have suggested that certain aspects of cognition, which they consider to be unique to humans (the cognitive skills of shared goals, joint attention, joint intentions, and cooperative communication), were driven by or were constituted of social cooperation. This cooperation is needed to create such things as complex technologies, cultural institutions, and systems of symbols. Unlike any

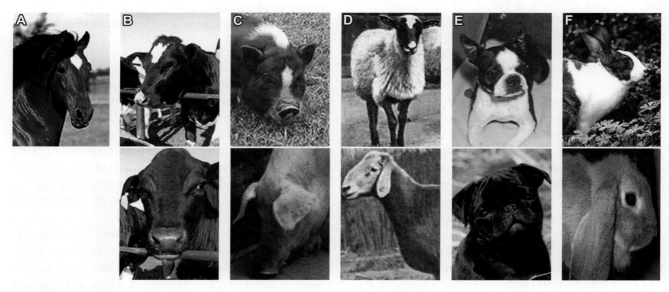

FIGURE 14.21 Morphological markers of domestication are seen in different animal families and orders.
White spotting (star depigmentation) on the head **(top row)** and floppy ears **(bottom row)**: A: Horse (*Equus caballus*); B: Cow (*Bos taurus*); C: Pig (*Sus scrofa domestica*); D: Sheep (*Ovis*); E: Dog (*Canis familiaris*); F: Rabbit (*Oryctolagus cuniculus*).

TABLE 14.1 Frequency Changes of Morphological Characteristics during "Domestication" of Foxes

| Characteristic | Animals per 100,000 with Trait | | Increase in Frequency (percent) |
	Domesticated Population	Nondomesticated Population	
Depigmentation (*Star*)	12,400	710	+1,646
Brown mottling	450	86	+423
Gray hairs	500	100	+400
Floppy ears	230	170	+35
Short tail	140	2	+6,900
Tail rolled in circle	9,400	830	+1,033

other species, humans cooperate with non-kin. This type of cooperation has been difficult to explain from an evolutionary standpoint, because cooperating individuals incur costs to themselves that benefit non-kin. This type of altruistic behavior doesn't make sense at the individual level. How can that be a strategy for success? Robert Trivers (1971; 2011) was the first to explain how altruistic behavior could be a successful strategy. As Steve Pinker (2012) succinctly puts it,

> It can be explained by an expectation of reciprocity and a concern with reputation. People punish those that are most likely to exploit them, choose to interact with partners who are least likely to free-ride, and cooperate and punish more, and free-ride less, when their reputations are on the line.

One way cooperation can arise is through the punishment of non-cooperators. Both theoretical models and experimental evidence show that in the absence of punishment, cooperation cannot sustain itself in the presence of **free-riders** and collapses. Free-riding individuals are those who do not cooperate or contribute, but exploit the efforts of others: They incur no costs and produce no benefits. For example, in the Public Goods game, each participant is given a number of tokens. Each decides how many tokens they will secretly put into a communal pot. They get to keep the rest. The experimenter figures the total of communal tokens, multiplies by a factor greater than one but fewer than the number of participants, and divides it evenly among the participants. The optimum strategy for the group would be for each person to contribute the maximum, whereas the optimum strategy for the individual is to be a free-rider: give none, and get a cut from all the people who donated. Obviously, free-riders fare better and are more successful because they do not pay the cost of contributing. Over multiple rounds, if punishment is not allowed, free-riding takes over and the

public contribution dwindles to zero. If punishment is allowed, however, cooperation increases (Figure 14.22; Fehr & Gächter, 1999, 2002). Thus, for cooperation to survive, the free-riders must be punished.

The interesting thing is that people will punish at a cost to themselves. In defiance of seemingly rational behavior, we humans engage in punishment even in one-time encounters. For instance, in the Ultimatum economic game, first conducted by Ariel Rubinstein (1982) and repeated in various forms, people will punish non-cooperators at personal cost, even in a one-shot game. In this game, two people are allowed only one turn. One person is given some money, say $20, and he has to split it with the other player, but he determines the percentage split. The other player determines if she will accept the amount that has been offered or not. Both players get to keep whatever amount of money is settled upon. If the player who is offered the money refuses the offer, however, then neither gets any. In a rational world, the player who offers the money need only offer a penny and the person who gets offered the money should take any offer, because that is the only way she will come out ahead. That, however, is not how people react. People tend to offer an even split, and people will accept the money only if they think it is a fair offer, ranging from at least $6 to $8. Anything less than that, and 80% of people will consider the deal unfair and refuse. In so doing, however, they actually incur a loss themselves. Punishing costs the punisher. Why, in one-shot encounters, are people overly generous? And why do people who have received lowball offers punish at a cost to themselves?

Evolutionary psychologists Andrew Delton and Max Krasnow, along with Leda Cosmides and John Tooby (Delton et al., 2011), explain initial cooperation by pointing out that individuals engaging in one-shot encounters must balance the cost of mistaking a one-shot interaction for a repeated interaction against the far greater cost of

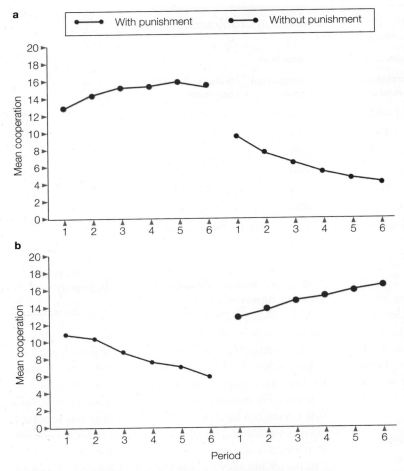

FIGURE 14.22 Cooperation is greater when punishment is an option.
(a) Participants have the opportunity to punish the other group members during the first six periods, but not in the second six periods. In **(b)**, the reverse is true. During the first six periods, punishment of other group is not allowed; but during the second six periods, it is. In both cases, cooperation increases when there is an opportunity to punish non-cooperators.

mistaking a repeated interaction for a one-shot interaction. You shake your head in wonder at the mechanic who overcharges, mistaking you for a tourist rather than a local resident. Now you will never return to his shop, but worse, you will tell all your friends about his overcharging. He has lost your repeat business and any word-of-mouth referrals, which is costing him much more than the amount that he padded his bill. The researchers used computer simulations to show that when neural decision systems for regulating dyadic reciprocity are selected for, generosity in one-shot encounters is the necessary by-product under conditions of uncertainty.

What's going on in this less than rational brain? Ernst Fehr and his colleagues (Knoch et al., 2007) used transcranial electric stimulation to disrupt brain functioning in the prefrontal cortex. They found that when the function of the right dorsolateral prefrontal cortex was disrupted, people would accept lower offers while still judging them to be unfair. They also found that suppression of this area increased selfish responses to unfair offers, suggesting that this area normally inhibits self-interest (taking any offer) and reduces the impact of the selfish urges on the decision-making processes. Thus, the right dorsolateral prefrontal cortex plays a key role in implementing behaviors that are fair.

Dominique de Quervain and her colleagues (2004) hypothesized that people derive satisfaction from punishing norm violations. They found evidence for this view by using positron emission tomography (PET). Their participants' brains underwent a PET scan while they learned about the abuse of trust in a game partner and determined if they were going to punish him and what the punishment would be—either monetarily real or simply symbolic. Real punishment activated the dorsal striatum, which has been implicated in the processing of goal-oriented rewards. Participants with stronger activations were willing to incur greater costs (lose money themselves) in order to punish. Meanwhile, symbolic punishment did not activate the dorsal striatum. We may punish because we are wired to do so, as a result of a selective process that enhanced human survival through cooperation.

Can you have cooperation and accountability without punishment? Clearly, our genome thinks punishment is important. Can we or should we rise above it? If we don't punish the offenders, will the non-cooperators take over and cooperative society fall apart?

Ultimately, if responsibility is a contract between two people rather than a property of a brain, then determinism has no meaning in this context. Human nature remains constant, but out in the social world, behavior can change. When multiple rounds of the Ultimatum game are played, punishing unfair offers results in a change in behavior: Fair offers increase, resulting in more cooperation. You may want to act selfishly and offer only $1 in the Ultimatum game so you can go home with $19, but you learned the hard way that it doesn't work. One person's behavior can affect that of another person. When the highway patrolman comes down the on ramp, you see him, check your speedometer, and slow down. Your doctor tells you that if you keep eating the way you do, you will develop diabetes, so you change your diet. You overcharge your customers, and they don't come back. We have to look at the whole picture, a brain in the midst

the appropriate use for a tool, even though still capable of producing the required movement. Compare *ideomotor apraxia*.

ideomotor apraxia   A form of apraxia in which the patient has difficulty executing the desired action properly. Patients with ideomotor apraxia appear to have a general idea about how the action should be performed and how tools are used, but they are unable to coordinate the movements to produce the action in a coherent manner. Compare *ideational apraxia*.

imitative behavior   The spontaneous and uncontrolled mimicking of another person's behavior that is sometimes exhibited by patients with frontal lobe damage.

inferior colliculus   A part of the midbrain that is involved in auditory processing. Compare *superior colliculus*.

inhibition of return (IOR)   A hypothesized process underlying the slowing of motor responses observed over time when attention is reflexively attracted to a location by a sensory event (i.e., reflexive cue). As the name implies, inhibition of return is conceptualized as inhibition of recently attended locations such that attention is inhibited in returning to that location (or object).

inhibitory control   The hypothesis that one aspect of executive functions is the regulation of habitual responses or environmentally dictated actions by active inhibition. A loss of inhibitory control is assumed to underlie the tendency of some patients with prefrontal lesions to produce socially inappropriate behavior.

insula   A part of cortex known to process gustatory information.

integrative agnosia   A form of agnosia associated with deficits in the recognition of objects due to the failure to group and integrate the component parts into a coherent whole. Patients with this deficit can faithfully reproduce drawings of objects; however, their percept is of isolated, unconnected parts or contours.

interaural time   The difference in time between when a sound reaches each of the two ears. This information is represented at various stages in the auditory pathway and provides an important cue for sound localization.

interoception   Physical sensations arising from inside the body such as pain, temperature, hunger, etc.

interpreter   A left-brain system that seeks explanations for internal and external events in order to produce appropriate response behaviors.

ion channel   A passageway in the cell membrane, formed by a transmembrane protein that creates a pore, through which ions (charged atoms in solution) of sodium, potassium, and chloride (Na^+, K^+, and Cl^-) might pass into or out of the cell.

ion pump   Proteins in the cellular membrane of neurons that are capable of transporting ions against their concentration gradient. The sodium-potassium pump transports sodium ions out of the neuron and potassium ions into the neuron.

joint attention   The ability to monitor someone else's attention by observing that person's gaze or actions and directing one's own attention similarly.

knockout procedure   A technique for creating a genetically altered version of a species. In the knockout species, specific genes are altered or eliminated. Knockout procedures can be used to study behavioral changes occurring in animals that have developed without the targeted gene, or to observe how genes code the development of the nervous system.

late selection   The theoretical model positing that all inputs are equally processed perceptually, but attention acts to differentially filter these inputs at later stages of information processing. Compare *early selection*.

lateral fissure   See *Sylvian fissure*.

lateral geniculate nucleus (LGN)   The thalamic nucleus that is the main target of axons of the optic tract. Output from the LGN is directed primarily to the primary visual cortex (Brodmann area 17). Compare *medial geniculate nucleus*.

lateral occipital complex (or cortex) (LOC)   A region of extrastriate cortex that is part of the ventral pathway. Processing in LOC is essential for shape perception and recognition.

lateral prefrontal cortex (LPFC)   The region of the cerebral cortex that lies anterior to Brodmann area 6, along the lateral surface. This region has been implicated in various executive functions, such as working memory and response selection.

layer   A common organizational cluster of neurons in the central nervous sytem.

learning   The process of acquiring new information.

lexical access   The process by which perceptual inputs activate word information in the mental lexicon, including semantic and syntactic information about the word.

lexical integration   The function of words being integrated into a full sentence, discourse, or large current context to discern the message.

lexical selection   The process of selecting from a collection of representations the activated word that best matches the sensory input.

LGN   See *lateral geniculate nucleus*.

limbic system   Several structures that form a border (*limbus* in Latin) around the brainstem, named the *grand lobe limbique* ("limbic lobe") by Paul Broca. The limbic system is the emotional network that includes the amygdala, orbitofrontal cortex, and portions of the basal ganglia.

limited capacity   The concept that the stages of information processing have a finite processing capability, leading to the need for the system to select high-priority information for access to these stages of analysis.

long-term memory   The retention of information over the long term, from hours to days and years. Compare *sensory memory* and *short-term memory*.

M1   See *primary motor cortex*.

magnetic resonance imaging (MRI)   A neuroimaging technique that exploits the magnetic properties of organic tissue. Certain atoms are especially sensitized to magnetic forces because of the number of protons and neutrons in their nuclei. The orientation of these atoms can be altered by the presence of a strong magnetic field. A radio frequency signal can be used to knock these aligned atoms from their orientation in the magnetic field. The atoms will then realign with the magnetic field and give off a radio frequency signal that can be measured by sensitive detectors. Structural MRI studies usually measure variations in the density of hydrogen ions in the tissue being scanned. Functional MRI measures changes over time in the signal intensity of the targeted atom.

magnetoencephalography (MEG)   A measure of the magnetic signals generated by the brain. The electrical activity of neurons also produces small magnetic fields, which can be measured by sensitive magnetic detectors placed along the scalp, similar to the way EEG measures the surface electrical activity. MEG can be used in an event-related manner similar to ERP studies, with similar temporal resolution. The spatial resolution, in theory, can be superior with MEG because magnetic signals are minimally distorted by organic tissue such as the brain or skull.

materialism A major philosophical approach to describing consciousness, based on the theory that the mind and brain are both physical mediums. Variations include: philosophical behaviorism, reductive materialism, and functionalism.

medial frontal cortex (MFC) The medial region of the frontal cortex that includes parts of areas 24, 32, and inferior aspects of 6 and 8. The medial frontal cortex is associated with cognitive control—in particular, monitoring functions for error detection and resolving conflict.

medial geniculate nucleus (MGN) A collection of cell bodies in the medial portion of the thalamus involved in processing auditory information. Output from the MGN is directed primarily to the primary auditory cortex. Compare *lateral geniculate nucleus*.

medulla Also *myelencephalon*. The brainstem's most caudal portion. The medulla is continuous with the spinal cord and contains the prominent, dorsally positioned nuclear groups known as the *gracile* and *cuneate nuclei*, which relay somatosensory information from the spinal cord to the brain, and the ventral pyramidal tracts, containing descending projection axons from the brain to the spinal cord. Various sensory and motor nuclei are found in the medulla.

MEG See *magnetoencephalography*.

memory The persistence of learning in a state that can be revealed later.

mental lexicon A mental store of information about words, including semantic information (meanings of the words), syntactic information (rules for using the words), and the details of word forms (spellings and sound patterns).

mesocortical pathway A path through which dopaminergic projections travel to reach the neocortex.

MGN See *medial geniculate nucleus*.

microstimulation Injection of electrical current in the vicinity of a group of neurons of interest, in order to induce neural activity. Microstimulation allows the experimenter to manipulate normal neural activity and observe the consequences on behavior.

midbrain The part of the brain consisting of the *tectum* (meaning "roof," and representing the dorsal portion of the mesencephalon), *tegmentum* (the main portion of the midbrain), and ventral regions occupied by large fiber tracts (*crus cerebri*) from the forebrain to the spinal cord (corticospinal tract), cerebellum, and brainstem (corticobulbar tract). The midbrain contains neurons that participate in visuomotor functions (e.g., superior colliculus, oculomotor nucleus, trochlear nucleus), visual reflexes (e.g., pretectal region), auditory relays (inferior colliculus), and the mesencephalic tegmental nuclei involved in motor coordination (red nucleus). It is bordered anteriorly by the diencephalon, and caudally by the pons.

mirror neuron Neurons that show similar responses when an animal is performing an action or observing that action produced by another organism. Mirror neurons are hypothesized to provide a strong link between perception and action, perhaps providing an important basis for the development of conceptual knowledge.

mirror system A distributed network of neurons that respond not only to one's own action but also to *perceived* actions. For instance, a mirror neuron responds when you pick up a pencil and when you watch someone else pick up a pencil.

module A specialized processing unit of the nervous system. Modules are hypothesized to perform specific computations; for example, some theorists believe there are dedicated modules for speech perception, distinct from those used for auditory perception.

monitoring The executive function associated with evaluating whether current representations and/or actions are conducive to the achievement of current goals. Errors can be avoided or corrected by a monitoring system. One of the hypothesized operations of a supervisory attentional system.

Montreal procedure Created by Wilder Penfield and Herbert Jasper, a procedure to treat epilepsy in which the neurons that produced seizures were surgically destroyed.

morpheme Morphemes are the smallest grammatical units of a language that carry bits of meaning. They may or may not be whole words; for example, *dog*, *spit*, *un-* and *-ly* are morphemes.

multiple realizability A philosophy of mind thesis that contends that a single mental state or event (such as pain) can be realized by many different physical states or events.

MRI See *magnetic resonance imaging*.

multisensory integration The integration of information from more than one sensory modality. Watching someone speak requires the integration of auditory and visual information.

multiunit recording A physiological procedure in which an array of electrodes is inserted in the brain such that the activity of many cells can be recorded simultaneously.

myelencephalon See *medulla*.

myelin A fatty substance that surrounds the axons of many neurons and increases the effective membrane resistance, helping to speed the conduction of action potentials.

N400 response Also simply "the N400." A negative-polarity event-related potential that is elicited by words, and that is larger in amplitude for words that do not fit well into the sentence context. Compare *P600 response*.

neglect See *unilateral spatial neglect*.

neocortex The portion of the cortex that typically contains six main cortical layers (with sublayers) and has a high degree of specialization of neuronal organization. The neocortex is composed of areas like the primary sensory and motor cortex and association cortex, and as its name suggests, is the most modern (evolved) type of cortex.

neural circuit Groups of interconnected neurons that process specific kinds of information.

neural network Computer model in which processing is distributed over units whose inputs and outputs represent specific features. For example, they may indicate whether a stimulus contains a visual feature, such as a vertical or horizontal line.

neural system Groups of neural circuits that combine to form larger systems for processing information. For example, the visual system is a system comprising many smaller more specialized neural circuits.

neuroeconomics An emerging field of brain science that combines economics and cognitive neuroscience with the goal of understanding the neural mechanisms involved in decision making.

neuron   One of two cell types (along with the *glial cell*) in the nervous system. Neurons are responsible for processing sensory, motor, cognitive, and affective information.

neuron doctrine   The concept proposed by the great Spanish neuroanatomist Santiago Ramon y Cajal in the 19th century that the neuron is the fundamental unit of the nervous system, and that the nervous system is composed of billions of these units (neurons) connected to process information.

neurophysiology   The study of the physiological processes of the nervous system. Neural activity is characterized by physiological changes that can be described both electrically and chemically. The changes can be observed at many different levels, ranging from the gross changes recorded with EEG, to the firing of individual neurons, to the molecular changes that occur at the synapse.

neurotransmitter   A chemical substance that transmits the signal between neurons at chemical synapses.

nociceptors   The somatosensory receptors that convey pain information.

node of Ranvier   A location at which myelin is interrupted between successive patches of axon, and where an action potential can be generated.

nondeclarative memory   Knowledge to which we typically have no conscious access, such as motor and cognitive skills (procedural knowledge). For example, the ability to ride a bicycle is a nondeclarative form of knowledge. Although we can describe the action itself, the actual information one needs to ride a bicycle is not easy to describe. Compare *declarative memory.*

normative decision theory   A theory of how actions are selected in which the basic premise is that the agent makes the optimal choice, having considered the possible rewards and costs associated with each option.

nucleus (pl. nuclei)   1. In neuroanatomy, a collection of cell bodies in the central nervous system—for example, the lateral geniculate nucleus. 2. In biology, a cellular organelle where DNA is stored.

nucleus accumbens   The ventral part of the striatum, one of the nuclei of the basal ganglia. The nucleus accumbens is associated with the reward system of the brain, showing changes in activity in response to both primary and secondary reinforcers.

object constancy   The ability to recognize invariant properties of an object across a wide range of contexts. For example, although the size of the retinal image changes dramatically when a car recedes in the distance, our percept is that the car remains the same size. Similarly, we are able to recognize that an object is the same when seen from different perspectives.

occipital lobe   A cortical lobe located at the posterior of the cerebral cortex that primarily contains neurons involved in visual information processing.

odorant   A molecule conducted through the air that leads to activation of the olfactory receptors and may be perceived as having a smell when processed through the olfactory system. Compare *tastant.*

optic ataxia   A neurological syndrome in which the patient has great difficulty using visual information to guide her actions, even though she is unimpaired in her ability to recognize objects. Optic ataxia is associated with lesions of the parietal lobe.

optogenetics   A procedure in which a genetic manipulation is performed that will result in the expression of a photosensitive protein. The experimenter can then activate the neurons by exposing the tissue to light. The genetic manipulation can be modified such that the protein expression is limited to particular neural regions.

orbitofrontal cortex (OFC)   A region of the frontal lobe, located above the orbits of the eyes, that is implicated in a range of functions, including perceptual processes associated with olfaction and taste, as well as those associated with monitoring whether one's behavior is appropriate.

overt attention   Turning one's head to orient towards a stimulus, be it visual, auditory, olfactory, etc.

P600 response   Also *syntactic positive shift.* A positive-polarity event-related potential elicited when words violate syntactic rules in sentences. Compare *N400 response.*

parahippocampal place area (PPA)   A functionally defined area of the brain (usually with fMRI), located in the parahippocampal region of the temporal lobe that shows a preferential response to stimuli depicting scenes or places.

parietal lobe   A cortical lobe located posterior to the central sulcus, anterior to the occipital lobe, and superior to the posterior temporal cortex. This cortical region contains a variety of neurons, including the somatosensory cortex, gustatory cortex, and parietal association cortex, which includes regions involved in visuomotor orienting, attention, and representation of space.

Parkinson's disease   A degenerative disorder of the basal ganglia in which the pathology results from the loss of dopaminergic cells in the substantia nigra. Primary symptoms include difficulty in initiating movement, slowness of movement, poorly articulated speech, and, in some cases, resting tremor. Compare *Huntington's disease.*

perceptual representation system (PRS)   A form of nondeclarative memory, acting within the perceptual system, in which the structure and form of objects and words can be primed by prior experience and can be revealed later through implicit memory tests.

peripheral nervous system (PNS)   A courier network that delivers sensory information to the CNS and then conducts the motor commands of the CNS to control muscles of the body; anything outside the brain and spinal cord. Compare *central nervous system.*

permeability   The extent to which ions can cross a neuronal membrane.

perseveration   The tendency to produce a particular response on successive trials, even when the context has changed such that the response is no longer appropriate. Commonly observed in patients with prefrontal damage, perseveration is thought to reflect a loss of inhibitory control.

PET   See *positron emission tomography.*

pharmacological studies   Experimental method in which the independent variable involves the administration of a chemical agent or drug. An example would be when people are given drugs that act as dopamine agonists and observations are made on their performance in decision-making tasks.

phoneme   The smallest perceived units of sound in a language, of which, for example, there are 40 in the English language.

phonology   The way sounds of a language are organized to create meaning.

photoreceptor   A specialized cell in the retina that transduces light energy into changes in membrane potential. The photoreceptors are the interface for the visual system between the external world and the nervous system.

phrenology   The study of the physical shape of the human head, based on the belief that variations in the skull's surface can reveal specific intellectual and personality traits. Today phrenology is understood to lack validity.

PiB A radioactive compound that is used as a tracer in PET studies to label beta-amyloid, a substance that is associated with Alzheimer's Disease. The discovery of PiB provided an important biomarker for identifying people at risk for developing this disease.

pituitary gland Controlled by the hypothalamus, the pituitary gland helps maintain the normal state of the body (homeostasis).

planum temporale The surface area of the temporal lobe that includes Wernicke's area. The planum temporale has long been believed to be larger in the left hemisphere because of the lateralization of language function, although this theory is currently controversial.

PNS See *peripheral nervous system.*

pons A region in the brain that includes the pontine tegmental regions on the floor of the fourth ventricle, and the pons itself, a vast system of fiber tracts interspersed with pontine nuclei. The fibers are continuations of the cortical projections to the spinal cord, brainstem, and cerebellar regions. The pons also includes the primary sensory nuclear groups for auditory and vestibular inputs, and somatosensory inputs from, and motor nuclei projecting to, the face and mouth. Neurons of the reticular formation can also be found in the anterior regions of the pons.

population vector A statistical procedure to represent the activity across a group of neurons. Population vectors reflect the aggregate activity across the cells, providing a better correlation with behavior than that obtained from the analysis of individual neurons. For example, the population vector calculated from neurons in the motor cortex can predict the direction of a limb movement.

positron emission tomography (PET) A neuroimaging method that measures metabolic activity or blood flow changes in the brain by monitoring the distribution of a radioactive tracer. The PET scanner measures the photons that are produced during the decay of a tracer. A popular tracer for cognitive neuroscience studies is O^{15} because its decay time is rapid and the distribution of oxygen increases to neural regions that are active.

posterior commissure Located above the cerebral aqueduct at the junction of the third ventricle, this carries interhemispheric fibers that contribute to the papillary light reflex.

postsynaptic Referring to the neuron located after the synapse with respect to information flow. Compare *presynaptic.*

prediction error A theoretical construct in theories of reinforcement learning that is defined as the difference between an expected and actual outcome or reward. If the reward is greater than expected, a positive prediction occurs which can be used to increase the likelihood of the behavior. If the reward is less than expected, the negative prediction can be used to decrease the likelihood of the behavior.

preferred direction A property of cells in the motor pathway, referring to the direction of movement that results in the highest firing rate of the neuron. Voxels have also been shown to have preferred directions in fMRI studies, indicating that such preferences can even be measured at the cell population level of analysis.

prefrontal cortex (PFC) A region of cortex that takes part in the higher aspects of motor control and the planning and execution of behavior, perhaps especially tasks that require the integration of information over time and thus mandate the involvement of working memory mechanisms. The prefrontal cortex has three or more main areas that are commonly referred to in descriptions of the gross anatomy of the frontal lobe: the dorsolateral prefrontal cortex, the anterior cingulate and medial frontal regions, and the orbitofrontal cortex.

premotor cortex A secondary motor area that includes the lateral aspect of Brodmann area 6, just anterior to the primary motor cortex. Although some neurons in the premotor cortex project to the corticospinal tract, many terminate on neurons in the primary motor cortex and help shape the forthcoming movement.

presynaptic Referring to the neuron located before the synapse with respect to information flow. Compare *postsynaptic.*

primary auditory cortex (A1) The initial cortical processing area of the auditory system.

primary gustatory cortex The initial cortical processing area for gustation, located in the insula and operculum.

primary motor cortex (M1) A region of the cerebral cortex that lies along the anterior bank of the central sulcus and precentral gyrus, forming Brodmann area 4. Some axons originating in the primary motor cortex form the majority of the corticospinal tract; others project to cortical and subcortical regions involved in motor control. The primary motor cortex contains a prominent somatotopic representation of the body.

primary olfactory cortex The initial cortical processing area for olfaction, located at the ventral junction of the frontal and temporal cortices, near the limbic cortex.

primary reinforcer A reward or outcome that has a direct benefit for survival. The classic examples are food, water, and sex, since without these, the individual or the species would not survive.

primary somatosensory cortex (S1) The initial cortical processing area for somatosensation, including Brodmann areas 1, 2, and 3. This area of the brain contains a somatotopic representation of the body called the sensory *homunculus.*

primary visual cortex (V1) The initial cortical processing area for vision, located in the most posterior portion of the occipital lobe, known as Brodmann area 17.

priming A form of learning in which behavior or a physiological response is altered because of some recent stimulus or state. Priming usually refers to changes that occur over a short-time scale; for example, hearing the word "river" primes the word "water."

procedural memory A form of nondeclarative memory that involves the learning of a variety of motor skills (e.g., knowledge of how to ride a bike) and cognitive skills (e.g., knowledge of how to read).

proprioception The awareness of the position of one's own body parts, such as limbs. This awareness arises from the information provided by specialized nerve cells at the linkage of the muscles and tendons.

prosopagnosia A neurological syndrome characterized by a deficit in the ability to recognize faces. Some patients will show a selective deficit in face perception, a type of category-specific deficit. In others, the prosopagnosia is one part of a more general agnosia. Prosopagnosia is frequently associated with bilateral lesions in the ventral pathway, although it can also occur with unilateral lesions of the right hemisphere.

PRS See *perceptual representation system.*

pulvinar A large region of the posterior thalamus comprising many nuclei having interconnections with specific regions of the cortex.

qualia A philosophical term referring to an individual's personal perception or experience of something.

quantum theory The study of the smallest particles that make up atoms in order to understand the fundamental properties of matter.

rationalism The idea that, through right thinking and rejection of unsupportable or superstitious beliefs, true beliefs can be determined.

rCBF See *regional cerebral blood flow.*

reappraisal An early cognitive strategy to reassess an emotion.

recency memory Memory for the temporal order of previous events. Recency memory is a form of episodic memory in that it involves remembering when a specific event took place. Patients with prefrontal lesions do poorly on tests of recency memory, even though their long-term memory is relatively intact.

receptive field The area of external space within which a stimulus that must be presented in order to activate a cell. For example, cells in the visual cortex respond to stimuli that appear within a restricted region of space. In addition to spatial position, the cells may be selective to other stimulus features, such as color or shape. Cells in the auditory cortex also have receptive fields. The cell's firing rate increases when the sound comes from the region of space that defines its receptive field.

reflexive attention The automatic orienting of attention induced by bottom-up, or stimulus-driven, effects, such as when a flash of light in the periphery captures one's attention. Compare *voluntary attention.*

reflexive cuing See *exogenous cuing.*

refractory period The short period of time following an action potential during which the neuron may not be able to generate action potentials or may be able to do so only with larger-than-normal depolarizing currents.

regional cerebral blood flow (rCBF) The distribution of the brain's blood supply, which can be measured with various imaging techniques. In PET scanning, rCBF is used as a measure of metabolic changes following increased neural activity in restricted regions of the brain.

relational memory Memory that relates the individual pieces of information relevant to a particular memory and that supports episodic memories.

repetition suppression effect The phenomenon seen during functional MRI in which the BOLD response to a stimulus decreases with each subsequent stimulus repetition.

response conflict A situation in which more than one response is activated, usually because of some ambiguity in the stimulus information. It has been hypothesized that the anterior cingulate monitors the level of response conflict and modulates processing in active systems when conflict is high.

resting membrane potential The difference in voltage across the neuronal membrane at rest, when the neuron is not signaling.

restorative justice An attempt to restore the harm done by involving the perpetrator, the victim and the community in the resolution.

retina A layer of neurons along the back surface of the eye. The retina contains a variety of cells, including photoreceptors (the cells that respond to light) and ganglion cells (the cells whose axons form the optic nerve).

retinotopic Referring to a topographic map of visual space across a restricted region of the brain. Activation across the retina is determined by the reflectance of light from the environment. A retinotopic map in the brain is a representation in which some sort of orderly spatial relationship is maintained. Multiple retinotopic maps have been identified in the cortex and subcortex.

retinotopic map A topographic representation in the nervous system that reflects spatial properties of the environment in an eye-based reference frame. For example, primary visual cortex contains a retinotopic map of the contralateral side of space, relative to the center of gaze.

retributive justice Justice that imposes punishment commiserate with the magnitude of the crime as the best response to a crime.

retrieval The utilization of stored information to create a conscious representation or to execute a learned behavior like a motor act. Compare *encoding.*

retrograde amnesia The loss of memory for events that happened in the past. Compare *anterograde amnesia.*

Ribot's Law See *temporal gradient.*

reversal learning An attempt to teach someone to respond in the opposite way in which they were previously taught.

S1 See *primary somatosensory cortex.*

S2 See *secondary somatosensory cortex.*

saltatory conduction The mode of conduction in myelinated neurons, in which action potentials are generated down the axon only at nodes of Ranvier. Measurement of the propagation of the action potential gives it the appearance of jumping from node to node—hence the term *saltatory*, which comes from the Latin *saltare*, meaning "to jump."

SAS See *supervisory attentional system.*

scotoma A region in external space in which a person or animal fails to perceive a stimulus following neural damage. Scotomas occur following lesions of primary visual cortex or partial lesions of ascending visual pathways. The size and location of scotomas vary depending on the extent and location of the lesions.

secondary reinforcer Rewards that do not have intrinsic, or direct value, but have acquired their desirability as part of social and cultural norms. Money and social status are important secondary reinforcers.

secondary somatosensory cortex (S2) The area of the brain that receives inputs from primary somatosensory cortex and processes higher level somatosensory information.

selective attention The ability to focus one's concentration on a subset of sensory inputs, trains of thought, or actions, while simultaneously ignoring others. Selective attention can be distinguished from nonselective attention, which includes simple behavioral arousal (i.e., being generally more versus less attentive).

self-knowledge A philosophical term referring to an individual's knowledge of their own personal nature such as beliefs, abilities and desires.

self-reference effect An effect rooted in the theoretical perspective that the recall of information is related to how deeply the information was initially processed.

Specifically, the self-reference effect is the superior memory for information that is encoded in relation to oneself.

semantic The way that meaning is represented in the words of a language.

semantic memory Knowledge that is based on facts one has learned, but does not include knowledge of the context in which the learning occurred. A form of declarative memory. Contrast with *episodic memory*.

semantic paraphasia The production of a word related in meaning to the intended word (e.g., *horse* for *cow*) instead of the intended word itself. Wernicke's aphasia patients often produce semantic paraphasias.

sensorimotor adaptation A form of motor learning in which a learned skill is modified due to some change in the environment or agent. For example, a soccer player who adjusts her shot to compensate for a strong cross-wind is exhibiting a form of motor adaptation.

sensorimotor learning A term that refers to the acquisition of a new motor skill or capability. Motor learning can arise from maturation processes (e.g, infants crawling) or intense, dedicated practice (e.g, piano playing).

sensory memory The short-lived retention of sensory information, measurable in milliseconds to seconds, as when we recover what was said to us a moment before when we were not paying close attention to the speaker. Sensory memory for audition is called *echoic memory*; sensory memory for vision is called *iconic memory*. Compare *short-term memory* and *long-term memory*.

sentience The ability to be conscious and experience subjectivity.

short-term memory The retention of information over seconds to minutes. See also *working memory*. Compare *long-term memory* and *sensory memory*.

simulation A method used in computer modeling to mimic a certain behavior or process. Simulations require a program that explicitly specifies the manner in which information is represented and processed. The resulting model can be tested to see if its output matches the simulated behavior or process. The program can then be used to generate new predictions.

simulation theory A theoretical account of how we understand other people's minds. From this perspective, we try to make inferences about other people's minds by considering what we might do if we were in their position.

single-cell recording A neurophysiological method used to monitor the activity of individual neurons. The procedure requires positioning a small recording electrode either inside a cell or, more typically, near the outer membrane of a neuron. The electrode measures changes in the membrane potential and can be used to determine the conditions that cause the cell to respond.

single dissociation A method used to develop functional models of mental and/or neural processes. Evidence of a single dissociation requires a minimum of two groups and two tasks. A single dissociation is present when the groups differ in their performance on one task but not the other. Single dissociations provide weak evidence of functional specialization since it is possible that the two tasks differ in terms of their sensitivity to detect group differences. Compare *double dissociation*.

SMA See *supplementary motor area*.

smoothing Data processing technique used in functional imaging studies. Given that the signal being measured in small, relative to the noise (random variation), signal processing techniques provide a more robust measure by performing a weighted average of the signal from the observed location with its spatial neighbors.

social cognitive neuroscience An emerging field of brain science that combines social-personality psychology and cognitive neuroscience with the goal of understanding the neural mechanisms involved in social interaction in humans.

soma (pl. somata) The cell body of a neuron.

somatic marker A physiological-emotional mechanism that was once theorized to help us sort through possible options and make a decision. Somatic markers were thought to provide a common metric for evaluating options with respect to their potential benefit.

somatotopy A point-for-point representation of the body surface in the nervous system. In the somatosensory cortex, regions of the body near one another (e.g., the index and middle fingers) are represented by neurons located near one another. Regions that are farther apart on the body surface (e.g., the nose and the big toe) are coded by neurons located farther apart in the somatosensory cortex.

spike-triggering zone The location, at the juncture of the soma and the axon of a neuron, where currents from synaptic inputs on the soma and distant dendrites are summed and where voltage-gated Na^+ channels are located that can be triggered to generate action potentials that can propagate down the axon.

spinal interneurons A neuron found in the spinal cord. Many descending axons from the pyramidal and extrapyramidal tracts synapse on interneurons which, in turn, synapse on other interneurons or alpha motorneurons.

spine A little knob attached by a small neck to the surface of a dendrite. Synapses are located on spines.

splenium The posterior area of the corpus callosum that interconnects the occipital lobe.

split-brain research The study of patients who have had the corpus callosum severed, typically as a radical treatment for intractable epilepsy.

stimulus-driven Describing behavior that is dictated by the environmental context and fails to incorporate an animal's or person's goals. For example, a person with a lesion of prefrontal cortex might drink from a glass placed in front of him even if he isn't thirsty.

storage The result of the acquisition and consolidation of information, which create and maintain, respectively, a permanent record.

striatum One of the nuclei of the basal ganglia. The striatum is the main receiving zone of the basal ganglia, receiving extensive inputs from the cerebral cortex and other subcortical structures. The striatum in humans is composed of the caudate and putamen nuclei.

stimulus–response decision Behavior in which the response is tightly linked to the stimulus, usually through extensive experience. See also *habit*.

subliminal perception When a stimulus, which is not consciously perceived, nevertheless influences one's conscious state.

substantia nigra One of the nuclei that form the basal ganglia. The substantia nigra is composed of two parts: The axons of the substantia nigra *pars compacta* provide the primary source of the neurotransmitter dopamine and terminate in the striatum (caudate and putamen). The substantia nigra *pars reticularis* is one of the output nuclei from the basal ganglia.

sulcus (pl. sulci)   Also *fissure*. An invaginated region that appears as a line or crease of the surface of the cerebral cortex. Compare *gyrus*.

superior colliculus   A subcortical visual structure located in the midbrain. The superior colliculus receives input from the retinal system and is interconnected with the subcortical and cortical systems. It plays a key role in visuomotor processes and may be involved in the inhibitory component of reflexive attentional orienting. Compare *inferior colliculus*.

supervisory attentional system (SAS)   The psychological model used to explain how response selection is achieved in a flexible manner. Without the SAS, behavior is dictated by context, with the selected action being the one that has been produced most often in the current context. The SAS allows for flexible behavior by biasing certain actions based on current goals or helping to determine actions in unfamiliar situations.

supplementary motor area (SMA)   A secondary motor area that includes the medial aspect of Brodmann area 6, just anterior to the primary motor cortex. The SMA plays an important role in the production of sequential movements, especially those that have been well learned.

suppression   Intentionally excluding a thought or feeling from conscious awareness.

Sylvian (lateral) fissure   Also *lateral fissure*. A large fissure (sulcus) on the lateral surface of the cerebral cortex first described by the anatomist Franciscus Sylvius. The Sylvian fissure separates the frontal cortex from the temporal lobe below.

symmetry breaking   A term in physics, which describes the phenomenon that occurs when small fluctuations acting on a system at a critical point determine which of several equally likely outcomes will occur.

synapse   The specialized site on the neural membrane where a neuron comes in close position to another neuron to transmit information. Synapses include both presynaptic (e.g., synaptic vesicles with neurotransmitter) and postsynaptic (e.g., receptors) specializations in the neurons that are involved in chemical transmission. Electrical synapses involve special structures called gap junctions that make direct cytoplasmic connections between neurons.

synapse elimination   The elimination of some synaptic contacts between neurons during development, including postnatally.

synaptic cleft   The gap between neurons at synapses.

synaptic potential   The voltage difference across the membrane at the synapse during synaptic transmission.

synaptogenesis   The formation of synaptic connections between neurons in the developing nervous system.

syncytium (pl. syncytia)   A continuous mass of tissue that shares a common cytoplasm.

synesthesia   A mixing of the senses whereby stimulation of one sense (e.g., touch) automatically causes an illusory perceptual experience in the same or another sense (e.g., vision).

syntactic parsing   The assignment of a syntactic structure to a word in a sentence (e.g., this word is the object of the sentence, and this word is the action).

syntax   The rules that constrain word combinations and sequences in a sentence.

Talairach coordinate   An anatomical referencing system in which a brain location is defined in three spatial dimensions (x,y,z). The Talairach atlas was devised from the detailed analysis of one human brain and has been used to provide a reference for comparing across individuals in neuroimaging studies.

tastant   A food molecule that stimulates a receptor in a taste cell to initiate the sensory transduction of gustation. Compare *odorant*.

temporal gradient   The effect in which some cases of retrograde amnesia tend to be greatest for the most recent events.

temporal lobe   Lateral ventral portions of the cerebral cortex bounded superiorly by the Sylvian fissure and posteriorly by the anterior edge of the occipital lobe and ventral portion of the parietal lobe. The ventromedial portions contain the hippocampal complex and amygdala. The lateral neocortical regions are involved in higher order vision (object analysis), the representation of conceptual information about the visual world, and linguistic representations. The superior portions within the depths of the Sylvian fissure contain auditory cortex.

temporally limited amnesia   Retrograde amesia following brain damage that extents backwards from the time of the damage, but does not include the entire life of the individual.

thalamic reticular nucleus (TRN)   A thin layer of neurons surrounding the nuclei of the thalamus, which receives inputs from the cortex and subcortical structures and sends projections to the thalamic relay nuclei.

thalamus   A group of nuclei, primarily major sensory relay nuclei for somatosensory, gustatory, auditory, visual, and vestibular inputs to the cerebral cortex. The thalamus also contains nuclei involved in basal ganglia–cortical loops, and other specialized nuclear groups. It is a part of the diencephalon, a subcortical region, located in the center of the mass of the forebrain. Each hemisphere contains one thalamus, and they are connected at the midline in most humans by the massa intermedia.

theory of mind   Also *mentalizing*. The ability to self-reflect and think about the mental states of others, which allows predictions of what others can understand, and how they will interact and behave in a given situation. This trait is considered unique to the human species.

theory theory   A scientific theory where one makes an assessment of other's mental states based on their own theories of the outside world.

threshold   The membrane potential value to which the membrane must be depolarized for an action potential to be initiated.

time-frequency analysis   Signal processing technique for analyzing the content of a stimulus and how that content changes over time. For example, in ECoG, a time frequency analysis describes the power of the neural activity at different frequencies over time.

TMS   See *transcranial magnetic stimulation*.

topography   The systematic relationship between a particular property of the external world and the neural representation of that property. Examples of topographic representations include retinotopic maps in the visual cortex, tonotopic maps in the auditory cortex, and somatosensory maps in the motor and sensory cortices.

tract   A bundle of axons in the central nervous system.

transcortical   Pertaining to communication between locations in the cortex. For example, transcortical fibers connect the frontal cortex to the temporal cortex.

transcranial direct current stimulation (tDCS) A non-invasive method in which a low voltage electrical current is created across the brain by applying two electrodes to the scalp. tDCS is hypothesized to potentiate neurons near the anodal electrode and hyperpolarize neurons near the cathodal electrode.

transcranial magnetic stimulation (TMS) A noninvasive method used to stimulate neurons in the intact human brain. A strong electrical current is rapidly generated in a coil placed over the targeted region. This current generates a magnetic field that causes the neurons in the underlying region to discharge. TMS is used in clinical settings to evaluate motor function by direct stimulation of the motor cortex. Experimentally, the procedure is used to transiently disrupt neural processing, thus creating brief, reversible lesions.

transient global amnesia A sudden, dramatic, but transient (lasting only hours) amnesia that is both anterograde and retrograde.

traumatic brain injury (TBI) A form of brain injury resulting from an accident such as a diving accident, bullet wound, or blast injury. The damage in TBI is usually diffuse with damage to both grey and white matter tracts from the accelerative forces experienced at the time of the injury.

unilateral spatial neglect Also simply *neglect*. A behavioral pattern exhibited by neurological patients with lesions to the forebrain, in which they fail at or are slowed in acknowledging that objects or events exist in the hemispace opposite their lesion. Neglect is most closely associated with damage to the right parietal cortex.

utilitarian justice Also known as consequentialism, is justice that is forward looking and is concerned about the greater future good for society. This may or may not involve punishment, deterrence, incapacitation, rehabilitation, and may or may not be "fair."

utilization behavior An extreme dependency on the prototypical use of an object without regard for its use in a particular context.

V1 See *primary visual cortex.*

value An abstract entity referring to the overall preference given to a stimulus or action. The value is assumed to reflect the combination of a number of different attributes such as how much reward will be received, the likelihood of that reward, and the efforts and costs required to achieve the reward.

ventral (occipitotemporal) stream The visual pathway that traverses the occipital and temporal lobes. This pathway is associated with object recognition and visual memory.

ventral tegmental area A part of the dopamine system. Dopaminergic neurons originating here project through either the mesolimbic pathway, or the mesocortical pathway.

vesicle A small intracellular organelle, located in the presynaptic terminals at synapses, that contains neurotransmitter.

view-dependent frame of reference A theory based on the idea that perception involves recognizing an object from a certain viewpoint. View-dependent theories assume that visual memory is based on previous experiences with objects in specific orientations and that the recognition of an object in a novel orientation involves an approximation process to the stored representations of specific perspectives. Compare *view-invariant frame of reference.*

view-invariant frame of reference A theory based on the idea that perception involves recognizing certain properties of an object that remain invariant, or constant across different perspectives. In this view, these properties form the basis of visual memory, and recognition entails matching the perceived properties to this knowledge base. Compare *view-dependent frame of reference.*

visual agnosia A failure of perception that is limited to the visual modality. In visual agnosia, the patient is relatively good at perceiving properties such as color, shape, or motion yet cannot recognize objects or identify their uses.

visuomotor adaptation A form of sensorimotor adaptation in which the visual feedback is altered, resulting in a mismatch between proprioception and vision. With practice, the motor system adjusts to compensate for the mismatch.

voltage-gated ion channel A transmembrane ion channel that changes molecular conformation when the membrane potential changes, changing the conductance of the channel for specific ions such as sodium, potassium or chloride.

voluntary attention The volitional, or intentional, focusing of attention on a source of input, train of thought, or action. Compare *reflexive attention.*

voxel The smallest unit of three-dimensional data that can be represented in an MRI.

Wada test A clinical procedure in which a barbituate is injected to temporarily disrupt function in one of the cerebral hemispheres. This procedure, used to identify the source of epileptic seizures provided important initial insights into hemispheric specialization.

Wernicke's aphasia A language deficit usually caused by brain lesions in the posterior parts of the left hemisphere, resulting in comprehension deficits. Compare *Broca's aphasia.*

Wernicke's area Area of human left posterior superior temporal gyrus: Identified by Carl Wernicke in the 19th century.

white matter Regions of the nervous system composed of millions of individual axons, each surrounded by myelin. The myelin is what gives the fibers their whitish color—hence the name *white matter*. Compare *gray matter.*

working memory Transient representations of task-relevant information. These representations may be related to information that has just been activated from long-term memory or something recently experienced. Representations in working memory guide behavior in the present, constituting what has been called, "the blackboard of the mind." See also *short-term memory.*

References

Aboitiz F., Scheibel, A. B., Fisher, R. S., & Zaidel, E. (1992). Fiber composition of the human corpus callosum. *Brain Research, 598,* 143–153.

Ackermann, H., & Riecker, A. (2010). Cerebral control of motor aspects of speech production: neurophysiological and functional imaging data. In B. Maassen & P.H.H.M. van Lieshout (Eds.), *Speech motor control: New developments in basic and applied research* (pp 117–134). Oxford: OxfordUniversity Press.

Ackermann, H. & Ziegler, W. (2010). Brain mechanisms underlying speech motor control. In W.J. Hardcastle, J. Laver, & F.E. Gibbon (Eds.), *The handbook of phonetic sciences,* 2nd Edition (pp 202–250). Malden, MA: Wiley-Blackwell.

Adachi, I., Chou, D., & Hampton, R. (2009). Thatcher effect in monkeys demonstrates conservation of face perception across primates. *Current Biology, 19,* 1270–1273.

Addante, R. J., Watrous, A. J., Yonelinas, A. P., Ekstrom, A. D., Ranganath, C. (2011). Prestimulus theta activity predicts correct source memory retrieval. *Proceedings of the National Academy of Science USA, 108,* 10702–10707.

Adolphs, R. (2008). Fear, faces, and the human amygdala. *Current Opinion in Neurobiology, 18,* 166–172.

Adolphs, R. (2009). The social brain: Neural basis of social knowledge. *Annual Review of Psychology, 60,* 693–716.

Adolphs, R. (2010). What does the amygdala contribute to social cognition? *Annals of the New York Academy of Science, 1191*(1), 42–61.

Adolphs, R., Gosselin, F., Buchanan, T. W., Tranel, D., Schyns, P., & Damasio, A. R. (2005). A mechanism for impaired fear recognition after amygdala damage. *Nature, 433,* 68–72.

Adolphs, R., & Tranel, D. (1999). Intact recognition of emotional prosody following amygdala damage. *Neuropsychologia, 37,* 1285–1292.

Adolphs, R., & Tranel, D. (2004). Impaired judgments of sadness but not happiness following bilateral amygdala damage. *Journal of Cognitive Neuroscience, 16,* 453–462.

Adolphs, R., Tranel, D., & Damasio, A. R. (2003). Dissociable neural systems for recognizing emotions. *Brain and Cognition, 52,* 61–69.

Adolphs, R. A., Tranel, D., Damasio, H., & Damasio, A. R. (1994). Impaired recognition of emotion in facial expressions following bilateral amygdala damage to the human amygdala. *Nature, 372,* 669–672.

Adolphs, R., Tranel, D., Damasio, H., & Damasio, A. R. (1995). Fear and the human amygdala. *Journal of Neuroscience, 75,* 5879–5891.

Adolphs, R., Tranel, D., & Damasio, A. R. (1998). The human amygdala in social judgment. *Nature, 393,* 470–74.

Adolphs, R., Tranel, D., & Denburg, N. (2000). Impaired emotional declarative memory following unilateral amygdala damage. *Learning & Memory, 7,* 180–186.

Adolphs, R., Tranel, D., Hamann, S., Young, A. W., Calder, A. J., Phelps, E. A., et al. (1999). Recognition of facial emotion in nine individuals with bilateral amygdala damage. *Neuropsychologia, 37,* 1111–1117.

Afraz, S., Kiani, R., & Esteky, H. (2006). Microstimulation of inferotemporal cortex influences face categorization. *Nature, 442,* 692–695.

Aggleton, J. P. & Brown, M. W. (1999). Episodic memory amnesia and the hippocampal-anterior thalamic axis. *Behavioral and Brain Sciences, 22,* 425–444.

Aglioti, S. M., Cesari, P., Romani, M., & Urgesi, C. (2008). Action anticipation and motor resonance in elite basketball players. *Nature Neuroscience, 11,* 1109–1116.

Agosta, F., Henry, R. G., Migliaccio, R., Neuhaus, J., Miller, B. L., Dronkers, N. F., et al. (2010). Language networks in semantic dementia. *Brain, 133*(1), 286–299.

Aguirre, G. K., & D'Esposito, M. E. (1999). Topographical disorientation: A synthesis and taxonomy. *Brain, 122,* 1613–1628.

Airan, R. D., Thompson, K. R., Fenno, L. E., Bernstein, H., & Deisseroth, K. (2009). Temporally precise *in vivo* control of intracellular signaling. *Nature, 458,* 1025–1029.

Akelaitis, A. J. (1941). Studies on the corpus callosum: Higher visual functions in each homonymous visual field following complete section of corpus callosum. *Archives of Neurology and Psychiatry, 45,* 788.

Akelaitis, A. J. (1943). Studies on the corpus callosum. *Journal of Neuropathology & Experimental Neurology, 2*(3), 226–262.

Alexander, R. D. (1990). *How did humans evolve? Reflections on the uniquely unique species.* Ann Arbor: Museum of Zoology, the University of Michigan Special Publication No. 1

Allen, G., Buxton, R. B., Wong, E. C., & Courchesne, E. (1997). Attentional activation of the cerebellum independent of motor involvement. *Science, 275,* 1940–1943.

Allen, M. (1983). Models of hemisphere specialization. *Psychological Bulletin, 93,* 73–104.

Alloway, T. P., & Alloway, R. G. (2010). Investigating the predictive roles of working memory and IQ in academic attainment. *Journal of Experimental Child Psychology, 80*(2), 606–621.

Amedi, A., Floel, A., Knecht, S., Zohary, E., & Cohen, L. G. (2004). Transcranial magnetic stimulation of the occipital pole interferes with verbal processing in blind subjects. *Nature Neuroscience, 7,* 1266–1270.

Amsterdam, B. K. (1972). Mirror self-image reactions before age two. *Developmental Psychobiology, 5,* 297–305.

Amunts, K., Lenzen, M., Friederici, A.D., Schleicher, A., Morosan, P., Palomero-Gallagher, N., & Zilles, K. (2010). Broca's region: novel organizational principles and multiple receptor mapping. *PLoS Biology, 8,* e1000489.

Anders, S., Eippert, F., Weiskopf, N., & Veit, R. (2008). The human amygdala is sensitive to the valence of pictures and sounds irrespective of arousal: An fMRI study. *Social Cognitive and Affective Neuroscience, 3,* 233–243.

Andersen, R. A., & Buneo, C. A. (2002). Intentional maps in posterior parietal cortex. *Annual Review of Neuroscience, 25,* 189–220. [Epub, March 27]

Anderson, A. K., Christoff, K., Stappen, I., Panitz, D., Ghahremani, D. G., Glover, G., et al. (2003). Dissociated neural representations of intensity and valence in human olfaction. *Nature Neuroscience, 6,* 196–202.

Anderson, A. K. (2005). Affective influences on the attentional dynamics supporting awareness. *Journal of Experimental Psychology: General, 134*(2), 258–281.

ANDERSON, A. K., & PHELPS, E. A. (1998). Intact recognition of vocal expressions of fear following bilateral lesions of the human amygdala. *NeuroReport, 9*, 3607–3613.

ANDERSON, A. K., & PHELPS, E. A. (2000). Expression without recognition: Contributions of the human amygdala to emotional communication. *Psychological Science, 11*, 106–111.

ANDERSON, A. K., & PHELPS, E. A. (2001). Lesions of the human amygdala impair enhanced perception of emotionally salient events. *Nature, 411*, 305–309.

ANDERSON, M. C., & LEVY, B. J. (2009). Suppressing unwanted memories. *Current Directions in Psychological Science, 18*(4), 184–194.

ANDERSON, P. A. (1972). More is different. *Science, 177*(4047), 393–396.

ANDERSON, S. R. (in press). What is special about the human language faculty, and how did it get that way? In R. Botha & M. Everaert (Eds.), *The Evolutionary Emergence of Human Language.* Oxford: Oxford University Press.

ANDERSON, S. W., BECHARA, A., DAMASIO, H., TRANEL, D., & DAMASIO, A. R. (1999). Impairment of social and moral behavior related to early damage in human prefrontal cortex. *Nature Neuroscience, 2*, 1032–1037.

ANDINO, S.L. G. & MENENDEZ, R. G. DE P. (2012). Coding of saliency by ensemble bursting in the amygdala of primates. *Frontiers in Behavioral Neuroscience, 6*(38), 1–16.

ANDREWS, K., MURPHY, L., MUNDAY, R., & LITTLEWOOD, C. (1996). Misdiagnosis of the vegetative state: Retrospective study in a rehabilitation unit. *British Medical Journal, 313*(7048), 13–16.

ANGRILLI, A., MARUI, A., PALOMBA, D., FLOR, H., BIRBAUMER, N., SARTORI, G., ET AL. (1996). Startle reflex and emotion modulation impairment after a right amygdala lesion. *Brain, 119*, 1991–2000.

ANNETT, M. (2002). *Handedness and brain asymmetry: The right shift theory.* Hove, England: Psychology Press.

ARAVANIS, A. M., WANG, L. P., ZHANG, F., MELTZER, L. A., MOGRI, Z. M., SCHNEIDER, M. B., ET AL. (2007). An optical neural interface: In vivo control of rodent motor cortex with integrated fiberoptic and optogenetic technology. *Journal of Neural Engineering, 4*(3), S143–S156.

ARON, A., FISHER, H., MASHEK, D., STRONG, G., LI, H., & BROWN, L.L. (2005). Reward,motivation and emotion systems associated with early-stage intense romantic love. *Journal of Neurophysiology, 94*, 327–337.

ARON, A. R., BEHRENS, T. E., SMITH, S., FRANK, M. J., & POLDRACK, R. A. (2007). Triangulating a cognitive control network using diffusion-weighted magnetic resonance imaging (MRI) and functional MRI. *Journal of Neuroscience, 27*, 3743–3752.

ARON, A. R., & POLDRACK, R. A. (2006). Cortical and subcortical contributions to Stop signal response inhibition: Role of the subthalamic nucleus. *Journal of Neuroscience, 26*, 2424–2433.

ARMSTRONG, K. M., SCHAFER, R. J., CHANG, M. H., & MOORE, T. (2012). Attention and action in the frontal eye field. In R. Mangun (Ed.), *The neuroscience of attention* (pp.151–166). Oxford: Oxford University Press.

ARVANITAKI, A. (1939). Recherches sur la résponse oscillatoire locale de l'axone géant isolé de 'Sepia.' *Archives Internationales de Physiologie, 49*, 209–256.

ATKINSON, R. C., & SHIFFRIN, R. M. (1968). Human memory: A proposed system and its control processes. In K. W. Spence & J. T. Spence (Eds.), *The psychology of learning and motivation* (Vol. 2, pp. 89–195). New York: Academic Press.

ATKINSON, R. C., & SHIFFRIN, R. M. (1971). The control of short-term memory. *Scientific American, 225*(2), 82–90.

AUGUSTINE, J. R. (1996). Circuitry and functional aspects of the insular lobe in primates including humans. *Brain Research Reviews, 22*, 229–244.

AVENANTI, A., BUETI, D., GALATI, G., & AGLIOTI, S. M. (2005). Transcranial magnetic stimulation highlights the sensorimotor side of empathy for pain. *Nature Reviews Neuroscience, 8*, 955–960.

AZEVEDO, F. A. C., CARVALHO, L. R. B., GRINBERG, L. T., FARFEL, J. M., FERRETTI, R. E. L., LEITE, ET AL. (2009). Equal numbers of neuronal and nonneuronal cells make the human brain an isometrically scaled-up primate brain. *Journal of Comparative Neurology, 513*(5), 532–541.

BADDELEY, A. (1995). Working memory. In M. S. Gazzaniga (Ed.), *The cognitive neurosciences* (pp. 755–764). Cambridge, MA: MIT Press.

BADDELEY, A. (2003). Working memory: Looking back and looking forward. *Nature Reviews Neuroscience, 4*, 829–839.

BADDELEY, A., & HITCH, G. (1974). Working memory. In G. H. Bower (Ed.), *The psychology of learning and motivation* (Vol. 8, pp. 47–89). New York: Academic Press.

BADRE, D., & D'ESPOSITO, M. (2007). Functional magnetic resonance imaging evidence for a hierarchical organization of the prefrontal cortex. *Journal of Cognitive Neuroscience, 19*(12), 2082–2099.

BADRE, D., HOFFMAN, J. COONEY, J. W., & D'ESPOSITO, M. (2009). Hierarchical cognitive control deficits following damage to the human frontal lobe. *Nature Neuroscience, 12*(4), 515–522.

BAIRD, A. A., COLVIN, M. K., VANHORN, J. D., INATI, S., & GAZZANIGA, M. S. (2005). Functional connectivity: Integrating behavioral, diffusion tensor imaging, and functional magnetic resonance imaging data sets. *Journal of Cognitive Neuroscience, 17*, 687–693.

BAKIN, J., S., SOUTH, D. A., & WEINBERGER, N. M. (1996). Induction of receptive field plasticity in the auditory cortex of the guinea pig during instrumental avoidance conditioning. *Behavioral Neuroscience, 110*, 905–913.

BANDYOPADHYAY, S., SHAMMA , S. A., & KANOLD, P. O. (2010). Dichotomy of functional organization in the mouse auditory cortex. *Nature Neuroscience, 13*, 361–368.

BANNERMAN, D.M., BUS, T., TAYLOR, A., SANDERSON, D.J., SCHWARZ, I., JENSEN, V., HVALBY, Ø., RAWLINS, J.N.P., SEEBURG, P.H., & SPRENGEL, R. (2012). Dissecting spatial knowledge from spatial choice by hippocampal NMDA receptor deletion. *Nature Neuroscience, 15*, 1153–1159.

BANNERMAN, D. M., GOOD, M. A., BUTCHER, S. P., RAMSAY, M., & MORRIS, R. G. M. (1995). Distinct components of spatial learning revealed by prior training and NMDA receptor blockade. *Nature, 378*, 182–186.

BANSAFI, M., ZELANO, C., JOHNSON, B., MAINLAND, J., KHAN, R., & SOBEL, N. (2004). Olfaction: From sniff to percept. In M. S. Gazzaniga (Ed.), *The cognitive neurosciences III* (pp. 259–280). Cambridge, MA: MIT Press

BARBUR, J. L., WATSON, J. D. G., FRACKOWIAK, R. S. J., & ZEKI, S. (1993). Conscious visual perception without V1. *Brain, 116*, 1293–1302.

BARCELÓ, F., SUWAZONO, S., & KNIGHT, R. T. (2000). Prefrontal modulation of visual processing in humans. *Nature Neuroscience, 3*(4), 399–403.

BARON-COHEN, S. (1995). *Mindblindness: An essay on autism and theory of mind.* Cambridge, MA: MIT Press.

BARON-COHEN, S., BURT, L., SMITH-LAITTAN, F., HARRISON, J., & BOLTON, P. (1996). Synaesthesia: Prevalence and familiality. *Perception, 25*, 1073–1079.

BARON-COHEN, S., LESLIE, A. M., & FRITH, U. (1985). Does the autistic child have a "theory of mind"? *Cognition, 21*, 37–46.

BARON-COHEN, S., LESLIE, A. M., & FRITH, U. (1986). Mechanical, behavioural and intentional understanding of picture stories in autistic children. *British Journal of Developmental Psychology, 4*, 113–125.

BARRASH, J., TRANEL, D., & ANDERSON, S. W. (2000). Acquired personality disturbances associated with bilateral damage to the ventromedial prefrontal region. *Developmental Neuropsychology, 18,* 355–381.

BARRETT, A. M., CRUCIAN, G. P., RAYMER, A. M., & HEILMAN, K. M. (1999). Spared comprehension of emotional prosody in a patient with global aphasia. *Neuropsychiatry, Neuropsychology, and Behavioral Neurology, 12,* 117–120.

BARRETT, L. F. (2006a). Are emotions natural kinds? *Perspectives on Psychological Science, 1*(1), 28–58.

BARRETT, L. F. (2006b). Solving the emotional paradox: Categorization and the experience of emotion. *Personality and Social Psychology Review, 10,* 20–46.

BARRETT, L. F. (2009). Variety is the spice of life: A psychological construction approach to understanding variability in emotion. *Cognition & Emotion, 23,* 1284–1306.

BARRETT, L. F., QUIGLEY, K. S., BLISS-MOREAU, E. & ARONSON, K. R. (2004). Interoceptive sensitivity and self-reports of emotional experience. *Journal of Personality and Social Psychology, 87,* 684–697.

BARTHOLOMEUS, B. (1974). Effects of task requirements on ear superiority for sung speech. *Cortex, 10,* 215–223.

BARTOSHUK, L. M., DUFFY, V. B., & MILLER, I. J. (1994). PTC/PROP tasting: Anatomy, psychophysics and sex effects. *Physiology and Behavior, 56,* 1165–1171.

BARTSCH, T. & DEUSCHL, G. (2010). Transient global amnesia: functional anatomy and clinical implications. *Lancet Neurology, 9,* 205–214.

BASSETT, D. S., & BULLMORE, E. (2006). Small-world brain networks. *Neuroscientist, 12*(6), 512–524.

BASSETT, D. S., & BULLMORE, E. (2009). Human brain networks in health and disease. *Current Opinions in Neurology, 22,* 340–347.

BASSETT, D. S., BULLMORE, E., MEYER-LINDENBERG, A., WEINBERGER, D. R., COPPOLA, R. (2009). Cognitive fitness of cost efficient brain functional networks. *Proceedings of the National Academy of Sciences, USA, 106,* 11747–11752.

BASSETT, D. S., & GAZZANIGA, M. S. (2011). Understanding complexity in the human brain. *Trends in Cognitive Sciences, 15*(5), 200–209.

BATISTA, A. P., BUNEO, C. A., SNYDER, L. H., & ANDERSON, R. A. (1999). Reach plans in eye-centered coordinates. *Science, 285,* 257–260.

BAUER, P. J., & WEWERKA, S. S. (1995). One- to two-year-olds' recall of events: The more expressed, the more impressed. *Journal of Experimental Child Psychology, 59,* 475–496.

BAUMANN, M. A., FLUET, M. C., & SCHERBERGER, H. (2009). Context-specific grasp movement representation in the macaque anterior intraparietal area. *Journal of Neuroscience, 29*(20), 6436–6448.

BAUMEISTER, R. F., MASICAMPO, E. J., & DEWALL, C. N. (2009). Prosocial benefits of feeling free: Disbelief in free will increases aggression and reduces helpfulness. *Personality and Social Psychology Bulletin, 35*(2), 260–268.

BAXTER, M. G., PARKER, A., LINDNER, C. C., IZQUIERDO, A. D., & MURRAY, E. A. (2000). Control of response selection by reinforcer value requires interaction of amygdala and orbital prefrontal cortex. *Journal of Neuroscience, 20,* 4311–4319.

BAYLIS, G. C., ROLLS, E. T., & LEONARD, C. M. (1985). Selectivity between faces in the responses of a population of neurons in the cortex in the superior temporal sulcus of the monkey. *Brain Research, 342,* 91–102.

BEAR, M. F., CONNORS, B. W., & PARADISO, M. A. (1996). *Neuroscience: Exploring the brain.* Baltimore, MD: Williams & Wilkins.

BECHARA, A., DAMASIO, A.R., DAMASIO, H., & ANDERSON, S.W. (1994). Insensitivity to future consequences following damage to human prefrontal cortex. *Cognition, 50,* 7–12.

BECHARA, A., DAMASIO, H., TRANEL, D., & DAMASIO, A. R. (1997). Deciding advantageously before knowing the advantageous strategy. *Science, 275,* 1293–1295.

BECHARA, A., TRANEL, D., DAMASIO, H., ADOLPHS, R., ROCKLAND, C., & DAMASIO, A. R. (1995). Double dissociation of conditioning and declarative knowledge relative to the amygdala and hippocampus in human. *Science, 269,* 1115–1118.

BECHARA, A., TRANEL, D., DAMASIO, H., & DAMASIO, A. R. (1996). Failure to respond autonomically to anticipated future outcomes following damage to prefrontal cortex. *Cerebral Cortex, 6,* 215–225.

BECKMANN, M., JOHANSEN-BERG, H., & RUSHWORTH, M. F. S. (2009). Connectivity-based parcellation of human cingulate cortex and its relation to functional specialization. *Journal of Neuroscience, 29*(4), 1175–1190.

BEER, J. S. (2007). The default self: Feeling good or being right? *Trends in Cognitive Sciences, 11,* 187–189.

BEER, J. S., HEEREY, E. H., KELTNER, D., SCABINI, D., & KNIGHT, R. T. (2003). The regulatory function of self-conscious emotion: Insights from patients with orbitofrontal damage. *Journal of Personality and Social Psychology, 85,* 594–604.

BEER, J. S., JOHN, O. P., SCABINI, D., & KNIGHT, R. T. (2006). Orbitofrontal cortex and social behavior: Integrating self-monitoring and emotion-cognition interactions. *Journal of Cognitive Neuroscience, 18,* 871–880.

BEHRENS, T. E., WOOLRICH, M. W., JENKINSON, M., JOHANSEN-BERG, H., NUNES, R. G., CLARE, S., ET AL. (2003). Characterization and propagation of uncertainty in diffusion-weighted MR imaging. *Magnetic Resonance in Medicine, 50,* 1077–1088.

BEHRMANN, M., MOSCOVITCH, M., & WINOCUR, G. (1994). Intact visual imagery and impaired visual perception in a patient with visual agnosia. *Journal of Experimental Psychology. Human Perception and Performance, 20,* 1068–1087.

BELLIVEAU, J. W., ROSEN, B. R., KANTOR, H. L., RZEDZIAN, R. R., KENNEDY, D. N., McKINSTRY, R.C., ET AL. (1990). Functional cerebral imaging by susceptibility-contrast NMR. *Magnetic Resonance in Medicine, 14,* 538–546.

BELLUGI, U., KLIMA, E.S., & HICKOK, G. (2010). Brain organization: Clues from deaf signers with left or right hemisphere lesions. In L. Clara (Ed.), *Of Gesture and Word.* Lisbon, Portugal (in press).

BELYAEV, D. (1979). Destabilizing selection as a factor in domestication. *Journal of Heredity, 70,* 301–308.

BENDESKY, A., TSUNOZAKI, M., ROCKMAN, M. V., KRUGLYAK, L., & BARGMANN, C. I. (2011). Catecholamine receptor polymorphisms affect decision making in *C. elegans. Nature, 472,* 313–318.

BENTIN, S., DEOUELL, L. Y., & SOROKER, N. (1999). Selective visual streaming in face recognition: Evidence from developmental prosopagnosia. *NeuroReport, 10,* 823–827.

BERMAN, R. A., HEISER, L. M., SAUNDERS, R. C., & COLBY, C. L. (2005). Dynamic circuitry for updating spatial representations. I. Behavioral evidence for interhemispheric transfer in the split-brain macaque. *Journal of Neurophysiology, 94,* 3228–3248.

BERMOND, B., NIEUWENHUYSEDR, B., FASOTTI, L., & SCHUERMAN, J. (1991). Spinal cord lesions, peripheral feedback and intensities of emotional feelings. *Cognition and Emotion, 5,* 201–220.

BERNARD, C. (1865). *An introduction to the study of experimental medicine.* First English translation by Henry Copley Greene, published by Macmillan & Co., Ltd., 1927; reprinted in 1949. The Dover Edition of 1957 is a reprint of the original translation with a new foreword by I. Bernard Cohen of Harvard University.

BERNS, G. S., McCLURE, S. M., PAGNONI, G., & MONTAGUE, P. R. (2001). Predictability modulates human brain response to reward. *Journal of Neuroscience, 21*(8), 2793–2798.

BERNS, G. S., & SEJNOWSKI, T. (1996). How the basal ganglia makes decisions. In A. Damasio, H. Damasio, & Y. Christen (Eds.), *The neurobiology of decision making* (pp. 101–113). Cambridge, MA: MIT Press.

BERNTSON, G. G., BECHARA, A., DAMASIO, H., TRANEL, D., & CACIOPPO, J. T. (2007). Amygdala contribution to selective dimensions of emotion. *Social Cognitive Affective Neuroscience, 2*(2), 123–129.

BERNTSON, G. G., NORMAN, G. J., BECHARA, A., BRUSS, J., TRANEL, D., & CACIOPPO, J. T. (2011). The insula and evaluative processes. *Psychological Science, 22,* 80–86.

BERRIDGE, K. C. (2007). The debate over dopamine's role in reward: The case for incentive salience. *Psychopharmacology, 191,* 391–431.

BERRIDGE, K. C., & KRINGELBACK, M. L. (2008). Affective neuroscience of pleasure: Reward in humans and animals. *Psychopharmacology, 199*(3), 457–480.

BERRIDGE, K. C., & ROBINSON, T. E. (1998). What is the role of dopamine in reward: hedonic impact, reward learning, or incentive salience? *Brain Research Reviews, 28*(3), 309–369.

BERTOLINO, A., CAFORIO, G., BLASI, G., DE CANDIA, M., LATORRE, V., PETRUZZELLA, V., ET AL. (2004). Interaction of COMT (Val(108/158)Met) genotype and olanzapine treatment on prefrontal cortical function in patients with schizophrenia. *American Journal of Psychiatry, 161,* 1798–1805.

BESTMANN, S., RUFF, C., BLAKEMORE, C., DRIVER, J., & THILO, K. (2007). Spatial attention changes excitability of human visual cortex to direct stimulation. *Current Biology, 17,* 134–139.

BIANCHI, L. (1922). *The mechanism of the brain.* (J. H. MacDonald, Trans.) Edinburgh, Scotland: E. & S. Livingstone.

BIANCHI-DEMICHELI, F., GRAFTON, S. T., & ORTIGUE, S. (2006). The power of love on the human brain. *Social Neuroscience, 1*(2), 90–103.

BINDER, J., & PRICE, C. J. (2001). Functional neuroimaging of language processes. In R. Cabeza & A. Kingstone (Eds.), *Handbook of functional neuroimaging of cognition* (pp. 187–251). Cambridge, MA: MIT Press.

BINDER, J. R., FROST, J. A., HAMMEKE, T. A., BELLGOWAN, P. S. F., RAO, S. M., & COX, J. A. (1999). Conceptual processing during the conscious resting state: A functional MRI study. *Journal of Cognitive Neuroscience, 11,* 80–93.

BINDER, J. R., FROST, J. A., HAMMEKE, T. A., BELLGOWAN, P. S. F., SPRINGER, J. A., KAUFMAN, J. N., ET AL. (2000). Human temporal lobe activation by speech and non-speech sounds. *Cerebral Cortex, 10,* 512–528.

BINKOFSKI, F., & BUCCINO, G. (2004). Motor functions of the Broca's region. *Brain & Language, 89,* 362–389.

BISIACH, E., & LUZZATTI, C. (1978). Unilateral neglect of representational space. *Cortex, 14,* 129–133.

BISLEY, J. W., & GOLDBERG, M. E. (2006). Neural correlates of attention and distractibility in the lateral intraparietal area. *Journal of Neurophysiology, 95,* 1696–1717.

BITTERMAN, Y., MUKAMEL, R., MALACH, T., FRIED, I., & NELKEN, I. (2007). Ultra-fine frequency tuning reveled in single neurons of human auditory cortex. *Nature, 451,* 197–201.

BIZZI, E., ACCORNERO, N., CHAPPLE, W., & HOGAN, N. (1984). Posture control and trajectory formation during arm movement. *Journal of Neuroscience, 4,* 2738–2744.

BLACKFORD, J. U., BUCKHOLTZ, J. W., AVERY, S. N., & ZALD, D. H. (2010). A unique role for human amygdala in novelty detection. *NeuroImage, 50,* 1188–1193.

BLAIR, R. J. R., MORRIS, J. S., FRITH, C. D., PERRETT, D. I., & DOLAN, R. J. (1999). Dissociable neural responses to facial expressions of sadness and anger. *Brain, 122,* 883–893.

BLAKE, R. (1993) Cats perceive biological motion. *Psychological Science, 4,* 54–57.

BLAKESLEE, S. (2006, January 10). Cells that read minds. *New York Times.*

BLANKE O., ORTIGUE, S., LANDIS, T., & SEECK, M. (2002). Neuropsychology: Stimulating illusory own-body perceptions. *Nature, 419,* 269–270.

BLEULER, E. (1911). *Dementia praecox: Oder die Gruppe der Schizofrenien* (Handbuch der Psychiatrie. Spezieller Teil, Abt. 4, Hälfte 1). Leipzig, Germany: Deuticke.

BLISS, T. V. P., & LØMO, T. (1973). Long-lasting potentiation of synaptic transmission in the dentate area of the anaesthetized rabbit following stimulation of the perforant pathway. *Journal of Physiology, 232,* 331–356.

BLOCK, J. R., & YUKER, H. E. (1992). *Can you believe your eyes? Over 250 illusions and other visual oddities.* Mattituck, NY: Amereon.

BLONDERS, L. X., BOWERS, D., & HEILMAN, K. M. (1991). The role of the right hemisphere in emotional communication. *Brain, 114,* 1115–1127.

BOGGIO, P. S., NUNES, A., RIGONATTI, S. P., NITSCHE, M. A., PASCUAL-LEONE, A., & FREGNI, F. (2007). Repeated sessions of noninvasive brain DC stimulation is associated with motor function improvement in stroke patients. *Restorative Neurology and Neuroscience, 25*(2), 123–129.

BOHR, M. (1937). Causality and complementarity. *Philosophy of Science, 4*(3), 289–298.

BOLGER, D. J., PERFETTI, C. A., & SCHNEIDER, W. (2005). Cross-cultural effect on the brain revisited: Universal structures plus writing system variation. *Human Brain Mapping, 25,* 92–104.

BOLY, M., FAYMONVILLE, M. E., SCHNAKERS, C., PEIGNEUX, P., LAMBERMONT, B., PHILLIPS, C., ET AL. (2008). Perception of pain in the minimally conscious state with PET activation: An observational study. *Lancet Neurology, 7,* 1013–1020.

BONDA, E., PETRIDES, M., OSTRY, D., & EVANS, A. (1996). Specific involvement of human parietal systems and the amygdala in the perception of biological motion. *Journal of Neuroscience, 16,* 3737–3744.

BOOKHEIMER, S. (2002). Functional MRI of language: New approaches to understanding the cortical organization of semantic processing. *Annual Review of Neuroscience, 25,* 151–188.

BORIA, S., FABBRI-DESTRO, M., CATTANEO, L., SPARACI, L., SINIGAGLIA, C., SANTELLI, E., ET AL. (2009). Intention understanding in autism. *PLoS One 4*(5), e5596. doi:10.1371/journal.pone.0005596

BOTVINICK, M., NYSTROM, L. E., FISSELL, K., CARTER, C. S., & COHEN, J. D. (1999). Conflict monitoring versus selection-for-action in anterior cingulate cortex. *Nature, 402,* 179–181.

BOWER, J. M. (1997). Control of sensory data acquisition. *International Review of Neurobiology, 41,* 489–513.

BOYDEN, E. S. (2011). A history of optogenetics: The development of tools for controlling brain circuits with light. *F1000Prime Reports Biology, 3*(11). Retrieved from http://f1000.com/reports/b/3/1

BOYDEN, E. S., ZHANG, F., BAMBERG, E., NAGEL, G., & DEISSEROTH, K. (2005). Millisecond-timescale, genetically targeted optical control of neural activity. *Nature Neuroscience, 8,* 1263–1268.

BRADSHAW, J. L., & NETTLETON, N. C. (1981). The nature of hemispheric specialization in man. *Behavioral and Brain Sciences, 4,* 51–91.

BRADSHAW, J. L., & ROGERS, L. J. (1993). *The evolution of lateral asymmetries, language, tool use, and intellect.* San Diego, CA: Academic Press.

BRAITENBERG, V. (1984). *Vehicles: Experiments in synthetic psychology.* Cambridge, MA: MIT Press.

BRANSFORD, J. D., & JOHNSON, M. K. (1972). Contextual prerequisites for understanding: Some investigations of comprehension and recall. *Journal of Verbal Learning and Verbal Behavior, 11,* 717–726.

BRAVER, T. (2012). The variable nature of cognitive control: A dual mechanisms framework. *Trends in Cognitive Science, 16*(2), 106–113.

BREITER, H. C., ETCOFF, H. L., WHALAN, P. J., KENNEDY, W. A., RAUCH, S. L., BUCKNER, R. L., ET AL. (1996). Response and habituation of the human amygdala during visual processing of facial expression. *Neuron, 17*, 875–887.

BREMNER, J. D., RANDALL, P., VERMETTEN, E., STAIB, L., BRONEN, R. A., MAZURE, C., ET AL. (1997). Magnetic resonance imaging-based measurement of hippocampal volume in posttraumatic stress disorder to childhood physical and sexual abuse: A preliminary report. *Biological Psychiatry, 41*, 23–32.

BROADBENT, D. A. (1958). *Perception and communication.* New York: Pergamon.

BRODAL, A. (1982). *Neurological anatomy.* New York: Oxford University Press.

BRODMANN, K. (1960). On the comparative localization of the cortex (translated from the French and German). In G. von Bonin, *Some papers on the cerebral cortex* (pp. 201–230). Springfield, IL: Thomas, 1960. (Original work published 1909)

BROMBERG-MARTIN, E. S., MATSUMOTO, M., & HIKOSAKA, O. (2010). Dopamine in motivational control: Rewarding, aversive, and alerting. *Neuron, 68*, 815–834.

BROTCHIE, P., IANSEK, R., & HORNE, M. K. (1991). Motor function of the monkey globus pallidus. *Brain, 114*, 1685–1702.

BROWN, J. W., & BRAVER, T. S. (2005). Learned predictions of error likelihood in the anterior cingulate cortex. *Science, 307*, 1118–1121.

BROWN, T. (1911). The intrinsic factors in the act of progression in the mammal. *Proceedings of the Royal Society of London, Series B, 84*, 308–319.

BRYDEN, M. P. (1982). *Laterality: Functional asymmetry in the intact human brain.* New York: Academic Press.

BUCHANAN, T. W., TRANEL, D., & ADOLPHS, R. (2006). Memories for emotional autobiographical events following unilateral damage to medial temporal lobe. *Brain, 129*, 115–127.

BUCHSBAUM, M. S., BUCHSBAUM, B. R., CHOKRON, S., TANG, C., WEI, T. C., & BYNE, W. (2006). Thalamocortical circuits: fMRI assessment of the pulvinar and medial dorsal nucleus in normal volunteers. *Neuroscience Letters, 404*, 282–287.

BUCKHOLTZ, J. W., ASPLUND, C. L., DUX, P. E., ZALD, D. H., GORE, J. C., JONES, O. D., ET AL. (2008). The neural correlates of third-party punishment. *Neuron, 60*, 930–940.

BUCKNER, R. L., ANDREWS-HANNA, J. R., & SCHACTER, D. L. (2008) The brain's default network. Anatomy, function, and relevance to disease. *Annals of the New York Academy of Science, 1124*, 1–38.

BUCKNER, R. L., & CARROLL, D. C. (2007). Self-projection and the brain. *Trends in Cognitive Science, 11*, 49–57.

BUCKNER, R. L., KELLEY, W. M., & PETERSEN, S. E. (1999). Frontal cortex contributes to human memory formation. *Nature Reviews Neuroscience, 2*, 311–314.

BUDGE, J. (1862). *Lehrbuch der speciellen Physiologie des Menschen.* Leipzig, Germany: Voigt & Günther.

BULLMORE, E. T., & BASSETT, D. S. (2011). Brain graphs: Graphical models of the human brain connectome. *Annual Review of Clinical Psychology, 7*, 113–140.

BULLOCK, T. H. (1984). Comparative neuroscience holds promise for a quiet revolution. *Science, 225*, 473–478.

BULLOCK, T. H. (1993). How are more complex brains different? One view and an agenda for comparative neurobiology. *Brain, Behavior and Evolution, 41*, 88–96.

BUNGE, M. (2010). *Matter and mind.* Berlin: Springer.

BUNGE, S. A. (2004). How we use rules to select actions: A review of evidence from cognitive neuroscience. *Cognitive, Affective & Behavioral Neuroscience, 4*, 564–579.

BURGESS, G. C., GRAY, J. R., CONWAY, A. R. A., & BRAVER, T. S. (2011). Neural mechanisms of interference control underlie the relationship between fluid intelligence and working memory span. *Journal of Experimental Psychology: General, 140*(4), 674–692.

BURNS, J. K. (2006). Psychosis: A costly by-product of social brain evolution in *Homo sapiens. Progress in Neuropsychopharmacological and Biological Psychiatry, 30*, 797–814.

BUSH, G., LUU, P., & POSNER, M. I. (2000). Cognitive and emotional influences in anterior cingulate cortex. *Trends in Cognitive Sciences, 4*, 215–222.

BUTTELMANN, D., CARPENTER, M., & TOMASELLO, M. (2009). Eighteen-month-olds show false belief understanding in an active helping paradigm. *Cognition, 112*, 337–342.

BYRNE, R. B., & WHITEN, A. (1988). *Machiavellian Intelligence.* Oxford, England: Clarendon Press.

CABEZA, R. (2008). Role of posterior parietal regions in episodic memory retrieval: The dual attentional processes hypothesis. *Neuropsychologia, 46*, 1813–1827.

CABEZA, R., RAO, S. M., WAGNER, A. D., MAYER, A. R., & SCHACTER, D. L. (2001). Can medial temporal lobe regions distinguish true from false? An event-related fMRI study of veridical and illusory recognition memory. *Proceedings of the National Academy of Sciences, USA, 98*, 4805–4810.

CAGNIARD, B., BALSAM, P. D., BRUNNER, D., & ZHUANG, X. (2005). Mice with chronically elevated dopamine exhibit enhanced motivation, but not learning, for a food reward. *Neuropsychopharmacology, 31*(7), 1362–1370.

CAHILL, L., BABINSKY, R., MARKOWITSCH, H. J., & McGAUGH, J. L. (1995). The amygdala and emotional memory. *Science, 377*, 295–296.

CAHILL, L., HAIER, R. J., FALLON, J., ALKIRE, M. T., TANG, C., KEATOR, D., ET AL. (1996). Amygdala activity at encoding correlated with long-term, free recall of emotional information. *Proceedings of the National Academy of Sciences, USA, 93*, 8016–8021.

CALDER, A. J., KEANE, J., MANES, F., ANTOUN, N., & YOUNG, A. W. (2000). Impaired recognition and experience of disgust following brain injury. *Nature Neuroscience, 3*, 1077–1078.

CALL, J., & TOMASELLO, M. (2008). Does the chimpanzee have a theory of mind? 30 years later. *Trends in Cognitive Science, 12*, 187–192.

CALTON, J. L., DICKINSON, A. R., & SNYDER, L. H. (2002). Non-spatial, motor-specific activation in posterior parietal cortex. *Nature Neuroscience, 5*, 580–588.

CALVERT, G. A., BULLMORE, E. T., BRAMMER, M. J., CAMPBELL, R., WILLIAMS, S. C., McGUIRE, P. K., ET AL. (1997). Activation of auditory cortex during silent lipreading. *Science, 276*, 593–596.

CALVO-MERINO, B., GLASER, D. E., GRÈZES, J., PASSINGHAM, R. E., & HAGGARD, P. (2005). Action observation and acquired motor skills: An fMRI study with expert dancers. *Cerebral Cortex, 15*, 1243–1249.

CAMERON, I. G., COE, B., WATANABE, M., STROMAN, P. W., & MUNOZ, D. P. (2009). Role of the basal ganglia in switching a planned response. *European Journal of Neuroscience, 29*(12), 2413–2425.

CAMILLE, N., CORICELLI, G., SALLET, J., PRADAT-DIEHL, P., DUHAMEL, J. R., & SIRIGU, A. (2004). The involvement of the orbitofrontal cortex in the experience of regret. *Science, 304*, 1167–1170.

CANNON, C. M., & BSEIKRI, M. R. (2004). Is dopamine required for natural reward? *Physiology and Behavior, 81*, 741–748.

CANNON, C. M., & PALMITER, R. D. (2003). Reward without dopamine. *Journal of Neuroscience, 23*, 10827–10831.

CANOLTY, R. T., SOLTANI, M., DALAL, S. S., EDWARDS, E., DRONKERS, M. F., NAGARAJAN, S. S., ET AL. (2007). Spatiotemporal dynamics of word processing in the human brain. *Frontiers in Neuroscience, 1*(1), 185–196.

CAPLAN, D. (1994). Language and the brain. In M. A. Gernsbacher (Ed.), *Handbook of psycholinguistics* (pp. 1023–1053). San Diego, CA: Academic Press.

CAPLAN, D., ALPERT, N., WATERS, G., & OLIVIERI, A. (2000). Activation of Broca's area by syntactic processing under conditions of concurrent articulation. *Human Brain Mapping, 9*, 65–71.

CARAMAZZA, A. (1992). Is cognitive neuropsychology possible? *Journal of Cognitive Neuroscience, 4*, 80–95.

CARAMAZZA, A. (1996). The brain's dictionary. *Nature, 380*, 485–486.

CARAMAZZA, A., & SHELTON, J. (1998). Domain-specific knowledge systems in the brain: The animate-inanimate distinction. *Journal of Cognitive Neuroscience, 10*, 1–34.

CARLSMITH, K. M. (2006). The roles of retribution and utility in determining punishment. *Journal of Experimental Social Psychology, 42*, 437–451.

CARLSMITH, K. M. (2008). On justifying punishment: The discrepancy between works and actions. *Social Justice Research, 21*, 119–137.

CARLSMITH, K. M., & DARLEY, J. M. (2008). Psychological aspects of retributive justice. In M. P. Zanna (Ed.), *Advances in experimental social psychology* (Vol. 40, pp. 193–236). San Diego, CA: Elsevier.

CARMEL, D., & BENTIN, S. (2002). Domain specificity versus expertise: Factors influencing distinct processing of faces. *Cognition, 83*, 1–29.

CARMENA, J. M., LEBEDEV, M. A., CRIST, R. E., O'DOHERTY, J. E., SANTUCCI, D. M., DIMITROV, D. F., ET AL. (2003). Learning to control a brain–machine interface for reaching and grasping by primates. *PLoS Biology, 1*(2), E42. [Epub, October 13]

CARPENTER, M. (1976). *Human neuroanatomy* (7th ed.). Baltimore, MD: Williams & Wilkins.

CASPI, A., MCCLAY, J., MOFFITT, T. E., MILL, J., MARTIN, J., CRAIG, I. W., ET AL. (2002). Role of genotype in the cycle of violence in maltreated children. *Science, 297*, 851–854.

CASANOVA, M. F., BUXHOEVEDEN, D., SWITALA, A., & ROY, E. (2002). Minicolumnar pathology in autism. *Neurology, 58*, 428–432.

CASANOVA, M. F., CHRISTENSEN, J. D., GIEDD, J., RUMSEY, J. M., GARVER, D. L., & POSTEL, G. C. (2005). Magnetic resonance imaging study of brain asymmetries in dyslexic patients. *Journal of Child Neurology, 20*, 842–847.

CASANOVA, M. F., & TILLQUIST, C. R. (2008). Encephalization, emergent properties, and psychiatry: A minicolumnar perspective. *Neuroscientist, 14*, 101–118.

CASANOVA, M. F., VAN KOOTEN, I. A. J., SWITALA, A. E., VAN ENGELAND, H., HEINSEN, H., STEINBUSCH, H. W. M., ET AL. (2006). Minicolumnar abnormalities in autism. *Acta Neuropoathologica, 112*(3), 287–303.

CASEY, B. J., SOMERVILLE, L. H., GOTLIB, I. H., AYDUK, O., FRANKLIN, N. T. ASKREN, M. K., ET AL. (2011). Behavioral and neural correlates of delay of gratification 40 years later. *Proceedings of the National Academy of Sciences, 108*(36), 14998–15003.

CASTAIGNE, P., LHERMITTE, F., SIGNORET, J. L., & ABELANET, R. (1980). Description et étude scannographique du cerveau de Leborgne: La découverte de Broca. *Revue Neurologique, 136*, 563–583.

CASTRIOTA-SCANDERBEG, A., HAGBERG, G. E., CERASA, A., COMMITTERI, G., GALATI, G., PATRIA, F., ET AL. (2005). The appreciation of wine by sommeliers: A functional magnetic resonance study of sensory integration. *NeuroImage, 25*, 570–578.

CATANI, M., FFYTCHE, D. H. (2005). The rises and falls of disconnection syndromes. *Brain, 128*, 2224–22239.

CATANIA, K. C., & KAAS, J. H. (1995). Organization of the somatosensory cortex of the star-nosed mole. *Journal of Comparative Neurology, 351*, 549–567.

CATANIA, K. C., NORTHCUTT, R. G., KAAS, J. H., & BECK, P. D. (1993). Nose stars and brain stripes. *Nature, 364*, 493.

CATTANEO, L., FABBRI-DESTRO, M., BORIA, S., PIERACCINI, C., MONTI, A., COSSU, G., ET AL. (2007). Impairment of actions chains in autism and its possible role in intention understanding. *Proceedings of the National Academy of Sciences, USA, 104*, 17825–17830.

CELEBRINI, S., & NEWSOME, W. T. (1995). Microstimulation of extrastriate area MST influences performance on a direction discrimination task. *Journal of Neurophysiology, 73*, 437–448.

CERF, M., THIRUVENGADAM, M., MORMANN, F., KRASKOV, A., QUIROGA, R.Q., KOCH, C., & FRIED, I. (2010). On-line, voluntary control of human temporal lobe neurons. *Nature, 467*, 1104–1110.

CHABRIS, C. F., & HAMILTON, S. E. (1992). Hemispheric specialization for skilled perceptual organization by chess masters. *Neuropsychologia, 30*, 4–57.

CHAKRAVARTHY, V.S., JOSEPH, D., & BAPI, R. S. (2009). What do the basal ganglia do? A modeling perspective. *Biological Cybernetics, 103*, 237–253.

CHANGIZI, M. A., ZHANG, Q., YE, H., & SHIMOJO, S. (2006). The structures of letters and symbols throughout human history are selected to match those found in objects in natural scenes. *The American Naturalist, 167*(5), E117–E139.

CHAO, L. L., & MARTIN, A. (2000). Representation of manipulable man-made objects in the dorsal stream. *NeuroImage, 12*, 478–484.

CHAPIN, J. K., MOXON, K. A., MARKOWITZ, R. S., & NICOLELIS, M. A. (1999). Real-time control of a robot arm using simultaneously recorded neurons in the motor cortex. *Nature Neuroscience, 2*, 664–670.

CHAPPELL, M. H., ULUG, A. M., ZHANG, L., HEITGER, M. H., JORDAN, B. D., ZIMMERMAN, R. D., ET AL. (2006). Distribution of microstructural damage in the brains of professional boxers: A diffusion MRI study. *Journal of Magnetic Resonance Imaging, 24*, 537–542.

CHARNOV, E. (1974). Optimal foraging: The marginal value theorem. *Theoretical Population Biology, 9*(2), 129–136.

CHAWLA, D., LUMER, E. D., & FRISTON, K. J. (1999). The relationship between synchronization among neuronal populations and their mean activity levels. *Neural Computation, 11*, 1389–1411.

CHENG, Y., LIN, C. P., LIU, H. L., HSU, Y. Y., LIM, K. E., HUNG, D., ET AL. (2007). Expertise modulates the perception of pain in others. *Current Biology, 17*, 1708–1713.

CHERRY, E. C. (1953). Some experiments on the recognition of speech, with one and two ears. *Journal of the Acoustical Society of America, 25*, 975–979.

CHIARELLO, C. (1991). Interpretation of word meanings by the cerebral hemispheres: One is not enough. In P. J. Schwanenflugel (Ed.), *The psychology of word meanings* (pp. 251–278). Hillsdale, NJ: Erlbaum.

CHILDS, N. L., MERCER, W. N., & CHILDS, H. W. (1993). Accuracy of diagnosis of persistent vegetative state. *Neurology, 43*(8), 1465–1467.

CHOMSKY, N. (1956). Three models for the description of language. *IEEE Transactions on Information Theory, 2*(3), 113–124.

CHOMSKY, N. (1957). *Syntactic structures.* The Hague, Netherlands: Mouton.

CHOMSKY, N. (1975). *Reflections on language.* New York: Pantheon.

CHOMSKY, N. (2006). *Language and mind* (3rd ed.). Cambridge: Cambridge University Press.

CHRISTIANSON, S. A. (1992). *The handbook of emotion and memory: Research and theory.* Hillsdale, NJ: Erlbaum.

CHUGANI, H. T. (1998). A critical period of brain development: Studies of cerebral glucose utilization with PET. *Preventive Medicine, 27*, 184–188.

CHURA, L. R., LOMBARDO, M. V., ASHWIN, E., AUYEUNG, B., CHAKRABARTI, B., BULLMORE, E. T., & BARON-COHEN, S. (2010). Organizational effects of fetal testosterone on human corpus callosum size and asymmetry. *Psychoneuroendocrinology, 35*, 122–132.

CHURCHILL, W. (1930). *My early life: A roving commission.* New York: Scribner.

CHURCHLAND, M. M., CUNNINGHAM, J. P., KAUFMAN, M. T., RYU, S. I, & SHENOY, K. V. (2010). Cortical preparatory activity:

Representation of movement or first cog in a dynamical machine? *Neuron, 68*, 387–400.

CHURCHLAND, M. M., CUNNINGHAM, J. P., KAUFMAN, M. T., FOSTER, J. D., NUYUJUKIAN, P., RYI, S. I., ET AL. (2012). Neural population dynamics during reaching. *Nature, 487*, 51–56. doi:10.1038/nature11129

CHWALISZ, K., DIENER, E., & GALLAGHER, D. (1988). Autonomic arousal feedback and emotional experience: Evidence from the spinal cord injured. *Journal of Personality and Social Psychology, 54*, 820–828.

CIKARA, M., BOTVINICK, M. M., & FISKE, S. T. (2011). Us versus them: Social identity shapes neural responses to intergroup competition and harm. *Psychological Science, 22*(3), 306–313.

CISEK, P. (2007). Cortical mechanisms of action selection: The affordance competition hypothesis. *Philosophical Transactions of the Royal of Society London, Series B: Biological Science, 362*(1485), 1585–99.

CISEK, P., & KALASCA, J. F. (2010). Neural mechanisms for interacting with a world full of action choices. *Annual Review of Neuroscience, 33*, 269–298.

CLARK, D. D., & SOKOLOFF, L. (1999). Circulation and energy metabolism of the brain. In G. J. Siegel, B. W. Agranoff, R. W. Albers, S. K. Fisher, & M. D. Uhler (Eds.), *Basic neurochemistry: Molecular, cellular and medical aspects* (6th ed., pp. 637–670). Philadelphia: Lippincott-Raven.

CLARK, R. E., & SQUIRE, L. R. (1998). Classical conditioning and brain systems: The role of awareness. *Science, 280*, 77–81.

CLASSEN, J., LIEPERT, J., WISE, S. P., HALLETT, M., & COHEN, L. G. (1998). Rapid plasticity of human cortical movement representation induced by practice. *Journal of Neurophysiology, 79*, 1117–1123.

COHEN, A., & IVRY, R. (1989). Illusory conjunctions inside and outside the focus of attention. *Journal of Experimental Psychology. Human Perception and Performance, 15*, 650–663.

COHEN, J. D., BOTVINICK, M., & CARTER, C. S. (2000). Anterior cingulate and prefrontal cortex: Who's in control? *Nature Neuroscience, 3*, 421–423.

COHEN, L., DEHAENE, S., NACCACHE, L., LEHÉRICY, S., DEHAENE-LAMBERTZ, G., HÉNAFF, M. A., & MICHEL, F. (2000). The visual word form area: spatial and temporal characterization of an initial stage of reading in normal subjects and posterior split-brain patients. *Brain, 123*, 291–307.

COHEN, L., LEHERICY, S., CHOCHON, F., LEMER, C., RIVAUD, S., & DEHAENE, S. (2002). Language-specific tuning of visual cortex? Functional properties of the visual word form area. *Brain, 125*(Pt. 5), 1054–1069.

COHEN, N. J., & EICHENBAUM, H. (1993). *Memory, amnesia and the hippocampal system.* Cambridge, MA: MIT Press.

COLLINS, A. M., & LOFTUS, E. F. (1975). A spreading-activation theory of semantic processing. *Psychological Review, 82*, 407–428.

COLTHEART, M., CURTIS, B., ATKINS, P., & HALLER, M. (1993). Models of reading aloud: Dual route and parallel-distributed-processing approaches. *Psychological Review, 100*, 589–608.

CORBALLIS, M. C. (1991). *The lopsided ape: Evolution of the generative mind.* New York: Oxford University Press.

CORBALLIS, M. C. (2009). The evolution of language. *Annals of the New York Academy of Sciences, 1156*(1), 19–43.

CORBALLIS, P. M., FENDRICH, R., SHAPLEY, R. M., & GAZZANIGA, M. S. (1999). Illusory contour perception and amodal boundary completion: Evidence of a dissociation following callosotomy. *Journal of Cognitive Neuroscience, 11*, 459–466.

CORBETT, B. A., CARMEAN, V., RAVIZZA ,S., WENDELKEN, G., HENRY, M. L. CARTER, C., & RIVERA, S. M. (2009). A functional and structural study of emotion and face processing in children with autism. *Psychiatry Research: Neuroimaging, 173*, 196–205.

CORBETTA, M., KINCADE, J. M., LEWIS, C., SNYDER, A. Z., & SAPIR, A. (2005). Neural basis and recovery of spatial attention deficits in spatial neglect. *Nature Neuroscience, 8*, 1603–1610.

CORBETTA, M., KINCADE, J. M., OLLINGER, J. M., McAVOY, M. P., & SHULMAN, G. L. (2000). Voluntary orienting is dissociated from target detection in human posterior parietal cortex. *Nature Neuroscience, 3*, 292–297.

CORBETTA, M., MIEZIN, F. M., DOBMEYER, S., SHULMAN, G. L., & PETERSEN, S. E. (1991). Selective and divided attention during visual discriminations of shape, color and speed: Functional anatomy by positron emission tomography. *Journal of Neuroscience, 11*, 2383–2402.

CORBETTA, M., & SHULMAN, G. (2002). Control of goal-directed and stimulus-driven attention in the brain. *Nature Reviews Neuroscience, 3*, 201–215.

CORBETTA, M., & SHULMAN, G. (2011). Spatial neglect and attention networks. *Annual Review of Neuroscience, 34*, 569–599.

COREN, S., WARD, L. M., & ENNS, J. T. (1994). *Sensation and perception* (4th ed.). Ft. Worth, TX: Harcourt Brace.

CORKIN, S. (2002). What's new with the amnesic patient H.M.? *Nature Reviews Neuroscience, 3*, 153–160.

CORKIN, S., AMARAL, D., GONZALEZ, R., JOHNSON, K., & HYMAN, B. T. (1997). H.M.'s medial temporal lobe lesion: Findings from magnetic resonance imaging. *Journal of Neuroscience, 17*, 3964–3979.

CORICELLI, G., CRITCHLEY, H. D., JOFFILY, M., O'DOHERTY, J. P., SIRIGU, A., & DOLAN, R. J. (2005). Regret and its avoidance: A neuroimaging study of choice behavior. *Nature Neuroscience, 8*, 1255–1262.

CORTHOUT, E., UTTL, B., ZIEMANN, U., COWEY, A., & HALLETT, M. (1999). Two periods of processing in the (circum)striate visual cortex as revealed by transcranial magnetic stimulation. *Neuropsychologia, 37*, 137–145.

COSMIDES, L. (1984). The logic of social exchange: Has natural selection shaped how humans reason? Studies with the Wason selection task. *Cognition, 31*, 187–276.

COSMIDES, L., & TOOBY, J. (1992). Cognitive adaptations for social exchange. In J. H. Barkow, L. Cosmides, & J. Tooby (Eds.), *The adapted mind* (pp. 163–228). New York: Oxford University Press.

COSMIDES, L., & TOOBY, J. (2000). Evolutionary psychology and the emotions. In M. Lewis & J. M. Haviland-Jones (Eds.), *Handbook of emotions* (2nd ed.). New York: Guilford.

COUDÉ, G., FERRARI, P.F., RODÀ, F., MARANESI, M., BORELLI, E., VERONI, B., MONTI, F., ROZZI, S. & FOGASSI, L. (2011) Neurons controlling voluntary vocalization in the macaque ventral premotor crtex. *PLoS ONE 6*(11): e26822.

COURCHESNE, E., & PIERCE, K. (2005a). Brain overgrowth in autism during a critical time in development: Implications for frontal pyramidal neuron and interneuron development and connectivity. *International Journal of Developmental Neuroscience, 23*(2–3), 153–170.

COURCHESNE, E., & PIERCE, K. (2005b). Why the frontal cortex in autism might be talking only to itself: Local over-connectivity but long-distance disconnection. *Current Opinions in Neurobiology, 15*(2), 225–230.

COWEY, A. (2010). The blindsight saga. *Experimental Brain Research, 200*, 3–24.

CRAIG, A. D. (2009). How do you feel—now? The anterior insula and human awareness. *Nature Reviews Neuroscience, 10*, 59–70.

CRAIK, F. I. M., & LOCKHART, R. S. (1972). Levels of processing: A framework for memory research. *Journal of Verbal Learning and Verbal Behavior, 11*, 671–684.

CRICK, F. (1992). Function of the thalamic reticular complex: The searchlight hypothesis. In S. M. Kosslyn & R. A. Andersen (Eds.), *Frontiers in cognitive neuroscience* (pp. 366–372). Cambridge, MA: MIT Press.

CRICK, F. (1999). The impact of molecular biology on neuroscience. *Philosophical Transactions of the Royal Society of London, Series B: Biological Sciences, 354*(1392), 2021–2025.

CRITCHLEY, H. D. (2009). Psychophysiology of neural, cognitive and affective integration: fMRI and autonomic indicants. *International Journal of Psychophysiology, 73*, 88–94.

CRITCHLEY, H. D., MATHIAS, C. J., JOSEPHS, O., O'DOHERTY, J., ZANINI, S., DEWAR, B. K., ET AL. (2003). Human cingulate cortex and autonomic control: Converging neuroimaging and clinical evidence. *Brain, 126*, 2139–2152.

CRITCHLEY, H. D., WIENS, S., ROTHSTEIN, P., ÖHMAN, A., & DOLAN, R. J. (2004). Neural systems supporting interoceptive awareness. *Nature Neuroscience, 7*, 189–195.

CROXSON, P. L., WALTON, M. E., O'REILLY, J. X., BEHRENS, T. E. J., & RUSHWORTH, M. F. S. (2009). Effort based cost-benefit valuation and the human brain. *Journal of Neuroscience, 29*, 4531–4541.

CSIKSZENTMIHALYI, M. (1990). *Flow: The psychology of optimal experience.* New York: Harper & Row.

CSIKSZENTMIHALYI, M. & LEFEVRE, J. (1989). Optimal experience in work and leisure. *Journal of Personality and Social Psychology, 56*, 815–822.

CUI, H., & ANDERSEN, R. A. (2007). Posterior parietal cortex encodes autonomously selected motor plans. *Neuron, 56*, 552–559.

CULHAM, J. C., DANCKERT, S. L., DESOUZA, J. F., GATI, J. S., MENON, R. S., & GOODALE, M. A. (2003). Visually guided grasping produces fMRI activation in dorsal but not ventral stream brain areas. *Experimental Brain Research, 153*, 180–189.

CUNNINGHAM, W. A., JOHNSON, M. K., RAYE, C. L., GATENBY, J. C., GORE, J. C., & BANAJI, M. R. (2004). Separable neural components in the processing of black and white faces. *Psychological Science, 15*, 806–813.

DALTON, K. M., NACEWICZ, B. M., JOHNSTONE, T., SCHAEFER, H. S., GERNSBACHER, M. A., GOLDSMITH, H. H., ET AL. (2005). Gaze fixation and the neural circuitry of face processing in autism. *Nature Neuroscience, 8*, 519–526.

DAMASIO, A. R. (1990). Category-related recognition defects as a clue to the neural substrates of knowledge. *Trends in Neurosciences, 13*, 95–98.

DAMASIO, A. R. (1994). *Descartes' error: Emotion, reason, and the human brain.* New York: Putnam.

DAMASIO, A. R. (1998). Investigating the biology of consciousness. *Philosophical Transactions of the Royal Society of London, 353*, 1879–1882.

DAMASIO, A. R. (2011). Thinking about brain and consciousness. In S. Dehaene & Y. Christen (Eds.), *Characterizing consciousness: From cognition to the clinic?* Berlin: Springer-Verlag.

DAMASIO, A. R., & MEYER, K. (2008). Consciousness: An overview of the phenomenon and of its possible neural basis. In S. Laureys & G. Tononi (Eds.), *The neurology of consciousness* (pp. 3–14). London: Elsevier.

DAMASIO, A. R., TRANEL, D., & DAMASIO, H. (1990). Individuals with sociopathic behavior caused by frontal damage fail to respond auto-nomically to social stimuli. *Behavioral Brain Research, 41*, 81–94.

DAMASIO, H., GRABOWSKI, T., FRANK, R., GALABURDA, A. M., & DAMASIO, A. R. (1994). The return of Phineas Gage: Clues about the brain from the skull of a famous patient. *Science, 264*, 1102–1105.

DAMASIO, H., GRABOWSKI, T. J., TRANEL, D., HICHWA, R. D., & DAMA-SIO, A. R. (1996). A neural basis for lexical retrieval. *Nature, 380*, 499–505.

DAMASIO, H., TRANEL, D., GRABOWSKI, T., ADOLPHS, R., & DAMASIO, A. (2004). Neural systems behind word and concept retrieval. *Cognition, 92*, 179–229.

DARLEY, J. M., CARLSMITH, K. M., & ROBINSON, P. H. (2000). Incapacitation and just deserts as motives for punishment. *Law and Human Behavior, 24*, 659–683.

DARWIN, C. (1859). *On the origin of species.* London: Murray. (Reprint, Cambridge, MA: Harvard University Press)

DARWIN, C. (1871). *The descent of man and selection in relation to sex.* London: Murray.

DARWIN, C. (1873). *The expression of the emotions in man and animals.* Oxford: Oxford University Press.

DARWIN, C., EKMAN, P., & PRODGER, P. (1998). *The expression of the emotions in man and animals* (3rd ed.). Oxford: Oxford University Press.

DASELAAR, S. M., PRINCE, S. E., DENNIS, N. A., HAYES, S. M., KIM, H., & CABEZA R. (2009). Posterior midline and ventral parietal activity is associated with retrieval success and encoding failure. *Frontiers in Human Neuroscience, 3*, 13.

DASILVA, A. F., TUCH, D. S., WIEGELL, M. R., & HADJIKHANI, N. (2003). A primer on diffusion tensor imaging of anatomical sub-structures. *Neurosurgical Focus, 15*, E4.

DAVACHI, L. (2006). Item, context and relational episodic encoding in humans. *Current Opinions in Neurobiology, 16*, 693–700.

DAVACHI, L., MITCHELL, J. P., & WAGNER, A. D. (2003). Multiple routes to memory: distinct medial temporal lobe processes build item and source memories. *Proceedings of the National Academy of Science U.S.A., 100*, 2157–2162.

DAVACHI, L. & WAGNER, A. D. (2002). Hippocampal contributions to episodic encoding: insights from relational and item-based learning. *Journal of Neurophysiology, 88*, 982–990.

DAVIDSON, R. J. (1995). Cerebral asymmetry, emotion, and affective style. In R. J. Davidson & K. Hugdahl (Eds.), *Brain asymmetry* (pp. 361–387). Cambridge, MA: MIT Press.

DAVIDSON, R. J. (2012). *The emotional life of your brain.* New York: Hudson Street Press.

DAVIDSON, R. J., EKMAN, P., SARON, C., SENULIS, J., & FRIESEN, W. V. (1990). Approach-withdrawal and cerebral asymmetry: Emotional expression and brain physiology. *Journal of Personality and Social Psychology, 58*, 330–341.

DAVIDSON, R. J., JACKSON, D. C., & KALIN, N. H. (2000). Emotion, plasticity, context, and regulation: Perspectives from affective neuroscience. *Psychological Bulletin, 126*, 890–909.

DAVIDSON, R.J., PUTNAM, K.M., & LARSON, C.L. (2000). Dysfunction in the neural circuitry of emotion regulation—a possible prelude to violence. *Science, 289*, 591–594.

DAVIES, R.R., GRAHAM, K.S., XUEREB, J.H., WILLIAMS, G.B. & HODGES, J.R. (2004). The human perirhinal cortex and semantic memory. *European Journal of Neuroscience, 20*, 2441–2446.

DAVIS, M. (1992). The role of the amygdala in conditioned fear. In J. P. Aggleton (Ed.), *The amygdala: Neurobiological aspects of emotion, memory and mental dysfunction* (pp. 255–306). New York: Wiley-Liss.

DAW, N. D., O'DOHERTY, J. P., DAYAN, P., SEYMOUR, B., & DOLAN, R. J. (2006). Cortical substrates for exploratory decisions in humans. *Nature, 441*, 876–879.

DAWKINS, R. (1976). *The selfish gene.* New York: Oxford University Press.

DAWSON, J. L. M., CHEUNG, Y. M., & LAU, R. T. S. (1973). Effects of neonatal sex hormones on sex-based cognitive abilities in the white rat. *Psychologia, 16*, 17–24.

DAYAN, P., & NIV, Y. (2008). Reinforcement learning: The good, the bad and the ugly. *Current Opinion in Neurobiology, 18*, 185–196.

DEARMOND, S., FUSCO, M., & DEWEY, M. (1976). *A photographic atlas: Structure of the human brain* (2nd ed.). New York: Oxford University Press.

De Bie, R. M., de Haan, R. J., Schuurman, P. R., Esselink, R. A., Bosch, D. A., & Speelman, J. D. (2002). Morbidity and mortality following pallidotomy in Parkinson's disease: A systematic review. *Neurology, 58*, 1008–1012.

Debiec, J., LeDoux, J. E., & Nader, K. (2002). Cellular and systems reconsolidation in the hippocampus. *Neuron, 36*, 527–538.

Decety, J. (2011). The neuroevolution of empathy. *Annals of the New York Academy of Sciences, 1231*, 35-45.

Decety, J., & Grezes, J. (1999). Neural mechanisms subserving the perception of human actions. *Trends in Cognitive Sciences, 3*, 172–178.

Decety, J., & Jackson, P. L. (2004). The functional architecture of human empathy. *Behavioral and Cognitive Neuroscience Reviews, 3*, 71–100.

Decety, J., Yang, C.-Y., & Cheng, Y. (2010). Physicians down-reguate their pain empathy response: An event–related brain potential study. *NeuroImage, 50*, 1676–1682.

Deep-Brain Stimulation for Parkinson's Disease Study Group. (2001). Deep-brain stimulation of the subthalamic nucleus or the pars interna of the globus pallidus in Parkinson's disease. *New England Journal of Medicine, 345*, 956–963.

De Fockert, J. W., Rees, G., Frith, C. D., & Lavie, N. (2001). The role of working memory in visual selective attention. *Science, 291*, 1803–1806.

Dehaene, S., Changeux, J. P., Naccache, L., Sackur, J., & Sergent, C. (2006). Conscious, preconscious, and subliminal processing: A testable taxonomy. *Trends in Cognitive Sciences, 10*, 204–211.

Dehaene, S. & Cohen, L. (2011). The unique role of the visual word form area in reading. *Trends in Cognitive Sciences, 15*(6), 254–261.

Dehaene, S., Le Clec'H, G., Poline, J.-B., Le Bihan, D., & Cohen (2002) The visual word form area: a prelexical representation of visual words in the fusiform gyrus. *Neuroreport, 13*, 321–325.

Dehaene, S., & Naccache, L. (2001). Towards a cognitive neuroscience of consciousness: Basic evidence and a workspace framework. *Cognition, 79*, 1–37.

Dehaene, S., Posner, M. I., & Tucker, D. M. (1994). Localization of a neural system for error detection and compensation. *Psychological Science, 5*, 303–305.

Dehaene-Lambertz, G., & Dehaene, S. 1994. Speed and cerebral correlates of syllable discrimination in infants. *Nature, 370*(6487), 292–95.

Deibert, E., Kraut, M., Kremen, S., & Hart, J., Jr. (1999). Neural pathways in tactile object recognition. *Neurology, 52*, 1413–1417.

Deisseroth, K. (2010, October 20). Optogenetics: Controlling the brain with light [extended version]. *Scientific American*.

Deisseroth, K., Feng, G., Majewska, A. K., Miesenböck, G., Ting, A., & Schnitzer, M. J. (2006). Next-generation optical technologies for illuminating genetically targeted brain circuits. *Journal of Neuroscience 26*(41), 10380–10386.

Déjerine, J. (1892) Contribution á l'étude anatomo-pathologique et clinique des différentes variétés de cécité verbale. *Mémoires de la Société de Biologie, 4*, 61–90.

Delbrück, M. (1986). *Mind from matter? An essay on evolutionary epistemology*. London: Blackwell.

Delis, D., Robertson, L., & Efron, R. (1986). Hemispheric specialization of memory for visual hierarchical stimuli. *Neuropsychologia, 24*, 205–214.

Dell, G. S. (1986). A spreading activation theory of retrieval in sentence production. *Psychological Review, 93*, 283–321.

DeLong, M. R. (1990). Primate models of movement disorders of basal ganglia origin. *Trends in Neurosciences, 13*, 281–285.

Delton, A. W., Krasnow, M. M., Tooby, J., & Cosmides, L. (2011). The evolution of direct reciprocity under uncertainty can explain human generosity in one-shot encounters. *Proceedings of the National Academy of Sciences, USA, 108*(44), 13335–13340.

De Martino, B., Kumaran, D., Seymour, & Dolan, R. J. (2006). Frames, biases, and rational decision-making in the human brain. *Science, 313*, 684–687.

Démonet, J. F., Chollet, F., Ramsay, S., Cerdebat, D., Nespoules, J. D., Wise, R., et al. (1992). The anatomy of phonological and semantic processing in normal subjects. *Brain, 115*, 1753–1768.

Démonet, J. F., Fiez, J. A., Paulesu, E, Petersen, S. E., & Zatorre, R. J. (1996). PET sutdies of phonological processing: A critical reply to Poeppe, *Brain and Language, 55*, 352–379.

Démonet, J. F., Price, C. J., Wise, R., & Frackowiak, R. S. J. (1994). Differential activation of right and left posterior Sylvian regions by semantic and phonological tasks: A positron emission tomography study. *Neuroscience Letters, 182*, 25–28.

Dennett, D. (1995). *Darwin's dangerous idea*. New York: Simon and Schuster.

Denny, B.T., Silvers, J.A., & Ochsner, K.N. (2009). How we heel what we don't want to feel. In A.M. Kring & D.M. Sloan (Eds.), *Emotion Regulation and Psychopathology: A Transdiagnostic Approach to Etiology and Treatment* (pp. 59–87). New York: Guilford.

De Quervain, D. J.-F., Fischbacher, U., Treyer, V., Schellhammer, M., Schnyder, U., Buck, A., & Fehr, E. (2004). The neural basis of altruistic punishment. *Science, 305*, 1254–1258.

De Renzi, E., Perani, D., Carlesimo, G. A., Silveri, M. C., & Fazio, F. (1994). Prosopagnosia can be associated with damage confined to the right hemisphere—An MRI and PET study and a review of the literature. *Neuropsychologia, 32*, 893–902.

Desimone, R. (1991). Face-selective cells in the temporal cortex of monkeys. *Journal of Cognitive Neuroscience, 3*, 1–8.

Desimone, R. (1996). Neural mechanisms for visual memory and their role in attention. *Proceedings of the National Academy of Sciences, USA, 93*, 13494–13499.

Desimone, R., Albright, T. D., Gross, C. G., & Bruce, C. (1984). Stimulus-selective properties of inferior temporal neurons in the macaque. *Journal of Neuroscience, 4*, 2051–2062.

Desimone, R., Wessinger, M., Thomas, L., & Schneider, W. (1990). Attentional control of visual perception: Cortical and subcortical mechanisms. *Cold Spring Harbor Symposia on Quantitative Biology, 55*, 963–971.

Desmurget, M., Epstein, C. M., Turner, R. S., Prablanc, C., Alexander, G. E., & Grafton, S. T. (1999). Role of the posterior parietal cortex in updating reaching movements to a visual target. *Nature Neuroscience, 2*, 563–567.

Desmurget, M., Reilly, K. T., Richard, N., Szathmari, A., Mottolese, C., & Sirigu, A. (2009). Movement intention after parietal cortex stimulation in humans. *Science, 324*, 811–813.

Devinsky, O., Morrell, M. J., & Vogt, B. A. (1995). Contributions of anterior cingulate cortex to behavior. *Brain, 118*, 279–306.

DeWitt, I., & Rauschecker, J.P. (2012). Phoneme and word recognition in the auditory ventral stream. *Proceedings of the National Academy of Sciences, 109*(8), E505–E514.

Diamond, A. (1990). The development and neural bases of memory functions as indexed by the A(not)B and delayed response tasks in human infants and infant monkeys. In A. Diamond (Ed.), *The development and neural bases of higher cognitive functions* (pp. 267–317). New York: New York Academy of Sciences.

Diana, R. A., Yonelinas, A. P., & Ranganath, C. (2007). Imaging recollection and familiarity in the medial temporal lobe: A three-component model. *Trends in Cognitive Sciences, 11*, 379–386.

Ditterich, J., Mazurek, M. E., & Shadlen, M. N. (2003). Microstimulation of visual cortex affects the speed of perceptual decisions. *Nature Neuroscience, 6*(8), 891–898.

DOLCOS, F., LABAR, K. S., & CABEZA, R. (2004). Interaction between the amygdala and the medial temporal lobe memory system predicts better memory for emotional events. *Neuron, 42,* 855–863.

DOWNING, P., CHAN, A. W.-Y., PEELEN, M. V., DODDS, C. M., & KANWISHER, N. (2006). Domain specificity in visual cortex. *Cerebral Cortex, 16,* 1453–1461.

DOWNING, P., JIANG, Y., SHUMAN, M., & KANWISHER, N. (2001). A cortical area selective for visual processing of the human body. *Science, 293,* 2470–2473.

DOYLE, D., CABRAL, J., PFUETZNER, R., KUO, A., GULBIS, J., COHEN, S., ET AL. (1998). The structure of the potassium channel: Molecular basis of K+ conduction and selectivity. *Science, 280,* 69–77.

DOYLE, J. & CSETE, M. (2011). Architecture, constrains, and behavior. *Proceedings of the National Academy of Sciences, USA, 108*(Supplement 3), 15624–15630.

DRACHMAN, D. A., & ARBIT, J. (1966). Memory and the hippocampal complex. II. Is memory a multiple process? *Archives of Neurology, 15,* 52–61.

DRAGANSKI, B., GASER, C., BUSCH, V., SCHUIERER, G., BOGDAHN, U., & MAY, A. (2004). Neuroplasticity: Changes in grey matter induced by training. *Nature, 427*(6972), 311–312.

DREVETS, W. C. (1998). Functional neuroimaging studies of depression: The anatomy of melancholia. *Annual Review of Medicine, 49,* 341–361.

DRIVER, J., & NOESSELT, T. (2007). Multisensory interplay reveals crossmodal influences on "sensory-specific" brain regions, neural responses, and judgments. *Neuron, 57,* 11–23.

DRONKERS, N. F. (1996). A new brain region for coordinating speech articulation. *Nature, 384,* 159–161.

DRONKERS, N. F., PLAISANT, O., IBA-ZIZEN, M. T., & CABANIS, E. A. (2007). Paul Broca's historic cases: High-resolution MR imaging of the brains of Leborgne and Lelong. *Brain, 130*(5), 1432–1441.

DRONKERS, N. F., WILKINS, D. P., VAN VALIN, R. D., REDFERN, B. B., & JAEGER, J. J. (1994). A reconsideration of the brain areas involved in the disruption of morphosyntactic comprehension. *Brain and Language, 47,* 461–462.

DRUZGAL, T. J., & D'ESPOSITO, M. (2003). Dissecting contributions of prefrontal cortex and fusiform face area to face working memory. *Journal of Cognitive Neuroscience, 15,* 771–784.

DUM, R. P., & STRICK, P. L. (2002). Motor areas in the frontal lobe of the primate. *Physiology & Behavior, 77,* 677–682.

DUNCAN, J. (1984). Selective attention and the organization of visual information. *Journal of Experimental Psychology. General, 113,* 501–517.

DUNCAN, J. (1995). Attention, intelligence, and the frontal lobes. In M. S. Gazzaniga (Ed.), *The cognitive neurosciences* (pp. 721–733). Cambridge, MA: MIT Press.

DUNCAN, S., & BARRETT, L. F. (2007). Affect is a form of cognition: A neurobiological analysis. *Cognition & Emotion, 21,* 1184–1211.

DUNN, B. B., DALGLEISH, T., & LAWRENCE, A. D. (2006). The somatic marker hypothesis: A critical evaluation. *Neuroscience and Biobehavioral Reviews, 30,* 239–271.

DUONG, T. Q., KIM, D. S., UGURBIL, K., & KIM, S. G. (2000). Spatio-temporal dynamics of the BOLD fMRI signals: Toward mapping submillimeter cortical columns using the early negative response. *Magnetic Resonance in Medicine, 44,* 231–242.

DUX, P. E., TOMBU, M. N., HARRISON, S., ROGERS, B. P., TONG, F., & MAROIS, R. (2009). Training improves multitasking performance by increasing the speed of information processing in human prefrontal cortex. *Neuron, 63,* 127–138.

EASON, R., HARTER, M., & WHITE, C. (1969). Effects of attention and arousal on visually evoked cortical potentials and reaction time in man. *Physiology & Behavior, 4,* 283–289.

EFRON, R. (1990). *The decline and fall of hemispheric specialization.* Hillsdale, NJ: Erlbaum.

EGLY, R., DRIVER, J., & RAFAL, R. D. (1994). Shifting visual attention between objects and locations—Evidence from normal and parietal lesion subjects. *Journal of Experimental Psychology. General, 123,* 161–177.

EICHELE, T., DEBENER, S., CALHOUN, V. D., SPECHT, K., ENGEL, A. K., HUGDAH, K., ET AL. (2008). Prediction of human errors by maladaptive changes in event-related brain networks. *Proceedings of the National Academy of Sciences, USA, 105,* 6173–6178.

EICHENBAUM, H. (2000). A cortical-hippocampal system for declarative memory. *Nature Reviews. Neuroscience, 1,* 41–50.

EICHENBAUM, H., DUDCHENKO, P., WOOD, E., SHAPIRO, M., & TANILA, H. (1999). The hippocampus, memory, and place cells: Is it spatial memory or a memory space? *Neuron, 23,* 209–226.

EICHENBAUM, H., STEWART, C., & MORRIS, R. G. M. (1990). Hippocampal representation in spatial learning. *Journal of Neuroscience, 10,* 331–339.

EICHENBAUM, H., YONELINAS, A. P., & RANGANATH, C. (2007). The medial temporal lobe and recognition memory. *Annual Review of Neuroscience, 30,* 123–152.

EIMER, M., & HOLMES, A. (2006). Event-related brain potential correlates with emotional face processing. *Neuropsychologia, 45*(1), 15–31.

EISENBERG, J. F. (1981). *The mammalian radiations: An analysis of trends in evolution, adaptation and behavior.* Chicago: University of Chicago Press.

EKMAN, P. (1992). An argument for basic emotions. *Cognition and Emotion, 6,* 169–200.

EKMAN, P. (1973). Cross-cultural studies in facial expression. In P. Ekman (Ed.), *Darwin and facial expressions: A century of research in review.* New York: Academic Press.

EKMAN, P. (1992). An argument for basic emotions. *Cognition and Emotion, 6,* 169–200.

EKMAN, P. (1994). All emotions are basic. In P. Ekman and R. J. Davidson (Eds.), *The nature of emotion: Fundamental questions.* New York: Oxford Univeristy Press.

EKMAN, P. (1999). Basic emotions. In T. Dalgleish & M. Power (Eds.), *Handbook of cognition and emotion.* New York: Wiley.

EKMAN, P. (2003). Darwin, deception and facial expressions. *Annals of the New York Academy of Science, 1000,* 205–221.

EKMAN, P., & FRIESEN, W. V. (1971). Constants across cultures in the face and emotion. *Journal of Personality and Social Psychology, 17,* 124–129.

ELBERT, T., PANTEV, C., WIENBRUCH, C., ROCKSTROH, B., & TAUB, E. (1995). Increased cortical representation of the fingers of the left hand in string players. *Science, 270,* 305–307.

ELDRIDGE, L. L., KNOWLTON, B. J., FURMANSKI, C. S., BOOKHEIMER, S. Y., & ENGEL, S. A. (2000). Remembering episodes: A selective role for the hippocampus during retrieval. *Nature Neuroscience, 3,* 1149–1152.

EMLER, N. (1994). Gossip, reputation and adaptation. In R. F. Goodman & A. Ben-Ze'ev (Eds.). *Good gossip* (pp. 117–138). Lawrence: University of Kansas Press.

ENARD, W., PRZEWORSKI, M., FISHER, S. E., LAI, C. S., WIEBE, V., KITANO, T., MONACO, A. P., & PAABO, S. (2002). Molecular evolution of FOXP2, a gene involved in speech and language. *Nature, 418,* 869–872.

ENGEL, A. K., KREITER, A. K., KONIG, P., & SINGER, W. (1991). Synchronization of oscillatory neuronal responses between striate and extrastriate visual cortical areas of the cat. *Proceedings of the National Academy of Sciences, USA, 88,* 6048–6052.

EPSTEIN, R., & KANWISHER, N. (1998). A cortical representation of the local visual environment. *Nature, 392,* 598–601.

ERICSSON, K. A., KRAMPE, R. T., & TESCH-ROMER, C. (1993). The role of deliberate practice in the acquisition of expert performance. *Psychology Review, 100,* 363–406.

ERIKSEN, C. W., & ERIKSEN, B. (1971). Visual perceptual processing rates and backward and forward masking. *Journal of Experimental Psychology, 89*, 306–313.

ERIKSSON, P. S., PERFILIEVA, E., BJÖRK-ERIKSSON, T., ALBORN, A., NORDBORG, C., PETERSON, D., ET AL. (1998). Neurogenesis in the adult human hippocampus. *Nature Medicine, 4*, 1313–1317.

ESLINGER, P. J., & DAMASIO, A. R. (1985). Severe disturbance of higher cognition after bilateral frontal lobe ablation: Patient EVR. *Neurology, 35*, 1731–1741.

ESTERMAN, M., VERSTYNEN, T., IVRY, R. B., & ROBERTSON, L. C. (2006). Coming unbound: Disrupting automatic integration of synesthetic color and graphemes by transcranial magnetic stimulation of the right parietal lobe. *Journal of Cognitive Neuroscience, 18*, 1570–1576.

ETCOFF, N. L., EKMAN, P., MAGEE, J. J., & FRANK, M. G. (2000). Lie detection and language comprehension. *Nature, 405*, 139.

FARAH, M. J. (1988). Is visual imagery really visual? Overlooked evidence from neuropsychology. *Psychological Review, 95*, 307–317.

FARAH, M. J. (1994). Specialization within visual object recognition: Clues from prosopagnosia and alexia. In M. J. Farah & G. Ratcliff (Eds.), *The neuropsychology of high-level vision: Collected tutorial essays* (pp. 133–146). Hillsdale, NJ: Erlbaum.

FARAH, M. (2004). *Visual agnosia* (2nd ed.). Cambridge, MA: MIT Press.

FARAH, M. J., & MCCLELLAND, J. L. (1991). A computational model of semantic memory impairment: Modality specificity and emergent category specificity. *Journal of Experimental Psychology. General, 120*, 339–357.

FARADAY, M. (1933). *Faraday's Diary. Being the various philosophical notes of experiment investigation during the years 1820–1862.* London: George Bell and Sons.

FEHR, E., & GÄCHTER, S. (1999). Cooperation and punishment in public goods experiments. *American Economic Review, 90*(4), 980–994.

FEHR, E., & GÄCHTER, S. (2002). Altruistic punishment in humans. *Nature, 415*, 137–140.

FEINSTEIN, J. S., ADOLPHS, R., DAMASIO, A., & TRANEL, D. (2011). The human amygdala and the induction and experience of fear. *Current Biology, 21*, 34–38.

FELLOWS, L. K., & FARAH, M. J. (2005). Is anterior cingulate cortex necessary for cognitive control? *Brain, 128*, 788–796.

FELLOWS, L. K., & FARAH, M. J. (2007). The role of ventromedial prefrontal cortex in decision making: Judgment under uncertainty or judgment per se? *Cerebral Cortex, 17*, 2669–2674.

FENDRICH, R., WESSINGER, C. M., & GAZZANIGA, M. S. (1992). Residual vision in a scotoma: Implications for blindsight. *Science, 258*, 1489–1491.

FEREDOES, E., HEINEN, K., WEISKOPF, N., RUFF, C., & DRIVER, J. (2011). Causal evidence for frontal involvement in memory target maintenance by posterior brain areas during distracter interference of visual working memory. *Proceedings of the National Academy of Sciences, USA, 108*, 17510–17515.

FERRY, B., & MCGAUGH, J. L. (2000). Role of amygdala norepinephrine in mediating stress hormone regulation of memory storage. *Acta Pharmacologica Sinica, 21*, 481–493.

FEYNMAN, R. (1998). *The meaing of it all.* New York: Perseus Books Group.

FEYNMAN, R. P., LEIGHTON, R. B., & SANDS, M. (1995). *Six easy pieces: Essentials of physics explained by its most brilliant teacher.* New York: Basic Books.

FIORILLO, C. D., TOBLER, P. N., & SCHULTZ, W. (2003). Discrete coding of reward probability and uncertainty by dopamine neurons. *Science, 299*, 1898–1902.

FINGER, S. (1994). *Origins of neuroscience.* New York: Oxford University Press.

FISHER, S.E. (2005). Dissection of molecular mechanisms underlying speech and language disorders. *Applied Psycholinguistics, 26*, 111–128.

FISHER, S. E., VARGHA-KHADEM, F., WATKINS, K. E., MONACO, A. P. & PEMBREY, M. E. (1998). Localization of a gene implicated in a severe speech and language disorder. *Nature Genetics, 18*, 168–170.

FLACK, J. C., KRAKAUER, D. C., & DE WAAL, F. B. M. (2005). Robustness mechanisms in primate societies: A perturbation study. *Proceedings of the Royal Society of London, Series B, 272*(1568), 1091–1099.

FLORENCE, S. L., & KAAS, J. H. (1995). Large-scale reorganization at multiple levels of the somatosensory pathway follows therapeutic amputation of the hand in monkeys. *Journal of Neuroscience, 15*, 8083–8095.

FLOURENS, M.-J. P. (1824). *Recherches expérimentales sur les proprieties et les functiones du systeme nerveux dans le animaux vertébrés.* Paris: Ballière.

FODOR, J. A. (1983). *The modularity of mind.* Cambridge, MA: MIT Press.

FORSTER, B., CORBALLIS, P. M., & CORBALLIS, M. C. (2000). The perception of sequentiality following callosotomy. *Neuropsychologia.* In press 2000.

FOSTER, D., & WILSON, M. (2006). Reverse replay of behavioral sequences in hippocampal place cells during the awake state. *Nature, 440*, 680–683.

FOX, P. T., MIEZIN, F. M., ALLMAN, J. M., VAN ESSEN, D. C., & RAICHLE, M. E. (1987). Retinotopic organization of human visual cortex mapped with positron-emission tomography. *Journal of Neuroscience, 7*, 913–922.

FOX, P. T., MINTUN, M. A., REIMAN, E. M., & RAICHLE, M. E. (1988). Enhanced detection of focal brain responses using intersubject average and change-distribution subtracted PET images. *Journal of Cerebral Blood Flow and Metabolism, 8*, 642-653.

FOX, P. T., & RAICHLE, M. E. (1986). Focal physiological uncoupling of cerebral blood flow and oxidative metabolism during somatosensory stimulation in human subjects. *Proceedings of the National Academy of Sciences, USA, 83*, 1140–1144.

FOX, P. T., RAICHLE, M. E., MINTUN, M. A., & DENCE, C. (1988). Nonoxidative glucose consumption during focal physiologic neural activity. *Science, 241*, 462–464.

FRANCO, M. I., TURIN, L., MERSHIN, A., & SKOULAKIS, E. M. C. (2011). Molecular vibration-sensing component in *Drosophila melanogaster* olfaction. *Proceedings of the National Academy of Sciences, 108*(9), 3797–3802.

FRANK, M. J., & FOSSELLA, J. A. (2011). Neurogenetics and pharmacology of learning, motivation and cognition. *Neuropsychopharmacology, 36*, 133–152.

FRANK, M. J., SAMANTA, J., MOUSTAFA, A. A., & SHERMAN, S. J. (2007). Hold your horses: Impulsivity, deep brain stimulation, and medication in parkinsonism. *Science, 318*, 1309–1312.

FRANZ, E., ELIASSEN, J., IVRY, R., & GAZZANIGA, M. (1996). Dissociation of spatial and temporal coupling in the bimanual movements of callosotomy patients. *Psychological Science, 7*, 306–310.

FRAZIER, L. (1987). Structure in auditory word recognition. *Cognition, 25*, 157–187.

FREEDMAN, D. J., RIESENHUBER, M., POGGIO, T., & MILLER, E. K. (2001). Categorical representations of visual stimuli in the primate prefrontal cortex. *Science, 291*, 312–316.

FREEMAN, W., & WATTS, J. W. (1950). *Psychosurgery: In the treatment of mental disorders and intractable pain* (2nd ed.). Springfield, IL: Charles C. Thomas.

FREGNI, F., BOGGIO, P., MANSUR, C., WAGNER, T., FERREIRA, M., LIMA, M. C., ET AL. (2005). Transcranial direct current stimulation of the unaffected hemisphere in stroke patients. *NeuroReport, 16*(14), 1551–1555.

FREUD, S. (1882) *Über den Bau der Nervenfasern und Nervenzellen beim Flusskrebs* (Sitzungsberichte der Kaiserliche Akademie der Wissenschaften, Mathematisch-Naturwissenschaftliche Classe, v. 85). [Vienna: K. K. Hof- und Staatsdruckerei].

FREY, S. H., FUNNELL, M. G., GERRY, V. E., & GAZZANIGA, M. S. (2005). A dissociation between the representation of tool-use skills and hand dominance: Insights from left- and right-handed callosotomy patients. *Journal of Cognitive Neuroscience, 17,* 262–272.

FRICKER-GATES, R. A., SHIN, J. J., TAI, C. C., CATAPANO, L. A., & MACKLIS, J. D. (2002). Late-stage immature neocortical neurons reconstruct interhemispheric connections and form synaptic contacts with increased efficiency in adult mouse cortex undergoing targeted neurodegeneration. *Journal of Neuroscience, 22,* 4045–4056.

FRIEDRICH, F. J., EGLY, R., RAFAL, R. D., & BECK, D. (1998). Spatial attention deficits in humans: A comparison of superior parietal and temporal-parietal junction lesions. *Neuropsychology, 12,* 193–207.

FRIEDERICI, A. D. (2011). The brain basis of language processing: From structure to function. *Physiological Reviews, 91,* 1357–1392.

FRIEDERICI, A. D. (2012a). Language development and the ontogeny of the dorsal pathway. *Frontiers in Evolutionary Neuroscience, 4,* 1–7.

FRIEDERICI, A. D. (2012b). The cortical language circuit: From auditory perception to sentence comprehension. *Trends in Cognitive Science, 16*(5), 262–268.

FRIEDERICI, A., PFEIFER, E., & HAHNE, A. (1993). Event-related brain potentials during natural speech processing: Effects of semantic, morphological and syntactic violations. *Cognitive Brain Research, 1,* 183–192.

FRIEDERICI, A.D., BAHLMANN, J., HEIM, S., SCHUBOTZ, R.I., & ANWANDER, A. (2006) The brain differentiates human and non-human grammars: Functional localization and structural connectivity. *Proceedings of the National Academy of Science U.S.A., 103,* 2458–2463.

FRITH, C. (2003). What do imaging studies tell us about the neural basis of autism? *Novartis Foundation Symposium, 251,* 149–166.

FRITH, C. D. (2000). The role of the dorsolateral prefrontal cortex in the selection of action as revealed by functional imaging. In S. Monsell & J. Driver (Eds.), *Attention and performance: Vol. 18. Control of cognitive processes* (pp. 549–565). Cambridge, MA: MIT Press.

FRITSCH, G., & HITZIG, E. (1870). Uber die elektrische Erregbarkeit des Grosshirns (On the electrical excitability of the cerebrum). *Archiv fur Anatomie, Physiologie und wissenschaftliche Medizin, 37,* 300–332.

FRUHMANN, B. M., JOHANNSEN, L., & KARNATH, H. O. (2008). Time course of eye and head deviation in spatial neglect. *Neuropsychology, 22,* 697–702.

FUKUDA, K., AWH, E., & VOGEL. E. K. (2010). Discrete capacity limits in visual working memory. *Current Opinions in Neurobiology, 20*(2), 177–182.

FULTON, J. F. (1928). Observations upon the vascularity of the human occipital lobe during visual activity. *Brain, 51,* 310–320.

FUNAYAMA, E. S., GRILLON, C. G., DAVIS, M., & PHELPS, E. A. (2001). A double dissociation in the affective modulation of startle in humans: Effects of unilateral temporal lobectomy. *Journal of Cognitive Neuroscience, 13,* 721–729.

FUNNELL, M., METCALFE, J., & TSAPKINI, K. (1996) In the mind but not on the tongue: Feeling of knowing in an anomic patient. In Lynne M. Reder (Ed.), *Implicit Memory and Metacognition*: Chap. 7 (pp. 171–194). Mahwah, NJ: Lawrence Erlbaum Associates, Inc.

FUSAR-POLI, P., PLACENTINO, A., CARLETTI, F., LANDI, P., ALLEN, P., SURGULADZE, S., ET AL. (2009). Functional atlas of emotional faces processing: A voxel-based meta-analysis of 105 functional magnetic resonance imaging studies. *Journal of Psychiatry & Neuroscience, 34,* 418–432.

FUSTER, J. M. (1989). *The prefrontal cortex: Anatomy, physiology, and neuropsychology of the frontal lobe* (2nd ed.). New York: Raven.

GABRIELI, J.D.E., FLEISCHMAN, D. A., KEANE, M. M., REMINGER, S.L., & MORRELL, F. (1995). Double dissociation between memory systems underlying explicit and implicit memory in the human brain. *Psychological Science, 6,* 76–82.

GAFFAN, D., & HARRISON, S. (1987). Amygdalectomy and disconnection in visual learning for auditory secondary reinforcement by monkeys. *Journal of Neuroscience, 7,* 2285–2292.

GAFFAN, D., & HORNAK, J. (1997). Visual neglect in the monkey. Representation and disconnection. *Brain, 120*(Pt. 9), 1647–1657.

GAILLIOT, M. T., BAUMEISTER, R. F., DEWALL, C. N., MANER, J. K., PLANT, E. A., TICE, D. M., ET AL. (2007). Self-control relies on glucose as a limited energy source: Willpower is more than a metaphor. *Journal of Personality and Social Psychology, 92,* 325–336.

GALEA, J. M., VAZQUEZ, A., PASRICHA, N., DE XIVRY, J. J. O., & CELNIK, P. (2011). Dissociating the roles of the cerebellum and motor cortex during adaptive learning: The motor cortex retains what the cerebellum learns. *Cerebral Cortex, 21*(8), 1761–1770.

GALL, F. J., & SPURZHEIM, J. (1810–1819). *Anatomie et physiologie du système nerveux en général, et du cerveau en particulier.* Paris: Schoell.

GALLAGHER, M., & HOLLAND, P. C. (1992). Understanding the function of the central nucleus: Is simple conditioning enough? In J. P. Aggleton (Ed.), *The amygdala: Neurobiological aspects of emotion, memory, and mental dysfunction* (pp. 307–321). New York: Wiley-Liss.

GALLANT, J. L., SHOUP, R. E., & MAZER, J. A. (2000). A human extrastriate area functionally homologous to macaque V4. *Neuron, 27,* 227–235.

GALLISTEL, C. R. (1995). The replacement of general-purpose theories with adaptive specializations. In M. S. Gazzaniga (Ed.), *The cognitive neurosciences* (pp. 1255–1267). Cambridge, MA: MIT Press.

GALLUP, G. G., JR. (1970). Chimpanzees: Self-recognition. Science, 2, 86–87.

GALLUP, G. G., JR. (1982). Self-awareness and the emergence of mind in primates. *American Journal of Primatology, 2,* 237–248.

GALUSKE, R. A., SCHLOTE, W., BRATZKE, H., & SINGER, W. (2000). Interhemispheric asymmetries of the modular structure in human temporal cortex. *Science, 289,* 1946–1949.

GALVAN, A. (2010, February 12). Adolescent development of the reward system. *Frontiers in Human Neuroscience, 4* [PubMed: 20198130].

GAMER, M. & BUCHEL, C. (2009).Amygdala activation predicts gaze toward fearful eyes. *Journal of Neuroscience, 29,* 9123–9126.

GANGULY, K., & CARMENA, J. M. (2009). Emergence of a stable cortical map for neuroprosthetic control. *PLoS Biology 7*(7), e1000153. doi:10.1371/ journal.pbio.1000153

GANGULY, K., DIMITROV, D. F., WALLIS, J. D., & CARMENA, J. M. (2011). Reversible large-scale modification of cortical networks during neuroprosthetic control. *Nature Neuroscience, 14*(5), 662–669.

GANIS, G., THOMPSON, W. L., & KOSSLYN, S. M. (2004). Brain areas underlying visual mental imagery and visual perception: An fMRI study. *Brain Research: Cognitive Brain Research, 20*(2), 226–241.

GAO, J. H., PARSONS, L. M., BOWER, J. M., XIONG, J., LI, J., & FOX, P. T. (1996). Cerebellum implicated in sensory acquisition and discrimination rather than motor control. *Science, 272,* 545–547.

GARDNER, R. A., & GARDNER, B. T. (1969). Teaching sign language to a chimpanzee. *Science, 165,* 664–672.

GASH, D. M., ZHANG, Z., OVADIA, A., CASS, W. A., YI, A., SIMMERMAN, L., ET AL. (1996). Functional recovery in parkinsonian monkeys treated with GDNF. *Nature, 380,* 252–255.

GATZ, M., REYNOLDS, C. A., FRATIGLIONI, L., JOHANSSON, B., MORTIMER, J. A., BERG, S., ET AL. (2006). Role of genes and environments for explaining Alzheimer disease. *Archives of General Psychiatry, 63,* 168–174.

GAULIN, S. J. C. (1995). Does evolutionary theory predict sex differences in the brain? In M. S. Gazzaniga (Ed.), *The cognitive neurosciences* (pp. 1211–1225). Cambridge, MA: MIT Press.

Gaulin, S. J. C., & Fitzgerald, R. W. (1989). Sexual selection for spatial-learning ability. *Animal Behaviour, 37,* 322–331.

Gauthier, I. L., Behrmann, M., & Tarr, M. J. (1999). Can face recognition really be dissociated from object recognition? *Journal of Cognitive Neuroscience, 11,* 349–370.

Gauthier, I., Skudlarski, P., Gore, J. C., & Anderson, A. W. (2000). Expertise for cars and birds recruits brain areas involved in face recognition. *Nature Neuroscience, 3,* 191–197.

Gauthier, I., Tarr, M. J., Anderson, A. W., Skudlarski, P., & Gore, J. C. (1999). Activation of the middle fusiform "face area" increases with expertise in recognizing novel objects. *Nature Neuroscience, 2,* 568–573.

Gazzaley, A., Cooney, J. W., McEvoy, K., Knight, R. T., & D'Esposito, M. (2005a). Top-down enhancement and suppression of the magnitude and speed of neural activity. *Journal of Cognitive Neuroscience, 17,* 507–517.

Gazzaley, A., Cooney, J. W., Rissman, J., & D'Esposito, M. (2005b). Top-down suppression deficit underlies working memory impairment in normal aging. *Nature Neuroscience, 8,* 1298–1300.

Gazzaniga, M. S. (1985). *The social brain.* New York: Basic Books.

Gazzaniga, M. S. (1992). *Nature's mind: The biological roots of thinking, emotions, sexuality, language, and intelligence.* New York: Basic Books.

Gazzaniga, M. S. (1995). Principles of human brain organization derived from split-brain studies. *Neuron, 14,* 217–228.

Gazzaniga, M. S. (2000). Cerebral specialization and interhemispheric communication: Does the corpus callosum enable the human condition? *Brain, 123,* 1293–1326.

Gazzaniga, M. S. (2005). Forty-five years of split brain research and still going strong. *Nature Reviews Neuroscience, 6,* 653–659.

Gazzaniga, M. S. (2011). *Who's in charge?* New York: Harper Collins.

Gazzaniga, M. S. (2013). Mental life and responsibility in real time with a determined brain. In W. Sinnott-Armstrong (Ed.), *Moral Psychology, Volume 4: Free Will and Moral Responsibility.* Cambridge, MA: MIT Press.

Gazzaniga, M. S., Bogen, J. E., & Sperry, R. (1962). Some functional effects of sectioning the cerebral commissures in man. *Proceedings of the National Academy of Sciences, USA, 48,* 1756–1769.

Gazzaniga, M. S., & LeDoux, J. E. (1978). *The integrated mind.* New York: Plenum.

Gazzaniga, M. S., & Smylie, C. S. (1983). Facial recognition and brain asymmetries: Clues to underlying mechanisms. *Annals of Neurology, 13,* 536–540.

Gazzaniga, M. S., & Smylie, C. S. (1984). Dissociation of language and cognition: A psychological profile of two disconnected right hemispheres. *Brain, 107,* 145–153.

Gazzaniga, M. S., & Smylie, C. S. (1990). Hemispheric mechanisms controlling voluntary and spontaneous facial expressions. *Journal of Cognitive Neuroscience, 2,* 239–245.

Gazzaniga, M. S., & Sperry, R. W. (1967). Language after section of the cerebral commissures. *Brain, 90,* 131–148.

Geary, D. C. (1995). Reflections of evolution and culture in children's cognition. Implications for mathematical development and instruction. *American Psychologist, 50,* 24–37.

Gehring, W. J., Goss, B., Coles, M. G. H., Meyer, D. E., & Donchin, E. (1993). A neural system for error detection and compensation. *Psychological Science, 4,* 385–390.

Gehring, W.J. & Knight, R. (2000). Prefrontal-cingulate interactions in action monitoring. *Nature Neuroscience, 3,* 516–50.

Georgopoulos, A. P. (1990). Neurophysiology of reaching. In M. Jeannerod (Ed.), *Attention and performance XIII: Motor representation and control* (pp. 227–263). Hillsdale, NJ: Erlbaum.

Georgopoulos, A. P. (1995). Motor cortex and cognitive processing. In M. S. Gazzaniga (Ed.), *The cognitive neurosciences* (pp. 507–517). Cambridge, MA: MIT Press.

Geraci, A., & Surian, L. (2010). *Sixteen-month-olds prefer agents that perform equal distributions.* Poster session presented at the annual meeting of the International Society of Infant Studies, Baltimore, MD.

Geraerts, W. P. M., Smit, A. B., & Li, K. W. (1994). Constraints and innovations in the molecular evolution of neuronal signaling: Implications for behavior. In R. J. Greenspan & C. P. Kyriacou (Eds.), *Flexibility and constraint in behavioral systems* (pp. 207–235). New York: Wiley.

Gerlach, C., Law, I., & Paulson, O. B. (2002). When action turns into words. Activation of motor-based knowledge during categorization of manipulable objects. *Journal of Cognitive Neuroscience, 14,* 1230–1239.

Gerloff, C., Corwell, B., Chen, R., Hallett, M., & Cohen, L. G. (1997). Stimulation over the human supplementary motor area interferes with the organization of future elements in complex motor sequences. *Brain, 120,* 1587–1602.

Geschwind, N. (1967). The varieties of naming errors. *Cortex, 3,* 97–112.

Geschwind, N., & Galaburda, A. M. (1987). *Cerebral lateralization: Biological mechanisms, associations, and pathology.* Cambridge, MA: MIT Press.

Geschwind, N., & Levitsky, W. (1968). Human brain: Left-right asymmetries in temporal speech region. *Science, 161,* 186–187.

Giard, M.-H., Fort, A., Mouchetant-Rostaing, Y., & Pernier, J. (2000). Neurophysiological mechanisms of auditory selective attention in humans. *Frontiers in Bioscience, 5,* D84–D94.

Gibson, J. J. (1979). *The ecological approach to visual perception.* Boston: Houghton Mifflin.

Gibson, J., Beierlein, M., & Connors, B. (1999). Two networks of electrically coupled inhibitory neurons in neocortex. *Nature, 402,* 75–79.

Giedd, J. N., Blumenthal, J., Jeffries, N. O., Castellanos, F. X., Liu, H., Zijdenbos, A., et al. (1999). Brain development during childhood and adolescence: A longitudinal MRI study. *Nature Neuroscience, 2,* 861–863.

Gierhan, S.M.E. (2013 in press). Connections for auditory language in the human brain. *Brain and Language.*

Gilbertson, M. W., Shenton, M. E., Ciszewski, A., Kasai, K., Lasko, N. B., Orr, S. P., et al. (2002). Smaller hippocampal volume predicts pathologic vulnerability to psychological trauma. *Nature Neuroscience, 5,* 1242–1247.

Gilboa, A., Ramirez, J., Köhler, S., Westmacott, R., Black, S. E., & Moscovitch, M. (2005). Retrieval of autobiographical memory in Alzheimer's disease: Relation to volumes of medial temporal lobe and other structures. *Hippocampus, 15,* 535–550.

Gilovich, T. (1991). *How we know what isn't so.* New York: Macmillan.

Glisky, E. L., Polster, M. R., & Routhuieaux, B. C. (1995). Double dissociation between item and source memory. *Neuropsychology, 9,* 229–235.

Goel, V., Grafman, J., Tajik, J., Gana, S., & Danto, D. (1997). A study of the performance of patients with frontal lobe lesions in a financial planning task. *Brain, 120,* 1805–1822.

Goldberg, G. (1985). Supplementary motor area structure and function: Review and hypothesis. *Behavioral and Brain Sciences, 8,* 567–616.

Goldin, P.R., McRae, K., Ramel, W., & Gross, J.J. (2008). The neural bases of emotion regulation: reappraisal and suppression of negative emotion. *Biological Psychiatry, 63,* 577–586.

Goldman-Rakic, P. S. (1987). Circuitry of primate prefrontal cortex and regulation of behavior by representational memory. In *Handbook of physiology. The nervous system* (Vol. V, pp. 373–417). Bethesda, MD: American Physiological Society.

Goldman-Rakic, P. S. (1992). Working memory and the mind. *Scientific American, 267*(3), 111–117.

GOLDMAN-RAKIC, P. S. (1995). Architecture of the prefrontal cortex and the central executive. In J. Grafman, K. J. Holyoak, & F. Boller (Eds.), *Structure and functions of the human prefrontal cortex* (pp. 71–83). New York: New York Academy of Sciences.

GOLDSBY, R. A. (1976). *Basic biology.* New York: Harper and Row.

GOLDSTEIN, J. (1999). Emergence as a construct: History and issues. *Emergence: Complexity and Organization, 1(1),* 49–72.

GOLGI, C. (1894). *Untersuchungen über den feineren Bau des centralen und peripherischen Nervensystems.* Jena, Germany: Fischer.

GOODALE, M. A., & MILNER, A. D. (1992). Separate visual pathways for perception and action. *Trends in Neurosciences, 15,* 22–25.

GOODALE, M. A., & MILNER, A. D. (2004). *Sight unseen: An exploration of conscious and unconscious vision.* Oxford: Oxford University Press.

GOODALL, J. (1986). *The chimpanzees of Gombe: Patterns of behavior.* Harvard University Press.

GOODMAN, G., QUAS, J., BATTERMAN-FAUNEE, J., RIDDLESBERGER, M., & KUHN, J. (1994). Predictors of accurate and inaccurate memories of traumatic events experienced in childhood. *Consciousness and Cognition, 3,* 269–294.

GRABOWECKY, M., ROBERTSON, L. C., & TREISMAN, A. (1993). Preattentive processes guide visual search. *Journal of Cognitive Neuroscience, 5,* 288–302.

GRADINARU, V., MOGRI, M., THOMPSON, K. R., HENDERSON, J. M., & DEISSEROTH, K. (2009). Optical deconstruction of parkinsonian neural circuitry. *Science, 324,* 354–359.

GRAEF, S., BIELE, G., KRUGEL, L. K., MARZINZIK, F., WAHL, M., WOTKA, J., KLOSTERMAN, F., & HEEKEREN, H. R. (2010). Differential influence of levodopa on reward-base learning in Parkinson's disease. *Frontiers in Human Neuroscience, 4,* 169.

GRAFTON, S. T., FADIGA, L., ARBIB, M. A., & RIZZOLATTI, G. (1997). Premotor cortex activation during observation and naming of familiar tools. *NeuroImage, 6,* 231–236.

GRAFTON, S. T., HAZELTINE, E., & IVRY, R. (1995). Functional mapping of sequence learning in normal humans. *Journal of Cognitive Neuroscience, 7,* 497–510.

GRAHAM, J., CARLSON, G. R., & GERARD, R. W. (1942). Membrane and injury potentials of single muscle fibers. *Federation Proceedings, 1,* 31.

GRATTON, G., & FABIANI, M. (1998). Dynamic brain imaging: Event-related optical signal (EROS) measures of the time course and localization of cognitive-related activity. *Psychonomic Bulletin & Review, 5,* 535–563.

GRAY, C. M., KONIG, P., ENGEL, A. K., & SINGER, W. (1989). Oscillatory responses in cat visual cortex exhibit inter-columnar synchronization which reflects global stimulus properties. *Nature, 338,* 334–337.

GRAZIANO, M. S. A., & AFLALO, T. N. (2007). Mapping behavioral repertoire onto the cortex. *Neuron, 56,* 239–251.

GRAZIANO, M. S. A., COOKE, D. F., TAYLOR, C. S. R., & MOORE, T. (2004). Distribution of hand location in monkeys during spontaneous behavior. *Experimental Brain Research, 155,* 30–36.

GRAZIANO, M. S. A., & GROSS, C. G. (1994). Mapping space with neurons. *Current Directions in Psychological Science, 3,* 164–167.

GRAZIANO, M. S. A., TAYLOR, C. S. R., & MOORE, T. (2002). Complex movements evoked by microstimulation of precentral cortex. *Neuron, 34,* 841–851.

GREENBERG, J. O. (1995). *Neuroimaging: A companion to Adams and Victor's Principles of neurology.* New York: McGraw-Hill.

GREENE, J. D., NYSTROM, L. E., ENGELL, A. D., DARLEY, J. M., & COHEN, J. D. (2004). The neural bases of cognitive conflict and control in moral judgment. *Neuron, 44,* 389–400.

GREENE, J. D., SOMMERVILLE, R. B., NYSTROM, L. E., DARLEY, J. M., & COHEN, J. D. (2001). An fMRI investigation of emotional engagement in moral judgment. *Science, 293,* 2105–2108.

GREENFIELD, P. M. (1991). Language, tool and brain: The ontogeny and phylogeny of hierarchically organized sequential behavior. *Behavioral Brain Science, 14,* 531–595.

GREENWALD, A. G., McGHEE, J. L., & SCHWARTZ, J. L. (1998). Measuring individual differences in social cognition: The Implicit Association Test. *Journal of Personality and Social Psychology, 74,* 1474–1480.

GREFKES, C., & FINK, G. R. (2005). The functional organization of the intraparietal sulcus in humans and monkeys. *Journal of Anatomy, 207,* 3–17.

GRICE, H.P. (1957). Meaning. *Philosophical Review, 66,* 377–88.

GRIFFITHS, J. D., MARSLEN-WILSON, W. D., STAMATAKIS, E. A., & TYLER, L. K. (2013). Functional organization of the neural language system: Dorsal and ventral pathways are critical for syntax. *Cerebral Cortex, 23(1),* 139–147.

GRILL-SPECTOR, K., KNOUF, N., & KANWISHER, N. (2004). The fusiform face area subserves face perception, not generic within-category identification. *Nature Neuroscience, 7,* 555–562.

GRILL-SPECTOR, K., KOURTZI, Z., & KANWISHER, N. (2001). The lateral occipital complex and its role in object recognition. *Vision Research, 41,* 1409–1422.

GRINBAND, J., SAVITSKAYA, J., WAGER, T. D., TEICHERT, T., FERRERA, V. P., & HIRSCH, J. (2011a). The dorsal medial frontal cortex is sensitive to time on task, not response conflict or error likelihood. *NeuroImage, 57,* 303–311.

GRINBAND, J., SAVITSKAYA, J., WAGER, T. D., TEICHERT, T., FERRERA, V. P., & HIRSCH, J. (2011b). Conflict, error likelihood, and RT: Response to Brown & Yeung et al. *NeuroImage, 57,* 320–322.

GRINBAND, J., WAGER, T. D., LINDQUIST, M., FERRERA, V. P., & HIRSCH, J. (2008). Detection of time-varying signals in event-related fMRI designs. *NeuroImage, 43,* 509–520.

GROSS, J. (1998a). The emerging field of emotion regulation: An integrative review. *Review of General Psychology, 2(3),* 271–299.

GROSS, J. (1998b). Antecedent- and response-focused emotion regulation: Divergent consequences for experience, expression, and physiology. *Journal of Personality and Social Psychology, 74,* 224–237.

GROSSENBACHER, P. G., & LOVELACE, C. T. (2001). Mechanisms of synesthesia: Cognitive and physiological constraints. *Trends in Cognitive Sciences, 5,* 36–41.

GROSSMAN, M., ESLINGER, P. J., TROIANI, V., ANDERSON, C., AVANTS, B., GEE, J. C., ET AL. (2010). The role of ventral medial prefrontal cortex in social decisions: Converging evidence from fMRI and frontotemporal lobar degeneration. *Neuropsychologia, 48,* 3505–3512.

GROSSMANN, T., JOHNSON, M. H., FARRONI, T., & CSIBRA, G. (2007). Social perception in the infant brain: Gamma oscillatory activity in response to eye gaze. *Social, Cognitive, and Affective Neuroscience, 2,* 284–291.

GRUETER, M., GRUETER, T., BELL, V., HORST, J., LASKOWSKI, W., SPERLING, K., ET AL. (2007). Hereditary prosopagnosia: The first case series. *Cortex, 43(6),* 734–749.

GRZIMEK'S ENCYCLOPEDIA OF MAMMALS, Vol. 3. (1990). New York: McGraw-Hill.

GUR, R. C., SKOLNICK, B. E., & GUR, R. E. (1994). Effects of emotional discrimination tasks on cerebral blood flow: Regional activation and its relation to performance. *Brain and Cognition, 25,* 271–286.

GUSNARD, D. A., AKBUDAK, R., SHULMAN, G. L., & RAICHE, M. E. (2001). Medial prefrontal cortex and self-referential mental activity: Relation to a default mode of brain function. *Proceedings of the National Academy of Sciences, 98(7),* 4259–4264.

GUSNARD, D. A., & RAICHLE, M. E. (2001). Searching for a baseline: Functional imaging and the resting human brain. *Nature Reviews Neuroscience, 2,* 685–694.

HABEL, U., KLEIN, M., KELLERMANN, T., SHAH, N. J., & SCHNEIDER, F. (2005). Same or different? Neural correlates of happy and sad mood in healthy males. *NeuroImage, 26*, 206–214.

HABIB, M., & SIRIGU, A. (1987). Pure topographical disorientation: A definition and anatomical basis. *Cortex, 23*, 73–85.

HADAMARD, J. (1945). *An essay on the psychology of invention in the mathematical field.* Princeton, NJ: Princeton University Press.

HAERER, A. F. (1992). *DeJong's the neurologic examination* (5th ed.; rev. ed. of *The neurologic examination*, R. N. DeJong, 4th ed., 1979). Philadelphia: Lippincott.

HAEUSSER, M. (2000). The Hodgkin-Huxley theory of the action potential. *Nature Reviews. Neuroscience, 3*, 1165.

HAGOORT, P. (2005). On Broca, brain, and binding: A new framework. *Trends in Cognitive Neurosciences, 9*, 416–423.

HAGOORT, P., BROWN, C., & GROOTHUSEN, J. (1993). The syntactic positive shift (SPS) as an ERP measure of syntactic processing. *Language and Cognitive Processes, 8*, 439–483.

HAGOORT, P., BROWN, C., & SWAAB, T. (1996). Lexical semantic event-related potential effects in patients with left hemisphere lesions and aphasia, and patients with right hemisphere lesions without aphasia. *Brain, 119*, 627–649.

HAGOORT, P., HALD, L., BASTIAANSEN, M., & PETERSSON, K. (2004). Integration of word meaning and world knowledge in language comprehension. *Science, 403*, 438–441.

HALLIGAN, P. W., & MARSHALL, J. C. (1998). Neglect of awareness. *Conscious Cognition, 7*, 356–380.

HAMANI, C., NEIMAT, J., & LOZANO, A. M. (2006). Deep brain stimulation for the treatment of Parkinson's disease. *Journal of Neural Transmission, 70*(Suppl.), 393–399.

HAMANN, S. B., ELY, T. D., GRAFTON, S. T., & KILTS, C. D. (1999). Amygdala activity related to enhanced memory for pleasant and aversive stimuli. *Nature Neuroscience, 2*, 289–293.

HAMANN, S. B., ELY, T. D., HOFFMAN, J. M., & KILTS, C. D. (2002). Ecstasy and agony: Activation of the human amygdala in positive and negative emotion. *Psychological Science, 13*, 135–141.

HAMANN, S. B., & SQUIRE, L. R. (1995). On the acquisition of new declarative knowledge in amnesia. *Behavioral Neuroscience, 109*, 1027–1044.

HAMILTON, A. F. DE C., & GRAFTON, S. T. (2007). Action outcomes are represented in human inferior frontoparietal cortex. *Cerebral Cortex, 18*, 1160–1168.

HAMPTON, A. N., ADOLPHS, R., TYSZKA, J. M., & O'DOHERTY, J. P. (2007). Contributions of the amygdala to reward expectancy and choice signals in human prefrontal cortex. *Neuron, 55*, 545–555.

HAPPÉ, F. (1999). Cognitive deficit or cognitive style? *Trends in Cognitive Sciences, 3*(6), 216–222.

HARE, B., & KWETUENDA, S. (2010). Bonobos voluntarily share their own food with others. *Current Biology, 20*, 230–231.

HARE, B., PLYUSNINA, I., IGNACIO, N., SCHEPINA, O., STEPIKA, A., WRANGHAM, R., ET AL. (2005). Social cognitive evolution in captive foxes is a correlated by-product of experimental domestication. *Current Biology, 15*, 226–230.

HARE, B., & TOMASELLO, M. (2005). Human-like social skills in dogs? *Trends in Cognitive Science, 9*, 439–444.

HARE, B., WOBBER, V., & WRANGHAM, R. (2012). The self-domestication hypothesis: Evolution of bonobo psychology is due to selection against aggression. *Animal Behaviour.* doi:10.1016/j.anbehav.2011.12.007

HARE, T. A., CAMERER, C. F., & RANGER, A. (2009). Self-control in decision making involves modulation of the vmPFC valuation system. *Science, 324*, 646–648.

HAREL, N. Y., & STRITTMATTER, S. M. (2006). Can regenerating axons recapitulate developmental guidance during recovery from spinal cord injury? *Nature Reviews Neuroscience, 7*, 603–616.

HARKNESS, R. D., & MAROUDAS, N. G. (1985). Central place foraging by an ant (*Cataglyphis bicolor* Fab.): A model of searching. *Animal Behaviour, 33*, 916–928.

HARMON-JONES, E., & MILLS, J. (1999). *Cognitive dissonance: Progress on a pivotal theory in social psychology.* Washington, DC: American Psychological Association.

HARRIS, P. L. (1992). From simulation to folk psychology: The case for development. *Mind and Language, 7*, 120–144.

HARRIS, P. L., & NUNEZ, M. (1996). Understanding permission rules by preschool children. *Child Development, 67*(4), 1572–1591.

HART, J., BERNDT, R. S., & CARAMAZZA, A. (1985). Category-specific naming deficit following cerebral infarction. *Nature, 316*, 439–440.

HARTLINE, H. K. (1938). The response of single optic nerve fibers of the vertebrate eye to illumination of the retina. *American Journal of Physiology, 121*, 400–415.

HATFIELD, E., & RAPSON, R. L. (1987). Passionate love/sexual desire: Can the same paradigm explain both? *Archives of Sexual Behavior, 16*(3), 259–278.

HATSOPOULOS, N. G., & SUMINSKI, A. J. (2011). Sensing with the motor cortex. *Neuron, 72*, 477–487.

HATSOPOULOS, N. G., XU, Q., & AMIT, Y. (2007). Encoding of movement fragments in the motor cortex. *Journal of Neuroscience, 27*, 5105–5114.

HAXBY, J. V., HOFFMAN, E. A., & GOBBINI, M. I. (2000). The distributed human neural system for face perception. *Trends in Cognitive Science, 4*, 223–233.

HAYDEN, B., PEARSON, J. M., & PLATT, M. L. (2011). Neuronal basis of sequential foraging decision in a patchy environment. *Nature Neuroscience, 14*(7), 933–939.

HAYES, A., DAVIDSON, M., KEELE, S. W., & RAFAL, R. (1998). Toward a functional analysis of the basal ganglia. *Journal of Cognitive Neuroscience, 10*, 178–198.

HAYNES, J.-D., & REES, G. (2005). Predicting the orientation of invisible stimuli from activity in human primary visual cortex. *Nature Neuroscience, 8*(5), 686–691.

HAYNES, J.-D., & REES, G. (2006). Decoding mental states from rain activity in humans. *Nature Neuroscience, 7*, 523–534.

HAZELTINE, E., GRAFTON, S. T., & IVRY, R. (1997). Attention and stimulus characteristics determine the locus of motor-sequence encoding. A PET study. *Brain, 120*, 123–40.

HAZELTINE, E., TEAGUE, D., & IVRY, R. B. (2002). Simultaneous dual-task performance reveals parallel response selection after practice. *Journal of Experimental Psychology: Human Perception and Performance, 28*(3), 527–545.

HE, Z., & BAILLARGEON, R. (2010). *Reciprocity within but not across groups: 2.5-year-olds' expectations about ingroup and outgroup agents.* Poster session presented at the annual meeting of the International Society of Infant Studies, Baltimore, MD.

HEBB, D. (1949). *The organization of behavior: A neuropsychological theory.* New York: Wiley.

HEBERLEIN, A. S., & ADOLPHS, R. (2004). Impaired spontaneous anthropomorphizing despite intact perception and social knowledge. *Proceedings of the National Academy of Sciences, USA, 101*, 7487–7491.

HEEREY, E. A., CAPPS, L. M., KELTNER, D., & KRING, A. M. (2005). Understanding teasing: Lessons from children with autism. *Journal of Abnormal Child Psychology, 33*, 55–68.

HEIDER, F., & SIMMEL, M. (1944). An experimental study of apparent behavior. *American Journal of Psychology, 57*, 243–259.

HEILMAN, K. M., BOWERS, D., & WATSON, R. T. (1983). Performance on hemispatial pointing task by patients with neglect syndrome. *Neurology, 33*, 661–664.

HEILMAN, K. M., ROTHI, L. J., & VALENSTEIN, E. (1982). Two forms of ideomotor apraxia. *Neurology, 32*, 342–346.

HEILMAN, K. M., SCHOLES, R., & WATSON, R. T. (1975). Auditory affective agnosia: Disturbed comprehension of affective speech. *Journal of Neurology, Neurosurgery, and Psychiatry, 38*, 69–72.

HEINZE, H. J., MANGUN, G. R., BURCHERT, W., HINRICHS, H., SCHOLZ, M., MÜNTE, T. F., ET AL. (1994). Combined spatial and temporal imaging of brain activity during visual selective attention in humans. *Nature, 372*, 543–546.

HELMHOLTZ, H. VON. (1909–1911). *Handbuch der Physiologischen Optik* [Treatise on Physiological Optics]. Leipzig, Germany: L. Vos. (Translated in R. M. Warren and R. P. Warren, *Helmholtz on perception: Its physiology and development.* New York: Wiley, 1968.)

HELMHOLTZ, H. VON (1995). On the relation of natural science to science in general. In David Cahan (Ed.), *Science and culture: Popular and philosophical essays* (p. 93). Chicago: University of Chicago Press. (Original work published in 1862)

HELMS TILLERY, S. I., TAYLOR, D. M., & SCHWARTZ, A. B. (2003). The general utility of a neuroprosthetic device under direct cortical control. *Proceedings of the Engineering in Medicine and Biology Society 25th International Conference*, 2043–2046.

HENKE, K., MONDADORI, C.R.A TREYER, V., M., NITSCH, R. M., BUCK, A. & HOCK, C. (2003a). Nonconscious formation and reactivation of semantic associations by way of the medial temporal lobe. *Neuropsychologia, 41*, 863–876.

HENKE, K., TREYER, V., NAGY, E. T., KNEIFEL, S., DÜSTELER, M., NITSCH, R.M., & BUCK, A. (2003b). Active hippocampus during nonconscious memories. *Consciousness and Cognition, 12*, 31–48.

HENKE, K. (2010). A model for memory systems based on processing modes rather than consciousness. *Nature Reviews Neuroscience, 11*, 523–532.

HERNÁNDEZ-PEÓN, R., SCHERRER, H., & JOUVET, M. (1956). Modification of electrical activity in cochlear nucleus during attention in unanesthetized cats. *Science, 123*, 331–332.

HERRMANN, E., CALL, J., HERNÀNDEZ-LLOREDA, M. V., HARE, B., & TOMASELLO, M. (2007). Humans have evolved specialized skills of social cognition: The cultural intelligence hypothesis. *Science, 317*, 1360–1366.

HERRMANN, E., HARE, B., CALL, J., & TOMASELLO, M. (2010). Differences in the cognitive skills of bonobos and chimpanzees. *PloS One, 5*, e12438.

HERRICK, C. J. (1963). *Brains of rats and men.* New York: Hafner.

HERZ, R. S., ELIASSEN, J., BELAND, S., & SOUZA, T. (2004). Neuroimaging evidence for the emotional potency of odor-evoked memory. *Neuropsychologia, 42*, 371–378.

HICKOK, G., & POEPPEL, D. (2004) Dorsal and ventral streams: a framework for understanding aspects of the functional anatomy of language. *Cognition, 92*, 67–99.

HICKOK, G., & POEPPEL, D. (2007) The cortical organization of speech processing. *Nature Reviews Neuroscience, 8*, 393–402.

HIGO, T., MARS, R. B., BOORMAN, E. D., BUCH, E. R., & RUSHWORTH, M. F. (2011). Distributed and causal influence of frontal operculum in task control. *Proceedings of the National Academy of Sciences, USA, 108*, 4230–4235.

HIKOSAKA, K., IWAI, E., SAITO, H., & TANAKA, K. (1988). Polysensory properties of neurons in the anterior bank of the caudal superior temporal sulcus of the macaque monkey. *Journal of Neurophysiology, 60*, 1615–1637.

HIKOSAKA, O., BROMBERG-MARTIN, E., HONG, S., & MATSUMOTO, M. (2008). New insights on the subcortical representation of reward. *Current Opinions in Neurobiology, 18*, 203–208.

HILLIS, A. E. (2006). Neuroboiology of unilateral spatial neglect. *Neuroscientist, 12*, 153–163.

HILLIS, A. E., NEWHART, M., HEIDLER, J., BARKER, P. B., HERSKOVITS, E. H., & DEGAONKAR, M. (2005). Anatomy of spatial attention: Insights from perfusion imaging and hemispatial neglect in acute stroke. *Journal of Neuroscience, 25*, 3161–3167.

HILLIS, A. E., WORK, M., BARKER, P. B., JACOBS, M. A., BREESE, E. L., & MAURER, K. (2004). Re-examining the brain regions crucial for orchestrating speech articulation. *Brain, 127*, 1461–1462.

HILLYARD, S. A., HINK, R. F., SCHWENT, V. L., & PICTON, T. W. (1973). Electrical signs of selective attention in the human brain. *Science, 182*, 177–180.

HILLYARD, S., & MÜNTE, T. F. (1984). Selective attention to color and location: An analysis with event-related brain potentials. *Perception & Psychophysics, 36*(2), 185–198.

HILTS, P. J. (1995). *Memory's ghost: The strange tale of Mr. M. and the nature of memory.* New York: Simon & Schuster.

HIRSH, R. (1974). The hippocampus and contextual retrieval of information from memory: A theory. *Behavioral Biology, 12*, 421–444.

HOCHBERG, L. R., SERRUYA, M. D., FRIEHS, G. M., MUKAND, J. A., SALEH, M., CAPLAN, A. H., ET AL. (2006). Neuronal ensemble control of prosthetic devices by a human with tetraplegia. *Nature, 442*, 164–171.

HODGES, J.R., PATTERSON, K., OXBURY, S., & FUNNELL, E. (1992). Semantic dementia. Progressive fluent aphasia with temporal lobe atrophy. *Brain, 115*, 1783–1806.

HODGKIN, A. L., & HUXLEY, A. F. (1939). Action potentials recorded from inside a nerve fibre. *Nature, 144*, 710–711.

HODOS, W., & CAMPBELL, C. B. G. (1969). Scala naturae: Why there is no theory in comparative psychology. *Psychological Review, 76*, 337–350.

HOFER, H., & FRAHM, J. (2006). Topography of the human corpus callosum revisited—Comprehensive fiber tractography using diffusion tensor magnetic resonance imaging. *NeuroImage, 32*, 989–994.

HOFFER, R. (2009). *Something in the air.* New York: Simon & Schuster.

HOFSTADTER, D. (1979). *Gödel Escher, Bach: An eternal golden braid.* New York: Basic Books.

HOLBOURN, A. H. S. (1943). Mechanics of head injury. *Lancet, 2*, 438–441.

HOLLAND, P. C., & GALLAGHER, M. (1999). Amygdala circuitry in attentional and representational processes. *Trends in Cognitive Sciences, 3*, 65–73.

HOLMES, G. (1919). Disturbances of visual orientation. *British Journal of Ophthalmology, 2*, 449–468.

HOLMES, N. P., & SPENCE, C. (2005). Multisensory integration: Space, time and superadditivity. *Current Biology, 15*, R762–R764.

HOLTZMAN, J. D. (1984). Interactions between cortical and subcortical visual areas: Evidence from human commissurotomy patients. *Vision Research, 24*, 801–813.

HOLTZMAN, J. D., & GAZZANIGA, M. S. (1982). Dual task interactions due exclusively to limits in processing resources. *Science, 218*, 1325–1327.

HOLTZMAN, J. D., SIDTIS, J. J., VOLPE, B. T., WILSON, D. H., & GAZZANIGA, M. S. (1981). Dissociation of spatial information for stimulus localization and the control of attention. *Brain, 104*, 861–872.

HOMAE, F., WATANABE, H., NAKANO, T., ASAKAWA, K., & TAGA, G. (2006). The right hemisphere of sleeping infant perceives sentential prosody. *Neuroscience Research, 54*, 276–280.

HOPF, J. M., BOEHLER, C. N., LUCK, S. J., TSOTSOS, J. K., HEINZE, H. J., & SCHOENFELD, M. A. (2006). Direct neurophysiological evidence for spatial suppression surrounding the focus of attention in vision. *Proceedings of the National Academy of Sciences, USA, 103*(4), 1053–1058.

HOPF, J. M., BOELMANS, K., SCHOENFELD, M. A., LUCK, S. J., & HEINZE, H. J. (2004). Attention to features precedes attention to locations in visual search: Evidence from electromagnetic brain responses in humans. *Journal of Neuroscience, 24*, 1822–1832.

Hopf, J. M., Luck, S. J., Boelmans, K., Schoenfeld, M. A., Boehler, C. N., Rieger, J., et al. (2006). The neural site of attention matches the spatial scale of perception. *Journal of Neuroscience, 26,* 3532–3540.

Hopfinger, J. B., Buonocore, M. H., & Mangun, G. R. (2000). The neural mechanisms of top-down attentional control. *Nature Neuroscience, 3,* 284–291.

Hopfinger, J. B., & Mangun, G. R. (1998). Reflexive attention modulates visual processing in human extrastriate cortex. *Psychological Science, 9,* 441–447.

Hopfinger, J. B., & Mangun, G. R. (2001). Tracking the influence of reflexive attention on sensory and cognitive processing. *Cognitive, Affective & Behavioral Neuroscience, 1,* 56–65.

Hopkins, W.D., Taglialatela, J.P., & Leavens, D.A. (2007). Chimpanzees differentially produce novel vocalizations to capture the attention of a human. *Animal Behaviour, 73*(2), 281–286.

Hore, J., Wild, B., & Diener, H. (1991). Cerebellar dysmetria at the elbow, wrist, and fingers. *Journal of Neurophysiology, 65,* 563–571.

Horsley, V., & Clarke, R. H. (1908). The structure and functions of the cerebellum examined by a new method. *Brain, 31,* 45–124.

Hosp, J. A., Pekanovic, A., Rioult-Pedotti, M. S., & Luft, A. R. (2011). Dopaminergic projections from midbrain to primary motor cortex mediate motor skill learning. *Journal of Neuroscience, 31,* 2481–2487.

Huang, V. S., Haith, A., Mazzoni, P., & Krakauer, J. W. (2011). Rethinking motor learning and savings in adaptation paradigms: Model-free memory for successful actions combines with internal models. *Neuron, 70,* 787–801.

Huang, Y.-Y., Battistuzzi, C., Oquendo, M. A., Harkavy-Friedman, J., Greenhill, L., Zalsman, G., et al. (2004). Human 5-HT1A receptor C(−1019)G polymorphism and psychopathology. *International Journal of Neuropsychopharmacology, 7,* 441–451.

Hubel, D. H., & Wiesel, T. N. (1968). Receptive fields and functional architecture of monkey striate cortex. *Journal of Physiology, 195,* 215–243.

Hubel, D. H., & Wiesel, T. N. (1977). Ferrier lecture. Functional architecture of macaque monkey visual cortex. *Proceedings of the Royal Society of London, Series B, 198,* 1–59.

Humphrey, N. K. (1976). The social function of intellect. In P. P. G. Bateson & R. A. Hinde (Eds.), *Growing points in ethology.* Cambridge: Cambridge University Press.

Humphreys, G. W., & Riddoch, M. J. (1987). The fractionation of visual agnosia. In G. W. Humphreys & M. J. Riddoch (Eds.), *Visual object processing: A cognitive neuropsychological approach.* Hove, England: Erlbaum.

Humphreys, G. W., Riddoch, M. J., Donnelly, N., Freeman, T., Boucart, M., & Muller, H. M. (1994). Intermediate visual processing and visual agnosia. In M. J. Farah & G. Ratcliff (Eds.), *The neuropsychology of high-level vision: Collected tutorial essays* (pp. 63–102). Hillsdale, NJ: Erlbaum.

Humphreys, K., Hassan, U., Avidan, G., Minshew, N., Behrmann, M. (2008). Cortical patterns of category-selective activation for faces, places, and objects in adults with autism. *Autism Research, 1,* 52–83.

Hung, J., Driver, J., & Walsh, V. (2005). Visual selection and posterior parietal cortex: Effects of repetitive transcranial magnetic stimulation on partial report analyzed by Bundesen's theory of visual attention. *Journal of Neuroscience, 25,* 9602–9612.

Hurlburt, R. T., Happe, F., & Frith, U. (1994). Sampling the form of inner experience in three adults with Asperger syndrome. *Psychological Medicine, 24,* 385–395.

Hurst, J., Baraitser, M., Auger, E., Graham, F. & Norell, S. (1990). An extended family with a dominantly inherited speech disorder. *Devopmental Medicine and Child Neurology, 32,* 347–355.

Hutchison, W. D., Davis, K. D., Lozano, A. M., Tasker, R. R., & Dostrovsky, J.O. (1999). Pain-related neurons in the human cingulate cortex. *Nature Neuroscience, 2,* 403–405.

Hutchison, W. D., Dostrovsky, J. O., Walters, J. R., Courtemanche, R., Boraud, T., Goldberg, J., et al. (2004). Neuronal oscillations in the basal ganglia and movement disorders: Evidence from whole animal and human recordings. *Journal of Neuroscience, 24,* 9240–9243.

Hutsler, J., & Galuske, R. A. (2003). Hemispheric asymmetries in cerebral cortical networks. *Trends in Neuroscience, 26,* 429–435.

Huttenlocher, P. R., & Dabholkar, A. S. (1997). Regional differences in synaptogenesis in human cerebral cortex. *Journal of Comparative Neurology, 387,* 167–178.

Hyde, I. H (1921). A micro-electrode and unicellular stimulation. *Biological Bulletin, 40,* 130–133.

Ido, T., Wan, C. N, Casella, B., Fowler, J. S., Wolf, A. P., Reivich, M., et al. (1978). Labeled 2-deoxy-2-fluoro-D-glucose analogs. 18F-labeled 2-deoxy-2-fluoro-D-glucose, 2-deoxy-2-fluoro-D-mannose and C-14-2-deoxy-2-fluoro-D-glucose. *Journal of Labelled Compounds and Radiopharmaceuticals, 14,* 175–183.

Igaz, L. M., Bekinschtein, P., Vianna, M. M., Izquierdo, I., & Medina, J. H. (2004). Gene expression during memory formation. *Neurotoxicity Research, 6,* 189–204.

Illes, J., & Racine, E. (2005). Imaging or imagining? A neuroethics challenge informed by genetics. *American Journal of Bioethics, 5,* 1–14.

Imamizu, H., Miyauchi, S., Tamada, T., Sasaki, Y., Takino, R., Putz, B., et al. (2000). Human cerebellar activity reflecting an acquired internal model of a new tool. *Nature, 403,* 192–195.

Innocenti, G. M., Aggoun-Zouaoui, D., & Lehmann, P. (1995). Cellular aspects of callosal connections and their development. *Neuropsychologia, 33,* 961–987.

Irwin, W., Davidson, R. J., Lowe, M. J., Mock, B. J., Sorenson, J. A., & Turski, P. A. (1996). Human amygdala activation detected with echo-planar functional magnetic resonance imaging. *Neuroreport, 7,* 1765–1769.

Isaacson, W. (2007). *Einstein: His life and universe.* New York: Simon & Schuster.

Ito, M., Tamura, H., Fujita, I., & Tanaka, K. (1995). Size and position invariance of neuronal responses in monkey inferotemporal cortex. *Journal of Neurophysiology, 73,* 218–226.

Ivry, R. B., & Hazeltine, E. (1999). Subcortical locus of temporal coupling in the bimanual movements of a callosotomy patient. *Human Movement Science, 18,* 345–75.

Ivry, R. B., & Lebby, P. C. (1993). Hemispheric differences in auditory perception are similar to those found in visual perception. *Psychological Science, 4,* 41–45.

Ivry, R. B., & Robertson, L. C. (1998). *The two sides of perception.* Cambridge, MA: MIT Press.

Ivry, R. B., Spencer, R. M., Zelaznik, H. N., & Diedrichsen, J. (2002). The cerebellum and event timing. In S. M. Highstein & W. T. Thach (Eds.), *The cerebellum: Recent developments in cerebellar research* (Annals of the New York Academy of Sciences, vol. 978, pp. 302–317). New York: New York Academy of Sciences.

Jabbi, M., Swart, M., & Keysers, C. (2007). Empathy for positive and negative emotions in the gustatory cortex. *NeuroImage, 34,* 1744–1753.

Jack, C. R., Jr., Dickson, D. W., Parisi, J. E., Xu, Y. C., Cha, R. H., O'Brien, P. C., et al. (2002). Antemortem MRI findings correlate with hippocampal neuropathology in typical aging and dementia. *Neurology, 58,* 750–757.

Jackendoff, R. (1987). *Consiousness and the Computational Mind.* Cambridge MA: MIT Press.

Jackson, D. C, Burghy, C. A., Hanna, A. J., Larson, C. L., & Davidson, R. J. (2000). Resting frontal and anterior temporal EEG asymmetry predicts ability to regulate negative emotion. *Psychophysiology, 37,* S50.

JACKSON, D. C., MUELLER, C. J., DOLSKI, I., DALTON, K. M., NITSCHKE, J. B., URRY, H. L., ET AL. (2003). Now you feel it, now you don't: Frontal brain electrical asymmetry and individual differences in emotion regulation. *Psychological Science, 14,* 612–617.

JACKSON, J. H. (1876). Case of large cerebral tumor without optic neuritis and with left hemiplegia and imperceptions. *Royal Ophthalmological Hospital Reports, 8,* 434–444.

JACOB, F. (1977). Evolution and tinkering. *Science, 196,* 1161–1166.

JACOBS, L. F., GAULIN, S. J. C., SHERRY, D. F., & HOFFMAN, G. E. (1990). Evolution of spatial cognition: Sex-specific patterns of spatial behavior predict hippocampal size. *Proceedings of the National Academy of Sciences, USA, 87,* 6349–6352.

JAMES, T. W., CULHAM, J., HUMPHREY, G. K., MILNER, A. D., & GOODALE, M. A. (2003). Ventral occipital lesions impair object recognition but not object-directed grasping: An fMRI study. *Brain, 126*(Pt. 11), 2463–2475.

JAMES, W. (1884). What is an emotion? *Mind, 9*(34), 188–205.

JAMES, W. (1890). *Principles of psychology.* New York: Holt.

JANOWSKY, J. S., SHIMAMURA, A. P., & SQUIRE, L. R. (1989). Source memory impairment in patients with frontal lobe lesions. *Neuropsychologia, 27,* 1043–1056.

JASPER, H. H. (1995). A historical perspective: The rise and fall of prefrontal lobotomy. *Advances in Neurology, 66,* 97–114.

JASPER, H., & PENFIELD, W. (1954). *Epilepsy and the functional anatomy of the human brain* (2nd ed.). New York: Little, Brown.

JENKINS, I. H., BROOKS, D. J., NIXON, P. D., FRACKOWIAK, R. S. J., & PASSINGHAM, R. E. (1994). Motor sequence learning: A study with positron emission tomography. *Journal of Neuroscience, 14,* 3775–3790.

JENSEN, M. C., BRANT-ZAWADZKI, M. N., OBUCHOWSKI, N., MODIC, M. T., MALKASIAN, D., & ROSS, J. S. (1994). Magnetic resonance imaging of the lumbar spine in people without back pain. *New England Journal of Medicine, 331,* 69–73.

JIANG, Y., & HE, S. (2006). Cortical responses to invisible faces: Dissociating subsystems for facial-information processing. *Current Biology, 16,* 2023–2029.

JIANG, Y., ZHOU, K., & HE, S. (2007). Human visual cortex responds to invisible chromatic flicker. *Nature Neuroscience, 10*(5), 657–662.

JOBST, K. A., SMITH, A. D., SZATMARI, M., ESIRI, M. M., JASKOWSKI, A., HINDLEY, N., ET AL. (1994). Rapidly progressing atrophy of medial temporal lobe in Alzheimer's disease. *Lancet, 343,* 829–830.

JOHANSEN-BERG, H., DELLA-MAGGIORE, V., BEHRENS, T. E., SMITH, S. M., & PAUS, T. (2007). Integrity of white matter in the corpus callosum correlates with bimanual coordination skills. *NeuroImage, 36*(Suppl. 2), T16–T21.

JOHNSON, C., & WILBRECHT, L. (2011). Juvenile mice show greater flexibility in multiple choice reversal learning than adults. *Developmental Cognitive Neuroscience, 1*(4), 540–551.

JOHNSON, M. K., KIM, J. K., & RISSE, G. (1985). Do alcoholic Korsakoff's syndrome patients acquire affective reactions? *Journal of Experimental Psychology: Learning, Memory and Cognition, 11,* 22–36.

JOHNSON-FREY, S. H., NEWMAN-NORLUND, R., & GRAFTON, S. T. (2004). A distributed left hemisphere network active during planning of everyday tool use skills. *Cerebral Cortex, 15,* 681–695.

JOHNSRUDE, I. S., OWEN, A. M., WHITE, N. M., ZHAO, W. V., & BOH-BOT, V. (2000). Impaired preference conditioning after anterior temporal lobe resection in humans. *Journal of Neuroscience, 20,* 2649–2656.

JOLLY, A. (1966). Lemur social behaviour and primate intelligence. *Science, 153,* 501–506.

JONES, B., & MISHKIN, M. (1972). Limbic lesions and the problem of stimulus-reinforcement associations. *Experimental Neurology, 36,* 362–377.

JUSCZYK, P. W., HIRSH-PASEK, K., NELSON, D. G., KENNEDY, L. J., WOODWARD, A., & PIWOZ, J. (1992) Perception of acoustic correlates of major phrasal units by young infants. *Cognitive Psychology, 24,* 252–293.

JUST, M., CARPENTER, P., KELLER, T., EDDY, W., & THULBORN, K. (1996). Brain activation modulated by sentence comprehension. *Science, 274,* 114–116.

KAAS, J. H. (1995). The reorganization of sensory and motor maps in adult mammals. In M. S. Gazzaniga (Ed.), *The cognitive neurosciences* (pp. 51–71). Cambridge, MA: MIT Press.

KAAS, J. H. (1997). What comparative studies of neocortex tell us about the human brain. *Revista Brasileira de Biologia, 56,* 315–322.

KAAS, J. H. (1999). The transformation of association cortex into sensory cortex. *Brain Research Bulletin, 50,* 425.

KAAS, J. H., NELSON, R. J., SUR, M., DYKES, R. W., & MERZENICH, M. M. (1984). The somatotopic organization of the ventroposterior thalamus of the squirrel monkey, *Saimiri sciureus. Journal of Comparative Neurology, 226,* 111–140.

KABLE, J. W., & GLIMCHER, P. W. (2007). The neural correlates of subjective value during intertemporal choice. *Nature Neuroscience, 10*(12), 1625–1633.

KADISH, S. H. (1987). Excusing crime. *California Legal Review, 75,* 257.

KAKEI, S., HOFFMAN, D. S., & STRICK, P. L. (1999). Muscle and movement representations in the primary motor cortex. *Science, 285,* 2136–2139.

KAKEI, S., HOFFMAN, D. S., & STRICK P. L. (2001). Direction of action is represented in the ventral premotor cortex. *Nature Neuroscience, 4,* 1020–1025.

KALI, S., & DAYAN, P. (2004). Off-line replay maintains declarative memories in a model of hippocampal–neocortical interactions. *Nature Neuroscience, 7,* 286–294.

KANA, R. K., WADSWORTH, H. M., & TRAVERS, B. G. (2011). A systems level analysis of the mirror neuron hypothesis and imitation impairments in autism spectrum disorders. *Neuroscience & Biobehavioral Reviews, 53,* 894–902.

KANDEL, E. R., SCHWARTZ, J. H., & JESSELL, T. M. (EDS.). (1991). *Principles of neural science* (3rd ed.). New York: Elsevier.

KANWISHER, N. (2000). Domain specificity in face perception. *Nature Neuroscience, 3,* 759–763.

KANWISHER, N., MCDERMOTT, J., & CHUN, M. M. (1997a). The fusiform face area: A module in human extrastriate cortex specialized for face perception. *Journal of Neuroscience, 17,* 4302–4311.

KANWISHER, N., WOODS, R., IACOBONI, M., & MAZZIOTTA, J. C. (1997b). A locus in human extrastriate cortex for visual shape analysis. *Journal of Cognitive Neuroscience, 9,* 133–142.

KAPP, B. S., PASCOE, J. P., & BIXLER, M. A. (1984). The amygdala: A neuroanatomical systems approach to its contributions to aversive conditioning. In N. Butters & L. R. Squire (Eds.), *Neuropsychology of memory* (pp. 473–488). New York: Guilford.

KARNATH, H., FERBER, S., & HIMMELBACH, M. (2001). Spatial awareness is a function of the temporal lobe not the posterior parietal lobe. *Nature, 411,* 950–953.

KARNATH, H., FRUHMANN BERGER, M., KÜKER, W., & RORDEN, C. (2004). The anatomy of spatial neglect based on voxelwise statistical analysis: A study of 140 patients. *Cerebral Cortex, 14,* 1165–1172.

KARNATH, H., RÜTER, J., MANDLER, A., & HIMMELBACH, M. (2009). The anatomy of object recognition—visual form agnosia caused by medial occipitotemporal stroke. *Journal of Neuroscience, 29*(18), 5854–5862.

KARNATH, O. H., RENNIG, J., JOHANNSEN, L., & RORDEN, C. (2011). The anatomy underlying acute versus chronic spatial neglect. *Brain, 134*(Pt. 3), 903–912.

KARNI, A., MEYER, G., JEZZARD, P., ADAMS, M. M., TURNER, R., & UNGERLEIDER, L. G. (1995). Functional MRI evidence for adult motor cortex plasticity during motor skill learning. *Nature, 377,* 155–158.

KARNI, A., MEYER, G., REY-HIPOLITO, C., JEZZARD, P., ADAMS, M., TURNER, R., ET AL. (1998). The acquisition of skilled motor performance: Fast and slow experience-driven changes in primary motor cortex. *Proceedings of the National Academy of Sciences, USA, 95,* 861–868.

KASTNER, S., DEWEERD, P., DESIMONE, R., & UNGERLEIDER, L. C. (1998). Mechanisms of directed attention in the human extrastriate cortex as revealed by functional MRI. *Science, 282,* 108–111.

KASTNER, S., SCHNEIDER, K., & WUNDERLICH, K. (2006). Beyond a relay nucleus: Neuroimaging views on the human LGN. *Progress in Brain Research, 155,* 125–143.

KASTNER, S., & UNGERLEIDER, L. (2000). Mechanisms of visual attention in the human cortex. *Annual Review of Neuroscience, 23,* 315–341.

KAUFFMAN, T., THEORET, H., & PASCUAL-LEONE, A. (2002). Braille character discrimination in blindfolded human subjects. *NeuroReport, 13,* 571–574.

KAUFMAN, J. N., ROSS, T. J., STEIN, E. A., & GARAVAN, H. (2003). Cingulate hypoactivity in cocaine users during a GO-NOGO task as revealed by event-related functional magnetic resonance imaging. *Journal of Neuroscience, 23,* 7839–7843.

KAY, K. N., NASELARIS, T., PRENGER, R. J., & GALLANT, J. L. (2008). Identifying natural images from human brain activity. *Nature, 452,* 352–356.

KAYSER, C., PETKOV, C. I., AUGATH, M., & LOGOTHETIS, N. K. (2005). Integration of touch and sound in auditory cortex. *Neuron, 48,* 373–384.

KAYSER, C., PETKOV, C. I., AUGATH, M., & LOGOTHETIS, N. K. (2007). Functional imaging reveals visual modulation of specific fields in auditory cortex. *Journal of Neuroscience, 27,* 1824–1835.

KEELE, S. (1986). Motor control. In K. R. Boff, L. Kaufman, & J. P. Thomas (Eds.), *Handbook of perception and human performance* (Vol. 2, pp. 1–60). New York: Wiley.

KEELE, S. W., IVRY, R., MAYR, U., HAZELTINE, E., & HEUER, H. (2003). The cognitive and neural architecture of sequence representation. *Psychological Review, 110,* 316–339.

KEENAN, J. P., NELSON, A., O'CONNOR, M., & PASCUAL-LEONE, A. (2001). Self-recognition and the right hemisphere. *Nature, 409,* 305.

KELLENBACH, M. L., BRETT, M., & PATTERSON, K. (2003). Actions speak louder than functions: The importance of manipulability and action in tool representation. *Journal of Cognitive Neuroscience, 15,* 30–46.

KELLEY, W. M., MACRAE, C. N., WYLAND, C. L., CAGLAR, S., INATI, S., & HEATHERTON, T. F. (2002). Finding the self? An event-related fMRI study. *Journal of Cognitive Neuroscience, 14,* 785–794.

KENNEDY, D. P., & ADOLPHS, R. (2010). Impaired fixation to eyes following amygdala damage arises from abnormal bottom-up attention. *Neuropsychologia, 48*(12), 3392–3398.

KENNEDY, D. P., & COURCHESNE, E. (2008). Functional abnormalities of the default network during self- and other-reflection in autism. *Social Cognitive and Affective Neuroscience, 3,* 177–190.

KENNEDY, D. P., REDCAY, E., & COURCHESNE, E. (2006). Failing to deactivate: Resting functional abnormalities in autism. *Proceedings of the National Academy of Sciences, 103,* 8275–8280.

KENNEDY, H. (1996, August 6). Polly's smiling killer gets death sentence. *New York Daily News,.*

KENNERLEY, S. W., DAHMUBED, A. F., LARA, A. H., & WALLIS, J. D. (2009). Neurons in the frontal lobe encode the value of multiple decision variables. *Journal of Cognitive Neuroscience, 21*(6): 1162–1178.

KENNETT, S., EIMER, M., SPENCE, C., & DRIVER, J. (2001). Tactile-visual links in exogenous spatial attention under different postures: convergent evidence from psychophysics and ERPs. *Journal of Cognitive Neuroscience, 13,* 462–478.

KERETSZ, A., & HOOPER, P. (1982). Praxis and language: The extent and variety of apraxia in aphasia. *Neuropsychologia, 20,* 275–286.

KERNS, J. G., COHEN, J. D., MACDONALD, A. W., CHO, R. Y., STENGER, V. A., & CARTER, C. S. (2004). Anterior cingulate conflict monitoring and adjustments in control. *Science, 303,* 1023–1026.

KETY, S., & SCHMIDT, C. F. (1948). The nitrous oxide method for the quantitative determination of cerebral blood flow in man: Theory, procedure and normal values. *Journal of Clinical Investigation, 27,* 107–119.

KEYSERS, C., KAAS, J. H., & GAZZOLA, V. (2010). Somatosensation in social perception. *Nature Reviews Neuroscience, 11,* 417–428.

KEYSERS, C., WICKER, B., GAZZOLA, V., ANTON, J. L., FOGASSI, L., & GALLESE, V. (2004). A touching sight: SII/PV activation during the observation and experience of touch. *Neuron, 42,* 335–346.

KILLGORE, W. D. S., & YURGELUN-TODD, D. A. (2004). Activation of the amygdala and anterior cingulate during nonconscious processing of sad versus happy faces. *NeuroImage, 21,* 1215–1223.

KIHLSTROM, J. (1995). Memory and consciousness: An appreciation of Claparède and recognition et moïtè. *Consciousness and Cognition, 4*(4), 379–386.

KIM, A. & OSTERHOUT, L. (2005). The independence of combinatory sematic processing evidence from event-related potentials. *Journal of Memory and Language, 52,* 205–225.

KIM, S.-G., UGURBIL, K., & STRICK, P. L. (1994). Activation of a cerebellar output nucleus during cognitive processing. *Science, 265,* 949–951.

KIMBURG, D.Y., & FARAH, M. (1993). A unified account of cognitive impairments following frontal lobe damage: The role of working memory in complex, organized behavior. *Journal of Experimental Psychology, 122*(4), 411–428.

KIMURA, D. (1973). The asymmetry of the human brain. *Scientific American, 228*(3), 70–78.

KINGSTONE, A., ENNS, J., MANGUN, G. R., & GAZZANIGA, M. S. (1995). Guided visual search is a left hemisphere process in split-brain patients. *Psychological Science, 6,* 118–121.

KINGSTONE, A., FRIESEN, C. K., & GAZZANIGA, M. S. (2000). Reflexive joint attention depends on lateralized cortical connections. *Psychological Science, 11,* 159–166.

KINGSTONE, A., & GAZZANIGA, M. S. (1995). Subcortical transfer of higher order information: More illusory than real? *Neuropsychology, 9,* 321–328.

KINSBOURNE, M. (1982). Hemispheric specialization and the growth of human understanding. *American Psychologist, 37,* 411–420.

KIRCHER, T. T., SENIOR, C., PHILLIPS, M. L., RABE-HESKETH, S., BENSON, P. J., BULLMORE, E. T., ET AL. (2001). Recognizing one's own face. *Cognition, 78,* B1–B15.

KIRSCHBAUM, C., WOLF, O. T., MAY, M., WIPPICH, W., & HELLHAMMER, D. H. (1996). Stress- and treatment-induced elevations of cortisol levels associated with impaired declarative memory in healthy adults. *Life Sciences, 58,* 1475–1483.

KIRSCHNER, M., & GERHART, J. (1998). Evolvability. *Proceedings of the National Academy of Sciences, USA, 95,* 8420–8427.

KITTERLE, F., CHRISTMAN, S., & HELLIGE, J. (1990). Hemispheric differences are found in identification, but not detection of low versus high spatial frequencies. *Perception & Psychophysics, 48,* 297–306.

KLATT, D. H. (1989). Review of selected models of speech perception. In W. Marslen-Wilson (Ed.), *Lexical representation and process* (pp. 169–226). Cambridge, MA: MIT Press.

KLEIM, J. A., CHAN, S., PRINGLE, E., SCHALLERT, K., PROCACCIO, V., JIMENEZ, R., ET AL. (2006). BDNF val66met polymorphism is associated with modified experience-dependent plasticity in human motor cortex. *Nature Neuroscience, 9*, 735–737.

KLEIN, S. B., & KIHLSTROM, J. F. (1986). Elaboration, organization, and the self-reference effect in memory. *Journal of Experimental Psychology: General, 115*, 26–38.

KLEIN, S. B., & LAX, M. L. (2010). The unanticipated resilience of trait self-knowledge in the face of neural damage. *Memory, 18*, 918–948.

KLEIN, S. B., LOFTUS, J., & KIHLSTROM, J. F. (2002a). Memory and temporal experience: The effects of episodic memory loss on an amnesic patient's ability to remember the past and imagine the future. *Social Cognition, 20*, 353–379.

KLEIN, S. B., LOFTUS, J., & PLOG, A. E. (1992). Trait judgments about the self: Evidence from the encoding specificity paradigm. *Personality and Social Psychology Bulletin, 18*, 730–735.

KLEIN, S. B., ROZENDAL, K., & COSMIDES, L. (2002b). A social cognitive neuroscience analysis of the self. *Social Cognition, 20*, 105–135.

KLEINSMITH, L. J., & KAPLAN, S. (1963). Paired-associate learning as a function of arousal and interpolated interval. *Journal of Experimental Psychology, 65*, 190–193.

KLIN, A., JONES, W., SCHULTZ, R., VOLKMAR, F., & COHEN, D. (2002a). Defining and quantifying the social phenotype in autism. *American Journal of Psychiatry, 159*, 895–908.

KLIN, A., JONES, W., SCHULTZ, R., VOLKMAR, F., & COHEN, D. (2002b). Visual fixation patterns during viewing of naturalistic social situations as predictors of social competence in individuals with autism. *Archives of General Psychiatry, 59*, 809–816.

KLIN, A., SPARROW, S. S., DE BILDT, A., CICCHETTI, D. V., COHEN, D. J., & VOLKMAR F. R. (1999). A normed study of face recognition in autism and related disorders. *Journal of Autism and Developmental Disorders, 29*, 499–508.

KLINGBERG, T., HEDEHUS, M., TEMPLE, E., SALZ, T., GABRIELI, J. D., MOSELEY, M. E., ET AL. (2000). Microstructure of temporo-parietal white matter as a basis for reading ability: Evidence from diffusion tensor magnetic resonance imaging. *Neuron, 25*, 493–500.

KLUCHAREV, V., HYTÖNEN, K., RIJPKEMA, M., SMIDTS, A., & FERNÁNDEZ, G. (2009). Reinforcement learning signal predicts social conformity. *Neuron, 61*(1), 140–151.

KLUNK, W. E., ET AL. (2004). Imaging brain amyloid in Alzheimer's disease with Pittsburgh Compound-B. *Annals of Neurology, 55*(3), 306–319.

KLÜVER, H., & BUCY, P. C. (1939). Preliminary analysis of functions of the temporal lobes in monkeys. *Archives of Neurology, 42*, 979–1000.

KNIGHT, R. T., & GRABOWECKY, M. (1995). Escape from linear time: Prefrontal cortex and conscious experience. In M. S. Gazzaniga (Ed.), *The cognitive neurosciences* (pp. 1357–1371). Cambridge, MA: MIT Press.

KNOCH, D., PASCUAL-LEONE, A., MEYER, K., TREYER, V., & FEHR, E. (2007). Diminishing reciprocal fairness by disrupting the right prefrontal cortex. *Science, 314*, 829–832.

KNOWLTON, B. J., SQUIRE, L. R., PAULSEN, J. S., SWERDLOW, N. R., & SWENSON, M. (1996). Dissociations within nondeclarative memory in Huntington's disease. *Neuropsychology, 10*(4), 538–548.

KNUTSON, B., ADAMS, C. M., FONG, G. W., & HOMMER, D. (2001). Anticipation of increasing monetary reward selectively recruits nucleus accumbens. *Journal of Neuroscience, 21*(RC159), 1–5.

KOBAYASHI, H., & KOHSHIMA, S. (2001). Unique morphology of the human eye and its adaptive meaning: Comparative studies on external morphology of the primate eye. *Journal of Human Evolution, 40*, 419–435.

KOBAYASHI, S., & SCHULTZ, W. (2008). Influence of reward delays on responses of dopamine neurons. *Journal of Neuroscience, 28*(31), 7837–7846.

KOCH, C., & ULLMAN, S. (1985). Shifts in selective visual attention: Towards the underlying neural circuitry. *Human Neurobiology, 4*, 219–227.

KOECHLIN, E., ODY, C., & KONNEIHER, F. (2003). The architecture of cognitive control in the human prefrontal cortex. *Science, 302*, 1181–1185.

KOHLER, E., KEYSERS, C., UMILTA, A., FOGASSI, L., GALLESE, V., & RIZOLATT, G. (2002). Hearing sounds, understanding actions: Action representation in mirror neurons. *Science, 297*, 846–848.

KOHLER, S., KAPUR, S., MOSCOVITCH, M., WINOCUR, G., & HOULE, S. (1995). Dissociation of pathways for object and spatial vision: A PET study in humans. *NeuroReport, 6*, 1865–1868.

KOLB, B., & WHISHAW, I. Q. (1996). *Fundamentals of human neuropsychology* (4th ed.). New York: Freeman.

KOLLING, N., BEHRENS, T., MARS, R., & RUSHWORTH, M. (2012). Neural mechanisms of foraging. *Science, 336*(6077), 95–98.

KONISHI, M. (1993). Listening with two ears. *Scientific American, 268*(4), 66–73.

KONISHI, S., NAKAJIMA, K., UCHIDA, I., KAMEYAMA, M., NAKAHARA, K., SEKIHARA, K., ET AL. (1998). Transient activation of inferior prefrontal cortex during cognitive set shifting. *Nature Neuroscience, 1*, 80–84.

KONKEL, A., WARREN, D. E., DUFF, M. C., TRANEL, D. N., & COHEN, N. J. (2008). Hippocampal amnesia impairs all manner of relational memory. *Frontiers of Human Neuroscience, 2*, 15.

KORDOWER, J. H., FREEMAN, T. B., SNOW, B. J., VINGERHOETS, F. J., MUFSON, E. J., SANBERG, P. R., ET AL. (1995). Neuropathological evidence of graft survival and striatal reinnervation after the transplantation of fetal mesencephalic tissue in a patient with Parkinson's disease. *New England Journal of Medicine, 332*, 1118–1124.

KOVACS, A., TEGLAS, E., & ENDRESS, A. (2010). The social sense: Susceptibility to others' beliefs in human infants and adults. *Science, 330*, 1830–1834.

KOSSLYN, S. M., SHIN, L. M., THOMPSON, W. L., McNALLY, P. J., RAUCH, S. L., ET AL. (1996). Neural effects of visualizing and perceiving aversive stimuli: A PET investigation. *NeuroReport, 7*, 1569–1576.

KOTTER, R., & MEYER, N. (1992). The limbic system: A review of its empirical foundation. *Behavioural Brain Research, 52*, 105–127.

KOTZ, S. M. & SCHWARTZE, M. (2010). Cortical speech processing unplugged: a timely subcortico-cortical framework. *Trends Cognitive Sciences, 14*, 392–399.

KOUNEIHER, F., CHARRON, S., & KOECHLIN, E. (2008). Motivation and cognitive control in the human prefrontal cortex. *Nature Neuroscience, 12*(7), 939–947.

KOVACS, A., TEGLAS, E., & ENDRESS, A. (2010). The social sense: Susceptibility to others' beliefs in human infants and adults. *Science, 330*, 1830–1834.

KRACK, P., POLLAK, P., LIMOUSIN, P., HOFFMANN, D., XIE, J., BENAZZOUZ, A., ET AL. (1998). Subthalamic nucleus or internal pallidal stimulation in young onset Parkinson's disease. *Brain, 121*, 451–457.

KRAUSE, J., LALUEZA-FOX, C., ORLANDO, L., ENARD, W., GREEN, R. E., BURBANO, H. A., HUBLIN, J. J., HÄNNI, C., FORTEA, J., DE LA RASILLA, M., BERTRANPETIT, J., ROSAS, A., & PÄÄBO S. (2007). The derived FOXP2 variant of modern humans was shared with Neandertals. *Current Biology, 17*, 1908–1912.

KRAVITZ, A.V., FREEZE, B. S., PARKER, P. R., KAY, K., THWIN, M. T., DEISSEROTH, K., ET AL. (2010). Regulation of parkinsonian motor behaviours by optogenetic control of basal ganglia circuitry. *Nature, 466*(7306), 622–626.

KRAVITZ, A. V., TYE, L. D., & KREITZER, A. C. (2012). Distinct roles for direct and indirect pathway striatal neurons in reinforcement. *Nature Neuroscience, 15*(6), 816–818.

KROLAK-SALMON, P., HÉNAFF, M. A., ISNARD, J., TALLON-BAUDRY, C., GUÉNOT, M., VIGHETTO, A., ET AL. (2003). An attention modulated response to disgust in human ventral anterior insula. *Annals of Neurology, 53*, 446–453.

KRUBITZER, L. (1998). What can monotremes tell us about brain evolution? *Philosophical Transactions of the Royal Society of London, Series B: Biological Sciences, 353*, 1127–1146.

KRUBITZER, L. A. (2000). How does evolution build a complex brain? In G. R. Bock & G. Cardew (Eds.), *Novartis Foundation Symposium: Vol. 228. Evolutionary developmental biology of the cerebral cortex* (pp. 206–220). Chichester, England: Wiley.

KRUBITZER, L., MANGER, P., PETTIGREW, J., & CALFORD, M. (1995). The organization of somatosensory cortex in monotremes: In search of the prototypical plan. *Journal of Comparative Neurology, 351*, 261–306.

KUFFLER, S., & NICHOLLS, J. (1976). *From neuron to brain.* Sunderland, MA: Sinauer.

KUPERBERG, G. R. (2007). Neural mechanisms of language comprehension: Challenges to syntax. *Brain Research, 1146*, 23–49.

KUPERBERG, G. R., SITNIKOVA, T., CAPLAN, D., & HOLCOMB, P. (2003). Electrophysiological distinctions in processing conceptual relationships within simple sentences. *Cognitive Brain Research, 17*, 117–129.

KUPFERMANN, I. (1991). Localization of higher cognitive and affective functions: The association cortices. In E. R. Kandel, J. H. Schwartz, & T. M. Jessell (Eds.), *Principles of neural science* (pp. 821–838). Norwalk, CT: Appleton and Lange.

KURZBAN, R., TOOBY, J., & COSMIDES, L. (2001). Can race be erased? Coalitional computation and social categorization. *Proceedings of the National Academy of Sciences, USA, 98*, 15387–15392.

KUTAS, M., & FEDERMEIER, K. D. (2000). Electrophysiology reveals semantic memory use in language comprehension. *Trends in Cognitive Sciences, 4*, 463–470.

KUTAS, M., & HILLYARD, S. A. (1980). Reading senseless sentences: Brain potentials reflect semantic incongruity. *Science, 207*, 203–205.

KYLLIÄINEN, A., WALLACE, S., COUTANCHE, M. N., LEPPÄNEN, J. M., CUSACK, J., BAILEY, A. J., ET AL. (2012). Affective–motivational brain responses to direct gaze in children with autism spectrum disorder. *Journal of Child Psychology & Psychiatry.* doi:10.1111/j.1469-7610.2011.02522.x

LABAR, K. S., LEDOUX, J. E., SPENCER, D. D., & PHELPS, E. A. (1995). Impaired fear conditioning following unilateral temporal lobectomy in humans. *Journal of Neuroscience, 15*, 6846–6855.

LABAR, K. S., & PHELPS, E. A. (1998). Role of the human amygdala in arousal mediated memory consolidation. *Psychological Science, 9*, 490–493.

LABERGE, D. (1990). Thalamic and cortical mechanisms of attention suggested by recent positron emission tomographic experiments. *Journal of Cognitive Neuroscience, 2*, 358–372.

LADAVAS, E., PALADINI, R., & CUBELLI, R. (1993). Implicit associative priming in a patient with left visual neglect. *Neuropsychologia, 31*, 1307–1320.

LAI, C.S., FISHER, S. E., HURST, J. A., VARGHA-KHADERM, F., & MONACO, A.P. (2001). A novel forkhead-domain gene is mutated in a severe speech and language disorder. *Nature, 413*, 519–523.

LAMANTIA, A. S., & RAKIC, P. (1990). Cytological and quantitative characteristics of four cerebral commissures in the rhesus monkey. *Journal of Comparative Neurology, 291*, 520–537.

LAMME, V. (2003). Why visual attention and awareness are different. *Trends in Cognitive Sciences, 17*, 12–18.

LANDAU, W. M., FREYGANG, W. H., ROLAND, L. P., SOKOLOFF, L., & DETY, S. S. (1955). The local circulation of the living brain: Values in the unanesthetized and anesthetized cat. *Transactions of the American Neurological Association, 80*, 125–129.

LANE, R. D., FINK, G. R., CHAU, P. M., & DOLAN, R. J. (1997). Neural activation during selective attention to subjective emotional responses. *NeuroReport, 8*, 3969–3972.

LANE, R., REIMAN, E. M., AHERN, G. L., SCHWARTZ, G. E., & DAVIDSON, R. J. (1997). Neuroanatomical correlates of happiness, sadness, and disgust. *American Journal of Psychiatry, 154*, 926–933.

LANGSTON, W. J. (1984). I. MPTP neurotoxicity: An overview and characterization of phases of toxicity. *Life Sciences, 36*, 201–206.

LARSSON, J., & HEEGER, D. J. (2006). Two retinotopic visual areas in human lateral occipital cortex. *Journal of Neuroscience, 26*(51), 13128–13142.

LASHLEY, K. S. (1929). *Brain mechanisms and intelligence: A quantitative study of injuries to the brain.* Chicago: University of Chicago Press.

LASSEN, N.A., INGVAR, D. H., & SKINHØJ, E. (1978). Brain function and blood flow. *Scientific American, 239*, 62–71.

LAUGHLIN, R. B. (2006). *A different universe: Reinventing physics from the bottom down.* New York: Basic Books.

LAUREYS, S., FAYMONVILLE, M. E., PEIGNEUX, P., DAMAS, P., LAMBERMONT, B., DEL FIORE, G., ET AL. (2002). Cortical processing of noxious somatosensory stimuli in the persistent vegetative state. *NeuroImage, 17*(2), 732–741.

LAUTERBUR, P. (1973). Image formation by induced local interactions: Examples employing nuclear magnetic resonance. *Nature, 242*, 190–191.

LAZARUS, R. S. (1993). From psychological stress to emotions: A history of changing outlooks. *Annual Review of Psychology, 44*, 1–21.

LÊ, S., CARDEBAT, D., BOULANOUAR, K., HENAFF, M. A., MICHEL, F., MILNER, D., ET AL. (2002). Seeing, since childhood, without ventral stream: A behavioural study. *Brain, 125*(Pt. 1), 58–74.

LEBEDEV, M. A., & NICOLELIS, M. A. (2006). Brain-machine interfaces: Past, present and future. *Trends in Neurosciences, 29*, 536–546.

LE BIHAN, D. (2003). Looking into the functional architecture of the brain with diffusion MRI. *Nature Reviews Neuroscience, 4*, 469–480.

LEDOUX, J. E. (1991). Emotion and the limbic system concept. *Concepts in Neuroscience, 2*, 169–199.

LEDOUX, J. E. (1992). Emotion and the amygdala. In J. P. Aggleton (Ed.), *The amygdala: Neurobiological aspects of emotion, memory, and mental dysfunction* (pp. 339–351). New York: Wiley-Liss.

LEDOUX, J. E. (1994). Emotion, memory and the brain. *Scientific American, 270*(6), 50–57.

LEDOUX, J. E. (1995). In search of an emotional system in the brain: Leaping from fear to emotion and consciousness. In M. S. Gazzaniga (Ed.), *The cognitive neurosciences* (pp. 1047–1061). Cambridge, MA: MIT Press.

LEDOUX, J. E. (1996). *The emotional brain: The mysterious underpinnings of emotional life.* New York: Simon & Schuster.

LEDOUX, J. E. (2000). Emotion and the brain. *Annual Review of Neuroscience, 23*, 155–184.

LEDOUX, J. E. (2007). The amygdala. *Current Biology, 17*(20), R868–R874.

LEHMANN, H., LACANILAO, S., & SUTHERLAND, R. J. (2007). Complete or partial hippocampal damage produces equivalent retrograde amnesia for remote contextual fear memories. *European Journal of Neuroscience, 25*, 1278–1286.

LENNEBURG, E. (1967). *Biological Foundations of Language.* New York: John Wiley & Sons.

LESHIKAR, E. D. & DUARTE, A. (2012). Medial prefrontal cortex supports source memory accuracy for self-referenced items. *Social Neuroscience, 7*(2), 126–145.

LETTVIN, J. Y., MATURANA, H. R., McCULLOCH, W. S., & PITTS, W. H. (1959). What the frog's eye tells the frog's brain. *Proceedings of the Institute of Radio Engineers, 47*, 1940–1951.

LEVELT, W. J. M. (1989). *Speaking: From intention to articulation.* Cambridge, MA: MIT Press.

LEVELT, W. J. M. (1994). The skill of speaking. In P. Bertelson, P. Eelen, & G. d'Ydewalle (Eds.), *International perspectives on psychological science: Vol. 1. Leading themes* (pp. 89–103). Hove, England: Erlbaum.

LEVELT, W. J. M. (1999). Models of word production. *Trends in Cognitive Sciences, 3,* 223–232.

LEVELT, W. J. M., ROELOFS, A., & MEYER, A. S. (1999). A theory of lexical access in speech production. *Behavioral and Brain Sciences, 22,* 1–75.

LEVY, D. A., HOPKINS, R. O., & SQUIRE, L. R. (2004). Impaired odor recognition memory in patients with hippocampal lesions. *Learning and Memory, 11,* 794–796.

LEWIS, D. A., & LUND, J. S. (1990). Heterogeneity of chandelier neurons in monkey neocortex: Corticotropin-releasing factor and parvalbumin-immunoreactive populations. *Journal of Comparative Neurology, 293,* 599–615.

LEY, R. G., & BRYDEN, M. P. (1982). A dissociation of right and left hemispheric effects for recognizing emotional tone and verbal content. *Brain and Cognition, 1,* 3–9.

LEYTON, M., CASEY, K. F., DELANEY, J. S., KOLIVAKIS, T., & BENKELFAT, C. (2005). Cocaine craving, euphoria, and self-administration: A preliminary study of the effect of catecholamine precursor depletion. *Behavioral Neuroscience, 119,* 1619–1627.

LHERMITTE, F. (1983). "Utilization behaviour" and its relation to lesions of the frontal lobes. *Brain, 106,* 237–255.

LHERMITTE, F., PILLON, B., & SERDARU, M. (1986). Human autonomy and the frontal lobes. Part I: Imitation and utilization behavior: A neuropsychological study of 75 patients. *Annals of Neurology, 19,* 326–334.

LI, Y., LIU, Y., LI, J., QIN, W., LI, K., YU, C., ET AL. (2009). Brain anatomical networks and intelligence. *PLoS Computational Biology, 5*(5), e1000395.

LIBET, B. (1996). Neuronal processes in the production of conscious experience. In M. Velmans (Ed.). *The Science of Consciousness* (pp. 96-117). London: Routedge.

LIBET, B., GLEASON, C.A, WRIGHT, E.W., & PEARL, D.K. (1983). Time of conscious intention to act in relation to onset of cerebral activity (readiness potential): The unconscious initiation of a freely voluntary act. *Brain, 106*(3), 623–642.

LIBET, B., WRIGHT, E.W., FEINSTEIN, B. & PEARL, D.K. (1979). Subjective referral of the timing for a conscious sensory ecperience: A functional role for the somatosensory specific projection system in man. *Brain, 102*(1), 193–224.

LIEBAL, K., CALL, J., & TOMASELLO, M. (2004). Use of gesture sequences in chimpanzees. *American Journal of Primatology, 64,* 377–396.

LINDGREN, S.D., DE RENZI, E,.M & RICHMAN, L. C. (1985). Cross-national comparisons of developmental dyslexia in Italy and the United States. *Child Development, 56,* 1404-1417.

LINDQUIST, K. A., WAGER, T. D., KOBER, H., BLISS-MOREAU, E., & BARRETT, L. F. (2012). The brain basis of emotion: A meta-analytic review. *Behavioral and Brain Sciences, 35,* 121–143.

LINEBARGER, M., SCHWARTZ, M., & SAFFRAN, E. (1983). Sensitivity to grammatical structure in so-called agrammatic aphasics. *Cognition, 13,* 361–392.

LISSAUER, H. (1890). Ein Fall von Seelenblindheit nebst einem Beitrage zur Theorie derselben. *Archiv für Psychiatrie, 21,* 222–270.

LISZKOWSKI, U., CARPENTER, M., & TOMASELLO, M. (2008). Twelve-month-olds communicate helpfully and appropriately for knowledgeable and ignorant partners. *Cognition, 108,* 732–739.

LIU, T., STEVENS, S. T., & CARRASCO, M. (2007). Comparing the time course and efficacy of spatial and feature-based attention. *Vision Research, 47,* 108–113.

LLOYD-PIERCE, N. (1997, February 23). How we met Joe Simpson and Simon Yates. *Independent,* Retrieved from http://www.independent.co.uk/arts-entertainment/how-we-met-joe-simpson-and-simon-yates-1

LOCKHART, D. J., & BARLOW, C. (2001). Expressing what's on your mind: DNA arrays and the brain. *Nature Reviews Neuroscience, 2,* 63–68.

LOFTUS, E., & GREENE, E. (1980). Warning: Even memory for faces may be contagious. *Law and Human Behavior, 4,* 323–334.

LOFTUS, E., MILLER, D., & BURNS, H. (1978). Semantic integration of verbal information into visual memory. *Journal of Experimental Psychology. Human Learning and Memory, 4,* 19–31.

LOFTUS, W. C., TRAMO, M. J., THOMAS, C. E., GREEN, R. L., NORDGREN, R. A., & GAZZANIGA, M. S. (1993). Three-dimensional quantitative analysis of hemispheric asymmetry in the human superior temporal region. *Cerebral Cortex, 3,* 348–355.

LOGOTHETIS, M. K., PAULS, J., AUGATH, M., TRINATH, T., & OELTERMANN, A. (2001). Neurophysiological investigation of the basis of the fMRI signal. *Nature, 412,* 150–157.

LOMBARDO, M. V., CHAKRABARTI, B., BULLMORE, E. T., & BARON-COHEN, S. (2011). Specialization of right temporo-parietal junction for mentalizing and its association with social impairments in autism. *NeuroImage, 56,* 1832–1838.

LOMBER, S.G., & MALHOTRA, S. (2008). Double dissociation of "what" and "where" processing in auditory cortex. *Nature Neuroscience, 11*(5), 609–616.

LOOMIS, J. M., FUJITA, N., DA SILVA, J. A., & FUKUSIMA, S. S. (1992). Visual space perception and visually directed action. *Journal of Experimental Psychology, 18,* 906–921.

LORENZ, K., & TINBERGEN, N. (1957). Taxis and instinct: Taxis and instinctive action in the egg-retrieving behavior of the Graylag Goose. In C. H. Schiller (Ed. & Trans.), *Instinctive behavior: The development of a modern concept.* New York: International Universities Press. (Original work published in 1938 in *Zeitschrift für Tierpsychologie, 2,* 1–19.)

LOSIN, E. A., RUSSELL, J. L., FREEMAN, H., MEGUERDITCHIAN, A., & HOPKINS, W. D. (2008). Left hemisphere specialization for orofacial movements of learned vocal signals by captive chimpanzees. *PLos One, 3*(6), e2529.

LUCIANI, L. (1901–1911). *Fisiologia del Homo.* Firenze, Italy: Le Monnier.

LUCK, S. J., CHELAZZI, L., HILLYARD, S. A., & DESIMONE, R. (1997). Mechanisms of spatial selective attention in areas V1, V2, and V4 of macaque visual cortex. *Journal of Neurophysiology, 77,* 24–42.

LUCK, S. J., FAN, S., & HILLYARD, S. A. (1993). Attention-related modulation of sensory-evoked brain activity in a visual search task. *Journal of Cognitive Neuroscience, 5,* 188–195.

LUCK, S. J., & HILLYARD, S. A. (1994). Spatial filtering during visual search: Evidence from human electrophysiology. *Journal of Experimental Psychology. Human Perception and Performance, 20,* 1000–1014.

LUCK, S. J., HILLYARD, S. A., MANGUN, G. R., & GAZZANIGA, M. S. (1989). Independent hemispheric attentional systems mediate visual search in split-brain patients. *Nature, 342,* 543–545.

LUDERS, E., NARR, K. L., ZAIDEL, E., THOMPSON, P. M., JANCKE, L., & TOGA, A. W. (2006). Parasagittal asymmetries of the corpus callosum. *Cerebral Cortex, 16,* 346–354.

LUPIEN, S. J., FIOCCO, A., WAN, N., MAHEU, F., LORD, C., SCHRAMEK, T., ET AL. (2005). Stress hormones and human memory function across the life span. *Psychoneuroendocrinology, 30,* 225–242.

LYONS, M. K. (2011). Deep brain stimulation: Current and future clinical applications. *Mayo Clinic Proceedings, 86*(7), 662–672.

MACDONALD, A. W., COHEN, J. D., STENGER, V. A., & CARTER, C. S. (2000). Dissociating the role of the dorsolateral prefrontal and anterior cingulate cortex in cognitive control. *Science, 288,* 1835–1838.

MacGregor, L.J., Pulvermuller, F., van Casteren, M., & Shtyrov, Y. (2012) Ultra-rapid access to words in the brain. *Nature Communications, 3*(711), http://dx.doi.org/10.1038/ncomms1715.

MacKay, D. G. (1987). *The organization of perception and action: A theory for language and other cognitive skills.* New York: Springer.

MacLean, P. D. (1949). Psychosomatic disease and the "visceral brain": Recent developments bearing on the Papez theory of emotion. *Psychosomatic Medicine, 11,* 338–353.

MacLean, P. D. (1952). Some psychiatric implications of physiological studies on frontotemporal portion of limbic system (visceral brain). *Electroencephalography and Clinical Neurophysiology, 4,* 407–418.

MacLeod, C. (1991). Half a century of research on the Stroop effect: An integrative review. *Psychological Bulletin, 109,* 163–203.

MacMillan, M. B. (1986). A wonderful journey through skull and brains: The travels of Mr. Gage's tamping iron. *Brain and Cognition, 5,* 67–107.

MacMillan, M. (2000). *An odd kind of fame: Stories of Phineas Gage.* Cambridge, MA: MIT Press.

Macrae, C. N., Moran, J. M., Heatherton, T. F., Banfield, J. F., & Kelley, W. M. (2004). Medial prefrontal activity predicts memory for self. *Cerebral Cortex, 14,* 647–654.

Magno, E., & Allan, K. (2007). Self-reference during explicit memory retrieval: An event-related potential analysis. *Psychological Science, 18,* 672–677.

Mahon, B., Anzellotti, S., Schwarzbach, J., Zampini, M., & Caramazza, A. (2009). Category-specific organization in the human brain does not require visual experience. *Neuron, 63,* 397–405.

Mainland, J., & Sobel, N. (2006). The sniff is part of the olfactory percept. *Chemical Senses, 31,* 181–196. [Epub, December 8, 2005]

Malhotra, P., Coulthard, E. J., & Husain, M. (2009). Role of right posterior parietal cortex in maintaining attention to spatial locations over time. *Brain, 132,* 645–660.

Malmo, R. (1942). Interference factors in delayed response in monkeys after removal of frontal lobes. *Journal of Neurophysiology, 5,* 295–308.

Mampe, B., Friederici, A. D., Christophe, A. & Wermke, K. (2009). Newborns'cry melody is shaped by their native language. *Current Biology, 19,* 1994–1997.

Mangun, G. R., & Hillyard, S. A. (1991). Modulations of sensory-evoked brain potentials indicate changes in perceptual processing during visual-spatial priming. *Journal of Experimental Psychology. Human Perception and Performance, 17,* 1057–1074.

Mangun, G. R., Hopfinger, J., Kussmaul, C., Fletcher, E., & Heinze, H. J. (1997). Covariations in PET and ERP measures of spatial selective attention in human extrastriate visual cortex. *Human Brain Mapping, 5,* 273–279.

Mann, J. J. (2003). Neurobiology of suicidal behavior. *Nature Reviews Neuroscience, 4,* 819–828.

Manser, M. B. Bell, M. B., & Fletcher, L. B. (2001).The information that receivers extract form alarm calls in suricates. *Proceedings of the Royal Society B, 268,* 2485–2491.

Marcel, A. (1983a). Conscious and unconscious perception: Experiments on visual masking and word recognition. *Cognitive Psychology, 15,* 197–237.

Marcel, A. (1983b). Conscious and unconscious perception: An approach to the relations between phenomenal experience and perceptual process. *Cognitive Psychology, 15,* 238–300.

Markowitsch, H. J., Kalbe, E., Kessler, J., von Stockhausen, H. M., Ghaemi, M., & Heiss, W. D. (1999). Short-term memory deficit after focal parietal damage. *Journal of Clinical and Experimental Neuropsychology, 21,* 784–797.

Markus, H. (1977). Self-schemata processing information about the self. *Journal of Personality and Social Research, 35,* 63–78.

Marler, P. (1991). Song-learning behavior: The interface with neuroethology. *Trends in Neurosciences, 14,* 199–206.

Marois, R., Yi, D. J., & Chun, M. M. (2004). The neural fate of consciously perceived and missed events in the attentional blink. *Neuron, 41,* 465–472.

Marr, D. (1982). *Vision: A computational investigation into the human representation and processing of visual information.* San Francisco: Freeman.

Marsh, E. B., & Hillis, A. E. (2008). Dissociation between egocentric and allocentric visuospatial and tactile neglect in acute stroke. *Cortex, 44,* 1215–1220.

Marshall, A. J., Wrangham, R. W., & Arcadi, A. C. (1991). Does learning affect the structure of vocalizations in chimpanzees? *Animal Behaviour, 58*(4), 825–830.

Marslen-Wilson, W., & Tyler, L. K. (1980). The temporal structure of spoken language understanding. *Cognition, 8,* 1–71.

Martin, A., Wiggs, C. L., Ungerleider, L. G., & Haxby, J. V. (1996). Neural correlates of category specific behavior. *Nature, 379,* 649–652.

Martin, S. J., De Hoz, L., & Morris, R. G. (2005). Retrograde amnesia: Neither partial nor complete hippocampal lesions in rats result in preferential sparing of remote spatial memory, even after reminding. *Neuropsychologia, 43,* 609–624.

Martin, T. A., Keating, J. G., Goodkin, H. P., Bastian, A. J., & Thach, W. T. (1996). Throwing while looking through prisms. I. Focal olivocerebellar lesions impair adaptation. *Brain, 119,* 1183–1198.

Martin, V. C., Schacter, D. L., Corballis, M. C., & Addis, D. R. (2011). A role for the hippocampus in encoding simulations of future events. *Proceedings of the National Academy of Science, USA, 108,* 13858–13863.

Martinez, A., Anllo-Vento, L., Sereno, M. I., Frank, L. R., Buxton, R. B., Dubowitz, D. J., et al. (1999). Involvement of striate and extrastriate visual cortical areas in spatial attention. *Nature Neuroscience, 2,* 364–369.

Mather, M., Henkel, L. A., & Johnson, M. K. (1997). Evaluating characteristics of false memories: Remember/know judgments and memory characteristics questionnaire compared. *Memory and Cognition, 25,* 826–837.

Matsumoto, M., & Hikosaka, O. (2007). Lateral habenula as a source of negative reward signals in dopamine neurons. *Nature, 447,* 1111–1117.

Matsumoto, M., & Hikosaka, O. (2009a). Representation of negative motivational value in the primate lateral habenula. *Nature Neuroscience, 12*(1), 77–84.

Matsumoto, M., & Hikosaka, O. (2009b). Two types of dopamine neuron distinctly convey positive and negative motivational signals. *Nature, 459,* 837–841.

Matsuno-Yagi, A., & Mukohata, Y. (1977). Two possible roles of bacteriorhodopsin: A comparative study of strains of *Halobacterium halobium* differing in pigmentation. *Biochemical and Biophysical Research Communication, 78,* 237–243.

Mattingley, J. B., Rich, A. N., Yelland, G., & Bradshaw, J. L. (2001). Unconscious priming eliminates automatic binding of colour and alphanumeric form in synaesthesia. *Nature, 410,* 580–582.

Matyas, F., Sreenivasan, V., Marbach, F., Wacongne, C., Barsy, B., Mateo, C., et al. (2010). Motor control by sensory cortex. *Science, 330,* 1240–1243.

Maunsell, J. H. R., & Van Essen, D. C. (1983). Functional properties of neurons in middle temporal visual area of the macaque monkey. I. Selectivity for stimulus direction, speed, and orientation. *Journal of Neurophysiology, 49,* 1127–1147.

Mayford, M. (2012). Navigating uncertain waters. *Nature Neuroscience, 15,* 1056–1057.

Mazoyer, B., Tzourio, N., Frak, V., Syrota, A., Murayama, N., Levier, O., et al. (1993). The cortical representation of speech. *Journal of Cognitive Neuroscience, 5,* 467–479.

McAdams, C. J., & Maunsell, J. H. R. (2000). Attention to both space and feature modulates neuronal responses in macaque area V4. *Journal of Neurophysiology, 83,* 1751–1755.

McAdams, C. J., & Reid, R. C. (2005). Attention modulates the responses of simple cells in monkey primary visual cortex. *Journal of Neuroscience, 25,* 11023–11033.

McAlonan, K., Cavanaugh, J., & Wurtz, R. H. (2008). Guarding the gateway to cortex with attention in visual thalamus. *Nature, 456,* 391–394.

McCarthy, G., Puce, A., Gore, J. C., & Allison, T. (1997). Face-specific processing in the human fusiform gyrus. *Journal of Cognitive Neuroscience, 9,* 605–610.

McCarthy, R., & Warrington, E. K. (1986). Visual associative agnosia: A clinico-anatomical study of a single case. *Journal of Neurology, Neurosurgery, and Psychiatry, 49,* 1233–1240.

McClelland, J. L. (2000). Connectionist models of memory. In E. Tulving & F. I. M. Craik (Eds.), *The Oxford handbook of memory* (pp. 583–596). New York: Oxford University Press.

McClelland, J. L., & Rumelhart, D. E. (1981). An interactive activation model of context effects in letter perception: Part 1. An account of the basic findings. *Psychological Review, 88,* 375–407.

McClelland, J. L., & Rumelhart, D. E. (1986). *Parallel distributed processing: Explorations in the microstructure of cognition: Vol. 2. Psychological and biological models.* Cambridge, MA: MIT Press.

McClelland, J. L., St. John, M., & Taraban, R. (1989). Sentence comprehension: A parallel distributed processing approach. *Language and Cognitive Processes, 4,* 287–335.

McGaugh, J. L., Cahill, L., & Roozendaal, B. (1996). Involvement of the amygdala in memory storage: Interaction with other brain systems. *Proceedings of the National Academy of Sciences, USA, 93,* 13508–13514.

McGaugh, J. L., Introini-Collision, I. B., Cahill, L., Munsoo, K., & Liang, K. C. (1992). Involvement of the amygdala in neuromodulatory influences on memory storage. In J. P. Aggleton (Ed.), *The amygdala: Neurobiological aspects of emotion, memory, and mental dysfunction* (pp. 431–451). New York: Wiley-Liss.

McHenry, L. C., Jr. (1969). *Garrison's history of neurology.* Springfield, IL: Thomas.

McIntosh, A. R. (2004). Contexts and catalysts: A resolution of the localization and integration of function in the brain. *Neuroinformatics, 2*(2), 175–181.

McIntosh, D. N., Reichmann-Decker, A., Winkielman, P., & Wilbarger, J. (2006). When the social mirror breaks: Deficits in automatic, but not voluntary, mimicry of emotional facial expressions in autism. *Developmental Science, 9*(3), 295–302.

McManus, C. (1999). Handedness, cerebral lateralization, and the evolution of handedness. In M. C. Corballis & S. E. G. Lea (Eds.), *The descent of mind* (pp. 194–217). Oxford: Oxford University Press.

McNeil, J. E., & Warrington, E. K. (1993). Prosopagnosia: A face-specific disorder. *Quarterly Journal of Experimental Psychology. A, Human Experimental Psychology, 46,* 1–10.

Meadows, J. C. (1974). Disturbed perception of colours associated with localized cerebral lesions. *Brain, 97,* 615–632.

Medina, J., Kannan, V., Pawlak, M. A., Kleinman, J. T., Newhart, M., Davis, C., et al. (2009). Neural substrates of visuospatial processing in distinct reference frames: Evidence from unilateral spatial neglect. *Journal of Cognitive Neuroscience, 21*(11), 2073–2084.

Meguerditchian, A., Molesti, S. & Vauclair, J. (2011). Right-handedness predominance in 162 baboons for gestural communication: Consistency across time and groups. *Behavioral Neuroscience, 125*(4), 653–660.

Meguerditchian, A., Vauclair, J., & Hopkins, W. D. (2010). Captive chimpanzees use their right hand to communicate with each other: Implications for the origin of the cerebral substrate for language. *Cortex, 46*(1), 40-48.

Meguerditchian, A. & Vauclair, J. (2006). Baboons communicate with their right hand. *Behavioural Brain Research, 171,* 170–174.

Mehler, J., Jusczyk, P., Lambertz, G., Halsted, N., Bertoncini, J. & Amieltison, C. (1988). A precursor of language acquisition in young infants. *Cognition, 29,* 143–178.

Meintzschel, F., & Ziemann, U. (2005). Modification of practice-dependent plasticity in human motor cortex by neuromodulators. *Cerebral Cortex, 16*(8), 1106–1115.

Meltzoff, A. N., & Prinz, W. (2002). *The imitative mind: Development, evolution and brain bases.* Cambridge: Cambridge University Press.

Merabet, L. B., Swisher, J. D., McMains, S. A., Halko, M. A., Amedi, A., Pascual-Leone, A., & Somers, D. C. (2007). Combined activation and deactivation of visual cortex during tactile sensory processing. *Journal of Neurophysiology, 97,* 1633–1641.

Merzenich, M. M., & Jenkins, W. M. (1995). Cortical plasticity, learning and learning dysfunction. In B. Julesz & I. Kovacs (Eds.), *Maturational windows and adult cortical plasticity* (pp. 1–24). Reading, MA: Addison-Wesley.

Merzenich, M. M., & Kaas, J. H. (1980). *Principles of organization of sensory-perceptual systems of mammals.* New York: Academic Press.

Merzenich, M. M., Kaas, J. H., Sur, M., & Lin, C. S. (1978). Double representation of the body surface within cytoarchitectonic areas 3b and 1 in "SI" in the owl monkey (*Aotus trivirgatus*). *Journal of Comparative Neurology, 181,* 41–73.

Merzenich, M. M., Recanzone, G., Jenkins, W. M., Allard, T. T., & Nudo, R. J. (1988). Cortical representational plasticity. In P. Rakic & W. Singer (Eds.), *Neurobiology of neocortex* (pp. 41–67). New York: Wiley.

Mesulam, M. M. (1981). A cortical network for directed attention and unilateral neglect. *Annuals of Neurology, 10,* 309–325.

Mesulam, M. M. (1998). From sensation to cognition. *Brain, 121,* 1013–1052.

Mesulam, M. M. (2000). *Principals of behavioral and cognitive neurology.* New York: Oxford University Press.

Metcalfe, J., Funnell, M., & Gazzaniga, M. S. (1995). Right hemisphere superiority: Studies of a split-brain patient. *Psychological Science, 6,* 157–164.

Meyer-Lindenberg, A., Buckholtz, J. W., Kolachana, B. R., Hariri, A., Pezawas, L., Blasi, G., et al. (2006). Neural mechanisms of genetic risk for impulsivity and violence in humans. *Proceedings of the National Academy of Sciences, USA, 103,* 6269–6274.

Miall, R. C., Christensen, L. O. D., Owen, C., & Stanley, J. (2007). Disruption of state estimation in the human lateral cerebellum. *PLoS Biology, 5,* e316.

Middleton, F. A., & Strick, P. L. (2000). Basal ganglia and cerebellar loops: Motor and cognitive circuits. *Brain Research. Brain Research Reviews, 31,* 236–250.

Migaud, M., Charlesworth, P., Dempster, M., Webster, L. C., Watabe, A. M., Makhinson, M., et al. (1998). Enhanced long-term potentiation and impaired learning in mice with mutant postsynaptic density-95 protein. *Nature, 396,* 433–439.

Miller, G. (1951). *Language and communication.* New York: McGraw-Hill.

Miller, G. (1956). The magical number seven, plus-or-minus two: Some limits on our capacity for processing information. *Psychological Review, 101,* 343–352.

Miller, G. (1962). *Psychology, the science of mental life.* New York: Harper & Row.

Miller, M. B., Kingstone, A., & Gazzaniga, M.S. (1997). HERA and the split-brain. *Society of Neuroscience Abstract, 23,* 1579.

MILLER, M. B., SINNOTT-ARMSTRONG, W., YOUNG, L., KING, D., PAGGI, A., FABRI, M., ET AL. (2010). Abnormal moral reasoning in complete and partial callosotomy patients. *Neuropsychologia*, 48(7), 2215–2220.

MILLER, M. B., VAN HORN, J. D., WOLFORD, G. L., HANDY, T. C., VALSANGKAR-SMYTH, M., INATI, S., ET AL. (2002). Extensive individual differences in brain activations associated with episodic retrieval are reliable over time. *Journal of Cognitive Neuroscience*, 14(8), 1200–1214.

MILNER, B. (1995). Aspects of human frontal lobe function. *Advances in Neurology*, 66, 67–84.

MILNER, B., CORKIN, S., & TEUBER, H. (1968). Further analysis of the hippocampal amnesic syndrome: 14-year follow-up study of HM. *Neuropsychologia*, 6, 215–234.

MILNER, B., CORSI, P., & LEONARD, G. (1991). Frontal-lobe contributions to recency judgements. *Neuropsychologia*, 29, 601–618.

MISCHEL, W., EBBESEN, E. B., & ZEISS, A. R. (1972). Cognitive and attentional mechanisms in delay of gratification. *Journal of Personality and Social Psychology*, 21(2), 204–218.

MISHKIN, M. (1978). Memory in monkeys severely impaired by combined but not by separate removal of amygdala and hippocampus. *Nature*, 273, 297–298.

MITCHELL, J. P. (2008). Activity in right temporo-parietal junction is not selective for theory-of-mind. *Cerebral Cortex*, 18, 262–271.

MITCHELL, J. P. (2009). Inferences about mental states. *Philosophical Transactions of the Royal Society of London, Series B*, 364(1521), 1309–1316.

MITCHELL, J. P. (2011). *The sovereignty of social cognition: Insights from neuroscience*. Unpublished manuscript.

MITCHELL, J. P., BANAJI, M. R., & MACRAE, C. N. (2005). General and specific contributions of the medial prefrontal cortex to knowledge about mental states. *NeuroImage*, 28, 757–762.

MITCHELL, J. P., MACRAE, C. N., & BANAJI, M.R. (2004). Encoding-specific effects of social cognition on the neural correlates of subsequent memory. *Journal of Neuroscience*, 24, 4912–4917.

MITCHELL, J. P., MACRAE, C. N., & BANAJI, M.R. (2006). Dissociable medial prefrontal contributions to judgments of similar and dissimilar others. *Neuron*, 50, 655–663.

MITCHELL, J. P., SCHIRMER, J., AMES, D. L., & GILBERT, D. T. (2011). Medial prefrontal cortex predicts intertemporal choice. *Journal of Cognitive Neuroscience*, 23(4), 1–10.

MITCHELL, R. W. (1994). Multiplicities of self. In S. T. Parker, R. W. Mitchell, & M. L. Boccia (Eds.), *Self-awareness in animals and humans*. Cambridge: Cambridge University Press.

MITCHELL, R. W. (1997). Kinesthetic-visual matching and the self-concept as explanations of mirror-self-recognition. *Journal for the Theory of Social Behavior*, 27, 101–123.

MOBBS, D., YU, R., MEYER, M., PASSAMONTI, L., SEYMOUR, B., CALDER, A. J., ET AL. (2009). A key role for similarity in vicarious reward. *Science*, 324(5929), 900.

MOLL, H., & TOMASELLO, M. (2007). Co-operation and human cognition: The Vygotskian intelligence hypothesis. *Philosophical Transactions of the Royal Society of London*, 362, 639–648.

MOLNAR, Z. (2004). Thomas Willis (1621–1645), the founder of clinical neuroscience. *Nature Reviews Neuroscience*, 5, 329–335.

MONCHI, O., PETRIDES, M., PETRE, V., WORSLEY, K., & DAGHER, A. (2001). Wisconsin card sorting revisited: Distinct neural circuits participating in different stages of the task identified by event-related functional magnetic resonance imaging. *Journal of Neuroscience*, 21, 7733–7741.

MONTALDI, D., SPENCER, T. J., ROBERTS, N., & MAYES, A. R. (2006). The neural system that mediates familiarity memory. *Hippocampus*, 16, 504–520.

MONTI, M. M., VANHAUDENHUYSE, A., COLEMAN, M. R., BOLY, M., PICKARD, J. D., TSHIBANDA, L., ET AL. (2010). Willful modulation of brain activity in disorders of consciousness. *New England Journal of Medicine*, 362, 579–589.

MOORE, T., & ARMSTRONG, K. M. (2003). Selective gating of visual signals by microstimulation of frontal cortex. *Nature*, 421, 370–373.

MOORE, T., & FALLAH, M. (2001). Control of eye movements and spatial attention. *Proceedings of the National Academy of Sciences*, 98, 1273–1276.

MORAN, J., & DESIMONE, R. (1985). Selective attention gates visual processing in extrastriate cortex. *Science*, 229, 782–784.

MORAN, J. M., MACRAE, C. N., HEATHERTON, T. F., WYLAND, C. L., & KELLEY, W. M. (2006). Neuroanatomical evidence for distinct cognitive and affective components of self. *Journal of Cognitive Neuroscience*, 18, 1586–1594.

MORAY, N. (1959). Attention in dichotic listening: Effective cues and the influence of instructions. *Quarterly Journal of Experimental Psychology*, 9, 56–60.

MORGAN, J.L. & DEMUTH, K., (1996). *Signal to Syntax*. Mahwah, NJ: Erlbaum.

MORGAN, M. A., & LEDOUX, J. E. (1999). Contribution of ventrolateral prefrontal cortex to the acquisition and extinction of conditioned fear in rats. *Neurobiology of Learning and Memory*, 72, 244–251.

MORIGUCHI, Y., NEGREIRA, A., WEIRERICH, M., DAUTOFF, R., DICKERSON, B. C., WRIGHT, C. I., ET AL. (2010). Differential hemodynamic response in affective circuitry with aging: Novelty, valence and arousal. *Journal of Cognitive Neuroscience*. Retrieved from http://www.mitpressjournals.org.ezpprod1.hul.harvard.edu/doi/pdf/10.1162/jocn.2010.21527

MORISHIMA, Y., AKAISHI, R., YAMADA, Y., OKUDA, J., TOMA, K., & SAKAI, K. (2009). Task-specific signal transmission from prefrontal cortex in visual selective attention. *Nature Neuroscience*, 12, 85–91.

MORMANN, F., DUBOIS, J., KORNBLITH, S., MILOSAVLJEVIC, M., CERF, M., ISON, M., ET AL. (2011). A category-specific response to animals in the right human amygdala. *Nature Neuroscience*. Retrieved from http://www.nature.com.proxy.library.ucsb.edu:2048/neuro/journal/vaop/ncurrent/full/nn.2899.html

MORRIS, J. S., BUCHEL, C., & DOLAN, R. J. (2001). Parallel neural responses in amygdala subregions and sensory cortex during implicit fear conditioning. *NeuroImage*, 13, 1044–1052.

MORRIS, J. S., FRISTON, K. J., BUCHEL, C., FRITH, C. D., YOUNG. A. W., ET AL. (1998). A neuromodulatory role for the human amygdala in processing emotional facial expressions. *Brain*, 121, 47–57.

MORRIS, R. G. (1981). Spatial localization does not require the presence of local cues. *Learning and Motivation*, 12, 239–260.

MORUZZI, G., & MAGOUN, H. W. (1949). Brainstem reticular formation and activation of the EEG. *Electroencephalography and Clinical Neurophysiology*, 1, 455–473.

MOSCOVITCH, M., WINOCUR, G., & BEHRMANN, M. (1997). What is special about face recognition? Nineteen experiments on a person with visual object agnosia and dyslexia but normal face recognition. *Journal of Cognitive Neuroscience*, 9, 555–604.

MOTTER, B. C. (1993). Focal attention produces spatially selective processing in visual cortical areas V1, V2, and V4 in the presence of competing stimuli. *Journal of Neurophysiology*, 70, 909–919.

MOTTRON, L. & BELLEVILE, S. (1993). A study of perceptual analysis in a high-level autistic subject with exceptional graphic abilities. *Brain and Cognition*, 23(2), 279–309.

MOUNTCASTLE, V. B. (1976). The world around us: Neural command functions for selective attention. *Neurosciences Research Program Bulletin*, 14(Suppl.), 1–47.

Mozell, M., Kent, P., & Murphy, S. (1991). The effect of flow rate upon the magnitude of the olfactory response differs for different odorants. *Chemical Senses, 16,* 631–649.

Mueller, C. M., & Dweck, C. S. (1998). Intelligence praise can undermine motivation and performance. *Journal of Personality and Social Psychology, 75,* 33–52.

Mueller, N. G., & Kleinschmidt, A. (2003). Dynamic interaction of object- and space-based attention in retinotopic visual areas. *Journal of Neuroscience, 23,* 9812–9816.

Münte, T. F., Heinze, H.-J., & Mangun, G. R. (1993). Dissociation of brain activity related to semantic and syntactic aspects of language. *Journal of Cognitive Neuroscience, 5,* 335–344.

Münte, T. F., Schilz, K., & Kutas, M. (1998). When temporal terms belie conceptual order. *Nature, 395,* 71–73.

Murphey, D. K., Yoshor, D., & Beauchamp, M. S. (2008). Perception matches selectivity in the human anterior color center. *Current Biology, 18,* 216–220.

Murray, R. J., Schaer, M., & Debbane, M. (2012). Degrees of separation: A quantitative neuroimaging meta-analysis investigating self-specificity and shared neural activation between self- and other-reflection. *Neuroscience & Biobehavioral Reviews, 36,* 1043–1059.

Mushiake, H., Masahiko, I., & Tanji, J. (1991). Neuronal activity in the primate premotor, supplementary, and precentral motor cortex during visually guided and internally determined sequential movements. *Journal of Neurophysiology, 66,* 705–718.

Nacewicz, B. M., Dalton, K. M., Johnstone, T., Long, M. T., McAuliff, E. M., Oakes, T. R., et al. (2006). Amygdala volume and nonverbal social impairment in adolescent and adult males with autism. *Archives of General Psychiatry, 63,* 1417–1428.

Nadel, L., & Hardt, O. (2011). Update on memory systems and processes. *Neuropsychopharmacology, 36,* 251–273.

Naeser, M. A., Palumbo, C. L., Helm-Estabrooks, N., Stiassny-Eder, D., & Albert, M. L. (1989). Severe non-fluency in aphasia: Role of the medial subcallosal fasciculus plus other white matter pathways in recovery of spontaneous speech. *Brain, 112,* 1–38.

Nagel, G., Ollig, D., Fuhrmann, M., Kateriya, S., Musti, A. M., Bambaer, E., et al. (2002). Channelrhodopsin-1: A light-gated proton channel in green algae. *Science, 296*(5577), 2395–2398.

Nagel, T. (1974), What is it like to be a bat? *Philosophical Review, 83*(4), 435–450.

Narain, C., Scott, S. K., Wise, R. J., Rosen, S., Leff, A., Iversen, S. D., & Matthews, P. M. (2003). Defining a left-lateralized response specific to intelligible speech using fMRI. *Cerebral Cortex, 13,* 1362–1368.

Naselaris, T., Prenger, R. J., Kay, K. N., Oliver, M., & Gallant, J. L. (2009). Bayesian reconstruction of natural images from human brain activity. *Neuron, 63,* 902–915.

Navon, D. (1977). Forest before trees: The precedence of global features in visual perception. *Cognitive Psychology, 9,* 353–383.

Nee, D. E. & Jonides, J. (2011). Dissociable contributions of prefrontal cortex and the hippocampus to short-term memory: Evidence for a 3-state model of memory. *Neuroimage, 54*(2), 1540–1548.

Netter, F. H. (1983). *The CIBA collection of medical illustrations: Vol. 1. Nervous system, Part 1: Anatomy and physiology.* Summit, NJ: CIBA Pharmaceutical.

Neville, H. J., & Lawson, D. L. (1987). Attention to central and peripheral visual space in a movement detection task. III. Separate effects of auditory deprivation and acquisition of a visual language. *Brain Research, 405,* 284–294.

Newsome, W. T., Britten, K. H., & Movshon, J. A. (1989). Neuronal correlates of a perceptual decision. *Nature, 341,* 52–54.

Newsome, W. T. & Pare, E. B. (1988). A selective impairment of motion perception following lesions of the middle temporal visual area (MT). *Journal of Neuroscience, 8,* 2201–2211.

Nieuwland, M., & Van Berkum, J. (2005). Testing the limits of the semantic illusion phenomenon: ERPs reveal temporary semantic change deafness in discourse comprehension. *Cognitive Brain Research, 24,* 691–701.

Nishimoto, S., Vu, A. T., Naselaris, T., Benjamini, Y., Yu, B., & Gallant, J. L. (2011). Reconstructing visual experiences from brain activity evoked by natural movies. *Current Biology, 21,* 1–6.

Nissen, M. J., Knopman, D. S., & Schacter, D. L. (1987). Neurochemical dissociation of memory systems. *Neurology, 37,* 789–794.

Niv, Y. (2007). Cost, benefit, tonic, phasic: What do response rates tell us about dopamine and motivation? *Annals of the New York Academy of Science, 1104,* 357–376.

Nobre, A. C. (2001). The attentive homunculus: Now you see it, now you don't. *Neuroscience and Biobehavioral Reviews, 25,* 477–496.

Nobre, A. C., Allison, T., & McCarthy, G. (1994). Word recognition in the human inferior temporal lobe. *Nature, 372,* 260–263.

Norman, D. A., & Shallice, T. (1986). Attention to action: Willed and automatic control of behavior. In R. J. Davidson, G. E. Schwartz, & D. Shapiro (Eds.), *Consciousness and self-regulation* (Vol. 4, pp. 1–18). New York: Plenum.

Norman, K. A., & Schacter, D. L. (1997). False recognition in younger and older adults: Exploring the characteristics of illusory memories. *Memory and Cognition, 25,* 838–848.

Norris, D., McQueen, J., & Cutler, A. (1995). Competition and segmentation in spoken word recognition. *Journal of Experimental Psychology. Learning, Memory, and Cognition, 21,* 1209–1228.

North, N. T., & O'Carroll, R. E. (2001). Decision making in patients with spinal cord damage: Afferent feedback and the somatic marker hypothesis. *Neuropsychologia, 39,* 521–524.

Northoff, G. (2005). Is emotion regulation self-regulation? *Trends in Cognitive Sciences, 9,* 408–409.

Nottebohm, F. (1980). Brain pathways for vocal learning in birds: A review of the first 10 years. *Progress in Psychobiology and Physiological Psychology, 9,* 85–124.

Nunn, J. A., Gregory, L. J., Brammer, M., Williams, S. C., Parslow, D. M., Morgan, M. J., et al. (2002). Functional magnetic resonance imaging of synesthesia: Activation of V4/V8 by spoken words. *Nature Neuroscience, 5,* 371–375.

Nyberg, L., Cabeza, R., & Tulving, E. (1996). PET studies of encoding and retrieval: The HERA model. *Psychonomic Bulletin & Review, 3,* 134–147.

Nyberg, L., Cabeza, R., & Tulving, E. (1998). Asymmetric frontal activation during episodic memory: What kind of specificity? *Trends in Cognitive Sciences, 2,* 419–420.

Nyberg, L., McIntosh, A., Cabeza, R., Habib, R., Houle, S., & Tulving, E. (1996). General and specific brain regions involved in encoding and retrieval of events: What, where, and when. *Proceedings of the National Academy of Sciences, USA, 93,* 11280–11285.

Oberauer, K. (2002). Access to information in working memory: Exploring the focus of attention. *Journal of Experimental Psychology Learning Memory and Cognition, 28,* 411–421.

Oberman, L. M., Ramachandran, V. S., & Pineda, J. A. (2008). Modulation of mu suppression in children with autism spectrum disorders in response to familiar or unfamiliar stimuli: The mirror neuron hypothesis. *Neuropsychologia, 46*(5), 1558–1565.

Ochsner, K.N. (2007a). How thinking controls feeling: A social cognitive neuroscience approach. In E. Harmon-Jones & P. Winkieleman (Eds.), *Social neuroscience: Integrating biological and psychological explanations of social behavior* (pp. 106–133). New York: Guilford Press.

Ochsner, K. N. (2007b). Social cognitive neuroscience: Historical development, core principles, and future promise. In A. Kruglanski & E. Higgins (Eds.), *Social psychology: A handbook of basic principles.* New York: Guilford.

OCHSNER, K. N., BEER, J. S., ROBERTSON, E. A., COOPER, J., GABRIELI, J. D. E., KIHLSTROM, J. F., ET AL. (2005). The neural correlates of direct and reflected self-knowledge. *NeuroImage, 28*, 797–814.

OCHSNER, K. N., BUNGE, S. A., GROSS, J. J., & GABRIELI, J.D. (2002). Rethinking feelings: an FMRI study of the cognitive regulation of emotion. *Journal of Cognitive Neuroscience, 14*(8), 1215–1229.

OCHSNER, K., & GROSS, J. (2005). The cognitive control of emotion. *Trends in Cognitive Sciences, 9*(5), 242–249.

OCHSNER, K. N., RAY, R. D., COOPER, J. C., ROBERTSON, E. R., CHOPRA, S., GABRIELI, J. D. E., ET AL. (2004). For better or for worse: Neural systems supporting the cognitive down- and up-regulation of negative emotion. *NeuroImage, 23*, 483–499.

OCHSNER, K., SILVERS, J., & BUHLE, J. T. (2012). Functional imaging studies of emotion regulation: a synthetic review and evolving model of the cognitive control of emotion. *Annals of the New York Academy of Sciences, 1251*, E1–E24, March.

O'CONNOR, D. H., FUKUI, M. M., PINSK, M. A., & KASTNER, S. (2002). Attention modulates responses in the human lateral geniculate nucleus. *Nature Neuroscience, 5*, 1203–1209.

O'CONNOR, J. J., & ROBERSON, E. F. (2008). *Edward Norton Lorenz.* Retrieved from http://www-history.mcs.st-andrews.ac.uk/Biographies/Lorenz_Edward.html

O'CRAVEN, K. M., DOWNING, P. E., & KANWISHER, N. (1999). fMRI evidence for objects as the units of attentional selection. *Nature, 401*, 584–587.

O'CRAVEN, K. M., & KANWISHER, N. (2000). Mental imagery of faces and places activates corresponding stimulus specific brain regions. *Journal of Cognitive Neuroscience, 12*, 1013–1023.

O'DOHERTY, J., DAYAN, P., SCHULTZ, J., DEICHMANN, R., FRISTON, K., & DOLAN, R. J. (2004). Dissociable roles of ventral and dorsal striatum in instrumental conditioning. *Science, 304*, 452–454.

O'DOHERTY, J. O., KRINGELBACH, M. L., ROLLS, E. T., HORNAK, J., & ANDREWS, C. (2001). Abstract reward and punishment representations in the human orbitofrontal cortex. *Nature Neuroscience, 4*, 95–102.

OESTERHELT, D., & STOECKENIUS, W. (1971). Rhodopsin-like protein from the purple membrane of *Halobacterium halobium. Nature New Biology, 233*, 149–152.

OGAWA, S., LEE, T. M., KAY, A. R., & TANK, D. W. (1990). Brain magnetic resonance imaging with contrast dependent on blood oxygenation. *Proceedings of the National Academy of Sciences, USA, 87*, 9868–9872.

OJEMANN, G., OJEMANN, J., LETTICH, E., & BERGER, M. (1989). Cortical language localization in left, dominant hemisphere. *Journal of Neurosurgery, 71*, 316–326.

O'KEEFE, J., & DOSTROVSKY, J. (1971). The hippocampus as a spatial map. Preliminary evidence from unit activity in the freely-moving rat. *Brain Research, 1*, 171–175.

O'KEEFE, J., & NADEL, L. (1978). *The hippocampus as a cognitive map.* Oxford: Oxford University Press.

OLDENDORF, W. H. (1961). Isolated flying spot detection of radiodensity discontinuities—displaying the internal structural pattern of a complex object. *BioMedical Electronics, IRE, 8*, 68–72.

OLIVEIRA, F.T., DIEDRICHSEN, J., VERSTYNEN, T., DUQUE, J., & IVRY, R. B. (2010). Transcranial magnetic stimulation of posterior parietal cortex affects decisions of hand choice. *Proceedings of the National Academy of Sciences, USA, 107*, 17751–17756.

OLDS, J., & MILNER, P. M. (1954). Positive reinforcement produced by electrical stimulation of septal area and other regions of rat brain. *Journal of Comparative Physiology and Psychology, 47*, 419–427.

ONISHI, K. H., & BAILLARGEON, R. (2005). Do 15-month-old infants understand false beliefs? *Science, 308*(5719), 255–258.

O'REILLY, R. (2010). The what and how of prefrontal cortical organization. *Trends in Neurosciences, 33*, 355–361.

ORTIGUE, S., & BIANCHI-DEMICHELI, F. (2008). The chronoarchitecture of human sexual desire: A high-density electrical mapping study. *NeuroImage, 43*(2), 337–345.

ORTIGUE, S., & BIANCHI-DEMICHELI, F. (2011). Intention, false beliefs, and delusional jealousy: Insights into the right hemisphere from neurological patients and neuroimaging studies. *Medical Science Monitor, 17*, RA1–RA11.

ORTIGUE, S., BIANCHI-DEMICHELI, F., PATEL, N., FRUM, C., & LEWIS, J. (2010a). Neuroimaging of love: fMRI meta-analysis evidence toward new perspectives in sexual medicine. *Journal of Sexual Medicine, 7*(11), 3541–3552.

ORTIGUE, S., PATEL, N., BIANCHI-DEMICHELI, F., & GRAFTON, S.T. (2010b). Implicit priming of embodied cognition on human motor intention understanding in dyads in love. *Journal of Social and Personal Relationships, 27*(7), 1001–1015.

OSBORN, A. G., BLASER, S., & SALZMAN, K. L. (2004). *Diagnostic imaging. Brain.* Salt Lake City, UT: Amirsys.

OSGOOD, C. E., SUCI, G. J., & TANNENGAUM, P. H. (1957). *The measurement of meaning.* Urbana: University of Illinois Press.

OSTERHOUT, L., & HOLCOMB, P. J. (1992). Event-related brain potentials elicited by syntactic anomaly. *Journal of Memory and Language, 31*, 785–806.

OWEN, A. M., COLEMAN, M. R., BOLY, M., DAVIS, M. H., LAUREYS, S., & PICKARD, J. (2006). Detecting awareness in the vegetative state. *Science, 313*, 1402.

PADOA-SCHIOPPA, C. (2011). Neurobiology of economic choice: A good-based model. *Annual Review of Neuroscience, 34*, 333–359.

PADOA-SCHIOPPA, C., & ASSAD, J. A. (2006). Neurons in the orbitofrontal cortex encode economic value. *Nature, 441*(7090), 223–226.

PALFREMAN, J., & LANGSTON, J. W. (1995). *The case of the frozen addicts.* New York: Pantheon.

PALLER, K., KUTAS, M., & MCISAAC, H. (1995). Monitoring conscious recollection via the electrical activity of the brain. *Psychological Science, 6*, 107–111.

PALLIS, C. A. (1955). Impaired identification of faces and places with agnosia for colors. *Journal of Neurology, Neurosurgery, and Psychiatry, 18*, 218–224.

PANKSEPP, J. (1998). *Affective neuroscience: The foundations of human and animal emotions.* New York: Oxford University Press.

PAPEZ, J. W. (1937). A proposed mechanism of emotion. *Archives of Neurology and Psychiatry, 79*, 217–224.

PASCUAL-LEONE, A., BARTRES-FAZ, D., & KEENAN, J. P. (1999). Transcranial magnetic stimulation: Studying the brain-behaviour relationship by induction of "virtual lesions." *Philosophical Transactions of the Royal Society of London, Series B:, Biological Sciences, 354*, 1229–1238.

PASSINGHAM, R. E. (1982). *The human primate.* Oxford, England: Freeman.

PASSINGHAM, R. E. (1993). *The frontal lobes and voluntary action.* New York: Oxford University Press.

PATTEE, H. H. (2001). Causation, control, and the evolution of complexity. In P. B. Andersen, P. V. Christiansen, C. Emmeche, & M. O. Finnermann (Eds.), *Downward causation: Minds, bodies and matter* (pp. 63–77). Copenhagen: Aarhus University Press.

PAULESU, E., FRITH, U., SNOWLING, M., GALLAGHER, A., MORTON, J., FRACKOWIAK, R. S. J., & FRITH, C. D. (1996). Is developmental dyslexia a disconnection syndrome?: Evidence from PET scanning. *Brain, 119*(1), 143–157.

PAULING, L., & CORYELL, C. D. (1936). The magnetic properties and structure of hemoglobin, oxyhemoglobin and carbonmonoxyhemoglobin. *Proceedings of the National Academy of Sciences, USA, 22*, 210–216.

PAYNE, J., & NADEL, L. (2004). Sleep, dreams, and memory consolidation: The role of the stress hormone cortisol. *Learning and Memory, 11*, 671–678.

PELPHREY, K. A., SINGERMAN, J. D., ALLISON, T., & MCCARTHY, G. (2003). Brain activation evoked by perception of gaze shifts: The influence of context. *Neuropsychologia, 41*, 156–170.

PELPHREY, K. A., VIOLA, R. J., & MCCARTHY, G. (2004). When strangers pass: Processing of mutual and averted social gaze in the superior temporal sulcus. *Psychological Science, 15*, 598–603.

PENFIELD, W., & JASPER, H. (1954). *Epilepsy and the functional anatomy of the human brain.* Boston: Little, Brown.

PERANI, D., DEHAENE, S., GRASS, F., COHEN, L., CAPP, S. F., DUPOUX, E., ET AL. (1996). Brain processes of native and foreign languages. *NeuroReport, 7*, 2439–2444.

PERANI, D., SACCUMAN, M. C., SCIFO, P., ANWANDER, A., SPADA, D., BALDOLI, C., ET AL. (2011). Neural language networks at birth. *Proceedings of the National Academy of Sciences, 108*(38).

PERETZ, I., KOLINSKY, R., TRAMO, M., LABRECQUE, R., HUBLET, C., DEMEURISSE, G., ET AL. (1994). Functional dissociations following bilateral lesions of auditory cortex. *Brain, 117*, 1283–1301.

PERLMUTTER, J. S., & MINK, J. W. (2006). Deep brain stimulation. *Annual Review of Neuroscience, 29*, 229–257.

PERNER, J., & RUFFMAN, T. (1995). Episodic memory and autonoetic consciousness: Developmental evidence and a theory of childhood amnesia. *Journal of Experimental Child Psychology, 59*, 516–548.

PERRETT, D. I., ORAM, M. W., HIETANEN, J. K., & BENSON, P. J. (1994). Issues of representations in object vision. In M. J. Farah & G. Ratcliff (Eds.), *The neuropsychology of high-level vision: Collected tutorial essays* (pp. 33–62). Hillsdale, NJ: Erlbaum.

PERRETT, S., RUIZ, B., & MAUK, M. (1993). Cerebellar cortex lesions disrupt learning-dependent timing of conditioned eyelid responses. *Journal of Neuroscience, 13*, 1708–1718.

PESSIGLIONE, M., SEYMOUR, B., FLANDIN, G., DOLAN, R. J., & FRITH, C. D. (2006) Dopamine-dependent prediction errors underpin reward-seeking behaviour in humans. *Nature, 442*(31), 1042–1045.

PESSOA, L. (2008). On the relationship between emotion and cognition. *Nature Reviews Neuroscience, 9*, 148–158.

PESSOA, L. (2011). Emotion and cognition and the amygdala: From "What is it?" to "What's to be done?" *Neuropsychologia, 49*(4), 3416–3429.

PETERS, B. L., & STRINGHAM, E. (2006). No booze? You may lose: Why drinkers earn more money than nondrinkers. *Journal of Labor Research, 27*, 411–422.

PETERS, E., VÄSTFJÄLL, D., GÄRLING, T., & SLOVIC, P. (2006). Affect and decision making: A "hot" topic. *Journal of Behavioral and Decision Making, 19*, 79–85.

PETERS, J., & BUCHEL, C. (2009). Overlapping and distinct neural systems code for subjective value during intertemporal and risky decision making. *Journal of Neuroscience, 29*, 15727–15734.

PETERSEN, S. E., FIEZ, J. A., & CORBETTA, M. (1992). Neuroimaging. *Current Opinion in Neurobiology, 2*, 217–222.

PETERSEN, S. E., ROBINSON, D. L., & MORRIS, J. D. (1987). Contributions of the pulvinar to visual spatial attention. *Neuropsychologia, 25*, 97–105.

PETERSEN, S. E., VAN MIER, H., FIEZ, J. A., & RAICHLE, M. E. (1998). The effects of practice on the functional anatomy of task performance. *Proceedings of the National Academy of Sciences USA, 95*, 853–860.

PETRIDES, M. (2000). Middorsolateral and midventrolateral prefrontal cortex: Two levels of executive control for the processing of mnemonic information. In S. Monsell & J. Driver (Eds.), *Control of cognitive processes: Attention and performance XVIII* (pp. 535–548). Cambridge, MA: MIT Press.

PETRIDES, M., & PANDYA, D. N. (2009). Distinct parietal and temporal pathways to the homologues of Broca's area in the monkey. *PLoS Biology, 7*(8), 1–16.

PFISTER, H. R., & BÖHM, G. (2008). The multiplicity of emotions: A framework of emotional functions in decision making. *Judgment and Decision Making, 3*, 5–17.

PHELPS, E. A., CANNISTRACI, C. J., & CUNNINGHAM, W. A. (2003). Intact performance on an indirect measure of race bias following amygdala damage. *Neuropsychologia, 41*, 203–208.

PHELPS, E. A., & GAZZANIGA, M. S. (1992). Hemispheric differences in mnemonic processing: The effects of left hemisphere interpretation. *Neuropsychologia, 30*, 293–297.

PHELPS, E. A., LABAR, D. S., ANDERSON, A. K., O'CONNOR, K. J., FULBRIGHT, R. K., & SPENCER, D. S. (1998). Specifying the contributions of the human amygdala to emotional memory: A case study. *Neurocase, 4*, 527–540.

PHELPS, E. A., O'CONNOR, K. J., CUNNINGHAM, W. A., FUNAYMA, E. S., GATENBY, J. C., GORE, J. C., ET AL. (2000). Performance on indirect measures of race evaluation predicts amygdala activity. *Journal of Cognitive Neuroscience, 12*, 729–738.

PHELPS, E. A., O'CONNOR, K. J., GATENBY, J. C., GRILLON, C., GORE, J. C., & DAVIS, M. (2001). Activation of the human amygdala to a cognitive representation of fear. *Nature Neuroscience, 4*, 437–441.

PHELPS, E. A., LING, S., & CARRASCO, M. (2006). Emotion facilitates perception and potentiates the perceptual benefit of attention. *Psychological Science, 17*, 292–299.

PHILLIPS, M. L., YOUNG, A. W., SCOTT, S. K., CALDER, A. J., ANDREW, C., GIAMPIETRO, V., ET AL. (1998). Neural responses to facial and vocal expressions of fear and disgust. *Proceedings of the Royal Society of London, Series B, 265*, 1809–1817.

PHILLIPS, M. L., YOUNG, A. W., SENIOR, C., BRAMMER, M., ANDREW, C., CALDER, A. J., ET AL. (1997). A specific neural substrate for perceiving facial expressions of disgust. *Nature, 389*, 495–498.

PIERCE, K., HAIST, F.. SEDAGAT, F., & COURCHESNE, E. (2004). The brain response to personally familiar faces in autism: Findings of fusiform activity and beyond. *Brain, 127*, 2703–2716.

PIERCE, K., MÜLLER, R. A., AMBROSE, J., ALLEN, G., & COURCHESNE, E. (2001). Face processing occurs outside the fusiform 'face area' in autism: evidence from functional MRI. *Brain, 124*, 2059–2073.

PIKA, S., LIEBAL, K., & TOMASELLO, M. (2003). Gestural communication in young gorillas (*Gorilla gorilla*): Gestural repertoire, and use. *American Journal of Primatology, 60*, 95–111.

PIKA, S., LIEBAL, K., & TOMASELLO, M. (2005). Gestural communication in subadult bonobos (*Pan paniscus*): Repertoire and use. *American Journal of Primatology, 65*, 39–61.

PINKER, S. (1994). *The language instinct.* New York: Morrow.

PINKER, S. (1997). *How the mind works.* New York: Norton.

PINKER, S. (2011). The better angels of our nature: Why violence has declined. New York: Viking Press.

PINKER, S. (2012). The false allure of group selection. *Edge.* Retrieved from http://edge.org/conversation/the-false-allure-of-group-selection

PINKER, S., & BLOOM, P. (1990). Natural language and natural selection. *Behavioral and Brain Sciences, 13*, 707–726.

PISELLA, L, GRÉA, H., TILIKETE, C., VIGHETTO, A., DESMURGET, M., RODE, G., ET AL. (2000). An "automatic pilot" for the hand in human posterior parietal cortex: Toward reinterpreting optic ataxia. *Nature Neuroscience, 3*, 729–736.

PITCHER, D., CHARLES, L., DEVLIN, J. T., WALSH, V., & DUCHAINE, B. (2009). Triple dissociation of faces, bodies, and objects in extrastriate cortex. *Current Biology, 19*, 1–6.

PLANT, G. T., LAXER, K. D., BARBARO, N. M., SCHIFFMAN, J. S., & NAKAYAMA, K. (1993). Impaired visual motion perception in the contralateral hemifield following unilateral posterior cerebral lesions in humans. *Brain*, 116, 1303–1335.

PLOMIN, R., CORLEY, R., DEFRIES, J. C., & FULKER, D. W. (1990). Individual differences in television viewing in early childhood: Nature as well as nurture. *Psychological Science*, 1, 371–377.

PLOOG, D. (2002). Is the neural basis of vocalisation different in non-human primates and *Homo sapiens*? In T. J. Crow (Ed.), *The Speciation of Modern* Homo sapiens (pp. 121–135). Oxford: Oxford University Press.

POEPPEL, D., EMMOREY, K., HICKOK, G., & PYLKKÄNEN, L. (2012). Towards new neurobioloy of language. *The Journal of Neeurosciencce*, 32(41), 14125–14131.

POEPPEL, D. & MONOHAN, P. J. (2008). Speech perception: Cognitive foundations and cortical implementation. *Current Directions in Psychological Science*, 17(2), 80–85.

POLLATOS, O., GRAMANN, K., & SCHANDRY, R. (2007). Neural systems connecting interoceptive awareness and feelings. *Human Brain Mapping*, 28, 9–18.

POHL, W. (1973). Dissociation of spatial discrimination deficits following frontal and parietal lesions in monkeys. *Journal of Comparative and Physiological Psychology*, 82, 227–239.

POSNER, M. I. (1986). *Chronometric explorations of mind*. New York: Oxford University Press.

POSNER, M. I., & RAICHLE, M. E. (1994). *Images of mind*. New York: Freeman.

POSNER, M., & ROTHBART, M. (2012). Willpower and brain networks. *Bulletin of the International Society for the Study of Behavioural Development (ISSBD)*, 61(1), 7–9.

POSNER, M. I., SNYDER, C. R. R., & DAVIDSON, J. (1980). Attention and the detection of signals. *Journal of Experimental Psychology. General*, 109, 160–174.

POSNER, M. I., WALKER, J. A., FRIEDRICH, F. J., & RAFAL, B. D. (1984). Effects of parietal injury on covert orienting of attention. *Journal of Neuroscience*, 4, 1863–1874.

POSTLE, B. R., & CORKIN, S. (1998). Impaired word-stem completion priming but intact perceptual identification priming with novel words: Evidence from the amnesic patient H.M. *Neuropsychologia*, 36, 421–440.

POVINELLI, D. J., RULF, A. R., LANDAU, K., & BIERSCHWALE, D. T. (1993). Self-recognition in chimpanzees (*Pan troglodytes*): Distribution, ontogeny, and patterns of emergence. *Journal of Comparative Psychology*, 107, 347–372.

POWELL, H. W. R., PARKER, G. J. M., ALEXANDER, D. C., SYMMS, M. R., BOULBY, P. A.,WHEELER-KINGSHOTT, C. A. M., ET AL. (2006). Hemispheric asymmetries inlanguage-related pathways: A combined functional MRI and tractography study. *NeuroImage*, 32(1), 388–399.

PRABHAKARAN, V., NARAYANAN, K., ZHAO, Z., & GABRIELI, J. D. (2000). Integration of diverse information in working memory within the frontal lobe. *Nature Neuroscience*, 3, 85–90.

PREMACK, D. (1972). Concordant preferences as a precondition for affective but not for symbolic communication (or how to do experimental anthropology). *Cognition*, 1, 251–264.

PREMACK, D., & WOODRUFF, G. (1978). Does the chimpanzee have a theory of mind? *Behavioral and Brain Sciences*, 1, 515–526.

PREUSS, T. (2001). The discovery of cerebral diversity: An unwelcome scientific revolution. In D. Falk & K. R. Gibson (Eds.), *Evolutionary anatomy of the primate cortex* (p. 154). Cambridge: Cambridge University Press.

PREUSS, T. (2012). Human brain evolution: From gene discovery to phenotype discovery. *Proceedings of the National Academy of Science USA*, 109 (Suppl 1), 10709–10716.

PREUSS, T. M., & COLEMAN, G. Q. (2002). Human-specific organization of primary visual cortex: Alternating compartments of dense

Cat-301 and calbindin immunoreactivity in layer 4A. *Cerebral Cortex*, 12, 671–691.

PREVIC, F. H. (1991). A general theory concerning the prenatal origins of cerebral lateralization in humans. *Psychological Review*, 98, 299–334.

PRICE, C. J. (2012) A review and synthesis of the first 20 years of PET and fMRI studies of heard speech, spoken language and reading. *Neuroimage*, 62, 816–847.

PRINZ, A. A., BUCHER, D., & MARDER, E. (2004). Similar network activity from disparate circuit parameters. *Nature Reviews Neuroscience*, 7(12), 1345–1352.

PROVINE, R. (2004). Laughing, tickling, and the evolution of speech and self. *Current Directions in Psychological Science*, 13, 215–218.

PROVINE, R. & YONG, Y. (1991). Laughter: A stereotyped human vocalization. *Ethology*, 89, 115–124.

PRUSZYNSKI, J. A., KURTZER, I., NASHED, J. Y., OMRANI, M., BROUWER, B., & SCOTT, S. H. (2011a). Primary motor cortex underlies multi-joint integration for fast feedback control. *Nature*, 478, 387–391.

PRUSZYNSKI, J. A., KURTZER, I., & SCOTT, S. H. (2011b). The long-latency reflex is composed of at least two functionally independent processes. *Journal of Neurophysiology*, 106, 449–459.

PUCE, A., ALLISON, T., ASGARI, M., GORE, J. C., & MCCARTHY, G. (1996). Differential sensitivity of human visual cortex to faces, letterstrings, and textures: A functional magnetic resonance imaging study. *Journal of Neuroscience*, 16, 5205–5215.

PURVES, D., AUGUSTINE, G., & FITZPATRICK, D. (2001). *Neuroscience* (2nd ed.). Sunderland, MA: Sinauer.

PUTMAN, M. C., STEVEN, M. S., DORON, C., RIGGALL, A. C., & GAZZANIGA, M. S. (2010). Cortical projection topography of the human splenium: Hemispheric asymmetry and individual difference. *Journal of Cognitive Neuroscience*, 22(8), 1662–1669.

QUIROGA, R. Q., REDDY, L., KERIMAN, G., KOCH, C., & FRIED, I. (2005). Invariant visual representation by single neurons in the human brain. *Nature*, 435, 1102–1107.

RAICHLE, M. (2008). A brief history of human brain mapping. *Trends in Neuroscience*, 32, 118–126.

RAICHLE, M. E. (1994). Visualizing the mind. *Scientific American*, 270(4), 58–64.

RAICHLE, M. E., FIEZ, J. A., VIDEEN, T. O., MacLEOD, A. K., PARDO, J. V., FOX, P. T., ET AL. (1994). Practice-related changes in human brain functional anatomy during nonmotor learning. *Cerebral Cortex*, 4, 8–26.

RAICHLE, M. E., MacLEOD, A. M., SNYDER, A. Z., POWERS, W. J., GUSNARD, D. A., ET AL. (2001). A default mode of brain function. *Proceedings of the National Academy of Science, USA*, 98, 676–682.

RAINE, A. (2002). Biosocial studies of antisocial and violent behavior in children and adults: A review. *Journal of Abnormal Child Psychology*, 30, 311–326.

RAINE, A., LENCZ, T., BIHRLE, S., LaCASSE, L., & COLLETTI, P. (2000). Reduced prefrontal gray matter volume and reduced autonomic activity in antisocial personality disorder. *Archives of General Psychiatry*, 57, 119–127.

RAKIC, P. (1995a). Corticogenesis in human and nonhuman primates. In M. S. Gazzaniga (Ed.), *The cognitive neurosciences* (pp. 127–146). Cambridge, MA: MIT Press.

RAMACHANDRAN, V. S. (1993). Behavioral and magnetoencephalographic correlates of plasticity in the adult human brain. *Proceedings of the National Academy of Sciences, USA*, 90, 10413–10420.

RAMACHANDRAN, V. S., & HUBBARD, E. M. (2001a). Psychophysical investigations into the neural basis of synaesthesia. *Proceedings of the Royal Society of London, Series B*, 268, 979–983.

RAMACHANDRAN, V. S., & HUBBARD, E. M. (2001b). Synaesthesia— A window into perception, thought and language. *Journal of Consciousness Studies*, 8, 3–34.

Ramachandran, V. S., & Hubbard, E. M. (2003). Hearing colors, tasting shapes. *Scientific American, 288*(5), 52–59.

Ramirez-Amaya, V., Marrone, D. F., Gage, F. H., Worley, P. F., & Barnes, C. A. (2006). Integration of new neurons into functional neural networks. *Journal of Neuroscience, 26,* 12237–12241.

Ramón y Cajal, S. (1909–1911). *Histologie du système nerveaux de l'homme et de vertébrés.* Paris: Maloine.

Rampon, C., Tang, Y. P., Goodhouse, J., Shimizu, E., Kyin, M., & Tsien, J. Z. (2000). Enrichment induces structural changes and recovery from nonspatial memory deficits in CA1 NMDAR1-knockout mice. *Nature Neuroscience, 3,* 238–244.

Ranganath, C. (2010). Binding items and contexts: The cognitive neuroscience of episodic memory. *Current Directions in Psychological Science, 19*(3), 131–137.

Ranganath, C., & Blumenfeld, R. S. (2005). Doubts about double dissociations between short- and long-term memory. *Trends in Cognitive Sciences, 9,* 374–380.

Ranganath, C., & Richey, M. (2012). Two cortical systems for memory guided behaviour. *Nature Reviews Neuroscience, 13,* 713–726.

Ranganath, C., Yonelinas, A. P., Cohen, M. X., Dy, C. J., Tom, S. M., & D'Esposito, M. (2004). Dissociable correlates of recollection and familiarity within the medial temporal lobes. *Neuropsychologia, 42,* 2–13.

Rangel, A., Camerer, C., & Montague, P. R. (2008). A framework for studying the neurobiology of value-based decision making. *Nature Reviews Neuroscience, 9*(7), 545–556.

Rao, S. C., Rainer, G., & Miller, E. K. (1997). Integration of what and where in the primate prefrontal cortex. *Science, 276,* 821–824.

Rathelot, J.-A., & Strick, P. L. (2009). Subdivisions of primary motor cortex based on cortico-motoneuronal cells. *Proceedings of the National Academy of Sciences, 106*(3), 918–923.

Reddy, L., Tsuchiya, N., & Serre, T. (2010). Reading the mind's eye: Decoding category information during mental imagery. *Neuro-Image, 50*(2), 818–825.

Reicher, G. M. (1969). Perceptual recognition as a function of meaningfulness of stimulus material. *Journal of Experimental Psychology, 81,* 275–280.

Reichert, H., & Boyan, G. (1997). Building a brain: Developmental insights in insects. *Trends in Neuroscience, 20,* 258–264.

Reinholz, J., & Pollmann, S. (2005). Differential activation of object-selective visual areas by passive viewing of pictures and words. *Brain Research. Cognitive Brain Research, 24,* 702–714.

Rentschler, I., Treutwein, B., & Landis, T. (1994). Dissociation of local and global processing in visual agnosia. *Vision Research, 34,* 963–971.

Reuter-Lorenz, P. A., & Fendrich, R. (1990). Orienting attention across the vertical meridian: Evidence from callosotomy patients. *Journal of Cognitive Neuroscience, 2,* 232–238.

Reverberi, C., Toraldo, A., d'Agostini, S., & Skrap, M. (2005). Better without (lateral) frontal cortex? Insight problems solved by frontal patients. *Brain, 128,* 2882–2890.

Reynolds, J. N. J., & Wickens, J. R. (2000). Substantia nigra dopamine regulates synaptic plasticity and membrane potential fluctuations in the rat neostriatum, in vivo. *Neuroscience, 99,* 199–203.

Rhodes, G., Byatt, G., Michie, P. T., & Puce, A. (2004). Is the fusiform face area specialized for faces, individuation, or expert individuation? *Journal of Cognitive Neuroscience, 16,* 189–203.

Rich, A. N., Williams, M. A., Puce, A., Syngeniotis, A., Howard, M. A., McGlone, F., et al. (2006). Neural correlates of imagined and synaesthetic colours. *Neuropsychologia, 44,* 2918–2925.

Ridderinkhof, K. R., de Vlugt, Y., Bramlage, A., Spaan, M., Elton, M., Snel, J., et al. (2002). Alcohol consumption impairs detection of performance errors in mediofrontal cortex. *Science, 298,* 2209–2211.

Ridderinkhof, K. R., Ullsperger, M., Crone, E. A., & Nieuwenhuis, S. (2004). The role of the medial frontal cortex in cognitive control. *Science, 306,* 443–447.

Riddoch, G. (1917). Dissociation of visual perceptions due to occipital injuries, with especial reference to appreciation of movement. *Brain, 40,* 15–47.

Riddoch, M. J., Humphreys, G. W., Gannon, T., Bott, W., & Jones, V. (1999). Memories are made of this: The effects of time on stored visual knowledge in a case of visual agnosia. *Brain, 122*(Pt. 3), 537–559.

Riley, B., & Kendler, K. S. (2006). Molecular genetic studies of schizophrenia. *European Journal of Human Genetics, 14,* 669–680.

Rilling, J. K., Glasser, M. F., Preuss, T. M., Ma, X., Zhao, T., Hu, X., et al. (2008). The evolution of the arcuate fasciculus revealed with comparative DTI. *Nature Neuroscience, 11*(4), 426–428.

Rilling, J. K., Gutman, D. A., Zeh, T. R., Pagnoni, G., Berns, G. S., & Kilts, C. D. (2002). A neural basis for social cooperation. *Neuron, 35,* 395–405.

Ringo, J. L., Doty, R. W., Demeter, S., & Simard, P. Y. (1994). Time is of the essence: A conjecture that hemispheric specialization arises from interhemispheric conduction delays. *Cerebral Cortex, 4,* 331–343.

Risse, G. L., Gates, J. R., & Fangman, M. C. (1997). A reconsideration of bilateral language representation based on the intracarotid amobarbital procedure. *Brain and Cognition, 33,* 118–132.

Ritchey M., Dolcos, F., Eddington, K. M., Strauman, T. J., & Cabeza, R. (2011). Neural correlates of emotional processing in depression: changes with cognitive behavioral therapy and predictors of treatment response. *Journal of Psychiatric Research, 45*(5), 577–587.

Ritchey, M., LaBar, K. S., & Cabeza, R. (2011). Level of processing modulates the neural correlates of emotional memory formation. *Journal of Cognitive Neuroscience, 23,* 757–771.

Rizzolatti, G., & Arbib, M. A. (1998). Language within our grasp. *Trends Cognitive Science, 21,* 188–194.

Rizzolatti, G., Fogassi, L., & Gallese, V. (2000). Cortical mechanisms subserving object grasping and action recognition: A new view on the cortical motor functions. In M. S. Gazzaniga (Ed.), *The cognitive neurosciences* (2nd ed., pp. 539–552). Cambridge, MA: MIT Press.

Rizzolatti, G., Gentilucci, M., Fogassi, L., Luppino, G., Matelli, M., & Camarda, R. (1988). Functional organization of inferior area 6 in the macaque monkey. *Experimental Brain Research, 71,* 465–490.

Ro, T., Farnè, A., & Chang, E. (2003). Inhibition of return and the human frontal eye fields. *Experimental Brain Research, 150,* 290–296.

Roberts, D. C., Loh, E. A., & Vickers, G. (1989). Self-administration of cocaine on a progressive ratio schedule in rats: Dose-response relationship and effect of haloperidol pretreatment. *Psychopharmacology, 97,* 535–538.

Roberts, T. P. L., Poeppel, D., & Rowley, H. A. (1998). Magnetoencephalography and magnetic source imaging. *Neuropsychiatry, Neuropsychology, and Behavioral Neurology, 11,* 49–64.

Robertson, I. H., Manly, T., Beschin, N., Daini, R., Haeske-Dewick, H., Hömberg, V., et al. (1997). Auditory sustained attention is a marker of unilateral spatial neglect. *Neuropsychologia, 35,* 1527–1532.

Robertson, L. C., Knight, R. T., Rafal, R., & Shimamura, A. P. (1993). Cognitive neuropsychology is more than single-case studies. *Journal of Experimental Psychology. Learning, Memory, and Cognition, 19,* 710–717.

Robertson, L. C., Lamb, M. R., & Knight, R. T. (1988). Effects of lesions of temporal–parietal junction on perceptual and attentional processing in humans. *Journal of Neuroscience, 8,* 3757–3769.

Robertson, L. C., Lamb, M. R., & Zaidel, E. (1993). Interhemispheric relations in processing hierarchical patterns: Evidence from normal and commissurotomized subjects. *Neuropsychology, 7,* 325–342.

Robinson, D. L., Goldberg, M. E., & Stanton, G. B. (1978). Parietal association cortex in the primate: Sensory mechanisms and behavioral modulation. *Journal of Neurophysiology, 41,* 910–932.

Robinson, D. L., & Petersen, S. (1992). The pulvinar and visual salience. *Trends in Neurosciences, 15,* 127–132.

Rodrigo, S., Naggara, O., Oppenheim, C., Golestani, N., Poupon, C., Cointepas, Y., et al. (2007). Human subinsular asymmetry studied by diffusion tensor imaging and fiber tracking. *American Journal of Neuroradiology, 28*(8), 1526–1531.

Rodrigues, S. M., Le Doux, J. E., & Sapolsky, R. M. (2009). The influence of stress hormones on fear circuitry. *Annual review of Neuroscience, 32,* 289–313.

Rodriguez-Oroz, M. C., Obeso, J. A., Lang, A. E., Houeto, J. L., Pollak, P., Rehncrona, S., et al. (2005) Bilateral deep brain stimulation in Parkinson's disease: A multicentre study with 4 years follow-up. *Brain, 128,* 2240–2249.

Roediger, H. L., & McDermott, K. B. (1995). Creating false memories: Remembering words not presented in lists. *Journal of Experimental Psychology. Learning, Memory, and Cognition, 21,* 803–814.

Rogers, R. D., Sahakian, R. A., Hodges, J. R., Polkey, C. E., Kennard, C., & Robbins, T. W. (1998). Dissociating executive mechanisms of task control following frontal lobe damage and Parkinson's disease. *Brain, 121,* 815–842.

Rogers, T. B., Kuiper, N. A., & Kirker, W. S. (1977). Self-reference and the encoding of personal information. *Journal of Personality and Social Psychology, 35,* 677–688.

Rolheiser, T., Stamatakis, E. A., & Tyler, L. K. (2011). Dynamic processing in the human language system: Synergy between the arcuate fascicle and extreme capsule. *The Journal of Neuroscience, 31*(47), 16949–16957.

Rolls, E. T. (1992). Neurophysiological mechanisms underlying face processing within and beyond the temporal cortical visual areas. *Philosophical Transactions of the Royal Society of London, Series B:, Biological Sciences, 335,* 11–20.

Rolls, E. T. (2004). The functions of the orbitofrontal cortex. *Brain Cognition, 55*(1), 11–29.

Rolls, E. T., Critchley, H. D., Mason, R., & Wakeman, E. A. (1996). Orbitofrontal cortex neurons: Role in olfactory and visual association learning. *Journal of Neurophysiology, 75,* 1970–1981.

Romei, V., Murray, M., Merabet, L. B., & Thut, G. (2007). Occipital transcranial magnetic stimulation has opposing effects on visual and auditory stimulus detection: Implications for multisensory interactions. *Journal of Neuroscience, 27*(43), 11465–11472.

Rose, J. E., Hind, J. E., Anderson, D. J., & Brugge, J. F. (1971). Some effects of stimulus intensity on response of auditory nerve fibers in the squirrel monkey. *Journal of Neurophysiology, 24,* 685–699.

Rosenbaum, D. A., Slotta, J. D., Vaughan, J., & Plamondon, R. (1991). Optimal movement selection. *Psychological Science, 2,* 86–91.

Rosenbaum, R. S., Kohler, S., Schacter, D. L., Moscovitch, M., Westmacott, R., Black, S. E., et al. (2005). The case of K.C.: Contributions of a memory-impaired person to memory theory. *Neuropsychologia, 43,* 989–1021.

Roser, M. E., Fugelsang, J. A., Dunbar, K. N., Corballis, P. M., & Gazzaniga, M. S. (2005). Dissociating processes supporting causal perception and causal inference in the brain. *Neuropsychology, 19,* 591–602.

Rothschild, G., Nelken, I., & Mizrahi, A. (2010). Functional organization and population dynamics in the mouse primary auditory cortex. *Nature Neuroscience, 13,* 353–360.

Rothwell, J. C., Traub, M. M., Day, B. L., Obeso, J. A., Thomas, P. K., & Marsden, C. D. (1982). Manual motor performance in a deafferented man. *Brain, 105,* 515–542.

Rouw, R., & Scholte, H. S. (2007). Increased structural connectivity in grapheme-color synesthesia. *Nature Neuroscience, 10*(6), 792–797.

Rowan, A. N., & Rollin, B. E. (1983). Animal research—For and against: A philosophical, social, and historical perspective. *Perspectives in Biology and Medicine, 27,* 1–17.

Rowe, D. C. (2001). *Biology of crime.* Los Angeles: Roxbury.

Rowland, L. P. (Ed.). (1989). *Merritt's textbook of neurology* (8th ed.). Philadelphia: Lea & Febiger.

Rubinstein, A. (1982). Perfect equilibrium in a bargaining model. *Econometrica, 50*(1), 97–109.

Ruff, C. C., Blankenburg, F., Bjoertomt, O., Bestmann, S., Freeman, E., Haynes, J.-D., et al. (2006). Concurrent TMS-fMRI and psychophysics reveal frontal influences on human retinotopic visual cortex. *Current Biology, 16,* 1479–1488.

Rumelhart, D. E., McClelland, J. L., & PDP Research Group. (1986). *Parallel distributed processing: Explorations in the microstructure of cognition: Vol. 1. Foundations.* Cambridge, MA: MIT Press.

Rushworth, M. F. S., Kolling, N., Sallet, J., & Mars, R. B. (2012). Valuation and decision-making in frontal cortex: One or many serial or parallel systems? *Current Opinion in Neurobiology, 22,* 1–10.

Russell, J. A. (1979). Affective space is bipolar. *Journal of Personality and Social Psychology, 37,* 345–356.

Russell, J. A. (2003). Core affect and the psychological construction of emotion. *Psychological Review, 110,* 145–172.

Ryan, J. D., Althoff, R. R., Whitlow, S., & Cohen, N. J. (2000). Amnesia is a deficit in relational memory. *Psychological Science, 11,* 454–461.

Sabini, J., & Silver, M. (2005). Ekman's basic emotions: Why not love and jealousy? *Cognition and Emotion, 19*(5), 693–712.

Sacks, O. W. (1995). *An anthropologist on Mars: Seven paradoxical tales.* New York: Knopf.

Sadato, N., Pascual-Leone, A., Grafman, J., Ibanez, V., Deiber, M-P., Dold, G., et al. (1996). Activation of the primary visual cortex by Braille reading in blind subjects. *Nature, 380,* 526–528.

Sagiv, N., & Bentin, S. (2001). Structural encoding of human and schematic faces: Holistic and part-based processes. *Journal of Cognitive Neuroscience, 13,* 937–951.

Sahin, N. T., Pinker, S., Cash, S. S., Schomer, D., & Halgren, E. (2009). Sequential processing of lexical, grammatical, and phonological information within Broca's Area. *Science, 326,* 445-449.

Said, C. P., Dotsch, R., & Todorov, A. (2010). The amygdala and FFA track both social and non-social face dimensions. *Neuropsychologia, 48,* 3596–3605.

Sakai, K., & Passingham, R. E. (2003). Prefrontal interactions reflect future task operations. *Nature Neuroscience, 6,* 75–81.

Sakarai, Y. (1996). Hippocampal and neocortical cell assemblies encode processes for different types of stimuli in the rat. *Journal of Neuroscience, 16*(8), 2809–2819.

Sakarai, U., Momose, T., Iwata, M., Sudo, Y., Ohtomo, K., & Kanazawa, I. (2000). Different cortical activity in reading Kanji words, Kana words and Kana nonwords. *Cognitive Brain Research, 9*(1), 111–115.

Salzman, C. D., Britten, K. H., & Newsome, W. T. (1990). Cortical microstimulation influences perceptual judgments of motion direction. *Nature, 346,* 174–177.

Samii, A., Turnbull, I. M., Kishore, A., Schulzer, M., Mak, E., Yardley, S., et al. (1999). Reassessment of unilateral pallidotomy in Parkinson's disease: A 2-year follow-up study. *Brain, 122,* 417–425.

Sams, M., Hari, R., Rif, J., & Knuutila, J. (1993). The human auditory sensory memory trace persists about 10 sec: Neuromagnetic evidence. *Journal of Cognitive Neuroscience, 5,* 363–370.

SANFEY, A. G., LOEWENSTEIN, G., MCCLURE, S., & COHEN, J. D. (2006). Neuroeconomics: Cross currents in research on decision-making. *Trends in Cognitive Sciences, 10*, 108–116.

SANFEY, A. G., RILLING, J. K., ARONSON, J. A., NYSTROM, L. E., & COHEN, J. D. (2003). The neural basis of economic decision-making in the ultimatum game. *Science, 300*, 1755–1758.

SAPER, C. B. (2002). The central autonomic nervous system: Conscious visceral perception and autonomic pattern generation. *Annual Review of Neuroscience, 25*, 433–469.

SAPIR, A., SOROKER, N., BERGER, A., & HENIK, A. (1999). Inhibition of return in spatial attention: Direct evidence for collicular generation. *Nature Neuroscience, 2*, 1053–1054.

SAPOLSKY, R. M. (1992). Stress, the aging brain, and the mechanisms of neuron death. Cambridge, MA: MIT Press.

SAPOLSKY, R. M., UNO, H., REBERT, C. S., & FINCH, C. E. (1990). Hippocampal damage associated with prolonged glucocorticoid exposure in primates. *Journal of Neuroscience, 10*, 2897–2902.

SASANUMA, S. (1980). Acquired dyslexia in Japanese: Clinical features and underlying mechamisms. In M. Coltheart, K. E. Patterson, & J. C. Marshall (Eds). *Deep Dyslexia* (pp. 91–118). London: Routledge & KeganPaul.

SATORI, G., & JOB, R. (1988). The oyster with four legs: A neuropsychological study on the interaction of visual and semantic information. *Cognitive Neuropsychology, 5*, 105–132.

SAUCIER, D., & CAIN, D. P. (1995). Spatial learning without NMDA receptor-dependent long-term potentiation. *Nature, 378*, 186–189.

SAUR, D., KREHER, B.W., SCHNELL, S., KÜMMERER, D., KELLMEYER, P., VRY, M.S., UMAROVA, R., MUSSO, M., GLAUCHE, V., ABEL, S., HUBER, W., RIJNTJES, M., HENNIG, J., & WEILLER, C. (2008). Ventral and dorsal pathways for language. *Proceedings of the National Academy Science USA, 105*, 18035–18040.

SAVAGE-RUMBAUGH, S. & LEWIN, R. (1994). *Kanzi: The Ape at the Brink of the Human Mind.* New York: John Wiley and Sons, Inc.

SAVER, J. L., & DAMASIO, A. R. (1991). Preserved access and processing of social knowledge in a patient with acquired sociopathy due to ventromedial frontal damage. *Neuropsychologia, 29*, 1241–1249.

SAXE, R., & POWELL, L. J. (2006). It's the thought that counts: Specific brain regions for one component of theory of mind. *Psychological Science, 17*, 692–699.

SAXE, R., & WEXLER, A. (2005). Making sense of another mind: The role of the right temporo-parietal junction. *Neuropsychologia, 43*, 1391–1399.

SAXE, R. R., WHITFIELD-GABRIELI, S., SCHOLZ, J., & PELPHREY, K. A. (2009). Brain regions for perceiving and reasoning about other people in school-aged children. *Child Development, 80*, 1197–1209.

SAYGIN, A. P., WILSON, S. M., DRONKERS, N. F., & BATES, E. (2004). Action comprehension in aphasia: Linguistic and non-linguistic deficits and their lesion correlates. *Neuropsychologia, 42*, 1788–1804.

SCALIA, A. (2002). *Akins v. Virginia* (00-8452) 536 U.S. 304. Retrieved from http://www.law.cornell.edu/supct/html/00-8452.Z

SCHACHTER, S., & SINGER, J. (1962). Cognitive, social and physiological determinants of emotional state. *Psychological Review, 69*, 379–399.

SCHACTER, D. L. (1987). Implicit memory: History and current status. *Journal of Experimental Psychology. Learning, Memory, and Cognition, 113*, 501–518.

SCHACTER, D. L., GILBERT, D. T., & WEGNER, D. M. (2007). *Psychology.* New York: Worth.

SCHEIBEL, A. B., PAUL, L. A., FRIED, I., FORSYTHE, A. B., TOMIYASU, U., WECHSLER, A., ET AL. (1985). Dendritic organization of the anterior speech area. *Experimental Neurology, 87*(1), 109–17.

SCHENK, F., & MORRIS, R. G. M. (1985). Dissociation between components of a spatial memory in rats after recovery from the effects of retrohippocampal lesion. *Experimental Brain Research, 58*, 11–28.

SCHINDLER, I., RICE, N. J., MCINTOSH, R.D., ROSSETTI, Y., VIGHETTO, A., & MILNER, A.D. (2004). Automatic avoidance of obstacles is a dorsal stream function: Evidence from optic ataxia. *Nature Neuroscience, 7*, 779–784.

SCHIRBER, M. (2005, February 18). Monkey's brain runs robotic arm. *LiveScience.* Retrieved from http://www.livescience.com/technology/050218 _monkey_arm.html

SCHMIDT, R. A. (1987). The acquisition of skill: Some modifications to the perception–action relationship through practice. In H. Heuer & A. F. Sanders (Eds.), *Perspectives on perception and action* (pp. 77–103). Hillsdale, NJ: Erlbaum.

SCHMITZ, W., & JOHNSON, S. C. (2007). Relevance to self: A brief review and framework of neural systems underlying appraisal. *Neuroscience & Biobehavioral Reviews, 31*(4), 585–596.

SCHNAKERS, C., VANHAUDENHUYSE, A., GIACINO, J., VENTURA, M., BOLY, M., MAJERUS, S., ET AL. (2009). Diagnostic accuracy of the vegetative and minimally conscious state: Clinical consensus versus standardized neurobehavioral assessment. *BMC Neurology, 9*(35). Retrieved from http://www.biomedcentral.com/1471-2377/9/35

SCHNEIDER, G. E. (1969). Two visual systems. *Science, 163*, 895–902.

SCHOENBAUM, G., SADDORIS, M. P., & STALNAKER, T. A. (2007). Reconciling the roles of orbitofrontal cortex in reversal learning and the encoding of outcome expectancies. *Annals of the New York Academy of Science, 1121*, 320–335.

SCHOENEMANN, P. T., SHEEHAN, M. J., & GLOTZER, L. D. (2005). Prefrontal white matter volume is disproportionately larger in humans than in other primates. *Nature Neuroscience, 8*, 242–252.

SCHOENFELD, M., HOPF, J. M., MARTINEZ, A., MAI, H., SATTLER, C., GASDE, A., ET AL. (2007). Spatio-temporal analysis of feature-based attention. *Cerebral Cortex, 17*(10), 2468–2477.

SCHOLZ, J., TRIANTAFYLLOU, C., WHITFIELD-GABRIELI, S., BROWN, E. N., & SAXE, R. (2009). Distinct regions of right temporo-parietal junction are selective for theory of mind and exogenous attention. *PLoS One, 4*(3), e4869.

SCHULTZ, W. (1998). Predictive reward signal of dopamine neurons. *Journal of Neurophysiology, 80*(1), 1–27.

SCHULTZ, W. (2002). Getting formal with dopamine and reward. *Neuron, 36*(2), 241–263.

SCHULTZ, W., DAYAN, P., & MONTAGUE, P.R. (1997) A neural substrate of prediction and reward. *Science, 275*, 1593–1599.

SCHUMACHER, E. H., SEYMOUR, T. L., GLASS, J. M., FENCSIK, D. E., LAUBER, E. J., KIERAS, D. E., & MEYER, D. E. (2001). Virtually perfect time sharing in dual-task performance: uncorking the central cognitive bottleneck. *Psychological Science, 12*(2), 101–8.

SCHUMMERS, J., YU, H., & SUR, M. (2008). Tuned responses of astrocytes and their influence on hemodynamic signals in the visual cortex. *Science, 320*, 1638–1643.

SCHWARZKOPF, D. S., SONG, C., & REES, G. (2011). The surface area of human V1 predicts the subjective experience of object size. *Nature Neuroscience, 14*(1), 28–30.

SCHWARZLOSE, R., BAKER, C., & KANWISHER, N. (2005). Separate face and body selectivity on the fusiform gyrus. *Journal of Neuroscience, 25*(47), 11055–11059.

SCHWEIMER, J., & HAUBER, W. (2006). Dopamine D1 receptors in the anterior cingulate cortex regulate effort-based decision making. *Learning and Memory, 13*, 777–782.

SCHWEIMER, J., SAFT, S., & HAUBER, W. (2005). Involvement of catecholamine neurotransmission in the rat anterior cingulate in effort-related decision making. *Behavioral Neuroscience, 119*, 1687–1692.

SCOTT, S. H. (2004). Optimal feedback control and the neural basis of volitional motor control. *Nature Reviews Neuroscience, 5*, 534–546.

Scott, S. K., Young, A. W., Calder, A. J., Hellawell, D. J., Aggleton, J. P., & Johnson, M. (1997). Impaired auditory recognition of fear and anger following bilateral amygdala lesions. *Nature, 385*, 254–257.

Scoville, W. B. (1954). The limbic lobe in man. *Journal of Neurosurgery, 11*, 64–66.

Scoville, W. B., & Milner, B. (1957). Loss of recent memory after bilateral hippocampal lesions. *Journal of Neurology, Neurosurgery, and Psychiatry, 20*, 11–21.

Sebanz, N., Bekkering, H., & Knoblich, G. (2006). Joint action: Bodies and minds moving together. *Trends in Cognitive Science, 10*, 70–76.

Seidenberg, M. S., & McClelland, J. L. (1989). A distributed, developmental model of word recognition and naming. *Psychological Review, 96*, 523–568.

Seidler, R. D., Noll, D. C., & Chintalapati, P. (2006). Bilateral basal ganglia activation associated with sensorimotor adaptation. *Experimental Brain Research, 175*, 544–555.

Sejnowski, T. J., & Churchland, P. S. (1989). Brain and cognition. In M. I. Posner (Ed.), *Foundations of cognitive science* (pp. 301–356). Cambridge, MA: MIT Press.

Sekuler, R., & Blake, R. (1990). *Perception* (2nd ed.). New York: McGraw-Hill.

Selfridge, O. G. (1959). Pandemonium: A paradigm for learning. In *Proceedings of a symposium on the mechanisation of thought processes* (pp. 511–526). London: H.M. Stationary Office.

Senju, A., Maeda, M., Kikuchi, Y., Hasegawa, T., Tojo, Y., & Osanai, H. (2007). Absence of contagious yawning in children with autism spectrum disorder. *Biology Letters, 3*(6), 706–708.

Sergent, J. (1982). The cerebral balance of power: Confrontation or cooperation: *Journal of Experimental Psychology. Human Perception and Performance, 8*, 253–272.

Sergent, J. (1985). Influence of task and input factors on hemispheric involvement in face processing. *Journal of Experimental Psychology. Human Perception and Performance, 11*, 846–861.

Senghas, A. (1995). The development of Nicaraguan Sign Language via the language acquisition process. In D. MacLaughlin & S. McEwen (Eds.), *Proceedings of the 19th Annual Boston University Conference on Language Development* (pp. 543–552). Boston: Cascadilla Press.

Servos, P., Engel, S. A., Gati, J., & Menon, R. (1999). fMRI evidence for an inverted face representation in human somatosensory cortex. *NeuroReport, 10*, 1393–1395.

Seyfarth, R. M., Cheney, D. L., & Marler, P. (1980). Vervet monkey alarm calls: semantic communication in a free-ranging primate. *Animal Behaviour, 28*, 1070–1094.

Seyfarth R. M. & Cheney, D. L. (1986.) Vocal development in vervet monkeys. *Animal Behaviour, 34*, 1640–58.

Seyfarth, R. M. & Cheney, D. L. (2003a). Signalers and receivers in animal communication. *Annual Review of Psychology, 54*, 145–173.

Seyfarth, R. M. & Cheney, D. L. (2003b). Meaning and emotion in animal vocalizations. *Annals of the NewYork Acadamy of Science, 1000*, 32–55.

Seymour, B., Daw, N., Dayan, P., Singer, T., & Dolan, R. (2007). Differential encoding of losses and gains in the human striatum. *Journal of Neuroscience, 27*, 4826–4831.

Shackleton, E. H. (1919). *South*. London: William Heinemann.

Shadmehr, R., & Holcomb, H. H. (1997). Neural correlates of motor memory consolidation. *Science, 277*, 821–825.

Shallice, T., & Burgess, P. W. (1991). Deficits in strategy application following frontal lobe damage in man. *Brain, 114*, 727–741.

Shallice, T., Burgess, P. W., Schon, F., & Baxter, D. M. (1989). The origins of utilization behaviour. *Brain, 112*, 1587–1598.

Shallice, T., & Warrington, E. (1969). Independent functioning of verbal memory stores: A neuropsychological study. *Quarterly Journal of Experimental Psychology, 22*, 261–273.

Shams, L., Kamitani, Y., & Shimojo, S. (2000). Illusions. What you see is what you hear. *Nature, 408*, 788.

Shariff, G. A. (1953). Cell counts in the primate cerebral cortex. *Journal of Comparative Neurology, 98*, 381–400.

Sharot, T., Riccardi, A. M., Raio, C. M., & Phelps, E. A. (2007). Neural mechanisms mediating optimism bias. *Nature, 450*, 102–105.

Shaw, P., Greenstein, D., Lerch, J., Clasen, L., Lenroot, R., Gogtay, N., et al. (2006). Intellectual ability and cortical development in children and adolescents. *Nature, 440*, 676–679.

Shaw, P., Kabani, N. J, Lerch, J. P, Eckstrand, K, Lenroot, R., et al. (2008). Neurodevelopmental trajectories of the human cerebral cortex. *Journal of Neuroscience, 28*, 3586–3594.

Sheinberg, D. L., & Logothetis, N. K. (1997). The role of temporal cortical areas in perceptual organization. *Proceedings of the National Academy of Sciences, USA, 94*, 3408–3413.

Shepherd, G. M. (1991). *Foundations of the neuron doctrine*. New York: Oxford University Press.

Shepherd, G. M., Woolf, T. B., & Carnevale, N. T. L. (1989). Comparisons between active properties and distal dendritic branches and spines: Implications for neuronal computations. *Journal of Cognitive Neuroscience, 1*, 273–286.

Sherrington, C. S. (1935). Santiago Ramón y Cajal 1852–1934. *Obituary Notices of Fellows of the Royal Society, 4*, 425–441.

Sherrington, C. S. (1947). *The integrative action of the nervous system* (2nd ed.). New Haven, CT: Yale University Press.

Sherrington, C. S. (1953). *Man on his nature*. Cambridge: Cambridge University Press.

Shi, F., Yap, P.-T., Smith, J. K., Giovanello, K. S., Goerger, C., Lin, W., et al. (2011). Disrupted anatomical brain connectivity in retired professional football players. *Proceedings of the International Society of Magnetic Resonance Medicine, 19*, 347.

Shi, R., Werker, J. F., & Morgan, J. L. (1999). Newborn infants' sensitivity to perceptual cues to lexical and grammatical words. *Cognition, 72*(2), B11–21.

Shimamura, A. P. (2000). The role of the prefrontal cortex in dynamic filtering. *Psychobiology, 28*, 207–218.

Shimamura, A. P. (2011). Episodic retrieval and the cortical binding of relational activity. *Cognitive Affective Behavioral Neuroscience, 11*, 277–291.

Shipp, S. (2004). The brain circuitry of attention. *Trends in Cognitive Science, 8*(5), 223–230.

Shmuelop, L., & Zohary, E. (2006). Dissociation between ventral and dorsal fMRI activation during object and action recognition. *Neuron, 47*, 457–470.

Shors, T. J. (2004). Memory traces of trace memories: Neurogenesis, synaptogenesis and awareness. *Trends in Neurosciences, 27*, 250–256.

Shulman, G. L., Astafiev, S. V., Franke, D., Pope, D. L., Snyder, A. Z., McAvoy, M., et al. (2009). Interaction of stimulus-driven reorienting and expectation in ventral and dorsal frontoparietal and basal ganglia-cortical networks. *Journal of Neuroscience, 29*, 4392–4407.

Shulman, G. L., Pope, D. L., Astafiev, S. V., McAvoy, M. P., Snyder, A. Z., & Corbetta, M. (2010). Right hemisphere dominance during spatial selective attention and target detection occurs outside the dorsal frontoparietal network. *Journal of Neuroscience, 30*, 3640–3651.

Sidtis, J. J., Volpe, B. T., Holtzman, J. D., Wilson, D. H., & Gazzaniga, M. S. (1981). Cognitive interaction after staged callosal section: Evidence for transfer of semantic activation. *Science, 212*, 344–346.

Simion, F., Regolin, L. & Bulf, H. (2008). A predisposition for biological motion in the newborn baby. *Proceedings of the National Academy of Science USA, 105*, 809–813.

Simpson, J. (1988). *Touching the Void*. New York: HarperCollings.

SINGER, T., SEYMOUR, B., O'DOHERTY, J., KAUBE, H., DOLAN, R. J., & FRITH, C. D. (2004). Empathy for pain involves the affective but not sensory components of pain. *Science, 303,* 1157–1162.

SINGER, T., SEYMOUR, B., O'DOHERTY, J., STEFAN, K. E., DOLAN, R. J., & FRITH, C. D. (2006). Empathic neural responses are modulated by the perceived fairness of others. *Nature, 439*(7075), 466–469.

SINGER, W. (2000). Phenomenal awareness and consciousness from a neurobiological perspective. In T. Metzinger (Ed.), *Neural correlates of consciousness* (pp. 121–137). Cambridge, MA: MIT Press.

SLOANE, S., & BAILLARGEON, R. (2010). *2.5-Year-olds divide resources equally between two identical non-human agents.* Poster session presented at the annual meeting of the International Society of Infant Studies, Baltimore, MD.

SMALL, D. M., ZATORRE, R. J., DAGHER, A., EVANS, A. C., & JONES-GOTMAN, M. (2001). Changes in brain activity related to eating chocolate. *Brain, 124,* 1720–1733.

SMILEK, D., DIXON, M. J., & MERIKLE, P. M. (2005). Synaesthesia: Discordant male monozygotic twins. *Neurocase, 11,* 363–370.

SMITH, A. P. R., STEPHAN, K. E., RUGG, M. D., & DOLAN, R. J. (2006). Task and content modulate amygdala–hippocampal connectivity in emotional retrieval. *Neuron, 49,* 631–638.

SMITH, E. E., JONIDES, J., & KOEPPE, R. A. (1996). Dissociating verbal and spatial working memory using PET. *Cerebral Cortex, 6,* 11–20.

SNODGRASS, J. G., & VANDERWART, M. (1980). A standardized set of 260 pictures: Norms for name agreement, image agreement, familiarity, and visual complexity. *Journal of Experimental Psychology. Human Learning and Memory, 6,* 174–215.

SOBEL, N., PRABHAKARAN, V., DESMOND, J. E., GLOVER, G. H., GOODE, R. L., SULLIVAN, E. V., ET AL. (1998). Sniffing and smelling: Separate subsystems in the human olfactory cortex. *Nature, 392,* 282–286.

SOLOMAN, R. C. (2008). The philosophy of emotions. In M. Lewis, J. M. Haviland-Jones, & L. F. Barrett (Eds.), *The handbook of emotions* (3rd ed., pp. 1–16). New York: Guilford.

SOON, C. S., BRASS, M., HEINZE, H.-J., & HAYNES, J.-D. (2008). Unconscious determinants of free decision in the human brain. *Nature Neuroscience, 11*(5), 543–545.

SOUTHGATE, V., CHEVALLIER, C., & CSIBRA, G. (2010). Seventeen-month-olds appeal to false beliefs to interpret others' referential communication. *Developmental Science, 13,* 907–912.

SPELKE, E., HIRST, W., & NEISSER, U. (1976). Skills of divided attention. *Cognition, 4,* 215–230.

SPERRY, R. (1984). Consciousness, personal identity and the divided brain. *Neuropsychologia, 22,* 661–673.

SPERRY, R. W., GAZZANIGA, M. S., & BOGEN, J. E. (1969). Interhemispheric relationships: The neocortical commissures; syndromes of hemisphere disconnection. In P. J. Vinken & G. W. Bruyn (Eds.), *Handbook of clinical neurology* (Vol. 4, pp. 273–290). Amsterdam: North-Holland.

SPEZIO, M. L., ADOLPHS, R., HURLEY, R. S. E., & PIVEN, J. (2007). Analysis of face gaze in autism using "Bubbles." *Neuropsychologia, 45,* 144–151.

SQUIRE, L. R. (1992). Memory and the hippocampus: A synthesis from findings with rats, monkeys, and humans. *Psychology Review, 99,* 195–231.

SQUIRE, L. R., BLOOM, F. E., MCCONNELL, S. K., ROBERTS, J. L., SPITZER, N. C., & ZIGMOND, M. J. (EDS.). (2003). *Fundamental neuroscience* (2nd ed.). Amsterdam: Academic Press.

SQUIRE, L. R., & KNOWLTON, B. J. (1995). Memory, hippocampus, and brain systems. In M. S. Gazzaniga (Ed.), *The cognitive neurosciences* (pp. 825–837). Cambridge, MA: MIT Press.

SQUIRE, L. R., & SLATER, P. (1983). Electroconvulsive therapy and complaints of memory dysfunction: A prospective three-year follow-up study. *British Journal of Psychiatry, 142,* 1–8.

STAFF WORKING PAPER. (2004). An overview of the impact of neuroscience evidence in criminal law. *The President's Council on Bioethics.* Retrieved from http://bioethics.georgetown.edu/pcbe/background/neuroscience_evidence.html

STAGG, C. J., & NITSCHE, M. A. (2011). Physiological basis of transcranial direct current stimulation. *Neuroscientist, 17*(1), 37–53.

STEIN, B., & MEREDITH, M. (1993). The merging of the senses. Cambridge, MA: MIT Press.

STEIN, B. E., STANFORD, T. R., WALLACE, M. T., VAUGHAN, J. W., & JIANG, W. (2004). Crossmodal spatial interactions in subcortical and cortical circuits. In C. Spence & J. Driver (Eds.), *Crossmodal space and crossmodal attention* (pp. 25–50). Oxford: Oxford University Press.

STEIN, M. B., KOVEROLA, C., HANNA, C., TORCHIA, M. G., & MCCLARTY, B. (1997). Hippocampal volume in woman victimized by childhood sexual abuse. *Psychological Medicine, 27,* 951–959.

STEPHENS, G. J., SILBERT, L. J., & HASSON, U. (2010). Speaker-listener neural coupling underlies successful communication. *PNAS.* Retrieved from http://www.pnas.org/content/early/2010/07/13/1008662107.full

STERELNY, K. (2012). Language, gesture, skill: the co-evolutionary foundations of language. *Philosphical Transactions of the Royal Society B, 367*(1599), 2141–2151.

STERNBERG, S. (1966). High speed scanning in human memory. *Science, 153,* 652–654.

STERNBERG, S. (1975). Memory scanning: New findings and current controversies. *Quarterly Journal of Experimental Psychology, 27,* 1–32.

STEVEN, M. S., DORON, K. W., GAZZANIGA, M. S., & COLVIN, M. K. (2006). Subregion parcellation and topographic connectivity mapping of the human corpus callosum using diffusion tensor imaging. Poster presented at the Cognitive Neuroscience Society 2006 Annual Meeting. Cognitive Neuroscience Society Abstracts, No. A4.

STEVEN, M. S., & PASCUAL-LEONE, A. (2006). Transcranial magnetic stimulation and the human brain: An ethical evaluation. In J. Illes (Ed.), *Neuroethics: Defining the issues in theory, practice, and policy* (pp. 201–212). Oxford: Oxford University Press.

STEVENS, L. K., MCGRAW, P. V., LEDGEWY, T., & SCHLUPPECK, D. (2009). Temporal characteristics of global motion processing revealed by transcranial magnetic stimulation. *European Journal of Neuroscience, 30,* 2415–2426.

STONE, V. E., BARON-COHEN, S., & KNIGHT, R. T. (1998). Frontal lobe contributions to theory of mind. *Journal of Cognitive Neuroscience, 10,* 640–656.

STRATTON, G. M. (1896). Some preliminary experiments on vision without inversion of the retinal image. *Psychological Review, 3*(6), 611–617.

STRICK, P. L. (2002). Stimulating research on motor cortex. *Nature Neuroscience, 5,* 714–715.

STRIEDTER, G. F. (2005). *Principles of brain evolution.* Sunderland, MA: Sinauer.

STROOP, J. (1935). Studies of interference in serial verbal reaction. *Journal of Experimental Psychology, 18,* 643–662.

STROMSWOLD, K., CAPLAN, D., ALPERT, N., & RAUCH S. (1996). Localization of syntactic comprehension by positron emission tomography. *Brain and Language, 52,* 452–473.

STUSS, D. T., LEVINE, B., ALEXANDER, M. P., HONG, J., PALUMBO, C., HAMER, L., ET AL. (2000). Wisconsin Card Sorting Test performance in patients with focal frontal and posterior brain damage: Effects of lesion location and test structure on separable cognitive processes. *Neuropsychologia, 38,* 388–402.

SUAREZ, S. D., & GALLUP, G. G., JR. (1981). Self-recognition in chimpanzees and orangutans, but not gorillas. *Journal of Human Evolution, 10,* 175–188.

Sun, F. T., Miller, L. M., & D'Esposito, M. (2004). Measuring interregional functional connectivity using coherence and partial coherence analyses of fMRI data. *NeuroImage, 21*, 647–658.

Sutherland, S. (1995). Consciousness. *The international dictionary of psychology* (2nd ed.). London: Macmillan.

Suzuki, W. A. & Amaral, D. G. (1994). Perirhinal and parahippocampal cortices of the macaque monkey: cortical afferents. *Journal of Comparative Neurology, 350*, 497–533.

Swaab, T. Y., Brown, C. M., & Hagoort, P. (1997). Spoken sentence comprehension in aphasia: Event-related potential evidence for a lexical integration deficit. *Journal of Cognitive Neuroscience, 9*, 39–66.

Swanson, L. W. (1983). The hippocampus and the concept of the limbic system. In W. Seifert (Ed.), *Neurobiology of the hippocampus* (pp. 3–19). London: Academic Press.

Swanson, L. W., & Petrovich, G. D. (1998). What is the amygdala? *Trends in Neurosciences, 21*, 323–331.

Swartz, K. B. (1997). What is mirror self-recognition in nonhuman primates, and what is it not? *Annals of the New York Academy of Sciences, 818*, 64–71.

Sweet, W. H., & Brownell, G. L. (1953). Localization of brain tumors with positron emitters. *Nucleonics, 11*, 40–45.

Talairach, J., & Tournoux, P. (1988). *Co-planar stereotaxic atlas of the human brain: 3-Dimensional proportional system—an approach to cerebral imaging.* New York: Thieme Medical Publishers.

Tamir, D. I. & Mitchell, J. (2011). The default network distinguishes construals of proximal versus distal events. *The Journal of Cognitive Neuroscience, 23*(10), 2945–2955.

Tanaka, J. W., & Farah, M. J. (1993). Parts and wholes in face recognition. *Quarterly Journal of Experimental Psychology. A:, Human Experimental Psychology, 46*, 225–245.

Tanaka, S. C., Schweighofer, N., Asahi, S., Shishida, K., Okamoto, Y., Yamawaki, S., et al. (2007). Serotonin differentially regulates short and long-term prediction of rewards in the ventral and dorsal striatum. *PLoS One, 2*, e1333.

Tarr, M. J., Buelthoff, H. H., Zabinski, M., & Blanz, V. (1997). To what extent do unique parts influence recognition across changes in viewpoint? *Psychological Science, 8*, 282–289.

Tarr, M. J., & Gauthier, I. (2000). FFA: A flexible fusiform area for subordinate-level visual processing automatized by expertise. *Nature Neuroscience, 3*, 764–769.

Taub, E., & Berman, A. J. (1968). Movement and learning in the absence of sensory feedback. In S. J. Freedman (Ed.), *The neuropsychology of spatially oriented behavior* (pp. 173–191). Homewood, IL: Dorsey.

Taylor, C. T., Wiggett, A. J., & Downing, P. E. (2007). Functional MRI analysis of body and body part representations in the extrastriate and fusiform body areas. *Journal of Neurophysiology, 98*, 1626–1633.

Taylor, D. M., Tillery, S. I., & Schwartz, A. B. (2002). Direct cortical control of 3D neuroprosthetic devices. *Science, 296*, 1829–1832.

Taylor, S. E., & Brown, J. D. (1988). Illusion and well-being: A social psychological perspective on mental health. *Psychological Bulletin, 103*, 193–210.

Teather, L. A., Packard, M. G., & Bazan, N. G. (1998). Effects of posttraining intrahippocampal injections of platelet-activating factor and PAF antagonists on memory. *Neurobiology of Learning and Memory, 70*, 349–363.

Templeton, C. N., Greene, E., & Davis, K. (2005). Allometry of alarm calls: black-capped chickadees encode information about predator size. *Science, 308*, 1934–1937.

Tennie, C., Call, J., & Tomasello, M. (2006). Push or pull: Imitation versus emulation in human children and great apes. *Ethology, 112*, 1159–1169.

Tennie, C., Call, J., & Tomasello, M. (2010). Evidence for emulation in chimpanzees in social settings using the floating peanut task. *PLoS One, 5*(5), e10544. doi:10.1371/journal.pone.0010544

Ter-Pogossian, M. M., Phelps, M. E., & Hoffman, E. J. (1975). A positron emission transaxial tomograph for nuclear medicine imaging (PETT). *Radiology, 114*, 89–98.

Ter-Pogossian, M. M., & Powers, W. E. (1958). The use of radioactive oxygen-15 in the determination of oxygen content in malignant neoplasms. In *Radioisotopes in scientific research*, Vol. 3. *Proceedings of the 1st UNESCO International Conference, Paris*. New York: Pergamon Press.

Thibault, C., Lai, C., Wilke, N., Duong, B., Olive, M. F., Rahman, S., et al. (2000). Expression profiling of neural cells reveals specific patterns of ethanol-responsive gene expression. *Molecular Pharmacology, 58*, 1593–1600.

Thiebaut de Schotten, M., Dell'Acqua, F., Valabregue, R., & Catani, M. (2012). Monkey to human comparative anatomy of the frontal lobe association tracts. *Cortex, 48*(1), 82–96.

Thompson, P. (1980). Margaret Thatcher: A new illusion. *Perception, 9*, 483–483.

Thompson, R. F. (2000). *The brain: A neuroscience primer* (3rd ed.). New York: Freeman.

Thompson-Schill, S. L., D'Esposito, M., Aguirre, G. K., & Farah, M. J. (1997). Role of left inferior prefrontal cortex in retrieval of semantic knowledge: A reevaluation. *Proceedings of the National Academy of Sciences, USA, 94*, 14792–14797.

Thompson-Schill, S. L., D'Esposito, M., & Kan, I. P. (1999). Effects of repetition and competition on activity in left prefrontal cortex during word generation. *Neuron, 23*, 513–522.

Thompson-Schill, S. L., Swick, D., Farah, M. J., D'Esposito, M., Kan, I. P., & Knight, R. T. (1998). Verb generation in patients with focal frontal lesions: A neuropsychological test of neuroimaging findings. *Proceedings of the National Academy of Sciences, USA, 95*, 15855–15860.

Thorndike, E. (1911). *Animal intelligence: An experimental study of the associative processes in animals.* New York: MacMillan.

Thulborn, K. R., Waterton, J. C., Matthews, P. M., & Radda, G. K. (1982). Oxygenation dependence of the transverse relaxation time of water protons in whole blood at high field. *Biochimica et Biophysica Acta, 714*, 265–270.

Thut, G., Nietzel, A., & Pascual-Leone, A. (2005). Dorsal posterior parietal rTMS affects voluntary orienting of visual-spatial attention. *Cerebral Cortex, 15*(5), 628–638.

Tignor, R. L. (2008). *Worlds together, worlds apart: A history of the world from the beginnings of humankind to the present* (2nd ed.). New York: Norton.

Tobler, P. N., Fiorillo, C. D., & Schultz, W. (2005). Adaptive coding of reward value by dopamine neurons. *Science, 307*, 1642–1645.

Tom, S. M., Fox, C. R., Trepel, C., & Poldrack, R. A. (2007). The neural basis of loss aversion in decision-making under risk. *Science, 315*(5811), 515–518.

Tomasello, M. (2007). If they are so good at grammar, then why don't they talk? Hints from apes and humans' use of gestures. *Language Learning and Development, 3*, 1–24.

Tomasello, M., Carpenter, M., Call, J., Behne, T., & Moll, H. (2005). Understanding and sharing intentions: The origins of cultural cognition. *Behavioral and Brain Sciences, 28*, 675–735.

Tomasello, M., Hare, B., Lehmann, H., & Call, J. (2007). Reliance on head versus eyes in the gaze following of great apes and human infants: The cooperative eye hypothesis. *Journal of Human Evolution, 52*, 314–320.

TOOLEY, K., TRAXLER, M., & SWAAB, T. (2009). Electrophysiological and behavioral evidence of syntactic priming in sentence comprehension. *Journal of Experimental Psychology: Language, Memory and Cognition, 35,* 19–45.

TOOTELL, R. B., HADJIKHANI, N., HALL, E. K., MARRETT, S., VANDUFFEL, W., VAUGHAN, J. T., ET AL. (1998). The retinotopy of visual spatial attention. *Neuron, 21,* 1409–1422.

TOOTELL, R. B., SILVERMAN, M. S., SWITKES, E., & DEVALOIS, R. L. (1982). Deoxyglucose analysis of retinotopic organization in primate striate cortex. *Science, 218,* 902–904.

TOSONI, A., GALATI, G., ROMANI, G. L., & CORBETTA, M. (2008). Sensory-motor mechanisms in human parietal cortex underlie arbitrary visual decisions. *Nature Neuroscience, 11,* 1446–1453.

TRACY, J., & MATSUMOTO, D. (2008). The spontaneous expression of pride and shame: Evidence for biologically innate nonverbal displays. *Proceedings of the National Academy of Science, USA, 105,* 11655–11660.

TRANEL, D., & HYMAN, B. T. (1990). Neuropsychological correlates of bilateral amygdala damage. *Archives of Neurology, 47,* 349–355.

TREISMAN, A. M. (1969). Strategies and models of selective attention. *Psychological Review, 76,* 282–299.

TREISMAN, A. (1991). Search, similarity, and integration of features between and within dimensions. *Journal of Experimental Psychology: Human Perception and Performance, 17,* 652–676.

TREISMAN, A., & GELADE, G. (1980). A feature-integration theory of attention. *Cognitive Psychology, 12,* 97–136.

TRIVERS, R. L. (1971). The evolution of reciprocal altruism. *Quarterly Review of Biology, 46,* 35–57.

TRIVERS, R. L. (2011). *The folly of fools: The logic of deceit and self-deception in human life.* New York: Penguin.

TRUT, L. (1999). Early canid domestication: The farm-fox experiment. *American Scientist, 87,* 160–169.

TRUT, L. OSKINA, I., & KHARLAMOVA, A. (2009). Animal evolution during domestication: The domesticated fox as a model. *BioEssays, 31*(3), 349–360.

TSAO, D. Y., FREIWALD, W. A., TOOTELL, R. B., & LIVINGSTONE, M. S. (2006). A cortical region consisting entirely of face-selective cells. *Science, 311,* 670–674.

TULVING, E. (1993). Self-knowledge of an amnesiac individual is represented abstractly. In T. K. Srull & R. S. Wyer (Eds.), *The mental representation of trait and autobiographical knowledge about the self* (pp. 147–156). Hillsdale, NJ: Erlbaum.

TULVING, E., HAYMAN, C. A., & MACDONALD, C. A. (1991). Long-lasting perceptual priming and semantic learning in amnesia. A case experiment. *Journal of Experimental Psychology, 17,* 595–617.

TULVING, E., KAPUR, S., CRAIK, F. I. M., MOSCOVITCH, M., & HOULE, S. (1994). Hemispheric encoding/retrieval asymmetry in episodic memory: Positron emission tomography findings. *Proceedings of the National Academy of Sciences, USA, 91,* 2016–2020.

TULVING, E., & SHACTER, D. L. (1990). Priming and human memory systems. *Science, 7,* 1–306.

TURIN, L. (1996). A spectroscopic mechanism for primary olfactory reception. *Chemical Senses, 21,* 773–791.

TURK, D. J. (2002). Mike or me? Self-recognition in a split-brain patient. *Nature Neuroscience, 5,* 841–842.

TVERSKY, A., & KAHNEMAN, D. (1988). Rational choice and the framing of decisions. In E. D. Bell, H. Raiffa, & A. Tversky (Eds.), *Decision making: Descriptive, normative, and prescriptive interactions* (pp. 167–192). Cambridge: Cambridge University Press.

TYE, K. M., PRAKASH, R., KIM, S.-Y., FENNO, L. E., GROSENICK, L., ZARABI, H., ET AL. (2011). Amygdala circuitry mediating reversible and bidirectional control of anxiety. *Nature, 471*(7338), 358–362.

TYLER, L. K. MARSLEN-WILSON, W. D., RANDALL, B., WRIGHT, P., DEVEREUX, B. J., ZHUANG, J., PAPOUTSI, M., & STAMATAKIS, E. A. (2011). Left inferior frontal cortex and syntax: function, structure and behaviour in patients with left hemisphere damage. *Brain, 134,* 415–431.

UMILTA, M. A., KOHLER, E., GALLESE, V., FOGASSI, L., FADIGA, L., KEYSERS, C., ET AL. (2001). I know what you are doing: A neurophysiological study. *Neuron, 31,* 155–165.

UNGERLEIDER, L. G., & MISHKIN, M. (1982). Two cortical visual systems. In D. J. Engle, M. A. Goodale, & R. J. Mansfield (Eds.), *Analysis of visual behavior* (pp. 549–586). Cambridge, MA: MIT Press.

VAISH, A., CARPENTER, M., & TOMASELLO, M. (2010). *Moral mediators of young children's prosocial behavior toward victims and perpetrators.* Poster session presented at the annual meeting of the International Society of Infant Studies, Baltimore, MD.

VALENSTEIN, E. S. (1986). *Great and desperate cures: The rise and decline of psychosurgery and other radical treatments for mental illness.* New York: Basic Books.

VALLAR, G., & PERANI, D. (1986). The anatomy of unilateral neglect after right-hemisphere stroke lesions. A clinical/CT-scan correlation study in man. *Neuropsychologia, 24,* 609–622.

VAN DEN HEUVEL, M. P., STAM, C. J., KAHN, R. S., & HULSHOFF POL, H. E. (2009). Efficiency of functional brain networks and intellectual performance. *Journal of Neuroscience, 29,* 7619–7624.

VANDER, A., SHERMAN, J., & LUCIANO, D. (2001). *Human physiology: The mechanisms of body function* (8th ed.). Boston: McGraw-Hill.

VANDUFFEL, W., TOOTELL, R. B. H., & ORBAN, G. G. (2000). Attention-dependent suppression of metabolic activity in the early stages of the macaque visual System *Cerebral Cortex, 10*(2), 109–126.

VAN KOOTEN, I. A., PALMEN, S. J., VON CAPPELN, P., STEINBUSCH, H. W., KORR, H., HEINSEN, H., ET AL. (2008). Neurons in the fusiform gyrus are fewer and smaller in autism. *Brain, 131,* 987–999.

VAN TURENNOUT, M., HAGOORT, P., & BROWN, C. M. (1999). Brain activity during speaking: From syntax to phonology in 40 milliseconds. *Science, 280,* 572–574.

VAN WAGENEN, W. P., & HERREN, R. Y. (1940). Surgical division of commissural pathways in the corpus callosum: Relation to spread of an epileptic seizure. *Archives of Neurology and Psychiatry, 44,* 740–759.

VARGHA-KHADEM, F., GADIAN, D. G., COPP, A., & MISHKIN, M. (2005). FOXP2 and the neuroanatomy of speech and language. *Nature Reviews Neuroscience, 6,* 131–138.

VARGHA-KHADEM, F., GADIAN, D. G., WATKINS, K. E., CONNELLY, A., VAN PAESSCHEN, W., & MISHKIN, M. (1997). Differential effects of early hippocampal pathology on episodic and semantic memory. *Science, 277,* 376–380.

VARGHA-KHADEM, F., WATKINS, K., ALCOCK, K., FLETCHER, P., & PASSINGHAM, R. (1995). Praxic and nonverbal cognitive deficits in a large family with a genetically transmitted speech and language disorder. *Proceedings of the National Academy of Science, USA, 92,* 930–933.

VELLISTE, M., PEREL, S., SPALDING, M. C., WHITFORD, A. S., & SCHWARTZ, A. B. (2008). Cortical control of a prosthetic arm for self-feeding. *Nature. 453,* 1098–1101.

VERDON, V., SCHWARTZ, S., LOVBLAD, K. O., HAUERT, C. A., & VUILLEUMIER, P. (2010). Neuroanatomy of hemispatial neglect and its functional components: A study using voxel-based lesion-symptom mapping. *Brain, 133,* 880–894.

VIJAYRAGHAVAN, S., WANG, M., BIRNBAUM, S. G., BRUCE, C. J., WILLIAMS, G. V., & ARNSTEN, A. F. T. (2007). Inverted-U dopamine D1 receptor actions on prefrontal neurons engaged in working memory. *Nature Neuroscience, 10,* 376–384.

VILBERG, K. L., & RUGG, M. D. (2008). Memory retrieval and the parietal cortex: A review of evidence from a dual-process perspective. *Neuropsychologia, 46,* 1787–1799.

VITALI, P., MIGLIACCIO, R., AGOSTA, F., ROSEN, H. J., & GESCHWIND, M. D. (2008). Neuroimaging in dementia. *Seminars in Neurology, 28*(4), 467–483.

Vohs, K. D., & Schooler, J. W. (2008). The value in believing in free will: Encouraging a belief in determinism increases cheating. *Psychological Science*, 19(1), 49–54.

Volfovsky, N., Parnas, H., Segal, M., & Korkotian, E. (1999). Geometry of dendritic spines affects calcium dynamics in hippocampal neurons: Theory and experiments. *Journal of Neurophysiology*, 82, 450–462.

Volpe, B. T., LeDoux, J. E., & Gazzaniga, M. S. (1979). Information processing of visual field stimuli in an "extinguished" field. *Nature*, 282, 722–724.

Vuilleumier, P., Armony, J. L., Driver, J., & Dolan, R. J. (2001). Effects of attention and emotion on face processing in the human brain: An event-related fMRI study. *Neuron*, 30, 829–841.

Vuilleumier, P., Henson, R. N., Driver, J., & Dolan, R. J. (2002). Multiple levels of visual object constancy revealed by event-related fMRI of repetition priming. *Nature Neuroscience*, 5, 491–499.

Vuilleumier, P., Richardson, M. P., Armony, J. L., Driver, J., & Dolan, R. J. (2004). Distant influences of amygdala lesion on visual cortical activation during emotional face processing. *Nature Neuroscience*, 7, 1271–1278.

Vytal, K., & Hamann, S. (2010). Neuroimaging support for discrete neural correlates of basic emotions: A voxel-based meta-analysis. *Journal of Cognitive Neuroscience*, 22(12), 2864–2885.

Wade, N. (2003, October 7). American and Briton win Nobel for using chemists' test for M.R.I.'s. *New York Times*.

Wager, T. D., & Smith, E. E. (2003). Neuroimaging studies of working memory: A meta-analysis. *Cognitive, Affective & Behavioral Neuroscience*, 3, 255–274.

Wagner, A., Shannon, B. J., Kahn, I., & Buckner, R. L. (2005). Parietal lobe contributions to episodic memory retrieval. *Trends in Cognitive Sciences*, 9(9), 445–453.

Wagner, A. D., Schacter, D. L., Rotte, M., Koutstaal, W., Maril, A., Dale, A. M., et al. (1998). Building memories: Remembering and forgetting of verbal experiences as predicted by brain activity. *Science*, 281, 1188–1191.

Wagner, G. P., Pavlicev, M., & Cheverud, J. M. (2007). The road to modularity. *Nature Reviews Genetics*, 8, 921–931.

Walker, E. P. (1983). *Walker's mammals of the world* (4th ed., Vol. 1). Baltimore, MD: Johns Hopkins University Press.

Wang, A. T., Lee, S. S., Sigman, M., & Dapretto, M. (2007). Reading affect in the face and voice: Neural correlates of interpreting communicative intent in children and adolescents with autism spectrum disorders. *Archives of General Psychiatry*, 64, 698–708.

Wang, X. T. (1996). Domain-specific rationality in human choices: Violations of utility axioms and social contexts. *Cognition*, 60, 31–63.

Wapner, W., Judd, T., & Gardner, H. (1978). Visual agnosia in an artist. *Cortex*, 14, 343–364.

Warrington, E. K. (1982). Neuropsychological studies of object recognition. *Philosophical Transactions of the Royal Society of London, Series B: Biological Sciences*, 298, 13–33.

Warrington, E. K. (1985). Agnosia: The impairment of object recognition. In P. J. Vinken, G. W. Bruyn, & H. L. Klawans (Eds.), *Handbook of clinical neurology* (pp. 333–349). New York: Elsevier.

Warrington, E. K., & McCarthy, R. A. (1994). Multiple meaning systems in the brain: A case for visual semantics. *Neuropsychologia*, 32, 1465–1473.

Warrington, E. K. & Rabin, P. (1970). Perceptual matching in patients with cerebral lesions. *Neuropsychologia*, 8, 475–487.

Warrington, E. K., & Shallice, T. (1984). Category specific semantic impairments. *Brain*, 107, 829–854.

Warrington, E. K., & Taylor, A. M. (1978). Two categorical stages of object recognition. *Perception*, 7, 695–705.

Watts, D. J., & Strogatz, S. H. (1998). Collective dynamics of "small-world" networks. *Nature*, 393, 440–442.

Weeks, S. J. & Hobson., R. P. (1987). The salience of facial expression for autistic children. *Journal of Child Psychology and Psychiatry*, 28(1), 137–152.

Wegiel, J., Krzysztof, I., Nowicki, K., Imaki, H., Wegiel, J., Marchi, E., et al. (2010). The neuropathology of autism: Defects of neurogenesis and neuronal migration, and dysplastic changes. *Acta Neuropathologica*, 119, 755–770.

Weickert, T. W., Goldberg, T. E., Mishara, A., Apud, J. A., Kolachana, B. S., Egan, M. F., et al. (2004). Catechol-O-methyltransferase val108/158met genotype predicts working memory response to antipsychotic medications. *Biological Psychiatry*, 56, 677–682.

Weierich, M. R., Wright, C. I., Negreira, A., Dickerson, B. C., & Barrett, L. F. (2010). Novelty as a dimension in the affective brain. *NeuroImage*, 49, 2871–2878.

Weinberger, D. R. (1988). Schizophrenia and the frontal lobes. *Trends in Neurosciences*, 11, 367–370.

Weinberger, N. M. (1995). Retuning the brain by fear conditioning. In M.S.Gazzaniga (Ed.), *The cognitive neurosciences* (pp. 1071–1089). Cambridge, MA: The MIT Press.

Weisberg, D. S., Keil, F. C., Goodstein, J., Rawson, E., & Gray, J. R. (2008). The seductive allure of neuroscience explanations. *Journal of Cognitive Neuroscience*, 20, 470–477.

Weiskrantz, L. (1956). Behavioral changes associated with ablation of the amygdaloid complex in monkeys. *Journal of Comparative and Physiological Psychology*, 49, 381–391.

Weiskrantz, L. (1974).Visual capacity in the hemianopic field following a restricted occipital ablation. *Brain*, 97, 709–728.

Weiskrantz, L. (1986). *Blindsight: A case study and implications*. Oxford: Oxford University Press.

Weller, W. L. (1993). SmI cortical barrels in an Australian marsupial, *Trichosurus vulpecula* (brush-tailed possum): Structural organization, patterned distribution, and somatotopic relationships. *Journal of Comparative Neurology*, 337, 471–492.

Werker, J. F. & Tees, R. C. (1999). Influences on infant speech processing: toward a new synthesis. *Annual Review of Psychology*, 50, 509–535.

Wernicke C. (1876). Das Urwindungssystem des menschlichen Gehirns. *Archiv für Psychiatrie und Nervenkrankheiten*, 6, 298–326.

Wessinger, C. M., Buonocore, M. H., Kussmaul, C. L., & Mangun, G. R. (1997). Tonotopy in human auditory cortex examined with functional magnetic resonance imaging. *Human Brain Mapping*, 5, 18–25.

Whalen, P. J. (2007). The uncertainty of it all. *Trends in Cognitive Sciences*, 11, 499–500.

Whalen, P. J., Kagan, J., Cook, R. G., Davis, F. C., Kim, H., Polis, S., et al. (2004). Human amygdala responsivity to masked fearful eye whites. *Science*, 306, 2061.

Whalen, P. J., Rauch, S. L., Etcoff, N. L., McInerney, S. C., Lee, M. B., & Jenike, M. A. (1998). Masked presentations of emotional facial expressions modulate amygdala activity without explicit knowledge. *Journal of Neuroscience*, 18, 411–418.

Wheeler, E. Z., & Fellows, L. K. (2008). The human ventromedial frontal lobe is critical for learning from negative feedback. *Brain*, 131(5), 1323–1331.

Wheeler, M. A., Stussl, D. T., & Tulving, E. (1997). Toward a theory of episodic memory: The frontal lobes and autonoetic consciousness. *Psychological Bulletin*, 121, 331–354.

Wheeler, M. E., Petersen, S. E., & Buckner, R. L. (2000). Memory's echo: Vivid remembering reactivates sensory-specific cortex. *Proceedings of the National Academy of Sciences, USA*, 97, 11125–11129.

WHEELER, M. E., SHULMAN, G. L., BUCKNER, R. L., MIEZIN, F. M., VELANOVA, K., & PETERSEN, S. E. (2006). Evidence for separate perceptual reactivation and search processes during remembering. *Cerebral Cortex, 16*, 949–959.

WICHMANN, T., & DELONG, M. R. (1996). Functional and pathophysiological models of the basal ganglia. *Current Opinion in Neurobiology, 6*, 751–758.

WICKELGREN, W. A. (1974). *How to solve problems.* San Francisco: Freeman.

WICKER, B., KEYSERS, C., PLAILLY, J., ROYET, J.-P., GALLESE, V., & RIZZOLATTI, G. (2003). Both of us disgusted in my insula: The common neural basis of seeing and feeling disgust. *Neuron, 40*, 655–664.

WIESENDANGER, M., ROUILLER, E. M., KAZENNIKOV, O., & PERRIG, S. (1996). Is the supplementary motor area a bilaterally organized system? *Advances in Neurology, 70*, 85–93.

WILLIAMS, G. C. (1966). *Adaptation and natural selection.* Princeton, NJ: Princeton University Press.

WILLIAMS, J. H., WHITEN, A., & SINGH, T. (2004). A systematic review of action imitation in autistic spectrum disorder. *Journal of Autism and Developmental Disorders, 34*, 285–299.

WILLIAMSON, A., SPENCER, D. D., & SHEPHERD, G. M. (1993). Comparisons between the membrane and synaptic properties of human and rodent dentate granule cells. *Brain Research, 622*, 194–202.

WILLIS, J., & TODOROV, A. (2006). First impressions: Making up your mind after a 100-ms exposure to a face. *Psychological Science, 17*, 592–598.

WILSON, E. O. (1975). *Sociobiology, the new synthesis.* Cambridge, MA: Belknap Press of Harvard University Press.

WILSON, F. A., SCALAIDHE, S. P., & GOLDMAN-RAKIC, P. S. (1993). Dissociation of object and spatial processing domains in primate prefrontal cortex. *Science, 260*, 1955–1958.

WILSON, M. A., & MCNAUGHTON, B. L. (1994). Reactivation of hippocampal ensemble memories during sleep. *Science, 265*, 676–679.

WILSON, M. A., & TONEGAWA, S. (1997). Synaptic plasticity, place cells, and spatial memory: Study with second generation knockouts. *Trends in Neurosciences, 20*, 102–106.

WILSON, S. M., GALANTUCCI, S., TARTAGLIA, M. C., & GORNO-TEMPINI, M. L. (2012). The neural basis of syntactic deficits in primary progressive aphasia. *Brain and Language.* http://dx.doi.org/10.1016/j.bandl.2012.04.005

WILTGEN, B. J., & SILVA, A. J. (2007). Memory for context becomes less specific with time. *Learning and Memory, 14*, 313–317.

WISE, R. J. (2003). Language systems in normal and aphasic human subjects: Functional imaging studies and inferences from animal studies. *British Medical Bulletin, 65*, 95–119.

WISE, S. P., DI PELLEGRINO, G., & BOUSSAOUD, D. (1996). The premotor cortex and nonstandard sensorimotor mapping. *Canadian Journal of Physiology and Pharmacology, 74*, 469–482.

WITELSON, S. F., KIGAR, D. L., & HARVEY, T. (1999). The exceptional brain of Albert Einstein. *Lancet, 353*, 2149–2153.

WITHERS, G. S., GEORGE, J. M., BANKER, G. A., & CLAYTON, D. F. (1997). Delayed localization of synelfin (synuclein, NACP) to presynaptic terminals in cultured rat hippocampal neurons. *Brain Research. Developmental Brain Research, 99*, 87–94.

WOLDORFF, M. G., GALLEN, C. C., HAMPSON, S. A., HILLYARD, S. A., PANTEV, C., SOBEL, D., ET AL. (1993). Modulation of early sensory processing in human auditory cortex during auditory selective attention. *Proceedings of the National Academy of Sciences, USA, 90*, 8722–8726.

WOLDORFF, M. G., HAZLETT, C. J., FICHTENHOLTZ, H. M., WEISSMAN, D. H., DALE, A. M., & SONG, A. W. (2004). Functional parcellation of attentional control regions of the brain. *Journal of Cognitive Neuroscience, 16*(1), 149–165.

WOLDORFF, M. G., & HILLYARD, S. A. (1991). Modulation of early auditory processing during selective listening to rapidly presented tones. *Electroencephalography and Clinical Neurophysiology, 79*, 170–191.

WOLF, S. L., WINSTEIN, C. J., MILLER, J. M., THOMPSON, P. A., TAUB, E., USWATTE, G., ET AL. (2008). Retention of upper limb function in stroke survivors who have received constraint-induced movement therapy: The EXCITE randomised trial. *Lancet Neurology, 7*, 33–40.

WOLFE, J. M., ALVAREZ, G. A., & HOROWITZ, T. S. (2000). Attention is fast but volition is slow. *Nature, 406*, 691.

WOLFORD, G., MILLER, M. B., & GAZZANIGA, M. (2000). The left hemisphere's role in hypothesis formation. *Journal of Neuroscience, 20*, RC64. Retrieved from http://www.jneurosci.org/cgi/content/full/20/6/RC64

WOLPAW, J. R., LOEB, G. E., ALLISON, B. Z., DONCHIN. E., DO NASCIMENTO, O. F., HEETDERKS, W. J., ET AL. (2006). BCI Meeting 2005—Workshop on signals and recording methods. *IEEE Transactions on Neural Systems and Rehabilitation Engineering, 14*, 138–141.

WOLPERT, D. M., MIALL, R. C., & KAWATO, M. (1998). Internal models in the cerebellum. *Trends in Cognitive Science, 2*, 338–347.

WOODARD, J. S. (1973). *Histologic neuropathology: A color slide set.* Orange: California Medical Publications.

WOOD, E. R., DUDCHENKO, P. A., & EICHENBAUM, H. (1999). The globalrecord of memory in hippocampal neuronal activity. *Nature, 397*, 613–616.

WOOLSEY, C. N. (1952). Pattern of localization in sensory and motor areas of the cerebral cortex. In *The biology of mental health and disease* (pp. 193–225). New York: Hoeber.

WOOLSEY, C. N. (1958). Organization of somatic sensory and motor areas of the cerebral cortex. In H. F. Harlow & C. N. Woolsey (Eds.), *Biological and biochemical bases of behavior* (pp. 63–81). Madison: University of Wisconsin Press.

WOOLSEY, T. A., WELKER, C., & SCHWARTZ, R. H. (1975). Comparative anatomical studies of the SmI face cortex with special reference to the occurrence of "barrels" in layer IV. *Journal of Comparative Neurology, 164*, 79–94.

WRIGHT, C. I., NEGREIRA, A., GOLD, A. L., BRITTON, J. C., WILLIAMS, D., & BARRETT, L. F. (2008). Neural correlates of novelty and face-age effects in young and elderly adults. *NeuroImage, 42*, 956–968.

WURTZ, R. H., GOLDBERG, M. E., & ROBINSON, D. L. (1982). Brain mechanisms of visual attention. *Scientific American, 246*(6), 124–135.

XU, Y., LIU, J., & KANWISHER, N. (2005). The M170 is selective for faces, not for expertise. *Neuropsychologia, 43*, 588–597.

XUE, G., LU, Z., LEVIN, I. P., & BECHARA, A. (2010). The impact of prior risk experiences on subsequent risky decision-making: The role of the insula. *NeuroImage, 50*, 709–716.

YACOUB, E., HAREL, N., & UǦURBIL, K. (2008). High-field fMRI unveils orientation columns in humans. *Proceedings of the National Academy of Sciences, 105*(30), 10607–10612.

YIN, H. H. & KNOWLTON, B. J. (2006). The role of the basal ganglia in habit formation. *Nature, 7*, 464–476.

YIN, H. H., ZHUANG, X., & BALLEINE, B. W. (2006b). Instrumental learning in hyperdopaminergic mice. *Neurobiology of Learning and Memory, 3*, 238–283.

YINGLING, C. D., & SKINNER, J. E. (1976). Selective regulation of thalamic sensory relay nuclei by nucleus reticularis thalami. *Electroencephalography and Clinical Neurophysiology, 41*, 476–482.

YONELINAS, A., KROLL, N., DOBBINS, I., LAZZARA, M., & KNIGHT, R. T. (1998). Recollection and familiarity deficits in amnesia: Convergence of remember-know, process dissociation, and receiver operating characteristic data. *Neuropsychology, 12*, 323–339.

ZAJONC, R. B. (1984). On the primacy of affect. *American Psychologist, 39*, 117–123.

ZAKI, J., & OCHSNER, K. (2011). Reintegrating the study of accuracy into social cognition research. *Psychological Inquiry, 22*, 159–182.

ZAMANILLO, D., SPRENGEL, R., HVALBY, O., JENSEN, V., BURNASHEV, N., ROZOV, A., ET AL. (1999). Importance of AMPA receptors for hippocampal synaptic plasticity but not for spatial learning. *Science, 284*, 1805–1811.

ZANGALADZE, A., EPSTEIN, C. M., GRAFTON, S. T., & SATHIAN, K. (1999). Involvement of visual cortex in tactile discrimination of orientation. *Nature, 401*, 587–590.

ZANTO, T. P., RUBENS, M. T., THANGAVEL, A., & GAZZALEY, A. (2011). Causal role of the prefrontal cortex in top-down modulation of visual processing and working memory. *Nature Neuroscience, 14*(5), 656–663.

ZAREI, M., JOHANSEN-BERG, H., SMITH, S., CICCARELLI, O., THOMPSON, A. J., & MATTHEWS, P. M. (2006). Functional anatomy of interhemispheric cortical connections in the human brain. *Journal of Anatomy, 209*(3), 311–320.

ZARKOS, J. (2004). Raising the bar. *Sun Valley Guide.* Retrieved from http://www.svguide.com/s04/s04_fosburyflop.htm

ZEMELMAN, B. V., LEE, G. A., NG, M., & MIESENBÖCK, G. (2002). Selective photostimulation of genetically chARGed neurons. *Neuron, 33*(1), 15–22.

ZEKI, S. (1993a). The mystery of Louis Verrey. *Gesnerus, 50*, 96–112.

ZEKI, S. (1993b). *A vision of the brain.* Oxford, England: Blackwell.

ZHANG, J., WEBB, D. M., & PODLAHA, O. (2002). Accelerated protein evolution and origins of human-specific features: Foxp2 as an example. *Genetics, 162*, 1825–1835.

ZHANG, W., & LUCK, S. J. (2009). Feature-based attention modulates feedforward visual processing. *Nature Neuroscience, 12*, 24–25.

ZHU, Q., SONG, Y., HU, S., LI, X., TIAN, M., ZHEN, Z., ET AL. (2010). Heritability of the specific cognitive ability of face perception. *Current Biology, 20*(2), 137–142.

ZIEMANN, U., MUELLBACHER, W., HALLETT, M., & COHEN, L. G. (2001). Full text modulation of practice-dependent plasticity in human motor cortex. *Brain, 124*, 1171–1181.

ZIHL, J., VON CRAMON, D., & MAI, N. (1983). Selective disturbance of movement vision after bilateral brain damage. *Brain, 106*, 313–340.

ZIMMER, C. (2004). *Soul made flesh: The discovery of the brain—and how it changed the world.* New York: Free Press.

ZOLA-MORGAN, S., & SQUIRE, L. (1993). Neuroanatomy of memory. *Annual Review of Neuroscience, 16*, 547–563.

ZOLA-MORGAN, S., SQUIRE, L. R., CLOWER, R. P., & REMPEL, N. L. (1993). Damage to the perirhinal cortex exacerbates memory impairment following lesions to the hippocampal formation. *Journal of Neuroscience, 13*, 251–265.

ZORAWSKI, M., BLANDING, N. Q., KUHN, C. M., & LABAR, K. S. (2006). Effects of sex and stress on acquisition and consolidation of human fear conditioning. *Learning & Memory, 13*, 441–450.

ZRENNER, E., BARTZ-SCHMIDT, K. U., BENAV, H., BESCH, D., BRUCKMANN, A., GABEL, V., ET AL. (2011). Subretinal electronic chips allow blind patients to read letters and combine them to words. *Proceedings of the Royal Society of London, Series B, 278*, 1489–1497.

ZUBERBÜHLER, K. (2001). A syntactic rule in forest monkey communication. *Animal Behavior, 63*(2), 293–299.

ZWITSERLOOD, P. (1989). The locus of the effects of sentential-semantic context in spoken-word processing. *Cognition, 32*, 25–64.

Acknowledgments for corrections, typos and suggestions: Carlos Avendaño, Annik Carson, Mette Clausen-Bruun

Abbreviations

2FDG ^{18}F-labeled fluorodeoxy-D-glucose
2-D two-dimensional
3-D three-dimensional
A1 primary auditory cortex
A2 secondary auditory cortex
ABR auditory brainstem response
ACC anterior cingulate cortex
ACh acetylcholine
AChE acetylcholinesterase
ACS aversive conditioned stimulus
ADHD attention deficit/hyperactivity disorder
AEP auditory evoked potential
AIDS acquired immunodeficiency syndrome
AP5 2-amino-5-phosphonopentanoate
APD antisocial personality disorder
ASD autism spectrum disorders
ATP adenosine triphosphate
BA Brodmann's area
BC brain control
BBB blood–brain barrier
BMI brain–machine interface
BOLD blood oxygen level–dependent
BrdU bromodeoxyuridine
cAMP cyclic adenosine monophosphate
CAPS Clinician-Administered PTSD Scale
cGMP cyclic guanosine monophosphate
ChR-2 channelrhodopsin-2
CIMT constraint-induced movement therapy
CNS central nervous system
COMT catechol-O-methyltransferase
CSF cerebrospinal fluid
CR conditioned response
CS conditioned stimulus
CT or CAT computer tomography or computerized axial tomography
dACC dorsal anterior cingulate cortex
DA dopaminergic
DBH dopamine beta-hydroxylase
DBS deep-brain stimulator; deep-brain stimulation
dLF dorsolateral frontal
dLO dorsolateral occipital cortex
DLPFC dorsolateral prefrontal cortex
DNA deoxyribonucleic acid
DTI diffusion tensor imaging
ECoG electrocorticogram
ECT electroconvulsive therapy
EEG electroencephalogram
EMG electromyogram
EPSP excitatory postsynaptic potential
ERF event-related field
ERN error-related negativity
ERP event-related potential
ESS experience sharing system
FA fractional anisotropy
FEF frontal eye field

FFA fusiform face area
fMRI functional magnetic resonance imaging
FP frontal pole
FTLD frontotemporal lobar degeneration
GABA gamma-aminobutyric acid
GAD generative assembling device
GFAP glial fibrillary acidic protein
GFP green fluorescent protein
GP$_e$ external segment of the globus pallidus
GP$_i$ internal segment of the globus pallidus
GTP guanosine triphosphate
HERA hemispheric encoding/retrieval asymmetry
HPA hypothalamic-pituitary-adrenal axis
HRP horseradish peroxidase
HIV human immunodeficiency virus
IAT Implicit Association Test
IC inferior colliculus
IFC inferior frontal cortex
IFJ inferior frontal junction
ILN intralaminar nuclei
IOR inhibition of return
IPL inferior parietal lobule
IPS intraparietal sulcus
IPSP inhibitory postsynaptic potential
ISI interstimulus interval
LAN left anterior negativity
LC locus coeruleus
LGN lateral geniculate nucleus of the thalamus
LIFG left inferior frontal gyrus
LIP lateral intraparietal
LOC lateral occipital cortex
LPFC lateral prefrontal cortex
LRP lateralized readiness potential
LTD long-term depression
LTP long-term potentiation
LVF left visual field
M1 primary motor cortex
MAO monoamine oxidase
MAOA monoamine oxidase A
MEG magnetoencephalography; magnetoencephalogram
MEP motor evoked potential
MFC medial frontal cortex
MGN medial geniculate nucleus of the thalamus
MIP medial intraparietal
MMF mismatch field
MMN mismatch negativity
MOG middle occipital gyrus
MPFC medial prefrontal cortex
MPTP 1-methyl-4-phenyl-1,2,3,6-tetrahydropyridine
MRC Medical Research Council
MRI magnetic resonance imaging
MS multiple sclerosis
MSAS mental state attribution system
MSR mirror self-recognition
MTL medial temporal lobe

NAcc   nucleus accumbens
NIMH   National Institute of Mental Health
NMDA   N-methyl-D-aspartate
NPE   negative prediction error
NSC   non-self-control group
OCB   olivocochlear bundle
OFC   orbitofrontal cortex
PAG   periacqueductal gray matter
PCC   posterior cingulate cortex
PE   prediction error
PET   positron emission tomography
PFC   prefrontal cortex
P$_i$ inorganic phosphate
PiB   Pittsburgh Compound B
PD   preferred direction
PICA   posterior inferior cerebellar artery
PMC   premotor cortex
PMLS   posteromedial lateral suprasylvian area
PNS   peripheral nervous system
PPA   parahippocampal place area
PPC   posterior parietal cortex
PPE   positive prediction error
preSMA   presupplementary motor area
PSP   progressive supranuclear palsy
PTA   phosphotungstic acid
PTSD   posttraumatic stress disorder
RAS   reticular activating system
rCBF   regional cerebral blood flow
RDK   random dot kinematogram
REM   rapid eye movement
RF   receptive field
RS   repetition suppression
RSVP   rapid serial visual presentation
RT   response time; reaction time
rTPJ   temporoparietal junction in the right hemisphere
RVF   right visual field
S1   primary somatosensory cortex
S2   secondary somatosensory cortex

SAS   supervisory attentional system
SCR   skin conductance response
SD   standard deviation
SE   standard error
SEM   standard error of the mean
SMA   supplementary motor area
SN$_c$ pars compacta of the substantia nigra
SN$_r$ pars reticularis of the substantia nigra
SOA   stimulus onset asynchrony
SPECT   single-photon-emission computed tomography
SPS   syntactic positive shift
SQUID   superconducting quantum interference device
SSRI   selective serotonin reuptake inhibitor
STG   superior temporal gyrus
STN   subthalamic nucleus
STS   superior temporal sulcus
TBSS   tract-based spatial statistics
tDCS   transcranial direct current stimulation
TfR   transferrin receptor
TGA   transient global amnesia
THC   tetrahydrocannabinol
TMS   transcranial magnetic stimulation
TOT   tip of the tongue state
TPJ   temporoparietal junction
UR   unconditioned response
US   unconditioned stimulus
V1   visual area 1 of the visual cortex
V2   visual area 2 of the visual cortex
V5   visual area 5 of the visual cortex
vACC   ventral anterior cingulate cortex
VLPFC   ventrolateral prefrontal cortex
VMF   ventromedial frontal lobe
VMPFC   ventromedial prefrontal cortex
VOR   vestibulo-ocular reflex
VPM   ventral posterior medial nucleus
VTA   ventral tegmental area
VWFA   visual word form area
WCST   Wisconsin Card Sorting Task

Credits

Chapter 1

Page 2: 3D4Medical.com; **1.1:** Reproduced with the permission of the Bodleian Library, University of Oxford; **1.2:** The Print Collector/Alamy; **1.3:** Reproduced with the permission of the Bodleian Library, University of Oxford; **1.4:** US National Library of Medicine; **1.5:** General Research Division, New York Public Library, Astor, Lenox and Tilden Foundations; **1.6:** Mary Evans Picture Library; **1.7:** Mary Evans Picture Library/Sigmund Freud Copyrights; **1.8a:** New York Academy of Medicine; **1.10:** akg-images/Interfoto; **1.11:** Everett Collection Historical/Alamy; **1.13a:** Science Scource; **1.14:** Everett Collection Historical/Alamy; **p. 11, fig 1a:** Science Source; **p. 11, fig 1b:** Erich Lessing/Art Resource, NY; **p. 11, fig 2:** Bettmann/Corbis; **1.15:** Courtesy of the National Library of Medicine; **1.16a:** Betttmann/Corbis; **1.16b:** Benjamin Harris/University of New Hampshire; **1.17:** Hipix/Alamy; **1.18:** McGill Reporter; **1.19:** Photo by Owen Egan, Courtesy of The Montreal Neurological Institute, McGill University; **1.20:** Courtesy of the late George A. Miller; **1.21:** Bettmann/Corbis; **1.22:** Robert A. Lisak; **1.24:** Fulton, J.F. (1928). Observations upon the vascularity of the human occipital lobe during visual activity. *Brain, 51*(3), 310–320. © Oxford University Press; **1.25:** Sokoloff (2000). Seymour S. Kety, M.D. *Journal of Cerebral Blood Flow & Metabolism.* © 2000, Rights Managed by Nature Publishing Group; **1.26:** DIZ Muenchen GmbH, Sueddeutsche Zeitung Photo/Alamy; **1.27:** Becker Medical Library, Washington University School of Medicine; **1.28:** Courtesy UCLA Health Sciences Media Relations; **1.29:** AP Photo; **1.30:** Seiji Ogawa et al. (1990). Oxygenation-sensitive contrast in magnetic resonance image of rodent brain at high magnetic fields, *Magnetic Resonance in Medicine, 1,* 68–78 ©Wiley-Liss, Inc; **1.31a:** Kwong et al. (1992). Dynamic magnetic resonance imaging of human brain activity during primary sensory stimulation. *PNAS.* 1992. Courtesy of K.K. Kwong; **1.31b** Marcus E. Raichle, Figure 19 in "Chapter 2: A Brief History of Functional Brain Mapping" from *Brain Mapping: The Systems,* pp. 33-75. Reprinted by permission of Academic Press, a division of Elsevier.

Chapter 2

Page 22: Dr. Thomas Deerinck/Visuals Unlimited/Corbis; **2.1:** Manuscripts and Archives, Yale University; **2.2, clockwise from top left:** C.J. Guerin, Ph.D. MRC Toxicology Unit/Photo Researchers; Robert S. McNeil/Baylor College of Medicine/Photo Researchers; Science Source/Getty Images; CNRI/Getty Images; Deco Images II/Alamy; Rick Stahl/Nikon Small World; **2.4b:** Thomas Deerinck/Visuals Unlimited; **2.5b:** doc-stock/Visuals Unlimited; **2.6:** Courtesy Dr. S. Halpain, University of California San Diego; **2.7:** CNRI/Science Source/Photo Researchers; **2.20b:** Courtesy of Allen Song, Duke University; **2.27b:** Courtesy of Allen Song, Duke University; **2.29b:** Courtesy of Allen Song, Duke University; **2.32c:** *The Brain: A Neuroscience Primer* by Richard F. Thompson. © 1985, 1993, 2000 by Worth Publishers. Used with permission; **2.36b:** Wessinger et al. (1997). Tonotopy in human auditory cortex examined with functional magnetic resonance imaging. *Human Brain Mapping, 5,* 18–25. New York: © Wiley-Liss, Inc.; **p. 59, fig 1:** Chimpanzee brain provided by Dr. Dean Falk. From Javier DeFelipe, The evolution of the brain, the human nature of cortical circuits, and intellectual creativity. *Frontiers in Neuroanatomy.,* 16 May 2011; All other brains from: Yáñez et al. (2005). Double bouquet cell in the human cerebral cortex and a comparison with other mammals. *Journal of Comparative Neurology,* 486(4): 344–360. ©2005 Wiley-Liss, Inc.; **2.39b:** Lennart Nilsson/Bonnier Alba AB; **2.24:** © Bryan Reading/ HYPERLINK "http://www.cartoonstock.com" www.cartoonstock.com; **2.43:** Erikson et al. (1998). Neurogenesis in the adult hippocampus, *Nature Medicine* 4: 1312–1317. © Nature Publishing Group; **2.44:** Erikson et al. (1998): Neurogenesis in the adult hippocampus, *Nature Medicine,* 4: 1312–1317. © Nature Publishing Group.

Chapter 3

Page 70: Deco/Alamy; **3.6:** DeArmond et al. *Structure of the Human Brain: A Photographic Atlas* 2nd edition. New York: Oxford University Press, 1976. ©1976 by Oxford University Press, Inc. Reprinted with permission; **3.7:** Woodward, J.S. Histologic Neuropathology: A Color Slide Set. Orange, CA: California Medical Publications, 1973; **3.8:** de Leeuw et al. (2005). Progression of cerebral white matter lesions in Alzheimer's disease. *Journal of Neurology, Neurosurgery and Psychiatry.* 76: 1286–1288. © 2005 BMJ Publishing Group; **3.9a:** Woodward, J.S., *Histologic Neuropathology: A Color Slide Set.* Orange, CA: California Medical Publications, 1973; **3.9b:** Holbourn, A.H.S., Mechanics of head injury, *The Lancet* 2: 177–180, © by The Lancet 1943; **3.10:** Chappell et al. (2006). Distribution of microstructural damage in the brains of professional boxers. *Journal of Magnetic Resonance Imaging* 24: 537–542. © 2006 Wiley-Liss, Inc.; **3.12** Pessiglione et al., Figure 1 from "Dopamine-dependent prediction errors underpin reward-seeking behavior in humans." *Nature,* 442(31), 1042–1045. Copyright © 2006 Nature Publishing Group. Reprinted with permission; **3.13a:** From chapter "Transcranial magnetic stimulation & the human brain" by Megan Steven & Alvaro Pascual-Leone in "Neuroethics: Defining the Issues in Theory, Practice & Policy" edited by Illes, Judith, (2005). By permission of Oxford University Press; **3.15a, b:** Rampon et al. (2000). Enrichment induces structural changes and recovery from nonspatial memory deficits in CA1 NMDAR1-knockout mice, *Nature Neuroscience* 3: 238–244. © 2000, Rights Managed by Nature Publishing Group; **3.16b:** Greenberg, J.O., and Adams, R.D. (Eds),

Neuroimaging: A Companion to Adams and Victor's Principles of Neurology. New York: McGraw-Hill, Inc., 1995. Reprinted by permission of McGraw-Hill, Inc; **3.17b:** Greenberg, J.O., and Adams, R.D. (Eds.), *Neuroimaging: A Companion to Adams and Victor's Principles of Neurology.* New York: McGraw-Hill, Inc., 1995. Reprinted by permission of McGraw-Hill, Inc; **3.18a, b:** Images courtesy of Dr. Megan S. Steven, Karl Doron, and Adam Riggall. Darmouth Brain Imaging Center at Darmouth College; **p. 96, fig 1:** Gonzalez et al. (2012). Coding of saliency by ensemble bursting in the amygdala of primates. *Frontiers in Behavioral Neuroscience,* 6(38), 1 © 2012 Gonzalez Andino and Grave de Peralta Menendez. Images courtesy of S. Gonzalez and R. Grave de Peralta of the Electrical Neuroimaging Group; **3.21:** Quiroga et al. 2005. Invariant visual representation by single neurons in the human brain, *Nature* 435(23): 1102–1107. © 2005 Nature Publishing Group; **3.22:** Ramare/AgeFotostock; **3.26:** Addante et al. (2011). Prestimulus theta activity predicts correct source memory retrieval. *Proceedings of the National Academy of Science* USA, 108, 10702–10707. © National Academy of Sciences, USA; **3.27a, c:** Roberts et al. (1998). Magnetoencephalography and magnetic source imaging, *Cognitive and Behavioral Neurology.* Wolters Kluwer Health, Jan 1, 1998. © 1998, Lippincott-Raven Publishers; **3.28:** Canolty et al. (2007). *Frontiers in Neuroscience* 1:1 185–196. Image courtesy of the authors; **3.29a:** Courtesy of Marcus Raichle, M.D. School of Medicine, Washington University in St. Louis; 3.30: Fox et al. (1987). Retinotopic organization of human visual cortex mapped with Position-emission Tomography. *The Journal of Neuroscience,* 7(3): 918 (1987). Reprinted with permission of The Society for Neuroscience; **3.31:** Vitali et al. (2008). Neuroimaging in dementia. *Seminars in Neurology,* 28(4): 467–483. Images courtesy Gil Rabinovici, UC San Francisco and William Jagust, UC Berkeley; **3.35a, b:** Wagner et al. (1998). Building memories: Remembering and forgetting of verbal experiences as predicted by brain activity, *Science,* 281: 1188–1191. © 1998, AAAS; **3.39a:** Deibert et al. (1999). Neural pathways in tactile object recognition, *Neurology,* 52(9): 1413–1417. © Lippincott Williams & Wilkins, Inc.–Journals; **3.40b:** Frank et al. (2011). Neurogenetics and pharmacology of learning, motivation, and cognition. *Neuropsychopharmacology* (6): 133–152. © 2010, Rights Managed by Nature Publishing Group.

Chapter 4
Page 120: Roger Harris/Science Photo Library/Getty Images; **4.3:** © The Photo Works; **4.5:** Arthur Toga and Paul M. Thompson (2003). Mapping Brain Asymmetry, *Nature Reviews Neuroscience* 4, 37–48. © 2003 Rights managed by Nature Publishing Group. Photo Courtesy Dr. Arthur W. Toga and Dr. Paul M. Thompson, Laboratory of Neuro Imaging at UCLA; **4.6:** Hutsler (2003). The specialized structure of human language cortex. *Brain and Language.* August 2003. © Elsevier; **4.8:** Sabine Hofer & Jens Frahm. (2006). Topography of the human corpus callosum revisited—Comprehensive fiber tractography using diffusion tensor magnetic resonance imaging. *NeuroImage, 32,* 989–994. ©2006 Elsevier; **4.10:** Courtesy of Pietro Gobbi and Daniele Di Motta,

Atlas of Anatomy Central Nervous System, HYPERLINK "http://www.biocfarm.unibo.it/aunsnc/Default.htm" http://www.biocfarm.unibo.it/aunsnc/Default.htm; **4.12:** Michael Gazzaniga; **4.14:** Michael Gazzaniga; **4.18:** Turk et al. (2002). Mike or me? Self-recognition in a split-brain patient. September 2002. *Nature Neuroscience,* 5 (9): 841–2. © 2002 Nature Publishing Group; **4.21:** DeJong et al. (1992). *The Neurologic Examination,* 5th edition. Philadelphia, PA: J.B. Lippincott Company; **4.22:** Kingstone et al. (1995). Subcortical transfer of higher order information: More illusory than real? *Neuropsychology, 9:* 321–328. ©2012 APA, all rights reserved; **4.29:** Phelps, E. A., and Gazzaniga, M. S. (1992). Hemispheric differences in mnemonic processing: The effects of left hemisphere interpretation. *Neuropsychologia, 30,* 293–297. ©2012 Elsevier Ltd. All rights reserved; **4.30:** Gazzaniga, M.S. 2000. Cerebral specialization and interhemispheric communication. Does the corpus callosum enable the human condition? *Brain, 123:* 1293–1326. © 2000 Oxford University Press; **4.32:** Efron, Robertson, & Delis, Figure from "Hemispheric Specialization of Memory for Visual Hierarchical Stimuli," *Neuropsychologia,* 24:2. © 1985 by Elsevier Science & Technology Journals. Reproduced with permission of Elsevier Science & Technology Journals in the format Textbook via Copyright Clearance Center.

Chapter 5
Page 162: Gabe Palmer/Corbis; **5.2a:** Seymour/Photo Researchers; **5.2b:** Bjorn Rorslett/Photo Researchers; **5.7a:** Roy Lawe/Alamy; **5.7b:** Musat/Dreamstime.com; **5.7c** Judith Collins/Alamy; **5.10:** Courtesy of N. Sobel. Sobel et al. (1998). Sniffing and smelling: separate subsystems in the human olfactory cortex. *Nature, 92:* 282–286. © 1998, Rights Managed by Nature Publishing Group; **5.13b:** Small et al. (2001). Changes in brain activity related to eating chocolate. *Brain, 124;* 1720–1733. ©2001 Oxford University Press; **5.17, left:** BrazilPhotos.com/Alamy; **5.17b:** LWA-Paul Chmielowiec/Corbis; **5.30** Larsson and Heeger, Figure 4a from "Two retinotopic visual areas in human lateral occipital cortex." *The Journal of Neuroscience,* 26(51), 13128–13142. © 2006 by the Society for Neuroscience. Reprinted with permission from the Society for Neuroscience; **p. 189, fig 1:** Zrenner et al., Figure 1, 2 and 3 from "Subretinal electronic chips allow blind patients to read letters and combine them to words." *Proceedings of the Royal Society B,* 278, 1489–1497. Reprinted by permission of the Royal Society; **5.31:** Yacoub et al. (2008). *PNAS,* 105(30): 1060–1062. ©2008 *National Academy of Sciences of the USA;* **5.33:** Haynes and Rees, Figure 2 from "Predicting the orientation of invisible stimuli from activity in human primary visual cortex." *Nature Neuroscience,* Vol. 8, No. 5, pp. 686-691. Reprinted by permission from Macmillan Publishers Ltd, Copyright © 2005, Nature Publishing Group; **5.37:** © manu-Fotolia.com; **5.38:** Gallant et al. (2000). A human extrastriate area functionally homologous to macaque V4, *Neuron,* 27: 227–235. © 2000, Elsevier; **5.39:** Gallant et al. (2000). A human extrastriate area functionally homologous to macaque V4, *Neuron,* 27: 227–235. © 2000, Elsevier; **5.40a:** Musée d'Orsay, Paris.

Photo: Giraudon/Art Resource; **5.40b:** © 2008 Estate of Pablo Picasso/Artists Rights Society (ARS), New York; **5.42:** Stevens et al., Figures 2, 4 and 3 from "Temporal characteristics of global motion processing revealed by transcranial magnetic stimulation." *European Journal of Neuroscience, 30,* pp. 2415–2426. Reprinted by permission of John Wiley & Sons, Inc.; **5.44:** Courtesy HYPERLINK "http://www.brainrules. net" www.brainrules.net; **5.46** Driver and Noesselt, Figure 2 from "Multisensory interplay reveals crossmodal influences on 'sensory-specific' brain regions, neural responses, and judgments." *Neuron, 57,* pp. 11–23. Copyright © 2008 by Elsevier Science & Technology Journals. Reproduced with permission of Elsevier Science & Technology Journals in the format Textbook via Copyright Clearance Center; **5.48:** Driver and Noesselt, Figure 5 from "Multisensory interplay reveals crossmodal influences on 'sensory-specific' brain regions, neural responses, and judgments." *Neuron, 57,* pp. 11–23. Copyright © 2008 by Elsevier Science & Technology Journals. Reproduced with permission of Elsevier Science & Technology Journals in the format Textbook via Copyright Clearance Center; **5.49:** Esterman (2006). Coming unbound: Disrupting automatic integration of synesthetic color and graphemes by Transcranial Magnetic Stimulation of the right parietal lobe. *Journal of Cognitive Neuroscience,* 18:1570–1576. © Society for Neuroscience; **5.50:** Romke Rouw and H. Steven Scholte, Increased structural connectivity in grapheme-color synesthesia. *Nature Neuroscience* 10 (6), 792–797 . Reprinted by permission from Macmillan Publishers Ltd, ©2007, Rights Managed by Nature Publishing Group; **5.51a:** Merabet et al. (2008) Rapid and reversible recruitment of early visual cortex for touch. *PLoS ONE* 3(8): e3046.

Chapter 6

Page **218:** Lonely Planet/Getty Images; **6.1a:** Adelrepeng/ Dreamstime.com; **6.1b:** Carl & Ann Purcell/Corbis; **6.2a:** Courtesy of the Laboratory of Neuro Imaging at UCLA and Martinos Center for Biomedical Imaging at MGH, Consortium of the Human Connectome Project HYPERLINK "http://www.humanconnectomeproject.org" www.human-connectomeproject.org; **6.6:** Culham et. al. (2003). Ventral occipital lesions impair object guarantors brain. *Brain,* 126: 243–247, by permission of Oxford University Press; **6.7:** Shmuelof et al. (2005). Dissociation between Ventral and Dorsal fMRI Activation during Object and Action Recognition, *Neuron,* 47: 457–470. © 2005 by Elsevier; **6.13b:** Kanwisher et al. (1997). A locus in human extrastriate cortex for visual shape analysis, *Journal of Cognitive Neuroscience* 9: 133–142. © 1997, Massachusetts Institute of Technology; **6.16:** Older Malagasy woman. Photo by Steve Evans; HYPERLINK "http://creativecommons.org/licenses/by/2.0/deed.en" http://creativecommons.org/licenses/by/2.0/deed.en; **6.19:** Behrmann, M., et al., Figure from "Intact visual imagery and impaired visual perception in a patient with visual agnosia", *Journal of Experimental Psychology: Human Perception and Performance,* 20. Copyright © 1994 by the American Psychological Association. Reprinted by permission; **6.20:** McCarthy, G., and Warrington, E.K. (1986). Visual associative agnosia:

A Clinico-anatomical study of a single case, *Journal of Neurology, Neurosurgery and Psychiatry* 49: 1233–1240. © 1986, British Medical Journal Publishing Group; **p. 242, fig 1:** Sacks, O.W., *An Anthropologist on Mars: Seven Paradoxical Tales.* New York: Knopf, 1995. Reprinted with permission; **p. 247, fig 1a:** Mahon et al. (2009). Category-specific organization in the human brain does not require visual experience. *Neuron,* 63(3): 397–405. © 2009 Elsevier; **p. 247, fig 1b:** van Kooten et al. (2008). Neurons in the fusiform gyrus are fewer and smaller in autism. *Brain* © Oxford University Press; **6.25:** Baylis et al. (1985). Selectivity between faces in the responses of a population of neurons in the cortex in the superior temporal sulcus of the monkey, *Brain Research,* 91–102. ©1985 Elsevier; **6.26:** Tsao, et al. (2006). A Cortical Region Consisting Entirely of Face-Selective Cells, *Science* 311: 670–674. Reprinted with permission from AAAS; **6.27:** McCarthy et al. (1997). Face-specific processing in the human fusiform gyrus, *Journal of Cognitive Neuroscience.* p. 605–610. © 1997 Massachusetts Institute of Technology; **6.28:** Jiang, Yi and He, Sheng (2006). Cortical Responses to Invisible Faces: Dissociating Subsystems for Facial-Information Processing. *Current Biology* 16: 2023–2029. © 2006 Reproduced with permission of Elsevier Science & Technology Journals in the format Textbook via Copyright Clearance Center; **6.29:** Reprinted from *Cognition,* 83:1, Bentin & Carmel, "Domain specificity versus expertise: factors influencing distinct processing of faces", pp. 1–29, Copyright © 2002, with permission from Elsevier; **6.30a:** Afraz et al. (2006). Microstimulation of inferotemporal cortex influences face categorization. *Nature* 442, 692-695. ©2006 Nature Publishing Group; **6.31:** Grill-Spector et al., Figure 6 from "The fusiform face area subserves face perception, not generic within-category identification." *Nature Neuroscience,* 7, pp. 555–562. Reprinted by permission from Macmillan Publishers Ltd, Copyright © 2004, Nature Publishing Group; **6.32:** Scala/Art Resource, NY; **6.33:** Cohen et al. (2000). The visual word form area Spatial and temporal characterization of an initial stage of reading in normal subjects and posterior split-brain patients. *Brain,* 123(2): 291–307. © 2000 Oxford University Press; **6.35:** Thompson (1980). Margaret Thatcher: A new illusion. *Perception* 9(4): 483–484. © Pion; **6.37:** Taylor et al. (2007) Functional MRI Analysis of Body and Body part Representations in the Extrasite and Fusiform Body Areas. *Journal of Neurophysiology,* 98(3): 1626–1633. © 2007 American Physiological Society; **6.38a:** Pitcher et al. (2009) Triple Dissociation of Faces, Bodies, and Objects in Extrastriate Cortex. *Current Biology,* 19(4): 319–324. © 2009 Elsevier; **6.39:** Kanwisher et al. (1997). A locus in human extrastriate cortex for visual shape analysis, *Journal of Cognitive Neuroscience* 9, 133–142. Copyright (c) 1997, Massachusetts Institute of Technology; **6.41:** Haynes and Rees. (2006) Neuroimaging: Decoding mental states from brain activity in humans. *Nature Reviews Neuroscience,* 7, 523–534 © 2006, Rights managed by Nature Publishing Group; **6.42 and 6.43:** Kay et al. (2008). Identifying natural images from human brain activity. *Nature,* 452: 352–355. (c) 2008, Nature Publishing Group; **6.44:** Courtesy Jack Gallant; **6.45:** Naselaris et al. (2009). Bayesian Reconstruction of natural Images from Human brain

Activity. *Neuron 63*(6): 902–915 © 2009 Elsevier; **6.46:** Owen et al. (2006). Detecting Awareness in the Vegetative State, *Science*, 313: 1402. © 2006 AAAS.

Chapter 7

Page 272: Alan Poulson Photography/Shutterstock; **7.2:** Courtesy National Library of Medicine, Bethesda, Maryland; **7.3:** © 2013 Artists Rights Society (ARS), New York/VG Bild-Kunst, Bonn; **7.4:** Corbetta and Shulman, Figure 1 from "Spatial neglect and attention networks." *Annual Review of Neuroscience. 34*, pp. 569–99. Reprinted with permission; **7.6:** Institute of Neurology and Institute of Cognitive Neuroscience, University College London, London, UK; **7.9a:** Bettmann/Corbis; **7.12:** Ronald C. James; **7.19:** McAdams et al. (2005). Attention Modulates the Responses of Simple Cells in Monkey Primary Visual Cortex. *Journal of Neuroscience, 25*(47): 11023–33. © 2005 by the Society for Neuroscience; reprinted with permission from the Society for Neuroscience; **7.20:** Hopfinger et al. (2000). The neural mechanism of top-down attentional control, *Nature Neuroscience, 3:* 284–291. © 2000, Rights Managed by Nature Publishing Group; **7.21** and **7.23:** Tootell et al. (1998). The retinotopy of visual spatial attention, *Neuron* 21: 1409–1422. © 1998, Elsevier; **7.24** and **7.25:** Hopf J.M., Luck, S.J., Boelmans, K., Schoenfeld, M.A., Boehler, C.N., Rieger, J., & Heinz, H. J. (2006). The neural site of attention matches the spatial scale of perception. *Journal of Neuroscience*, 26, 3532–3540. © Society for Neuroscience, reprinted with permission from the Society for Neuroscience; **7.27:** O'Connor et al. (2002). Attention modulates responses in the human lateral geniculate nucleus. *Nature Neuroscience* (11): 1203–9. © 2002, Rights Managed by Nature Publishing Group; **7.28:** McAlonan, K., Cavanaugh, J., & Wurtz, R.H., Adapted from figure 1b,c of "Guarding the gateway to cortex with attention in visual thalamus." *Nature*, 456, 391–394. © 2008 Nature Publishing Group. Reprinted with permission; **7.31:** Luck, S.J., Fan, S. & Hillyard, S. A., Adapted from Figure 1 "Attention-related modulation of sensory-evoked brain activity in a visual search task." *Journal of Cognitive Neuroscience, 5,* pp. 188–195. Reprinted by permission of MIT Press Journals; **7.32:** iStockphoto; **7.33:** Liu, et al., Figures from "Comparing the time course and efficacy of spatial and feature-based attention", *Vision Research*, 47:1. Copyright © 2007 by Elsevier Science & Technology Journals. Reproduced with permission of Elsevier Science & Technology Journals in the format Textbook via Copyright Clearance Center; **7.34:** Hillard, S. & Munte, T. F., Adapted from figures 3 and 5 of "Selective attention to color and location: An analysis with event-related brain potentials." *Perception & Psychophysics*, Vol. 36, No. 2, 185-198. Reprinted by permission of Springer Science + Business Media; **7.36:** M. Schoenfeld, JM Hopf, A. Martinez, H. Mai, C. Sattler, A. Gasde, HJ Heinze, S. Hillyard et al. (2007). Spatio-temporal Analysis of Feature-Based Attention," *Cerebral Cortex,* 17:10. Copyright 2007 by Oxford University Press- Journals. Reproduced with permission of Oxford University Press– Journals in the format Textbook via Copyright Clearance Center; **7.37:** Hopf et al. (2004). Attention to features precedes attention to locations in visual search; evidence from electro-magnetic brain responses in humans. *Journal of Neuroscience,* 24(8): 1822–32. © Society for Neuroscience; **7.38:** Zhang et al. (2008). Feature-based attention modulates feed forward visual processing. *Nature Neuroscience*, 12: 24–25. © 2009, Rights Managed by Nature Publishing; **7.39:** Mueller & Kleinschmidt, Figures from "Dynamic Interaction of Object- and Space-Based Attention in Retinotopic Visual Areas", *Journal of Neuroscience*, Vol. 23, No. 30, pp. 9812-6. Copyright 2003 by the Society for Neuroscience. Reprinted with permission from the Society for Neuroscience; **7.43:** Hopfinger et al. (2000) The neural mechanism of top-down attentional control, *Nature Neuroscience* 3: 284–291. © 2000, Rights Managed by Nature Publishing Group; **7.44:** Armstrong, K. M., Schafer, R.J., Chang, M. H. & Moore, T., Figure 7.3 from "Attention and action in the frontal eye field." In R. Mangun (Ed.), *The Neuroscience of Attention* (pp. 151–166). Oxford, England: Oxford University Press. Reprinted with permission; **7.45:** Morishima et al. (2009). Task-specific signal transmission from prefrontal cortex in visual selective attention. *Nature Neuroscience*, 12: 85–91. Reprinted by permission from Macmillan Publishers Ltd, © 2009, Rights Managed by Nature Publishing; **7.48:** Bisley JW, Goldberg ME, Figures from "Neural Correlates of Attention and Distractibility in the Lateral Intraparietal Area", *Journal of Neurophysiology*, 95:3. Copyright © 1996 by American Physiological Society. Reproduced with permission of American Physiological Society in the format Textbook via Copyright Clearance Center.

Chapter 8

Page 326: Ronald Martinez/Getty Images; **8.1a:** From Lewis P. Rowland (Ed.), *Merritt's Textbook of Neurology*, 8th edition. Philadelphia: Lea & Febiger, 1989, p. 661. Copyright © 1989 by Lea & Febiger; **8.1b:** Photo by Russ Lee; **8.15:** Churchland, M.M., Cunningham, J. P., Kaufman, M.T. Ryu, S.I. & Shenoy, K.V., Figure 2 from "Cortical preparatory activity: representation of movement or first cog in a dynamical machine?" *Neuron, 68*, pp. 387–400. Copyright © 2010 by Elsevier Science & Technology Journals. Reproduced with permission of Elsevier Science & Technology Journals in the format Textbook via Copyright Clearance Center; **8.16:** Cisek, P. & Kalasca, J. F., Figure 1 from Neural mechanisms for interacting with a world full of action choices. *Annual Review of Neuroscience, 33,* pp. 269–298. Reprinted with permission; **8.17:** Cisek, P. & Kalasca, J. F., Figure 2 from Neural mechanisms for interacting with a world full of action choices. *Annual Review of Neuroscience, 33,* pp. 269–298. Reprinted with permission; **8.18:** Hamilton et al. (2007). Action outcomes are represented in human inferior frontoparietal cortex. *Cerebral Cortex, 18,* 1160–1168. © 2008 Oxford University Press; **8.19:** Hamilton & Grafton, Figure 2 from "Action outcomes are represented in human inferior frontoparietal cortex." *Cerebral Cortex, 18,* pp. 1160–1168. Copyright © 2007 by Oxford University Press–Journals. Reproduced with permission of Oxford University Press–Journals in the format Textbook via Copyright Clearance Center; **8.21:** Ganguly, K. & Carmena, J. M., (2009) Figure 2 from "Emergence of a Stable Cortical Map for Neuroprosthetic Control." *PLoS Biology 7*(7): e1000153. doi:10.1371/

journal.pbio.1000153; **8.22a-d:** Hochberg et al. (2006). Neuronal ensemble control of prosthetic devices by a human with tetraplegia. *Nature*, 13(442): 164–171. © 2006, Rights Managed by Nature Publishing Group; **8.26:** Color plates 2 and 4 from Greenberg, J.O. and Adams, R.D. (Eds.), *Neuroimaging: A Companion to Adams and Victor's Principles of Neurology.* New York: McGraw-Hill, Inc., 1995. Reprinted by permission of McGraw-Hill, Inc; **8.29:** Calvo-Merino et al. (2005), Action Observation and Acquired Motor Skills: an fMRI Study with Expert Dancers. *Cerebral Cortex, 15:*1243–1249. Copyright Elsevier 2005; **8.30:** Aglioti et al. (2008). Action anticipation and motor resonance in elite basketball players. *Nature Neuroscience* 11: 1109–1116. Reprinted by permission from Macmillan Publishers Ltd, © 2008, Rights Mangaged by Nature Publishing Group; **8.31:** Courtesy of authors; **8.32:** Martin et al. (1996), Figure 1 from "Throwing while looking through prisms. I. Focal olivocerebellar lesions impair adaptation." *Brain, 119,* 1183–1198. Copyright © 1996 by Oxford University Press–Journals. Reproduced with permission of Oxford University Press–Journals in the format Textbook via Copyright Clearance Center; **8.33:** Martin et al. (1996), Figure 2 from "Throwing while looking through prisms. I. Focal olivocerebellar lesions impair adaptation." *Brain, 119,* 1183–1198. Copyright © 1996 by Oxford University Press–Journals. Reproduced with permission of Oxford University Press–Journals in the format Textbook via Copyright Clearance Center; **8.34:** Galea, J. M., Vazquez, A., Pasricha, N., Dexivry J. J. O. & Celnik, P. (2010), Figure 5 from "Dissociating the roles of the cerebellum and motor cortex during adaptive learning: The motor cortex retains what the cerebellum learns. *Cerebral Cortex,* December 10, online. Copyright © 2010 by Oxford University Press–Journals. Reproduced with permission of Oxford University Press–Journals in the format Textbook via Copyright Clearance Center; **8.35:** Hosp et al. (2011). Dopaminergic projections from midbrain to primary motor cortex mediate motor skill learning. *Journal of Neuroscience.* 31: 2481–2487. © Society for Neuroscience; **8.36:** Galea, J. M., Vazquez, A., Pasricha, N., Dexivry J. J. O. & Celnik, P. (2010), Figure 5 from "Dissociating the roles of the cerebellum and motor cortex during adaptive learning: The motor cortex retains what the cerebellum learns. *Cerebral Cortex,* December 10, online. Copyright © 2010 by Oxford University Press–Journals. Reproduced with permission of Oxford University Press–Journals in the format Textbook via Copyright Clearance Center; **8.38, top left:** Bigmax/Dreamstime.com; **8.38, top right:** Nalukai/Dreamstime.com; **8.38, bottom left:** Radub85/Dreamstime.com; **8.38, bottom right:** iStockphoto; **8.39:** Johansen-Berg, H., Della-Maggiore, V., Behrens, T. E., Smith, S. M. & Paus, T., (2007), "Integrity of white matter in the corpus callosum correlates with bimanual co-ordination skills." *Neuroimage, 36* (Suppl. 2), T16–T21. Copyright © 2007 by Elsevier Science & Technology Journals. Reproduced with permission of Elsevier Science & Technology Journals in the format Textbook via Copyright Clearance Center.

Chapter 9

Page 378: Blend Images/Alamy; **9.1:** Chowdhury et al. (2010). Microneurosurgical management of temporal lobe epilepsy by amygdalohippocampectomy. *Asian Journal of Neurosurgery,* 5(2): 10–18. Medknow Publications and Media Pvt. Ltd; **9.6:** Markowitsch et al. (1999). Short-term memory deficit after focal parietal damage, *Journal of Clinical & Experimental Neuropsychology* 21: 784–797. © 1999 Routledge; **9.9:** Jonides et al. (1998). Inhibition in verbal working memory revealed by brain activation. *PNAS, 95*(14). © 1998, The National Academy of Science; **9.10:** Drawing © Ruth Tulving, Courtesy the artist; **9.14:** Corkin et al. (1997). H.M.'s medial temporal lobe lesion: Findings from magnetic resonance imaging. *The Journal of Neuroscience* 17: 3964–3979, © 1997 Society of Neuroscience; **9.16:** Courtesy of Professor David Amaral; **9.24:** Ranganath, et al., Figure from "Dissociable correlates of recollection and familiarity within the medial temporal lobes," *Neuropsychologia,* 42:1. Copyright © 2003 by Elsevier Science & Technology Journals. Reproduced with permission of Elsevier Science & Technology Journals in the format Textbook via Copyright Clearance Center; **9.25:** Ranganath et. al. (2004). Dissociable correlates of recollection and familiarity within the medial temporal lobes *Neuropsychologia,* 42: 2–13 © 2004, Elsevier 2004; **9.26:** Eldridge et al. (2000). Remembering episode: a selective role for the hippocampus during retrieval. *Nature Neuroscience,* 3 (11):1149–52 © 2000, Rights Managed by Nature Publishing Group; **9.27:** Ranganath et. al. (2004). Dissociable correlates of recollection and familiarity within the medial temporal lobes *Neuropsychologia,* 42, 2–13 © 2004, Elsevier; **9.28:** Eichenbaum et al. (2007). The Medial Temporal Lobe and Recognition Memory, *CoAnnual Review of Neuroscience,* 30 © 2007 by Annual Reviews; **9.29:** Hannula et al. (2010). Worth a glance: using eye movements to investigate the cognitive neuroscience of memory. *Frontiers in Human Neuroscience.* 4: 1–16. © 2010 Hannula, Althoff, Warren, Riggs, Cohen and Ryan; **p. 409, fig 1:** McClelland, J.L., Connectionist Models of Memory. In Tulving, E. and Craik, F.I.M. (Eds.), The Oxford Handbook of Memory, pp. 583–596. Oxford University Press: New York, 2000; **9.30:** Wheeler et al. (2000). Memory's echo: Vivid remembering reactivates sensory-specific cortex, *Proceedings of the National Academy of Sciences,* 97(20): 11125–11129; **9.31:** Courtesy of Roberto Cabeza; **9.32:** Buckner et al. (1999). Frontal cortex contributes to human memory formation. *Nature Neuroscience.* April 311–314. © 1999, Rights Managed by Nature Publishing Group; **9.35:** Ranganath, C. & Richey, M. (2012), Figure 2 from "Two cortical systems for memory guided behaviour." *Nature Reviews Neuroscience,* 13, 713–726. Reprinted by permission from Macmillan Publishers Ltd, Copyright © 2012, Nature Publishing Group.

Chapter 10

Page 424: Tim Shaffer/Reuters/Landov; **10.1** and **10.2:** Adolphs et. al. (1995) Fear and the Human Amygdala. *The Journal of Neuroscience,* 15(9): 5878–5891. © Society for Neuroscience; **10.4:** © Paul Ekman; **10.6:** Reproduced with permission © 2004, Bob Willingham. Tracy JL and Matsumoto D. (2008). The spontaneous expression of pride and shame: Evidence for biologically innate nonverbal displays. *PNAS* 105:11655–11660; **10.11:** Anderson et al. (2001) Lesions of the human amygdala impair enhanced perception of emotionally salient events.

Nature. May 17; 41:305–309; © 2001, Rights Managed by Nature Publishing Group; **10.13a:** Phelps et al. (2001). Activation of the left amygdala to a cognitive representation of fear. *Nature Neuroscience*. 4: 37–41. © 2001 Rights Managed by Nature Publishing Group; **10.15:** R.J.R. Blair et. al. Dissociable neural responses to facial expressions of sadness and anger, *Brain*. 1999, 122, 883–893, by permission of Oxford University Press; **10.16:** Adolphs et al. (2005). A mechanism for impaired fear recognition after amygdala damage. *Nature*. 433:68–72; © 2005, Rights Managed by Nature Publishing Group; **10.17:** Whalen, et. al. (2004). Human Amygdala Responsivity to Masked Fearful Eye Whites. *Science* 306:, 2061. © AAAS; **10.18:** Cunningham et al. (2004). Separable neural components in the processing of Black and White Faces. *Psychological Science*, 15: 806–813. © 2004, Association for *Psychological Science*; **10.19:** Said et al. (2010). The amygdala and FFA track both social and non-social face dimensions. *Neuropsychologia*, 48: 3596-3605 © 2010 Elsevier; **10.20:** Ochsner, K., Silvers, J., & Buhle, J. T. (2012). Figure 2a from "Functional imaging studies of emotion regulation: a synthetic review and evolving model of the cognitive control of emotion." *Annals of the New York Academy of Sciences*, 1251, E1–E24, March. Reprinted with permission of The New York Academy of Sciences; **10.21:** Gross, J., Figure 1 from "Antecedent- and response-focused emotion regulation: Divergent consequences for experience, expression, and physiology." *Journal of Personality and Social Psychology*, 74, 224–237. Reprinted by permission of the American Psychological Association; **10.22:** Ochsner et al. (2004). For better or for worse: Neural systems supporting the cognitive down- and up-regulation of negative emotion. *Neurolmage*, 23, 483–499 © 2004 Elsevier, Inc. All rights reserved; **10.24:** Habel et al. May 2005. Same or different? Neural correlates of happy and sad mood in healthy males. *NeuroImage*, 26(1): 206–214. © 2005 Elsevier; **10.25 and 10.26:** Ortigue et al. (2010a). Neuroimaging of Love: fMRI Meta-analysis Evidence toward New Perspectives in Sexual Medicine. *Journal of Sexual Medicine*, 7(11): 3541–3552. © 2010 International Society for Sexual Medicine; **10.28:** Lindquist et al. (2012). The brain basis of emotion: A meta-analytic review. *Behavioral and Brain Sciences*. 35: 121–143. © Cambridge University Press 2012.

Chapter 11
Page 468: Colin Hawkins/cultura/Corbis; **11.1a:** Courtesy Musée Depuytren, Paris; **11.6:** Kirsten I. Taylor , Barry J. Devereux & Lorraine K. Tyler (2011), Figure 1 from "Conceptual structure: Towards an integrated neurocognitive account." *Language and Cognitive Processes*, 26(9), 1368-1401. Reprinted by permission of Taylor & Francis Group; **11.7:** Taylor, K. I., Moss, H. E. & Tyler, L .K. (2007). Figure from "The Conceptual Structure Account: A cognitive model of semantic memory and its neural instantiation." J. Hart & M. Kraut (eds.), *The Neural Basis of Semantic Memory*. Cambridge: Cambridge University Press. pp. 265–301. Reprinted with permission; **11.14:** McClelland, James L., David E. Rumelhart, and PDP Research Group., *Parallel Distributed Processing, Volume 2: Explorations in the Microstructure of Cognition: Psychological and Biological Models,*

figure: "Fragment of a Connectionist Network for Letter Recognition", © 1986 Massachusetts Institute of Technology, by permission of The MIT Press; **11.16:** Puce et al. (1996). Differential sensitivity of human visual cortex to faces, letterstrings, and textures: A functional magnetic resonance imaging study. *Journal of Neuroscience* 16 (1996) © 2013 by the Society for Neuroscience; **11.18:** Munte, Heinze and Mangun, Figure from "Dissociation of Brain Activity Related to Syntactic and Semantic Aspects of Language", *Journal of Cognitive Neuroscience*, 5:3, Summer 1993. Reprinted by permission of MIT Press Journals; **11.20:** Courtesy of Nina Dronkers; **11.22:** Robert C. Berwick, Angela D. Friederici, Noam Chomsky, Johan J. Bolhuis, Figure 2 from "Evolution, brain, and the nature of language," *Trends in Cognitive Science*, 16(5), 262–268. Copyright © 2012 by Elsevier Science & Technology Journals. Reproduced with permission of Elsevier Science & Technology Journals in the format Textbook via Copyright Clearance Center; Sahin, N.T., Pinker, S., Cash, S.S., Schomer, D., & Halgren, E. (2009). Figure 4a from "Sequential processing of lexical, grammatical, and phonological information within Broca's Area." *Science, 326*, 445-449. Reprinted by permission of the American Association for the Advancement of Science; **11.25:** Sahin, N.T., Pinker, S., Cash, S.S., Schomer, D., & Halgren, E. (2009). Figures 2a, 2b, 2c, and 4c from "Sequential processing of lexical, grammatical, and phonological information within Broca's Area." *Science, 326*, 445–449. Reprinted by permission of the American Association for the Advancement of Science.

Chapter 12
Page 506: Randy Faris/Corbis; **p. 514, fig 1:** Burgess, G. C., Gray, J. R., Conway, A. R. A., & Braver, T. S. (2011). Figure 2 from "Neural mechanisms of interference control underlie the relationship between fluid intelligence and working memory span." *Journal of Experimental Psychology:* General, 140(4), 674–692. Copyright © 2011 by the American Psychological Association. Reprinted by permission; **12.6:** Druzgal et al. (2003). Dissecting Contributions of Prefrontal Cortex and Fusiform Face, *Journal of Cognitive Neuroscience*, 15(6) © 2003, Massachusetts Institute of Technology–Journals. Reproduced with permission of MIT Press–Journals in the format Textbook via Copyright Clearance Center; **12.7:** Katsuyuki Sakai and Richard E. Passingham, Figures from "Prefrontal Interactions Reflect Future Task Operations," *Nature Neuroscience*, 6:1, January 2003. Reprinted by permission from Macmillan Publishers Ltd, Copyright © 2003, Nature Publishing Group; **12.9:** Koechlin et al. (2003). The Architecture of Cognitive Control in the Human Prefrontal Cortex, *Science*, 302(5648): 1181–1185. © 2003 AAAS; **12.11:** Kennerley et al. (2009). Neurons in the frontal lobe encode the value of multiple decision variables. *Journal of Cognitive Neuroscience*, 21(6): 1162–1178. ©2009, Massachusetts Institute of Technology; **12.12:** Hare et al. (2009). Self-control in decision-making involves modulation of the vmPFC valuation system. *Science*, 324, 646-648. ©2009, AAAS; **12.15:** Schultz, W. (1998), Figure 2 from "Predictive reward signal of dopamine neurons." *Journal of Neurophysiology*, 80(1), 1–27. Copyright © 1993 by American Physiological Society. Reproduced with

permission of American Physiological Society in the format Textbook via Copyright Clearance Center; **12.16a:** Fiorillo, C. D., Tobler, P. N. , & Schultz, W. (2003). Figure 2a from "Discrete coding of reward probability and uncertainty by dopamine neurons." *Science, 299,* 1898–1902. Reprinted by permission of the American Association for the Advancement of Science; **12.16b:** Kobayashi, S. & Schultz, W. (2008). Figure 4 from "Influence of reward delays on responses of dopamine neurons." *The Journal of Neuroscience, 28*(31), 7837–7846. Copyright © 2008 by the Society for Neuroscience. Reprinted with permission from the Society for Neuroscience; **12.17:** Seymour et al. (2007). Differential encoding of losses and gains in the human striatum. *Journal of Neuroscience 27*(18): 4826–4831. © Society for Neuroscience; **12.21:** Badre, D. & D'Esposito, M. (2007). Figure 4 from "Functional magnetic resonance imaging evidence for a hierarchical organization of the prefrontal cortex." *Journal of Cognitive Neuroscience, 19*(12), 2082–2099. © 2007 by the Massachusetts Institute of Technology. Reprinted by permission of MIT Press Journals; **12.23b:** Thompson-Schill et al. (1997). Role of left interior prefrontal cortex in retrieval of semantic knowledge: A reevaluation, *Proceedings National Academy of Sciences* 94: 14792–14797; **p. 540, fig 1a:** Burgess et al. (2011). Neural mechanisms of interference control underlie the relationship between fluid intelligence and working memory span. *Journal of Experimental Psychology,* 140(4), 674–692; **p. 540, fig1b, c:** Dux, P.E., Tombu, M.N., Harrison, S., Rogers, B.P., Tong, F., & Marois, R. (2009). Figures 3 and 5b from "Training improves multitasking performance by increasing the speed of information processing in human prefrontal cortex." *Neuron,* 63, 127–138. Copyright © 2009 by Elsevier Science & Technology Journals. Reproduced with permission of Elsevier Science & Technology Journals in the format Textbook via Copyright Clearance Center. **12.27a:** Gazzaley et al. (2005). Top-down Enhancement and Suppression *Journal of Cognitive Neuroscience.* © 2005, Massachusetts Institute of Technology; **12.28:** Zanto, T. P., Rubens, M. T., Thangavel, A., & Gazzaley, A. (2011). Figure 3a and 4 a and b from "Causal role of the prefrontal cortex in goal-based modulation of visual processing and working." *Nature Neuroscience, 14*(5) 656–663. Reprinted by permission from Macmillan Publishers Ltd, Copyright © 2011, Nature Publishing Group; **12.30:** Frank, M. J., Samanta, J., Moustafa, A. A., & Sherman, S. J. (2007). Figure 1a and 2a from "Hold your horses: impulsivity, deep brain stimulation, and medication in parkinsonism." *Science,* 318, 1309–1312. Reprinted by permission of the American Association for the Advancement of Science.

Chapter 13

Page 558: David J. Green/Alamy; **13.1:** Damasio et. al. (1994). The Return of Phineas Gage: Clues about the brain from the skull of a famous patient. *Science,* 264 (5162): 1102–1105. © 1994, AAAS; **p. 564, fig 1:** Cohen et al. (1988). From syndrome to illness: Delineating the pathophysiology of schizophrenia with PET. *Schizophrenia Bulletin.* 14(2): 169–176. © 1988, Oxford University Press; **p. 565, fig 2:** Bettmann/Corbis; **13.3:** Kelley et al. (2002). Finding the self? An eventrelated fMRI study. *Journal of Cognitive Neuroscience.* 14, 785–794. © 2002, Massachusetts Institute of Technology; **13.5:** Debra A. Gusnard,and Marcus E. Raichle (2001). Searching for a baseline: functional imaging and the resting human brain. *Nature Reviews Neuroscience,* 2(10): 685–694. © 2001 Rights Managed by Nature Publishing Group; **13.7:** Jennifer S. Beer, Oliver P. John, Donatella Scabini, and Robert T. Knight, Figure 5 from "Orbitofrontal Cortex and Social Behavior: Integrating Self-monitoring and Emotion-Cognition Interactions," *Journal of Cognitive Neuroscience,* 18:6 (June, 2006), pp. 871–879. © 2006 by the Massachusetts Institute of Technology. Reprinted by permission of MIT Press Journals; **13.10:** Phillips et al. (1997). A specific neural substrate for perceiving facial expressions of disgust. *Nature.* October 2; 389:495–498. ©1997, Rights Managed by Nature Publishing Group; **13.13:** Cikara, M., Botvinick, M.M., & Fiske, S.T. (2011). Figure 2 from "Us Versus Them: Social Identity Shapes Neural Responses to Intergroup Competition and Harm." *Psychological Science, 22* (3), 306–313. Copyright © 2011 by Association for Psychological Science. Reprinted with permission; **13.15:** Cikara, M., Botvinick, M.M., & Fiske, S.T. (2011). Figure 4 from "Us Versus Them: Social Identity Shapes Neural Responses to Intergroup Competition and Harm." *Psychological Science, 22* (3), 306–313. Copyright © 2011 by Association for Psychological Science. Reprinted with permission: **13.16b:** Mitchell et al. (2004). Encoding-Specific Effects of Social Cognition on the Neural Correlates of Subsequent Memory. *Journal of Neuroscience,* 24(21): 4912–4917. ©2004, Society for Neuroscience; **13.18c:** Saxe et al. (2006). It's the Thought That Counts: Specific Brain Regions for One Component of Theory of Mind, *Psychological Science 17*(8): 692–699. © 2006, APS; **13.19:** Pelphrey et al. (2006). Brain Mechanisms for interpreting the actions of others from Biological-Motion Cues. Current Directions in *Psychological Science.* 15(3): 136–140. © 2006, APS; **13.20:** Kylliainen et al. (2012). Affective–motivational brain responses to direct gaze in children with autism spectrum disorder. *Journal of Child Psychology and Psychiatry.* © 2012 The Authors. Journal of Child Psychology and Psychiatry © 2012 Association for Child and Adolescent Mental Health; **13.21:** Klin et al. (2002). Visual Fixation Patterns During Viewing of Naturalistic Social Situations as Predictors of Social Competence in Individuals with Autism. *Archives of General Psychiatry.* 59: 809–816. © 2002 American Medical Association; **13.22:** Cattaneo, et al., Figure 1 from "Impairment of actions chains in autism and its possible role in intention understanding." *Proceedings of the National Academy of Science USA., 104,* 17825–17830. Reprinted with permission; **13.26a:** Jennifer S. Beer (2007). The default self: feeling good or being right? *Trends in Cognitive Sciences.* 11(5): 187–189. © 2007, Elsevier 2007; **13.26b:** Beer et al. (2003) The Regulatory Function of Self-Conscious Emotion: Insights From Patients With Orbitofrontal Damage. *Journal of Personality and Social Psychology, 85*(4) 594–604. © 2003 by the APA; **13.26 and 13.27:** Grossman et al. (2010). The role of ventral medial prefrontal cortex in social decisions: Converging evidence from fMRI and frontotemporal lobar degeneration. *Neuropsychologia, 48,* 3505–3512. © 2010, Elsevier.

Chapter 14
Page 604: Shutterstock; **14.1:** AP Photo; **14.13:** Povinelli, D.J., et al. (1993) Self-recognition ion chimpanzees (Pan troglodytes): Distribution, ontogeny, and patterns of emergence. *Journal of Comparative Psychology.* 107:347–372. Photos © Daniel Povinelli; **14.15:** Prinz, A.A., Bucher, D., & Marder, E. (2004). Figure 5 from "Similar network activity from disparate circuit parameters." *Nature Neuroscience,* 7(12), 1345–1352. Reprinted by permission from Macmillan Publishers Ltd, Copyright © 2011, Nature Publishing Group; **14.17:** Miller, M.B., van Horn, J. D., Wolford, G. L., Handy, T. C., Valsangkar-Smyth, M., Inati, S., Grafton, S., & Gazzaniga, M.S. (2002). Figure 2 from "Extensive individual differences in brain activations associated with episodic retrieval are reliable over time." *Journal of Cognitive Neuroscience, 14*(8), 1200–1214. Reprinted by permission of MIT Press Journals; **14.19:** Belyaev, D. (1979). Destabilizing selection as a factor in domestication. *Journal of Heredity.* 70, 301–308. ©1979 Oxford University Press; **14.20:** Trut, L. (1999). Early canid domestication: The farm-fox experiment. *American Scientist, 87*(2): 160–169. Photo courtesy of Lyudmila Trut; **14.21:** Trut, L. Oskina, I., and Kharlamova, A. (2009). Animal evolution during domestication: the domesticated fox as a model. *Bioessays.* 31(3) 349–360. © 2009 Wiley Periodicals.

Index